# In Praise of *Engineering a Compiler* Second Edition

*Compilers are a rich area of study, drawing together the whole world of computer science in one, elegant construction. Cooper and Torczon have succeeded in creating a welcoming guide to these software systems, enhancing this new edition with clear lessons and the details you simply must get right, all the while keeping the big picture firmly in view.* Engineering a Compiler *is an invaluable companion for anyone new to the subject.*

**Michael D. Smith**
Dean of the Faculty of Arts and Sciences
John H. Finley, Jr. Professor of Engineering and Applied Sciences, Harvard University

*The Second Edition of* Engineering a Compiler *is an excellent introduction to the construction of modern optimizing compilers. The authors draw from a wealth of experience in compiler construction in order to help students grasp the big picture while at the same time guiding them through many important but subtle details that must be addressed to construct an effective optimizing compiler. In particular, this book contains the best introduction to Static Single Assignment Form that I've seen.*

**Jeffery von Ronne**
Assistant Professor
Department of Computer Science
The University of Texas at San Antonio

Engineering a Compiler *increases its value as a textbook with a more regular and consistent structure, and with a host of instructional aids: review questions, extra examples, sidebars, and marginal notes. It also includes a wealth of technical updates, including more on nontraditional languages, real-world compilers, and nontraditional uses of compiler technology. The optimization material—already a signature strength—has become even more accessible and clear.*

**Michael L. Scott**
Professor
Computer Science Department
University of Rochester
Author of *Programming Language Pragmatics*

*Keith Cooper and Linda Torczon present an effective treatment of the history as well as a practitioner's perspective of how compilers are developed. Theory as well as practical real world examples of existing compilers (i.e. LISP, FORTRAN, etc.) comprise a multitude of effective discussions and illustrations. Full circle discussion of introductory along with advanced "allocation" and "optimization" concepts encompass an effective "life-cycle" of compiler engineering. This text should be on every bookshelf of computer science students as well as professionals involved with compiler engineering and development.*

**David Orleans**
Nova Southeastern University

# Engineering a Compiler

## Second Edition

# About the Authors

**Keith D. Cooper** is the Doerr Professor of Computational Engineering at Rice University. He has worked on a broad collection of problems in optimization of compiled code, including interprocedural data-flow analysis and its applications, value numbering, algebraic reassociation, register allocation, and instruction scheduling. His recent work has focused on a fundamental reexamination of the structure and behavior of traditional compilers. He has taught a variety of courses at the undergraduate level, from introductory programming through code optimization at the graduate level. He is a Fellow of the ACM.

**Linda Torczon**, Senior Research Scientist, Department of Computer Science at Rice University, is a principal investigator on the Platform-Aware Compilation Environment project (PACE), a DARPA-sponsored project that is developing an optimizing compiler environment which automatically adjusts its optimizations and strategies to new platforms. From 1990 to 2000, Dr. Torczon served as executive director of the Center for Research on Parallel Computation (CRPC), a National Science Foundation Science and Technology Center. She also served as the executive director of HiPerSoft, of the Los Alamos Computer Science Institute, and of the Virtual Grid Application Development Software Project (VGrADS).

# Engineering a Compiler

## Second Edition

**Keith D. Cooper**

**Linda Torczon**

*Rice University*
*Houston, Texas*

AMSTERDAM • BOSTON • HEIDELBERG • LONDON
NEW YORK • OXFORD • PARIS • SAN DIEGO
SAN FRANCISCO • SINGAPORE • SYDNEY • TOKYO

Morgan Kaufmann Publishers is an imprint of Elsevier

ELSEVIER

Acquiring Editor: Todd Green
Development Editor: Nate McFadden
Project Manager: Andre Cuello
Designer: Alisa Andreola

*Cover Image*: "The Landing of the Ark," a vaulted ceiling-design whose iconography was narrated, designed, and drawn by John Outram of John Outram Associates, Architects and City Planners, London, England. To read more visit *www.johnoutram.com/rice.html*.

*Morgan Kaufmann* is an imprint of Elsevier.
30 Corporate Drive, Suite 400, Burlington, MA 01803, USA

**Notices**

Knowledge and best practice in this field are constantly changing. As new research and experience broaden our understanding, changes in research methods or professional practices may become necessary. Practitioners and researchers must always rely on their own experience and knowledge in evaluating and using any information or methods described herein. In using such information or methods they should be mindful of their own safety and the safety of others, including parties for whom they have a professional responsibility.

To the fullest extent of the law, neither the Publisher nor the authors, contributors, or editors, assume any liability for any injury and/or damage to persons or property as a matter of products liability, negligence or otherwise, or from any use or operation of any methods, products, instructions, or ideas contained in the material herein.

**Library of Congress Cataloging-in-Publication Data**
Application submitted

**British Library Cataloguing-in-Publication Data**
A catalogue record for this book is available from the British Library.

ISBN: 978-0-12-088478-0

For information on all Morgan Kaufmann publications
visit our website at *www.mkp.com*

Printed and bound by CPI Group (UK) Ltd, Croydon, CR0 4YY

Transferred to Digital Printing, 2013

*We dedicate this volume to*

- *our parents, who instilled in us the thirst for knowledge and supported us as we developed the skills to follow our quest for knowledge;*
- *our children, who have shown us again how wonderful the process of learning and growing can be; and*
- *our spouses, without whom this book would never have been written.*

# About the Cover

The cover of this book features a portion of the drawing, "The Landing of the Ark," which decorates the ceiling of Duncan Hall at Rice University. Both Duncan Hall and its ceiling were designed by British architect John Outram. Duncan Hall is an outward expression of architectural, decorative, and philosophical themes developed over Outram's career as an architect. The decorated ceiling of the ceremonial hall plays a central role in the building's decorative scheme. Outram inscribed the ceiling with a set of significant ideas—a creation myth. By expressing those ideas in an allegorical drawing of vast size and intense color, Outram created a signpost that tells visitors who wander into the hall that, indeed, this building is not like other buildings.

By using the same signpost on the cover of *Engineering a Compiler*, the authors intend to signal that this work contains significant ideas that are at the core of their discipline. Like Outram's building, this volume is the culmination of intellectual themes developed over the authors' professional careers. Like Outram's decorative scheme, this book is a device for communicating ideas. Like Outram's ceiling, it presents significant ideas in new ways.

By connecting the design and construction of compilers with the design and construction of buildings, we intend to convey the many similarities in these two distinct activities. Our many long discussions with Outram introduced us to the Vitruvian ideals for architecture: commodity, firmness, and delight. These ideals apply to many kinds of construction. Their analogs for compiler construction are consistent themes of this text: function, structure, and elegance. Function matters; a compiler that generates incorrect code is useless. Structure matters; engineering detail determines a compiler's efficiency and robustness. Elegance matters; a well-designed compiler, in which the algorithms and data structures flow smoothly from one pass to another, can be a thing of beauty.

We are delighted to have John Outram's work grace the cover of this book.

Duncan Hall's ceiling is an interesting technological artifact. Outram drew the original design on one sheet of paper. It was photographed and scanned at 1200 dpi yielding roughly 750 MB of data. The image was enlarged to form 234 distinct $2 \times 8$ foot panels, creating a $52 \times 72$ foot image. The panels were printed onto oversize sheets of perforated vinyl using a 12 dpi acrylic-ink printer. These sheets were precision mounted onto $2 \times 8$ foot acoustic tiles and hung on the vault's aluminum frame.

# Contents

# Preface to the Second Edition

The practice of compiler construction changes continually, in part because the designs of processors and systems change. For example, when we began to write *Engineering a Compiler* (EAC) in 1998, some of our colleagues questioned the wisdom of including a chapter on instruction scheduling because out-of-order execution threatened to make scheduling largely irrelevant. Today, as the second edition goes to press, the rise of multicore processors and the push for more cores has made in-order execution pipelines attractive again because their smaller footprints allow the designer to place more cores on a chip. Instruction scheduling will remain important for the near-term future.

At the same time, the compiler construction community continues to develop new insights and algorithms, and to rediscover older techniques that were effective but largely forgotten. Recent research has created excitement surrounding the use of chordal graphs in register allocation (see Section 13.5.2). That work promises to simplify some aspects of graph-coloring allocators. Brzozowski's algorithm is a DFA minimization technique that dates to the early 1960s but has not been taught in compiler courses for decades (see Section 2.6.2). It provides an easy path from an implementation of the subset construction to one that minimizes DFAs. A modern course in compiler construction might include both of these ideas.

How, then, are we to structure a curriculum in compiler construction so that it prepares students to enter this ever changing field? We believe that the course should provide each student with the set of base skills that they will need to build new compiler components and to modify existing ones. Students need to understand both sweeping concepts, such as the collaboration between the compiler, linker, loader, and operating system embodied in a linkage convention, and minute detail, such as how the compiler writer might reduce the aggregate code space used by the register-save code at each procedure call.

## ■ CHANGES IN THE SECOND EDITION

The second edition of *Engineering a Compiler* (EAC2e) presents both perspectives: big-picture views of the problems in compiler construction and detailed discussions of algorithmic alternatives. In preparing EAC2e, we focused on the usability of the book, both as a textbook and as a reference for professionals. Specifically, we

- Improved the flow of ideas to help the student who reads the book sequentially. Chapter introductions explain the purpose of the chapter, lay out the major concepts, and provide a high-level overview of the chapter's subject matter. Examples have been reworked to provide continuity across chapters. In addition, each chapter begins with a summary and a set of keywords to aid the user who treats EAC2e as a reference book.
- Added section reviews and review questions at the end of each major section. The review questions provide a quick check as to whether or not the reader has understood the major points of the section.

- Moved definitions of key terms into the margin adjacent to the paragraph where they are first defined and discussed.
- Revised the material on optimization extensively so that it provides broader coverage of the possibilities for an optimizing compiler.

Compiler development today focuses on optimization and on code generation. A newly hired compiler writer is far more likely to port a code generator to a new processor or modify an optimization pass than to write a scanner or parser. The successful compiler writer must be familiar with current best-practice techniques in optimization, such as the construction of static single-assignment form, and in code generation, such as software pipelining. They must also have the background and insight to understand new techniques as they appear during the coming years. Finally, they must understand the techniques of scanning, parsing, and semantic elaboration well enough to build or modify a front end.

Our goal for EAC2e has been to create a text and a course that exposes students to the critical issues in modern compilers and provides them with the background to tackle those problems. We have retained, from the first edition, the basic balance of material. Front ends are commodity components; they can be purchased from a reliable vendor or adapted from one of the many open-source systems. At the same time, optimizers and code generators are custom-crafted for particular processors and, sometimes, for individual models, because performance relies so heavily on specific low-level details of the generated code. These facts affect the way that we build compilers today; they should also affect the way that we teach compiler construction.

## ■ ORGANIZATION

EAC2e divides the material into four roughly equal pieces:

- The first major section, Chapters 2 through 4, covers both the design of a compiler front end and the design and construction of tools to build front ends.
- The second major section, Chapters 5 through 7, explores the mapping of source-code into the compiler's intermediate form—that is, these chapters examine the kind of code that the front end generates for the optimizer and back end.
- The third major section, Chapters 8 through 10, introduces the subject of code optimization. Chapter 8 provides an overview of optimization. Chapters 9 and 10 contain deeper treatments of analysis and transformation; these two chapters are often omitted from an undergraduate course.
- The final section, Chapters 11 through 13, focuses on algorithms used in the compiler's back end.

## ■ THE ART AND SCIENCE OF COMPILATION

The lore of compiler construction includes both amazing success stories about the application of theory to practice and humbling stories about the limits of what we can do. On the success side, modern scanners are built by applying the theory of regular languages to automatic construction of recognizers. LR parsers use the same techniques to perform the handle-recognition that drives a shift-reduce parser. Data-flow analysis applies lattice theory to the analysis of programs in clever and useful ways. The approximation algorithms used in code generation produce good solutions to many instances of truly hard problems.

On the other side, compiler construction exposes complex problems that defy good solutions. The back end of a compiler for a modern processor approximates the solution to two or more interacting NP-complete problems (instruction scheduling, register allocation, and, perhaps, instruction and data placement). These NP-complete problems, however, look easy next to problems such as algebraic reassociation of expressions (see, for example, Figure 7.1). This problem admits a huge number of solutions; to make matters worse, the desired solution depends on context in both the compiler and the application code. As the compiler approximates the solutions to such problems, it faces constraints on compile time and available memory. A good compiler artfully blends theory, practical knowledge, engineering, and experience.

Open up a modern optimizing compiler and you will find a wide variety of techniques. Compilers use greedy heuristic searches that explore large solution spaces and deterministic finite automata that recognize words in the input. They employ fixed-point algorithms to reason about program behavior and simple theorem provers and algebraic simplifiers to predict the values of expressions. Compilers take advantage of fast pattern-matching algorithms to map abstract computations to machine-level operations. They use linear diophantine equations and Pressburger arithmetic to analyze array subscripts. Finally, compilers use a large set of classic algorithms and data structures such as hash tables, graph algorithms, and sparse set implementations.

In EAC2e, we have tried to convey both the art and the science of compiler construction. The book includes a sufficiently broad selection of material to show the reader that real tradeoffs exist and that the impact of design decisions can be both subtle and far-reaching. At the same time, EAC2e omits some techniques that have long been part of an undergraduate compiler construction course, but have been rendered less important by changes in the marketplace, in the technology of languages and compilers, or in the availability of tools.

## ■ APPROACH

Compiler construction is an exercise in engineering design. The compiler writer must choose a path through a design space that is filled with diverse alternatives, each with distinct costs, advantages, and complexity. Each decision has an impact on the resulting compiler. The quality of the end product depends on informed decisions at each step along the way.

Thus, there is no single right answer for many of the design decisions in a compiler. Even within "well understood" and "solved" problems, nuances in design and implementation have an impact on both the behavior of the compiler and the quality of the code that it produces. Many considerations play into each decision. As an example, the choice of an intermediate representation for the compiler has a profound impact on the rest of the compiler, from time and space requirements through the ease with which different algorithms can be applied. The decision, however, is often given short shrift. Chapter 5 examines the space of intermediate representations and some of the issues that should be considered in selecting one. We raise the issue again at several points in the book—both directly in the text and indirectly in the exercises.

EAC2e explores the design space and conveys both the depth of the problems and the breadth of the possible solutions. It shows some ways that those problems have been solved, along with the constraints that made those solutions attractive. Compiler writers need to understand both the problems and their solutions, as well as the impact of those decisions on other facets of the compiler's design. Only then can they make informed and intelligent choices.

## ■ PHILOSOPHY

This text exposes our philosophy for building compilers, developed during more than twenty-five years each of research, teaching, and practice. For example, intermediate representations should expose those details that matter in the final code; this belief leads to a bias toward low-level representations. Values should reside in registers until the allocator discovers that it cannot keep them there; this practice produces examples that use virtual registers and store values to memory only when it cannot be avoided. Every compiler should include optimization; it simplifies the rest of the compiler. Our experiences over the years have informed the selection of material and its presentation.

## ■ A WORD ABOUT PROGRAMMING EXERCISES

A class in compiler construction offers the opportunity to explore software design issues in the context of a concrete application—one whose basic functions are well understood by any student with the background for a compiler construction course. In most versions of this course, the programming exercises play a large role.

We have taught this class in versions where the students build a simple compiler from start to finish—beginning with a generated scanner and parser and ending with a code generator for some simplified RISC instruction set. We have taught this class in versions where the students write programs that address well-contained individual problems, such as register allocation or instruction scheduling. The choice of programming exercises depends heavily on the role that the course plays in the surrounding curriculum.

In some schools, the compiler course serves as a capstone course for seniors, tying together concepts from many other courses in a large, practical, design and implementation project. Students in such a class might write a complete compiler for a simple language or modify an open-source compiler to add support for a new language feature or a new architectural feature. This class might present the material in a linear order that closely follows the text's organization.

In other schools, that capstone experience occurs in other courses or in other ways. In such a class, the teacher might focus the programming exercises more narrowly on algorithms and their implementation, using labs such as a local register allocator or a tree-height rebalancing pass. This course might skip around in the text and adjust the order of presentation to meet the needs of the labs. For example, at Rice, we have often used a simple local register allocator as the first lab; any student with assembly-language programming experience understands the basics of the problem. That strategy, however, exposes the students to material from Chapter 13 before they see Chapter 2.

In either scenario, the course should draw material from other classes. Obvious connections exist to computer organization, assembly-language programming, operating systems, computer architecture, algorithms, and formal languages. Although the connections from compiler construction to other courses may be less obvious, they are no less important. Character copying, as discussed in Chapter 7, plays a critical role in the performance of applications that include network protocols, file servers, and web servers. The techniques developed in Chapter 2 for scanning have applications that range from text editing through URL-filtering. The bottom-up local register allocator in Chapter 13 is a cousin of the optimal offline page replacement algorithm, MIN.

## ■ ADDITIONAL MATERIALS

Additional resources are available that can help you adapt the material presented in EAC2e to your course. These include a complete set of lectures from the authors' version of the course at Rice University and a set of solutions to the exercises. Your Elsevier representative can provide you with access.

# Acknowledgments

Many people were involved in the preparation of the first edition of EAC. Their contributions have carried forward into this second edition. Many people pointed out problems in the first edition, including Amit Saha, Andrew Waters, Anna Youssefi, Ayal Zachs, Daniel Salce, David Peixotto, Fengmei Zhao, Greg Malecha, Hwansoo Han, Jason Eckhardt, Jeffrey Sandoval, John Elliot, Kamal Sharma, Kim Hazelwood, Max Hailperin, Peter Froehlich, Ryan Stinnett, Sachin Rehki, Sağnak Taşırlar, Timothy Harvey, and Xipeng Shen. We also want to thank the reviewers of the second edition, who were Jeffery von Ronne, Carl Offner, David Orleans, K. Stuart Smith, John Mallozzi, Elizabeth White, and Paul C. Anagnostopoulos. The production team at Elsevier, in particular, Alisa Andreola, Andre Cuello, and Megan Guiney, played a critical role in converting the a rough manuscript into its final form. All of these people improved this volume in significant ways with their insights and their help.

Finally, many people have provided us with intellectual and emotional support over the last five years. First and foremost, our families and our colleagues at Rice have encouraged us at every step of the way. Christine and Carolyn, in particular, tolerated myriad long discussions on topics in compiler construction. Nate McFadden guided this edition from its inception through its publication with patience and good humor. Penny Anderson provided administrative and organizational support that was critical to finishing the second edition. To all these people go our heartfelt thanks.

# Overview of Compilation

## ■ CHAPTER OVERVIEW

Compilers are computer programs that translate a program written in one language into a program written in another language. At the same time, a compiler is a large software system, with many internal components and algorithms and complex interactions between them. Thus, the study of compiler construction is an introduction to techniques for the translation and improvement of programs, and a practical exercise in software engineering. This chapter provides a conceptual overview of all the major components of a modern compiler.

**Keywords:** Compiler, Interpreter, Automatic Translation

## 1.1 INTRODUCTION

The role of the computer in daily life grows each year. With the rise of the Internet, computers and the software that runs on them provide communications, news, entertainment, and security. Embedded computers have changed the ways that we build automobiles, airplanes, telephones, televisions, and radios. Computation has created entirely new categories of activity, from video games to social networks. Supercomputers predict daily weather and the course of violent storms. Embedded computers synchronize traffic lights and deliver e-mail to your pocket.

All of these computer applications rely on software computer programs that build virtual tools on top of the low-level abstractions provided by the underlying hardware. Almost all of that software is translated by a tool called a *compiler*. A compiler is simply a computer program that translates other computer programs to prepare them for execution. This book presents the fundamental techniques of automatic translation that are used

**Compiler**
a computer program that translates other computer programs

**Engineering a Compiler**

to build compilers. It describes many of the challenges that arise in compiler construction and the algorithms that compiler writers use to address them.

### Conceptual Roadmap

A compiler is a tool that translates software written in one language into another language. To translate text from one language to another, the tool must understand both the form, or syntax, and content, or meaning, of the input language. It needs to understand the rules that govern syntax and meaning in the output language. Finally, it needs a scheme for mapping content from the source language to the target language.

The structure of a typical compiler derives from these simple observations. The compiler has a front end to deal with the source language. It has a back end to deal with the target language. Connecting the front end and the back end, it has a formal structure for representing the program in an intermediate form whose meaning is largely independent of either language. To improve the translation, a compiler often includes an optimizer that analyzes and rewrites that intermediate form.

### Overview

Computer programs are simply sequences of abstract operations written in a *programming language*—a formal language designed for expressing computation. Programming languages have rigid properties and meanings—as opposed to natural languages, such as Chinese or Portuguese. Programming languages are designed for expressiveness, conciseness, and clarity. Natural languages allow ambiguity. Programming languages are designed to avoid ambiguity; an ambiguous program has no meaning. Programming languages are designed to specify computations—to record the sequence of actions that perform some task or produce some results.

Programming languages are, in general, designed to allow humans to express computations as sequences of operations. Computer processors, hereafter referred to as processors, microprocessors, or machines, are designed to execute sequences of operations. The operations that a processor implements are, for the most part, at a much lower level of abstraction than those specified in a programming language. For example, a programming language typically includes a concise way to print some number to a file. That single programming language statement must be translated into literally hundreds of machine operations before it can execute.

The tool that performs such translations is called a compiler. The compiler takes as input a program written in some language and produces as its output an equivalent program. In the classic notion of a compiler, the output program is expressed in the operations available on some specific processor, often called the target machine. Viewed as a black box, a compiler might look like this:

Typical "source" languages might be C, C++, FORTRAN, Java, or ML. The "target" language is usually the instruction set of some processor.

Some compilers produce a target program written in a human-oriented programming language rather than the assembly language of some computer. The programs that these compilers produce require further translation before they can execute directly on a computer. Many research compilers produce C programs as their output. Because compilers for C are available on most computers, this makes the target program executable on all those systems, at the cost of an extra compilation for the final target. Compilers that target programming languages rather than the instruction set of a computer are often called *source-to-source translators*.

Many other systems qualify as compilers. For example, a typesetting program that produces PostScript can be considered a compiler. It takes as input a specification for how the document should look on the printed page and it produces as output a PostScript file. PostScript is simply a language for describing images. Because the typesetting program takes an executable specification and produces another executable specification, it is a compiler.

The code that turns PostScript into pixels is typically an *interpreter*, not a compiler. An interpreter takes as input an executable specification and produces as output the result of executing the specification.

Some languages, such as Perl, Scheme, and APL, are more often implemented with interpreters than with compilers.

Some languages adopt translation schemes that include both compilation and interpretation. Java is compiled from source code into a form called *bytecode*, a compact representation intended to decrease download times for Java applications. Java applications execute by running the bytecode on the corresponding Java Virtual Machine (JVM), an interpreter for bytecode. To complicate the picture further, many implementations of the JVM include a

**Instruction set**
The set of operations supported by a processor; the overall design of an instruction set is often called an *instruction set architecture* or ISA.

**Virtual machine**
A virtual machine is a simulator for some processor. It is an *interpreter* for that machine's instruction set.

compiler that executes at runtime, sometimes called a *just-in-time compiler*, or JIT, that translates heavily used bytecode sequences into native code for the underlying computer.

Interpreters and compilers have much in common. They perform many of the same tasks. Both analyze the input program and determine whether or not it is a valid program. Both build an internal model of the structure and meaning of the program. Both determine where to store values during execution. However, interpreting the code to produce a result is quite different from emitting a translated program that can be executed to produce the result. This book focuses on the problems that arise in building compilers. However, an implementor of interpreters may find much of the material relevant.

### *Why Study Compiler Construction?*

A compiler is a large, complex program. Compilers often include hundreds of thousands, if not millions, of lines of code, organized into multiple subsystems and components. The various parts of a compiler interact in complex ways. Design decisions made for one part of the compiler have important ramifications for other parts. Thus, the design and implementation of a compiler is a substantial exercise in software engineering.

A good compiler contains a microcosm of computer science. It makes practical use of greedy algorithms (register allocation), heuristic search techniques (list scheduling), graph algorithms (dead-code elimination), dynamic programming (instruction selection), finite automata and push-down automata (scanning and parsing), and fixed-point algorithms (data-flow analysis). It deals with problems such as dynamic allocation, synchronization, naming, locality, memory hierarchy management, and pipeline scheduling. Few software systems bring together as many complex and diverse components. Working inside a compiler provides practical experience in software engineering that is hard to obtain with smaller, less intricate systems.

Compilers play a fundamental role in the central activity of computer science: preparing problems for solution by computer. Most software is compiled, and the correctness of that process and the efficiency of the resulting code have a direct impact on our ability to build large systems. Most students are not satisfied with reading about these ideas; many of the ideas must be implemented to be appreciated. Thus, the study of compiler construction is an important component of a computer science education.

Compilers demonstrate the successful application of theory to practical problems. The tools that automate the production of scanners and parsers apply results from formal language theory. These same tools are used for text searching, website filtering, word processing, and command-language interpreters. Type checking and static analysis apply results from lattice theory, number theory, and other branches of mathematics to understand and improve programs. Code generators use algorithms for tree-pattern matching, parsing, dynamic programming, and text matching to automate the selection of instructions.

Still, some problems that arise in compiler construction are open problems—that is, the current best solutions have room for improvement. Attempts to design high-level, universal, intermediate representations have foundered on complexity. The dominant method for scheduling instructions is a greedy algorithm with several layers of tie-breaking heuristics. While it is obvious that compilers should use commutativity and associativity to improve the code, most compilers that try to do so simply rearrange the expression into some canonical order.

Building a successful compiler requires expertise in algorithms, engineering, and planning. Good compilers approximate the solutions to hard problems. They emphasize efficiency, in their own implementations and in the code they generate. They have internal data structures and knowledge representations that expose the right level of detail—enough to allow strong optimization, but not enough to force the compiler to wallow in detail. Compiler construction brings together ideas and techniques from across the breadth of computer science and applies them in a constrained setting to solve some truly hard problems.

### The Fundamental Principles of Compilation

Compilers are large, complex, carefully engineered objects. While many issues in compiler design are amenable to multiple solutions and interpretations, there are two fundamental principles that a compiler writer must keep in mind at all times. The first principle is inviolable:

> *The compiler must preserve the meaning of the program being compiled.*

Correctness is a fundamental issue in programming. The compiler must preserve correctness by faithfully implementing the "meaning" of its input program. This principle lies at the heart of the social contract between the compiler writer and compiler user. If the compiler can take liberties with meaning, then why not simply generate a `nop` or a `return`? If an incorrect translation is acceptable, why expend the effort to get it right?

The second principle that a compiler must observe is practical:

> *The compiler must improve the input program in some discernible way.*

A traditional compiler improves the input program by making it directly executable on some target machine. Other "compilers" improve their input in different ways. For example, tpic is a program that takes the specification for a drawing written in the graphics language pic and converts it into LaTeX; the "improvement" lies in LaTeX's greater availability and generality. A source-to-source translator for c must produce code that is, in some measure, better than the input program; if it is not, why would anyone invoke it?

## 1.2 COMPILER STRUCTURE

A compiler is a large, complex software system. The community has been building compilers since 1955, and over the years, we have learned many lessons about how to structure a compiler. Earlier, we depicted a compiler as a simple box that translates a source program into a target program. Reality, of course, is more complex than that simple picture.

As the single-box model suggests, a compiler must both understand the source program that it takes as input and map its functionality to the target machine. The distinct nature of these two tasks suggests a division of labor and leads to a design that decomposes compilation into two major pieces: a *front end* and a *back end*.

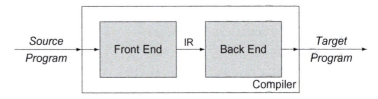

The front end focuses on understanding the source-language program. The back end focuses on mapping programs to the target machine. This separation of concerns has several important implications for the design and implementation of compilers.

The front end must encode its knowledge of the source program in some structure for later use by the back end. This *intermediate representation* (IR) becomes the compiler's definitive representation for the code it is translating. At each point in compilation, the compiler will have a definitive representation. It may, in fact, use several different IRs as compilation progresses, but at each point, one representation will be the definitive IR. We think of the definitive IR as the version of the program passed between independent phases of the compiler, like the IR passed from the front end to the back end in the preceding drawing.

In a two-phase compiler, the front end must ensure that the source program is well formed, and it must map that code into the IR. The back end must map

**IR**
A compiler uses some set of data structures to represent the code that it processes. That form is called an *intermediate representation*, or IR.

---

**MAY YOU STUDY IN INTERESTING TIMES**

This is an exciting era in the design and implementation of compilers. In the 1980s, almost all compilers were large, monolithic systems. They took as input one of a handful of languages and produced assembly code for some particular computer. The assembly code was pasted together with the code produced by other compilations—including system libraries and application libraries—to form an executable. The executable was stored on a disk, and at the appropriate time, the final code was moved from the disk to main memory and executed.

Today, compiler technology is being applied in many different settings. As computers find applications in diverse places, compilers must cope with new and different constraints. Speed is no longer the sole criterion for judging the compiled code. Today, code might be judged on how small it is, on how much energy it consumes, on how well it compresses, or on how many page faults it generates when it runs.

At the same time, compilation techniques have escaped from the monolithic systems of the 1980s. They are appearing in many new places. Java compilers take partially compiled programs (in Java "bytecode" format) and translate them into native code for the target machine. In this environment, success requires that the sum of compile time plus runtime must be less than the cost of interpretation. Techniques to analyze whole programs are moving from compile time to link time, where the linker can analyze the assembly code for the entire application and use that knowledge to improve the program. Finally, compilers are being invoked at runtime to generate customized code that capitalizes on facts that cannot be known any earlier. If the compilation time can be kept small and the benefits are large, this strategy can produce noticeable improvements.

---

the IR program into the instruction set and the finite resources of the target machine. Because the back end only processes IR created by the front end, it can assume that the IR contains no syntactic or semantic errors.

The compiler can make multiple passes over the IR form of the code before emitting the target program. This should lead to better code, as the compiler can, in effect, study the code in one phase and record relevant details. Then, in later phases, it can use these recorded facts to improve the quality of translation. This strategy requires that knowledge derived in the first pass be recorded in the IR, where later passes can find and use it.

Finally, the two-phase structure may simplify the process of *retargeting* the compiler. We can easily envision constructing multiple back ends for a single front end to produce compilers that accept the same language but target different machines. Similarly, we can envision front ends for different

**Retargeting**
The task of changing the compiler to generate code for a new processor is often called *retargeting* the compiler.

languages producing the same IR and using a common back end. Both scenarios assume that one IR can serve for several combinations of source and target; in practice, both language-specific and machine-specific details usually find their way into the IR.

Introducing an IR makes it possible to add more phases to compilation. The compiler writer can insert a third phase between the front end and the back end. This middle section, or *optimizer*, takes an IR program as its input and produces a semantically equivalent IR program as its output. By using the IR as an interface, the compiler writer can insert this third phase with minimal disruption to the front end and back end. This leads to the following compiler structure, termed a *three-phase compiler*.

**Optimizer**
The middle section of a compiler, called an *optimizer*, analyzes and transforms the IR to improve it.

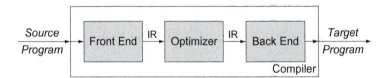

The optimizer is an IR-to-IR transformer that tries to improve the IR program in some way. (Notice that these transformers are, themselves, compilers according to our definition in Section 1.1.) The optimizer can make one or more passes over the IR, analyze the IR, and rewrite the IR. The optimizer may rewrite the IR in a way that is likely to produce a faster target program from the back end or a smaller target program from the back end. It may have other objectives, such as a program that produces fewer page faults or uses less energy.

Conceptually, the three-phase structure represents the classic optimizing compiler. In practice, each phase is divided internally into a series of passes. The front end consists of two or three passes that handle the details of recognizing valid source-language programs and producing the initial IR form of the program. The middle section contains passes that perform different optimizations. The number and purpose of these passes vary from compiler to compiler. The back end consists of a series of passes, each of which takes the IR program one step closer to the target machine's instruction set. The three phases and their individual passes share a common infrastructure. This structure is shown in Figure 1.1.

In practice, the conceptual division of a compiler into three phases, a front end, a middle section or optimizer, and a back end, is useful. The problems addressed by these phases are different. The front end is concerned with understanding the source program and recording the results of its analysis into IR form. The optimizer section focuses on improving the IR form.

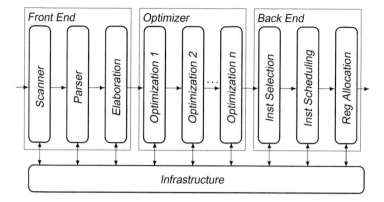

■ **FIGURE 1.1** Structure of a Typical Compiler.

The back end must map the transformed IR program onto the bounded resources of the target machine in a way that leads to efficient use of those resources.

Of these three phases, the optimizer has the murkiest description. The term *optimization* implies that the compiler discovers an optimal solution to some problem. The issues and problems that arise in optimization are so complex and so interrelated that they cannot, in practice, be solved optimally. Furthermore, the actual behavior of the compiled code depends on interactions among all of the techniques applied in the optimizer and the back end. Thus, even if a single technique can be proved optimal, its interactions with other techniques may produce less than optimal results. As a result, a good optimizing compiler can improve the quality of the code, relative to an unoptimized version. However, an optimizing compiler will almost always fail to produce optimal code.

The middle section can be a single monolithic pass that applies one or more optimizations to improve the code, or it can be structured as a series of smaller passes with each pass reading and writing IR. The monolithic structure may be more efficient. The multipass structure may lend itself to a less complex implementation and a simpler approach to debugging the compiler. It also creates the flexibility to employ different sets of optimization in different situations. The choice between these two approaches depends on the constraints under which the compiler is built and operates.

## 1.3 OVERVIEW OF TRANSLATION

To translate code written in a programming language into code suitable for execution on some target machine, a compiler runs through many steps.

**NOTATION**

Compiler books are, in essence, about notation. After all, a compiler translates a program written in one notation into an equivalent program written in another notation. A number of notational issues will arise in your reading of this book. In some cases, these issues will directly affect your understanding of the material.

*Expressing Algorithms* We have tried to keep the algorithms concise. Algorithms are written at a relatively high level, assuming that the reader can supply implementation details. They are written in a *slanted, sans-serif font*. Indentation is both deliberate and significant; it matters most in an *if-then-else* construct. Indented code after a *then* or an *else* forms a block. In the following code fragment

```
if Action [s,word] = "shift sᵢ" then
    push word
    push sᵢ
    word ← NextWord()
else if ···
```

all the statements between the *then* and the *else* are part of the *then* clause of the *if-then-else* construct. When a clause in an *if-then-else* construct contains just one statement, we write the keyword *then* or *else* on the same line as the statement.

*Writing Code* In some examples, we show actual program text written in some language chosen to demonstrate a particular point. Actual program text is written in a monospace font.

*Arithmetic Operators* Finally, we have forsaken the traditional use of * for × and of / for ÷, except in actual program text. The meaning should be clear to the reader.

To make this abstract process more concrete, consider the steps needed to generate executable code for the following expression:

```
a ← a × 2 × b × c × d
```

where a, b, c, and d are variables, ← indicates an assignment, and × is the operator for multiplication. In the following subsections, we will trace the path that a compiler takes to turn this simple expression into executable code.

## 1.3.1 The Front End

Before the compiler can translate an expression into executable target-machine code, it must understand both its form, or *syntax*, and its meaning, or *semantics*. The front end determines if the input code is well formed, in terms of both syntax and semantics. If it finds that the code is valid, it creates a representation of the code in the compiler's intermediate representation; if not, it reports back to the user with diagnostic error messages to identify the problems with the code.

### Checking Syntax

To check the syntax of the input program, the compiler must compare the program's structure against a definition for the language. This requires an appropriate formal definition, an efficient mechanism for testing whether or not the input meets that definition, and a plan for how to proceed on an illegal input.

Mathematically, the source language is a set, usually infinite, of strings defined by some finite set of rules, called a *grammar*. Two separate passes in the front end, called the scanner and the parser, determine whether or not the input code is, in fact, a member of the set of valid programs defined by the grammar.

Programming language grammars usually refer to words based on their parts of speech, sometimes called syntactic categories. Basing the grammar rules on parts of speech lets a single rule describe many sentences. For example, in English, many sentences have the form

> *Sentence* → *Subject* `verb` *Object* `endmark`

where `verb` and `endmark` are parts of speech, and *Sentence*, *Subject*, and *Object* are syntactic variables. *Sentence* represents any string with the form described by this rule. The symbol "→" reads "derives" and means that an instance of the right-hand side can be abstracted to the syntactic variable on the left-hand side.

Consider a sentence like "Compilers are engineered objects." The first step in understanding the syntax of this sentence is to identify distinct words in the input program and to classify each word with a part of speech. In a compiler, this task falls to a pass called the *scanner*. The scanner takes a stream of characters and converts it to a stream of classified words—that is, pairs of the form $(p,s)$, where $p$ is the word's *part of speech* and $s$ is its spelling. A scanner would convert the example sentence into the following stream of classified words:

**Scanner**
the compiler pass that converts a string of characters into a stream of words

> (`noun`,"Compilers"), (`verb`,"are"), (`adjective`,"engineered"),
> (`noun`,"objects"), (`endmark`,".")

In practice, the actual spelling of the words might be stored in a hash table and represented in the pairs with an integer index to simplify equality tests. Chapter 2 explores the theory and practice of scanner construction.

In the next step, the compiler tries to match the stream of categorized words against the rules that specify syntax for the input language. For example, a working knowledge of English might include the following grammatical rules:

| 1 | *Sentence* | → | *Subject* verb *Object* endmark |
|---|---|---|---|
| 2 | *Subject* | → | noun |
| 3 | *Subject* | → | *Modifier* noun |
| 4 | *Object* | → | noun |
| 5 | *Object* | → | *Modifier* noun |
| 6 | *Modifier* | → | adjective |
| | ... | | |

By inspection, we can discover the following *derivation* for our example sentence:

| Rule | Prototype Sentence |
|---|---|
| — | *Sentence* |
| 1 | *Subject* verb *Object* endmark |
| 2 | noun verb *Object* endmark |
| 5 | noun verb *Modifier* noun endmark |
| 6 | noun verb adjective noun endmark |

The derivation starts with the syntactic variable *Sentence*. At each step, it rewrites one term in the prototype sentence, replacing the term with a right-hand side that can be derived from that rule. The first step uses Rule 1 to replace *Sentence*. The second uses Rule 2 to replace *Subject*. The third replaces *Object* using Rule 5, while the final step rewrites *Modifier* with adjective according to Rule 6. At this point, the prototype sentence generated by the derivation matches the stream of categorized words produced by the scanner.

The derivation proves that the sentence "Compilers are engineered objects." belongs to the language described by Rules 1 through 6. The sentence is grammatically correct. The process of automatically finding derivations is called *parsing*. Chapter 3 presents the techniques that compilers use to parse the input program.

**Parser**
the compiler pass that determines if the input stream is a sentence in the source language

A grammatically correct sentence can be meaningless. For example, the sentence "Rocks are green vegetables" has the same parts of speech in the same order as "Compilers are engineered objects," but has no rational meaning. To understand the difference between these two sentences requires contextual knowledge about software systems, rocks, and vegetables.

The semantic models that compilers use to reason about programming languages are simpler than the models needed to understand natural language. A compiler builds mathematical models that detect specific kinds of inconsistency in a program. Compilers check for consistency of type; for example, the expression

$$a \leftarrow a \times 2 \times b \times c \times d$$

**Type checking**
the compiler pass that checks for type-consistent uses of names in the input program

might be syntactically well-formed, but if $b$ and $d$ are character strings, the sentence might still be invalid. Compilers also check for consistency of number in specific situations; for example, an array reference should have the same number of dimensions as the array's declared rank and a procedure call should specify the same number of arguments as the procedure's definition. Chapter 4 explores some of the issues that arise in compiler-based type checking and semantic elaboration.

## Intermediate Representations

The final issue handled in the front end of a compiler is the generation of an IR form of the code. Compilers use a variety of different kinds of IR, depending on the source language, the target language, and the specific transformations that the compiler applies. Some IRs represent the program as a graph. Others resemble a sequential assembly code program. The code in the margin shows how our example expression might look in a low-level, sequential IR. Chapter 5 presents an overview of the variety of kinds of IRs that compilers use.

$$t_0 \leftarrow a \times 2$$
$$t_1 \leftarrow t_0 \times b$$
$$t_2 \leftarrow t_1 \times c$$
$$t_3 \leftarrow t_2 \times d$$
$$a \leftarrow t_3$$

For every source-language construct, the compiler needs a strategy for how it will implement that construct in the IR form of the code. Specific choices affect the compiler's ability to transform and improve the code. Thus, we spend two chapters on the issues that arise in generation of IR for source-code constructs. Procedure linkages are, at once, a source of inefficiency in the final code and the fundamental glue that pieces together different source files into an application. Thus, we devote Chapter 6 to the issues that surround procedure calls. Chapter 7 presents implementation strategies for most other programming language constructs.

> **TERMINOLOGY**
>
> A careful reader will notice that we use the word *code* in many places where either *program* or *procedure* might naturally fit. Compilers can be invoked to translate fragments of code that range from a single reference through an entire system of programs. Rather than specify some scope of compilation, we will continue to use the ambiguous, but more general, term, *code*.

## 1.3.2 The Optimizer

When the front end emits IR for the input program, it handles the statements one at a time, in the order that they are encountered. Thus, the initial IR program contains general implementation strategies that will work in any surrounding context that the compiler might generate. At runtime, the code will execute in a more constrained and predictable context. The optimizer analyzes the IR form of the code to discover facts about that context and uses that contextual knowledge to rewrite the code so that it computes the same answer in a more efficient way.

Efficiency can have many meanings. The classic notion of optimization is to reduce the application's running time. In other contexts, the optimizer might try to reduce the size of the compiled code, or other properties such as the energy that the processor consumes evaluating the code. All of these strategies target efficiency.

Returning to our example, consider it in the context shown in Figure 1.2a. The statement occurs inside a loop. Of the values that it uses, only a and d change inside the loop. The values of 2, b, and c are invariant in the loop. If the optimizer discovers this fact, it can rewrite the code as shown in Figure 1.2b. In this version, the number of multiplications has been reduced from $4 \cdot n$ to $2 \cdot n + 2$. For $n > 1$, the rewritten loop should execute faster. This kind of optimization is discussed in Chapters 8, 9, and 10.

### Analysis

Most optimizations consist of an analysis and a transformation. The analysis determines where the compiler can safely and profitably apply the technique. Compilers use several kinds of analysis to support transformations. *Data-flow analysis* reasons, at compile time, about the flow of values at runtime. Data-flow analyzers typically solve a system of simultaneous set equations that are derived from the structure of the code being translated. *Dependence analysis* uses number-theoretic tests to reason about the values that can be

**Data-flow analysis**
a form of compile-time reasoning about the runtime flow of values

```
b ← ⋯                          b ← ⋯
c ← ⋯                          c ← ⋯
a ← 1                          a ← 1
for i = 1 to n                 t ← 2 × b × c
  read d                       for i = 1 to n
  a ← a × 2 × b × c × d          read d
  end                            a ← a × d × t
                                 end
```

(a) Original Code in Context        (b) Improved Code

■ **FIGURE 1.2** Context Makes a Difference.

assumed by subscript expressions. It is used to disambiguate references to array elements. Chapter 9 presents a detailed look at data-flow analysis and its application, along with the construction of static-single-assignment form, an IR that encodes information about the flow of both values and control directly in the IR.

### *Transformation*

To improve the code, the compiler must go beyond analyzing it. The compiler must use the results of analysis to rewrite the code into a more efficient form. Myriad transformations have been invented to improve the time or space requirements of executable code. Some, such as discovering loop-invariant computations and moving them to less frequently executed locations, improve the running time of the program. Others make the code more compact. Transformations vary in their effect, the scope over which they operate, and the analysis required to support them. The literature on transformations is rich; the subject is large enough and deep enough to merit one or more separate books. Chapter 10 covers the subject of scalar transformations—that is, transformations intended to improve the performance of code on a single processor. It presents a taxonomy for organizing the subject and populates that taxonomy with examples.

### 1.3.3 **The Back End**

The compiler's back end traverses the IR form of the code and emits code for the target machine. It selects target-machine operations to implement each IR operation. It chooses an order in which the operations will execute efficiently. It decides which values will reside in registers and which values will reside in memory and inserts code to enforce those decisions.

**ABOUT ILOC**

Throughout the book, low-level examples are written in a notation that we call ILOC—an acronym derived from "intermediate language for an optimizing compiler." Over the years, this notation has undergone many changes. The version used in this book is described in detail in Appendix A.

Think of ILOC as the assembly language for a simple RISC machine. It has a standard set of operations. Most operations take arguments that are registers. The memory operations, loads and stores, transfer values between memory and the registers. To simplify the exposition in the text, most examples assume that all data consists of integers.

Each operation has a set of operands and a target. The operation is written in five parts: an operation name, a list of operands, a separator, a list of targets, and an optional comment. Thus, to add registers 1 and 2, leaving the result in register 3, the programmer would write

$$\text{add } r_1, r_2 \Rightarrow r_3 \quad // \text{ example instruction}$$

The separator, $\Rightarrow$, precedes the target list. It is a visual reminder that information flows from left to right. In particular, it disambiguates cases where a person reading the assembly-level text can easily confuse operands and targets. (See loadAI and storeAI in the following table.)

The example in Figure 1.3 only uses four ILOC operations:

| ILOC Operation | Meaning |
|---|---|
| loadAI $\quad r_1, c_2 \Rightarrow r_3$ | Memory$(r_1 + c_2) \rightarrow r_3$ |
| loadI $\quad\; c_1 \quad\;\; \Rightarrow r_2$ | $c_1 \rightarrow r_2$ |
| mult $\quad\; r_1, r_2 \Rightarrow r_3$ | $r_1 \times r_2 \rightarrow r_3$ |
| storeAI $\quad r_1 \quad\;\; \Rightarrow r_2, c_3$ | $r_1 \rightarrow$ Memory$(r_2 + c_3)$ |

Appendix A contains a more detailed description of ILOC. The examples consistently use $r_{arp}$ as a register that contains the start of data storage for the current procedure, also known as the *activation record pointer*.

### Instruction Selection

The first stage of code generation rewrites the IR operations into target machine operations, a process called *instruction selection*. Instruction selection maps each IR operation, in its context, into one or more target machine operations. Consider rewriting our example expression, $a \leftarrow a \times 2 \times b \times c \times d$, into code for the ILOC virtual machine to illustrate the process. (We will use ILOC throughout the book.) The IR form of the expression is repeated in the margin. The compiler might choose the operations shown in Figure 1.3. This code assumes that a, b, c, and d

$$t_0 \leftarrow a \times 2$$
$$t_1 \leftarrow t_0 \times b$$
$$t_2 \leftarrow t_1 \times c$$
$$t_3 \leftarrow t_2 \times d$$
$$a \;\leftarrow t_3$$

```
loadAI   r_arp, @a ⇒ r_a        // load 'a'
loadI    2         ⇒ r_2        // constant 2 into r_2
loadAI   r_arp, @b ⇒ r_b        // load 'b'
loadAI   r_arp, @c ⇒ r_c        // load 'c'
loadAI   r_arp, @d ⇒ r_d        // load 'd'
mult     r_a, r_2  ⇒ r_a        // r_a ← a × 2
mult     r_a, r_b  ⇒ r_a        // r_a ← (a × 2) × b
mult     r_a, r_c  ⇒ r_a        // r_a ← (a × 2 × b) × c
mult     r_a, r_d  ⇒ r_a        // r_a ← (a × 2 × b × c) × d
storeAI  r_a       ⇒ r_arp,@a   // write r_a back to 'a'
```

■ **FIGURE 1.3** ILOC Code for a ← a × 2 × b × c × d.

are located at offsets @a, @b, @c, and @d from an address contained in the register $r_{arp}$.

The compiler has chosen a straightforward sequence of operations. It loads all of the relevant values into registers, performs the multiplications in order, and stores the result to the memory location for a. It assumes an unlimited supply of registers and names them with symbolic names such as $r_a$ to hold a and $r_{arp}$ to hold the address where the data storage for our named values begins. Implicitly, the instruction selector relies on the register allocator to map these symbolic register names, or *virtual registers*, to the actual registers of the target machine.

**Virtual register**
a symbolic register name that the compiler uses to indicate that a value can be stored in a register

The instruction selector can take advantage of special operations on the target machine. For example, if an immediate-multiply operation (multI) is available, it might replace the operation mult $r_a, r_2 ⇒ r_a$ with multI $r_a, 2 ⇒ r_a$, eliminating the need for the operation loadI $2 ⇒ r_2$ and reducing the demand for registers. If addition is faster than multiplication, it might replace mult $r_a, r_2 ⇒ r_a$ with add $r_a, r_a ⇒ r_a$, avoiding both the loadI and its use of $r_2$, as well as replacing the mult with a faster add. Chapter 11 presents two different techniques for instruction selection that use pattern matching to choose efficient implementations for IR operations.

## Register Allocation

During instruction selection, the compiler deliberately ignored the fact that the target machine has a limited set of registers. Instead, it used virtual registers and assumed that "enough" registers existed. In practice, the earlier stages of compilation may create more demand for registers than the hardware can support. The register allocator must map those virtual registers onto actual target-machine registers. Thus, the register allocator decides, at each point in the code, which values should reside in the target-machine registers. It then rewrites the code to reflect its decisions. For example, a register allocator might minimize register use by rewriting the code from Figure 1.3 as follows:

```
loadAI   r_arp, @a ⇒ r₁           // load 'a'
add      r₁, r₁   ⇒ r₁           // r₁ ← a × 2
loadAI   r_arp, @b ⇒ r₂           // load 'b'
mult     r₁, r₂    ⇒ r₁           // r₁ ← (a × 2) × b
loadAI   r_arp, @c ⇒ r₂           // load 'c'
mult     r₁, r₂    ⇒ r₁           // r₁ ← (a × 2 × b) × c
loadAI   r_arp, @d ⇒ r₂           // load 'd'
mult     r₁, r₂    ⇒ r₁           // r₁ ← (a × 2 × b × c) × d
storeAI  r₁        ⇒ r_arp, @a    // write r_a back to 'a'
```

This sequence uses three registers instead of six.

Minimizing register use may be counterproductive. If, for example, any of the named values, a, b, c, or d, are already in registers, the code should reference those registers directly. If all are in registers, the sequence could be implemented so that it required no additional registers. Alternatively, if some nearby expression also computed $a \times 2$, it might be better to preserve that value in a register than to recompute it later. This optimization would increase demand for registers but eliminate a later instruction. Chapter 13 explores the problems that arise in register allocation and the techniques that compiler writers use to solve them.

### Instruction Scheduling

To produce code that executes quickly, the code generator may need to reorder operations to reflect the target machine's specific performance constraints. The execution time of the different operations can vary. Memory access operations can take tens or hundreds of cycles, while some arithmetic operations, particularly division, take several cycles. The impact of these longer latency operations on the performance of compiled code can be dramatic.

Assume, for the moment, that a loadAI or storeAI operation requires three cycles, a mult requires two cycles, and all other operations require one cycle. The following table shows how the previous code fragment performs under these assumptions. The **Start** column shows the cycle in which each operation begins execution and the **End** column shows the cycle in which it completes.

| Start | End | | | |
|-------|-----|--|--|--|
| 1 | 3 | loadAI | $r_{arp}$, @a $\Rightarrow r_1$ | // load 'a' |
| 4 | 4 | add | $r_1$, $r_1$ $\Rightarrow r_1$ | // $r_1 \leftarrow a \times 2$ |
| 5 | 7 | loadAI | $r_{arp}$, @b $\Rightarrow r_2$ | // load 'b' |
| 8 | 9 | mult | $r_1$, $r_2$ $\Rightarrow r_1$ | // $r_1 \leftarrow (a \times 2) \times b$ |
| 10 | 12 | loadAI | $r_{arp}$, @c $\Rightarrow r_2$ | // load 'c' |
| 13 | 14 | mult | $r_1$, $r_2$ $\Rightarrow r_1$ | // $r_1 \leftarrow (a \times 2 \times b) \times c$ |
| 15 | 17 | loadAI | $r_{arp}$, @d $\Rightarrow r_2$ | // load 'd' |
| 18 | 19 | mult | $r_1$, $r_2$ $\Rightarrow r_1$ | // $r_1 \leftarrow (a \times 2 \times b \times c) \times d$ |
| 20 | 22 | storeAI | $r_1$ $\Rightarrow r_{arp}$, @a | // write $r_a$ back to 'a' |

This nine-operation sequence takes 22 cycles to execute. Minimizing register use did not lead to rapid execution.

Many processors have a property by which they can initiate new operations while a long-latency operation executes. As long as the results of a long-latency operation are not referenced until the operation completes, execution proceeds normally. If, however, some intervening operation tries to read the result of the long-latency operation prematurely, the processor delays the operation that needs the value until the long-latency operation completes. An operation cannot begin to execute until its operands are ready, and its results are not ready until the operation terminates.

The instruction scheduler reorders the operations in the code. It attempts to minimize the number of cycles wasted waiting for operands. Of course, the scheduler must ensure that the new sequence produces the same result as the original. In many cases, the scheduler can drastically improve the performance of "naive" code. For our example, a good scheduler might produce the following sequence:

| Start | End | | | |
|-------|-----|--|--|--|
| 1 | 3 | loadAI | $r_{arp}$, @a $\Rightarrow r_1$ | // load 'a' |
| 2 | 4 | loadAI | $r_{arp}$, @b $\Rightarrow r_2$ | // load 'b' |
| 3 | 5 | loadAI | $r_{arp}$, @c $\Rightarrow r_3$ | // load 'c' |
| 4 | 4 | add | $r_1$, $r_1$ $\Rightarrow r_1$ | // $r_1 \leftarrow a \times 2$ |
| 5 | 6 | mult | $r_1$, $r_2$ $\Rightarrow r_1$ | // $r_1 \leftarrow (a \times 2) \times b$ |
| 6 | 8 | loadAI | $r_{arp}$, @d $\Rightarrow r_2$ | // load 'd' |
| 7 | 8 | mult | $r_1$, $r_3$ $\Rightarrow r_1$ | // $r_1 \leftarrow (a \times 2 \times b) \times c$ |
| 9 | 10 | mult | $r_1$, $r_2$ $\Rightarrow r_1$ | // $r_1 \leftarrow (a \times 2 \times b \times c) \times d$ |
| 11 | 13 | storeAI | $r_1$ $\Rightarrow r_{arp}$, @a | // write $r_a$ back to 'a' |

**COMPILER CONSTRUCTION IS ENGINEERING**

A typical compiler has a series of passes that, together, translate code from some source language into some target language. Along the way, the compiler uses dozens of algorithms and data structures. The compiler writer must select, for each step in the process, an appropriate solution.

A successful compiler executes an unimaginable number of times. Consider the total number of times that GCC compiler has run. Over GCC's lifetime, even small inefficiencies add up to a significant amount of time. The savings from good design and implementation accumulate over time. Thus, the compiler writer must pay attention to compile time costs, such as the asymptotic complexity of algorithms, the actual running time of the implementation, and the space used by data structures. The compiler writer should have in mind a budget for how much time the compiler will spend on its various tasks.

For example, scanning and parsing are two problems for which efficient algorithms abound. Scanners recognize and classify words in time proportional to the number of characters in the input program. For a typical programming language, a parser can build derivations in time proportional to the length of the derivation. (The restricted structure of programming languages makes efficient parsing possible.) Because efficient and effective techniques exist for scanning and parsing, the compiler writer should expect to spend just a small fraction of compile time on these tasks.

By contrast, optimization and code generation contain several problems that require more time. Many of the algorithms that we will examine for program analysis and optimization will have complexities greater than $O(n)$. Thus, algorithm choice in the optimizer and code generator has a larger impact on compile time than it does in the compiler's front end. The compiler writer may need to trade precision of analysis and effectiveness of optimization against increases in compile time. He or she should make such decisions consciously and carefully.

This version of the code requires just 13 cycles to execute. The code uses one more register than the minimal number. It starts an operation in every cycle except 8, 10, and 12. Other equivalent schedules are possible, as are equal-length schedules that use more registers. Chapter 12 presents several scheduling techniques that are in widespread use.

### Interactions Among Code-Generation Components

Most of the truly hard problems that occur in compilation arise during code generation. To make matters more complex, these problems interact. For example, instruction scheduling moves `load` operations away from the arithmetic operations that depend on them. This can increase the period over which the values are needed and, correspondingly, increase the number of registers needed during that period. Similarly, the assignment of particular values to specific registers can constrain instruction scheduling by creating a "false" dependence between two operations. (The second operation cannot be scheduled until the first completes, even though the values in the common register are independent. Renaming the values can eliminate this false dependence, at the cost of using more registers.)

## 1.4 SUMMARY AND PERSPECTIVE

Compiler construction is a complex task. A good compiler combines ideas from formal language theory, from the study of algorithms, from artificial intelligence, from systems design, from computer architecture, and from the theory of programming languages and applies them to the problem of translating a program. A compiler brings together greedy algorithms, heuristic techniques, graph algorithms, dynamic programming, DFAS and NFAS, fixed-point algorithms, synchronization and locality, allocation and naming, and pipeline management. Many of the problems that confront the compiler are too hard for it to solve optimally; thus, compilers use approximations, heuristics, and rules of thumb. This produces complex interactions that can lead to surprising results—both good and bad.

To place this activity in an orderly framework, most compilers are organized into three major phases: a front end, an optimizer, and a back end. Each phase has a different set of problems to tackle, and the approaches used to solve those problems differ, too. The front end focuses on translating source code into some IR. Front ends rely on results from formal language theory and type theory, with a healthy dose of algorithms and data structures. The middle section, or optimizer, translates one IR program into another, with the goal of producing an IR program that executes efficiently. Optimizers analyze programs to derive knowledge about their runtime behavior and then use that knowledge to transform the code and improve its behavior. The back end maps an IR program to the instruction set of a specific processor. A back end approximates the answers to hard problems in allocation and scheduling, and the quality of its approximation has a direct impact on the speed and size of the compiled code.

This book explores each of these phases. Chapters 2 through 4 deal with the algorithms used in a compiler's front end. Chapters 5 through 7 describe background material for the discussion of optimization and code generation. Chapter 8 provides an introduction to code optimization. Chapters 9 and 10 provide more detailed treatment of analysis and optimization for the interested reader. Finally, Chapters 11 through 13 cover the techniques used by back ends for instruction selection, scheduling, and register allocation.

## ■ CHAPTER NOTES

The first compilers appeared in the 1950s. These early systems showed surprising sophistication. The original FORTRAN compiler was a multipass system that included a distinct scanner, parser, and register allocator, along with some optimizations [26, 27]. The Alpha system, built by Ershov and his colleagues, performed local optimization [139] and used graph coloring to reduce the amount of memory needed for data items [140, 141].

Knuth provides some interesting recollections of compiler construction in the early 1960s [227]. Randell and Russell describe early implementation efforts for Algol 60 [293]. Allen describes the history of compiler development inside IBM with an emphasis on the interplay of theory and practice [14].

Many influential compilers were built in the 1960s and 1970s. These include the classic optimizing compiler FORTRAN H [252, 307], the Bliss-11 and Bliss-32 compilers [72, 356], and the portable BCPL compiler [300]. These compilers produced high-quality code for a variety of CISC machines. Compilers for students, on the other hand, focused on rapid compilation, good diagnostic messages, and error correction [97, 146].

The advent of RISC architecture in the 1980s led to another generation of compilers; these focused on strong optimization and code generation [24, 81, 89, 204]. These compilers featured full-blown optimizers structured as shown in Figure 1.1. Modern RISC compilers still follow this model.

During the 1990s, compiler-construction research focused on reacting to the rapid changes taking place in microprocessor architecture. The decade began with Intel's $i860$ processor challenging compiler writers to manage pipelines and memory latencies directly. At its end, compilers confronted challenges that ranged from multiple functional units to long memory latencies to parallel code generation. The structure and organization of 1980s RISC compilers proved flexible enough for these new challenges, so researchers built new passes to insert into the optimizers and code generators of their compilers.

While Java systems use a mix of compilation and interpretation [63, 279], Java is not the first language to employ such a mix. Lisp systems have long included both native-code compilers and virtual-machine implementation schemes [266, 324]. The Smalltalk-80 system used a bytecode distribution and a virtual machine [233]; several implementations added just-in-time compilers [126].

## ■ EXERCISES

1. Consider a simple Web browser that takes as input a textual string in HTML format and displays the specified graphics on the screen. Is the display process one of compilation or interpretation?

2. In designing a compiler, you will face many tradeoffs. What are the five qualities that you, as a user, consider most important in a compiler that you purchase? Does that list change when you are the compiler writer? What does your list tell you about a compiler that you would implement?

3. Compilers are used in many different circumstances. What differences might you expect in compilers designed for the following applications?
   a. A just-in-time compiler used to translate user interface code downloaded over a network
   b. A compiler that targets the embedded processor used in a cellular telephone
   c. A compiler used in an introductory programming course at a high school
   d. A compiler used to build wind-tunnel simulations that run on a massively parallel processor (where all processors are identical)
   e. A compiler that targets numerically intensive programs to a large number of diverse machines

*Chapter* **2**

# Scanners

## ■ CHAPTER OVERVIEW

The scanner's task is to transform a stream of characters into a stream of words in the input language. Each word must be classified into a syntactic category, or "part of speech." The scanner is the only pass in the compiler to touch every character in the input program. Compiler writers place a premium on speed in scanning, in part because the scanner's input is larger, in some measure, than that of any other pass, and, in part, because highly efficient techniques are easy to understand and to implement.

This chapter introduces regular expressions, a notation used to describe the valid words in a programming language. It develops the formal mechanisms to generate scanners from regular expressions, either manually or automatically.

**Keywords:** Scanner, Finite Automaton, Regular Expression, Fixed Point

## 2.1 INTRODUCTION

Scanning is the first stage of a three-part process that the compiler uses to understand the input program. The scanner, or lexical analyzer, reads a stream of characters and produces a stream of words. It aggregates characters to form words and applies a set of rules to determine whether or not each word is legal in the source language. If the word is valid, the scanner assigns it a syntactic category, or part of speech.

The scanner is the only pass in the compiler that manipulates every character of the input program. Because scanners perform a relatively simple task, grouping characters together to form words and punctuation in the source language, they lend themselves to fast implementations. Automatic tools for scanner generation are common. These tools process a mathematical description of the language's lexical syntax and produce a fast recognizer. Alternatively, many compilers use hand-crafted scanners; because the task is simple, such scanners can be fast and robust.

### Conceptual Roadmap

This chapter describes the mathematical tools and programming techniques that are commonly used to construct scanners—both generated scanners and hand-crafted scanners. The chapter begins, in Section 2.2, by introducing a model for *recognizers*, programs that identify words in a stream of characters. Section 2.3 describes *regular expressions*, a formal notation for specifying syntax. In Section 2.4, we show a set of constructions to convert a regular expression into a recognizer. Finally, in Section 2.5 we present three different ways to implement a scanner: a table-driven scanner, a direct-coded scanner, and a hand-coded approach.

**Recognizer**
a program that identifies specific words in a stream of characters

Both generated and hand-crafted scanners rely on the same underlying techniques. While most textbooks and courses advocate the use of generated scanners, most commercial compilers and open-source compilers use hand-crafted scanners. A hand-crafted scanner can be faster than a generated scanner because the implementation can optimize away a portion of the overhead that cannot be avoided in a generated scanner. Because scanners are simple and they change infrequently, many compiler writers deem that the performance gain from a hand-crafted scanner outweighs the convenience of automated scanner generation. We will explore both alternatives.

### Overview

A compiler's scanner reads an input stream that consists of characters and produces an output stream that contains words, each labelled with its *syntactic category*—equivalent to a word's part of speech in English. To accomplish this aggregation and classification, the scanner applies a set of rules that describe the lexical structure of the input programming language, sometimes called its *microsyntax*. The microsyntax of a programming language specifies how to group characters into words and, conversely, how to separate words that run together. (In the context of scanning, we consider punctuation marks and other symbols as words.)

**Syntactic category**
a classification of words according to their grammatical usage

**Microsyntax**
the lexical structure of a language

Western languages, such as English, have simple microsyntax. Adjacent alphabetic letters are grouped together, left to right, to form a word. A blank space terminates a word, as do most nonalphabetic symbols. (The word-building algorithm can treat a hyphen in the midst of a word as if it were an alphabetic character.) Once a group of characters has been aggregated together to form a potential word, the word-building algorithm can determine its validity with a dictionary lookup.

Most programming languages have equally simple microsyntax. Characters are aggregated into words. In most languages, blanks and punctuation marks terminate a word. For example, Algol and its descendants define an *identifier* as a single alphabetic character followed by zero or more alphanumeric characters. The identifier ends with the first nonalphanumeric character. Thus, fee and f1e are valid identifiers, but 12fum is not. Notice that the set of valid words is specified by rules rather than by enumeration in a dictionary.

In a typical programming language, some words, called *keywords* or *reserved words*, match the rule for an identifier but have special meanings. Both while and static are keywords in both C and Java. Keywords (and punctuation marks) form their own syntactic categories. Even though static matches the rule for an identifier, the scanner in a C or Java compiler would undoubtedly classify it into a category that has only one element, the keyword static. To recognize keywords, the scanner can either use dictionary lookup or encode the keywords directly into its microsyntax rules.

**Keyword**
a word that is reserved for a particular syntactic purpose and, thus, cannot be used as an identifier

The simple lexical structure of programming languages lends itself to efficient scanners. The compiler writer starts from a specification of the language's microsyntax. She either encodes the microsyntax into a notation accepted by a scanner generator, which then constructs an executable scanner, or she uses that specification to build a hand-crafted scanner. Both generated and hand-crafted scanners can be implemented to require just $O(1)$ time per character, so they run in time proportional to the number of characters in the input stream.

## 2.2 RECOGNIZING WORDS

The simplest explanation of an algorithm to recognize words is often a character-by-character formulation. The structure of the code can provide some insight into the underlying problem. Consider the problem of recognizing the keyword new. Assuming the presence of a routine *NextChar* that returns the next character, the code might look like the fragment shown in Figure 2.1. The code tests for n followed by e followed by w. At each step, failure to match the appropriate character causes the code to reject the string and "try something else." If the sole purpose of the program was to recognize the word new, then it should print an error message or return failure. Because scanners rarely recognize only one word, we will leave this "error path" deliberately vague at this point.

The code fragment performs one test per character. We can represent the code fragment using the simple transition diagram shown to the right of the code. The transition diagram represents a recognizer. Each circle represents an abstract state in the computation. Each state is labelled for convenience.

```
c ← NextChar();
if (c = 'n')
    then begin;
        c ← NextChar();
        if (c = 'e')
            then begin;
                c ← NextChar();
                if (c = 'w')
                    then report success;
                    else try something else;
            end;
            else try something else;
    end;
    else try something else;
```

■ **FIGURE 2.1** Code Fragment to Recognize "new".

The initial state, or start state, is $s_0$. We will always label the start state as $s_0$. State $s_3$ is an accepting state; the recognizer reaches $s_3$ only when the input is new. Accepting states are drawn with double circles, as shown in the margin. The arrows represent transitions from state to state based on the input character. If the recognizer starts in $s_0$ and reads the characters n, e, and w, the transitions take us to $s_3$. What happens on any other input, such as n, o, and t? The n takes the recognizer to $s_1$. The o does not match the edge leaving $s_1$, so the input word is not new. In the code, cases that do not match new *try something else*. In the recognizer, we can think of this action as a transition to an error state. When we draw the transition diagram of a recognizer, we usually omit transitions to the error state. Each state has a transition to the error state on each unspecified input.

Using this same approach to build a recognizer for while would produce the following transition diagram:

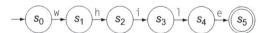

If it starts in $s_0$ and reaches $s_5$, it has identified the word while. The corresponding code fragment would involve five nested if-then-else constructs.

To recognize multiple words, we can create multiple edges that leave a given state. (In the code, we would begin to elaborate the *do something else* paths.)

One recognizer for both new and not might be

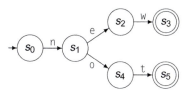

The recognizer uses a common test for n that takes it from $s_0$ to $s_1$, denoted $s_0 \xrightarrow{n} s_1$. If the next character is e, it takes the transition $s_1 \xrightarrow{e} s_2$. If, instead, the next character is o, it makes the move $s_1 \xrightarrow{o} s_4$. Finally, a w in $s_2$, causes the transition $s_2 \xrightarrow{w} s_3$, while a t in $s_4$ produces $s_4 \xrightarrow{t} s_5$. State $s_3$ indicates that the input was new while $s_5$ indicates that it was not. The recognizer takes one transition per input character.

We can combine the recognizer for new or not with the one for while by merging their initial states and relabeling all the states.

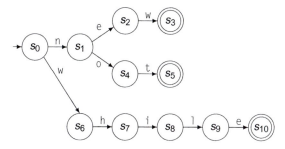

State $s_0$ has transitions for n and w. The recognizer has three accepting states, $s_3$, $s_5$, and $s_{10}$. If any state encounters an input character that does not match one of its transitions, the recognizer moves to an error state.

## 2.2.1 **A Formalism for Recognizers**

Transition diagrams serve as abstractions of the code that would be required to implement them. They can also be viewed as formal mathematical objects, called *finite automata*, that specify recognizers. Formally, a finite automaton (FA) is a five-tuple $(S, \Sigma, \delta, s_0, S_A)$, where

- $S$ is the finite set of states in the recognizer, along with an error state $s_e$.
- $\Sigma$ is the finite alphabet used by the recognizer. Typically, $\Sigma$ is the union of the edge labels in the transition diagram.

**Finite automaton**

a formalism for recognizers that has a finite set of states, an alphabet, a transition function, a start state, and one or more accepting states

- $\delta(s,c)$ is the recognizer's transition function. It maps each state $s \in S$ and each character $c \in \Sigma$ into some next state. In state $s_i$ with input character $c$, the FA takes the transition $s_i \xrightarrow{c} \delta(s_i,c)$.
- $s_0 \in S$ is the designated start state.
- $S_A$ is the set of accepting states, $S_A \subseteq S$. Each state in $S_A$ appears as a double circle in the transition diagram.

As an example, we can cast the FA for *new* or *not* or *while* in the formalism as follows:

$$S = \{s_0, s_1, s_2, s_3, s_4, s_5, s_6, s_7, s_8, s_9, s_{10}, s_e\}$$

$$\Sigma = \{e, h, i, l, n, o, t, w\}$$

$$\delta = \begin{cases} s_0 \xrightarrow{n} s_1, & s_0 \xrightarrow{w} s_6, & s_1 \xrightarrow{e} s_2, & s_1 \xrightarrow{o} s_4, & s_2 \xrightarrow{w} s_3, \\ s_4 \xrightarrow{t} s_5, & s_6 \xrightarrow{h} s_7, & s_7 \xrightarrow{i} s_8, & s_8 \xrightarrow{l} s_9, & s_9 \xrightarrow{e} s_{10} \end{cases}$$

$$s_0 = s_0$$

$$S_A = \{s_3, s_5, s_{10}\}$$

For all other combinations of state $s_i$ and input character $c$, we define $\delta(s_i, c) = s_e$, where $s_e$ is the designated error state. This quintuple is equivalent to the transition diagram; given one, we can easily re-create the other. The transition diagram is a picture of the corresponding FA.

An FA accepts a string $x$ if and only if, starting in $s_0$, the sequence of characters in the string takes the FA through a series of transitions that leaves it in an accepting state when the entire string has been consumed. This corresponds to our intuition for the transition diagram. For the string new, our example recognizer runs through the transitions $s_0 \xrightarrow{n} s_1$, $s_1 \xrightarrow{e} s_2$, and $s_2 \xrightarrow{w} s_3$. Since $s_3 \in S_A$, and no input remains, the FA accepts new. For the input string nut, the behavior is different. On n, the FA takes $s_0 \xrightarrow{n} s_1$. On u, it takes $s_1 \xrightarrow{u} s_e$. Once the FA enters $s_e$, it stays in $s_e$ until it exhausts the input stream.

More formally, if the string $x$ is composed of characters $x_1\ x_2\ x_3 \ldots x_n$, then the FA $(S, \Sigma, \delta, s_0, S_A)$ accepts $x$ if and only if

$$\delta(\delta(\ldots \delta(\delta(\delta(s_0, x_1), x_2), x_3) \ldots, x_{n-1}), x_n) \in S_A.$$

Intuitively, this definition corresponds to a repeated application of $\delta$ to a pair composed of some state $s \in S$ and an input symbol $x_i$. The base case, $\delta(s_0, x_1)$, represents the FA's initial transition, out of the start state, $s_0$, on the character $x_1$. The state produced by $\delta(s_0, x_1)$ is then used as input, along with $x_2$, to $\delta$ to produce the next state, and so on, until all the input has been consumed. The result of the final application of $\delta$ is, again, a state. If that state is an accepting state, then the FA accepts $x_1\,x_2\,x_3\ldots x_n$.

Two other cases are possible. The FA might encounter an error while processing the string—that is, some character $x_j$ might take it into the error state $s_e$. This condition indicates a lexical error; the string $x_1\,x_2\,x_3\ldots x_j$ is not a valid prefix for any word in the language accepted by the FA. The FA can also discover an error by exhausting its input and terminating in a nonaccepting state other than $s_e$. In this case, the input string is a proper prefix of some word accepted by the FA. Again, this indicates an error. Either kind of error should be reported to the end user.

In any case, notice that the FA takes one transition for each input character. Assuming that we can implement the FA efficiently, we should expect the recognizer to run in time proportional to the length of the input string.

### 2.2.2 **Recognizing More Complex Words**

The character-by-character model shown in the original recognizer for `not` extends easily to handle arbitrary collections of fully specified words. How could we recognize a number with such a recognizer? A specific number, such as 113.4, is easy.

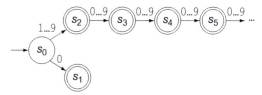

To be useful, however, we need a transition diagram (and the corresponding code fragment) that can recognize any number. For simplicity's sake, let's limit the discussion to unsigned integers. In general, an integer is either zero, or it is a series of one or more digits where the first digit is from one to nine, and the subsequent digits are from zero to nine. (This definition rules out leading zeros.) How would we draw a transition diagram for this definition?

The transition $s_0 \xrightarrow{0} s_1$ handles the case for zero. The other path, from $s_0$ to $s_2$, to $s_3$, and so on, handles the case for an integer greater than zero. This path, however, presents several problems. First, it does not end, violating the stipulation that $S$ is finite. Second, all of the states on the path beginning with $s_2$ are equivalent, that is, they have the same labels on their output transitions and they are all accepting states.

```
char ← NextChar( );
state ← s0 ;

while (char ≠ eof and state ≠ se) do
    state ← δ(state,char);
    char ← NextChar( );
end;

if (state ∈ SA)
    then report acceptance;
    else report failure;
```

$S = \{s_0, s_1, s_2, s_e\}$

$\Sigma = \{0, 1, 2, 3, 4, 5, 6, 7, 8, 9\}$

$$\delta = \begin{Bmatrix} s_0 \xrightarrow{0} s_1, & s_0 \xrightarrow{1\text{-}9} s_2 \\ s_2 \xrightarrow{0\text{-}9} s_2, & s_1 \xrightarrow{0\text{-}9} s_e \end{Bmatrix}$$

$S_A = \{s_1, s_2\}$

■ **FIGURE 2.2** A Recognizer for Unsigned Integers.

This FA recognizes a class of strings with a common property: they are all unsigned integers. It raises the distinction between the class of strings and the text of any particular string. The class "unsigned integer" is a syntactic category, or part of speech. The text of a specific unsigned integer, such as 113, is its *lexeme*.

**Lexeme**
the actual text for a word recognized by an FA

We can simplify the FA significantly if we allow the transition diagram to have cycles. We can replace the entire chain of states beginning at $s_2$ with a single transition from $s_2$ back to itself:

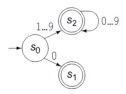

This cyclic transition diagram makes sense as an FA. From an implementation perspective, however, it is more complex than the acyclic transition diagrams shown earlier. We cannot translate this directly into a set of nested `if-then-else` constructs. The introduction of a cycle in the transition graph creates the need for cyclic control flow. We can implement this with a `while` loop, as shown in Figure 2.2. We can specify δ efficiently using a table:

| δ | 0 | 1 | 2 | 3 | 4 | 5 | 6 | 7 | 8 | 9 | Other |
|---|---|---|---|---|---|---|---|---|---|---|-------|
| $s_0$ | $s_1$ | $s_2$ | $s_2$ | $s_2$ | $s_2$ | $s_2$ | $s_2$ | $s_2$ | $s_2$ | $s_2$ | $s_e$ |
| $s_1$ | $s_e$ | $s_e$ | $s_e$ | $s_e$ | $s_e$ | $s_e$ | $s_e$ | $s_e$ | $s_e$ | $s_e$ | $s_e$ |
| $s_2$ | $s_2$ | $s_2$ | $s_2$ | $s_2$ | $s_2$ | $s_2$ | $s_2$ | $s_2$ | $s_2$ | $s_2$ | $s_e$ |
| $s_e$ | $s_e$ | $s_e$ | $s_e$ | $s_e$ | $s_e$ | $s_e$ | $s_e$ | $s_e$ | $s_e$ | $s_e$ | $s_e$ |

Changing the table allows the same basic code skeleton to implement other recognizers. Notice that this table has ample opportunity for compression.

The columns for the digits 1 through 9 are identical, so they could be represented once. This leaves a table with three columns: 0, 1 . . . 9, and *other*. Close examination of the code skeleton shows that it reports failure as soon as it enters $s_e$, so it never references that row of the table. The implementation can elide the entire row, leaving a table with just three rows and three columns.

We can develop similar FAS for signed integers, real numbers, and complex numbers. A simplified version of the rule that governs identifier names in Algol-like languages, such as C or Java, might be: *an identifier consists of an alphabetic character followed by zero or more alphanumeric characters.* This definition allows an infinite set of identifiers, but can be specified with the simple two-state FA shown to the left. Many programming languages extend the notion of "alphabetic character" to include designated special characters, such as the underscore.

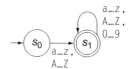

FAS can be viewed as specifications for a recognizer. However, they are not particularly concise specifications. To simplify scanner implementation, we need a concise notation for specifying the lexical structure of words, and a way of turning those specifications into an FA and into code that implements the FA. The remaining sections of this chapter develop precisely those ideas.

---

**SECTION REVIEW**

A character-by-character approach to scanning leads to algorithmic clarity. We can represent character-by-character scanners with a transition diagram; that diagram, in turn, corresponds to a finite automaton. Small sets of words are easily encoded in acyclic transition diagrams. Infinite sets, such as the set of integers or the set of identifiers in an Algol-like language, require cyclic transition diagrams.

---

**Review Questions**

Construct an FA to accept each of the following languages:

1. A six-character identifier consisting of an alphabetic character followed by zero to five alphanumeric characters
2. A string of one or more pairs, where each pair consists of an open parenthesis followed by a close parenthesis
3. A Pascal comment, which consists of an open brace, {, followed by zero or more characters drawn from an alphabet, $\Sigma$, followed by a close brace, }

## 2.3  REGULAR EXPRESSIONS

The set of words accepted by a finite automaton, $\mathcal{F}$, forms a language, denoted $L(\mathcal{F})$. The transition diagram of the FA specifies, in precise detail, that language. It is not, however, a specification that humans find intuitive. For any FA, we can also describe its language using a notation called a *regular expression* (RE). The language described by an RE is called a *regular language*.

Regular expressions are equivalent to the FAs described in the previous section. (We will prove this with a construction in Section 2.4.) Simple recognizers have simple RE specifications.

- The language consisting of the single word new can be described by an RE written as *new*. Writing two characters next to each other implies that they are expected to appear in that order.
- The language consisting of the two words new or while can be written as *new* or *while*. To avoid possible misinterpretation of *or*, we write this using the symbol | to mean *or*. Thus, we write the RE as *new* | *while*.
- The language consisting of new or not can be written as *new* | *not*. Other RES are possible, such as *n(ew* | *ot)*. Both RES specify the same pair of words. The RE *n(ew* | *ot)* suggests the structure of the FA that we drew earlier for these two words.

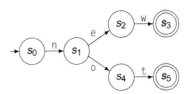

To make this discussion concrete, consider some examples that occur in most programming languages. Punctuation marks, such as colons, semicolons, commas, and various brackets, can be represented by their character representations. Their RES have the same "spelling" as the punctuation marks themselves. Thus, the following RES might occur in the lexical specification for a programming language:

$$: \quad ; \quad ? \quad => \quad ( \quad ) \quad \{ \quad \} \quad [ \quad ]$$

Similarly, keywords have simple RES.

$$if \quad while \quad this \quad integer \quad instanceof$$

To model more complex constructs, such as integers or identifiers, we need a notation that can capture the essence of the cyclic edge in an FA.

The FA for an unsigned integer, shown at the left, has three states: an initial state $s_0$, an accepting state $s_1$ for the unique integer zero, and another accepting state $s_2$ for all other integers. The key to this FA's power is the transition from $s_2$ back to itself that occurs on each additional digit. State $s_2$ folds the specification back on itself, creating a rule to derive a new unsigned integer from an existing one: add another digit to the right end of the existing number. Another way of stating this rule is: *an unsigned integer is either a zero, or a nonzero digit followed by zero or more digits.* To capture the essence of this FA, we need a notation for this notion of "zero or more occurrences" of an RE. For the RE $x$, we write this as $x^*$, with the meaning "zero or more occurrences of $x$." We call the * operator *Kleene closure*, or *closure* for short. Using the closure operator, we can write an RE for this FA:

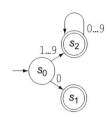

$$0 \mid (1 \mid 2 \mid 3 \mid 4 \mid 5 \mid 6 \mid 7 \mid 8 \mid 9) \ (0 \mid 1 \mid 2 \mid 3 \mid 4 \mid 5 \mid 6 \mid 7 \mid 8 \mid 9)^*.$$

### 2.3.1 **Formalizing the Notation**

To work with regular expressions in a rigorous way, we must define them more formally. An RE describes a set of strings over the characters contained in some alphabet, $\Sigma$, augmented with a character $\epsilon$ that represents the empty string. We call the set of strings a *language*. For a given RE, $r$, we denote the language that it specifies as $L(r)$. An RE is built up from three basic operations:

1. *Alternation* The alternation, or union, of two sets of strings, $R$ and $S$, denoted $R \mid S$, is $\{x \mid x \in R \text{ or } x \in S\}$.
2. *Concatenation* The concatenation oftwo sets $R$ and $S$, denoted $RS$, contains all strings formed by prepending an element of $R$ onto one from $S$, or $\{xy \mid x \in R \text{ and } y \in S\}$.
3. *Closure* The Kleene closure of a set $R$, denoted $R^*$, is $\bigcup_{i=0}^{\infty} R^i$. This is just the union of the concatenations of $R$ with itself, zero or more times.

For convenience, we sometimes use a notation for *finite closure*. The notation $R^i$ denotes from one to $i$ occurrences of $R$. A finite closure can be always be replaced with an enumeration of the possibilities; for example, $R^3$ is just $(R \mid RR \mid RRR)$. The *positive closure*, denoted $R^+$, is just $RR^*$ and consists of one or more occurrences of $R$. Since all these closures can be rewritten with the three basic operations, we ignore them in the discussion that follows.

**Finite closure**

For any integer $i$, the RE $R^i$ designates one to $i$ occurrences of $R$.

**Positive closure**

The RE $R^+$ denotes one or more occurrences of $R$, often written as $\bigcup_{i=1}^{\infty} R^i$.

Using the three basic operations, alternation, concatenation, and Kleene closure, we can define the set of REs over an alphabet $\Sigma$ as follows:

1. If $a \in \Sigma$, then $a$ is also an RE denoting the set containing only $a$.
2. If $r$ and $s$ are REs, denoting sets $L(r)$ and $L(s)$, respectively, then

**REGULAR EXPRESSIONS IN VIRTUAL LIFE**

Regular expressions are used in many applications to specify patterns in character strings. Some of the early work on translating REs into code was done to provide a flexible way of specifying strings in the "find" command of a text editor. From that early genesis, the notation has crept into many different applications.

Unix and other operating systems use the asterisk as a wildcard to match substrings against file names. Here, ∗ is a shorthand for the RE Σ*, specifying zero or more characters drawn from the entire alphabet of legal characters. (Since few keyboards have a Σ key, the shorthand has stayed with us.) Many systems use **?** as a wildcard that matches a single character.

The grep family of tools, and their kin in non-Unix systems, implement regular expression pattern matching. (In fact, grep is an acronym for global regular-expression pattern match and print.)

Regular expressions have found widespread use because they are easily written and easily understood. They are one of the techniques of choice when a program must recognize a fixed vocabulary. They work well for languages that fit within their limited rules. They are easily translated into an executable form, and the resulting recognizer is fast.

$r \mid s$ is an RE denoting the union, or alternation, of $L(r)$ and $L(s)$,

$rs$ is an RE denoting the concatenation of $L(r)$ and $L(s)$, respectively, and

$r^*$ is an RE denoting the Kleene closure of $L(r)$.

**3.** $\epsilon$ is an RE denoting the set containing only the empty string.

To eliminate any ambiguity, parentheses have highest precedence, followed by closure, concatenation, and alternation, in that order.

As a convenient shorthand, we will specify ranges of characters with the first and the last element connected by an ellipsis, "...". To make this abbreviation stand out, we surround it with a pair of square brackets. Thus, $[0 \ldots 9]$ represents the set of decimal digits. It can always be rewritten as $(0 \mid 1 \mid 2 \mid 3 \mid 4 \mid 5 \mid 6 \mid 7 \mid 8 \mid 9)$.

### 2.3.2 Examples

The goal of this chapter is to show how we can use formal techniques to automate the construction of high-quality scanners and how we can encode the microsyntax of programming languages into that formalism. Before proceeding further, some examples from real programming languages are in order.

1. The simplified rule given earlier for identifiers in Algol-like languages, an alphabetic character followed by zero or more alphanumeric characters, is just $([A...Z] | [a...z]) ([A...Z] | [a...z] | [0...9])^*$. Most languages also allow a few special characters, such as the underscore (_), the percent sign (%), or the ampersand (&), in identifiers.

   If the language limits the maximum length of an identifier, we can use the appropriate finite closure. Thus, identifiers limited to six characters might be specified as $([A...Z] | [a...z]) ([A...Z] | [a...z] | [0...9])^5$. If we had to write out the full expansion of the finite closure, the RE would be much longer.

2. An unsigned integer can be described as either zero or a nonzero digit followed by zero or more digits. The RE $0 | [1...9] [0...9]^*$ is more concise. In practice, many implementations admit a larger class of strings as integers, accepting the language $[0...9]^+$.

3. Unsigned real numbers are more complex than integers. One possible RE might be $(0 | [1...9] [0...9]^*) (\epsilon | . [0...9]^*)$ The first part is just the RE for an integer. The rest generates either the empty string or a decimal point followed by zero or more digits.

   Programming languages often extend real numbers to scientific notation, as in $(0 | [1...9] [0...9]^*) (\epsilon | . [0...9]^*) E (\epsilon | + | -)$
   $(0 | [1...9] [0...9]^*)$.

   This RE describes a real number, followed by an E, followed by an integer to specify the exponent.

4. Quoted character strings have their own complexity. In most languages, any character can appear inside a string. While we can write an RE for strings using only the basic operators, it is our first example where a complement operator simplifies the RE. Using complement, a character string in C or Java can be described as " $(\char`\^")^*$ ".

   C and C++ do not allow a string to span multiple lines in the source code—that is, if the scanner reaches the end of a line while inside a string, it terminates the string and issues an error message. If we represent newline with the escape sequence \n, in the C style, then the RE " $(\char`\^(" | \backslash n))^*$ " will recognize a correctly formed string and will take an error transition on a string that includes a newline.

5. Comments appear in a number of forms. C++ and Java offer the programmer two ways of writing a comment. The delimiter // indicates a comment that runs to the end of the current input line. The RE for this style of comment is straightforward: $// (\char`\^\backslash n)^* \backslash n$, where \n represents the newline character.

   Multiline comments in C, C++, and Java begin with the delimiter /* and end with */. If we could disallow * in a comment, the RE would be

**Complement operator**

The notation $\char`\^ c$ specifies the set $\{\Sigma - c\}$, the complement of $c$ with respect to $\Sigma$.

Complement has higher precedence than $*$, $|$, or $+$.

**Escape sequence**

Two or more characters that the scanner translates into another character. Escape sequences are used for characters that lack a glyph, such as newline or tab, and for ones that occur in the syntax, such as an open or close quote.

simple: $/*(^*)^**/$. With $*$, the RE is more complex: $/*(^*|*^+^/)^**/$. An FA to implement this RE follows.

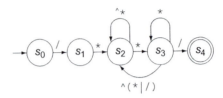

The correspondence between the RE and this FA is not as obvious as it was in the examples earlier in the chapter. Section 2.4 presents constructions that automate the construction of an FA from an RE. The complexity of the RE and FA for multiline comments arises from the use of multi-character delimiters. The transition from $s_2$ to $s_3$ encodes the fact that the recognizer has seen a $*$ so that it can handle either the appearance of a $/$ or the lack thereof in the correct manner. In contrast, Pascal uses single-character comment delimiters: { and }, so a Pascal comment is just $\{ \}^* \}$.

Trying to be specific with an RE can also lead to complex expressions. Consider, for example, that the register specifier in a typical assembly language consists of the letter $r$ followed immediately by a small integer. In ILOC, which admits an unlimited set of register names, the RE might be $r[0\ldots9]^+$, with the following FA:

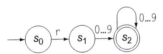

This recognizer accepts r29, and rejects s29. It also accepts r99999, even though no currently available computer has 100,000 registers.

On a real computer, however, the set of register names is severely limited— say, to 32, 64, 128, or 256 registers. One way for a scanner to check validity of a register name is to convert the digits into a number and test whether or not it falls into the range of valid register numbers. The alternative is to adopt a more precise RE specification, such as:

$$r([0\ldots2]([0\ldots9]|\epsilon)|[4\ldots9]|(3(0|1|\epsilon)))$$

This RE specifies a much smaller language, limited to register numbers 0 to 31 with an optional leading 0 on single-digit register names. It accepts r0, r00, r01, and r31, but rejects r001, r32, and r99999. The corresponding FA looks like:

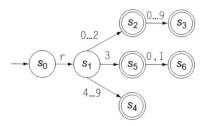

Which FA is better? They both make a single transition on each input character. Thus, they have the same cost, even though the second FA checks a more complex specification. The more complex FA has more states and transitions, so its representation requires more space. However, their operating costs are the same.

This point is critical: the cost of operating an FA is proportional to the length of the input, not to the length or complexity of the RE that generates the FA. More complex REs may produce FAS with more states that, in turn, need more space. The cost of generating an FA from an RE may also rise with increased complexity in the RE. But, the cost of FA operation remains one transition per input character.

Can we improve our description of the register specifier? The previous RE is both complex and counterintuitive. A simpler alternative might be:

r0 | r00 | r1 | r01 | r2 | r02 | r3 | r03 | r4 | r04 | r5 | r05 | r6 | r06 | r7 | r07 |
r8 | r08 | r9 | r09 | r10 | r11 | r12 | r13 | r14 | r15 | r16 | r17 | r18 | r19 | r20 |
r21 | r22 | r23 | r24 | r25 | r26 | r27 | r28 | r29 | r30 | r31

This RE is conceptually simpler, but much longer than the previous version. The resulting FA still requires one transition per input symbol. Thus, if we can control the growth in the number of states, we might prefer this version of the RE because it is clear and obvious. However, when our processor suddenly has 256 or 384 registers, enumeration may become tedious, too.

### 2.3.3 Closure Properties of REs

Regular expressions and the languages that they generate have been the subject of extensive study. They have many interesting and useful properties. Some of these properties play a critical role in the constructions that build recognizers from REs.

**Regular languages**

Any language that can be specified by a regular expression is called a *regular language*.

**PROGRAMMING LANGUAGES VERSUS NATURAL LANGUAGES**

Lexical analysis highlights one of the subtle ways in which programming languages differ from natural languages, such as English or Chinese. In natural languages, the relationship between a word's representation—its spelling or its pictogram—and its meaning is not obvious. In English, *are* is a verb while *art* is a noun, even though they differ only in the final character. Furthermore, not all combinations of characters are legitimate words. For example, *arz* differs minimally from *are* and *art*, but does not occur as a word in normal English usage.

A scanner for English could use FA-based techniques to recognize potential words, since all English words are drawn from a restricted alphabet. After that, however, it must look up the prospective word in a dictionary to determine if it is, in fact, a word. If the word has a unique part of speech, dictionary lookup will also resolve that issue. However, many English words can be classified with several parts of speech. Examples include *buoy* and *stress*; both can be either a noun or a verb. For these words, the part of speech depends on the surrounding context. In some cases, understanding the grammatical context suffices to classify the word. In other cases, it requires an understanding of meaning, for both the word and its context.

In contrast, the words in a programming language are almost always specified lexically. Thus, any string in $[1 \ldots 9][0 \ldots 9]^*$ is a positive integer. The RE $[a \ldots z]([a \ldots z] \mid [0 \ldots 9])^*$ defines a subset of the Algol identifiers; *arz*, *are* and *art* are all identifiers, with no lookup needed to establish the fact. To be sure, some identifiers may be reserved as keywords. However, these exceptions can be specified lexically, as well. No context is required.

This property results from a deliberate decision in programming language design. The choice to make spelling imply a unique part of speech simplifies scanning, simplifies parsing, and, apparently, gives up little in the expressiveness of the language. Some languages have allowed words with dual parts of speech—for example, PL/I has no reserved keywords. The fact that more recent languages abandoned the idea suggests that the complications outweighed the extra linguistic flexibility.

Regular expressions are closed under many operations—that is, if we apply the operation to an RE or a collection of REs, the result is an RE. Obvious examples are concatenation, union, and closure. The concatenation of two REs $x$ and $y$ is just $xy$. Their union is $x \mid y$. The Kleene closure of $x$ is just $x^*$. From the definition of an RE, all of these expressions are also REs.

These closure properties play a critical role in the use of REs to build scanners. Assume that we have an RE for each syntactic category in the source language, $a_0, a_1, a_2, \ldots, a_n$. Then, to construct an RE for all the valid words in the language, we can join them with alternation as $a_0 \mid a_1 \mid a_2 \mid \ldots \mid a_n$. Since REs are closed under union, the result is an RE. Anything that we can do to an RE for a single syntactic category will be equally applicable to the RE for all the valid words in the language.

Closure under union implies that any finite language is a regular language. We can construct an RE for any finite collection of words by listing them in a large alternation. Because the set of REs is closed under union, that alternation is an RE and the corresponding language is regular.

Closure under concatenation allows us to build complex REs from simpler ones by concatenating them. This property seems both obvious and unimportant. However, it lets us piece together REs in systematic ways. Closure ensures that *ab* is an RE as long as both *a* and *b* are REs. Thus, any techniques that can be applied to either *a* or *b* can be applied to *ab*; this includes constructions that automatically generate a recognizer from REs.

Regular expressions are also closed under both Kleene closure and the finite closures. This property lets us specify particular kinds of large, or even infinite, sets with finite patterns. Kleene closure lets us specify infinite sets with concise finite patterns; examples include the integers and unbounded-length identifiers. Finite closures let us specify large but finite sets with equal ease.

The next section shows a sequence of constructions that build an FA to recognize the language specified by an RE. Section 2.6 shows an algorithm that goes the other way, from an FA to an RE. Together, these constructions establish the equivalence of REs and FAS. The fact that REs are closed under alternation, concatenation, and closure is critical to these constructions.

The equivalence between REs and FAS also suggests other closure properties. For example, given a complete FA, we can construct an FA that recognizes all words *w* that are not in $L(\text{FA})$, called the complement of $L(\text{FA})$. To build this new FA for the complement, we can swap the designation of accepting and nonaccepting states in the original FA. This result suggests that REs are closed under complement. Indeed, many systems that use REs include a complement operator, such as the ^ operator in `lex`.

**Complete FA**
an FA that explicitly includes all error transitions

---

**SECTION REVIEW**

Regular expressions are a concise and powerful notation for specifying the microsyntax of programming languages. REs build on three basic operations over finite alphabets: alternation, concatenation, and Kleene closure. Other convenient operators, such as finite closures, positive closure, and complement, derive from the three basic operations. Regular expressions and finite automata are related; any RE can be realized in an FA and the language accepted by any FA can be described with RE. The next section formalizes that relationship.

---

**Review Questions**

1. Recall the RE for a six-character identifier, written using a finite closure.

$$([A\ldots Z] \mid [a\ldots z]) \, ([A\ldots Z] \mid [a\ldots z] \mid [0\ldots 9])^5$$

Rewrite it in terms of the three basic RE operations: alternation, concatenation, and closure.

2. In PL/I, the programmer can insert a quotation mark into a string by writing two quotation marks in a row. Thus, the string

```
The quotation mark, ", should be typeset in italics
```

would be written in a PL/I program as

```
"The quotation mark, "", should be typeset in italics."
```

Design an RE and an FA to recognize PL/I strings. Assume that strings begin and end with quotation marks and contain only symbols drawn from an alphabet, designated as $\Sigma$. Quotation marks are the only special case.

---

## 2.4 FROM REGULAR EXPRESSION TO SCANNER

The goal of our work with finite automata is to automate the derivation of executable scanners from a collection of REs. This section develops the constructions that transform an RE into an FA that is suitable for direct implementation and an algorithm that derives an RE for the language accepted by an FA. Figure 2.3 shows the relationship between all of these constructions.

To present these constructions, we must distinguish between *deterministic* FAS, or DFAS, and *nondeterministic* FAS, or NFAS, in Section 2.4.1. Next,

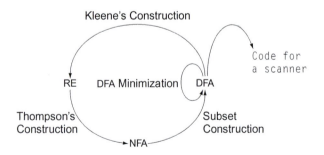

■ **FIGURE 2.3** The Cycle of Constructions.

we present the construction of a deterministic FA from an RE in three steps. Thompson's construction, in Section 2.4.2, derives an NFA from an RE. The subset construction, in Section 2.4.3, builds a DFA that simulates an NFA. Hopcroft's algorithm, in Section 2.4.4, minimizes a DFA. To establish the equivalence of REs and DFAS, we also need to show that any DFA is equivalent to an RE; Kleene's construction derives an RE from a DFA. Because it does not figure directly into scanner construction, we defer that algorithm until Section 2.6.1.

### 2.4.1 **Nondeterministic Finite Automata**

Recall from the definition of an RE that we designated the empty string, $\epsilon$, as an RE. None of the FAS that we built by hand included $\epsilon$, but some of the REs did. What role does $\epsilon$ play in an FA? We can use transitions on $\epsilon$ to combine FAS and form FAS for more complex REs. For example, assume that we have FAS for the REs $m$ and $n$, called $FA_m$ and $FA_n$, respectively.

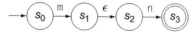

We can build an FA for $mn$ by adding a transition on $\epsilon$ from the accepting state of $FA_m$ to the initial state of $FA_n$, renumbering the states, and using $FA_n$'s accepting state as the accepting state for the new FA.

**$\epsilon$-transition**
a transition on the empty string, $\epsilon$, that does not advance the input

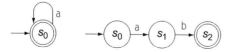

With an $\epsilon$-transition, the definition of acceptance must change slightly to allow one or more $\epsilon$-transitions between any two characters in the input string. For example, in $s_1$, the FA takes the transition $s_1 \xrightarrow{\epsilon} s_2$ without consuming any input character. This is a minor change, but it seems intuitive. Inspection shows that we can combine $s_1$ and $s_2$ to eliminate the $\epsilon$-transition.

Merging two FAS with an $\epsilon$-transition can complicate our model of how FAS work. Consider the FAS for the languages $a^*$ and $ab$.

We can combine them with an $\epsilon$-transition to form an FA for $a^*ab$.

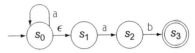

The $\epsilon$ transition, in effect, gives the FA two distinct transitions out of $s_0$ on the letter a. It can take the transition $s_0 \xrightarrow{a} s_0$, or the two transitions $s_0 \xrightarrow{\epsilon} s_1$ and $s_1 \xrightarrow{a} s_2$. Which transition is correct? Consider the strings aab and ab. The DFA should accept both strings. For aab, it should move $s_0 \xrightarrow{a} s_0$, $s_0 \xrightarrow{\epsilon} s_1$, $s_1 \xrightarrow{a} s_2$, and $s_2 \xrightarrow{b} s_3$. For ab, it should move $s_0 \xrightarrow{\epsilon} s_1$, $s_1 \xrightarrow{a} s_2$, and $s_2 \xrightarrow{b} s_3$.

**Nondeterministic FA**
an FA that allows transitions on the empty string, $\epsilon$, and states that have multiple transitions on the same character

As these two strings show, the correct transition out of $s_0$ on a depends on the characters that follow the a. At each step, an FA examines the current character. Its state encodes the left context, that is, the characters that it has already processed. Because the FA must make a transition before examining the next character, a state such as $s_0$ violates our notion of the behavior of a sequential algorithm. An FA that includes states such as $s_0$ that have multiple transitions on a single character is called a *nondeterministic finite automaton* (NFA). By contrast, an FA with unique character transitions in each state is called a *deterministic finite automaton* (DFA).

**Deterministic FA**
A DFA is an FA where the transition function is single-valued. DFAs do not allow $\epsilon$-transitions.

To make sense of an NFA, we need a set of rules that describe its behavior. Historically, two distinct models have been given for the behavior of an NFA.

1. Each time the NFA must make a nondeterministic choice, it follows the transition that leads to an accepting state for the input string, if such a transition exists. This model, using an omniscient NFA, is appealing because it maintains (on the surface) the well-defined accepting mechanism of the DFA. In essence, the NFA guesses the correct transition at each point.

2. Each time the NFA must make a nondeterministic choice, the NFA clones itself to pursue each possible transition. Thus, for a given input character, the NFA is in a specific set of states, taken across all of its clones. In this model, the NFA pursues all paths concurrently.

   At any point, we call the specific set of states in which the NFA is active its *configuration*. When the NFA reaches a configuration in which it has exhausted the input and one or more of the clones has reached an accepting state, the NFA accepts the string.

**Configuration of an NFA**
the set of concurrently active states of an NFA

In either model, the NFA $(S, \Sigma, \delta, s_0, S_A)$ accepts an input string $x_1\ x_2\ x_3 \ldots x_k$ if and only if there exists at least one path through the transition diagram that starts in $s_0$ and ends in some $s_k \in S_A$ such that the edge labels along the path match the input string. (Edges labelled with $\epsilon$ are omitted.) In other words, the $i^{th}$ edge label must be $x_i$. This definition is consistent with either model of the NFA's behavior.

### Equivalence of NFAs and DFAs

NFAS and DFAS are equivalent in their expressive power. Any DFA is a special case of an NFA. Thus, an NFA is at least as powerful as a DFA. Any NFA can be simulated by a DFA—a fact established by the subset construction in Section 2.4.3. The intuition behind this idea is simple; the construction is a little more complex.

Consider the state of an NFA when it has reached some point in the input string. Under the second model of NFA behavior, the NFA has some finite set of operating clones. The number of these configurations can be bounded; for each state, the configuration either includes one or more clones in that state or it does not. Thus, an NFA with $n$ states produces at most $|\Sigma|^n$ configurations.

To simulate the behavior of the NFA, we need a DFA with a state for each configuration of the NFA. As a result, the DFA may have exponentially more states than the NFA. While $S_{DFA}$, the set of states in the DFA, might be large, it is finite. Furthermore, the DFA still makes one transition per input symbol. Thus, the DFA that simulates the NFA still runs in time proportional to the length of the input string. The simulation of an NFA on a DFA has a potential space problem, but not a time problem.

**Powerset of $N$**
the set of all subsets of $N$, denoted $2^N$

Since NFAS and DFAS are equivalent, we can construct a DFA for $a^*ab$:

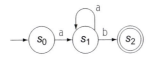

It relies on the observation that $a^*ab$ specifies the same set of words as $aa^*b$.

### 2.4.2 **Regular Expression to NFA: Thompson's Construction**

The first step in moving from an RE to an implemented scanner must derive an NFA from the RE. *Thompson's construction* accomplishes this goal in a straightforward way. It has a template for building the NFA that corresponds to a single-letter RE, and a transformation on NFAS that models the effect of each basic RE operator: concatenation, alternation, and closure. Figure 2.4

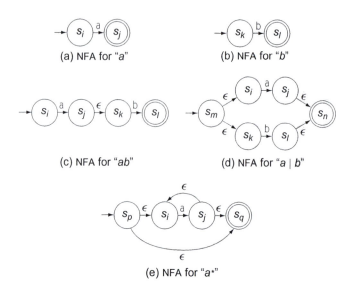

(a) NFA for "a"

(b) NFA for "b"

(c) NFA for "ab"

(d) NFA for "a | b"

(e) NFA for "a*"

■ **FIGURE 2.4**  Trivial NFAs for Regular Expression Operators.

shows the trivial NFAS for the RES $a$ and $b$, as well as the transformations to form NFAS for the RES $ab$, $a|b$, and $a^*$ from the NFAS for $a$ and $b$. The transformations apply to arbitrary NFAS.

The construction begins by building trivial NFAS for each character in the input RE. Next, it applies the transformations for alternation, concatenation, and closure to the collection of trivial NFAS in the order dictated by precedence and parentheses. For the RE $a(b|c)^*$, the construction would first build NFAS for $a$, $b$, and $c$. Because parentheses have highest precedence, it next builds the NFA for the expression enclosed in parentheses, $b|c$. Closure has higher precedence than concatenation, so it next builds the closure, $(b|c)^*$. Finally, it concatenates the NFA for $a$ to the NFA for $(b|c)^*$.

The NFAS derived from Thompson's construction have several specific properties that simplify an implementation. Each NFA has one start state and one accepting state. No transition, other than the initial transition, enters the start state. No transition leaves the accepting state. An $\epsilon$-transition always connects two states that were, earlier in the process, the start state and the accepting state of NFAS for some component RES. Finally, each state has at most two entering and two exiting $\epsilon$-moves, and at most one entering and one exiting move on a symbol in the alphabet. Together, these properties simplify the representation and manipulation of the NFAS. For example, the construction only needs to deal with a single accepting state, rather than iterating over a set of accepting states in the NFA.

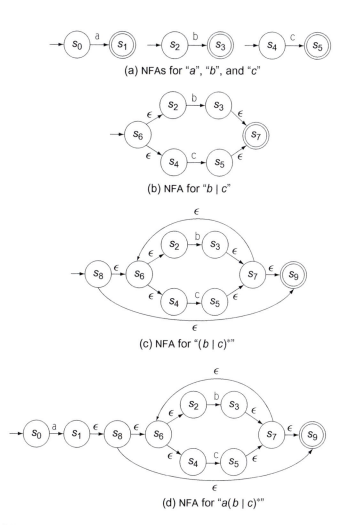

(a) NFAs for "*a*", "*b*", and "*c*"

(b) NFA for "*b | c*"

(c) NFA for "(*b | c*)*"

(d) NFA for "*a(b | c)*"

■ **FIGURE 2.5** Applying Thompson's Construction to $a(b|c)^*$.

Figure 2.5 shows the NFA that Thompson's construction builds for $a(b|c)^*$. It has many more states than the DFA that a human would likely produce, shown at left. The NFA also contains many $\epsilon$-moves that are obviously unneeded. Later stages in the construction will eliminate them.

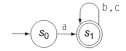

## 2.4.3 **NFA to DFA: The Subset Construction**

Thompson's construction produces an NFA to recognize the language specified by an RE. Because DFA execution is much easier to simulate than NFA execution, the next step in the cycle of constructions converts the NFA built

**REPRESENTING THE PRECEDENCE OF OPERATORS**

Thompson's construction must apply its three transformations in an order that is consistent with the precedence of the operators in the regular expression. To represent that order, an implementation of Thompson's construction can build a tree that represents the regular expression and its internal precedence. The RE $a(b|c)^*$ produces the following *tree*:

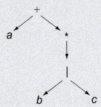

where + represents concatenation, | represents alternation, and $\star$ represents closure. The parentheses are folded into the structure of the tree and, thus, have no explicit representation.

The construction applies the individual transformations in a postorder walk over the tree. Since transformations correspond to operations, the postorder walk builds the following sequence of NFAs: $a, b, c, b|c, (b|c)^*$, and, finally, $a(b|c)^*$. Chapters 3 and 4 show how to build expression trees.

by Thompson's construction into a DFA that recognizes the same language. The resulting DFAs have a simple execution model and several efficient implementations. The algorithm that constructs a DFA from an NFA is called the *subset construction*.

The subset construction takes as input an NFA, $(N, \Sigma, \delta_N, n_0, N_A)$. It produces a DFA, $(D, \Sigma, \delta_D, d_0, D_A)$. The NFA and the DFA use the same alphabet, $\Sigma$. The DFA's start state, $d_0$, and its accepting states, $D_A$, will emerge from the construction. The complex part of the construction is the derivation of the set of DFA states $D$ from the NFA states $N$, and the derivation of the DFA transition function $\delta_D$.

**Valid configuration**
configuration of an NFA that can be reached by some input string

The algorithm, shown in Figure 2.6, constructs a set $Q$ whose elements, $q_i$ are each a subset of $N$, that is, each $q_i \in 2^N$. When the algorithm halts, each $q_i \in Q$ corresponds to a state, $d_i \in D$, in the DFA. The construction builds the elements of $Q$ by following the transitions that the NFA can make on a given input. Thus, each $q_i$ represents a valid configuration of the NFA.

The algorithm begins with an initial set, $q_0$, that contains $n_0$ and any states in the NFA that can be reached from $n_0$ along paths that contain only

```
q₀ ← ε-closure({n₀});
Q ← q₀;
WorkList ← {q₀};

while (WorkList ≠ Ø ) do
    remove q from WorkList;
    for each character c ∈ Σ do
        t ← ε-closure(Delta(q,c));
        T[q,c] ← t;
        if t ∉ Q then
            add t to Q and to WorkList;
    end;
end;
```

■ **FIGURE 2.6** The Subset Construction.

$\epsilon$-transitions. Those states are equivalent since they can be reached without consuming input.

To construct $q_0$ from $n_0$, the algorithm computes $\epsilon\text{-}closure(n_0)$. It takes, as input, a set $S$ of NFA states. It returns a set of NFA states constructed from $S$ as follows: $\epsilon\text{-}closure$ examines each state $s_i \in S$ and adds to $S$ any state reachable by following one or more $\epsilon$-transitions from $s_i$. If $S$ is the set of states reachable from $n_0$ by following paths labelled with abc, then $\epsilon\text{-}closure(S)$ is the set of states reachable from $n_0$ by following paths labelled abc$\epsilon^*$. Initially, $Q$ has only one member, $q_0$ and the WorkList contains $q_0$.

The algorithm proceeds by removing a set $q$ from the worklist. Each $q$ represents a valid configuration of the original NFA. The algorithm constructs, for each character $c$ in the alphabet $\Sigma$, the configuration that the NFA would reach if it read $c$ while in configuration $q$. This computation uses a function Delta$(q,c)$ that applies the NFA's transition function to each element of $q$. It returns $\cup_{s \in q_i} \delta_N(s,c)$.

The while loop repeatedly removes a configuration $q$ from the worklist and uses Delta to compute its potential transitions. It augments this computed configuration with any states reachable by following $\epsilon$-transitions, and adds any new configurations generated in this way to both $Q$ and the worklist. When it discovers a new configuration $t$ reachable from $q$ on character $c$, the algorithm records that transition in the table $T$. The inner loop, which iterates over the alphabet for each configuration, performs an exhaustive search.

Notice that $Q$ grows monotonically. The while loop adds sets to $Q$ but never removes them. Since the number of configurations of the NFA is bounded and each configuration only appears once on the worklist, the while loop must halt. When it halts, $Q$ contains all of the valid configurations of the NFA and $T$ holds all of the transitions between them.

$Q$ can become large—as large as $|2^N|$ distinct states. The amount of nondeterminism found in the NFA determines how much state expansion occurs. Recall, however, that the result is a DFA that makes exactly one transition per input character, independent of the number of states in the DFA. Thus, any expansion introduced by the subset construction does not affect the running time of the DFA.

### From Q to D

When the subset construction halts, it has constructed a model of the desired DFA, one that simulates the original NFA. Building the DFA from $Q$ and $T$ is straightforward. Each $q_i \in Q$ needs a state $d_i \in D$ to represent it. If $q_i$ contains an accepting state of the NFA, then $d_i$ is an accepting state of the DFA. We can construct the transition function, $\delta_D$, directly from $T$ by observing the mapping from $q_i$ to $d_i$. Finally, the state constructed from $q_0$ becomes $d_0$, the initial state of the DFA.

### Example

Consider the NFA built for $a(b|c)^*$ in Section 2.4.2 and shown in Figure 2.7a, with its states renumbered. The table in Figure 2.7b sketches the steps that the subset construction follows. The first column shows the name of the set in $Q$ being processed in a given iteration of the while loop. The second column shows the name of the corresponding state in the new DFA. The third column shows the set of NFA states contained in the current set from $Q$. The final three columns show results of computing the $\epsilon$-$closure$ of $Delta$ on the state for each character in $\Sigma$.

The algorithm takes the following steps:

1. The initialization sets $q_0$ to $\epsilon$-$closure(\{n_0\})$, which is just $n_0$. The first iteration computes $\epsilon$-$closure(Delta(q_0,a))$, which contains six NFA states, and $\epsilon$-$closure(Delta(q_0,b))$ and $\epsilon$-$closure(Delta(q_0,c))$, which are empty.
2. The second iteration of the while loop examines $q_1$. It produces two configurations and names them $q_2$ and $q_3$.
3. The third iteration of the while loop examines $q_2$. It constructs two configurations, which are identical to $q_2$ and $q_3$.
4. The fourth iteration of the while loop examines $q_3$. Like the third iteration, it reconstructs $q_2$ and $q_3$.

Figure 2.7c shows the resulting DFA; the states correspond to the DFA states from the table and the transitions are given by the $Delta$ operations that

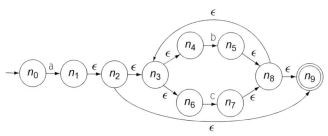

(a) NFA for "$a(b \mid c)^{*}$" (With States Renumbered)

| Set Name | DFA States | NFA States | $\epsilon$-closure(Delta($q,*$)) | | |
|---|---|---|---|---|---|
| | | | a | b | c |
| $q_0$ | $d_0$ | $n_0$ | $\{n_1, n_2, n_3,$ $n_4, n_6, n_9\}$ | – none – | – none – |
| $q_1$ | $d_1$ | $\{n_1, n_2, n_3,$ $n_4, n_6, n_9\}$ | – none – | $\{n_5, n_8, n_9,$ $n_3, n_4, n_6\}$ | $\{n_7, n_8, n_9,$ $n_3, n_4, n_6\}$ |
| $q_2$ | $d_2$ | $\{n_5, n_8, n_9,$ $n_3, n_4, n_6\}$ | – none – | $q_2$ | $q_3$ |
| $q_3$ | $d_3$ | $\{n_7, n_8, n_9,$ $n_3, n_4, n_6\}$ | – none – | $q_2$ | $q_3$ |

(b) Iterations of the Subset Construction

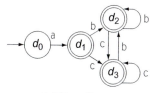

(a) Resulting DFA

■ **FIGURE 2.7** Applying the Subset Construction to the NFA from Figure 2.5.

generate those states. Since the sets $q_1$, $q_2$ and $q_3$ all contain $n_9$ (the accepting state of the NFA), all three become accepting states in the DFA.

### Fixed-Point Computations

The subset construction is an example of a *fixed-point computation*, a particular style of computation that arises regularly in computer science. These

**Monotone function**

a function $f$ on domain $D$ is *monotone* if, $\forall x, y \in D, x \leq y \Rightarrow f(x) \leq f(y)$

computations are characterized by the iterated application of a monotone function to some collection of sets drawn from a domain whose structure is known. These computations terminate when they reach a state where further iteration produces the same answer—a "fixed point" in the space of successive iterates. Fixed-point computations play an important and recurring role in compiler construction.

Termination arguments for fixed-point algorithms usually depend on known properties of the domain. For the subset construction, the domain $D$ is $2^{2^N}$, since $Q = \{q_0, q_1, q_2, \ldots, q_k\}$ where each $q_i \in 2^N$. Since $N$ is finite, $2^N$ and $2^{2^N}$ are also finite. The while loop adds elements to $Q$; it cannot remove an element from $Q$. We can view the while loop as a monotone increasing function $f$, which means that for a set $x, f(x) \geq x$. (The comparison operator $\geq$ is $\supseteq$.) Since $Q$ can have at most $|2^N|$ distinct elements, the while loop can iterate at most $|2^N|$ times. It may, of course, reach a fixed point and halt more quickly than that.

### Computing $\epsilon$-closure Offline

An implementation of the subset construction could compute $\epsilon$-*closure()* by following paths in the transition graph of the NFA as needed. Figure 2.8 shows another approach: an offline algorithm that computes $\epsilon$-*closure({n})* for each state $n$ in the transition graph. The algorithm is another example of a fixed-point computation.

For the purposes of this algorithm, consider the transition diagram of the NFA as a graph, with nodes and edges. The algorithm begins by creating a set $E$ for each node in the graph. For a node $n$, $E(n)$ will hold the current

```
for each state n ∈ N do
    E(n) ← {n};
end;
WorkList ← N;
while (WorkList≠∅) do
    remove n from WorkList;
    t ← {n} ∪ ⋃ₙ→ᵖ∈δₙ E(p);
    if t ≠ E(n)
        then begin;
            E(n) ← t;
            WorkList ← WorkList ∪ {m | m→n ∈ δₙ};
        end;
end;
```

■ **FIGURE 2.8** An Offline Algorithm for $\epsilon$-closure.

approximation to $\epsilon$-*closure(n)*. Initially, the algorithm sets $E(n)$ to $\{n\}$, for each node $n$, and places each node on the worklist.

Each iteration of the while loop removes a node $n$ from the worklist, finds all of the $\epsilon$-transitions that leave $n$, and adds their targets to $E(n)$. If that computation changes $E(n)$, it places $n$'s predecessors along $\epsilon$-transitions on the worklist. (If $n$ is in the $\epsilon$-closure of its predecessor, adding nodes to $E(n)$ must also add them to the predecessor's set.) This process halts when the worklist becomes empty.

Using a bit-vector set for the worklist can ensure that the algorithm does not have duplicate copies of a node's name on the worklist.

See Appendix B.2.

The termination argument for this algorithm is more complex than that for the algorithm in Figure 2.6. The algorithm halts when the worklist is empty. Initially, the worklist contains every node in the graph. Each iteration removes a node from the worklist; it may also add one or more nodes to the worklist.

The algorithm only adds a node to the worklist if the $E$ set of its successor changes. The $E(n)$ sets increase monotonically. For a node $x$, its successor $y$ along an $\epsilon$-transition can place $x$ on the worklist at most $|E(y)| \leq |N|$ times, in the worst case. If $x$ has multiple successors $y_i$ along $\epsilon$-transitions, each of them can place $x$ on the worklist $|E(y_i)| \leq |N|$ times. Taken over the entire graph, the worst case behavior would place nodes on the worklist $k \cdot |N|$ times, where $k$ is the number of $\epsilon$-transitions in the graph. Thus, the worklist eventually becomes empty and the computation halts.

### 2.4.4 **DFA to Minimal DFA: Hopcroft's Algorithm**

As a final refinement to the RE→DFA conversion, we can add an algorithm to minimize the number of states in the DFA. The DFA that emerges from the subset construction can have a large set of states. While this does not increase the time needed to scan a string, it does increase the size of the recognizer in memory. On modern computers, the speed of memory accesses often governs the speed of computation. A smaller recognizer may fit better into the processor's cache memory.

To minimize the number of states in a DFA, $(D, \Sigma, \delta, d_0, D_A)$, we need a technique to detect when two states are equivalent—that is, when they produce the same behavior on any input string. The algorithm in Figure 2.9 finds equivalence classes of DFA states based on their behavior. From those equivalence classes, we can construct a minimal DFA.

The algorithm constructs a set partition, $P = \{p_1, p_2, p_3, \ldots p_m\}$, of the DFA states. The particular partition, $P$, that it constructs groups together DFA states by their behavior. Two DFA states, $d_i, d_j \in p_s$, have the same behavior in response to all input characters. That is, if $d_i \xrightarrow{c} d_x$, $d_j \xrightarrow{c} d_y$, and $d_i, d_j \in p_s$,

**Set partition**

A *set partition* of $S$ is a collection of nonempty, disjoint subsets of $S$ whose union is exactly $S$.

```
T ← {D_A,  {D − D_A} };          Split(S) {
P ← Ø                                for each c ∈ Σ do
while (P ≠ T) do                         if c splits S into s₁ and s₂
   P ← T;                                   then return {s₁,s₂};
   T ← Ø;                            end;
   for each set p ∈ P do            return S;
      T ← T ∪ Split(p);          }
   end;
end;
```

■ **FIGURE 2.9** DFA Minimization Algorithm.

then $d_x$ and $d_y$ must be in the same set $p_t$. This property holds for every set $p_s \in P$, for every pair of states $d_i, d_j \in p_s$, and for every input character, $c$. Thus, the states in $p_s$ have the same behavior with respect to input characters and the remaining sets in $P$.

To minimize a DFA, each set $p_s \in P$ should be as large as possible, within the constraint of behavioral equivalence. To construct such a partition, the algorithm begins with an initial rough partition that obeys all the properties *except* behavioral equivalence. It then iteratively refines that partition to enforce behavioral equivalence. The initial partition contains two sets, $p_0 = D_A$ and $p_1 = \{D − D_A\}$. This separation ensures that no set in the final partition contains both accepting and nonaccepting states, since the algorithm never combines two partitions.

The algorithm refines the initial partition by repeatedly examining each $p_s \in P$ to look for states in $p_s$ that have different behavior for some input string. Clearly, it cannot trace the behavior of the DFA on every string. It can, however, simulate the behavior of a given state in response to a single input character. It uses a simple condition for refining the partition: a symbol $c \in \Sigma$ must produce the same behavior for every state $d_i \in p_s$. If it does not, the algorithm splits $p_s$ around $c$.

This splitting action is the key to understanding the algorithm. For $d_i$ and $d_j$ to remain together in $p_s$, they must take equivalent transitions on each character $c \in \Sigma$. That is, $\forall c \in \Sigma, d_i \overset{c}{\to} d_x$ and $d_j \overset{c}{\to} d_y$, where $d_x, d_y \in p_t$. Any state $d_k \in p_s$ where $d_k \overset{c}{\to} d_z, d_z \notin p_t$, cannot remain in the same partition as $d_i$ and $d_j$. Similarly, if $d_i$ and $d_j$ have transitions on $c$ and $d_k$ does not, it cannot remain in the same partition as $d_i$ and $d_j$.

Figure 2.10 makes this concrete. The states in $p_1 = \{d_i, d_j, d_k\}$ are equivalent if and only if their transitions, $\forall c \in \Sigma$, take them to states that are, themselves, in an equivalence class. As shown, each state has a transition on a: $d_i \overset{a}{\to} d_x$, $d_j \overset{a}{\to} d_y$, and $d_k \overset{a}{\to} d_z$. If $d_x$, $d_y$, and $d_z$ are all in the same set in

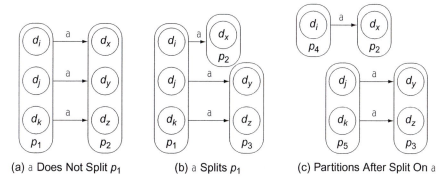

(a) a Does Not Split $p_1$   (b) a Splits $p_1$   (c) Partitions After Split On a

■ **FIGURE 2.10** Splitting a Partition around a.

the current partition, as shown on the left, then $d_i$, $d_j$, and $d_k$ should remain together and a does not split $p_1$.

On the other hand, if $d_x$, $d_y$, and $d_z$ are in two or more different sets, then a splits $p_1$. As shown in the center drawing of Figure 2.10, $d_x \in p_2$ while $d_y$ and $d_z \in p_3$, so the algorithm must split $p_1$ and construct two new sets $p_4 = \{d_i\}$ and $p_5 = \{d_j, d_k\}$ to reflect the potential for different outcomes with strings that begin with the symbol a. The result is shown on the right side of Figure 2.10. The same split would result if state $d_i$ had no transition on a.

To refine a partition $P$, the algorithm examines each $p \in P$ and each $c \in \Sigma$. If $c$ splits $p$, the algorithm constructs two new sets from $p$ and adds them to $T$. (It could split $p$ into more than two sets, all having internally consistent behavior on $c$. However, creating one consistent state and lumping the rest of $p$ into another state will suffice. If the latter state is inconsistent in its behavior on $c$, the algorithm will split it in a later iteration.) The algorithm repeats this process until it finds a partition where it can split no sets.

To construct the new DFA from the final partition $p$, we can create a single state to represent each set $p \in P$ and add the appropriate transitions between these new representative states. For the state representing $p_l$, we add a transition to the state representing $p_m$ on $c$ if some $d_j \in p_l$ has a transition on $c$ to some $d_k \in p_m$. From the construction, we know that if $d_j$ has such a transition, so does every other state in $p_l$; if this were not the case, the algorithm would have split $p_l$ around $c$. The resulting DFA is minimal; the proof is beyond our scope.

### Examples

Consider a DFA that recognizes the language *fee | fie*, shown in Figure 2.11a. By inspection, we can see that states $s_3$ and $s_5$ serve the same purpose. Both

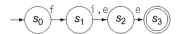

(a) DFA for "*fee | fie*"

| | Current | Examines | | |
|---|---|---|---|---|
| **Step** | **Partition** | **Set** | **Char** | **Action** |
| 0 | {ﾠ{$s_3,s_5$}, {$s_0,s_1,s_2,s_4$}ﾠ} | — | — | — |
| 1 | {ﾠ{$s_3,s_5$}, {$s_0,s_1,s_2,s_4$}ﾠ} | {$s_3,s_5$} | all | none |
| 2 | {ﾠ{$s_3,s_5$}, {$s_0,s_1,s_2,s_4$}ﾠ} | {$s_0,s_1,s_2,s_4$} | e | split {$s_2,s_4$} |
| 3 | {ﾠ{$s_3,s_5$}, {$s_0,s_1$}, {$s_2,s_4$}ﾠ} | {$s_0,s_1$} | f | split {$s_1$} |
| 4 | {ﾠ{$s_3,s_5$}, {$s_0$}, {$s_1$}, {$s_2,s_4$}ﾠ} | all | all | none |

(b) Critical Steps in Minimizing the DFA

(c) The Minimal DFA (States Renumbered)

■ **FIGURE 2.11** Applying the DFA Minimization Algorithm.

are accepting states entered only by a transition on the letter e. Neither has a transition that leaves the state. We would expect the DFA minimization algorithm to discover this fact and replace them with a single state.

Figure 2.11b shows the significant steps that occur in minimizing this DFA. The initial partition, shown as step 0, separates accepting states from nonaccepting states. Assuming that the while loop in the algorithm iterates over the sets of $P$ in order, and over the characters in $\Sigma = \{e, f, i\}$ in order, then it first examines the set {$s_3,s_5$}. Since neither state has an exiting transition, the state does not split on any character. In the second step, it examines {$s_0,s_1,s_2,s_4$}; on the character e, it splits {$s_2,s_4$} out of the set. In the third step, it examines {$s_0,s_1$} and splits it around the character f. At that point, the partition is {ﾠ{$s_3,s_5$}, {$s_0$}, {$s_1$}, {$s_2,s_4$}ﾠ}. The algorithm makes one final pass over the sets in the partition, splits none of them, and terminates.

To construct the new DFA, we must build a state to represent each set in the final partition, add the appropriate transitions from the original DFA, and designate initial and accepting state(s). Figure 2.11c shows the result for this example.

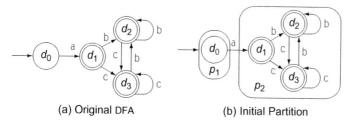

(a) Original DFA       (b) Initial Partition

■ **FIGURE 2.12** DFA for $a(b|c^*)$.

As a second example, consider the DFA for $a(b|c)^*$ produced by Thompson's construction and the subset construction, shown in Figure 2.12a. The first step of the minimization algorithm constructs an initial partition $\{\{d_0\}, \{d_1, d_2, d_3\}\}$, as shown on the right. Since $p_1$ has only one state, it cannot be split. When the algorithm examines $p_2$, it finds no transitions on a from any state in $p_2$. For both b and c, each state has a transition back into $p_2$. Thus, no symbol in $\Sigma$ splits $p_2$, and the final partition is $\{\{d_0\}, \{d_1, d_2, d_3\}\}$.

The resulting minimal DFA is shown in Figure 2.12b. Recall that this is the DFA that we suggested a human would derive. After minimization, the automatic techniques produce the same result.

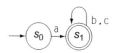

This algorithm is another example of a fixed-point computation. $P$ is finite; at most, it can contain $|D|$ elements. The while loop splits sets in $P$, but never combines them. Thus, $|P|$ grows monotonically. The loop halts when some iteration splits no sets in $P$. The worst-case behavior occurs when each state in the DFA has different behavior; in that case, the while loop halts when $P$ has a distinct set for each $d_i \in D$. This occurs when the algorithm is applied to a minimal DFA.

### 2.4.5 Using a DFA as a Recognizer

Thus far, we have developed the mechanisms to construct a DFA implementation from a single RE. To be useful, a compiler's scanner must recognize all the syntactic categories that appear in the grammar for the source language. What we need, then, is a recognizer that can handle all the REs for the language's microsyntax. Given the REs for the various syntactic categories, $r_1, r_2, r_3, \ldots, r_k$, we can construct a single RE for the entire collection by forming $(r_1 \mid r_2 \mid r_3 \mid \ldots \mid r_k)$.

If we run this RE through the entire process, building an NFA, constructing a DFA to simulate the NFA, minimizing it, and turning that minimal DFA into executable code, the resulting scanner recognizes the next word that matches one of the $r_i$'s. That is, when the compiler invokes it on some input, the scanner will examine characters one at a time and accept the string if it is in an accepting state when it exhausts the input. The scanner should return both the text of the string and its syntactic category, or part of speech. Since most real programs contain more than one word, we need to transform either the language or the recognizer.

At the language level, we can insist that each word end with some easily recognizable delimiter, like a blank or a tab. This idea is deceptively attractive. Taken literally, it requires delimiters surrounding all operators, as +, -, (, ), and the comma.

At the recognizer level, we can change the implementation of the DFA and its notion of acceptance. To find the longest word that matches one of the RES, the DFA should run until it reaches the point where the current state, $s$, has no outgoing transition on the next character. At that point, the implementation must decide which RE it has matched. Two cases arise; the first is simple. If $s$ is an accepting state, then the DFA has found a word in the language and should report the word and its syntactic category.

If $s$ is not an accepting state, matters are more complex. Two cases occur. If the DFA passed through one or more accepting states on its way to $s$, the recognizer should back up to the most recent such state. This strategy matches the longest valid prefix in the input string. If it never reached an accepting state, then no prefix of the input string is a valid word and the recognizer should report an error. The scanners in Section 2.5.1 implement both these notions.

As a final complication, an accepting state in the DFA may represent several accepting states in the original NFA. For example, if the lexical specification includes RES for keywords as well as an RE for identifiers, then a keyword such as new might match two RES. The recognizer must decide which syntactic category to return: identifier or the singleton category for the keyword new.

Most scanner-generator tools allow the compiler writer to specify a priority among patterns. When the recognizer matches multiple patterns, it returns the syntactic category of the highest-priority pattern. This mechanism resolves the problem in a simple way. The lex scanner generator, distributed with many Unix systems, assigns priorities based on position in the list of RES. The first RE has highest priority, while the last RE has lowest priority.

As a practical matter, the compiler writer must also specify RES for parts of the input stream that do not form words in the program text. In most programming languages, blank space is ignored, but every program contains it. To handle blank space, the compiler writer typically includes an RE that matches blanks, tabs, and end-of-line characters; the action on accepting blank space is to invoke the scanner, recursively, and return its result. If comments are discarded, they are handled in a similar fashion.

---

**SECTION REVIEW**

Given a regular expression, we can derive a minimal DFA to recognize the language specified by the RE using the following steps: (1) apply Thompson's construction to build an NFA for the RE; (2) use the subset construction to derive a DFA that simulates the behavior of the RE; and (3) use Hopcroft's algorithm to identify equivalent states in the DFA and construct a minimal DFA. This trio of constructions produces an efficient recognizer for any language that can be specified with an RE.

Both the subset construction and the DFA minimization algorithm are fixed-point computations. They are characterized by repeated application of a monotone function to some set; the properties of the domain play an important role in reasoning about the termination and complexity of these algorithms. We will see more fixed-point computations in later chapters.

---

**Review Questions**

1. Consider the RE *who* | *what* | *where*. Use Thompson's construction to build an NFA from the RE. Use the subset construction to build a DFA from the NFA. Minimize the DFA.

2. Minimize the following DFA:

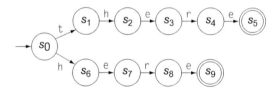

## 2.5 **IMPLEMENTING SCANNERS**

Scanner construction is a problem where the theory of formal languages has produced tools that can automate implementation. For most languages, the compiler writer can produce an acceptably fast scanner directly from a set of regular expressions. The compiler writer creates an RE for each syntactic category and gives the REs as input to a scanner generator. The generator constructs an NFA for each RE, joins them with $\epsilon$-transitions, creates a corresponding DFA, and minimizes the DFA. At that point, the scanner generator must convert the DFA into executable code.

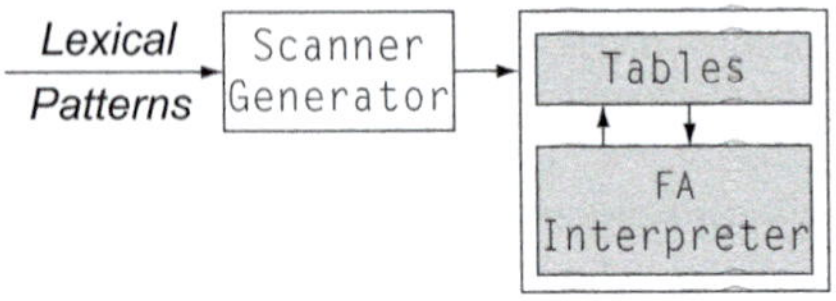

■ **FIGURE 2.13** Generating a Table-Driven Scanner.

This section discusses three implementation strategies for converting a DFA into executable code: a table-driven scanner, a direct-coded scanner, and a hand-coded scanner. All of these scanners operate in the same manner, by simulating the DFA. They repeatedly read the next character in the input and simulate the DFA transition caused by that character. This process stops when the DFA recognizes a word. As described in the previous section, that occurs when the current state, $s$, has no outbound transition on the current input character.

If $s$ is an accepting state, the scanner recognizes the word and returns a lexeme and its syntactic category to the calling procedure. If $s$ is a nonaccepting state, the scanner must determine whether or not it passed through an accepting state on the way to $s$. If the scanner did encounter an accepting state, it should roll back its internal state and its input stream to that point and report success. If it did not, it should report the failure.

These three implementation strategies, table driven, direct coded, and hand coded, differ in the details of their runtime costs. However, they all have the same asymptotic complexity—constant cost per character, plus the cost of roll back. The differences in the efficiency of well-implemented scanners change the constant costs per character but not the asymptotic complexity of scanning.

The next three subsections discuss implementation differences between table-driven, direct-coded, and hand-coded scanners. The strategies differ in how they model the DFA's transition structure and how they simulate its operation. Those differences, in turn, produce different runtime costs. The final subsection examines two different strategies for handling reserved keywords.

### 2.5.1 Table-Driven Scanners

The table-driven approach uses a skeleton scanner for control and a set of generated tables that encode language-specific knowledge. As shown in Figure 2.13, the compiler writer provides a set of lexical patterns, specified

```
NextWord()
  state ← s₀ ;
  lexeme ← " ";
  clear stack;
  push(bad);

  while (state≠sₑ) do
    NextChar(char);
    lexeme ← lexeme + char;

    if state ∈ Sₐ
        then clear stack;
    push(state);

    cat ← CharCat[char];
    state ← δ[state,cat];
  end;

  while(state ∉ Sₐ and
         state≠bad) do
    state ← pop();
    truncate lexeme;
    RollBack();
  end;

  if state ∈ Sₐ
     then return Type[state];
     else return invalid;
```

| r | 0,1,2,...,9 | EOF | **Other** |
|---|---|---|---|
| Register | Digit | Other | Other |

The Classifier Table, *CharCat*

|  | **Register** | **Digit** | **Other** |
|---|---|---|---|
| $s_0$ | $s_1$ | $s_e$ | $s_e$ |
| $s_1$ | $s_e$ | $s_2$ | $s_e$ |
| $s_2$ | $s_e$ | $s_2$ | $s_e$ |
| $s_e$ | $s_e$ | $s_e$ | $s_e$ |

The Transition Table, $\delta$

| $s_0$ | $s_1$ | $s_2$ | $s_e$ |
|---|---|---|---|
| invalid | invalid | register | invalid |

The Token Type Table, *Type*

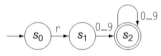

The Underlying DFA

■ **FIGURE 2.14** A Table-Driven Scanner for Register Names.

as regular expressions. The scanner generator then produces tables that drive the skeleton scanner.

Figure 2.14 shows a table-driven scanner for the RE $r[0\ldots9]^+$, which was our first attempt at an RE for ILOC register names. The left side of the figure shows the skeleton scanner, while the right side shows the tables for $r[0\ldots9]^+$ and the underlying DFA. Notice the similarity between the code here and the recognizer shown in Figure 2.2 on page 32.

The skeleton scanner divides into four sections: initializations, a scanning loop that models the DFA's behavior, a roll back loop in case the DFA overshoots the end of the token, and a final section that interprets and reports the results. The scanning loop repeats the two basic actions of a scanner: read a character and simulate the DFA's action. It halts when the DFA enters the error state, $s_e$. Two tables, $CharCat$ and $\delta$, encode all knowledge about the DFA. The roll back loop uses a stack of states to revert the scanner to its most recent accepting state.

The skeleton scanner uses the variable $state$ to hold the current state of the simulated DFA. It updates $state$ using a two-step, table-lookup process. First, it classifies $char$ into one of a small set of categories using the $Char\text{-}Cat$ table. The scanner for $r[0\ldots9]^{+}$ has three categories: *Register, Digit,* or *Other.* Next, it uses the current state and the character category as indices into the transition table, $\delta$.

For small examples, such as $r[0\ldots9]^{+}$, the classifier table is larger than the complete transition table. In a realistically sized example, that relationship should be reversed.

This two-step translation, character to category, then state and category to new state, lets the scanner use a compressed transition table. The tradeoff between direct access into a larger table and indirect access into the compressed table is straightforward. A complete table would eliminate the mapping through $CharCat$, but would increase the memory footprint of the table. The uncompressed transition table grows as the product of the number of states in the DFA and the number of characters in $\Sigma$; it can grow to the point where it will not stay in cache.

With a small, compact character set, such as ASCII, $CharCat$ can be represented as a simple table lookup. The relevant portions of $CharCat$ should stay in the cache. In that case, table compression adds one cache reference per input character. As the character set grows (e.g. Unicode), more complex implementations of $CharCat$ may be needed. The precise tradeoff between the per-character costs of both compressed and uncompressed tables will depend on properties of both the language and the computer that runs the scanner.

To provide a character-by-character interface to the input stream, the skeleton scanner uses a macro, $NextChar$, which sets its sole parameter to contain the next character in the input stream. A corresponding macro, $RollBack$, moves the input stream back by one character. (Section 2.5.3 looks at $NextChar$ and $RollBack$.)

If the scanner reads too far, $state$ will not contain an accepting state at the end of the first while loop. In that case, the second while loop uses the state trace from the stack to roll the state, lexeme, and input stream back to the most recent accepting state. In most languages, the scanner's overshoot will be limited. Pathological behavior, however, can cause the scanner to examine individual characters many times, significantly increasing the overall cost of scanning. In most programming languages, the amount of roll back is small relative to the word lengths. In languages where significant amounts of roll back can occur, a more sophisticated approach to this problem is warranted.

### Avoiding Excess Roll Back

Some regular expressions can produce quadratic calls to roll back in the scanner shown in Figure 2.14. The problem arises from our desire to have the scanner return the longest word that is a prefix of the input stream.

Consider the RE *ab* | (*ab*)* *c*. The corresponding DFA, shown in the margin, recognizes either *ab* or any number of occurrences of *ab* followed by a final *c*. On the input string ababababc, a scanner built from the DFA will read all the characters and return the entire string as a single word. If, however, the input is abababab, it must scan all of the characters before it can determine that the longest prefix is ab. On the next invocation, it will scan ababab to return ab. The third call will scan abab to return ab, and the final call will simply return ab without any roll back. In the worst, case, it can spend quadratic time reading the input stream.

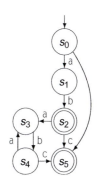

Figure 2.15 shows a modification to the scanner in Figure 2.14 that avoids this problem. It differs from the earlier scanner in three important ways. First, it has a global counter, *InputPos*, to record position in the input stream. Second, it has a bit-array, *Failed*, to record dead-end transitions as the scanner finds them. *Failed* has a row for each state and a column for each position in the input stream. Third, it has an initialization routine that

```
NextWord()
    state ← s0 ;
    lexeme ← " ";
    clear stack;
    push(⟨bad, bad⟩);

    while (state≠se) do
        NextChar(char);
        InputPos ← InputPos + 1;
        lexeme ← lexeme + char;
        if Failed[state,InputPos]
            then break;
        if state ∈ SA
            then clear stack;
        push((state,InputPos));
        cat ← CharCat[char];
        state ← δ[state,cat];
    end;
```

```
    while(state ∉ SA and state≠bad ) do
        Failed[state,InputPos] ← true;
        (state,InputPos) ← pop();
        truncate lexeme;
        RollBack();
    end;

    if state ∈ SA
        then return TokenType[state];
        else return bad;


InitializeScanner()
    InputPos = 0;

    for each state s in the DFA do
        for i=0 to |input stream| do
            Failed[s,i] ← false;
        end;
    end;
```

■ **FIGURE 2.15** The Maximal Munch Scanner.

must be called before `NextWord()` is invoked. That routine sets `InputPos` to zero and sets `Failed` uniformly to false.

This scanner, called the *maximal munch scanner*, avoids the pathological behavior by marking dead-end transitions as they are popped from the stack. Thus, over time, it records specific ⟨*state,input position*⟩ pairs that cannot lead to an accepting state. Inside the scanning loop, the first while loop, the code tests each ⟨*state,input position*⟩ pair and breaks out of the scanning loop whenever a failed transition is attempted.

Optimizations can drastically reduce the space requirements of this scheme. (See, for example, Exercise 16 on page 82.) Most programming languages have simple enough microsyntax that this kind of quadratic roll back cannot occur. If, however, you are building a scanner for a language that can exhibit this behavior, the scanner can avoid it for a small additional overhead per character.

### Generating the Transition and Classifier Tables

Given a DFA, the scanner generator can generate the tables in a straightforward fashion. The initial table has one column for every character in the input alphabet and one row for each state in the DFA. For each state, in order, the generator examines the outbound transitions and fills the row with the appropriate states. The generator can collapse identical columns into a single instance; as it does so, it can construct the character classifier. (Two characters belong in the same class if and only if they have identical columns in $\delta$.) If the DFA has been minimized, no two rows can be identical, so row compression is not an issue.

### Changing Languages

To model another DFA, the compiler writer can simply supply new tables. Earlier in the chapter, we worked with a second, more constrained specification for ILOC register names, given by the RE: $r([0...2]([0...9]|\epsilon) | [4...9] | (3(0|1|\epsilon)))$. That RE gave rise to the following DFA:

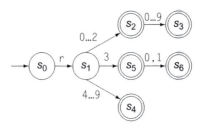

Because it has more states and transitions than the RE for $r[0...9]^+$, we should expect a larger transition table.

| | r | 0,1 | 2 | 3 | 4...9 | Other |
|---|---|---|---|---|---|---|
| $s_0$ | $s_1$ | $s_e$ | $s_e$ | $s_e$ | $s_e$ | $s_e$ |
| $s_1$ | $s_e$ | $s_2$ | $s_2$ | $s_5$ | $s_4$ | $s_e$ |
| $s_2$ | $s_e$ | $s_3$ | $s_3$ | $s_3$ | $s_3$ | $s_e$ |
| $s_3$ | $s_e$ | $s_e$ | $s_e$ | $s_e$ | $s_e$ | $s_e$ |
| $s_4$ | $s_e$ | $s_e$ | $s_e$ | $s_e$ | $s_e$ | $s_e$ |
| $s_5$ | $s_e$ | $s_6$ | $s_e$ | $s_e$ | $s_e$ | $s_e$ |
| $s_6$ | $s_e$ | $s_e$ | $s_e$ | $s_e$ | $s_e$ | $s_e$ |
| $s_e$ | $s_e$ | $s_e$ | $s_e$ | $s_e$ | $s_e$ | $s_e$ |

As a final example, the minimal DFA for the RE $a\,(b|c)^*$ has the following table:

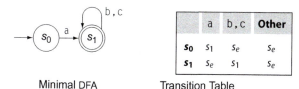

| | a | b,c | Other |
|---|---|---|---|
| $s_0$ | $s_1$ | $s_e$ | $s_e$ |
| $s_1$ | $s_e$ | $s_1$ | $s_e$ |

Minimal DFA    Transition Table

The character classifier has three classes: a, b or c, and all other characters.

### 2.5.2 Direct-Coded Scanners

To improve the performance of a table-driven scanner, we must reduce the cost of one or both of its basic actions: read a character and compute the next DFA transition. Direct-coded scanners reduce the cost of computing DFA transitions by replacing the explicit representation of the DFA's state and transition graph with an implicit one. The implicit representation simplifies the two-step, table-lookup computation. It eliminates the memory references entailed in that computation and allows other specializations. The resulting scanner has the same functionality as the table-driven scanner, but with a lower overhead per character. A direct-coded scanner is no harder to generate than the equivalent table-driven scanner.

The table-driven scanner spends most of its time inside the central while loop; thus, the heart of a direct-coded scanner is an alternate implementation of that while loop. With some detail abstracted, that loop performs the following actions:

```
while (state ≠ sₑ) do
    NextChar(char);
    cat ← CharCat[char];
    state ← δ[state,cat];
end;
```

---

**REPRESENTING STRINGS**

The scanner classifies words in the input program into a small set of categories. From a functional perspective, each word in the input stream becomes a pair (*word,type*), where *word* is the actual text that forms the word and *type* represents its syntactic category.

For many categories, having both *word* and *type* is redundant. The words +, ×, and for have only one spelling. For identifiers, numbers, and character strings, however, the compiler will repeatedly use the *word*. Unfortunately, many compilers are written in languages that lack an appropriate representation for the *word* part of the pair. We need a representation that is compact and offers a fast equality test for two words.

A common practice to address this problem has the scanner create a single hash table (see Appendix B.4) to hold all the distinct strings used in the input program. The compiler then uses either the string's index in this "string table" or a pointer to its stored image in the string table as a proxy for the string. Information derived from the string, such as the length of a character constant or the value and type of a numerical constant, can be computed once and referenced quickly through the table. Since most computers have storage-efficient representations for integers and pointers, this reduces the amount of memory used internally in the compiler. By using the hardware comparison mechanisms on the integer or pointer proxies, it also simplifies the code used to compare them.

---

Notice the variable $state$ that explicitly represents the DFA's current state and the tables $CharCat$ and $\delta$ that represent the DFA's transition diagram.

### Overhead of Table Lookup

For each character, the table-driven scanner performs two table lookups, one in $CharCat$ and another in $\delta$. While both lookups take $\mathbf{O}(1)$ time, the table abstraction imposes constant-cost overheads that a direct-coded scanner can avoid. To access the $i^{th}$ element of $CharCat$, the code must compute its address, given by

$$@CharCat_0 + i \times w$$

Detailed discussion of code for array addressing starts on page 359 in Section 7.5.

where $@CharCat_0$ is a constant related to the starting address of $CharCat$ in memory and $w$ is the number of bytes in each element of $CharCat$. After computing the address, the code must load the data found at that address in memory.

Because $\delta$ has two dimensions, the address calculation is more complex. For the reference $\delta(state, cat)$, the code must compute

```
@δ₀ + (state × number of columns in δ + cat) × w
```

where $@\delta_0$ is a constant related to the starting address of $\delta$ in memory and $w$ is the number of bytes per element of $\delta$. Again, the scanner must issue a load operation to retrieve the data stored at this address.

Thus, the table-driven scanner performs two address computations and two load operations for each character that it processes. The speed improvements in a direct-coded scanner come from reducing this overhead.

### Replacing the Table-Driven Scanner's While Loop

Rather than represent the current DFA state and the transition diagram explicitly, a direct-coded scanner has a specialized code fragment to implement each state. It transfers control directly from state-fragment to state-fragment to emulate the actions of the DFA. Figure 2.16 shows a direct-coded scanner

```
s_init :   lexeme ← " ";
           clear stack;
           push(bad);
           goto s₀ ;

s₀ :       NextChar(char);
           lexeme ← lexeme + char;
           if state ∈ S_A
               then clear stack;
           push(state);
           if (char = 'r')
               then goto s₁ ;
               else goto s_out ;

s₁ :       NextChar(char);
           lexeme ← lexeme + char;
           if state ∈ S_A
               then clear stack;
           push(state);
           if ('0' ≤ char ≤ '9')
               then goto s₂ ;
               else goto s_out ;

s₂ :       NextChar(char);
           lexeme ← lexeme + char;
           if state ∈ S_A
               then clear stack;
           push(state);
           if '0' ≤ char ≤ '9'
               then goto s₂ ;
               else goto s_out

s_out :    while (state ∉ S_A and
                    state ≠ bad) do
               state ← pop();
               truncate lexeme;
               RollBack();
           end;
           if state ∈ S_A
               then return Type[state];
               else return invalid ;
```

■ **FIGURE 2.16** A Direct-Coded Scanner for $r[0...9]^+$.

for $r[0...9]^+$; it is equivalent to the table-driven scanner shown earlier in Figure 2.14.

Consider the code for state $s_1$. It reads a character, concatenates it onto the current word, and advances the character counter. If *char* is a digit, it jumps to state $s_2$. Otherwise, it jumps to state $s_{out}$. The code requires no complicated address calculations. The code refers to a tiny set of values that can be kept in registers. The other states have equally simple implementations.

The code in Figure 2.16 uses the same mechanism as the table-driven scanner to track accepting states and to roll back to them after an overrun. Because the code represents a specific DFA, we could specialize it further. In particular, since the DFA has just one accepting state, the stack is unneeded and the transitions to $s_{out}$ from $s_0$ and $s_1$ can be replaced with *report failure*. In a DFA where some transition leads from an accepting state to a nonaccepting state, the more general mechanism is needed.

A scanner generator can directly emit code similar to that shown in Figure 2.16. Each state has a couple of standard assignments, followed by branching logic that implements the transitions out of the state. Unlike the table-driven scanner, the code changes for each set of REs. Since that code is generated directly from the REs, the difference should not matter to the compiler writer.

Code in the style of Figure 2.16 is often called *spaghetti code* in honor of its tangled control flow.

Of course, the generated code violates many of the precepts of structured programming. While small examples may be comprehensible, the code for a complex set of regular expressions may be difficult for a human to follow. Again, since the code is generated, humans should not need to read or debug it. The additional speed obtained from direct coding makes it an attractive option, particularly since it entails no extra work for the compiler writer. Any extra work is pushed into the implementation of the scanner generator.

### Classifying Characters

The continuing example, $r[0...9]^+$, divides the alphabet of input characters into just four classes. An r falls in class *Register*. The digits 0, 1, 2, 3, 4, 5, 6, 7, 8, and 9 fall in class *Digit*, the special character returned when *NextChar* exhausts its input falls in class *EndOfFile*, and anything else falls in class *Other*.

**Collating sequence**
the "sorting order" of the characters in an alphabet, determined by the integers assigned each character

The scanner can easily and efficiently classify a given character, as shown in Figure 2.16. State $s_0$ uses a direct test on 'r' to determine if *char* is in *Register*. Because all the other classes have equivalent actions in the DFA, the scanner need not perform further tests. States $s_1$ and $s_2$ classify *char* into either *Digit* or anything else. They capitalize on the fact that the digits 0 through 9 occupy adjacent positions in the ASCII collating sequence, corresponding to the integers 48 to 57.

In a scanner where character classification is more involved, the translation-table approach used in the table-driven scanner may be less expensive than directly testing characters. In particular, if a class contains multiple characters that do not occupy adjacent slots in the collating sequence, a table lookup may be more efficient than direct testing. For example, a class that contained the arithmetic operators +, -, *, \, and ^ (43, 45, 42, 48, and 94 in the ASCII sequence) would require a moderately long series of comparisons. Using a translation table, such as *CharCat* in the table-driven example, might be faster than the comparisons if the translation table stays in the processor's primary cache.

### 2.5.3 **Hand-Coded Scanners**

Generated scanners, whether table-driven or direct-coded, use a small, constant amount of time per character. Despite this fact, many compilers use hand-coded scanners. In an informal survey of commercial compiler groups, we found that a surprisingly large fraction used hand-coded scanners. Similarly, many of the popular open-source compilers rely on hand-coded scanners. For example, the *flex* scanner generator was ostensibly built to support the *gcc* project, but *gcc 4.0* uses hand-coded scanners in several of its front ends.

The direct-coded scanner reduced the overhead of simulating the DFA; the hand-coded scanner can reduce the overhead of the interfaces between the scanner and the rest of the system. In particular, a careful implementation can improve the mechanisms used to read and manipulate characters on input and the operations needed to produce a copy of the actual lexeme on output.

#### *Buffering the Input Stream*

While character-by-character I/O leads to clean algorithmic formulations, the overhead of a procedure call per character is significant relative to the cost of simulating the DFA in either a table-driven or a direct-coded scanner. To reduce the I/O cost per character, the compiler writer can use buffered I/O, where each read operation returns a longer string of characters, or buffer, and the scanner then indexes through the buffer. The scanner maintains a pointer into the buffer. Responsibility for keeping the buffer filled and tracking the current location in the buffer falls to *NextChar*. These operations can be performed inline; they are often encoded in a macro to avoid cluttering the code with pointer dereferences and increments.

The cost of reading a full buffer of characters has two components, a large fixed overhead and a small per-character cost. A buffer and pointer scheme amortizes the fixed costs of the read over many single-character fetches. Making the buffer larger reduces the number of times that the scanner incurs this cost and reduces the per-character overhead.

Using a buffer and pointer also leads to a simple and efficient implementation of the $RollBack$ operation that occurs at the end of both the generated scanners. To roll the input back, the scanner can simply decrement the input pointer. This scheme works as long as the scanner does not decrement the pointer beyond the start of the buffer. At that point, however, the scanner needs access to the prior contents of the buffer.

**Double buffering**
A scheme that uses two input buffers in a modulo fashion to provide bounded roll back is often called *double buffering*.

In practice, the compiler writer can bound the roll-back distance that a scanner will need. With bounded roll back, the scanner can simply use two adjacent buffers and increment the pointer in a modulo fashion, as shown below:

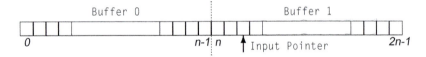

To read a character, the scanner increments the pointer, modulo *2n* and returns the character at that location. To roll back a character, the program decrements the input pointer, modulo *2n*. It must also manage the contents of the buffer, reading additional characters from the input stream as needed.

Both $NextChar$ and $RollBack$ have simple, efficient implementations, as shown in Figure 2.17. Each execution of $NextChar$ loads a character, increments the $Input$ pointer, and tests whether or not to fill the buffer. Every $n$ characters, it fills the buffer. The code is small enough to be included inline, perhaps generated from a macro. This scheme amortizes the cost of filling the buffer over $n$ characters. By choosing a reasonable size for $n$, such as 2048, 4096, or more, the compiler writer can keep the I/O overhead low.

$RollBack$ is even less expensive. It performs a test to ensure that the buffer contents are valid and then decrements the input pointer. Again, the implementation is sufficiently simple to be expanded inline. (If we used this implementation of $NextChar$ and $RollBack$ in the generated scanners, $RollBack$ would need to truncate the final character away from $lexeme$.)

```
Char ← Buffer[Input];
Input ← (Input+1) mod 2n;

if (Input mod n = 0)
   then begin;
      fill Buffer[Input : Input+n-1];
      Fence ← (Input+n) mod 2n;
   end;

return Char;
```

Implementing *NextChar*

```
Input ← 0;
Fence ← 0;
fill Buffer[0:n];
```

Initialization

```
if (Input = Fence)
   then signal roll back error;

Input ← (Input-1) mod 2n;
```

Implementing *RollBack*

■ **FIGURE 2.17** Implementing *NextChar* and *RollBack*.

As a natural consequence of using finite buffers, *RollBack* has a limited history in the input stream. To keep it from decrementing the pointer beyond the start of that context, *NextChar* and *RollBack* cooperate. The pointer *Fence* always indicates the start of the valid context. *NextChar* sets *Fence* each time it fills a buffer. *RollBack* checks *Fence* each time it tries to decrement the *Input* pointer.

After a long series of *NextChar* operations, say, more than $n$ of them, *RollBack* can always back up at least $n$ characters. However, a sequence of calls to *NextChar* and *RollBack* that work forward and backward in the buffer can create a situation where the distance between *Input* and *Fence* is less than $n$. Larger values of $n$ decrease the likelihood of this situation arising. Expected backup distances should be a consideration in selecting the buffer size, $n$.

### Generating Lexemes

The code shown for the table-driven and direct-coded scanners accumulated the input characters into a string *lexeme*. If the appropriate output for each syntactic category is a textual copy of the lexeme, then those schemes are efficient. In some common cases, however, the parser, which consumes the scanner's output, needs the information in another form.

For example, in many circumstances, the natural representation for a register number is an integer, rather than a character string consisting of an 'r' and a sequence of digits. If the scanner builds a character representation, then somewhere in the interface, that string must be converted to an integer. A typical way to accomplish that conversion uses a library routine, such as atoi in the standard C library, or a string-based I/O routine, such as sscanf. A more efficient way to solve this problem would be to accumulate the integer's value one digit at a time.

In the continuing example, the scanner could initialize a variable, *RegNum*, to zero in its initial state. Each time that it recognized a digit, it could multiply *RegNum* by 10 and add the new digit. When it reached an accepting state, *RegNum* would contain the needed value. To modify the scanner in Figure 2.16, we can delete all statements that refer to *lexeme*, add *RegNum* ← *0*; to $s_{init}$, and replace the occurrences of goto $s_2$ in states $s_1$ and $s_2$ with:

```
begin;
  RegNum ← RegNum × 10 + (char - '0');
  goto s₂;
end;
```

where both *char* and *'0'* are treated as their ordinal values in the ASCII collating sequence. Accumulating the value this way likely has lower overhead than building the string and converting it in the accepting state.

For other words, the lexeme is implicit and, therefore, redundant. With singleton words, such as a punctuation mark or an operator, the syntactic category is equivalent to the lexeme. Similarly, many scanners recognize comments and white space and discard them. Again, the set of states that recognize the comment need not accumulate the lexeme. While the individual savings are small, the aggregate effect is to create a faster, more compact scanner.

This issue arises because many scanner generators let the compiler writer specify actions to be performed in an accepting state, but do not allow actions on each transition. The resulting scanners must accumulate a character copy of the lexeme for each word, whether or not that copy is needed. If compile time matters (and it should), then attention to such minor algorithmic details leads to a faster compiler.

### 2.5.4 Handling Keywords

We have consistently assumed that keywords in the input language should be recognized by including explicit REs for them in the description that generates the DFA and the recognizer. Many authors have proposed an alternative strategy: having the DFA classify them as identifiers and testing each identifier to determine whether or not it is a keyword.

This strategy made sense in the context of a hand-implemented scanner. The additional complexity added by checking explicitly for keywords causes a significant expansion in the number of DFA states. This added implementation burden matters in a hand-coded program. With a reasonable hash table (see Appendix B.4), the expected cost of each lookup should be constant. In fact, this scheme has been used as a classic application for *perfect hashing*. In perfect hashing, the implementor ensures, for a fixed set of keys, that the hash function generates a compact set of integers with no collisions. This lowers the cost of lookup on each keyword. If the table implementation takes into account the perfect hash function, a single probe serves to distinguish keywords from identifiers. If it retries on a miss, however, the behavior can be much worse for nonkeywords than for keywords.

If the compiler writer uses a scanner generator to construct the recognizer, then the added complexity of recognizing keywords in the DFA is handled by the tools. The extra states that this adds consume memory, but not compile time. Using the DFA mechanism to recognize keywords avoids a table lookup on each identifier. It also avoids the overhead of implementing a keyword table and its support functions. In most cases, folding keyword recognition into the DFA makes more sense than using a separate lookup table.

---

**SECTION REVIEW**

Automatic construction of a working scanner from a minimal DFA is straightforward. The scanner generator can adopt a table-driven approach, wherein it uses a generic skeleton scanner and language-specific tables, or it can generate a direct-coded scanner that threads together a code fragment for each DFA state. In general, the direct-coded approach produces a faster scanner because it has lower overhead per character.

Despite the fact that all DFA-based scanners have small constant costs per characters, many compiler writers choose to hand code a scanner. This approach lends itself to careful implementation of the interfaces between the scanner and the I/O system and between the scanner and the parser.

---

**Review Questions**

1. Given the DFA shown to the left, complete the following:

   a. Sketch the character classifier that you would use in a table-driven implementation of this DFA.

   b. Build the transition table, based on the transition diagram and your character classifier.

   c. Write an equivalent direct-coded scanner.

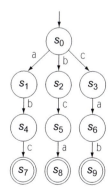

2. An alternative implementation might use a recognizer for $(a|b|c)(a|b|c)(a|b|c)$, followed by a lookup in a table that contains the three words abc, bca, and cab.

   a. Sketch the DFA for this language.

   b. Show the direct-coded scanner, including the call needed to perform keyword lookup.

   c. Contrast the cost of this approach with those in question 1 above.

3. What impact would the addition of transition-by-transition actions have on the DFA-minimization process? (Assume that we have a linguistic mechanism of attaching code fragments to the edges in the transition graph.)

## 2.6 ADVANCED TOPICS

### 2.6.1 DFA to Regular Expression

The final step in the cycle of constructions, shown in Figure 2.3, is to construct an RE from a DFA. The combination of Thompson's construction and the subset construction provide a constructive proof that DFAS are at least as powerful as REs. This section presents Kleene's construction, which builds an RE to describe the set of strings accepted by an arbitrary DFA. This algorithm establishes that REs are at least as powerful as DFAS. Together, they show that REs and DFAS are equivalent.

Consider the transition diagram of a DFA as a graph with labelled edges. The problem of deriving an RE that describes the language accepted by the DFA corresponds to a path problem over the DFA's transition diagram. The set of strings in $L(\text{DFA})$ consists of the set of edge labels for every path from $d_0$ to $d_i$, $\forall\, d_i \in D_A$. For any DFA with a cyclic transition graph, the set of such paths is infinite. Fortunately, REs have the Kleene closure operator to handle this case and summarize the complete set of subpaths created by a cycle.

Figure 2.18 shows one algorithm to compute this path expression. It assumes that the DFA has states numbered from 0 to $|D| - 1$, with $d_0$ as the start state. It generates an expression that represents the labels along all paths between two nodes, for each pair of nodes in the transition diagram. As a final step, it combines the expressions for each path that leaves $d_0$ and reaches some accepting state, $d_i \in D_A$. In this way, it systematically constructs the path expressions for all paths.

The algorithm computes a set of expressions, denoted $R_{ij}^k$, for all the relevant values of $i$, $j$, and $k$. $R_{ij}^k$ is an expression that describes all paths through the transition graph from state $i$ to state $j$, without going through a state

```
for i = 0 to |D| - 1
    for j = 0 to |D| - 1
        R_ij^-1 = { a | δ(d_i, a) = d_j }
        if (i = j) then
            R_ij^-1 = R_ij^-1 | { ε }
for k = 0 to |D| - 1
    for i = 0 to |D| - 1
        for j = 0 to |D| - 1
            R_ij^k = R_ik^{k-1}(R_kk^{k-1})*R_kj^{k-1} | R_ij^{k-1}
L = |_{s_j ∈ D_A}  R_0j^{|D|-1}
```

■ **FIGURE 2.18**  Deriving a Regular Expression from a DFA.

numbered higher than $k$. Here, *through* means both entering and leaving, so that $R^2_{1,16}$ can be nonempty if an edge runs directly from 1 to 16.

Initially, the algorithm places all of the direct paths from $i$ to $j$ in $R_{ij}^{-1}$, with $\{\epsilon\}$ added to $R_{ij}^{-1}$ if $i = j$. Over successive iterations, it builds up longer paths to produce $R_{ij}^k$ by adding to $R_{ij}^{k-1}$ the paths that pass through $k$ on their way from $i$ to $j$. Given $R_{ij}^{k-1}$, the set of paths added by going from $k-1$ to $k$ is exactly the set of paths that run from $i$ to $k$ using no state higher than $k-1$, concatenated with the paths from $k$ to itself that pass through no state higher than $k-1$, followed by the paths from $k$ to $j$ that pass through no state higher than $k-1$. That is, each iteration of the loop on $k$ adds the paths that pass through $k$ to each set $R_{ij}^{k-1}$ to produce $R_{ij}^k$.

When the $k$ loop terminates, the various $R_{ij}^k$ expressions account for all paths through the graph. The final step computes the set of paths that start with $d_0$ and end in some accepting state, $d_j \in d_A$, as the alternation of the path expressions.

Traditional statements of this algorithm assume that node names range from 1 to $n$, rather than from 0 to $n-1$. Thus, they place the direct paths in $R_{ij}^0$.

### 2.6.2  **Another Approach to DFA Minimization: Brzozowski's Algorithm**

If we apply the subset construction to an NFA that has multiple paths from the start state for some prefix, the construction will group the states involved in those duplicate prefix paths together and will create a single path for that prefix in the DFA. The subset construction always produces DFAs that have no duplicate prefix paths. Brzozowski used this observation to devise an alternative DFA minimization algorithm that directly constructs the minimal DFA from an NFA.

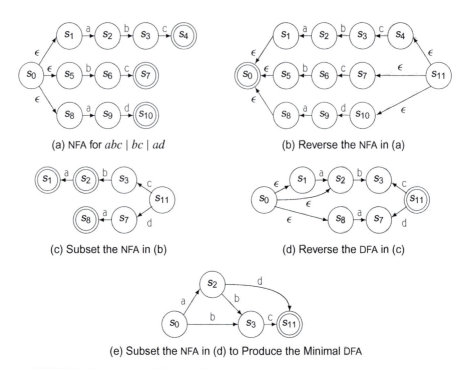

(a) NFA for *abc | bc | ad*

(b) Reverse the NFA in (a)

(c) Subset the NFA in (b)

(d) Reverse the DFA in (c)

(e) Subset the NFA in (d) to Produce the Minimal DFA

■ **FIGURE 2.19** Minimizing a DFA with Brzozowski's Algorithm.

For an NFA *n*, let *reverse(n)* be the NFA obtained by reversing the direction of all the transitions, making the initial state into a final state, adding a new initial state, and connecting it to all of the states that were final states in *n*. Further, let *reachable(n)* be a function that returns the set of states and transitions in *n* that are reachable from its initial state. Finally, let *subset(n)* be the DFA produced by applying the subset construction to *n*.

Now, given an NFA *n*, the minimal equivalent DFA is just

> *reachable( subset( reverse( reachable( subset( reverse(n))) ))).*

The inner application of *subset* and *reverse* eliminates duplicate suffixes in the original NFA. Next, *reachable* discards any states and transitions that are no longer interesting. Finally, the outer application of the triple, *reachable, subset,* and *reverse,* eliminates any duplicate prefixes in the NFA. (Applying *reverse* to a DFA can produce an NFA.)

The example in Figure 2.19 shows the steps of the algorithm on a simple NFA for the RE *abc | bc | ad*. The NFA in Figure 2.19a is similar to the one that Thompson's construction would produce; we have removed the $\epsilon$-transitions that "glue" together the NFAs for individual letters. Figure 2.19b shows the result of applying *reverse* to that NFA. Figure 2.19c depicts the DFA that *subset* constructs from the *reverse* of the NFA. At this point, the algorithm applies *reachable* to remove any unreachable states; our example NFA has none. Next, the algorithm applies *reverse* to the DFA, which produces the NFA in Figure 2.19d. Applying *subset* to that NFA produces the DFA in Figure 2.19e. Since it has no unreachable states, it is the minimal DFA for $abc \mid bc \mid cd$.

This technique looks expensive, because it applies *subset* twice and we know that *subset* can construct an exponentially large set of states. Studies of the running times of various FA minimization techniques suggest, however, that this algorithm performs reasonably well, perhaps because of specific properties of the NFA produced by the first application of *reachable (subset( reverse(n)))*. From a software-engineering perspective, it may be that implementing *reverse* and *reachable* is easier than debugging the partitioning algorithm.

### 2.6.3 Closure-Free Regular Expressions

One subclass of regular languages that has practical application beyond scanning is the set of languages described by closure-free regular expressions. Such REs have the form $w_1 \mid w_2 \mid w_3 \mid \ldots \mid w_n$ where the individual words, $w_i$, are just concatenations of characters in the alphabet, $\Sigma$. These REs have the property that they produce DFAs with acyclic transition graphs.

These simple regular languages are of interest for two reasons. First, many pattern recognition problems can be described with a closure-free RE. Examples include words in a dictionary, URLs that should be filtered, and keys to a hash table. Second, the DFA for a closure-free RE can be built in a particularly efficient way.

To build the DFA for a closure-free RE, begin with a start state $s_0$. To add a word to the existing DFA, the algorithm follows the path for the new word until it either exhausts the pattern or finds a transition to $s_e$. In the former case, it designates the final state for the new word as an accepting state. In the latter, it adds a path for the new word's remaining suffix. The resulting DFA can be encoded in tabular form or in direct-coded form (see Section 2.5.2). Either way, the recognizer uses constant time per character in the input stream.

In this algorithm, the cost of adding a new word to an existing DFA is proportional to the length of the new word. The algorithm also works incrementally; an application can easily add new words to a DFA that is in use. This property makes the acyclic DFA an interesting alternative for

$s_0$

d    f    s

$s_1$    $s_5$    $s_9$

e    e    e

$s_2$    $s_6$    $s_{10}$

e    e    e

$s_3$    $s_7$    $s_{11}$

d    d    d

$s_4$    $s_8$    $s_{12}$

implementing a perfect hash function. For a small set of keys, this technique produces an efficient recognizer. As the number of states grows (in a direct-coded recognizer) or as key length grows (in a table-driven recognizer), the implementation may slow down due to cache-size constraints. At some point, the impact of cache misses will make an efficient implementation of a more traditional hash function more attractive than incremental construction of the acyclic DFA.

The DFAs produced in this way are not guaranteed to be minimal. Consider the acyclic DFA that it would produce for the REs *deed, feed*, and *seed*, shown to the left. It has three distinct paths that each recognize the suffix *eed*. Clearly, those paths can be combined to reduce the number of states and transitions in the DFA. Minimization will combine states ($s_2$, $s_6$, $s_{10}$), states ($s_3$, $s_7$, $s_{11}$), and states ($s_4$, $s_8$, $s_{12}$) to produce a seven state DFA.

The algorithm builds DFAs that are minimal with regard to prefixes of words in the language. Any duplication takes the form of multiple paths for the same suffix.

## 2.7 CHAPTER SUMMARY AND PERSPECTIVE

The widespread use of regular expressions for searching and scanning is one of the success stories of modern computer science. These ideas were developed as an early part of the theory of formal languages and automata. They are routinely applied in tools ranging from text editors to web filtering engines to compilers as a means of concisely specifying groups of strings that happen to be regular languages. Whenever a finite collection of words must be recognized, DFA-based recognizers deserve serious consideration.

The theory of regular expressions and finite automata has developed techniques that allow the recognition of regular languages in time proportional to the length of the input stream. Techniques for automatic derivation of DFAs from REs and for DFA minimization have allowed the construction of robust tools that generate DFA-based recognizers. Both generated and hand-crafted scanners are used in well-respected modern compilers. In either case, a careful implementation should run in time proportional to the length of the input stream, with a small overhead per character.

## ■ CHAPTER NOTES

Originally, the separation of lexical analysis, or scanning, from syntax analysis, or parsing, was justified with an efficiency argument. Since the cost of scanning grows linearly with the number of characters, and the constant costs are low, pushing lexical analysis from the parser into a separate scanner lowered the cost of compiling. The advent of efficient parsing techniques weakened this argument, but the practice of building scanners persists because it provides a clean separation of concerns between lexical structure and syntactic structure.

Because scanner construction plays a small role in building an actual compiler, we have tried to keep this chapter brief. Thus, the chapter omits many theorems on regular languages and finite automata that the ambitious reader might enjoy. The many good texts on this subject can provide a much deeper treatment of finite automata and regular expressions, and their many useful properties [194, 232, 315].

Kleene [224] established the equivalence of REs and FAs. Both the Kleene closure and the DFA to RE algorithm bear his name. McNaughton and Yamada showed one construction that relates REs to NFAs [262]. The construction shown in this chapter is patterned after Thompson's work [333], which was motivated by the implementation of a textual search command for an early text editor. Johnson describes the first application of this technology to automate scanner construction [207]. The subset construction derives from Rabin and Scott [292]. The DFA minimization algorithm in Section 2.4.4 is due to Hopcroft [193]. It has found application to many different problems, including detecting when two program variables always have the same value [22].

The idea of generating code rather than tables, to produce a direct-coded scanner, appears to originate in work by Waite [340] and Heuring [189]. They report a factor of five improvement over table-driven implementations. Ngassam et al. describe experiments that characterize the speedups possible in hand-coded scanners [274]. Several authors have examined tradeoffs in scanner implementation. Jones [208] advocates direct coding but argues for a structured approach to control flow rather than the spaghetti code shown in Section 2.5.2. Brouwer et al. compare the speed of 12 different scanner implementations; they discovered a factor of 70 difference between the fastest and slowest implementations [59].

The alternative DFA minimization technique presented in Section 2.6.2 was described by Brzozowski in 1962 [60]. Several authors have compared DFA minimization techniques and their performance [328, 344]. Many authors have looked at the construction and minimization of acyclic DFAs [112, 343, 345].

## ■ EXERCISES

**1.** Describe informally the languages accepted by the following FAS:

**a.**

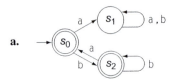

**b.**

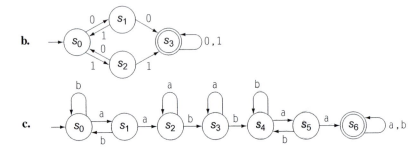

**c.**

**2.** Construct an FA accepting each of the following languages:
   **a.** $\{w \in \{a, b\}^* \mid w$ starts with '$a$' and contains '$baba$' as a substring$\}$
   **b.** $\{w \in \{0, 1\}^* \mid w$ contains '111' as a substring and does not contain '00' as a substring$\}$
   **c.** $\{w \in \{a, b, c\}^* \mid$ in $w$ the number of '$a$'s modulo 2 is equal to the number of '$b$'s modulo 3$\}$

**3.** Create FAS to recognize (a) words that represent complex numbers and (b) words that represent decimal numbers written in scientific notation.

**4.** Different programming languages use different notations to represent integers. Construct a regular expression for each one of the following:
   **a.** Nonnegative integers in C represented in bases 10 and 16.
   **b.** Nonnegative integers in VHDL that may include underscores (an underscore cannot occur as the first or last character).
   **c.** Currency, in dollars, represented as a positive decimal number rounded to the nearest one-hundredth. Such numbers begin with the character $, have commas separating each group of three digits to the left of the decimal point, and end with two digits to the right of the decimal point, for example, $8,937.43 and $7,777,777.77.

**Hint**
Not all the specifications describe regular languages.

**5.** Write a regular expression for each of the following languages:
   **a.** Given an alphabet $\Sigma = \{0, 1\}$, L is the set of all strings of alternating pairs of 0s and pairs of 1s.

**b.** Given an alphabet $\Sigma = \{0, 1\}$, L is the set of all strings of 0s and 1s that contain an even number of 0s or an even number of 1s.

**c.** Given the lowercase English alphabet, L is the set of all strings in which the letters appear in ascending lexicographical order.

**d.** Given an alphabet $\Sigma = \{a, b, c, d\}$, L is the set of strings *xyzwy*, where *x* and *w* are strings of one or more characters in $\Sigma$, *y* is any single character in $\Sigma$, and *z* is the character z, taken from outside the alphabet. (Each string xyzwy contains two words *xy* and *wy* built from letters in $\Sigma$. The words end in the same letter, *y*. They are separated by *z*.)

**e.** Given an alphabet $\Sigma = \{+, -, \times, \div, (, ), \text{id}\}$, L is the set of algebraic expressions using addition, subtraction, multiplication, division, and parentheses over ids.

**6.** Write a regular expression to describe each of the following programming language constructs:

**a.** Any sequence of tabs and blanks (sometimes called *white space*)

**b.** Comments in the programming language c

**c.** String constants (without escape characters)

**d.** Floating-point numbers

**7.** Consider the three regular expressions: Section 2.4

$(ab \mid ac)^*$

$(0 \mid 1)^*\ 1100\ \ 1^*$

$(01 \mid 10 \mid 00)^*\ \ 11$

**a.** Use Thompson's construction to construct an NFA for each RE.

**b.** Convert the NFAS to DFAS.

**c.** Minimize the DFAS.

**8.** One way of proving that two RES are equivalent is to construct their minimized DFAS and then compare them. If they differ only by state names, then the RES are equivalent. Use this technique to check the following pairs of RES and state whether or not they are equivalent.

**a.** $(0 \mid 1)^*$ and $(0^* \mid 10^*)^*$

**b.** $(ba)^+\ (a^*\ b^* \mid a^*)$ and $(ba)^*\ ba^+\ (b^* \mid \epsilon)$

**9.** In some cases, two states connected by an $\epsilon$-move can be combined.

**a.** Under what set of conditions can two states connected by an $\epsilon$-move be combined?

**b.** Give an algorithm for eliminating $\epsilon$-moves.

**c.** How does your algorithm relate to the $\epsilon$-closure function used to implement the subset construction?

10. Show that the set of regular languages is closed under intersection.

11. The DFA minimization algorithm given in Figure 2.9 is formulated to enumerate all the elements of $P$ and all of the characters in $\Sigma$ on each iteration of the while loop.
    **a.** Recast the algorithm so that it uses a worklist to hold the sets that must still be examined.
    **b.** Recast the $Split$ function so that it partitions the set around all of the characters in $\Sigma$.
    **c.** How does the expected case complexity of your modified algorithms compare to the expected case complexity of the original algorithm?

Section 2.5

12. Construct a DFA for each of the following C language constructs, and then build the corresponding table for a table-driven implementation for each of them:
    **a.** Integer constants
    **b.** Identifiers
    **c.** Comments

13. For each of the DFAs in the previous exercise, build a direct-coded scanner.

14. This chapter describes several styles of DFA implementations. Another alternative would use mutually recursive functions to implement a scanner. Discuss the advantages and disadvantages of such an implementation.

15. To reduce the size of the transition table, the scanner generator can use a character classification scheme. Generating the classifier table, however, seems expensive. The obvious algorithm would require $O(|\Sigma|^2 \cdot |states|)$ time. Derive an asymptotically faster algorithm for finding identical columns in the transition table.

16. Figure 2.15 shows a scheme that avoids quadratic roll back behavior in a scanner built by simulating a DFA. Unfortunately, that scheme requires that the scanner know in advance the length of the input stream and that it maintain a bit-matrix, $Failed$, of size $|states| \times |input|$. Devise a scheme that uses less space than the scheme shown in Figure 2.15. How does your technique affect the size of the $Failed$ table in cases where the worst case input does not occur?

# Parsers

## ■ CHAPTER OVERVIEW

The parser's task is to determine if the input program, represented by the stream of classified words produced by the scanner, is a valid sentence in the programming language. To do so, the parser attempts to build a derivation for the input program, using a grammar for the programming language.

This chapter introduces context-free grammars, a notation used to specify the syntax of programming languages. It develops several techniques for finding a derivation, given a grammar and an input program.

**Keywords:** Parsing, Grammar, LL(1), LR(1), Recursive Descent

## 3.1 INTRODUCTION

Parsing is the second stage of the compiler's front end. The parser works with the program as transformed by the scanner; it sees a stream of words where each word is annotated with a syntactic category (analogous to its part of speech). The parser derives a syntactic structure for the program, fitting the words into a grammatical model of the source programming language. If the parser determines that the input stream is a valid program, it builds a concrete model of the program for use by the later phases of compilation. If the input stream is not a valid program, the parser reports the problem and appropriate diagnostic information to the user.

As a problem, parsing has many similarities to scanning. The formal problem has been studied extensively as part of formal language theory; that work forms the theoretical basis for the practical parsing techniques used in most compilers. Speed matters; all of the techniques that we will study take time proportional to the size of the program and its representation. Low-level detail affects performance; the same implementation tradeoffs arise in parsing as in scanning. The techniques in this chapter are amenable to implementation as table-driven parsers, direct-coded parsers, and hand-coded parsers. Unlike scanners, where hand-coding is common, tool-generated parsers are more common than hand-coded parsers.

### Conceptual Roadmap

The primary task of the parser is to determine whether or not the input program is a syntactically valid sentence in the source language. Before we can build parsers that answer this question, we need both a formal mechanism for specifying the syntax of the source language and a systematic method of determining membership in this formally specified language. By restricting the form of the source language to a set of languages called context-free languages, we can ensure that the parser can efficiently answer the membership question. Section 3.2 introduces context-free grammars (CFGs) as a notation for specifying syntax.

Many algorithms have been proposed to answer the membership question for CFGs. This chapter examines two different approaches to the problem. Section 3.3 introduces top-down parsing in the form of recursive-descent parsers and LL(1) parsers. Section 3.4 examines bottom-up parsing as exemplified by LR(1) parsers. Section 3.4.2 presents the detailed algorithm for generating canonical LR(1) parsers. The final section explores several practical issues that arise in parser construction.

### Overview

A compiler's parser has the primary responsibility for recognizing syntax—that is, for determining if the program being compiled is a valid sentence in the syntactic model of the programming language. That model is expressed as a formal grammar $G$; if some string of words $s$ is in the language defined by $G$ we say that $G$ *derives* $s$. For a stream of words $s$ and a grammar G, the parser tries to build a constructive proof that $s$ can be derived in $G$—a process called *parsing*.

**Parsing**
given a stream $s$ of words and a grammar $G$, find a derivation in $G$ that produces $s$

Parsing algorithms fall into two general categories. Top-down parsers try to match the input stream against the productions of the grammar by predicting the next word (at each point). For a limited class of grammars, such prediction can be both accurate and efficient. Bottom-up parsers work from low-level detail—the actual sequence of words—and accumulate context until the derivation is apparent. Again, there exists a restricted class of grammars for which we can generate efficient bottom-up parsers. In practice, these restricted sets of grammars are large enough to encompass most features of interest in programming languages.

## 3.2 **EXPRESSING SYNTAX**

The task of the parser is to determine whether or not some stream of words fits into the syntax of the parser's intended source language. Implicit in this description is the notion that we can describe syntax and check it; in practice, we need a notation to describe the syntax of languages that people might use to program computers. In Chapter 2, we worked with one such notation, regular expressions. They provide a concise notation for describing syntax and an efficient mechanism for testing the membership of a string in the language described by an RE. Unfortunately, REs lack the power to describe the full syntax of most programming languages.

For most programming languages, syntax is expressed in the form of a context-free grammar. This section introduces and defines CFGs and explores their use in syntax-checking. It shows how we can begin to encode meaning into syntax and structure. Finally, it introduces the ideas that underlie the efficient parsing techniques described in the following sections.

### 3.2.1 **Why Not Regular Expressions?**

To motivate the use of CFGs, consider the problem of recognizing algebraic expressions over variables and the operators $+$, $-$, $\times$, and $\div$. We can define "variable" as any string that matches the RE $[a \dots z] ([a \dots z] \mid [0 \dots 9])^*$, a simplified, lowercase version of an Algol identifier. Now, we can define an expression as follows:

$$[a \dots z] ([a \dots z] \mid [0 \dots 9])^* \quad ((+ \mid - \mid \times \mid \div) \ [a \dots z] ([a \dots z] \mid [0 \dots 9])^* )^*$$

This RE matches "a+b×c" and "fee÷fie×foe". Nothing about the RE suggests a notion of operator precedence; in "a+b×c," which operator executes first, the + or the ×? The standard rule from algebra suggests × and ÷ have precedence over + and -. To enforce other evaluation orders, normal algebraic notation includes parentheses.

Adding parentheses to the RE in the places where they need to appear is somewhat tricky. An expression can start with a '(', so we need the option for an initial (. Similarly, we need the option for a final ).

We will underline ( and ) so that they are visually distinct from the ( and ) used for grouping in REs.

$$( ( \mid \epsilon) \ [a \dots z] ([a \dots z] \mid [0 \dots 9])^*$$
$$(( + \mid - \mid \times \mid \div) \ [a \dots z] ([a \dots z] \mid [0 \dots 9])^* )^* \ ( ) \mid \epsilon)$$

This RE can produce an expression enclosed in parentheses, but not one with internal parentheses to denote precedence. The internal instances of ( all occur before a variable; similarly, the internal instances of ) all occur after a variable. This observation suggests the following RE:

$$( ( ( |\epsilon) \, [a \ldots z] \, ([a \ldots z] \, | \, [0 \ldots 9])^*$$
$$( (+ | - | \times | \div) \, [a \ldots z] \, ([a \ldots z] \, | \, [0 \ldots 9])^* \, ( ) | \epsilon ) \, )^*$$

Notice that we simply moved the final ) inside the closure.

This RE matches both "a+b×c" and "(a+b)×c." It will match any correctly parenthesized expression over variables and the four operators in the RE. Unfortunately, it also matches many syntactically incorrect expressions, such as "a+(b×c" and "a+b)×c)." In fact, we cannot write an RE that will match all expressions with balanced parentheses. (Paired constructs, such as begin and end or then and else, play an important role in most programming languages.) This fact is a fundamental limitation of REs; the corresponding recognizers cannot count because they have only a finite set of states. The language $(^m \, )^n$ where $m = n$ is not regular. In principle, DFAS cannot count. While they work well for microsyntax, they are not suitable to describe some important programming language features.

### 3.2.2 Context-Free Grammars

To describe programming language syntax, we need a more powerful notation than regular expressions that still leads to efficient recognizers. The traditional solution is to use a context-free grammar (CFG). Fortunately, large subclasses of the CFGs have the property that they lead to efficient recognizers.

**Context-free grammar**

For a language L, its CFG defines the sets of strings of symbols that are valid sentences in L.

A context-free grammar, G, is a set of rules that describe how to form sentences. The collection of sentences that can be derived from G is called the *language defined by G*, denoted G. The set of languages defined by context-free grammars is called the set of context-free languages. An example may help. Consider the following grammar, which we call *SN*:

**Sentence**

a string of symbols that can be derived from the rules of a grammar

$$SheepNoise \; \rightarrow \; \text{baa } SheepNoise$$
$$| \; \text{baa}$$

**Production**

Each rule in a CFG is called a *production*.

**Nonterminal symbol**

a syntactic variable used in a grammar's productions

**Terminal symbol**

a word that can occur in a sentence

A word consists of a lexeme and its syntactic category. Words are represented in a grammar by their syntactic category

The first rule, or *production* reads "*SheepNoise* can derive the word baa followed by more *SheepNoise*." Here *SheepNoise* is a syntactic variable representing the set of strings that can be derived from the grammar. We call such a syntactic variable a *nonterminal symbol*. Each word in the language defined by the grammar is a *terminal symbol*. The second rule reads "*SheepNoise* can also derive the string baa."

To understand the relationship between the *SN* grammar and *L(SN)*, we need to specify how to apply rules in *SN* to derive sentences in *L(SN)*. To begin, we must identify the *goal symbol* or *start symbol* of *SN*. The goal symbol

---

**BACKUS-NAUR FORM**

The traditional notation used by computer scientists to represent a context-free grammar is called *Backus-Naur form*, or BNF. BNF denoted non-terminal symbols by wrapping them in angle brackets, like (SheepNoise). Terminal symbols were underlined. The symbol ::= means "derives," and the symbol | means "also derives." In BNF, the sheep noise grammar becomes:

$$\langle SheepNoise \rangle \quad ::= \quad \underline{baa} \; \langle SheepNoise \rangle$$
$$| \quad \underline{baa}$$

This is completely equivalent to our grammar *SN*.

BNF has its origins in the late 1950s and early 1960s [273]. The syntactic conventions of angle brackets, underlining, ::=, and | arose from the limited typographic options available to people writing language descriptions. (For example, see David Gries' book *Compiler Construction for Digital Computers*, which was printed entirely on a standard lineprinter [171].) Throughout this book, we use a typographically updated form of BNF. Nonterminals are written in *italics*. Terminals are written in the typewriter font. We use the symbol → for "derives."

---

represents the set of all strings in $L(SN)$. As such, it cannot be one of the words in the language. Instead, it must be one of the nonterminal symbols introduced to add structure and abstraction to the language. Since *SN* has only one nonterminal, *SheepNoise* must be the goal symbol.

To derive a sentence, we start with a prototype string that contains just the goal symbol, *SheepNoise*. We pick a nonterminal symbol, $\alpha$, in the prototype string, choose a grammar rule, $\alpha \rightarrow \beta$, and rewrite $\alpha$ with $\beta$. We repeat this rewriting process until the prototype string contains no more nonterminals, at which point it consists entirely of words, or terminal symbols, and is a sentence in the language.

**Derivation**
a sequence of rewriting steps that begins with the grammar's start symbol and ends with a sentence in the language

At each point in this derivation process, the string is a collection of terminal or nonterminal symbols. Such a string is called a *sentential form* if it occurs in some step of a valid derivation. Any sentential form can be derived from the start symbol in zero or more steps. Similarly, from any sentential form we can derive a valid sentence in zero or more steps. Thus, if we begin with *SheepNoise* and apply successive rewrites using the two rules, at each step in the process the string is a sentential form. When we have reached the point where the string contains only terminal symbols, the string is a sentence in $L(SN)$.

**Sentential form**
a string of symbols that occurs as one step in a valid derivation

**CONTEXT-FREE GRAMMARS**

Formally, a context-free grammar $G$ is a quadruple $(T, NT, S, P)$ where:

$T$  is the set of terminal symbols, or words, in the language $L(G)$. Terminal symbols correspond to syntactic categories returned by the scanner.

$NT$  is the set of nonterminal symbols that appear in the productions of $G$. Nonterminals are syntactic variables introduced to provide abstraction and structure in the productions.

$S$  is a nonterminal designated as the *goal symbol* or *start symbol* of the grammar. $S$ represents the set of sentences in $L(G)$.

$P$  is the set of productions or rewrite rules in $G$. Each rule in $P$ has the form $NT \rightarrow (T \cup NT)^+$; that is, it replaces a single nonterminal with a string of one or more grammar symbols.

The sets $T$ and $NT$ can be derived directly from the set of productions, $P$. The start symbol may be unambiguous, as in the *SheepNoise* grammar, or it may not be obvious, as in the following grammar:

$$Paren \rightarrow ( \; Bracket \; ) \qquad\qquad Bracket \rightarrow [ \; Paren \; ]$$
$$| \; ( \quad ) \qquad\qquad\qquad\qquad | \; [ \quad ]$$

In this case, the choice of start symbol determines the shape of the outer brackets. Using *Paren* as $S$ ensures that every sentence has an outermost pair of parentheses, while using *Bracket* forces an outermost pair of square brackets. To allow either, we would need to introduce a new symbol *Start* and the productions *Start* → *Paren* | *Bracket*.

Some tools that manipulate grammars require that $S$ not appear on the right-hand side of any production, which makes $S$ easy to discover.

To derive a sentence in *SN*, we start with the string that consists of one symbol, *SheepNoise*. We can rewrite *SheepNoise* with either rule 1 or rule 2. If we rewrite *SheepNoise* with rule 2, the string becomes baa and has no further opportunities for rewriting. The rewrite shows that baa is a valid sentence in $L(SN)$. The other choice, rewriting the initial string with rule 1, leads to a string with two symbols: baa *SheepNoise*. This string has one remaining nonterminal; rewriting it with rule 2 leads to the string baa baa, which is a sentence in $L(SN)$. We can represent these derivations in tabular form:

| Rule | Sentential Form |
|------|-----------------|
|      | *SheepNoise*    |
| 2    | baa             |

| Rule | Sentential Form |
|------|-----------------|
|      | *SheepNoise*    |
| 1    | baa *SheepNoise* |
| 2    | baa baa         |

Rewrite with Rule 2　　　　　Rewrite with Rules 1 Then 2

As a notational convenience, we will use $\rightarrow^+$ to mean "derives in one or more steps." Thus, *SheepNoise* $\rightarrow^+$ baa and *SheepNoise* $\rightarrow^+$ baa baa.

Rule 1 lengthens the string while rule 2 eliminates the nonterminal *SheepNoise*. (The string can never contain more than one instance of *SheepNoise*.) All valid strings in *SN* are derived by zero or more applications of rule 1, followed by rule 2. Applying rule 1 $k$ times followed by rule 2 generates a string with $k + 1$ baas.

### 3.2.3 More Complex Examples

The *SheepNoise* grammar is too simple to exhibit the power and complexity of CFGs. Instead, let's revisit the example that showed the shortcomings of RES: the language of expressions with parentheses.

$$
\begin{array}{rlll}
1 & \textit{Expr} & \rightarrow & (\ \textit{Expr}\ ) \\
2 & & | & \textit{Expr Op}\ \text{name} \\
3 & & | & \text{name} \\
4 & \textit{Op} & \rightarrow & + \\
5 & & | & - \\
6 & & | & \times \\
7 & & | & \div \\
\end{array}
$$

Beginning with the start symbol, *Expr*, we can generate two kinds of sub-terms: parenthesized subterms, with rule 1, or plain subterms, with rule 2. To generate the sentence "(a+b)×c", we can use the following rewrite sequence (2,6,1,2,4,3), shown on the left. Remember that the grammar deals with syntactic categories, such as name rather than lexemes such as a, b, or c.

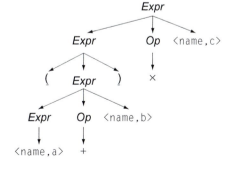

| Rule | Sentential Form |
|------|-----------------|
|      | *Expr* |
| 2    | *Expr Op* name |
| 6    | *Expr* × name |
| 1    | ( *Expr* ) × name |
| 2    | ( *Expr Op* name ) × name |
| 4    | ( *Expr* + name ) × name |
| 3    | ( name + name ) × name |

Rightmost Derivation of ( a + b ) × c          Corresponding Parse Tree

The tree on the right, called a *parse tree*, represents the derivation as a graph.

**Parse tree or syntax tree**
a graph that represents a derivation

This simple CFG for expressions cannot generate a sentence with unbalanced or improperly nested parentheses. Only rule 1 can generate an open parenthesis; it also generates the matching close parenthesis. Thus, it cannot generate strings such as "a + ( b×c" or "a+b )×c)," and a parser built from the grammar will not accept the such strings. (The best RE in Section 3.2.1 matched both of these strings.) Clearly, CFGs provide us with the ability to specify constructs that REs do not.

**Rightmost derivation**

a derivation that rewrites, at each step, the rightmost nonterminal

The derivation of (a+b)×c rewrote, at each step, the rightmost remaining nonterminal symbol. This systematic behavior was a choice; other choices are possible. One obvious alternative is to rewrite the leftmost nonterminal at each step. Using leftmost choices would produce a different derivation sequence for the same sentence. The leftmost derivation of (a+b)×c would be:

**Leftmost derivation**

a derivation that rewrites, at each step, the leftmost nonterminal

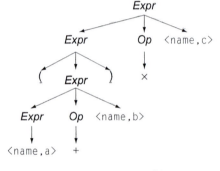

| Rule | Sentential Form |
|------|----------------|
|      | *Expr* |
| 2    | *Expr Op* name |
| 1    | ( *Expr* ) *Op* name |
| 2    | ( *Expr Op* name ) *Op* name |
| 3    | ( name *Op* name ) *Op* name |
| 4    | ( name + name ) *Op* name |
| 6    | ( name + name ) × name |

Leftmost Derivation of ( a + b ) x c

Corresponding Parse Tree

The leftmost and rightmost derivations use the same set of rules; they apply those rules in a different order. Because a parse tree represents the rules applied, but not the order of their application, the parse trees for the two derivations are identical.

From the compiler's perspective, it is important that each sentence in the language defined by a CFG has a unique rightmost (or leftmost) derivation. If multiple rightmost (or leftmost) derivations exist for some sentence, then, at some point in the derivation, multiple distinct rewrites of the rightmost (or leftmost) nonterminal lead to the same sentence. A grammar in which multiple rightmost (or leftmost) derivations exist for a sentence is called an *ambiguous* grammar. An ambiguous grammar can produce multiple derivations and multiple parse trees. Since later stages of translation will associate meaning with the detailed shape of the parse tree, multiple parse trees imply multiple possible meanings for a single program—a bad property for a programming language to have. If the compiler cannot be sure of the meaning of a sentence, it cannot translate it into a definitive code sequence.

**Ambiguity**

A grammar G is *ambiguous* if some sentence in L(G) has more than one rightmost (or leftmost) derivation.

The classic example of an ambiguous construct in the grammar for a programming language is the if-then-else construct of many Algol-like languages. The straightforward grammar for if-then-else might be

|   |            |               |                                             |
|---|------------|---------------|---------------------------------------------|
| 1 | *Statement* | $\rightarrow$ | if *Expr* then *Statement* else *Statement* |
| 2 |            | \|            | if *Expr* then *Statement*                  |
| 3 |            | \|            | *Assignment*                                |
| 4 |            | \|            | ... *other statements* ...                  |

This fragment shows that the else is optional. Unfortunately, the code fragment

if *Expr*$_1$ then if *Expr*$_2$ then *Assignment*$_1$ else *Assignment*$_2$

has two distinct rightmost derivations. The difference between them is simple. The first derivation has *Assignment*$_2$ controlled by the inner if, so *Assignment*$_2$ executes when *Expr*$_1$ is true and *Expr*$_2$ is false:

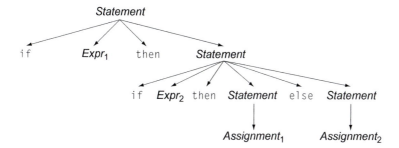

The second derivation associates the else clause with the first if, so that *Assignment*$_2$ executes when *Expr*$_1$ is false, independent of the value of *Expr*$_2$:

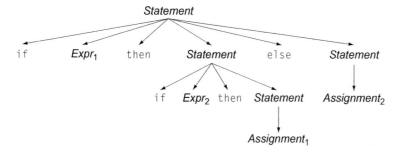

Clearly, these two derivations produce different behaviors in the compiled code.

To remove this ambiguity, the grammar must be modified to encode a rule that determines which `if` controls an `else`. To fix the `if-then-else` grammar, we can rewrite it as

| 1 | *Statement* | → | `if` *Expr* `then` *Statement* |
|---|---|---|---|
| 2 | | \| | `if` *Expr* `then` *WithElse* `else` *Statement* |
| 3 | | \| | *Assignment* |
| 4 | *WithElse* | → | `if` *Expr* `then` *WithElse* `else` *WithElse* |
| 5 | | \| | *Assignment* |

The solution restricts the set of statements that can occur in the `then` part of an `if-then-else` construct. It accepts the same set of sentences as the original grammar, but ensures that each `else` has an unambiguous match to a specific `if`. It encodes into the grammar a simple rule—bind each `else` to the innermost unclosed `if`. It has only one rightmost derivation for the example.

| Rule | Sentential Form |
|---|---|
| | *Statement* |
| 1 | `if` *Expr* `then` *Statement* |
| 2 | `if` *Expr* `then` `if` *Expr* `then` *WithElse* `else` *Statement* |
| 3 | `if` *Expr* `then` `if` *Expr* `then` *WithElse* `else` *Assignment* |
| 5 | `if` *Expr* `then` `if` *Expr* `then` *Assignment* `else` *Assignment* |

The rewritten grammar eliminates the ambiguity.

The `if-then-else` ambiguity arises from a shortcoming in the original grammar. The solution resolves the ambiguity in a way by imposing a rule that is easy for the programmer to remember. (To avoid the ambiguity entirely, some language designers have restructured the `if-then-else` construct by introducing `elseif` and `endif`.) In Section 3.5.3, we will look at other kinds of ambiguity and systematic ways of handling them.

### 3.2.4 Encoding Meaning into Structure

The `if-then-else` ambiguity points out the relationship between meaning and grammatical structure. However, ambiguity is not the only situation where meaning and grammatical structure interact. Consider the parse tree that would be built from a rightmost derivation of the simple expression `a + b x c`.

| Rule | Sentential Form |
|------|-----------------|
|  | *Expr* |
| 2 | *Expr Op* name |
| 6 | *Expr* x name |
| 2 | *Expr Op* name x name |
| 4 | *Expr* + name x name |
| 3 | name + name x name |

Derivation of a + b x c

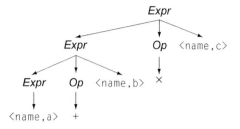

Corresponding Parse Tree

One natural way to evaluate the expression is with a simple postorder tree-walk. It would first compute a + b and then multiply that result by c to produce the result (a + b) x c. This evaluation order contradicts the classic rules of algebraic precedence, which would evaluate it as a + (b x c). Since the ultimate goal of parsing the expression is to produce code that will implement it, the expression grammar should have the property that it builds a tree whose "natural" treewalk evaluation produces the correct result.

The real problem lies in the structure of the grammar. It treats all of the arithmetic operators in the same way, without any regard for precedence. In the parse tree for (a + b) x c, the fact that the parenthetic subexpression was forced to go through an extra production in the grammar adds a level to the parse tree. The extra level, in turn, forces a postorder treewalk to evaluate the parenthetic subexpression before it evaluates the multiplication.

We can use this effect to encode operator precedence levels into the grammar. First, we must decide how many levels of precedence are required. In the simple expression grammar, we have three levels of precedence: highest precedence for ( ), medium precedence for x and ÷, and lowest precedence for + and -. Next, we group the operators at distinct levels and use a nonterminal to isolate the corresponding part of the grammar. Figure 3.1

| 0 | *Goal* | → | *Expr* |
|---|--------|---|--------|
| 1 | *Expr* | → | *Expr* + *Term* |
| 2 | | &#124; | *Expr* - *Term* |
| 3 | | &#124; | *Term* |
| 4 | *Term* | → | *Term* x *Factor* |
| 5 | | &#124; | *Term* ÷ *Factor* |
| 6 | | &#124; | *Factor* |
| 7 | *Factor* | → | ( *Expr* ) |
| 8 | | &#124; | num |
| 9 | | &#124; | name |

■ **FIGURE 3.1** The Classic Expression Grammar.

shows the resulting grammar; it includes a unique start symbol, *Goal*, and a production for the terminal symbol num that we will use in later examples.

In the classic expression grammar, *Expr*, represents the level for + and -, *Term* represents the level for × and ÷, and *Factor* represents the level for ( ). In this form, the grammar derives a parse tree for a + b × c that is consistent with standard algebraic precedence, as shown below.

| Rule | Sentential Form |
|------|-----------------|
|  | *Expr* |
| 1 | *Expr* + *Term* |
| 4 | *Expr* + *Term* × *Factor* |
| 6 | *Expr* + *Term* × name |
| 9 | *Expr* + *Factor* × name |
| 9 | *Expr* + name × name |
| 3 | *Term* + name × name |
| 6 | *Factor* + name × name |
| 9 | name + name × name |

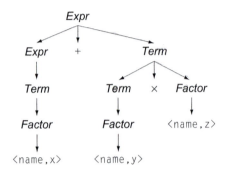

Derivation of a + b × c          Corresponding Parse Tree

A postorder treewalk over this parse tree will first evaluate b × c and then add the result to a. This implements the standard rules of arithmetic precedence. Notice that the addition of nonterminals to enforce precedence adds interior nodes to the tree. Similarly, substituting the individual operators for occurrences of *Op* removes interior nodes from the tree.

Other operations require high precedence. For example, array subscripts should be applied before standard arithmetic operations. This ensures, for example, that a + b[i] evaluates b[i] to a value before adding it to a, as opposed to treating i as a subscript on some array whose location is computed as a + b. Similarly, operations that change the type of a value, known as *type casts* in languages such as C or Java, have higher precedence than arithmetic but lower precedence than parentheses or subscripting operations.

If the language allows assignment inside expressions, the assignment operator should have low precedence. This ensures that the code completely evaluates both the left-hand side and the right-hand side of the assignment before performing the assignment. If assignment (←) had the same precedence as addition, for example, the expression a ← b + c would assign b's value to a before performing the addition, assuming a left-to-right evaluation.

**CLASSES OF CONTEXT-FREE GRAMMARS AND THEIR PARSERS**

We can partition the universe of context-free grammars into a hierarchy based on the difficulty of parsing the grammars. This hierarchy has many levels. This chapter mentions four of them, namely, arbitrary CFGs, LR(1) grammars, LL(1) grammars, and regular grammars (RGs). These sets nest as shown in the diagram.

Arbitrary CFGs require more time to parse than the more restricted LR(1) or LL(1) grammars. For example, Earley's algorithm parses arbitrary CFGs in $\mathbf{O}(n^3)$ time, worst case, where $n$ is the number of words in the input stream. Of course, the actual running time may be better. Historically, compiler writers have shied away from "universal" techniques because of their perceived inefficiency.

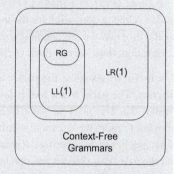

Context-Free Grammars

The LR(1) grammars include a large subset of the unambiguous CFGs. LR(1) grammars can be parsed, bottom-up, in a linear scan from left to right, looking at most one word ahead of the current input symbol. The widespread availability of tools that derive parsers from LR(1) grammars has made LR(1) parsers "everyone's favorite parsers."

The LL(1) grammars are an important subset of the LR(1) grammars. LL(1) grammars can be parsed, top-down, in a linear scan from left to right, with a one-word lookahead. LL(1) grammars can be parsed with either a hand-coded recursive-descent parser or a generated LL(1) parser. Many programming languages can be written in an LL(1) grammar.

Regular grammars (RGs) are CFGs that generate regular languages. A regular grammar is a CFG where productions are restricted to two forms, either $A \rightarrow a$ or $A \rightarrow aB$, where $A, B \in NT$ and $a \in T$. Regular grammars are equivalent to regular expressions; they encode precisely those languages that can be recognized by a DFA. The primary use for regular languages in compiler construction is to specify scanners.

Almost all programming-language constructs can be expressed in LR(1) form and, often, in LL(1) form. Thus, most compilers use a fast-parsing algorithm based on one of these two restricted classes of CFG.

## 3.2.5  Discovering a Derivation for an Input String

We have seen how to use a CFG $G$ as a rewriting system to generate sentences that are in $L(G)$. In contrast, a compiler must infer a derivation for a given input string, or determine that no such derivation exists. The process of constructing a derivation from a specific input sentence is called *parsing*.

A parser takes, as input, an alleged program written in some source language.

The parser sees the program as it emerges from the scanner: a stream of words annotated with their syntactic categories. Thus, the parser would see a + b x c as ⟨name,a⟩ + ⟨name,b⟩ x ⟨name,c⟩. As output, the parser needs to produce either a derivation for the input program or an error message for an invalid program. For an unambiguous language, a parse tree is equivalent to a derivation; thus, we can think of the parser's output as a parse tree.

It is useful to visualize the parser as building a syntax tree for the input program. The parse tree's root is known; it represents the grammar's start symbol. The leaves of the parse tree are known; they must match, in order from left to right, the stream of words returned by the scanner. The hard part of parsing lies in discovering the grammatical connection between the leaves and the root. Two distinct and opposite approaches for constructing the tree suggest themselves:

1. *Top-down parsers* begin with the root and grow the tree toward the leaves. At each step, a top-down parser selects a node for some nonterminal on the lower fringe of the tree and extends it with a subtree that represents the right-hand side of a production that rewrites the nonterminal.

2. *Bottom-up parsers* begin with the leaves and grow the tree toward the root. At each step, a bottom-up parser identifies a contiguous substring of the parse tree's upper fringe that matches the right-hand side of some production; it then builds a node for the rule's left-hand side and connects it into the tree.

In either scenario, the parser makes a series of choices about which productions to apply. Most of the intellectual complexity in parsing lies in the mechanisms for making these choices. Section 3.3 explores the issues and algorithms that arise in top-down parsing, while Section 3.4 examines bottom-up parsing in depth.

## 3.3 **TOP-DOWN PARSING**

A top-down parser begins with the root of the parse tree and systematically extends the tree downward until its leaves match the classified words returned by the scanner. At each point, the process considers a partially built parse tree. It selects a nonterminal symbol on the lower fringe of the tree and extends it by adding children that correspond to the right-hand side of some production for that nonterminal. It cannot extend the frontier from a terminal. This process continues until either

a. the fringe of the parse tree contains only terminal symbols, and the input stream has been exhausted, or
b. a clear mismatch occurs between the fringe of the partially built parse tree and the input stream.

In the first case, the parse succeeds. In the second case, two situations are possible. The parser may have selected the wrong production at some earlier step in the process, in which case it can backtrack, systematically reconsidering earlier decisions. For an input string that is a valid sentence, backtracking will lead the parser to a correct sequence of choices and let it construct a correct parse tree. Alternatively, if the input string is not a valid sentence, backtracking will fail and the parser should report the syntax error to the user.

One key insight makes top-down parsing efficient: *a large subset of the context-free grammars can be parsed without backtracking.* Section 3.3.1 shows transformations that can often convert an arbitrary grammar into one suitable for backtrack-free top-down parsing. The two sections that follow it introduce two distinct techniques for constructing top-down parsers: hand-coded recursive-descent parsers and generated LL(1) parsers.

Figure 3.2 shows a concrete algorithm for a top-down parser that constructs a leftmost derivation. It builds a parse tree, anchored at the variable *root*. It uses a stack, with access functions *push( )* and *pop( )*, to track the unmatched portion of the fringe.

The main portion of the parser consists of a loop that focuses on the leftmost unmatched symbol on the partially-built parse tree's lower fringe. If the focus symbol is a nonterminal, it expands the parse tree downward; it chooses a production, builds the corresponding part of the parse tree, and moves the focus to the leftmost symbol on this new portion of the fringe. If the focus symbol is a terminal, it compares the focus against the next word in the input. A match moves both the focus to the next symbol on the fringe and advances the input stream.

If the focus is a terminal symbol that does not match the input, the parser must backtrack. First, it systematically considers alternatives for the most recently chosen rule. If it exhausts those alternatives, it moves back up the parse tree and reconsiders choices at a higher level in the parse tree. If this process fails to match the input, the parser reports a syntax error. Backtracking increases the asymptotic cost of parsing; in practice, it is an expensive way to discover syntax errors.

```
root ← node for the start symbol, S;
focus ← root;
push(null);

word ← NextWord();

while (true) do;
    if (focus is a nonterminal) then begin;
        pick next rule to expand focus (A → β₁,β₂,...,βₙ);
        build nodes for β₁,β₂...βₙ as children of focus;
        push(βₙ,βₙ₋₁,...,β₂);
        focus ← β₁;
    end;
    else if (word matches focus) then begin;
        word ← NextWord();
        focus ← pop()
    end;
    else if (word = eof and focus = null)
        then accept the input and return root;
        else backtrack;
end;
```

■ **FIGURE 3.2** A Leftmost, Top-Down Parsing Algorithm.

The implementation of "backtrack" is straightforward. It sets focus to its parent in the partially-built parse tree and disconnects its children. If an untried rule remains with focus on its left-hand side, the parser expands focus by that rule. It builds children for each symbol on the right-hand side, pushes those symbols onto the stack in right-to-left order, and sets focus to point at the first child. If no untried rule remains, the parser moves up another level and tries again. When it runs out of possibilities, it reports a syntax error and quits.

To facilitate finding the "next" rule, the parser can store the rule number in a nonterminal's node when it expands that node.

When it backtracks, the parser must also rewind the input stream. Fortunately, the partial parse tree encodes enough information to make this action efficient. The parser must place each matched terminal in the discarded production back into the input stream, an action it can take as it disconnects them from the parse tree in a left-to-right traversal of the discarded children.

### 3.3.1 Transforming a Grammar for Top-Down Parsing

The efficiency of a top-down parser depends critically on its ability to pick the correct production each time that it expands a nonterminal. If the parser always makes the right choice, top-down parsing is efficient. If it makes poor choices, the cost of parsing rises. For some grammars, the worst case behavior is that the parser does not terminate. This section examines two structural issues with CFGs that lead to problems with top-down parsers and presents transformations that the compiler writer can apply to the grammar to avoid these problems.

### A Top-Down Parser with Oracular Choice

As an initial exercise, consider the behavior of the parser from Figure 3.2 with the classic expression grammar in Figure 3.1 when applied to the string a + b x c. For the moment, assume that the parser has an oracle that picks the correct production at each point in the parse. With oracular choice, it might proceed as shown in Figure 3.3. The right column shows the input string, with a marker ↑ to indicate the parser's current position in the string. The symbol → in the rule column represents a step in which the parser matches a terminal symbol against the input string and advances the input. At each step, the sentential form represents the lower fringe of the partially-built parse tree.

With oracular choice, the parser should take a number of steps proportional to the length of the derivation plus the length of the input. For a + b x c the parser applied eight rules and matched five words.

Notice, however, that oracular choice means inconsistent choice. In both the first and second steps, the parser considered the nonterminal *Expr*. In the first step, it applied rule 1, *Expr → Expr + Term*. In the second step, it applied rule 3, *Expr → Term*. Similarly, when expanding *Term* in an attempt to match a, it applied rule 6, *Term → Factor*, but when expanding *Term* to match b,

| Rule | Sentential Form | Input |
|------|-----------------|-------|
| | *Expr* | ↑ name + name x name |
| 1 | *Expr + Term* | ↑ name + name x name |
| 3 | *Term + Term* | ↑ name + name x name |
| 6 | *Factor + Term* | ↑ name + name x name |
| 9 | name + *Term* | ↑ name + name x name |
| → | name + *Term* | name ↑ + name x name |
| → | name + *Term* | name + ↑ name x name |
| 4 | name + *Term* x *Factor* | name + ↑ name x name |
| 6 | name + *Factor* x *Factor* | name + ↑ name x name |
| 9 | name + name x *Factor* | name + ↑ name x name |
| → | name + name x *Factor* | name + name ↑ x name |
| → | name + name x *Factor* | name + name x ↑ name |
| 9 | name + name x name | name + name x ↑ name |
| → | name + name x name | name + name x name ↑ |

■ **FIGURE 3.3** Leftmost, Top-Down Parse of a + b x c with Oracular Choice.

it applied rule 4, *Term* → *Term* × *Factor*. It would be difficult to make the top-down parser work with consistent, algorithmic choice when using this version of the expression grammar.

### Eliminating Left Recursion

One problem with the combination of the classic expression grammar and a leftmost, top-down parser arises from the structure of the grammar. To see the difficulty, consider an implementation that always tries to apply the rules in the order in which they appear in the grammar. Its first several actions would be:

| Rule | Sentential Form | Input |
|------|-----------------|-------|
| | *Expr* | ↑ name + name × name |
| 1 | *Expr* + *Term* | ↑ name + name × name |
| 1 | *Expr* + *Term* + *Term* | ↑ name + name × name |
| 1 | ... | ↑ name + name × name |

It starts with *Expr* and tries to match a. It applies rule 1 to create the sentential form *Expr* + *Term* on the fringe. Now, it faces the nonterminal *Expr* and the input word a, again. By consistent choice, it applies rule 1 to replace *Expr* with *Expr* + *Term*. Of course, it still faces *Expr* and the input word a. With this grammar and consistent choice, the parser will continue to expand the fringe indefinitely because that expansion never generates a leading terminal symbol.

**Left recursion**

A rule in a CFG is left recursive if the first symbol on its right-hand side is the symbol on its left-hand side or can derive that symbol.

The former case is called *direct* left recursion, while the latter case is called *indirect* left recursion.

This problem arises because the grammar uses *left recursion* in productions 1, 2, 4, and 5. With left-recursion, a top-down parser can loop indefinitely without generating a leading terminal symbol that the parser can match (and advance the input). Fortunately, we can reformulate a left-recursive grammar so that it uses right recursion—any recursion involves the rightmost symbol in a rule.

The translation from left recursion to right recursion is mechanical. For direct left recursion, like the one shown below to the left, we can rewrite the individual productions to use right recursion, shown on the right.

$$
\begin{aligned}
\textit{Fee} \;\to\;& \textit{Fee } \alpha \\
\mid\;& \beta
\end{aligned}
\qquad\qquad
\begin{aligned}
\textit{Fee} \;\to\;& \beta \textit{ Fee}' \\
\textit{Fee}' \;\to\;& \alpha \textit{ Fee}' \\
\mid\;& \epsilon
\end{aligned}
$$

The transformation introduces a new nonterminal, *Fee'*, and transfers the recursion onto *Fee'*. It also adds the rule *Fee'*→ϵ, where ϵ represents the empty string. This ϵ-*production* requires careful interpretation in the parsing algorithm. To expand the production *Fee'*→ϵ, the parser simply sets *focus* ← *pop( )*, which advances its attention to the next node, terminal or nonterminal, on the fringe.

In the classic expression grammar, direct left recursion appears in the productions for both *Expr* and *Term*.

| Original | | | Transformed | | |
|---|---|---|---|---|---|
| *Expr* | → | *Expr + Term* | *Expr* | → | *Term* Expr′ |
| | \| | *Expr - Term* | *Expr′* | → | + *Term* Expr′ |
| | \| | *Term* | | \| | - *Term* Expr′ |
| | | | | \| | ε |
| *Term* | → | *Term* x *Factor* | *Term* | → | *Factor Term′* |
| | \| | *Term* ÷ *Factor* | *Term′* | → | x *Factor Term′* |
| | \| | *Factor* | | \| | ÷ *Factor Term′* |
| | | | | \| | ε |

Plugging these replacements back into the classic expression grammar yields a right-recursive variant of the grammar, shown in Figure 3.4. It specifies the same set of expressions as the classic expression grammar.

The grammar in Figure 3.4 eliminates the problem with nontermination. It does not avoid the need for backtracking. Figure 3.5 shows the behavior of the top-down parser with this grammar on the input a + b x c. The example still assumes oracular choice; we will address that issue in the next subsection. It matches all 5 terminals and applies 11 productions—3 more than it did with the left-recursive grammar. All of the additional rule applications involve productions that derive $\epsilon$.

This simple transformation eliminates direct left recursion. We must also eliminate indirect left recursion, which occurs when a chain of rules such as $\alpha{\rightarrow}\beta$, $\beta{\rightarrow}\gamma$, and $\gamma{\rightarrow}\alpha\delta$ creates the situation that $\alpha{\rightarrow}^{+}\alpha\delta$. Such indirect left recursion is not always obvious; it can be obscured by a long chain of productions.

| | | | | | | | |
|---|---|---|---|---|---|---|---|
| 0 | *Goal* | → | *Expr* | 6 | *Term′* | → | x *Factor Term′* |
| 1 | *Expr* | → | *Term Expr′* | 7 | | \| | ÷ *Factor Term′* |
| 2 | *Expr′* | → | + *Term Expr′* | 8 | | \| | ε |
| 3 | | \| | - *Term Expr′* | 9 | *Factor* | → | ( *Expr* ) |
| 4 | | \| | ε | 10 | | \| | num |
| 5 | *Term* | → | *Factor Term′* | 11 | | \| | name |

■ **FIGURE 3.4** Right-Recursive Variant of the Classic Expression Grammar.

| Rule | Sentential Form | Input |
|------|-----------------|-------|
|      | *Expr* | ↑ name + name x name |
| 1    | *Term Expr'* | ↑ name + name x name |
| 5    | *Factor Term' Expr'* | ↑ name + name x name |
| 11   | name *Term' Expr'* | ↑ name + name x name |
| →    | name *Term' Expr'* | name ↑ + name x name |
| 8    | name *Expr'* | name ↑ + name x name |
| 2    | name + *Term Expr'* | name ↑ + name x name |
| →    | name + *Term Expr'* | name + ↑ name x name |
| 5    | name + *Factor Term' Expr'* | name + ↑ name x name |
| 11   | name + name *Term' Expr'* | name + ↑ name x name |
| →    | name + name *Term' Expr'* | name + name ↑ x name |
| 6    | name + name x *Factor Term' Expr'* | name + name ↑ x name |
| →    | name + name x *Factor Term' Expr'* | name + name x ↑ name |
| 11   | name + name x name *Term' Expr'* | name + name x ↑ name |
| →    | name + name x name *Term' Expr'* | name + name x name ↑ |
| 8    | name + name x name *Expr'* | name + name x name ↑ |
| 4    | name + name x name | name + name x name ↑ |

■ **FIGURE 3.5** Leftmost, Top-Down Parse of a + b x c with the Right-Recursive Expression Grammar.

To convert indirect left recursion into right recursion, we need a more systematic approach than inspection followed by application of our transformation. The algorithm in Figure 3.6 eliminates all left recursion from a grammar by thorough application of two techniques: forward substitution to convert indirect left recursion into direct left recursion and rewriting direct left recursion as right recursion. It assumes that the original grammar has no cycles ($A \rightarrow^+ A$) and no $\epsilon$-productions.

The algorithm imposes an arbitrary order on the nonterminals. The outer loop cycles through the nonterminals in this order. The inner loop looks for any production that expands $A_i$ into a right-hand side that begins with $A_j$, for $j < i$. Such an expansion may lead to an indirect left recursion. To avoid this, the algorithm replaces the occurrence of $A_j$ with all the alternative right-hand sides for $A_j$. That is, if the inner loop discovers a production $A_i \rightarrow A_j\gamma$, and $A_j \rightarrow \delta_1|\delta_2|\cdots|\delta_k$, then the algorithm replaces $A_i \rightarrow A_j\gamma$ with a set of productions $A_i \rightarrow \delta_1\gamma|\delta_2\gamma|\cdots|\delta_k\gamma$. This process eventually converts each indirect left recursion into a direct left recursion. The final step in the outer loop converts any direct left recursion on $A_i$ to right recursion using the simple transformation shown earlier. Because new nonterminals are added at the end and only involve right recursion, the loop can ignore them—they do not need to be checked and converted.

```
impose an order on the nonterminals, A₁, A₂, ..., Aₙ

for i ← 1 to n do;
    for j ← 1 to i - 1 do;
        if ∃ a production Aᵢ→Aⱼγ
            then replace Aᵢ→Aⱼγ with one or more
                productions that expand Aⱼ
    end;
    rewrite the productions to eliminate
        any direct left recursion on Aᵢ
end;
```

■ **FIGURE 3.6** Removal of Indirect Left Recursion.

Considering the loop invariant for the outer loop may make this clearer. At the start of the $i^{th}$ outer loop iteration

$\forall k < i$, no production expanding $A_k$ has $A_l$ in its rhs, for $l < k$.

At the end of this process, $(i = n)$, all indirect left recursion has been eliminated through the repetitive application of the inner loop, and all immediate left recursion has been eliminated in the final step of each iteration.

## Backtrack-Free Parsing

The major source of inefficiency in the leftmost, top-down parser arises from its need to backtrack. If the parser expands the lower fringe with the wrong production, it eventually encounters a mismatch between that fringe and the parse tree's leaves, which correspond to the words returned by the scanner. When the parser discovers the mismatch, it must undo the actions that built the wrong fringe and try other productions. The act of expanding, retracting, and re-expanding the fringe wastes time and effort.

In the derivation of Figure 3.5, the parser chose the correct rule at each step. With consistent choice, such as considering rules in order of appearance in the grammar, it would have backtracked on each name, first trying *Factor* → *( Expr )* and then *Factor* → num before deriving name. Similarly, the expansions by rules 4 and 8 would have considered the other alternatives before expanding to $\epsilon$.

For this grammar, the parser can avoid backtracking with a simple modification. When the parser goes to select the next rule, it can consider both the focus symbol and the next input symbol, called the *lookahead symbol*. Using a one symbol lookahead, the parser can disambiguate all of the choices that arise in parsing the right-recursive expression grammar. Thus, we say that the grammar is *backtrack free* with a lookahead of one symbol. A backtrack-free grammar is also called a *predictive grammar*.

**Backtrack-free grammar**
a CFG for which the leftmost, top-down parser can always predict the correct rule with lookahead of at most one word

```
for each α ∈ (T∪eof∪ε) do;
    FIRST(α) ← α;
end;
for each A ∈ NT do;
    FIRST(A) ← Ø ;
end;

while (FIRST sets are still changing) do;
    for each p∈P, where p has the form A→β do;
        if β is β₁β₂...βₖ, where βᵢ ∈ T∪NT, then begin;
            rhs ← FIRST(β₁) − {ε};
            i ← 1;
            while (ε ∈ FIRST(βᵢ) and i ≤ k-1) do;
                rhs ← rhs ∪ (FIRST(βᵢ₊₁)−{ε}) ;
                i ← i + 1;
            end;
        end;
        if i = k and ε ∈ FIRST(βₖ)
            then rhs ← rhs ∪ {ε};
        FIRST(A) ← FIRST(A) ∪ rhs;
    end;
end;
```

■ **FIGURE 3.7** Computing FIRST Sets for Symbols in a Grammar.

We can formalize the property that makes the right-recursive expression grammar backtrack free. At each point in the parse, the choice of an expansion is obvious because each alternative for the leftmost nonterminal leads to a distinct terminal symbol. Comparing the next word in the input stream against those choices reveals the correct expansion.

**FIRST set**

For a grammar symbol $\alpha$, FIRST($\alpha$) is the set of terminals that can appear at the start of a sentence derived from $\alpha$.

The intuition is clear, but formalizing it will require some notation. For each grammar symbol $\alpha$, define the set FIRST($\alpha$) as the set of terminal symbols that can appear as the first word in some string derived from $\alpha$. The domain of FIRST is the set of grammar symbols, $T \cup NT \cup \{\epsilon, \text{eof}\}$ and its range is $T \cup \{\epsilon, \text{eof}\}$. If $\alpha$ is either a terminal, $\epsilon$, or eof, then FIRST($\alpha$) has exactly one member, $\alpha$. For a nonterminal $A$, FIRST($A$) contains the complete set of terminal symbols that can appear as the leading symbol in a sentential form derived from $A$.

eof occurs implicitly at the end of every sentence in the grammar. Thus, it is in both the domain and range of FIRST.

Figure 3.7 shows an algorithm that computes the FIRST sets for each symbol in a grammar. As its initial step, the algorithm sets the FIRST sets for the simple cases, terminals, $\epsilon$, and eof. For the right-recursive expression grammar shown in Figure 3.4 on page 101, that initial step produces the following FIRST sets:

| | num | name | + | - | × | ÷ | ( | ) | eof | $\epsilon$ |
|---|---|---|---|---|---|---|---|---|---|---|
| FIRST | num | name | + | - | x | ÷ | ( | ) | eof | $\epsilon$ |

Next, the algorithm iterates over the productions, using the FIRST sets for the right-hand side of a production to derive the FIRST set for the nonterminal on its left-hand side. This process halts when it reaches a fixed point. For the right-recursive expression grammar, the FIRST sets of the nonterminals are:

| | *Expr* | *Expr'* | *Term* | *Term'* | *Factor* |
|---|---|---|---|---|---|
| FIRST | (, name, num | +, -, $\epsilon$ | (, name, num | x, ÷, $\epsilon$ | (, name, num |

We defined FIRST sets over single grammar symbols. It is convenient to extend that definition to strings of symbols. For a string of symbols, $s = \beta_1 \beta_2 \beta_3 \ldots \beta_k$, we define FIRST$(s)$ as the union of the FIRST sets for $\beta_1, \beta_2, \ldots, \beta_n$, where $\beta_n$ is the first symbol whose FIRST set does not contain $\epsilon$, and $\epsilon \in$ FIRST$(s)$ if and only if it is in the set for each of the $\beta_i$, $1 \leq i \leq k$. The algorithm in Figure 3.7 computes this quantity into the variable rhs.

Conceptually, FIRST sets simplify implementation of a top-down parser. Consider, for example, the rules for *Expr'* in the right-recursive expression grammar:

$$
\begin{array}{llll}
2 & Expr' & \rightarrow & + \ Term \ Expr' \\
3 & & | & - \ Term \ Expr' \\
4 & & | & \epsilon
\end{array}
$$

When the parser tries to expand an *Expr'*, it uses the lookahead symbol and the FIRST sets to choose between rules 2, 3, and 4. With a lookahead of +, the parser expands by rule 2 because + is in FIRST$(+ \ Term \ Expr')$ and not in FIRST$(- \ Term \ Expr')$ or FIRST$(\epsilon)$. Similarly, a lookahead of - dictates a choice of rule 3.

Rule 4, the $\epsilon$-production, poses a slightly harder problem. FIRST$(\epsilon)$ is just $\{\epsilon\}$, which matches no word returned by the scanner. Intuitively, the parser should apply the $\epsilon$ production when the lookahead symbol is not a member of the FIRST set of any other alternative. To differentiate between legal inputs

```
for each A ∈ NT do;
    FOLLOW(A) ← ∅ ;
end;

FOLLOW(S) ← {eof};

while (FOLLOW sets are still changing) do;
    for each p ∈ P of the form A → β₁β₂···βₖ do;
        TRAILER ← FOLLOW(A);
        for i ← k down to 1 do;
            if βᵢ ∈ NT then begin;
                FOLLOW(βᵢ) ← FOLLOW(βᵢ) ∪ TRAILER;
                if ε ∈ FIRST(βᵢ)
                    then TRAILER ← TRAILER ∪ (FIRST(βᵢ) − ε);
                    else TRAILER ← FIRST(βᵢ);
            end;
            else TRAILER ← FIRST(βᵢ);    // is {βᵢ}
        end;
    end;
end;
```

■ **FIGURE 3.8** Computing FOLLOW Sets for Non-Terminal Symbols.

and syntax errors, the parser needs to know which words can appear as the leading symbol after a valid application of rule 4—the set of symbols that can follow an *Expr'*.

**FOLLOW set**

For a nonterminal $\alpha$, FOLLOW($\alpha$) contains the set of words that can occur immediately after $\alpha$ in a sentence.

To capture that knowledge, we define the set FOLLOW(*Expr'*) to contain all of the words that can occur to the immediate right of a string derived from *Expr'*. Figure 3.8 presents an algorithm to compute the FOLLOW set for each nonterminal in a grammar; it assumes the existence of FIRST sets. The algorithm initializes each FOLLOW set to the empty set and then iterates over the productions, computing the contribution of the partial suffixes to the FOLLOW set of each symbol in each right-hand side. The algorithm halts when it reaches a fixed point. For the right-recursive expression grammar, the algorithm produces:

|  | **Expr** | **Expr'** | **Term** | **Term'** | **Factor** |
|---|---|---|---|---|---|
| FOLLOW | eof, ) | eof, ) | eof, +, -, ) | eof, +, -, ) | eof, +, -, ×, ÷, ) |

The parser can use FOLLOW(*Expr'*) when it tries to expand an *Expr'*. If the lookahead symbol is +, it applies rule 2. If the lookahead symbol is -, it applies rule 3. If the lookahead symbol is in FOLLOW(*Expr'*), which contains eof and ), it applies rule 4. Any other symbol causes a syntax error.

Using FIRST and FOLLOW, we can specify precisely the condition that makes a grammar backtrack free for a top-down parser. For a production $A \to \beta$, define its augmented FIRST set, $\text{FIRST}^+$, as follows:

$$\text{FIRST}^+(A \to \beta) = \begin{cases} \text{FIRST}(\beta) & \text{if } \epsilon \notin \text{FIRST}(\beta) \\ \text{FIRST}(\beta) \cup \text{FOLLOW}(A) & \text{otherwise} \end{cases}$$

Now, a backtrack-free grammar has the property that, for any nonterminal $A$ with multiple right-hand sides, $A \to \beta_1 \mid \beta_2 \mid \cdots \mid \beta_n$

$$\text{FIRST}^+(A \to \beta_i) \cap \text{FIRST}^+(A \to \beta_j) = \emptyset, \ \forall \ 1 \leq i, j \leq n, \ i \neq j.$$

Any grammar that has this property is *backtrack free*.

For the right-recursive expression grammar, only productions 4 and 8 have $\text{FIRST}^+$ sets that differ from their FIRST sets.

| | Production | FIRST set | FIRST$^+$ set |
|---|---|---|---|
| 4 | $Expr' \to \epsilon$ | $\{\epsilon\}$ | $\{\epsilon, \texttt{eof}, \texttt{)}\}$ |
| 8 | $Term' \to \epsilon$ | $\{\epsilon\}$ | $\{\epsilon, \texttt{eof}, \texttt{+}, \texttt{-}, \texttt{)}\}$ |

Applying the backtrack-free condition pairwise to each set of alternate right-hand sides proves that the grammar is, indeed, backtrack free.

### Left-Factoring to Eliminate Backtracking

Not all grammars are backtrack free. For an example of such a grammar, consider extending the expression grammar to include function calls, denoted with parentheses, $\texttt{(}$ and $\texttt{)}$, and array-element references, denoted with square brackets, $\texttt{[}$ and $\texttt{]}$. To add these options, we replace production 11, *Factor* → $\texttt{name}$, with a set of three rules, plus a set of right-recursive rules for argument lists.

| 11 | *Factor* | → | $\texttt{name}$ |
|---|---|---|---|
| 12 | | \| | $\texttt{name}$ $\texttt{[}$ *ArgList* $\texttt{]}$ |
| 13 | | \| | $\texttt{name}$ $\texttt{(}$ *ArgList* $\texttt{)}$ |
| 15 | *ArgList* | → | *Expr MoreArgs* |
| 16 | *MoreArgs* | → | , *Expr MoreArgs* |
| 17 | | \| | $\epsilon$ |

Because productions 11, 12, and 13 all begin with $\texttt{name}$, they have identical $\text{FIRST}^+$ sets. When the parser tries to expand an instance of *Factor* with a lookahead of $\texttt{name}$, it has no basis to choose among 11, 12, and 13. The compiler writer can implement a parser that chooses one rule and backtracks when it is wrong. As an alternative, we can transform these productions to create disjoint $\text{FIRST}^+$ sets.

A two-word lookahead would handle this case. However, for any finite lookahead we can devise a grammar where that lookahead is insufficient.

The following rewrite of productions 11, 12, and 13 describes the same language but produces disjoint FIRST$^+$ sets:

| 11 | *Factor* | $\rightarrow$ | name *Arguments* |
|----|----------|---------------|------------------|
| 12 | *Arguments* | $\rightarrow$ | [ *ArgList* ] |
| 13 | | \| | ( *ArgList* ) |
| 14 | | \| | $\epsilon$ |

**Left factoring**

the process of extracting and isolating common prefixes in a set of productions

The rewrite breaks the derivation of *Factor* into two steps. The first step matches the common prefix of rules 11, 12, and 13. The second step recognizes the three distinct suffixes: [ *Expr* ], ( *Expr* ), and $\epsilon$. The rewrite adds a new nonterminal, *Arguments*, and pushes the alternate suffixes for *Factor* into right-hand sides for *Arguments*. We call this transformation *left factoring*.

We can left factor any set of rules that has alternate right-hand sides with a common prefix. The transformation takes a nonterminal and its productions:

$$A \rightarrow \alpha\beta_1 \mid \alpha\beta_2 \mid \cdots \mid \alpha\beta_n \mid \gamma_1 \mid \gamma_2 \mid \cdots \mid \gamma_j$$

where $\alpha$ is the common prefix and the $\gamma_i$'s represent right-hand sides that do not begin with $\alpha$. The transformation introduces a new nonterminal $B$ to represent the alternate suffixes for $\alpha$ and rewrites the original productions according to the pattern:

$$A \rightarrow \alpha B \mid \gamma_1 \mid \gamma_2 \mid \cdots \mid \gamma_j$$
$$B \rightarrow \beta_1 \mid \beta_2 \mid \cdots \mid \beta_n$$

To left factor a complete grammar, we must inspect each nonterminal, discover common prefixes, and apply the transformation in a systematic way. For example, in the pattern above, we must consider factoring the right-hand sides of $B$, as two or more of the $\beta_i$'s could share a prefix. The process stops when all common prefixes have been identified and rewritten.

Left-factoring can often eliminate the need to backtrack. However, some context-free languages have no backtrack-free grammar. Given an arbitrary CFG, the compiler writer can systematically eliminate left recursion and use left-factoring to eliminate common prefixes. These transformations may produce a backtrack-free grammar. In general, however, it is undecidable whether or not a backtrack-free grammar exists for an arbitrary context-free language.

### 3.3.2 Top-Down Recursive-Descent Parsers

Backtrack-free grammars lend themselves to simple and efficient parsing with a paradigm called *recursive descent*. A recursive-descent parser is

---

**PREDICTIVE PARSERS VERSUS DFAs**

Predictive parsing is the natural extension of DFA-style reasoning to parsers. A DFA transitions from state to state based solely on the next input character. A predictive parser chooses an expansion based on the next word in the input stream. Thus, for each nonterminal in the grammar, there must be a unique mapping from the first word in any acceptable input string to a specific production that leads to a derivation for that string. The real difference in power between a DFA and a predictively parsable grammar derives from the fact that one prediction may lead to a right-hand side with many symbols, whereas in a regular grammar, it predicts only a single symbol. This lets predictive grammars include productions such as $p \rightarrow (p)$, which are beyond the power of a regular expression to describe. (Recall that a regular expression can recognize $(^+ \Sigma^*)^+$, but this does not specify that the numbers of opening and closing parentheses must match.)

Of course, a hand-coded, recursive-descent parser can use arbitrary tricks to disambiguate production choices. For example, if a particular left-hand side cannot be predicted with a single-symbol lookahead, the parser could use two symbols. Done judiciously, this should not cause problems.

---

structured as a set of mutually recursive procedures, one for each non-terminal in the grammar. The procedure corresponding to nonterminal $A$ recognizes an instance of $A$ in the input stream. To recognize a nonterminal $B$ on some right-hand side for $A$, the parser invokes the procedure corresponding to $B$. Thus, the grammar itself serves as a guide to the parser's implementation.

Consider the three rules for *Expr'* in the right-recursive expression grammar:

|   | Production | FIRST$^+$ |
|---|---|---|
| 2 | *Expr'* $\rightarrow$ + *Term Expr'* | $\{+\}$ |
| 3 |      \|  - *Term Expr'* | $\{-\}$ |
| 4 |      \|  $\epsilon$ | $\{\epsilon, \texttt{eof}, \underline{)}\}$ |

To recognize instances of *Expr'*, we will create a routine `EPrime()`. It follows a simple scheme: choose among the three rules (or a syntax error) based on the FIRST$^+$ sets of their right-hand sides. For each right-hand side, the code tests directly for any further symbols.

To test for the presence of a nonterminal, say $A$, the code invokes the procedure that corresponds to $A$. To test for a terminal symbol, such as `name`, it performs a direct comparison and, if successful, advances the input stream

```
EPrime( )
   /* Expr' → + Term Expr' | - Term Expr' */
   if (word = + or word = -) then begin;
      word ← NextWord( );
      if (Term( ))
         then return EPrime( );
         else return false;
   end;
   else if (word = ) or word = eof)      /* Expr' → ε */
      then return true;
      else begin;                         /* no match */
         report a syntax error;
         return false;
      end;
```

■ **FIGURE 3.9** An Implementation of E Prime( ).

by calling the scanner, *NextWord( )*. If it matches an ε-production, the code does not call *NextWord( )*. Figure 3.9 shows a straightforward implementation of *EPrime( )*. It combines rules 2 and 3 because they both end with the same suffix, *Term Expr'*.

The strategy for constructing a complete recursive-descent parser is clear. For each nonterminal, we construct a procedure to recognize its alternative right-hand sides. These procedures call one another to recognize nonterminals. They recognize terminals by direct matching. Figure 3.10 shows a top-down recursive-descent parser for the right-recursive version of the classic expression grammar shown in Figure 3.4 on page 101. The code for similar right-hand sides has been combined.

For a small grammar, a compiler writer can quickly craft a recursive-descent parser. With a little care, a recursive-descent parser can produce accurate, informative error messages. The natural location for generating those messages is when the parser fails to find an expected terminal symbol—inside *EPrime*, *TPrime*, and *Factor* in the example.

### 3.3.3 Table-Driven LL(1) Parsers

Following the insights that underlie the FIRST$^+$ sets, we can automatically generate top-down parsers for backtrack-free grammars. The tool constructs FIRST, FOLLOW, and FIRST$^+$ sets. The FIRST$^+$ sets completely dictate the parsing decisions, so the tool can then emit an efficient top-down parser. The resulting parser is called an LL(1) parser. The name LL(1) derives from the fact that these parsers scan their input left to right, construct a leftmost

```
Main( )
    /* Goal → Expr */
    word ← NextWord( );
    if (Expr( ))
        then if (word = eof )
            then report success;
            else Fail( );

Fail( )
    report syntax error;
    attempt error recovery or exit;

Expr( )
    /* Expr → Term Expr' */
    if (Term( ))
        then return EPrime( );
        else Fail();

EPrime( )
    /* Expr' → + Term Expr' */
    /* Expr' → - Term Expr' */
    if (word = + or word = - )
        then begin;
            word ← NextWord( );
            if (Term( ))
                then return EPrime( );
                else Fail();
        end;
    else if (word = ) or word = eof )
        /* Expr' → ε */
        then return true;
        else Fail();

Term( )
    /* Term → Factor Term' */
    if (Factor( ))
        then return TPrime( );
        else Fail();
```

```
TPrime( )
    /* Term' → × Factor Term' */
    /* Term' → ÷ Factor Term' */
    if (word = × or word = ÷ )
        then begin;
            word ← NextWord( );
            if (Factor( ))
                then return TPrime( );
                else Fail();
        end;
    else if (word = + or word = - or
            word = ) or word = eof)
        /* Term' → ε */
        then return true;
        else Fail();

Factor( )
    /* Factor → ( Expr ) */
    if (word = ( ) then begin;
        word ← NextWord( );
        if (not Expr( ))
            then Fail();
        if (word ≠ ) )
            then Fail();
        word ← NextWord( );
        return true;
    end;
    /* Factor → num */
    /* Factor → name */
    else if (word = num or
            word = name )
        then begin;
            word ← NextWord( );
            return true;
        end;
    else Fail();
```

■ **FIGURE 3.10** Recursive-Descent Parser for Expressions.

```
word ← NextWord( );
push eof onto Stack;
push the start symbol, S, onto Stack;
focus ← top of Stack;
loop forever;
   if (focus = eof and word = eof )
      then report success and exit the loop;

   else if (focus ∈ T or focus = eof) then begin;
      if focus matches word then begin;
         pop Stack;
         word ← NextWord( );
      end;

      else report an error looking for symbol at top of stack;
   end;

   else begin; /* focus is a nonterminal */
      if Table[focus,word] is A → B₁B₂···Bₖ then begin;
         pop Stack;
         for i ← k to 1 by -1 do;
            if (Bᵢ ≠ ϵ)
               then push Bᵢ onto Stack;
         end;
      end;

      else report an error expanding focus;
   end;

   focus ← top of Stack;
end;
```

(a) The Skeleton LL(1) Parser

| | eof | + | - | × | ÷ | ( | ) | name | num |
|---|---|---|---|---|---|---|---|---|---|
| **Goal** | — | — | — | — | — | 0 | — | 0 | 0 |
| **Expr** | — | — | — | — | — | 1 | — | 1 | 1 |
| **Expr′** | 4 | 2 | 3 | — | — | — | 4 | — | — |
| **Term** | — | — | — | — | — | 5 | — | 5 | 5 |
| **Term′** | 8 | 8 | 8 | 6 | 7 | — | 8 | — | — |
| **Factor** | — | — | — | — | — | 9 | — | 11 | 10 |

(b) The LL(1) Parse Table for Right-Recursive Expression Grammar

■ **FIGURE 3.11** An LL(1) Parser for Expressions.

```
build FIRST, FOLLOW, and FIRST⁺ sets;

for each nonterminal A do;
    for each terminal w do;
        Table[A ,w] ← error;
    end;
    for each production p of the form A → β do;
        for each terminal w ∈ FIRST⁺(A → β) do;
            Table[A ,w] ← p;
            end;
        if eof ∈ FIRST⁺(A → β)
            then Table[A ,eof] ← p;
    end;
end;
```

■ **FIGURE 3.12** LL(1) Table-Construction Algorithm.

derivation, and use a lookahead of 1 symbol. Grammars that work in an LL(1) scheme are often called LL(1) grammars. LL(1) grammars are, by definition, backtrack free.

To build an LL(1) parser, the compiler writer provides a right-recursive, backtrack-free grammar and a *parser generator* constructs the actual parser. The most common implementation technique for an LL(1) parser generator uses a table-driven skeleton parser, such as the one shown at the top of Figure 3.11. The parser generator constructs the table, `Table`, which codifies the parsing decisions and drives the skeleton parser. The bottom of Figure 3.11 shows the LL(1) table for the right-recursive expression grammar shown in Figure 3.4 on page 101.

**Parser generator**
a tool that builds a parser from specifications, usually a grammar in a BNF-like notation

Parser generators are also called *compiler compilers*.

In the skeleton parser, the variable `focus` holds the next grammar symbol on the partially built parse tree's lower fringe that must be matched. (`focus` plays the same role in Figure 3.2.) The parse table, `Table`, maps pairs of nonterminals and lookahead symbols (terminals or `eof`) into productions. Given a nonterminal $A$ and a lookahead symbol $w$, `Table[A,w]` specifies the correct expansion.

The algorithm to build `Table` is straightforward. It assumes that FIRST, FOLLOW, and FIRST⁺ sets are available for the grammar. It iterates over the grammar symbols and fills in `Table`, as shown in Figure 3.12. If the grammar meets the backtrack free condition (see page 107), the construction will produce a correct table in $\mathbf{O}(|P| \times |T|)$ time, where $P$ is the set of productions and $T$ is the set of terminals.

If the grammar is not backtrack free, the construction will assign more than one production to some elements of `Table`. If the construction assigns to

| Rule | Stack | Input |
|------|-------|-------|
| — | eof *Goal* | ↑ name + name × name |
| 0 | eof *Expr* | ↑ name + name × name |
| 1 | eof *Expr′ Term* | ↑ name + name × name |
| 5 | eof *Expr′ Term′ Factor* | ↑ name + name × name |
| 11 | eof *Expr′ Term′* name | ↑ name + name × name |
| → | eof *Expr′ Term′* | name ↑ + name × name |
| 8 | eof *Expr′* | name ↑ + name × name |
| 2 | eof *Expr′ Term* + | name ↑ + name × name |
| → | eof *Expr′ Term* | name + ↑ name × name |
| 5 | eof *Expr′ Term′ Factor* | name + ↑ name × name |
| 11 | eof *Expr′ Term′* name | name + ↑ name × name |
| → | eof *Expr′ Term′* | name + name ↑ × name |
| 6 | eof *Expr′ Term′ Factor* × | name + name ↑ × name |
| → | eof *Expr′ Term′ Factor* | name + name × ↑ name |
| 11 | eof *Expr′ Term′* name | name + name × ↑ name |
| → | eof *Expr′ Term′* | name + name × name ↑ |
| 8 | eof *Expr′* | name + name × name ↑ |
| 4 | eof | name + name × name ↑ |

■ **FIGURE 3.13** Actions of the LL(1) Parser on a + b × c.

`Table[A,w]` multiple times, then two or more alternative right-hand sides for $A$ have $w$ in their FIRST$^+$ sets, violating the backtrack-free condition. The parser generator can detect this situation with a simple test on the two assignments to `Table`.

The example in Figure 3.13 shows the actions of the LL(1) expression parser for the input string a + b × c. The central column shows the contents of the parser's stack, which holds the partially completed lower fringe of the parse tree. The parse concludes successfully when it pops *Expr′* from the stack, leaving eof exposed on the stack and eof as the next symbol, implicitly, in the input stream.

Now, consider the actions of the LL(1) parser on the illegal input string x + ÷ y, shown in Figure 3.14 on page 115. It detects the syntax error when it attempts to expand a *Term* with lookahead symbol ÷. `Table[`*Term*`,÷]` contains "—", indicating a syntax error.

Alternatively, an LL(1) parser generator could emit a direct-coded parser, in the style of the direct-coded scanners discussed in Chapter 2. The parser generator would build FIRST, FOLLOW, and FIRST$^+$ sets. Next, it would iterate through the grammar, following the same scheme used by the table-construction algorithm in Figure 3.12. Rather than emitting table entries, it would generate, for each nonterminal, a procedure to recognize

| Rule | Stack | Input |
|:---:|:---|:---|
| — | eof *Goal* | ↑ name + ÷ name |
| 0 | eof *Expr* | ↑ name + ÷ name |
| 1 | eof *Expr′ Term* | ↑ name + ÷ name |
| 5 | eof *Expr′ Term′ Factor* | ↑ name + ÷ name |
| 11 | eof *Expr′ Term′* name | ↑ name + ÷ name |
| → | eof *Expr′ Term′* | name ↑ + ÷ name |
| 8 | eof *Expr′* | name ↑ + ÷ name |
| 2 | eof *Expr′ Term* + | name ↑ + ÷ name |
| → | eof *Expr′* ⌐Term¬ | name +⌐↑ ÷¬name |

*syntax error at this point*

■ **FIGURE 3.14** Actions of the LL(1) Parser on x + ÷ y.

each of the possible right-hand sides for that nonterminal. This process would be guided by the FIRST$^+$ sets. It would have the same speed and locality advantages that accrue to direct-coded scanners and recursive-descent parsers, while retaining the advantages of a grammar-generated system, such as a concise, high-level specification and reduced implementation effort.

---

**SECTION REVIEW**

Predictive parsers are simple, compact, and efficient. They can be implemented in a number of ways, including hand-coded, recursive-descent parsers and generated LL(1) parsers, either table driven or direct coded. Because these parsers know, at each point in the parse, the set of words that can occur as the next symbol in a valid input string, they can produce accurate and useful error messages.

Most programming-language constructs can be expressed in a backtrack-free grammar. Thus, these techniques have widespread application. The restriction that alternate right-hand sides for a nonterminal have disjoint FIRST$^+$ sets does not seriously limit the utility of LL(1) grammars. As we will see in Section 3.5.4, the primary drawback of top-down, predictive parsers lies in their inability to handle left recursion. Left-recursive grammars model the left-to-right associativity of expression operators in a more natural way than right-recursive grammars.

---

**Review Questions**

1. To build an efficient top-down parser, the compiler writer must express the source language in a somewhat constrained form. Explain the restrictions on the source-language grammar that are required to make it amenable to efficient top-down parsing.

**2.** Name two potential advantages of a hand-coded recursive-descent parser over a generated, table-driven LL(1) parser, and two advantages of the LL(1) parser over the recursive-descent implementation.

■

## 3.4 **BOTTOM-UP PARSING**

Bottom-up parsers build a parse tree starting from its leaves and working toward its root. The parser constructs a leaf node in the tree for each word returned by the scanner. These leaves form the lower fringe of the parse tree. To build a derivation, the parser adds layers of nonterminals on top of the leaves in a structure dictated by both the grammar and the partially completed lower portion of the parse tree.

At any stage in the parse, the partially-completed parse tree represents the state of the parse. Each word that the scanner has returned is represented by a leaf. The nodes above the leaves encode all of the knowledge that the parser has yet derived. The parser works along the upper frontier of this partially-completed parse tree; that frontier corresponds to the current sentential form in the derivation being built by the parser.

To extend the frontier upward, the parser looks in the current frontier for a substring that matches the right-hand side of some production $A \rightarrow \beta$. If it finds $\beta$ in the frontier, with its right end at $k$, it can replace $\beta$ with $A$, to create a new frontier. If replacing $\beta$ with $A$ at position $k$ is the next step in a valid derivation for the input string, then the pair $\langle A \rightarrow \beta, k \rangle$ is a *handle* in the current derivation and the parser should replace $\beta$ with $A$. This replacement is called a *reduction* because it reduces the number of symbols on the frontier, unless $|\beta| = 1$. If the parser is building a parse tree, it builds a node for $A$, adds that node to the tree, and connects the nodes representing $\beta$ as $A$'s children.

**Handle**
a pair, $\langle A \rightarrow \beta, k \rangle$, such that $\beta$ appears in the frontier with its right end at position $k$ and replacing $\beta$ with $A$ is the next step in the parse

**Reduction**
reducing the frontier of a bottom-up parser by $A \rightarrow \beta$ replaces $\beta$ with $A$ in the frontier

Finding handles is the key issue that arises in bottom-up parsing. The techniques presented in the following sections form a particularly efficient handle-finding mechanism. We will return to this issue periodically throughout Section 3.4. First, however, we will finish our high-level description of bottom-up parsers.

The bottom-up parser repeats a simple process. It finds a handle $\langle A \rightarrow \beta, k \rangle$ on the frontier. It replaces the occurrence of $\beta$ at $k$ with $A$. This process continues until either: (1) it reduces the frontier to a single node that represents the grammar's goal symbol, or (2) it cannot find a handle. In the first case, the parser has found a derivation; if it has also consumed all the words in the input stream (i.e. the next word is eof), then the parse succeeds. In the second case, the parser cannot build a derivation for the input stream and it should report that failure.

A successful parse runs through every step of the derivation. When a parse fails, the parser should use the context accumulated in the partial derivation to produce a meaningful error message. In many cases, the parser can recover from the error and continue parsing so that it discovers as many syntactic errors as possible in a single parse (see Section 3.5.1).

The relationship between the derivation and the parse plays a critical role in making bottom-up parsing both correct and efficient. The bottom-up parser works from the final sentence toward the goal symbol, while a derivation starts at the goal symbol and works toward the final sentence. The parser, then, discovers the steps of the derivation in reverse order. For a derivation:

$$Goal = \gamma_0 \rightarrow \gamma_1 \rightarrow \gamma_2 \rightarrow \cdots \rightarrow \gamma_{n-1} \rightarrow \gamma_n = sentence,$$

the bottom-up parser discovers $\gamma_i \rightarrow \gamma_{i+1}$ before it discovers $\gamma_{i-1} \rightarrow \gamma_i$. The way that it builds the parse tree forces this order. The parser must add the node for $\gamma_i$ to the frontier before it can match $\gamma_i$.

The scanner returns classified words in left-to-right order. To reconcile the left-to-right order of the scanner with the reverse derivation constructed by the scanner, a bottom-up parser looks for a rightmost derivation. In a rightmost derivation, the leftmost leaf is considered last. Reversing that order leads to the desired behavior: leftmost leaf first and rightmost leaf last.

At each point, the parser operates on the frontier of the partially constructed parse tree; the current frontier is a prefix of the corresponding sentential form in the derivation. Because each sentential form occurs in a rightmost derivation, the unexamined suffix consists entirely of terminal symbols. When the parser needs more right context, it calls the scanner.

With an unambiguous grammar, the rightmost derivation is unique. For a large class of unambiguous grammars, $\gamma_{i-1}$ can be determined directly from $\gamma_i$ (the parse tree's upper frontier) and a limited amount of lookahead in the input stream. In other words, given a frontier $\gamma_i$ and a limited number of additional classified words, the parser can find the handle that takes $\gamma_i$ to $\gamma_{i-1}$. For such grammars, we can construct an efficient handle-finder, using a technique called LR parsing. This section examines one particular flavor of LR parser, called a *table-driven* LR(1) parser.

An LR(1) parser scans the input from left to right to build a rightmost derivation in reverse. At each step, it makes decisions based on the history of the parse and a lookahead of, at most, one symbol. The name LR(1) derives from these properties: Left-to-right scan, Reverse rightmost derivation, and 1 symbol of lookahead.

Informally, we will say that a language has the LR(1) property if it can be parsed in a single left-to-right scan, to build a reverse-rightmost derivation, using only one symbol of lookahead to determine parsing actions. In practice, the simplest test to determine if a grammar has the LR(1) property is to let a parser generator attempt to build the LR(1) parser. If that process fails, the grammar lacks the LR(1) property. The remainder of this section introduces LR(1) parsers and their operation. Section 3.4.2 presents an algorithm to build the tables that encode an LR(1) parser.

### 3.4.1  **The LR(1) Parsing Algorithm**

The critical step in a bottom-up parser, such as a table-driven LR(1) parser, is to find the next handle. Efficient handle finding is the key to efficient bottom-up parsing. An LR(1) parser uses a handle-finding automaton, encoded into two tables, called `Action` and `Goto`. Figure 3.15 shows a simple table-driven LR(1) parser.

The skeleton LR(1) parser interprets the `Action` and `Goto` tables to find successive handles in the reverse rightmost derivation of the input string. When it finds a handle $\langle A \rightarrow \beta, k \rangle$, it reduces $\beta$ at $k$ to $A$ in the current sentential form—the upper frontier of the partially completed parse tree. Rather than build an explicit parse tree, the skeleton parser keeps the current upper frontier of the partially constructed tree on a stack, interleaved with states from the handle-finding automaton that let it thread together the reductions into a parse. At any point in the parse, the stack contains a prefix of the current frontier. Beyond this prefix, the frontier consists of leaf nodes. The variable *word* holds the first word in the suffix that lies beyond the stack's contents; it is the *lookahead symbol*.

Using a stack lets the LR(1) parser make the position, $k$, in the handle be constant and implicit.

To find the next handle, the LR(1) parser shifts symbols onto the stack until the automaton finds the right end of a handle at the stack top. Once it has a handle, the parser reduces by the production in the handle. To do so, it pops the symbols in $\beta$ from the stack and pushes the corresponding left-hand side, $A$, onto the stack. The `Action` and `Goto` tables thread together shift and reduce actions in a grammar-driven sequence that finds a reverse rightmost derivation, if one exists.

To make this concrete, consider the grammar shown in Figure 3.16a, which describes the language of properly nested parentheses. Figure 3.16b shows the `Action` and `Goto` tables for this grammar. When used with the skeleton LR(1) parser, they create a parser for the parentheses language.

```
push $;
push start state, s₀;
word ← NextWord( );
while (true) do;
    state ← top of stack;
    if Action[state,word] = "reduce A → β" then begin;
        pop 2 × |β| symbols;
        state ← top of stack;
        push A;
        push Goto[state, A];
    end;
    else if Action[state,word] = "shift sᵢ" then begin;
        push word;
        push sᵢ;
        word ← NextWord( );
    end;
    else if Action[state,word] = "accept"
        then break;
    else Fail( );
end;
report success;    /* executed break on "accept" case */
```

■ **FIGURE 3.15** The Skeleton LR(1) Parser.

To understand the behavior of the skeleton LR(1) parser, consider the sequence of actions that it takes on the input string "( )".

| Iteration | State | word | Stack | Handle | Action |
|---|---|---|---|---|---|
| *initial* | — | ( | $ 0 | — *none* — | — |
| 1 | 0 | ( | $ 0 | — *none* — | *shift 3* |
| 2 | 3 | ) | $ 0 ( 3 | — *none* — | *shift 7* |
| 3 | 7 | eof | $ 0 ( 3 ) 7 | ( ) | *reduce 5* |
| 4 | 2 | eof | $ 0 *Pair* 2 | *Pair* | *reduce 3* |
| 5 | 1 | eof | $ 0 *List* 1 | *List* | *accept* |

The first line shows the parser's initial state. Subsequent lines show its state at the start of the while loop, along with the action that it takes. At the start of the first iteration, the stack does not contain a handle, so the parser shifts the lookahead symbol, (, onto the stack. From the Action table, it knows to shift and move to state 3. At the start of the second iteration, the stack still

|       | *Action* **Table** |       |       | *Goto* **Table** |        |
|-------|--------------------|-------|-------|------------------|--------|
| **State** | eof            | (     | )     | *List*           | *Pair* |
| 0     |                    | s 3   |       | 1                | 2      |
| 1     | acc                | s 3   |       |                  | 4      |
| 2     | r 3                | r 3   |       |                  |        |
| 3     |                    | s 6   | s 7   |                  | 5      |
| 4     | r 2                | r 2   |       |                  |        |
| 5     |                    |       | s 8   |                  |        |
| 6     |                    | s 6   | s 10  |                  | 9      |
| 7     | r 5                | r 5   |       |                  |        |
| 8     | r 4                | r 4   |       |                  |        |
| 9     |                    |       | s 11  |                  |        |
| 10    |                    |       | r 5   |                  |        |
| 11    |                    |       | r 4   |                  |        |

| 1 | *Goal* → *List* |
| 2 | *List* → *List Pair* |
| 3 |        | *Pair* |
| 4 | *Pair* → ( *Pair* ) |
| 5 |        | ( ) |

(a) Parentheses Grammar         (b) *Action* and *Goto* Tables

■ **FIGURE 3.16** The Parentheses Grammar.

does not contain a handle, so the parser shifts ) onto the stack to build more context. It moves to state 7.

In the third iteration, the situation has changed. The stack contains a handle, $\langle Pair \rightarrow ( ) \rangle,t$, where $t$ is the stack top. The *Action* table directs the parser to reduce ( ) to *Pair*. Using the state beneath *Pair* on the stack, 0, and *Pair*, the parser moves to state 2 (specified by *Goto[0,Pair]*). In state 2, with *Pair* atop the stack and eof as its lookahead, the parser finds the handle $\langle List \rightarrow Pair,t \rangle$ and reduces, which leaves the parser in state 1 (specified by *Goto[0,List]*). Finally, in state 1, with *List* atop the stack and eof as its lookahead, the parser discovers the handle $\langle Goal \rightarrow List,t \rangle$. The *Action* table encodes this situation as an *accept* action, so the parse halts.

In an LR parser, the handle is always positioned at stacktop and the chain of handles produces a reverse rightmost derivation.

This parse required two shifts and three reduces. LR(1) parsers take time proportional to the length of the input (one shift per word returned from the scanner) and the length of the derivation (one reduce per step in the derivation). In general, we cannot expect to discover the derivation for a sentence in any fewer steps.

Figure 3.17 shows the parser's behavior on the input string, "( ( ) ) ( )." The parser performs six shifts, five reduces, and one accept on this input. Figure 3.18 shows the state of the partially-built parse tree at the start of each iteration of the parser's while loop. The top of each drawing shows an iteration number and a gray bar that contains the partial parse tree's upper frontier. In the LR(1) parser, this frontier appears on the stack.

| Iteration | State | *word* | Stack | Handle | Action |
|:---:|:---:|:---:|:---|:---:|:---:|
| *initial* | — | ( | $ 0 | — none — | — |
| 1 | 0 | ( | $ 0 | — none — | shift 3 |
| 2 | 3 | ( | $ 0 ( 3 | — none — | shift 6 |
| 3 | 6 | ) | $ 0 ( 3 ( 6 | — none — | shift 10 |
| 4 | 10 | ) | $ 0 ( 3 ( 6 ) 10 | ( ) | reduce 5 |
| 5 | 5 | ) | $ 0 ( 3 *Pair* 5 | — none — | shift 8 |
| 6 | 8 | ( | $ 0 ( 3 *Pair* 5 ) 8 | ( *Pair* ) | reduce 4 |
| 7 | 2 | ( | $ 0 *Pair* 2 | *Pair* | reduce 3 |
| 8 | 1 | ( | $ 0 *List* 1 | — none — | shift 3 |
| 9 | 3 | ) | $ 0 *List* 1 ( 3 | — none — | shift 7 |
| 10 | 7 | eof | $ 0 *List* 1 ( 3 ) 7 | ( ) | reduce 5 |
| 11 | 4 | eof | $ 0 *List* 1 *Pair* 4 | *List Pair* | reduce 2 |
| 12 | 1 | eof | $ 0 *List* 1 | *List* | accept |

■ **FIGURE 3.17** States of the LR(1) Parser on ( ( ) ) ( ).

## Handle Finding

The parser's actions shed additional light on the process of finding handles. Consider the parser's actions on the string "( )", as shown in the table on page 119. The parser finds a handle in each of iterations 3, 4, and 5. In iteration 3, the frontier of ( ) clearly matches the right-hand side of production 5. From the *Action* table, we see that a lookahead of either eof or ( implies a reduce by production 5. Then, in iteration 4, the parser recognizes that *Pair*, followed by a lookahead of either eof or ( constitutes a handle for the reduction by *List* → *Pair*. The final handle of the parse, *List* with lookahead of eof in state 1, triggers the accept action.

To understand how the states preserved on the stack change the parser's behavior, consider the parser's actions on our second input string, "( ( ) ) ( )," as shown in Figure 3.17. Initially, the parser shifts (, (, and ) onto the stack, in iterations 1 to 3. In iteration 4, the parser reduces by production 5; it replaces the top two symbols on the stack, ( and ), with *Pair* and moves to state 5.

Between these two examples, the parser recognized the string ( ) at stacktop as a handle three times. It behaved differently in each case, based on the prior left context encoded in the stack. Comparing these three situations exposes how the stacked states control the future direction of the parse.

With the first example, ( ), the parser was in $s_7$ with a lookahead of eof when it found the handle. The reduction reveals $s_0$ beneath ( ), and $Goto[s_0, Pair]$ is $s_2$. In $s_2$, a lookahead of eof leads to another reduction followed by an accept action. A lookahead of ) in $s_2$ produces an error.

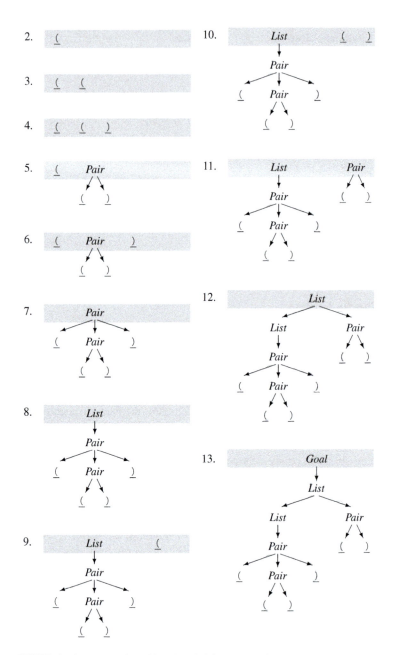

■ **FIGURE 3.18** The Sequence of Partial Parse Trees Built for ( ( ) ) ( ).

The second example, $\underline{(\;(\;\;)\;)\;(\;\;)}$, encounters a handle for $(\;\;)$ twice. The first handle occurs in iteration 4. The parser is in $s_{10}$ with a lookahead of $)$. It has previously shifted $\underline{(}$, $\underline{(}$, and $\underline{)}$ onto the stack. The `Action` table indicates "r 5," so the parser reduces by *Pair* $\rightarrow$ $(\;\;)$. The reduction reveals $s_3$ beneath $(\;\;)$ and $Goto[s_3,Pair]$ is $s_5$, a state in which further $)$'s are legal. The second time it finds $(\;\;)$ as a handle occurs in iteration 10. The reduction reveals $s_1$ beneath $(\;\;)$ and takes the parser to $s_4$. In $s_4$, a lookahead of either `eof` or $\underline{(}$ triggers a reduction of *List Pair* to *List*, while a lookahead of $)$ is an error.

The `Action` and `Goto` tables, along with the stack, cause the parser to track prior left context and let it take different actions based on that context. Thus, the parser handles correctly each of the three instances in which it found a handle for $(\;\;)$. We will revisit this issue when we examine the construction of `Action` and `Goto`.

### Parsing an Erroneous Input String

To see how an LR(1) parser discovers a syntax error, consider the sequence of actions that it takes on the string "$\underline{(\;)\;)}$", shown below:

| Iteration | State | *word* | Stack | Handle | Action |
|---|---|---|---|---|---|
| *initial* | — | $\underline{(}$ | $ 0 | — *none* — | — |
| 1 | 0 | $\underline{(}$ | $ 0 | — *none* — | shift 3 |
| 2 | 3 | $\underline{)}$ | $ 0 $\underline{(}$ 3 | — *none* — | shift 7 |
| 3 | 7 | $\underline{)}$ | $ 0 $\underline{(}$ 3 $\underline{)}$ 7 | — *none* — | error |

The first two iterations of the parse proceed as in the first example, "$\underline{(\;)}$". The parser shifts $\underline{(}$ and $\underline{)}$. In the third iteration of the while loop, it looks at the `Action` table entry for state 7 and $\underline{)}$. That entry contains neither shift, reduce, nor accept, so the parser interprets it as an error.

The LR(1) parser detects syntax errors through a simple mechanism: the corresponding table entry is invalid. The parser detects the error as soon as possible, before reading any words beyond those needed to prove the input erroneous. This property allows the parser to localize the error to a specific point in the input. Using the available context and knowledge of the grammar, we can build LR(1) parsers that provide good diagnostic error messages.

### Using LR Parsers

The key to LR parsing lies in the construction of the `Action` and `Goto` tables. The tables encode all of the legal reduction sequences that can arise in a reverse rightmost derivation for the given grammar. While the number of such sequences is huge, the grammar itself constrains the order in which reductions can occur.

The compiler writer can build *Action* and *Goto* tables by hand. However, the table-construction algorithm requires scrupulous bookkeeping; it is a prime example of the kind of task that should be automated and relegated to a computer. Programs that automate this construction are widely available. The next section presents one algorithm that can be used to construct LR(1) parse tables.

With an LR(1) parser generator, the compiler writer's role is to define the grammar and to ensure that the grammar has the LR(1) property. In practice, the LR(1) table generator identifies those productions that are ambiguous or that are expressed in a way that requires more than one word of lookahead to distinguish between a shift action and a reduce action. As we study the table-construction algorithm, we will see how those problems arise, how to cure them, and how to understand the kinds of diagnostic information that LR(1) parser generators produce.

### Using More Lookahead

The ideas that underlie LR(1) parsers actually define a family of parsers that vary in the amount of lookahead that they use. An LR(k) parser uses, at most, k lookahead symbols. Additional lookahead allows an LR(2) parser to recognize a larger set of grammars than an LR(1) parsing system. Almost paradoxically, however, the added lookahead does not increase the set of languages that these parsers can recognize. LR(1) parsers accept the same set of languages as LR(k) parsers for $k > 1$. The LR(1) grammar for a language may be more complex than an LR(k) grammar.

### 3.4.2 Building LR(1) Tables

To construct *Action* and *Goto* tables, an LR(1) parser generator builds a model of the handle-recognizing automaton and uses that model to fill in the tables. The model, called the *canonical collection of sets of LR(1) items*, represents all of the possible states of the parser and the transitions between those states. It is reminiscent of the subset construction from Section 2.4.3.

To illustrate the table-construction algorithm, we will use two examples. The first is the parentheses grammar given in Figure 3.16a. It is small enough to use as a running example, but large enough to exhibit some of the complexities of the process.

$$
\begin{array}{ll}
1 & \textit{Goal} \rightarrow \textit{List} \\
2 & \textit{List} \;\; \rightarrow \textit{List Pair} \\
3 & \qquad \mid \textit{Pair} \\
4 & \textit{Pair} \rightarrow \underline{(} \; \textit{Pair} \; \underline{)} \\
5 & \qquad \mid \underline{(} \; \underline{)}
\end{array}
$$

Our second example, in Section 3.4.3, is an abstracted version of the classic `if-then-else` ambiguity. The table construction fails on this grammar because of its ambiguity. The example highlights the situations that lead to failures in the table-construction process.

## LR(1) Items

In an LR(1) parser, the `Action` and `Goto` tables encode information about the potential handles at each step in the parse. The table-construction algorithm, therefore, needs a concrete representation for both handles and potential handles, and their associated lookahead symbols. We represent each potential handle with an LR(1) item. An LR(1) item $[A \rightarrow \beta \bullet \gamma, a]$ consists of a production $A \rightarrow \beta\gamma$; a placeholder, $\bullet$, that indicates the position of the stacktop in the production's right-hand side; and a specific terminal symbol, a, as a lookahead symbol.

**LR(1) item**
$[A \rightarrow \beta \bullet \gamma, a]$ where $A \rightarrow \beta\gamma$ is a grammar production, $\bullet$ represents the position of the parser's stacktop, and a is a terminal symbol in the grammar

The table-construction algorithm uses LR(1) items to build a model of the sets of valid states for the parser, the canonical collection of sets of LR(1) items. We designate the canonical collection $\mathcal{CC} = \{cc_0, cc_1, cc_2, \ldots, cc_n\}$. The algorithm builds $\mathcal{CC}$ by following possible derivations in the grammar; in the final collection, each set $cc_i$ in $\mathcal{CC}$ contains the set of potential handles in some possible parser configuration. Before we delve into the table construction, further explanation of LR(1) items is needed.

For a production $A \rightarrow \beta\gamma$ and a lookahead symbol a, the placeholder can generate three distinct items, each with its own interpretation. In each case, the presence of the item in some set $cc_i$ in the canonical collection indicates input that the parser has seen is consistent with the occurrence of an $A$ followed by an a in the grammar. The position of $\bullet$ in the item distinguishes between the three cases.

1. $[A \rightarrow \bullet\beta\gamma, a]$ indicates that an $A$ would be valid and that recognizing a $\beta$ next would be one step toward discovering an $A$. We call such an item a *possibility*, because it represents a possible completion for the input already seen.
2. $[A \rightarrow \beta \bullet \gamma, a]$ indicates that the parser has progressed from the state $[A \rightarrow \bullet\beta\gamma, a]$ by recognizing $\beta$. The $\beta$ is consistent with recognizing

$[Goal \rightarrow \bullet List, \texttt{eof}]$

$[Goal \rightarrow List \bullet, \texttt{eof}]$

| | | |
|---|---|---|
| $[List \rightarrow \bullet List\ Pair, \texttt{eof}]$ | $[List \rightarrow \bullet List\ Pair, \underline{(}\ ]$ | |
| $[List \rightarrow List \bullet Pair, \texttt{eof}]$ | $[List \rightarrow List \bullet Pair, \underline{(}\ ]$ | |
| $[List \rightarrow List\ Pair \bullet, \texttt{eof}]$ | $[List \rightarrow List\ Pair \bullet, \underline{(}\ ]$ | |

$[List \rightarrow \bullet Pair, \texttt{eof}\ ]$      $[List \rightarrow \bullet Pair, \underline{(}\ ]$

$[List \rightarrow Pair \bullet, \texttt{eof}\ ]$      $[List \rightarrow Pair \bullet, \underline{(}\ ]$

| | | |
|---|---|---|
| $[Pair \rightarrow \bullet \underline{(}\ Pair\ \underline{)}, \texttt{eof}\ ]$ | $[Pair \rightarrow \bullet \underline{(}\ Pair\ \underline{)}, \underline{)}]$ | $[Pair \rightarrow \bullet \underline{(}\ Pair\ \underline{)}, \underline{(}]$ |
| $[Pair \rightarrow \underline{(} \bullet Pair\ \underline{)}, \texttt{eof}\ ]$ | $[Pair \rightarrow \underline{(} \bullet Pair\ \underline{)}, \underline{)}]$ | $[Pair \rightarrow \underline{(} \bullet Pair\ \underline{)}, \underline{(}]$ |
| $[Pair \rightarrow \underline{(}\ Pair \bullet \underline{)}, \texttt{eof}\ ]$ | $[Pair \rightarrow \underline{(}\ Pair \bullet \underline{)}, \underline{)}]$ | $[Pair \rightarrow \underline{(}\ Pair \bullet \underline{)}, \underline{(}]$ |
| $[Pair \rightarrow \underline{(}\ Pair\ \underline{)} \bullet, \texttt{eof}\ ]$ | $[Pair \rightarrow \underline{(}\ Pair\ \underline{)} \bullet, \underline{)}]$ | $[Pair \rightarrow \underline{(}\ Pair\ \underline{)} \bullet, \underline{(}]$ |
| $[Pair \rightarrow \bullet \underline{(}\ \underline{)}, \texttt{eof}]$ | $[Pair \rightarrow \bullet \underline{(}\ \underline{)}, \underline{(}]$ | $[Pair \rightarrow \bullet \underline{(}\ \underline{)}, \underline{)}]$ |
| $[Pair \rightarrow \underline{(} \bullet \underline{)}, \texttt{eof}]$ | $[Pair \rightarrow \underline{(} \bullet \underline{)}, \underline{(}]$ | $[Pair \rightarrow \underline{(} \bullet \underline{)}, \underline{)}]$ |
| $[Pair \rightarrow \underline{(}\ \underline{)} \bullet, \texttt{eof}]$ | $[Pair \rightarrow \underline{(}\ \underline{)} \bullet, \underline{(}]$ | $[Pair \rightarrow \underline{(}\ \underline{)} \bullet, \underline{)}]$ |

■ **FIGURE 3.19** LR(1) Items for the Parentheses Grammar.

an $A$. One valid next step would be to recognize a $\gamma$. We call such an item *partially complete*.

3. $[A \rightarrow \beta\gamma \bullet, \texttt{a}]$ indicates that the parser has found $\beta\gamma$ in a context where an $A$ followed by an $\texttt{a}$ would be valid. If the lookahead symbol is $\texttt{a}$, then the item is a handle and the parser can reduce $\beta\gamma$ to $A$. Such an item is *complete*.

In an LR(1) item, the $\bullet$ encodes some local left context—the portions of the production already recognized. (Recall, from the earlier examples, that the states pushed onto the stack encode a summary of the context to the left of the current LR(1) item—in essence, the history of the parse so far.) The lookahead symbol encodes one symbol of legal right context. When the parser finds itself in a state that includes $[A \rightarrow \beta\gamma \bullet, \texttt{a}]$ with a lookahead of $\texttt{a}$, it has a handle and should reduce $\beta\gamma$ to $A$.

Figure 3.19 shows the complete set of LR(1) items generated by the parentheses grammar. Two items deserve particular notice. The first, $[Goal \rightarrow \bullet List, \texttt{eof}]$, represents the initial state of the parser—looking for a string that reduces to *Goal*, followed by $\texttt{eof}$. Every parse begins in this state. The second, $[Goal \rightarrow List \bullet, \texttt{eof}]$, represents the desired final state of the parser—finding a string that reduces to *Goal*, followed by $\texttt{eof}$. This item represents every successful parse. All of the possible parses result from stringing together parser states in a grammar-directed way, beginning with $[Goal \rightarrow \bullet List, \texttt{eof}]$ and ending with $[Goal \rightarrow List \bullet, \texttt{eof}]$.

### Constructing the Canonical Collection

To build the canonical collection of sets of LR(1) items, $\mathcal{CC}$, a parser generator must start from the parser's initial state, $[Goal \rightarrow \bullet List, \texttt{eof}]$, and construct a model of all the potential transitions that can occur. The algorithm represents each possible configuration, or state, of the parser as a set of LR(1) items. The algorithm relies on two fundamental operations on these sets of LR(1) items: taking a closure and computing a transition.

- The closure operation completes a state; given some core set of LR(1) items, it adds to that set any related LR(1) items that they imply. For example, anywhere that $Goal \rightarrow List$ is legal, the productions that derive a *List* are legal, too. Thus, the item $[Goal \rightarrow \bullet List, \texttt{eof}]$ implies both $[List \rightarrow \bullet List \ Pair, \texttt{eof}]$ and $[List \rightarrow \bullet Pair, \texttt{eof}]$. The `closure` procedure implements this function.
- To model the transition that the parser would make from a given state on some grammar symbol, $x$, the algorithm computes the set of items that would result from recognizing an $x$. To do so, the algorithm selects the subset of the current set of LR(1) items where $\bullet$ precedes $x$ and advances the $\bullet$ past the $x$ in each of them. The `goto` procedure implements this function.

To simplify the task of finding the goal symbol, we require that the grammar have a unique goal symbol that does not appear on the right-hand side of any production. In the parentheses grammar, that symbol is *Goal*.

The item $[Goal \rightarrow \bullet List, \texttt{eof}]$ represents the parser's initial state for the parentheses grammar; every valid parse recognizes *Goal* followed by `eof`. This item forms the core of the first state in $\mathcal{CC}$, labelled $cc_0$. If the grammar has multiple productions for the goal symbol, each of them generates an item in the initial core of $cc_0$.

### The `closure` Procedure

To compute the complete initial state of the parser, $cc_0$, from its core, the algorithm must add to the core all of the items implied by the items in the core. Figure 3.20 shows an algorithm for this computation. *Closure* iterates over all the items in set $s$. If the placeholder $\bullet$ in an item immediately precedes some nonterminal $C$, then `closure` must add one or more items for each production that can derive $C$. Closure places the $\bullet$ at the initial position of each item that it builds this way.

The rationale for `closure` is clear. If $[A \rightarrow \beta \bullet C\delta, a] \in s$, then a string that reduces to $C$, followed by $\delta a$ will complete the left context. Recognizing a $C$ followed by $\delta a$ should cause a reduction to $A$, since it completes the

```
closure(s)
    while (s is still changing)
        for each item [A→β•Cδ,a] ∈ s
            for each production C→γ ∈ P
                for each b ∈ FIRST(δa)
                    s ← s ∪ {[C→•γ,b]}
    return s
```

■ **FIGURE 3.20** The *closure* Procedure.

production's right-hand side ($C\delta$) and follows it with a valid lookahead symbol.

To build the items for a production $C \rightarrow \gamma$, *closure* inserts the placeholder before $\gamma$ and adds the appropriate lookahead symbols—each terminal that can appear as the initial symbol in $\delta$a. This includes every terminal in FIRST($\delta$). If $\epsilon \in$ FIRST($\delta$), it also includes a. The notation FIRST($\delta$a) in the algorithm represents this extension of the FIRST set to a string in this way. If $\delta$ is $\epsilon$, this devolves into FIRST(a) = { a }.

In our experience, this use of FIRST($\delta$a) is the point in the process where a human is most to likely make a mistake.

For the parentheses grammar, the initial item is [*Goal* → • *List*,eof]. Applying *closure* to that set adds the following items:

> [*List* → • *List Pair*,eof], [*List* → • *List Pair*,( ], [*List* → • *Pair*,eof ],
> [*List* → • *Pair*,( ], [*Pair* → • ( *Pair* ),eof ], [*Pair* → • ( *Pair* ),( ],
> [*Pair* → • ( ),eof] [*Pair* → • ( ),( ]

These eight items, along with [*Goal* → • *List*,eof], constitute set $cc_0$ in the canonical collection. The order in which *closure* adds the items will depend on how the set implementation manages the interaction between the "*for each item*" iterator and the set union in the innermost loop.

*Closure* is another fixed-point computation. The triply-nested loop either adds items to *s* or leaves *s* intact. It never removes an item from *s*. Since the set of LR(1) items is finite, this loop must halt. The triply nested loop looks expensive. However, close examination reveals that each item in *s* needs to be processed only once. A worklist version of the algorithm could capitalize on that fact.

### The goto *Procedure*

The second fundamental operation that the construction uses is the *goto* function. *Goto* takes as input a model of a parser state, represented as a set $cc_i$ in the canonical collection, and a grammar symbol *x*. It computes, from $cc_i$ and *x*, a model of the parser state that would result from recognizing an *x* in state *i*.

```
goto(s,x)
   moved ← Ø
   for each item i ∈ s
         if the form of i is [α→β•xδ, a] then
               moved ← moved ∪ {[α→βx•δ, a]}
   return closure(moved)
```

■ **FIGURE 3.21** The *goto* Function.

The *goto* function, shown in Figure 3.21, takes a set of LR(1) items *s* and a grammar symbol *x* and returns a new set of LR(1) items. It iterates over the items in *s*. When it finds an item in which the • immediately precedes *x*, it creates a new item by moving the • rightward past *x*. This new item represents the parser's configuration after recognizing *x*. *Goto* places these new items in a new set, takes its *closure* to complete the parser state, and returns that new state.

Given the initial set for the parentheses grammar,

$$\text{cc}_0 = \begin{cases} [Goal \to \bullet List, \text{eof}] & [List \to \bullet List\ Pair, \text{eof}] & [List \to \bullet List\ Pair, \underline{(}] \\ [List \to \bullet Pair, \text{eof}] & [List \to \bullet Pair, \underline{(}] & [Pair \to \bullet\ \underline{(}\ Pair\ \underline{)}, \text{eof}] \\ [Pair \to \bullet\ \underline{(}\ Pair\ \underline{)},\underline{(}] & [Pair \to \bullet\ \underline{(}\ \underline{)}, \text{eof}] & [Pair \to \bullet\ \underline{(}\ \underline{)},\underline{(}] \end{cases}$$

we can derive the state of the parser after it recognizes an initial $\underline{(}$ by computing $goto(\text{cc}_0,\underline{(}\ )$. The inner loop finds four items that have • before $\underline{(}$. *Goto* creates a new item for each, with the • advanced beyond $\underline{(}$. Closure adds two more items, generated from the items with • before *Pair*. These items introduce the lookahead symbol $\underline{)}$. Thus, $goto(\text{cc}_0,\underline{(}\ )$ returns

$$\begin{cases} [Pair \to \underline{(} \bullet Pair\ \underline{)},\text{eof}] & [Pair \to \underline{(} \bullet Pair\ \underline{)},\underline{(}] & [Pair \to \underline{(} \bullet\underline{)},\text{eof}] \\ [Pair \to \underline{(} \bullet\underline{)},\underline{(}] & [Pair \to \bullet\ \underline{(}\ Pair\ \underline{)},\underline{)}] & [Pair \to \bullet\ \underline{(}\ \underline{)},\underline{)}] \end{cases}.$$

To find the set of states that derive directly from some state such as $\text{cc}_0$, the algorithm can compute $goto(\text{cc}_0,x)$ for each *x* that occurs after a • in an item in $\text{cc}_0$. This produces all the sets that are one symbol away from $\text{cc}_0$. To compute the complete canonical collection, we simply iterate this process to a fixed point.

### The Algorithm

To construct the canonical collection of sets of LR(1) items, the algorithm computes the initial set, $\text{cc}_0$, and then systematically finds all of the sets of LR(1) items that are reachable from $\text{cc}_0$. It repeatedly applies *goto* to the new sets in $\mathcal{CC}$; *goto*, in turn, uses *closure*. Figure 3.22 shows the algorithm.

For a grammar with the goal production $S' \to S$, the algorithm begins by initializing $\mathcal{CC}$ to contain $\text{cc}_0$, as described earlier. Next, it systematically

$$\text{CC}_0 \;\leftarrow\; closure(\{[S' \rightarrow \bullet S, \text{eof}]\})$$
$$\mathcal{CC} \;\leftarrow\; \{\text{CC}_0\}$$

```
while (new sets are still being added to CC)
    for each unmarked set CCᵢ ∈ CC
        mark CCᵢ as processed
            for each x following a • in an item in CCᵢ
                temp ← goto(CCᵢ,x)
                if temp ∉ CC
                    then CC ← CC∪{temp}
                record transition from CCᵢ to temp on x
```

■ **FIGURE 3.22** The Algorithm to Build $\mathcal{CC}$.

extends $\mathcal{CC}$ by looking for any transition from a state in $\mathcal{CC}$ to a state not yet in $\mathcal{CC}$. It does this constructively, by building each possible state, `temp`, and testing `temp` for membership in $\mathcal{CC}$. If `temp` is new, it adds `temp` to $\mathcal{CC}$. Whether or not `temp` is new, it records the transition from $\text{CC}_i$ to `temp` for later use in building the parser's `Goto` table.

To ensure that the algorithm processes each set $\text{CC}_i$ just once, it uses a simple marking scheme. It creates each set in an unmarked condition and marks the set as it is processed. This drastically reduces the number of times that it invokes `goto` and `closure`.

This construction is a fixed-point computation. The canonical collection, $\mathcal{CC}$, is a subset of the powerset of the LR(1) items. The while loop is monotonic; it adds new sets to $\mathcal{CC}$ and never removes them. If the set of LR(1) items has $n$ elements, then $\mathcal{CC}$ can grow no larger than $2^n$ items, so the computation must halt.

This upper bound on the size of $\mathcal{CC}$ is quite loose. For example, the parentheses grammar has 33 LR(1) items and produces just 12 sets in $\mathcal{CC}$. The upper bound would be $2^{33}$, a much larger number. For more complex grammars, $|\mathcal{CC}|$ is a concern, primarily because the `Action` and `Goto` tables grow with $|\mathcal{CC}|$. As described in Section 3.6, both the compiler writer and the parser-generator writer can take steps to reduce the size of those tables.

### The Canonical Collection for the Parentheses Grammar

As a first complete example, consider the problem of building $\mathcal{CC}$ for the parentheses grammar. The initial set, $\text{CC}_0$, is computed as $closure([Goal \rightarrow \bullet List, \text{eof}])$.

| Iteration | Item | *Goal* | *List* | *Pair* | ( | ) | eof |
|-----------|------|--------|--------|--------|---|---|-----|
| 0 | $CC_0$ | Ø | $CC_1$ | $CC_2$ | $CC_3$ | Ø | Ø |
| 1 | $CC_1$ | Ø | Ø | $CC_4$ | $CC_3$ | Ø | Ø |
|   | $CC_2$ | Ø | Ø | Ø | Ø | Ø | Ø |
|   | $CC_3$ | Ø | Ø | $CC_5$ | $CC_6$ | $CC_7$ | Ø |
| 2 | $CC_4$ | Ø | Ø | Ø | Ø | Ø | Ø |
|   | $CC_5$ | Ø | Ø | Ø | Ø | $CC_8$ | Ø |
|   | $CC_6$ | Ø | Ø | $CC_9$ | $CC_6$ | $CC_{10}$ | Ø |
|   | $CC_7$ | Ø | Ø | Ø | Ø | Ø | Ø |
| 3 | $CC_8$ | Ø | Ø | Ø | Ø | Ø | Ø |
|   | $CC_9$ | Ø | Ø | Ø | Ø | $CC_{11}$ | Ø |
|   | $CC_{10}$ | Ø | Ø | Ø | Ø | Ø | Ø |
| 4 | $CC_{11}$ | Ø | Ø | Ø | Ø | Ø | Ø |

■ **FIGURE 3.23** Trace of the LR(1) Construction on the Parentheses Grammar.

$$CC_0 = \begin{cases} [Goal \rightarrow \bullet\, List, \texttt{eof}] & [List \rightarrow \bullet\, List\ Pair, \texttt{eof}] & [List \rightarrow \bullet\, List\ Pair, \texttt{(}] \\ [List \rightarrow \bullet\, Pair, \texttt{eof}] & [List \rightarrow \bullet\, Pair, \texttt{(}] & [Pair \rightarrow \bullet\ \texttt{(}\ Pair\ \texttt{)}, \texttt{eof}] \\ [Pair \rightarrow \bullet\ \texttt{(}\ Pair\ \texttt{)}, \texttt{(}] & [Pair \rightarrow \bullet\ \texttt{(}\ \texttt{)}, \texttt{eof}] & [Pair \rightarrow \bullet\ \texttt{(}\ \texttt{)}, \texttt{(}] \end{cases}$$

Since each item has the • at the start of its right-hand side, $CC_0$ contains only possibilities. This is appropriate, since it is the parser's initial state. The first iteration of the *while* loop produces three sets, $CC_1$, $CC_2$, and $CC_3$. All of the other combinations in the first iteration produce empty sets, as indicated in Figure 3.23, which traces the construction of $CC$.

*goto*($CC_0$, *List*) is $CC_1$.

$$CC_1 = \begin{cases} [Goal \rightarrow List\ \bullet, \texttt{eof}] & [List \rightarrow List\ \bullet\ Pair, \texttt{eof}] & [List \rightarrow List\ \bullet\ Pair, \texttt{(}] \\ [Pair \rightarrow \bullet\ \texttt{(}\ Pair\ \texttt{)}, \texttt{eof}] & [Pair \rightarrow \bullet\ \texttt{(}\ Pair\ \texttt{)}, \texttt{(}] & [Pair \rightarrow \bullet\ \texttt{(}\ \texttt{)}, \texttt{eof}] \\ & [Pair \rightarrow \bullet\ \texttt{(}\ \texttt{)}, \texttt{(}] & \end{cases}$$

$CC_1$ represents the parser configurations that result from recognizing a *List*. All of the items are possibilities that lead to another pair of parentheses, except for the item [*Goal* → *List* •, eof]. It represents the parser's accept state—a reduction by *Goal* → *List*, with a lookahead of eof.

*goto*($CC_0$, *Pair*) is $CC_2$.

$$CC_2 = \left\{ [List \rightarrow Pair\ \bullet, \texttt{eof}] \quad [List \rightarrow Pair\ \bullet, \texttt{(}] \right\}$$

$CC_2$ represents the parser configurations after it has recognized an initial *Pair*. Both items are handles for a reduction by *List* → *Pair*.

$goto(cc_0, \lfloor)$ is $cc_3$.

$$cc_3 = \begin{cases} [Pair \rightarrow \bullet \, (\, Pair\, ),\, )] & [Pair \rightarrow (\bullet Pair\, ),\, \text{eof}] & [Pair \rightarrow (\bullet Pair\, ),\, (] \\ [Pair \rightarrow \bullet \, (\, ),\, )] & [Pair \rightarrow (\bullet\, ),\, \text{eof}] & [Pair \rightarrow (\bullet\, ),\, (] \end{cases}$$

$cc_3$ represents the parser's configuration after it recognizes an initial $($. When the parser enters state 3, it must recognize a matching $)$ at some point in the future.

The second iteration of the $\texttt{while}$ loop tries to derive new sets from $cc_1$, $cc_2$, and $cc_3$. Five of the combinations produce nonempty sets, four of which are new.

$goto(cc_1, Pair)$ is $cc_4$.

$$cc_4 = \left\{ [List \rightarrow List\ Pair \bullet,\, \text{eof}] \quad [List \rightarrow List\ Pair \bullet,\, (] \right\}$$

The left context for this set is $cc_1$, which represents a state where the parser has recognized one or more occurrences of *List*. When it then recognizes a *Pair*, it enters this state. Both items represent a reduction by $List \rightarrow List\ Pair$.

$goto(cc_1, \lfloor)$ is $cc_3$, which represents the future need to find a matching $)$.

$goto(cc_3, Pair)$ is $cc_5$.

$$cc_5 = \left\{ [Pair \rightarrow (\, Pair \bullet\, ),\, \text{eof}] \quad [Pair \rightarrow (\, Pair \bullet\, ),\, (] \right\}$$

$cc_5$ consists of two partially complete items. The parser has recognized a $($ followed by a *Pair*; it now must find a matching $)$. If the parser finds a $)$, it will reduce by rule 4, $Pair \rightarrow (\, Pair\, )$.

$goto(cc_3, \lfloor)$ is $cc_6$.

$$cc_6 = \begin{cases} [Pair \rightarrow \bullet\, (\, Pair\, ),\, )] & [Pair \rightarrow (\bullet Pair\, ),\, )] \\ [Pair \rightarrow \bullet\, (\, ),\, )] & [Pair \rightarrow (\bullet\, ),\, )] \end{cases}$$

The parser arrives in $cc_6$ when it encounters a $($ and it already has at least one $($ on the stack. The items show that either a $($ or a $)$ lead to valid states.

$goto(cc_3, \rfloor)$ is $cc_7$.

$$cc_7 = \left\{ [Pair \rightarrow (\, )\, \bullet,\, \text{eof}] \quad [Pair \rightarrow (\, )\, \bullet,\, (] \right\}$$

If, in state 3, the parser finds a $)$, it takes the transition to $cc_7$. Both items specify a reduction by $Pair \rightarrow (\, )$.

The third iteration of the $\texttt{while}$ loop tries to derive new sets from $cc_4$, $cc_5$, $cc_6$, and $cc_7$. Three of the combinations produce new sets, while one produces a transition to an existing state.

$goto(cc_5, \underline{)})$ is $cc_8$.

$$cc_8 = \left\{ [Pair \rightarrow ( \ Pair \ ) \ \bullet, \texttt{eof}] \quad [Pair \rightarrow ( \ Pair \ ) \ \bullet, \underline{(}] \right\}$$

When it arrives in state 8, the parser has recognized an instance of rule 4, $Pair \rightarrow ( \ Pair \ )$. Both items specify the corresponding reduction.

$goto(cc_6, Pair)$ is $cc_9$.

$$cc_9 = \left\{ [Pair \rightarrow ( \ Pair \ \bullet \ ), \underline{)}] \right\}$$

In $cc_9$, the parser needs to find a $\underline{)}$ to complete rule 4.

$goto(cc_6, \underline{(})$ is $cc_6$. In $cc_6$, another $\underline{(}$ will cause the parser to stack another state 6 to represent the need for a matching $\underline{)}$.

$goto(cc_6, \underline{)})$ is $cc_{10}$.

$$cc_{10} = \left\{ [Pair \rightarrow ( \ ) \ \bullet, \underline{)}] \right\}$$

This set contains one item, which specifies a reduction to *Pair*.

The fourth iteration of the `while` loop tries to derive new sets from $cc_8$, $cc_9$, and $cc_{10}$. Only one combination creates a nonempty set.

$goto(cc_9, \underline{)})$ is $cc_{11}$.

$$cc_{11} = \left\{ [Pair \rightarrow ( \ Pair \ ) \ \bullet, \underline{)}] \right\}$$

State 11 calls for a reduction by $Pair \rightarrow ( \ Pair \ )$.

The final iteration of the `while` loop tries to derive new sets from $cc_{11}$. It finds only empty sets, so the construction halts with 12 sets, $cc_0$ through $cc_{11}$.

### Filling in the Tables

Given the canonical collection of sets of LR(1) items for a grammar, the parser generator can fill in the `Action` and `Goto` tables by iterating through $CC$ and examining the items in each $cc_j \in CC$. Each $cc_j$ becomes a parser state. Its items generate the nonempty elements of one row of `Action`; the corresponding transitions recorded during construction of $CC$ specify the nonempty elements of `Goto`. Three cases generate entries in the `Action` table:

1. An item of the form $[A \rightarrow \beta \bullet c\gamma, a]$ indicates that encountering the terminal symbol c would be a valid next step toward discovering the nonterminal $A$. Thus, it generates a *shift* item on c in the current state. The next state for the recognizer is the state generated by computing goto on the current state with the terminal c. Either $\beta$ or $\gamma$ can be $\epsilon$.
2. An item of the form $[A \rightarrow \beta \bullet, a]$ indicates that the parser has recognized a $\beta$, and if the lookahead is a, then the item is a handle. Thus, it generates a *reduce* item for the production $A \rightarrow \beta$ on a in the current state.
3. An item of the form $[S' \rightarrow S \bullet, eof]$ where $S'$ is the goal symbol indicates the accepting state for the parser; the parser has recognized an input stream that reduces to the goal symbol and the lookahead symbol is eof. This item generates an *accept* action on eof in the current state.

Figure 3.24 makes this concrete. For an LR(1) grammar, it should uniquely define the nonerror entries in the *Action* and *Goto* tables.

The table-filling actions can be integrated into the construction of $\mathcal{CC}$.

Notice that the table-filling algorithm essentially ignores items where the $\bullet$ precedes a nonterminal symbol. Shift actions are generated when $\bullet$ precedes a terminal. Reduce and accept actions are generated when $\bullet$ is at the right end of the production. What if $cc_i$ contains an item $[A \rightarrow \beta \bullet \gamma \delta, a]$, where $\gamma \in NT$? While this item does not generate any table entries itself, its presence in the set forces the *closure* procedure to include items that generate table entries. When *closure* finds a $\bullet$ that immediately precedes a nonterminal symbol $\gamma$, it adds productions that have $\gamma$ as their left-hand side, with a $\bullet$ preceding their right-hand sides. This process instantiates FIRST($\gamma$) in $cc_i$. The *closure* procedure will find each $x \in$ FIRST($\gamma$) and add the items into $cc_i$ to generate shift items for each $x$.

```
for each CC_i ∈ CC
    for each item I ∈ CC_i
        if I is [A→β•cγ,a] and goto(CC_i,c) = CC_j then
            Action[i,c] ← "shift j"
        else if I is [A→β•,a] then
            Action[i,a] ← "reduce A→β"
        else if I is [S'→S•,eof] then
            Action[i,eof] ← "accept"
    for each n ∈ NT
        if goto(CC_i,n) = CC_j then
            Goto[i,n] ← j
```

■ **FIGURE 3.24** LR(1) Table-Filling Algorithm.

For the parentheses grammar, the construction produces the `Action` and `Goto` tables shown in Figure 3.16b on page 120. As we saw, combining the tables with the skeleton parser in Figure 3.15 creates a functional parser for the language.

In practice, an LR(1) parser generator must produce other tables needed by the skeleton parser. For example, when the skeleton parser in Figure 3.15 on page 119 reduces by $A \rightarrow \beta$, it pops "$2 \times |\beta|$" symbols from the stack and pushes $A$ onto the stack. The table generator must produce data structures that map a production from the reduce entry in the `Action` table, say $A \rightarrow \beta$, into both $|\beta|$ and $A$. Other tables, such as a map from the integer representing a grammar symbol into its textual name, are needed for debugging and for diagnostic messages.

### Handle Finding, Revisited

LR(1) parsers derive their efficiency from a fast handle-finding mechanism embedded in the `Action` and `Goto` tables. The canonical collection, $\mathcal{CC}$, represents a handle-finding DFA for the grammar. Figure 3.25 shows the DFA for our example, the parentheses grammar.

How can the LR(1) parser use a DFA to find the handles, when we know that the language of parentheses is not a regular language? The LR(1) parser relies on a simple observation: *the set of handles is finite.* The set of handles is precisely the set of complete LR(1) items—those with the placeholder • at the right end of the item's production. Any language with a finite set of sentences can be recognized by a DFA. Since the number of productions and the number of lookahead symbols are both finite, the number of complete items is finite, and the language of handles is a regular language.

The LR(1) parser makes the handle's position implicit, at stacktop. This design decision drastically reduces the number of possible handles.

When the LR(1) parser executes, it interleaves two kinds of actions: shifts and reduces. The shift actions simulate steps in the handle-finding DFA. The

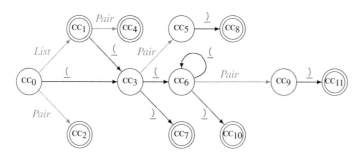

■ **FIGURE 3.25** Handle-Finding DFA for the Parentheses Grammar.

parser performs one shift action per word in the input stream. When the handle-finding DFA reaches a final state, the LR(1) parser performs a reduce action. The reduce actions reset the state of the handle-finding DFA to reflect the fact that the parser has recognized a handle and replaced it with a non-terminal. To accomplish this, the parser pops the handle and its state off the stack, revealing an older state. The parser uses that older state, the look-ahead symbol, and the *Goto* table to discover the state in the DFA from which handle-finding should continue.

The reduce actions tie together successive handle-finding phases. The reduction uses left context—the state revealed by the reduction summarizes the prior history of the parse—to restart the handle-finding DFA in a state that reflects the nonterminal that the parser just recognized. For example, in the parse of "<u>( ( ) ) ( )</u>", the parser stacked an instance of state 3 for every <u>(</u> that it encounters. These stacked states allow the algorithm to match up the opening and closing parentheses.

Notice that the handle-finding DFA has transitions on both terminal and non-terminal symbols. The parser traverses the nonterminal edges only on a reduce action. Each of these transitions, shown in gray in Figure 3.25, corresponds to a valid entry in the *Goto* table. The combined effect of the terminal and nonterminal actions is to invoke the DFA recursively each time it must recognize a nonterminal.

### 3.4.3 Errors in the Table Construction

As a second example of the LR(1) table construction, consider the ambiguous grammar for the classic `if-then-else` construct. Abstracting away the details of the controlling expression and all other statements (by treating them as terminal symbols) produces the following four-production grammar:

| | | | |
|---|---|---|---|
| 1 | *Goal* | → | *Stmt* |
| 2 | *Stmt* | → | `if expr then` *Stmt* |
| 3 | | \| | `if expr then` *Stmt* `else` *Stmt* |
| 4 | | \| | `assign` |

It has two nonterminal symbols, *Goal* and *Stmt*, and six terminal symbols, `if`, `expr`, `then`, `else`, `assign`, and the implicit `eof`.

The construction begins by initializing $cc_0$ to the item [*Goal* → • *Stmt*, `eof`] and taking its *closure* to produce the first set.

| | Item | Goal | Stmt | if | expr | then | else | assign | eof |
|---|---|---|---|---|---|---|---|---|---|
| 0 | $CC_0$ | ∅ | $CC_1$ | $CC_2$ | ∅ | ∅ | ∅ | $CC_3$ | ∅ |
| 1 | $CC_1$ | ∅ | ∅ | ∅ | ∅ | ∅ | ∅ | ∅ | ∅ |
| | $CC_2$ | ∅ | ∅ | ∅ | $CC_4$ | ∅ | ∅ | ∅ | ∅ |
| | $CC_3$ | ∅ | ∅ | ∅ | ∅ | ∅ | ∅ | ∅ | ∅ |
| 2 | $CC_4$ | ∅ | ∅ | ∅ | ∅ | $CC_5$ | ∅ | ∅ | ∅ |
| 3 | $CC_5$ | ∅ | $CC_6$ | $CC_7$ | ∅ | ∅ | ∅ | $CC_8$ | ∅ |
| 4 | $CC_6$ | ∅ | ∅ | ∅ | ∅ | ∅ | $CC_9$ | ∅ | ∅ |
| | $CC_7$ | ∅ | ∅ | ∅ | $CC_{10}$ | ∅ | ∅ | ∅ | ∅ |
| | $CC_8$ | ∅ | ∅ | ∅ | ∅ | ∅ | ∅ | ∅ | ∅ |
| 5 | $CC_9$ | ∅ | $CC_{11}$ | $CC_2$ | ∅ | ∅ | ∅ | $CC_3$ | ∅ |
| | $CC_{10}$ | ∅ | ∅ | ∅ | ∅ | $CC_{12}$ | ∅ | ∅ | ∅ |
| 6 | $CC_{11}$ | ∅ | ∅ | ∅ | ∅ | ∅ | ∅ | ∅ | ∅ |
| | $CC_{12}$ | ∅ | $CC_{13}$ | $CC_7$ | ∅ | ∅ | ∅ | $CC_8$ | ∅ |
| 7 | $CC_{13}$ | ∅ | ∅ | ∅ | ∅ | ∅ | $CC_{14}$ | ∅ | ∅ |
| 8 | $CC_{14}$ | ∅ | $CC_{15}$ | $CC_7$ | ∅ | ∅ | ∅ | $CC_8$ | ∅ |
| 9 | $CC_{15}$ | ∅ | ∅ | ∅ | ∅ | ∅ | ∅ | ∅ | ∅ |

■ **FIGURE 3.26** Trace of the LR(1) Construction on the *If-Then-Else* Grammar.

$$CC_0 = \left\{ \begin{array}{ll} [Goal \rightarrow \bullet\ Stmt, \text{eof}] & [Stmt \rightarrow \bullet\ \text{if expr then } Stmt, \text{eof}] \\ [Stmt \rightarrow \bullet\ \text{assign}, \text{eof}] & [Stmt \rightarrow \bullet\ \text{if expr then } Stmt \text{ else } Stmt, \text{eof}] \end{array} \right\}$$

From this set, the construction begins deriving the remaining members of the canonical collection of sets of LR(1) items.

Figure 3.26 shows the progress of the construction. The first iteration examines the transitions out of $CC_0$ for each grammar symbol. It produces three new sets for the canonical collection from $CC_0$: $CC_1$ for *Stmt*, $CC_2$ for if, and $CC_3$ for assign. These sets are:

$$CC_1 = \left\{ [Goal \rightarrow Stmt\ \bullet, \text{eof}] \right\}$$

$$CC_2 = \left\{ \begin{array}{l} [Stmt \rightarrow \text{if} \bullet \text{expr then } Stmt, \text{eof}], \\ [Stmt \rightarrow \text{if} \bullet \text{expr then } Stmt \text{ else } Stmt, \text{eof}] \end{array} \right\}$$

$$CC_3 = \left\{ [Stmt \rightarrow \text{assign} \bullet, \text{eof}] \right\}$$

The second iteration examines transitions out of these three new sets. Only one combination produces a new set, looking at $CC_2$ with the symbol expr.

$$CC_4 = \left\{ \begin{array}{l} [Stmt \rightarrow \text{if expr} \bullet \text{then } Stmt, \text{eof}], \\ [Stmt \rightarrow \text{if expr} \bullet \text{then } Stmt \text{ else } Stmt, \text{eof}] \end{array} \right\}$$

The next iteration computes transitions from $CC_4$; it creates $CC_5$ as $goto(CC_4, \text{then})$.

$$CC_5 = \left\{\begin{array}{l} [\textit{Stmt} \rightarrow \texttt{if expr then} \bullet \textit{Stmt}, \texttt{eof}], \\ [\textit{Stmt} \rightarrow \texttt{if expr then} \bullet \textit{Stmt} \texttt{ else } \textit{Stmt}, \texttt{eof}], \\ [\textit{Stmt} \rightarrow \bullet \texttt{ if expr then } \textit{Stmt}, \{\texttt{eof}, \texttt{else}\}], \\ [\textit{Stmt} \rightarrow \bullet \texttt{ assign}, \{\texttt{eof}, \texttt{else}\}], \\ [\textit{Stmt} \rightarrow \bullet \texttt{ if expr then } \textit{Stmt} \texttt{ else } \textit{Stmt}, \{\texttt{eof}, \texttt{else}\}] \end{array}\right\}$$

The fourth iteration examines transitions out of $CC_5$. It creates new sets for *Stmt*, for if, and for assign.

$$CC_6 = \left\{\begin{array}{l} [\textit{Stmt} \rightarrow \texttt{if expr then } \textit{Stmt} \bullet, \texttt{eof}], \\ [\textit{Stmt} \rightarrow \texttt{if expr then } \textit{Stmt} \bullet \texttt{ else } \textit{Stmt}, \texttt{eof}] \end{array}\right\}$$

$$CC_7 = \left\{\begin{array}{l} [\textit{Stmt} \rightarrow \texttt{if} \bullet \texttt{ expr then } \textit{Stmt}, \{\texttt{eof}, \texttt{else}\}], \\ [\textit{Stmt} \rightarrow \texttt{if} \bullet \texttt{ expr then } \textit{Stmt} \texttt{ else } \textit{Stmt}, \{\texttt{eof}, \texttt{else}\}] \end{array}\right\}$$

$$CC_8 = \{[\textit{Stmt} \rightarrow \texttt{assign} \bullet, \{\texttt{eof}, \texttt{else}\}]\}$$

The fifth iteration examines $CC_6$, $CC_7$, and $CC_8$. While most of the combinations produce the empty set, two combinations lead to new sets. The transition on else from $CC_6$ leads to $CC_9$, and the transition on expr from $CC_7$ creates $CC_{10}$.

$$CC_9 = \left\{\begin{array}{l} [\textit{Stmt} \rightarrow \texttt{if expr then } \textit{Stmt} \texttt{ else } \bullet \textit{ Stmt}, \texttt{eof}], \\ [\textit{Stmt} \rightarrow \bullet \texttt{ if expr then } \textit{Stmt}, \texttt{eof}], \\ [\textit{Stmt} \rightarrow \bullet \texttt{ if expr then } \textit{Stmt} \texttt{ else } \textit{Stmt}, \texttt{eof}], \\ [\textit{Stmt} \rightarrow \bullet \texttt{ assign}, \texttt{eof}] \end{array}\right\}$$

$$CC_{10} = \left\{\begin{array}{l} [\textit{Stmt} \rightarrow \texttt{if expr} \bullet \texttt{ then } \textit{Stmt}, \{\texttt{eof}, \texttt{else}\}], \\ [\textit{Stmt} \rightarrow \texttt{if expr} \bullet \texttt{ then } \textit{Stmt} \texttt{ else } \textit{Stmt}, \{\texttt{eof}, \texttt{else}\}] \end{array}\right\}$$

When the sixth iteration examines the sets produced in the fifth iteration, it creates two new sets, $CC_{11}$ from $CC_9$ on *Stmt* and $CC_{12}$ from $CC_{10}$ on then. It also creates duplicate sets for $CC_2$ and $CC_3$ from $CC_9$.

$$CC_{11} = \{[\textit{Stmt} \rightarrow \texttt{if expr then } \textit{Stmt} \texttt{ else } \textit{Stmt} \bullet, \texttt{eof}]\}$$

$$CC_{12} = \left\{\begin{array}{l} [\textit{Stmt} \rightarrow \texttt{if expr then} \bullet \textit{ Stmt}, \{\texttt{eof}, \texttt{else}\}], \\ [\textit{Stmt} \rightarrow \texttt{if expr then} \bullet \textit{ Stmt} \texttt{ else } \textit{Stmt}, \{\texttt{eof}, \texttt{else}\}], \\ [\textit{Stmt} \rightarrow \bullet \texttt{if expr then } \textit{Stmt}, \{\texttt{eof}, \texttt{else}\}], \\ [\textit{Stmt} \rightarrow \bullet \texttt{if expr then } \textit{Stmt} \texttt{ else } \textit{Stmt}, \{\texttt{eof}, \texttt{else}\}], \\ [\textit{Stmt} \rightarrow \bullet \texttt{assign}, \{\texttt{eof}, \texttt{else}\}] \end{array}\right\}$$

Iteration seven creates $CC_{13}$ from $CC_{12}$ on *Stmt*. It recreates $CC_7$ and $CC_8$.

$$CC_{13} = \begin{cases} [Stmt \rightarrow \texttt{if expr then } Stmt \bullet \texttt{,\{eof,else\}],} \\ [Stmt \rightarrow \texttt{if expr then } Stmt \bullet \texttt{else } Stmt, \texttt{\{eof,else\}]} \end{cases}$$

Iteration eight finds one new set, $CC_{14}$ from $CC_{13}$ on the transition for `else`.

$$CC_{14} = \begin{cases} [Stmt \rightarrow \texttt{if expr then } Stmt \texttt{ else } \bullet \; Stmt, \texttt{\{eof,else\}],} \\ [Stmt \rightarrow \bullet \texttt{ if expr then } Stmt, \texttt{\{eof,else\}],} \\ [Stmt \rightarrow \bullet \texttt{ if expr then } Stmt \texttt{ else } Stmt, \texttt{\{eof,else\}],} \\ [Stmt \rightarrow \bullet \texttt{ assign,\{eof,else\}]} \end{cases}$$

Iteration nine generates $CC_{15}$ from $CC_{14}$ on the transition for *Stmt*, along with duplicates of $CC_7$ and $CC_8$.

$$CC_{15} = \{[Stmt \rightarrow \texttt{if expr then } Stmt \texttt{ else } Stmt \bullet, \texttt{\{eof,else\}]}\}$$

The final iteration looks at $CC_{15}$. Since the $\bullet$ lies at the end of every item in $CC_{15}$, it can only generate empty sets. At this point, no additional sets of items can be added to the canonical collection, so the algorithm has reached a fixed point. It halts.

The ambiguity in the grammar becomes apparent during the table-filling algorithm. The items in states $CC_0$ through $CC_{12}$ generate no conflicts. State $CC_{13}$ contains four items:

1. $[Stmt \rightarrow \texttt{if expr then } Stmt \; \bullet \texttt{, else}]$
2. $[Stmt \rightarrow \texttt{if expr then } Stmt \; \bullet \texttt{, eof}]$
3. $[Stmt \rightarrow \texttt{if expr then } Stmt \; \bullet \texttt{ else } Stmt, \texttt{else}]$
4. $[Stmt \rightarrow \texttt{if expr then } Stmt \; \bullet \texttt{ else } Stmt, \texttt{eof}]$

Item 1 generates a reduce entry for $CC_{13}$ and the lookahead `else`. Item 3 generates a shift entry for the same location in the table. Clearly, the table entry cannot hold both actions. This *shift-reduce conflict* indicates that the grammar is ambiguous. Items 2 and 4 generate a similar shift-reduce conflict with a lookahead of `eof`. When the table-filling algorithm encounters such a conflict, the construction has failed. The table generator should report the problem—a fundamental ambiguity between the productions in the specific $LR(1)$ items—to the compiler writer.

A typical error message from a parser generator includes the $LR(1)$ items that generate the conflict; another reason to study the table construction.

In this case, the conflict arises because production 2 in the grammar is a prefix of production 3. The table generator could be designed to resolve this conflict in favor of shifting; that forces the parser to recognize the longer production and binds the `else` to the innermost `if`.

An ambiguous grammar can also produce a *reduce-reduce conflict*. Such a conflict can occur if the grammar contains two productions $A \rightarrow \gamma \delta$ and $B \rightarrow \gamma \delta$, with the same right-hand side $\gamma \delta$. If a state contains the items $[A \rightarrow \gamma \delta \bullet, a]$ and $[B \rightarrow \gamma \delta \bullet, a]$, then it will generate two conflicting reduce actions for the lookahead a—one for each production. Again, this conflict reflects a fundamental ambiguity in the underlying grammar; the compiler writer must reshape the grammar to eliminate it (see Section 3.5.3).

Since parser generators that automate this process are widely available, the method of choice for determining whether a grammar has the LR(1) property is to invoke an LR(1) parser generator on it. If the process succeeds, the grammar has the LR(1) property.

Exercise 12 shows an LR(1) grammar that has no equivalent LL(1) grammar.

As a final example, the LR tables for the classic expression grammar appear in Figures 3.31 and 3.32 on pages 151 and 152.

---

**SECTION REVIEW**

LR(1) parsers are widely used in compilers built in both industry and academia. These parsers accept a large class of languages. They use time proportional to the size of the derivation that they construct. Tools that generate an LR(1) parser are widely available in a broad variety of implementation languages.

The LR(1) table-construction algorithm is an elegant application of theory to practice. It systematically builds up a model of the handle-recognizing DFA and then translates that model into a pair of tables that drive the skeleton parser. The table construction is a complex undertaking that requires painstaking attention to detail. It is precisely the kind of task that should be automated—parser generators are better at following these long chains of computations than are humans. That notwithstanding, a skilled compiler writer should understand the table-construction algorithms because they provide insight into how the parsers work, what kinds of errors the parser generator can encounter, how those errors arise, and how they can be remedied.

---

**Review Questions**

1. Show the steps that the skeleton LR(1) parser, with the tables for the parentheses grammar, would take on the input string "( ( ) ( ) ) ( )."

2. Build the LR(1) tables for the *SheepNoise* grammar, given in Section 3.2.2 on page 86, and show the skeleton parser's actions on the input "baa baa baa."

## 3.5 **PRACTICAL ISSUES**

Even with automatic parser generators, the compiler writer must manage several issues to produce a robust, efficient parser for a real programming language. This section addresses several issues that arise in practice.

### 3.5.1 **Error Recovery**

Programmers often compile code that contains syntax errors. In fact, compilers are widely accepted as the fastest way to discover such errors. In this application, the compiler must find as many syntax errors as possible in a single attempt at parsing the code. This requires attention to the parser's behavior in error states.

All of the parsers shown in this chapter have the same behavior when they encounter a syntax error: they report the problem and halt. This behavior prevents the compiler from wasting time trying to translate an incorrect program. However, it ensures that the compiler finds at most one syntax error per compilation. Such a compiler would make finding all the syntax errors in a file of program text a potentially long and painful process.

A parser should find as many syntax errors as possible in each compilation. This requires a mechanism that lets the parser recover from an error by moving to a state where it can continue parsing. A common way of achieving this is to select one or more words that the parser can use to synchronize the input with its internal state. When the parser encounters an error, it discards input symbols until it finds a synchronizing word and then resets its internal state to one consistent with the synchronizing word.

In an Algol-like language, with semicolons as statement separators, the semicolon is often used as a synchronizing word. When an error occurs, the parser calls the scanner repeatedly until it finds a semicolon. It then changes state to one that would have resulted from successful recognition of a complete statement, rather than an error.

In a recursive-descent parser, the code can simply discard words until it finds a semicolon. At that point, it can return control to the point where the routine that parses statements reports success. This may involve manipulating the runtime stack or using a nonlocal jump like C's setjmp and longjmp.

In an LR(1) parser, this kind of resynchronization is more complex. The parser discards input until it finds a semicolon. Next, it scans backward down the parse stack until it finds a state *s* such that Goto[*s*, *Statement*] is a valid, nonerror entry. The first such state on the stack represents the statement that contains the error. The error recovery routine then discards entries on the stack above that state, pushes the state Goto[*s*, *Statement*] onto the stack and resumes normal parsing.

In a table-driven parser, either LL(1) or LR(1), the compiler needs a way of telling the parser generator where to synchronize. This can be done using error productions—a production whose right-hand side includes a reserved word that indicates an error synchronization point and one or more synchronizing tokens. With such a construct, the parser generator can construct error-recovery routines that implement the desired behavior.

Of course, the error-recovery routines should take steps to ensure that the compiler does not try to generate and optimize code for a syntactically invalid program. This requires simple handshaking between the error-recovery apparatus and the high-level driver that invokes the various parts of the compiler.

### 3.5.2 Unary Operators

The classic expression grammar includes only binary operators. Algebraic notation, however, includes unary operators, such as unary minus and absolute value. Other unary operators arise in programming languages, including autoincrement, autodecrement, address-of, dereference, boolean complement, and typecasts. Adding such operators to the expression grammar requires some care.

Consider adding a unary absolute-value operator, ‖, to the classic expression grammar. Absolute value should have higher precedence than either × or ÷.

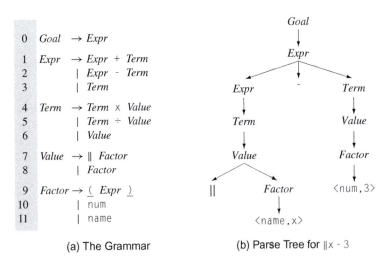

| 0 | *Goal* | → *Expr* |
| 1 | *Expr* | → *Expr* + *Term* |
| 2 | | \| *Expr* - *Term* |
| 3 | | \| *Term* |
| 4 | *Term* | → *Term* × *Value* |
| 5 | | \| *Term* ÷ *Value* |
| 6 | | \| *Value* |
| 7 | *Value* | → ‖ *Factor* |
| 8 | | \| *Factor* |
| 9 | *Factor* | → ( *Expr* ) |
| 10 | | \| num |
| 11 | | \| name |

(a) The Grammar

(b) Parse Tree for ‖x - 3

■ **FIGURE 3.27** Adding Unary Absolute Value to the Classic Expression Grammar.

However, it needs a lower precedence than *Factor* to force evaluation of parenthetic expressions before application of ‖. One way to write this grammar is shown in Figure 3.27. With these additions, the grammar is still LR(1). It lets the programmer form the absolute value of a number, an identifier, or a parenthesized expression.

Figure 3.27b shows the parse tree for the string ‖x - 3. It correctly shows that the code must evaluate ‖x before performing the subtraction. The grammar does not allow the programmer to write ‖‖x, as that makes little mathematical sense. It does, however, allow ‖(‖x), which makes as little sense as ‖‖x.

The inability to write ‖‖x hardly limits the expressiveness of the language. With other unary operators, however, the issue seems more serious. For example, a C programmer might need to write **p to dereference a variable declared as char **p;. We can add a dereference production for *Value* as well: *Value* → * *Value*. The resulting grammar is still an LR(1) grammar, even if we replace the x operator in *Term* → *Term* x *Value* with *, overloading the operator "*" in the way that C does. This same approach works for unary minus.

### 3.5.3 **Handling Context-Sensitive Ambiguity**

Using one word to represent two different meanings can create a syntactic ambiguity. One example of this problem arose in the definitions of several early programming languages, including FORTRAN, PL/I, and Ada. These languages used parentheses to enclose both the subscript expressions of an array reference and the argument list of a subroutine or function. Given a textual reference, such as fee(i,j), the compiler cannot tell if fee is a two-dimensional array or a procedure that must be invoked. Differentiating between these two cases requires knowledge of fee's declared type. This information is not syntactically obvious. The scanner undoubtedly classifies fee as a name in either case. A function call and an array reference can appear in many of the same situations.

Neither of these constructs appears in the classic expression grammar. We can add productions that derive them from *Factor*.

$$
\begin{aligned}
\textit{Factor} &\rightarrow \textit{FunctionReference} \\
&\mid \textit{ArrayReference} \\
&\mid \text{( } \textit{Expr} \text{ )} \\
&\mid \texttt{num} \\
&\mid \texttt{name} \\
\textit{FunctionReference} &\rightarrow \texttt{name ( } \textit{ArgList} \text{ )} \\
\textit{ArrayReference} &\rightarrow \texttt{name ( } \textit{ArgList} \text{ )}
\end{aligned}
$$

Since the last two productions have identical right-hand sides, this grammar is ambiguous, which creates a reduce-reduce conflict in an LR(1) table builder.

Resolving this ambiguity requires extra-syntactic knowledge. In a recursive-descent parser, the compiler writer can combine the code for *FunctionReference* and *ArrayReference* and add the extra code required to check the name's declared type. In a table-driven parser built with a parser generator, the solution must work within the framework provided by the tools.

Two different approaches have been used to solve this problem. The compiler writer can rewrite the grammar to combine both the function invocation and the array reference into a single production. In this scheme, the issue is deferred until a later step in translation, when it can be resolved with information from the declarations. The parser must construct a representation that preserves all the information needed by either resolution; the later step will then rewrite the reference to its appropriate form as an array reference or as a function invocation.

Alternatively, the scanner can classify identifiers based on their declared types, rather than their microsyntactic properties. This classification requires some hand-shaking between the scanner and the parser; the coordination is not hard to arrange as long as the language has a define-before-use rule. Since the declaration is parsed before the use occurs, the parser can make its internal symbol table available to the scanner to resolve identifiers into distinct classes, such as variable-name and function-name. The relevant productions become:

$$\begin{aligned} \textit{FunctionReference} &\rightarrow \texttt{function-name} \ ( \ \textit{ArgList} \ ) \\ \textit{ArrayReference} &\rightarrow \texttt{variable-name} \ ( \ \textit{ArgList} \ ) \end{aligned}$$

Rewritten in this way, the grammar is unambiguous. Since the scanner returns a distinct syntactic category in each case, the parser can distinguish the two cases.

### 3.5.4 Left versus Right Recursion

As we have seen, top-down parsers need right-recursive grammars rather than left-recursive ones. Bottom-up parsers can accommodate either left or right recursion. Thus, the compiler writer must choose between left and right recursion in writing the grammar for a bottom-up parser. Several factors play into this decision.

## Stack Depth

In general, left recursion can lead to smaller stack depths. Consider two alternate grammars for a simple list construct, shown in Figures 3.28a and 3.28b. (Notice the similarity to the *SheepNoise* grammar.) Using these grammars to produce a five-element list leads to the derivations shown in Figures 3.28c and 3.28d, respectively. An LR(1) parser would construct these sequences in reverse. Thus, if we read the derivation from the bottom line to the top line, we can follow the parsers's actions with each grammar.

1. *Left-recursive grammar* This grammar shifts $elt_1$ onto its stack and immediately reduces it to *List*. Next, it shifts $elt_2$ onto the stack and reduces it to *List*. It proceeds until it has shifted each of the five $elt_i$s onto the stack and reduced them to *List*. Thus, the stack reaches a maximum depth of two and an average depth of $\frac{10}{6} = 1\frac{2}{3}$.
2. *Right-recursive grammar* This version shifts all five $elt_i$s onto its stack. Next, it reduces $elt_5$ to *List* using rule two, and the remaining

$$
\begin{aligned}
List &\rightarrow List\ \text{elt} \\
&\mid\ \text{elt}
\end{aligned}
$$

(a) Left-Recursive Grammar

$$
\begin{aligned}
List &\rightarrow \text{elt}\ List \\
&\mid\ \text{elt}
\end{aligned}
$$

(b) Right-Recursive Grammar

*List*

*List* elt$_5$

*List* elt$_4$ elt$_5$

*List* elt$_3$ elt$_4$ elt$_5$

*List* elt$_2$ elt$_3$ elt$_4$ elt$_5$

elt$_1$ elt$_2$ elt$_3$ elt$_4$ elt$_5$

(c) Derivation with Left Recursion

*List*

elt$_1$ *List*

elt$_1$ elt$_2$ *List*

elt$_1$ elt$_2$ elt$_3$ *List*

elt$_1$ elt$_2$ elt$_3$ elt$_4$ *List*

elt$_1$ elt$_2$ elt$_3$ elt$_4$

elt$_5$ *List*

(d) Derivation with Right Recursion

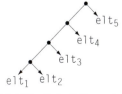

(e) AST with Left Recursion

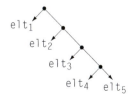

(f) AST with Right Recursion

■ **FIGURE 3.28** Left- and Right-Recursive List Grammars.

elt$_i$s using rule one. Thus, its maximum stack depth will be five and its average will be $\frac{20}{6} = 3\frac{1}{3}$.

The right-recursive grammar requires more stack space; its maximum stack depth is bounded only by the length of the list. In contrast, the maximum stack depth with the left-recursive grammar depends on the grammar rather than the input stream.

For short lists, this is not a problem. If, however, the list represents the statement list in a long run of straight-line code, it might have hundreds of elements. In this case, the difference in space can be dramatic. If all other issues are equal, the smaller stack height is an advantage.

### Associativity

**Abstract syntax tree**
An AST is a contraction of the parse tree. See Section 5.2.1 on page 227.

Left recursion naturally produces left associativity, and right recursion naturally produces right associativity. In some cases, the order of evaluation makes a difference. Consider the abstract syntax trees (ASTs) for the two five-element lists, shown in Figures 3.28e and 3.28f. The left-recursive grammar reduces elt$_1$ to a *List*, then reduces *List* elt$_2$, and so on. This produces the AST shown on the left. Similarly, the right-recursive grammar produces the AST shown on the right.

For a list, neither of these orders is obviously incorrect, although the right-recursive AST may seem more natural. Consider, however, the result if we replace the list constructor with arithmetic operations, as in the grammars

$$
\begin{array}{lll}
\textit{Expr} & \rightarrow & \textit{Expr} \; + \; \texttt{Operand} \\
& | & \textit{Expr} \; - \; \texttt{Operand} \\
& | & \texttt{Operand}
\end{array}
\qquad
\begin{array}{lll}
\textit{Expr} & \rightarrow & \texttt{Operand} \; + \; \textit{Expr} \\
& | & \texttt{Operand} \; - \; \textit{Expr} \\
& | & \texttt{Operand}
\end{array}
$$

For the string $x_1 + x_2 + x_3 + x_4 + x_5$ the left-recursive grammar implies a left-to-right evaluation order, while the right-recursive grammar implies a right-to-left evaluation order. With some number systems, such as floating-point arithmetic, these two evaluation orders can produce different results.

Since the mantissa of a floating-point number is small relative to the range of the exponent, addition can become an identity operation with two numbers that are far apart in magnitude. If, for example, $x_4$ is much smaller than $x_5$, the processor may compute $x_4 + x_5 = x_5$ With well-chosen values, this effect can cascade and yield different answers from left-to-right and right-to-left evaluations.

Similarly, if any of the terms in the expression is a function call, then the order of evaluation may be important. If the function call changes the value of a variable in the expression, then changing the evaluation order might change the result.

In a string with subtractions, such as $x_1 - x_2 + x_3$, changing the evaluation order can produce incorrect results. Left associativity evaluates, in a postorder tree walk, to $(x_1 - x_2) + x_3$, the expected result. Right associativity, on the other hand, implies an evaluation order of $x_1 - (x_2 + x_3)$. The compiler must, of course, preserve the evaluation order dictated by the language definition. The compiler writer can either write the expression grammar so that it produces the desired order or take care to generate the intermediate representation to reflect the correct order and associativity, as described in Section 4.5.2.

---

**SECTION REVIEW**

Building a compiler involves more than just transcribing the grammar from some language definition. In writing down the grammar, many choices arise that have an impact on both the function and the utility of the resulting compiler. This section dealt with a variety of issues, ranging from how to perform error recovery through the tradeoff between left recursion and right recursion.

---

**Review Questions**

1. The programming language C uses square brackets to indicate an array subscript and parentheses to indicate a procedure or function argument list. How does this simplify the construction of a parser for C?

2. The grammar for unary absolute value introduced a new terminal symbol as the unary operator. Consider adding a unary minus to the classic expression grammar. Does the fact that the same terminal symbol occurs as either a unary minus or a binary minus introduce complications? Justify your answer.

---

## 3.6 **ADVANCED TOPICS**

To build a satisfactory parser, the compiler writer must understand the basics of engineering a grammar and a parser. Given a working parser, there are often ways of improving its performance. This section looks at two specific issues in parser construction. First, we examine transformations on the grammar that reduce the length of a derivation to produce a faster parse. These

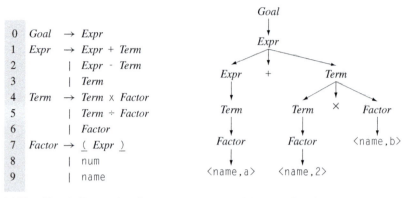

| | | |
|---|---|---|
| 0 | *Goal* | → *Expr* |
| 1 | *Expr* | → *Expr* + *Term* |
| 2 | | \| *Expr* - *Term* |
| 3 | | \| *Term* |
| 4 | *Term* | → *Term* × *Factor* |
| 5 | | \| *Term* ÷ *Factor* |
| 6 | | \| *Factor* |
| 7 | *Factor* | → ( *Expr* ) |
| 8 | | \| num |
| 9 | | \| name |

(a) The Classic Expression Grammar  (b) Parse Tree for a + 2 x b

■ **FIGURE 3.29** The Classic Expression Grammar, Revisited.

ideas apply to both top-down and bottom-up parsers. Second, we discuss transformations on the grammar and the `Action` and `Goto` tables that reduce table size. These techniques apply only to LR parsers.

### 3.6.1 Optimizing a Grammar

While syntax analysis no longer consumes a major share of compile time, the compiler should not waste undue time in parsing. The actual form of a grammar has a direct effect on the amount of work required to parse it. Both top-down and bottom-up parsers construct derivations. A top-down parser performs an expansion for every production in the derivation. A bottom-up parser performs a reduction for every production in the derivation. A grammar that produces shorter derivations takes less time to parse.

The compiler writer can often rewrite the grammar to reduce the parse tree height. This reduces the number of expansions in a top-down parser and the number of reductions in a bottom-up parser. Optimizing the grammar cannot change the parser's asymptotic behavior; after all, the parse tree must have a leaf node for each symbol in the input stream. Still, reducing the constants in heavily used portions of the grammar, such as the expression grammar, can make enough difference to justify the effort.

Consider, again, the classic expression grammar from Section 3.2.4. (The LR(1) tables for the grammar appear in Figures 3.31 and 3.32.) To enforce the desired precedence among operators, we added two nonterminals, *Term* and *Factor*, and reshaped the grammar into the form shown in Figure 3.29a. This grammar produces rather large parse trees, even for simple expressions. For example, the expression a + 2 x b, the parse tree has 14 nodes, as shown

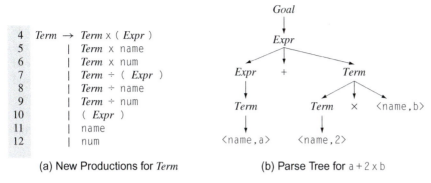

| 4 | *Term* | $\rightarrow$ | *Term* x ( *Expr* ) |
| 5 | | \| | *Term* x name |
| 6 | | \| | *Term* x num |
| 7 | | \| | *Term* ÷ ( *Expr* ) |
| 8 | | \| | *Term* ÷ name |
| 9 | | \| | *Term* ÷ num |
| 10 | | \| | ( *Expr* ) |
| 11 | | \| | name |
| 12 | | \| | num |

(a) New Productions for *Term*          (b) Parse Tree for a + 2 x b

■ **FIGURE 3.30**  Replacement Productions for *Term*.

in Figure 3.29b. Five of these nodes are leaves that we cannot eliminate. (Changing the grammar cannot shorten the input program.)

Any interior node that has only one child is a candidate for optimization. The sequence of nodes *Expr* to *Term* to *Factor* to ⟨name, a⟩ uses four nodes for a single word in the input stream. We can eliminate at least one layer, the layer of *Factor* nodes, by folding the alternative expansions for *Factor* into *Term*, as shown in Figure 3.30a. It multiplies by three the number of alternatives for *Term*, but shrinks the parse tree by one layer, shown in Figure 3.30b.

In an LR(1) parser, this change eliminates three of nine reduce actions, and leaves the five shifts intact. In a top-down recursive-descent parser for an equivalent predictive grammar, it would eliminate 3 of 14 procedure calls.

In general, any production that has a single symbol on its right-hand side can be folded away. These productions are sometimes called *useless pro-ductions*. Sometimes, useless productions serve a purpose—making the grammar more compact and, perhaps, more readable, or forcing the deriva-tion to assume a particular shape. (Recall that the simplest of our expression grammars accepts a + 2 x b but does not encode any notion of precedence into the parse tree.) As we shall see in Chapter 4, the compiler writer may include a useless production simply to create a point in the derivation where a particular action can be performed.

Folding away useless productions has its costs. In an LR(1) parser, it can make the tables larger. In our example, eliminating *Factor* removes one col-umn from the Goto table, but the extra productions for *Term* increase the size of $CC$ from 32 sets to 46 sets. Thus, the tables have one fewer column, but an extra 14 rows. The resulting parser performs fewer reductions (and runs faster), but has larger tables.

In a hand-coded, recursive-descent parser, the larger grammar may increase the number of alternatives that must be compared before expanding some left-hand side. The compiler writer can sometimes compensate for the increased cost by combining cases. For example, the code for both nontrivial expansions of *Expr'* in Figure 3.10 is identical. The compiler writer could combine them with a test that matches word against either + or -. Alternatively, the compiler writer could assign both + and - to the same syntactic category, have the parser inspect the syntactic category, and use the lexeme to differentiate between the two when needed.

### 3.6.2  Reducing the Size of LR(1) Tables

Unfortunately, the LR(1) tables generated for relatively small grammars can be large. Figures 3.31 and 3.32 show the canonical LR(1) tables for the classic expression grammar. Many techniques exist for shrinking such tables, including the three approaches to reducing table size described in this section.

#### *Combining Rows or Columns*

If the table generator can find two rows, or two columns, that are identical, it can combine them. In Figure 3.31, the rows for states 0 and 7 through 10 are identical, as are rows 4, 14, 21, 22, 24, and 25. The table generator can implement each of these sets once, and remap the states accordingly. This would remove nine rows from the table, reducing its size by 28 percent. To use this table, the skeleton parser needs a mapping from a parser state to a row index in the Action table. The table generator can combine identical columns in the analogous way. A separate inspection of the Goto table will yield a different set of state combinations—in particular, all of the rows containing only zeros should condense to a single row.

In some cases, the table generator can prove that two rows or two columns differ only in cases where one of the two has an "error" entry (denoted by a blank in our figures). In Figure 3.31, the columns for eof and for num differ only where one or the other has a blank. Combining such columns produces the same behavior on correct inputs. It does change the parser's behavior on erroneous inputs and may impede the parser's ability to provide accurate and helpful error messages.

Combining rows and columns produces a direct reduction in table size. If this space reduction adds an extra indirection to every table access, the cost of those memory operations must trade off directly against the savings in memory. The table generator could also use other techniques to represent sparse matrices—again, the implementor must consider the tradeoff of memory size against any increase in access costs.

| State | eof | + | − | × | ÷ | ( | ) | num | name |
|---|---|---|---|---|---|---|---|---|---|
| | | | | | *Action* **Table** | | | | |
| 0 | | | | | | s 4 | | s 5 | s 6 |
| 1 | acc | s 7 | s 8 | | | | | | |
| 2 | r 4 | r 4 | r 4 | s 9 | s 10 | | | | |
| 3 | r 7 | r 7 | r 7 | r 7 | r 7 | | | | |
| 4 | | | | | | s 14 | | s 15 | s 16 |
| 5 | r 9 | r 9 | r 9 | r 9 | r 9 | | | | |
| 6 | r 10 | r 10 | r 10 | r 10 | r 10 | | | | |
| 7 | | | | | | s 4 | | s 5 | s 6 |
| 8 | | | | | | s 4 | | s 5 | s 6 |
| 9 | | | | | | s 4 | | s 5 | s 6 |
| 10 | | | | | | s 4 | | s 5 | s 6 |
| 11 | | s 21 | s 22 | | | | s 23 | | |
| 12 | | r 4 | r 4 | s 24 | s 25 | | r 4 | | |
| 13 | | r 7 | r 7 | r 7 | r 7 | | r 7 | | |
| 14 | | | | | | s 14 | | s 15 | s 16 |
| 15 | | r 9 | r 9 | r 9 | r 9 | | r 9 | | |
| 16 | | r 10 | r 10 | r 10 | r 10 | | r 10 | | |
| 17 | r 2 | r 2 | r 2 | s 9 | s 10 | | | | |
| 18 | r 3 | r 3 | r 3 | s 9 | s 10 | | | | |
| 19 | r 5 | r 5 | r 5 | r 5 | r 5 | | | | |
| 20 | r 6 | r 6 | r 6 | r 6 | r 6 | | | | |
| 21 | | | | | | s 14 | | s 15 | s 16 |
| 22 | | | | | | s 14 | | s 15 | s 16 |
| 23 | r 8 | r 8 | r 8 | r 8 | r 8 | | | | |
| 24 | | | | | | s 14 | | s 15 | s 16 |
| 25 | | | | | | s 14 | | s 15 | s 16 |
| 26 | | s 21 | s 22 | | | | s 31 | | |
| 27 | | r 2 | r 2 | s 24 | s 25 | | r 2 | | |
| 28 | | r 3 | r 3 | s 24 | s 25 | | r 3 | | |
| 29 | | r 5 | r 5 | r 5 | r 5 | | r 5 | | |
| 30 | | r 6 | r 6 | r 6 | r 6 | | r 6 | | |
| 31 | | r 8 | r 8 | r 8 | r 8 | | r 8 | | |

■ **FIGURE 3.31** Action Table for the Classic Expression Grammar.

## Shrinking the Grammar

In many cases, the compiler writer can recode the grammar to reduce the number of productions it contains. This usually leads to smaller tables. For example, in the classic expression grammar, the distinction between a number and an identifier is irrelevant to the productions for *Goal*, *Expr*, *Term*, and *Factor*. Replacing the two productions *Factor* → num and *Factor* →

| | Goto **Table** | | | | | Goto **Table** | | |
|---|---|---|---|---|---|---|---|---|
| **State** | **Expr** | **Term** | **Factor** | | **State** | **Expr** | **Term** | **Factor** |
| 0 | 1 | 2 | 3 | | 16 | | | |
| 1 | | | | | 17 | | | |
| 2 | | | | | 18 | | | |
| 3 | | | | | 19 | | | |
| 4 | 11 | 12 | 13 | | 20 | | | |
| 5 | | | | | 21 | | 27 | 13 |
| 6 | | | | | 22 | | 28 | 13 |
| 7 | | 17 | 3 | | 23 | | | |
| 8 | | 18 | 3 | | 24 | | | 29 |
| 9 | | | 19 | | 25 | | | 30 |
| 10 | | | 20 | | 26 | | | |
| 11 | | | | | 27 | | | |
| 12 | | | | | 28 | | | |
| 13 | | | | | 29 | | | |
| 14 | 26 | 12 | 13 | | 30 | | | |
| 15 | | | | | 31 | | | |

■ **FIGURE 3.32** $Goto$ Table for the Classic Expression Grammar.

name with a single production *Factor* → val shrinks the grammar by a production. In the $Action$ table, each terminal symbol has its own column. Folding num and name into a single symbol, val, removes a column from the $Action$ table. To make this work, in practice, the scanner must return the same syntactic category, or word, for both num and name.

Similar arguments can be made for combining x and ÷ into a single terminal muldiv, and for combining + and - into a single terminal addsub. Each of these replacements removes a terminal symbol and a production. These three changes produce the reduced expression grammar shown in Figure 3.33a. This grammar produces a smaller $CC$, removing rows from the table. Because it has fewer terminal symbols, it has fewer columns as well.

The resulting $Action$ and $Goto$ tables are shown in Figure 3.33b. The $Action$ table contains 132 entries and the $Goto$ table contains 66 entries, for a total of 198 entries. This compares favorably with the tables for the original grammar, with their 384 entries. Changing the grammar produced a 48 percent reduction in table size. The tables still contain opportunities for further reductions. For example, rows 0, 6, and 7 in the $Action$ table are identical, as are rows 4, 11, 15, and 17. Similarly, the $Goto$ table has many

$$
\begin{array}{rll}
1 & Goal & \rightarrow Expr \\
2 & Expr & \rightarrow Expr\ \texttt{addsub}\ Term \\
3 & & |\ Term \\
4 & Term & \rightarrow Term\ \texttt{muldiv}\ Factor \\
5 & & |\ Factor \\
6 & Factor & \rightarrow (\ Expr\ ) \\
7 & & |\ \texttt{val}
\end{array}
$$

(a) The Reduced Expression Grammar

| | Action Table | | | | | | Goto Table | | |
|---|---|---|---|---|---|---|---|---|---|
| | eof | addsub | muldiv | ( | ) | val | *Expr* | *Term* | *Factor* |
| 0 | | | | s 4 | | s 5 | 1 | 2 | 3 |
| 1 | acc | s 6 | | | | | | | |
| 2 | r 3 | r 3 | s 7 | | | | | | |
| 3 | r 5 | r 5 | r 5 | | | | | | |
| 4 | | | | s 11 | | s 12 | 8 | 9 | 10 |
| 5 | r 7 | r 7 | r 7 | | | | | | |
| 6 | | | | s 4 | | s 5 | | 13 | 3 |
| 7 | | | | s 4 | | s 5 | | | 14 |
| 8 | | s 15 | | | s 16 | | | | |
| 9 | | r 3 | s 17 | | r 3 | | | | |
| 10 | | r 5 | r 5 | | r 5 | | | | |
| 11 | | | | s 11 | | s 12 | 18 | 9 | 10 |
| 12 | | r 7 | r 7 | | r 7 | | | | |
| 13 | r 2 | r 2 | s 7 | | | | | | |
| 14 | r 4 | r 4 | r 4 | | | | | | |
| 15 | | | | s 11 | | s 12 | | 19 | 10 |
| 16 | r 6 | r 6 | r 6 | | | | | | |
| 17 | | | | s 11 | | s 12 | | | 20 |
| 18 | | s 15 | | | s 21 | | | | |
| 19 | | r 2 | s 17 | | r 2 | | | | |
| 20 | | r 4 | r 4 | | r 4 | | | | |
| 21 | | r 6 | r 6 | | r 6 | | | | |

(b) *Action* and *Goto* Tables for the Reduced Expression Grammar

■ **FIGURE 3.33** The Reduced Expression Grammar and its Tables.

rows that only contain the error entry. If table size is a serious concern, rows and columns can be combined after shrinking the grammar.

Other considerations may limit the compiler writer's ability to combine productions. For example, the × operator might have multiple uses that make combining it with ÷ impractical. Similarly, the parser might use separate productions to let the parser handle two syntactically similar constructs in different ways.

### Directly Encoding the Table

As a final improvement, the parser generator can abandon the table-driven skeleton parser in favor of a hard-coded implementation. Each state becomes a small case statement or a collection of if—then—else statements that test the type of the next symbol and either shift, reduce, accept, or report an error. The entire contents of the *Action* and *Goto* tables can be encoded in this way. (A similar transformation for scanners is discussed in Section 2.5.2.)

The resulting parser avoids directly representing all of the "don't care" states in the *Action* and *Goto* tables, shown as blanks in the figures. This space savings may be offset by larger code size, since each state now includes more code. The new parser, however, has no parse table, performs no table lookups, and lacks the outer loop found in the skeleton parser. While its structure makes it almost unreadable by humans, it should execute more quickly than the corresponding table-driven parser. With appropriate code-layout techniques, the resulting parser can exhibit strong locality in both the instruction cache and the paging system. For example, we should place all the routines for the expression grammar together on a single page, where they cannot conflict with one another.

### Using Other Construction Algorithms

Several other algorithms to construct LR-style parsers exist. Among these techniques are the SLR(1) construction, for simple LR(1), and the LALR(1) construction, for lookahead LR(1). Both of these constructions produce smaller tables than the canonical LR(1) algorithm.

The SLR(1) algorithm accepts a smaller class of grammars than the canonical LR(1) construction. These grammars are restricted so that the lookahead symbols in the LR(1) items are not needed. The algorithm uses FOLLOW sets to distinguish between cases in which the parser should shift and those in which it should reduce. This mechanism is powerful enough to resolve many grammars of practical interest. By using FOLLOW sets, the algorithm eliminates the need for lookahead symbols. This produces a smaller canonical collection and a table with fewer rows.

The LALR(1) algorithm capitalizes on the observation that some items in the set representing a state are critical and that the remaining ones can be derived from the critical items. The LALR(1) table construction only represents the critical items; again, this produces a canonical collection that is equivalent to the one produced by the SLR(1) construction. The details differ, but the table sizes are the same.

The canonical LR(1) construction presented earlier in the chapter is the most general of these table-construction algorithms. It produces the largest tables, but accepts the largest class of grammars. With appropriate table reduction techniques, the LR(1) tables can approximate the size of those produced by the more limited techniques. However, in a mildly counterintuitive result, any language that has an LR(1) grammar also has an LALR(1) grammar and an SLR(1) grammar. The grammars for these more restrictive forms will be shaped in a way that allows their respective construction algorithms to resolve the situations in which the parser should shift and those in which it should reduce.

## 3.7 **SUMMARY AND PERSPECTIVE**

Almost every compiler contains a parser. For many years, parsing was a subject of intense interest. This led to the development of many different techniques for building efficient parsers. The LR(1) family of grammars includes all of the context-free grammars that can be parsed in a deterministic fashion. The tools produce efficient parsers with provably strong error-detection properties. This combination of features, coupled with the widespread availability of parser generators for LR(1), LALR(1), and SLR(1) grammars, has decreased interest in other automatic parsing techniques such as operator precedence parsers.

Top-down, recursive-descent parsers have their own set of advantages. They are, arguably, the easiest hand-coded parsers to construct. They provide excellent opportunities to detect and repair syntax errors. They are efficient; in fact, a well-constructed top-down, recursive-descent parser can be faster than a table-driven LR(1) parser. (The direct encoding scheme for LR(1) may overcome this speed advantage.) In a top-down, recursive-descent parser, the compiler writer can more easily finesse ambiguities in the source language that might trouble an LR(1) parser—such as a language in which keyword names can appear as identifiers. A compiler writer who wants to construct a hand-coded parser, for whatever reason, is well advised to use the top-down, recursive-descent method.

In choosing between LR(1) and LL(1) grammars, the choice becomes one of available tools. In practice, few, if any, programming-language constructs fall in the gap between LR(1) grammars and LL(1) grammars. Thus, starting with an available parser generator is always better than implementing a parser generator from scratch.

More general parsing algorithms are available. In practice, however, the restrictions placed on context-free grammars by the LR(1) and LL(1) classes do not cause problems for most programming languages.

## ■ CHAPTER NOTES

The earliest compilers used hand-coded parsers [27, 227, 314]. The syntactic richness of Algol 60 challenged early compiler writers. They tried a variety of schemes to parse the language; Randell and Russell give a fascinating overview of the methods used in a variety of Algol 60 compilers [293, Chapter 1].

Irons was one of the first to separate the notion of syntax from translation [202]. Lucas appears to have introduced the notion of recursive-descent parsing [255]. Conway applies similar ideas to an efficient single-pass compiler for COBOL [96].

The ideas behind LL and LR parsing appeared in the 1960s. Lewis and Stearns introduced LL(k) grammars [245]; Rosenkrantz and Stearns described their properties in more depth [305]. Foster developed an algorithm to transform a grammar into LL(1) form [151]. Wood formalized the notion of left-factoring a grammar and explored the theoretical issues involved in transforming a grammar to LL(1) form [353, 354, 355].

Knuth laid out the theory behind LR(1) parsing [228]. DeRemer and others developed techniques, the SLR and LALR table-construction algorithms, that made the use of LR parser generators practical on the limited-memory computers of the day [121, 122]. Waite and Goos describe a technique for automatically eliminating useless productions during the LR(1) table-construction algorithm [339]. Penello suggested direct encoding of the tables into executable code [282]. Aho and Ullman [8] is a definitive reference on both LL and LR parsing. Bill Waite provided the example grammar in exercise 3.7.

Several algorithms for parsing arbitrary context-free grammars appeared in the 1960s and early 1970s. Algorithms by Cocke and Schwartz [91], Younger [358], Kasami [212], and Earley [135] all had similar computational complexity. Earley's algorithm deserves particular note because of its similarity to the LR(1) table-construction algorithm. Earley's algorithm derives the set of possible parse states at parse time, rather than at runtime, where the LR(1) techniques precompute these in a parser generator. From a high-level view, the LR(1) algorithms might appear as a natural optimization of Earley's algorithm.

## ■ EXERCISES

1. Write a context-free grammar for the syntax of regular expressions.

2. Write a context-free grammar for the Backus-Naur form (BNF) notation for context-free grammars.

3. When asked about the definition of an *unambiguous context-free grammar* on an exam, two students gave different answers. The first defined it as "a grammar where each sentence has a unique syntax tree by leftmost derivation." The second defined it as "a grammar where each sentence has a unique syntax tree by any derivation." Which one is correct?

4. The following grammar is not suitable for a top-down predictive parser. Identify the problem and correct it by rewriting the grammar. Show that your new grammar satisfies the LL(1) condition.

$$
\begin{array}{lll}
L \rightarrow R\,\text{a} & R \rightarrow \text{aba} & Q \rightarrow \text{bbc} \\
\quad | \quad Q\,\text{ba} & \quad | \quad \text{caba} & \quad | \quad \text{bc} \\
& \quad | \quad R\,\text{bc} &
\end{array}
$$

5. Consider the following grammar:

$$
\begin{array}{ll}
A \rightarrow B\,\text{a} & C \rightarrow \text{c}\,B \\
B \rightarrow \text{dab} & \quad | \quad A\,\text{c} \\
\quad | \quad C\,\text{b} &
\end{array}
$$

Does this grammar satisfy the LL(1) condition? Justify your answer. If it does not, rewrite it as an LL(1) grammar for the same language.

6. Grammars that can be parsed top-down, in a linear scan from left to right, with a $k$ word lookahead are called LL($k$) grammars. In the text, the LL(1) condition is described in terms of FIRST sets. How would you define the FIRST sets necessary to describe an LL($k$) condition?

7. Suppose an elevator is controlled by two commands: ↑ to move the elevator up one floor and ↓ to move the elevator down one floor. Assume that the building is arbitrarily tall and that the elevator starts at floor $x$.

   Write an LL(1) grammar that generates arbitrary command sequences that (1) never cause the elevator to go below floor $x$ and (2) always return the elevator to floor $x$ at the end of the sequence. For example, ↑↑↓↓ and ↑↓↑↓ are valid command sequences, but ↑↓↓↑ and ↑↓↓ are not. For convenience, you may consider a null sequence as valid. Prove that your grammar is LL(1).

**Section 3.4**

**8.** Top-down and bottom-up parsers build syntax trees in different orders. Write a pair of programs, TopDown and BottomUp, that take a syntax tree and print out the nodes in order of construction. TopDown should display the order for a top-down parser, while BottomUp should show the order for a bottom-up parser.

**9.** The *ClockNoise* language (*CN*) is represented by the following grammar:

$$
\begin{array}{rcl}
Goal & \rightarrow & ClockNoise \\
ClockNoise & \rightarrow & ClockNoise \; \texttt{tick tock} \\
& | & \texttt{tick tock}
\end{array}
$$

**a.** What are the LR(1) items of *CN*?
**b.** What are the FIRST sets of *CN*?
**c.** Construct the Canonical Collection of Sets of LR(1) Items for *CN*.
**d.** Derive the Action and Goto tables.

**10.** Consider the following grammar:

$$
\begin{array}{rcl}
Start & \rightarrow & S \\
S & \rightarrow & A \; \texttt{a} \\
A & \rightarrow & B \; C \\
& | & B \; C \; \texttt{f} \\
B & \rightarrow & \texttt{b} \\
C & \rightarrow & \texttt{c}
\end{array}
$$

**a.** Construct the canonical collection of sets of LR(1) items for this grammar.
**b.** Derive the Action and Goto tables.
**c.** Is the grammar LR(1)?

**11.** Consider a robot arm that accepts two commands: $\triangledown$ puts an apple in the bag and $\triangle$ takes an apple out of the bag. Assume the robot arm starts with an empty bag.

A valid command sequence for the robot arm should have no prefix that contains more $\triangle$ commands than $\triangledown$ commands. As examples, $\triangledown\triangledown\triangle\triangle$ and $\triangledown\triangle\triangledown$ are valid command sequences, but $\triangledown\triangle\triangle\triangledown$ and $\triangledown\triangle\triangledown\triangle\triangle$ are not.

**a.** Write an LR(1) grammar that represents all the value command sequences for the robot arm.
**b.** Prove that the grammar is LR(1).

**12.** The following grammar has no known LL(1) equivalent:

$$
\begin{array}{llll}
0 & Start & \rightarrow & A \\
1 & & | & B \\
2 & A & \rightarrow & \underline{(}\ A\ \underline{)} \\
3 & & | & \underline{a} \\
4 & B & \rightarrow & \underline{(}\ B\ \underline{>} \\
5 & & | & \underline{b}
\end{array}
$$

Show that the grammar is LR(1).

**13.** Write a grammar for expressions that can include binary operators (+ and ×), unary minus (-), autoincrement (++), and autodecrement (- -) with their customary precedence. Assume that repeated unary minuses are not allowed, but that repeated autoincrement and autodecrement operators are allowed.

Section 3.6

**14.** Consider the task of building a parser for the programming language Scheme. Contrast the effort required for a top-down recursive-descent parser with that needed for a table-driven LR(1) parser. (Assume that you already have an LR(1) table generator.)

Section 3.7

**15.** The text describes a manual technique for eliminating useless productions in a grammar.
  **a.** Can you modify the LR(1) table-construction algorithm so that it automatically eliminates the overhead from useless productions?
  **b.** Even though a production is syntactically useless, it may serve a practical purpose. For example, the compiler writer might associate a syntax-directed action (see Chapter 4) with the useless production. How should your modified table-construction algorithm handle an action associated with a useless production?

# Context-Sensitive Analysis

## ■ CHAPTER OVERVIEW

An input program that is grammatically correct may still contain serious errors that would prevent compilation. To detect such errors, a compiler performs a further level of checking that involves considering each statement in its actual context. These checks find errors of type and of agreement.

This chapter introduces two techniques for context-sensitive checking. Attribute grammars are a functional formalism for specifying context-sensitive computation. Ad hoc syntax-directed translation provides a simple framework where the compiler writer can hang arbitrary code snippets to perform these checks.

**Keywords:** Semantic Elaboration, Type Checking, Attribute Grammars, Ad Hoc Syntax Directed Translation

## 4.1 INTRODUCTION

The compiler's ultimate task is to translate the input program into a form that can execute directly on the target machine. For this purpose, it needs knowledge about the input program that goes well beyond syntax. The compiler must build up a large base of knowledge about the detailed computation encoded in the input program. It must know what values are represented, where they reside, and how they flow from name to name. It must understand the structure of the computation. It must analyze how the program interacts with external files and devices. All of these facts can be derived from the source code, using contextual knowledge. Thus, the compiler must perform deeper analysis than is typical for a scanner or a parser.

These kinds of analysis are either performed alongside parsing or in a post-pass that traverses the IR produced by the parser. We call this analysis either "context-sensitive analysis," to differentiate it from parsing, or "semantic elaboration," since its elaborates the IR. This chapter explores two techniques for organizing this kind of analysis in a compiler: an automated approach based on attribute grammars and an ad hoc approach that relies on similar concepts.

### Conceptual Roadmap

To accumulate the contextual knowledge needed for further translation, the compiler must develop ways of viewing the program other than syntax. It uses abstractions that represent some aspect of the code, such as a type system, a storage map, or a control-flow graph. It must understand the program's name space: the kinds of data represented in the program, the kinds of data that can be associated with each name and each expression, and the mapping from a name's appearance in the code back to a specific instance of that name. It must understand the flow of control, both within procedures and across procedures. The compiler will have an abstraction for each of these categories of knowledge.

This chapter focuses on mechanisms that compilers use to derive context-sensitive knowledge. It introduces one of the abstractions that the compiler manipulates during semantic elaboration, the type system. (Others are introduced in later chapters.) Next, the chapter presents a principled automatic approach to implementing these computations in the form of *attribute grammars*. It then presents the most widely used technique, *ad hoc syntax-directed translation*, and compares the strengths and weaknesses of these two tools. The advanced topics section includes brief descriptions of situations that present harder problems in type inference, along with a final example of ad hoc syntax-directed translation.

### Overview

Consider a single name used in the program being compiled; let's call it $x$. Before the compiler can emit executable target-machine code for computations involving $x$, it must have answers to many questions.

- *What kind of value is stored in x?* Modern programming languages use a plethora of data types, including numbers, characters, boolean values, pointers to other objects, sets (such as {red, yellow, green}), and others. Most languages include compound objects that aggregate individual values; these include arrays, structures, sets, and strings.
- *How big is x?* Because the compiler must manipulate $x$, it needs to know the length of $x$'s representation on the target machine. If $x$ is a number, it might be one word (an integer or floating-point number), two

words (a double-precision floating-point number or a complex number), or four words (a quad-precision floating-point number or a double-precision complex number). For arrays and strings, the number of elements might be fixed at compile time or it might be determined at runtime.

■ *If x is a procedure, what arguments does it take? What kind of value, if any, does it return?* Before the compiler can generate code to invoke a procedure, it must know how many arguments the code for the called procedure expects, where it expects to find those arguments, and what kind of value it expects in each argument. If the procedure returns a value, where will the calling routine find that value, and what kind of data will it be? (The compiler must ensure that the calling procedure uses the value in a consistent and safe manner. If the calling procedure assumes that the return value is a pointer that it can dereference, and the called procedure returns an arbitrary character string, the results may not be predictable, safe, or consistent.)

■ *How long must x's value be preserved?* The compiler must ensure that $x$'s value remains accessible for any part of the computation that can legally reference it. If $x$ is a local variable in Pascal, the compiler can easily overestimate $x$'s interesting lifetime by preserving its value for the duration of the procedure that declares $x$. If $x$ is a global variable that can be referenced anywhere, or if it is an element of a structure explicitly allocated by the program, the compiler may have a harder time determining its lifetime. The compiler can always preserve $x$'s value for the entire computation; however, more precise information about $x$'s lifetime might let the compiler reuse its space for other values with nonconflicting lifetimes.

■ *Who is responsible for allocating space for x (and initializing it)?* Is space allocated for $x$ implicitly, or does the program explicitly allocate space for it? If the allocation is explicit, then the compiler must assume that $x$'s address cannot be known until the program runs. If, on the other hand, the compiler allocates space for $x$ in one of the runtime data structures that it manages, then it knows more about $x$'s address. This knowledge may let it generate more efficient code.

The compiler must derive the answers to these questions, and more, from the source program and the rules of the source language. In an Algol-like language, such as Pascal or C, most of these questions can be answered by examining the declarations for $x$. If the language has no declarations, as in APL, the compiler must either derive this kind of information by analyzing the program, or it must generate code that can handle any case that might arise.

Many, if not all, of these questions reach beyond the context-free syntax of the source language. For example, the parse trees for $x \leftarrow y$ and $x \leftarrow z$ differ only in the text of the name on the right-hand side of the assignment. If $x$ and $y$ are integers while $z$ is a character string, the compiler may need to emit different code for $x \leftarrow y$ than for $x \leftarrow z$. To distinguish between these cases, the compiler must delve into the program's meaning. Scanning and parsing deal solely with the program's form; the analysis of meaning is the realm of *context-sensitive analysis*.

To see this difference between syntax and meaning more clearly, consider the structure of a program in most Algol-like languages. These languages require that every variable be declared before it is used and that each use of a variable be consistent with its declaration. The compiler writer can structure the syntax to ensure that all declarations occur before any executable statement. A production such as

$$ProcedureBody \rightarrow Declarations\ Executables$$

where the nonterminals have the obvious meanings, ensures that all declarations occur before any executable statements. This syntactic constraint does nothing to check the deeper rule—that the program actually declares each variable before its first use in an executable statement. Neither does it provide an obvious way to handle the rule in c++ that requires declaration before use for some categories of variables, but lets the programmer intermix declarations and executable statements.

To solve this particular problem, the compiler typically creates a table of names. It inserts a name on declaration; it looks up the name at each reference. A lookup failure indicates a missing declaration.

This ad hoc solution bolts onto the parser, but uses mechanisms well outside the scope of context-free languages.

Enforcing the "declare before use" rule requires a deeper level of knowledge than can be encoded in the context-free grammar. The context-free grammar deals with syntactic categories rather than specific words. Thus, the grammar can specify the positions in an expression where a variable name may occur. The parser can recognize that the grammar allows a variable name to occur, and it can tell that one has occurred. However, the grammar has no way to match one instance of a variable name with another; that would require the grammar to specify a much deeper level of analysis—an analysis that can account for context and that can examine and manipulate information at a deeper level than context-free syntax.

## 4.2 AN INTRODUCTION TO TYPE SYSTEMS

**Type**
an abstract category that specifies properties held in common by all its members

Common types include *integer*, *list*, and *character*.

Most programming languages associate a collection of properties with each data value. We call this collection of properties the value's *type*. The type specifies a set of properties held in common by all values of that type. Types can be specified by membership; for example, an integer might be any whole number $i$ in the range $-2^{31} \leq i < 2^{31}$, or red might be a value in an enumerated type colors, defined as the set {red, orange, yellow, green, blue, brown, black, white}. Types can be specified by rules; for example, the declaration of a structure in c defines a type. In this case, the type includes any object with the declared fields in the declared order; the individual fields have types that specify the allowable ranges of values and their interpretation. (We represent the type of a structure as the product of the types of its constituent fields, in order.) Some types are predefined by a programming language; others are constructed by the programmer. The set of types in a programming language, along with the rules that use types to specify program behavior, are collectively called a *type system*.

## 4.2.1 **The Purpose of Type Systems**

Programming-language designers introduce type systems so that they can specify program behavior at a more precise level than is possible in a context-free grammar. The type system creates a second vocabulary for describing both the form and behavior of valid programs. Analyzing a program from the perspective of its type system yields information that cannot be obtained using the techniques of scanning and parsing. In a compiler, this information is typically used for three distinct purposes: safety, expressiveness, and runtime efficiency.

### *Ensuring Runtime Safety*

A well-designed type system helps the compiler detect and avoid runtime errors. The type system should ensure that programs are well behaved—that is, the compiler and runtime system can identify all ill-formed programs before they execute an operation that causes a runtime error. In truth, the type system cannot catch all ill-formed programs; the set of ill-formed programs is not computable. Some runtime errors, such as dereferencing an out-of-bounds pointer, have obvious (and often catastrophic) effects. Others, such as mistakenly interpreting an integer as a floating-point number, can have subtle and cumulative effects. The compiler should eliminate as many runtime errors as it can using type-checking techniques.

To accomplish this, the compiler must first infer a type for each expression. These inferred types expose situations in which a value is incorrectly interpreted, such as using a floating-point number in place of a boolean value. Second, the compiler must check the types of the operands of each operator against the rules that define what the language allows. In some cases, these rules might require the compiler to convert values from one representation to another. In other circumstances, they may forbid such a conversion and simply declare that the program is ill formed and, therefore, not executable.

**Type inference**

the process of determining a type for each name and each expression in the code

| + | integer | real | double | complex |
|---|---------|------|--------|---------|
| integer | integer | real | double | complex |
| real | real | real | double | complex |
| double | double | double | double | *illegal* |
| complex | complex | complex | *illegal* | complex |

■ **FIGURE 4.1** Result Types for Addition in FORTRAN 77.

**Implicit conversion**

Many languages specify rules that allow an operator to combine values of different type and require that the compiler insert conversions as needed.

The alternative is to require the programmer to write an *explicit conversion* or *cast*.

In many languages, the compiler can infer a type for every expression. FORTRAN 77 has a particularly simple type system with just a handful of types. Figure 4.1 shows all the cases that can arise for the + operator. Given an expression a + b and the types of a and b, the table specifies the type of a + b. For an integer a and a double-precision b, a + b produces a double-precision result. If, instead, a were complex, a + b would be illegal. The compiler should detect this situation and report it before the program executes—a simple example of type safety.

For some languages, the compiler cannot infer types for all expressions. APL, for example, lacks declarations, allows a variable's type to change at any assignment, and lets the user enter arbitrary code at input prompts. While this makes APL powerful and expressive, it ensures that the implementation must do some amount of runtime type inference and checking. The alternative, of course, is to assume that the program behaves well and ignore such checking. In general, this leads to bad behavior when a program goes awry. In APL, many of the advanced features rely heavily on the availability of type and dimension information.

Safety is a strong reason for using typed languages. A language implementation that guarantees to catch most type-related errors before they execute can simplify the design and implementation of programs. A language in which every expression can be assigned an unambiguous type is called a *strongly typed* language. If every expression can be typed at compile time, the language is *statically typed*; if some expressions can only be typed at runtime, the language is *dynamically typed*. Two alternatives exist: an *untyped* language, such as assembly code or BCPL, and a *weakly typed* language—one with a poor type system.

## Improving Expressiveness

A well-constructed type system allows the language designer to specify behavior more precisely than is possible with context-free rules. This capability lets the language designer include features that would be impossible to specify in a context-free grammar. An excellent example is *operator overloading*, which gives context-dependent meanings to an operator. Many programming languages use + to signify several kinds of addition. The interpretation of + depends on the types of its operands. In typed languages, many operators are overloaded. The alternative, in an untyped language, is to provide lexically different operators for each case.

**Operator overloading**
An operator that has different meanings based on the types of its arguments is "overloaded."

For example, in BCPL, the only type is a "cell." A cell can hold any bit pattern; the interpretation of that bit pattern is determined by the operator applied to the cell. Because cells are essentially untyped, operators cannot be overloaded. Thus, BCPL uses + for integer addition and #+ for floating-point addition. Given two cells a and b, both a + b and a #+ b are valid expressions, neither of which performs any conversion on its operands.

In contrast, even the oldest typed languages use overloading to specify complex behavior. As described in the previous section, FORTRAN has a single addition operator, +, and uses type information to determine how it should be implemented. ANSI C uses function prototypes—declarations of the number and type of a function's parameters and the type of its returned value—to convert arguments to the appropriate types. Type information determines the effect of autoincrementing a pointer in C; the amount of the increment is determined by the pointer's type. Object-oriented languages use type information to select the appropriate implementation at each procedure call. For example, Java selects between a default constructor and a specialized one by examining the constructor's argument list.

### Generating Better Code

A well-designed type system provides the compiler with detailed information about every expression in the program—information that can often be used to produce more efficient translations. Consider implementing addition in FORTRAN 77. The compiler can completely determine the types of all expressions, so it can consult a table similar to the one in Figure 4.2. The code on the right shows the ILOC operation for the addition, along with the conversions specified in the FORTRAN standard for each mixed-type expression. The full table would include all the cases from Figure 4.1.

In a language with types that cannot be wholly determined at compile time, some of this checking might be deferred until runtime. To accomplish this, the compiler would need to emit code similar to the pseudo-code in Figure 4.3. The figure only shows the code for two numeric types, integer and real. An actual implementation would need to cover the entire set of possibilities. While this approach ensures runtime safety, it adds significant

| Type of | | | Code |
|---|---|---|---|
| a | b | a + b | |
| integer | integer | integer | iADD $r_a$, $r_b$ ⇒ $r_{a+b}$ |
| integer | real | real | i2f $f_a$ ⇒ $r_{a_f}$ |
| | | | fADD $r_{a_f}$, $r_b$ ⇒ $r_{a_f+b}$ |
| integer | double | double | i2d $r_a$ ⇒ $r_{a_d}$ |
| | | | dADD $r_{a_d}$, $r_b$ ⇒ $r_{a_d+b}$ |
| real | real | real | fADD $r_a$, $r_b$ ⇒ $r_{a+b}$ |
| real | double | double | r2d $r_a$ ⇒ $r_{a_d}$ |
| | | | dADD $r_{a_d}$, $r_b$ ⇒ $r_{a_d+b}$ |
| double | double | double | dADD $r_a$, $r_b$ ⇒ $r_{a+b}$ |

■ **FIGURE 4.2** Implementing Addition in FORTRAN 77.

overhead to each operation. One goal of compile-time checking is to provide such safety without the runtime cost.

Notice that runtime type checking requires a runtime representation for type. Thus, each variable has both a value field and a tag field. The code that performs runtime checking—the nested if-then-else structure in Figure 4.3—relies on the tag fields, while the arithmetic uses the value fields. With tags, each data item needs more space, that is, more bytes in memory. If a variable is stored in a register, both its value and its tag will need registers. Finally, tags must be initialized, read, compared, and written at runtime. All of those activities add overhead to a simple addition operation.

The benefit of keeping a in a register comes from speed of access. If a's tag is in RAM, that benefit is lost.

An alternative is to use part of the space in a to store the tag and to reduce the range of values that a can hold.

Runtime type checking imposes a large overhead on simple arithmetic and on other operations that manipulate data. Replacing a single addition, or a conversion and an addition, with the nest of if-then-else code in Figure 4.3 has a significant performance impact. The size of the code in Figure 4.3 strongly suggests that operators such as addition be implemented as procedures and that each instance of an operator be treated as a procedure call. In a language that requires runtime type checking, the costs of runtime checking can easily overwhelm the costs of the actual operations.

Performing type inference and checking at compile time eliminates this kind of overhead. It can replace the complex code of Figure 4.3 with the fast, compact code of Figure 4.2. From a performance perspective, compile-time checking is *always* preferable. However, language design determines whether or not that is possible.

```
// partial code for "a+b ⇒ c"
if (tag(a) = integer) then
    if (tag(b) = integer) then
        value(c) = value(a) + value(b);
        tag(c) = integer;
    else if (tag(b) = real) then
        temp = ConvertToReal(a);
        value(c) = temp + value(b);
        tag(c) = real;
    else if (tag(b) = ...) then
        // handle all other types ...
    else
        signal runtime type fault
else if (tag(a) = real) then
    if (tag(b) = integer) then
        temp = ConvertToReal(b);
        value(c) = value(a) + temp;
        tag(c) = real;
    else if (tag(b) = real) then
        value(c) = value(a) + value(b);
        tag(c) = real;
    else if (tag(b) = ...) then
        // handle all other types ...
    else
        signal runtime type fault
else if (tag(a) = ...) then
    // handle all other types ...
else
    signal illegal tag value;
```

■ **FIGURE 4.3** Schema for Implementing Addition with Runtime Type Checking.

## Type Checking

To avoid the overhead of runtime type checking, the compiler must analyze the program and assign a type to each name and each expression. It must check these types to ensure that they are used in contexts where they are legal. Taken together, these activities are often called *type checking*. This is an unfortunate misnomer, because it lumps together the separate activities of type inference and identifying type-related errors.

The programmer should understand how type checking is performed in a given language and compiler. A strongly typed, statically checkable language might be implemented with runtime checking (or with no checking). An untyped language might be implemented in a way that catches certain kinds of errors. Both ML and Modula-3 are good examples of strongly typed languages that can be statically checked. Common Lisp has a strong type system that must be checked dynamically. ANSI C is a typed language, but some implementations do a poor job of identifying type errors.

The theory underlying type systems encompasses a large and complex body of knowledge. This section provides an overview of type systems and introduces some simple problems in type checking. Subsequent sections use simple problems of type inference as examples of context-sensitive computations.

## 4.2.2 Components of a Type System

A type system for a typical modern language has four major components: a set of base types, or built-in types; rules for constructing new types from the existing types; a method for determining if two types are equivalent or compatible; and rules for inferring the type of each source-language expression. Many languages also include rules for the implicit conversion of values from one type to another based on context. This section describes each of these in more detail, with examples from popular programming languages.

### *Base Types*

Most programming languages include base types for some, if not all, of the following kinds of data: numbers, characters, and booleans. These types are directly supported by most processors. Numbers typically come in several forms, such as integers and floating-point numbers. Individual languages add other base types. Lisp includes both a rational number type and a recursive type cons. Rational numbers are, essentially, pairs of integers interpreted as ratios. A cons is defined as either the designated value nil or (cons first rest) where first is an object, rest is a cons, and cons creates a list from its arguments.

The precise definitions for base types, and the operators defined for them, vary across languages. Some languages refine these base types to create more; for example, many languages distinguish between several types of numbers in their type systems. Other languages lack one or more of these base types. For example, C has no string type, so C programmers use an array of characters instead. Almost all languages include facilities to construct more complex types from their base types.

## Numbers

Almost all programming languages include one or more kinds of numbers as base types. Typically, they support both limited-range integers and approximate real numbers, often called *floating-point* numbers. Many programming languages expose the underlying hardware implementation by creating distinct types for different hardware implementations. For example, C, C++, and Java distinguish between signed and unsigned integers.

FORTRAN, PL/I, and C expose the size of numbers. Both C and FORTRAN specify the length of data items in relative terms. For example, a `double` in FORTRAN is twice the length of a `real`. Both languages, however, give the compiler control over the length of the smallest category of number. In contrast, PL/I declarations specify a length in bits. The compiler maps this desired length onto one of the hardware representations. Thus, the IBM 370 implementation of PL/I mapped both a `fixed binary(12)` and a `fixed binary(15)` variable to a 16-bit integer, while a `fixed binary(31)` became a 32-bit integer.

Some languages specify implementations in detail. For example, Java defines distinct types for signed integers with lengths of 8, 16, 32, and 64 bits. Respectively, they are `byte`, `short`, `int`, and `long`. Similarly, Java's `float` type specifies a 32-bit IEEE floating-point number, while its `double` type specifies a 64-bit IEEE floating-point number. This approach ensures identical behavior on different architectures.

Scheme takes a different approach. The language defines a hierarchy of number types but lets the implementor select a subset to support. However, the standard draws a careful distinction between exact and inexact numbers and specifies a set of operations that should return an exact number when all of its arguments are exact. This provides a degree of flexibility to the implementer, while allowing the programmer to reason about when and where approximation can occur.

## Characters

Many languages include a character type. In the abstract, a character is a single letter. For years, due to the limited size of the Western alphabets, this led to a single-byte (8-bit) representation for characters, usually mapped into the ASCII character set. Recently, more implementations—both operating system and programming language—have begun to support larger character sets expressed in the Unicode standard format, which requires 16 bits. Most languages assume that the character set is ordered, so that standard comparison operators, such as $<$, $=$, and $>$, work intuitively, enforcing lexicographic ordering. Conversion between a character and an integer appears in some languages. Few other operations make sense on character data.

**Booleans**

Most programming languages include a boolean type that takes on two values: `true` and `false`. Standard operations provided for booleans include `and`, `or`, `xor`, and `not`. Boolean values, or boolean-valued expressions, are often used to determine the flow of control. C considers boolean values as a subrange of the unsigned integers, restricted to the values zero (`false`) and one (`true`).

## *Compound and Constructed Types*

While the base types of a programming language usually provide an adequate abstraction of the actual kinds of data handled directly by the hardware, they are often inadequate to represent the information domain needed by programs. Programs routinely deal with more complex data structures, such as graphs, trees, tables, arrays, records, lists, and stacks. These structures consist of one or more objects, each with its own type. The ability to construct new types for these compound or aggregate objects is an essential feature of many programming languages. It lets the programmer organize information in novel, program-specific ways. Tying these organizations to the type system improves the compiler's ability to detect ill-formed programs. It also lets the language express higher-level operations, such as a whole-structure assignment.

Take, for example, Lisp, which provides extensive support for programming with lists. Lisp's list is a constructed type. A list is either the designated value `nil` or `(cons first rest)` where `first` is an object, `rest` is a list, and `cons` is a constructor that creates a list from its two arguments. A Lisp implementation can check each call to `cons` to ensure that its second argument is, in fact, a list.

**Arrays**

Arrays are among the most widely used aggregate objects. An array groups together multiple objects of the same type and gives each a distinct name—albeit an implicit, computed name rather than an explicit, programmer-designated, name. The C declaration `int a[100][200];` sets aside space for $100 \times 200 = 20,000$ integers and ensures that they can be addressed using the name `a`. The references `a[1][17]` and `a[2][30]` access distinct and independent memory locations. The essential property of an array is that the program can compute names for each of its elements by using numbers (or some other ordered, discrete type) as subscripts.

Support for operations on arrays varies widely. FORTRAN 90, PL/I, and APL all support assignment of whole or partial arrays. These languages support element-by-element application of arithmetic operations to arrays. For

$10 \times 10$ arrays x, y, and z, indexed from 1 to 10, the statement x = y + z would overwrite each x[i,j] with y[i,j]+z[i,j] for all $1 \leq i, j \leq 10$. APL takes the notion of array operations further than most languages; it includes operators for inner product, outer product, and several kinds of reductions. For example, the sum reduction of y, written x $\leftarrow +/y$, assigns x the scalar sum of the elements of y.

An array can be viewed as a constructed type because we construct an array by specifying the type of its elements. Thus, a $10 \times 10$ array of integers has type *two-dimensional array of integers*. Some languages include the array's dimensions in its type; thus a $10 \times 10$ array of integers has a different type than a $12 \times 12$ array of integers. This lets the compiler catch array operations in which dimensions are incompatible as a type error. Most languages allow arrays of any base type; some languages allow arrays of constructed types as well.

### Strings

Some programming languages treat strings as a constructed type. PL/I, for example, has both bit strings and character strings. The properties, attributes, and operations defined on both of these types are similar; they are properties of a string. The range of values allowed in any position differs between a bit string and a character string. Thus, viewing them as *string of bit* and *string of character* is appropriate. (Most languages that support strings limit the built-in support to a single string type—the character string.) Other languages, such as C, support character strings by handling them as arrays of characters.

A true string type differs from an array type in several important ways. Operations that make sense on strings, such as concatenation, translation, and computing the length, may not have analogs for arrays. Conceptually, string comparison should work from lexicographic order, so that "a" < "boo" and "fee" < "fie". The standard comparison operators can be overloaded and used in the natural way. Implementing comparison for an array of characters suggests an equivalent comparison for an array of numbers or an array of structures, where the analogy to strings may not hold. Similarly, the actual length of a string may differ from its allocated size, while most uses of an array use all the allocated elements.

### Enumerated Types

Many languages allow the programmer to create a type that contains a specific set of constant values. An *enumerated type*, introduced in Pascal, lets the programmer use self-documenting names for small sets of constants. Classic examples include days of the week and months. In C syntax, these might be

```
enum WeekDay {Monday, Tuesday, Wednesday,
              Thursday, Friday, Saturday, Sunday};

enum Month {January, February, March, April,
            May, June, July, August, September,
            October, November, December};
```

The compiler maps each element of an enumerated type to a distinct value. The elements of an enumerated type are ordered, so comparisons between elements of the same type make sense. In the examples, Monday < Tuesday and June < July. Operations that compare different enumerated types make no sense—for example, Tuesday > September should produce a type error, Pascal ensures that each enumerated type behaves as if it were a sub-range of the integers. For example, the programmer can declare an array indexed by the elements of an enumerated type.

### Structures and Variants

Structures, or *records*, group together multiple objects of arbitrary type. The elements, or members, of the structure are typically given explicit names. For example, a programmer implementing a parse tree in C might need nodes with both one and two children.

```
struct Node1 {                    struct Node2 {
   struct   Node1 *left;             struct   Node2 *left;
   unsigned Operator;                struct   Node2 *right;
   int      Value                    unsigned Operator;
}                                     int      Value
                                  }
```

The type of a structure is the ordered product of the types of the individual elements that it contains. Thus, we might describe the type of a Node1 as (Node1 *) × unsigned × int, while a Node2 would be (Node2 *) × (Node2 *) × unsigned × int. These new types should have the same essential properties that a base type has. In C, autoincrementing a pointer to a Node1 or casting a pointer into a Node1 * has the desired effect—the behavior is analogous to what happens for a base type.

Many programming languages allow the creation of a type that is the union of other types. For example, some variable x can have the type integer or boolean or WeekDay. In Pascal, this is accomplished with variant records—a *record* is the Pascal term for a structure. In C, this is accomplished with a union. The type of a union is the alternation of its component types; thus our variable x has type integer ∪ boolean ∪ WeekDay. Unions can also

---

**AN ALTERNATIVE VIEW OF STRUCTURES**

The classical view of structures treats each kind of structure as a distinct type. This approach to structure types follows the treatment of other aggregates, such as arrays and strings. It seems natural. It makes distinctions that are useful to the programmer. For example, a tree node with two children probably should have a different type than a tree node with three children; presumably, they are used in different situations. A program that assigns a three-child node to a two-child node should generate a type error and a warning message to the programmer.

From the perspective of the runtime system, however, treating each structure as a distinct type complicates the picture. With distinct structure types, the heap contains an arbitrary set of objects drawn from an arbitrary set of types. This makes it difficult to reason about programs that deal directly with the objects on the heap, such as a garbage collector. To simplify such programs, their authors sometimes take a different approach to structure types.

This alternate model considers all structures in the program as a single type. Individual structure declarations each create a variant form of the type *structure*. The type *structure*, itself, is the union of all these variants. This approach lets the program view the heap as a collection of objects of a single type, rather than a collection of many types. This view makes code that manipulates the heap much simpler to analyze and optimize.

---

include structures of distinct types, even when the individual structure types have different lengths. The language must provide a mechanism to reference each field unambiguously.

## Pointers

Pointers are abstract memory addresses that let the programmer manipulate arbitrary data structures. Many languages include a pointer type. Pointers let a program save an address and later examine the object that it addresses. Pointers are created when objects are created (new in Java or malloc in C). Some languages provide an operator that returns the address of an object, such as C's & operator.

The address operator, when applied to an object of type $t$, returns a value of type *pointer to t*.

To protect programmers from using a pointer to type $t$ to reference a structure of type $s$, some languages restrict pointer assignment to "equivalent" types. In these languages, the pointer on the left-hand side of an assignment must have the same type as the expression on the right-hand side. A program can legally assign a *pointer to integer* to a variable declared as *pointer to integer* but not to one declared as *pointer to pointer to integer* or *pointer to boolean*.

**Polymorphism**

A function that can operate on arguments of different types is a *polymorphic* function.

If the set of types must be specified explicitly, the function uses *ad hoc polymorphism*; if the function body does not specify types, it uses *parametric polymorphism*.

These latter assignments are either illegal or require an explicit conversion by the programmer.

Of course, the mechanism for creating new objects should return an object of the appropriate type. Thus, Java's `new` explicitly creates a typed object; other languages use a polymorphic routine that takes the return type as a parameter. ANSI C handles this in an unusual way: The standard allocation routine `malloc` returns a *pointer to* `void`. This forces the programmer to cast the value returned by each call to `malloc`.

Some languages allow direct manipulation of pointers. Arithmetic on pointers, including autoincrement and autodecrement, allow the program to construct new pointers. C uses the type of a pointer to determine autoincrement and decrement magnitudes. The programmer can set a pointer to the start of an array; autoincrementing advances the pointer from one element in the array to the next element.

Type safety with pointers relies on an implicit assumption that addresses correspond to typed objects. The ability to construct new pointers seriously reduces the ability of both the compiler and its runtime system to reason about pointer-based computations and to optimize such code. (See, for example, Section 8.4.1.)

### Type Equivalence

A critical component of any type system is the mechanism that it uses to decide whether or not two different type declarations are equivalent. Consider the two declarations in C shown in the margin. Are `Tree` and `STree` the same type? Are they equivalent? Any programming language with a nontrivial type system must include an unambiguous rule to answer this question for arbitrary types.

```
struct Tree {
  struct Tree *left;
  struct Tree *right;
  int value
}

struct STree {
  struct STree *left;
  struct STree *right;
  int value
}
```

Historically, two general approaches have been tried. The first, *name equivalence*, asserts that two types are equivalent if and only if they have the same name. Philosophically, this rule assumes that the programmer can select any name for a type; if the programmer chooses different names, the language and its implementation should honor that deliberate act. Unfortunately, the difficulty of maintaining consistent names grows with the size of the program, the number of authors, and the number of distinct files of code.

The second approach, *structural equivalence*, asserts that two types are equivalent if and only if they have the same structure. Philosophically, this rule asserts that two objects are interchangeable if they consist of the same set of fields, in the same order, and those fields all have equivalent types. Structural equivalence examines the essential properties that define the type.

---

**REPRESENTING TYPES**

As with most objects that a compiler must manipulate, types need an internal representation. Some languages, such as FORTRAN 77, have a small fixed set of types. For these languages, a small integer tag is both efficient and sufficient. However, many modern languages have open-ended type systems. For these languages, the compiler writer needs to design a structure that can represent arbitrary types.

If the type system is based on name equivalence, any number of simple representations will suffice, as long as the compiler can use the representation to trace back to a representation of the actual structure. If the type system is based on structural equivalence, the representation of the type must encode its structure. Most such systems build trees to represent types. They construct a tree for each type declaration and compare tree structures to test for equivalence.

---

Each policy has strengths and weaknesses. Name equivalence assumes that identical names occur as a deliberate act; in a large programming project, this requires discipline to avoid unintentional clashes. Structural equivalence assumes that interchangeable objects can be used safely in place of one another; if some of the values have "special" meanings, this can create problems. (Imagine two hypothetical, structurally identical types. The first holds a system I/O control block, while the second holds the collection of information about a bit-mapped image on the screen. Treating them as distinct types would allow the compiler to detect a misuse—passing the I/O control block to a screen refresh routine—while treating them as the same type would not.)

### Inference Rules

In general, type inference rules specify, for each operator, the mapping between the operand types and the result type. For some cases, the mapping is simple. An assignment, for example, has one operand and one result. The result, or left-hand side, must have a type that is compatible with the type of the operand, or right-hand side. (In Pascal, the subrange 1..100 is compatible with the integers since any element of the subrange can be assigned safely to an integer.) This rule allows assignment of an integer value to an integer variable. It forbids assignment of a structure to an integer variable, without an explicit conversion that makes sense of the operation.

The relationship between operand types and result types is often specified as a recursive function on the type of the expression tree. The function computes the result type of an operation as a function of the types of its operands. The functions might be specified in tabular form, similar to the table in Figure 4.1. Sometimes, the relationship between operand types and result types is specified by a simple rule. In Java, for example, adding two integer types of different precision produces a result of the more precise (longer) type.

The inference rules point out type errors. Mixed-type expressions may be illegal. In FORTRAN 77, a program cannot add a `double` and a `complex`. In Java, a program cannot assign a number to a character. These combinations should produce a type error at compile time, along with a message that indicates how the program is ill formed.

Some languages require the compiler to perform implicit conversions. The compiler must recognize certain combinations of mixed-type expressions and handle them by inserting the appropriate conversions. In FORTRAN, adding an integer and a floating-point number forces conversion of the integer to floating-point form before the addition. Similarly, Java mandates implicit conversions for integer addition of values with different precision. The compiler must coerce the less precise value to the form of the more precise value before addition. A similar situation arises in Java with integer assignment. If the right-hand side is less precise, it is converted to the more precise type of the left-hand side. If, however, the left-hand side is less precise than the right-hand side, the assignment produces a type error unless the programmer inserts an explicit cast operation to change its type and coerce its value.

### Declarations and Inference

As previously mentioned, many programming languages include a "declare before use" rule. With mandatory declarations, each variable has a well-defined type. The compiler needs a way to assign types to constants. Two approaches are common. Either a constant's form implies a specific type—for example, 2 is an integer and 2.0 is a floating-point number—or the compiler infers a constant's type from its usage—for example, $sin(2)$ implies that 2 is a floating-point number, while $x \leftarrow 2$, for integer x, implies that 2 is an integer. With declared types for variables, implied types for constants, and a complete set of type-inference rules, the compiler can assign types to any expression over variables and constants. Function calls complicate the picture, as we shall see.

This scheme overloads 2 with different meanings in different contexts. Experience suggests that programmers are good at understanding this kind of overloading.

Some languages absolve the programmer from writing any declarations. In these languages, the problem of type inference becomes substantially more intricate. Section 4.5 describes some of the problems that this creates and some of the techniques that compilers use to address them.

**CLASSIFYING TYPE SYSTEMS**

Many terms are used to describe type systems. In the text, we have introduced the terms *strongly typed*, *untyped*, and *weakly typed* languages. Other distinctions between type systems and their implementations are important.

*Checked versus Unchecked Implementations* The implementation of a programming language may elect to perform enough checking to detect and to prevent all runtime errors that result from misuse of a type. (This may actually exclude some value-specific errors, such as division by zero.) Such an implementation is called *strongly checked*. The opposite of a strongly checked implementation is an *unchecked implementation*—one that assumes a well-formed program. Between these poles lies a spectrum of *weakly checked implementations* that perform partial checking.

*Compile Time versus Runtime Activity* A strongly typed language may have the property that all inference and all checking can be done at compile time. An implementation that actually does all this work at compile time is called *statically typed* and *statically checked*. Some languages have constructs that must be typed and checked at runtime. We term these languages *dynamically typed* and *dynamically checked*. To confuse matters further, of course, a compiler writer can implement a strongly typed, statically typed language with dynamic checking. Java is an example of a language that could be statically typed and checked, except for an execution model that keeps the compiler from seeing all the source code at once. This forces it to perform type inference as classes are loaded and to perform some of the checking at runtime.

## Inferring Types for Expressions

The goal of type inference is to assign a type to each expression that occurs in a program. The simplest case for type inference occurs when the compiler can assign a type to each base element in an expression—that is, to each leaf in the parse tree for an expression. This requires declarations for all variables, inferred types for all constants, and type information about all functions.

Conceptually, the compiler can assign a type to each value in the expression during a simple postorder tree walk. This should let the compiler detect every violation of an inference rule, and report it *at compile time*. If the language lacks one or more of the features that make this simple style of inference possible, the compiler will need to use more sophisticated techniques. If compile time type inference becomes too difficult, the compiler writer may need to move some of the analysis and checking to runtime.

Type inference for expressions, in this simple case, directly follows the expression's structure. The inference rules describe the problem in terms of the source language. The evaluation strategy operates bottom up on the parse tree. For these reasons, type inference for expressions has become a classic example problem to illustrate context-sensitive analysis.

### Interprocedural Aspects of Type Inference

Type inference for expressions depends, inherently, on the other procedures that form the executable program. Even in the simplest type systems, expressions contain function calls. The compiler must check each of those calls. It must ensure that each actual parameter is type compatible with the corresponding formal parameter. It must determine the type of any returned value for use in further inference.

**Type signature**
a specification of the types of the formal parameters and return value(s) of a function

To analyze and understand procedure calls, the compiler needs a *type signature* for each function. For example, the strlen function in C's standard library takes an operand of type char * and returns an int that contains its length in bytes, excluding the terminating character. In C, the programmer can record this fact with a *function prototype* that looks like:

**Function prototype**
The C language includes a provision that lets the programmer declare functions that are not present. The programmer includes a skeleton declaration, called a *function prototype*.

```
unsigned int strlen(const char *s);
```

This prototype asserts that strlen takes an argument of type char *, which it does not modify, as indicated by the const attribute. The function returns a nonnegative integer. Writing this in a more abstract notation, we might say that

$$strlen : const\ char\ * \rightarrow unsigned\ int$$

which we read as "strlen is a function that takes a constant-valued character string and returns an unsigned integer." As a second example, the classic Scheme function filter has the type signature

$$filter: (\alpha \rightarrow boolean) \times list\ of\ \alpha \rightarrow list\ of\ \alpha$$

That is, filter is a function that takes two arguments. The first should be a function that maps some type $\alpha$ into a boolean, written $(\alpha \rightarrow boolean)$, and the second should be a list whose elements are of the same type $\alpha$. Given arguments of those types, filter returns a list whose elements have type $\alpha$. The function filter exhibits *parametric polymorphism*: its result type is a function of its argument types.

To perform accurate type inference, the compiler needs a type signature for every function. It can obtain that information in several ways. The compiler can eliminate separate compilation, requiring that the entire program be presented for compilation as a unit. The compiler can require the programmer to provide a type signature for each function; this usually takes the form of mandatory function prototypes. The compiler can defer type checking until either link time or runtime, when all such information is available. Finally, the compiler writer can embed the compiler in a program-development system that gathers the requisite information and makes it available to the compiler on demand. All of these approaches have been used in real systems.

---

**SECTION REVIEW**

A type system associates with each value in the program some textual name, a type, that represents a set of common properties held by all values of that type. The definition of a programming language specifies interactions between objects of the same type, such as legal operations on values of a type, and between objects of different type, such as mixed-type arithmetic operations. A well-designed type system can increase the expressiveness of a programming language, allowing safe use of features such as overloading. It can expose subtle errors in a program long before they become puzzling runtime errors or wrong answers. It can let the compiler avoid runtime checks that waste time and space.

A type system consists of a set of base types, rules for constructing new types from existing ones, a method for determining equivalence of two types, and rules for inferring the types of each expression in a program. The notions of base types, constructed types, and type equivalence should be familiar to anyone who has programmed in a high-level language. Type inference plays a critical role in compiler implementation.

---

**Review Questions**

1. For your favorite programming language, write down the base types in its type system. What rules and constructs does the language allow to build aggregate types? Does it provide a mechanism for creating a procedure that takes a variable number of arguments, such as `printf` in the C standard I/O library?

2. What kinds of information must the compiler have to ensure type safety at procedure calls? Sketch a scheme based on the use of function prototypes. Sketch a scheme that can check the validity of those function prototypes.

## 4.3  **THE ATTRIBUTE-GRAMMAR FRAMEWORK**

One formalism that has been proposed for performing context-sensitive analysis is the *attribute grammar*, or attributed context-free grammar. An attribute grammar consists of a context-free grammar augmented by a set of rules that specify computations. Each rule defines one value, or *attribute*, in terms of the values of other attributes. The rule associates the attribute with a specific grammar symbol; each instance of the grammar symbol that occurs in a parse tree has a corresponding instance of the attribute. The rules are functional; they imply no specific evaluation order and they define each attribute's value uniquely.

**Attribute**
a value attached to one or more of the nodes in a parse tree

To make these notions concrete, consider a context-free grammar for signed binary numbers. Figure 4.4 defines the grammar $SBN = (T,NT,S,P)$. *SBN* generates all signed binary numbers, such as `-101`, `+11`, `-01`, and `+11111001100`. It excludes unsigned binary numbers, such as `10`.

From *SBN*, we can build an attribute grammar that annotates *Number* with the value of the signed binary number that it represents. To build an attribute grammar from a context-free grammar, we must decide what attributes each node needs, and we must elaborate the productions with rules that define values for these attributes. For our attributed version of *SBN*, the following attributes are needed:

| Symbol | Attributes |
|--------|-----------|
| *Number* | `value` |
| *Sign* | `negative` |
| *List* | `position, value` |
| *Bit* | `position, value` |

In this case, no attributes are needed for the terminal symbols.

Figure 4.5 shows the productions of *SBN* elaborated with attribution rules. Subscripts are added to grammar symbols whenever a specific symbol

$$
P = \left\{
\begin{array}{lcl}
Number & \rightarrow & Sign\ List \\
Sign & \rightarrow & + \\
 & | & - \\
List & \rightarrow & List\ Bit \\
 & | & Bit \\
Bit & \rightarrow & 0 \\
 & | & 1
\end{array}
\right\}
\qquad
\begin{array}{lcl}
T & = & \{+,\ -,\ 0,\ 1\} \\
\\
NT & = & \{Number,\ Sign,\ List,\ Bit\} \\
\\
S & = & \{Number\}
\end{array}
$$

■ **FIGURE 4.4**  An Attribute Grammar for Signed Binary Numbers.

| | Production | Attribution Rules |
|---|---|---|
| 1 | *Number* → *Sign List* | *List*.$position$ ← $0$<br>if *Sign*.$negative$<br>    then *Number*.$value$ ← -*List*.$value$<br>    else *Number*.$value$ ← *List*.$value$ |
| 2 | *Sign* → + | *Sign*.$negative$ ← $false$ |
| 3 | *Sign* → - | *Sign*.$negative$ ← $true$ |
| 4 | *List* → *Bit* | *Bit*.$position$ ← *List*.$position$<br>*List*.$value$ ← *Bit*.$value$ |
| 5 | *List*$_0$ → *List*$_1$ *Bit* | *List*$_1$.$position$ ← *List*$_0$.$position$+$1$<br>*Bit*.$position$ ← *List*$_0$.$position$<br>*List*$_0$.$value$ ← *List*$_1$.$value$+*Bit*.$value$ |
| 6 | *Bit* → 0 | *Bit*.$value$ ← $0$ |
| 7 | *Bit* → 1 | *Bit*.$value$ ← $2^{Bit.position}$ |

■ **FIGURE 4.5** Attribute Grammar for Signed Binary Numbers.

appears multiple times in a single production. This practice disambiguates references to that symbol in the rules. Thus, the two occurrences of *List* in production 5 have subscripts, both in the production and in the corresponding rules.

The rules add attributes to the parse tree nodes by their names. An attribute mentioned in a rule must be instantiated for every occurrence of that kind of node.

Each rule specifies the value of one attribute in terms of literal constants and the attributes of other symbols in the production. A rule can pass information from the production's left-hand side to its right-hand side; a rule can also pass information in the other direction. The rules for production 4 pass information in both directions. The first rule sets *Bit*.$position$ to *List*.$position$, while the second rule sets *List*.$value$ to *Bit*.$value$. Simpler attribute grammars can solve this particular problem; we have chosen this one to demonstrate particular features of attribute grammars.

Given a string in the *SBN* grammar, the attribution rules set *Number*.$value$ to the decimal value of the binary input string. For example, the string -101 causes the attribution shown in Figure 4.6a. (The names for $value$, $number$, and $position$ are truncated in the figure.) Notice that *Number*.$value$ has the value -5.

To evaluate an attributed parse tree for some sentence in $L(SBN)$, the attributes specified in the various rules are instantiated for each node in the parse tree. This creates, for example, an attribute instance for both *value* and *position* in each *List* node. Each rule implicitly defines a set of dependences; the attribute being defined depends on each argument to the rule. Taken over the entire parse tree, these dependences form an *attribute-dependence graph*. Edges in the graph follow the flow of values in the evaluation of a rule; an edge from $node_i.field_j$ to $node_k.field_l$ indicates that the rule defining $node_k.field_l$ uses the value of $node_i.field_j$ as one of its inputs. Figure 4.6b shows the attribute-dependence graph induced by the parse tree for the string -101.

The bidirectional flow of values that we noted earlier (in, for example, production 4) shows up in the dependence graph, where arrows indicate both flow upward toward the root (*Number*) and flow downward toward the leaves. The *List* nodes show this effect most clearly. We distinguish between attributes based on the direction of value flow. *Synthesized attributes* are defined by bottom-up information flow; a rule that defines an attribute for the production's left-hand side creates a synthesized attribute. A synthesized attribute can draw values from the node itself, its descendants in the parse tree, and constants. *Inherited attributes* are defined by top-down and lateral information flow; a rule that defines an attribute for the production's right-hand side creates an inherited attribute. Since the attribution rule can name any symbol used in the corresponding production, an inherited attribute can draw values from the node itself, its parent and its siblings in the parse tree,

**Synthesized attribute**
an attribute defined wholly in terms of the attributes of the node, its children, and constants

**Inherited attribute**
an attribute defined wholly in terms of the node's own attributes and those of its siblings or its parent in the parse tree (plus constants)

The rule *node.field* ← 1 can be treated as either synthesized or inherited.

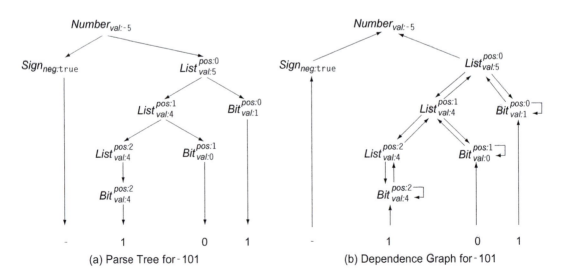

(a) Parse Tree for -101        (b) Dependence Graph for -101

■ **FIGURE 4.6** Attributed Tree for the Signed Binary Number −101.

and constants. Figure 4.6b shows that the `value` and `negative` attributes are synthesized, while the `position` attribute is inherited.

Any scheme for evaluating attributes must respect the relationships encoded implicitly in the attribute-dependence graph. Each attribute must be defined by some rule. If that rule depends on the values of other attributes, it cannot be evaluated until all those values have been defined. If the rule depends on no other attribute values, then it must produce its value from a constant or some external source. As long as no rule relies on its own value, the rules should uniquely define each value.

Of course, the syntax of the attribution rules allows a rule to reference its own result, either directly or indirectly. An attribute grammar containing such rules is ill formed. We say that such rules are *circular* because they can create a cycle in the dependence graph. For the moment, we will ignore circularity; Section 4.3.2 addresses this issue.

**Circularity**
An attribute grammar is circular if it can, for some inputs, create a cyclic dependence graph.

The dependence graph captures the flow of values that an evaluator must respect in evaluating an instance of an attributed tree. If the grammar is noncircular, it imposes a partial order on the attributes. This partial order determines when the rule defining each attribute can be evaluated. Evaluation order is unrelated to the order in which the rules appear in the grammar.

Consider the evaluation order for the rules associated with the uppermost *List* node—the right child of *Number*. The node results from applying production five, *List* → *List Bit*; applying that production adds three rules to the evaluation. The two rules that set inherited attributes for the *List* node's children must execute first. They depend on the value of *List*.`position` and set the `position` attributes for the node's subtrees. The third rule, which sets the *List* node's `value` attribute, cannot execute until the two subtrees both have defined `value` attributes. Since those subtrees cannot be evaluated until the first two rules at the *List* node have been evaluated, the evaluation sequence will include the first two rules early and the third rule much later.

To create and use an attribute grammar, the compiler writer determines a set of attributes for each symbol in the grammar and designs a set of rules to compute their values. These rules specify a computation for any valid parse tree. To create an implementation, the compiler writer must create an evaluator; this can be done with an ad hoc program or by using an evaluator generator—the more attractive option. The evaluator generator takes as input the specification for the attribute grammar. It produces the code for an evaluator as its output. This is the attraction of attribute grammars for the compiler writer; the tools take a high-level, nonprocedural specification and automatically produce an implementation.

One critical insight behind the attribute-grammar formalism is the notion that the attribution rules can be associated with productions in the context-free grammar. Since the rules are functional, the values that they produce are independent of evaluation order, for any order that respects the relationships embodied in the attribute-dependence graph. In practice, any order that evaluates a rule only after all of its inputs have been defined respects the dependences.

### 4.3.1 Evaluation Methods

The attribute-grammar model has practical use only if we can build evaluators that interpret the rules to evaluate an instance of the problem automatically—a specific parse tree, for example. Many attribute evaluation techniques have been proposed in the literature. In general, they fall into three major categories.

1. *Dynamic Methods* These techniques use the structure of a particular attributed parse tree to determine the evaluation order. Knuth's original paper on attribute grammars proposed an evaluator that operated in a manner similar to a dataflow computer architecture—each rule "fired" as soon as all its operands were available. In practical terms, this might be implemented using a queue of attributes that are ready for evaluation. As each attribute is evaluated, its successors in the attribute dependence graph are checked for "readiness" (see Section 12.3). A related scheme would build the attribute dependence graph, topologically sort it, and use the topological order to evaluate the attributes.

2. *Oblivious Methods* In these methods, the order of evaluation is independent of both the attribute grammar and the particular attributed parse tree. Presumably, the system's designer selects a method deemed appropriate for both the attribute grammar and the evaluation environment. Examples of this evaluation style include repeated left-to-right passes (until all attributes have values), repeated right-to-left passes, and alternating left-to-right and right-to-left passes. These methods have simple implementations and relatively small runtime overheads. They lack, of course, any improvement that can be derived from knowledge of the specific tree being attributed.

3. *Rule-Based Methods* Rule-based methods rely on a static analysis of the attribute grammar to construct an evaluation order. In this framework, the evaluator relies on grammatical structure; thus, the parse tree guides the application of the rules. In the signed binary number example, the evaluation order for production 4 should use the first rule to set *Bit.position*, recurse downward to *Bit*, and, on return, use *Bit.value* to set *List.value*. Similarly, for production 5, it should evaluate the first

two rules to define the *position* attributes on the right-hand side, then recurse downward to each child. On return, it can evaluate the third rule to set the *List.value* field of the parent *List* node. Tools that perform the necessary static analysis offline can produce fast rule-based evaluators.

### 4.3.2 **Circularity**

Circular attribute grammars can give rise to cyclic attribute-dependence graphs. Our models for evaluation fail when the dependence graph contains a cycle. A failure of this kind in a compiler causes serious problems—for example, the compiler might not be able to generate code for its input. The catastrophic impact of cycles in the dependence graph suggests that this issue deserves close attention.

If a compiler uses attribute grammars, it must handle circularity in an appropriate way. Two approaches are possible.

1. *Avoidance* The compiler writer can restrict the attribute grammar to a class that cannot give rise to circular dependence graphs. For example, restricting the grammar to use only synthesized and constant attributes eliminates any possibility of a circular dependence graph. More general classes of noncircular attribute grammars exist; some, like *strongly noncircular attribute grammars,* have polynomial-time tests for membership.
2. *Evaluation* The compiler writer can use an evaluation method that assigns a value to every attribute, even those involved in cycles. The evaluator might iterate over the cycle and assign appropriate or default values. Such an evaluator would avoid the problems associated with a failure to fully attribute the tree.

In practice, most attribute-grammar systems restrict their attention to noncircular grammars. The rule-based evaluation methods may fail to construct an evaluator if the attribute grammar is circular. The oblivious methods and the dynamic methods will attempt to evaluate a circular dependence graph; they will simply fail to define some of the attribute instances.

### 4.3.3 **Extended Examples**

To better understand the strengths and weaknesses of attribute grammars as a tool, we will work through two more detailed examples that might arise in a compiler: inferring types for expression trees in a simple, Algol-like language, and estimating the execution time, in cycles, for a straight-line sequence of code.

### Inferring Expression Types

Any compiler that tries to generate efficient code for a typed language must confront the problem of inferring types for every expression in the program. This problem relies, inherently, on context-sensitive information; the type associated with a name or num depends on its identity—its textual name—rather than its syntactic category.

Consider a simplified version of the type inference problem for expressions derived from the classic expression grammar given in Chapter 3. Assume that the expressions are represented as parse trees, and that any node representing a name or num already has a *type* attribute. (We will return to the problem of getting the type information into these *type* attributes later in the chapter.) For each arithmetic operator in the grammar, we need a function that maps the two operand types to a result type. We will call these functions $\mathcal{F}_+$, $\mathcal{F}_-$, $\mathcal{F}_\times$, and $\mathcal{F}_\div$; they encode the information found in tables such as the one shown in Figure 4.1. With these assumptions, we can write simple attribution rules that define a *type* attribute for each node in the tree. Figure 4.7 shows the attribution rules.

If a has type integer (denoted $\mathcal{I}$) and c has type real (denoted $\mathcal{R}$), then this scheme generates the following attributed parse tree for the input string a - 2 × c:

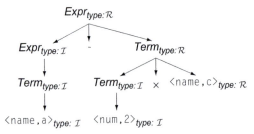

The leaf nodes have their *type* attributes initialized appropriately. The remainder of the attributes are defined by the rules from Figure 4.7, with the assumption that $\mathcal{F}_+$, $\mathcal{F}_-$, $\mathcal{F}_\times$, and $\mathcal{F}_\div$ reflect the FORTRAN 77 rules.

A close look at the attribution rules shows that all the attributes are synthesized attributes. Thus, all the dependences flow from a child to its parent in the parse tree. Such grammars are sometimes called *S-attributed grammars*. This style of attribution has a simple, rule-based evaluation scheme. It meshes well with bottom-up parsing; each rule can be evaluated when the parser reduces by the corresponding right-hand side. The attribute-grammar paradigm fits this problem well. The specification is short. It is easily understood. It leads to an efficient evaluator.

Careful inspection of the attributed expression tree shows two cases in which an operation has an operand whose type is different from the type of the

| Production | Attribution Rules |
|---|---|
| $Expr_0 \rightarrow Expr_1 + Term$ | $Expr_0.\texttt{type} \leftarrow \mathcal{F}_+(Expr_1.\texttt{type}, Term.\texttt{type})$ |
| $\mid Expr_1 - Term$ | $Expr_0.\texttt{type} \leftarrow \mathcal{F}_-(Expr_1.\texttt{type}, Term.\texttt{type})$ |
| $\mid Term$ | $Expr_0.\texttt{type} \leftarrow Term.\texttt{type}$ |
| $Term_0 \rightarrow Term_1 \ Factor$ | $Term_0.\texttt{type} \leftarrow \mathcal{F}_\times(Term_1.\texttt{type}, Factor.\texttt{type})$ |
| $\mid Term_1 \ Factor$ | $Term_0.\texttt{type} \leftarrow \mathcal{F}_\div(Term_1.\texttt{type}, Factor.\texttt{type})$ |
| $\mid Factor$ | $Term_0.\texttt{type} \leftarrow Factor.\texttt{type}$ |
| $Factor \rightarrow (Expr)$ | $Factor.\texttt{type} \leftarrow Expr.\texttt{type}$ |
| $\mid \texttt{num}$ | $\texttt{num.type}$ *is already defined* |
| $\mid \texttt{name}$ | $\texttt{name.type}$ *is already defined* |

■ **FIGURE 4.7** Attribute Grammar to Infer Expression Types.

operation's result. In FORTRAN 77, this requires the compiler to insert a conversion operation between the operand and the operator. For the *Term* node that represents the multiplication of 2 and c, the compiler would convert 2 from an integer representation to a real representation. For the *Expr* node at the root of the tree, the compiler would convert a from an integer to a real. Unfortunately, changing the parse tree does not fit well into the attribute-grammar paradigm.

To represent these conversions in the attributed tree, we could add an attribute to each node that holds its converted type, along with rules to set the attributes appropriately. Alternatively, we could rely on the process that generates code from the tree to compare the two types—parent and child—during the traversal and insert the necessary conversion. The former approach adds some work during attribute evaluation, but localizes all of the information needed for a conversion to a single parse-tree node. The latter approach defers that work until code generation, but does so at the cost of distributing the knowledge about types and conversions across two separate parts of the compiler. Either approach will work; the difference is largely a matter of taste.

### A Simple Execution-Time Estimator

As a second example, consider the problem of estimating the execution time of a sequence of assignment statements. We can generate a sequence of assignments by adding three new productions to the classic expression grammar:

$$
\begin{aligned}
Block &\rightarrow Block \ Assign \\
&\mid Assign \\
Assign &\rightarrow \texttt{name} = Expr;
\end{aligned}
$$

| Production | Attribution Rules |
|---|---|
| $Block_0 \rightarrow Block_1$ $Assign$ | { $Block_0.cost \leftarrow Block_1.cost + Assign.cost$ } |
| $\mid$ $Assign$ | { $Block_0.cost \leftarrow Assign.cost$ } |
| $Assign \rightarrow$ name $= Expr;$ | { $Assign.cost \leftarrow Cost(\text{store}) + Expr.cost$ } |
| $Expr_0 \rightarrow Expr_1 + Term$ | { $Expr_0.cost \leftarrow Expr_1.cost + Cost(\text{add}) + Term.cost$ } |
| $\mid$ $Expr_1 - Term$ | { $Expr_0.cost \leftarrow Expr_1.cost + Cost(\text{sub}) + Term.cost$ } |
| $\mid$ $Term$ | { $Expr_0.cost \leftarrow Term.cost$ } |
| $Term_0 \rightarrow Term_1 \times Factor$ | { $Term_0.cost \leftarrow Term_1.cost + Cost(\text{mult}) + Factor.cost$ } |
| $\mid$ $Term_1 \div Factor$ | { $Term_0.cost \leftarrow Term_1.cost + Cost(\text{div}) + Factor.cost$ } |
| $\mid$ $Factor$ | { $Term_0.cost \leftarrow Factor.cost$ } |
| $Factor \rightarrow$ ( $Expr$ ) | { $Factor.cost \leftarrow Expr.cost$ } |
| $\mid$ num | { $Factor.cost \leftarrow Cost(\text{loadI})$ } |
| $\mid$ name | { $Factor.cost \leftarrow Cost(\text{load})$ } |

■ **FIGURE 4.8** Simple Attribute Grammar to Estimate Execution Time.

where *Expr* is from the expression grammar. The resulting grammar is simplistic in that it allows only simple identifiers as variables and it contains no function calls. Nonetheless, it is complex enough to convey the issues that arise in estimating runtime behavior.

Figure 4.8 shows an attribute grammar that estimates the execution time of a block of assignment statements. The attribution rules estimate the total cycle count for the block, assuming a single processor that executes one operation at a time. This grammar, like the one for inferring expression types, uses only synthesized attributes. The estimate appears in the $cost$ attribute of the topmost *Block* node of the parse tree. The methodology is simple. Costs are computed bottom up; to read the example, start with the productions for *Factor* and work your way up to the productions for *Block*. The function $Cost$ returns the latency of a given ILOC operation.

### Improving the Execution-Cost Estimator

To make this example more realistic, we can improve its model for how the compiler handles variables. The initial version of our cost-estimating attribute grammar assumes that the compiler naively generates a separate load operation for each reference to a variable. For the assignment $x = y + y$, the model counts two load operations for y. Few compilers would generate a redundant load for y. More likely, the compiler would generate a sequence such as:

```
loadAI   r_arp, @y  ⇒ r_y
add      r_y, r_y   ⇒ r_x
storeAI  r_x        ⇒ r_arp, @x
```

that loads y once. To approximate the compiler's behavior better, we can modify the attribute grammar to charge only a single load for each variable used in the block. This requires more complex attribution rules.

To account for loads more accurately, the rules must track references to each variable by the variable's name. These names are extra-grammatical, since the grammar tracks the syntactic category name rather than individual names such as x, y, and z. The rule for name should follow the general outline:

```
if ( name has not been loaded )
    then Factor.cost ← Cost(load);
    else Factor.cost ← 0;
```

The key to making this work is the test "name has not been loaded."

To implement this test, the compiler writer can add an attribute that holds the set of all variables already loaded. The production *Block → Assign* can initialize the set. The rules must thread the expression trees to pass the set through each assignment. This suggests augmenting each node with two sets, *Before* and *After*. The *Before* set for a node contains the lexemes of all names that occur earlier in the *Block*; each of these must have been loaded already. A node's *After* set contains all the names in its *Before* set, plus any names that would be loaded in the subtree rooted at that node.

The expanded rules for *Factor* are shown in Figure 4.9. The code assumes that it can obtain the textual name—the lexeme—of each name. The first production, which derives ( *Expr* ), copies the *Before* set down into the *Expr* subtree and copies the *After* set up to the *Factor*. The second production, which derives num, simply copies its parent's *Before* set into its parent's *After* set. num must be a leaf in the tree; therefore, no further actions are needed. The final production, which derives name, performs the critical work. It tests the *Before* set to determine whether or not a load is needed and updates the parent's cost and *After* attributes accordingly.

To complete the specification, the compiler writer must add rules that copy the *Before* and *After* sets around the parse tree. These rules, sometimes called *copy rules*, connect the *Before* and *After* sets of the various *Factor* nodes. Because the attribution rules can reference only local attributes—defined as the attributes of a node's parent, its siblings, and its children—the attribute grammar must explicitly copy values around the parse tree to

| Production | Attribution Rules |
|---|---|
| $Factor \rightarrow (Expr)$ | $\{ Factor.cost \leftarrow Expr.cost ;$ <br> $Expr.Before \leftarrow Factor.Before ;$ <br> $Factor.After \leftarrow Expr.After \}$ |
| $\vert$ num | $\{ Factor.cost \leftarrow \texttt{Cost(loadI)} ;$ <br> $Factor.After \leftarrow Factor.Before \}$ |
| $\vert$ name | $\{ if\ (\texttt{name}.lexeme \notin Factor.Before)$ <br> $\quad then$ <br> $\qquad Factor.cost \leftarrow \texttt{Cost(load)} ;$ <br> $\qquad Factor.After \leftarrow Factor.Before$ <br> $\qquad \cup \{ \texttt{name}.lexeme \}$ <br> $\quad else$ <br> $\qquad Factor.cost \leftarrow 0 ;$ <br> $\qquad Factor.After \leftarrow Factor.Before \}$ |

■ **FIGURE 4.9** Rules to Track Loads in *Factor* Productions.

ensure that they are local. Figure 4.10 shows the required rules for the other productions in the grammar. One additional rule has been added; it initializes the *Before* set of the first *Assign* statement to ∅.

This model is much more complex than the simple model. It has over three times as many rules; each rule must be written, understood, and evaluated. It uses both synthesized and inherited attributes, so the simple bottom-up evaluation strategy will no longer work. Finally, the rules that manipulate the *Before* and *After* sets require a fair amount of attention—the kind of low-level detail that we would hope to avoid by using a system based on high-level specifications.

### Back to Inferring Expression Types

In the initial discussion about inferring expression types, we assumed that the attributes name.*type* and num.*type* were already defined by some external mechanism. To fill in those values using an attribute grammar, the compiler writer would need to develop a set of rules for the portion of the grammar that handles declarations.

Those rules would need to record the type information for each variable in the productions associated with the declaration syntax. The rules would need to collect and aggregate that information so that a small set of attributes contained the necessary information on all the declared variables. The rules would need to propagate that information up the parse tree to a node that is an ancestor of all the executable statements, and then to copy it downward into each expression. Finally, at each leaf that is a name or num, the rules would need to extract the appropriate facts from the aggregated information.

| Production | Attribution Rules |
|---|---|
| $Block_0 \rightarrow Block_1\ Assign$ | $\{\ Block_0.cost \leftarrow Block_1.cost + Assign.cost;$ <br> $Assign.Before \leftarrow Block_1.After;$ <br> $Block_0.After \leftarrow Assign.After$ |
| $\mid\ Assign$ | $\{\ Block_0.cost \leftarrow Assign.cost;$ <br> $Assign.Before \leftarrow \emptyset;$ <br> $Block_0.After \leftarrow Assign.After\ \}$ |
| $Assign \rightarrow \text{name} = Expr;$ | $\{\ Assign.cost \leftarrow Cost(\text{store}) + Expr.cost;$ <br> $Expr.Before \leftarrow Assign.Before;$ <br> $Assign.After \leftarrow Expr.After\ \}$ |
| $Expr_0 \rightarrow Expr_1 + Term$ | $\{\ Expr_0.cost \leftarrow Expr_1.cost + Cost(\text{add}) + Term.cost;$ <br> $Expr_1.Before \leftarrow Expr_0.Before;$ <br> $Term.Before \leftarrow Expr_1.After;$ <br> $Expr_0.After \leftarrow Term.After\ \}$ |
| $\mid\ Expr_1 - Term$ | $\{\ Expr_0.cost \leftarrow Expr_1.cost + Cost(\text{sub}) + Term.cost;$ <br> $Expr_1.Before \leftarrow Expr_0.Before;$ <br> $Term.Before \leftarrow Expr_1.After;$ <br> $Expr_0.After \leftarrow Term.After\ \}$ |
| $\mid\ Term$ | $\{\ Expr_0.cost \leftarrow Term.cost;$ <br> $Term.Before \leftarrow Expr_0.Before;$ <br> $Expr_0.After \leftarrow Term.After\ \}$ |
| $Term_0 \rightarrow Term_1 \times Factor$ | $\{\ Term_0.cost \leftarrow Term_1.cost + Cost(\text{mult}) + Factor.cost;$ <br> $Term_1.Before \leftarrow Term_0.Before;$ <br> $Factor.Before \leftarrow Term_1.After;$ <br> $Term_0.After \leftarrow Factor.After\ \}$ |
| $\mid\ Term_1 \div Factor$ | $\{\ Term_0.cost \leftarrow Term_1.cost + Cost(\text{div}) + Factor.cost;$ <br> $Term_1.Before \leftarrow Term_0.Before;$ <br> $Factor.Before \leftarrow Term_1.After;$ <br> $Term_0.After \leftarrow Factor.After\ \}$ |
| $\mid\ Factor$ | $\{\ Term_0.cost \leftarrow Factor.cost;$ <br> $Factor.Before \leftarrow Term_0.Before;$ <br> $Term_0.After \leftarrow Factor.After\ \}$ |

■ **FIGURE 4.10** Copy Rules to Track Loads.

The resulting set of rules would be similar to those that we developed for tracking loads but would be more complex at the detailed level. These rules also create large, complex attributes that must be copied around the parse tree. In a naive implementation, each instance of a copy rule would create a new copy. Some of these copies could be shared, but many of the versions created by merging information from multiple children will differ (and, thus, need to be distinct copies). The same problem arises with the *Before* and *After* sets in the previous example.

### A Final Improvement to the Execution-Cost Estimator

While tracking loads improved the fidelity of the estimated execution costs, many further refinements are possible. Consider, for example, the impact of finite register sets on the model. So far, our model has assumed that the target computer provides an unlimited set of registers. In reality, computers provide small register sets. To model the capacity of the register set, the estimator could limit the number of values allowed in the `Before` and `After` sets.

As a first step, we must replace the implementation of `Before` and `After`. They were implemented with arbitrarily sized sets; in this refined model, the sets should hold exactly $k$ values, where $k$ is the number of registers available to hold the values of variables. Next, we must rewrite the rules for the production *Factor* → name to model register occupancy. If a value has not been loaded, and a register is available, it charges for a simple load. If a load is needed, but no register is available, it can evict a value from some register and charge for the load. The choice of which value to evict is complex; it is discussed in Chapter 13. Since the rule for *Assign* always charges for a store, the value in memory will be current. Thus, no store is needed when a value is evicted. Finally, if the value has already been loaded and is still in a register, then no cost is charged.

This model complicates the rule set for *Factor* → name and requires a slightly more complex initial condition (in the rule for *Block* → *Assign*). It does not, however, complicate the copy rules for all the other productions. Thus, the accuracy of the model does not add significantly to the complexity of using an attribute grammar. All of the added complexity falls into the few rules that directly manipulate the model.

### 4.3.4 Problems with the Attribute-Grammar Approach

The preceding examples illustrate many of the computational issues that arise in using attribute grammars to perform context-sensitive computations on parse trees. Some of these pose particular problems for the use of attribute grammars in a compiler. In particular, most applications of attribute grammars in the front end of a compiler assume that the results of attribution must be preserved, typically in the form of an attributed parse tree. This section details the impact of the problems that we have seen in the preceding examples.

### Handling Nonlocal Information

Some problems map cleanly onto the attribute-grammar paradigm, particularly those problems in which all information flows in the same direction. However, problems with a complex pattern of information flow can be difficult to express as attribute grammars. An attribution rule can name only values associated with a grammar symbol that appears in the same production; this constrains the rule to using only nearby, or local, information. If the computation requires a nonlocal value, the attribute grammar must include copy rules to move those values to the points where they are used.

Copy rules can swell the size of an attribute grammar; compare Figures 4.8, 4.9, and 4.10. The implementor must write each of those rules. In the evaluator, each of the rules must be executed, creating new attributes and additional work. When information is aggregated, as in the declare-before-use rule or the framework for estimating execution times, a new copy of the information must be made each time a rule changes an aggregate's value. These copy rules add another layer of work to the tasks of writing and evaluating an attribute grammar.

### Storage Management

For realistic examples, evaluation produces large numbers of attributes. The use of copy rules to move information around the parse tree can multiply the number of attribute instances that evaluation creates. If the grammar aggregates information into complex structures—to pass declaration information around the parse tree, for example—the individual attributes can be large. The evaluator must manage storage for attributes; a poor storage-management scheme can have a disproportionately large negative impact on the resource requirements of the evaluator.

If the evaluator can determine which attribute values can be used after evaluation, it may be able to reuse some of the attribute storage by reclaiming space for values that can never again be used. For example, an attribute grammar that evaluated an expression tree to a single value might return that value to the process that invoked it. In this scenario, the intermediate values calculated at interior nodes might be dead—never used again—and, thus, candidates for reclamation. On the other hand, if the tree resulting from attribution is persistent and subject to later inspection—as might be the case in an attribute grammar for type inference—then the evaluator must assume that a later phase of the compiler can traverse the tree and inspect arbitrary attributes. In this case, the evaluator cannot reclaim the storage for any of the attribute instances.

This problem reflects a fundamental clash between the functional nature of the attribute-grammar paradigm and the imperative use to which it might be put in the compiler. The possible uses of an attribute in later phases of the compiler have the effect of adding dependences from that attribute to uses not specified in the attribute grammar. This bends the functional paradigm and removes one of its strengths: the ability to automatically manage attribute storage.

### Instantiating the Parse Tree

An attribute grammar specifies a computation relative to the parse tree for a valid sentence in the underlying grammar. The paradigm relies, inherently, on the availability of the parse tree. The evaluator might simulate the parse tree, but it must behave as if the parse tree exists. While the parse tree is useful for discussions of parsing, few compilers actually build a parse tree.

Some compilers use an abstract syntax tree (AST) to represent the program being compiled. The AST has the essential structure of the parse tree but eliminates many of the internal nodes that represent nonterminal symbols in the grammar (see the description starting on page 226 of Section 5.2.1). If the compiler builds an AST, it could use an attribute grammar tied to a grammar for the AST. However, if the compiler has no other use for the AST, then the programming effort and compile-time cost associated with building and maintaining the AST must be weighed against the benefits of using the attribute-grammar formalism.

### Locating the Answers

One final problem with attribute-grammar schemes for context-sensitive analysis is more subtle. The result of attribute evaluation is an attributed tree. The results of the analysis are distributed over that tree, in the form of attribute values. To use these results in later passes, the compiler must traverse the tree to locate the desired information.

The compiler can use carefully constructed traversals to locate a particular node, which requires walking from the root of the parse tree down to the appropriate location—on each access. This makes the code both slower and harder to write, because the compiler must execute each of these traversals and the compiler writer must construct each of them. The alternative is to copy the important answers to a point in the tree where they are easily found, typically the root. This introduces more copy rules, exacerbating that problem.

### Breakdown of the Functional Paradigm

One way to address all of these problems is to add a central repository for attributes. In this scenario, an attribute rule can record information directly into a global table, where other rules can read the information. This hybrid approach can eliminate many of the problems that arise from nonlocal information. Since the table can be accessed from any attribution rule, it has the effect of providing local access to any information already derived.

Adding a central repository for facts complicates matters in another way. If two rules communicate through a mechanism other than an attribution rule, the implicit dependence between them is removed from the attribute dependence graph. The missing dependence should constrain the evaluator to ensure that the two rules are processed in the correct order; without it, the evaluator may be able to construct an order that, while correct for the grammar, has unintended behavior because of the removed constraint. For example, passing information between the declaration syntax and an executable expression through a table might allow the evaluator to process declarations after some or all of the expressions that use the declared variables. If the grammar uses copy rules to propagate that same information, those rules constrain the evaluator to orders that respect the dependences embodied by those copy rules.

---

**SECTION REVIEW**

Attribute grammars provide a functional specification that can be used to solve a variety of problems, including many of the problems that arise in performing context-sensitive analysis. In the attribute-grammar approach, the compiler writer produces succinct rules to describe the computation; the attribute-grammar evaluator then provides the mechanisms to perform the actual computation. A high-quality attribute-grammar system would simplify the construction of the semantic elaboration section of a compiler.

The attribute-grammar approach has never achieved widespread popularity for a number of mundane reasons. Large problems, such as the difficulty of performing nonlocal computation and the need to traverse the parse tree to discover answers to simple questions, have discouraged the adoption of these ideas. Small problems, such as space management for short-lived attributes, evaluator efficiency, and the lack of widely-available, open-source attribute-grammar evaluators have also made these tools and techniques less attractive.

---

### Review Questions

1. From the "four function calculator" grammar given in the margin, construct an attribute-grammar scheme that attributes each *Calc* node with the specified computation, displaying the answer on each reduction to *Expr*.

2. The "define-before-use" rule specifies that each variable used in a procedure must be declared before it appears in the text. Sketch an attribute-grammar scheme for checking that a procedure conforms with this rule. Is the problem easier if the language requires that all declarations precede any executable statement?

$$
\begin{aligned}
Calc &\rightarrow Expr \\
Expr &\rightarrow Expr + Term \\
&\mid Expr - Term \\
&\mid Term \\
Term &\rightarrow Term \times num \\
&\mid Term \div num \\
&\mid num
\end{aligned}
$$

Four Function Calculator

## 4.4 **AD HOC SYNTAX-DIRECTED TRANSLATION**

The rule-based evaluators for attribute grammars introduce a powerful idea that serves as the basis for the ad hoc techniques used for context-sensitive analysis in many compilers. In the rule-based evaluators, the compiler writer specifies a sequence of actions that are associated with productions in the grammar. The underlying observation, that the actions required for context-sensitive analysis can be organized around the structure of the grammar, leads to a powerful, albeit ad hoc, approach to incorporating this kind of analysis into the process of parsing a context-free grammar. We refer to this approach as ad hoc syntax-directed translation.

In this scheme, the compiler writer provides snippets of code that execute at parse time. Each snippet, or *action*, is directly tied to a production in the grammar. Each time the parser recognizes that it is at a particular place in the grammar, the corresponding action is invoked to perform its task. To implement this in a top-down, recursive-descent parser, the compiler writer simply adds the appropriate code to the parsing routines. The compiler writer has complete control over when the actions execute. In a bottom-up, shift-reduce parser, the actions are performed each time the parser performs a reduce action. This is more restrictive, but still workable.

To make this concrete, consider reformulating the signed binary number example in an ad hoc syntax-directed translation framework. Figure 4.11 shows one such framework. Each grammar symbol has a single value associated with it, denoted `val` in the code snippets. The code snippet for each rule defines the value associated with the symbol on the rule's left-hand side. Rule 1 simply multiplies the value for *Sign* with the value for *List*. Rules 2 and 3 set the value for *Sign* appropriately, just as rules 6 and 7 set the value for each instance of *Bit*. Rule 4 simply copies the value from *Bit* to *List*. The real work occurs in rule 5, which multiplies the accumulated value of the leading bits (in *List*. `val`) by two, and then adds in the next bit.

So far, this looks quite similar to an attribute grammar. However, it has two key simplifications. Values flow in only one direction, from leaves to root. It allows only a single value per grammar symbol. Even so, the scheme in Figure 4.11 correctly computes the value of the signed binary number. It leaves that value at the root of the tree, just like the attribute grammar for signed binary numbers.

These two simplifications make possible an evaluation method that works well with a bottom-up parser, such as the LR(1) parsers described in Chapter 3. Since each code snippet is associated with the right-hand side of a specific production, the parser can invoke the action each time it reduces by

| | Production | Code Snippet |
|---|---|---|
| 1 | *Number* → *Sign List* | *Number*.val ← *Sign*.val × *List*.val |
| 2 | *Sign* → + | *Sign*.val ← 1 |
| 3 | *Sign* → - | *Sign*.val ← -1 |
| 4 | *List* → *Bit* | *List*.val ← *Bit*.val |
| 5 | $List_0$ → $List_1$ *Bit* | $List_0$.val ← 2 × $List_1$.val + *Bit*.val |
| 6 | *Bit* → 0 | *Bit*.val ← 0 |
| 7 | *Bit* → 1 | *Bit*.val ← 1 |

■ **FIGURE 4.11** Ad Hoc Syntax-Directed Translation for Signed Binary Numbers.

that production. This requires minor modifications to the reduce action in the skeleton LR(1) parser shown in Figure 3.15.

```
else if Action[s,word] = "reduce A→β" then
    invoke the appropriate reduce action
    pop 2 × |β| symbols
    s ← top of stack
    push A
    push Goto[s,A]
```

The parser generator can gather the syntax-directed actions together, embed them in a case statement that switches on the number of the production being reduced, and place the case statement just before it pops the right-hand side from the stack.

The translation scheme shown in Figure 4.11 is simpler than the scheme used to explain attribute grammars. Of course, we can write an attribute grammar that applies the same strategy. It would use only synthesized attributes. It would have fewer attribution rules and fewer attributes than the one shown in Figure 4.5. We chose the more complex attribution scheme to illustrate the use of both synthesized and inherited attributes.

### 4.4.1 Implementing Ad Hoc Syntax-Directed Translation

To make ad hoc syntax-directed translation work, the parser must include mechanisms to pass values from their definitions in one action to their uses in another, to provide convenient and consistent naming, and to allow for actions that execute at other points in the parse. This section describes mechanisms for handling these issues in a bottom-up, shift-reduce parser.

Analogous ideas will work for top-down parsers. We adopt a notation introduced in the Yacc system, an early and popular LALR(1) parser generator distributed with the Unix operating system. The Yacc notation has been adopted by many subsequent systems.

### Communicating between Actions

To pass values between actions, the parser must have a methodology for allocating space to hold the values produced by the various actions. The mechanism must make it possible for an action that uses a value to find it. An attribute grammar associates the values (attributes) with nodes in the parse tree; tying the attribute storage to the tree nodes' storage makes it possible to find attribute values in a systematic way. In ad hoc syntax-directed translation, the parser may not construct the parse tree. Instead, the parser can integrate the storage for values into its own mechanism for tracking the state of the parse—its internal stack.

Recall that the skeleton LR(1) parser stored two values on the stack for each grammar symbol: the symbol and a corresponding state. When it recognizes a handle, such as a *List Bit* sequence to match the right-hand side of rule 5, the first pair on the stack represents the *Bit*. Underneath that lies the pair representing the *List*. We can replace these ⟨*symbol, state*⟩ pairs with triples, ⟨*value, symbol, state*⟩. This provides a single value attribute per grammar symbol—precisely what the simplified scheme needs. To manage the stack, the parser pushes and pops more values. On a reduction by $A \rightarrow \beta$, it pops $3 \times |\beta|$ items from the stack, rather than $2 \times |\beta|$ items. It pushes the value along with the symbol and state.

This approach stores the values at easily computed locations relative to the top of the stack. Each reduction pushes its result onto the stack as part of the triple that represents the left-hand side. The action reads the values for the right-hand side from their relative positions in the stack; the $i^{th}$ symbol on the right-hand side has its value in the $i^{th}$ triple from the top of the stack. Values are restricted to a fixed size; in practice, this limitation means that more complex values are passed using pointers to structures.

To save storage, the parser could omit the actual grammar symbols from the stack. The information necessary for parsing is encoded in the state. This shrinks the stack and speeds up the parse by eliminating the operations that stack and unstack those symbols. On the other hand, the grammar symbol can help in error reporting and in debugging the parser. This trade-off is usually decided in favor of not modifying the parser that the tools produce—such modifications must be reapplied each time the parser is regenerated.

## Naming Values

To simplify the use of stack-based values, the compiler writer needs a notation for naming them. Yacc introduced a concise notation to address this problem. The symbol $$ refers to the result location for the current production. Thus, the assignment $$ = 0; would push the integer value zero as the result corresponding to the current reduction. This assignment could implement the action for rule 6 in Figure 4.11. For the right-hand side, the symbols $1, $2, ..., $n refer to the locations for the first, second, through $n^{th}$ symbols in the right-hand side, respectively.

Rewriting the example from Figure 4.11 in this notation produces the following specification:

| | Production | | | Code Snippet |
|---|---|---|---|---|
| 1 | *Number* | $\to$ | *Sign List* | $$ \gets $1 \times $2 |
| 2 | *Sign* | $\to$ | + | $$ \gets 1 |
| 3 | *Sign* | $\to$ | - | $$ \gets -1 |
| 4 | *List* | $\to$ | *Bit* | $$ \gets $1 |
| 5 | *List*$_0$ | $\to$ | *List*$_1$ *Bit* | $$ \gets 2 \times $1 + $2 |
| 6 | *Bit* | $\to$ | 0 | $$ \gets 0 |
| 7 | *Bit* | $\to$ | 1 | $$ \gets 1 |

Notice how compact the code snippets are. This scheme has an efficient implementation; the symbols translate directly into offsets from the top of the stack. The notation $1 indicates a location $3 \times |\beta|$ slots below the top of the stack, while a reference to $i$ designates the location $3 \times (|\beta| - i + 1)$ slots from the top of the stack. Thus, the positional notation allows the action snippets to read and write the stack locations directly.

## Actions at Other Points in the Parse

Compiler writers might also need to perform an action in the middle of a production or on a shift action. To accomplish this, compiler writers can transform the grammar so that it performs a reduction at each point where an action is needed. To reduce in the middle of a production, they can break the production into two pieces around the point where the action should execute. A higher-level production that sequences the first part, then the second part, is added. When the first part reduces, the parser invokes the action. To force actions on shifts, a compiler writer can either move them into the scanner or add a production to hold the action. For example, to perform an action whenever the parser shifts the terminal symbol *Bit*, a compiler writer can add a production

$ShiftedBit \rightarrow Bit$

and replace every occurrence of *Bit* with *ShiftedBit*. This adds an extra reduction for every terminal symbol. Thus, the additional cost is directly proportional to the number of terminal symbols in the program.

### 4.4.2 Examples

To understand how ad hoc syntax-directed translation works, consider rewriting the execution-time estimator using this approach. The primary drawback of the attribute-grammar solution lies in the proliferation of rules to copy information around the tree. This creates many additional rules in the specification and duplicates attribute values at many nodes.

To address these problems in an ad hoc syntax-directed translation scheme, the compiler writer typically introduces a central repository for information about variables, as suggested earlier. This eliminates the need to copy values around the trees. It also simplifies the handling of inherited values. Since the parser determines evaluation order, we do not need to worry about breaking dependences between attributes.

Most compilers build and use such a repository, called a *symbol table*. The symbol table maps a name into a variety of annotations such as a type, the size of its runtime representation, and the information needed to generate a runtime address. The table may also store a number of type-dependent fields, such as the type signature of a function or the number of dimensions and their bounds for an array. Section 5.5 and Appendix B.4 delve into symbol-table design more deeply.

#### *Load Tracking, Revisited*

Consider, again, the problem of tracking load operations that arose as part of estimating execution costs. Most of the complexity in the attribute grammar for this problem arose from the need to pass information around the tree. In an ad hoc syntax-directed translation scheme that uses a symbol table, the problem is easy to handle. The compiler writer can set aside a field in the table to hold a boolean that indicates whether or not that identifier has already been charged for a load. The field is initially set to *false*. The critical code is associated with the production *Factor* → name. If the name's symbol table entry indicates that it has not been charged for a load, then cost is updated and the field is set to *true*.

| Production | Syntax-Directed Actions |
|---|---|
| $Block_0 \rightarrow Block_1$ *Assign* | |
|     &#124;  *Assign* | |
| *Assign* $\rightarrow$ name = *Expr* ; | { $cost = cost + Cost(store)$ } |
| *Expr* $\rightarrow$ *Expr* + *Term* | { $cost = cost + Cost(add)$ } |
|     &#124;  *Expr* − *Term* | { $cost = cost + Cost(sub)$ } |
|     &#124;  *Term* | |
| *Term* $\rightarrow$ *Term* × *Factor* | { $cost = cost + Cost(mult)$ } |
|     &#124;  *Term* ÷ *Factor* | { $cost = cost + Cost(div)$ } |
|     &#124;  *Factor* | |
| *Factor* $\rightarrow$ ( *Expr* ) | |
|     &#124;  num | { $cost = cost + Cost(loadI)$ } |
|     &#124;  name | { *if* name's *symbol table field* *indicates that it has not been loaded* *then*    $cost = cost + Cost(load)$    *set the field to true* } |

■ **FIGURE 4.12** Tracking Loads with Ad Hoc Syntax-Directed Translation.

Figure 4.12 shows this case, along with all the other actions. Because the actions can contain arbitrary code, the compiler can accumulate $cost$ in a single variable, rather than creating a $cost$ attribute at each node in the parse tree. This scheme requires fewer actions than the attribution rules for the simplest execution model, even though it can provide the accuracy of the more complex model.

Notice that several productions have no actions. The remaining actions are simple, except for the action taken on a reduction by name. All of the complication introduced by tracking loads falls into that single action; contrast that with the attribute-grammar version, where the task of passing around the *Before* and *After* sets came to dominate the specification. The ad hoc version is cleaner and simpler, in part because the problem fits nicely into the evaluation order dictated by the reduce actions in a shift-reduce parser. Of course, the compiler writer must implement the symbol table or import it from some library of data-structure implementations.

Clearly, some of these strategies could also be applied in an attribute-grammar framework. However, they violate the functional nature of the attribute grammar. They force critical parts of the work out of the attribute-grammar framework and into an ad hoc setting.

The scheme in Figure 4.12 ignores one critical issue: initializing cost. The grammar, as written, contains no production that can appropriately initialize cost to zero. The solution, as described earlier, is to modify the grammar in a way that creates a place for the initialization. An initial production, such as *Start → CostInit Block*, along with *CostInit → ε*, does this. The framework can perform the assignment cost ← 0 on the reduction from ε to *CostInit*.

### Type Inference for Expressions, Revisited

The problem of inferring types for expressions fit well into the attribute-grammar framework, as long as we assumed that leaf nodes already had type information. The simplicity of the solution shown in Figure 4.7 derives from two principal facts. First, because expression types are defined recursively on the expression tree, the natural flow of information runs bottom up from the leaves to the root. This biases the solution toward an *S*-attributed grammar. Second, expression types are defined in terms of the syntax of the source language. This fits well with the attribute-grammar framework, which implicitly requires the presence of a parse tree. All the type information can be tied to instances of grammar symbols, which correspond precisely to nodes in the parse tree.

We can reformulate this problem in an ad hoc framework, as shown in Figure 4.13. It uses the type inference functions introduced with Figure 4.7. The resulting framework looks similar to the attribute grammar for the same purpose from Figure 4.7. The ad hoc framework provides no real advantage for this problem.

| Production | | Syntax-Directed Actions |
|---|---|---|
| *Expr* | → *Expr − Term* | $\{ \$\$ \leftarrow \mathcal{F}_+(\$1,\$3) \}$ |
| | \| *Expr − Term* | $\{ \$\$ \leftarrow \mathcal{F}_-(\$1,\$3) \}$ |
| | \| *Term* | $\{ \$\$ \leftarrow \$1 \}$ |
| *Term* | → *Term × Factor* | $\{ \$\$ \leftarrow \mathcal{F}_\times(\$1,\$3) \}$ |
| | \| *Term ÷ Factor* | $\{ \$\$ \leftarrow \mathcal{F}_\div(\$1,\$3) \}$ |
| | \| *Factor* | $\{ \$\$ \leftarrow \$1 \}$ |
| *Factor* | → ( *Expr* ) | $\{ \$\$ \leftarrow \$2 \}$ |
| | \| num | $\{ \$\$ \leftarrow$ *type of the* num $\}$ |
| | \| name | $\{ \$\$ \leftarrow$ *type of the* name $\}$ |

■ **FIGURE 4.13** Ad Hoc Framework for Inferring Expression Types.

| Production | Syntax-Directed Actions |
|---|---|
| *Expr* $\rightarrow$ *Expr* + *Term* | { $\$\$ \leftarrow$ *MakeNode*$_2$ *(plus,$1,$3)*;<br>$\$\$.type \leftarrow \mathcal{F}_+(\$1.type,\$3.type)$ } |
| \| *Expr* − *Term* | { $\$\$ \leftarrow$ *MakeNode*$_2$*(minus,$1,$3)*;<br>$\$\$.type \leftarrow \mathcal{F}_-(\$1.type,\$3.type)$ } |
| \| *Term* | { $\$\$ \leftarrow$ *$1* } |
| *Term* $\rightarrow$ *Term* × *Factor* | { $\$\$ \leftarrow$ *MakeNode*$_2$*(times,$1,$3)*;<br>$\$\$.type \leftarrow \mathcal{F}_\times(\$1.type,\$3.type)$ } |
| \| *Term* ÷ *Factor* | { $\$\$ \leftarrow$ *MakeNode*$_2$*(divide,$1,$3)*;<br>$\$\$.type \leftarrow \mathcal{F}_\div(\$1.type,\$3.type)$ } |
| \| *Factor* | { $\$\$ \leftarrow$ *$1* } |
| *Factor* $\rightarrow$ ( *Expr* ) | { $\$\$ \leftarrow$ *$2* } |
| \| num | { $\$\$ \leftarrow$ *MakeNode*$_0$*(number)*;<br>$\$\$.text \leftarrow$ *scanned text*;<br>$\$\$.type \leftarrow$ *type of the number* } |
| \| name | { $\$\$ \leftarrow$ *MakeNode*$_0$*(identifier)*;<br>$\$\$.text \leftarrow$ *scanned text*;<br>$\$\$.type \leftarrow$ *type of the identifier* } |

■ **FIGURE 4.14** Building an Abstract Syntax Tree and Inferring Expression Types.

## Building an Abstract Syntax Tree

Compiler front ends must build an intermediate representation of the program for use in the compiler's middle part and its back end. Abstract syntax trees are a common form of tree-structured IR. The task of building an AST fits neatly into an ad hoc syntax-directed translation scheme.

Assume that the compiler has a series of routines named *MakeNode*$_i$, for $0 \leq i \leq 3$. The routine takes, as its first argument, a constant that uniquely identifies the grammar symbol that the new node will represent. The remaining $i$ arguments are the nodes that head each of the $i$ subtrees. Thus, *MakeNode*$_0$ *(number)* constructs a leaf node and marks it as representing a num. Similarly,

The *MakeNode* routines can implement the tree in any appropriate way. For example, they might map the structure onto a binary tree, as discussed in Section B.3.1.

> *MakeNode*$_2$*(Plus,MakeNode*$_0$*(number,) MakeNode*$_0$*(number))*

builds an AST rooted in a node for *plus* with two children, each of which is a leaf node for num.

To build an abstract syntax tree, the ad hoc syntax-directed translation scheme follows two general principles:

1. For an operator, it creates a node with a child for each operand. Thus, 2 + 3 creates a binary node for + with the nodes for 2 and 3 as children.
2. For a useless production, such as *Term* → *Factor*, it reuses the result from the *Factor* action as its own result.

In this manner, it avoids building tree nodes that represent syntactic variables, such as *Factor*, *Term*, and *Expr*. Figure 4.14 shows a syntax-directed translation scheme that incorporates these ideas.

### Generating ILOC *for Expressions*

As a final example of manipulating expressions, consider an ad hoc framework that generates ILOC rather than an AST. We will make several simplifying assumptions. The example limits its attention to integers; handling other types adds complexity, but little insight. The example also assumes that all values can be held in registers—both that the values fit in registers and that the ILOC implementation provides more registers than the computation will use.

Code generation requires the compiler to track many small details. To abstract away most of these bookkeeping details (and to defer some deeper issues to following chapters), the example framework uses four supporting routines.

1. *Address* takes a variable name as its argument. It returns the number of a register that contains the value specified by name. If necessary, it generates code to load that value.
2. *Emit* handles the details of creating a concrete representation for the various ILOC operations. It might format and print them to a file. Alternatively, it might build an internal representation for later use.
3. *NextRegister* returns a new register number. A simple implementation could increment a global counter.
4. *Value* takes a number as its argument and returns a register number. It ensures that the register contains the number passed as its argument. If necessary, it generates code to move that number into the register.

Figure 4.15 shows the syntax-directed framework for this problem. The actions communicate by passing register names in the parsing stack. The actions pass these names to *Emit* as needed, to create the operations that implement the input expression.

| Production | Syntax-Directed Actions |
|---|---|
| Expr → Expr + Term | { $$ ← *NextRegister*; *Emit*(*add*, $1, $3, $$) } |
| \| Expr − Term | { $$ ← *NextRegister*; *Emit*(*sub*, $1, $3, $$) } |
| \| Term | { $$ ← $1 } |
| Term → Term × Factor | { $$ ← *NextRegister*; *Emit*(*mult*, $1, $3, $$) } |
| \| Term ÷ Factor | { $$ ← *NextRegister*; *Emit*(*div*, $1, $3, $$) } |
| \| Factor | { $$ ← $1 } |
| Factor → ( Expr ) | { $$ ← $2 } |
| \| num | { $$ ← *Value(scanned text);* } |
| \| name | { $$ ← *Address(scanned text);* } |

■ **FIGURE 4.15** Emitting ɪʟᴏᴄ for Expressions.

## Processing Declarations

Of course, the compiler writer can use syntax-directed actions to fill in much of the information that resides in the symbol table. For example, the grammar fragment shown in Figure 4.16 describes a limited subset of the syntax for declaring variables in C. (It omits typedefs, structs, unions, the type qualifiers const, restrict, and volatile, as well as the details of the initialization syntax. It also leaves several nonterminals unelaborated.) Consider the actions required to build symbol-table entries for each declared variable. Each *Declaration* begins with a set of one or more qualifiers that specify the variable's type and storage class. These qualifiers are followed by a list of one or more variable names; each variable name can include specifications about indirection (one or more occurrences of ⋆), about array dimensions, and about initial values for the variable.

For example, the *StorageClass* production allows the programmer to specify information about the lifetime of a variable's value; an auto variable has a lifetime that matches the lifetime of the block that declares it, while static variables have lifetimes that span the program's entire execution. The register specifier suggests to the compiler that the value should be kept in a location that can be accessed quickly—historically, a hardware register. The extern specifier tells the compiler that declarations of the same name in different compilation units are to be linked as a single object.

| | | |
|---|---|---|
| *DeclarationList* | → | *DeclarationList Declaration* |
| | \| | *Declaration* |
| *Declaration* | → | *SpecifierList InitDeclaratorList* ; |
| *SpecifierList* | → | *Specifier SpecifierList* |
| | \| | *Specifier* |
| *Specifier* | → | *StorageClass* |
| | \| | *TypeSpecifier* |
| *StorageClass* | → | `auto` |
| | \| | `static` |
| | \| | `extern` |
| | \| | `register` |
| *TypeSpecifier* | → | `void` |
| | \| | `char` |
| | \| | `short` |
| | \| | `int` |
| | \| | `long` |
| | \| | `signed` |
| | \| | `unsigned` |
| | \| | `float` |
| | \| | `double` |
| *InitDeclaratorList* | → | *InitDeclaratorList* , *InitDeclarator* |
| | \| | *InitDeclarator* |
| *InitDeclarator* | → | *Declarator = Initializer* |
| | \| | *Declarator* |
| *Declarator* | → | *Pointer DirectDeclarator* |
| | \| | *DirectDeclarator* |
| *Pointer* | → | * |
| | \| | * *Pointer* |
| *DirectDeclarator* | → | `ident` |
| | \| | ( *Declarator* ) |
| | \| | *DirectDeclarator* ( ) |
| | \| | *DirectDeclarator* ( *ParameterTypeList* ) |
| | \| | *DirectDeclarator* ( *IdentifierList* ) |
| | \| | *DirectDeclarator* [ ] |
| | \| | *DirectDeclarator* [ *ConstantExpr* ] |

■ **FIGURE 4.16**  A Subset of C's Declaration Syntax.

While such restrictions can be encoded in the grammar, the standard writers chose to leave it for semantic elaboration to check, rather than complicate an already large grammar.

The compiler must ensure that each declared name has at most one storage class attribute. The grammar places the specifiers before a list of one or more names. The compiler can record the specifiers as it processes them and apply them to the names when it later encounters them. The grammar admits an arbitrary number of *StorageClass* and *TypeSpecifier* keywords; the standard limits the ways that the actual keywords can be combined. For example, it allows only one *StorageClass* per declaration. The compiler must enforce

**WHAT ABOUT CONTEXT-SENSITIVE GRAMMARS?**

Given the progression of ideas from the previous chapters, it might seem natural to consider the use of context-sensitive languages to perform context-sensitive checks, such as type inference. After all, we used regular languages to perform lexical analysis and context-free languages to perform syntax analysis. A natural progression might suggest the study of context-sensitive languages and their grammars. Context-sensitive grammars can express a larger family of languages than can context-free grammars.

However, context-sensitive grammars are not the right answer for two distinct reasons. First, the problem of parsing a context-sensitive grammar is P-Space complete. Thus, a compiler that used such a technique could run *very* slowly. Second, many of the important questions are difficult, if not impossible, to encode in a context-sensitive grammar. For example, consider the issue of declaration before use. To write this rule into a context-sensitive grammar would require the grammar to encode each distinct combination of declared variables. With a sufficiently small name space (for example, Dartmouth BASIC limited the programmer to single-letter names, with an optional single digit), this might be manageable; in a modern language with a large name space, the set of names is too large to encode in a context-sensitive grammar.

this restriction through context-sensitive checking. Similar restrictions apply to *TypeSpecifiers*. For example, short is legal with int but not with float.

To process declarations, the compiler must collect the attributes from the qualifiers, add any indirection, dimension, or initialization attributes, and enter the variable in the table. The compiler writer might set up a properties structure whose fields correspond to the properties of a symbol-table entry. At the end of a *Declaration*, it can initialize the values of each field in the structure. As it reduces the various productions in the declaration syntax, it can adjust the values in the structure accordingly.

- On a reduction of auto to *StorageClass*, it can check that the field for storage class has not already been set, and then set it to auto. Similar actions for static, extern, and register complete the handling of those properties of a name.
- The type specifier productions will set other fields in the structure. They must include checks to insure that only valid combinations occur.
- Reduction from ident to *DirectDeclarator* should trigger an action that creates a new symbol-table entry for the name and copies the current settings from the properties structure into that entry.

■ Reducing by the production

$$InitDeclaratorList \rightarrow InitDeclaratorList \ , \ InitDeclarator$$

can reset the properties fields that relate to the specific name, including those set by the *Pointer*, *Initializer*, and *DirectDeclarator* productions.

By coordinating a series of actions across the productions in the declaration syntax, the compiler writer can arrange to have the properties structure contain the appropriate settings each time a name is processed.

When the parser finishes building the *DeclarationList*, it has built a symbol-table entry for each variable declared in the current scope. At that point, it may need to perform some housekeeping chores, such as assigning storage locations to declared variables. This can be done in an action for the production that reduces the *DeclarationList*. If necessary, that production can be split to create a convenient point for the action.

---

**SECTION REVIEW**

The introduction of parser generators created the need for a mechanism to tie context-sensitive actions to the parse-time behavior of the compiler. Ad hoc syntax-directed translation, as described in this section, evolved to fill that need. It uses some of the same intuitions as the attribute-grammar approach. It allows only one evaluation order. It has a limited name space for use in the code snippets that form semantic actions.

Despite these limitations, the power of allowing arbitrary code in semantic actions, coupled with support for this technique in widely used parser generators, has led to widespread use of ad hoc syntax-directed translation. It works well in conjunction with global data structures, such as a symbol table, to perform nonlocal communication. It efficiently and effectively solves a class of problems that arise in building a compiler's front end.

---

$Calc \rightarrow Expr$

$Expr \rightarrow Expr + Term$
$\quad | \quad Expr - Term$
$\quad | \quad Term$

$Term \rightarrow Term \times num$
$\quad | \quad Term \div num$
$\quad | \quad num$

Four function calculator

Hint: Recall that an attribute grammar does not specify order of evaluation.

**Review Questions**

1. Consider the problem of adding ad hoc actions to an LL(1) parser generator. How would you modify the LL(1) skeleton parser to include user-defined actions for each production?

2. In review question 1 for Section 4.3, you built an attribute-grammar framework to compute values in the "four function calculator" grammar. Now, consider implementing a calculator widget for the desktop on your personal computer. Contrast the utility of your attribute grammar and your ad hoc syntax-directed translation scheme for the calculator implementation.

## 4.5 **ADVANCED TOPICS**

This chapter has introduced the basic notions of type theory and used them as one motivating example for both attribute-grammar frameworks and for ad hoc syntax-directed translation. A deeper treatment of type theory and its applications could easily fill an entire volume.

The first subsection lays out some language design issues that affect the way that a compiler must perform type inference and type checking. The second subsection looks at a problem that arises in practice: rearranging a computation during the process of building the intermediate representation for it.

### 4.5.1 **Harder Problems in Type Inference**

Strongly typed, statically checked languages can help the programmer produce valid programs by detecting large classes of erroneous programs. The same features that expose errors can improve the compiler's ability to generate efficient code for a program by eliminating runtime checks and exposing where the compiler can specialize special case code for some construct to eliminate cases that cannot occur at runtime. These facts account, in part, for the growing role of type systems in modern programming languages.

Our examples, however, have made assumptions that do not hold in all programming languages. For example, we assumed that variables and procedures are declared—the programmer writes down a concise and binding specification for each name. Varying these assumptions can radically change the nature of both the type-checking problem and the strategies that the compiler can use to implement the language.

Some programming languages either omit declarations or treat them as optional information. Scheme programs lack declarations for variables. Smalltalk programs declare classes, but an object's class is determined only when the program instantiates that object. Languages that support separate compilation—compiling procedures independently and combining them at link time to form a program—may not require declarations for independently compiled procedures.

In the absence of declarations, type checking is harder because the compiler must rely on contextual clues to determine the appropriate type for each name. For example, if i is used as an index for some array a, that might constrain i to have a numeric type. The language might allow only integer subscripts; alternatively, it might allow any type that can be converted to an integer.

Typing rules are specified by the language definition. The specific details of those rules determine how difficult it is to infer a type for each variable.

This, in turn, has a direct effect on the strategies that a compiler can use to implement the language.

### Type-Consistent Uses and Constant Function Types

Consider a declaration-free language that requires consistent use of variables and functions. In this case, the compiler can assign each name a general type and narrow that type by examining each use of the name in context. For example, a statement such as $a \leftarrow b \times 3.14159$ provides evidence that $a$ and $b$ are numbers and that $a$ must have a type that allows it to hold a decimal number. If $b$ also appears in contexts where an integer is expected, such as an array reference $c(b)$, then the compiler must choose between a noninteger number (for $b \times 3.14159$) and an integer (for $c(b)$). With either choice, it will need a conversion for one of the uses.

If functions have return types that are both known and constant—that is, a function $fee$ always returns the same type—then the compiler can solve the type inference problem with an iterative fixed-point algorithm operating over a lattice of types.

### Type-Consistent Uses and Unknown Function Types

Map can also handle functions with multiple arguments. To do so, it takes multiple argument lists and treats them as lists of arguments, in order.

If the type of a function varies with the function's arguments, then the problem of type inference becomes more complex. This situation arises in Scheme, for example. Scheme's library procedure $map$ takes as arguments a function and a list. It returns the result of applying the function argument to each element of the list. That is, if the argument function takes type $\alpha$ to $\beta$, then $map$ takes a list of $\alpha$ to a list of $\beta$. We would write its type signature as

$$map: (\alpha \rightarrow \beta) \times \text{list of } \alpha \rightarrow \text{list of } \beta$$

Since $map$'s return type depends on the types of its arguments, a property known as *parametric polymorphism*, the inference rules must include equations over the space of types. (With known, constant return types, functions return values in the space of types.) With this addition, a simple iterative fixed-point approach to type inference is not sufficient.

The classic approach to checking these more complex systems relies on unification, although clever type-system design and type representations can permit the use of simpler or more efficient techniques.

### Dynamic Changes in Type

If a variable's type can change during execution, other strategies may be required to discover where type changes occur and to infer appropriate types.

In principle, a compiler can rename the variables so that each definition site corresponds to a unique name. It can then infer types for those names based on the context provided by the operation that defines each name.

To infer types successfully, such a system would need to handle points in the code where distinct definitions must merge due to the convergence of different control-flow paths, as with $\phi$-functions in static single assignment form (see Sections 5.4.2 and 9.3). If the language includes parametric polymorphism, the type-inference mechanism must handle it, as well.

The classic approach to implementing a language with dynamically changing types is to fall back on interpretation. Lisp, Scheme, Smalltalk, and APL all have similar problems. The standard implementation practice for these languages involves interpreting the operators, tagging the data with their types, and checking for type errors at runtime.

In APL, the programmer can easily write a program where a×b multiplies integers the first time it executes and multiplies multidimensional arrays of floating-point numbers the next time. This led to a body of research on check elimination and check motion. The best APL systems avoided most of the checks that a naive interpreter would need.

## 4.5.2 **Changing Associativity**

As we saw in Section 3.5.4, associativity can make a difference in numerical computation. Similarly, it can change the way that data structures are built. We can use syntax-directed actions to build representations that reflect a different associativity than the grammar would naturally produce.

In general, left-recursive grammars naturally produce left associativity, while right-recursive grammars naturally produce right associativity. To see this, consider the left-recursive and right-recursive list grammars, augmented with syntax-directed actions to build lists, shown at the top of Figure 4.17. The actions associated with each production build a list representation. Assume that $L(x,y)$ is a list constructor; it can be implemented as $MakeNode_2(cons,x,y)$. The lower part of the figure shows the result of applying the two translation schemes to an input consisting of five elts.

The two trees are, in many ways, equivalent. An in-order traversal of both trees visits the leaf nodes in the same order. If we add parentheses to reflect the tree structure, the left-recursive tree is $((((elt_1,elt_2),elt_3),elt_4),elt_5)$ while the right-recursive tree is $(elt_1,(elt_2,(elt_3,(elt_4,elt_5))))$. The ordering produced by left recursion corresponds to the classic left-to-right ordering for algebraic operators. The ordering produced by right recursion corresponds to the notion of a list found in Lisp and Scheme.

| Production | Actions |
|---|---|
| *List* → *List* elt | {$$ ← L($1,$2)} |
| \| elt | {$$ ← $1} |

| Production | Actions |
|---|---|
| *List* → elt *List* | {$$ ← L($1,$2)} |
| \| elt | {$$ ← $1} |

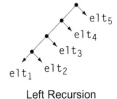

Left Recursion

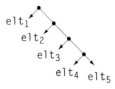

Right Recursion

■ **FIGURE 4.17** Recursion versus Associativity.

Sometimes, it is convenient to use different directions for recursion and associativity. To build the right-recursive tree from the left-recursive grammar, we could use a constructor that adds successive elements to the end of the list. A straightforward implementation of this idea would have to walk the list on each reduction, making the constructor itself take $\mathbf{O}(n^2)$ time, where $n$ is the length of the list. To avoid this overhead, the compiler can create a list header node that contains pointers to both the first and last nodes in the list. This introduces an extra node to the list. If the system constructs many short lists, the overhead may be a problem.

A solution that we find particularly appealing is to use a list header node during construction and discard it after the list has been built. Rewriting the grammar to use an $\epsilon$-production makes this particularly clean.

| Grammar | Actions |
|---|---|
| *List* → $\epsilon$ | { $$ ← *MakeListHeader* ( ) } |
| \| *List* elt | { $$ ← *AddToEnd*($1, $2) } |
| *Quux* → *List* | { $$ ← *RemoveListHeader*($1) } |

A reduction with the $\epsilon$-production creates the temporary list header node; with a shift-reduce parser, this reduction occurs first. The *List* → *List* elt production invokes a constructor that relies on the presence of the temporary header node. When *List* is reduced on the right-hand side of any other production, the corresponding action invokes a function that discards the temporary header and returns the first element of the list.

This approach lets the parser reverse the associativity at the cost of a small constant overhead in both space and time. It requires one more reduction per list, for the $\epsilon$-production. The revised grammar admits an empty list, while the original grammar did not. To remedy this problem, `RemoveListHeader` can explicitly check for the empty case and report the error.

## 4.6  SUMMARY AND PERSPECTIVE

In Chapters 2 and 3, we saw that much of the work in a compiler's front end can be automated. Regular expressions work well for lexical analysis. Context-free grammars work well for syntax analysis. In this chapter, we examined two ways to perform context-sensitive analysis: attribute-grammar formalism and an ad hoc approach. For context-sensitive analysis, unlike scanning and parsing, formalism has not displaced the ad hoc approach.

The formal approach, using attribute grammars, offers the hope of writing high-level specifications that produce reasonably efficient executables. While attribute grammars are not the solution to every problem in context-sensitive analysis, they have found application in several domains, ranging from theorem provers to program analysis. For problems in which the attribute flow is mostly local, attribute grammars work well. Problems that can be formulated entirely in terms of one kind of attribute, either inherited or synthesized, often produce clean, intuitive solutions when cast as attribute grammars. When the problem of directing the flow of attributes around the tree with copy rules comes to dominate the grammar, it is probably time to step outside the functional paradigm of attribute grammars and introduce a central repository for facts.

The ad hoc technique, syntax-directed translation, integrates arbitrary snippets of code into the parser and lets the parser sequence the actions and pass values between them. This approach has been widely embraced because of its flexibility and its inclusion in most parser-generator systems. The ad hoc approach sidesteps the practical problems that arise from nonlocal attribute flow and from the need to manage attribute storage. Values flow in one direction alongside the parser's internal representation of its state (synthesized values for bottom-up parsers and inherited for top-down parsers). These schemes use global data structures to pass information in the other direction and to handle nonlocal attribute flow.

In practice, the compiler writer often tries to solve several problems at once, such as building an intermediate representation, inferring types, and assigning storage locations. This tends to create significant attribute flows in both directions, pushing the implementor toward an ad hoc solution that uses some central repository for facts, such as a symbol table. The justification for solving many problems in one pass is usually compile-time efficiency. However, solving the problems in separate passes can often produce solutions that are easier to understand, to implement, and to maintain.

This chapter introduced the ideas behind type systems as an example of the kind of context-sensitive analysis that a compiler must perform. The study of type theory and type-system design is a significant scholarly activity with a deep literature of its own. This chapter scratched the surface of type inference and type checking, but a deeper treatment of these issues is beyond the scope of this text. In practice, the compiler writer needs to study the type system of the source language thoroughly and to engineer the implementation of type inference and type checking carefully. The pointers in this chapter are a start, but a realistic implementation requires more study.

## ■ CHAPTER NOTES

Type systems have been an integral part of programming languages since the original FORTRAN compiler. While the first type systems reflected the resources of the underlying machine, deeper levels of abstraction soon appeared in type systems for languages such as Algol 68 and Simula 67. The theory of type systems has been actively studied for decades, producing a string of languages that embodied important principles. These include Russell [45] (parametric polymorphism), CLU [248] (abstract data types), Smalltalk [162] (subtyping through inheritance), and ML [265] (thorough and complete treatment of types as first-class objects). Cardelli has written an excellent overview of type systems [69]. The APL community produced a series of classic papers that dealt with techniques to eliminate runtime checks [1, 35, 264, 349].

Attribute grammars, like many ideas in computer science, were first proposed by Knuth [229, 230]. The literature on attribute grammars has focused on evaluators [203, 342], on circularity testing [342], and on applications of attribute grammars [157, 298]. Attribute grammars have served as the basis for several successful systems, including Intel's Pascal compiler for the 80286 [142, 143], the Cornell Program Synthesizer [297] and the Synthesizer Generator [198, 299].

Ad hoc syntax-directed translation has always been a part of the development of real parsers. Irons described the basic ideas behind syntax-directed translation to separate a parser's actions from the description of its syntax [202]. Undoubtedly, the same basic ideas were used in hand-coded precedence parsers. The style of writing syntax-directed actions that we describe was introduced by Johnson in Yacc [205]. The same notation has been carried forward into more recent systems, including `bison` from the Gnu project.

## ■ EXERCISES

Section 4.2

**1.** In Scheme, the + operator is overloaded. Given that Scheme is dynamically typed, describe a method to type check an operation of the form (+ a b) where a and b may be of any type that is valid for the + operator.

**2.** Some languages, such as APL or PHP, neither require variable declarations nor enforce consistency between assignments to the same variable. (A program can assign the integer 10 to × and later assign the string value "book" to × in the same scope.) This style of programming is sometimes called *type juggling*.

Suppose that you have an existing implementation of a language that has no declarations but requires type-consistent uses. How could you modify it to allow type juggling?

Section 4.3

**3.** Based on the following evaluation rules, draw an annotated parse tree that shows how the syntax tree for a - (b + c) is constructed.

| Production | Evaluation Rules |
|---|---|
| $E_0 \rightarrow E_1 + T$ | { $E_0.nptr \leftarrow mknode(+, E_1.nptr, T.nptr)$ } |
| $E_0 \rightarrow E_1 - T$ | { $E_0.nptr \leftarrow mknode(-, E_1.nptr, T.nptr)$ } |
| $E_0 \rightarrow T$ | { $E_0.nptr \leftarrow T.nptr$ } |
| $T \rightarrow (E)$ | { $T.nptr \leftarrow E.nptr$ } |
| $T \rightarrow id$ | { $T.nptr \leftarrow mkleaf(id, id.entry)$ } |

**4.** Use the attribute-grammar paradigm to write an interpreter for the classic expression grammar. Assume that each name has a value attribute and a lexeme attribute. Assume that all attributes are already defined and that all values will always have the same type.

**5.** Write a grammar to describe all binary numbers that are multiples of four. Add attribution rules to the grammar that will annotate the start symbol of a syntax tree with an attribute value that contains the decimal value of the binary number.

**6.** Using the grammar defined in the previous exercise, build the syntax tree for the binary number 11100.
  **a.** Show all the attributes in the tree with their corresponding values.
  **b.** Draw the attribute dependence graph for the syntax tree and classify all attributes as being either synthesized or inherited.

**Section 4.4**

7. A Pascal program can declare two integer variables a and b with the syntax

$$\text{var a, b: int}$$

This declaration might be described with the following grammar:

$$
\begin{aligned}
VarDecl &\rightarrow \text{var } IDList : TypeID \\
IDList &\rightarrow IDList, ID \\
&\mid ID
\end{aligned}
$$

where *IDList* derives a comma-separated list of variable names and *TypeID* derives a valid Pascal type. You may find it necessary to rewrite the grammar.

a. Write an attribute grammar that assigns the correct data type to each declared variable.

b. Write an ad hoc syntax-directed translation scheme that assigns the correct data type to each declared variable.

c. Can either scheme operate in a single pass over the syntax tree?

8. Sometimes, the compiler writer can move an issue across the boundary between context-free and context-sensitive analysis. Consider, for example, the classic ambiguity that arises between function invocation and array references in FORTRAN 77 (and other languages). These constructs might be added to the classic expression grammar using the productions:

$$
\begin{aligned}
Factor &\rightarrow \text{name } ( ExprList ) \\
ExprList &\rightarrow ExprList , Expr \\
&\mid Expr
\end{aligned}
$$

Here, the only difference between a function invocation and an array reference lies in how the name is declared.

In previous chapters, we have discussed using cooperation between the scanner and the parser to disambiguate these constructs. Can the problem be solved during context-sensitive analysis? Which solution is preferable?

9. Sometimes, a language specification uses context-sensitive mechanisms to check properties that can be tested in a context-free way. Consider the grammar fragment in Figure 4.16 on page 208. It allows an arbitrary number of *StorageClass* specifiers when, in fact, the standard restricts a declaration to a single *StorageClass* specifier.

a. Rewrite the grammar to enforce the restriction grammatically.

b. Similarly, the language allows only a limited set of combinations of *TypeSpecifier*. long is allowed with either int or float; short is allowed only with int. Either signed or unsigned can appear with any form of `int`. `signed` may also appear on `char`. Can these restrictions be written into the grammar?

**c.** Propose an explanation for why the authors structured the grammar as they did.

**d.** Do your revisions to the grammar change the overall speed of the parser? In building a parser for C, would you use the grammar like the one in Figure 4.16, or would you prefer your revised grammar? Justify your answer.

Hint: The scanner returned a single token type for any of the *StorageClass* values and another token type for any of the *TypeSpecifiers*.

**10.** Object-oriented languages allow operator and function overloading. In these languages, the function name is not always a unique identifier, since you can have multiple related definitions, as in

**Section 4.5**

```
void Show(int);
void Show(char *);
void Show(float);
```

For lookup purposes, the compiler must construct a distinct identifier for each function. Sometimes, such overloaded functions will have different return types, as well. How would you create distinct identifiers for such functions?

**11.** Inheritance can create problems for the implementation of object-oriented languages. When object type *A* is a parent of object type *B*, a program can assign a "pointer to *B*" to a "pointer to *A*," with syntax such as a ← b. This should not cause problems since everything that *A* can do, *B* can also do. However, one cannot assign a "pointer to *A*" to a "pointer to *B*," since object class *B* can implement methods that object class *A* does not.

Design a mechanism that can use ad hoc syntax-directed translation to determine whether or not a pointer assignment of this kind is allowed.

# Intermediate Representations

## ■ CHAPTER OVERVIEW

The central data structure in a compiler is the intermediate form of the program being compiled. Most passes in the compiler read and manipulate the IR form of the code. Thus, decisions about what to represent and how to represent it play a crucial role in both the cost of compilation and its effectiveness. This chapter presents a survey of IR forms that compilers use, including graphical IR, linear IRs, and symbol tables.

**Keywords:** Intermediate Representation, Graphical IR, Linear IR, SSA Form, Symbol Table

## 5.1 INTRODUCTION

Compilers are typically organized as a series of passes. As the compiler derives knowledge about the code it compiles, it must convey that information from one pass to another. Thus, the compiler needs a representation for all of the facts that it derives about the program. We call this representation an *intermediate representation*, or IR. A compiler may have a single IR, or it may have a series of IRs that it uses as it transforms the code from source language into its target language. During translation, the IR form of the input program is the definitive form of the program. The compiler does not refer back to the source text; instead, it looks to the IR form of the code. The properties of a compiler's IR or IRs have a direct effect on what the compiler can do to the code.

Almost every phase of the compiler manipulates the program in its IR form. Thus, the properties of the IR, such as the mechanisms for reading and writing specific fields, for finding specific facts or annotations, and for navigating around a program in IR form, have a direct impact on the ease of writing the individual passes and on the cost of executing those passes.

## Conceptual Roadmap

This chapter focuses on the issues that surround the design and use of an IR in compilation. Section 5.1.1 provides a taxonomic overview of IRs and their properties. Many compiler writers consider trees and graphs as the natural representation for programs; for example, parse trees easily capture the derivations built by a parser. Section 5.2 describes several IRs based on trees and graphs. Of course, most processors that compilers target have linear assembly languages as their native language. Accordingly, some compilers use linear IRs with the rationale that those IRs expose properties of the target machine's code that the compiler should explicitly see. Section 5.3 examines linear IRs.

The final sections of this chapter deal with issues that relate to IRs but are not, strictly speaking, IR design issues. Section 5.4 explores issues that relate to naming: the choice of specific names for specific values. Naming can have a strong impact on the kind of code generated by a compiler. That discussion includes a detailed look at a specific, widely used IR called *static single-assignment form*, or SSA. Section 5.5 provides a high-level overview of how the compiler builds, uses, and maintains *symbol tables*. Most compilers build one or more symbol tables to hold information about names and values and to provide efficient access to that information.

*Appendix B.4 provides more material on symbol table implementation.*

## Overview

To convey information between its passes, a compiler needs a representation for all of the knowledge that it derives about the program being compiled. Thus, almost all compilers use some form of intermediate representation to model the code being analyzed, translated, and optimized. Most passes in the compiler consume IR; the scanner is an exception. Most passes in the compiler produce IR; passes in the code generator can be exceptions. Many modern compilers use multiple IRs during the course of a single compilation. In a pass-structured compiler, the IR serves as the primary and definitive representation of the code.

A compiler's IR must be expressive enough to record all of the useful facts that the compiler might need to transmit between passes. Source code is insufficient for this purpose; the compiler derives many facts that have no representation in source code, such as the addresses of variables and constants or the register in which a given parameter is passed. To record all of the detail that the compiler must encode, most compiler writers augment the IR with tables and sets that record additional information. We consider these tables part of the IR.

Selecting an appropriate IR for a compiler project requires an understanding of the source language, the target machine, and the properties of the applications that the compiler will translate. For example, a source-to-source translator might use an IR that closely resembles the source code, while a compiler that produces assembly code for a microcontroller might obtain better results with an assembly-code-like IR. Similarly, a compiler for C might need annotations about pointer values that are irrelevant in a compiler for Perl, and a Java compiler keeps records about the class hierarchy that have no counterpart in a C compiler.

Implementing an IR forces the compiler writer to focus on practical issues. The compiler needs inexpensive ways to perform the operations that it does frequently. It needs concise ways to express the full range of constructs that might arise during compilation. The compiler writer also needs mechanisms that let humans examine the IR program easily and directly. Self-interest should ensure that compiler writers pay heed to this last point. Finally, compilers that use an IR almost always make multiple passes over the IR for a program. The ability to gather information in one pass and use it in another improves the quality of code that a compiler can generate.

The $\Rightarrow$ symbol in ILOC serves no purpose except to improve readability.

### 5.1.1 **A Taxonomy of Intermediate Representations**

Compilers have used many kinds of IR. We will organize our discussion of IRs along three axes: structural organization, level of abstraction, and naming discipline. In general, these three attributes are independent; most combinations of organization, abstraction, and naming have been used in some compiler.

Broadly speaking, IRs fall into three structural categories:

- *Graphical IRs* encode the compiler's knowledge in a graph. The algorithms are expressed in terms of graphical objects: nodes, edges, lists, or trees. The parse trees used to depict derivations in Chapter 3 are a graphical IR.
- *Linear IRs* resemble pseudo-code for some abstract machine. The algorithms iterate over simple, linear sequences of operations. The ILOC code used in this book is a form of linear IR.
- *Hybrid IRs* combine elements of both graphical and linear IRs, in an attempt to capture their strengths and avoid their weaknesses. A common hybrid representation uses a low-level linear IR to represent blocks of straight-line code and a graph to represent the flow of control among those blocks.

The structural organization of an IR has a strong impact on how the compiler writer thinks about analysis, optimization, and code generation. For example, treelike IRs lead naturally to passes structured as some form of treewalk. Similarly, linear IRs lead naturally to passes that iterate over the operations in order.

The second axis of our IR taxonomy is the level of abstraction at which the IR represents operations. The IR can range from a near-source representation in which a single node might represent an array access or a procedure call to a low-level representation in which several IR operations must be combined to form a single target-machine operation.

To illustrate the possibilities, assume that $A[1...10, 1...10]$ is an array of four-byte elements stored in row-major order and consider how the compiler might represent the array reference $A[i,j]$ in a source-level tree and in ILOC.

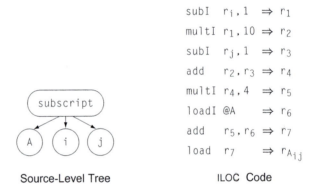

```
subI   r_i,1  ⇒ r_1
multI  r_1,10 ⇒ r_2
subI   r_j,1  ⇒ r_3
add    r_2,r_3 ⇒ r_4
multI  r_4,4  ⇒ r_5
loadI  @A     ⇒ r_6
add    r_5,r_6 ⇒ r_7
load   r_7    ⇒ r_Aij
```

Source-Level Tree · ILOC Code

In the source-level tree, the compiler can easily recognize the computation as an array reference; the ILOC code obscures that fact fairly well. In a compiler that tries to determine when two different references can touch the same memory location, the source-level tree makes it easy to find and compare references. By contrast, the ILOC code makes those tasks hard. Optimization only makes the situation worse; in the ILOC code, optimization might move parts of the address computation elsewhere. The tree node will remain intact under optimization.

On the other hand, if the goal is to optimize the target-machine code generated for the array access, the ILOC code lets the compiler optimize details that remain implicit in the source-level tree. For this purpose, a low-level IR may prove better.

Not all tree-based IRs use a near-source-level of abstraction. To be sure, parse trees are implicitly related to the source code, but trees with other levels of abstraction have been used in many compilers. Many C compilers, for example, have used low-level expression trees. Similarly, linear IRs can have relatively high-level constructs, such as a `max` or a `min` operator, or a string-copy operation.

The third axis of our IR taxonomy deals with the name space used to represent values in the code. In translating source code to a lower-level form, the compiler must choose names for a variety of distinct values. For example, to evaluate a - 2 × b in a low-level IR, the compiler might generate a sequence of operations such as those shown in the margin. Here, the compiler has used four names, $t_1$ through $t_4$. An equally valid scheme would replace the occurrences of $t_2$ and $t_4$ with $t_1$, which cuts the number of names in half.

$$t_1 \leftarrow b$$
$$t_2 \leftarrow 2 \times t_1$$
$$t_3 \leftarrow a$$
$$t_4 \leftarrow t_3 - t_2$$

The choice of a naming scheme has a strong effect on how optimization can improve the code. If the subexpression 2 - b has a unique name, the compiler might find other evaluations of 2 - b that it can replace with a reference to the value produced here. If the name is reused, the current value may not be available at the subsequent, redundant evaluation. The choice of a naming scheme also has an impact on compile time, because it determines the sizes of many compile-time data structures.

As a practical matter, the costs of generating and manipulating an IR should concern the compiler writer, since they directly affect a compiler's speed. The data-space requirements of different IRs vary over a wide range. Since the compiler typically touches all of the space that it allocates, data space usually has a direct relationship to running time. To make this discussion concrete, consider the IRs used in two different research systems that we built at Rice University.

■ The $\mathcal{R}^n$ Programming Environment built an abstract syntax tree for FORTRAN. Nodes in the tree occupied 92 bytes each. The parser built an average of eleven nodes per FORTRAN source line, for a size of just over 1,000 bytes per source-code line.

■ The MSCP research compiler used a full-scale implementation of ILOC. (The ILOC in this book is a simple subset.) ILOC operations occupy 23 to 25 bytes. The compiler generates an average of roughly fifteen ILOC operations per source-code line, or about 375 bytes per source-code line. Optimization reduces the size to just over three operations per source-code line, or fewer than 100 bytes per source-code line.

Finally, the compiler writer should consider the expressiveness of the IR—its ability to accommodate all the facts that the compiler needs to record. The IR for a procedure might include the code that defines it, the results of static analysis, profile data from previous executions, and maps to let the debugger understand the code and its data. All of these facts should be expressed in a way that makes clear their relationship to specific points in the IR.

## 5.2 GRAPHICAL IRS

Many compilers use IRs that represent the underlying code as a graph. While all the graphical IRs consist of nodes and edges, they differ in their level of abstraction, in the relationship between the graph and the underlying code, and in the structure of the graph.

### 5.2.1 Syntax-Related Trees

The parse trees shown in Chapter 3 are graphs that represent the source-code form of the program. Parse trees are one specific form of treelike IRs. In most treelike IRs, the structure of the tree corresponds to the syntax of the source code.

#### Parse Trees

As we saw in Section 3.2.2, the *parse tree* is a graphical representation for the derivation, or parse, that corresponds to the input program. Figure 5.1 shows the classic expression grammar alongside a parse tree for $a \times 2 + a \times 2 \times b$. The parse tree is large relative to the source text because it represents the complete derivation, with a node for each grammar symbol in the derivation. Since the compiler must allocate memory for each node and each edge, and it must traverse all those nodes and edges during compilation, it is worth considering ways to shrink this parse tree.

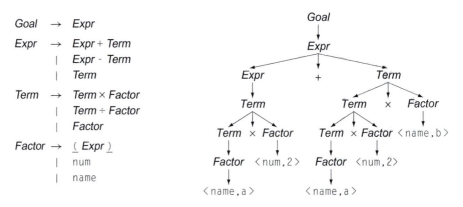

(a) Classic Expression Grammar          (b) Parse Tree for $a \times 2 + a \times 2 \times b$

■ **FIGURE 5.1** Parse Tree for $a \times 2 + a \times 2 \times b$ Using the Classic Expression Grammar.

Minor transformations on the grammar, as described in Section 3.6.1, can eliminate some of the steps in the derivation and their corresponding syntax-tree nodes. A more effective technique is to abstract away those nodes that serve no real purpose in the rest of the compiler. This approach leads to a simplified version of the parse tree, called an abstract syntax tree.

Parse trees are used primarily in discussions of parsing, and in attribute-grammar systems, where they are the primary IR. In most other applications in which a source-level tree is needed, compiler writers tend to use one of the more concise alternatives, described in the remainder of this subsection.

### Abstract Syntax Trees

The *abstract syntax tree* (AST) retains the essential structure of the parse tree but eliminates the extraneous nodes. The precedence and meaning of the expression remain, but extraneous nodes have disappeared. Here is the AST for $a \times 2 + a \times 2 \times b$:

**Abstract syntax tree**
An AST is a contraction of the parse tree that omits most nodes for nonterminal symbols.

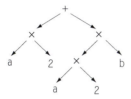

The AST is a near-source-level representation. Because of its rough correspondence to a parse tree, the parser can built an AST directly (see Section 4.4.2).

ASTs have been used in many practical compiler systems. Source-to-source systems, including syntax-directed editors and automatic parallelization tools, often use an AST from which source code can easily be regenerated. The S-expressions found in Lisp and Scheme implementations are, essentially, ASTs.

Even when the AST is used as a near-source-level representation, representation choices affect usability. For example, the AST in the $\mathcal{R}^n$ Programming Environment used the subtree shown in the margin to represent a `complex` constant in FORTRAN, written $(c_1, c_2)$. This choice worked well for the syntax-directed editor, in which the programmer was able to change $c_1$ and $c_2$ independently; the `pair` node corresponded to the parentheses and the comma.

This pair format, however, proved problematic for the compiler. Each part of the compiler that dealt with constants needed special-case code for complex constants. All other constants were represented with a single

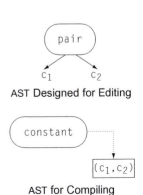

AST Designed for Editing

AST for Compiling

---

**STORAGE EFFICIENCY AND GRAPHICAL REPRESENTATIONS**

Many practical systems have used abstract syntax trees to represent the source text being translated. A common problem encountered in these systems is the size of the AST relative to the input text. Large data structures can limit the size of programs that the tools can handle.

The AST nodes in the $\mathcal{R}^n$ Programming Environment were large enough that they posed a problem for the limited memory systems of 1980s workstations. The cost of disk I/O for the trees slowed down all the $\mathcal{R}^n$ tools.

No single problem leads to this explosion in AST size. $\mathcal{R}^n$ had only one kind of node, so that structure included all the fields needed by any node. This simplified allocation but increased the node size. (Roughly half the nodes were leaves, which need no pointers to children.) In other systems, the nodes grow through the addition of myriad minor fields used by one pass or another in the compiler. Sometimes, the node size increases over time, as new features and passes are added.

Careful attention to the form and content of the AST can shrink its size. In $\mathcal{R}^n$, we built programs to analyze the contents of the AST and how the AST was used. We combined some fields and eliminated others. (In some cases, it was less expensive to recompute information than to write it and read it.) In a few cases, we used hash linking to record unusual facts—using one bit in the field that stores each node's type to indicate the presence of additional information stored in a hash table. (This scheme reduced the space devoted to fields that were rarely used.) To record the AST on disk, we converted it to a linear representation with a preorder treewalk; this eliminated the need to record any internal pointers.

In $\mathcal{R}^n$, these changes reduced the size of ASTs in memory by roughly 75 percent. On disk, after the pointers were removed, the files were about half the size of their memory representation. These changes let $\mathcal{R}^n$ handle larger programs and made the tools more responsive.

---

node that contained a pointer to the constant's actual text. Using a similar format for complex constants would have complicated some operations, such as editing the complex constants and loading them into registers. It would have simplified others, such as comparing two constants. Taken over the entire system, the simplifications would likely have outweighed the complications.

Abstract syntax trees have found widespread use. Many compilers and interpreters use them; the level of abstraction that those systems need varies widely. If the compiler generates source code as its output, the AST typically has source-level abstractions. If the compiler generates assembly code, the final version of the AST is usually at or below the abstraction level of the machine's instruction set.

## Directed Acyclic Graphs

While the AST is more concise than a syntax tree, it faithfully retains the structure of the original source code. For example, the AST for a × 2 + a × 2 × b contains two distinct copies of the expression a × 2. A *directed acyclic graph* (DAG) is a contraction of the AST that avoids this duplication. In a DAG, nodes can have multiple parents, and identical subtrees are reused. Such sharing makes the DAG more compact than the corresponding AST.

For expressions without assignment, textually identical expressions must produce identical values. The DAG for a × 2 + a × 2 × b, shown to the left, reflects this fact by sharing a single copy of a × 2. The DAG encodes an explicit hint for evaluating the expression. If the value of a cannot change between the two uses of a, then the compiler should generate code to evaluate a × 2 once and use the result twice. This strategy can reduce the cost of evaluation. However, the compiler must prove that a's value cannot change. If the expression contains neither assignment nor calls to other procedures, the proof is easy. Since an assignment or a procedure call can change the value associated with a name, the DAG construction algorithm must invalidate subtrees as the values of their operands change.

DAGS are used in real systems for two reasons. If memory constraints limit the size of programs that the compiler can handle, using a DAG can help by reducing the memory footprint. Other systems use DAGS to expose redundancies. Here, the benefit lies in better compiled code. These latter systems tend to use the DAG as a derivative IR—building the DAG, transforming the definitive IR to reflect the redundancies, and discarding the DAG.

## Level of Abstraction

All of our example trees so far have shown near-source IRs. Compilers also use low-level trees. Tree-based techniques for optimization and code generation, in fact, may require such detail. As an example, consider the statement w ← a - 2 × b. A source-level AST creates a concise form, as shown in Figure 5.2a. However, the source-level tree lacks much of the detail needed to translate the statement into assembly code. A low-level tree, shown in Figure 5.2b, can make that detail explicit. This tree introduces four new node types. A val node represents a value already in a register. A num node represents a known constant. A lab node represents an assembly-level label, typically a relocatable symbol. Finally, ◆ is an operator that dereferences a value; it treats the value as a memory address and returns the contents of the memory at that address.

**Directed acyclic graph**
A DAG is an AST with sharing. Identical subtrees are instantiated once, with multiple parents.

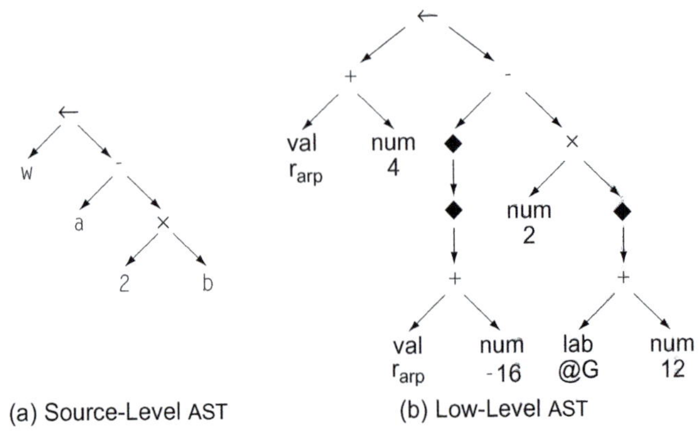

(a) Source-Level AST    (b) Low-Level AST

■ **FIGURE 5.2** Abstract Syntax Trees with Different Levels of Abstraction.

**Data area**

The compiler groups together storage for values that have the same lifetime and visibility. We call these blocks of storage *data areas*.

The low-level tree reveals the address calculations for the three variables. w is stored at offset 4 from the pointer in $r_{arp}$, which holds the pointer to the data area for the current procedure. The double dereference of a shows that it is a call-by-reference formal parameter accessed through a pointer stored 16 bytes before $r_{arp}$. Finally, b is stored at offset 12 after the label @G.

The level of abstraction matters because the compiler can, in general, only optimize details that are exposed in the IR. Properties that are implicit in the IR are hard to change, in part because the compiler would need to translate implicit facts in different, instance-specific ways. For example, to customize the code generated for an array reference, the compiler must rewrite the related IR expressions. In a real program, different array references are optimized in different ways, each according to the surrounding context. For the compiler to tailor those references, it must be able to write down the improvements in the IR.

As a final point, notice that the representations for the variable references in the low-level tree reflect the different interpretations that occur on the right and left side of the assignment. On the left-hand side, w evaluates to an address, while both a and b evaluate to values because of the ◆ operator.

### 5.2.2 Graphs

While trees provide a natural representation for the grammatical structure of the source code discovered by parsing, their rigid structure makes them less useful for representing other properties of programs. To model these aspects of program behavior, compilers often use more general graphs as IRs. The DAG introduced in the previous section is one example of a graph.

### Control-Flow Graph

The simplest unit of control flow in a program is a *basic block*—a maximal length sequence of straightline, or branch-free, code. A basic block is a sequence of operations that always execute together, unless an operation raises an exception. Control always enters a basic block at its first operation and exits at its last operation.

**Basic block**
a maximal-length sequence of branch-free code

It begins with a labelled operation and ends with a branch, jump, or predicated operation.

A *control-flow graph* (CFG) models the flow of control between the basic blocks in a program. A CFG is a directed graph, $G = (N, E)$. Each node $n \in N$ corresponds to a basic block. Each edge $e = (n_i, n_j) \in E$ corresponds to a possible transfer of control from block $n_i$ to block $n_j$.

**Control-flow graph**
A CFG has a node for every basic block and an edge for each possible control transfer between blocks.

We use the acronym CFG for both *context-free grammar* (see page 86) and *control-flow graph*. The meaning should be clear from context.

To simplify the discussion of program analysis in Chapters 8 and 9, we assume that each CFG has a unique entry node, $n_0$, and a unique exit node, $n_f$. In the CFG for a procedure, $n_0$ corresponds to the procedure's entry point. If a procedure has multiple entries, the compiler can insert a unique $n_0$ and add edges from $n_0$ to each actual entry point. Similarly, $n_f$ corresponds to the procedure's exit. Multiple exits are more common than multiple entries, but the compiler can easily add a unique $n_f$ and connect each of the actual exits to it.

The CFG provides a graphical representation of the possible runtime control-flow paths. The CFG differs from the syntax-oriented IRs, such as an AST, in which the edges show grammatical structure. Consider the following CFG for a while loop:

The edge from *stmt*$_1$ back to the loop header creates a cycle; the AST for this fragment would be acyclic. For an if-then-else construct, the CFG is acyclic:

It shows that control always flows from *stmt*$_1$ and *stmt*$_2$ to *stmt*$_3$. In an AST, that connection is implicit, rather than explicit.

Compilers typically use a CFG in conjunction with another IR. The CFG represents the relationships among blocks, while the operations inside a block

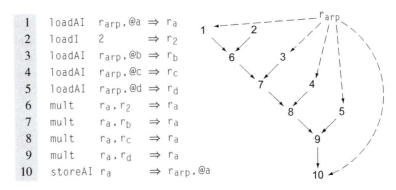

```
 1   loadAI   r_arp,@a  ⇒  r_a
 2   loadI    2         ⇒  r_2
 3   loadAI   r_arp,@b  ⇒  r_b
 4   loadAI   r_arp,@c  ⇒  r_c
 5   loadAI   r_arp,@d  ⇒  r_d
 6   mult     r_a,r_2   ⇒  r_a
 7   mult     r_a,r_b   ⇒  r_a
 8   mult     r_a,r_c   ⇒  r_a
 9   mult     r_a,r_d   ⇒  r_a
10   storeAI  r_a       ⇒  r_arp,@a
```

■ **FIGURE 5.3** An ILOC Basic Block and Its Dependence Graph.

are represented with another IR, such as an expression-level AST, a DAG, or one of the linear IRs. The resulting combination is a hybrid IR.

Some authors recommend building CFGs in which each node represents a shorter segment of code than a basic block. The most common alternative block is a *single-statement block*. Using single-statement blocks can simplify algorithms for analysis and optimization.

**Single-statement blocks**
a block of code that corresponds to a single source-level statement

The tradeoff between a CFG built with single-statement blocks and one built with basic blocks revolves around time and space. A CFG built on single-statement blocks has more nodes and edges than a CFG built with basic blocks. The single-statement version uses more memory and takes longer to traverse than the basic-block version of a CFG. More important, as the compiler annotates the nodes and edges in the CFG, the single-statement CFG has many more sets than the basic-block CFG. The time and space spent in constructing and using these annotations undoubtedly dwarfs the cost of CFG construction.

Many parts of the compiler rely on a CFG, either explicitly or implicitly. Analysis to support optimization generally begins with control-flow analysis and CFG construction (Chapter 9). Instruction scheduling needs a CFG to understand how the scheduled code for individual blocks flows together (Chapter 12). Global register allocation relies on a CFG to understand how often each operation might execute and where to insert loads and stores for spilled values (Chapter 13).

### Dependence Graph

**Data-dependence graph**
a graph that models the flow of values from definitions to uses in a code fragment

Compilers also use graphs to encode the flow of values from the point where a value is created, a *definition*, to any point where it is used, a *use*. A *data-dependence graph* embodies this relationship. Nodes in a data-dependence

```
1    x ← 0
2    i ← 1
3    while (i < 100)
4      if (a[i] > 0)
5        then x ← x + a[i]
6        i ← i + 1
7    print x
```

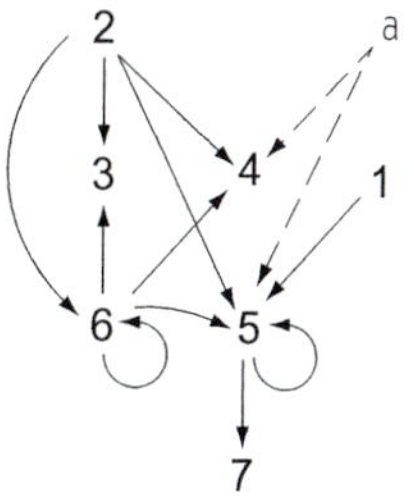

**■ FIGURE 5.4** Interaction between Control Flow and the Dependence Graph.

graph represent operations. Most operations contain both definitions and uses. An edge in a data-dependence graph connects two nodes, one that defines a value and another that uses it. We draw dependence graphs with edges that run from definition to use.

To make this concrete, Figure 5.3 reproduces the example from Figure 1.3 and shows its data-dependence graph. The graph has a node for each statement in the block. Each edge shows the flow of a single value. For example, the edge from 3 to 7 reflects the definition of $r_b$ in statement 3 and its subsequent use in statement 7. $r_{arp}$ contains the starting address of the local data area. Uses of $r_{arp}$ refer to its implicit definition at the start of the procedure; they are shown with dashed lines.

The edges in the graph represent real constraints on the sequencing of operations—a value cannot be used until it has been defined. However, the dependence graph does not fully capture the program's control flow. For example, the graph requires that 1 and 2 precede 6. Nothing, however, requires that 1 or 2 precedes 3. Many execution sequences preserve the dependences shown in the code, including $\langle 1, 2, 3, 4, 5, 6, 7, 8, 9, 10 \rangle$ and $\langle 2, 1, 6, 3, 7, 4, 8, 5, 9, 10 \rangle$. The freedom in this partial order is precisely what an "out-of-order" processor exploits.

At a higher level, consider the code fragment shown in Figure 5.4. References to a[i] are shown deriving their values from a node representing prior definitions of a. This connects all uses of a together through a single node. Without sophisticated analysis of the subscript expressions, the compiler cannot differentiate between references to individual array elements.

This dependence graph is more complex than the previous example. Nodes 5 and 6 both depend on themselves; they use values that they may have defined in a previous iteration. Node 6, for example, can take the value of i from either 2 (in the initial iteration) or from itself (in any subsequent iteration). Nodes 4 and 5 also have two distinct sources for the value of i: nodes 2 and 6.

Data-dependence graphs are often used as a derivative IR—constructed from the definitive IR for a specific task, used, and then discarded. They play a central role in instruction scheduling (Chapter 12). They find application in a variety of optimizations, particularly transformations that reorder loops to expose parallelism and to improve memory behavior; these typically require sophisticated analysis of array subscripts to determine more precisely the patterns of access to arrays. In more sophisticated applications of the data-dependence graph, the compiler may perform extensive analysis of array subscript values to determine when references to the same array can overlap.

### Call Graph

**Interprocedural**

Any technique that examines interactions across multiple procedures is called *interprocedural*.

**Intraprocedural**

Any technique that limits its attention to a single procedure is called *intraprocedural*.

**Call graph**

a graph that represents the calling relationships among the procedures in a program

The call graph has a node for each procedure and an edge for each call site.

To address inefficiencies that arise across procedure boundaries, some compilers perform *interprocedural* analysis and optimization. To represent the runtime transfers of control between procedures, compilers use a *call graph*. A call graph has a node for each procedure and an edge for each distinct procedure call site. Thus, the code calls $q$ from three textually distinct sites in $p$; the call graph has three edges $(p, q)$, one for each call site.

Both software-engineering practice and language features complicate the construction of a call graph.

- Separate compilation, the practice of compiling small subsets of a program independently, limits the compiler's ability to build a call graph and to perform interprocedural analysis and optimization. Some compilers build partial call graphs for all of the procedures in a compilation unit and perform analysis and optimization across that set. To analyze and optimize the whole program in such a system, the programmer must present it all to the compiler at once.
- Procedure-valued parameters, both as input parameters and as return values, complicate call-graph construction by introducing ambiguous call sites. If fee takes a procedure-valued argument and invokes it, that site has the potential to call a different procedure on each invocation of fee. The compiler must perform an interprocedural analysis to limit the set of edges that such a call induces in the call graph.
- Object-oriented programs with inheritance routinely create ambiguous procedure calls that can only be resolved with additional type information. In some languages, interprocedural analysis of the class hierarchy can provide the information needed to disambiguate these calls. In other languages, that information cannot be known until runtime. Runtime resolution of ambiguous calls poses a serious problem for call graph construction; it also creates significant runtime overheads on the execution of the ambiguous calls.

Section 9.4 discusses practical techniques for call graph construction.

**SECTION REVIEW**

Graphical IRs present an abstract view of the code being compiled. They differ in the meaning imputed to each node and each edge.

- In a parse tree, nodes represent syntactic elements in the source-language grammar, while the edges tie those elements together into a derivation.
- In an abstract syntax tree or a dag, nodes represent concrete items from the source-language program, and edges tie those together in a way that indicates control-flow relationships and the flow of data.
- In a control-flow graph, nodes represent blocks of code and edges represent transfers of control between blocks. The definition of a block may vary, from a single statement through a basic block.
- In a dependence graph, the nodes represent computations and the edges represent the flow of values from definitions to uses; as such, edges also imply a partial order on the computations.
- In a call graph, the nodes represent individual procedures and the edges represent individual call sites. Each call site has a distinct edge to provide a representation for call-site specific knowledge, such as parameter bindings.

Graphical IRs encode relationships that may be difficult to represent in a linear IR. A graphical IR can provide the compiler with an efficient way to move between logically connected points in the program, such as the definition of a variable and its use, or the source of a conditional branch and its target.

**Review Questions**

1. Compare and contrast the difficulty of writing a *prettyprinter* for a parse tree, an AST and a DAG. What additional information would be needed to reproduce the original code's format precisely?

2. How does the number of edges in a dependence graph grow as a function of the input program's size?

**Prettyprinter**
a program that walks a syntax tree and writes out the original code

## 5.3 LINEAR IRS

The alternative to a graphical IR is a linear IR. An assembly-language program is a form of linear code. It consists of a sequence of instructions that execute in their order of appearance (or in an order consistent with that order). Instructions may contain more than one operation; if so, those operations execute in parallel. The linear IRs used in compilers resemble the assembly code for an abstract machine.

The logic behind using a linear form is simple. The source code that serves as input to the compiler is a linear form, as is the target-machine code that it emits. Several early compilers used linear IRs; this was a natural notation for their authors, since they had previously programmed in assembly code.

Linear IRs impose a clear and useful ordering on the sequence of operations. For example, in Figure 5.3, contrast the ILOC code with the data-dependence graph. The ILOC code has an implicit order; the dependence graph imposes a partial ordering that allows many different execution orders.

If a linear IR is used as the definitive representation in a compiler, it must include a mechanism to encode transfers of control among points in the program. Control flow in a linear IR usually models the implementation of control flow on the target machine. Thus, linear codes usually include conditional branches and jumps. Control flow demarcates the basic blocks in a linear IR; blocks end at branches, at jumps, or just before labelled operations.

**Taken branch**
In most ISAs, conditional branches use one label. Control flows either to the label, called the *taken branch*, or to the operation that follows the label, called the *not-taken* or *fall-through branch*.

In the ILOC used throughout this book, we include a branch or jump at the end of every block. In ILOC, the branch operations specify a label for both the taken path and the not-taken path. This eliminates any fall-through paths at the end of a block. Together, these stipulations make it easier to find basic blocks and to reorder them.

Many kinds of linear IRs have been used in compilers.

- One-address codes model the behavior of accumulator machines and stack machines. These codes expose the machine's use of implicit names so that the compiler can tailor the code for it. The resulting code is quite compact.

**Destructive operation**
an operation in which one of the operands is always redefined with the result

- Two-address codes model a machine that has destructive operations. These codes fell into disuse as memory constraints became less important; a three-address code can model destructive operations explicitly.
- Three-address codes model a machine where most operations take two operands and produce a result. The rise of RISC architectures in the 1980s and 1990s made these codes popular, since they resemble a simple RISC machine.

The remainder of this section describes two linear IRs that remain popular: stack-machine code and three-address code. Stack-machine code offers a compact, storage-efficient representation. In applications where IR size matters, such as a Java applet transmitted over a network before execution, stack-machine code makes sense. Three-address code models the instruction format of a modern RISC machine; it has distinct names for two operands and a result. You are already familiar with one three-address code: the ILOC used in this book.

### 5.3.1 **Stack-Machine Code**

Stack-machine code, a form of one-address code, assumes the presence of a stack of operands. Most operations take their operands from the stack and push their results back onto the stack. For example, an integer subtract operation would remove the top two elements from the stack and push their difference onto the stack. The stack discipline creates a need for some new operations. Stack IRs usually include a `swap` operation that interchanges the top two elements of the stack. Several stack-based computers have been built; this IR seems to have appeared in response to the demands of compiling for these machines. Stack-machine code for the expression $a - 2 \times b$ appears in the margin.

```
push  2
push  b
multiply
push  a
subtract
```
Stack-Machine Code

Stack-machine code is compact. The stack creates an implicit name space and eliminates many names from the IR. This shrinks the size of a program in IR form. Using the stack, however, means that all results and arguments are transitory, unless the code explicitly moves them to memory.

Stack-machine code is simple to generate and to execute. Smalltalk 80 and Java both use bytecodes, a compact IR similar in concept to stack-machine code. The bytecodes either run in an interpreter or are translated into target-machine code just prior to execution. This creates a system with a compact form of the program for distribution and a reasonably simple scheme for porting the language to a new target machine (implementing the interpreter).

**Bytecode**
an IR designed specifically for its compact form; typically code for an abstract stack machine

The name derives from its limited size; opcodes are limited to one byte or less.

### 5.3.2 **Three-Address Code**

In three-address code most operations have the form $i \leftarrow j$ op $k$, with an operator (op), two operands (j and k) and one result (i). Some operators, such as an immediate load and a jump, will need fewer arguments. Sometimes, an operation with more than three addresses is needed. Three address code for $a - 2 \times b$ appears in the margin. ILOC is another example of a three-address code.

$$t_1 \leftarrow 2$$
$$t_2 \leftarrow b$$
$$t_3 \leftarrow t_1 \times t_2$$
$$t_4 \leftarrow a$$
$$t_5 \leftarrow t_4 - t_3$$
Three-Address Code

Three-address code is attractive for several reasons. First, three-address code is reasonably compact. Most operations consist of four items: an operation and three names. Both the operation and the names are drawn from limited sets. Operations typically require 1 or 2 bytes. Names are typically represented by integers or table indices; in either case, 4 bytes is usually enough. Second, separate names for the operands and the target give the compiler freedom to control the reuse of names and values; three-address code has no destructive operations. Three-address code introduces a new set of compiler-generated names—names that hold the results of the various operations. A carefully chosen name space can reveal new opportunities to improve the code. Finally, since many modern processors implement three-address operations, a three-address code models their properties well.

Within three-address codes, the set of specific supported operators and their level of abstraction can vary widely. Often, a three-address IR will contain mostly low-level operations, such as jumps, branches, and simple memory operations, alongside more complex operations that encapsulate control flow, such as `max` or `min`. Representing these complex operations directly makes them easier to analyze and optimize.

For example, `mvcl` (<u>mo</u>ve <u>c</u>haracters <u>l</u>ong) takes a source address, a destination address, and a character count. It copies the specified number of characters from memory beginning at the source address to memory beginning at the destination address. Some machines, like the IBM 370, implement this functionality in a single instruction (`mvcl` is a 370 opcode). On machines that do not implement the operation in hardware, it may require many operations to perform such a copy.

Adding `mvcl` to the three-address code lets the compiler use a compact representation for this complex operation. It allows the compiler to analyze, optimize, and move the operation without concern for its internal workings. If the hardware supports an `mvcl`-like operation, then code generation will map the IR construct directly to the hardware operation. If the hardware does not, then the compiler can translate `mvcl` into a sequence of lower-level IR operations or a procedure call before final optimization and code generation.

### 5.3.3 Representing Linear Codes

Many data structures have been used to implement linear IRs. The choices that a compiler writer makes affect the costs of various operations on IR code. Since a compiler spends most of its time manipulating the IR form of the code, these costs deserve some attention. While this discussion focuses on three-address codes, most of the points apply equally to stack-machine code (or any other linear form).

Three-address codes are often implemented as a set of quadruples. Each quadruple is represented with four fields: an operator, two operands (or sources), and a destination. To form blocks, the compiler needs a mechanism to connect individual quadruples. Compilers implement quadruples in a variety of ways.

$$t_1 \leftarrow 2$$
$$t_2 \leftarrow b$$
$$t_3 \leftarrow t_1 \times t_2$$
$$t_4 \leftarrow a$$
$$t_5 \leftarrow t_4 - t_3$$

Three-Address Code

Figure 5.5 shows three different schemes for implementing the three-address code for $a - 2 \times b$, repeated in the margin. The simplest scheme, in

| Target | Op | Arg₁ | Arg₂ |
|--------|-----|------|------|
| $t_1$ | ← | 2 | |
| $t_2$ | ← | b | |
| $t_3$ | × | $t_1$ | $t_2$ |
| $t_4$ | ← | a | |
| $t_5$ | - | $t_4$ | $t_3$ |

(a) Simple Array     (b) Array of Pointers     (c) Linked List

■ **FIGURE 5.5** Implementations of Three-Address Code for $a - 2 \times b$.

Figure 5.5a, uses a short array to represent each basic block. Often, the compiler writer places the array inside a node in the CFG. (This may be the most common form of hybrid IR.) The scheme in Figure 5.5b uses an array of pointers to group quadruples into a block; the pointer array can be contained in a CFG node. The final scheme, in Figure 5.5c, links the quadruples together to form a list. It requires less storage in the CFG node, at the cost of restricting accesses to sequential traversals.

Consider the costs incurred in rearranging the code in this block. The first operation loads a constant into a register; on most machines this translates directly into an immediate load operation. The second and fourth operations load values from memory, which on most machines might incur a multicycle delay unless the values are already in the primary cache. To hide some of the delay, the instruction scheduler might move the loads of b and a in front of the immediate load of 2.

In the simple array scheme, moving the load of b ahead of the immediate load requires saving the four fields of the first operation, copying the corresponding fields from the second slot into the first slot, and overwriting the fields in the second slot with the saved values for the immediate load. The array of pointers requires the same three-step approach, except that only the pointer values must be changed. Thus, the compiler saves the pointer to the immediate load, copies the pointer to the load of b into the first slot in the array, and overwrites the second slot in the array with the saved pointer to the immediate load. For the linked list, the operations are similar, except that the complier must save enough state to let it traverse the list.

Now, consider what happens in the front end when it generates the initial round of IR. With the simple array form and the array of pointers, the compiler must select a size for the array—in effect, the number of quadruples that it expects in a block. As it generates the quadruples, it fills in the array. If the array is too large, it wastes space. If it is too small, the compiler must

**INTERMEDIATE REPRESENTATIONS IN ACTUAL USE**

In practice, compilers use a variety of IRs. Legendary FORTRAN compilers of yore, such as IBM's FORTRAN H compilers, used a combination of quadruples and control-flow graphs to represent the code for optimization. Since FORTRAN H was written in FORTRAN, it held the IR in an array.

For a long time, GCC relied on a very low-level IR, called register transfer language (RTL). In recent years, GCC has moved to a series of IRs. The parsers initially produce a near-source tree; these trees can be language specific but are required to implement parts of a common interface. That interface includes a facility for lowering the trees to the second IR, GIMPLE. Conceptually, GIMPLE consists of a language-independent, tree-like structure for control-flow constructs, annotated with three-address code for expressions and assignments. It is designed, in part, to simplify analysis. Much of GCC's new optimizer uses GIMPLE; for example, GCC builds static single-assignment form on top of GIMPLE. Ultimately, GCC translates GIMPLE into RTL for final optimization and code generation.

The LLVM compiler uses a single low-level IR; in fact, the name LLVM stands for "low-level virtual machine." LLVM's IR is a linear three-address code. The IR is fully typed and has explicit support for array and structure addresses. It provides support for vector or SIMD data and operations. Scalar values are maintained in SSA form throughout the compiler. The LLVM environment uses GCC front ends, so LLVM IR is produced by a pass that performs GIMPLE-to-LLVM translation.

The Open64 compiler, an open-source compiler for the IA-64 architecture, uses a family of five related IRs, called WHIRL. The initial translation in the parser produces a near-source-level WHIRL. Subsequent phases of the compiler introduce more detail to the WHIRL program, lowering the level of abstraction toward the actual machine code. This lets the compiler use a source-level AST for dependence-based transformations on the source text and a low-level IR for the late stages of optimization and code generation.

reallocate it to obtain a larger array, copy the contents of the "too small" array into the new, larger array, and deallocate the small array. The linked list, however, avoids these problems. Expanding the list just requires allocating a new quadruple and setting the appropriate pointer in the list.

A multipass compiler may use different implementations to represent the IR at different points in the compilation process. In the front end, where the focus is on generating the IR, a linked list might both simplify the implementation and reduce the overall cost. In an instruction scheduler, with its focus on rearranging the operations, either of the array implementations might make more sense.

Notice that some information is missing from Figure 5.5. For example, no labels are shown because labels are a property of the block rather than any individual quadruple. Storing a list of labels with the block saves space in each quadruple; it also makes explicit the property that labels occur only on the first operation in a basic block. With labels attached to a block, the compiler can ignore them when reordering operations inside the block, avoiding one more complication.

### 5.3.4 Building a Control-Flow Graph from a Linear Code

Compilers often must convert between different IRS, often different styles of IRS. One routine conversion is to build a CFG from a linear IR such as ILOC. The essential features of a CFG are that it identifies the beginning and end of each basic block and connects the resulting blocks with edges that describe the possible transfers of control among blocks. Often, the compiler must build a CFG from a simple, linear IR that represents a procedure.

As a first step, the compiler must find the beginning and the end of each basic block in the linear IR. We will call the initial operation of a block a *leader*. An operation is a leader if it is the first operation in the procedure, or if it has a label that is, potentially, the target of some branch. The compiler can identify leaders in a single pass over the IR, shown in Figure 5.6a. It iterates over the operations in the program, in order, finds the labelled statements, and records them as leaders.

**Ambiguous jump**
a branch or jump whose target cannot be determined at compile time; typically, a jump to an address in a register

If the linear IR contains labels that are not used as branch targets, then treating labels as leaders may unnecessarily split blocks. The algorithm could

```
next ← 1
Leader[next++] ← 1
for i ← 1 to n
  if op_i has a label l_i then
    Leader[next++] ← i
    create a CFG node for l_i
```

```
for i ← 1 to next - 1
  j ← Leader[i] + 1
  while ( j ≤ n and op_j ∉ Leader)
    j ← j + 1
  j ← j - 1
  Last[i] ← j
  if op_j is "cbr r_k → l_1, l_2" then
    add edge from j to node for l_1
    add edge from j to node for l_2
  else if op_j is "jumpI → l_1" then
    add edge from j to node for l_1
  else if op_j is "jump → r_1" then
    add edges from j to all labelled statements
```

(a) Finding Leaders    (b) Finding Last and Adding Edges

■ **FIGURE 5.6**  Building a Control-Flow Graph.

**COMPLICATIONS IN CFG CONSTRUCTION**

Features of the IR, the target machine, and the source language can complicate CFG construction.

Ambiguous jumps may force the compiler to introduce edges that are never feasible at runtime. The compiler writer can improve this situation by including features in the IR that record potential jump targets. ILOC includes the `tbl` pseudo-operation to let the compiler record the potential targets of an ambiguous jump. Anytime the compiler generates a `jump`, it should follow the `jump` with a set of `tbl` operations that record the possible branch targets. CFG construction can use these hints to avoid spurious edges.

If the compiler builds a CFG from target-machine code, features of the target architecture can complicate the process. The algorithm in Figure 5.6 assumes that all leaders, except the first, are labelled. If the target machine has fall-through branches, the algorithm must be extended to recognize unlabeled statements that receive control on a fall-through path. PC-relative branches cause a similar set of problems.

Branch delay slots introduce several problems. A labelled statement that sits in a branch delay slot is a member of two distinct blocks. The compiler can cure this problem by replication—creating new (unlabeled) copies of the operations in the delay slots. Delay slots also complicate finding the end of a block. The compiler must place operations located in delay slots into the block that precedes the branch or jump.

If a branch or jump can occur in a branch delay slot, the CFG builder must walk forward from the leader to find the block-ending branch—the first branch it encounters. Branches in the delay slot of a block-ending branch can, themselves, be pending on entry to the target block. They can split the target block and force creation of new blocks and new edges. This kind of behavior seriously complicates CFG construction.

Some languages allow jumps to labels outside the current procedure. In the procedure containing the branch, the branch target can be modelled with a new CFG node created for that purpose. The complication arises on the other end of the branch. The compiler must know that the target label is the target of a nonlocal branch, or else subsequent analysis may produce misleading results. For this reason, languages such as Pascal or Algol restricted nonlocal gotos to labels in visible outer lexical scopes. C requires the use of the functions `setjmp` and `longjmp` to expose these transfers.

track which labels are jump targets. However, if the code contains any ambiguous jumps, then it must treat all labelled statements as leaders anyway.

The second pass, shown in Figure 5.6b, finds every block-ending operation. It assumes that every block ends with a branch or a jump and that branches specify labels for both outcomes—a "branch taken" label and a "branch not taken" label. This simplifies the handling of blocks and allows the compiler's back end to choose which path will be the "fall through" case of a branch. (For the moment, assume branches have no delay slots.)

To find the end of each block, the algorithm iterates through the blocks, in order of their appearance in the `Leader` array. It walks forward through the IR until it finds the leader of the next block. The operation immediately before that leader ends the current block. The algorithm records that operation's index in `Last[i]`, so that the pair ⟨`Leader[i]`, `Last[i]`⟩ describes block $i$. It adds edges to the CFG as needed.

For a variety of reasons, the CFG should have a unique entry node $n_0$ and a unique exit node $n_f$. The underlying code should have this shape. If it does not, a simple postpass over the graph can create $n_0$ and $n_f$.

---

**SECTION REVIEW**

Linear IRs represent the code being compiled as an ordered sequence of operations. Linear IRs can vary in their level of abstraction; the source code for a program in a plain text file is a linear form, as is the assembly code for that same program. Linear IRs lend themselves to compact, human-readable representations.

Two widely used linear IRs are bytecodes, generally implemented as a one-address code with implicit names on many operations, and three-address code, generally implemented as a set of binary operations that have distinct name fields for two operands and one result.

---

**Review Questions**

1. Consider the expression $a \times 2 + a \times 2 \times b$. Translate it into stack machine code and into three address code. Compare and contrast the number of operations and the number of operands in each form. How do they compare against the trees in Figure 5.1?

2. Sketch an algorithm to build control-flow graphs from ILOC for programs that include spurious labels and ambiguous jumps.

---

## 5.4 MAPPING VALUES TO NAMES

The choice of a specific IR and a level of abstraction helps determine what operations the compiler can manipulate and optimize. For example, a source-level AST makes it easy to find all the references to an array ×. At the same time, it hides the details of the address calculations required to access an element of ×. In contrast, a low-level, linear IR such as ILOC exposes the details of the address calculation, at the cost of obscuring the fact that a specific reference relates to ×.

Similarly, the discipline that the compiler uses to assign internal names to the various values computed during execution has an effect on the code that it can generate. A naming scheme can expose opportunities for optimization or it can obscure them. The compiler must invent names for many, if not all, of the intermediate results that the program produces when it executes. The choices that it makes with regard to names determines, to a large extent, which computations can be analyzed and optimized.

### 5.4.1 Naming Temporary Values

The IR form of a program usually contains more detail than does the source version. Some of those details are implicit in the source code; others result from deliberate choices in the translation. To see this, consider the four-line block of source code shown in Figure 5.7a. Assume that the names refer to distinct values.

The block deals with just four names, $\{ a, b, c, d \}$. It refers to more than four values. Each of $b$, $c$, and $d$ have a value before the first statement executes. The first statement computes a new value, $b+c$, as does the second, which computes $a - d$. The expression $b+c$ in the third statement computes

| | | |
|---|---|---|
| | $t_1 \leftarrow b$ | $t_1 \leftarrow b$ |
| | $t_2 \leftarrow c$ | $t_2 \leftarrow c$ |
| | $t_3 \leftarrow t_1 + t_2$ | $t_3 \leftarrow t_1 + t_2$ |
| | $a \quad \leftarrow t_3$ | $a \quad \leftarrow t_3$ |
| | $t_4 \leftarrow d$ | $t_4 \leftarrow d$ |
| | $t_1 \leftarrow t_3 - t_4$ | $t_5 \leftarrow t_3 - t_4$ |
| | $b \quad \leftarrow t_1$ | $b \quad \leftarrow t_5$ |
| $a \leftarrow b + c$ | $t_2 \leftarrow t_1 + t_2$ | $t_6 \leftarrow t_5 + t_2$ |
| $b \leftarrow a - d$ | $c \quad \leftarrow t_2$ | $c \quad \leftarrow t_6$ |
| $c \leftarrow b + c$ | $t_4 \leftarrow t_3 - t_4$ | $t_5 \leftarrow t_3 - t_4$ |
| $d \leftarrow a - d$ | $d \quad \leftarrow t_4$ | $d \quad \leftarrow t_5$ |
| (a) Source Code | (b) Source Names | (c) Value Names |

■ **FIGURE 5.7** Naming Leads to Different Translations.

a different value than the earlier b + c, unless c = d initially. Finally, the last statement computes a - d; its result is always identical to that produced by the second statement.

The source code names tell the compiler little about the values that they hold. For example, the use of b in the first and third statements refer to distinct values (unless c = d). The reuse of the name b conveys no information; in fact, it might mislead a casual reader into thinking that the code sets a and c to the same value.

When the compiler names each of these expressions, it can chose names in ways that specifically encode useful information about their values. Consider, for example, the translations shown in Figures 5.7b and 5.7c. These two variants were generated with different naming disciplines.

The code in Figure 5.7b uses fewer names than the code in 5.7c. It follows the source code names, so that a reader can easily relate the code back to the code in Figure 5.7a. The code in Figure 5.7c uses more names than the code in 5.7b. Its naming discipline reflects the computed values and ensures that textually identical expressions produce the same result. This scheme makes it obvious that a and c may receive different values, while b and d must receive the same value.

As another example of the impact of names, consider again the representation of an array reference, A[i,j]. Figure 5.8 shows two IR fragments that represent the same computation at very different levels of abstraction. The high-level IR, in Figure 5.8a, contains all the essential information and is easy to identify as a subscript reference. The low-level IR, in Figure 5.8b,

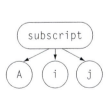

$$
\begin{array}{lll}
\text{load} & 1 & \Rightarrow r_1 \\
\text{sub} & r_j, r_1 & \Rightarrow r_2 \\
\text{loadI} & 10 & \Rightarrow r_3 \\
\text{mult} & r_2, r_3 & \Rightarrow r_4 \\
\text{sub} & r_i, r_1 & \Rightarrow r_5 \\
\text{add} & r_4, r_5 & \Rightarrow r_6 \\
\text{loadI} & @A & \Rightarrow r_7 \\
\text{add} & r_7, r_6 & \Rightarrow r_8 \\
\text{load} & r_8 & \Rightarrow r_{A_{ij}} \\
\end{array}
$$

(a) Source-Level Abstract Syntax Tree     (b) Low-Level Linear Code (ILOC)

■ **FIGURE 5.8** Different Levels of Abstraction for an Array Subscript Reference .

exposes many details to the compiler that are implicit in the high-level AST fragment. All of the details in the low-level IR can be inferred from the source-level AST.

In the low-level IR, each intermediate result has its own name. Using distinct names exposes those results to analysis and transformation. In practice, most of the improvement that compilers achieve in optimization arises from capitalizing on context. To make that improvement possible, the IR must expose the context. Naming can hide context, as when it reuses one name for many distinct values. It can also expose context, as when it creates a correspondence between names and values. This issue is not specifically a property of linear codes; the compiler could use a lower-level AST that exposed the entire address computation.

## 5.4.2 Static Single-Assignment Form

**SSA form**

an IR that has a value-based name system, created by renaming and use of pseudo-operations called $\phi$-functions

SSA encodes both control and value flow. It is used widely in optimization (see Section 9.3).

*Static single-assignment form* (SSA) is a naming discipline that many modern compilers use to encode information about both the flow of control and the flow of data values in the program. In SSA form, names correspond uniquely to specific definition points in the code; each name is defined by one operation, hence the name static single assignment. As a corollary, each use of a name as an argument in some operation encodes information about where the value originated; the textual name refers to a specific definition point. To reconcile this single-assignment naming discipline with the effects of control flow, SSA form inserts special operations, called $\phi$-functions, at points where control-flow paths meet.

**$\phi$-function**

A $\phi$-function takes several names and merges them, defining a new name.

A program is in SSA form when it meets two constraints: (1) each definition has a distinct name; and (2) each use refers to a single definition. To transform an IR program to SSA form, the compiler inserts $\phi$-functions at points where different control-flow paths merge and it then renames variables to make the single-assignment property hold.

To clarify the impact of these rules, consider the small loop shown on the left side of Figure 5.9. The right column shows the same code in SSA form. Variable names include subscripts to create a distinct name for each definition. $\phi$-functions have been inserted at points where multiple distinct values can reach the start of a block. Finally, the while construct has been rewritten with two distinct tests, to reflect the fact that the initial test refers to $x_0$ while the end-of-loop test refers to $x_2$.

The $\phi$-function's behavior depends on context. It defines its target SSA name with the value of its argument that corresponds to the edge along which

```
                                    x₀ ← ...
                                    y₀ ← ...
                                    if (x₀ ≥ 100) goto next
      x ← ...
                              loop: x₁ ← φ(x₀,x₂)
      y ← ...
                                    y₁ ← φ(y₀,y₂)
      while(x < 100)
                                    x₂ ← x₁ + 1
        x ← x + 1
                                    y₂ ← y₁ + x₂
        y ← y + x
                                    if (x₂ < 100) goto loop
                              next: x₃ ← φ(x₀,x₂)
                                    y₃ ← φ(y₀,y₂)

     (a) Original Code              (b) Code in SSA Form
```

■ **FIGURE 5.9** A Small Loop in SSA Form.

control entered the block. Thus, when control flows into the loop from the block above the loop, the $\phi$-functions at the top of the loop body copy the values of $x_0$ and $y_0$ into $x_1$ and $y_1$, respectively. When control flows into the loop from the test at the loop's bottom, the $\phi$-functions select their other arguments, $x_2$ and $y_2$.

On entry to a basic block, all of its $\phi$-functions execute concurrently, before any other statement. First, they all read the values of the appropriate arguments, then they all define their target SSA names. Defining their behavior in this way allows the algorithms that manipulate SSA form to ignore the ordering of $\phi$-functions at the top of a block—an important simplification. It can complicate the process of translating SSA form back into executable code, as we shall see in Section 9.3.5.

SSA form was intended for code optimization. The placement of $\phi$-functions in SSA form encodes information about both the creation of values and their uses. The single-assignment property of the name space allows the compiler to sidestep many issues related to the lifetimes of values; for example, because names are never redefined or killed, the value of a name is available along any path that proceeds from that operation. These two properties simplify and improve many optimization techniques.

The example exposes some oddities of SSA form that bear explanation. Consider the $\phi$-function that defines $x_1$. Its first argument, $x_0$, is defined in the block that precedes the loop. Its second argument, $x_2$, is defined later in the block labelled loop. Thus, when the $\phi$ first executes, one of its arguments is undefined. In many programming-language contexts, this would cause problems. Since the $\phi$-function reads only one argument, and that argument

**THE IMPACT OF NAMING**

In the late 1980s, we experimented with naming schemes in a FORTRAN compiler. The first version generated a new temporary register for each computation by bumping a simple counter. It produced large name spaces, for example, 985 names for a 210-line implementation of the singular value decomposition (SVD). The name space seemed large for the program size. It caused speed and space problems in the register allocator, where the size of the name space governs the size of many data structures. (Today, we have better data structures and faster machines with more memory.)

The second version used an allocate/free protocol to manage names. The front end allocated temporaries on demand and freed them when the immediate uses were finished. This scheme used fewer names; for example, SVD used roughly 60 names. It sped up allocation, reducing, for example, the time to find live variables in SVD by 60 percent.

Unfortunately, associating multiple expressions with a single temporary name obscured the flow of data and degraded the quality of optimization. The decline in code quality overshadowed any compile-time benefits.

Further experimentation led to a short set of rules that yielded strong optimization while mitigating growth in the name space.

1. Each textual expression received a unique name, determined by entering the operator and operands into a hash table. Thus, each occurrence of an expression, for example, $r_{17}+r_{21}$, targeted the same register.
2. In $\langle op\rangle$ $r_i$, $r_j$ $\Rightarrow$ $r_k$, k was chosen so that $i,j<k$.
3. Register copy operations (i2i $r_i \Rightarrow r_j$ in ILOC) were allowed to have $i>j$ only if $r_j$ corresponded to a scalar program variable. The registers for such variables were only defined by copy operations. Expressions evaluated into their "natural" register and then were moved into the register for the variable.
4. Each store operation (store $r_i \Rightarrow r_j$ in ILOC) is followed by a copy from $r_i$ into the variable's named register. (Rule 1 ensures that loads from that location always target the same register. Rule 4 ensures that the virtual register and memory location contain the same value.)

This name-space scheme used about 90 names for SVD, but exposed all the optimizations found with the first name-space scheme. The compiler used these rules until we adopted SSA form, with its discipline for names.

corresponds to the most recently taken edge in the CFG, it can never read the undefined value.

$\phi$-functions do not conform to a three-address model. A $\phi$-function takes an arbitrary number of operands. To fit SSA form into a three-address IR, the

---

**BUILDING SSA**

Static single-assignment form is the only IR we describe that does not have an obvious construction algorithm. Section 9.3 presents the algorithm in detail. However, a sketch of the construction process will clarify some of the issues. Assume that the input program is already in ILOC form. To convert it to an equivalent linear form of SSA, the compiler must first insert $\phi$-functions and then rename the ILOC virtual registers.

The simplest way to insert $\phi$-functions adds one for each ILOC virtual register at the start of each basic block that has more than one predecessor in the control-flow graph. This inserts many unneeded $\phi$-functions; most of the complexity in the full algorithm is aimed at reducing the number of extraneous $\phi$-functions.

To rename the ILOC virtual registers, the compiler can process the blocks, in a depth-first order. For each virtual register, it keeps a counter. When the compiler encounters a definition of $r_j$, it increments the counter for $r_j$, say to k, and rewrites the definition with the name $r_{j_k}$. As the compiler traverses the block, it rewrites each use of $r_j$ with $r_{j_k}$ until it encounters another definition of $r_j$. (That definition bumps the counter to $k+1$.) At the end of a block, the compiler looks down each control-flow edge and rewrites the appropriate $\phi$-function parameter for $r_j$ in each block that has multiple predecessors.

After renaming, the code conforms to the two rules of SSA form. Each definition creates a unique name. Each use refers to a single definition. Several better SSA construction algorithms exist; they insert fewer $\phi$-functions than this simple approach.

---

compiler writer must include a mechanism for representing operations with longer operand lists. Consider the block at the end of a case statement as shown in the margin.

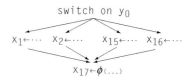

The $\phi$-function for $x_{17}$ must have an argument for each case. A $\phi$-operation has one argument for each entering control-flow path; thus, it does not fit into the fixed-arity, three-address scheme.

In a simple array representation for three-address code, the compiler writer must either use multiple slots for each $\phi$-operation or use a side data structure to hold the $\phi$-operations' arguments. In the other two schemes for implementing three-address code shown in Figure 5.5, the compiler can insert tuples of varying size. For example, the tuples for load and load immediate might have space for just two names, while the tuple for a $\phi$-operation could be large enough to accommodate all its operands.

### 5.4.3 **Memory Models**

Just as the mechanism for naming temporary values affects the information that can be represented in an IR version of a program, so, too, does the compiler's choice of a storage location for each value. The compiler must determine, for each value computed in the code, where that value will reside. For the code to execute, the compiler must assign a specific location, such as register $r_{13}$ or 16 bytes from the label L0089. Before the final stages of code generation, however, the compiler may use symbolic addresses that encode a level in the memory hierarchy, for example, registers or memory, but not a specific location within that level.

Consider the ILOC examples used throughout this book. A symbolic memory address is denoted by prefixing it with the character @. Thus, @x is the offset of $\times$ from the start of the storage area containing it. Since $r_{arp}$ holds the activation record pointer, an operation that uses @x and $r_{arp}$ to compute an address depends, implicitly, on the decision to store the variable $\times$ in the memory reserved for the current procedure's activation record.

In general, compilers work from one of two memory models.

1. *Register-to-Register Model*   Under this model, the compiler keeps values in registers aggressively, ignoring any limitations imposed by the size of the machine's physical register set. Any value that can legally be kept in a register for most of its lifetime is kept in a register. Values are stored to memory only when the semantics of the program require it—for example, at a procedure call, any local variable whose address is passed as a parameter to the called procedure must be stored back to memory. A value that cannot be kept in a register for most of its lifetime is stored in memory. The compiler generates code to store its value each time it is computed and to load its value at each use.

2. *Memory-to-Memory Model*   Under this model, the compiler assumes that all values are kept in memory locations. Values move from memory to a register just before they are used. Values move from a register to memory just after they are defined. The number of registers named in the IR version of the code can be small compared to the register-to-register model. In this model, the designer may find it worthwhile to include memory-to-memory operations, such as a memory-to-memory add, in the IR.

The choice of memory model is mostly orthogonal to the choice of IR. The compiler writer can build a memory-to-memory AST or a memory-to-memory version of ILOC just as easily as register-to-register versions of either of these

**THE HIERARCHY OF MEMORY OPERATIONS IN ILOC 9X**

The ILOC used in this book is abstracted from an IR named ILOC 9X that was used in a research compiler project at Rice University. ILOC 9X includes a hierarchy of memory operations that the compiler uses to encode knowledge about values. At the bottom of the hierarchy, the compiler has little or no knowledge about the value; at the top of the hierarchy, it knows the actual value. These operations are as follows:

| Operation | Meaning |
|---|---|
| Immediate load | Loads a known constant value into a register. |
| Nonvarying load | Loads a value that does not change during execution. The compiler does not know the value, but can prove that it is not defined by a program operation. |
| Scalar load & store | Operate on a scalar value, not an array element, a structure element, or a pointer-based value. |
| General load & store | Operate on a value that may be an array element, a structure element, or a pointer-based value. This is the general-case operation. |

By using this hierarchy, the front end can encode knowledge about the target value directly into the ILOC 9X code. As other passes discover additional information, they can rewrite operations to change a value from using a general-purpose load to a more restricted form. If the compiler discovers that some value is a known constant, it can replace a general load or a scalar load of that value with an immediate load. If an analysis of definitions and uses discovers that some location cannot be defined by any executable store operation, loads of that value can be rewritten to use a non-varying load.

Optimizations can capitalize on the knowledge encoded in this fashion. For example, a comparison between the result of a non-varying load and a constant must itself be invariant—a fact that might be difficult or impossible to prove with a scalar load or a general load.

IRS. (Stack-machine code and code for an accumulator machine might be exceptions; they contain their own unique memory models.)

The choice of memory model has an impact on the rest of the compiler. With a register-to-register model, the compiler typically uses more registers than the target machine provides. Thus, the register allocator must map the set of *virtual registers* used in the IR program onto the physical registers provided by the target machine. This often requires insertion of extra load, store, and copy operations, making the code slower and larger. With a memory-to-memory model, however, the IR version of the code typically uses fewer registers than a modern processor provides. Here, the register allocator looks for memory-based values that it can hold in registers for longer periods of time. In this model, the allocator makes the code faster and smaller by removing loads and stores.

Compilers for RISC machines tend to use the register-to-register model for two reasons. First, the register-to-register model more closely reflects the instruction sets of RISC architectures. RISC machines do not have a full complement of memory-to-memory operations; instead, they implicitly assume that values can be kept in registers. Second, the register-to-register model allows the compiler to encode directly in the IR some of the subtle facts that it derives. The fact that a value is kept in a register means that the compiler, at some earlier point, had proof that keeping it in a register is safe. Unless it encodes that fact in the IR, the compiler will need to prove it, again and again.

To elaborate, if the compiler can prove that only one name provides access to a value, it can keep that value in a register. If multiple names might exist, the compiler must behave conservatively and keep the value in memory. For example, a local variable $x$ can be kept in a register, unless it can be referenced in another scope. In a language that supports nested scopes, like Pascal or Ada, this reference can occur in a nested procedure. In C, this can occur if the program takes $x$'s address, &x, and accesses the value through that address. In Algol or PL/I, the program can pass $x$ as a call-by-reference parameter to another procedure.

---

**SECTION REVIEW**

The schemes used to name values in a compiler's IR have a direct effect on the compiler's ability to optimize the IR and to generate quality assembly code from the IR. The compiler must generate internal names for all values, from variables in the source language program to the intermediate values computed as part of an address expression for a subscripted array reference. Careful use of names can encode and expose facts for late use in optimization; at the same time, proliferation of names can slow the compiler by forcing it to use larger data structures.

The name space generated in SSA form has gained popularity because it encodes useful properties; for example, each name corresponds to a unique definition in the code. This precision can aid in optimization, as we will see in Chapter 8.

The name space can also encode a memory model. A mismatch between the memory model and the target machine's instruction set can complicate subsequent optimization and code generation, while a close match allows the compiler to tailor carefully to the target machine.

---

**Review Questions**

1. Consider the function `fib` shown in the margin. Write down the ILOC that a compiler's front end might generate for this code under a register-to-register model and under a memory-to-memory model. How do the two compare? Under what circumstances might each memory be desirable?

2. Convert the register-to-register code that you generated in the previous question into SSA form. Are there $\phi$-functions whose output value can never be used?

```
int fib(int n) {
  int x = 1;
  int y = 1;
  int z = 1;

  while(n > 1)
    z = x + y;
    x = y;
    y = z;
    n = n - 1;
  return z;
}
```

## 5.5 SYMBOL TABLES

As part of translation, a compiler derives information about the various entities manipulated by the program being translated. It must discover and store many distinct kinds of information. It encounters a wide variety of names—variables, defined constants, procedures, functions, labels, structures, and files. As discussed in the previous section, the compiler also generates many names. For a variable, it needs a data type, its storage class, the name and lexical level of its declaring procedure, and a base address and offset in memory. For an array, the compiler also needs the number of dimensions and the upper and lower bounds for each dimension. For records or structures, it needs a list of the fields, along with the relevant information for each field. For functions and procedures, it needs the number of parameters and their types, as well as the types of any returned values; a more sophisticated translation might record information about what variables a procedure can reference or modify.

The compiler must either record this information in the IR or re-derive it on demand. For the sake of efficiency, most compilers record facts rather than recompute them. These facts can be recorded directly in the IR. For example, a compiler that builds an AST might record information about variables as annotations (or attributes) of the node representing each variable's declaration. The advantage of this approach is that it uses a single representation for the code being compiled. It provides a uniform access method and a single implementation. The disadvantage of this approach is that the single access method may be inefficient—navigating the AST to find the appropriate declaration has its own costs. To eliminate this inefficiency, the compiler can thread the IR so that each reference has a link back to the corresponding declaration. This adds space to the IR and overhead to the IR builder.

When the compiler writes the IR to disk, it may be cheaper to recompute facts than to write them and then read them.

The alternative, as we saw in Chapter 4, is to create a central repository for these facts and provide efficient access to it. This central repository, called a symbol table, becomes an integral part of the compiler's IR. The symbol table localizes information derived from potentially distant parts of the source code. It makes such information easily and efficiently available, and it simplifies the design and implementation of any code that must refer to information about variables derived earlier in compilation. It avoids the expense of searching the IR to find the portion that represents a variable's declaration; using a symbol table often eliminates the need to represent the declarations directly in the IR. (An exception occurs in source-to-source translation. The compiler may build a symbol table for efficiency and preserve the declaration syntax in the IR so that it can produce an output program that closely resembles the input program.) It eliminates the overhead of making each reference contain a pointer to the declaration. It replaces both of these with a computed mapping from the textual name to the stored information. Thus, in some sense, the symbol table is simply an efficiency trick.

At many places in this text, we refer to "the symbol table." As we shall see in Section 5.5.4, the compiler may include several distinct, specialized symbol tables. A careful implementation might use the same access methods for all these tables.

Symbol-table implementation requires attention to detail. Because nearly every aspect of translation refers to the symbol table, efficiency of access is critical. Because the compiler cannot predict, before translation, the number of names that it will encounter, expanding the symbol table must be both graceful and efficient. This section provides a high-level treatment of the issues that arise in designing a symbol table. It presents the compiler-specific aspects of symbol-table design and use. For deeper implementation details and design alternatives, see Section B.4 in Appendix B.

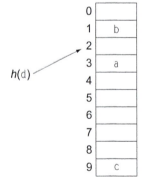

### 5.5.1 **Hash Tables**

A compiler accesses its symbol table frequently. Thus, efficiency is a key issue in the design of a symbol table. Because hash tables provide constant-time expected-case lookups, they are the method of choice for implementing symbol tables. Hash tables are conceptually elegant. They use a *hash function*, $h$, to map names to small integers, and use the small integer to index the table. With a hashed symbol table, the compiler stores all the information that it derives about the name $n$ in the table in slot $h(n)$. The figure in the margin shows a simple ten-slot hash table. It is a vector of records, each record holding the compiler-generated description of a single name. The names a, b, and c have already been inserted. The name d is being inserted, at $h(\mathsf{d}) = 2$.

The primary reason to use hash tables is to provide a constant-time expected-case lookup keyed by a textual name. To achieve this, $h$ must be inexpensive to compute. Given an appropriate function $h$, accessing the record for $n$ requires computing $h(n)$ and indexing into the table at $h(n)$. If $h$ maps two or more symbols to the same small integer, a "collision" occurs. (In the marginal figure, this would occur if $h(\mathsf{d}) = 3$.) The implementation must handle this situation gracefully, preserving both the information and the lookup time. In this section, we assume that $h$ is a perfect hash function, that is, it never produces a collision. Furthermore, we assume that the compiler knows, in advance, how large to make the table. Appendix B.4 describes hash-table implementation in more detail, including hash functions, collision handling, and schemes for expanding a hash table.

Hash tables can be used as an efficient representation for sparse graphs. Given two nodes, $x$ and $y$, an entry for the key $xy$ indicates that an edge $(x, y)$ exists. (This scheme requires a hash function that generates a good distribution from a pair of small integers; both the multiplicative and universal hash functions described in Appendix B.4.1 work well.) A well-implemented hash table can provide fast insertion and a fast test for the presence of a specific edge. Additional information is required to answer questions such as "What nodes are adjacent to $x$?"

### 5.5.2 Building a Symbol Table

The symbol table defines two interface routines for the rest of the compiler.

1. `LookUp(name)` returns the record stored in the table at $h(name)$ if one exists. Otherwise, it returns a value indicating that *name* was not found.
2. `Insert(name,record)` stores the information in `record` in the table at $h(name)$. It may expand the table to accommodate the record for *name*.

The compiler can use separate functions for `LookUp` and `Insert`, or they can be combined by passing `LookUp` a flag that specifies whether or not to insert the name. This ensures, for example, that a `LookUp` of an undeclared variable will fail—a property useful for detecting a violation of the declare-before-use rule in syntax-directed translation schemes or for supporting nested lexical scopes.

This simple interface fits directly into the ad hoc syntax-directed translation schemes described in Chapter 4. In processing declaration syntax, the compiler builds up a set of attributes for each variable. When the parser recognizes a production that declares some variable, it can enter the name and

**AN ALTERNATIVE TO HASHING**

Hashing is the method most widely used to organize a compiler's symbol table. Multiset discrimination is an interesting alternative that eliminates any possibility of worst-case behavior. The critical insight behind multiset discrimination is that the index can be constructed offline in the scanner.

To use multiset discrimination, the compiler writer must take a different approach to scanning. Instead of processing the input incrementally, the compiler scans the entire program to find the complete set of identifiers. As it discovers each identifier, it creates a tuple ⟨*name,position*⟩, where *name* is the text of the identifier and *position* is its ordinal position in the list of classified words, or *tokens*. It enters all the tuples into a large set.

The next step sorts the set lexicographically. In effect, this creates a set of subsets, one per identifier. Each of these subsets holds the tuples for all the occurrences of its identifier. Since each tuple refers to a specific token, through its *position* value, the compiler can use the sorted set to modify the token stream. The compiler makes a linear scan over the set, processing each subset. It allocates a symbol-table index for the entire subset, then rewrites the tokens to include that index. This augments the identifier tokens with their symbol-table indices. If the compiler needs a textual lookup function, the resulting table is ordered alphabetically for a binary search.

The price for using this technique is an extra pass over the token stream, along with the cost of the lexicographic sort. The advantages, from a complexity perspective, are that it avoids any possibility of hashing's worst-case behavior and that it makes the initial size of the symbol table obvious, even before parsing. This technique can be used to replace a hash table in almost any application in which an offline solution will work.

attributes into the symbol table using `Insert`. If a variable name can appear in only one declaration, the parser can call `LookUp` first to detect a repeated use of the name. When the parser encounters a variable name outside the declaration syntax, it uses `LookUp` to obtain the appropriate information from the symbol table. `LookUp` fails on any undeclared name. The compiler writer, of course, may need to add functions to initialize the table, to store it to and retrieve it from external media, and to finalize it. For a language with a single name space, this interface suffices.

### 5.5.3 Handling Nested Scopes

Few programming languages provide a single unified name space. Most languages allow a program to declare names at multiple levels. Each of these levels has a *scope*, or a region in the program's text where the name can be used. Each of these levels has a *lifetime*, or a period at runtime where the value is preserved.

If the source language allows scopes to be nested one inside another, then the front end needs a mechanism to translate a reference, such as *x*, to the proper scope and lifetime. The primary mechanism that compilers use to perform this translation is a scoped symbol table.

For the purposes of this discussion, assume that a program can create an arbitrary number of scopes nested one within another. We will defer an in-depth discussion of lexical scoping until Section 6.3.1; however, most programmers have enough experience with the concept for this discussion. Figure 5.10 shows a c program that creates five distinct scopes. We will label the scopes with numbers that indicate the nesting relationships among them. The level *0* scope is the outermost scope, while the level *3* scope is the innermost one.

The table on the right side of the figure shows the names declared in each scope. The declaration of b at level *2a* hides the level *1* declaration from any code inside the block that creates level *2a*. Inside level *2b*, a reference to b again refers to the level *1* parameter. In a similar way, the declarations

```
static int w;        /* level 0 */
int x;

void example(int a, int b) {
  int c;             /* level 1 */
  {
    int b, z;        /* level 2a */
    ...
  }
  {
    int a, x;        /* level 2b */
    ...
    {
      int c, x; /* level 3 */
      b = a + b + c + w;
    }
  }
}
```

| Level | Names |
|-------|-------|
| 0 | w, x, example |
| 1 | a, b, c |
| 2a | b, z |
| 2b | a, x |
| 3 | c, x |

■ **FIGURE 5.10**  Simple Lexical Scoping Example in C.

of a and $\times$ in level *2b* hide their earlier declarations (at level *1* and level *0*, respectively).

This context creates the naming environment in which the assignment statement executes. Subscripting names to show their level, we find that the assignment refers to

$$b_1 = a_{2b} + b_1 + c_3 + w_0$$

Notice that the assignment cannot use the names declared in level *2a* because that block closes, along with its scope, before level *2b* opens.

To compile a program that contains nested scopes, the compiler must map each variable reference to its specific declaration. This process, called *name resolution*, maps each reference to the lexical level at which it is declared. The mechanism that compilers use to accomplish this name resolution is a lexically scoped symbol table. The remainder of this section describes the design and implementation of lexically scoped symbol tables. The corresponding runtime mechanisms, which translate the lexical level of a reference to an address, are described in Section 6.4.3. Scoped symbol tables also have direct application in code optimization. For example, the superlocal value-numbering algorithm presented in Section 8.5.1 relies on a scoped hash table for efficiency.

### The Concept

To manage nested scopes, the parser must change, slightly, its approach to symbol-table management. Each time the parser enters a new lexical scope, it can create a new symbol table for that scope. This scheme creates a sheaf of tables, linked together in an order that corresponds to the lexical nesting levels. As it encounters declarations in the scope, it enters the information into the current table. *Insert* operates on the current symbol table. When it encounters a variable reference, *LookUp* must first check the table for the current scope. If the current table does not hold a declaration for the name, it checks the table for the surrounding scope. By working its way through the symbol tables for successively lower-numbered lexical levels, it either finds the most recent declaration for the name, or fails in the outermost scope, indicating that the variable has no declaration visible in the current scope.

Figure 5.11 shows the symbol table built in this fashion for our example program, at the point where the parser has reached the assignment statement. When the compiler invokes the modified *LookUp* function for the name b, it will fail in level *3*, fail in level *2*, and find the name in level *1*. This corresponds exactly to our understanding of the program—the most recent

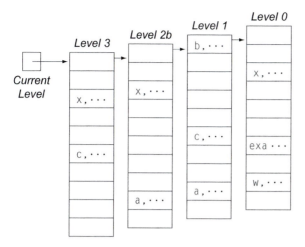

**■ FIGURE 5.11** Simple "Sheaf-of-Tables" Implementation.

declaration for b is as a parameter to example, at level *1*. Since the first block at level *2*, block *2a*, has already closed, its symbol table is not on the search chain. The level where the symbol is found, *1* in this case, forms the first part of an address for b. If the symbol-table record includes a storage off-set for each variable, then the pair ⟨*level, offset*⟩ specifies where to find b in memory—at *offset* from the start of storage for the *level* scope. We call this pair b's *static coordinate*.

### The Details

To handle this scheme, two additional calls are required. The compiler needs a call that initializes a new symbol table for a scope and one that finalizes the table for a scope.

1. *InitializeScope()* increments the current level and creates a new symbol table for that level. It links the new table to the enclosing level's table and updates the current level pointer used by *LookUp* and *Insert*.
2. *FinalizeScope()* changes the current-level pointer so that it points to the table for the scope surrounding the current level and then decrements the current level. If the compiler needs to preserve the level-by-level tables for later use, *FinalizeScope* can either leave the table intact in memory or write the table to external media and reclaim its space.

To account for lexical scoping, the parser calls *InitializeScope* each time it enters a new lexical scope and *FinalizeScope* each time it exits a lexical

**Static coordinate**

a pair, <*l,o*>, that records address information about some variable *x*

*l* specifies the lexical level where *x* is declared; *o* specifies the offset within the data area for that level.

scope. This scheme produces the following sequence of calls for the program in Figure 5.10:

| | | |
|---|---|---|
| 1. *InitializeScope* | 10. *Insert(b)* | 19. *LookUp(b)* |
| 2. *Insert(w)* | 11. *Insert(z)* | 20. *LookUp(a)* |
| 3. *Insert(x)* | 12. *FinalizeScope* | 21. *LookUp(b)* |
| 4. *Insert(example)* | 13. *InitializeScope* | 22. *LookUp(c)* |
| 5. *InitializeScope* | 14. *Insert(a)* | 23. *LookUp(w)* |
| 6. *Insert(a)* | 15. *Insert(x)* | 24. *FinalizeScope* |
| 7. *Insert(b)* | 16. *InitializeScope* | 25. *FinalizeScope* |
| 8. *Insert(c)* | 17. *Insert(c)* | 26. *FinalizeScope* |
| 9. *InitializeScope* | 18. *Insert(x)* | 27. *FinalizeScope* |

As it enters each scope, the compiler calls *InitializeScope*. It adds each name to the table using *Insert*. When it leaves a given scope, it calls *FinalizeScope* to discard the declarations for that scope. For the assignment statement, it looks up each of the names, as encountered. (The order of the *LookUp* calls will vary, depending on how the assignment statement is traversed.)

If *FinalizeScope* retains the symbol tables for finalized levels in memory, the net result of these calls will be the symbol table shown in Figure 5.12. The current level pointer is set to a null value. The tables for all levels are left in memory and linked together to reflect lexical nesting. The compiler can provide subsequent passes of the compiler with access to the relevant symbol-table information by storing a pointer to the appropriate table in the

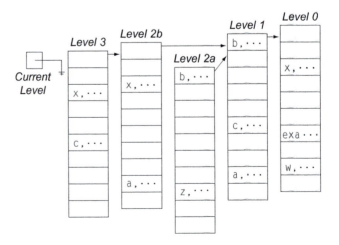

■ **FIGURE 5.12** Final Table for the Example.

IR at the start of each new level. Alternatively, identifiers in the IR can point directly to their symbol-table entries.

### 5.5.4 The Many Uses for Symbol Tables

The preceding discussion focused on a central symbol table, albeit one that might be composed of several tables. In reality, compilers build multiple symbol tables that they use for different purposes.

#### Structure Table

The textual strings used to name fields in a structure or record exist in a distinct name space from the variables and procedures. The name `size` might occur in several different structures in a single program. In many programming languages, such as C or Ada, using `size` as a field in a structure does not preclude its use as a variable or function name.

For each field in a structure, the compiler needs to record its type, its size, and its offset inside the record. It gleans this information from the declarations, using the same mechanisms that it uses for processing variable declarations. It must also determine the overall size for the structure, usually computed as the sum of the field sizes, plus any overhead space required by the runtime system.

There are several approaches for managing the name space of field names:

1. *Separate Tables*   The compiler can maintain a separate symbol table for each record definition. This is the cleanest idea, conceptually. If the overhead for using multiple tables is small, as in most object-oriented implementations, then using a separate table and associating it with the symbol table entry for the structure's name makes sense.
2. *Selector Table*   The compiler can maintain a separate table for field names. To avoid clashes between fields with identical names in different structures, it must use qualified names—concatenate either the name of the structure or something that uniquely maps to the structure, such as the structure name's symbol-table index, to the field name. For this approach, the compiler must somehow link together the individual fields associated with each structure.
3. *Unified Table*   The compiler can store field names in its principal symbol table by using qualified names. This decreases the number of tables, but it means that the principal symbol table must support all of the fields required for variables and functions, as well as all of the fields needed for each field-selector in a structure. Of the three options, this is probably the least attractive.

The separate table approach has the advantage that any scoping issues—such as reclaiming the symbol table associated with a structure—fit naturally into the scope management framework for the principal symbol table. When the structure can be seen, its internal symbol table is accessible through the corresponding structure record.

In the latter two schemes, the compiler writer will need to pay careful attention to scoping issues. For example, if the current scope declares a structure fee and an enclosing scope already has defined fee, then the scoping mechanism must correctly map fee to the structure (and its corresponding field entries). This may also introduce complications into the creation of qualified names. If the code contains two definitions of fee, each with a field named size, then fee.size is not a unique key for either field entry. This problem can be solved by associating a unique integer, generated from a global counter, with each structure name.

### Linked Tables for Name Resolution in an Object-Oriented Language

In an object-oriented language, the name scoping rules are governed by the structure of the data as much as by the structure of the code. This creates a more complicated set of rules; it also leads to a more complicated set of symbol tables. Java, for example, needs tables for the code being compiled, for any external classes that are both known and referenced in the code, and for the inheritance hierarchy above the class containing the code.

A simple implementation attaches a symbol table to each class, with two nesting hierarchies: one for lexical scoping inside individual methods and the other following the inheritance hierarchy for each class. Since a single class can serve as superclass to several subclasses, this latter hierarchy is more complicated than the simple sheaf-of-tables drawing suggests. However, it is easily managed.

To resolve a name fee when compiling a method m in class $C$, the compiler first consults the lexically scoped symbol table for m. If it does not find fee in this table, it then searches the scopes for the various classes in the inheritance hierarchy, starting with $C$ and proceeding up the chain of superclasses from $C$. If this lookup fails to find fee, the search then checks the global symbol table for a class or symbol table of that name. The global table must contain information on both the current package and any packages that have been used.

Thus, the compiler needs a lexically scoped table for each method, built while it compiles the methods. It needs a symbol table for each class, with links upward through the inheritance hierarchy. It needs links to the other classes in its package and to a symbol table for package-level variables. It needs access to the symbol tables for each used class. The lookup process is more complex, because it must follow these links in the correct order and examine only names that are visible. However, the basic mechanisms required to implement and manipulate the tables are already familiar.

### 5.5.5 Other Uses for Symbol Table Technology

The basic ideas that underlie symbol table implementation have widespread application, both inside a compiler and in other domains. Hash tables are used to implement sparse data structures; for example, a sparse array can be implemented by constructing a hash key from the indices and only storing non-zero values. Runtime systems for LISP-like languages have reduced their storage requirements by having the `cons` operator hash its arguments— effectively enforcing a rule that textually identical objects share a single instance in memory. Pure functions, those that always return the same values on the same input parameters, can use a hash table to produce an implementation that behaves as a *memo function*.

**Memo function**
a function that stores results in a hash table under a key built from its arguments and uses the hash table to avoid recomputation of prior results

---

**SECTION REVIEW**

Several tasks inside a compiler require efficient mappings from noninteger data into a compact set of integers. Symbol table technology provides an efficient and effective way to implement many of these mappings. The classic examples map a textual string, such as the name of a variable or temporary, into an integer. Key considerations that arise in symbol table implementation include scalability, space efficiency, and cost of creation, insertion, deletion, and destruction, both for individual entries and for new scopes.

This section presented a simple and intuitive approach to implementing a symbol table: linked sheaves of hash tables. (Section B.4, in Appendix B, presents several alternative implementation schemes.) In practice, this simple scheme works well in many applications inside a compiler, ranging from the parser's symbol table to tracking information for superlocal value numbering (see Section 8.5.1).

---

**Review Questions**

1. Using the "sheaf-of-tables" scheme, what is the complexity of inserting a new name into the table at the current scope? What is the complexity of looking up a name declared at an arbitrary scope? What is, in your experience, the maximum lexical-scope nesting level for programs that you write?

**2.** When the compiler initializes a scope, it may need to provide an initial symbol table size. How might you estimate that initial symbol table size in the parser? How might you estimate it in subsequent passes of the compiler?

## 5.6 **SUMMARY AND PERSPECTIVE**

The choice of an intermediate representation has a major impact on the design, implementation, speed, and effectiveness of a compiler. None of the intermediate forms described in this chapter are, definitively, the right answer for all compilers or all tasks in a given compiler. The designer must consider the overall goals of a compiler project when selecting an intermediate form, designing its implementation, and adding auxiliary data structures such as symbol and label tables.

Contemporary compiler systems use all manner of intermediate representations, ranging from parse trees and abstract syntax trees (often used in source-to-source systems) through lower-than-machine-level linear codes (used, for example, in the Gnu compiler systems). Many compilers use multiple IRs—building a second or third one to perform a particular analysis or transformation, then modifying the original, and definitive, one to reflect the result.

## ■ **CHAPTER NOTES**

The literature on intermediate representations and experience with them is sparse. This is somewhat surprising because of the major impact that decisions about IRs have on the structure and behavior of a compiler. The classic IR forms have been described in a number of textbooks [7, 33, 147, 171]. Newer forms like SSA [50, 110, 270] are described in the literature on analysis and optimization. Muchnick provides a modern treatment of the subject and highlights the use of multiple levels of IR in a single compiler [270].

The idea of using a hash function to recognize textually identical operations dates back to Ershov [139]. Its specific application in Lisp systems seems to appear in the early 1970s [124, 164]; by 1980, it was common enough that McCarthy mentions it without citation [259].

Cai and Paige introduced multiset discrimination as an alternative to hashing [65]. Their intent was to provide an efficient lookup mechanism with guaranteed constant time behavior. Note that closure-free regular expressions, described in Section 2.6.3, can be applied to achieve a similar effect. The work on shrinking the size of $\mathcal{R}^n$'s AST was done by David Schwartz and Scott Warren.

In practice, the design and implementation of an IR has an inordinately large impact on the eventual characteristics of the completed compiler. Large, complex IRs seem to shape systems in their own image. For example, the large ASTs used in early 1980s programming environments like $\mathcal{R}^n$ limited the size of programs that could be analyzed. The RTL form used in GCC has a low level of abstraction. Accordingly, the compiler does a fine job of managing details such as those needed for code generation, but has few, if any, transformations that require source-like knowledge, such as loop blocking to improve memory hierarchy behavior.

## ■ EXERCISES

1. A parse tree contains much more information than an abstract syntax tree.

   **a.** In what circumstances might you need information that is found in the parse tree but not the abstract syntax tree?

   **b.** What is the relationship between the size of the input program and its parse tree? Its abstract syntax tree?

   **c.** Propose an algorithm to recover a program's parse tree from its abstract syntax tree.

Section 5.2

2. Write an algorithm to convert an expression tree into a DAG.

3. Show how the following code fragment

   ```
   if (c[i] ≠ 0)
       then a[i] ← b[i] ÷ c[i];
       else a[i] ← b[i];
   ```

   might be represented in an abstract syntax tree, in a control-flow graph, and in quadruples. Discuss the advantages of each representation. For what applications would one representation be preferable to the others?

Section 5.3

4. Examine the code fragment shown in Figure 5.13. Draw its CFG and show its SSA form as a linear code.

5. Show how the expression $x - 2 \times y$ might be translated into an abstract syntax tree, one-address code, two-address code, and three-address code.

6. Given a linear list of ILOC operations, develop an algorithm that finds the basic blocks in the ILOC code. Extend your algorithm to build a control-flow graph to represent the connections between blocks.

7. For the code shown in Figure 5.14, find the basic blocks and construct the CFG.

Section 5.4

```
            ...
            x ← ...
            y ← ...
            a ← y + 2
            b ← 0
            while(x < a)
               if (y < x)
                  x ← y + 1
                  y ← b × 2
               else
                  x ← y + 2
                  y ← a ÷ 2;
               w ← x + 2
               z ← y × a
               y ← y + 1
```

■ **FIGURE 5.13** Code Fragment for Exercise 4.

```
L01: add      ra,rb    ⇒ r1          L05: add      r9,rb     ⇒ r11
     add      rc,rd    ⇒ r2               add      ra,rb     ⇒ r12
     add      r1,r2    ⇒ r3               add      rc,rd     ⇒ r13
     add      ra,rb    ⇒ r4               i2i      ra        ⇒ r13
     cmp_LT   r1,r2    ⇒ r5               add      r13,rb    ⇒ r14
     cbr      r5       → L02,L04          multI    r12,17    ⇒ r15
L02: add      ra,rb    ⇒ r6               jumpI              → L03
     multI    r6,17    ⇒ r7          L06: add      r1,r2     ⇒ r16
     jumpI             → L03              i2i      r2        ⇒ r17
L03: add      ra,rb    ⇒ r22              i2i      r1        ⇒ r18
     multI    r22,17   ⇒ r23              add      r17,r18   ⇒ r19
     jumpI             → L07              add      r18,r17   ⇒ r20
L04: add      rc,rd    ⇒ r8               multI    r1,17     ⇒ r21
     i2i      ra       ⇒ r9               jumpI              → L03
     cmp_LT   r9,rd    ⇒ r10         L07: nop
     cbr      r10      → L05,L06
```

■ **FIGURE 5.14** Code Fragment for Exercise 7.

8. Consider the three c procedures shown in Figure 5.15.
   a. Suppose a compiler uses a register-to-register memory model. Which variables in procedures A, B, and C would the compiler be forced to store in memory? Justify your answers.
   b. Suppose a compiler uses a memory-to-memory model. Consider the execution of the two statements that are in the if clause of the

```
static int max = 0;
void A(int b, int e)
{
  int a, c, d, p;
  a = B(b);
  if (b > 100) {
     c = a + b;
     d = c * 5 + e;
  }
  else
     c = a * b;
  p = c;
  C(&p);
}

int B(int k)
{
  int x, y;
  x = pow(2, k);
  y = x * 5;
  return y;
}

void C(int *p)
{
  if (*p > max)
     max = *p;
}
```

■ **FIGURE 5.15** Code for Exercise 8.

if-else construct. If the compiler has two registers available at that point in the computation, how many loads and stores would the compiler need to issue in order to load values in registers and store them back to memory during execution of those two statements? What if the compiler has three registers available?

9. In FORTRAN, two variables can be forced to begin at the same storage location with an equivalence statement. For example, the following statement forces a and b to share storage:

$$\text{equivalence } (a,b)$$

Can the compiler keep a local variable in a register throughout the procedure if that variable appears in an equivalence statement? Justify your answer.

10. Some part of the compiler must be responsible for entering each identifier into the symbol table.

   **a.** Should the scanner or the parser enter identifiers into the symbol table? Each has an opportunity to do so.

   **b.** Is there an interaction between this issue, declare-before-use rules, and disambiguation of subscripts from function calls in a language with the FORTRAN 77 ambiguity?

11. The compiler must store information in the IR version of the program that allows it to get back to the symbol table entry for each name. Among the options open to the compiler writer are pointers to the

Section 5.5

```
1    procedure main
2        integer a, b, c;
3        procedure f1(w,x);
4            integer a,x,y;
5            call f2(w,x);
6            end;
7        procedure f2(y,z)
8            integer a,y,z;
9            procedure f3(m,n)
10               integer b, m, n;
11               c = a * b * m * n;
12               end;
13           call f3(c,z);
14           end;
15       ...
16       call f1(a,b);
17       end;
```

■ **FIGURE 5.16** Program for Exercise 12.

original character strings and subscripts into the symbol table. Of course, the clever implementor may discover other options. What are the advantages and disadvantages of each of these representations for a name? How would you represent the name?

12. You are writing a compiler for a simple lexically-scoped language. Consider the example program shown in Figure 5.16.
   a. Draw the symbol table and its contents at line 11.
   b. What actions are required for symbol table management when the parser enters a new procedure and when it exits a procedure?

13. The most common implementation technique for a symbol table uses a hash table, where insertion and deletion are expected to have **O**(1) cost.
   a. What is the worst-case cost for insertion and for deletion in a hash table?
   b. Suggest an alternative implementation scheme that guarantees **O**(1) insertion and deletion.

# The Procedure Abstraction

## ■ CHAPTER OVERVIEW

Procedures play a critical role in the development of software systems. They provide abstractions for control flow and naming. They provide basic information hiding. They are the building block on which systems provide interfaces. They are one of the principal forms of abstraction in Algol-like languages; object-oriented languages rely on procedures to implement their methods or code members.

This chapter provides an in-depth look at the implementation of procedures and procedure calls, from the perspective of a compiler writer. Along the way, it highlights the implementation similarities and differences between Algol-like languages and object-oriented languages.

**Keywords:** Procedure Calls, Parameter Binding, Linkage Conventions

## 6.1 INTRODUCTION

The procedure is one of the central abstractions in most modern programming languages. Procedures create a controlled execution environment; each procedure has its own private named storage. Procedures help define interfaces between system components; cross-component interactions are typically structured through procedure calls. Finally, procedures are the basic unit of work for most compilers. A typical compiler processes a collection of procedures and produces code for them that will link and execute correctly with other collections of compiled procedures.

This latter feature, often called separate compilation, allows us to build large software systems. If the compiler needed the entire text of a program for each compilation, large software systems would be untenable. Imagine recompiling a multimillion line application for each editing change made during development! Thus, procedures play as critical a role in system design and engineering as they do in language design and compiler implementation. This chapter focuses on how compilers implement the procedure abstraction.

### Conceptual Roadmap

To translate a source-language program into executable code, the compiler must map all of the source-language constructs that the program uses into operations and data structures on the target processor. The compiler needs a strategy for each of the abstractions supported by the source language. These strategies include both algorithms and data structures that are embedded into the executable code. These runtime algorithms and data structures combine to implement the behavior dictated by the abstraction. These runtime strategies also require support at compile time in the form of algorithms and data structures that run inside the compiler.

This chapter explains the techniques used to implement procedures and procedure calls. Specifically, it examines the implementation of control, of naming, and of the call interface. These abstractions encapsulate many of the features that make programming languages usable and that enable construction of large-scale systems.

### Overview

The procedure is one of the central abstractions that underlie most modern programming languages. Procedures create a controlled execution environment. Each procedure has its own private named storage. Statements executed inside the procedure can access the private, or local, variables in that private storage. A procedure executes when it is invoked, or called, by another procedure (or the operating system). The callee may return a value to its caller, in which case the procedure is termed a *function*. This interface between procedures lets programmers develop and test parts of a program in isolation; the separation between procedures provides some insulation against problems in other procedures.

**Callee**

In a procedure call, we refer to the procedure that is invoked as the *callee*.

**Caller**

In a procedure call, we refer to the calling procedure as the *caller*.

Procedures play an important role in the way that programmers develop software and that compilers translate programs. Three critical abstractions that procedures provide allow the construction of nontrivial programs.

1. *Procedure Call Abstraction* Procedural languages support an abstraction for procedure calls. Each language has a standard mechanism to invoke a procedure and map a set of arguments, or parameters, from the caller's name space to the callee's name space. This abstraction typically includes a mechanism to return control to the

caller and continue execution at the pointimmediately after the call. Most languages allow a procedure to return one or more values to the caller. The use of standard linkage conventions, sometimes referred to as *calling sequences*, lets the programmer invoke code written and compiled by other people and at other times; it lets the application invoke library routines and system services.

**Linkage convention**
an agreement between the compiler and operating system that defines the actions taken to call a procedure or function

2. *Name Space* In most languages, each procedure creates a new and protected name space. The programmer can declare new names, such as variables and labels, without concern for the surrounding context. Inside the procedure, those local declarations take precedence over any earlier declarations for the same names. The programmer can create parameters for the procedure that allow the caller to map values and variables in the caller's name space into formal parameters in the callee's name space. Because the procedure has a known and separate name space, it can function correctly and consistently when called from different contexts. Executing a call instantiates the callee's name space. The call must create storage for the objects declared by the callee. This allocation must be both automatic and efficient—a consequence of calling the procedure.

**Actual parameter**
A value or variable passed as a parameter at a call site is an *actual parameter* of the call.

**Formal parameter**
A name declared as a parameter of some procedure *p* is a *formal parameter* of *p*.

3. *External Interface* Procedures define the critical interfaces among the parts of large software systems. The linkage convention defines rules that map names to values and locations, that preserve the caller's runtime environment and create the callee's environment, and that transfer control from caller to callee and back. It creates a context in which the programmer can safely invoke code written by other people. The existence of uniform calling sequences allows the development and use of libraries and system calls. Without a linkage convention, both the programmer and the compiler would need detailed knowledge about the implementation of the callee at each procedure call.

Thus, the procedure is, in many ways, the fundamental abstraction that underlies Algol-like languages. It is an elaborate facade created collaboratively by the compiler and the underlying hardware, with assistance from the operating system. Procedures create named variables and map them to virtual addresses; the operating system maps virtual addresses to physical addresses. Procedures establish rules for visibility of names and addressability; the hardware typically provides several variants of load and store operations. Procedures let us decompose large software systems into components; linkers and loaders knit these together into an executable program that the hardware can execute by advancing its program counter and following branches.

---

**A WORD ABOUT TIME**

This chapter deals with both compile-time and runtime mechanisms. The distinction between events that occur at compile time and those that occur at runtime can be confusing. The compiler generates all the code that executes at runtime. As part of the compilation process, the compiler analyzes the source code and builds data structures that encode the results of the analysis. (Recall the discussion of lexically scoped symbol tables in Section 5.5.3.) The compiler determines much of the storage layout that the program will use at runtime. It then generates the code needed to create that layout, to maintain it during execution, and to access both data objects and code in memory. When the compiled code runs, it accesses data objects and calls procedures or methods. All of the code is generated at compile time; all of the accesses occur at runtime.

---

A large part of the compiler's task is putting in place the code needed to realize the various pieces of the procedure abstraction. The compiler must dictate the layout of memory and encode that layout in the generated program. Since it may compile the different components of the program at different times, without knowing their relationships to one another, this memory layout and all the conventions that it induces must be standardized and uniformly applied. The compiler must also use the various interfaces provided by the operating system, to handle input and output, manage memory, and communicate with other processes.

This chapter focuses on the procedure as an abstraction and the mechanisms that the compiler uses to establish its control abstraction, name space, and interface to the outside world.

## 6.2 PROCEDURE CALLS

In Algol-like languages (ALLs), procedures have a simple and clear call/return discipline. A procedure call transfers control from the call site in the caller to the start of the callee; on exit from the callee, control returns to the point in the caller that immediately follows its invocation. If the callee invokes other procedures, they return control in the same way. Figure 6.1a shows a Pascal program with several nested procedures, while Figures 6.1b and 6.1c show the program's call graph and its *execution history*, respectively.

The call graph shows the set of potential calls among the procedures. Executing Main can result in two calls to Fee: one from Foe and another from Fum. The execution history shows that both calls occur at runtime. Each

```
program Main(input, output);
   var x,y,z: integer;
   procedure Fee;
      var x: integer;
      begin { Fee }
         x := 1;
         y := x * 2 + 1
      end;

   procedure Fie;
      var y: real;
      procedure Foe;
         var z: real;
            procedure Fum;
               var y: real;
               begin { Fum }
                  x := 1.25 * z;
                  Fee;
                  writeln('x = ',x)
               end;
            begin { Foe }
               z := 1;
               Fee;
               Fum
            end;
         begin { Fie }
            Foe;
            writeln('x = ',x)
         end;
      begin { Main }
         x := 0;
      Fie
   end.
```

(a) Example Pascal Program

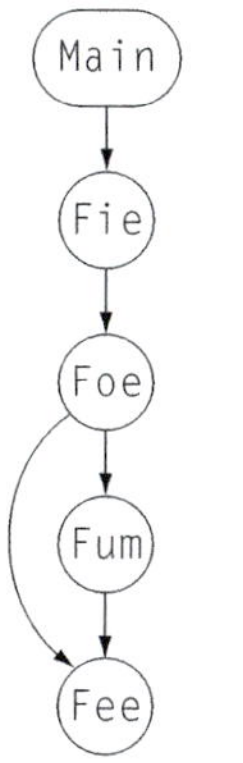

(b) Call Graph

1. Main **calls** Fie
2. Fie **calls** Foe
3. Foe **calls** Fee
4. Fee **returns to** Foe
5. Foe **calls** Fum
6. Fum **calls** Fee
7. Fee **returns to** Fum
8. Fum **returns to** Foe
9. Foe **returns to** Fie
10. Fie **returns to** Main

(c) Execution History

■ **FIGURE 6.1** Nonrecursive Pascal Program and Its Execution History.

of these calls creates a distinct instance, or *activation*, of Fee. By the time that Fum is called, the first instance of Fee is no longer active. It was created by the call from Foe (event 3 in the execution history), and destroyed after it returned control back to Foe (event 4). When control returns to Fee, from the call in Fum (event 6), it creates a new activation of Fee. The return from Fee to Fum destroys that activation.

**Activation**

A call to a procedure *activates* it; thus, we call an instance of its execution an *activation*.

```
(define (fact k)
  (cond
    [(<= k 1) 1]
    [else (* (fact (sub1 k)) k)]
  ))
```

■ **FIGURE 6.2** Recursive Factorial Program in Scheme.

When the program executes the assignment x := 1 in the first invocation of Fee, the active procedures are Fee, Foe, Fie, and Main. These all lie on a path in the call graph from Main to Fee. Similarly, when it executes the second invocation of Fee, the active procedures (Fee, Fum, Foe, Fie, and Main) lie on a path from Main to Fee. Pascal's call and return mechanism ensures that, at any point during execution, the procedure activations instantiate some rooted path through the call graph.

When the compiler generates code for calls and returns, that code must preserve enough information so that calls and returns operate correctly. Thus, when Foe calls Fum, the code must record the address in Foe to which Fum should return control. Fum may *diverge*, or not return, due to a runtime error, an infinite loop, or a call to another procedure that does not return. Still, the call mechanism must preserve enough information to allow execution to resume in Foe if Fum returns.

**Diverge**
A computation that does not terminate normally is said to *diverge*.

The call and return behavior of ALLs can be modelled with a stack. As Fie calls Foe, it pushes the return address in Fie onto the stack. When Foe returns, it pops that address off the stack and jumps to the address. If all procedures use the same stack, popping a return address exposes the next one.

**Return address**
When *p* calls *q*, the address in *p* where execution should continue after *p*'s return is called its *return address*.

The stack mechanism handles recursion as well. The call mechanism, in effect, unrolls the cyclic path through the call graph and creates a distinct activation for each call to a procedure. As long as the recursion terminates, this path will be finite and the stack of return addresses will correctly capture the program's behavior.

To make this concrete, consider the recursive factorial computation shown in Figure 6.2. When invoked to compute (fact 5), it generates a series of recursive calls: (fact 5) calls (fact 4) calls (fact 3) calls (fact 2) calls (fact 1). At that point, the cond statement executes the clause for (<= k 1), terminating the recursion. The recursion unwinds in the reverse order, with the call to (fact 1) returning the value 1 to (fact 2). It, in turn, returns the value 2 to (fact 3), which returns 6 to (fact 4). Finally, (fact 4) returns 24 to (fact 5), which multiplies 24 times 5 to return the answer 120. The recursive program exhibits last-in, first-out behavior, so the stack mechanism correctly tracks all of the return addresses.

## Control Flow in Object-Oriented Languages

From the perspective of procedure calls and returns, object-oriented languages (OOLs) are similar to ALLS. The primary differences between procedure calls in an OOL and an ALL lie in the mechanism used to name the callee and in the mechanisms used to locate the callee at runtime.

## More Complex Control Flow

Following Scheme, many programming languages allow a program to encapsulate a procedure and its runtime context into an object called a *closure*. When the closure is invoked, the procedure executes in the encapsulated runtime context. A simple stack is inadequate to implement this control abstraction. Instead, the control information must be saved in some more general structure that can represent the more complex control-flow relationship. Similar problems arise if the language allows references to local variables that outlast a procedure's activation.

**Closure**
a procedure and the runtime context that defines its free variables

---

**SECTION REVIEW**

In Algol-like languages, procedures are invoked with a call and they terminate in a return, unless the procedure diverges. To translate calls and returns, the compiler must arrange for the code to record, at each call, the appropriate return address and to use, at each return, the return address that corresponds to the correct call. Using a stack to hold return addresses correctly models the last-in, first-out behavior of return addresses.

One key data structure used to analyze caller–callee relationships is the call graph. It represents the set of calls between procedures, with an edge from Foe to Fum for each call site in Foe that invokes Fum. Thus, it captures the static relationship between callers and callees defined by the source code. It does not capture the dynamic, or runtime, relationship between procedures; for example, it cannot tell how many times the recursive factorial program in Figure 6.2 calls itself.

---

**Review Questions**

1. Many programming languages include a direct transfer of control, often called a `goto`. Compare and contrast a procedure call and a `goto`.

2. Consider the factorial program shown in Figure 6.2. Write down the execution history of a call to (`fact 5`). Explicitly match up the calls and returns. Show the value of k and of the return value.

## 6.3 NAME SPACES

**Scope**

In an Algol-like language, *scope* refers to a name space. The term is often used in discussions of the visibility of names.

In most procedural languages, a complete program will contain multiple name spaces. Each name space, or *scope*, maps a set of names to a set of values and procedures over some set of statements in the code. This range might be the whole program, some collection of procedures, a single procedure, or a small set of statements. The scope may inherit some names from other scopes. Inside a scope, the programmer can create names that are inaccessible outside the scope. Creating a name, fee, inside a scope can obscure definitions of fee in surrounding scopes, in effect making them inaccessible inside the scope. Thus, scope rules give the programmer control over access to information.

### 6.3.1 Name Spaces of Algol-like Languages

Most programming languages inherit many of the conventions that were defined for Algol 60. This is particularly true of the rules that govern the visibility of names. This section explores the notion of naming that prevails in ALLs, with particular emphasis on the hierarchical scope rules that apply in such languages.

#### Nested Lexical Scopes

**Lexical scope**

Scopes that nest in the order that they are encountered in the program are often called *lexical scopes*.

In lexical scoping, a name refers to the definition that is lexically closest to its use—that is, the definition in the closest surrounding scope.

Most ALLs allow the programmer to nest scopes inside one another. The limits of a scope are marked by specific terminal symbols in the programming language. Typically, each new procedure defines a scope that covers its entire definition. Pascal demarcated scopes with a begin at the start and an end at the finish. C uses curly braces, { and }, to begin and end a *block*; each block defines a new scope.

Pascal popularized nested procedures. Each procedure defines a new scope, and the programmer can declare new variables and procedures in each scope. It uses the most common scoping discipline, called *lexical scoping*. The general principle behind lexical scoping is simple:

> In a given scope, each name refers to its lexically closest
> declaration.

Thus, if *s* is used in the current scope, it refers to the *s* declared in the current scope, if one exists. If not, it refers to the declaration of *s* that occurs in the closest enclosing scope. The outermost scope contains global variables.

To make lexical scoping concrete, consider the Pascal program shown in Figure 6.3. It contains five distinct scopes, one corresponding to the program Main and one for each of the procedures Fee, Fie, Foe, and Fum. Each procedure declares some set of variables drawn from the set of names x, y, and z.

```
program Main₀(input, output);
  var x₁,y₁,z₁: integer;
  procedure Fee₁;
    var x₂: integer;
    begin { Fee₁ }
      x₂ := 1;
      y₁ := x₂ * 2 + 1
    end;

  procedure Fie₁;
    var y₂: real;
    procedure Foe₂;
      var z₃: real;
        procedure Fum₃
          var y₄: real;
          begin { Fum₃ }
            x₁ := 1.25 * z₃;
            Fee₁;
            writeln('x = ',x₁)
          end;
      begin { Foe₂ }
        z₃ := 1;
        Fee₁;
        Fum₃
      end;
    begin { Fie₁ }
      Foe₂;
      writeln('x = ',x₁)
    end;
  begin { Main₀ }
    x₁ := 0;
    Fie₁
end.
```

(a) Pascal Program

| Scope | x | y | z |
|-------|------|------|------|
| Main | ⟨1,0⟩ | ⟨1,4⟩ | ⟨1,8⟩ |
| Fee | ⟨2,0⟩ | ⟨1,4⟩ | ⟨1,8⟩ |
| Fie | ⟨1,0⟩ | ⟨2,0⟩ | ⟨1,8⟩ |
| Foe | ⟨1,0⟩ | ⟨2,0⟩ | ⟨3,0⟩ |
| Fum | ⟨1,0⟩ | ⟨4,0⟩ | ⟨3,0⟩ |

(b) Static Coordinates

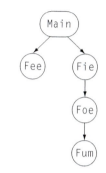

(c) Nesting Relationships

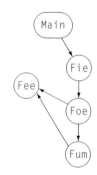

(d) Calling Relationships

■ **FIGURE 6.3** Nested Lexical Scopes in Pascal.

The figure shows each name with a subscript that indicates its level number. Names declared in a procedure always have a level that is one more than the level of the procedure name. Thus, if Main has level 0, as shown, names declared directly in Main, such as x, y, z, Fee, and Fie all have level 1.

To represent names in a lexically scoped language, the compiler can use the *static coordinate* for each name. The static coordinate is a pair $\langle l, o \rangle$, where

**Static coordinate**

For a name x declared in scope s, its static coordinate is a pair $\langle l, o \rangle$ where *l* is the lexical nesting level of s and o is the offset where x is stored in the scope's data area.

---

**DYNAMIC SCOPING**

The alternative to lexical scoping is dynamic scoping. The distinction between lexical and dynamic scoping only matters when a procedure refers to a variable that is declared outside the procedure's own scope, often called a *free variable*.

With lexical scoping, the rule is simple and consistent: a free variable is bound to the declaration for its name that is lexically closest to the use. If the compiler starts in the scope containing the use, and checks successive surrounding scopes, the variable is bound to the first declaration that it finds. The declaration always comes from a scope that encloses the reference.

With dynamic scoping, the rule is equally simple: a free variable is bound to the variable by that name that was most recently created at runtime. Thus, when execution encounters a free variable, it binds that free variable to the most recent instance of that name. Early implementations created a runtime stack of names, on which every name was pushed as its declaration was encountered. To bind a free variable, the running code searched the name stack from its top downward until a variable with the right name was found. Later implementations are more efficient.

While many early Lisp systems used dynamic scoping, lexical scoping has become the dominant choice. Dynamic scoping is easy to implement in an interpreter and somewhat harder to implement efficiently in a compiler. It can create bugs that are difficult to detect and hard to understand. Dynamic scoping still appears in some languages; for example, Common Lisp still allows the program to specify dynamic scoping.

---

$l$ is the name's lexical nesting level and $o$ is the its offset in the data area for level $l$. To obtain $l$, the front end uses a lexically scoped symbol table, as described in Section 5.5.3. The offset, $o$, should be stored with the name and its level in the symbol table. (Offsets can be assigned when declarations are processed during context-sensitive analysis.) The table on the right side of Figure 6.3 shows the static coordinate for each variable name in each procedure.

The second part of name translation occurs during code generation. The compiler must use the static coordinate to locate the value at runtime. Given a coordinate $\langle l,o \rangle$, the code generator must emit code that translates $l$ into the runtime address of the appropriate data area. Then, it can use the offset $o$ to compute the address for the variable corresponding to $\langle l,o \rangle$. Section 6.4.3 describes two different ways to accomplish this task.

## Scope Rules across Various Languages

Programming language scope rules vary idiosyncratically from language to language. The compiler writer must understand the specific rules of a source language and must adapt the general translation schemes to work with these specific rules. Most ALLs have similar scope rules. Consider the rules for the languages FORTRAN, C, and Scheme:

- FORTRAN has a simple name space. A FORTRAN program creates a single global scope, along with a local scope for each procedure or function. Global variables are grouped together in a "common block"; each common block consists of a name and a list of variables. The global scope holds the names of procedures and common blocks. Global names have lifetimes that match the lifetime of the program. A procedure's scope holds parameter names, local variables, and labels. Local names obscure global names if they conflict. Names in the local scope have, by default, lifetimes that match an invocation of the procedure, The programmer can give a local variable the lifetime of a global variable by listing it in a `save` statement.

- C has more complex rules. A C program has a global scope for procedure names and global variables. Each procedure has a local scope for variables, parameters, and labels. The language definition does not allow nested procedures, although some compilers have implemented this feature as an extension. Procedures can contain blocks (set off with left and right braces) that create separate local scopes; blocks can be nested. Programmers often use a block-level scope to create temporary storage for code generated by a preprocessor macro or to create a local variable whose scope is the body of a loop.

  C introduces another scope: the file-level scope. This scope includes names declared as `static` that not enclosed in a procedure. Thus, `static` procedures and functions are in the file-level scope, as are any `static` variables declared at the outermost level in the file. Without the `static` attribute, these names would be global variables. Names in the file-level scope are visible to any procedure in the file, but are not visible outside the file. Both variables and procedures can be declared static.

- Scheme has a simple set of scope rules. Almost all objects in Scheme reside in a single global space. Objects can be data or executable expressions. System-provided functions, such as `cons`, live alongside user-written code and data items. Code, which consists of an executable expression, can create private objects by using a `let` expression. Nesting `let` expressions inside one another can create nested lexical scopes of arbitrary depth.

Separate compilation makes it hard for FORTRAN compilers to detect different declarations for a common block in distinct files. Thus, the compiler must translate common-block references into ⟨*block, offset*⟩ pairs to produce correct behavior.

**Static name**
A variable declared as *static* retains its value across invocations of its defining procedure.

Variables that are not static are called *automatic*.

### 6.3.2 **Runtime Structures to Support Algol-like Languages**

To implement the twin abstractions of procedure calls and scoped name spaces, the translation must establish a set of runtime structures. The key data structure involved in both control and naming is the *activation record* (AR), a private block of memory associated with a specific invocation of a specific procedure. In principle, every procedure call gives rise to a new AR.

**Activation record**
a region of storage set aside to hold control information and data storage associated with a single instance of a single procedure

- The compiler must arrange for each call to store the return address where the callee can find it. The return address goes into the AR.
- The compiler must map the actual parameters at the call site into the formal parameter names by which they are known in the callee. To do so, it stores ordered parameter information in the AR.
- The compiler must create storage space for variables declared in the callee's local scope. Since these values have lifetimes that match the lifetime of the return address, it is convenient to store them in the AR.
- The callee needs other information to connect it to the surrounding program, and to allow it to interact safely with other procedures. The compiler arranges to store that information in the callee's AR.

Since each call creates a new AR, when multiple instances of a procedure are active, each has its own AR. Thus, recursion gives rise to multiple ARs, each of which holds the local state for a different invocation of the recursive procedure.

Figure 6.4 shows how the contents of an AR might be laid out. The entire AR is addressed through an *activation record pointer* (ARP), with various fields in the AR found at positive and negative offsets from the ARP. The ARs in Figure 6.4 have a number of fields.

**Activation record pointer**
To locate the current AR the compiler arranges to keep a pointer to the AR, the *activation record pointer*, in a designated register.

- The parameter area holds actual parameters from the call site, in an order that corresponds to their order of appearance at the call.
- The register save area contains enough space to hold registers that the procedure must preserve due to procedure calls.
- The return-value slot provides space to communicate data from the callee back to the caller, if needed.
- The return-address slot holds the runtime address where execution should resume when the callee terminates.
- The "addressability" slot holds information used to allow the callee to access variables in surrounding lexical scopes (not necessarily the caller).
- The slot at the callee's ARP stores the caller's ARP. The callee needs this pointer so that it can restore the caller's environment when it terminates.
- The local data area holds variables declared in the callee's local scope.

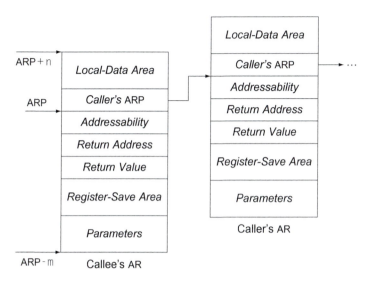

**FIGURE 6.4** Typical Activation Records.

For the sake of efficiency, some of the information shown in Figure 6.4 may be kept in dedicated registers.

### Local Storage

The AR for an invocation of procedure $q$ holds the local data and state information for that invocation. Each separate call to $q$ generates a separate AR. All data in the AR is accessed through the ARP. Because procedures typically access their AR frequently, most compilers dedicate a hardware register to hold the ARP of the current procedure. In ILOC, we refer to this dedicated register as $r_{arp}$.

The ARP always points to a designated location in the AR. The central part of the AR has a static layout; all the fields have known fixed lengths. This ensures that the compiled code can access those items at fixed offsets from the ARP. The ends of the AR are reserved for storage areas whose sizes may change from one invocation to another; typically one holds parameter storage while the other holds local data.

#### Reserving Space for Local Data

Each local data item may need space in the AR. The compiler should assign each such item an appropriately sized area and record the current lexical level and its offset from the ARP in the symbol table. This pair, the lexical level and offset, become the item's static coordinate. Then, the variable can be accessed using an operation like loadAO, with $r_{arp}$ and the offset as its arguments, to provide efficient access to local variables.

The compiler may not know the sizes of some local variables at compile time. For example, the program might read the size of an array from external media or determine it from work done in an earlier phase of the computation. For such variables, the compiler can leave space in the local data area for a pointer to the actual data or to a descriptor for an array (see Section 7.5.3 on page 362). The compiler arranges to allocate the actual storage elsewhere, at runtime, and to fill the reserved slot with the address of the dynamically allocated memory. In this case, the static coordinate leads the compiler to the pointer's location, and the actual access either uses the pointer directly or uses the pointer to calculate an appropriate address in the variable-length data area.

### Initializing Variables

If the source language allows the program to specify an initial value for a variable, the compiler must arrange for that initialization to occur. If the variable is allocated statically—that is, it has a lifetime that is independent of any procedure—and the initial value is known at compile time, the data can be inserted directly into the appropriate locations by the loader. (Static variables are usually stored outside all ARs. Having one instance of such a variable provides the needed semantics—a single value preserved across all the calls. Using a separate static data area—either one per procedure or one for the entire program—lets the compiler use the initialization features commonly found in loaders.)

Local variables, on the other hand, must be initialized at runtime. Because a procedure may be invoked multiple times, the only feasible way to set initial values is to generate instructions that store the necessary values to the appropriate locations. In effect, these initializations are assignments that execute before the procedure's first statement, each time it is invoked.

### Space for Saved Register Values

When $p$ calls $q$, one of them must save the register values that $p$ needs after the call. It may be necessary to save all the register values; on the other hand, a subset may suffice. On return to $p$, these saved values must be restored. Since each activation of $p$ stores a distinct set of values, it makes sense to store these saved registers in the AR of either $p$ or $q$, or both. If the callee saves a register, its value is stored in the callee's register save area. Similarly, if the caller saves a register, its value is stored in the caller's register save area. For a caller $p$, only one call inside $p$ can be active at a time. Thus, a single register save area in $p$'s AR suffices for all the calls that $p$ can make.

### *Allocating Activation Records*

When $p$ calls $q$ at runtime, the code that implements the call must allocate an AR for $q$ and initialize it with the appropriate values. If all the fields shown in Figure 6.4 are stored in memory, then the AR must be available to the caller, $p$, so that it can store the actual parameters, return address, caller's ARP, and addressability information. This forces allocation of $q$'s AR into $p$, where the size of its local data area may not be known. On the other hand, if these values are passed in registers, actual allocation of the AR can be performed in the callee, $q$. This lets $q$ allocate the AR, including any space required for the local data area. After allocation, it may store into its AR some of the values passed in registers.

The compiler writer has several options for allocating activation records. This choice affects both the cost of procedure calls and the cost of implementing advanced language features, such as building a closure. It also affects the total amount of memory needed for activation records.

### Stack Allocation of Activation Records

In many cases, the contents of an AR are only of interest during the lifetime of the procedure whose activation causes the AR's creation. In short, most variables cannot outlive the procedure that creates them, and most procedure activations cannot outlive their callers. With these restrictions, calls and returns are balanced; they follow a last-in, first-out (LIFO) discipline. A call from $p$ to $q$ eventually returns, and any returns that occur between the call from $p$ to $q$ and the return from $q$ to $p$ must result from calls made (either directly or indirectly) by $q$. In this case, the activation records also follow the LIFO ordering; thus, they can be allocated on a stack. Pascal, C, and Java are typically implemented with stack-allocated ARs.

Keeping activation records on a stack has several advantages. Allocation and deallocation are inexpensive; each requires one arithmetic operation on the value that marks the stack's top. The caller can begin the process of setting up the callee's AR. It can allocate all the space up to the local data area. The callee can extend the AR to include the local data area by incrementing the top-of-stack (TOS) pointer. It can use the same mechanism to extend the current AR incrementally to hold variable-size objects, as shown in Figure 6.5. Here, the callee has copied the TOS pointer into the local data area slot for $A$ and then incremented the TOS pointer by the size of $A$. Finally, with stack-allocated ARs, a debugger can walk the stack from its top to its base to produce a snapshot of the currently active procedures.

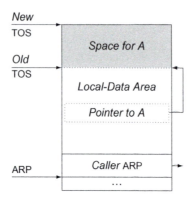

■ **FIGURE 6.5** Stack Allocation of a Dynamically Sized Array.

### Heap Allocation of Activation Records

If a procedure can outlive its caller, the stack discipline for allocating ARS breaks down. Similarly, if a procedure can return an object, such as a closure, that includes, explicitly or implicitly, references to its local variables, stack allocation is inappropriate because it will leave behind dangling pointers. In these situations, ARS can be kept in heap storage (see Section 6.6). Implementations of Scheme and ML typically use heap-allocated ARS.

A modern memory allocator can keep the cost of heap allocation low. With heap-allocated ARS, variable-size objects can be allocated as separate objects on the heap. If heap objects need explicit deallocation, then the code for procedure return must free the AR and its variable-size extensions. With implicit deallocation (see Section 6.6.2), the garbage collector frees them when they are no longer useful.

### Static Allocation of Activation Records

**Leaf procedure**
a procedure that contains no calls

If a procedure $q$ calls no other procedures, then $q$ can never have multiple active invocations. We call $q$ a *leaf procedure* since it terminates a path through a graph of the possible procedure calls. The compiler can statically allocate activation records for leaf procedures. This eliminates the runtime costs of AR allocation. If the calling convention requires the caller to save its own registers, then $q$'s AR needs no register save area.

If the language does not allow closures, the compiler can do better than allocating a static AR for each leaf procedure. At any point during execution, only one leaf procedure can be active. (To have two such procedures active, the first one would need to call another procedure, so it would not be a leaf.) Thus, the compiler can allocate a single static AR for use by all of the leaf procedures. The static AR must be large enough to accommodate any of the program's leaf procedures. The static variables declared in any of the leaf procedures can be laid out together in that single AR. Using a single static AR for leaf procedures reduces the space overhead of separate static ARs for each leaf procedure.

### Coalescing Activation Records

If the compiler discovers a set of procedures that are always invoked in a fixed sequence, it may be able to combine their activation records. For example, if a call from $p$ to $q$ always results in calls to $r$ and $s$, the compiler may find it profitable to allocate the ARs for $q$, $r$, and $s$ at the same time. Combining ARs can save on the costs of allocation; the benefits will vary directly with allocation costs. In practice, this optimization is limited by separate compilation and the use of function-valued parameters. Both limit the compiler's ability to determine the calling relationships that actually occur at runtime.

## 6.3.3 Name Spaces of Object-Oriented Languages

Much has been written about object-oriented design, object-oriented programming, and object-oriented languages. Languages such as Simula, Smalltalk, C++, and Java all support object-oriented programming. Many other languages have extensions that provide them with features to support object-oriented programming. Unfortunately, the term *object-oriented* has been given so many different meanings and implementations that it has come to signify a wide range of language features and programming paradigms.

As we shall see, not all OOLs can be compiled, in the traditional sense of a translation that finalizes all of the details about the executable program. Features of some OOLs create name spaces that cannot be understood until runtime. Implementations of these languages rely on runtime mechanisms that run from interpretation to runtime compilation (so-called *just-in-time compilers* or JITs). Because interpreters and JITs use many of the same structures as a compiler, we describe the problem as it might be implemented in a traditional compiler.

**Just-in-time compiler**
Schemes that perform some of the tasks of a traditional compiler at runtime are often called *just-in-time* compilers or JITs.

In a JIT, compile time becomes part of runtime, so JITs place an emphasis on compile-time efficiency.

From the compiler's perspective, OOLs reorganize the program's name space. Most OOLs retain the procedure-oriented lexical scoping conventions of an ALL for use within procedural code. They augment this classic naming scheme with a second set of conventions for naming, one organized around the layout of data—specifically, the definitions of objects. This data-centric naming discipline leads to a second hierarchy of scopes and a second mechanism for resolving names—that is, for mapping a source-language name into a runtime address so that the compiled code can access the data associated with that name.

---

**TERMINOLOGY FOR OBJECT-ORIENTED LANGUAGES**

The diversity of object-oriented languages has led to some ambiguity in the terms that we use to discuss them. To make the discussion in this chapter concrete, we will use the following terms:

1. *Object* An object is an abstraction with one or more members. Those members can be data items, code that manipulates those data items, or other objects. An object with code members is a *class*. Each object has internal state—data whose lifetimes match the object's lifetime.
2. *Class* A class is a collection of objects with the same abstract structure and characteristics. A class defines the set of data members in each *instance* of the class and defines the code members (*methods*) that are local to that class. Some methods are *public*, or externally visible, others are *private*, or invisible outside the class.
3. *Inheritance* Inheritance refers to a relationship among classes that defines a partial order on the name scopes of classes. Each class may have a *superclass* from which it inherits both code and data members. If *a* is the superclass of *b*, *b* is a subclass of *a*. Some languages allow a class to have multiple superclasses.
4. *Receiver* Methods are invoked relative to some object, called the method's receiver. The receiver is known by a designated name, such as this or self, inside the method.

The complexity and the power of an OOL arise, in large part, from the organizational possibilities presented by its multiple name spaces.

---

The syntax and terminology used to specify subclasses varies between languages. In Java, a subclass *extends* its superclass, while in C++, a subclass is *derived* from its superclass.

Inheritance imposes an ancestor relation on the classes in an application. Each class has, by declaration, one or more parent classes, or superclasses. Inheritance changes both the name space of the application and the mapping of method names to implementations. If $\alpha$ is a superclass of $\beta$, then $\beta$ is a subclass of $\alpha$ and any method defined in $\alpha$ must operate correctly on an object of class $\beta$, if it is visible in $\beta$. The converse is not true; a method declared in class $\beta$ cannot be applied to an object of its superclass $\alpha$, as the method from $\beta$ may need fields present in an object of class $\beta$ that are absent from an object of class $\alpha$.

### Visibility

When a method runs, it can reference names defined in multiple scope hierarchies. The method is a procedure, with its own name space defined by the set of lexical scopes in which it is declared; the method can access names in those scopes using the familiar conventions defined for ALLS. The method was invoked relative to some receiver; it can access that object's own members. The method is defined in the receiver's class. The method can access the members of that class and, by inheritance, of its superclasses. Finally, the program creates some global name space and executes in it. The running method can access any names that are contained in that global name space.

To make these issues concrete, consider the abstracted example shown in Figure 6.6. It defines a class, Point, of objects with integer fields x and y and methods draw and move. ColorPoint is a subclass of Point that extends Point with an additional field c of type Color. It uses Point's method for move, overrides its method for draw and defines a new method test that performs some computation and then invokes draw. Finally, class C defines local fields and methods and uses ColorPoint.

Now, consider the names that are visible inside method m of class C. Method m maps x and y to their declarations in C. It expressly references the class names Point and ColorPoint. The assignment y = p.x takes its right-hand side from the field x in the object p, which p has by inheritance from class Point. The left-hand side refers to m's local variable y. The call to draw maps to the method defined in ColorPoint. Thus, m refers to definitions from all three classes in the example.

```
class Point {
    public int x, y;
    public void draw() {...};
    public void move() {...};
}

class ColorPoint extends Point {      // inherits x, y, & move()
    Color c;                          // local field of ColorPoint
    public void draw() {...};         // hide Point's draw()
    public void test() {...; draw();};  // local method
}

class C {
    int x, y;                         // local fields
    public void m() {                 // local method
        int y;                        // local variable of m
        Point p = new ColorPoint();   // uses ColorPoint and, by
        y = p.x                       // inheritance, Point
        p.draw()
    }
}
```

■ **FIGURE 6.6** Definitions for Point and ColorPoint.

To translate this example, the compiler must track the hierarchy of names and scopes established both by the scope rules inside methods and classes and by the hierarchy of classes and superclasses established by `extends`. Name resolution in this environment depends on both the details of the code definitions and the class structure of the data definitions. To translate an OOL, the compiler needs to model both the name space of the code and the name spaces associated with the class hierarchy. The complexity of that model depends on details of the specific OOL.

In Java, `public` makes a name visible everywhere while `private` makes the name visible only within its own class.

To add a final complication, some OOLs provide attributes for individual names that change their visibility. For example, a Java name can have the attributes `public` or `private`. Similarly, some OOLs provide a mechanism to reference names obscured by nesting. In c++, the :: operator allows the code to name a scope while in Java the programmer can use a fully qualified name.

### Naming in the Class Hierarchy

The class hierarchy defines a set of nested name scopes, just as a set of nested procedures and blocks does in an ALL. In an ALL, lexical position defines the relationship between those name scopes—if procedure $d$ is declared inside procedure $c$, then $d$'s name space is nested inside $c$'s name space. In an OOL, the class declarations can be lexically disjoint and the subclass relation is specified by explicit declarations.

**Direct superclass**

If class $\alpha$ extends $\beta$, then $\beta$ is $\alpha$'s direct superclass. If $\beta$ has a superclass $\gamma$, then $\gamma$ is, by transitivity, a superclass of $\alpha$, but it is not $\alpha$'s direct superclass.

To find the declaration of a name, the compiler must search the lexical hierarchy, the class hierarchy, and the global name space. For a name x in a method m, the compiler first searches the lexical scopes that surround the reference in m. If that lookup fails, it searches the class hierarchy for the class that contains m. Conceptually, it searches m's declared class, then m's direct superclass, then that class' direct superclass, and so on until it finds the name or exhausts the class hierarchy. If the name is not found in either the lexical hierarchy or the class hierarchy, the compiler searches the global name space.

To support the more complex naming environment of an OOL, the compiler writer uses the same basic tools used with an ALL: a linked set of symbol tables (see Section 5.5.3). In an OOL, the compiler simply has more tables than in an ALL and it must use those tables in a way that reflects the naming environment. It can link the tables together in the appropriate order, or it can keep the three kinds of tables separate and search them in the appropriate order.

The major complication that arises with some OOLs derives not from the presence of a class hierarchy, but rather from when that hierarchy is defined. If the OOL requires that class definitions be present at compile time and that

---

**TRANSLATING JAVA**

The Java programming language was designed to be portable, to be secure, and to have a compact representation for transmission over networks. These design goals led directly to a two-stage translation scheme for Java that is followed in almost all Java implementations.

Java code is first compiled, in the traditional sense, from Java source into an IR called Java bytecode. Java bytecode is compact. Java bytecode forms the instruction set for the Java Virtual Machine (JVM). The JVM has been implemented with an interpreter that can be compiled on almost any target platform, providing portability. Because Java code executes inside the JVM, the JVM can control interactions between the Java code and the system, limiting the ability of a Java program to gain illicit access to system resources—a strong security feature.

This design implies a specific translation scheme. Java code is first compiled into Java bytecode. The bytecode is then interpreted by the JVM. Because interpretation adds runtime overhead, many JVM implementations include a just-in-time compiler that translates heavily used bytecode sequences into native code for the underlying hardware. As a result, Java translation is a combination of compilation and interpretation.

---

class definitions not change after compile time, then name resolution inside methods can be performed at compile time. We say that such a language has a *closed class structure*. On the other hand, if the language allows the running program to change its class structure, either by importing classes as in Java or by editing classes as in Smalltalk, then the language has an *open class structure*.

Given a method m, the compiler can map a name that appears in m to either a declaration in some nested scope of m, or to the class definition that contains m. If the name is declared in a superclass, the compiler's ability to determine which superclass declares the name depends on whether the class structure is open or closed. With a closed class structure, the compiler has the complete class hierarchy, so it can resolve all names back to their declarations and, with appropriate runtime structures to support naming, can generate code to access any name. With an open class structure, the compiler may not know the class structure until runtime. Such languages require runtime mechanisms to resolve names in the class hierarchy; that requirement, in turn, typically leads to implementations that rely on interpretation or runtime compilation. Similar situations can arise from explicit or implicit conversions in a language with a closed class structure; for example virtual functions in c++ may require runtime support.

**Closed class structure**
If the class structure of an application is fixed at compile time, the OOL has a *closed hierarchy*.

**Open class structure**
If an application can change its class structure at runtime, it has an *open hierarchy*.

c++ has a closed class structure. Any functions, other than virtual functions, can be resolved at compile time. Virtual functions require runtime resolution.

### 6.3.4 **Runtime Structures to Support Object-Oriented Languages**

Just as Algol-like languages need runtime structures to support their lexical name spaces, so too do object-oriented languages need runtime structures to support both their lexical hierarchy and their class hierarchy. Some of those structures are identical to the ones found in an ALL. For example, the control information for methods, as well as storage for method-local names, is stored in ARS. Other structures are designed to address specific problems introduced by the OOL. For example, object lifetimes need not match the invocation of any particular method, so their persistent state cannot be stored in some AR. Thus, each object needs its own object record (OR) to hold its state. The ORS of classes instantiate the inheritance hierarchy; they play a critical role in translation and execution.

The amount of runtime support that an OOL needs depends heavily on features of the OOL. To explain the range of possibilities, we will begin with the structures that might be generated for the definitions in Figure 6.6, assuming a language with single inheritance and an open class structure. From that base case, we will explore the simplifications and optimizations that a closed class structure allows.

Figure 6.7 shows the runtime structures that might result from instantiating three objects using the definitions from Figure 6.6. SimplePoint instantiates Point, while both LeftCorner and RightCorner instantiate ColorPoint. Each of object has its own OR, as do the classes Point and

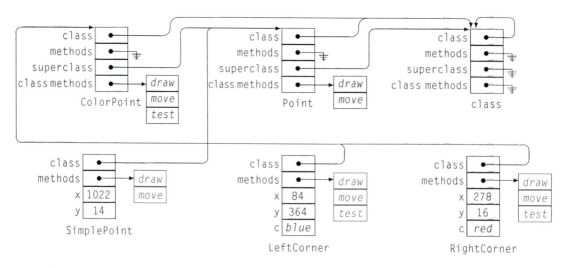

■ **FIGURE 6.7** Runtime Structures for the ColorPoint Example.

ColorPoint. For completeness, the diagram shows an OR for class class. Depending on the language, an implementation may avoid representing some of these fields, method vectors, and pointers.

The OR for a simple object, such as LeftCorner, contains a pointer to the class that defined LeftCorner, a pointer to the method vector for that class, and space for its fields, x, y, and c, Notice that the inherited fields in a ColorPoint and in its method vector have the same offset that they would in the base class Point. The OR for ColorPoint literally extends the OR for Point. The resulting consistency allows a superclass method such as Point.move to operate correctly on a subclass object, such as LeftCorner.

The OR for a class contains a pointer to its class, class, a pointer to the method vector for class, and its local fields which include superclass and class methods. In the figure, all method vectors are drawn as complete method vectors—that is, they include all of the methods for the class, both local and inherited. The superclass field records the inheritance hierarchy, which may be necessary in an open class structure. The class methods field points to the method vector used members of the class.

To avoid a confusing tangle of lines in the figure, we have simplified the method vectors in several ways. The drawing shows separate method vectors rather than pointers to a shared copy of the class methods vectors. The copies are drawn in gray. Class class has null pointers for both its methods and its class methods fields. In a real implementation, these would likely have some methods, which would, in turn, cause non-null pointers in the methods field of both Point and ColorPoint.

### Method Invocation

How does the compiler generate code to invoke a method such as draw? Methods are always invoked relative to an object, say RightCorner, as receiver. For the invocation to be legal, RightCorner must be visible at the point of the call, so the compiler can discover how to find RightCorner with a symbol-table lookup. The compiler first looks in the method's lexical hierarchy, then in the class hierarchy, and, finally, in the global scope. That lookup provides enough information to let the compiler emit code to obtain a pointer to RightCorner's OR.

Once the compiler has emitted code to obtain the OR pointer, it locates the method vector pointer at offset 4 in the OR pointer. It uses draw's offset, which is 0 relative to the method vector pointer, to obtain a pointer to the desired implementation of draw. It uses that code pointer in a standard procedure call, with one twist—it passes RightCorner's OR pointer as the implicit first parameter to draw. Because it located draw from RightCorner's OR, which contains a pointer to ColorPoint's class methods vector, the code sequence locates the proper implementation of draw. If the invocation had been SimplePoint.draw, the same process would have found Point's method vector pointer and called Point.draw.

The example assumes that each class has a complete method vector. Thus, the slot for move in ColorPoint's method vector points to Point.move while the slot for draw points to ColorPoint.draw. This scheme produces the desired result—an object of class x invokes the implementation of a method that is visible inside the definition for class x. The alternative scheme would represent only ColorPoint's locally defined methods in its class method vector, and would locate an inherited method by chasing ORs up the superclass chain in a manner analogous to access links for lexical scoping and ARs.

### Object-Record Layout

"Implementation" might be a compiler, an interpreter, or a JIT. The layout problem is the same.

One subtle point in the example is that an implementation must maintain consistent offsets, by name, up and down the superclass hierarchy. Fields, such as x and y, must appear at the same offset in an OR of class Point and ColorPoint for a method such as move to operate correctly on ORs of either its class or its superclasses. For the same reason, methods must appear at the same offsets in the method vectors of related classes.

Without inheritance, the compiler can assign offsets in arbitrary order to the class' fields and methods. It compiles those offsets directly into the code. The code uses the receiver's pointer (e.g. this) and the offsets to locate any desired field in the OR or any method in the method vector.

With single inheritance, OR layout is straightforward. Since each class has only one direct superclass, the compiler appends the new fields to the end of the superclass OR layout, extending the OR layout. This approach, called *prefixing*, ensures consistent offsets up and down the superclass hierarchy. When an object is cast to one of its superclasses, the fields in the OR are in their expected locations. The ORs in Figure 6.7 follow this scheme.

In a language with a closed class structure, object-record layout can be done at compile time, as soon as all the superclasses are known. In a language with an open class structure, object-record layout must be done between the time when the superclass structure is known and the time when ORs are allocated. If the class structure is unknown at compile time but cannot change at runtime, these issues can be resolved at linktime or at the start of execution. If the class structure can change at runtime, as in either Java or Smalltalk, then the runtime environment must be prepared to adjust object layouts and the class hierarchy.

- If classes change infrequently, the overhead for adjusting object-record layouts can be small. The runtime environment, either an interpreter or a JIT and an interpreter, can compute object record layouts and build method vectors for each affected class when the class structure changes.

In Java, for example, classes only change when the class loader runs. Thus, the class loader could trigger the rebuilding process.

- If classes change often, the compiler must still compute object-record layouts and adjust them. However, it may be more efficient for the implementation to use incomplete method vectors and search rather than rebuilding class method vectors at each change. (See the next subsection.)

As a final issue, consider what happens if the language allows changes to the structure of a class that has instantiated objects. Adding a field or a method to a class with instantiated objects necessitates visiting those objects, building them new ORs, and connecting those ORs back into the runtime environment in a seamless way. (Typically, the latter requirement requires an extra level of indirection on references to ORs.) To avoid these complications, most languages forbid changes to classes that already have instantiated objects.

### Static versus Dynamic Dispatch

The runtime structures shown in Figure 6.7 suggest that every method call requires one or more load operations to locate the method's implementation. In a language with a closed class structure, the compiler can avoid this overhead for most calls. In C++, for example, the compiler can resolve any method to a concrete implementation at compile time, unless the method is declared as a *virtual method*—meaning, essentially, that the programmer wants to locate the implementation relative to the receiver's class.

**Dispatch**
The process of calling a method is often called *dispatch*, a term derived from the message-passing model of OOLs such as Smalltalk.

With a virtual method, dispatch is done through the appropriate method vector. The compiler emits code to locate the method's implementation at runtime using the object's `method` vector, a process called *dynamic dispatch*. If, however, the C++ compiler can prove that some virtual method call has a known invariant receiver class, it can generate a direct call, sometimes called *static dispatch*.

Languages with open class structures may need to rely on dynamic dispatch. If the class structure can change at runtime, the compiler cannot resolve method names to implementations; instead, it must defer this process to runtime. The techniques used to address this problem range from recomputing method vectors at each change in the class hierarchy to runtime name resolution and search in the class hierarchy.

- If the class hierarchy changes infrequently, the implementation may simply rebuild method vectors for the affected classes after each change. In this scheme, the runtime system must traverse the superclass

**METHOD CACHES**

To support an open class hierarchy, the compiler may need to produce a search key for each method name and retain a mapping of keys to implementations that it can search at runtime. The map from method name to search key can be simple—using the method name or a hash index for that name—or it can be complex—assigning each method name an integer from a compact set using some link-time mechanism. In either case, the compiler must include tables that can be searched at runtime to locate the implementation of a method in the most recent ancestor of the receiver's class.

To improve method lookup in this environment, the runtime system can implement a *method cache*—a software analog of the hardware data cache found in most processors. The method cache has a small number of entries, say 1000. Each cache entry consists of a key, a class, and a pointer to a method implementation. A dynamic dispatch begins with a lookup in the method cache; if it finds an entry with the receiver's class and method key, it returns the cached method pointer. If the lookup fails, the dispatch performs a complete search up the superclass chain, starting with the receiver's class. It caches the result that it finds and returns the method pointer.

Of course, creating a new entry may force eviction of some other cache entry. Standard cache replacement policies, such as least recently used or round robin, can select the method to evict. Larger caches retain more information, but require more memory and may take longer to search. When the class structure changes, the implementation can clear the method cache to prevent incorrect results on future lookups.

To capture type locality at individual calls, some implementations use an *inline method cache*, a single entry cache located at the actual call site. The cache stores the receiver's class and the method pointer from the last invocation at that site. If the current receiver class matches the previous receiver class, the call uses the cached method pointer. A change to the class hierarchy must invalidate the cache, either by changing the class' tag or by overwriting the class tags at each inline cache. If the current class does not match the cached class, a full lookup is used, and that lookup writes its results into the inline cache.

hierarchy to locate method implementations and build subclass method vectors.

■ If the class hierarchy changes often, the implementor may choose to keep incomplete method vectors in each class—record just the local methods. In this scheme, a call to a superclass method triggers a runtime search in the class hierarchy for the first method of that name.

Either of these schemes requires that the language runtime retain lookup tables of method names—either source level names or search keys derived from those names. Each class needs a small dictionary in its OR. Runtime name resolution looks up the method name in the dictionaries through the hierarchy, in a manner analogous to the chain of symbol tables described in Section 5.5.3.

OOL implementations try to reduce the cost of dynamic dispatch through one of two general strategies. They can perform analysis to prove that a given method invocation always uses a receiver of the same known class, in which case they can replace dynamic dispatch with static dispatch. For calls where they cannot discover the receiver's class, or where the class varies at runtime, the implementations can cache search results to improve performance. In this scheme, the search consults a method cache before it searches the class hierarchy. If the method cache contains the mapping for the receiver's class and the method name, the call uses the cached method pointer and avoids the search.

## Multiple Inheritance

Some OOLs allow multiple inheritance, meaning a new class may inherit from several superclasses that have inconsistent object layouts. This situation poses a new problem: the compiled code for a superclass method uses offsets based on the OR layout for that superclass. Of course, different immediate superclasses may assign conflicting offsets to their fields. To reconcile these competing offsets, the compiler must adopt a slightly more complex scheme: it must use different OR pointers with methods from different superclasses.

Consider a class $\alpha$ that inherits from multiple superclasses, $\beta$, $\gamma$, and $\delta$. To lay out the OR for an object of class $\alpha$, the implementation must first impose an order on $\alpha$'s superclasses—say $\beta$, $\gamma$, $\delta$. It lays out the OR for class $\alpha$ as the entire OR, including class pointer and method vector, for $\beta$, followed by the entire OR for $\gamma$, followed by the entire OR for $\delta$. To this layout, it appends any fields declared locally in the declaration of $\alpha$. It constructs the method vector for $\alpha$ by appending $\alpha$'s methods to the method vector for the first superclass.

The drawing in the margin shows the resulting OR layout for class $\alpha$, We assume that $\alpha$ defines two local fields, $\alpha_1$ and $\alpha_2$, and that the fields of $\beta$, $\gamma$, and $\delta$ are named similarly. The OR for $\alpha$ divides into four logical sections: the OR for $\beta$, the OR for $\gamma$, the OR for $\delta$, and the space for fields declared in $\alpha$. Methods declared in $\alpha$ are appended to the method vector for the first section. The "shadow" class pointers and method vectors, whose

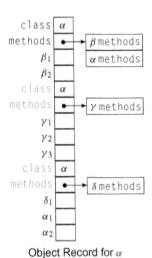

Object Record for $\alpha$

labels appear in gray, exist to allow those superclass methods to receive the environment that they expect—the OR layout of the corresponding superclass.

The remaining complication involved in multiple inheritance lies in the fact that the OR pointer must be adjusted when a superclass method is invoked using one of the shadow class pointers and method vectors. The invocation must adjust the pointer by the distance between the class pointer at the top of the OR and the shadow class pointer. The simplest mechanism to accomplish this adjustment is to insert a *trampoline function* between the method vector and the actual method. The trampoline adjusts the OR pointer, invokes the method with all of the parameters, and readjusts the OR pointer on return.

---

**SECTION REVIEW**

Algol-like languages typically use lexical scoping, in which names spaces are properly nested and new instances of a name obscure older ones. To hold data associated with its local scope, a procedure has an activation record for each invocation. In contrast, while object-oriented languages may use lexical scopes for procedure-local names, they also rely on a hierarchy of scopes defined by the data—by the hierarchy of class definitions. This dual-hierarchy name space leads to more complex interactions among names and to more complex implementations.

Both styles of naming require runtime structures that both reflect and implement the naming hierarchy. In an ALL, the activation records can capture the structure of the name space, provide the necessary storage for most values, and preserve the state necessary for correct execution. In an OOL, the activation records of running code still capture the lexically scoped portion of the name space and the state of execution; however, the implementation also needs a hierarchy of object records and class records to model the object-based portion of the name space.

---

**Review Questions**

1. In C, setjmp and longjmp provide a mechanism for interprocedural transfer of control. setjmp creates a data structure; invoking longjmp on the data structure created by a setjmp causes execution to continue immediately after the setjmp, with the context present when the setjmp executed. What information must setjmp preserve? How does the implementation of setjmp change between stack-allocated and heap-allocated ARs?

2. Consider the example from Figure 6.7. If the compiler encounters a reference to LeftCorner with a cast to class Point, which implementation of the method draw would that cast reference invoke? How could the programmer refer to the other implementation of draw?

■

## 6.4 COMMUNICATING VALUES BETWEEN PROCEDURES

The central notion underlying the concept of a procedure is abstraction. The programmer abstracts common operations relative to a small set of names, or formal parameters, and encapsulates those operations in a procedure. To use the procedure, the programmer invokes it with an appropriate *binding* of values, or actual parameters, to those formal parameters. The callee executes, using the formal parameter names to access the values passed as actual parameters. If the programmer desires, the procedure can return a result.

### 6.4.1 Passing Parameters

Parameter binding maps the actual parameters at a call site to the callee's formal parameters. It lets the programmer write a procedure without knowledge of the contexts in which it will be called. It lets the programmer invoke the procedure from many distinct contexts without exposing details of the procedure's internal operation in each caller. Thus, parameter binding plays a critical role in our ability to write abstract, modular code.

Most modern programming languages use one of two conventions for mapping actual parameters to formal parameters: *call-by-value* binding and *call-by-reference* binding. These techniques differ in their behavior. The distinction between them may be best explained by understanding their implementations.

### *Call by Value*

Consider the following procedure, written in C, and several call sites that invoke it:

```
int fee(int x, int y) {        c = fee(2,3);
    x = 2 * x;                 a = 2;
    y = x + y;                 b = 3;
    return y;                  c = fee(a,b);
}                              a = 2;
                               b = 3;
                               c = fee(a,a);
```

**Call by value**
a convention where the caller evaluates the actual parameters and passes their values to the callee

Any modification of a value parameter in the callee is not visible in the caller.

Consider the earlier example, rewritten in PL/I, which uses call-by-reference parameter binding.

```
fee: procedure (x,y)                    c = fee(2,3);
         returns fixed binary;          a = 2;
     declare x, y fixed binary;         b = 3;
     x = 2 * x;                         c = fee(a,b);
     y = x + y;                         a = 2;
     return y;                          b = 3;
     end fee;                           c = fee(a,a);
```

With call-by-reference parameter binding, the example produces different results. The first call is straightforward. The second call redefines both a and b; those changes would be visible in the caller. The third call causes x and y to refer to the same location, and thus, the same value. This *alias* changes fee's behavior. The first assignment gives a the value 4. The second assignment then gives a the value 8, and fee returns 8, where fee(2,2) would return 6.

**Alias**

When two names can refer to the same location, they are said to be *aliases*.

In the example, the third call creates an alias between x and y inside fee.

| Call by<br>Reference | a<br>in | <br>out | b<br>in | <br>out | Return<br>Value |
|---|---|---|---|---|---|
| fee(2,3) | - | - | - | - | 7 |
| fee(a,b) | 2 | 4 | 3 | 7 | 7 |
| fee(a,a) | 2 | 8 | 3 | 3 | 8 |

### Space for Parameters

The size of the representation for a parameter has an impact on the cost of procedure calls. Scalar values, such as variables and pointers, are stored in registers or in the parameter area of the callee's AR. With call-by-value parameters, the actual value is stored; with call-by-reference parameters, the address of the parameter is stored. In either case, the cost per parameter is small.

Large values, such as arrays, records, or structures, pose a problem for call by value. If the language requires that large values be copied, the overhead of copying them into the callee's parameter area will add significant cost to the procedure call. (In this case, the programmer may want to model call by reference and pass a pointer to the object rather than the object.) Some languages allow the implementation to pass such objects by reference. Others include provisions that let the programmer specify that passing a particular parameter by reference is acceptable; for example, the `const` attribute in C assures the compiler that a parameter with the attribute is not modified.

### 6.4.2 **Returning Values**

To return a value from a function the compiler must set aside space for the returned value. Because the return value, by definition, is used after the callee terminates, it needs storage outside the callee's AR. If the compiler writer can ensure that the return value is of small fixed size, then it can store the value either in the caller's AR or in a designated register.

With call-by-value parameters, linkage conventions often designate the register reserved for the first parameter as the register to hold the return value.

All of our pictures of the AR have included a slot for a returned value. To use this slot, the caller allocates space for the returned value in its own AR, and stores a pointer to that space in the return slot of its own AR. The callee can load the pointer from the caller's return-value slot (using the copy of the caller's ARP that it has in the callee's AR). It can use the pointer to access the storage set aside in the caller's AR for the returned value. As long as both caller and callee agree about the size of the returned value, this works.

If the caller cannot know the size of the returned value, the callee may need to allocate space for it, presumably on the heap. In this case, the callee allocates the space, stores the returned value there, and stores the pointer in the return-value slot of the caller's AR. On return, the caller can access the return value using the pointer that it finds in its return-value slot. The caller must free the space allocated by the callee.

If the return value is small—the size of the return-value slot or less—then the compiler can eliminate the indirection. For a small return value, the callee can store the value directly into the return value slot of the caller's AR. The caller can then use the value directly from its AR. This improvement requires, of course, that the compiler handle the value in the same way in both the caller and the callee. Fortunately, type signatures for procedures can ensure that both compiles have the requisite information.

### 6.4.3 **Establishing Addressability**

As part of the linkage convention, the compiler must ensure that each procedure can generate an address for each variable that it needs to reference. In an ALL, a procedure can refer to global variables, local variables, and any variable declared in a surrounding lexical scope. In general, the address calculation consists of two portions: finding the *base address* of the appropriate *data area* for the scope that contains the value, and finding the correct offset within that data area. The problem of finding base addresses divides into two

**Data area**
The region in memory that holds the data for a specific scope is called its *data area*.

**Base address**
The address of the start of a data area is often called a *base address*.

cases: data areas with static base addresses and those whose address cannot be known until runtime.

### Variables with Static Base Addresses

Compilers typically arrange for global data areas and static data areas to have static base addresses. The strategy to generate an address for such a variable is simple: compute the data area's base address into a register and add its offset to the base address. The compiler's IR will typically include address modes to represent this calculation; for example, in ILOC, loadAI represents a "register + immediate offset" mode and loadAO represents a "register + register" mode.

To generate the runtime address of a static base address, the compiler attaches a symbolic, assembly-level label to the data area. Depending on the target machine's instruction set, that label might be used in a load immediate operation or it might be used to initialize a known location, in which case it can be moved into a register with a standard load operation.

**Name mangling**

The process of constructing a unique string from a source-language name is called *name mangling*.

If &fee. is too long for an immediate load, the compiler may need to use multiple operations to load the address.

The compiler constructs the label for a base address by *mangling* the name. Typically, it adds a prefix, a suffix, or both to the original name, using characters that are legal in the assembly code but not in the source language. For example, mangling the global variable name fee might produce the label &fee.; the label is then attached to an assembly-language pseudo-operation that reserves space for fee. To move the address into a register, the compiler might emit an operation such as loadI &fee. $\Rightarrow$ $r_j$. Subsequent operations can then use $r_j$ to access the memory location for fee. The label becomes a relocatable symbol for the assembler and the loader, which convert it into a runtime virtual address.

Global variables may be labelled individually or in larger groups. In FORTRAN, for example, the language collects global variables into common blocks. A typical FORTRAN compiler establishes one label for each common block. It assigns an offset to each variable in each common block and generates load and store operations relative to the common block's label. If the data area is larger than the offset allowed in a "register + offset" operation, it may be advantageous to have multiple labels for parts of the data area.

Similarly, the compiler may combine all the static variables in a single scope into one data area. This reduces the likelihood of an unexpected naming conflict; such conflicts are discovered during linking or loading and can be confusing to the programmer. To avoid such conflicts, the compiler can base the label on a globally visible name associated with the scope. This strategy decreases the number of base addresses in use at any time, reducing demand for registers. Using too many registers to hold base addresses may adversely affect overall runtime performance.

### Variables with Dynamic Base Addresses

As described in Section 6.3.2, local variables declared within a procedure are typically stored in the procedure's AR. Thus, they have dynamic base addresses. To access these values, the compiler needs a mechanism to find the addresses of various ARs. Fortunately, lexical scoping rules limit the set of ARs that can be accessed from any point in the code to the current AR and the ARs of lexically enclosing procedures.

### Local Variable of the Current Procedure

Accessing a local variable of the current procedure is trivial. Its base address is simply the address of the current AR, which is stored in the ARP. Thus, the compiler can emit code that adds its offset to the ARP and uses the result as the value's address. (This offset is the same value as the offset in the value's static coordinate.) In ILOC the compiler might use a `loadAI` (an "address + immediate offset" operation) or a `loadAO` (an "address + offset" operation). Most processors provide efficient support for these common operations.

In some cases, a value is not stored at a constant offset from the ARP. The value might reside in a register, in which case loads and stores are not needed. If the variable has an unpredictable or changing size, the compiler will store it in an area reserved for variable-size objects, either at the end of the AR or in the heap. In this case, the compiler can reserve space in the AR for a pointer to the variable's actual location and generate one additional load to access the variable.

### Local Variables of Other Procedures

To access a local variable of some enclosing lexical scope, the compiler must arrange for the construction of runtime data structures that map a static coordinate, produced using a lexically-scoped symbol table in the parser, into a runtime address.

For example, assume that procedure fee, at lexical level $m$, references variable a from fee's lexical ancestor fie, at level $n$. The parser converts this reference into a static coordinate $\langle n,o \rangle$, where $o$ is a's offset in the AR for fie. The compiler can compute the number of lexical levels between fee and fie as $m-n$. (The coordinate $\langle m-n,o \rangle$ is sometimes called the *static-distance coordinate* of the reference.)

The compiler needs a mechanism to convert $\langle n,o \rangle$ into a runtime address. In general, that scheme will use runtime data structures to find the ARP of the most recent level $n$ procedure, and use that ARP as the base address in its computation. It adds the offset $o$ to that base address to produce a runtime address for the value whose static coordinate is $\langle n,o \rangle$. The complication lies in building and traversing the runtime data structures to find the base address. The following subsections examine two common methods: use of access links and use of a global display.

### Access Links

The intuition behind access links is simple. The compiler ensures that each AR contains a pointer, called an *access link* or a *static link*, to the AR of its immediate lexical ancestor. The access links form a chain that includes all the lexical ancestors of the current procedure, as shown in Figure 6.8. Thus, any local variable of another procedure that is visible to the current procedure is stored in an AR on the chain of access links that begins in the current procedure.

To access a value $\langle n,o \rangle$ from a level $m$ procedure, the compiler emits code to walk the chain of links and find the level $n$ ARP. Next, it emits a load that uses the level $n$ ARP and $o$. To make this concrete, consider the program represented by Figure 6.8. Assume that $m$ is 2 and that the access link is stored at an offset of $-4$ from the ARP. The following table shows a set of

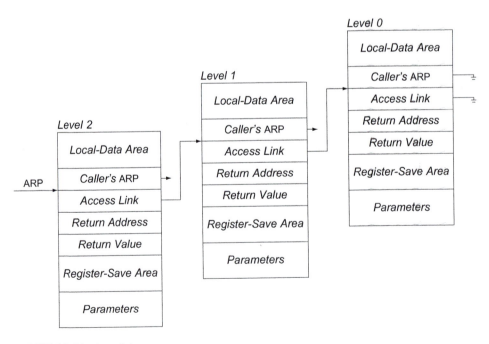

■ **FIGURE 6.8** Using Access Links.

three different static coordinates alongside the ILOC code that a compiler might generate for them. Each sequence leaves the result in $r_2$.

| Coordinate | Code |
|---|---|
| $\langle 2,24 \rangle$ | loadAI $r_{arp}$, 24 $\Rightarrow$ $r_2$ |
| $\langle 1,12 \rangle$ | loadAI $r_{arp}$, -4 $\Rightarrow$ $r_1$ |
| | loadAI $r_1$, 12 $\quad\Rightarrow$ $r_2$ |
| $\langle 0,16 \rangle$ | loadAI $r_{arp}$, -4 $\Rightarrow$ $r_1$ |
| | loadAI $r_1$, -4 $\quad\Rightarrow$ $r_1$ |
| | loadAI $r_1$, 16 $\quad\Rightarrow$ $r_2$ |

Since the compiler has the static coordinate for each reference, it can compute the static distance $(m-n)$. The distance tells it how many chain-following loads to generate, so the compiler can emit the correct sequence for each nonlocal reference. The cost of the address calculation is proportional to the static distance. If programs exhibit shallow lexical nesting, the difference in cost between accessing two variables at different levels will be fairly small.

To maintain access links, the compiler must add code to each procedure call that finds the appropriate ARP and stores it as the callee's access link. For a caller at level $m$ and a callee at level $n$, three cases arise. If $n = m + 1$, the callee is nested inside the caller, and the callee can use the caller's ARP as its access link. If $n = m$, the callee's access link is the same as the caller's access link. Finally, if $n < m$, the callee's access link is the level $n - 1$ access link for the caller. (If $n$ is zero, the access link is null.) The compiler can generate a sequence of $m - n + 1$ loads to find this ARP and store that pointer as the callee's access link.

### Global Display

In this scheme, the compiler allocates a single global array, called the *display*, to hold the ARP of the most recent activation of a procedure at each lexical level. All references to local variables of other procedures become indirect references through the display. To access a variable $\langle n,o \rangle$, the compiler uses the ARP from element $n$ of the display. It uses $o$ as the offset and generates the appropriate load operation. Figure 6.9 shows this situation.

Returning to the static coordinates used in the discussion of access links, the following table shows code that the compiler might emit for a display-based

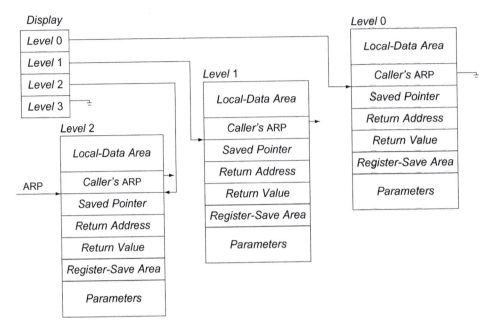

■ **FIGURE 6.9** Using a Global Display.

implementation. Assume that the current procedure is at lexical level 2, and that the label _disp gives the address of the display.

| Coordinate | Code |
|---|---|
| $\langle 2,24 \rangle$ | loadAI $r_{arp}$, 24 $\Rightarrow r_2$ |
| $\langle 1,12 \rangle$ | loadI _disp $\Rightarrow r_1$ <br> loadAI $r_1$, 4 $\Rightarrow r_1$ <br> loadAI $r_1$, 12 $\Rightarrow r_2$ |
| $\langle 0,16 \rangle$ | loadI _disp $\Rightarrow r_1$ <br> loadAI $r_1$, 16 $\Rightarrow r_2$ |

With a display, the cost of nonlocal access is fixed. With access links, the compiler generates a series of $m-n$ loads; with a display, it uses $n \times l$ as offset into the display, where $l$ is the length of a pointer (4 in the example). Local access is still cheaper than nonlocal access, but with a display, the penalty for nonlocal access is constant, rather than variable.

Of course, the compiler must insert code where needed to maintain the display. Thus, when procedure $p$ at level $n$ calls some procedure $q$ at level $n+1$, $p$'s ARP becomes the display entry for level $n$. (While $p$ is executing, that entry is unused.) The simplest way to keep the display current is to have $p$ update the level $n$ entry when control enters $p$ and to restore it on exit from $p$. On entry, $p$ can copy the level $n$ display entry to the reserved addressability slot in its AR and store its own ARP in the level $n$ slot of the display.

Many of these display updates can be avoided. The only procedures that can use the ARP stored by a procedure $p$ are procedures $q$ that $p$ calls (directly or indirectly), where $q$ is nested inside $p$'s scope. Thus, any $p$ that does not call a procedure nested inside itself need not update the display. This eliminates all updates in leaf procedures, as well as many other updates.

---

**SECTION REVIEW**

If the fundamental purpose of a procedure is abstraction, then the ability to communicate values between procedures is critical to their utility. The flow of values between procedures occurs with two different mechanisms: the use of parameters and the use of values that are visible in multiple procedures. In each of these cases, the compiler writer must arrange access conventions and runtime structures to support the access. For parameter binding, two particular mechanisms have emerged as the common cases: call by value and call by reference. For nonlocal accesses, the compiler must emit code to compute the appropriate base addresses. Two mechanisms have emerged as the common cases: access links and a display.

The most confusing aspect of this material is the distinction between actions that happen at compile time, such as the parser finding static coordinates for a variable, and those that happen at runtime, such as the executing program tracing up a chain of access links to find the ARP of some surrounding scope. In the case of compile-time actions, the compiler performs the action directly. In the case of runtime actions, the compiler emits code that will perform the action at runtime.

---

**Review Questions**

1. An early FORTRAN implementation had an odd bug. The short program in the margin would print, as its result, the value 16. What did the compiler do that led to this result? What should it have done instead? (FORTRAN uses call-by-reference parameter binding.)

2. Compare and contrast the costs involved in using access links versus global displays to establish addresses for references to variables declared in surrounding scopes. Which would you choose? Do language features affect your choice?

```
subroutine change(n)
  integer n
  n = n * 2
end

program test
  call change(2)
  print *, 2 * 2
end
```

## 6.5 **STANDARDIZED LINKAGES**

The procedure linkage is a contract between the compiler, the operating system, and the target machine that clearly divides responsibility for naming, allocation of resources, addressability, and protection. The procedure linkage ensures interoperability of procedures between the user's code, as translated by the compiler, and code from other sources, including system libraries, application libraries, and code written in other programming languages. Typically, all of the compilers for a given combination of target machine and operating system use the same linkage, to the extent possible.

The linkage convention isolates each procedure from the different environments found at call sites that invoke it. Assume that procedure $p$ has an integer parameter $x$. Different calls to $p$ might bind $x$ to a local variable stored in the caller's stack frame, to a global variable, to an element of some static array, and to the result of evaluating an integer expression such as $y + 2$. Because the linkage convention specifies how to evaluate the actual parameter and store its value, as well as how to access $x$ in the callee, the compiler can generate code for the callee that ignores the differences between the runtime environments at the different calls sites. As long as all the procedures obey the linkage convention, the details will mesh to create the seamless transfer of values promised by the source-language specification.

The linkage convention is, of necessity, machine dependent. For example, it depends implicitly on information such as the number of registers available on the target machine and the mechanisms for executing a call and a return.

Figure 6.10 shows how the pieces of a standard procedure linkage fit together. Each procedure has a *prologue sequence* and an *epilogue sequence*. Each call site includes both a *precall sequence* and a *postreturn sequence*.

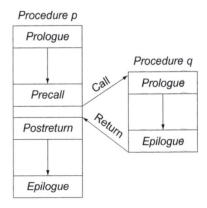

■ **FIGURE 6.10** A Standard Procedure Linkage.

- *Precall Sequence* The precall sequence begins the process of constructing the callee's environment. It evaluates the actual parameters, determines the return address, and, if necessary, the address of space reserved to hold a return value. If a call-by-reference parameter is currently allocated to a register, the precall sequence needs to store it into the caller's AR so that it can pass that location's address to the callee.

  Many of the values shown in the diagrams of the AR can be passed to the callee in registers. The return address, an address for the return value, and the caller's ARP are obvious candidates. The first $k$ actual parameters can be passed in registers as well—a typical value for $k$ might be 4. If the call has more than $k$ parameters, the remaining actual parameters must be stored in either the callee's AR or the caller's AR.

- *Postreturn Sequence* The postreturn sequence undoes the actions of the precall sequence. It must restore any call-by-reference and call-by-value-result parameters that need to be returned to registers. It restores any caller-saved registers from the register save area. It may need to deallocate all or part of the callee's AR.

- *Prologue Sequence* The prologue for a procedure completes the task of creating the callee's runtime environment. It may create space in the callee's AR to store some of the values passed by the caller in registers. It must create space for local variables and initialize them, as necessary. If the callee references a procedure-specific static data area, it may need to load the label for that data area into a register.

- *Epilogue Sequence* The epilogue for a procedure begins the process of dismantling the callee's environment and reconstructing the caller's environment. It may participate in deallocating the callee's AR. If the procedure returns a value, the epilogue may be responsible for storing the value into the address specified by the caller. (Alternatively, the code generated for a return statement may perform this task.) Finally, it restores the caller's ARP and jumps to the return address.

This framework provides general guidance for building a linkage convention. Many of the tasks can be shifted between caller and callee. In general, moving work into the prologue and epilogue code produces more compact code. The precall and postreturn sequences are generated for each call, while the prologue and epilogue occur once per procedure. If procedures are called, on average, more than once, then there are fewer prologue and epilogue sequences than precall and postreturn sequences.

---

**MORE ABOUT TIME**

In a typical system, the linkage convention is negotiated between the compiler implementors and the operating-system implementors at an early stage of the system's development. Thus, issues such as the distinction between caller-saves and callee-saves registers are decided at design time. When the compiler runs, it must emit procedure prologue and epilogue sequences for each procedure, along with precall and postreturn sequences for each call site. This code executes at runtime. Thus, the compiler cannot know the return address that it should store into a callee's AR. (Neither can it know, in general, the address of that AR.) It can, however, include a mechanism that will generate the return address at link time (using a relocatable assembly language label) or at runtime (using some offset from the program counter) and store it into the appropriate location in the callee's AR.

Similarly, in a system that uses a display to provide addressability for local variables of other procedures, the compiler cannot know the runtime addresses of the display or the AR. Nonetheless, it emits code to maintain the display. The mechanism that achieves this requires two pieces of information: the lexical nesting level of the current procedure and the address of the global display. The former is known at compile time; the latter can be determined at link time by using a relocatable assembly language label. Thus, the prologue can simply load the current display entry for the procedure's level (using a loadAO from the display address) and store it into the AR (using a storeAO relative to the ARP). Finally, it stores the address of the new AR into the display slot for the procedure's lexical level.

---

### Saving Registers

At some point in the call sequence, any register values that the caller expects to survive across the call must be saved into memory. Either the caller or the callee can perform the actual save; there is an advantage to either choice. If the caller saves registers, it can avoid saving values that it knows are not useful across the call; that knowledge might allow it to preserve fewer values. Similarly, if the callee saves registers, it can avoid saving values of registers that it does not use; again, that knowledge might result in fewer saved values.

**Caller-saves registers**
The registers designated for the caller to save are *caller-saves registers*.

**Callee-saves registers**
The registers designated for the callee to save are *callee-saves registers*.

In general, the compiler can use its knowledge of the procedure being compiled to optimize register save behavior. For any specific division of labor between caller and callee, we can construct programs for which it works well and programs for which it does not. Most modern systems take a middle ground and designate a portion of the register set for caller-saves treatment and a portion for callee-saves treatment. In practice, this seems to work well. It encourages the compiler to put long-lived values in callee-saves registers, where they will be stored only if the callee actually needs the register. It encourages the compiler to put short-lived values in caller-saves registers, where it may avoid saving them at a call.

### Allocating the Activation Record

In the most general case, both the caller and the callee need access to the callee's AR. Unfortunately, the caller cannot know, in general, how large the callee's AR must be (unless the compiler and linker can contrive to have the linker paste the appropriate values into each call site).

With stack-allocated ARs, a middle ground is possible. Since allocation consists of incrementing the stack-top pointer, the caller can begin the creation of the callee's AR by bumping the stack top and storing values into the appropriate places. When control passes to the callee, it can extend the partially built AR by incrementing the stack top to create space for local data. The postreturn sequence can then reset the stack-top pointer, performing the entire deallocation in a single step.

With heap-allocated ARs, it may not be possible to extend the callee's AR incrementally. In this situation, the compiler writer has two choices.

1. The compiler can pass the values that it must store in the callee's AR in registers; the prologue sequence can then allocate an appropriately sized AR and store the passed values in it. In this scheme, the compiler writer reduces the number of values that the caller passes to the callee by arranging to store the parameter values in the caller's AR. Access to those parameters uses the copy of the caller's ARP that is stored in the callee's AR.
2. The compiler writer can split the AR into multiple distinct pieces, one to hold the parameter and control information generated by the caller and the others to hold space needed by the callee but unknown to the caller. The caller cannot, in general, know how large to make the local data area. The compiler can store this number for each callee using mangled labels; the caller can then load the value and use it. Alternatively, the callee can allocate its own local data area and keep its base address in a register or in a slot in the AR created by the caller.

Heap-allocated ARs add to the overhead cost of a procedure call. Care in the implementation of the calling sequence and the allocator can reduce those costs.

### Managing Displays and Access Links

Either mechanism for managing nonlocal access requires some work in the calling sequence. Using a display, the prologue sequence updates the display record for its own level and the epilogue sequence restores it. If the procedure never calls a more deeply nested procedure, it can skip this step. Using access links, the precall sequence must locate the appropriate first access link for the callee. The amount of work varies with the difference in lexical level between caller and callee. As long as the callee is known at compile time, either scheme is reasonably efficient. If the callee is unknown (if it is, for example, a function-valued parameter), the compiler may need to emit special-case code to perform the appropriate steps.

---

**SECTION REVIEW**

The procedure linkage ties together procedures. The linkage convention is a social contract between the compiler, the operating system, and the underlying hardware. It governs the transfer of control between procedures, the preservation of the caller's state and the creation of the callee's state, and the rules for passing values between them.

Standard procedure linkages allow us to assemble executable programs from procedures that have different authors, that are translated at different times, and that are compiled with different compilers. Procedure linkages allow each procedure to operate safely and correctly. The same conventions allow application code to invoke system and library calls. While the details of the linkage convention vary from system to system, the basic concepts are similar across most combinations of target machine, operating system, and compiler.

---

**Review Questions**

1. What role does the linkage convention play in the construction of large programs? Of interlanguage programs? What facts would the compiler need to know in order to generate code for an interlanguage call?
2. If the compiler knows, at a procedure call, that the callee does not, itself, contain any procedure calls, what steps might it omit from the calling sequence? Are there any fields in the AR that the callee would never need?

## 6.6 ADVANCED TOPICS

The compiler must arrange for the allocation of space to hold the various runtime structures discussed in Section 6.3. For some languages, those structures have lifetimes that do not fit well into the first-in first-out discipline of a stack. In such cases, the language implementation allocates space in the runtime heap—a region of memory set aside for such objects and managed by routines in a runtime support library. The compiler must also arrange storage for other objects that have lifetimes unrelated to the flow of control, such as many lists in a Scheme program or many objects in a Java program.

We assume a simple interface to the heap, namely, a routine `allocate(size)` and a routine `free(address)`. The `allocate` routine takes an integer argument `size` and returns the address of a block of space in the heap that contains at least `size` bytes. The `free` routine takes the address of a block of previously allocated space in the heap and returns it to the pool of free space. The critical issues that arise in designing algorithms for explicitly managing the heap are the speeds of both `allocate` and `free` and the extent to which the pool of free space becomes fragmented into small blocks.

This section sketches the algorithms involved in allocation and reclamation of space in a runtime heap. Section 6.6.1 focuses on techniques for explicit management of the heap. Along the way, it describes how to implement `free` for each of the schemes. Section 6.6.2 examines implicit deallocation—techniques that avoid the need for `free`.

## 6.6.1 **Explicit Heap Management**

Most language implementations include a runtime system that provides support functions for the code generated by the compiler. The runtime system typically includes provision for management of a runtime heap. The actual routines that implement the heap may be language specific, as in a Scheme interpreter or a Java virtual machine, or they may be part of the underlying operating system, as in the POSIX implementations of `malloc` and `free`.

While many techniques have been proposed to implement `allocate` and `free`, most of those implementations share common strategies and insights. This section explores a simple strategy, *first-fit allocation*, that exposes most of the issues, and then shows how a strategy such as first fit is used to implement a modern allocator.

### *First-Fit Allocation*

The goal of a first-fit allocator is to allocate and free space in the heap quickly. First fit emphasizes speed over memory utilization. Every block in the heap has a hidden field that holds its size. In general, the size field is located in the word preceding the address returned by `allocate`, as shown in Figure 6.11a. Blocks available for allocation reside on a list called the *free list*. In addition to the mandatory size field, blocks on the free list have additional fields, as shown in Figure 6.11b. Each free block has a pointer to the next block on the free list (set to null in the last block) and a pointer to the block itself in the last word of the block. To initialize the heap, the allocator creates a free list that contains a single large unallocated block.

(a) Allocated Block     (b) Free Block

■ **FIGURE 6.11** Blocks in a First-Fit Allocator.

A call allocate($k$) causes the following sequence of events: The allocate routine walks the free list until it discovers a block with size greater than or equal to $k$ plus one word for the size field. Assume it finds an appropriate block, $b_i$. It removes $b_i$ from the free list. If $b_i$ is larger than necessary, allocate creates a new free block from the excess space at the end of $b_i$ and places that block on the free list. The allocate routine returns a pointer to the second word of $b_i$.

If allocate fails to find a large enough block, it tries to extend the heap. If it succeeds in extending the heap, it returns a block of appropriate size from this newly allocated portion of the heap. If extending the heap fails, allocate reports failure (typically by returning a null pointer).

To deallocate a block, the program calls free with the address of the block, $b_j$. The simplest implementation of free adds $b_j$ to the head of the free list and returns. This produces a fast free routine. Unfortunately, it leads to an allocator that, over time, fragments memory into small blocks.

To overcome this flaw, the allocator can use the pointer at the end of a freed block to coalesce adjacent free blocks. The free routine loads the word preceding $b_j$'s size field, which is the end-of-block pointer for the block that immediately precedes $b_j$ in memory. If that word contains a valid pointer, and it points to a matching block header (one whose address plus size field points to the start of $b_j$), then both $b_j$ and its predecessor are free. The free routine can combine them by increasing the predecessor's size field and storing the appropriate pointer at the end of $b_j$. Combining these blocks lets free avoid updating the free list.

To make this scheme work, allocate and free must maintain the end-of-block pointers. Each time that free processes a block, it must update that pointer with the address of the head of the block. The allocate routine must invalidate either the next pointer or the end-of-block pointer to prevent free from coalescing a freed block with an allocated block in which those fields have not been overwritten.

The free routine can also try to combine $b_j$ with its successor in memory, $b_k$. It can use $b_j$'s size field to locate the start of $b_k$. It can use $b_k$'s size field and end-of-block pointer to determine if $b_k$ is free. If $b_k$ is free, then free

**ARENA-BASED ALLOCATION**

Inside the compiler itself, the compiler writer may find it profitable to use a specialized allocator. Compilers have phase-oriented activity. This lends itself well to an arena-based allocation scheme.

With an arena-based allocator, the program creates an arena at the beginning of an activity. It uses the arena to hold allocated objects that are related in their use. Calls to allocate objects in the arena are satisfied in a stacklike fashion; an allocation involves incrementing a pointer to the arena's high-water mark and returning a pointer to the newly allocated block. No call is used to deallocate individual objects; they are freed when the arena that contains them is deallocated.

The arena-based allocator is a compromise between traditional allocators and garbage-collecting allocators. With an arena-based allocator, the calls to `allocate` can be made lightweight (as in the modern allocator). No freeing calls are needed; the program frees the entire arena in a single call when it finishes the activity for which the arena was created.

can combine the two blocks, removing $b_k$ from the free list, adding $b_j$ to the free list, and updating $b_j$'s size field and end-of-block pointer appropriately. To make the free-list update efficient, the free list should be a doubly linked list. Of course, the pointers are stored in unallocated blocks, so the space overhead is irrelevant. Extra time required to update the doubly linked free list is minimal.

As described, the coalescing scheme depends on the fact that the relationship between the final pointer and the size field in a free block are absent in an allocated block. While it is extremely unlikely that the allocator will identify an allocated block as free, this can happen. To ensure against this unlikely event, the implementor can make the end-of-block pointer a field that exists in both allocated and free blocks. On allocation, the pointer is set to contain an address outside the heap, such as zero. On freeing, the pointer is set to the block's own address. The cost of this added assurance is an extra field in each allocated block and an extra store for each allocation.

Many variations on first-fit allocation have been tried. They trade off the cost of `allocate`, the cost of `free`, the amount of fragmentation produced by a long series of allocations, and the amount of space wasted by returning blocks larger than requested.

### Multipool Allocators

Modern allocators are derived from first-fit allocation but simplified by a couple of observations about the behavior of programs. As memory sizes grew in the early 1980s, it became reasonable to waste some space if doing so led to faster allocation. At the same time, studies of program behavior suggested that real programs allocate memory frequently in a few common sizes and infrequently in large or unusual sizes.

Modern allocators use separate memory pools for several common sizes. Typically, selected sizes are powers of two, starting with a small block size (such as 16 bytes) and running up to the size of a virtual-memory page (typically 4096 or 8192 bytes). Each pool has only one size of block, so `allocate` can return the first block on the appropriate free list, and `free` can simply add the block to the head of the appropriate free list. For requests larger than a page, a separate first-fit allocator is used. Allocators based on these ideas are fast. They work particularly well for heap allocation of activation records.

These changes simplify both `allocate` and `free`. The `allocate` routine must check for an empty free list and adds a new page to the free list if it is empty. The `free` routine inserts the freed block at the head of the free list for its size. A careful implementation could determine the size of a freed block by checking its address against the memory segments allocated for each pool. Alternative schemes include using a size field as before, and, if the allocator places all the storage on a page into a single pool, storing the size of the blocks in a page in the first word of the page.

### Debugging Help

Programs written with explicit allocation and deallocation are notoriously difficult to debug. It appears that programmers have difficulty deciding when to free heap-allocated objects. If the allocator can quickly distinguish between an allocated object and a free object, then the heap-management software can provide the programmer with some help in debugging.

For example, to coalesce adjacent free blocks, the allocator needs a pointer from the end of a block back to its head. If an allocated block has that pointer set to an invalid value, then the deallocation routine can check that field and report a runtime error when the program attempts to deallocate a free block or an illegal address—a pointer to anything other than the start of an allocated block.

For a modest additional overhead, heap-management software can provide additional help. By linking together allocated blocks, the allocator can create an environment for memory-allocation debugging tools. A snapshot tool can walk the list of allocated blocks. Tagging blocks by the call site that created them lets the tool expose memory leaks. Timestamping them allows the tool to provide the programmer with detailed information about memory use. Tools of this sort can provide invaluable help in locating blocks that are never deallocated.

## 6.6.2 **Implicit Deallocation**

Many programming languages support implicit deallocation of heap objects. The implementation deallocates memory objects automatically when they are no longer in use. This requires some care in the implementation of both the allocator and the compiled code. To perform implicit deallocation, or *garbage collection*, the compiler and runtime system must include a mechanism for determining when an object is no longer of interest, or *dead*, and a mechanism for reclaiming and recycling the dead space.

**Garbage collection**
the implicit deallocation of objects that reside on the runtime heap

The work associated with garbage collection can be performed incrementally, for individual statements, or it can be performed as a batch-oriented task that runs on demand, when the free-space pool is exhausted. Reference counting is a classic way to perform incremental garbage collection. Mark-sweep collection is a classic approach to performing batch-oriented collection.

### *Reference Counting*

This technique adds a counter to each heap-allocated object. The counter tracks the number of outstanding pointers that refer to the object. When the allocator creates the object, it sets the reference count to one. Each assignment to a pointer variable adjusts two reference counts. It decrements the reference count of the pointer's preassignment value and increments the reference count of the pointer's postassignment value. When an object's reference count drops to zero, no pointer exists that can reach the object, so the system may safely free the object. Freeing an object can, in turn, discard pointers to other objects. This must decrement the reference counts of those objects. Thus, discarding the last pointer to an abstract syntax tree should free the entire tree. When the root node's reference count drops to zero, it is freed and its descendant's reference counts are decremented. This, in turn, should free the descendants, decrementing the counts of their children. This process continues until the entire AST has been freed.

The presence of pointers in allocated objects creates problems for reference-counting schemes, as follows:

1. The running code needs a mechanism to distinguish pointers from other data. It may either store extra information in the header field for each object or limit the range of pointers to less than a full word and use the

remaining bits to "tag" the pointer. Batch collectors face the same problem and use the same solutions.

2. The amount of work done for a single decrement can grow quite large. If external constraints require bounded deallocation times, the runtime system can adopt a more complex protocol that limits the number of objects deallocated for each pointer assignment. By keeping a queue of objects that must be freed and limiting the number handled on each reference-count adjustment, the system can distribute the cost of freeing objects over a larger set of operations. This amortizes the cost of freeing over the set of all assignments to heap-allocated objects and bounds the work done per assignment.

3. The program might form cyclic graphs with pointers. The reference counts for a cyclic data structure cannot be decremented to zero. When the last external pointer is discarded, the cycle becomes both unreachable and nonrecyclable. To ensure that all such objects are freed, the programmer must break the cycle before discarding the last pointer to the cycle. (The alternative, to perform reachability analysis on the pointers at runtime, would make reference counting prohibitively expensive.) Many categories of heap-allocated objects, such as variable-length strings and activation records, cannot be involved in such cycles.

Reference counting incurs additional cost on every pointer assignment. The amount of work done for a specific pointer assignment can be bounded; in any well-designed scheme, the total cost can be limited to some constant factor times the number of pointer assignments executed plus the number of objects allocated. Proponents of reference counting argue that these over-heads are small enough and that the pattern of reuse in reference-counting systems produces good program locality. Opponents of reference counting argue that real programs do more pointer assignments than allocations, so that garbage collection achieves equivalent functionality with less total work.

### *Batch Collectors*

Batch collectors consider deallocation only when the free-space pool has been exhausted. When the allocator fails to find needed space, it invokes the batch collector. The collector pauses the program's execution, examines the pool of allocated memory to discover unused objects, and reclaims their space. When the collector terminates, the free-space pool is usually nonempty. The allocator can finish its original task and return a newly allocated object to the caller. (As with reference counting, schemes exist that perform collection incrementally to amortize the cost over longer periods of execution.)

If the collector cannot free any space, then it must request additional space from the system. If none is available, allocation fails.

Logically, batch collectors proceed in two phases. The first phase discovers the set of objects that can be reached from pointers stored in program variables and compiler-generated temporaries. The collector conservatively assumes that any object reachable in this manner is live and that the remainder are dead. The second phase deallocates and recycles dead objects. Two commonly used techniques are *mark-sweep* collectors and *copying* collectors. They differ in their implementation of the second phase of collection—recycling.

### Identifying Live Data

Collecting allocators discover live objects by using a marking algorithm. The collector needs a bit for each object in the heap, called a *mark bit*. This bit can be stored in the object's header, alongside tag information used to record pointer locations or object size. Alternatively, the collector can create a dense bit map for the heap when needed. The initial step clears all the mark bits and builds a worklist that contains all the pointers stored in registers and in variables accessible to current or pending procedures. The second phase of the algorithm walks forward from these pointers and marks every object that is reachable from this set of visible pointers.

Figure 6.12 presents a high-level sketch of a marking algorithm. It is a simple fixed-point computation that halts because the heap is finite and the marks prevent a pointer contained in the heap from entering the `Worklist` more than once. The cost of marking is, in the worst case, proportional to the number of pointers contained in program variables and temporaries plus the size of the heap.

The marking algorithm can be either precise or conservative. The difference lies in how the algorithm determines that a specific data value is a pointer in the final line of the `while` loop.

- In a precise collector, the compiler and runtime system know the type and layout of each object. This information can be recorded in object headers, or it can be known implicitly from the type system. Either way, the marking phase only follows real pointers.
- In a conservative marking phase, the compiler and runtime system may be unsure about the type and layout of some objects. Thus, when an object is marked, the system considers each field that may be a possible pointer. If its value might be a pointer, it is treated as a pointer. Any value that does not represent a word-aligned address might be excluded, as might values that fall outside the known boundaries of the heap.

Conservative collectors have limitations. They fail to reclaim some objects that a precise collector would find. Nonetheless, conservative collectors have

```
Clear all marks
Worklist ← { pointer values from activation records & registers }
while (Worklist ≠ Ø)
    remove p from the Worklist
    if (p→object is unmarked)
        mark p→object
        add pointers from p→object to Worklist
```

■ **FIGURE 6.12** A Simple Marking Algorithm.

been successfully retrofitted into implementations for languages such as c that do not normally support garbage collection.

When the marking algorithm halts, any unmarked object must be unreachable from the program. Thus, the second phase of the collector can treat that object as dead. Some objects marked as live may also be dead. However, the collector lets them survive because it cannot prove them dead. As the second phase traverses the heap to collect the garbage, it can reset the mark fields to "unmarked." This lets the collector avoid the initial traversal of the heap in the marking phase.

### Mark-Sweep Collectors

Mark-sweep collectors reclaim and recycle objects by making a linear pass over the heap. The collector adds each unmarked object to the free list (or one of the free lists), where the allocator will find it and reuse it. With a single free list, the same collection of techniques used to coalesce blocks in the first-fit allocator applies. If compaction is desirable, it can be implemented by incrementally shuffling live objects downward during the sweep, or with a postsweep compaction pass.

### Copying Collectors

Copying collectors divide memory into two pools, an *old* pool and a *new* pool. The allocator always operates from the old pool. The simplest type of copying collector is called *stop and copy*. When an allocation fails, a stop and copy collector copies all the live data from the old pool into the new pool and swaps the identities of the old and new pools. The act of copying live data compacts it; after collection, all the free space is in a single contiguous block. Collection can be done in two passes, like mark sweep, or it can be done incrementally, as live data is discovered. An incremental scheme can mark objects in the old pool as it copies them to avoid copying the same object multiple times.

An important family of copying collectors are the *generational collectors*. These collectors capitalize on the observation that an object that survives one collection is more likely to survive subsequent collections. To capitalize on this observation, generational collectors periodically repartition their "new" pool into a "new" and an "old" pool. In this way, successive collections examine only newly allocated objects. Generational schemes vary in how often they declare a new generation, freezing the surviving objects and exempting them from the next collection, and whether or not they periodically re-examine the older generations.

### Comparing the Techniques

Garbage collection frees the programmer from needing to worry about when to release memory and from tracking down the inevitable storage leaks that result from attempting to manage allocation and deallocation explicitly. The individual schemes have their strengths and weaknesses. In practice, the benefits of implicit deallocation outweigh the disadvantages of either scheme for most applications.

Reference counting distributes the cost of deallocation more evenly across program execution than does batch collection. However, it increases the cost of every assignment that involves a heap-allocated value—even if the program never runs out of free space. In contrast, batch collectors incur no cost until the allocator fails to find needed space. At that point, however, the program incurs the full cost of collection. Thus, any allocation can provoke a collection.

Mark-sweep collectors examine the entire heap, while copying collectors only examine the live data. Copying collectors actually move every live object, while mark-sweep collectors leave them in place. The tradeoff between these costs will vary with the application's behavior and with the actual costs of various memory references.

Reference-counting implementations and conservative batch collectors have problems recognizing cyclic structures, because they cannot distinguish between references from within the cycle and those from without. The mark-sweep collectors start from an external set of pointers, so they discover that a dead cyclic structure is unreachable. The copying collectors, starting from the same set of pointers, simply fail to copy the objects involved in the cycle.

Copying collectors compact memory as a natural part of the process. The collector can either update all the stored pointers, or it can require use of an indirection table for each object access. A precise mark-sweep collector can compact memory, too. The collector would move objects from one end of memory into free space at the other end. Again, the collector can either rewrite the existing pointers or mandate use of an indirection table.

In general, a good implementor can make both mark sweep and copying work well enough that they are acceptable for most applications. In applications that cannot tolerate unpredictable overhead, such as real-time controllers, the runtime system must incrementalize the process, as the amortized reference-counting scheme does. Such collectors are called *real-time collectors*.

## 6.7 SUMMARY AND PERSPECTIVE

The primary rationale for moving beyond assembly language is to provide a more abstract programming model and, thus, raise both programmer productivity and the understandability of programs. Each abstraction that a programming language supports needs a translation to the target machine's instruction set. This chapter has explored the techniques commonly used to translate some of these abstractions.

Procedural programming was invented early in the history of programming. Some of the first procedures were debugging routines written for early computers; the availability of these prewritten routines allowed programmers to understand the runtime state of an errant program. Without such routines, tasks that we now take for granted, such as examining the contents of a variable or asking for a trace of the call stack, required the programmer to enter long machine-language sequences without error.

The introduction of lexical scoping in languages like Algol 60 influenced language design for decades. Most modern programming languages carry forward some of Algol's philosophy toward naming and addressability. Techniques developed to support lexical scoping, such as access links and displays, reduced the runtime cost of this abstraction. These techniques are still used today.

Object-oriented languages take the scoping concepts of ALLs and reorient them in data-directed ways. The compiler for an object-oriented language uses both compile-time and runtime structures invented for lexical scoping to implement the naming discipline imposed by the inheritance hierarchy of a specific program.

Modern languages have added some new twists. By making procedures first-class objects, languages like Scheme have created new control-flow paradigms. These require variations on traditional implementation techniques—for example, heap allocation of activation records. Similarly, the growing acceptance of implicit deallocation requires occasional conservative treatment of a pointer. If the compiler can exercise a little more care and free the programmer from ever deallocating storage again, that appears to be a good tradeoff. (Generations of experience suggest that programmers are not effective at freeing all the storage that they allocate. They also free objects to which they retain pointers.)

As new programming paradigms emerge, they will introduce new abstractions that require careful thought and implementation. By studying the successful techniques of the past and understanding the constraints and costs involved in real implementations, compiler writers will develop strategies that decrease the runtime penalty for using higher levels of abstraction.

## ■ CHAPTER NOTES

Much of the material in this chapter comes from the accumulated experience of the compiler-construction community. The best way to learn more about the name-space structures of various languages is to consult the language definitions themselves. These documents are a necessary part of a compiler writer's library.

Procedures appeared in the earliest high-level languages—that is, languages that were more abstract than assembly language. FORTRAN [27] and Algol 60 [273] both had procedures with most of the features found in modern languages. Object-oriented languages appeared in the late 1960s with SIMULA 67 [278] followed by Smalltalk 72 [233].

Lexical scoping was introduced in Algol 60 and has persisted to the present day. The early Algol compilers introduced most of the support mechanisms described in this chapter, including activation records, access links, and parameter-passing techniques. Much of the material from Sections 6.3 through 6.5 was present in these early systems [293]. Optimizations quickly appeared, like folding storage for a block-level scope into the containing procedure's activation record. The IBM 370 linkage conventions recognized the difference between leaf procedures and others; they avoided allocating a register save area for leaf routines. Murtagh took a more complete and systematic approach to coalescing activation records [272].

The classic reference on memory allocation schemes is Knuth's *Art of Computer Programming* [231, § 2.5]. Modern multipool allocators appeared in the early 1980s. Reference counting dates to the early 1960s and has been used in many systems [95, 125]. Cohen and later Wilson, provide broad surveys of the literature on garbage collection [92, 350]. Conservative collectors were introduced by Boehm and Weiser [44, 46, 120]. Copying collectors appeared in response to virtual memory systems [79, 144]; they led, somewhat naturally, to the generational collectors in widespread use today [247, 337]. Hanson introduced the notion of arena-based allocation [179].

## ■ EXERCISES

1. Show the call tree and execution history for the following C program:

```c
int Sub(int i, int j) {
   return i - j;
}
int Mul(int i, int j) {
   return i * j;
}
int Delta(int a, int b, int c) {
   return Sub(Mul(b,b), Mul(Mul(4,a),c));
}
void main() {
   int a, b, c, delta;
   scanf("%d %d %d", &a, &b, &c);
   delta = Delta(a, b, c);
   if (delta == 0)
     puts("Two equal roots");
   else if (delta > 0)
     puts("Two different roots");
   else
     puts("No root");
}
```

2. Show the call tree and execution history for the following C program:

```c
void Output(int n, int x) {
   printf("The value of %d! is %s.\n", n, x);
}
int Fat(int n) {
   int x;
     if (n > 1)
   x = n * Fat(n - 1);
   else
     x = 1;
   Output(n, x);
   return x;
}
void main() {
   Fat(4);
}
```

**3.** Consider the following Pascal program, in which only procedure calls and variable declarations are shown:

```
1   program Main(input, output);
2     var a, b, c : integer;
3     procedure P4; forward;
4     procedure P1;
5       procedure P2;
6         begin
7         end;
8       var b, d, f : integer;
9       procedure P3;
10        var a, b : integer;
11        begin
12          P2;
13          end;
14      begin
15        P2;
16        P4;
17        P3;
18        end;
19    var d, e : integer;
20    procedure P4;
21      var a, c, g : integer;
22      procedure P5;
23        var c, d : integer;
24        begin
25          P1;
26          end;
27      var d : integer;
28      begin
29        P1;
30        P5;
31        end;
32    begin
33      P1;
34      P4;
35      end.
```

**a.** Construct a static coordinate table, similar to the one in Figure 6.3.
**b.** Construct a graph to show the nesting relationships in the program.
**c.** Construct a graph to show the calling relationships in the program.

4. Some programming languages allow the programmer to use functions in the initialization of local variables but not in the initialization of global variables.

   a. Is there an implementation rationale to explain this seeming quirk of the language definition?

   b. What mechanisms would be needed to allow initialization of a global variable with the result of a function call?

5. The compiler writer can optimize the allocation of ARs in several ways. For example, the compiler might:

   a. Allocate ARs for leaf procedures statically.

   b. Combine the ARs for procedures that are always called together. (When $\alpha$ is called, it always calls $\beta$.)

   c. Use an arena-style allocator in place of heap allocation of ARs.

   For each scheme, consider the following questions:

   a. What fraction of the calls might benefit? In the best case? In the worst case?

   b. What is the impact on runtime space utilization?

6. Draw the structures that the compiler would need to create to support an object of type Dumbo, defined as follows:

   ```
   class Elephant {
       private int Length;
       private int Weight;
       static int type;

       public int GetLen();
       public int GetTyp();
   }

   class Dumbo extends Elephant {
       private int EarSize;
       private boolean Fly;

       public boolean CanFly();
   }
   ```

7. In a programming language with an open class structure, the number of method invocations that need runtime name resolution, or dynamic dispatch, can be large. A method cache, as described in Section 6.3.4, can reduce the runtime cost of these lookups by short-circuiting them. As an alternative to a global method cache, the implementation might maintain a single entry method cache at each call site—an inline

```
 1   procedure main;
 2     var a : array[1...3] of int;
 3         i : int;
 4     procedure p2(e : int);
 5       begin
 6         e := e + 3;
 7         a[i] := 5;
 8         i := 2;
 9         e := e + 4;
10         end;
11       begin
12         a := [1, 10, 77];
13         i := 1;
14         p2(a[i]);
15         for i := 1 to 3 do
16           print(a[i]);
17         end.
```

■ **FIGURE 6.13** Program for Problem 8.

method cache that records record the address of the method most recently dispatched from that site, along with its class.
Develop pseudocode to use and maintain such an inline method cache. Explain the initialization of the inline method caches and any modifications to the general method lookup routine required to support inline method caches.

8. Consider the program written in Pascal-like pseudo code shown in Figure 6.13. Simulate its execution under call-by-value, call-by-reference, call-by-name, and call-by-value-result parameter binding rules. Show the results of the print statements in each case.

Section 6.4

9. The possibility that two distinct variables refer to the same object (memory area) is considered undesirable in programming languages. Consider the following Pascal procedure, with parameters passed by reference:

```
procedure mystery(var x, y : integer);
  begin
    x := x + y;
    y := x - y;
    x := x - y;
  end;
```

```
1      program main(input, output);
2        procedure P1( function g(b: integer): integer);
3          var a: integer;
4          begin
5            a := 3;
6            writeln(g(2))
7          end;
8        procedure P2;
9          var a: integer;
10         function F1(b: integer): integer;
11           begin
12             F1 := a + b
13           end;
14         procedure P3;
15           var a:integer;
16           begin
17             a := 7;
18             P1(F1)
19           end;
20         begin
21           a := 0;
22           P3
23         end;
24       begin
25         P2
26       end.
```

(a) Example Pascal Program

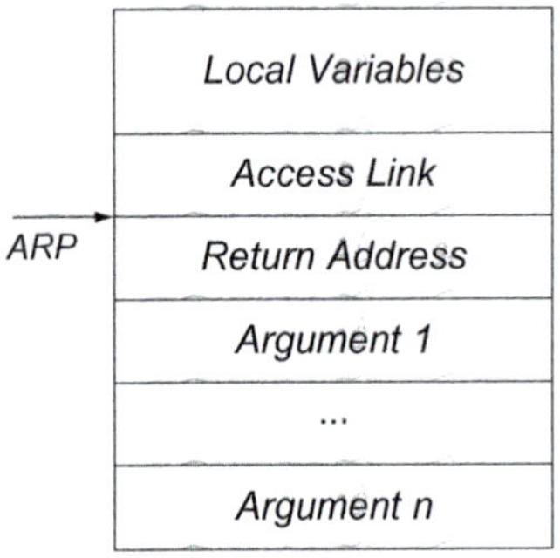

| Local Variables |
|:---:|
| Access Link |
| Return Address |
| Argument 1 |
| ... |
| Argument n |

ARP → (points to Return Address row)

(b) Activation Record Structure

| Access Link (0) |
|:---:|
| Return Address (0) |

ARP → (points to Access Link (0) row)

(c) Initial Activation Record

■ **FIGURE 6.14** Program for Problem 10.

If no overflow or underflow occurs during the arithmetic operations:

**a.** What result does mystery produce when it is called with two distinct variables, a and b?

**b.** What would be the expected result if mystery is invoked with a single variable a passed to both parameters? What is the actual result in this case?

**Section 6.5**

**10.** Consider the Pascal program shown in Figure 6.14a. Suppose that the implementation uses ARS as shown in Figure 6.14b. (Some fields have been omitted for simplicity.) The implementation stack allocates the ARS, with the stack growing toward the top of the page. The ARP is the only pointer to the AR, so access links are previous values of the ARP. Finally, Figure 6.14c shows the initial AR for a computation. For the example program in Figure 6.14a, draw the set of its ARs just prior to the return from function F1. Include all entries in the ARs. Use line numbers for return addresses. Draw directed arcs for access links. Label the values of local variables and parameters. Label each AR with its procedure name.

**11.** Assume that the compiler is capable of analyzing the code to determine facts such as *"from this point on, variable* v *is not used again in this procedure"* or *"variable* v *has its next use in line 11 of this procedure,"* and that the compiler keeps all local variables in registers for the following three procedures:

```
procedure main
    integer a, b, c
    b = a + c;
    c = f1(a,b);
    call print(c);
    end;
procedure f1(integer x, y)
    integer v;
    v = x * y;
    call print(v);
    call f2(v);
    return -x;
    end;
procedure f2(integer q)
    integer k, r;
    ...
    k = q / r;
    end;
```

**a.** Variable x in procedure f1 is live across two procedure calls. For the fastest execution of the compiled code, should the compiler keep it in a caller-saves or callee-saves register? Justify your answer.

**b.** Consider variables a and c in procedure main. Should the compiler keep them in caller-saves or callee-saves registers, again assuming that the compiler is trying to maximize the speed of the compiled code? Justify your answer.

12. Consider the following Pascal program. Assume that the ARs follow the same layout as in problem 10,with the same initial condition, *except* that the implementation uses a global display rather than access links.

```
1    program main(input, output);
2      var x : integer;
3          a : float;
4      procedure p1();
5        var g:character;
6        begin
7          ...
8          end;
9      procedure p2();
10       var h:character;
11       procedure p3();
12         var h,i:integer;
13         begin
14           p1();
15           end;
16       begin
17         p3();
18         end;
19     begin
20       p2();
21     end
```

Draw the set of ARs that are on the runtime stack when the program reaches line 7 in procedure p1.

# Code Shape

## ■ CHAPTER OVERVIEW

To translate an application program, the compiler must map each source-language statement into a sequence of one or more operations in the target machine's instruction set. The compiler must chose among many alternative ways to implement each construct. Those choices have a strong and direct impact on the quality of the code that the compiler eventually produces.

This chapter explores some of the implementation strategies that the compiler can employ for a variety of common programming-language constructs.

**Keywords:** Code Generation, Control Structures, Expression Evaluation

## 7.1 INTRODUCTION

When the compiler translates application code into executable form, it faces myriad choices about specific details, such as the organization of the computation and the location of data. Such decisions often affect the performance of the resulting code. The compiler's decisions are guided by information that it derives over the course of translation. When information is discovered in one pass and used in another, the compiler must record that information for its own later use.

Often, compilers encode facts in the IR form of the program—facts that are hard to re-derive unless they are encoded. For example, the compiler might generate the IR so that every scalar variable that can safely reside in a register is stored in a virtual register. In this scheme, the register allocator's job is to decide which virtual registers it should demote to memory. The alternative, generating the IR with scalar variables stored in memory and having the allocator promote them into registers, requires much more complex analysis.

Encoding knowledge into the IR name space in this way both simplifies the later passes and improves the compiler's effectiveness and efficiency.

### Conceptual Roadmap

The translation of source code constructs into target-machine operations is one of the fundamental acts of compilation. The compiler must produce target code for each source-language construct. Many of the same issues arise when generating IR in the compiler's front end and generating assembly code for a real processor in its back end. The target processor may, due to finite resources and idiosyncratic features, present a more difficult problem, but the principles are the same.

This chapter focuses on ways to implement various source-language constructs. In many cases, specific details of the implementation affect the compiler's ability to analyze and to improve the code in later passes. The concept of "code shape" encapsulates all of the decisions, large and small, that the compiler writer makes about how to represent the computation in both IR and assembly code. Careful attention to code shape can both simplify the task of analyzing and improving the code, and improve the quality of the final code that the compiler produces.

### Overview

In general, the compiler writer should focus on shaping the code so that the various passes in the compiler can combine to produce outstanding code. In practice, a compiler can implement most source-language constructs many ways on a given processor. These variations use different operations and different approaches. Some of these implementations are faster than others; some use less memory; some use fewer registers; some might consume less energy during execution. We consider these differences to be matters of *code shape*.

Code shape has a strong impact both on the behavior of the compiled code and on the ability of the optimizer and back end to improve it. Consider, for example, the way that a c compiler might implement a `switch` statement that switched on a single-byte character value. The compiler might use a cascaded series of `if-then-else` statements to implement the `switch` statement. Depending on the layout of the tests, this could produce different results. If the first test is for zero, the second for one, and so on, then this approach devolves to linear search over a field of 256 keys. If characters are uniformly distributed, the character searches will require an average of 128 tests and branches per character—an expensive way to implement a case statement. If, instead, the tests perform a binary search, the average case would involve eight tests and branches, a more palatable number. To trade

| | Source Code | Low-Level, Three-Address Code |
|---|---|---|
| **Code** | $x + y + z$ | $\begin{array}{lll} r_1 \leftarrow r_x + r_y & r_1 \leftarrow r_x + r_z & r_1 \leftarrow r_y + r_z \\ r_2 \leftarrow r_1 + r_z & r_2 \leftarrow r_1 + r_y & r_2 \leftarrow r_1 + r_x \end{array}$ |
| **Tree** | | |

■ **FIGURE 7.1** Alternate Code Shapes for $x + y + z$.

data space for speed, the compiler can construct a table of 256 labels and interpret the character by loading the corresponding table entry and jumping to it—with a constant overhead per character.

All of these are legal implementations of the switch statement. Deciding which one makes sense for a particular switch statement depends on many factors. In particular, the number of cases and their relative execution frequencies are important, as is detailed knowledge of the cost structure for branching on the processor. Even when the compiler cannot determine the information that it needs to make the best choice, it must make a choice. The differences among the possible implementations, and the compiler's choice, are matters of code shape.

As another example, consider the simple expression $x + y + z$, where $x$, $y$, and $z$ are integers. Figure 7.1 shows several ways of implementing this expression. In source-code form, we may think of the operation as a ternary add, shown on the left. However, mapping this idealized operation into a sequence of binary additions exposes the impact of evaluation order. The three versions on the right show three possible evaluation orders, both as three-address code and as abstract syntax trees. (We assume that each variable is in an appropriately named register and that the source language does not specify the evaluation order for such an expression.) Because integer addition is both commutative and associative, all the orders are equivalent; the compiler must choose one to implement.

Left associativity would produce the first binary tree. This tree seems "natural" in that left associativity corresponds to our left-to-right reading style. Consider what happens if we replace $y$ with the literal constant 2 and $z$ with 3. Of course, $x + 2 + 3$ is equivalent to $x + 5$. The compiler should detect the computation of $2 + 3$, evaluate it, and fold the result directly into the code. In the left-associative form, however, $2 + 3$ never occurs. The order $x + z + y$ hides it, as well. The right-associative version exposes the opportunity for improvement. For each prospective tree, however, there is an assignment of variables and constants to x, y, and z that does not expose the constant expression for optimization.

As with the switch statement, the compiler cannot choose the best shape for this expression without understanding the context in which it appears. If, for example, the expression x + y has been computed recently and neither the values of x nor y have changed, then using the leftmost shape would let the compiler replace the first operation, $r_1 \leftarrow r_x + r_y$, with a reference to the previously computed value. Often, the best evaluation order depends on context from the surrounding code.

This chapter explores the code-shape issues that arise in implementing many common source-language constructs. It focuses on the code that should be generated for specific constructs, while largely ignoring the algorithms required to pick specific assembly-language instructions. The issues of instruction selection, register allocation, and instruction scheduling are treated separately, in later chapters.

## 7.2 ASSIGNING STORAGE LOCATIONS

As part of translation, the compiler must assign a storage location to each value produced by the code. The compiler must understand the value's type, its size, its visibility, and its lifetime. The compiler must take into account the runtime layout of memory, any source-language constraints on the layout of data areas and data structures, and any target-processor constraints on placement or use of data. The compiler addresses these issues by defining and following a set of conventions.

A typical procedure computes many values. Some of them, such as variables in an Algol-like language, have explicit names in the source code. Other values have implicit names, such as the value i - 3 in the expression A[i - 3, j + 2].

- The lifetime of a named value is defined by source-language rules and actual use in the code. For example, a static variable's value must be preserved across multiple invocations of its defining procedure, while a local variable of the same procedure is only needed from its first definition to its last use in each invocation.
- In contrast, the compiler has more freedom in how it treats unnamed values, such as i - 3. It must handle them in ways that are consistent with the meaning of the program, but it has great leeway in determining where these values reside and how long to retain them.

Compilation options may also affect placement; for example, code compiled to work with a debugger should preserve all values that the debugger can name—typically named variables.

The compiler must also decide, for each value, whether to keep it in a register or to keep it in memory. In general, compilers adopt a "memory model"—a set of rules to guide it in choosing locations for values. Two common policies are a memory-to-memory model and a register-to-register model. The choice between them has a major impact on the code that the compiler produces.

With a memory-to-memory model, the compiler assumes that all values reside in memory. Values are loaded into registers as needed, but the code stores them back to memory after each definition. In a memory-to-memory model, the IR typically uses *physical register* names. The compiler ensures that demand for registers does not exceed supply at each statement.

**Physical register**
a named register in the target ISA

In a register-to-register model, the compiler assumes that it has enough registers to express the computation. It invents a distinct name, a *virtual register*, for each value that can legally reside in a register. The compiled code will store a virtual register's value to memory only when absolutely necessary, such as when it is passed as a parameter or a return value, or when the register allocator spills it.

**Virtual register**
a symbolic name used in the IR in place of a physical register name

Choice of memory model also affects the compiler's structure. For example, in a memory-to-memory model, the register allocator is an optimization that improves the code. In a register-to-register memory model, the register allocator is a mandatory phase that reduces demand for registers and maps the virtual register names onto physical register names.

## 7.2.1 **Placing Runtime Data Structures**

To perform storage assignment, the compiler must understand the system-wide conventions on memory allocation and use. The compiler, the operating system, and the processor cooperate to ensure that multiple programs can execute safely on an interleaved (time-sliced) basis. Thus, many of the decisions about how to lay out, manipulate, and manage a program's address space lie outside the purview of the compiler writer. However, the decisions have a strong impact on the code that the compiler generates. Thus, the compiler writer must have a broad understanding of these issues.

Figure 7.2 shows a typical layout for the address space used by a single compiled program. The layout places fixed size regions of code and data at the low end of the address space. Code sits at the bottom of the address space; the adjacent region, labelled *Static*, holds both static and global data areas, along with any fixed size data created by the compiler. The region above

The compiler may create additional static data areas to hold constant values, jump tables, and debugging information.

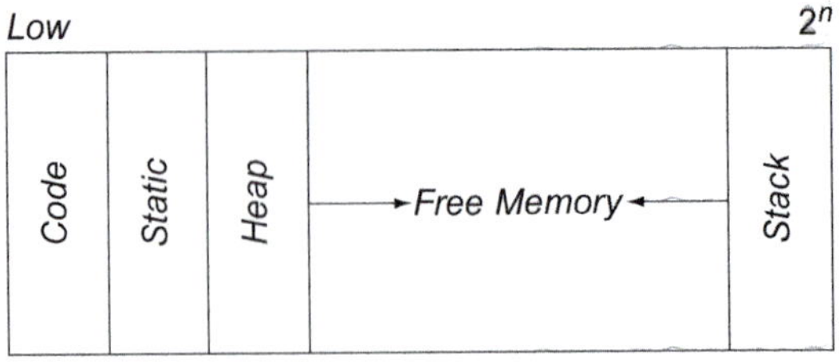

■ **FIGURE 7.2** Logical Address-Space Layout.

these static data areas is devoted to data areas that expand and contract. If the compiler can stack-allocate ARs, it will need a runtime stack. In most languages, it will also need a heap for dynamically allocated data structures. To allow for efficient space utilization, the heap and the stack should be placed at opposite ends of the open space and grow towards each other. In the drawing, the heap grows toward higher addresses, while the stack grows toward lower addresses. The opposite arrangement works equally well.

From the compiler's perspective, this logical address space is the whole picture. However, modern computer systems typically execute many programs in an interleaved fashion. The operating system maps multiple logical address spaces into the single physical address space supported by the processor. Figure 7.3 shows this larger picture. Each program is isolated in its own logical address space; each can behave as if it has its own machine.

**Page**
the unit of allocation in a virtual address space

The operating system maps virtual pages into physical page frames.

A single logical address space can occupy disjoint pages in the physical address space; thus, the addresses 100,000 and 200,000 in the program's logical address space need not be 100,000 bytes apart in physical memory. In fact, the physical address associated with the logical address 100,000 may be larger than the physical address associated with the logical address 200,000. The mapping from logical addresses to physical addresses is maintained cooperatively by the hardware and the operating system. It is, in almost all respects, beyond the compiler's purview.

## 7.2.2 Layout for Data Areas

For convenience, the compiler groups together the storage for values with the same lifetimes and visibility; it creates distinct data areas for them. The placement of these data areas depends on language rules about lifetimes and visibility of values. For example, the compiler can place procedure-local automatic storage inside the procedure's activation record, precisely because the lifetimes of such variables matches the AR's lifetime. In contrast, it must place procedure-local static storage where it will exist across invocations—in the "static" region of memory. Figure 7.4 shows a typical

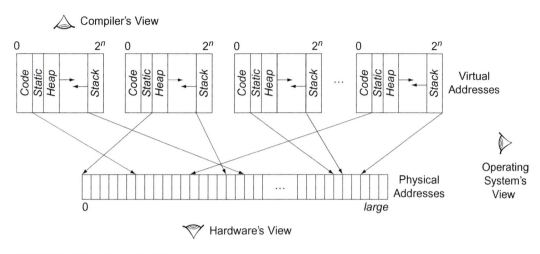

■ **FIGURE 7.3** Different Views of the Address Space.

> *if x is declared locally in procedure p, and*
>     *its value is <u>not</u> preserved across distinct invocations of p*
>         *then assign it to procedure-local storage*
>
>     *if its value is preserved across invocations of p*
>         *then assign it to procedure-local static storage*
>
> *if x is declared as globally visible*
>         *then assign it to global storage*
>
> *if x is allocated under program control*
>         *then assign it to the runtime heap*

■ **FIGURE 7.4** Assigning Names to Data Areas.

set of rules for assigning a variable to a specific data area. Object-oriented languages follow different rules, but the problems are no more complex.

Placing local automatic variables in the AR leads to efficient access. Since the code already needs the ARP in a register, it can use ARP-relative offsets to access these values, with operations such as `loadAI` or `loadAO`. Frequent access to the AR will likely keep it in the data cache. The compiler places variables with either static lifetimes or global visibility into data areas in the "static" region of memory. Access to these values takes slightly more work at runtime; the compiler must ensure that it has an address for the data area in a register.

To establish the address of a static or global data area, the compiler typically loads a relocatable assembly language label.

Values stored in the heap have lifetimes that the compiler cannot easily predict. A value can be placed in the heap by two distinct mechanisms.

**A PRIMER ON CACHE MEMORIES**

One way that architects try to bridge the gap between processor speed and memory speed is through the use of *cache memories*. A cache is a small, fast memory placed between the processor and main memory. The cache is divided into a series of equal-sized *frames*. Each frame has an address field, called its *tag*, that holds a main-memory address.

The hardware automatically maps memory locations to cache frames. The simplest mapping, used in a direct-mapped cache, computes the cache address as the main memory address modulo the size of the cache. This partitions the memory into a linear set of blocks, each the size of a cache frame. A *line* is a memory block that maps to a frame. At any point in time, each cache frame holds a copy of the data from one of its blocks. Its tag field holds the address in memory where that data normally resides.

On each read access to memory, the hardware checks to see if the requested word is already in its cache frame. If so, the requested bytes are returned to the processor. If not, the block currently in the frame is evicted and the requested block is brought into the cache.

Some caches use more complex mappings. A set-associative cache uses multiple frames for each cache line, typically two or four frames per line. A fully associative cache can place any block in any frame. Both these schemes use an associative search over the tags to determine if a block is in the cache. Associative schemes use a policy to determine which block to evict; common schemes are random replacement and least-recently-used (LRU) replacement.

In practice, the effective memory speed is determined by memory bandwidth, cache block length, the ratio of cache speed to memory speed, and the percentage of accesses that hit in the cache. From the compiler's perspective, the first three are fixed. Compiler-based efforts to improve memory performance focus on increasing the ratio of cache hits to cache misses, called the hit ratio.

Some architectures provide instructions that allow a program to give the cache hints as to when specific blocks should be brought into memory (*prefetched*) and when they are no longer needed (*flushed*).

The programmer can explicitly allocate storage from the heap; the compiler should not override that decision. The compiler can place a value on the heap when it detects that the value might outlive the procedure that created it. In either case, a value in the heap is represented by a full address, rather than an offset from some base address.

## Assigning Offsets

In the case of local, static, and global data areas, the compiler must assign each name an offset inside the data area. Target ISAs constrain the placement of data items in memory. A typical set of constraints might specify that 32-bit integers and 32-bit floating-point numbers begin on word (32-bit) boundaries, that 64-bit integer and floating-point data begin on doubleword (64-bit) boundaries, and that string data begin on halfword (16-bit) boundaries. We call these alignment rules.

Some processors provide operations to implement procedure calls beyond a simple jump operation. Such support often adds further alignment constraints. For example, the ISA might dictate the format of the AR and the alignment of the start of each AR. The DEC VAX computers had a particularly elaborate call instruction; it stored registers and other parts of the processor state based on a call-specific bit mask that the compiler produced.

For each data area, the compiler must compute a layout that assigns each variable in the data area its offset. That layout must comply with the ISA's alignment rules. The compiler may need to insert padding between some variables to obtain the proper alignments. To minimize wasted space, the compiler should order the variables into groups, from those with the most restrictive alignment rules to those with the least. (For example, doubleword alignment is more restrictive than word alignment.) The compiler then assigns offsets to the variables in the most restricted category, followed by the next most restricted class, and so on, until all variables have offsets. Since alignment rules almost always specify a power of two, the end of each category will naturally fit the restriction for the next category.

Most assembly languages have directives to specify the alignment of the start of a data area, such as a doubleword boundary.

## Relative Offsets and Cache Performance

The widespread use of cache memories in modern computer systems has subtle implications for the layout of variables in memory. If two values are used in proximity in the code, the compiler would like to ensure that they can reside in the cache at the same time. This can be accomplished in two ways. In the best situation, the two values would share a single cache block, which guarantees that the values are fetched from memory to the cache together. If they cannot share a cache block, the compiler would like to ensure that the two variables map to different cache lines. The compiler can achieve this by controlling the distance between their addresses.

If we consider just two variables, controlling the distance between them seems manageable. When all the active variables are considered, however, the problem of optimal arrangement for a cache is NP-complete. Most variables have interactions with many other variables; this creates a web of relationships that the compiler may not be able to satisfy concurrently. If we consider a loop that uses several large arrays, the problem of arranging mutual noninterference becomes even worse. If the compiler can discover the relationship between the various array references in the loop, it can add padding between the arrays to increase the likelihood that the references hit different cache lines and, thus, do not interfere with each other.

As we saw previously, the mapping of the program's logical address space to the hardware's physical address space need not preserve the distance between specific variables. Carrying this thought to its logical conclusion, the reader should ask how the compiler can ensure anything about relative offsets that are larger than the size of a virtual-memory page. The processor's cache may use either virtual addresses or physical addresses in its tag fields. A virtually addressed cache preserves the spacing between values that the compiler creates; with such a cache, the compiler may be able to plan noninterference between large objects. With a physically addressed cache, the distance between two locations in different pages is determined by the page mapping (unless cache size $\leq$ page size). Thus, the compiler's decisions about memory layout have little, if any, effect, except within a single page. In this situation, the compiler should focus on getting objects that are referenced together into the same page and, if possible, the same cache line.

### 7.2.3 Keeping Values in Registers

In a register-to-register memory model, the compiler tries to assign as many values as possible to virtual registers. In this approach, the compiler relies on the register allocator to map virtual registers in the IR to physical registers on the processor and to *spill* to memory any virtual register that it cannot keep in a physical register. If the compiler keeps a static value in a register, it must load the value before its first use in the procedure and store it back to memory before leaving the procedure, either at the procedure's exit or at any call site within the procedure.

**Spill**
When the register allocator cannot assign some virtual register to a physical register, it *spills* the value by storing it to RAM after each definition and loading it into a temporary register before each use.

In most of the examples in this book, we follow a simple method for assigning virtual registers to values. Each value receives its own virtual register with a distinct subscript. This discipline exposes the largest set of values to subsequent analysis and optimization. It may, in fact, use too many names. (See the digression, "The Impact of Naming" on page 248.) However, this scheme has three principal advantages. It is simple. It can improve the results of analysis and optimization. It prevents the compiler writer from working processor-specific constraints into the code before optimization, thus enhancing portability. A strong register allocator can manage the name space and tailor it precisely to the needs of the application and the resources available on the target processor.

A value that the compiler can keep in a register is called an *unambiguous value*; a value that can have more than one name is called an *ambiguous value*. Ambiguity arises in several ways. Values stored in pointer-based variables are often ambiguous. Interactions between call-by-reference formal parameters and name scoping rules can make the formal parameters ambiguous. Many compilers treat array-element values as ambiguous values because the compiler cannot tell if two references, such as A[i,j] and A[m,n], can ever refer to the same location. In general, the compiler cannot keep an ambiguous value in a register across either a definition or a use of another ambiguous value.

**Unambiguous value**
A value that can be accessed with just one name is *unambiguous*.

**Ambiguous value**
Any value that can be accessed by multiple names is *ambiguous*.

With careful analysis, the compiler can disambiguate some of these cases. Consider the sequence of assignments in the margin, assuming that both a and b are ambiguous. If a and b refer to the same location, then c gets the value 26; otherwise it receives $m+n+13$. The compiler cannot keep a in a register across an assignment to another ambiguous variable unless it can prove that the set of locations to which the two names can refer are disjoint. This kind of comparative pairwise analysis is expensive, so compilers typically relegate ambiguous values to memory, with a load before each use and a store after each definition.

$$a \leftarrow m + n;$$
$$b \leftarrow 13;$$
$$c \leftarrow a + b;$$

Analysis of ambiguity therefore focuses on proving that a given value is not ambiguous. The analysis might be cursory and local. For example, in C, any local variable whose address is never taken is unambiguous in the procedure where it is declared. More complex analyses build sets of possible names for each pointer variable; any variable whose set has just one element is unambiguous. Unfortunately, analysis cannot resolve all ambiguities. Thus, the compiler must be prepared to handle ambiguous values cautiously and correctly.

Language features can affect the compiler's ability to analyze ambiguity. For example, ANSI C includes two keywords that directly communicate information about ambiguity. The restrict keyword informs the compiler that a pointer is unambiguous. It is often used when a procedure passes an address directly at a call site. The volatile keyword lets the programmer declare that the contents of a variable may change arbitrarily and without notice. It is used for hardware device registers and for variables that might be modified by interrupt service routines or other threads of control in an application.

**SECTION REVIEW**

The compiler must determine, for each value computed in the program, where it must be stored: in memory or a register and, in either case, the specific location. It must assign to each value a location that is consistent with both its lifetime (see Section 6.3) and its addressability (see Section 6.4.3). Thus, the compiler will group together values into data areas in which each value has the same storage class.

Storage assignment provides the compiler with a key opportunity to encode information into the IR for use by later passes. Specifically, the distinction between an ambiguous value and an unambiguous value can be hard to derive by analysis of the IR. If, however, the compiler assigns each unambiguous value its own virtual register for its entire lifetime, subsequent phases of the compiler can use a value's storage location to determine whether or not a reference is ambiguous. This knowledge simplifies subsequent optimization.

```
void fee() {
  int a, *b;
    ...
  b = &a;
    ...
}
```

**Review Questions**

1. Sketch an algorithm that assigns offsets to a list of static variables in a single file from a C program. How does it order the variables? What alignment restrictions might your algorithm encounter?

2. Consider the short C fragment in the margin. It mentions three values: a, b, and *b. Which values are ambiguous? Which are unambiguous?

## 7.3 ARITHMETIC OPERATORS

Modern processors provide broad support for evaluating expressions. A typical RISC machine has a full complement of three-address operations, including arithmetic operators, shifts, and boolean operators. The three-address form lets the compiler name the result of any operation and preserve it for later reuse. It also eliminates the major complication of the two-address form: destructive operations.

To generate code for a trivial expression, such as $a + b$, the compiler first emits code to ensure that the values of a and b are in registers, say $r_a$ and $r_b$. If a is stored in memory at offset @a in the current AR, the resulting code might be

```
loadI   @a        ⇒ r₁
loadAO  r_arp,r₁  ⇒ r_a
```

If, however, the value of a is already in a register, the compiler can simply use that register in place of $r_a$. The compiler follows a similar chain of decisions for b. Finally, it emits an instruction to perform the addition, such as

```
add ra,rb ⇒ rt
```

If the expression is represented in a tree-like IR, this process fits into a post-order tree walk. Figure 7.5a shows the code for a tree walk that generates code for simple expressions. It relies on two routines, *base* and *offset*, to hide some of the complexity. The *base* routine returns the name of a register holding the base address for an identifier; if needed, it emits code to get that address into a register. The *offset* routine has a similar function; it returns the name of a register holding the identifier's offset relative to the address returned by *base*.

```
expr(node) {
  int result, t1, t2;
  switch(type(node)) {
    case ×, ÷, +, -:
      t1 ← expr(LeftChild(node));
      t2 ← expr(RightChild(node));
      result ← NextRegister();
      emit(op(node), t1, t2, result);
      break;

    case IDENT:
      t1 ← base(node);
      t2 ← offset(node);
      result ← NextRegister();
      emit(loadAO, t1, t2, result);
      break;

    case NUM:
      result ← NextRegister();
      emit(loadI, val(node), none,
           result);
      break;
  }
  return result;
}
```

(a) Treewalk Code Generator

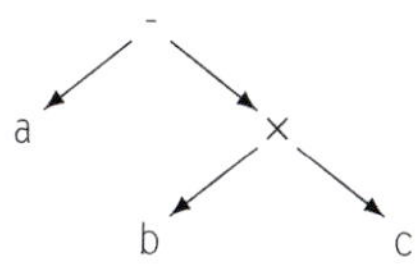

(b) Abstract Syntax Tree for

a - b x c

(c) Naive Code

```
loadI   @a         ⇒ r1
loadAO  rarp,r1    ⇒ r2
loadI   @b         ⇒ r3
loadAO  rarp,r3    ⇒ r4
loadI   @c         ⇒ r5
loadAO  rarp,r5    ⇒ r6
mult    r4,r6      ⇒ r7
sub     r2,r7      ⇒ r8
```

■ **FIGURE 7.5** Simple Treewalk Code Generator for Expressions.

The same code handles +, -, ×, and ÷. From a code-generation perspective, these operators are interchangeable, ignoring commutativity. Invoking the routine *expr* from Figure 7.5a on the AST for a - b × c shown in part b of the figure produces the results shown in part c of the figure. The example assumes that a, b, and c are not already in registers and that each resides in the current AR.

Notice the similarity between the treewalk code generator and the ad hoc syntax-directed translation scheme shown in Figure 4.15. The treewalk makes more details explicit, including the handling of terminals and the evaluation order for subtrees. In the syntax-directed translation scheme, the order of evaluation is controlled by the parser. Still, the two schemes produce roughly equivalent code.

### 7.3.1 **Reducing Demand for Registers**

Many issues affect the quality of the generated code. For example, the choice of storage locations has a direct impact, even for this simple expression. If a were in a global data area, the sequence of instructions needed to get a into a register might require an additional loadI to obtain the base address and a register to hold that value for a brief time. Alternatively, if a were in a register, the two instructions used to load it into $r_2$ could be omitted, and the compiler would use the name of the register holding a directly in the sub instruction. Keeping the value in a register avoids both the memory access and any address calculation. If a, b, and c were already in registers, the seven-instruction sequence could be shortened to a two-instruction sequence.

Code-shape decisions encoded into the treewalk code generator have an effect on demand for registers. The naive code in the figure uses eight registers, plus $r_{arp}$. It is tempting to assume that the register allocator, when it runs late in compilation, can reduce the number of registers to a minimum. For example, the register allocator could rewrite the code as shown in Figure 7.6a, which drops register use from eight registers to three, plus $r_{arp}$. The maximum demand for registers occurs in the sequence that loads c and performs the multiply.

A different code shape can reduce the demand for registers. The treewalk code generator loads a before it computes b × c, an artifact of the decision to use a left-to-right tree walk. Using a right-to-left tree walk would produce the code shown in Figure 7.6b. While the initial code uses the same number of registers as the code generated left-to-right, register allocation reveals that the code actually needs one fewer registers, as shown in Figure 7.6c.

```
loadI    @a        ⇒ r₁        loadI    @c        ⇒ r₁        loadI    @c        ⇒ r₁
loadAO   rarp,r₁   ⇒ r₁        loadAO   rarp,r₁   ⇒ r₂        loadAO   rarp,r₁   ⇒ r₁
loadI    @b        ⇒ r₂        loadI    @b        ⇒ r₃        loadI    @b        ⇒ r₂
loadAO   rarp,r₂   ⇒ r₂        loadAO   rarp,r₃   ⇒ r₄        loadAO   rarp,r₂   ⇒ r₂
loadI    @c        ⇒ r₃        mult     r₂,r₄     ⇒ r₅        mult     r₁,r₂     ⇒ r₁
loadAO   rarp,r₃   ⇒ r₃        loadI    @a        ⇒ r₆        loadI    @a        ⇒ r₂
mult     r₂,r₃     ⇒ r₂        loadAO   rarp,r₆   ⇒ r₇        loadAO   rarp,r₂   ⇒ r₂
sub      r₁,r₂     ⇒ r₂        sub      r₇,r₅     ⇒ r₈        sub      r₂,r₁     ⇒ r₁

  (a) Example After Allocation    (b) Evaluating b x c First      (c) After Register Allocation
```

■ **FIGURE 7.6** Rewriting a - b x c to Reduce Demand for Registers.

Of course, right-to-left evaluation is not a general solution. For the expression a x b + c, left-to-right evaluation produces the lower demand for registers. Some expressions, such as a + (b + c) x d, defy a simple static rule. The evaluation order that minimizes register demand is a + ( (b + c) x d ).

To choose an evaluation order that reduces demand for registers, the code generator must alternate between right and left children; it needs information about the detailed register needs of each subtree. As a rule, the compiler can minimize register use by evaluating first, at each node, the subtree that needs the most registers. The generated code must preserve the value of the first subtree that it evaluates across the evaluation of the second subtree; thus, handling the less demanding subtree first increases the demand for registers in the more demanding subtree by one register. This approach requires an initial pass over the code to compute demand for registers, followed by a pass that emits the actual code.

This approach, analysis followed by transformation, applies in both code generation and optimization [150].

### 7.3.2 **Accessing Parameter Values**

The code generator in Figure 7.5 implicitly assumes that a single access method works for all identifiers. Formal parameters may need different treatment. A call-by-value parameter passed in the AR can be handled as if it were a local variable. A call-by-reference parameter passed in the AR requires one additional indirection. Thus, for the call-by-reference parameter d, the compiler might generate

```
loadI    @d        ⇒ r₁
loadAO   rarp,r₁   ⇒ r₂
load     r₂        ⇒ r₃
```

to obtain d's value. The first two operations move the address of the parameter's value into $r_2$. The final operation moves the value itself into $r_3$.

**GENERATING LOAD ADDRESS IMMEDIATE**

A careful reader might notice that the code in Figure 7.5 never generates ILOC's load address-immediate instruction, loadAI. Instead, it generates a load immediate (loadI), followed by a load address-offset (loadAO):

$$\begin{array}{l} \texttt{loadI} \;\; \texttt{@a} \qquad\;\; \Rightarrow r_1 \\ \texttt{loadAO} \;\; r_{arp}, r_1 \Rightarrow r_2 \end{array} \quad \textit{instead of} \quad \texttt{loadAI} \;\; r_{arp}, \texttt{@a} \Rightarrow r_2$$

Throughout the book, the examples assume that it is preferable to generate this two-operation sequence, rather than the single operation. Three factors suggest this course.

**1.** The longer code sequence gives an explicit name to @a. If @a is reused in other contexts, that name can be reused.
**2.** The offset @a may not fit in the immediate field of a loadAI. That determination is best made in the instruction selector.
**3.** The two-operation sequence leads to a clean functional decomposition in the code generator, shown Figure 7.5.

The compiler can convert the two-operation sequence into a single operation during optimization, if appropriate (e.g. either @a is not reused or it is cheaper to reload it). The best course, however, may be to defer the issue to instruction selection, thus isolating the machine-dependent constant length into a part of the compiler that is already highly machine dependent.

If the compiler writer wants to generate the loadAI earlier, two simple approaches work. The compiler writer can refactor the treewalk code generator in Figure 7.5 and pull the logic hidden in *base* and *offset* into the case for *IDENT*. Alternatively, the compiler writer can have *emit* maintain a small instruction buffer, recognize this special case, and emit the loadAI. Using a small buffer makes this approach practical (see Section 11.5).

Many linkage conventions pass the first few parameters in registers. As written, the code in Figure 7.5 cannot handle a value that is permanently kept in a register. The necessary extensions, however, are easy to implement.

■ *Call-by-value parameters* The *IDENT* case must check if the value is already in a register. If so, it just assigns the register number to *result*. Otherwise, it uses the standard mechanisms to load the value from memory.
■ *Call-by-reference parameter* If the address resides in a register, the compiler simply loads the value into a register. If the address resides in the AR, it must load the address before it loads the value.

---

**COMMUTATIVITY, ASSOCIATIVITY, AND NUMBER SYSTEMS**

The compiler can often take advantage of algebraic properties of the operators. Addition and multiplication are commutative and associative, as are the boolean operators. Thus, if the compiler sees a code fragment that computes $a + b$ and then computes $b + a$, with no intervening assignments to either a or b, it should recognize that they compute the same value. Similarly, if it sees the expressions $a + b + c$ and $d + a + b$, it should recognize that $a + b$ is a common subexpression. If it evaluates both expressions in strict left-to-right order, it will never recognize the common subexpression, since it will compute the second expression as $d + a$ and then $(d + a) + b$.

The compiler should use commutativity and associativity to improve the quality of code that it generates. Reordering expressions can expose additional opportunities for many transformations.

*Due to limitations in precision, floating-point numbers on a computer represent only a subset of the real numbers, one that does not preserve associativity. For this reason, compilers should <u>not</u> reorder floating-point expressions unless the language definition specifically allows it.*

Consider the following example: computing $a - b - c$. We can assign floating-point values to a, b, and c such that

$$b, c < a \qquad a - b = a \qquad a - c = a$$

but $a - (b + c) \neq a$. In that case, the numerical result depends on the order of evaluation. Evaluating $(a - b) - c$ produces a result identical to a, while evaluating $b + c$ first and subtracting that quantity from a produces a result that is distinct from a.

This problem arises from the approximate nature of floating-point numbers; the mantissa is small relative to the range of the exponent. To add two numbers, the hardware must normalize them; if the difference in exponents is larger than the precision of the mantissa, the smaller number will be truncated to zero. The compiler cannot easily work its way around this issue, so it should, in general, avoid reordering float-point computations.

---

In either case, the code fits nicely into the treewalk framework. Note that the compiler cannot keep the value of a call-by-reference parameter in a register across an assignment, unless the compiler can prove that the reference is unambiguous, across all calls to the procedure.

If the actual parameter is a local variable of the caller and its address is never taken, the corresponding formal is unambiguous.

### 7.3.3 **Function Calls in an Expression**

So far, we have assumed that all the operands in an expression are variables, constants, and temporary values produced by other subexpressions. Function calls also occur as operands in expressions. To evaluate a function call, the compiler simply generates the calling sequence needed to invoke the function and emits the code necessary to move the returned value to a register (see Section 7.9). The linkage convention limits the callee's impact on the caller.

The presence of a function call may restrict the compiler's ability to change an expression's evaluation order. The function may have side effects that modify the values of variables used in the expression. The compiler must respect the implied evaluation order of the source expression, at least with respect to the call. Without knowledge about the possible side effects of a call, the compiler cannot move references across the call. The compiler must assume the worst case—that the function both modifies and uses every variable that it can access. The desire to improve on worst-case assumptions, such as this one, has motivated much of the work in interprocedural analysis (see Section 9.4).

### 7.3.4 **Other Arithmetic Operators**

To handle other arithmetic operations, we can extend the treewalk model. The basic scheme remains the same: get the operands into registers, perform the operation, and store the result. Operator precedence, from the expression grammar, ensures the correct evaluation order. Some operators require complex multioperation sequences for their implementation (e.g. exponentiation and trigonometric functions). These may be expanded inline or implemented with a call to a library routine supplied by the compiler or the operating system.

### 7.3.5 **Mixed-Type Expressions**

One complication allowed by many programming languages is an operation with operands of different types. (Here, we are concerned primarily with base types in the source language, rather than programmer-defined types.) As described in Section 4.2, the compiler must recognize this situation and insert the conversion code required by each operator's conversion table. Typically, this involves converting one or both operands to a more general type and performing the operation in that more general type. The operation that consumes the result value may need to convert it to yet another type.

Some processors provide explicit conversion operators; others expect the compiler to generate complex, machine-dependent code. In either case, the compiler writer may want to provide conversion operators in the IR. Such an operator encapsulates all the details of the conversion, including any control flow, and lets the compiler subject it to uniform optimization. Thus, code motion can pull an invariant conversion out of a loop without concern for the loop's internal control flow.

Typically, the programming-language definition specifies a formula for each conversion. For example, to convert `integer` to `complex` in FORTRAN 77, the compiler first converts the `integer` to a `real`. It uses the resulting number as the real part of the complex number and sets the imaginary part to a `real` zero.

For user-defined types, the compiler will not have conversion tables that define each specific case. However, the source language still defines the meaning of the expression. The compiler's task is to implement that meaning; if a conversion is illegal, then it should be prevented. As seen in Chapter 4, many illegal conversions can be detected and prevented at compile time. When a compile-time check is either impossible or inconclusive, the compiler should generate a runtime check that tests for illegal cases. When the code attempts an illegal conversion, the check should raise a runtime error.

### 7.3.6 **Assignment as an Operator**

Most Algol-like languages implement assignment with the following simple rules:

1. Evaluate the right-hand side of the assignment to a value.
2. Evaluate the left-hand side of the assignment to a location.
3. Store the right-hand side value into the left-hand side location.

Thus, in a statement such as $a \leftarrow b$, the two expressions $a$ and $b$ are evaluated differently. Since $b$ appears to the right of the assignment operator, it is evaluated to produce a value; if $b$ is an integer variable, that value is an integer. Since $a$ is to the left of the assignment operator, it is evaluated to produce a location; if $a$ is an integer variable, that value is the location of an integer. That location might be an address in memory, or it might be a register. To distinguish between these modes of evaluation, we sometimes refer to the result of evaluation on the right-hand side of an assignment as an *rvalue* and the result of evaluation on the left-hand side of an assignment as an *lvalue*.

**Rvalue**
An expression evaluated to a value is an *rvalue*.

**Lvalue**
An expression evaluated to a location is an *lvalue*.

In an assignment, the type of the lvalue can differ from the type of the rvalue. Depending on the language and the specific types, this situation may require either a compiler-inserted conversion or an error message. The typical source-language rule for conversion has the compiler evaluate the rvalue to its natural type and then convert the result to the type of the lvalue.

---

**SECTION REVIEW**

A postorder treewalk provides a natural way to structure a code generator for expression trees. The basic framework is easily adapted to handle a variety of complications, including multiple kinds and locations of values, function calls, type conversions, and new operators. To improve the code further may require multiple passes over the code.

Some optimizations are hard to fit into a treewalk framework. In particular, making good use of processor address modes (see Chapter 11), ordering operations to hide processor-specific delays (see Chapter 12), and register allocation (see Chapter 13) do not fit well into the treewalk framework. If the compiler uses a treewalk to generate IR, it may be best to keep the IR simple and allow the back end to address these issues with specialized algorithms.

---

**Review Questions**

1. Sketch the code for the two support routines, *base* and *offset*, used by the treewalk code generator in Figure 7.5.

2. How might you adapt the treewalk code generator to handle an unconditional jump operation, such as C's `goto` statement?

---

## 7.4 BOOLEAN AND RELATIONAL OPERATORS

Most programming languages operate on a richer set of values than numbers. Usually, this includes the results of boolean and relational operators, both of which produce boolean values. Because most programming languages have relational operators that produce boolean results, we treat the boolean and relational operators together. A common use for boolean and relational expressions is to alter the program's control flow. Much of the power of modern programming languages derives from the ability to compute and test such values.

The grammar uses the symbols ¬ for not, ∧ for and, and ∨ for or to avoid confusion with ILOC operators.

The type checker must ensure that each expression applies operators to names, numbers, and expressions of appropriate types.

Figure 7.7 shows the standard expression grammar augmented with boolean and relational operators. The compiler writer must, in turn, decide how to represent these values and how to compute them. For arithmetic expressions, such design decisions are largely dictated by the target architecture, which provides number formats and instructions to perform basic arithmetic. Fortunately, processor architects appear to have reached a widespread agreement about how to support arithmetic. Similarly, most architectures provide a rich set of boolean operations. However, support for relational operators varies widely from one architecture to another. The compiler writer must use an evaluation strategy that matches the needs of the language to the available instruction set.

$$
\begin{array}{rcl}
Expr & \rightarrow & Expr \vee AndTerm \\
 & | & AndTerm \\
AndTerm & \rightarrow & AndTerm \wedge RelExpr \\
 & | & RelExpr \\
RelExpr & \rightarrow & RelExpr < NumExpr \\
 & | & RelExpr \leq NumExpr \\
 & | & RelExpr = NumExpr \\
 & | & RelExpr \neq NumExpr \\
 & | & RelExpr \geq NumExpr \\
 & | & RelExpr > NumExpr \\
 & | & NumExpr
\end{array}
$$

$$
\begin{array}{rcl}
NumExpr & \rightarrow & NumExpr + Term \\
 & | & NumExpr - Term \\
 & | & Term \\
Term & \rightarrow & Term \times Value \\
 & | & Term \div Value \\
 & | & Factor \\
Value & \rightarrow & \neg\ Factor \\
 & | & Factor \\
Factor & \rightarrow & (Expr) \\
 & | & \texttt{num} \\
 & | & \texttt{name}
\end{array}
$$

■ **FIGURE 7.7** Adding Booleans and Relationals to the Expression Grammar.

### 7.4.1 Representations

Traditionally, two representations have been proposed for boolean values: a numerical encoding and a positional encoding. The former assigns specific values to true and false and manipulates them using the target machine's arithmetic and logical operations. The latter approach encodes the value of the expression as a position in the executable code. It uses comparisons and conditional branches to evaluate the expression; the different control-flow paths represent the result of evaluation. Each approach works well for some examples, but not for others.

### Numerical Encoding

When the program stores the result of a boolean or relational operation into a variable, the compiler must ensure that the value has a concrete representation. The compiler writer must assign numerical values to true and false that work with the hardware operations such as and, or, and not. Typical values are zero for false and either one or a word of ones, $\neg$false, for true.

For example, if b, c, and d are all in registers, the compiler might produce the following code for the expression $b \vee c \wedge \neg d$:

```
not  rd      ⇒ r1
and  rc, r1  ⇒ r2
or   rb, r2  ⇒ r3
```

For a comparison, such as $a < b$, the compiler must generate code that compares a and b and assigns the appropriate value to the result. If the target machine supports a comparison operation that returns a boolean, the code is trivial:

```
cmp_LT  ra, rb  ⇒ r1
```

ILOC contains syntax to implement both styles of compare and branch. A normal IR would choose one; ILOC includes both so that it can express the code in this section.

If, on the other hand, the comparison defines a condition code that must be read with a branch, the resulting code is longer and more involved. This style of comparison leads to a messier implementation for $a < b$.

```
        comp    ra,rb  ⇒ cc1
        cbr_LT  cc1    → L1,L2
L1: loadI   true   ⇒ r1
        jumpI          → L3
L2: loadI   false  ⇒ r1
        jumpI          → L3
L3: nop
```

Implementing $a < b$ with condition-code operations requires more operations than using a comparison that returns a boolean.

### Positional Encoding

In the previous example, the code at $L_1$ creates the value true and the code at $L_2$ creates the value false. At each of those points, the value is known. In some cases, the code need not produce a concrete value for the expression's result. Instead, the compiler can encode that value in a location in the code, such as $L_1$ or $L_2$.

Figure 7.8a shows the code that a treewalk code generator might emit for the expression $a < b \lor c < d \land e < f$. The code evaluates the three subexpressions, $a < b$, $c < d$, and $e < f$, using a series of comparisons and jumps. It then combines the result of the three subexpression evaluations using the boolean operations at $L_9$. Unfortunately, this produces a sequence of operations in which every path takes 11 operations, including three branches and three jumps. Some of the complexity of this code can be eliminated by representing the subexpression values implicitly and generating code that short circuits the evaluation, as in Figure 7.8b. This version of the code evaluates $a < b \lor c < d \land e < f$ with fewer operations because it does not create values to represent the subexpressions.

Positional encoding makes sense if an expression's result is never stored. When the code uses the result of an expression to determine control flow, positional encoding often avoids extraneous operations. For example, in the code fragment

```
if (a < b)
    then statement₁
    else statement₂
```

the sole use for $a < b$ is to determine whether *statement*₁ or *statement*₂ executes. Producing an explicit value for $a < b$ serves no direct purpose.

(a) Naive Encoding

```
        comp    ra,rb  ⇒ cc1     // a < b
        cbr_LT  cc1    → L1,L2
L1:     loadI   true   ⇒ r1
        jumpI          → L3
L2:     loadI   false  ⇒ r1
        jumpI          → L3

L3:     comp    rc,rd  ⇒ cc2     // c < d
        cbr_LT  cc2    → L4,L5
L4:     loadI   true   ⇒ r2
        jumpI          → L6
L5:     loadI   false  ⇒ r2
        jumpI          → L6

L6:     comp    re,rf  ⇒ cc3     // e < f
        cbr_LT  cc3    → L7,L8
L7:     loadI   true   ⇒ r3
        jumpI          → L9
L8:     loadI   false  ⇒ r3
        jumpI          → L9

L9:     and     r2,r3  ⇒ r4
        or      r1,r4  ⇒ r5
```

(b) Positional Encoding with Short-Circuit Evaluation

```
        comp    ra,rb  ⇒ cc1     // a < b
        cbr_LT  cc1    → L3,L1
L1:     comp    rc,rd  ⇒ cc2     // c < d
        cbr_LT  cc2    → L2,L4
L2:     comp    re,rf  ⇒ cc3     // e < f
        cbr_LT  cc3    → L3,L4
L3:     loadI   true   ⇒ r5
        jumpI          → L5
L4:     loadI   false  ⇒ r5
        jumpI          → L5
L5:     nop
```

■ **FIGURE 7.8** Encoding a < b ∨ c < d ∧ e < f.

On a machine where the compiler must use a comparison and a branch to produce a value, the compiler can simply place the code for *statement*₁ and *statement*₂ in the locations where naive code would assign true and false. This use of positional encoding leads to simpler, faster code than using numerical encoding.

```
        comp    ra,rb  ⇒ cc1     // a < b
        cbr_LT  cc1    → L1,L2
L1:     code for statement1
        jumpI          → L6
L2:     code for statement2
        jumpI          → L6
L6:     nop
```

Here, the code to evaluate a < b has been combined with the code to select between *statement*₁ and *statement*₂. The code represents the result of a < b as a position, either L₁ or L₂.

### 7.4.2 **Hardware Support for Relational Operations**

Specific, low-level details in the target machine's instruction set strongly influence the choice of a representation for relational values. In particular,

**SHORT-CIRCUIT EVALUATION**

In many cases, the value of a subexpression determines the value of the entire expression. For example, the code shown in Figure 7.8a, evaluates c < d ∧ e < f, even if it has already determined that a < b, in which case the entire expression evaluates to true. Similarly, if both a ≥ b and c ≥ d, then the value of e < f does not matter. The code in Figure 7.8b uses these relationships to produce a result as soon as the expression's value can be known. This approach to expression evaluation, in which the code evaluates the minimal amount of the expression needed to determine its final value, is called *short-circuit evaluation*. Short-circuit evaluation relies on two boolean identities:

$$\forall x, \quad \text{false} \land x = \text{false}$$
$$\forall x, \quad \text{true} \lor x = \text{true}$$

To generate the short-circuit code, the compiler must analyze the expression in light of these two identities and find the set of minimal conditions that determine its value. If clauses in the expression contain expensive operators or if the evaluation uses branches, as do many of the schemes discussed in this section, then short-circuit evaluation can significantly reduce the cost of evaluating boolean expressions.

Some programming languages, like C, require the compiler to use short-circuit evaluation. For example, the expression

```
(x != 0 && y / x > 0.001)
```

in C relies on short-circuit evaluation for safety. If x is zero, y / x is not defined. Clearly, the programmer intends to avoid the hardware exception triggered by division by zero. The language definition specifies that this code will never perform the division if x has the value zero.

the compiler writer must pay attention to the handling of condition codes, compare operations, and conditional move operations, as they have a major impact on the relative costs of the various representations. We will consider four schemes for supporting relational expressions: straight condition codes, condition codes augmented with a conditional move operation, boolean-valued comparisons, and predicated operations. Each scheme is an idealized version of a real implementation.

Figure 7.9 shows two source-level constructs and their implementations under each of these schemes. Figure 7.9a shows an if-then-else that controls a pair of assignment statements. Figure 7.9b shows the assignment of a boolean value.

| Source Code | `if (x < y)`<br>`    then a ← c + d`<br>`    else a ← e + f` |
|---|---|

ILOC Code:

```
          comp    rx,ry  ⇒ cc1                cmp_LT  rx,ry  ⇒ r1
          cbr_LT  cc1    → L1,L2              cbr     r1     → L1,L2

    L1: add       rc,rd  ⇒ ra          L1: add       rc,rd  ⇒ ra
        jumpI            → Lout            jumpI            → Lout

    L2: add       re,rf  ⇒ ra          L2: add       re,rf  ⇒ ra
        jumpI            → Lout            jumpI            → Lout

    Lout: nop                          Lout: nop
        Straight Condition Codes            Boolean Compare
```

```
    comp    rx,ry        ⇒ cc1              cmp_LT  rx,ry  ⇒ r1
    add     rc,rd        ⇒ r1              not     r1     ⇒ r2
    add     re,rf        ⇒ r2       (r1)?  add     rc,rd  ⇒ ra
    i2i_LT  cc1,r1,r2    ⇒ ra       (r2)?  add     re,rf  ⇒ ra
        Conditional Move                      Predicated Execution
```

(a) Using a Relational Expression to Govern Control Flow

| Source Code | `x ← a < b ∧ c < d` |
|---|---|

ILOC Code:

```
                                           comp    ra,rb        ⇒ cc1
                                           i2i_LT  cc1,rT,rF    ⇒ r1
                                           comp    rc,rd        ⇒ cc2
                                           i2i_LT  cc2,rT,rF    ⇒ r2
          comp    ra, rb  ⇒ cc1            and     r1,r2        ⇒ rx
          cbr_LT  cc1     → L1,L2              Conditional Move

    L1: comp    rc, rd  ⇒ cc2
        cbr_LT  cc2     → L3,L2            cmp_LT  ra, rb  ⇒ r1
                                           cmp_LT  rc, rd  ⇒ r2
    L2: loadI   false   ⇒ rx              and     r1, r2  ⇒ rx
        jumpI           → Lout
                                              Boolean Compare
    L3: loadI   true    ⇒ rx
        jumpI           → Lout            cmp_LT  ra, rb  ⇒ r1
                                           cmp_LT  rc, rd  ⇒ r2
    Lout: nop                             and     r1, r2  ⇒ rx
        Straight Condition Codes
                                              Predicated Execution
```

(b) Using a Relational Expression to Produce a Value

■ **FIGURE 7.9** Implementing Boolean and Relational Operators.

## Straight Condition Codes

In this scheme, the comparison operation sets a condition-code register. The only instruction that interprets the condition code is a conditional branch, with variants that branch on each of the six relations ($<$, $\leq$, $=$, $\geq$, $>$, and $\neq$). These instructions may exist for operands of several types.

---

**SHORT-CIRCUIT EVALUATION AS AN OPTIMIZATION**

Short-circuit evaluation arose from a positional encoding of the values of boolean and relational expressions. On processors that use condition codes to record the result of a comparison and use conditional branches to interpret the condition code, short circuiting makes sense.

As processors include features like conditional move, boolean-valued comparisons, and predicated execution, the advantages of short-circuit evaluation will likely fade. With branch latencies growing, the cost of the conditional branches required for short circuiting grows too. When the branch costs exceed the savings from avoiding evaluation, short circuiting will no longer be an improvement. Instead, full evaluation will be faster.

When the language requires short-circuit evaluation, as does C, the compiler may need to perform some analysis to determine when it is safe to substitute full evaluation for short-circuit evaluation. Thus, future C compilers may include analysis and transformation to replace short circuiting with full evaluation, just as compilers in the past have performed analysis and transformation to replace full evaluation with short-circuit evaluation.

---

The compiler must use conditional branches to interpret the value of a condition code. If the sole use of the result is to determine control flow, as in Figure 7.9a, then the conditional branch that the compiler uses to read the condition code can often implement the source-level control-flow construct, as well. If the result is used in a boolean operation, or it is preserved in a variable, as in Figure 7.9b, the code must convert the result into a concrete representation of a boolean, as do the two `loadI` operations in Figure 7.9b. Either way, the code has at least one conditional branch per relational operator.

The advantage of condition codes comes from another feature that processors usually implement alongside condition codes. Typically, arithmetic operations on these processors set the condition code to reflect their computed results. If the compiler can arrange to have the arithmetic operations that must be performed also set the condition code needed to control the branch, then the comparison operation can be omitted. Thus, advocates of this architectural style argue that it allows a more efficient encoding of the program—the code may execute fewer instructions than it would with a comparator that puts a boolean value in a general-purpose register.

### Conditional Move

This scheme adds a conditional move instruction to the straight condition-code model. In ILOC, a conditional move looks like:

```
i2i_LT  cc_i, r_j, r_k  ⇒  r_m
```

If the condition code $cc_i$ matches LT, then the value of $r_j$ is copied to $r_m$. Otherwise, the value of $r_k$ is copied to $r_m$. The conditional move operation typically executes in a single cycle. It leads to faster code by allowing the compiler to avoid branches.

Conditional move retains the principal advantage of using condition codes— avoiding a comparison when an earlier operation has already set the condition code. As shown in Figure 7.9a, it lets the compiler encode simple conditional operations with branches. Here, the compiler speculatively evaluates the two additions. It uses conditional move for the final assignment. This is safe as long as neither addition can raise an exception.

If the compiler has values for true and false in registers, say $r_T$ for true and $r_F$ for false, then it can use conditional move to convert the condition code into a boolean. Figure 7.9b uses this strategy. It compares a and b and places the boolean result in $r_1$. It computes the boolean for c < d into $r_2$. It computes the final result as the logical and of $r_1$ and $r_2$.

### Boolean-Valued Comparisons

This scheme avoids condition codes entirely. The comparison operator returns a boolean value in a register. The conditional branch takes that result as an argument that determines its behavior.

Boolean-valued comparisons do not help with the code in Figure 7.9a. The code is equivalent to the straight condition-code scheme. It requires comparisons, branches, and jumps to evaluate the if-then-else construct.

Figure 7.9b shows the strength of this scheme. The boolean compare lets the code evaluate the relational operator without a branch and without converting comparison results to boolean values. The uniform representation of boolean and relational values leads to concise, efficient code for this example.

A weakness of this model is that it requires explicit comparisons. Whereas the condition-code models can sometimes avoid the comparison by arranging to set the appropriate condition code with an earlier arithmetic operation, the boolean-valued comparison model always needs an explicit comparison.

### Predicated Execution

Architectures that support *predicated execution* let the compiler avoid some conditional branches. In ILOC, we write a predicated instruction by including a predicate expression before the instruction. To remind the reader of

**Predicated execution**
an architectural feature in which some operations take a boolean-valued operand that determines whether or not the operation takes effect

the predicate's purpose, we enclose it in parentheses and follow it with a question mark. For example,

$$(r_{17})? \ \text{add} \ r_a, r_b \ \Rightarrow \ r_c$$

indicates an add operation ($r_a + r_b$) that executes if and only if $r_{17}$ contains true.

The example in Figure 7.9a shows the strength of predicated execution. The code is simple and concise. It generates two predicates, $r_1$ and $r_2$. It uses them to control the code in the then and else parts of the source construct. In Figure 7.9b, predication leads to the same code as the boolean-comparison scheme.

The processor can use predication to avoid executing the operation, or it can execute the operation and use the predicate to avoid assigning the result. As long as the idled operation does not raise an exception, the differences between these two approaches are irrelevant to our discussion. Our examples show the operations required to produce both the predicate and its complement. To avoid the extra computation, a processor could provide comparisons that return two values, both the boolean value and its complement.

---

**SECTION REVIEW**

The implementation of boolean and relational operators involves more choices than the implementation of arithmetic operators. The compiler writer must choose between a numerical encoding and a positional encoding. The compiler must map those decisions onto the set of operations provided by the target processor's ISA.

In practice, compilers choose between numerical and positional encoding based on context. If the code instantiates the value, numerical encoding is necessary. If the value's only use is to determine control flow, positional encoding often produces better results.

---

**Review Questions**

1. If the compiler assigns the value zero to false, what are the relative merits of each of the following values for true? One? Any non-zero number? A word composed entirely of ones?

2. How might the treewalk code generation scheme be adapted to generate positional code for boolean and relational expressions? Can you work short-circuit evaluation into your approach?

## 7.5 STORING AND ACCESSING ARRAYS

So far, we have assumed that variables stored in memory contain scalar values. Many programs need arrays or similar structures. The code required to locate and reference an element of an array is surprisingly complex. This section shows several schemes for laying out arrays in memory and describes the code that each scheme produces for an array reference.

### 7.5.1 Referencing a Vector Element

The simplest form of an array has a single dimension; we call it a *vector*. Vectors are typically stored in contiguous memory, so that the $i^{th}$ element immediately precedes the $i+1^{st}$ element. Thus, a vector V[3...10] generates the following memory layout, where the number below a cell indicates its index in the vector:

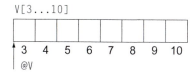

When the compiler encounters a reference, like V[6], it must use the index into the vector, along with facts available from the declaration of V, to generate an offset for V[6]. The actual address is then computed as the sum of the offset and a pointer to the start of V, which we write as @V.

As an example, assume that V has been declared as V[*low...high*], where *low* and *high* are the vector's lower and upper bounds. To translate the reference V[i], the compiler needs both a pointer to the start of storage for V and the offset of element i within V. The offset is simply $(i - low) \times w$, where $w$ is the length of a single element of V. Thus, if *low* is 3, i is 6, and $w$ is 4, the offset is $(6 - 3) \times 4 = 12$. Assuming that $r_i$ holds the value of i, the following code fragment computes the address of V[i] into $r_3$ and loads its value into $r_V$:

```
loadI @V      ⇒ r@V  // get V's address
subI  r_i,3   ⇒ r_1  // (offset - lower bound)
multI r_1,4   ⇒ r_2  // x element length (4)
add   r@V,r_2 ⇒ r_3  // address of V[i]
load  r_3     ⇒ r_V  // value of V[i]
```

Notice that the simple reference V[i] introduces three arithmetic operations. The compiler can improve this sequence. If $w$ is a power of two, the multiply can be replaced with an arithmetic shift; many base types in real programming languages have this property. Adding the address and offset seems unavoidable; perhaps this explains why most processors include an addressing mode that takes a base address and an offset and accesses the location at base address + offset. In ILOC, we write this as loadAO.

```
loadI    @V       ⇒ r@V    // get V's address
subI     r_i,3    ⇒ r_1    // (offset - lower bound)
lshiftI  r_1,2    ⇒ r_2    // x element length (4)
loadAO   r@V,r_2  ⇒ r_V    // value of V[i]
```

**False zero**

The false zero of a vector V is the address where V[0] would be.

In multiple dimensions, it is the location of a zero in each dimension.

Using a lower bound of zero eliminates the subtraction. If the compiler knows the lower bound of V, it can fold the subtraction into @V. Rather than using @V as the base address for V, it can use $V_0 = @V - low \times w$. We call $@V_0$ the *false zero* of V.

Using $@V_0$ and assuming that i is in $r_i$, the code for accessing V[i] becomes

```
loadI    @V_0      ⇒ r@V_0  // adjusted address for V
lshiftI  r_i, 2    ⇒ r_1    // x element length (4)
loadAO   r@V_0, r_1 ⇒ r_V   // value of V[i]
```

This code is shorter and, presumably, faster. A good assembly-language programmer might write this code. In a compiler, the longer sequence may produce better results by exposing details such as the multiply and add to optimization. Low-level improvements, such as converting the multiply into a shift and converting the add–load sequence into with loadAO, can be done late in compilation.

If the compiler does not know an array's bounds, it might calculate the array's false zero at runtime and reuse that value in each reference to the array. It might compute the false zero on entry to a procedure that references elements of the array multiple times. An alternative strategy, employed in languages like C, forces the use of zero as a lower bound, which ensures that $@V_0 = @V$ and simplifies all array-address calculations. However, attention to detail in the compiler can achieve the same results without restricting the programmer's choice of a lower bound.

## 7.5.2 **Array Storage Layout**

Accessing an element of a multidimensional array requires more work. Before discussing the code sequences that the compiler must generate, we must consider how the compiler will map array indices to memory locations. Most implementations use one of three schemes: *row-major order, column-major order*, or *indirection vectors*. The source-language definition usually specifies one of these mappings.

The code required to access an array element depends on the way that the array is mapped to memory. Consider the array A[1...2,1...4]. Conceptually, it looks like

$$
A \quad
\begin{array}{|c|c|c|c|}
\hline
1,1 & 1,2 & 1,3 & 1,4 \\
\hline
2,1 & 2,2 & 2,3 & 2,4 \\
\hline
\end{array}
$$

In linear algebra, the *row* of a two-dimensional matrix is its first dimension, and the *column* is its second dimension. In row-major order, the elements of a are mapped onto consecutive memory locations so that adjacent elements of a single row occupy consecutive memory locations. This produces the following layout:

$$
\begin{array}{|c|c|c|c|c|c|c|c|}
\hline
1,1 & 1,2 & 1,3 & 1,4 & 2,1 & 2,2 & 2,3 & 2,4 \\
\hline
\end{array}
$$

The following loop nest shows the effect of row-major order on memory access patterns:

```
for i ← 1 to 2
    for j ← 1 to 4
        A[i,j] ← A[i,j] + 1
```

In row-major order, the assignment statement steps through memory in sequential order, beginning with A[1,1], A[1,2], A[1,3], and on through A[2,4]. This sequential access works well with most memory hierarchies. Moving the i loop inside the j loop produces an access sequence that jumps between rows, accessing A[1,1], A[2,1], A[1,2],..., A[2,4]. For a small array like a, this is not a problem. For arrays that are larger than the cache, the lack of sequential access could produce poor performance in the memory hierarchy. As a general rule, row-major order produces sequential access when the rightmost subscript, j in this example, varies fastest.

The obvious alternative to row-major order is column-major order. It keeps the columns of a in contiguous locations, producing the following layout:

| 1,1 | 2,1 | 1,2 | 2,2 | 1,3 | 2,3 | 1,4 | 2,4 |
|-----|-----|-----|-----|-----|-----|-----|-----|

Column-major order produces sequential access when the leftmost subscript varies fastest. In our doubly nested loop, having the i loop in the outer position produces nonsequential access, while moving the i loop to the inner position would produce sequential access.

A third alternative, not quite as obvious, has been used in several languages. This scheme uses indirection vectors to reduce all multidimensional arrays to a set of vectors. For our array a, this would produce

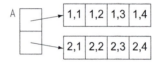

Each row has its own contiguous storage. Within a row, elements are addressed as in a vector. To allow systematic addressing of the row vectors, the compiler allocates a vector of pointers and initializes it appropriately. A similar scheme can create column-major indirection vectors.

Indirection vectors appear simple, but they introduce their own complexity. First, indirection vectors require more storage than either of the contiguous storage schemes, as shown graphically in Figure 7.10. Second, this scheme requires that the application initialize, at runtime, all of the indirection pointers. An advantage of the indirection vector approach is that it allows easy implementation of ragged arrays, that is, arrays where the length of the last dimension varies.

Each of these schemes has been used in a popular programming language. For languages that store arrays in contiguous storage, row-major order has been the typical choice; the one notable exception is FORTRAN, which uses column-major order. Both BCPL and Java support indirection vectors.

### 7.5.3 **Referencing an Array Element**

Programs that use arrays typically contain references to individual array elements. As with vectors, the compiler must translate an array reference into a base address for the array's storage and an offset where the element is located relative to the starting address.

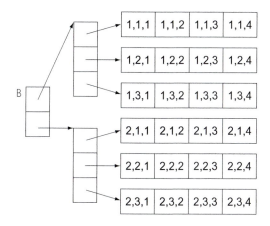

■ **FIGURE 7.10** Indirection Vectors in Row-Major Order for B[1...2,1...3,1...4].

This section describes the address calculations for arrays stored as a contiguous block in row-major order and as a set of indirection vectors. The calculations for column-major order follow the same basic scheme as those for row-major order, with the dimensions reversed. We leave those equations for the reader to derive.

### Row-Major Order

In row-major order, the address calculation must find the start of the row and then generate an offset within the row as if it were a vector. Extending the notation that we used to describe the bounds of a vector, we add subscripts to *low* and *high* that specify a dimension. Thus, $low_1$ refers to the lower bound of the first dimension, and $high_2$ refers to the upper bound of the second dimension. In our example A[1...2,1...4], $low_1$ is 1 and $high_2$ is 4.

To access element A[i,j], the compiler must emit code that computes the address of row i and follow that with the offset for element j, which we know from Section 7.5.1 will be $(j - low_2) \times w$. Each row contains four elements, computed as $high_2 - low_2 + 1$, where $high_2$ is the highest-numbered column and $low_2$ is the lowest-numbered column—the upper and lower bounds for the second dimension of A. To simplify the exposition, let $len_k = high_k - low_k + 1$, the length of the $k^{th}$ dimension. Since rows are laid out consecutively, row i begins at $(i - low_1) \times len_2 \times w$ from the start of A. This suggests the address computation

$$@A + (i - low_1) \times len_2 \times w + (j - low_2) \times w$$

Substituting actual values for $i$, $j$, $low_1$, $high_2$, $low_2$, and $w$, we find that A[2,3] lies at offset

$$(2 - 1) \times (4 - 1 + 1) \times 4 + (3 - 1) \times 4 = 2$$

from A[1,1] (assuming that @A points at A[1,1], at offset 0). Looking at A in memory, we find that the address of A[1,1] $+ 24$ is, in fact, the address of A[2,3].

In the vector case, we were able to simplify the calculation when upper and lower bounds were known at compile time. Applying the same algebra to create a false zero in the two-dimensional case produces

$$@A + (i \times len_2 \times w) - (low_1 \times len_2 \times w) + (j \times w) - (low_2 \times w), \text{ or}$$

$$@A + (i \times len_2 \times w) + (j \times w) - (low_1 \times len_2 \times w + low_2 \times w)$$

The last term, $(low_1 \times len_2 \times w + low_2 \times w)$, is independent of $i$ and $j$, so it can be factored directly into the base address

$$@A_0 = @A - (low_1 \times len_2 \times w + low_2 \times w) = @A - 20$$

Now, the array reference is simply

$$@A_0 + i \times len_2 \times w + j \times w$$

Finally, we can refactor and move the $w$ outside, saving an extraneous multiply

$$@A_0 + (i \times len_2 + j) \times w$$

For the address of A[2,3], this evaluates to

$$@A_0 + (2 \times 4 + 3) \times 4 = @A_0 + 44$$

Since $@A_0$ is just $@A - 20$, this is equivalent to $@A - 20 + 44 = @A + 24$, the same location found with the original version of the array address polynomial.

If we assume that i and j are in $r_i$ and $r_j$, and that $len_2$ is a constant, this form of the polynomial leads to the following code sequence:

```
loadI  @A₀      ⇒ r@A₀   // adjusted base for A
multI  rᵢ,len₂  ⇒ r₁     // i × len₂
add    r₁,rⱼ    ⇒ r₂     // + j
multI  r₂,4     ⇒ r₃     // x element length, 4
loadAO r@A₀,r₃  ⇒ rₐ     // value of A[i,j]
```

In this form, we have reduced the computation to two multiplications and two additions (one in the loadAO). The second multiply can be rewritten as a shift.

If the compiler does not have access to the array bounds, it must either compute the false zero at runtime or use the more complex polynomial that includes the subtractions that adjust for lower bounds. The former option can be profitable if the elements of the array are accessed multiple times in a procedure; computing the false zero on entry to the procedure lets the code use the less expensive address computation. The more complex computation makes sense only if the array is accessed infrequently.

The ideas behind the address computation for arrays with two dimensions generalize to arrays of higher dimension. The address polynomial for an array stored in column-major order can be derived in a similar fashion. The optimizations that we applied to reduce the cost of address computations apply equally well to the address polynomials for these other kinds of arrays.

### Indirection Vectors

Using indirection vectors simplifies the code generated to access an individual element. Since the outermost dimension is stored as a set of vectors, the final step looks like the vector access described in Section 7.5.1. For B[i,j,k], the final step computes an offset from k, the outermost dimension's lower bound, and the length of an element for B. The preliminary steps derive the starting address for this vector by following the appropriate pointers through the indirection-vector structure.

Thus, to access element B[i,j,k] in the array B shown in Figure 7.10, the compiler uses @B₀, i, and the length of a pointer, to find the vector for the subarray B[i,*,*]. Next, it uses that result, along with j and the length of a pointer to find the vector for the subarray B[i,j,*]. Finally, it uses that base address in the vector-address computation with k and element length $w$ to find the address of B[i,j,k].

If the current values for i,j, and k exist in registers $r_i$,$r_j$, and $r_k$, respectively, and $@B_0$ is the zero-adjusted address of the first dimension, then B[i,j,k] can be referenced as follows:

```
loadI   @B₀      ⇒ r@B₀   // false zero of B
multI   rᵢ,4     ⇒ r₁     // assume pointer is 4 bytes
loadAO  r@B₀,r₁  ⇒ r₂     // get @B[i,*,*]

multI   rⱼ,4     ⇒ r₃     // pointer is 4 bytes
loadAO  r₂,r₃    ⇒ r₄     // get @B[i,j,*]

multI   rₖ,4     ⇒ r₅     // assume element length is 4
loadAO  r₄,r₅    ⇒ rᵦ     // value of B[i,j,k]
```

This code assumes that the pointers in the indirection structure have already been adjusted to account for nonzero lower bounds. If that is not the case, then the values in $r_j$ and $r_k$ must be decremented by the corresponding lower bounds. The multiplies can be replaced by shifts in this example.

Using indirection vectors, the reference requires just two operations per dimension. This property made the indirection-vector scheme efficient on systems in which memory access is fast relative to arithmetic—for example, on most computer systems prior to 1985. As the cost of memory accesses has increased relative to arithmetic, this scheme has lost its advantage in speed.

On cache-based machines, locality is critical to performance. When arrays grow to be much larger than the cache, storage order affects locality. Row-major and column-major storage schemes produce good locality for some array-based operations. The locality properties of an array implemented with indirection vectors are harder for the compiler to predict and, perhaps, to optimize.

### Accessing Array-Valued Parameters

When an array is passed as a parameter, most implementations pass it by reference. Even in languages that use call by value for all other parameters, arrays are usually passed by reference. Consider the mechanism required to pass an array by value. The caller would need to copy each array element's value into the activation record of the callee. Passing the array as a reference parameter can greatly reduce the cost of each call.

If the compiler is to generate array references in the callee, it needs information about the dimensions of the array that is bound to the parameter. In FORTRAN, for example, the programmer is required to declare the array using either constants or other formal parameters to specify its dimensions. Thus, FORTRAN gives the programmer responsibility for passing to the callee the information that it needs to address correctly a parameter array.

Other languages leave the task of collecting, organizing, and passing the necessary information to the compiler. The compiler builds a descriptor that contains both a pointer to the start of the array and the necessary information for each dimension. The descriptor has a known size, even when the array's size cannot be known at compile time. Thus, the compiler can allocate space for the descriptor in the AR of the callee procedure. The value passed in the array's parameter slot is a pointer to this descriptor, which is called a *dope vector*.

**Dope vector**

a descriptor for an actual parameter array

Dope vectors may also be used for arrays whose bounds are determined at runtime.

When the compiler generates a reference to a formal-parameter array, it must extract the information from the dope vector. It generates the same address polynomial that it would use for a reference to a local array, loading values out of the dope vector as needed. The compiler must decide, as a matter of policy, which form of the address polynomial it will use. With the naive address polynomial, the dope vector contains a pointer to the start of the array, the lower bound of each dimension, and the sizes of all but one of the dimensions. With the address polynomial based on the false zero, the lower-bound information is unneeded. Because it may compile caller and callee separately, the compiler must be consistent in its usage. In most cases, the code to build the actual dope vector can be moved away from the call site and placed in the caller's prologue code. For a call inside a loop, this move reduces the call overhead.

One procedure might be invoked from multiple call sites, each passing a different array. The PL/I procedure `main` in Figure 7.11a contains two calls to procedure `fee`. The first passes the array `x`, while the second passes `y`. Inside `fee`, the actual parameter (`x` or `y`) is bound to the formal parameter `A`. The code in `fee` for a reference to `A` needs a dope vector to describe the actual parameter. Figure 7.11b shows the respective dope vectors for the two call sites, based on the false-zero version of the address polynomial.

Notice that the cost of accessing an array-valued parameter or a dynamically sized array is higher than the cost of accessing a local array with fixed bounds. At best, the dope vector introduces additional memory references to access the relevant entries. At worst, it prevents the compiler from performing optimizations that rely on complete knowledge of an array's declaration.

### 7.5.4 Range Checking

Most programming-language definitions assume, either explicitly or implicitly, that a program refers only to array elements within the defined bounds of an array. A program that references an out-of-bounds element is, by definition, not well formed. Some languages (for example, Java and Ada) require that out-of-bounds accesses be detected and reported. In other

```
program main;
  begin;
    declare x(1:100,1:10,2:50),
        y(1:10,1:10,15:35) float;
    ...
    call fee(x)
    call fee(y);
  end main;

procedure fee(A)
  declare A(*,*,*) float;
  begin;
    declare x float;
      declare i, j, k fixed binary;
    ...
    x = A(i,j,k);
    ...
  end fee;
```

```
A ──▶ ┌──────┐
      │ @x_0 │
      ├──────┤
      │ 100  │
      ├──────┤
      │ 10   │
      ├──────┤
      │ 49   │
      └──────┘
   At the First Call

A ──▶ ┌──────┐
      │ @y_0 │
      ├──────┤
      │ 10   │
      ├──────┤
      │ 10   │
      ├──────┤
      │ 21   │
      └──────┘
   At the Second Call
```

(a) Code that Passes Whole Arrays        (b) Dope Vectors for the Call Sites

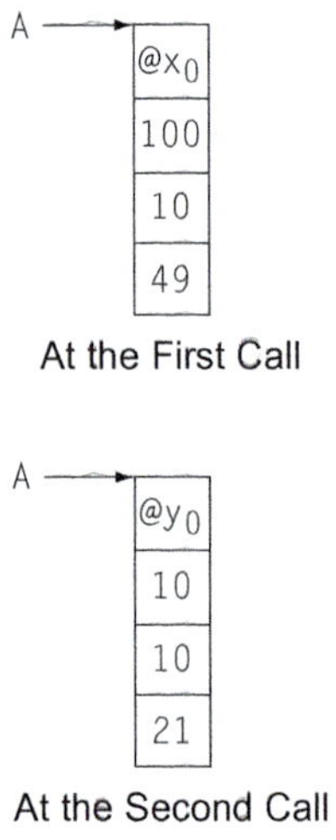

■ **FIGURE 7.11** Dope Vectors.

languages, compilers have included optional mechanisms to detect and report out-of-bounds array accesses.

The simplest implementation of *range checking*, as this is called, inserts a test before each array reference. The test verifies that each index value falls in the valid range for the dimension in which it is used. In an array-intensive program, the overhead of such checks can be significant. Many improvements on this simple scheme are possible. The least expensive alternative is to prove, in the compiler, that a given reference cannot generate an out-of-bounds reference.

If the compiler intends to insert range checks for array-valued parameters, it may need to include additional information in the dope vectors. For example, if the compiler uses the address polynomial based on the array's false zero, it has length information for each dimension, but not upper and lower bound information. It might perform an imprecise test by checking the offset against the array's overall length. However, to perform a precise test, the compiler must include the upper and lower bounds for each dimension in the dope vector and test against them.

When the compiler generates runtime code for range checking, it inserts many copies of the code to report an out-of-range subscript. Optimizing compilers often contain techniques that improve range-checking code.

Checks can be combined. They can be moved out of loops. They can be proved redundant. Taken together, such optimizations can radically reduce the overhead of range checking.

---

**SECTION REVIEW**

Programming language implementations store arrays in a variety of formats. The primary ones are contiguous arrays in either row-major or column-major order and disjoint arrays using indirection vectors. Each format has a distinct formula for computing the address of a given element. The address polynomials for contiguous arrays can be optimized with simple algebra to reduce their evaluation costs.

Parameters passed as arrays require cooperation between the caller and the callee. The caller must create a dope vector to hold the information that the callee requires. The caller and callee must agree on the dope vector format.

---

**Review Questions**

1. For a two-dimensional array A stored in column-major order, write down the address polynomial for the reference A[i,j]. Assume that A is declared with dimensions $(l_1 : h_1)$ and $(l_2 : h_2)$ and that elements of A occupy *w* bytes.

2. Given an array of integers with dimensions A[0:99,0:89,0:109], how many words of memory are used to represent A as a compact row-major order array? How many words are needed to represent A using indirection vectors? Assume that both pointers and integers require one word each.

## 7.6 CHARACTER STRINGS

The operations that programming languages provide for character data are different from those provided for numerical data. The level of programming-language support for character strings ranges from C's level of support, where most manipulation takes the form of calls to library routines, to PL/I's level of support, where the language provides first-class mechanisms to assign individual characters, specify arbitrary substrings, and concatenate strings to form new strings. To illustrate the issues that arise in string implementation, this section discusses string assignment, string concatenation, and the string-length computation.

String operations can be costly. Older CISC architectures, such as the IBM S/370 and the DEC VAX, provide extensive support for string manipulation. Modern RISC machines rely more heavily on the compiler to code these complex operations using a set of simpler operations. The basic operation, copying bytes from one location to another, arises in many different contexts.

### 7.6.1 **String Representations**

The compiler writer must choose a representation for strings; the details of that representation have a strong impact on the cost of string operations. To see this point, consider two common representations of a string b. The one on the left is traditional in c implementations. It uses a simple vector of characters, with a designated character ('\0') serving as a terminator. The glyph ∅ represents a blank. The representation on the right stores the length of the string (8) alongside its contents. Many language implementations have used this approach.

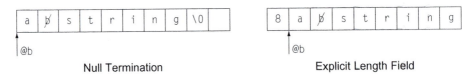

Null Termination                    Explicit Length Field

If the length field takes more space than the null terminator, then storing the length will marginally increase the size of the string in memory. (Our examples assume the length is 4 bytes; in practice, it might be smaller.) However, storing the length simplifies several operations on strings. If a language allows varying-length strings to be stored inside a string allocated with some fixed length, the implementor might also store the allocated length with the string. The compiler can use the allocated length for runtime bounds checking on assignment and concatenation.

### 7.6.2 **String Assignment**

String assignment is conceptually simple. In c, an assignment from the third character of b to the second character of a can be written as a[1]=b[2];. On a machine with character-sized memory operations (cload and cstore), this translates into the simple code shown in the margin. (Recall that the first character in a is a[0] because c uses zero as the lower bound of all arrays.)

```
loadI    @b       ⇒ r@b
cloadAI  r@b,2 ⇒ r2
loadI    @a       ⇒ r@a
cstoreAI r2       ⇒ r@a,1
```

If, however, the underlying hardware does not support character-oriented memory operations, the compiler must generate more complex code. Assuming that both a and b begin on word boundaries, that a character occupies 1 byte, and that a word is 4 bytes, the compiler might emit the following code:

```
loadI  0x0000FF00  ⇒ rC2    // mask for 2nd char
loadI  0xFF00FFFF  ⇒ rC124  // mask for chars 1, 2, & 4
```

```
loadI    @b        ⇒ r@b   // address of b
load     r@b       ⇒ r1    // get 1st word of b

and      r1,rC2    ⇒ r2    // mask away others
lshiftI  r2,8      ⇒ r3    // move it over 1 byte

loadI    @a        ⇒ r@a   // address of a
load     r@a       ⇒ r4    // get 1st word of a

and      r4,rC124  ⇒ r5    // mask away 2nd char
or       r3,r5     ⇒ r6    // put in new 2nd char
store    r6        ⇒ r@a   // put it back in a
```

This code loads the word that contains b[2], extracts the character, shifts it into position, masks it into the proper position in the word that contains a[1], and stores the result back into place. In practice, the masks that the code loads into $r_{C2}$ and $r_{C124}$ would likely be stored in statically initialized storage or computed. The added complexity of this code sequence may explain why character-oriented load and store operations are common.

The code is similar for longer strings. PL/I has a string assignment operator. The programmer can write a statement such as a = b; where a and b have been declared as character strings. Assume that the compiler uses the explicit length representation. The following simple loop will move the characters on a machine with byte-oriented cload and cstore operations:

```
              loadI    @b       ⇒ r@b
              loadAI   r@b,-4   ⇒ r1      // get b's length
              loadI    @a       ⇒ r@a
              loadAI   r@a,-4   ⇒ r2      // get a's length
              cmp_LT   r2,r1    ⇒ r3      // will b fit in a?
              cbr      r3       → Lsov,L1 // raise overflow

        L1:   loadI    0        ⇒ r4      // counter
              cmp_LT   r4,r1    ⇒ r5      // more to copy?
              cbr      r5       → L2,L3

a = b;  L2:   cloadAO  r@b,r4   ⇒ r6      // get char from b
              cstoreAO r6       ⇒ r@a,r4  // put it in a
              addI     r4,1     ⇒ r4      // increment offset
              cmp_LT   r4,r1    ⇒ r7      // more to copy?
              cbr      r7       → L2,L3

        L3:   storeAI  r1       ⇒ r@a,-4  // set length
```

Notice that this code tests the lengths of a and b to avoid overrunning a. (With an explicit length representation, the overhead is small.) The label $L_{sov}$ represents a runtime error handler for string-overflow conditions.

In c, which uses null termination for strings, the same assignment would be written as a character-copying loop.

```
t₁ = a;
t₂ = b;
do {
  *t₁++ = *t₂++;
} while (*t₂ != '\0')
```

```
        loadI  @b        ⇒ r@b    // get pointers
        loadI  @a        ⇒ r@a
        loadI  NULL      ⇒ r₁     // terminator
        cload  r@b       ⇒ r₂     // get next char
L₁:     cstore r₂        ⇒ r@a    // store it
        addI   r@b,1     ⇒ r@b    // bump pointers
        addI   r@a,1     ⇒ r@a
        cload  r@b       ⇒ r₂     // get next char
        cmp_NE r₁,r₂     ⇒ r₄
        cbr    r₄        → L₁,L₂
L₂:     nop                       // next statement
```

If the target machine supports autoincrement on load and store operations, the two adds in the loop can be performed in the cload and cstore operations, which reduces the loop to four operations. (Recall that C was originally implemented on the DEC PDP/11, which supported auto-postincrement.) Without autoincrement, the compiler would generate better code by using cloadAO and cstoreAO with a common offset. That strategy would only use one add operation inside the loop.

To achieve efficient execution for long word-aligned strings, the compiler can generate code that uses whole-word loads and stores, followed by a character-oriented loop to handle any leftover characters at the end of the string.

If the processor lacks character-oriented memory operations, the code is more complex. The compiler could replace the load and store in the loop body with a generalization of the scheme for masking and shifting single characters shown in the single character assignment. The result is a functional, but ugly, loop that requires many more instructions to copy b into a.

The advantages of the character-oriented loops are simplicity and generality. The character-oriented loop handles the unusual but complex cases, such as overlapping substrings and strings with different alignments. The disadvantage of the character-oriented loop is its inefficiency relative to a loop that moves larger blocks of memory on each iteration. In practice, the compiler might well call a carefully optimized library routine to implement the nontrivial cases.

## 7.6.3 **String Concatenation**

Concatenation is simply a shorthand for a sequence of one or more assignments. It comes in two basic forms: appending string b to string a, and creating a new string that contains a followed immediately by b.

The former case is a length computation followed by an assignment. The compiler emits code to determine the length of a. Space permitting, it then performs an assignment of b to the space that immediately follows the contents of a. (If sufficient space is not available, the code raises an error at runtime.) The latter case requires copying each character in a and each character in b. The compiler treats the concatenation as a pair of assignments and generates code for the assignments.

In either case, the compiler should ensure that enough space is allocated to hold the result. In practice, either the compiler or the runtime system must know the allocated length of each string. If the compiler knows those lengths, it can perform the check during code generation and avoid the runtime check. In cases where the compiler cannot know the lengths of a and b, it must generate code to compute the lengths at runtime and to perform the appropriate test and branch.

### 7.6.4 **String Length**

Programs that manipulate strings often need to compute a character string's length. In C programs, the function strlen in the standard library takes a string as its argument and returns the string's length, expressed as an integer. In PL/I, the built-in function length performs the same function. The two string representations described previously lead to radically different costs for the length computation.

1. *Null Terminated String* The length computation must start at the beginning of the string and examine each character, in order, until it reaches the null character. The code is similar to the C character-copying loop. It requires time proportional to the length of the string.
2. *Explicit Length Field* The length computation is a memory reference. In ILOC, this becomes a loadI of the string's starting address into a register, followed by a loadAI to obtain the length. The cost is constant and small.

The tradeoff between these representations is simple. Null termination saves a small amount of space, but requires more code and more time for the length computation. An explicit length field costs one more word per string, but makes the length computation take constant time.

A classic example of a string optimization problem is finding the length that would result from the concatenation of two strings, a and b. In a language with string operators, this might be written as length(a+b), where + signifies concatenation. This expression has two obvious implementations: construct the concatenated string and compute its length (strlen(strcat(a,b)) in C), and sum the lengths of a and b (strlen(a)+strlen(b) in c). The latter solution, of course, is desired. With an explicit length field, the operation can be optimized to use two loads and an add.

---

**SECTION REVIEW**

In principle, string operations are similar to operations on vectors. The details of string representation and the complications introduced by issues of alignment and a desire for efficiency can complicate the code that the compiler must generate. Simple loops that copy one character at a time are easy to generate, to understand, and to prove correct. More complex loops that move multiple characters per iteration can be more efficient; the cost of that efficiency is additional code to handle the end cases. Many compilers simply fall back on a system supplied string-copy routine, such as the Linux strcpy or memmove routines, for the complex cases.

---

**Review Questions**

1. Write the ILOC code for the string assignment a ← b using word-length loads and stores. (Use character-length loads and stores in a post loop to clean up the end cases.) Assume that a and b are word aligned and nonoverlapping.

2. How does your code change if a and b are character aligned rather than word aligned? What complications would overlapping strings introduce?

## 7.7 STRUCTURE REFERENCES

Most programming languages provide a mechanism to aggregate data together into a structure. The c structure is typical; it aggregates individually named elements, often of different types. A list implementation, in c, might, for example, use the following structure to create lists of integers:

```
struct node {
  int value;
  struct node *next;
};

struct node NILNode = {0, (struct node*) 0};
struct node *NIL = &NILNode;
```

Each node contains a single integer and a pointer to another node. The final declarations creates a node, NILNode, and a pointer, NIL. They initialize NILNode with value zero and an illegal next pointer, and set NIL to point at NILNode. (Programs often use a designated NIL pointer to denote the end of a list.) The introduction of structures and pointers creates two distinct problems for the compiler: *anonymous values* and *structure layout*.

### 7.7.1  Understanding Structure Layouts

When the compiler emits code for structure references, it needs to know both the starting address of the structure instance and the offset and length of each structure element. To maintain these facts, the compiler can build a separate table of structure layouts. This compile-time table must include the textual name for each structure element, its offset within the structure, and its source-language data type. For the list example on page 374, the compiler might build the tables shown in Figure 7.12. Entries in the element table use fully qualified names to avoid conflicts due to reuse of a name in several distinct structures.

With this information, the compiler can easily generate code for structure references. Returning to the list example, the compiler might translate the reference p1->next, for a pointer to node p1, into the following ILOC code:

```
loadI  4        ⇒ r₁  // offset of next
loadAO r_p1,r₁ ⇒ r₂  // value of p1->next
```

Structure Layout Table

| Name | Length | 1st Element |
|------|--------|-------------|
| node | 8 | • |
| ... | ... | • |

Structure Element Table

| Name | Length | Offset | Type | Next |
|------|--------|--------|------|------|
| node.value | 4 | 0 | int | • |
| node.next | 4 | 4 | struct node * | • |
| ... | ... | ... | ... | ... |

■ **FIGURE 7.12** Structure Tables for the List Example.

Here, the compiler finds the offset of `next` by following the table from the `node` entry in the structure table to the chain of entries for `node` in the element table. Walking that chain, it finds the entry for `node.next` and its offset, 4.

In laying out a structure and assigning offsets to its elements, the compiler must obey the alignment rules of the target architecture. This may force it to leave unused space in the structure. The compiler confronts this problem when it lays out the structure declared on the left:

```
struct example {
    int fee;
    double fie;
    int foe;
    double fum;
};
```

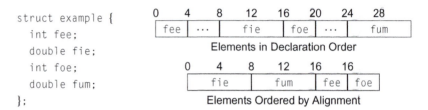

The top-right drawing shows the structure layout if the compiler is constrained to place the elements in declaration order. Because `fie` and `fum` must be doubleword aligned, the compiler must insert padding after `fee` and `foe`. If the compiler could order the elements in memory arbitrarily, it could use the layout shown on the bottom left, which needs no padding. This is a language-design issue: the language definition specifies whether or not the layout of a structure is exposed to the user.

### 7.7.2 Arrays of Structures

Many programming languages allow the user to declare an array of structures. If the user is allowed to take the address of a structure-valued element of an array, then the compiler must lay out the data in memory as multiple copies of the structure layout. If the programmer cannot take the address of a structure-valued element of an array, the compiler might lay out the structure as if it were a structure composed of elements that are, themselves, arrays. Depending on how the surrounding code accesses the data, these two strategies may have strikingly different performance on a system with cache memory.

To address an array of structures laid out as multiple copies of the structure, the compiler uses the array-address polynomials described in Section 7.5. The overall length of the structure, including any needed padding, becomes the element size $w$ in the address polynomial. The polynomial generates the address of the start of the structure instance. To obtain the value of a specific element, the element's offset is added to the instance's address.

If the compiler has laid out the structure with elements that are arrays, it must compute the starting location of the element array using the offset-table information and the array dimension. This address can then be used as the starting point for an address calculation using the appropriate array-address polynomial.

### 7.7.3 **Unions and Runtime Tags**

Many languages allow the programmer to create a structure with multiple, data-dependent interpretations. In C, the union construct has this effect. Pascal achieved the same effect with its variant records.

Unions and variants present one additional complication. To emit code for a reference to an element of a union, the compiler must resolve the reference to a specific offset. Because a union is built from multiple structure definitions, the possibility exists that element names are not unique. The compiler must resolve each reference to a unique offset and type in the runtime object.

This problem has a linguistic solution. The programming language can force the programmer to make the reference unambiguous. Consider the C declarations shown in Figure 7.13. Panel a shows declarations for two kinds of node, one that holds an integer value and another that holds a floating-point value.

The code in panel b declares a union named one that is either an n1 or an n2. To reference an integer value, the programmer specifies u1.inode.value. To reference a floating-point value, the programmer specifies u1.fnode.value. The fully qualified name resolves any ambiguity.

```
struct n1 {            union one {            union two {
   int kind;              struct n1 inode;       struct {
   int value;            struct n2 fnode;          int kind;
};                     } u1;                      int value;
                                                } inode;
struct n2 {                                     struct {
   int kind;                                       int kind;
   float value;                                    float value;
};                                              } fnode;
                                              } u2;
```

(a) Basic Structures      (b) Union of Structures      (c) Union of Implicit Structures

■ **FIGURE 7.13** Union Declarations in C.

The code in panel c declares a union named `two` that has the same properties as `one`. The declaration of `two` explicitly declares its internal structure. The linguistic mechanism for disambiguating a reference to value, however, is the same—the programmer specifies a fully qualified name.

As an alternative, some systems have relied on runtime discrimination. Here, each variant in the union has a field that distinguishes it from all other variants—a "tag." (For example, the declaration of `two`, might initialize `kind` to one for `inode` and to two for `fnode`.) The compiler can then emit code to check the value of the tag field and ensure that each object is handled correctly. In essence, it emits a case statement based on the tag's value. The language may require that the programmer define the tag field and its values; alternatively, the compiler could generate and insert tags automatically. In this latter case, the compiler has a strong motivation to perform type checking and remove as many checks as possible.

### 7.7.4 Pointers and Anonymous Values

A c program creates an instance of a structure in one of two ways. It can declare a structure instance, as with `NilNode` in the earlier example. Alternatively, the code can explicitly allocate a structure instance. For a variable `fee` declared as a pointer to node, the allocation would look like:

```
fee = (struct node *) malloc(sizeof(node));
```

The only access to this new `node` is through the pointer `fee`. Thus, we think of it as an anonymous value, since it has no permanent name.

Because the only name for an anonymous value is a pointer, the compiler cannot easily determine if two pointer references specify the same memory location. Consider the code fragment

```
1  p1 = (node *) malloc(sizeof(node));
2  p2 = (node *) malloc(sizeof(node));
3  if (...)
4     then p3 = p1;
5     else p3 = p2;
6  p1->value = ...;
7  p3->value = ...;
8  ...   = p1->value;
```

The first two lines create anonymous `nodes`. Line 6 writes through `p1` while line 7 writes through `p3`. Because of the `if-then-else`, `p3` can refer to either the node allocated in line 1 or in line 2. Finally, line 8 references `p1->value`.

The use of pointers limits the compiler's ability to keep values in registers. Consider the sequence of assignments in lines 6 through 8. Line 8 reuses either the value assigned in line 6 or the value assigned in line 7. As a matter of efficiency, the compiler should avoid storing that value to memory and reloading it. However, the compiler cannot easily determine which value line 8 uses. The answer to that question depends on the value of the conditional expression in line 3.

While it may be possible to know the value of the conditional expression in certain specific instances (for example, $1 > 2$), it is undecidable in the general case. Unless the compiler knows the value of the conditional expression, it must emit conservative code for the three assignments. It must load the value used in line 8 from memory, even though it recently had the value in a register.

The uncertainty introduced by pointers prevents the compiler from keeping values used in pointer-based references in registers. Anonymous objects further complicate the problem because they introduce an unbounded set of objects to track. As a result, statements that involve pointer-based references are often less efficient than the corresponding computations on unambiguous local values.

A similar effect occurs for code that makes intensive use of arrays. Unless the compiler performs an in-depth analysis of the array subscripts, it may not be able to determine whether two array references overlap. When the compiler cannot distinguish between two references, such as `a[i,j,k]` and `a[i,j,l]`, it must treat both references conservatively. The problem of disambiguating array references, while challenging, is easier than the problem of disambiguating pointer references.

Analysis to disambiguate pointer references and array references is a major source of potential improvement in program performance. For pointer-intensive programs, the compiler may perform an interprocedural data-flow analysis aimed at discovering, for each pointer, the set of objects to which it can point. For array-intensive programs, the compiler may use data-dependence analysis to understand the patterns of array references.

Data-dependence analysis is beyond the scope of this book. See [352, 20, 270].

---

**SECTION REVIEW**

To implement structures and arrays of structures, the compiler must establish a layout for each structure and must have a formula to calculate the offset of any structure element. In a language where the declarations dictate the relative position of data elements, structure layout simply requires the compiler to calculate offsets. If the language allows the compiler to determine the relative position of the data elements, then the layout problem is similar to data-area layout (see Section 7.2.2). The address computation for a structure element is a simple application of the schemes used for scalar variables (e.g. base + offset) and for array elements.

Two features related to structures introduce complications. If the language permits unions or variant structures, then input code must specify the desired element in an unambiguous way. The typical solution to this problem is the use of fully qualified names for structure elements in a union. The second issue arises from runtime allocation of structures. The use of pointers to hold addresses of dynamically allocated objects introduces ambiguities that complicate the issue of which values can be kept in registers.

---

**Review Questions**

1. When the compiler lays out a structure, it must ensure that each element of the structure is aligned on the appropriate boundary. The compiler may need to insert padding (blank space) between elements to meet alignment restrictions. Write a set of "rules of thumb" that a programmer could use to reduce the likelihood of compiler-inserted padding.

2. If the compiler has the freedom to rearrange structures and arrays, it can sometimes improve performance. What programming language features inhibit the compiler's ability to perform such rearrangement?

## 7.8 CONTROL-FLOW CONSTRUCTS

A basic block is just a maximal-length sequence of straight-line, unpredicated code. Any statement that does not affect control flow can appear inside a block. Any control-flow transfer ends the block, as does a labelled statement since it can be the target of a branch. As the compiler generates code, it can build up basic blocks by simply aggregating consecutive, unlabeled, non-control-flow operations. (We assume that a labelled statement is not labelled gratuitously, that is, every labelled statement is the target of some branch.) The representation of a basic block need not be complex. For example, if the compiler has an assembly-like representation held in a simple linear array, then a block can be described by a pair, ⟨*first,last*⟩, that holds the indices of the instruction that begins the block and the instruction that ends the block. (If the block indices are stored in ascending numerical order, an array of *firsts* will suffice.)

To tie a set of blocks together so that they form a procedure, the compiler must insert code that implements the control-flow operations of the source program. To capture the relationships among blocks, many compilers build a control-flow graph (CFG, see Sections 5.2.2 and 8.6.1) and use it for analysis, optimization, and code generation. In the CFG, nodes represent basic blocks and edges represent possible transfers of control between blocks. Typically, the CFG is a derivative representation that contains references to a more detailed representation of each block.

The code to implement control-flow constructs resides in the basic blocks—at or near the end of each block. (In ILOC, there is no fall-through case on a branch, so every block ends with a branch or a jump. If the IR models delay slots, then the control-flow operation may not be the last operation in the block.) While many different syntactic conventions have been used to express control flow, the number of underlying concepts is small. This section examines many of the control-flow constructs found in modern programming languages.

### 7.8.1 **Conditional Execution**

Most programming languages provide some version of an `if-then-else` construct. Given the source text

```
if expr
    then statement₁
    else statement₂
statement₃
```

the compiler must generate code that evaluates *expr* and branches to *statement₁* or *statement₂*, based on the value of *expr*. The ILOC code that implements the two statements must end with a jump to *statement₃*. As we saw in Section 7.4, the compiler has many options for implementing `if-then-else` constructs.

The discussion in Section 7.4 focused on evaluating the controlling expression. It showed how the underlying instruction set influenced the strategies for handling both the controlling expression and, in some cases, the controlled statements.

Programmers can place arbitrarily large code fragments inside the `then` and `else` parts. The size of these code fragments has an impact on the compiler's strategy for implementing the `if-then-else` construct. With trivial `then` and `else` parts, as shown in Figure 7.9, the primary consideration for the compiler is matching the expression evaluation to the underlying hardware. As the `then` and `else` parts grow, the importance of efficient execution inside the `then` and `else` parts begins to outweigh the cost of executing the controlling expression.

For example, on a machine that supports predicated execution, using predicates for large blocks in the `then` and `else` parts can waste execution cycles. Since the processor must issue each predicated instruction to one of its functional units, each operation with a false predicate has an opportunity cost—it ties up an issue slot. With large blocks of code under both the `then` and `else` parts, the cost of unexecuted instructions may outweigh the overhead of using a conditional branch.

Figure 7.14 illustrates this tradeoff. It assumes that both the `then` and `else` parts contain 10 independent ILOC operations and that the target machine can issue two operations per cycle.

Figure 7.14a shows code that might be generated using predication; it assumes that the value of the controlling expression is in $r_1$. The code issues two instructions per cycle. One of them executes in each cycle. All of the `then` part's operations are issued to Unit 1, while the `then` part's operations are issued to Unit 2. The code avoids all branching. If each operation

| Unit 1 | Unit 2 |
|--------|--------|
| $comparison \Rightarrow r_1$ | |
| $(r_1)$ op$_1$   $(\neg r_1)$ op$_{11}$ | |
| $(r_1)$ op$_2$   $(\neg r_1)$ op$_{12}$ | |
| $(r_1)$ op$_3$   $(\neg r_1)$ op$_{13}$ | |
| $(r_1)$ op$_4$   $(\neg r_1)$ op$_{14}$ | |
| $(r_1)$ op$_5$   $(\neg r_1)$ op$_{15}$ | |
| $(r_1)$ op$_6$   $(\neg r_1)$ op$_{16}$ | |
| $(r_1)$ op$_7$   $(\neg r_1)$ op$_{17}$ | |
| $(r_1)$ op$_8$   $(\neg r_1)$ op$_{18}$ | |
| $(r_1)$ op$_9$   $(\neg r_1)$ op$_{19}$ | |
| $(r_1)$ op$_{10}$   $(\neg r_1)$ op$_{20}$ | |

| Unit 1 | Unit 2 |
|--------|--------|
| $compare$ & $branch$ | |
| $L_1$: op$_1$ | op$_2$ |
| op$_3$ | op$_4$ |
| op$_5$ | op$_6$ |
| op$_7$ | op$_8$ |
| op$_9$ | op$_{10}$ |
| jumpI | $\rightarrow L_3$ |
| $L_2$: op$_{11}$ | op$_{12}$ |
| op$_{13}$ | op$_{14}$ |
| op$_{15}$ | op$_{16}$ |
| op$_{17}$ | op$_{18}$ |
| op$_{19}$ | op$_{20}$ |
| jumpI | $\rightarrow L_3$ |
| $L_3$: nop | |

(a) Using Predicates

(b) Using Branches

■ **FIGURE 7.14** Predication versus Branching.

**BRANCH PREDICTION BY USERS**

One urban compiler legend concerns branch prediction. FORTRAN has an arithmetic if statement that takes one of three branches, based on whether the controlling expression evaluates to a negative number, to zero, or to a positive number. One early compiler allowed the user to supply a weight for each label that reflected the relative probability of taking that branch. The compiler then used the weights to order the branches in a way that minimized total expected delay from branching.

After the compiler had been in the field for a year, the story goes, a maintainer discovered that the branch weights were being used in the reverse order, maximizing the expected delay. No one had complained. The story is usually told as a fable about the value of programmers' opinions about the behavior of code they have written. (Of course, no one reported the improvement, if any, from using the branch weights in the correct order.)

takes a single cycle, it takes 10 cycles to execute the controlled statements, independent of which branch is taken.

Figure 7.14b shows code that might be generated using branches; it assumes that control flows to $L_1$ for the then part or to $L_2$ for the else part. Because the instructions are independent, the code issues two instructions per cycle. Following the then path takes five cycles to execute the operations for the taken path, plus the cost of the terminal jump. The cost for the else part is identical.

The predicated version avoids the initial branch required in the unpredicated code (to either $L_1$ or $L_2$ in the figure), as well as the terminal jumps (to $L_3$). The branching version incurs the overhead of a branch and a jump, but may execute faster. Each path contains a conditional branch, five cycles of operations, and the terminal jump. (Some of the operations may be used to fill delay slots on jumps.) The difference lies in the effective issue rate—the branching version issues roughly half the instructions of the predicated version. As the code fragments in the then and else parts grow larger, this difference becomes larger.

Choosing between branching and predication to implement an if-then-else requires some care. Several issues should be considered, as follows:

1. *Expected frequency of execution* If one side of the conditional executes significantly more often, techniques that speed execution of that path may produce faster code. This bias may take the form of predicting a branch, of executing some instructions speculatively, or of reordering the logic.

2. *Uneven amounts of code* If one path through the construct contains many more instructions than the other, this may weigh against predication or for a combination of predication and branching.
3. *Control flow inside the construct* If either path contains nontrivial control flow, such as an `if-then-else`, loop, case statement, or call, then predication may be a poor choice. In particular, nested `if` constructs create complex predicates and lower the fraction of issued operations that are useful.

To make the best decision, the compiler must consider all these factors, as well as the surrounding context. These factors may be difficult to assess early in compilation; for example, optimization may change them in significant ways.

### 7.8.2 Loops and Iteration

Most programming languages include loop constructs to perform iteration. The first FORTRAN compiler introduced the `do` loop to perform iteration. Today, loops are found in many forms. For the most part, they have a similar structure.

Consider the C `for` loop as an example. Figure 7.15 shows how the compiler might lay out the code. The `for` loop has three controlling expressions: $e_1$, which provides for initialization; $e_2$, which evaluates to a boolean and governs execution of the loop; and $e_3$, which executes at the end of each iteration and, potentially, updates the values used in $e_2$. We will use this figure as the basic schema to explain the implementation of several kinds of loops.

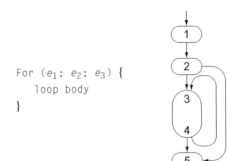

```
For (e₁; e₂; e₃) {
    loop body
}
```

| Step | Purpose |
|------|---------|
| 1 | Evaluate $e_1$ |
| 2 | If $(\neg e_2)$ <br> Then goto 5 |
| 3 | *Loop Body* |
| 4 | Evaluate $e_3$ <br> If $(e_2)$ <br> Then goto 3 |
| 5 | *Code After Loop* |

(a) Example Code for Loop      (b) Schema for Implementing Loop

■ **FIGURE 7.15** General Schema for Layout of a `for` Loop.

If the loop body consists of a single basic block—that is, it contains no other control flow—then the loop that results from this schema has an initial branch plus one branch per iteration. The compiler might hide the latency of this branch in one of two ways. If the architecture allows the compiler to predict whether or not the branch is taken, the compiler should predict the branch in step 4 as being taken (to start the next iteration). If the architecture allows the compiler to move instructions into the delay slot(s) of the branch, the compiler should attempt to fill the delay slot(s) with instruction(s) from the loop body.

### *For Loops*

To map a `for` loop into code, the compiler follows the general schema from Figure 7.15. To make this concrete, consider the following example. Steps 1 and 2 produce a single basic block, as shown in the following code:

```
                          loadI   1        ⇒ rᵢ      // Step 1
                          loadI   100      ⇒ r₁      // Step 2
                          cmp_GT  rᵢ,r₁    ⇒ r₂
for (i=1; i<=100; i++) {  cbr     r₂       → L₂,L₁
    loop body         L₁: loop body                  // Step 3
}
                          addI    rᵢ,1     ⇒ rᵢ .    // Step 4
next statement            cmp_LE  rᵢ,r₁    ⇒ r₃
                          cbr     r₃       → L₁,L₂
                      L₂: next statement             // Step 5
```

The code produced in steps 1, 2, and 4 is straightforward. If the loop body (step 3) either consists of a single basic block or it ends with a single basic block, then the compiler can optimize the update and test produced in step 4 with the loop body. This may lead to improvements in the code—for example, the instruction scheduler might use operations from the end of step 3 to fill delay slots in the branch from step 4.

The compiler can also shape the loop so that it has only one copy of the test— the one in step 2. In this form, step 4 evaluates $e_3$ and then jumps to step 2. The compiler would replace `cmp_LE`, `cbr` sequence at the end of the loop with a `jumpI`. This form of the loop is one operation smaller than the two-test form. However, it creates a two-block loop for even the simplest loops, and it lengthens the path through the loop by at least one operation. When code size is a serious consideration, consistent use of this more compact loop form might be worthwhile. As long as the loop-ending jump is an immediate jump, the hardware can take steps to minimize any disruption that it might cause.

The canonical loop shape from Figure 7.15 also sets the stage for later optimization. For example, if $e_1$ and $e_2$ contain only known constants, as in the example, the compiler can fold the value from step 1 into the test in step 2 and either eliminate the compare and branch (if control enters the loop) or eliminate the loop body (if control never enters the loop). In the single-test loop, the compiler cannot do this. Instead, the compiler finds two paths leading to the test—one from step 1 and one from step 4. The value used in the test, $r_i$, has a varying value along the edge from step 4, so the test's outcome is not predictable.

### FORTRAN's do *Loop*

In FORTRAN, the iterative loop is a do loop. It resembles the c for loop, but has a more restricted form.

```
              loadI   1       ⇒ rⱼ      // j ← 1
              loadI   1       ⇒ rᵢ      // Step 1
 j = 1        loadI   100     ⇒ r₁      // Step 2
 do 10 i = 1, 100   cmp_GT  rᵢ,r₁  ⇒ r₂
    loop body       cbr     r₂       → L₂,L₁
       j = j + 2   L₁: loop body            // Step 3
 10    continue     addI    rⱼ,2   ⇒ rⱼ     // j ← j+2
                    addI    rᵢ,1   ⇒ rᵢ     // Step 4
    next statement  cmp_LE  rᵢ,r₁  ⇒ r₃
                    cbr     r₃       → L₁,L₂

                L₂: next statement           // Step 5
```

The comments map portions of the ILOC code back to the schema in Figure 7.15.

The definition of FORTRAN, like that of many languages, has some interesting quirks. One such peculiarity relates to do loops and their index variables. The number of iterations of a loop is fixed before execution enters the loop. If the program changes the index variable's value, that change does not affect the number of iterations that execute. To ensure the correct behavior, the compiler may need to generate a hidden induction variable, called a *shadow index variable*, to control the iteration.

### *While Loops*

A while loop can also be implemented with the loop schema in Figure 7.15. Unlike the c for loop or the FORTRAN do loop, a while loop has no initialization. Thus, the code is even more compact.

```
                      cmp_LT  rₓ,rᵧ  ⇒ r₁    // Step 2
 while (x < y) {      cbr     r₁      → L₁,L₂
    loop body        L₁: loop body            // Step 3
                         cmp_LT  rₓ,rᵧ  ⇒ r₂   // Step 4
 }                       cbr     r₂      → L₁,L₂
 next statement
                      L₂: next statement       // Step 5
```

Replicating the test in step 4 creates the possibility of a loop with a single basic block. The same benefits that accrue to a `for` loop from this structure also occur for a `while` loop.

### Until Loops

An `until` loop iterates as long as the controlling expression is false. It checks the controlling expression after each iteration. Thus, it always enters the loop and performs at least one iteration. This produces a particularly simple loop structure, since it avoids steps 1 and 2 in the schema:

```
{                          L₁: loop body              // Step 3
    loop body                  cmp_LT rₓ,r_y ⇒ r₂     // Step 4
} until (x < y)                cbr    r₂    → L₂,L₁
                           L₂: next statement          // Step 5
next statement
```

C does not have an `until` loop. Its `do` construct is similar to an `until` loop, except that the sense of the condition is reversed. It iterates as long as the condition evaluates to true, where the `until` iterates as long as the condition is false.

### Expressing Iteration as Tail Recursion

In Lisp-like languages, iteration is often implemented (by programmers) using a stylized form of recursion. If the last action executed by a function is a call, that call is known as a *tail call*. For example, to find the last element of a list in Scheme, the programmer might write the following simple function:

```
(define (last alon)
    (cond
        ((empty? alon) empty)
        ((empty? (cdr alon)) (car alon))
        (else (last (cdr alon)))))
```

**Tail call**

A procedure call that occurs as the last action in some procedure is termed a tail call. A self-recursive tail call is termed a *tail recursion*.

Compilers often subject tail calls to special treatment, because the compiler can generate particularly efficient call for them (see Section 10.4.1). Tail recursion can be used to achieve the same effects as iteration, as in the following Scheme code:

```
(define (count alon ct)
    (cond
        ((empty? alon) ct)
        (else (count (cdr alon) (+ ct 1)))))

(define (len alon)
    (count alon 0))
```

Invoking `len` on a list returns the list's length. `len` relies on `count`, which implements a simple counter using tail calls.

### Break Statements

Several languages implement variations on a `break` or `exit` statement. The `break` statement is a structured way to exit a control-flow construct. In a loop, `break` transfers control to the first statement following the loop. For nested loops, a `break` typically exits the innermost loop. Some languages, such as Ada and Java, allow an optional label on a `break` statement. This causes the `break` statement to exit from the enclosing construct specified by that label. In a nested loop, a labelled `break` allows the program to exit several loops at once. C also uses `break` in its `switch` statement, to transfer control to the statement that follows the `switch` statement.

These actions have simple implementations. Each loop and each case statement should end with a label for the statement that follows it. A `break` would be implemented as an immediate jump to that label. Some languages include a `skip` or `continue` statement that jumps to the next iteration of a loop. This construct can be implemented as an immediate jump to the code that reevaluates the controlling expression and tests its value. Alternatively, the compiler can simply insert a copy of the evaluation, test, and branch at the point where the `skip` occurs.

## 7.8.3 Case Statements

Many programming languages include some variant of a case statement. FORTRAN has its computed goto. Algol-W introduced the case statement in its modern form. BCPL and C have a `switch` construct, while PL/I has a generalized construct that maps well onto a nested set of `if-then-else` statements. As the introduction to this chapter hinted, implementing a case statement efficiently is complex.

Consider the implementation of C's `switch` statement. The basic strategy is straightforward: (1) evaluate the controlling expression; (2) branch to the selected case; and (3) execute the code for that case. Steps 1 and 3 are well understood, as they follow from discussions elsewhere in this chapter. In C, the individual cases usually end with a `break` statement that exits the `switch` statement.

The complex part of case-statement implementation lies in choosing an efficient method to locate the designated case. Because the desired case is not known until runtime, the compiler must emit code that will use the value of the controlling expression to locate the corresponding case. No single

```
switch (e₁) {

  case 0:  block₀;
           break;
  case 1:  block₁;
           break;
  case 3:  block₃;
           break;
  default: block_d;
           break;
}
```

$$t_1 \leftarrow e_1$$
```
if (t₁ = 0)
    then block₀
    else if (t₁ = 1)
       then block₁
       else if (t₁ = 2)
          then block₂
          else if (t₁ = 3)
             then block₃
             else block_d
```

(a) Switch Statement          (b) Implemented as a Linear Search

■ **FIGURE 7.16** Case Statement Implemented with Linear Search.

method works well for all case statements. Many compilers have provision for several different search schemes and choose between them based on the specific details of the set of cases.

This section examines three strategies: a linear search, a binary search, and a computed address. Each strategy is appropriate under different circumstances.

### Linear Search

The simplest way to locate the appropriate case is to treat the case statement as the specification for a nested set of if-then-else statements. For example, the switch statement shown in Figure 7.16a can be translated into the nest of statements shown in Figure 7.16b. This translation preserves the meaning of the switch statement, but makes the cost of reaching individual cases dependent on the order in which they are written. With a linear search strategy, the compiler should attempt to order the cases by estimated execution frequency. Still, when the number of cases is small—say three or four—this strategy can be efficient.

### Directly Computing the Address

If the case labels form a compact set, the compiler can do better than binary search. Consider the switch statement shown in Figure 7.17a. It has case labels from zero to nine, plus a default case. For this code, the compiler can build a compact vector, or *jump table*, that contains the block labels, and find the appropriate label by index into the table. The jump table is shown

**Jump table**
a vector of labels used to transfer control based on a computed index into the table

```
switch (e₁) {
    case 0:   block₀
              break;
    case 1:   block₁
              break;
    case 2:   block₂
              break;
    ...
    case 9:   block₉
              break;
    default:  block_d
              break;
}
```

| Label |
|-------|
| $LB_0$ |
| $LB_1$ |
| $LB_2$ |
| $LB_3$ |
| $LB_4$ |
| $LB_5$ |
| $LB_6$ |
| $LB_7$ |
| $LB_8$ |
| $LB_9$ |

```
t₁ ← e₁
if (0 > t₁ or t₁ > 9)
    then jump to LB_d
    else
        t₂ ←@Table + t₁ x 4
        t₃ ← memory(t₂)
        jump to t₃
```

(a) Switch Statement      (b) Jump Table      (c) Code for Address Computation

■ **FIGURE 7.17** Case Statement Implemented with Direct Address Computation.

in Figure 7.17b, while the code to compute the correct case's label is shown in Figure 7.17c. The search code assumes that the jump table is stored at @Table and that each label occupies four bytes.

For a dense label set, this scheme generates compact and efficient code. The cost is small and constant—a brief calculation, a memory reference, and a jump. If a few holes exist in the label set, the compiler can fill those slots with the label for the default case. If no default case exists, the appropriate action depends on the language. In C, for example, the code should branch to the first statement after the switch, so the compiler can place that label in each hole in the table. If the language treats a missing case as an error, as PL/I did, the compiler can fill holes in the jump table with the label of a block that throws the appropriate runtime error.

### Binary Search

As the number of cases rises, the efficiency of linear search becomes a problem. In a similar way, as the label set becomes less dense and less compact, the size of the jump table can become a problem for the direct address computation. The classic solutions that arise in building an efficient search apply in this situation. If the compiler can impose an order on the case labels, it can use binary search to obtain a logarithmic search rather than a linear one.

The idea is simple. The compiler builds a compact ordered table of case labels, along with their corresponding branch labels. It uses binary search to

```
switch (e₁) {
    case 0:   block₀
              break;
    case 15:  block₁₅
              break;
    case 23:  block₂₃
              break;
    ...

    case 99:  block₉₉
              break;
    default:  blockₔ
              break;
}
```

| Value | Label |
|:-----:|:-----:|
| 0 | $LB_0$ |
| 15 | $LB_{15}$ |
| 23 | $LB_{23}$ |
| 37 | $LB_{37}$ |
| 41 | $LB_{41}$ |
| 50 | $LB_{50}$ |
| 68 | $LB_{68}$ |
| 72 | $LB_{72}$ |
| 83 | $LB_{83}$ |
| 99 | $LB_{99}$ |

```
t₁ ← e₁
down ← 0   // lower bound
up   ← 10  // upper bound + 1
while (down + 1 < up) {
    middle ← (up + down) ÷ 2
    if (Value [middle] ≤ t₁)
        then down ← middle
        else up ← middle
}

if (Value [down] = t₁
    then jump to Label[down]
    else jump to LBₔ
```

(a) Switch Statement        (b) Search Table        (c) Code for Binary Search

■ **FIGURE 7.18**  Case Statement Implemented with Binary Search.

discover a matching case label, or the absence of a match. Finally, it either branches to the corresponding label or to the `default` case.

Figure 7.18a shows our example case statement, rewritten with a different set of labels. For the figure, we will assume case labels of 0, 15, 23, 37, 41, 50, 68, 72, 83, and 99, as well as a default case. The labels could, of course, cover a much larger range. For such a case statement, the compiler might build a search table such as the one shown in Figure 7.18b, and generate a binary search, as in Figure 7.18c, to locate the desired case. If fall-through behavior is allowed, as in C, the compiler must ensure that the blocks appear in memory in their original order.

The exact form of the search loop might vary. For example, the code in the figure does not short circuit the case when it finds the label early. Empirical testing of several variants written in the target machine's assembly code is needed to find the best choices.

In a binary search or direct address computation, the compiler writer should ensure that the set of potential targets of the jump are visible in the IR, using a construct such as the ILOC `tbl` pseudo-operation (see Appendix A.4.2). Such hints both simplify later analysis and make its results more precise.

---

**SECTION REVIEW**
Programming languages include a variety of features to implement control flow. The compiler needs a schema for each control-flow construct in the source languages that it accepts. In some cases, such as a loop, one approach serves for a variety of different constructs. In others, such as a case statement, the compiler should choose an implementation strategy based on the specific properties of the code at hand.

```
do 10 i = 1, 100
    loop body
    i = i + 2
10  continue
```

**Review Questions**

1. Write the ILOC code for the FORTRAN loop shown in the margin. Recall that the loop body must execute 100 iterations, even though the loop modifies the value of i.

2. Consider the tradeoff between implementing a C switch statement with a direct address computation and with a binary search. At what point should the compiler switch from direct address computation to a binary search? What properties of the actual code should play a role in that determination?

## 7.9 PROCEDURE CALLS

The implementation of procedure calls is, for the most part, straightforward. As shown in Figure 7.19, a procedure call consists of a precall sequence and a postreturn sequence in the caller, and a prologue and an epilogue in the callee. A single procedure can contain multiple call sites, each with its own precall and postreturn sequences. In most languages, a procedure has one entry point, so it has one prologue sequence and one epilogue sequence. (Some languages allow multiple entry points, each of which has its own prologue sequence.) Many of the details involved in these sequences are described in Section 6.5. This section focuses on issues that affect the compiler's ability to generate efficient, compact, and consistent code for procedure calls.

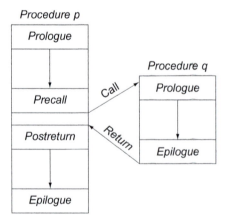

■ **FIGURE 7.19** A Standard Procedure Linkage.

As a general rule, moving operations from the precall and postreturn sequences into the prologue and epilogue sequences should reduce the overall size of the final code. If the call from $p$ to $q$ shown in Figure 7.19 is the only call to $q$ in the entire program, then moving an operation from the precall sequence in $p$ to the prologue in $q$ (or from the postreturn sequence in $p$ to the epilogue in $q$) has no impact on code size. If, however, other call sites invoke $q$ and the compiler moves an operation from the caller to the callee (at all the call sites), it should reduce the overall code size by replacing multiple copies of an operation with a single one. As the number of call sites that invoke a given procedure rises, the savings grow. We assume that most procedures are called from several locations; if not, both the programmer and the compiler should consider including the procedure inline at the point of its only invocation.

From the code-shape perspective, procedure calls are similar in Algol-like languages and object-oriented languages. The major difference between them lies in the technique used to name the callee (see Section 6.3.4). In addition, a call in an object-oriented language typically adds an implicit actual parameter, that is, the receiver's object record.

### 7.9.1 Evaluating Actual Parameters

When it builds the precall sequence, the compiler must emit code to evaluate the actual parameters to the call. The compiler treats each actual parameter as an expression. For a call-by-value parameter, the precall sequence evaluates the expression and stores its value in a location designated for that parameter—either in a register or in the callee's AR. For a call-by-reference parameter, the precall sequence evaluates the parameter to an address and stores the address in a location designated for that parameter. If a call-by-reference parameter has no storage location, then the compiler may need to allocate space to hold the parameter's value so that it has an address to pass to the callee.

If the source language specifies an order of evaluation for the actual parameters, the compiler must, of course, follow that order. Otherwise, it should use a consistent order—either left to right or right to left. The evaluation order matters for parameters that might have side effects. For example, a program that used two routines `push` and `pop` to manipulate a stack would produce different results for the sequence `subtract(pop(), pop())` under left-to-right and right-to-left evaluation.

Procedures typically have several implicit arguments. These include the procedure's ARP, the caller's ARP, the return address, and any information needed to establish addressability. Object-oriented languages pass the receiver as an implicit parameter. Some of these arguments are passed in registers while others usually reside in memory. Many architectures have an operation like

$$jsr\ label_1 \Rightarrow r_i$$

that transfers control to $label_1$ and places the address of the operation that follows the jsr into $r_i$.

Procedures passed as actual parameters may require special treatment. If $p$ calls $q$, passing procedure $r$ as an argument, $p$ must pass to $q$ more information than $r$'s starting address. In particular, if the compiled code uses access links to find nonlocal variables, the callee needs $r$'s lexical level so that a subsequent call to $r$ can find the correct access link for $r$'s level. The compiler can construct an ⟨*address,level*⟩ pair and pass it (or its address) in place of the procedure-valued parameter. When the compiler constructs the precall sequence for a procedure-valued parameter, it must insert the extra code to fetch the lexical level and adjust the access link accordingly.

### 7.9.2  Saving and Restoring Registers

Under any calling convention, one or both of the caller and the callee must preserve register values. Often, linkage conventions use a combination of caller-saves and callee-saves registers. As both the cost of memory operations and the number of registers have risen, the cost of saving and restoring registers at call sites has increased, to the point where it merits careful attention.

In choosing a strategy to save and restore registers, the compiler writer must consider both efficiency and code size. Some processor features impact this choice. Features that spill a portion of the register set can reduce code size. Examples of such features include register windows on the SPARC machines, the multiword load and store operations on the Power architectures, and the high-level call operation on the VAX. Each offers the compiler a compact way to save and restore some portion of the register set.

While larger register sets can increase the number of registers that the code saves and restores, in general, using these additional registers improves the speed of the resulting code. With fewer registers, the compiler would be forced to generate loads and stores throughout the code; with more registers, many of these spills occur only at a call site. (The larger register set should reduce the total number of spills in the code.) The concentration of saves and restores at call sites presents the compiler with opportunities to handle them in better ways than it might if they were spread across an entire procedure.

- *Using multi-register memory operations* When saving and restoring adjacent registers, the compiler can use a multiregister memory operation. Many ISAs support doubleword and quadword load and store operations. Using these operations can reduce code size; it may also improve execution speed. Generalized multiregister memory operations can have the same effect.

- *Using a library routine* As the number of registers grows, the precall and postreturn sequences both grow. The compiler writer can replace the sequence of individual memory operations with a call to a compiler-supplied save or restore routine. Done across all calls, this strategy can produce a significant savings in code size. Since the save and restore routines are known only to the compiler, they can use minimal call sequence to keep the runtime cost low.

  The save and restore routines can take an argument that specifies which registers must be preserved. It may be worthwhile to generate optimized versions for common cases, such as preserving all the caller-saves or callee-saves registers.

- *Combining responsibilities* To further reduce overhead, the compiler might combine the work for caller-saves and callee-saves registers. In this scheme, the caller passes a value to the callee that specifies which registers it must save. The callee adds the registers it must save to the value and calls the appropriate compiler-provided save routine. The epilogue passes the same value to the restore routine so that it can reload the needed registers. This approach limits the overhead to one call to save registers and one to restore them. It separates responsibility (caller saves versus callee saves) from the cost to call the routine.

The compiler writer must pay close attention to the implications of the various options on code size and runtime speed. The code should use the fastest operations for saves and restores. This requires a close look at the costs of single-register and multiregister operations on the target architecture. Using library routines to perform saves and restores can save space; careful implementation of those library routines may mitigate the added cost of invoking them.

---

**SECTION REVIEW**

The code generated for procedure calls is split between the caller and the callee, and between the four pieces of the linkage sequence (prologue, epilogue, precall, and postreturn). The compiler coordinates the code in these multiple locations to implement the linkage convention, as discussed in Chapter 6. Language rules and parameter binding conventions dictate the order of evaluation and the style of evaluation for actual parameters. System-wide conventions determine responsibility for saving and restoring registers.

Compiler writers pay particular attention to the implementation of procedure calls because the opportunities are difficult for general optimization techniques (see Chapters 8 and 10) to discover. The many-to-one nature of the caller-callee relationship complicates analysis and transformation, as does the distributed nature of the cooperating code sequences. Equally important, minor deviations from the defined linkage convention can cause incompatibilities in code compiled with different compilers.

---

**Review Questions**

1. When a procedure saves registers, either callee-saves registers in its prologue or caller-saves registers in a precall sequence, where should it save those registers? Are all of the registers saved for some call stored in the same AR?

2. In some situations, the compiler must create a storage location to hold the value of a call-by-reference parameter. What kinds of parameters may not have their own storage locations? What actions might be required in the precall and postcall sequences to handle these actual parameters correctly?

## 7.10 SUMMARY AND PERSPECTIVE

One of the more subtle tasks that confronts the compiler writer is selecting a pattern of target-machine operations to implement each source-language construct. Multiple implementation strategies are possible for almost any source-language statement. The specific choices made at design time have a strong impact on the code that the compiler generates.

In a compiler that is not intended for production use—a debugging compiler or a student compiler—the compiler writer might select easy to implement translations for each strategy that produce simple, compact code. In an optimizing compiler, the compiler writer should focus on translations that expose as much information as possible to the later phases of the compiler—low-level optimization, instruction scheduling, and register allocation. These two different perspectives lead to different shapes for loops, to different disciplines for naming temporary variables, and, possibly, to different evaluation orders for expressions.

The classic example of this distinction is the `case` statement. In a debugging compiler, the implementation as a cascaded series of `if-then-else` constructs is fine. In an optimizing compiler, the inefficiency of the myriad tests and branches makes a more complex implementation scheme worthwhile. The effort to improve the `case` statement must be made when the IR is generated; few, if any, optimizers will convert a cascaded series of conditionals into a binary search or a direct jump table.

## ■ CHAPTER NOTES

The material contained in this chapter falls, roughly, into two categories: generating code for expressions and handling control-flow constructs. Expression evaluation is well explored in the literature. Discussions of how to handle control flow are rarer; much of the material on control flow in this chapter derives from folklore, experience, and careful reading of the output of compilers.

Floyd presented the first multipass algorithm for generating code from expression trees [150]. He points out that both redundancy elimination and algebraic reassociation have the potential to improve the results of his algorithm. Sethi and Ullman [311] proposed a two-pass algorithm that is optimal for a simple machine model; Proebsting and Fischer extended this work to account for small memory latencies [289]. Aho and Johnson [5] introduced dynamic programming to find least-cost implementations.

The predominance of array calculations in scientific programs led to work on array-addressing expressions and to optimizations (like strength reduction, Section 10.7.2) that improve them. The computations described in Section 7.5.3 follow Scarborough and Kolsky [307].

Harrison used string manipulation as a motivating example for the pervasive use of inline substitution and specialization [182]. The example mentioned at the end of Section 7.6.4 comes from that paper.

Mueller and Whalley describe the impact of different loop shapes on performance [271]. Bernstein provides a detailed discussion of the options that arise in generating code for case statements [40]. Calling conventions are best described in processor-specific and operating-system-specific manuals.

Optimization of range checks has a long history. The PL/.8 compiler insisted on checking every reference; optimization lowered the overhead [257]. More recently, Gupta and others have extended these ideas to increase the set of checks that can be moved to compile time [173].

## ■ EXERCISES

1. Memory layout affects the addresses assigned to variables. Assume that character variables have no alignment restriction, short integer variables must be aligned to halfword (2 byte) boundaries, integer variables must be aligned to word (4 byte) boundaries, and long integer variables must be aligned to doubleword (8 byte) boundaries. Consider the following set of declarations:

```
char a;
long int b;
int c;
short int d;
long int e;
char f;
```

Draw a memory map for these variables:
   a. Assuming that the compiler cannot reorder the variables
   b. Assuming the compiler can reorder the variables to save space

2. As demonstrated in the previous question, the compiler needs an algorithm to lay out memory locations within a data area. Assume that the algorithm receives as input a list of variables, their lengths, and their alignment restrictions, such as

$$\langle a, 4, 4 \rangle, \langle b, 1, 3 \rangle, \langle c, 8, 8 \rangle, \langle d, 4, 4 \rangle, \langle e, 1, 4 \rangle, \langle f, 8, 16 \rangle, \langle g, 1, 1 \rangle.$$

The algorithm should produce, as output, a list of variables and their offsets in the data area. The goal of the algorithm is to minimize unused, or wasted, space.
   a. Write down an algorithm to lay out a data area with minimal wasted space.
   b. Apply your algorithm to the example list above and two other lists that you design to demonstrate the problems that can arise in storage layout.
   c. What is the complexity of your algorithm?

3. For each of the following types of variable, state where in memory the compiler might allocate the space for such a variable. Possible

answers include registers, activation records, static data areas (with different visibilities), and the runtime heap.

**a.** A variable local to a procedure

**b.** A global variable

**c.** A dynamically allocated global variable

**d.** A formal parameter

**e.** A compiler-generated temporary variable

4. Use the treewalk code-generation algorithm from Section 7.3 to generate naive code for the following expression tree. Assume an unlimited set of registers.

Section 7.3

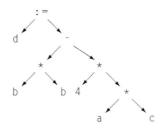

5. Find the minimum number of registers required to evaluate the following trees using the ILOC instruction set. For each nonleaf node, indicate which of its children must be evaluated first in order to achieve this minimum number of registers.

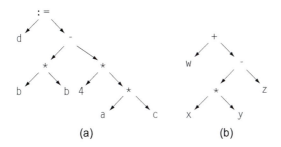

6. Build expression trees for the following two arithmetic expressions, using standard precedence and left-to-right evaluation. Compute the minimum number of registers required to evaluate each of them using the ILOC instruction set.

**a.** `((a + b) + (c + d)) + ((e + f) + (g + h))`

**b.** `a + b + c + d + e + f + g + h`

**Section 7.4**

**7.** Generate predicated ILOC for the following code sequence. (No branches should appear in the solution.)

```
if (x < y)
    then z = x * 5;
    else z = y * 5;
w = z + 10;
```

**8.** As mentioned in Section 7.4, short-circuit code for the following expression in C avoids a potential division-by-zero error:

```
a != 0 && b / a > 0.5
```

If the source-language definition does not specify short-circuit evaluation for boolean-valued expressions, can the compiler generate short-circuit code as an optimization for such expressions? What problems might arise?

**Section 7.5**

**9.** For a character array A[10...12,1...3] stored in row-major order, calculate the address of the reference A[i,j], using at most four arithmetic operations in the generated code.

**10.** What is a dope vector? Give the contents of the dope vector for the character array in the previous question. Why does the compiler need a dope vector?

**11.** When implementing a C compiler, it might be advisable to have the compiler perform range checking for array references. Assuming range checks are used and that all array references in a C program have successfully passed them, is it possible for the program to access storage outside the range of an array, for example, accessing A[-1] for an array declared with lower bound zero and upper bound N?

**Section 7.6**

**12.** Consider the following character-copying loop from Section 7.6.2:

```
                        loadI   @b      ⇒ r@b    // get pointers
                        loadI   @a      ⇒ r@a
                        loadI   NULL    ⇒ r1     // terminator
do {              L1: cload   r@b     ⇒ r2     // get next char
    *a++ = *b++;          cstore  r2      ⇒ r@a    // store it
                        addI    r@b,1   ⇒ r@b    // bump pointers
} while (*b!='\0')        addI    r@a,1   ⇒ r@a
                        cmp_NE  r1,r2   ⇒ r4
                        cbr     r4       → L1,L2

                  L2: nop                      // next stmt
```

Modify the code so that it branches to an error handler at $L_{SOV}$ on any attempt to overrun the allocated length of a. Assume that the allocated length of a is stored as an unsigned four-byte integer at an offset of −8 from the start of a.

13. Arbitrary string assignments can generate misaligned cases.
    a. Write the ILOC code that you would like your compiler to emit for an arbitrary PL/I-style character assignment, such as

       ```
       fee(i:j) = fie(k:l);
       ```

       where $j-i = l-k$. This statement copies the characters in fie, starting at location k and running through location l into the string fee, starting at location i and running through location j.

       Include versions using character-oriented memory operations and versions using word-oriented memory operations. You may assume that fee and fie do not overlap in memory.
    b. The programmer can create character strings that overlap. In PL/I, the programmer might write

       ```
       fee(i:j) = fee(i+1:j+1);
       ```

       or, even more diabolically,

       ```
       fee(i+k:j+k) = fee(i:j);
       ```

       How does this complicate the code that the compiler must generate for the character assignment?
    c. Are there optimizations that the compiler could apply to the various character-copying loops that would improve runtime behavior? How would they help?

14. Consider the following type declarations in C:

    ```
    struct S2 {        union U {          struct S1 {
        int i;             float r;           int a;
        int f;             struct S2;         double b;
    };                 };                     union U;
                                              int d;
                                          };
    ```

    Build a structure-element table for S1. Include in it all the information that a compiler would need to generate references to elements of a

Section 7.7

variable of type S1, including the name, length, offset, and type of each element.

15. Consider the following declarations in C:

```
struct record {
    int StudentId;
    int CourseId;
    int Grade;
} grades[1000];
int g, i;
```

Show the code that a compiler would generate to store the value in variable g as the grade in the $i^{th}$ element of grades, assuming the following:
   **a.** The array grades is stored as an array of structures.
   **b.** The array grades is stored as a structure of arrays.

**Section 7.8**

16. As a programmer, you are interested in the efficiency of the code that you produce. You recently implemented, by hand, a scanner. The scanner spends most of its time in a single while loop that contains a large case statement.
   **a.** How would the different case statement implementation techniques affect the efficiency of your scanner?
   **b.** How would you change your source code to improve the runtime performance under each of the case statement implementation strategies?

17. Convert the following C tail-recursive function to a loop:

```
List * last(List *l) {
    if (l == NULL)
        return NULL;
    else if (l->next == NULL)
        return l;
    else
        return last(l->next); }
```

**Section 7.9**

18. Assume that $x$ is an unambiguous, local, integer variable and that $x$ is passed as a call-by-reference actual parameter in the procedure where it is declared. Because it is local and unambiguous, the compiler might try to keep it in a register throughout its lifetime. Because it is

passed as a call-by-reference parameter, it must have a memory address at the point of the call.

**a.** Where should the compiler store $x$?

**b.** How should the compiler handle $x$ at the call site?

**c.** How would your answers change if $x$ was passed as a call-by-value parameter?

19. The linkage convention is a contract between the compiler and any outside callers of the compiled code. It creates a known interface that can be used to invoke a procedure and obtain any results that it returns (while protecting the caller's runtime environment). Thus, the compiler should only violate the linkage convention when such a violation cannot be detected from outside the compiled code.

**a.** Under what circumstances can the compiler be certain that using a variant linkage is safe? Give examples from real programming languages.

**b.** In these circumstances, what might the compiler change about the calling sequence and the linkage convention?

# Introduction to Optimization

**CHAPTER OVERVIEW**

To improve the quality of the code that it generates, an optimizing compiler analyzes the code and rewrites it into a more efficient form. This chapter introduces the problems and techniques of code optimization and presents key concepts through a series of example optimizations. Chapter 9 expands on this material with a deeper exploration of program analysis. Chapter 10 provides a broader coverage of optimizing transformations.

**Keywords:** Optimization, Safety, Profitability, Scope of Optimization, Analysis, Transformation

## 8.1 INTRODUCTION

The compiler's front end translates the source-code program into some intermediate representation (IR). The back end translates the IR program into a form where it can execute directly on the target machine, either a hardware platform such as a commodity microprocessor or a virtual machine as in Java. Between these processes sits the compiler's middle section, its optimizer. The task of the optimizer is to transform the IR program produced by the front end in a way that will improve the quality of the code produced by the back end. "Improvement" can take on many meanings. Often, it implies faster execution for the compiled code. It can also mean an executable that uses less energy when it runs or that occupies less space in memory. All of these goals fall into the realm of optimization.

This chapter introduces the subject of code optimization and provides examples of several different techniques that attack different kinds of inefficiencies and operate on different regions in the code. Chapter 9 provides a deeper treatment of some of the techniques of program analysis that are used to support optimization. Chapter 10 describes additional code-improvement transformations.

### Conceptual Roadmap

The goal of code optimization is to discover, at compile time, information about the runtime behavior of the program and to use that information to improve the code generated by the compiler. Improvement can take many forms. The most common goal of optimization is to make the compiled code run faster. For some applications, however, the size of the compiled code outweighs its execution speed; consider, for example, an application that will be committed to read-only memory, where code size affects the cost of the system. Other objectives for optimization include reducing the energy cost of execution, improving the code's response to real-time events, or reducing total memory traffic.

Optimizers use many different techniques to improve code. A proper discussion of optimization must consider the inefficiencies that can be improved and the techniques proposed for doing so. For each source of inefficiency, the compiler writer must choose from multiple techniques that claim to improve efficiency. The remainder of this section illustrates some of the problems that arise in optimization by looking at two examples that involve inefficiencies in array-address calculations.

**Safety**

A transformation is *safe* when it does not change the results of running the program.

**Profit**

A transformation is *profitable* to apply at some point when the result is an actual improvement.

Before implementing a transformation, the compiler writer must understand when it can be *safely* applied and when to expect *profit* from its application. Section 8.2 explores safety and profitability. Section 8.3 lays out the different granularities, or scopes, over which optimization occurs. The remainder of the chapter uses select examples to illustrate different sources of improvement and different scopes of optimization. This chapter has no "Advanced Topics" section; Chapters 9 and 10 serve that purpose.

### Overview

Opportunities for optimization arise from many sources. A major source of inefficiency arises from the implementation of source-language abstractions. Because the translation from source code into IR is a local process—it occurs without extensive analysis of the surrounding context—it typically generates IR to handle the most general case of each construct. With contextual knowledge, the optimizer can often determine that the code does not need that full generality; when that happens, the optimizer can rewrite the code in a more restricted and more efficient way.

A second significant source of opportunity for the optimizer lies with the target machine. The compiler must understand, in detail, the properties of the target that affect performance. Issues such as the number of functional units and their capabilities, the latency and bandwidth to various levels of the memory hierarchy, the various addressing modes supported in the instruction set, and the availability of unusual or complex operations all affect the kind of code that the compiler should generate for a given application.

Historically, most optimizing compilers have focused on improving the runtime speed of the compiled code. Improvement can, however, take other forms. In some applications, the size of the compiled code is as important as its speed. Examples include code that will be committed to read-only memory, where size is an economic constraint, or code that will be transmitted over a limited-bandwidth communications channel before it executes, where size has a direct impact on time to completion. Optimization for these applications should produce code that occupies less space. In other cases, the user may want to optimize for criteria such as register use, memory use, energy consumption, or response to real-time events.

Optimization is a large and detailed subject whose study could fill one or more complete courses (and books). This chapter introduces the subject and some of the critical ideas from optimization that play a role in Chapters 11, 12, and 13. The next two chapters delve more deeply into the analysis and transformation of programs. Chapter 9 presents an overview of static analysis. It describes some of the analysis problems that an optimizing compiler must solve and presents practical techniques that have been used to solve them. Chapter 10 examines so-called scalar optimizations—those intended for a uniprocessor—in a more systematic way.

## 8.2 BACKGROUND

Until the early 1980s, many compiler writers considered optimization as a feature that should be added to the compiler only after its other parts were working well. This led to a distinction between *debugging compilers* and *optimizing compilers*. A debugging compiler emphasized quick compilation at the expense of code quality. These compilers did not significantly rearrange the code, so a strong correspondence remained between the source code and the executable code. This simplified the task of mapping a runtime error to a specific line of source code; hence the term *debugging* compiler. In contrast, an optimizing compiler focuses on improving the running time of the executable code at the expense of compile time. Spending more time in compilation often produces better code. Because the optimizer often moves operations around, the mapping from source code to executable code is less transparent, and debugging is, accordingly, harder.

As RISC processors have moved into the marketplace (and as RISC implementation techniques were applied to CISC architectures), more of the burden for runtime performance has fallen on compilers. To increase performance, processor architects have turned to features that require more support from the compiler. These include delay slots following branches, nonblocking memory operations, increased use of pipelines, and increased numbers of functional units. These features make processors more performance sensitive to both high-level issues of program layout and structure and to low-level details of scheduling and resource allocation. As the gap between processor speed and application performance has grown, the demand for optimization has grown to the point where users expect every compiler to perform optimization.

The routine inclusion of an optimizer, in turn, changes the environment in which both the front end and the back end operate. Optimization further insulates the front end from performance concerns. To an extent, this simplifies the task of IR generation in the front end. At the same time, optimization changes the code that the back end processes. Modern optimizers assume that the back end will handle resource allocation; thus, they typically target an idealized machine that has an unlimited supply of registers, memory, and functional units. This, in turn, places more pressure on the techniques used in the compiler's back end.

If compilers are to shoulder their share of responsibility for runtime performance, they must include optimizers. As we shall see, the tools of optimization also play a large role in the compiler's back end. For these reasons, it is important to introduce optimization and explore some of the issues that it raises before discussing the techniques used in a compiler's back end.

### 8.2.1 Examples

To provide a focus for this discussion, we will begin by examining two examples in depth. The first, a simple two-dimensional array-address calculation, shows the role that knowledge and context play in the kind of code that the compiler can produce. The second, a loop nest from the routine dmxpy in the widely-used LINPACK numerical library, provides insight into the transformation process itself and into the challenges that transformed code can present to the compiler.

#### *Improving an Array-Address Calculation*

Consider the IR that a compiler's front end might generate for an array reference, such as m(i,j) in FORTRAN. Without specific knowledge about m, i, and j, or the surrounding context, the compiler must generate the full expression for addressing a two-dimensional array stored in column-major order. In Chapter 7, we saw the calculation for row-major order; FORTRAN's column-major order is similar:

$$@m + (j - low_2(m)) \times (high_1(m) - low_1(m) + 1) \times w + (i - low_1(m)) \times w$$

where @m is the runtime address of the first element of m, $low_i(m)$ and $high_i(m)$ are the lower and upper bounds, respectively, of m's $i^{th}$ dimension, and $w$ is the size of an element of m. The compiler's ability to reduce the cost of that computation depends directly on its analysis of the code and the surrounding context.

If m is a local array with lower bounds of one in each dimension and known upper bounds, then the compiler can simplify the calculation to

$$@m + (j - 1) \times hw + (i - 1) \times w$$

where $hw$ is $high_1(m) \times w$. If the reference occurs inside a loop where j runs from 1 to $k$, the compiler might use *operator strength reduction* to replace the term $(j - 1) \times hw$ with a sequence $j'_1, j'_2, j'_3, \ldots j'_k$, where $j'_1 = (1 - 1) \times hw = 0$ and $j'_i = j'_{i-1} + hw$. If i is also the induction variable of a loop running from 1 to $l$, then strength reduction can replace $(i - 1) \times w$ with the sequence $i'_1, i'_2, i'_3, \ldots i'_l$, where $i'_1 = 0$ and $i'_j = i'_{j-1} + w$. After these changes, the address calculation is just

$$@m + j' + i'$$

**Strength reduction**
a transformation that rewrites a series of operations, for example

$$i \cdot c, (i+1) \cdot c, \ldots, (i+k) \cdot c$$

with an equivalent series

$$i'_1, i'_2, \ldots, i'_{k'}$$

where $i'_1 = i \cdot c$ and $i'_j = i'_{j-1} + c$

See Section 10.7.2.

The j loop must increment $j'$ by $hw$ and the i loop must increment $i'$ by $w$. If the j loop is the outer loop, then the computation of @m + $j'$ can be moved out of the inner loop. At this point, the address computation in the inner loop contains an add and the increment for $i'$, while the outer loop contains an add and the increment for $j'$. Knowing the context around the reference to m(i,j) allows the compiler to significantly reduce the cost of array addressing.

If m is an actual parameter to the procedure, then the compiler may not know these facts at compile time. In fact, the upper and lower bounds for m might change on each call to the procedure. In such cases, the compiler may be unable to simplify the address calculation as shown.

## *Improving a Loop Nest in LINPACK*

As a more dramatic example of context, consider the loop nest shown in Figure 8.1. It is the central loop nest of the FORTRAN version of the routine dmxpy from the LINPACK numerical library. The code wraps two loops around a single long assignment. The loop nest forms the core of a

```
          subroutine dmxpy (n1, y, n2, ldm, x, m)
          double precision y(*), x(*), m(ldm,*)

            . . .
          jmin = j+16
          do 60 j = jmin, n2, 16
             do 50 i = 1, n1
                y(i) = (((((((((((((( (y(i))
     $            + x(j-15)*m(i,j-15)) + x(j-14)*m(i,j-14))
     $            + x(j-13)*m(i,j-13)) + x(j-12)*m(i,j-12))
     $            + x(j-11)*m(i,j-11)) + x(j-10)*m(i,j-10))
     $            + x(j- 9)*m(i,j- 9)) + x(j- 8)*m(i,j- 8))
     $            + x(j- 7)*m(i,j- 7)) + x(j- 6)*m(i,j- 6))
     $            + x(j- 5)*m(i,j- 5)) + x(j- 4)*m(i,j- 4))
     $            + x(j- 3)*m(i,j- 3)) + x(j- 2)*m(i,j- 2))
     $            + x(j- 1)*m(i,j- 1)) + x(j) *m(i,j)
  50         continue
  60      continue

            . . .
          end
```

■ **FIGURE 8.1** Excerpt from dmxpy in LINPACK.

routine to compute $y + x \times m$, for vectors $x$ and $y$ and matrix $m$. We will consider the code from two different perspectives: first, the transformations that the author hand-applied to improve performance, and second, the challenges that the compiler faces in translating this loop nest to run efficiently on a specific processor.

Before the author hand-transformed the code, the loop nest performed the following simpler version of the same computation:

```
       do 60 j = 1, n2
          do 50 i = 1, n1
             y(i) = y(i) + x(j) * m(i,j)
  50      continue
  60 continue
```

**Loop unrolling**

This replicates the loop body for distinct iterations and adjusts the index calculations to match.

To improve performance, the author *unrolled* the outer loop, the j loop, 16 times. That rewrite created 16 copies of the assignment statement with distinct values for j, ranging from j through j-15. It also changed the increment on the outer loop from 1 to 16. Next, the author merged the 16 assignments into a single statement, eliminating 15 occurrences of y(i) = y(i) + ⋯; that eliminates 15 additions and most of the loads and stores of y(i). Unrolling the loop eliminates some scalar operations. It often improves cache locality, as well.

To handle the cases where the the array bounds are not integral multiples of 16, the full procedure has four versions of the loop nest that precede the one shown in Figure 8.1. These "setup loops" process up to 15 columns of m, leaving j set to a value for which n2 - j is an integral multiple of 16. The first loop handles a single column of m, corresponding to an odd n2. The other three loop nests handle two, four and eight columns of m. This guarantees that the final loop nest, shown in Figure 8.1, can process the columns 16 at a time.

Ideally, the compiler would automatically transform the original loop nest into this more efficient version, or into whatever form is most appropriate for a given target machine. However, few compilers include all of the optimizations needed to accomplish that goal. In the case of dmxpy, the author performed the optimizations by hand to produce good performance across a wide range of target machines and compilers.

From the compiler's perspective, mapping the loop nest shown in Figure 8.1 onto the target machine presents some hard challenges. The loop nest contains 33 distinct array-address expressions, 16 for m, 16 for x, and one for y that it uses twice. Unless the compiler can simplify those address calculations, the loop will be awash in integer arithmetic.

Consider the references to x. They do not change during execution of the inner loop, which varies i. The optimizer can move the address calculations and the loads for x out of the inner loop. If it can keep the x values in registers, it can eliminate a large part of the overhead from the inner loop. For a reference such as x(j-12), the address calculation is just $@x + (j - 12) \times w$. To further simplify matters, the compiler can refactor all 16 references to x into the form $@x + jw - c_k$, where $jw$ is $j \cdot w$ and $c_k$ is $k \cdot w$ for each $0 \leq k \leq 15$. In this form, each load uses the same base address, $@x + jw$, with a different constant offset, $c_k$.

To map this efficiently onto the target machine requires knowledge of the available addressing modes. If the target has the equivalent of ILOC's loadAI operation (a register base address plus a small constant offset), then all the accesses to x can be written to use a single induction variable. Its initial value is $@x + jmin \cdot w$. Each iteration of the j loop increments it by $w$.

The 16 values of m used in the inner loop change on each iteration. Thus, the inner loop must compute addresses and load 16 elements of m on each iteration. Careful refactoring of the address expressions, combined with strength reduction, can reduce the overhead of accessing m. The value

@m + j · $high_1$(m) · $w$ can be computed in the j loop. (Notice that $high_1$(m) is the only concrete dimension declared in dmxpy's header.) The inner loop can produce a base address by adding it to $(i − 1) · w$. Then, the 16 loads can use distinct constants, $c_k · high_1$(m), where $c_k$ is $k · w$ for each $0 \leq k \leq 15$.

To achieve this code shape, the compiler must refactor the address expressions, perform strength reduction, recognize loop-invariant calculations and move them out of inner loops, and choose the appropriate addressing mode for the loads. Even with these improvements, the inner loop must perform 16 loads, 16 floating-point multiplies, and 16 floating-point adds, plus one store. The resulting block will present a challenge to the instruction scheduler.

If the compiler fails in some part of this transformation sequence, the resulting code might be substantially worse than the original. For example, if it cannot refactor the address expressions around a common base address for x and one for m, the code might maintain 33 distinct induction variables—one for each distinct address expression for x, m, and y. If the resulting demand for registers forces the register allocator to spill, it will insert additional loads and stores into the loop (which is already likely to be memory bound). In cases such as this one, the quality of code produced by the compiler depends on an orchestrated series of transformations that all must work; when one fails to achieve its purpose, the overall sequence may produce lower quality code than the user expects.

## 8.2.2 Considerations for Optimization

In the previous example, the programmer applied the transformations in the belief that they would make the program run faster. The programmer had to believe that they would preserve the meaning of the program. (After all, if transformations need not preserve meaning, why not replace the entire procedure with a single nop?)

Two issues, safety and profitability, lie at the heart of every optimization. The compiler must have a mechanism to prove that each application of the transformation is safe—that is, it preserves the program's meaning. The compiler must have a reason to believe that applying the transformation is profitable—that is, it improves the program's performance. If either of these is not true—that is, applying the transformation will change the program's meaning or will make its performance worse—the compiler should not apply the transformation.

### Safety

How did the programmer know that this transformation was safe? That is, why did the programmer believe that the transformed code would produce the same results as the original code? Close examination of the loop nest

**DEFINING SAFETY**

Correctness is the single most important criterion that a compiler must meet—the code that the compiler produces must have the same meaning as the input program. Each time the optimizer applies a transformation, that action must preserve the correctness of the translation.

Typically, *meaning* is defined as the observable behavior of the program. For a batch program, this is the memory state after it halts, along with any output it generates. If the program terminates, the values of all visible variables immediately before it halts should be the same under any translation scheme. For an interactive program, behavior is more complex and difficult to capture.

Plotkin formalized this notion as *observational equivalence.*

*For two expressions, M and N, we say that M and N are observationally equivalent if and only if, in any context C where both M and N are closed (that is, have no free variables), evaluating C[M] and C[N] either produces identical results or neither terminates [286].*

Thus, two expressions are observationally equivalent if their impacts on the visible, external environment are identical.

In practice, compilers use a simpler and looser notion of equivalence than Plotkin's, namely, that if, in their actual program context, two different expressions $e$ and $e'$ produce identical results, then the compiler can substitute $e'$ for $e$. This standard deals only with contexts that actually arise in the program; tailoring code to context is the essence of optimization. It does not mention what happens when a computation goes awry, or diverges.

In practice, compilers take care not to introduce divergence—the original code would work correctly, but the optimized code tries to divide by zero, or loops indefinitely. The opposite case, where the original code would diverge, but the optimized code does not, is rarely mentioned.

---

shows that the only interaction between successive iterations occurs through the elements of $y$.

- A value computed as $y(i)$ is not reused until the next iteration of the outer loop. The iterations of the inner loop are independent of each other, because each iteration defines precisely one value and no other iteration references that value. Thus, the iterations can execute in any order. (For example, if we run the inner loop from $n1$ to $1$ it produces the same results.)
- The interaction through $y$ is limited in its effect. The $i^{th}$ element of $y$ accumulates the sum of all the $i^{th}$ iterations of the inner loop. This pattern of accumulation is safely reproduced in the unrolled loop.

A large part of the analysis done in optimization goes toward proving the safety of transformations.

### Profitability

Why did the programmer think that loop unrolling would improve performance? That is, why is the transformation profitable? Several different effects of unrolling might speed up the code.

■ The total number of loop iterations is reduced by a factor of 16. This reduces the overhead operations due to loop control: adds, compares, jumps, and branches. If the loop executes frequently, these savings become significant.

This effect might suggest unrolling by an even larger factor. Finite resource limits probably dictated the choice of 16. For example, the inner loop uses the same 16 values of x for all the iterations of the inner loop. Many processors have only 32 registers that can hold a floating-point number. Unrolling by 32, the next power of two, would create enough of these "loop-invariant" values that they could not fit in the register set. Spilling them to memory would add loads and stores to the inner loop and undo the benefits of unrolling.

■ The array-address computations contain duplicated work. Consider the use of y(i). The original code computed y(i)'s address once per multiplication of x and m; the transformed code computes it once per 16 multiplications. The unrolled code does $\frac{1}{16}$ as much work to address y(i). The 16 references to m, and to a lesser extent x, should include common portions that the loop can compute once and reuse, as well.

■ The transformed loop performs more work per memory operation, where "work" excludes the overhead of implementing the array and loop abstractions. The original loop performed two arithmetic operations for three memory operations, while the unrolled loop performs 32 arithmetic operations for 18 memory operations, assuming that all the x values stay in registers. Thus, the unrolled loop is less likely to be *memory bound*. It has enough independent arithmetic to overlap the loads and hide some of their latencies.

**Memory bound**

A loop where loads and stores take more cycles than does computation is considered *memory bound*.

To determine if a loop is memory bound requires detailed knowledge about both the loop and the target machine.

Unrolling can help with other machine-dependent effects. It increases the amount of code in the inner loop, which may provide the instruction scheduler with more opportunities to hide latencies. If the end-of-loop branch has a long latency, the longer loop body may let the compiler fill more of that branch's delay slots. On some processors, unused delay slots must be filled with nops, in which case loop unrolling can decrease the number of nops fetched, reduce memory traffic and, perhaps, reduce the energy used to execute the program.

### Risk

If transformations intended to improve performance make it harder for the compiler to generate good code for the program, those potential problems should be considered as profitability issues. The hand transformations performed on dmxpy create new challenges for a compiler, including the following:

- *Demand for registers* The original loop needs only a handful of registers to hold its active values. Only x(j), some part of the address calculations for x, y, and m, and the loop index variables need registers across loop iterations, while y(i) and m(i,j) need registers briefly. In contrast, the transformed loop has 16 elements of x to keep in registers across the loop, along with the 16 values of m and y(i) that need registers briefly.
- *Form of address calculation* The original loop deals with three addresses, one each for y, x, and m. Because the transformed loop references many more distinct locations in each iteration, the compiler must shape the address calculations carefully to avoid repeated calculations and excessive demand for registers. In the worst case, the code might use independent calculations for all 16 elements of x, all 16 elements of m, and the one element of y.

  If the compiler shapes the address calculations appropriately, it can use a single pointer for m and another for x, each with 16 constant-valued offsets. It can rewrite the loop to use that pointer in the end-of-loop test, obviating the need for another register and eliminating another update. Planning and optimization make the difference.

Other problems of a machine-specific nature arise as well. For example, the 17 loads and one store, the 16 multiplies, the 16 adds, plus the address calculations and loop-overhead operations in each iteration must be scheduled with care. The compiler may need to issue some of the load operations in a previous iteration so that it can schedule the initial floating-point operations in a timely fashion.

## 8.2.3 **Opportunities for Optimization**

As we have seen, the task of optimizing a simple loop can involve complex considerations. In general, optimizing compilers capitalize on opportunities that arise from several distinct sources.

1. *Reducing the overhead of abstraction* As we saw for the array-address calculation at the beginning of the chapter, the data structures and types introduced by programming languages require runtime support. Optimizers use analysis and transformation to reduce this overhead.

2. *Taking advantage of special cases* Often, the compiler can use knowledge about the context in which an operation executes to specialize that operation. As an example, a C++ compiler can sometimes determine that a call to a virtual function always uses the same implementation. In that case, it can remap the call and reduce the cost of each invocation.

3. *Matching the code to system resources* If the resource requirements of a program differ from the processor's capacities, the compiler may transform the program to align its needs more closely with available resources. The transformations applied to dmxpy have this effect; they decrease the number of memory accesses per floating-point operation.

These are broad areas, described in sweeping generality. As we discuss specific analysis and transformation techniques, in Chapters 9 and 10, we will fill in these areas with more detailed examples.

---

**SECTION REVIEW**

Most compiler-based optimization works by specializing general purpose code to its specific context. For some code transformations, the benefits accrue from local effects, as with the improvements in the array-address calculations. Other transformations require broad knowledge of larger regions in the code and accrue their benefits from effects that occur over larger swaths of the code.

In considering any optimization, the compiler writer must worry about the following:

1. Safety, for example, does the transformation not change the meaning of the code?
2. Profitability, for example, how will the transformation improve the code?
3. Finding opportunities, for example, how can the compiler quickly locate places in the code where applying the given transformation is both safe and profitable?

---

**Review Questions**

1. In the code fragment from dmxpy in LINPACK, why did the programmer choose to unroll the outer loop rather than the inner loop? How would you expect the results to differ had she unrolled the inner loop?
2. In the c fragment shown below, what facts would the compiler need to discover before it could improve the code beyond a simple byte-oriented, load/store implementation?

```
MemCopy(char *source, char *dest, int length) {
    int i;
    for (i=1; i≤length; i++)
        { *dest++ = *source++; }
}
```

■

## 8.3 SCOPE OF OPTIMIZATION

Optimizations operate at different granularities or scopes. In the previous section, we looked at optimization of a single array reference and of an entire loop nest. The different scopes of these optimizations presented different opportunities to the optimizer. Reformulating the array reference improved performance for the execution of that array reference. Rewriting the loop improved performance across a larger region. In general, transformations and the analyses that support them operate on one of four distinct scopes: local, regional, global, or whole program.

**Scope of optimization**
The region of code where an optimization operates is its *scope of optimization*.

### Local Methods

Local methods operate over a single basic block: a maximal-length sequence of branch-free code. In an ILOC program, a basic block begins with a labelled operation and ends with a branch or a jump. In ILOC, the operation after a branch or jump must be labelled or else it cannot be reached; other notations allow a "fall-through" branch so that the operation after a branch or jump need not be labelled. The behavior of straight-line code is easier to analyze and understand than is code that contains branches and cycles.

Inside a basic block, two important properties hold. First, statements are executed sequentially. Second, if any statement executes, the entire block executes, unless a runtime exception occurs. These two properties let the compiler prove, with relatively simple analyses, facts that may be stronger than those provable for larger scopes. Thus, local methods sometimes make improvements that simply cannot be obtained for larger scopes. At the same time, local methods are limited to improvements that involve operations that all occur in the same block.

### Regional Methods

Regional methods operate over scopes larger than a single block but smaller than a full procedure. In the example control-flow graph (CFG) in the margin, the compiler might consider the entire loop, $\{B_0, B_1, B_2, B_3, B_4, B_5, B_6\}$, as a single region. In some cases, considering a subset of the code for the full procedure produces sharper analysis and better transformation results

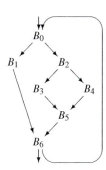

than would occur with information from the full procedure. For example, inside a loop nest, the compiler may be able to prove that a heavily used pointer is invariant (single-valued), even though it is modified elsewhere in the procedure. Such knowledge can enable optimizations such as keeping in a register the value referenced through that pointer.

The compiler can choose regions in many different ways. A region might be defined by some source-code control structure, such as a loop nest. The compiler might look at the subset of blocks in the region that form an *extended basic block* (EBB). The example CFG contains three EBBS: $\{B_0, B_1, B_2, B_3, B_4\}$, $\{B_5\}$, and $\{B_6\}$. While the two single-block EBBS provide no advantage over a purely local view, the large EBB may offer opportunities for optimization (see Section 8.5.1). Finally, the compiler might consider a subset of the CFG defined by some graph-theoretic property, such as a *dominator relation* or one of the strongly connected components in the CFG.

**Extended basic block**

a set of blocks $\beta_1, \beta_2, \ldots, \beta_n$ where $\beta_1$ has multiple CFG predecessors and each other $\beta_i$ has just one, which is some $\beta_j$ in the set

**Dominator**

In a CFG, $x$ *dominates* $y$ if and only if every path from the root to $y$ includes $x$.

Regional methods have several strengths. Limiting the scope of a transformation to a region smaller than the entire procedure allows the compiler to focus its efforts on heavily executed regions—for example, the body of a loop typically executes much more frequently than the surrounding code. The compiler can apply different optimization strategies to distinct regions. Finally, the focus on a limited area in the code often allows the compiler to derive sharper information about program behavior which, in turn, exposes opportunities for improvement.

### Global Methods

These methods, also called *intraprocedural methods*, use an entire procedure as context. The motivation for global methods is simple: decisions that are locally optimal may have bad consequences in some larger context. The procedure provides the compiler with a natural boundary for both analysis and transformation. Procedures are abstractions that encapsulate and insulate runtime environments. At the same time, they serve as units of separate compilation in many systems.

Global methods typically operate by building a representation of the procedure, such as a CFG, analyzing that representation, and transforming the underlying code. If the CFG can have cycles, the compiler must analyze the entire procedure before it understands what facts hold on entrance to any specific block. Thus, most global transformations have separate analysis and transformation phases. The analytical phase gathers facts and reasons about them. The transformation phase uses those facts to determine the safety and profitability of a specific transformation. By virtue of their global view,

**INTRAPROCEDURAL VERSUS INTERPROCEDURAL**

Few terms in compilation create as much confusion as the word *global*. Global analysis and optimization operate on an entire procedure. The modern English connotation, however, suggests an all-encompassing scope, as does the use of global in discussions of lexical scoping rules. In analysis and optimization, however, global means pertaining to a single procedure.

Interest in analysis and optimization across procedure boundaries necessitated terminology to differentiate between *global* analysis and analysis over larger scopes. The term *interprocedural* was introduced to describe analysis that ranged from two procedures to a whole program. Accordingly, authors began to use the term *intraprocedural* for single-procedure techniques. Since these words are so close in spelling and pronunciation, they are easy to confuse and awkward to use.

Perkin-Elmer Corporation tried to remedy this confusion when it introduced its "universal" FORTRAN VIIZ optimizing compiler for the PE 3200; the system performed extensive inlining followed by aggressive global optimization on the resulting code. Universal did not stick. We prefer the term *whole program* and use it whenever possible. It conveys the right distinction and reminds the reader and listener that "global" is not "universal."

these methods can discover opportunities that neither local nor regional methods can.

## Interprocedural Methods

These methods, sometimes called *whole-program methods*, consider scopes larger than a single procedure. We consider any transformation that involves more than one procedure to be an interprocedural transformation. Just as moving from a local scope to a global scope exposes new opportunities, so moving from single procedures to the multiple procedures can expose new opportunities. It also raises new challenges. For example, parameter-binding rules introduce significant complications into the analysis that supports optimization.

Interprocedural analysis and optimization occurs, at least conceptually, on the program's call graph. In some cases, these techniques analyze the entire program; in other cases the compiler may examine just a subset of the source code. Two classic examples of interprocedural optimizations are inline substitution, which replaces a procedure call with a copy of the body of the callee, and interprocedural constant propagation, which propagates and folds information about constants throughout the entireprogram.

---

**SECTION REVIEW**

Compilers perform both analysis and transformation over a variety of scopes, ranging from single basic blocks (local methods) to entire programs (whole-program methods). In general, the number of opportunities for improvement grows with the scope of optimization. However, analyzing larger scopes often results in less precise knowledge about the code's behavior. Thus, no simple relationship exits between scope of optimization and quality of the resulting code. It would be intellectually pleasing if a larger scope of optimization led, in general, to better code quality. Unfortunately, that relationship does not necessarily hold true.

---

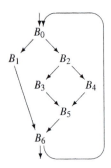

**Review Questions**

1. Basic blocks have the property that if one instruction executes, every instruction in the block executes, in a specified order (unless an exception occurs). State the weaker property that holds for a block in an extended basic block, other than the entry block, such as block $B_2$ in the EBB $\{B_0, B_1, B_2, B_3, B_4\}$, for the control-flow graph shown in the margin.

2. What kinds of improvement might the compiler find with whole-program compilation? Name several inefficiencies that can only be addressed by examining code across procedure boundaries. How does interprocedural optimization interact with the desire to compile procedures separately?

## 8.4 LOCAL OPTIMIZATION

Optimizations that operate over a local scope—a single basic block—are among the simplest techniques that the compiler can use. The simple execution model of a basic block leads to reasonably precise analysis in support of optimization. Thus, these methods are surprisingly effective.

**Redundant**

An expression $e$ is *redundant* at $p$ if it has already been evaluated on every path that leads to $p$.

This section presents two local methods as examples. The first, *value numbering*, finds redundant expressions in a basic block and replaces the redundant evaluations with reuse of a previously computed value. The second, *tree-height balancing*, reorganizes expression trees to expose more instruction-level parallelism.

### 8.4.1 Local Value Numbering

Consider the four-statement basic block shown in the margin. We will refer to the block as $B$. An expression, such as b + c or a - d, is redundant in $B$ if and only if it has been previously computed in $B$ and no intervening

operation redefines one of its constituent arguments. In *B*, the occurrence of
b + c in the third operation is not redundant because the second operation
redefines b. The occurrence of a - d in the fourth operation is redundant
because *B* does not redefine a or d between the second and fourth operations.

The compiler can rewrite this block so that it computes a - d once, as shown
in the margin. The second evaluation of a - d is replaced with a copy from b.
An alternative strategy would replace subsequent uses of d with uses of b.
However, that approach requires analysis to determine whether or not b is
redefined before some use of d. In practice, it is simpler to have the optimizer
insert a copy and let a subsequent pass determine which copy operations
are, in fact, necessary and which ones can have their source and destination
names combined.

In general, replacing redundant evaluations with references to previously
computed values is profitable—that is, the resulting code runs more quickly
than the original. However, profitability is not guaranteed. Replacing
d ← a - d with d ← b has the potential to extend the lifetime of b and to
shorten the lifetimes of either a or d or both—depending, in each case, on
where the last use of the value lies. Depending on the precise details, each
rewrite can increase demand for registers, decrease demand for registers, or
leave it unchanged. Replacing a redundant computation with a reference is
likely to be unprofitable if the rewrite causes the register allocator to spill a
value in the block.

In practice, the optimizer cannot consistently predict the behavior of the register allocator, in part because the code will be further transformed before it
reaches the allocator. Therefore, most algorithms for removing redundancy
assume that rewriting to avoid redundancy is profitable.

In the previous example, the redundant expression was textually identical to
the earlier instance. Assignment can, of course, produce a redundant expression that differs textually from its predecessor. Consider the block shown in
the margin. The assignment of b to d makes the expression d × c produce
the same value as b × c. To recognize this case, the compiler must track the
flow of values through names. Techniques that rely on textual identity do
not detect such cases.

Programmers will protest that they do not write code that contains redundant
expressions like those in the example. In practice, redundancy elimination finds many opportunities. Translation from source code to IR elaborates many details, such as address calculations, and introduces redundant
expressions.

Many techniques that find and eliminate redundancies have been developed. *Local value numbering* is one of the oldest and most powerful of

```
a  ←  b  +  c
b  ←  a  -  d
c  ←  b  +  c
d  ←  a  +  d
```
*Original Block*

```
a  ←  b  +  c
b  ←  a  -  d
c  ←  b  +  c
d  ←  b
```
*Rewritten Block*

**Lifetime**
The lifetime of a name is the region of code
between its definitions and its uses. Here,
definition means assignment.

```
a  ←  b  ×  c
d  ←  b
e  ←  d  ×  c
```
*Effect of Assignment*

these transformations. It discovers such redundancies within a basic block and rewrites the block to avoid them. It provides a simple and efficient framework for other local optimizations, such as constant folding and simplification using algebraic identities.

### The Algorithm

The idea behind value numbering is simple. The algorithm traverses a basic block and assigns a distinct number to each value that the block computes. It chooses the numbers so that two expressions, $e_i$ and $e_j$, have the same value number if and only $e_i$ and $e_j$ have provably equal values for all possible operands of the expressions.

Figure 8.2 shows the basic local value numbering algorithm (LVN). LVN takes as input a block with $n$ binary operations, each of the form $T_i \leftarrow L_i\ Op_i\ R_i$. LVN examines each operation, in order. LVN uses a hash table to map names, constants, and expressions into distinct value numbers. The hash table is initially empty.

To process the $i^{th}$ operation, LVN obtains value numbers for $L_i$ and $R_i$ by looking for them in the hash table. If it finds an entry, LVN uses the value number of that entry. If not, it creates one and assigns a new value number.

Given value numbers for $L_i$ and $R_i$, called $VN(L_i)$ and $VN(R_i)$, LVN constructs a hash key from $\langle VN(L_i), Op_i, VN(R_i)\rangle$ and looks up that key in the table. If an entry exists, the expression is redundant and can be replaced by a reference to the previously computed value. If not, operation $i$ is the first computation of the expression in this block, so LVN creates an entry for its hash key and assigns that entry a new value number. It also assigns the hash key's value number, whether new or pre-existing, to the table entry for $T_i$. Because LVN uses value numbers to construct the expression's hash

```
for i ← 0 to n-1, where the block has n operations    "Tᵢ ← Lᵢ Opᵢ Rᵢ"

    1. get the value numbers for Lᵢ and Rᵢ

    2. construct a hash key from Opᵢ and the value numbers for Lᵢ and Rᵢ

    3. if the hash key is already present in the table then
            replace operation i with a copy of the value into Tᵢ and
            associate the value number with Tᵢ
       else
            insert a new value number into the table at the hash key location
            record that new value number for Tᵢ
```

■ **FIGURE 8.2** Value Numbering a Single Block.

**THE IMPORTANCE OF ORDER**

The specific order in which expressions are written has a direct impact on the ability of optimizations to analyze and transform them. Consider the following distinct encodings of $v \leftarrow a \times b \times c$:

$$t_0 \leftarrow a \times b \qquad\qquad t_0 \leftarrow b \times c$$
$$v \;\leftarrow t_0 \times c \qquad\qquad v \;\leftarrow a \times t_0$$

The encoding on the left assigns value numbers to $a \times b$, to $(a \times b) \times c$ and to $v$, while the encoding on the right assigns value numbers to $b \times c$, to $a \times (b \times c)$ and to $v$. Depending on the surrounding context, one or the other encoding may be preferable. For example, if $b \times c$ occurs later in the block but $a \times b$ does not, then the right-hand encoding produces redundancy while the left does not.

In general, using commutativity, associativity, and distributivity to reorder expressions can change the results of optimization. Similar effects can be seen with constant folding; if we replace a with 3 and c with 5, neither ordering produces the constant operation $3 \times 5$, which can be folded.

Because the number of ways to reorder expressions is prohibitively large, compilers use heuristic techniques to find good orderings for expressions. For example, the IBM FORTRAN H compiler generated array-address computations in an order that tended to improve other optimizations. Other compilers have sorted the operands of commutative and associative operations into an order that corresponds to the loop nesting level at which they are defined. Because so many solutions are possible, heuristic solutions for this problem often require experimentation and tuning to discover what is appropriate for a specific language, compiler, and coding style.

key, rather than names, it can effectively track the flow of values through copy and assignment operations, such as the small example labelled "Effect of Assignment" on the previous page. Extending LVN to expressions of arbitrary arity is straightforward.

To see how LVN works, consider our original example block, shown on page 421. The version in the margin shows the value numbers that LVN assigns as superscripts. In the first operation, with an empty value table, b and c get new value numbers, 0 and 1 respectively. LVN constructs the textual string "$0 + 1$" as a hash key for the expression $a + b$ and performs a lookup. It does not find an entry for that key, so the lookup fails. Accordingly, LVN creates a new entry for "$0 + 1$" and assigns it value number 2. LVN then creates an entry for a and assigns it the value number of the expression, namely 2. Repeating this process for each operation, in sequential order, produces the rest of the value numbers shown in the margin.

$$a^2 \leftarrow b^0 + c^1$$
$$b^4 \leftarrow a^2 - d^3$$
$$c^5 \leftarrow b^4 + c^1$$
$$d^4 \leftarrow a^2 - d^3$$

```
a ← b + c
b ← a - d
c ← b + c
d ← b
```

The value numbers reveal, correctly, that the two occurrences of b + c produce different values, due to the intervening redefinition of b. On the other hand, the two occurrences of a - d produce the same value, since they have the same input value numbers and the same operator. LVN discovers this and records it by assigning b and d the same value number, namely 4. That knowledge lets LVN rewrite the fourth operation with a d ← b as shown in the margin. Subsequent passes may eliminate the copy.

### Extending the Algorithm

LVN provides a natural framework to perform several other local optimizations.

- *Commutative operations* Commutative operations that differ only in the order of their operands, such as a × b and b × a, should receive the same value numbers. As LVN constructs a hash key for the right-hand side of the current operation, it can sort the operands using some convenient scheme, such as ordering them by value number. This simple action will ensure that commutative variants receive the same value number.

- *Constant folding* If all the operands of an operation have known constant values, LVN can perform the operation and fold the answer directly into the code. LVN can store information about constants in the hash table, including their value. Before hash-key formation, it can test the operands and, if possible, evaluate them. If LVN discovers a constant expression, it can replace the operation with an immediate load of the result. Subsequent copy folding will clean up the code.

- *Algebraic identities* LVN can apply algebraic identities to simplify the code. For example, x + 0 and x should receive the same value number. Unfortunately, LVN needs special-case code for each identity. A series of tests, one per identity, can easily become long enough to produce an unacceptable slowdown in the algorithm. To ameliorate this problem, LVN should organize the tests into operator-specific decision trees. Since each operator has just a few identities, this approach keeps the overhead low. Figure 8.3 shows some of the identities that can be handled in this way.

$$
\begin{array}{llll}
a + 0 = a & a - 0 = a & a - a = 0 & 2 \times a = a + a \\
a \times 1 = a & a \times 0 = 0 & a \div 1 = a & a \div a = 1, a \neq 0 \\
a^1 = a & a^2 = a \times a & a \gg 0 = a & a \ll 0 = a \\
a\ \text{AND}\ a = a & a\ \text{OR}\ a = a & \text{MAX}\ (a,a) = a & \text{MIN}\ (a,a) = a
\end{array}
$$

■ **FIGURE 8.3** Algebraic Identities for Value Numbering.

```
for i ← 0 to n-1, where the block has n operations    "Tᵢ ← Lᵢ Opᵢ Rᵢ"

  1.  get the value numbers for Lᵢ and Rᵢ

  2.  if Lᵢ and Rᵢ are both constant then evaluate Lᵢ Opᵢ Rᵢ,
          assign the result to Tᵢ, and mark Tᵢ as constant

  3.  if Lᵢ Opᵢ Rᵢ matches an identity in Figure 8.3, then replace it with
          a copy operation or an assignment

  4.  construct a hash key from Opᵢ and the value numbers for Lᵢ and Rᵢ,
          using the value numbers in ascending order, if Opᵢ commutes

  5.  if the hash key is already present in the table then
            replace operation i with a copy into Tᵢ and
            associate the value number with Tᵢ
      else
            insert a new value number into the table at the hash key location
            record that new value number for Tᵢ
```

■ **FIGURE 8.4** Local Value Numbering with Extensions.

A clever implementor will discover other identities, including some that are type specific. The exclusive-or of two identical values should yield a zero of the appropriate type. Numbers in IEEE floating-point format have their own special cases introduced by the explicit representations of $\infty$ and NaN; for example, $\infty - \infty = \text{NaN}$, $\infty - \text{NaN} = \text{NaN}$, and $\infty \div \text{NaN} = \text{NaN}$.

**NaN**
Not a Number, a defined constant that represents an invalid or meaningless result in the IEEE standard for floating-point arithmetic

Figure 8.4 shows LVN with these extensions. Steps 1 and 5 appeared in the original algorithm. Step 2 evaluates and folds constant-valued operations. Step 3 checks for algebraic identities using the decision trees mentioned earlier. Step 4 reorders the operands of commutative operations. Even with these extensions, the cost per IR operation remains extremely low. Each step has an efficient implementation.

### The Role of Naming

The choice of names for variables and values can limit the effectiveness of value numbering. Consider what happens when LVN is applied to the block shown in the margin. Again, the superscripts indicate the value numbers assigned to each name and value.

$$a^3 \leftarrow x^1 + y^2$$
$$b^3 \leftarrow x^1 + y^2$$
$$a^4 \leftarrow 17^4$$
$$c^3 \leftarrow x^1 + y^2$$

In the first operation, LVN assigns 1 to $x$, 2 to $y$ and 3 to both $x + y$ and to $a$. At the second operation, it discovers that $x + y$ is redundant, with value number 3. Accordingly, it rewrites $b \leftarrow x + y$ with $b \leftarrow a$. The third operation is both straightforward and nonredundant. At the fourth operation, it again discovers that $x + y$ is redundant, with value number 3. It cannot, however, rewrite the operation as $c \leftarrow a$ because $a$ no longer has value number 3.

We can cure this problem in two distinct ways. We can modify LVN so that it keeps a mapping from value numbers to names. At an assignment to some name, say $a$, it must remove $a$ from the list for its old value number and add $a$ to the list for its new value number. Then, at a replacement, it can use any name that currently contains that value number. This approach adds some cost to the processing of each assignment and clutters up the code for the basic algorithm.

$$a_0^3 \leftarrow x_0^1 + y_0^2$$

$$b_0^3 \leftarrow x_0^1 + y_0^2$$

$$a_1^4 \leftarrow 17^4$$

$$c_0^3 \leftarrow x_0^1 + y_0^2$$

As an alternative, the compiler can rewrite the code in a way that gives each assignment a distinct name. Adding a subscript to each name for uniqueness, as shown in the margin, is sufficient. With these new names, the code defines each value exactly once. Thus, no value is ever redefined and lost, or *killed*. If we apply LVN to this block, it produces the desired result. It proves that the second and fourth operations are redundant; each can be replaced with a copy from $a_0$.

However, the compiler must now reconcile these subscripted names with the names in surrounding blocks to preserve the meaning of the original code. In our example, the original name $a$ should refer to the value from the subscripted name $a_1$ in the rewritten code. A clever implementation would map the new $a_1$ to the original $a$, $b_0$ to the original $b$, $c_0$ to the original $c$, and rename $a_0$ to a new temporary name. That solution reconciles the name space of the transformed block with the surrounding context without introducing copies.

This naming scheme approximates one property of the name space created for static single-assignment form, or SSA, introduced in Section 5.4.2. Section 9.3 explores translation from linear code into SSA form and from SSA form back into linear code. The algorithms that it presents for name-space translation are more general than needed for a single block, but will certainly handle the single-block case and will attempt to minimize the number of copy operations that must be inserted.

### The Impact of Indirect Assignments

The previous discussion assumes that assignments are direct and obvious, as in $a \leftarrow b \times c$. Many programs contain indirect assignments, where the compiler may not know which values or locations are modified. Examples include assignment through a pointer, such as $*p = 0$; in C, or assignment to a structure element or an array element, such as $a(i,j) = 0$ in FORTRAN. Indirect assignments complicate value numbering and other optimizations

**RUNTIME EXCEPTIONS AND OPTIMIZATION**

Some abnormal runtime conditions can raise exceptions. Examples include out-of-bounds memory references, undefined arithmetic operations such as division by zero, and ill-formed operations. (One way for a debugger to trigger a breakpoint is to replace the instruction with an ill-formed one and to catch the exception.) Some languages include features for handling exceptions, for both predefined and programmer-defined situations.

Typically, a runtime exception causes a transfer of control to an exception handler. The handler may cure the problem, re-execute the offending operation, and return control to the block. Alternatively, it may transfer control elsewhere or terminate execution.

The optimizer must understand which operations can raise an exception and must consider the impact of an exception on program execution. Because an exception handler might modify the values of variables or transfer control, the compiler must treat exception-raising operations conservatively. For example, every exception-raising operation might force termination of the current basic block. Such treatment can severely limit the optimizer's ability to improve the code.

To optimize exception-laden code, the compiler needs to understand and model the effects of exception handlers. To do so, it needs access to the code for the exception handlers and it needs a model of overall execution to understand which handlers might be in place when a specific exception-raising operation executes.

because they create imprecisions in the compiler's understanding of the flow of values.

Consider value numbering with the subscripted naming scheme presented in the previous section. To manage the subscripts, the compiler maintains a map from the base variable name, say a, to its current subscript. On an assignment, such as $a \leftarrow b + c$, the compiler simply increments the current subscript for a. Entries in the value table for the previous subscript remain intact. On an indirect assignment, such as $*p \leftarrow 0$, the compiler may not know which base-name subscripts to increment. Without specific knowledge of the memory locations to which p can refer, the compiler must increment the subscript of every variable that the assignment could possibly modify—potentially, the set of all variables. Similarly, an assignment such as $a(i,j) = 0$, where the value of either i or j is unknown, must be treated as if it changes the value of every element of a.

> Hint: The hash table of value numbers must reflect subscripted names. The compiler can use a second, smaller table to map base names to subscripts.

While this sounds drastic, it shows the true impact of an ambiguous indirect assignment on the set of facts that the compiler can derive. The compiler can perform analysis to disambiguate pointer references—that is, to narrow the

**Ambiguous reference**

A reference is *ambiguous* if the compiler cannot isolate it to a single memory location.

set of variables that the compiler believes a pointer can address. Similarly, it can use a variety of techniques to understand the patterns of element access in an array—again, to shrink the set of locations that it must assume are modified by an assignment to one element.

### 8.4.2 Tree-Height Balancing

As we saw in Chapter 7, the specific details of how the compiler encodes a computation can affect the compiler's ability to optimize that computation. Many modern processors have multiple functional units so that they can execute multiple independent operations in each cycle. If the compiler can arrange the instruction stream so that it contains independent operations, encoded in the appropriate, machine-specific way, then the application will run more quickly.

Consider the code for $a + b + c + d + e + f + g + h$ shown in the margin. A left-to-right evaluation would produce the left-associative tree in Figure 8.5a. Other permissible trees include those in Figure 8.5b and c. Each distinct tree implies constraints on the execution order that are not required by the rules of addition. The left-associative tree implies that the program must evaluate $a + b$ before it can perform the additions involving either $g$ or $h$. The corresponding right-associative tree, created by a right-recursive grammar, implies that $g + h$ must precede additions involving $a$ or $b$. The balanced tree imposes fewer constraints, but it still implies an evaluation order with more constraints than the actual arithmetic.

If the processor can perform more than one addition at a time, then the balanced tree should let the compiler produce a shorter schedule for the computation. Figure 8.6 shows possible schedules for the balanced tree and the left-associative tree on a computer with two single-cycle adders. The balanced tree can execute in four cycles, with one unit idle in the fourth cycle.

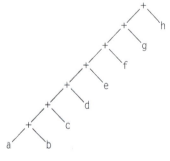

(a) Left-Associative Tree

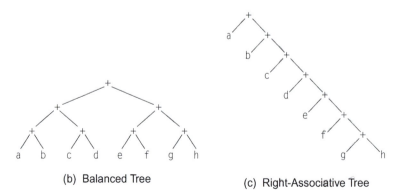

(b) Balanced Tree

(c) Right-Associative Tree

■ **FIGURE 8.5** Potential Tree Shapes for $a + b + c + d + e + f + g + h$.

| | Balanced Tree | | | Left-Associative Tree | |
|---|---|---|---|---|---|
| | **Unit 0** | **Unit 1** | | **Unit 0** | **Unit 1** |
| 1 | $t_1 \leftarrow a + b$ | $t_2 \leftarrow c + d$ | 1 | $t_1 \leftarrow a + b$ | — |
| 2 | $t_3 \leftarrow e + f$ | $t_4 \leftarrow g + h$ | 2 | $t_2 \leftarrow t_1 + c$ | — |
| 3 | $t_5 \leftarrow t_1 + t_2$ | $t_6 \leftarrow t_3 + t_4$ | 3 | $t_3 \leftarrow t_2 + d$ | — |
| 4 | $t_7 \leftarrow t_5 + t_6$ | — | 4 | $t_4 \leftarrow t_3 + e$ | — |
| 5 | — | — | 5 | $t_5 \leftarrow t_4 + f$ | — |
| 6 | — | — | 6 | $t_6 \leftarrow t_5 + g$ | — |
| 7 | — | — | 7 | $t_7 \leftarrow t_6 + h$ | — |

■ **FIGURE 8.6** Schedules from Different Tree Shapes for $a + b + c + d + e + f + g + h$.

In contrast, the left-associative tree requires seven cycles, leaving the second adder idle throughout the computation. The shape of the left-associative tree forces the compiler to serialize the additions. The right-associative tree will produce a similar effect.

This small example suggests an important optimization: using the commutative and associative laws of arithmetic to expose additional parallelism in expression evaluation. The remainder of this section presents an algorithm for rewriting code to create expressions whose tree form approximates a balanced tree. This particular transformation aims to improve execution time by exposing more concurrent operations, or *instruction-level parallelism*, to the compiler's instruction scheduler.

To formalize these notions into an algorithm, we will follow a simple scheme.

1. The algorithm identifies candidate expression trees in the block. All of the operators in a candidate tree must be identical; they must also be commutative and associative. Equally important, each name that labels an interior node of the candidate tree must be used exactly once.
2. For each candidate tree, the algorithm finds all its operands, assigns them a rank, and enters them into a priority queue, ordered by ascending rank. From this queue, the algorithm then reconstructs a tree that approximates a balanced binary tree.

This two phase scheme, analysis followed by transformation, is common in optimization.

### Finding Candidate Trees

A basic block consists of one or more intermixed computations. The compiler can interpret a block, in linear code, as a dependence graph (see Section 5.2.2); the graph captures both the flow of values and the ordering

$t_1 \leftarrow a \times b$
$t_2 \leftarrow c - d$
$y \leftarrow t_1 + t_2$
$z \leftarrow t_1 \times t_2$
Short Basic Block

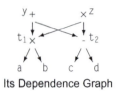

Its Dependence Graph

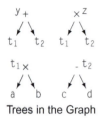

Trees in the Graph

**Observable value**
A value is *observable*, with respect to a code fragment (block, loop, etc.), if it is read outside that fragment.

constraints on the operations. In the short block shown in the margin, the code must compute $a \times b$ before it can compute either $t_1 + t_2$ or $t_1 \times t_2$.

The dependence graph does not, in general, form a single tree. Instead, it consists of multiple, intertwined, connected trees. The candidate expression trees that the balancing algorithm needs each contain a subset of the nodes in the block's dependence graph. Our example block is too short to have nontrivial trees, but it has four distinct trees—one for each operation, as shown in the margin.

When the algorithm rearranges operands, larger candidate trees provide more opportunities for rearrangement. Thus, the algorithm tries to construct maximal-sized candidate trees. Conceptually, the algorithm finds candidate trees that can be considered as a single $n$-ary operator, for as large a value of $n$ as possible. Several factors limit the size of a candidate tree.

1. The tree can be no larger than the block that it represents. Other transformations can increase the size of a basic block (see Section 10.6.1).
2. The rewritten code cannot change the *observable values* of the block—that is, any value used outside the block must be computed and preserved as it was in the original code. Similarly, any value used multiple times in the block must be preserved; in the example, both $t_1$ and $t_2$ have this property.
3. The tree cannot extend backward past the start of the block. In our marginal example, a, b, c, and d all receive their values before the start of the block. Thus, they become leaves in the tree.

The tree-finding phase also needs to know, for each name $T_i$ defined in the block, where $T_i$ is referenced. It assumes a set $\text{Uses}(T_i)$ that contains the index in the block of each use of $T_i$. If $T_i$ is used after the block, then $\text{Uses}(T_i)$ should contain two additional entries—arbitrary integers greater than the number of operations in the block. This trick ensures that $|\text{Uses}(x)| = 1$ if and only if $x$ is used as a local temporary variable. We leave the construction of the Uses sets as an exercise for the reader (see Problem 8.8 on page 473); it relies on LiveOut sets (see Section 8.6.1).

Figures 8.7 and 8.8 present the algorithm for balancing a basic block. Phase 1 of the algorithm, in Figure 8.7, is deceptively simple. It iterates over the operations in the block. It tests each operation to see if that operation must be the root of its own tree. When it finds a root, it adds the name defined by that operation to a priority queue of names, ordered by precedence of the root's operator.

```
// Rebalance a block b of n operations, each of form "Tᵢ ← Lᵢ Opᵢ Rᵢ"
// Phase 1: build a queue, Roots, of the candidate trees
Roots ← new queue of names
for i ← 0 to n-1
    Rank(Tᵢ) ← -1;
    if Opᵢ is commutative and associative and
        (|USES(Tᵢ)| > 1 or (|USES(Tᵢ)| = 1 and Op_USES(Tᵢ) ≠ Opᵢ)) then
            mark Tᵢ as a root
            Enqueue(Roots, Tᵢ, precedence of Opᵢ)

// Phase 2: remove a tree from Roots and rebalance it
while (Roots is not empty)
    var ← Dequeue(Roots)
    Balance(var)


Balance(root)    // Create balanced tree from its root, Tᵢ in "Tᵢ ← Lᵢ Opᵢ Rᵢ"
    if Rank(root) ≥ 0
        then return    // have already processed this tree

    q ← new queue of names                    // First, flatten the tree
    Rank(root) ← Flatten(Lᵢ, q) + Flatten(Rᵢ, q)
    Rebuild(q, Opᵢ)                           //Then, rebuild a balanced tree


Flatten(var,q)    // Flatten computes a rank for var & builds the queue
    if var is a constant                      // Cannot recur further
        then
            Rank(var) ← 0
            Enqueue(q, var, Rank(var))
        else if var∈UEVAR(b)                  // Cannot recur past top of block
                then
                    Rank(var) ← 1
                    Enqueue(q, var, Rank(var))
                else if var is a root
                        then                  // New queue for new root
                            Balance(var)      // Recur to find its rank
                            Enqueue(q, var, Rank(var))
                        else                  // var is Tⱼ in jᵗʰ op in block
                            Flatten(Lⱼ, q)    // Recur on left operand
                            Flatten(Rⱼ, q)    // Recur on right operand
    return Rank(var)
```

■ **FIGURE 8.7** Tree-Height Balancing Algorithm, Part I.

```
Rebuild(q,op)                                  // Build a balanced expression

    while (q is not empty)
        NL ← Dequeue(q)                        // Get a left operand
        NR ← Dequeue(q)                        // Get a right operand

        if NL and NR are both constants then   // Fold expression if constant
            NT ← Fold(op, NL, NR)
            if q is empty
                then
                    Emit("root ← NT")
                    Rank(root) = 0;
                else
                    Enqueue(q, NT, 0)
                    Rank(NT) = 0;

        else                                   // op is not a constant expression
            if q is empty                      // Get a name for result
                then NT ← root
                else NT ← new name

            Emit("NT ← NL op NR")

            Rank(NT) ← Rank(NL) + Rank(NR)     // Compute its rank

            if q is not empty                  // More ops in q ⇒ add NT to q
                then Enqueue(q, NT, r)
```

■ **FIGURE 8.8** Tree-Height Balancing Algorithm, Part II.

The test to identify a root has two parts. Assume that operation $i$ has the form $T_i \leftarrow L_i\ Op_i\ R_i$. First, $Op_i$ must be both commutative and associative. Second, one of the following two conditions must hold:

1. If $T_i$ is used more than once, then operation $i$ must be marked as a root to ensure that $T_i$ is available for all of its uses. Multiple uses make $T_i$ observable.

2. If $T_i$ is used just once, in operation $j$, but $Op_i \neq Op_j$, then operation $i$ must be a root, because it cannot be part of the tree that contains $Op_j$.

In either case, phase 1 marks $Op_i$ as a root and enqueues it.

### Rebuilding the Block in Balanced Form

Phase 2 takes the queue of candidate-tree roots and builds, from each root, an approximately balanced tree. Phase 2 starts with a while loop that calls *Balance* on each candidate tree root. *Balance*, *Flatten*, and *Rebuild* implement phase two.

*Balance* is invoked on a candidate-tree root. Working with *Flatten*, it creates a priority queue that holds all the operands of the current tree. *Balance* allocates a new queue and then invokes *Flatten* to recursively walk the tree, assign ranks to each operand, and enqueue them. Once the candidate tree has been flattened and ranked, *Balance* invokes *Rebuild* (see Figure 8.8) to reconstruct the code.

*Rebuild* uses a simple algorithm to construct the new code sequence. It repeatedly removes the two lowest ranked items from the tree. It emits an operation to combine them. It ranks the result and inserts the ranked result back into the priority queue. This process continues until the queue is empty.

Several details of this scheme are important.

1. When traversing a candidate tree, *Flatten* can encounter the root of another tree. At that point, it recurs on *Balance* rather than on *Flatten*, to create a new priority queue for the root's candidate tree and to ensure that it emits the code for the higher precedence subtree before the code that references the subtree's value. Recall that phase 1 ranked the *Roots* queue in increasing precedence order, which forces the correct order of evaluation here.

2. The block contains three kinds of references: constants, names defined in the block before their use in the block, and *upward-exposed names*. The routine *Flatten* handles each case separately. It relies on the set UEVAR($b$) that contains all the upwards-exposed names in block $b$. The computation of UEVAR is described in Section 8.6.1 and shown in Figure 8.14a.

   **Upward exposed**
   A name $x$ is *upward exposed* in block $b$ if the first use of $x$ in $b$ refers to a value computed before entering $b$.

3. Phase 2 ranks operands in a careful way. Constants receive rank zero, which forces them to the front of the queue, where *Fold* evaluates constant-valued operations, creates new names for the results, and works the results into the tree. Leaves receive rank one. Interior nodes receive the sum of their subtree ranks, which is equal to the number of nonconstant operands in the subtree. This ranking produces an approximation to a balanced binary tree.

## Examples

Consider what happens when we apply the algorithm to our original example in Figure 8.5. Assume that $t_7$ is live on exit from the block, that $t_1$ through $t_6$ are not, and that *Enqueue* inserts before the first equal-priority element. In that case, phase 1 finds a single root, $t_7$, and phase 2 invokes *Balance* on $t_7$. *Balance*, in turn, invokes *Flatten* followed by *Rebuild*. *Flatten* builds the queue:

$$\{ \langle h,1 \rangle, \langle g,1 \rangle, \langle f,1 \rangle, \langle e,1 \rangle, \langle d,1 \rangle, \langle c,1 \rangle, \langle b,1 \rangle, \langle a,1 \rangle \}.$$

*Rebuild* dequeues $\langle h,1 \rangle$ and $\langle g,1 \rangle$, emits "$n_0 \leftarrow h + g$", and enqueues $\langle n_0,2 \rangle$. Next, it dequeues $\langle f,1 \rangle$ and $\langle e,1 \rangle$, emits "$n_1 \leftarrow f + e$", and enqueues $\langle n_1,2 \rangle$. It dequeues $\langle d,1 \rangle$ and $\langle c,1 \rangle$, emits "$n_2 \leftarrow d + c$", and enqueues $\langle n_2,2 \rangle$. It then dequeues $\langle b,1 \rangle$ and $\langle a,1 \rangle$, emits "$n_3 \leftarrow b + a$", and enqueues $\langle n_3,2 \rangle$.

$$n_0 \leftarrow h + g$$
$$n_1 \leftarrow f + e$$
$$n_2 \leftarrow d + c$$
$$n_3 \leftarrow b + a$$
$$n_4 \leftarrow n_3 + n_2$$
$$n_5 \leftarrow n_1 + n_0$$
$$t_7 \leftarrow n_5 + n_4$$

At this point, *Rebuild* has produced partial sums with all eight of the original values. The queue now contains $\{ \langle n_3,2 \rangle, \langle n_2,2 \rangle, \langle n_1,2 \rangle, \langle n_0,2 \rangle \}$. The next iteration dequeues $\langle n_3,2 \rangle$ and $\langle n_2,2 \rangle$, emits "$n_4 \leftarrow n_3 + n_2$" and enqueues $\langle n_4,4 \rangle$. Next, it dequeues $\langle n_1,2 \rangle$ and $\langle n_0,2 \rangle$, emits "$n_5 \leftarrow n_1 + n_0$" and enqueues $\langle n_5,4 \rangle$. The final iteration dequeues $\langle n_5,4 \rangle$ and $\langle n_4,4 \rangle$, and emits "$t_7 \leftarrow n_5 + n_4$". The complete code sequence, shown the margin, matches to the balanced tree shown in Figure 8.5c; the resulting code can be scheduled as in the left side of Figure 8.6.

As a second example, consider the basic block shown in Figure 8.9a. This code might result from local value numbering; constants have been folded and redundant computations eliminated. The block contains several intertwined computations. Figure 8.9b shows the expression trees in the block. Note that $t_3$ and $t_7$ are reused by name. The longest path chain of computation is the tree headed by $t_6$ which has six operations.

When we apply phase 1 of the tree-height balancing algorithm to the block in Figure 8.9, it finds five roots, shown boxed in Figure 8.9c. It marks $t_3$ and $t_7$ because they have multiple uses. It marks $t_6$, $t_{10}$, and $t_{11}$ because they are in LIVEOUT($b$). At the end of phase 1, the priority queue *Roots*

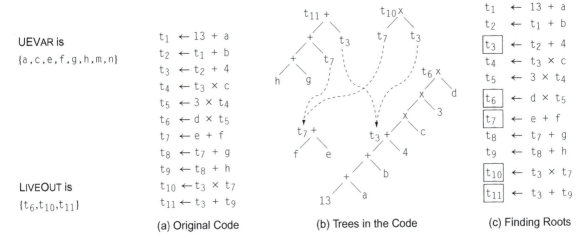

UEVAR is
$\{a,c,e,f,g,h,m,n\}$

LIVEOUT is
$\{t_6,t_{10},t_{11}\}$

| | |
|---|---|
| $t_1$ | $\leftarrow 13 + a$ |
| $t_2$ | $\leftarrow t_1 + b$ |
| $t_3$ | $\leftarrow t_2 + 4$ |
| $t_4$ | $\leftarrow t_3 \times c$ |
| $t_5$ | $\leftarrow 3 \times t_4$ |
| $t_6$ | $\leftarrow d \times t_5$ |
| $t_7$ | $\leftarrow e + f$ |
| $t_8$ | $\leftarrow t_7 + g$ |
| $t_9$ | $\leftarrow t_8 + h$ |
| $t_{10}$ | $\leftarrow t_3 \times t_7$ |
| $t_{11}$ | $\leftarrow t_3 + t_9$ |

(a) Original Code

(b) Trees in the Code

| | |
|---|---|
| $t_1$ | $\leftarrow 13 + a$ |
| $t_2$ | $\leftarrow t_1 + b$ |
| $t_3$ | $\leftarrow t_2 + 4$ |
| $t_4$ | $\leftarrow t_3 \times c$ |
| $t_5$ | $\leftarrow 3 \times t_4$ |
| $t_6$ | $\leftarrow d \times t_5$ |
| $t_7$ | $\leftarrow e + f$ |
| $t_8$ | $\leftarrow t_7 + g$ |
| $t_9$ | $\leftarrow t_8 + h$ |
| $t_{10}$ | $\leftarrow t_3 \times t_7$ |
| $t_{11}$ | $\leftarrow t_3 + t_9$ |

(c) Finding Roots

■ **FIGURE 8.9** Example of Tree-Height Balancing.

contains:

$$\{\ \langle t_{11}, 1\rangle,\ \langle t_7, 1\rangle,\ \langle t_3, 1\rangle,\ \langle t_{10}, 2\rangle,\ \langle t_6, 2\rangle\ \},$$

assuming that the precedence of $+$ is 1, the precedence of $\times$ is 2.

Phase 2 of the algorithm repeatedly removes a node from the *Roots* queue and calls *Balance* to process it. *Balance*, in turn, uses *Flatten* to create a priority queue of operands and then uses *Rebuild* to create a balanced computation from the operands. (Remember that each tree contains just one kind of operation.)

Phase 2 begins by calling *Balance* on $t_{11}$. Recall from Figure 8.9 that $t_{11}$ is the sum of $t_3$ and $t_7$. *Balance* calls *Flatten* on each of those nodes, which are, themselves, roots of other trees. Thus, the call to *Flatten*$(t_3, q)$ invokes *Balance* on $t_3$ and then invokes it on $t_7$.

*Balance*$(t_3)$ flattens that tree into the queue $\{\ \langle 4,0\rangle,\ \langle 13,0\rangle,\ \langle b,1\rangle,\ \langle a,1\rangle\ \}$ and invokes *Rebuild* on that queue. *Rebuild* dequeues $\langle 4,0\rangle$ and $\langle 13,0\rangle$, combines them, and enqueues $\langle 17,0\rangle$. Next, it dequeues $\langle 17,0\rangle$ and $\langle b,1\rangle$, emits "$n_0 \leftarrow 17 + b$", and adds $\langle n_0,1\rangle$ to the queue. On the final iteration for the $t_3$ tree, it dequeues $\langle n_0,1\rangle$ and $\langle a,1\rangle$, and emits "$t_3 \leftarrow n_0 + a$". It marks $t_3$ with rank 2 and returns.

$$n_0 \leftarrow 17 + b$$
$$t_3 \leftarrow n_0 + a$$

Invoking *Balance* on $t_7$ builds a trivial queue, $\{\ \langle e,1\rangle,\ \langle f,1\rangle\ \}$ and emits the operation "$t_7 \leftarrow e + f$". That completes the first iteration of the while loop in phase 2.

$$t_7 \leftarrow e + f$$

Next, phase 2 invokes *Balance* on the tree at $t_{11}$. It calls *Flatten*, which builds the queue $\{\ \langle h,1\rangle,\ \langle g,1\rangle,\ \langle t_7,2\rangle,\ \langle t_3,2\rangle\ \}$. Then, *Rebuild* emits the code "$n_1 \leftarrow h + g$" and enqueues $n_1$ with rank 2. Next, it emits the code "$n_2 \leftarrow n_1 + t_7$" and enqueues $n_2$ with rank 4. Finally, it emits the code "$t_{11} \leftarrow n_2 + t_3$" and marks $t_{11}$ with rank 6.

$$n_1 \leftarrow h + g$$
$$n_2 \leftarrow n_1 + t_7$$
$$t_{11} \leftarrow n_2 + t_3$$

The next two items that phase 2 dequeues from the *Roots* queue, $t_7$ and $t_3$, have already been processed, so they have nonzero ranks. Thus, *Balance* returns immediately on each of them.

The final call to *Balance* from phase 2 passes it the root $t_6$. For $t_6$, *Flatten* constructs the queue: $\{\ \langle 3,0\rangle,\ \langle d,1\rangle,\ \langle c,1\rangle,\ \langle t_3,2\rangle\ \}$. *Rebuild* emits the code "$n_3 \leftarrow 3 + d$" and enqueues $n_3$ with rank 1. Next, it emits "$n_4 \leftarrow n_3 + c$" and enqueues $n_4$ with rank 2. Finally, it emits "$t_6 \leftarrow n_4 + t_3$" and marks $t_3$ with rank 4.

$$n_3 \leftarrow 3 + d$$
$$n_4 \leftarrow n_3 + c$$
$$t_6 \leftarrow n_4 + t_3$$

The resulting tree is shown in Figure 8.10. Note that the tree rooted at $t_6$ now has a height of three operations, instead of six.

$$
\begin{aligned}
n_0 &\leftarrow 17 + b \\
t_3 &\leftarrow n_0 + a \\
t_7 &\leftarrow f + e \\
n_1 &\leftarrow h + g \\
n_2 &\leftarrow n_1 + t_7 \\
t_{11} &\leftarrow n_2 + t_3 \\
t_{10} &\leftarrow t_7 \times t_3 \\
n_3 &\leftarrow 3 \times c \\
n_4 &\leftarrow n_3 \times d \\
t_6 &\leftarrow n_4 \times t_3
\end{aligned}
$$

(a) Transformed Code

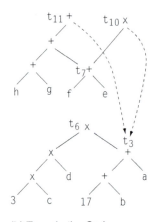

(b) Trees in the Code

■ **FIGURE 8.10** Code Structure after Balancing.

**SECTION REVIEW**

Local optimization operates on the code for a single basic block. The techniques rely on the information available in the block to rewrite that block. In the process, they must maintain the block's interactions with the surrounding execution context. In particular, they must preserve any observable values computed in the block.

Because they limit their scope to a single block, local optimizations can rely on properties that only hold true in straightline code. For example, local value numbering relies on the fact that all the operations in the block execute in an order that is consistent with straightline execution. Thus, it can build a model of prior context that exposes redundancies and constant-valued expressions. Similarly, tree-height balancing relies on the fact that a block has just one exit to determine which subexpressions in the block it must preserve and which ones it can rearrange.

**Review Questions**

1. Sketch an algorithm to find the basic blocks in a procedure expressed in ILOC. What data structures might you use to represent the basic block?

2. The tree-height balancing algorithm given in Figures 8.7 and 8.8 ranks a node $n$ in the final expression tree with the number of nonconstant leaves below it in the final tree. How would you modify the algorithm to produce ranks that correspond to the height of $n$ in the tree? Would that change the code that the algorithm produces?

## 8.5 REGIONAL OPTIMIZATION

Inefficiencies are not limited to single blocks. Code that executes in one block may provide the context for improving the code in another block. Thus, most optimizations examine a larger context than a single block.

This section examines two techniques that operate over regions of code that include multiple blocks but do not, typically, extend to an entire procedure. The primary complication that arises in the shift from local optimization to regional optimization is the need to handle more than one possibility for the flow of control. An if-then-else can take one of two paths. The branch at the end of a loop can jump back to another iteration or it can jump to the code that follows the loop.

To illustrate regional techniques, we present two of them. The first, superlocal value numbering, is an extension of local value numbering to larger regions. The second is a loop optimization that appeared in our discussion of the dmxpy loop nest: loop unrolling.

### 8.5.1 Superlocal Value Numbering

To improve the results of local value numbering, the compiler can extend its scope from a single basic block to an extended basic block, or EBB. To process an EBB, the algorithm should value number each path through the EBB. Consider, for example, the code shown in Figure 8.11a. Its CFG, shown in Figure 8.11b, contains one nontrivial EBB, $(B_0, B_1, B_2, B_3, B_4)$, and two trivial EBBs, $(B_5)$ and $(B_6)$. We call the resulting algorithm *superlocal value numbering* (SVN).

In the large EBB, SVN could treat each of the three paths as if it were a single block. That is, it could behave as if each of $(B_0, B_1)$, $(B_0, B_2, B_3)$, and $(B_0, B_2, B_4)$ were straightline code. To process $(B_0, B_1)$, the compiler can apply LVN to $B_0$ and use the resulting hash table as a starting point when it applies LVN to $B_1$. The same approach would handle $(B_0, B_2, B_3)$ and $(B_0, B_2, B_4)$ by processing the blocks for each in order and carrying the hash tables forward. The effect of this scheme is to treat a path as if it were a single block. For example, it would optimize $(B_0, B_2, B_3)$ as if it had the code as shown in Figure 8.11c. Any block with multiple predecessors, such as $B_5$ and $B_6$, must be handled as in local value numbering—without context from any predecessors.

This approach can find redundancies and constant-valued expressions that a strictly local value numbering algorithm would miss.

- In $(B_0, B_1)$, LVN discovers that the assignments to $n_0$ and $r_0$ are redundant. SVN discovers the same redundancies.

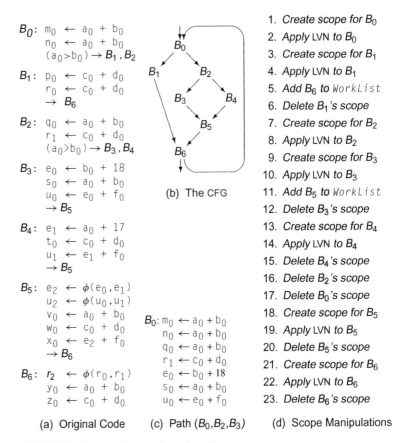

$B_0:$ $m_0 \leftarrow a_0 + b_0$
$n_0 \leftarrow a_0 + b_0$
$(a_0 > b_0) \rightarrow B_1, B_2$

$B_1:$ $p_0 \leftarrow c_0 + d_0$
$r_0 \leftarrow c_0 + d_0$
$\rightarrow B_6$

$B_2:$ $q_0 \leftarrow a_0 + b_0$
$r_1 \leftarrow c_0 + d_0$
$(a_0 > b_0) \rightarrow B_3, B_4$

$B_3:$ $e_0 \leftarrow b_0 + 18$
$s_0 \leftarrow a_0 + b_0$
$u_0 \leftarrow e_0 + f_0$
$\rightarrow B_5$

$B_4:$ $e_1 \leftarrow a_0 + 17$
$t_0 \leftarrow c_0 + d_0$
$u_1 \leftarrow e_1 + f_0$
$\rightarrow B_5$

$B_5:$ $e_2 \leftarrow \phi(e_0, e_1)$
$u_2 \leftarrow \phi(u_0, u_1)$
$v_0 \leftarrow a_0 + b_0$
$w_0 \leftarrow c_0 + d_0$
$x_0 \leftarrow e_2 + f_0$
$\rightarrow B_6$

$B_6:$ $r_2 \leftarrow \phi(r_0, r_1)$
$y_0 \leftarrow a_0 + b_0$
$z_0 \leftarrow c_0 + d_0$

(a) Original Code

(b) The CFG

$B_0:$ $m_0 \leftarrow a_0 + b_0$
$n_0 \leftarrow a_0 + b_0$
$q_0 \leftarrow a_0 + b_0$
$r_1 \leftarrow c_0 + d_0$
$e_0 \leftarrow b_0 + 18$
$s_0 \leftarrow a_0 + b_0$
$u_0 \leftarrow e_0 + f_0$

(c) Path $(B_0, B_2, B_3)$

1. *Create scope for $B_0$*
2. *Apply* LVN *to $B_0$*
3. *Create scope for $B_1$*
4. *Apply* LVN *to $B_1$*
5. *Add $B_6$ to* WorkList
6. *Delete $B_1$'s scope*
7. *Create scope for $B_2$*
8. *Apply* LVN *to $B_2$*
9. *Create scope for $B_3$*
10. *Apply* LVN *to $B_3$*
11. *Add $B_5$ to* WorkList
12. *Delete $B_3$'s scope*
13. *Create scope for $B_4$*
14. *Apply* LVN *to $B_4$*
15. *Delete $B_4$'s scope*
16. *Delete $B_2$'s scope*
17. *Delete $B_0$'s scope*
18. *Create scope for $B_5$*
19. *Apply* LVN *to $B_5$*
20. *Delete $B_5$'s scope*
21. *Create scope for $B_6$*
22. *Apply* LVN *to $B_6$*
23. *Delete $B_6$'s scope*

(d) Scope Manipulations

■ **FIGURE 8.11** Superlocal Value Numbering Example.

- In $(B_0, B_2, B_3)$, LVN finds that the assignment to $n_0$ is redundant. SVN also finds that the assignments to $q_0$ and $s_0$ are redundant.
- In $(B_0, B_2, B_4)$, LVN finds that the assignment to $n_0$ is redundant. SVN also finds that the assignments to $q_0$ and $t_0$ are redundant.
- In $B_5$ and $B_6$, SVN degenerates to LVN.

The difficulty in this approach lies in making the process efficient. The obvious approach is to treat each path as if it were a single block, pretending, for example, that the code for $(B_0, B_2, B_3)$ looks like the code in Figure 8.11c. Unfortunately, this approach analyzes a block once for each path that includes it. In the example, this approach would analyze $B_0$ three times and $B_2$ twice. While we want the optimization benefits that come from examining increased context, we also want to minimize compile-time costs.

For this reason, superlocal algorithms often capitalize on the tree structure of the EBB.

To make SVN efficient, the compiler must reuse the results of blocks that occur as prefixes on multiple paths through the EBB. It needs a way to undo the effects of processing a block. After processing $(B_0, B_2, B_3)$ it must recreate the state for the end of $(B_0, B_2)$ so that it can reuse that state to process $B_4$.

Among the many ways that the compiler can accomplish this effect are:

- It can record the state of the table at each block boundary and restore that state when needed.
- It can unwind the effects of a block by walking the block backward and, at each operation, undoing the work of the forward pass.
- It can implement the value table using the mechanisms developed for lexically scoped hash tables. As it enters a block, it creates a new scope. To retract the block's effects, it deletes that block's scope.

While all three schemes will work, using a scoped value table can produce the simplest and fastest implementation, particularly if the compiler can reuse an implementation from the front end (see Section 5.5.3).

Figure 8.12 shows a high-level sketch of the SVN algorithm, using a scoped value table. It assumes that the LVN algorithm has been parameterized to accept a block and a scoped value table. At each block $b$, it allocates a value table for $b$, links the value tables of the predecessor block as if it were a surrounding scope, and invokes LVN on block $b$ with this new table. When LVN returns, SVN must decide what to do with each of $b$'s successors.

The "sheaf-of-tables" implementation shown in Section 5.5.3 has the right properties for SVN. SVN can easily estimate the size of each table. The deletion mechanism is both simple and fast.

For a successor $s$ of $b$, two cases arise. If $s$ has exactly one predecessor, $b$, then it should be processed with the accumulated context from $b$. Accordingly, SVN recurs on $s$ with the table containing $b$'s context. If $s$ has multiple predecessors, then $s$ must start with an empty context. Thus, SVN adds $s$ to the *WorkList* where the outer loop will later find it and invoke SVN on it and the empty table.

One complication remains. A name's value number is recorded in the value table associated with the first operation in the EBB that defines it. This effect can defeat our use of the scoping mechanism. In our example CFG, if a name $x$ were defined in each of $B_0$, $B_3$, and $B_4$, its value number would be recorded in the scoped table for $B_0$. When SVN processed $B_3$, it would record $x$'s new value number from $B_3$ in the table for $B_0$. When SVN deleted the table for $B_3$ and created a new table for $B_4$, the value number from the definition in $B_3$ would remain.

```
// Start the process
WorkList ← { entry block }
Empty ← new table

while (WorkList is not empty)
    remove b from WorkList
    SVN(b, Empty)


// Superlocal value numbering algorithm
SVN(Block, Table)
    t ← new table for Block
    link Table as the surrounding scope for t
    LVN(Block, t)

    for each successor s of Block do
        if s has only 1 predecessor
            then SVN(s, t)

        else if s has not been processed
            then add s to WorkList

    deallocate t
```

■ **FIGURE 8.12** Superlocal Value Numbering Algorithm.

To avoid this complication, the compiler can run SVN on a representation that defines each name once. As we saw in Section 5.4.2, SSA form has the requisite property; each name is defined at exactly one point in the code. Using SSA form ensures that SVN records the value number for a definition in the table that corresponds to the block containing the definition. With SSA form, deleting the table for a block undoes all of its effects and reverts the value table to its state at the exit of the block's CFG predecessor. As discussed in Section 8.4.1, using SSA form can also make LVN more effective.

Applying the algorithm from Figure 8.12 to the code from Figure 8.11a produces the sequence of actions shown in Figure 8.11d. It begins with $B_0$ and proceeds down to $B_1$. At the end of $B_1$, it visits $B_6$, realizes that $B_6$ has multiple predecessors, and adds it to the worklist. Next, it backs up and processes $B_2$ and then $B_3$. At the end of $B_3$, it adds $B_5$ to the worklist. It then backs up to $B_2$ and processes $B_4$. At that point, control returns to the while loop, which invokes SVN on the two singleton blocks from the worklist, $B_5$ and $B_6$.

In terms of effectiveness, SVN discovers and removes redundant computations that LVN cannot. As mentioned earlier in the section, it finds that the assignments to $q_0$, $s_0$, and $t_0$ are redundant because of definitions in earlier blocks. LVN, with its purely local scope, cannot find these redundancies.

On the other hand, SVN has its own limitations. It fails to find redundancies in $B_5$ and $B_6$. The reader can tell, by inspection, that each assignment in these two blocks is redundant. Because those blocks have multiple predecessors, SVN cannot carry context into them. Thus, it misses those opportunities; to catch them, we need an algorithm that can consider a larger amount of context.

### 8.5.2 **Loop Unrolling**

Loop unrolling is, perhaps, the oldest and best-known loop transformation. To unroll a loop, the compiler replicates the loop's body and adjusts the logic that controls the number of iterations performed. To see this, consider the loop nest from dmxpy used as an example in Section 8.2.

```
    do 60 j = 1, n2
        do 50 i = 1, n1
            y(i) = y(i) + x(j) * m(i,j)
50      continue
60  continue
```

The compiler can unroll either the inner loop or the outer loop. The result of inner-loop unrolling is shown in Figure 8.13a. Unrolling the outer loop produces four inner loops; if the compiler then combines those inner-loop bodies—a transformation called *loop fusion*—it will produce code similar to that shown in Figure 8.13b. The combination of outer-loop unrolling and subsequent fusion of the inner loops is often called *unroll-and-jam*.

In each case, the transformed code needs a short prologue loop that peels off enough iterations to ensure that the unrolled loop processes an integral multiple of four iterations. If the respective loop bounds are all known at compile time, the compiler can determine whether or not the prologue is necessary.

These two distinct strategies, inner-loop unrolling and outer-loop unrolling, produce different results for this particular loop nest. Inner loop unrolling produces code that executes many fewer test-and-branch sequences than did the original code. In contrast, outer-loop unrolling followed by fusion of the inner loops not only reduces the number of test-and-branch sequences, but also produces reuse of y(i) and sequential access to both x and m. The increased reuse fundamentally changes the ratio of arithmetic operations to

**Loop fusion**

The process of combining two loop bodies into one is called *fusion*.

Fusion is safe when each definition and each use in the resulting loop has the same value that it did in the original loops.

Access to m is sequential because FORTRAN stores arrays in column-major order.

```
    do 60 j = 1, n2                            nextra = mod(n2,4)
      nextra = mod(n1,4)                       if (nextra .ge. 1) then
      if (nextra .ge. 1) then                    do 59 j = 1, nextra
        do 49 i = 1, nextra                        do 49 i = 1, n1
          y(i) = y(i) + x(j) * m(i,j)                y(i) = y(i) + x(j) * m(i,j)
49        continue                         49      continue
                                           59    continue

      do 50 i = nextra + 1, n1, 4            do 60 j = nextra+1, n2, 4
        y(i)   = y(i) + x(j) * m(i,j)          do 50 i = 1, n1
        y(i+1) = y(i+1) + x(j) * m(i+1,j)        y(i) = y(i) + x(j) * m(i,j)
        y(i+2) = y(i+2) + x(j) * m(i+2,j)        y(i) = y(i) + x(j+1) * m(i,j+1)
        y(i+3) = y(i+3) + x(j) * m(i+3,j)        y(i) = y(i) + x(j+2) * m(i,j+2)
50      continue                                 y(i) = y(i) + x(j+3) * m(i,j+3)
60    continue                             50    continue
                                           60  continue
```

|  (a) Unroll Inner Loop by Four  |  (b) Unroll Outer Loop by Four, Fuse Inner Loops  |

■ **FIGURE 8.13** Unrolling dmxpy's Loop Nest.

memory operations in the loop; undoubtedly, the author of dmxpy had that effect in mind when he hand-optimized the code. As discussed below, each approach may also accrue indirect benefits.

### Sources of Improvement and Degradation

Loop unrolling has both direct and indirect effects on the code that the compiler can produce for a given loop. The final performance of the loop depends on all of the effects, direct and indirect.

In terms of direct benefits, unrolling should reduce the number of operations required to complete the loop. The control-flow changes reduce the total number of test-and-branch sequences. Unrolling can create reuse within the loop body, reducing memory traffic. Finally, if the loop contains a cyclic chain of copy operations, unrolling can eliminate the copies (see Exercise 5 in this chapter).

As a hazard, though, unrolling increases program size, both in its IR form and in its final form as executable code. Growth in IR increases compile time; growth in executable code has little effect until the loop overflows the instruction cache—at which time the degradation probably overwhelms any direct benefits.

The compiler can also unroll for indirect effects, which can affect performance. The key side effect of unrolling is to increase the number of operations inside the loop body. Other optimizations can capitalize on this change in several ways:

- Increasing the number of independent operations in the loop body can lead to better instruction schedules. With more operations, the scheduler has a better chance to keep multiple functional units busy and to hide the latency of long-duration operations such as branches and memory accesses.

- Unrolling can move consecutive memory accesses into the same loop iteration, where the compiler can schedule them together. That may improve locality or allow the use of multiword operations.

- Unrolling can expose cross-iteration redundancies that are harder to discover in the original code. For example, both versions of the code shown in Figure 8.13 reuse address expressions across iterations of the original loop. In the unrolled loop, local value numbering would find and eliminate those redundancies. In the original, it would miss them.

- The unrolled loop may optimize in a different way than the original loop. For example, increasing the number of times that a variable occurs inside the loop can change the weights used in spill code selection within the register allocator (see Section 13.4). Changing the pattern of register spills can radically affect the speed of the final code for the loop.

- The unrolled loop body may have a greater demand for registers than the original loop body. If the increased demand for registers induces additional register spills (stores and reloads), then the resulting memory traffic may overwhelm the potential benefits of unrolling.

These indirect interactions are much harder to characterize and understand than the direct effects. They can produce significant performance improvements. They can also produce performance degradations. The difficulty of predicting such indirect effects has led some researchers to advocate an adaptive approach to choosing unroll factors; in such systems, the compiler tries several unroll factors and measures the performance of the resulting code.

---

**SECTION REVIEW**

Optimizations that focus on regions larger than a block and smaller than a whole procedure can provide improved performance for a modest increase in compile-time cost. For some transformations, the analysis needed to support the transformation and the impact that it has on the compiled code are both limited in scope.

Superlocal transformations have a rich history in both the literature and the practice of code optimization. Many local transformations adapt easily and efficiently to extended basic blocks. Superlocal extensions to instruction scheduling have been a staple of optimizing compilers for many years (see Section 12.4).

Loop-based optimizations, such as unrolling, can produce significant improvements, primarily because so many programs spend a significant fraction of their execution time inside loops. That simple fact makes loops and loop nests into rich targets for analysis and transformation. Improvements made inside a loop have a much larger impact than those made in code outside all loop nests. A regional approach to loop optimization makes sense because different loop nests can have radically different performance characteristics. Thus, loop optimization has been a major focus of optimization research for decades.

**Review Questions**

1. Superlocal value numbering extends local value numbering to extended basic blocks through clever use of a scoped hash table. Consider the issues that might arise in extending the tree-height balancing algorithm to a superlocal scope.

   **a.** How would you handle a single path through an EBB, such as $(B_0, B_2, B_3)$ in the control-flow graph shown in the margin?

   **b.** What complications arise when the algorithm tries to process $(B_0, B_2, B_4)$ after processing $(B_0, B_2, B_3)$?

2. The following code fragment computes a three-year trailing average:

```
TYTA(float *Series; float *TYTAvg; int count) {
    int i;
    float Minus2, Minus1;

    Minus2 = Series++;
    Minus1 = Series++;

    for (i=1; i ≤ count; i++) {
        Current = Series++;
        TYTAvg++ = (Current + Minus1 + Minus2)/3;
        Minus2 = Minus1;
        Minus1 = Current;
    }
}
```

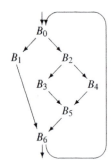

Hint: Compare possible improvements with unroll factors of two and three.

What improvements would accrue from unrolling the loop? How would the unroll factor affect the benefits?

## 8.6 GLOBAL OPTIMIZATION

Global optimizations operate on an entire procedure or method. Because their scope includes cyclic control-flow constructs such as loops, these methods typically perform an analysis phase before modifying the code.

This section presents two examples of global analysis and optimization. The first, finding uninitialized variables with live information, is not strictly an optimization. Rather, it uses global data-flow analysis to discover useful information about the flow of values in a procedure. We will use the discussion to introduce the computation of *live variables* information, which plays a role in many optimization techniques, including tree-height balancing (Section 8.4.2), the construction of SSA information (Section 9.3), and register allocation (Chapter 13). The second, global code placement, uses profile information gathered from running the compiled code to rearrange the layout of the executable code.

### 8.6.1 Finding Uninitialized Variables with Live Information

If a procedure $p$ can use the value of some variable $v$ before $v$ has been assigned a value, we say that $v$ is uninitialized at that use. Use of an uninitialized variable almost always indicates a logical error in the procedure being compiled. If the compiler can identify these situations, it should alert the programmer to their existence.

We can find potential uses of uninitialized variables by computing information about *liveness*. A variable $v$ is live at point $p$ if and only if there exists a path in the CFG from $p$ to a use of $v$ along which $v$ is not redefined. We encode live information by computing, for each block $b$ in the procedure, a set LiveOut($b$) that contains all the variables that are live on exit from $b$. Given a LiveOut set for the CFG's entry node $n_0$, each variable in LiveOut($n_0$) has a potentially uninitialized use.

The computation of LiveOut sets is an example of *global data-flow analysis*, a family of techniques for reasoning, at compile time, about the flow of values at runtime. Problems in data-flow analysis are typically posed as a set of simultaneous equations over sets associated with the nodes and edges of a graph.

**Data-flow analysis**
a form of compile-time analysis for reasoning about the flow of values at runtime

### *Defining the Data-Flow Problem*

Computing LiveOut sets is a classic problem in global data-flow analysis. The compiler computes, for each node $n$ in the procedure's CFG, a set LiveOut($n$) that contains all the variables that are live on exit from the block corresponding to $n$. For each node $n$ in the procedure's CFG, LiveOut($n$) is defined by an equation that uses the LiveOut sets of $n$'s successors in the CFG, and two sets UEVar($n$) and VarKill($n$) that encode facts about the block associated with $n$. We can solve the equations using an iterative fixed-point method, similar to the fixed-point methods that we saw in earlier chapters such as the subset construction in Section 2.4.3.

The defining equation for LiveOut is:

$$\text{LiveOut}(n) = \bigcup_{m \in succ(n)} (\text{UEVar}(m) \cup (\text{LiveOut}(m) \cap \overline{\text{VarKill}(m)}))$$

UEVar($m$) contains the upward-exposed variables in $m$—those variables that are used in $m$ before any redefinition in $m$. VarKill($m$) contains all the variables that are defined in $m$ and the overline on VarKill($m$) indicates its logical complement, the set of all variables not defined in $m$. Because LiveOut($n$) is defined in terms of $n$'s successors, the equation describes a *backward data-flow problem.*

**Backward data-flow problem**

a problem in which information flows backward over graph edges

**Forward data-flow problem**

a problem in which information flows along the graph edges

The equation encodes the definition in an intuitive way. LiveOut($n$) is just the union of those variables that are live at the head of some block $m$ that immediately follows $n$ in the CFG. The definition requires that a value be live on some path, not on all paths. Thus, the contributions of the successors of $n$ in the CFG are unioned together to form LiveOut($n$). The contribution of a specific successor $m$ of $n$ is:

$$\text{UEVar}(m) \cup (\text{LiveOut}(m) \cap \overline{\text{VarKill}(m)}).$$

A variable, $v$, is live on entry to $m$ under one of two conditions. It can be referenced in $m$ before it is redefined in $m$, in which case $v \in \text{UEVar}(m)$. It can be live on exit from $m$ and pass unscathed through $m$ because $m$ does not redefine it, in which case $v \in \text{LiveOut}(m) \cap \overline{\text{VarKill}(m)}$. Combining these two sets, with $\cup$, gives the necessary contribution of $m$ to LiveOut($n$). To compute LiveOut($n$), the analyzer combines the contributions of all $n$'s successors denoted $succ(n)$.

### Solving the Data-Flow Problem

To compute the LiveOut sets for a procedure and its CFG, the compiler can use a three-step algorithm.

1. *Build a CFG* This step is conceptually simple, although language and architecture features can complicate the problem (see Section 5.3.4).
2. *Gather initial information* The analyzer computes a UEVar and VarKill set for each block $b$ in a simple walk, as shown in Figure 8.14a.

3. *Solve the equations to produce* LiveOut(b) *for each block b* Figure 8.14b shows a simple iterative fixed-point algorithm that will solve the equations.

The following sections work through an example computation of LiveOut. Section 9.2 delves into data-flow computations in more depth.

## Gathering Initial Information

To compute LiveOut, the analyzer needs UEVar and VarKill sets for each block. A single pass can compute both. For each block, the analyzer initializes these sets to Ø. Next, it walks the block, in order from top to bottom, and updates both UEVar and VarKill to reflect the impact of each operation. Figure 8.14a shows the details of this computation.

Consider the CFG with a simple loop that contains an `if-then` construct, shown in Figure 8.15a. The code abstracts away many details. Figure 8.15b shows the corresponding UEVar and VarKill sets.

## Solving the Equations for LiveOut

Given the UEVar and VarKill sets, the compiler applies the algorithm from Figure 8.14b to compute LiveOut sets for each node in the CFG. It initializes all of the LiveOut sets to Ø. Next, it computes the LiveOut set for each block, in order from $B_0$ to $B_4$. It repeats the process, computing LiveOut for each node in order until the LiveOut sets no longer change.

```
// assume block b has k operations
// of form "x ← y op z"
for each block b
    Init(b)

Init(b)
    UEVar(b) ← Ø
    VarKill(b) ← Ø
    for i ← 1 to k
        if y ∉ VarKill(b)
            then add y to UEVar(b)
        if z ∉ VarKill(b)
            then add z to UEVar(b)
        add x to VarKill(b)
```

(a) Gathering Initial Information

```
// assume CFG has N blocks
// numbered 0 to N-1

for i ← 0 to N-1
    LiveOut(i) ← Ø

changed ← true

while (changed)
    changed ← false
    for i ← 0 to N-1
        recompute LiveOut(i)
        if LiveOut(i) changed then
            changed ← true
```

(b) Solving the Equations

■ **FIGURE 8.14** Iterative Live Analysis.

The table in Figure 8.15c shows the values of the LIVEOUT sets at each iteration of the solver. The row labelled *Initial* shows the initial values. The first iteration computes an initial approximation to the LIVEOUT sets. Because it processes the blocks in ascending order of their labels, $B_0, B_1$, and $B_2$ receive values based solely on the UEVAR sets of their CFG successors. When the algorithm reaches $B_3$, it has already computed an approximation for LIVEOUT($B_1$), so the value that it computes for $B_3$ reflects the contribution of the new value for LIVEOUT($B_1$). LIVEOUT($B_4$) is empty, as befits the exit block.

In the second iteration, the value s is added to LIVEOUT($B_0$) as a consequence of its presence in the approximation of LIVEOUT($B_1$). No other changes occur. The third iteration does not change the values of the LIVEOUT sets and halts.

The order in which the algorithm processes the blocks affects the values of the intermediate sets. If the algorithm visited the blocks in descending

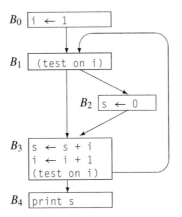

$B_0$ `i ← 1`

$B_1$ `(test on i)`

$B_2$ `s ← 0`

$B_3$ `s ← s + i`
`i ← i + 1`
`(test on i)`

$B_4$ `print s`

(a) Example Control-Flow Graph

|        | UEVAR | VARKILL |
|--------|-------|---------|
| $B_0$  | Ø     | {i}     |
| $B_1$  | {i}   | Ø       |
| $B_2$  | Ø     | {s}     |
| $B_3$  | {s,i} | {s,i}   |
| $B_4$  | {s}   | Ø       |

(b) Initial Information

| | LIVEOUT($n$) | | | | |
|---------|-------|-------|-------|-------|-------|
| Iteration | $B_0$ | $B_1$ | $B_2$ | $B_3$ | $B_4$ |
| Initial | Ø | Ø | Ø | Ø | Ø |
| 1 | {i} | {s,i} | {s,i} | {s,i} | Ø |
| 2 | {s,i} | {s,i} | {s,i} | {s,i} | Ø |
| 3 | {s,i} | {s,i} | {s,i} | {s,i} | Ø |

(c) Progress of the Solution

■ **FIGURE 8.15** Example LIVEOUT Computation.

order of their labels, it would require one fewer pass. The final values of the LiveOut sets are independent of the evaluation order. The iterative solver in Figure 8.14 computes a fixed-point solution to the equations for LiveOut.

The algorithm will halt because the LiveOut sets are finite and the recomputation of the LiveOut set for a block can only increase the number of names in that set. The only mechanism in the equation for excluding a name is the intersection with $\overline{\text{VarKill}}$. Since VarKill does not change during the computation, the update to each LiveOut set increases monotonically and, thus, the algorithm must eventually halt.

### *Finding Uninitialized Variables*

Once the compiler has computed LiveOut sets for each node in the procedure's CFG, finding uses of variables that may be uninitialized is straightforward. Consider some variable $v$. If $v \in \text{LiveOut}(n_0)$, where $n_0$ is the entry node of the procedure's CFG, then, by the construction of $\text{LiveOut}(n_0)$, there exists a path from $n_0$ to a use of $v$ along which $v$ is not defined. Thus, $v \in \text{LiveOut}(n_0)$ implies that $v$ has a use that may receive an uninitialized value.

This approach will identify variables that have a potentially uninitialized use. The compiler should recognize that situation and report it to the programmer. However, this approach may yield false positives for several reasons.

- If $v$ is accessible through another name and initialized through that name, live analysis will not connect the initialization and the use. This situation can arise when a pointer is set to the address of a local variable, as in the code fragment shown in the margin.

```
. . .
p = &x;
*p = 0;
. . .
x = x + 1;
```

- If $v$ exists before the current procedure is invoked, then it may have been previously initialized in a manner invisible to the analyzer. This case can arise with static variables of the current scope or with variables declared outside the current scope.
- The equations for live analysis may discover a path from the procedure's entry to a use of $v$ along which $v$ is not defined. If that path is not feasible at runtime, then $v$ will appear in $\text{LiveOut}(n_0)$ even though no execution will ever use the uninitialized value. For example, the C program in the margin always initializes s before its use, yet s $\in$ $\text{LiveOut}(n_0)$.

```
main() {
  int i, n, s;
  scanf("%d", &n);
  i = 1;
  while (i<=n) {
    if (i==1)
      s = 0;
    s = s + i++;
  }
}
```

If the procedure contains a procedure call and $v$ is passed to that procedure in a way that allows modification, then the analyzer must account for possible side effects of the call. In the absence of specific information about the callee, the analyzer must assume that every variable that might be modified is modified and that any variable that might be used is used. Such assumptions are safe, in that they represent the worst-case behavior.

The marginal example with the while loop illustrates one of the fundamental limits of data-flow analysis: it assumes that all paths through the CFG are feasible at runtime. That assumption can be overly conservative, as in the example. The only path in the CFG leading to an uninitialized use leads from entry of main into the loop, bypasses the initialization of s, and hits the increment of s. That path can never occur, because i must have the value 1 on the loop's first iteration. The equations for LIVEOUT cannot discover that fact.

The assumption that all paths in the CFG are feasible greatly reduces the cost of the analysis. At the same time, the assumption produces a loss of precision in the computed sets. To discover that s is initialized on the first iteration of the for loop, the compiler would need to combine an analysis that tracked individual paths with some form of constant propagation and with live analysis. To solve the problem in general would require symbolic evaluation of parts of the code during the analysis, a much more expensive prospect.

### *Other Uses for Live Variables*

Compilers use liveness in many contexts other than finding uninitialized variables.

- Live-variable information plays a critical role in global register allocation (see Section 13.4). The register allocator need not keep values in registers unless they are live; when a value makes the transition from being live to being not live, the allocator can reuse its register for another purpose.
- Live-variable information is used to improve the SSA construction; a value does not need a $\phi$-function in any block where it is not live. Using live information in this way can significantly reduce the number of $\phi$-functions that the compiler must insert when building the SSA form of a program.
- The compiler can use live information to discover useless store operations. At an operation that stores $v$ to memory, if $v$ is not live then the store is useless. This simple technique works well for unambiguous scalar variables—that is, variables known by only one name.

In different contexts, liveness is calculated for different sets of names. We have discussed LIVEOUT with an implicit domain of variable names. In register allocation, the compiler will compute LIVEOUT sets over the domain of register names or over contiguous subranges of those register names.

## 8.6.2 **Global Code Placement**

Many processors have asymmetric branch costs; the cost of a fall-through branch is less than the cost of a taken branch. Each branch has two successor basic blocks; the compiler can choose which block lies on the fall-through path and which lies on the taken path. The global code placement optimization relies, implicitly, on the observation that some branches have lopsided behavior—that the fall-through path has a lower cost than the taken path.

Consider the CFG shown in the margin. $(B_0, B_2)$ executes 100 times more often than $(B_0, B_1)$. With asymmetric branch costs, the compiler should use the less expensive branch for $(B_0, B_2)$. If $(B_0, B_1)$ and $(B_0, B_2)$ had roughly equal execution frequencies, then block placement would have little impact for this code.

Two different layouts for this code are shown to the left. The "slow" layout uses the fall-through branch to implement $(B_0, B_1)$ and the taken branch for $(B_0, B_2)$. The "fast" layout reverses this decision. If the fall-through branch is faster than the taken branch, then the "fast" layout uses the faster branch 100 times more often.

The compiler can take advantage of asymmetric branch costs. If the compiler knows the expected relative execution frequencies of the branches in a procedure, it can select a code layout that improves runtime performance.

To perform global code placement, the compiler reorders the basic blocks of a procedure to optimize the use of fall-through branches. It follows two principles. First, the compiler should make the most likely execution paths use fall-through branches. Thus, whenever possible, block should be followed immediately by its most frequent successor. Second, the compiler should move code that executes infrequently to the end of the procedure. Taken together, these principles produce longer sequences that execute without a disruptive (e.g. taken) branch.

We expect two beneficial effects from this execution order. The code should execute a larger proportion of fall-through branches, which may directly improve performance. That pattern should lead to more efficient instruction cache use.

Code placement, like most optimizations at the global scope, has separate analysis and transformation phases. The analysis phase must gather estimates of each branch's relative execution frequency. The transformation uses those branch frequencies, expressed as weights on edges in the CFG, to build a model of the frequently executed paths. It then orders the basic blocks from that model.

**Fall-through branch**
A one-address branch is either *taken* or execution *falls through* to the next operation in sequence.

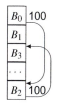 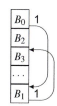

Slow Layout     Fast Layout

**GATHERING PROFILE DATA**

If the compiler understands the relative execution frequencies of the various parts of the program, it can use that information to improve the program's performance. Profile data can play an important role in optimizations such as global code placement (Section 8.6.2) or inline substitution (Section 8.7.1). Several approaches are used to gather profile data.

- *Instrumented executables* In this scheme, the compiler generates code to count specific events, such as procedure entries and exits or taken branches. At runtime, the data is written to an external file and processed offline by another tool.
- *Timer interrupts* Tools that use this approach interrupt program execution at frequent, regular intervals. The tool constructs a histogram of program counter locations where the interrupts occurred. Post-processing constructs a profile from the histogram.
- *Performance counters* Many processors offer some form of hardware counters to record hardware events, such as total cycles, cache misses, or taken branches. If counters are available, the runtime system can use them to construct highly accurate profile-like data.

These approaches produce somewhat different information and have distinct costs. An instrumented executable can measure almost any property of the execution; careful engineering can limit the overhead costs. A timer-interrupt system has lower overhead, but only pinpoints frequently executed statements (not the paths taken to reach them). Hardware counters are accurate and efficient, but depend in idiosyncratic ways on the specific processor architecture and implementation.

All of these approaches have proven successful at focusing optimization. Each of them requires cooperation between the compiler and the profiling tool on issues such as data formats, code layout, and methods for mapping runtime locations to program-based names.

### Obtaining Profile Data

For global code placement, the compiler needs estimates of the relative execution frequency of each edge in the CFG. It can obtain that information from a profiling run of the code: compile the entire program, run it under a profiling tool on representative data, and give the compiler access to the resulting profile data. It can obtain that information from a model of program execution; such models range from simple to elaborate, with a range of accuracies.

Example CFG

Specifically, the compiler needs execution counts for the CFG edges. The CFG in the margin illustrates why edge counts are superior to block counts for code placement. From the execution counts, shown as labels on the edges, we see that blocks $B_0$ and $B_5$ each execute ten times. The path $(B_0, B_1, B_3, B_5)$ executes more than any other path in this CFG fragment. The edge counts suggest, for example, that making the branch $(B_1, B_3)$ the fall-through case is better than making it the taken case. Relying on execution counts for blocks, however, the compiler would deduce that blocks $B_3$ and $B_4$ are of equal importance; it might well choose the less important edge, $(B_1, B_4)$, as the fall-through case. The code-placement algorithm uses profile data to rank the CFG edges by frequency of execution. Thus, accurate edge data has a direct effect on the quality of the results.

### Constructing Chains as Hot Paths in the CFG

To determine how it should lay out the code, the compiler constructs a set of CFG paths that include the most frequently executed edges—so-called *hot paths*. Each path is a chain of one or more blocks. Each path has a priority that will be used to construct the final code layout.

The compiler can use a greedy algorithm to find hot paths. Figure 8.16 shows one such algorithm. To begin, it creates a degenerate chain from each block that contains exactly that block. It sets the priority for each degenerate chain to a large number, such as the number of edges in the CFG or the largest available integer.

Next, the algorithm iterates over the edges in the CFG and builds up chains that model the hot paths. It takes the edges in order of execution frequency, with the most heavily used edges first. For an edge, $\langle x, y \rangle$, the algorithm merges the chain containing $x$ with the chain containing $y$ if and only if $x$ is the last node in its chain and $y$ is the first node in its chain. If either condition is not true, it leaves the chains that contain $x$ and $y$ alone.

The algorithm ignores self loops, $\langle x, x \rangle$, because they do not affect placement decisions.

```
E ← |edges|
for each block b
    make a degenerate chain, d, for b
    priority(d) ← E
P ← 0
for each CFG edge ⟨x,y⟩, x ≠ y, in decreasing frequency order
    if x is the tail of chain a and y is the head of chain b then
        t ← priority(a)
        append b onto a
        priority(a) ← min(t,priority(b),P++)
```

■ **FIGURE 8.16** Building Hot Paths.

If it merges the chains for $x$ and $y$, the algorithm must assign the new chain an appropriate priority. It computes that priority as the minimum of the priorities of the chains for $x$ and $y$. If both $x$ and $y$ are degenerate chains with their initial high priority, it sets the priority of the new chain to the ordinal number of merges that the algorithm has considered, denoted as P. This value places the chain behind chains constructed from higher-frequency edges and ahead of those constructed from lower-frequency edges.

The algorithm halts after it examines every edge. It produces a set of chains that model the hot paths in the CFG. Each node belongs to exactly one chain. Edges in chains execute more often than edges that cross from one chain to another. The priority values of each chain encode an order for relative layout of the chains that approximates the maximal number of executed forward branches.

**Forward branch**

A branch whose target has a higher address than its source is called a *forward branch*. In some architectures, forward branches are less disruptive than backward branches.

To illustrate the algorithm's operation, consider its behavior when applied to the example CFG from the previous section, repeated in the margin. The algorithm proceeds as follows:

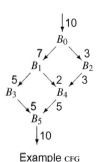

Example CFG

| Edge | Set of Chains | P |
|---|---|---|
| — | $(B_0)_E$, $(B_1)_E$, $(B_2)_E$, $(B_3)_E$, $(B_4)_E$, $(B_5)_E$ | 0 |
| $(B_0, B_1)$ | $(B_0, B_1)_0$, $(B_2)_E$, $(B_3)_E$, $(B_4)_E$, $(B_5)_E$ | 1 |
| $(B_3, B_5)$ | $(B_0, B_1)_0$, $(B_2)_E$, $(B_3, B_5)_1$, $(B_4)_E$ | 2 |
| $(B_4, B_5)$ | $(B_0, B_1)_0$, $(B_2)_E$, $(B_3, B_5)_1$, $(B_4)_E$ | 2 |
| $(B_1, B_3)$ | $(B_0, B_1, B_3, B_5)_0$, $(B_2)_E$, $(B_4)_E$ | 3 |
| $(B_0, B_2)$ | $(B_0, B, B_3, B_5)_0$, $(B_2)_E$, $(B_4)_E$ | 3 |
| $(B_2, B_4)$ | $(B_0, B_1, B_3, B_5)_0$, $(B_2, B_4)_3$ | 4 |
| $(B_1, B_4)$ | $(B_0, B_1, B_3, B_5)_0$, $(B_2, B_4)_3$ | 4 |

Priorities are shown as subscripts on the chain and $E$ is the number of edges in the CFG, as in Figure 8.16.

Breaking ties among equal-priority edges in a different way can produce a different set of chains. For example, if the algorithm considers $(B_4, B_5)$ before $(B_3, B_5)$, then it produces two chains: $(B_0, B_1, B_3)_0$ and $(B_2, B_4, B_5)_1$. Different chains may produce different code layouts. The layout algorithm still produces good results, even with a nonoptimal ordering for the equal-weight edges.

### Performing Code Layout

The set of chains produced by the algorithm in Figure 8.16 constitutes a partial order on the set of basic blocks. To produce an executable image of

```
t ← chain headed by the CFG entry node
WorkList ← {(t,priority(t))}
while (Worklist ≠ ∅)
    remove a chain c of lowest priority from WorkList
    for each block x in c in chain order
        place x at the end of the executable code
    for each block x in c
        for each edge ⟨x,y⟩ where y is unplaced
            t ← chain containing ⟨x,y⟩
            if (t,priority(t)) ∉ WorkList
                then WorkList ← WorkList ∪ { (t,priority(t))}
```

■ **FIGURE 8.17** Code-Layout Algorithm.

the code, the compiler must place all of the blocks into a fixed linear order. Figure 8.17 shows an algorithm that computes a linear layout from the set of chains. It encodes two simple heuristics: (1) place the blocks of a chain in order, so that fall-through branches implement the chain's edges, and (2) chose among alternatives using the priority number recorded for the chains.

The algorithm represents a chain with a pair $(c, p)$ where $c$ is the chain's name and $p$ is its priority. For the sake of efficiency, the test that avoids placing a chain on the worklist twice can be eliminated if we implement the worklist with a sparse set (see Appendix B.2.3). The following table shows the algorithm's behavior on the first set of chains produced for the example CFG:

| Step | WorkList | Code Layout |
|------|----------|-------------|
| — | $(B_0, B_1, B_3, B_5)_0$ | |
| 1 | $(B_2, B_4)_3$ | $B_0, B_1, B_3, B_5$ |
| 2 | $\emptyset$ | $B_0, B_1, B_3, B_5, B_2, B_4$ |

The first line shows the initial state. It puts the chain that contains $B_0$ on the worklist. The first iteration of the while loop places all the blocks in that chain. As it processes the edges leaving the placed blocks, it adds the other chain, $(B_2, B_4)$ on the worklist. The second iteration places those two blocks; it adds nothing to the worklist, so the algorithm halts.

We noted that a change in tie breaking could produce a change in the set of chains produced for the example. Taking the edge $(B_4, B_5)$ before $(B_3, B_5)$

produced the chains $(B_0, B_1, B_3)_0$ and $(B_2, B_4, B_5)_1$. Working from those chains, the code-layout algorithm behaves as follows:

| Step | WorkList | Code Layout |
|------|----------|-------------|
| — | $(B_0, B_1, B_3)_0$ | |
| 1 | $(B_2, B_4, B_5)_1$ | $B_0, B_1, B_3$ |
| 2 | | $B_0, B_1, B_3, B_2, B_4, B_5$ |

If we assume that the estimated execution frequences are correct, there is no reason to prefer one layout over the other.

### A Final Example

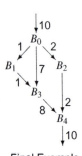

Final Example

Consider how the global code-placement algorithm treats the CFG shown in the margin. The chain-construction algorithm proceeds as follows:

| Edge | Set of Chains | P |
|------|---------------|---|
| — | $(B_0)_E$, $(B_1)_E$, $(B_2)_E$, $(B_3)_E$, $(B_4)_E$ | 0 |
| $(B_3, B_4)$ | $(B_0)_E$, $(B_1)_E$, $(B_2)_E$, $(B_3, B_4)_0$ | 1 |
| $(B_0, B_3)$ | $(B_0, B_3, B_4)_0$, $(B_1)_E$, $(B_2)_E$ | 2 |
| $(B_2, B_4)$ | $(B_0, B_3, B_4)_0$, $(B_1)_E$, $(B_2)_E$ | 2 |
| $(B_0, B_2)$ | $(B_0, B_3, B_4)_0$, $(B_1)_E$, $(B_2)_E$ | 2 |
| $(B_1, B_3)$ | $(B_0, B_3, B_4)_0$, $(B_1)_E$, $(B_2)_E$ | 2 |
| $(B_0, B_1)$ | $(B_0, B_3, B_4)_0$, $(B_1)_E$, $(B_2)_E$ | 2 |

On this graph, the algorithm halts with one multinode chain and two degenerate chains, both of which have their initial high priority.

The layout algorithm first places $(B_0, B_3, B_4)$. When it examines the outbound edges from the placed nodes, it adds both of the degenerate blocks to the worklist. The next two iterations remove the degenerate blocks, in arbitrary order, and place them. There is no reason to prefer one order over the other.

---

**SECTION REVIEW**

Optimizations that examine an entire procedure have opportunities for improvement that are not available at smaller scopes. Because the global, or procedure-wide, scope includes cyclic paths and backward branches, global optimizations usually need global analysis. As a consequence, these algorithms have an offline flavor; they consist of an analysis phase followed by a transformation phase.

This section highlighted two distinct kinds of analysis: global data-flow analysis and runtime collection of profile data. Data-flow analysis is a compile-time technique that accounts, mathematically, for the effects along all possible paths through the code. In contrast, profile data records what actually happened on a single run of the code, with a single set of input data. Data-flow analysis is conservative, in that it accounts for all possibilities. Runtime profiling is aggressive, in that it assumes that future runs will share runtime characteristics with the profiling run. Both can play an important role in optimization.

**Review Questions**

1. In some situations, the compiler needs to know that a variable is live along *all* paths that leave a block, rather than live along *some* path. Reformulate the equations for LiveOut so that they compute the set of names that are used before definition along every path from the end of the block to the CFG's exit node, $n_f$.

2. To collect accurate edge-count profiles, the compiler can instrument each edge in the profiled procedure's CFG. A clever implementation can instrument a subset of those edges and deduce the counts for the rest. Devise a scheme that derives accurate edge-count data without instrumenting each branch. On what principles does your scheme rely?

## 8.7 INTERPROCEDURAL OPTIMIZATION

As discussed in Chapter 6, procedure calls form boundaries in software systems. The division of a program into multiple procedures has both positive and negative impacts on the compiler's ability to generate efficient code. On the positive side, it limits the amount of code that the compiler considers at any one time. This effect keeps compile-time data structures small and limits the cost of various compile-time algorithms by limiting the problem sizes.

On the negative side, the division of the program into procedures limits the compiler's ability to understand what happens inside a call. For example, consider a call from `fee` to `fie` that passes a variable $x$ as a call-by-reference parameter. If the compiler knows that $x$ has the value 15 before the call, it cannot use that fact after the call, unless it knows that the call cannot change $x$. To use the value of $x$ after the call, the compiler must prove that the formal parameter corresponding to $x$ is not modified by `fie` or any procedure that it calls, directly or indirectly.

A second major source of inefficiency introduced by procedure calls arises from the fact that each call entails executing a precall and a postreturn sequence in the caller and a prolog and an epilog sequence in the callee. The operations implemented in these sequences take time. The transitions between these sequences require (potentially disruptive) jumps. These operations are all overhead needed in the general case to implement the abstractions of the source language. At any specific call, however, the compiler may be able to tailor the sequences or the callee to the local runtime environment and achieve better performance.

These effects, on compile-time knowledge and on runtime actions, can introduce inefficiencies that intraprocedural optimization cannot address. To reduce the inefficiencies introduced by separate procedures, the compiler may analyze and transform multiple procedures together, using interprocedural analysis and optimization. These techniques are equally important in Algol-like languages and in object-oriented languages.

In this section, we will examine two different interprocedural optimizations: inline substitution of procedure calls and procedure placement for improved code locality. Because whole-program optimization requires that the compiler have access to the code being analyzed and transformed, the decision to perform whole-program optimization has implications for compiler structure. Thus, the final subsection discusses the structural issues that arise in a system that includes interprocedural analysis and optimization.

### 8.7.1 Inline Substitution

As we saw in Chapters 6 and 7, the code that the compiler must generate to implement a procedure call involves a significant number of operations. The code must allocate an activation record, evaluate each actual parameter, preserve the caller's state, create the callee's environment, transfer control from caller to callee and back, and, if necessary, return values from callee to caller. In a sense, these runtime actions are part of the overhead of using a programming language; they maintain programming-language abstractions but are not strictly necessary to compute the results. Optimizing compilers try to reduce the cost of such overheads.

In some cases, the compiler can improve the efficiency of the final code by replacing the call site with a copy of the callee's body, appropriately tailored to the specific call site. This transformation, called *inline substitution*, allows the compiler to avoid most of the procedure linkage code and to tailor the new copy of the callee's body to the caller's context. Because the transformation moves code from one procedure to another and alters the program's call graph, inline substitution is considered an interprocedural transformation.

As with many optimizations, inline substitution has a natural partition into two subproblems: the actual transformation and a decision procedure that chooses call sites to inline. The transformation itself is relatively simple. The decision procedure is more complex and has a direct impact on performance.

---

The term "whole program" clearly implies analyzing all the code. We prefer the term "interprocedural" when we talk about analyzing some, but not all, of the procedures.

**Inline substitution**

a transformation that replaces a call site with a copy of the callee's body, rewritten to reflect parameter bindings

### The Transformation

To perform inline substitution, the compiler rewrites a call site with the body of the callee, while making appropriate modifications to model the effects of parameter binding. Figure 8.18 shows two procedures, fee and fie, both of which call a third procedure, foe. Figure 8.19 depicts the control flow after inlining the call from fie to foe. The compiler has created a copy of foe and moved it inside fie, connected fie's precall sequence directly to the prolog of its internal copy of foe and connected the epilog to the postcall sequence in a similar fashion. Some of the resulting blocks can be merged, enabling improvement with subsequent optimization.

Of course, the compiler must use an IR that can represent the inlined procedure. Some source-language constructs can create arbitrary and unusual control-flow constructs in the resulting code. For example, a callee with multiple premature returns may generate a complex control-flow graph. Similarly, FORTRAN's *alternate return* construct allows the caller to pass labels into the callee; the callee can then cause control to return to any of those labels. In either case, the resulting control-flow graph may be hard to represent in a near-source AST.

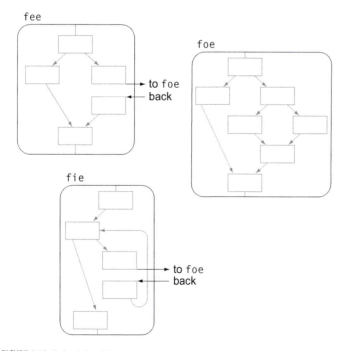

■ **FIGURE 8.18** Before Inline Substitution.

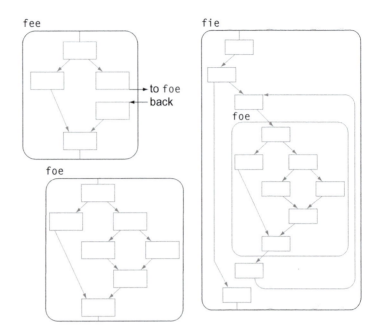

■ **FIGURE 8.19** After Inline Substitution.

In the implementation, the compiler writer should pay attention to the proliferation of local variables. A simple implementation would create one new local variable in the caller for each local variable in the callee. If the compiler inlines several procedures, or several call sites to the same callee, the local name space can grow quite large. While growth in the name space is not a correctness issue, it can increase the cost of compiling the transformed code and, in some cases, it can hurt performance in the final code. Attention to this detail can easily avoid the problem by reusing names across multiple inlined callees.

### The Decision Procedure

Choosing which call sites to inline is a complex task. Inlining a given call site can improve performance; unfortunately, it can also degrade performance. To make intelligent choices, the compiler must consider a broad range of characteristics of the caller, the callee, and the call site. The compiler must also understand its own strengths and weaknesses.

The primary sources of improvement from inlining are direct elimination of operations and improved effectiveness of other optimizations. The former effect can occur when parts of the linkage sequence can be eliminated;

for example, register save and restore code might be eliminated in favor of allowing the register allocator make those decisions. Knowledge from the caller may prove other code inside the callee dead or useless as well. The latter effect arises from having more contextual information in global optimization.

The primary source of degradation from inline substitution is decreased effectiveness of code optimization on the resulting code. Inlining the callee can increase code size and the name space size. It can increase demand for registers in the neighborhood of the original call site. Eliminating the register save and restore code changes the problem seen by the register allocator. In practice, any of these can lead to a decrease in optimization effectiveness.

Changes in architecture, such as larger register sets, can increase the cost of a procedure call. That change can, in turn, make inlining more attractive.

At each call site, the compiler must decide whether or not to inline the call. To complicate matters, a decision made at one call site affects the decision at other call sites. For example, if *a* calls *b* which calls *c*, choosing to inline *c* into *b* changes both the characteristics of the procedure that might be inlined into *a* and the call graph of the underlying program. Furthermore, inlining has effects, such as code size growth, that must be viewed across the whole program; the compiler writer may want to limit the overall growth in code size.

Decision procedures for inline substitution examine a variety of criteria at each call site. These include:

- *Callee size* If the callee is smaller than the procedure linkage code (pre-call, post-return, prolog, and epilog), then inlining the callee should reduce code size and execute fewer operations. This situation arises surprisingly often.
- *Caller size* The compiler may limit the overall size of any procedure to mitigate increases in compile time and decreases in optimization effectiveness.
- *Dynamic call count* An improvement at a frequently executed call site provides greater benefit than the same improvement at an infrequently executed call site. In practice, compilers use either profile data or simple estimates, such as 10 times the loop nesting depth.
- *Constant-valued actual parameters* The use of actual parameters that have known-constant values at a call site creates the potential for improvement as those constants are folded into the body of the callee.
- *Static call count* Compilers often track the number of distinct sites that call a procedure. Any procedure called from just one call site can be

```
Inline any call site that matches one of the following:
(1)  The callee uses more than t₀ percent of execution time, and
     (a) the callee contains no calls, or
     (b) the static call count is one, or
     (c) the call site has more than t₁ constant-valued parameters.
(2)  The call site represents more than t₂ percent of all calls, and
     (a) the callee is smaller than t₃, or
     (b)  inlining the call will produce a procedure smaller than t₄
```

■ **FIGURE 8.20** A Typical Decision Heuristic for Inline Substitution.

inlined without any code space growth. The compiler should update this metric as it inlines, to detect procedures that it reduces to one call site.

■ *Parameter count* The number of parameters can serve as a proxy for the cost of the procedure linkage, as the compiler must generate code to evaluate and store each actual parameter.

■ *Calls in the procedure* Tracking the number of calls in a procedure provides an easy way to detect leaves in the call graph—they contain no calls. Leaf procedures are often good candidates for inlining.

■ *Loop nesting depth* Call sites in loops execute more frequently than call sites outside loops. They also disrupt the compiler's ability to schedule the loop as a single unit (see Section 12.4).

■ *Fraction of execution time* Computing the fraction of execution time spent in each procedure from profile data can prevent the compiler from inlining routines that cannot have a significant impact on performance.

In practice, compilers precompute some or all of these metrics and then apply a heuristic or set of heuristics to determine which call sites to inline. Figure 8.20 shows a typical heuristic. It relies on a series of threshold parameters, named $t_0$ through $t_4$. The specific values chosen for the parameters will govern much of the heuristic's behavior; for example, $t_3$ should undoubtedly have a value greater than the size of the standard precall and postreturn sequences. The best settings for these parameters is undoubtedly program specific.

## 8.7.2 Procedure Placement

The global code placement technique from Section 8.6.2 rearranged blocks within a single procedure. An analogous problem exists on the interprocedural scale: rearranging procedures within an executable image.

*Given the call graph for a program, annotated with either measured or estimated execution frequencies for each call site, rearrange the procedures to reduce virtual-memory working-set sizes and to limit the potential for call-induced conflicts in the instruction cache.*

The principle is simple. If procedure $p$ calls $q$, we would like $p$ and $q$ to occupy adjacent locations in memory.

To solve this problem, we can treat the call graph as a set of constraints on the relative placement of procedures in the executable code. Each call-graph edge, $(p,q)$, specifies an adjacency that should occur in the executable code. Unfortunately, the compiler cannot satisfy all of those adjacencies. For example, if $p$ calls $q$, $r$, and $s$, the compiler cannot place all three of them next to $p$. Thus, compilers that perform procedure placement tend to use a greedy approximate technique to find a good placement, rather than trying to compute an optimal placement.

Recall that a program's call graph has a node for each procedure and an edge $(x,y)$ for each call from $x$ to $y$.

Procedure placement differs subtly from the global code placement problem discussed in Section 8.6.2. That algorithm improves the code by ensuring that hot paths can be implemented with fall-through branches. Thus, the chain-construction algorithm in Figure 8.16 ignores any CFG edge unless it runs from the tail of one chain to the head of another. In contrast, as the procedure placement algorithm builds chains of procedures, it can use edges that run between procedures that lie in the middles of their chains because its goal is simply to place procedures near each other—to reduce working set sizes and to reduce interference in the instruction cache. If $p$ calls $q$ and the distance from $p$ to $q$ is less than the size of the instruction cache, placement succeeds. Thus, in some sense, the procedure placement algorithm has more freedom than the block-layout algorithm.

Procedure placement consists of two phases: analysis and transformation. The analysis operates on the program's call graph. It repeatedly selects two nodes in the call graph and combines them. The order of combination is driven by execution frequency data, either measured or estimated. The order of combination determines the final layout. The layout phase is straightforward; it simply rearranges the code for the procedures into the order chosen by the analysis phase.

Figure 8.21 shows a greedy algorithm for the analysis phase of procedure placement. It operates over the program's call graph and iteratively constructs a placement by considering edges in order of their estimated execution frequency. As a first step, it builds the call graph, assigns each edge a weight that corresponds to its estimated execution frequency, and combines all the edges between two nodes into a single edge. As the final part of its

```
// Initialization work
build the call multi-graph G
initialize Q as a priority queue            // Order Q highest to lowest

for each edge (x,y) ∈ G                      // Add weights to the edges
   if (x = y)                                // Self loop is irrelevant
      then delete (x,y) from G
      else weight((x,y)) ← estimated execution frequency for (x,y)

for each node x ∈ G
   list(x) ← {x}                             // Initialize placement lists

   if multiple edges exist from x to y
      then combine them and their weights

   for each edge (x,z) ∈ G                   // Put each edge into Q
      Enqueue(Q,(x,z),weight((x,z)))


// Iterative reduction of the graph
while Q is not empty
   (x,y) ← Dequeue(Q)                        // Take highest priority edge

   for each edge (y,z) ∈ G                   // Move source from y to x
      ReSource((y,z),x)

   for each edge (z,y) ∈ G                   // Move target from y to x
      ReTarget((z,y),x)

   append list(y) to list(x)                 // Update the placement list

   delete y and its edges from G             // Clean up G
```

■ **FIGURE 8.21** Procedure Placement Algorithm.

initialization work, it builds a priority queue of the call-graph edges, ordered by their weights.

The second half of the algorithm iteratively builds up an order for procedure placement. The algorithm associates with each node in the graph an ordered list of procedures. These lists specify a linear order among the named procedures. When the algorithm halts, the lists will specify a total order on the procedures that can be used to place them in the executable code.

The algorithm uses the call-graph edge weights to guide the process. It repeatedly selects the highest-weight edge, say $(x,y)$, from the priority queue and combines its source $x$ and its sink $y$. Next, it must update the call graph to reflect the change.

1. For each edge $(y, z)$, it calls *ReSource* to replace $(y, z)$ with $(x, z)$ and to update the priority queue. If $(x, z)$ already exists, *ReSource* combines them.

2. For each edge $(z, y)$, it calls `ReTarget` to replace $(z, y)$ with $(z, x)$ and to update the priority queue. If $(z, x)$ already exists, `ReTarget` combines them.

To affect the placement of $y$ after $x$, the algorithm appends `list(y)` to `list(x)`. Finally, it deletes $y$ and its edges from the call graph.

The algorithm halts when the priority queue is empty. The final graph will have one node for each of the connected components of the original call graph. If all nodes were reachable from the node that represents the program's entry, the final graph will consist of a single node. If some procedures were not reachable, either because no path exists in the program that calls them or because those paths are obscured by ambiguous calls, then the final graph will consist of multiple nodes. Either way, the compiler and linker can use the lists associated with nodes in the final graph to specify the relative placement of procedures.

### Example

To see how the procedure placement algorithm works, consider the example call graph shown in panel 0 of Figure 8.22. The edge from $P_5$ to itself is shown in gray because it only affects the algorithm by changing the execution frequencies. A self loop cannot affect placement since its source and sink are identical.

Panel 0 shows the state of the algorithm immediately before the iterative reduction begins. Each node has the trivial list that contains its own name. The priority queue has every edge, except the self loop, ranked by execution frequency.

Panel 1 shows the state of the algorithm after the first iteration of the while loop. The algorithm collapsed $P_6$ into $P_5$, and updated both the list for $P_5$ and the priority queue.

In panel 2, the algorithm has collapsed $P_4$ into $P_5$. It retargeted $(P_1, P_4)$ onto $P_5$ and changed the corresponding edge name in the priority queue. In addition, it removed $P_4$ from the graph and updated the list for $P_5$.

The other iterations proceed in a similar fashion. Panel 4 shows a situation where it combined edges. When it collapsed $P_5$ into $P_1$, it retargeted $(P_0, P_5)$ onto $P_1$. Since $(P_0, P_1)$ already existed, it simply combined their weights and updated the priority queue by deleting $(P_0, P_5)$ and changing the weight on $(P_0, P_1)$.

At the end of the iterations, the graph has been collapsed to a single node, $P_0$. While this example constructed a layout that begins with the entry node, that happened because of the edge weights rather than by algorithmic design.

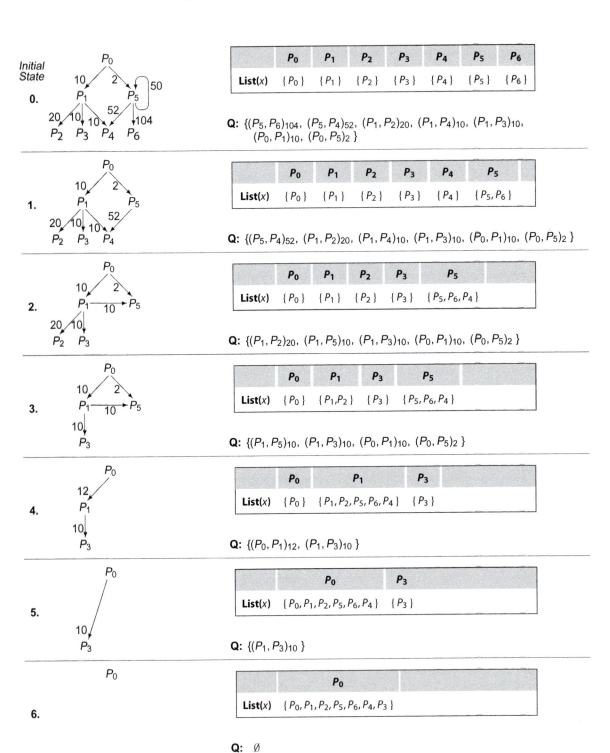

### 8.7.3 **Compiler Organization for Interprocedural Optimization**

Building a compiler that performs analysis and optimization across two or more procedures fundamentally changes the relationship between the compiler and the code that it produces. Traditional compilers have compilation units of a single procedure, a single class, or a single file of code; the resulting code depends solely on the contents of that compilation unit. Once the compiler uses knowledge about one procedure to optimize another, the correctness of the resulting code depends on the state of both procedures.

Consider the impact of inline substitution on the validity of the optimized code. Assume that the compiler inlines `fie` into `fee`. Any subsequent editing change to `fie` will necessitate recompilation of `fee`—a dependence that results from an optimization decision rather than from any relationship exposed in the source code.

If the compiler collects and uses interprocedural information, similar problems can arise. For example, `fee` may call `fie`, which calls `foe`; assume that the compiler relies on the fact that the call to `fie` does not change the known constant value of the global variable $x$. If the programmer subsequently edits `foe` so that it modifies $x$, that change can invalidate the prior compilation of both `fee` and `fie`, by changing the facts upon which optimization relies. Thus, a change to `foe` can necessitate a recompilation of other procedures in the program.

To address this fundamental issue, and to provide the compiler with access to all the source code that it needs, several different structures have been proposed for compilers that perform whole-program or interprocedural optimization: enlarging the compilation units, embedding the compiler in an integrated development environment, and performing the optimization at link time.

- *Enlarging Compilation Units*  The simplest solution to the practical problems introduced by interprocedural optimization is to enlarge the compilation units. If the compiler only considers optimization and analysis within a compilation unit, and those units are consistently applied, then it can sidestep the problems. It can only analyze and optimize code that is compiled together; thus, it cannot introduce dependences between compilation units and it should not require access to either source code or facts about other units. The IBM PL/I optimizing compiler took this approach; code quality improved as related procedures were grouped together in the same file.

  Of course, this approach limits the opportunities for interprocedural optimization. It also encourages the programmer to create larger

**Compilation unit**
The portion of a program presented to the compiler is often called a *compilation unit*.

compilation units and to group together procedures that call one another. Both of these may introduce practical problems in a system with multiple programmers. Still, as a practical matter, this organization is attractive because it least disturbs our model of the compiler's behavior.

■ *Integrated Development Environments* If the design embeds the compiler inside an integrated development environment (IDE), the compiler can access code as needed through the IDE. The IDE can notify the compiler when source code changes, so that the compiler can determine if recompilation is needed. This model shifts ownership of both the source code and the compiled code from the developer to the IDE. Collaboration between the IDE and the compiler then ensures that appropriate actions are taken to guarantee consistent and correct optimization.

■ *Link-time Optimization* The compiler writer can shift interprocedural optimization into the linker, where it will have access to all of the *statically* linked code. To obtain the benefits of interprocedural optimization, the linker may also need to perform subsequent global optimization. Since the results of link-time optimization are only recorded in the executable, and that executable is discarded on the next compilation, this strategy sidesteps the recompilation problem. It almost certainly performs more analysis and optimization that the other approaches, but it offers both simplicity and obvious correctness.

Many modern systems make use of runtime, or *dynamic*, linking for shared libraries. Runtime linking limits the opportunities for link-time optimization.

---

**SECTION REVIEW**

Analysis and optimization across procedure boundaries can reveal new opportunities for code improvement. Examples include tailoring the procedure linkage (precall, prolog, epilog, and postcall sequences) to a specific call site through exposing constant values or redundant values across a call. Many techniques have been proposed to recognize and exploit these opportunities; inline substitution is one of the best known and broadly effective of these techniques.

A compiler that applies interprocedural analysis and optimization must take care to ensure that the executables it builds are based on a consistent view of the entire program. Using facts from one procedure to modify the code in another can introduce subtle dependences between the code in distant procedures, dependences that the compiler must recognize and respect. Several strategies have been proposed to mitigate these effects; perhaps the simplest is to perform interprocedural transformations at link time.

**Review Questions**

1. Suppose procedure *a* invokes *b* and *c*. If the compiler inlines the call to *b*, what code space and data space savings might arise? If it inlines *c* as well, are further data-space savings possible?

2. In procedure placement, what happens to a procedure whose incoming edges all have estimated execution frequencies of zero? Where should the algorithm place such a procedure? Does the treatment of such a procedure affect execution time performance? Can the compiler eliminate them as useless?

## 8.8 SUMMARY AND PERSPECTIVE

The optimizer in a modern compiler contains a collection of techniques that try to improve the performance of the compiled code. While most optimizations try to improve runtime speed, optimizations can also target other measures, such as code size or energy consumption. This chapter has shown a variety of techniques that operate over scopes that range from single basic blocks through entire programs.

Optimizations improve performance by tailoring general translation schemes to the specific details of the code at hand. The transformations in an optimizer try to remove the overhead introduced in support of source-language abstractions, including data structures, control structures, and error checking. They try to recognize special cases that have efficient implementations and rewrite the code to realize those savings. They try to match the resource needs of the program against the actual resources available on the target processor, including functional units, the capacity and bandwidth of each level in the memory hierarchy (registers, cache, translation lookaside buffers, and memory), and instruction-level parallelism.

Before the optimizer can apply a transformation, it must determine that the proposed rewrite of the code is safe—that it preserves the code's original meaning. Typically, this requires that the optimizer analyze the code. In this chapter, we saw a number of approaches to proving safety, ranging from the bottom-up construction of the value table in local value numbering through computing LiveOut sets to detect uninitialized variables.

Once the optimizer has determined that it can safely apply a transformation, it must decide whether or not the rewrite will improve the code. Some techniques, such a local value numbering, simply assume that the rewrites they use are profitable. Other techniques, such as inline substitution, require complicated decision procedures to determine when a transformation might improve the code.

This chapter provided a basic introduction to the field of compiler-based code optimization. It introduced many of the terms and issues that arise in optimization. It does not include an "Advanced Topics" section; instead, the interested reader will find additional material on static analysis in support of optimization in Chapter 9 and on optimizing transformations in Chapter 10.

## ■ CHAPTER NOTES

The field of code optimization has a long and detailed literature. For a deeper treatment, the reader should consider some of the specialized books on the subject [20, 268, 270]. It would be intellectually pleasing if code optimization had developed in a logical and disciplined way, beginning with local techniques, extending them first to regions, then entire procedures, and finally entire programs. As it happened, however, development has occurred in a more haphazard fashion. For example, the original Fortran compiler [27] performed both local and global optimization—the former on expression trees and the latter for register allocation. Interest in both regional techniques, such as loop optimization [252], and whole-program techniques, such as inline substitution, crops up early in the literature, as well [16].

Local value numbering, with its extensions for algebraic simplifications and constant folding, is usually credited to Balke in the late 1960s [16, 87], although it is clear that Ershov achieved similar effects in a much earlier system [139]. Similarly, Floyd mentioned the potential for both local redundancy elimination and application of commutativity [150]. The extension to EBBS in superlocal value numbering is natural and has, undoubtedly, been invented and reinvented in many compilers. Our treatment derives from Simpson [53].

The tree-height balancing algorithm is due to Hunt [200]; it uses a rank function inspired by Huffman codes, but is easily adapted to other metrics. The classic algorithm for balancing instruction trees is due to Baer and Bovet [29]. The entire issue of finding and exploiting instruction-level parallelism is intimately related to instruction scheduling (see Chapter 12).

Loop unrolling is the simplest of loop nest optimizations. It has a long history in the literature [16]. The use of unrolling to eliminate register-to-register copy operations as in review question 2 for Section 8.5 on page 444 is due to Kennedy [214]. Unrolling can have subtle and surprising effects [108]. Selection of unroll factors has also been studied [114, 325].

The ideas that underlie live analysis have been around as long as compilers have been automatically allocating storage locations for values [242]. Beatty first defined live analysis in an internal IBM technical report [15]. Lowry and Medlock discuss "busy" variables [p. 16, 252] and the use of this information in both the elimination of dead code and in reasoning about interference (see Chapter 13). The analysis was formulated as a global data-flow analysis problem by 1971 [13, 213]. Live analysis will appear again in the construction of SSA form in Chapter 9 and in the discussion of register allocation in Chapter 13.

The code-placement algorithms, at both the global and whole-program scopes, are taken from Pettis and Hansen [284]. Subsequent work on this problem has focused on collecting better profile data and improving the placements [161, 183]. Later work includes work on branch alignment [66, 357] and code layout [78, 93, 161].

Inline substitution has been discussed in the literature for decades [16]. While the transformation is straightforward, its profitability has been the subject of many studies [31, 99, 119, 301].

Interprocedural analysis and optimization has been discussed in the literature for decades [18, 34, 322]. Inline substitution has a long history in the literature [16]. All of the scenarios mentioned in Section 8.7.3 have been explored in real systems [104, 322, 341]. Recompilation analysis is treated in depth by Burke and Torczon [64, 335]. See the notes for Chapter 9 for more references on interprocedural analysis.

## ■ EXERCISES

**1.** Apply the algorithm from Figure 8.4 to each of the following blocks:

Section 8.4

$$t_1 \leftarrow a + b$$
$$t_2 \leftarrow t_1 + c$$
$$t_3 \leftarrow t_2 + d$$
$$t_4 \leftarrow b + a$$
$$t_5 \leftarrow t_3 + e$$
$$t_6 \leftarrow t_4 + f$$
$$t_7 \leftarrow a + b$$
$$t_8 \leftarrow t_4 - t_7$$
$$t_9 \leftarrow t_8 \star t_6$$

Block $b_0$

$$t_1 \leftarrow a \times b$$
$$t_2 \leftarrow t_1 \times 2$$
$$t_3 \leftarrow t_2 \times c$$
$$t_4 \leftarrow 7 + t_3$$
$$t_5 \leftarrow t_4 + d$$
$$t_6 \leftarrow t_5 + 3$$
$$t_7 \leftarrow t_4 + e$$
$$t_8 \leftarrow t_6 + f$$
$$t_9 \leftarrow t_1 + 6$$

Block $b_1$

2. Consider a basic block, such as $b_0$ or $b_1$ in question Section 8.8 above. It has $n$ operations, numbered 0 to $n-1$.

   a. For a name $x$, USES($x$) contains the index in $b$ of each operation that uses $x$ as an operand. Write an algorithm to compute the USES set for every name mentioned in block $b$. If $x \in$ LIVEOUT($b$), then add two dummy entries ($> n$) to USES($x$).

   b. Apply your algorithm to blocks $b_0$ and $b_1$ above.

   c. For a reference to $x$ in operation $i$ of block $b$, DEF($x,i$) is the index in $b$ where the value of $x$ visible at operation $i$ was defined. Write an algorithm to compute DEF($x,i$) for each reference $x$ in $b$. If $x$ is upward exposed at $i$, then DEF($x,i$) should be $-1$.

   d. Apply your algorithm to blocks $b_0$ and $b_1$ above.

3. Apply the tree-height balancing algorithm from Figures 8.7 and 8.8 to the two blocks in problem 1. Use the information computed in problem 2b above. In addition, assume that LIVEOUT($b_0$) is $\{t_3, t_9\}$, that LIVEOUT($b_1$) is $\{t_7, t_8, t_9\}$, and that the names a through f are upward-exposed in the blocks.

Section 8.5

4. Consider the following control-flow graph:

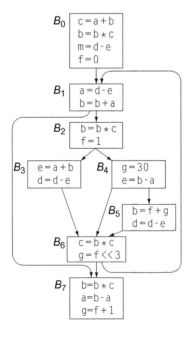

a. Find the extended basic blocks and list their distinct paths.
b. Apply local value numbering to each block.
c. Apply superlocal value numbering to the EBBS and note any improvements that it finds beyond those found by local value numbering.

5. Consider the following simple five-point stencil computation:

```
do 20 i = 2, n-1, 1
    t1 = A(i,j-1)
    t2 = A(i,j)
    do 10 j = 2, m-1, 1
        t3 = A(i,j+1)
        A(i,j) = 0.2 × (t1 + t2 + t3 + A(i-1,j) + A(i+1,j))
        t1 = t2
        t2 = t3
10      continue
20 continue
```

Each iteration of the loop executes two copy operations.
a. Loop unrolling can eliminate the copy operations. What unroll factor is needed to eliminate all copy operations in this loop?
b. In general, if a loop contains multiple cycles of copy operations, how can you compute the unroll factor needed to eliminate all of the copy operations?

6. At some point $p$, LIVE($p$) is the set of names that are *live* at $p$. LIVEOUT($b$) is just the LIVE set at the end of block $b$.
a. Develop an algorithm that takes as input a block $b$ and its LIVEOUT set and produces as output the LIVE set for each operation in the block.
b. Apply your algorithm to blocks $b_0$ and $b_1$ in problem 1, using LIVEOUT($b_0$) = $\{t_3, t_9\}$ and LIVEOUT($b_1$) = $\{t_7, t_8, t_9\}$.

Section 8.6

7. Figure 8.16 shows an algorithm for constructing hot paths in the CFG.
a. Devise an alternate hot-path construction that pays attention to ties among equal-weight edges.
b. Construct two examples where your algorithm leads to a code layout that improves on the layout produced by the book's algorithm. Use the code-layout algorithm from Figure 8.17 with the chains constructed by your algorithm and those built by the book's algorithm.

**Section 8.7**

**8.** Consider the following code fragment. It shows a procedure `fee` and two call sites that invoke `fee`.

```
static int A[1000,1000], B[1000];

    . . .

x = A[i,j] + y;
call fee(i,j,1000);

    . . .

call fee(1,1,0);

    . . .

fee(int row; int col; int ub) {
    int i, sum;

    sum = A[row,col];

    for (i=0; i<ub; i++) {
        sum = sum + B[i];
    }
}
```

**a.** What optimization benefits would you expect from inlining `fee` at each of the call sites? Estimate the fraction of `fee`'s code that would remain after inlining and subsequent optimization.

**b.** Based on your experience in part a, sketch a high-level algorithm for estimating the benefits of inlining a specific call site. Your technique should consider both the call site and the callee.

**9.** In Problem 8, features of the call site and its context determined the extent to which the optimizer could improve the inlined code. Sketch, at a high level, a procedure for estimating the improvements that might accrue from inlining a specific call site. (With such an estimator, the compiler could inline the call sites with the highest estimated profit, stopping when it reached some threshold on procedure size or total program size.)

**10.** When the procedure placement algorithm, shown in Figure 8.21, considers an edge $\langle p,q \rangle$ it always places $p$ before $q$.

**a.** Formulate a modification of the algorithm that would consider placing the sink of an edge before its source.

**b.** Construct an example where this approach places two procedures closer together than the original algorithm. Assume that all procedures are of uniform size.

# Data-Flow Analysis

**CHAPTER OVERVIEW**

Compilers analyze the IR form of the program being compiled to identify opportunities where the code can be improved and to prove the safety and profitability of transformations that might improve the code. Data-flow analysis is the classic technique for compile-time program analysis. It allows the compiler to reason about the runtime flow of values in the program.

This chapter explores iterative data-flow analysis, which uses a simple fixed-point algorithm. From the basics of data-flow analysis, it builds up the construction of static single-assignment (SSA) form, illustrates the use of SSA form, and introduces interprocedural analysis.

**Keywords:** Data-flow Analysis, SSA Form, Dominance, Constant Propagation

## 9.1 INTRODUCTION

As we saw in Chapter 8, optimization is the process of analyzing a program and transforming it in ways that improve its runtime behavior. Before the compiler can improve the code, it must locate points in the program where changing the code is likely to improve it, *and* the compiler must prove that changing the code at those points is safe. Both of these tasks require a deeper understanding of the code than the compiler's front end typically derives. To gather the information needed to locate opportunities for optimization and to justify those optimizations, compilers use some form of static analysis.

In general, static analysis involves compile-time reasoning about the runtime flow of values. This chapter explores techniques that compilers use to analyze programs in support of optimization. It presents data-flow analysis at a deeper level than provided in Chapter 8. Next, Section 9.3 presents algorithms for the construction and destruction of static single-assignment form. Section 9.4 discusses issues in whole-program analysis. The advanced topics section presents further material on computing dominance and a discussion of graph reducibility.

### Conceptual Roadmap

Compilers use static analysis to determine where optimizing transformations can be safely and profitably applied. In Chapter 8, we saw that optimizations operate on different scopes, from local to interprocedural. In general, a transformation needs analytical information that covers at least as large a scope as the transformation; that is, a local optimization needs at least local information, while a whole-procedure, or global, optimization needs global information.

Static analysis generally begins with control-flow analysis—analyzing the IR form of the code to understand the flow of control between operations. The result of control-flow analysis is a control-flow graph. Next, compilers analyze the details of how values flow through the code. They use the resulting information to find opportunities for improvement and to prove the safety of transformations. The optimization community developed global data-flow analysis to answer these questions.

Static single assignment form is an intermediate representation that unifies the results of control-flow analysis and data-flow analysis in a single sparse data structure. It has proven useful in both analysis and transformation and has become a standard representation used in both research and production compilers.

### Overview

Chapter 8 introduced the subject of analysis and transformation of programs by examining local methods, regional methods, global methods, and interprocedural methods. Value numbering is algorithmically simple, even though it achieves complex effects; it finds redundant expressions, simplifies code based on algebraic identities and zero, and propagates known constant values. In contrast, finding an uninitialized variable is conceptually simple but requires that the compiler analyze the entire procedure to track definitions and uses.

**Join point**

In a CFG, a *join point* is a node that has multiple predecessors.

The difference between these two problems lies in the kinds of control flows that each method must understand. Local and superlocal value numbering only deal with subsets of the CFG that form trees. To identify an uninitialized variable, the compiler must reason about the entire CFG, including cycles and *join points*, both of which complicate the analysis. In general, methods that restrict themselves to control-flow graphs that can be expressed as trees are amenable to online solutions, while those that must deal with cycles in the CFG require offline solutions—the entire analysis must complete before rewriting can begin.

Static, or compile-time, analysis is a collection of techniques that compilers use to prove the safety and profitability of a potential transformation. Static analysis over single blocks or trees of blocks is typically straightforward. This chapter focuses on global analysis, where the CFG can contain both cycles and join points. It will mention several problems in interprocedural analysis; these problems operate over the program's call graph or some related graph. To perform interprocedural analysis, the compiler must have access to information about other procedures in the program.

In simple cases, static analysis can produce precise results—the compiler can know exactly what will happen when the code executes. If the compiler can derive precise information, it might replace the runtime evaluation of an expression or function with an immediate load of the result. On the other hand, if the code reads values from any external source, involves even modest amounts of control flow, or encounters any ambiguous memory references (from pointers, array references, or call-by-reference parameters), then static analysis becomes much harder and the results of the analysis are less precise.

This chapter begins by examining classic problems in data-flow analysis. We focus on an iterative algorithm for solving these problems because it is simple, robust, and easy to understand. Section 9.3 presents an algorithm for constructing a static single-assignment form for a procedure. The construction relies heavily on results from data-flow analysis. The "Advanced Topics" section explores the notion of flow-graph reducibility, presents a faster approach to calculating dominators, and provides an introduction to interprocedural data-flow analysis.

## 9.2 ITERATIVE DATA-FLOW ANALYSIS

Compilers use data-flow analysis, a collection of techniques for compile-time reasoning about the runtime flow of values, to locate opportunities for optimization and to prove the safety of specific transformations. As we saw with live analysis in Section 8.6.1, problems in data-flow analysis take the form of a set of simultaneous equations defined over sets associated with the nodes and edges of a graph that represents the code being analyzed. Live analysis is formulated as a global data-flow problem that operates on the control-flow graph (CFG) of a procedure.

In this section, we will explore the properties of global data-flow problems and their solutions in more depth than was possible in Chapter 8. We will focus on one specific solution technique: an iterative fixed-point algorithm. It has the twin advantages of simplicity and robustness. As an initial example, we will examine the computation of dominance information. When we need a more complex example, we will return to consideration of LiveOut sets.

### 9.2.1 **Dominance**

**Dominance**

In a flow graph with entry node $b_0$, node $b_i$ *dominates* node $b_j$, written $b_i \gg b_j$, if and only if $b_i$ lies on every path from $b_0$ to $b_j$. By definition, $b_i \gg b_i$.

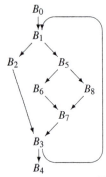

Many optimization techniques must reason about the structural properties of the underlying code and its control-flow graph. A key tool that compilers use to reason about the shape and structure of the CFG is the notion of *dominators*. As we will see, dominators play a key role in the construction of static single-assignment form. While many algorithms have been proposed to compute dominance information, an extremely simple data-flow problem will suffice to annotate each node $b_i$ in the CFG, which represents a basic block, with a set $\text{Dom}(b_i)$ that contains the names of all nodes that dominate $b_i$.

To make this notion of dominance concrete, consider the node $B_6$ in the CFG shown in the margin. (Note that this CFG differs slightly from the example in Chapter 8.) Nodes $B_0$, $B_1$, $B_5$, and $B_6$ all lie on every path from $B_0$ to $B_6$, so $\text{Dom}(B_6)$ is $\{B_0, B_1, B_5, B_6\}$. The full set of Dom sets for the CFG are as follows:

| | $B_0$ | $B_1$ | $B_2$ | $B_3$ | $B_4$ | $B_5$ | $B_6$ | $B_7$ | $B_8$ |
|---|---|---|---|---|---|---|---|---|---|
| **Dom($n$)** | {0} | {0,1} | {0,1,2} | {0,1,3} | {0,1,3,4} | {0,1,5} | {0,1,5,6} | {0,1,5,7} | {0,1,5,8} |

To compute these sets, the compiler can solve the following data-flow problem:

$$\text{Dom}(n) = \{n\} \cup \left( \bigcap_{m \in preds(n)} \text{Dom}(m) \right)$$

with the initial conditions that $\text{Dom}(n_0) = \{n_0\}$, and $\forall n \neq n_0$, $\text{Dom}(n) = N$, where $N$ is the set of all nodes in the CFG. These equations concisely capture the notion of dominance. Given an arbitrary flow graph—that is, a directed graph with a single entry and a single exit—the equations will correctly compute the Dom set for each node. Because they compute $\text{Dom}(n)$ as a function of $n$'s predecessors, denoted $preds(n_i)$, these equations form a forward data-flow problem.

```
n ← |N| - 1
Dom(0) ← {0}
for i ← 1 to n
    Dom(i) ← N

changed ← true
while (changed)
    changed ← false
    for i ← 1 to n
        temp ← {i} ∪ ( ⋂_{j∈preds(i)} Dom(j) )

        if temp ≠ Dom(i) then
            Dom(i) ← temp
            changed ← true
```

■ **FIGURE 9.1** Iterative Solver for Dominance.

To use the equations, the compiler can use the same three-step procedure used for live analysis in Section 8.6.1. It must (1) build a CFG, (2) gather initial information for each block, and (3) solve the equations to produce the DOM sets for each block. For DOM, step 2 is trivial. Recall that the equations for LIVEOUT used two sets per block: UEVAR($b$) and VARKILL($b$). Since dominance deals only with the structure of the graph and not with the behavior of the code in each block, the only local information needed for a block $b_i$ is its name, $i$.

Figure 9.1 shows a round-robin iterative solver for the dominance equations. It considers the nodes in order by their CFG name, $B_0$, $B_1$, $B_2$, and so on. It initializes the DOM set for each node, then repeatedly recomputes those DOM sets until they stop changing. It produces the following values in the DOM sets for our example:

| | **DOM(n)** | | | | | | | | |
|---|---|---|---|---|---|---|---|---|---|
| | $B_0$ | $B_1$ | $B_2$ | $B_3$ | $B_4$ | $B_5$ | $B_6$ | $B_7$ | $B_8$ |
| — | {0} | N | N | N | N | N | N | N | N |
| 1 | {0} | {0,1} | {0,1,2} | {0,1,2,3} | {0,1,2,3,4} | {0,1,5} | {0,1,5,6} | {0,1,5,6,7} | {0,1,5,8} |
| 2 | {0} | {0,1} | {0,1,2} | {0,1,3} | {0,1,3,4} | {0,1,5} | {0,1,5,6} | {0,1,5,7} | {0,1,5,8} |
| 3 | {0} | {0,1} | {0,1,2} | {0,1,3} | {0,1,3,4} | {0,1,5} | {0,1,5,6} | {0,1,5,7} | {0,1,5,8} |

The first column shows the iteration number; the row marked with a dash shows the initial values for the DOM sets. The first iteration computes correct DOM sets for any node with a single path from $B_0$, but computes overly large DOM sets for $B_3$, $B_4$, and $B_7$. In the second iteration, the smaller DOM set for $B_7$ corrects the set for $B_3$, which, in turn shrinks DOM($B_4$). Similarly, the set for $B_8$ corrects the set for $B_7$. The third iteration is required to recognize that the algorithm has reached a fixed point. Note that the final DOM sets agree with our earlier table.

Three critical questions arise regarding this solution procedure. First, does the algorithm halt? It iterates until the DOM sets stop changing, so the argument for termination is not obvious. Second, does it produce correct DOM sets? The answer is critical if we are to use DOM sets in optimization. Finally, how fast is the solver? Compiler writers should avoid algorithms that are unnecessarily slow.

### Termination

Iterative calculation of the DOM sets halts because the sets that approximate DOM shrink monotonically throughout the computation. The algorithm initializes the DOM set for $n_0$ to $\{0\}$, for the entry node $n_0$, and it initializes all the other DOM sets to $N$, the set of all nodes. A DOM set can be no smaller than one node name and can be no larger than $|N|$. Careful reasoning about the while loop shows that a DOM set, say $\text{DOM}(n_i)$, cannot grow from iteration to iteration. Either it shrinks, as the DOM set of one of its predecessors shrinks, or it remains unchanged.

The while loop halts as soon as it makes a pass over the nodes in which no DOM set changes. Since the DOM sets can only change by shrinking and the DOM sets are bounded in size, the while loop must eventually halt. When it halts, it has found a fixed point for this particular instance of the DOM computation.

### Correctness

Recall the definition of a dominator. Node $n_i$ dominates $n_j$ if every path from the entry node $n_0$ to $n_j$ contains $n_i$. Dominance is a property of paths in the CFG.

$\text{DOM}(n_j)$ contains $i$ if and only if $i \in \text{DOM}(n_k)$ for all $k \in preds(j)$, or if $i = j$. The algorithm computes $\text{DOM}(n_j)$ as the intersection of the DOM sets of all $n_j$'s predecessors, plus $n_j$ itself. How does this local computation over individual edges relate to the dominance property defined over all paths through the CFG?

**Meet operator**
In the theory of data-flow analysis, the *meet operator* is used to combine facts at the confluence of two paths.

The DOM sets computed by the iterative algorithm form a fixed-point solution to the equations for dominance. The theory of iterative data-flow analysis, which is beyond the scope of this text, assures us that a fixed point exists for these particular equations and that the fixed point is unique [210]. The all-paths solution of the definition is also a fixed-point for the equations, called the *meet-over-all-paths* solution. The uniqueness of the fixed point guarantees that the solution found by the iterative algorithm is the meet-over-all-paths solution.

## *Efficiency*

The uniqueness of the fixed-point solution to the DOM equations for a specific CFG ensures that the solution is independent of the order in which the solver computes those sets. Thus, the compiler writer is free to choose an order of evaluation that improves the analyzer's running time.

A *reverse postorder* (RPO) traversal of the graph is particularly effective for the iterative algorithm. A postorder traversal visits as many of a node's children as possible, in a consistent order, before visiting the node. (In a cyclic graph, a node's child may also be its ancestor.) An RPO traversal is the opposite—it visits as many of a node's predecessors as possible before visiting the node itself. A node's RPO number is simply $|N| + 1$ minus its postorder number, where $N$ is the set of nodes in the graph. Most interesting graphs will have multiple reverse postorder numberings; from the perspective of the iterative algorithm, they are equivalent.

For a forward data-flow problem, such as DOM, the iterative algorithm should use an RPO computed on the CFG. For a backward data-flow problem, such as LIVEOUT, the algorithm should use an RPO computed on the *reverse* CFG.

To see the impact of ordering, consider the impact of an RPO traversal on our example DOM computation. One RPO numbering for the example CFG is:

Postorder

Reverse Postorder

**Postorder number**
Label the nodes in the graph with their visitation order in a postorder traversal.

**Reverse CFG**
The CFG with its edges reversed; the compiler may need to add a unique exit node so that the reverse CFG has a unique entry node.

|        | $B_0$ | $B_1$ | $B_2$ | $B_3$ | $B_4$ | $B_5$ | $B_6$ | $B_7$ | $B_8$ |
|--------|-------|-------|-------|-------|-------|-------|-------|-------|-------|
| RPO($n$) | 0     | 1     | 6     | 7     | 8     | 2     | 4     | 5     | 3     |

Visiting the nodes in this order produces the following iterations and values:

| | DOM($n$) | | | | | | | | |
|---|---|---|---|---|---|---|---|---|---|
| | $B_0$ | $B_1$ | $B_2$ | $B_3$ | $B_4$ | $B_5$ | $B_6$ | $B_7$ | $B_8$ |
| — | {0} | N | N | N | N | N | N | N | N |
| 1 | {0} | {0,1} | {0,1,2} | {0,1,3} | {0,1,3,4} | {0,1,5} | {0,1,5,6} | {0,1,5,7} | {0,1,5,8} |
| 2 | {0} | {0,1} | {0,1,2} | {0,1,3} | {0,1,3,4} | {0,1,5} | {0,1,5,6} | {0,1,5,7} | {0,1,5,8} |

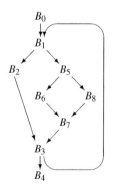

Working in RPO, the algorithm computes accurate DOM sets for this graph on the first iteration and halts after the second iteration. Using RPO, the algorithm halts in two passes over the graph rather than three. As we shall see, it does not compute accurate DOM sets in the first pass for all graphs.

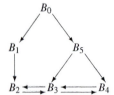

As a second example, consider the CFG shown in the margin. Its structure is more complex than the earlier CFG. It has two loops, $(B_2,B_3)$ and $(B_3,B_4)$, with multiple entries. In particular, $(B_2,B_3)$ has entries from both $(B_0,B_1,B_2)$ and $(B_0,B_5,B_3)$, while $(B_3,B_4)$ has entries from $(B_0,B_5,B_3)$ and $(B_0,B_5,B_4)$. This property makes the graph more difficult to analyze (see Section 9.5.1).

To apply the iterative algorithm, we need a reverse postorder numbering. One RPO numbering for this CFG is:

|        | $B_0$ | $B_1$ | $B_2$ | $B_3$ | $B_4$ | $B_5$ |
|--------|-------|-------|-------|-------|-------|-------|
| RPO(*n*) | 0     | 2     | 3     | 4     | 5     | 1     |

With this RPO numbering, the algorithm executes the following iterations:

|   | DOM(*n*) | | | | | |
|---|-------|-------|-------|-------|-------|-------|
|   | $B_0$ | $B_1$ | $B_2$ | $B_3$ | $B_4$ | $B_5$ |
| — | {0}   | N     | N     | N     | N     | N     |
| 1 | {0}   | {0,1} | {0,1,2} | {0,3} | {0,4} | {0,5} |
| 2 | {0}   | {0,1} | {0,2} | {0,3} | {0,4} | {0,5} |
| 3 | {0}   | {0,1} | {0,2} | {0,3} | {0,4} | {0,5} |

The algorithm requires two iterations to compute the correct DOM sets. The final iteration recognizes that the computation has reached a fixed point.

The dominance calculation relies only on the structure of the graph. It ignores the behavior of the code in any of the CFG's blocks. As such, it might be considered a form of control-flow analysis. Most data-flow problems involve reasoning about the behavior of the code and the flow of data between operations. As an example of this kind of calculation, we will revisit the analysis of live variables.

## 9.2.2 Live-Variable Analysis

In Section 8.6.1, we used the results of live analysis to identify uninitialized variables. Compilers use live information for many other purposes, such as register allocation and construction of some variants of SSA form. We formulated live analysis as a global data-flow problem with the equation:

$$\text{LIVEOUT}(n) = \bigcup_{m \in succ(n)} (\text{UEVAR}(m) \cup (\text{LIVEOUT}(m) \cap \overline{\text{VARKILL}(m)}))$$

and the initial condition that $\text{LIVEOUT}(n) = \emptyset, \forall n$.

**NAMING SETS IN DATA-FLOW EQUATIONS**

In writing the data-flow equations for classic problems, we have renamed many of the sets that contain local information. The original papers used more intuitive set names. Unfortunately, those names clash with each other across problems. For example, available expressions, live variables, reaching definitions, and anticipable expressions all use some notion of a *kill* set. These four problems, however, are defined over three distinct domains: expressions (AVAILOUT and ANTOUT), definition points (REACHES), and variables (LIVEOUT). Thus, using a single set name, such as KILL or KILLED, leads to confusion across problems.

The names that we have adopted encode both the domain and a hint as to the set's meaning. Thus, VARKILL($n$) contains the set of variables killed in block $n$, while EXPRKILL($n$) contains the set of expressions killed in the same block. Similarly, UEVAR($n$) contains the set of upward-exposed variables in block $n$, while UEEXPR($n$) contains the set of upward-exposed expressions. While these names are somewhat awkward, they make explicit the distinction between the notion of kill used in available expressions (EXPRKILL) and the one used in reaching definitions (DEFKILL).

Comparing the equations for LIVEOUT and DOM reveals differences between the problems. LIVEOUT is a backward data-flow problem, in that LIVEOUT($n$) is computed as a function of the information known on entry to each of $n$'s successors in the CFG. DOM is a forward data-flow problem, in that DOM($n$) is computed as a function of the information known at the end of each of $n$'s predecessors in the CFG. LIVEOUT looks for a future use on *any path* in the CFG; thus, it joins information from multiple paths with the union operator. DOM looks for predecessors that lie on *all paths* from the entry node; thus it joins information from multiple paths with the intersection operator. Finally, LIVEOUT reasons about the effects of operations. For this reason, it uses the block-specific constant sets UEVAR and VARKILL that are derived from the code for each block. By contrast, DOM only deals with the CFG's structure. Accordingly, its block-specific constant set contains only the name of the block.

Despite these differences, the framework for solving an instance of LIVEOUT is the same as for an instance of DOM. The compiler must:

1. Perform control-flow analysis to build a CFG, as in Figure 5.6 on page 241.
2. Compute the values of the initial sets, as in Figure 8.14a on page 447.
3. Apply the iterative algorithm, as in Figure 8.14b on page 447.

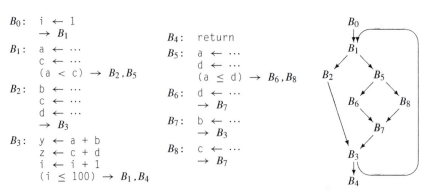

$B_0$:    i ← 1
      → $B_1$

$B_1$:    a ← …
      c ← …
      (a < c) → $B_2$, $B_5$

$B_2$:    b ← …
      c ← …
      d ← …
      → $B_3$

$B_3$:    y ← a + b
      z ← c + d
      i ← i + 1
      (i ≤ 100) → $B_1$, $B_4$

$B_4$:    return

$B_5$:    a ← …
      d ← …
      (a ≤ d) → $B_6$, $B_8$

$B_6$:    d ← …
      → $B_7$

$B_7$:    b ← …
      → $B_3$

$B_8$:    c ← …
      → $B_7$

(a) Code for the Basic Blocks

(b) Control-Flow Graph

| | $B_0$ | $B_1$ | $B_2$ | $B_3$ | $B_4$ | $B_5$ | $B_6$ | $B_7$ | $B_8$ |
|---|---|---|---|---|---|---|---|---|---|
| **UEVAR** | Ø | Ø | Ø | {a,b,c,d,i} | Ø | Ø | Ø | Ø | Ø |
| **VARKILL** | {i} | {a,c} | {b,c,d} | {y,z,i} | Ø | {a,d} | {d} | {b} | {c} |

(c) Initial Information

■ **FIGURE 9.2** Live Analysis Example.

To see the issues that arise in solving instances of LIVEOUT, consider the example in Figure 9.2. It fleshes out the example CFG that we have used throughout this chapter. Figure 9.2a shows code for each basic block. Figure 9.2b shows the CFG and Figure 9.2c shows the UEVAR and VARKILL sets for each block.

Figure 9.3 shows the progress of the iterative solver on the example from Figure 9.2, using the same RPO that we used in the DOM computation, namely $B_0$, $B_1$, $B_5$, $B_8$, $B_6$, $B_7$, $B_2$, $B_3$, $B_4$. Although the equations for LIVEOUT are more complex than those for DOM, the arguments for termination, correctness, and efficiency are similar to those for the dominance equations.

### Termination

Recall that in DOM the sets shrink monotonically.

Iterative live-variable analysis halts because the sets grow monotonically. Each time that the algorithm evaluates the LIVEOUT equation at a node in the CFG, that LIVEOUT set either grows or it remains the same. The equation cannot shrink the LIVEOUT set. On each iteration, one or more LIVEOUT sets grows in size, unless they all remain unchanged. Once the complete set of LIVEOUT sets remain unchanged in one iteration, they will not change in subsequent iterations. It will have reached a fixed point.

| | | | | | LIVEOUT($n$) | | | | |
|---|---|---|---|---|---|---|---|---|---|
| | $B_0$ | $B_1$ | $B_2$ | $B_3$ | $B_4$ | $B_5$ | $B_6$ | $B_7$ | $B_8$ |
| — | ∅ | ∅ | ∅ | ∅ | ∅ | ∅ | ∅ | ∅ | ∅ |
| 1 | ∅ | ∅ | {a,b,c,d,i} | ∅ | ∅ | ∅ | ∅ | {a,b,c,d,i} | ∅ |
| 2 | ∅ | {a,i} | {a,b,c,d,i} | {i} | ∅ | ∅ | {a,c,d,i} | {a,b,d,c,i} | {a,c,d,i} |
| 3 | {i} | {a,i} | {a,b,c,d,i} | {i} | ∅ | {a,c,d,i} | {a,c,d,i} | {a,b,c,d,i} | {a,c,d,i} |
| 4 | {i} | {a,c,i} | {a,b,c,d,i} | {i} | ∅ | {a,c,d,i} | {a,c,d,i} | {a,b,c,d,i} | {a,c,d,i} |
| 5 | {i} | {a,c,i} | {a,b,c,d,i} | {i} | ∅ | {a,c,d,i} | {a,c,d,i} | {a,b,c,d,i} | {a,c,d,i} |

■ **FIGURE 9.3** Progress of the Iterative Live Solver on the Example From Figure 9.2.

We know that the algorithm will reach a fixed point because the LIVEOUT sets are finite. The size of any LIVEOUT set is bounded by the number of variables, $|V|$; any LIVEOUT set is either $V$ or a proper subset of $V$. In the worst case, one LIVEOUT set would grow by one element in each iteration; that behavior would halt after $n \cdot |V|$ iterations, where $n$ is the number of nodes in the CFG.

$V$ is {a, b, c, d, i, y, z} in the code from Figure 9.2. $|V|$ is seven.

This property, the termination of the iterative algorithm because of the combination of monotonicity and the finite number of possible values for the underlying sets, is often called the *finite descending chain property*. In the dominance problem, the DOM sets shrink monotonically and the DOM sets are bounded by the number of nodes in the CFG. That combination, monotonicity and bounded size, again guarantees termination.

### Correctness

Iterative live analysis is correct if and only if it finds all the variables that satisfy the definition of liveness at the end of each block. Recall the definition: A variable $v$ is *live* at point $p$ if and only if there is a path from $p$ to a use of $v$ along which $v$ is not redefined. Thus, liveness is defined in terms of paths in the CFG. A path that contains no definitions of $v$ must exist from $p$ to a use of $v$. We call such a path a $v$-clear path.

LIVEOUT($n$) should contain $v$ if and only if $v$ is live at the end of block $n$. To form LIVEOUT($n$), the iterative solver computes the contribution to LIVEOUT($n$) of each successor of $n$ in the CFG. It combines these contributions using union because $v \in$ LIVEOUT($n$) if $v$ is live on *any* path leaving $n$. How does this local computation over individual edges relate to liveness defined over all paths?

The LIVEOUT sets computed by the iterative solver are a fixed-point solution to the live equations. Again, the theory of iterative data-flow analysis

---

**STATIC ANALYSIS VERSUS DYNAMIC ANALYSIS**

The notion of static analysis leads directly to the question, What about dynamic analysis? By definition, static analysis tries to estimate, at compile time, what will happen at runtime. In many situations, the compiler cannot tell what will happen, even though the answer might be obvious with knowledge of one or more runtime values.

Consider, for example, the C fragment

```
x = y * z + 12;
*p = 0;
q = y * z + 13;
```

It contains a redundant expression, y * z, if and only if p does not contain the address of either y or z. At compile time, the value of p and the address of y and z may be unknown. At runtime, they are known and can be tested. Testing these values at runtime would allow the code to avoid recomputing y * z, where compile-time analysis might be unable to answer the question.

However, the cost of testing whether p == &y or p == &z or neither and acting on the result is likely to exceed the cost of recomputing y * z. For dynamic analysis to make sense, it must be a priori profitable—that is, the savings must exceed the cost of the analysis. This happens in some cases; in most cases, it does not. In contrast, the cost of static analysis can be amortized over multiple runs of the executable code, so it is more attractive, in general.

---

assures us that these particular equations have a unique fixed point [210]. The uniqueness of the fixed point guarantees that the fixed-point solution computed by the iterative algorithms is identical to the meet-over-all-paths solution called for by the definition.

### Efficiency

It is tempting to think that RPO on the reverse CFG is equivalent to reverse preorder on the CFG. See Exercise 4 at the end of the chapter for a counter-example.

For a backward problem, such as LIVEOUT, the solver should use an RPO traversal on the reverse CFG, as shown in Figure 9.4. The iterative evaluation shown earlier used RPO on the CFG. For the example CFG, one RPO on the reverse CFG is

| | $B_0$ | $B_1$ | $B_2$ | $B_3$ | $B_4$ | $B_5$ | $B_6$ | $B_7$ | $B_8$ |
|---|---|---|---|---|---|---|---|---|---|
| RPO($n$) | 8 | 7 | 6 | 1 | 0 | 5 | 4 | 2 | 3 |

```
for i ← 0 to |N| - 1
    LIVEOUT( i ) ← ∅
changed ← true
while (changed)
  changed ← false
  for i ← 1 to |N| - 1
      j ← RPO[i]        // Computed on reverse CFG
      LIVEOUT(j) ← ⋃ₖ∈ₛᵤcc(j) UEVAR(k) ∪ (LIVEOUT(k) ∩ VARKILL(k))
      if LIVEOUT(j) has changed then
          changed ← true
```

■ **FIGURE 9.4** Round-Robin, Reverse Postorder Solver for LIVEOUT.

| | | | | | | LIVEOUT($n$) | | | |
|---|---|---|---|---|---|---|---|---|---|
| | $B_0$ | $B_1$ | $B_2$ | $B_3$ | $B_4$ | $B_5$ | $B_6$ | $B_7$ | $B_8$ |
| — | ∅ | ∅ | ∅ | ∅ | ∅ | ∅ | ∅ | ∅ | ∅ |
| 1 | {i} | {a,c,i} | {a,b,c,d,i} | ∅ | ∅ | {a,c,d,i} | {a,c,d,i} | {a,b,c,d,i} | {a,c,d,i} |
| 2 | {i} | {a,c,i} | {a,b,c,d,i} | {i} | ∅ | {a,c,d,i} | {a,c,d,i} | {a,b,c,d,i} | {a,c,d,i} |
| 3 | {i} | {a,c,i} | {a,b,c,d,i} | {i} | ∅ | {a,c,d,i} | {a,c,d,i} | {a,b,c,d,i} | {a,c,d,i} |

■ **FIGURE 9.5** Iterations of Live Analysis Using RPO on the Reverse CFG.

Visiting the nodes in RPO on the reverse CFG produces the iterations shown in Figure 9.5. Now, the algorithm halts in three iterations, rather than the five iterations required with a traversal ordered by RPO on the CFG. Comparing this table against the earlier computation, we can see why. On the first iteration, the algorithm computed correct LIVEOUT sets for all nodes except $B_3$. It took a second iteration for $B_3$ because of the back edge—the edge from $B_3$ to $B_1$. The third iteration is needed to recognize that the algorithm has reached its fixed point.

## 9.2.3 Limitations on Data-Flow Analysis

There are limits to what a compiler can learn from data-flow analysis. In some cases, the limits arise from the assumptions underlying the analysis. In other cases, the limits arise from features of the language being analyzed. To make informed decisions, the compiler writer must understand what data-flow analysis can do and what it cannot do.

```
x ← f(17)
if (y < x) then
    z ← x + 3
x ← 0
```

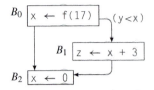

(a) Simple If-Then Construct          (b) Corresponding Control-Flow Graph

■ **FIGURE 9.6** Control Flow Limits the Precision of Data-Flow Analysis.

When it computes the LIVEOUT set for a node $n$ in the CFG, the iterative algorithm uses the sets LIVEOUT, UEVAR, and VARKILL for all of $n$'s successors in the CFG. This implicitly assumes that execution can reach all of those successors; in practice, one or more of them may not be reachable. Consider the code fragment shown in Figure 9.6 along with its CFG.

The assignment to $x$ in $B_0$ is live because of the use of $x$ in $B_1$. The assignment to $x$ in $B_2$ kills the value set in $B_0$. If $B_1$ cannot execute, then $x$'s value from $B_0$ is not live past the comparison with $y$, and $x \notin \text{LIVEOUT}(B_0)$. If the compiler can prove that the test $(y < x)$ is always false, then control will never transfer to block $B_1$ and the assignment to $z$ will never execute. If the call to $f$ has no side effects, the entire statement in $B_0$ is useless and need not be executed. Since the test's result is known, the compiler can completely eliminate both blocks $B_0$ and $B_1$.

The equations for LIVEOUT, however, take the union over all successors of the block, not just the block's executable successors. Thus, the analyzer computes LIVEOUT($B_0$) as

$$\text{UEVAR}(B_1) \cup (\text{LIVEOUT}(B_1) \cap \overline{\text{VARKILL}(B_1)}) \bigcup$$
$$\text{UEVAR}(B_2) \cup (\text{LIVEOUT}(B_2) \cap \overline{\text{VARKILL}(B_2)})$$

Data-flow analysis assumes that all paths through the CFG are feasible. Thus, the information that they compute summarizes the possible data-flow events, assuming that each path can be taken. This limits the precision of the resulting information; we say that the information is precise "up to symbolic execution." With this assumption, $x \in \text{LIVEOUT}(B_0)$ and both $B_0$ and $B_1$ must be preserved.

Another way that imprecision creeps into the results of data-flow analysis comes from the treatment of arrays, pointers, and procedure calls. An array reference, such as A[i,j,k], refers to a single element of A. However, without analysis that reveals the values of i, j, and k, the compiler cannot tell which element of A is being accessed. For this reason, compilers have traditionally lumped together all references to an array A. Thus, a use of A[x,y,z] counts as a use of A, and a definition of A[c,d,e] counts as a definition of A.

Some care must be taken, however, to avoid making too strong an inference. The compiler, knowing that its information on arrays is imprecise, must interpret that information conservatively. Thus, if the goal of the analysis is to determine where a value is no longer live (that is, the value must have been killed), a definition of A[i,j,k] does not kill the value of A. If the goal is to recognize where a value *might* not survive, then a definition of A[i,j,k] *might* define any element of A.

Pointers add another level of imprecision to the results of static analysis. Explicit arithmetic on pointers makes matters worse. Without an analysis that specifically tracks the values of pointers, the compiler must interpret an assignment to a pointer-based variable as a potential definition for every variable that the pointer might reach. Type safety can limit the set of objects potentially defined by an assignment through a pointer; a pointer declared as pointing to an object of type *t* can only be used to modify objects of type *t*. Without analysis of pointer values or a guarantee of type safety, assignment to a pointer-based variable can force the analyzer to assume that every variable has been modified. In practice, this effect often prevents the compiler from keeping the value of a pointer-based variable in a register across any pointer-based assignment. Unless the compiler can specifically prove that the pointer used in the assignment cannot refer to the memory location corresponding to the enregistered value, it cannot safely keep the value in a register.

The complexity of analyzing pointer use leads many compilers to avoid keeping values in registers if they can be the target of a pointer. Usually, some variables can be exempted from this treatment—such as a local variable whose address has never been explicitly taken. The alternative is to perform data-flow analysis aimed at disambiguating pointer-based references—reducing the set of possible variables that a pointer might reference at each point in the code. If the program can pass pointers as parameters or use them as global variables, pointer disambiguation becomes inherently interprocedural.

Procedure calls provide a final source of imprecision. To understand the data flow in the current procedure, the compiler must know what the callee can do to each variable that is accessible to both caller and callee. The callee may, in turn, call other procedures that have their own potential side effects.

Unless the compiler computes accurate summary information for each procedure call, it must estimate their worst-case behavior. While the specific assumptions vary from problem to problem, the general rule is to assume that the callee both uses and modifies every variable that it can address and that call-by-reference parameters create ambiguous references. Since few procedures exhibit this behavior, this assumption typically overestimates the effects of a call and introduces further imprecision into the results of data-flow analysis.

### 9.2.4 Other Data-Flow Problems

Compilers use data-flow analyses to prove the safety of applying transformations in particular situations. Thus, many distinct data-flow problems have been proposed, each to drive a particular optimization.

#### *Available Expressions*

To identify redundant expressions, the compiler can compute information about the *availability* of expressions. An expression $e$ is *available* at point $p$ in a procedure if and only if on every path from the procedure's entry to $p$, $e$ is evaluated and none of its constituent subexpressions is redefined between that evaluation and $p$. This analysis annotates each node $n$ in the CFG with a set AVAILIN($n$), which contains the names of all expressions in the procedure that are available on entry to the block corresponding to $n$. To compute AVAILIN, the compiler initially sets

$$\text{AVAILIN}(n_0) = \emptyset$$

$$\text{AVAILIN}(n) = \{\, all\ expressions\,\}, \forall n \neq n_0$$

Next, it solves the following equations:

$$\text{AVAILIN}(n) = \bigcap_{m \in preds(n)} (\text{DEEXPR}(m) \cup (\text{AVAILIN}(m) \cap \overline{\text{EXPRKILL}(m)}))$$

Here, DEEXPR($n$) is the set of downward exposed expressions in $n$. An expression $e \in$ DEEXPR($n$) if and only if block $n$ evaluates $e$ and none of $e$'s operands is defined between the last evaluation of $e$ in $n$ and the end of $n$. EXPRKILL($n$) contains all those expressions that are "killed" by a definition in $n$. An expression is killed if one or more of its operands are redefined in the block. Note that the equation defines a forward data-flow problem.

An expression $e$ is available on entry to $n$ if and only if it is available on exit from each of $n$'s predecessors in the CFG. As the equation states, an expression $e$ is available on exit from some block $m$ if one of two conditions holds: either $e$ is downward exposed in $m$, or it is available on entry to $m$ and is not killed in $m$.

AVAILIN sets can be used to perform global redundancy elimination, sometimes called *global common subexpression elimination*. Perhaps the simplest way to achieve this effect is to compute AVAILIN sets for each block and use them in local value numbering (see Section 8.4.1). The compiler can simply initialize the hash table for a block $b$ to AVAILIN($b$) before value numbering $b$. Lazy code motion is a stronger form of common subexpression elimination that also uses availability (see Section 10.3.1).

### Reaching Definitions

In some cases, the compiler needs to know where an operand was defined. If multiple paths in the CFG lead to the operation, then multiple definitions may provide the value of the operand. To find the set of definitions that reach a block, the compiler can compute *reaching definitions*. The domain of REACHES is the set of definitions in the procedure. A definition $d$ of some variable $v$ *reaches* operation $i$ if and only if $i$ reads the value of $v$ and there exists a path from $d$ to $i$ that does not define $v$.

The compiler annotates each node $n$ in the CFG with a set REACHES($n$), computed as a forward data-flow problem:

$$\text{REACHES}(n) = \emptyset, \forall n$$

$$\text{REACHES}(n) = \bigcup_{m \in preds(n)} (\text{DEDEF}(m) \cup (\text{REACHES}(m) \cap \overline{\text{DEFKILL}(m)}))$$

DEDEF($m$) is the set of downward-exposed definitions in $m$: those definitions in $m$ for which the defined name is not subsequently redefined in $m$. DEFKILL($m$) contains *all* the definition points that are obscured by a definition of the same name in $m$; $d \in \text{DEFKILL}(m)$ if $d$ defines some name $v$ and $m$ contains a definition that also defines $v$. Thus $\overline{\text{DEFKILL}(m)}$ consists of the definition points that are not obscured in $m$.

DEDEF and DEFKILL are both defined over the set of definition points, but computing each of them requires a mapping from names (variables and compiler-generated temporaries) to definition points. Thus, gathering the initial information for reaching definitions is more complex than it is for live variables.

### Anticipable Expressions

An expression $e$ is considered *anticipable*, or *very busy*, on exit from block $b$ if and only if (1) every path that leaves $b$ evaluates and subsequently uses $e$, and (2) evaluating $e$ at the end of $b$ would produce the same result as

**IMPLEMENTING DATA-FLOW FRAMEWORKS**

The equations for many global data-flow problems show a striking similarity. For example, available expressions, live variables, reaching definitions, and anticipable expressions all have propagation functions of the form

$$f(x) = c_1 \ op_1 \ (x \ op_2 \ c_2)$$

where $c_1$ and $c_2$ are constants determined by the actual code and $op_1$ and $op_2$ are standard set operations such as $\cup$ and $\cap$. This similarity shows up in the problem descriptions. It should also show up in their implementations.

The compiler writer can easily abstract away the details in which these problems differ and implement a single, parameterized analyzer. The analyzer needs functions to compute $c_1$ and $c_2$, implementations of the operators, and an indication of the problem's direction. In return, it produces the desired data-flow information.

This implementation strategy encourages code reuse. It hides the low-level details of the solver. At the same time, it creates a situation in which the compiler writer can profitably invest effort in optimizing the implementation. For example, a scheme that allows the framework to implement $f(x) = c_1 \ op_1 \ (x \ op_2 \ c_2)$ as a single function may outperform an implementation that uses $f_1(x) = c_1 \ op_1 \ x$ and $f_2(x) = x \ op_1 \ c_2$ and computes $f(x)$ as $f_1(f_2(x))$. This scheme lets all the client transformations benefit from optimizing set representations and operator implementations.

the first evaluation of $e$ along each of those paths. The term "anticipable" derives from the second condition, which implies that an evaluation of $e$ at $b$ anticipates the subsequent evaluations along all paths. The set of expressions anticipable on output from a block can be computed as a backward data-flow problem on the CFG. The domain of the problem is the set of expressions.

$$\text{ANTOUT}(n_f) = \emptyset$$

$$\text{ANTOUT}(n) = \{ \text{ all expressions } \}, \forall n \neq n_f$$

$$\text{ANTOUT}(n) = \bigcap_{m \in succ(n)} (\text{UEEXPR}(m) \cup (\text{ANTOUT}(m) \cap \overline{\text{EXPRKILL}(m)}))$$

Here $\text{UEEXPR}(m)$ is the set of upward-exposed expressions—those used in $m$ before they are killed. $\text{EXPRKILL}(m)$ is the set of expressions defined in $m$; it is the same set that appears in the equations for available expressions.

The results of anticipability analysis are used in code motion both to decrease execution time, as in lazy code motion, and to shrink the size of the compiled code, as in code hoisting. Both transformations are discussed in Section 10.3.

### Interprocedural Summary Problems

When analyzing a single procedure, the compiler must account for the impact of each procedure call. In the absence of specific information about the call, the compiler must make worst-case assumptions that account for all the possible actions of the callee, or any procedures that it, in turn, calls. These worst-case assumptions can seriously degrade the quality of the global data-flow information. For example, the compiler must assume that the callee modifies every variable that it can access; this assumption essentially stops the propagation of facts across a call site for all global variables, module-level variables, and call-by-reference parameters.

To limit such impact, the compiler can compute summary information on each call site. The classic summary problems compute the set of variables that might be modified as a result of the call and that might be used as a result of the call. The compiler can then use these computed summary sets in place of its worst case assumptions.

The *interprocedural may modify problem* annotates each call site with a set of names that the callee, and procedures it calls, might modify. May modify is one of the simplest problems in interprocedural analysis, but it can have a significant impact on the quality of information produced by other analyses, such as global constant propagation. May modify is posed as a set of data-flow equations over the program's call graph that annotate each procedure with a MayMod set.

$$
\text{MayMod}(p) = \text{LocalMod}(p) \cup \left( \bigcup_{e=(p,q)} \mathit{unbind}_e(\text{MayMod}(q)) \right)
$$

where $e = (p,q)$ is an edge from $p$ to $q$ in the call graph. The function $\mathit{unbind}_e$ maps one set of names into another. For a call-graph edge $e = (p,q)$, $\mathit{unbind}_e(x)$ maps each name in $x$ from the name space of $q$ to the name space of $p$, using the bindings at the specific call site that corresponds to $e$. Finally, $\text{LocalMod}(p)$ contains all the names modified locally in $p$ that are visible outside $p$. It is computed as the set of names defined in $p$ minus any names that are strictly local to $p$.

To solve for MayMod, the compiler can set $\text{MayMod}(p)$ to $\text{LocalMod}(p)$, for all procedures $p$, and then iteratively evaluate the equation for MayMod until it reaches a fixed point. Given the MayMod sets for each procedure, the compiler can compute the set of names that might be modified at a specific call, $e = (p,q)$, by computing a set $S$ as $\mathit{unbind}_e(\text{MayMod}(q))$ and then adding to $S$ any names that are aliased inside procedure $p$ to names in $S$.

**Flow insensitive**

This formulation of MayMod ignores control flow inside procedures. Such a formulation is said to be *flow insensitive*.

The compiler can also compute information on what variables might be referenced as a result of executing a procedure call, the *interprocedural may reference problem*. The equations to annotate each procedure $p$ with a set MAYREF($p$) are similar to the equations for MAYMOD.

---

**SECTION REVIEW**

Iterative data-flow analysis works by repeatedly re-evaluating the data-flow equation at each node in the underlying graph until the sets defined by the equations reach a fixed point. Many data-flow problems have a unique fixed point, which ensures a correct solution independent of the evaluation order evaluation, and the finite descending chain property, which guarantees termination independent of the evaluation order. Since the analyzer can choose any order, it should choose one that produces rapid termination. For most forward data-flow problems, that order is reverse postorder; for most backward problems, that order is reverse postorder on the reverse CFG. These orders force the iterative algorithm to evaluate as many predecessors (for forward problems) or successors (for backward problems) as possible before it evaluates a node $n$.

Many data-flow problems appear in the literature and in modern compilers. Examples include live analysis, used in register allocation; availability and anticipability, used in redundancy elimination and code motion; and interprocedural summary information, used to sharpen the results of single-procedure data-flow analysis. SSA form, described in the next section, provides a unifying structure that encodes both data-flow information, such as reaching definitions, and control-flow information, such as dominance. Many modern compilers use SSA form as an alternative to solving multiple distinct data-flow problems.

---

**Review Questions**

1. Compute DOM sets for the CFG shown in the margin, evaluating the nodes in the order $\{B_4, B_2, B_1, B_5, B_3, B_0\}$. Explain why this calculation takes a different number of iterations than the version shown on page 482.

2. Before a compiler can compute interprocedural data-flow information, it must build a call graph for the program. Just as ambiguous jumps complicate CFG construction, so too can ambiguous calls complicate call-graph construction. What language features might lead to an ambiguous call site—one where the compiler was uncertain as to the identify of the callee?

## 9.3 STATIC SINGLE-ASSIGNMENT FORM

Over time, many different data-flow problems have been formulated. If each transformation uses its own idiosyncratic analysis, the amount of time and effort spent implementing, debugging, and maintaining the analysis passes can grow unreasonably large. To limit the number of analyses that the compiler writer must implement and that the compiler must run, it is desirable to use a single analysis to perform multiple transformations.

One strategy for implementing such a "universal" analysis involves building a variant form of the program that encodes both data flow and control flow directly in the IR. SSA form, introduced in Sections 5.4.2 and 8.5.1, has this property. It can serve as the basis for a large set of transformations. From a single implementation that translates the code into SSA form, a compiler can perform many of the classic scalar optimizations.

Consider the various uses of the variable $x$ in the code fragment shown in Figure 9.7a. The gray lines show which definitions can reach each use of $x$. Figure 9.7b shows the same fragment, rewritten to convert $x$ to SSA form. Definitions of $x$ have been renamed, with subscripts, to ensure that each definition has a unique SSA name. For simplicity, we have left the references to other variables unchanged.

The SSA form of the code includes new assignments (to $x_3$, $x_5$, and $x_6$) that reconcile the distinct SSA names for $x$ with the uses of $x$ (in the assignments to $s$ and $z$). These assignments ensure that, along each edge in the CFG, the current value of $x$ has been assigned a unique name, independent of which path brought control to the edge. The right sides of these assignments contain a special function, a $\phi$-function, that combines the values from distinct edges.

A $\phi$-function takes as arguments the SSA names for the values associated with each edge that enters the block. When control enters a block, all the $\phi$-functions in the block execute, concurrently. They evaluate to the argument that corresponds to the edge along which control entered the block. Notationally, we write the arguments left-to-right to correspond to the edges left-to-right. On the printed page, this is easy. In an implementation, it requires some bookkeeping.

The SSA construction inserts $\phi$-functions after each point in the CFG where multiple paths converge—each join point. At join points, distinct SSA names must be reconciled to a single name. After the entire procedure has been converted to SSA form, two rules hold: (1) each definition in the procedure creates a unique name, and (2) each use refers to a single definition.

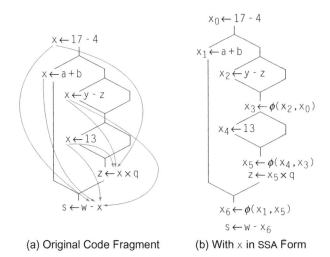

(a) Original Code Fragment　　(b) With $x$ in SSA Form

■ **FIGURE 9.7** SSA: Encoding Control Flow into Data Flow.

To transform a procedure into SSA form, the compiler must insert the appropriate $\phi$-functions for each variable into the code, and it must rename variables with subscripts to make the two rules hold. This simple, two-step plan produces the basic SSA construction algorithm.

### 9.3.1 A Simple Method for Building SSA Form

To construct the SSA form of a program, the compiler must insert $\phi$-functions at join points in the CFG, and it must rename variables and temporary values to conform with the rules that govern the SSA name space. The algorithm follows this outline:

1. *Inserting $\phi$-functions* At the start of each block that has multiple predecessors, insert a $\phi$-function, such as $y \leftarrow \phi(y, y)$, for every name $y$ that the code either defines or uses in the current procedure. The $\phi$-function should have one argument for each predecessor block in the CFG. This rule inserts a $\phi$-function in every case where one is needed. It also inserts many extraneous $\phi$-functions.

   The algorithm can insert the $\phi$-functions in arbitrary order. The definition of $\phi$-functions requires that all the $\phi$-functions at the top of a block execute concurrently—that is, they all read their input parameters simultaneously, then write their output values simultaneously. This lets the algorithm avoid many minor details that an ordering might introduce.

2. *Renaming* After $\phi$-functions have been inserted, the compiler can compute reaching definitions (see Section 9.2.4). Because the inserted $\phi$-functions are also definitions, they ensure that only one definition reaches any use. Next, the compiler can rename each use, both the variables and the temporaries, to reflect the definition that reaches it.

   The compiler must sort out the definitions that reach each $\phi$-function and make the names correspond to the paths along which they reach the block that contains the $\phi$-function. While conceptually simple, this task requires some bookkeeping.

This algorithm constructs a correct SSA form for the program. Each variable is defined exactly once, and each reference uses the name of a distinct definition. However, it produces SSA form that has, potentially, many more $\phi$-functions than necessary. The extra $\phi$-functions are problematic. They decrease the precision of some kinds of analysis when performed over SSA form. They occupy space, so the compiler wastes memory representing $\phi$-functions that are either redundant (that is, $x_j \leftarrow \phi(x_i, x_i)$) or are not live. They increase the cost of any algorithm that uses the resulting SSA form, since it must traverse all the extraneous $\phi$-functions.

We call this version of SSA *maximal* SSA *form*. To build SSA form with fewer $\phi$-functions requires more work; in particular, the compiler must analyze the code to determine where potentially distinct values converge in the CFG. This computation relies on the dominance information described in Section 9.2.1.

The next three subsections present, in detail, an algorithm to build *semipruned* SSA *form*—a version with fewer $\phi$-functions. Section 9.3.2 shows how dominance information introduced in Section 9.2.1 can be used to compute *dominance frontiers* to guide insertion of $\phi$-functions. Section 9.3.3 gives an algorithm to insert $\phi$-functions, and Section 9.3.4 shows how to rewrite variable names to complete the construction of SSA form. Section 9.3.5 discusses the difficulties that can arise in converting the code back into an executable form.

## 9.3.2 **Dominance Frontiers**

The primary problem with maximal SSA form is that it contains too many $\phi$-functions. To reduce their number, the compiler must determine more carefully where they are required. The key to placing $\phi$-functions lies in understanding which variables need a $\phi$-function at each join point. To solve this problem efficiently and effectively, the compiler can turn the question around. It can determine, for each block $i$, the set of blocks that will need a

$\phi$-function for any definition in block $i$. Dominance plays a critical role in this computation.

Consider a definition in node $n$ of the CFG. That value could potentially reach every node $m$ where $n \in \text{DOM}(m)$ without need for a $\phi$-function, since every path that reaches $m$ passes through $n$. The only way that the value does not reach $m$ is if another definition of the same name intervenes—that is, it occurs in some node $p$ between $n$ and $m$. In this case, the definition in $n$ does not force the presence of a $\phi$-function; instead, the redefinition in $p$ does.

A definition in node $n$ forces a $\phi$-function at join points that lie just outside the region of the CFG that $n$ dominates. More formally, a definition in node $n$ forces a corresponding $\phi$-function at any join point $m$ where (1) $n$ dominates a predecessor of $m$ ($q \in preds(m)$ and $n \in \text{DOM}(q)$), and (2) $n$ does not *strictly dominate m.* (Using strict dominance rather than dominance allows a $\phi$-function at the start of a single-block loop. In that case, $n = m$, and $m \notin \text{DOM}(n) - \{n\}$.) We call the collection of nodes $m$ that have this property with respect to $n$ the *dominance frontier* of $n$, denoted $\text{DF}(n)$.

**Strict dominance**

*a strictly dominates b if and only if $a \in \text{DOM}(b) - \{b\}$.*

Informally, $\text{DF}(n)$ contains the first nodes reachable from $n$ that $n$ does not dominate, on each CFG path leaving $n$. In the CFG of our continuing example, $B_5$ dominates $B_6$, $B_7$, and $B_8$, but does not dominate $B_3$. On every path leaving $B_5$, $B_3$ is the first node that $B_5$ does not dominate. Thus, $\text{DF}(B_5) = \{B_3\}$.

### Dominator Trees

**Dominator tree**

*a tree that encodes the dominance information for a flow graph*

Before giving an algorithm to compute dominance frontiers, we must introduce one further notion, the *dominator tree.* Given a node $n$ in a flow graph, the set of nodes that strictly dominate $n$ is given by $(\text{DOM}(n) - n)$. The node in that set that is closest to $n$ is called $n$'s immediate dominator, denoted $\text{IDOM}(n)$. The entry node of the flow graph has no immediate dominator.

The dominator tree of a flow graph contains every node of the flow graph. Its edges encode the IDOM sets in a simple way. If $m$ is $\text{IDOM}(n)$, then the dominator tree has an edge from $m$ to $n$. The dominator tree for our example CFG appears in the margin. Notice that $B_6$, $B_7$, and $B_8$ are all children of $B_5$, even though $B_7$ is not an immediate successor of $B_5$ in the CFG.

The dominator tree compactly encodes both the IDOM information and the complete DOM sets for each node. Given a node $n$ in the dominator tree, $\text{IDOM}(n)$ is just its parent in the tree. The nodes in $\text{DOM}(n)$ are exactly the nodes that lie on the path from the root of the dominator tree to $n$,

```
for all nodes, n, in the CFG
    DF(n) ← ∅
for all nodes, n, in the CFG
    if n has multiple predecessors then
        for each predecessor p of n
            runner ← p
            while runner ≠ IDom(n)
                DF(runner) ← DF(runner) ∪ {n}
                runner ← IDom(runner)
```

■ **FIGURE 9.8** Algorithm for Computing Dominance Frontiers.

inclusive of both the root and $n$. From the tree, we can read the following sets:

|        | $B_0$ | $B_1$   | $B_2$     | $B_3$     | $B_4$       | $B_5$     | $B_6$       | $B_7$       | $B_8$       |
|--------|-------|---------|-----------|-----------|-------------|-----------|-------------|-------------|-------------|
| **DOM**  | {0}   | {0,1}   | {0,1,2}   | {0,1,3}   | {0,1,3,4}   | {0,1,5}   | {0,1,5,6}   | {0,1,5,7}   | {0,1,5,8}   |
| **IDOM** | —     | 0       | 1         | 1         | 3           | 1         | 5           | 5           | 5           |

These DOM sets match those computed earlier;—indicates an undefined value.

### *Computing Dominance Frontiers*

To make $\phi$-insertion efficient, we need to calculate the dominance frontier for each node in the flow graph. We could formulate a data-flow problem to compute DF($n$) for each $n$ in the graph. Using both the dominator tree and the CFG, we can formulate a simple and direct algorithm, shown in Figure 9.8. Since only nodes that are join points in the CFG can be members of a dominance frontier, we first identify all of the join points in the graph. For a join point $j$, we examine each of its CFG predecessors.

The algorithm is based on three observations. First, nodes in a DF set must be join points in the graph. Second, for a join point $j$, each predecessor $k$ of $j$ must have $j \in$ DF($k$), since $k$ cannot dominate $j$ if $j$ has more than one predecessor. Finally, if $j \in$ DF($k$) for some predecessor $k$, then $j$ must also be in DF($l$) for each $l \in$ Dom($k$), unless $l \in$ Dom($j$).

The algorithm follows these observations. It locates nodes $j$ that are join points in the CFG. Then, for each predecessor $p$ of $j$, it walks up the dominator tree from $p$ until it finds a node that dominates $j$. From the second and third

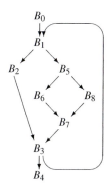

The Example CFG

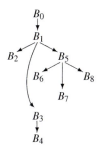

Its Dominator Tree

observations in the preceding paragraph, $j$ belongs in DF($l$) for each node $l$ that the algorithm traverses in this dominator-tree walk, except for the final node in the walk, since that node dominates $j$. A small amount of bookkeeping is needed to ensure that any $n$ is added to a node's dominance frontier only once.

To see how this works, consider again the example CFG and its dominance tree. The analyzer examines the nodes in some order, looking for nodes with multiple predecessors. Assuming that it takes the nodes in name order, it finds the join points as $B_1$, then $B_3$, then $B_7$.

1. $B_1$ For CFG-predecessor $B_0$, the algorithm finds that $B_0$ is IDom($B_1$), so it never enters the while loop. For CFG-predecessor $B_3$, it adds $B_1$ to DF($B_3$) and advances to $B_1$. It adds $B_1$ to DF($B_1$) and advances to $B_0$, where it halts.
2. $B_3$ For CFG-predecessor $B_2$, it adds $B_3$ to DF($B_2$), advances to $B_1$ which is IDom($B_3$), and halts. For CFG-predecessor $B_7$, it adds $B_3$ to DF($B_7$) and advances to $B_5$. It adds $B_3$ to DF($B_5$) and advances to $B_1$, where it halts.
3. $B_7$ For CFG-predecessor $B_6$, it adds $B_7$ to DF($B_6$), advances to $B_5$ which is IDom($B_7$), and halts. For CFG-predecessor $B_8$, it adds $B_7$ to DF($B_8$) and advances to $B_5$, where it halts.

Accumulating these results, we obtain the following dominance frontiers:

|  | $B_0$ | $B_1$ | $B_2$ | $B_3$ | $B_4$ | $B_5$ | $B_6$ | $B_7$ | $B_8$ |
|---|---|---|---|---|---|---|---|---|---|
| **DF** | $\emptyset$ | $\{B_1\}$ | $\{B_3\}$ | $\{B_1\}$ | $\emptyset$ | $\{B_3\}$ | $\{B_7\}$ | $\{B_3\}$ | $\{B_7\}$ |

### 9.3.3 Placing $\phi$-Functions

The naive algorithm placed a $\phi$-function for every variable at the start of every join node. With dominance frontiers, the compiler can determine more precisely where $\phi$-functions might be needed. The basic idea is simple. A definition of x in block $b$ forces a $\phi$-function at every node in DF($b$). Since that $\phi$-function is a new definition of x, it may, in turn, force the insertion of additional $\phi$-functions.

The compiler can further narrow the set of $\phi$-functions that it inserts. A variable that is only live within a single block can never have a live $\phi$-function. To apply this observation, the compiler can compute the set of names that

```
Globals ← ∅
Initialize all the Blocks sets to ∅
for each block b                          for each name x ∈ Globals
    VARKILL ← ∅                               WorkList ← Blocks(x)
    for each operation i in b, in order      for each block b ∈ WorkList
        assume that opᵢ is "x ← y op z"          for each block d in DF(b)
            if y ∉ VARKILL then                      if d has no φ-function for x then
                Globals ← Globals ∪ {y}                  insert a φ-function for x in d
            if z ∉ VARKILL then                          WorkList ← WorkList ∪ {d}
                Globals ← Globals ∪ {z}
            VARKILL ← VARKILL ∪ {x}
            Blocks(x) ← Blocks(x) ∪ {b}
```

|  |  |
|:---:|:---:|
| (a) Finding Global Names | (b) Rewriting the Code |

■ **FIGURE 9.9** φ-Function Insertion.

are live across multiple blocks—a set that we will call the *global names*. It can insert φ-functions for those names and ignore any name that is not in that set. (This restriction distinguishes semipruned SSA form from other varieties of SSA form.)

The word *global* is used here to mean of interest across the entire procedure.

The compiler can find the global names cheaply. In each block, it looks for names with upward-exposed uses—the UEVar set from the live-variables calculation. Any name that appears in one or more LiveOut sets must be in the UEVar set of some block. Taking the union of all the UEVar sets gives the compiler the set of names that are live on entry to one or more blocks and, hence, live in multiple blocks.

The algorithm, shown in Figure 9.9a, is derived from the obvious algorithm for computing UEVar. It constructs a single set, *Globals*, where the LiveOut computation must compute a distinct set for each block. As it builds the *Globals* set, it also constructs, for each name, a list of all blocks that contain a definition of that name. These block lists serve as an initial worklist for the φ-insertion algorithm.

The algorithm for inserting φ-functions is shown in Figure 9.9b. For each global name *x*, it initializes *WorkList* with *Blocks(x)*. For each block *b* on the *WorkList*, it inserts φ-functions at the head of every block *d* in *b*'s dominance frontier. Since all the φ-functions in a block execute concurrently, by definition, the algorithm can insert them at the head of *d* in any order. After

```
B₀: i ← 1                          B₄: return
    → B₁                           B₅: a ← ···
B₁: a ← ···                            d ← ···
    c ← ···                            (a ≤ d) → B₆,B₈
    (a < c) → B₂,B₅                B₆: d ← ···
B₂: b ← ···                            → B₇
    c ← ···                        B₇: b ← ···
    d ← ···                            → B₃
    → B₃                           B₈: c ← ···
B₃: y ← a + b                          → B₇
    z ← c + d
    i ← i + 1
    (i ≤ 100) → B₁,B₄
```

(a) Code for the Basic Blocks

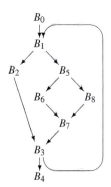

(b) Control-Flow Graph

|        | $B_0$ | $B_1$ | $B_2$ | $B_3$ | $B_4$ | $B_5$ | $B_6$ | $B_7$ | $B_8$ |
|--------|-------|-------|-------|-------|-------|-------|-------|-------|-------|
| **DF** | Ø | $\{B_1\}$ | $\{B_3\}$ | $\{B_1\}$ | Ø | $\{B_3\}$ | $\{B_7\}$ | $\{B_3\}$ | $\{B_7\}$ |

(c) Dominance Frontiers in the CFG

|            | a | b | c | d | i | y | z |
|------------|-----|-----|-------|---------|-------|-----|-----|
| **Blocks** | {1,5} | {2,7} | {1,2,8} | {2,5,6} | {0,3} | {3} | {3} |

(d) *Blocks* Sets for Each Name

(e) Dominator Tree

■ **FIGURE 9.10** Example SSA for $\phi$-function Insertion.

adding a $\phi$-function for $x$ to $d$, the algorithm adds $d$ to the WorkList to reflect the new assignment to $x$ in $d$.

### Example

Figure 9.10 recaps our running example. Panel a shows the code; panel b shows the CFG; panel c shows the dominance frontiers for each block; and panel e shows the dominator tree built from the CFG.

The first step in the $\phi$-function insertion algorithm finds global names and computes the *Blocks* set for each name. For the code in Figures 9.10a, the global names are $\{a,b,c,d,i\}$. Figure 9.10d shows the *Blocks* sets. Notice that the algorithm creates *Blocks* sets for $y$ and $z$, even though they are not in *Globals*. Separating the computation of *Globals* from that of

```
B₀: i ← 1
     → B₁
B₁: a ← φ(a,a)           B₃: a ← φ(a,a)
    b ← φ(b,b)               b ← φ(b,b)
    c ← φ(c,c)               c ← φ(c,c)           B₆: d ← ···
    d ← φ(d,d)               d ← φ(d,d)               → B₇
    i ← φ(i,i)               y ← a + b           B₇: c ← φ(c,c)
    a ← ···                  z ← c + d               d ← φ(d,d)
    c ← ···                  i ← i + 1               b ← ···
    (a < c) → B₂,B₅          (i ≤ 100) → B₁,B₄       → B₃
B₂: b ← ···             B₄: return              B₈: c ← ···
    c ← ···             B₅: a ← ···                 → B₇
    d ← ···                 d ← ···
    → B₃                    (a ≤ d) → B₆,B₈
```

■ **FIGURE 9.11** Example Code with $\phi$-Functions, Before Renaming.

*Blocks* would avoid instantiating these extra sets, at the cost of another pass over the code.

The $\phi$-function rewrite algorithm works on a name-by-name basis. Consider its actions for the variable a in the example. It initializes the worklist to *Blocks(a)*, which contains $B_1$ and $B_5$. The definition in $B_1$ causes it to insert a $\phi$-function at the start of each block in $\text{DF}(B_1) = \{B_1\}$. This action also enters $B_1$ back into the worklist. Next, it removes $B_5$ from the worklist and inserts a $\phi$-function in each block of $\text{DF}(B_5) = \{B_3\}$. The insertion at $B_3$ also places $B_3$ on the worklist. When $B_3$ comes off the worklist, it tries to add a $\phi$-function in $B_1$, because $B_1 \in \text{DF}(B_3)$. The algorithm notices that $B_1$ already has that $\phi$-function, so it does not perform an insertion. Thus, processing of a halts with an empty worklist. The algorithm follows the same logic for each name in *Globals*, to produce the following insertions:

| | a | b | c | d | i |
|---|---|---|---|---|---|
| **$\phi$-functions** | $\{B_1,B_3\}$ | $\{B_1,B_3\}$ | $\{B_1,B_3,B_7\}$ | $\{B_1,B_3,B_7\}$ | $\{B_1\}$ |

The resulting code appears in Figure 9.11.

Limiting the algorithm to global names lets it avoid inserting dead $\phi$-functions for x and y in block $B_1$. ($B_1 \in \text{DF}(B_3)$ and $B_3$ contains definitions of both x and y.) However, the distinction between local names and global names is not sufficient to avoid all dead $\phi$-functions. For example, the $\phi$-function for b in $B_1$ is not live because b is redefined before its value is used. To avoid inserting these $\phi$-functions, the compiler can construct

---

**THE DIFFERENT FLAVORS OF SSA FORM**

Several distinct flavors of SSA form have been proposed in the literature. The flavors differ in their criteria for inserting $\phi$-functions. For a given program, they can produce different sets of $\phi$-functions.

*Minimal SSA* inserts a $\phi$-function at any join point where two distinct definitions for the same original name meet. This is the minimal number consistent with the definition of SSA. Some of those $\phi$-functions, however, may be dead; the definition says nothing about the values being live when they meet.

*Pruned SSA* adds a liveness test to the $\phi$-insertion algorithm to avoid adding dead $\phi$-functions. The construction must compute LIVEOUT sets, so the cost of building pruned SSAs is higher than that of building minimal SSA.

*Semipruned SSA* is a compromise between minimal SSAs and pruned SSAs. Before inserting $\phi$-functions, the algorithm eliminates any names that are not live across a block boundary. This can shrink the name space and reduce the number of $\phi$-functions without the overhead of computing LIVEOUT sets. This is the algorithm given in Figure 9.9.

Of course, the number of $\phi$-functions depends on the specific program being converted into SSA form. For some programs, the reductions obtained by semipruned SSAs and pruned SSAs are significant. Shrinking the SSA form can lead to faster compilation, since passes that use SSA form then operate on programs that contain fewer operations—and fewer $\phi$-functions.

---

LIVEOUT sets and add a test based on liveness to the inner loop of the $\phi$-insertion algorithm. That modification causes the algorithm to produce *pruned* SSA *form*.

### Efficiency Improvements

To improve efficiency, the compiler should avoid two kinds of duplication. First, the algorithm should avoid placing any block on the worklist more than once per global name. It can keep a checklist of blocks that have already been processed. Since the algorithm must reset the checklist for each global name, the implementation should use a sparse set or a similar structure (see Appendix B.2.3).

Second, a given block can be in the dominance frontier of multiple nodes that appear on the `WorkList`. As shown in the figure, the algorithm must search the block to look for a pre-existing $\phi$-function. To avoid this search, the compiler can maintain a checklist of blocks that already contain $\phi$-functions for $x$. This takes a single sparse set, reinitialized along with `WorkList`.

### 9.3.4 **Renaming**

In the description of maximal SSA form, we stated that renaming variables was conceptually straightforward. The details, however, require some explanation.

In the final SSA form, each global name becomes a base name, and individual definitions of that base name are distinguished by the addition of a numerical subscript. For a name that corresponds to a source-language variable, say $x$, the algorithm uses $x$ as the base name. Thus, the first definition of $x$ that the renaming algorithm encounters will be named $x_0$ and the second will be $x_1$. For a compiler-generated temporary, the algorithm must generate a distinct base name.

The algorithm, shown in Figure 9.12, renames both definitions and uses in a preorder walk over the procedure's dominator tree. In each block, it first renames the values defined by $\phi$-functions at the head of the block, then it visits each operation in the block, in order. It rewrites the operands with current SSA names, then it creates a new SSA name for the result of the operation. This latter act makes the new name current. After all the operations in the block have been rewritten, the algorithm rewrites the appropriate $\phi$-function parameters in each CFG successor of the block, using the current SSA names. Finally, it recurs on any children of the block in the dominator tree. When it returns from those recursive calls, it restores the set of current SSA names to the state that existed before the current block was visited.

To manage this process, the algorithm uses a counter and a stack for each global name. A global name's stack holds the subscript of the name's current SSA name. At each definition, the algorithm generates a new subscript for the targeted name by pushing the value of its current counter onto the stack and incrementing the counter. Thus, the value on top of the stack for $n$ is always the subscript of $n$'s current SSA name. As the final step in processing a block, the algorithm pops all the names generated in that block off their respective stacks to restore the names that held at the end of that block's immediate dominator. Those names may be needed to process the block's remaining siblings in the dominator tree.

The stack and the counter serve distinct and separate purposes. As control in the algorithm moves up and down the dominator tree, the stack is managed to simulate the lifetime of the most recent definition in the current block.

```
for each global name i
    counter[i] ← 0
    stack[i] ← ∅
Rename(n₀)




NewName(n)
  i ← counter[n]
  counter[n] ← counter[n] + 1
  push i onto stack[n]
  return "nᵢ"
```

```
Rename(b)
  for each φ-function in b, "x ← φ(⋯)"
      rewrite x as NewName(x)

  for each operation "x ← y op z" in b
      rewrite y with subscript top(stack[y])
      rewrite z with subscript top(stack[z])
      rewrite x as NewName(x)

  for each successor of b in the CFG
      fill in φ-function parameters

  for each successor s of b in the dominator tree
      Rename(s)

  for each operation "x ← y op z" in b
      and each φ-function "x ← φ(⋯)"
      pop(stack[x])
```

■ **FIGURE 9.12** Renaming After $\phi$-Insertion.

The counter, on the other hand, grows monotonically to ensure that each successive definition receives a unique SSA name.

Figure 9.12 summarizes the algorithm. It initializes the stacks and counters, then calls *Rename* on the root of the dominator tree—the entry node of the CFG. *Rename* rewrites the block and recurs on successors in the dominator tree. To finish with the block, *Rename* pops any names that were pushed onto stacks while processing the block. The function *NewName* manipulates the counters and stacks to create new SSA names as needed.

One final detail remains. At the end of block $b$, *Rename* must rewrite $\phi$-function parameters in each of $b$'s CFG successors. The compiler must assign an ordinal parameter slot in those $\phi$-functions for $b$. When we draw the SSA form, we always assume a left-to-right order that matches the left-to-right order in which the edges are drawn. Internally, the compiler can number the edges and parameter slots in any consistent fashion that produces the desired result. This requires cooperation between the code that builds the SSA form and the code that builds the CFG. (For example, if the CFG implementation uses a list of edges leaving each block, the order of that list can determine the mapping.)

### Example

To finish the continuing example, let's apply the renaming algorithm to the code in Figure 9.11. Assume that $a_0$, $b_0$, $c_0$, and $d_0$ are defined on entry to $B_0$. Figure 9.13 shows the states of the counters and stacks for global names at various points during the process.

|          | a     | b     | c     | d     | i |
|----------|-------|-------|-------|-------|---|
| Counters | 1     | 1     | 1     | 1     | 0 |
| Stacks   | $a_0$ | $b_0$ | $c_0$ | $d_0$ |   |

(a) Initial Condition, Before $B_0$

|          | a     | b     | c     | d     | i     |
|----------|-------|-------|-------|-------|-------|
| Counters | 1     | 1     | 1     | 1     | 1     |
| Stacks   | $a_0$ | $b_0$ | $c_0$ | $d_0$ | $i_0$ |

(b) On Entry to $B_1$

|          | a     | b     | c     | d     | i     |
|----------|-------|-------|-------|-------|-------|
| Counters | 3     | 2     | 3     | 2     | 2     |
| Stacks   | $a_0$ | $b_0$ | $c_0$ | $d_0$ | $i_0$ |
|          | $a_1$ | $b_1$ | $c_1$ | $d_1$ | $i_1$ |
|          | $a_2$ |       | $c_2$ |       |       |

(c) On Entry to $B_2$

|          | a     | b     | c     | d     | i     |
|----------|-------|-------|-------|-------|-------|
| Counters | 3     | 3     | 4     | 3     | 2     |
| Stacks   | $a_0$ | $b_0$ | $c_0$ | $d_0$ | $i_0$ |
|          | $a_1$ | $b_1$ | $c_1$ | $d_1$ | $i_1$ |
|          | $a_2$ | $b_2$ | $c_2$ | $d_2$ |       |
|          |       |       | $c_3$ |       |       |

(d) End of $B_2$

|          | a     | b     | c     | d     | i     |
|----------|-------|-------|-------|-------|-------|
| Counters | 3     | 3     | 4     | 3     | 2     |
| Stacks   | $a_0$ | $b_0$ | $c_0$ | $d_0$ | $i_0$ |
|          | $a_1$ | $b_1$ | $c_1$ | $d_1$ | $i_1$ |
|          | $a_2$ |       | $c_2$ |       |       |

(e) On Entry to $B_3$

|          | a     | b     | c     | d     | i     |
|----------|-------|-------|-------|-------|-------|
| Counters | 4     | 4     | 5     | 4     | 3     |
| Stacks   | $a_0$ | $b_0$ | $c_0$ | $d_0$ | $i_0$ |
|          | $a_1$ | $b_1$ | $c_1$ | $d_1$ | $i_1$ |
|          | $a_2$ | $b_3$ | $c_2$ | $d_3$ | $i_2$ |
|          | $a_3$ |       | $c_4$ |       |       |

(f) At End of $B_3$

|          | a     | b     | c     | d     | i     |
|----------|-------|-------|-------|-------|-------|
| Counters | 4     | 4     | 5     | 4     | 3     |
| Stacks   | $a_0$ | $b_0$ | $c_0$ | $d_0$ | $i_0$ |
|          | $a_1$ | $b_1$ | $c_1$ | $d_1$ | $i_1$ |
|          | $a_2$ |       | $c_2$ |       |       |

(g) On Entry to $B_5$

|          | a     | b     | c     | d     | i     |
|----------|-------|-------|-------|-------|-------|
| Counters | 5     | 4     | 5     | 5     | 3     |
| Stacks   | $a_0$ | $b_0$ | $c_0$ | $d_0$ | $i_0$ |
|          | $a_1$ | $b_1$ | $c_1$ | $d_1$ | $i_1$ |
|          | $a_2$ |       | $c_2$ | $d_4$ |       |
|          | $a_4$ |       |       |       |       |

(h) Entry to $B_6$

|          | a     | b     | c     | d     | i     |
|----------|-------|-------|-------|-------|-------|
| Counters | 5     | 4     | 5     | 6     | 3     |
| Stacks   | $a_0$ | $b_0$ | $c_0$ | $d_0$ | $i_0$ |
|          | $a_1$ | $b_1$ | $c_1$ | $d_1$ | $i_1$ |
|          | $a_2$ |       | $c_2$ | $d_4$ |       |
|          | $a_4$ |       |       |       |       |

(i) Entry to $B_7$

|          | a     | b     | c     | d     | i     |
|----------|-------|-------|-------|-------|-------|
| Counters | 5     | 5     | 6     | 7     | 32    |
| Stacks   | $a_0$ | $b_0$ | $c_0$ | $d_0$ | $i_0$ |
|          | $a_1$ | $b_1$ | $c_1$ | $d_1$ | $i_1$ |
|          | $a_2$ |       | $c_2$ | $d_4$ |       |
|          | $a_4$ |       |       |       |       |

(j) On Entry to $B_8$

■ **FIGURE 9.13** States in the Renaming Example.

The algorithm makes a preorder walk over the dominator tree, which corresponds to visiting the nodes in ascending order by name, $B_0$ through $B_8$. The initial configuration of the stacks and counters appears in Figure 9.13a. As the algorithm proceeds through the blocks, it takes the following actions:

- *Block $B_0$* This block contains only one operation. *Rename* rewrites i with $i_0$, increments the counter, and pushes $i_0$ onto the stack for i. Next, it visits $B_0$'s CFG-successor, $B_1$, and rewrites the $\phi$-function parameters that correspond to $B_0$ with their current names: $a_0$, $b_0$, $c_0$, $d_0$, and $i_0$. It then recurs on $B_0$'s child in the dominator tree, $B_1$. After that, it pops the stack for i and returns.

- *Block $B_1$* *Rename* enters $B_1$ with the state shown in Figure 9.13b. It rewrites the $\phi$-function targets with new names, $a_1$, $b_1$, $c_1$, $d_1$, and $i_1$. Next, it creates new names for the definitions of a and c and rewrites them. It rewrites the uses of a and c in the comparison. Neither of $B_1$'s CFG successors have $\phi$-functions, so it recurs on $B_1$'s dominator-tree children, $B_2$, $B_3$, and $B_5$. Finally, it pops the stacks and returns.

- *Block $B_2$* *Rename* enters $B_2$ with the state shown in Figure 9.13c. This block has no $\phi$-functions to rewrite. *Rename* rewrites the definitions of b, c, and d, creating a new SSA name for each. It then rewrites $\phi$-function parameters in $B_2$'s CFG successor, $B_3$. Figure 9.13d shows the stacks and counters just before they are popped. Finally, it pops the stacks and returns.

- *Block $B_3$* *Rename* enters $B_3$ with the state shown in Figure 9.13e. Notice that the stacks have been popped to their state when *Rename* entered $B_2$, but the counters reflect the names created inside $B_2$. In $B_3$, *Rename* rewrites the $\phi$-function targets, creating new SSA names for each. Next, it rewrites each assignment in the block, using current SSA names for the uses and then creating new SSA names for the definition. (Since y and z are not global names, it leaves them intact.)

  $B_3$ has two CFG successors, $B_1$ and $B_4$. In $B_1$, it rewrites the $\phi$-function parameters that correspond to the edge from $B_3$, using the stacks and counters shown in Figure 9.13f. $B_4$ has no $\phi$-functions. Next, *Rename* recurs on $B_3$'s dominator-tree child, $B_4$. When that call returns, *Rename* pops the stacks and returns.

- *Block $B_4$* This block just contains a return statement. It has no $\phi$-functions, definitions, uses, or successors in either the CFG or the dominator tree. Thus, *Rename* performs no actions and leaves the stacks and counters unchanged.

$$B_0: \quad i_0 \leftarrow 1$$
$$\rightarrow B_1$$

$B_1: \quad a_1 \leftarrow \phi(a_0, a_3)$
$\quad\quad b_1 \leftarrow \phi(b_0, b_3)$
$\quad\quad c_1 \leftarrow \phi(c_0, c_4)$
$\quad\quad d_1 \leftarrow \phi(d_0, d_3)$
$\quad\quad i_1 \leftarrow \phi(i_0, i_2)$
$\quad\quad a_2 \leftarrow \cdots$
$\quad\quad c_2 \leftarrow \cdots$
$\quad\quad (a_2 < c_2) \rightarrow B_2, B_5$

$B_2: \quad b_2 \leftarrow \cdots$
$\quad\quad c_3 \leftarrow \cdots$
$\quad\quad d_2 \leftarrow \cdots$
$\quad\quad \rightarrow B_3$

$B_3: \quad a_3 \leftarrow \phi(a_2, a_4)$
$\quad\quad b_3 \leftarrow \phi(b_2, b_4)$
$\quad\quad c_4 \leftarrow \phi(c_3, c_5)$
$\quad\quad d_3 \leftarrow \phi(d_2, d_6)$
$\quad\quad y \leftarrow a_3 + b_3$
$\quad\quad z \leftarrow c_4 + d_3$
$\quad\quad i_2 \leftarrow i_1 + 1$
$\quad\quad (i_2 \leq 100) \rightarrow B_1, B_4$

$B_4: \quad$ return

$B_5: \quad a_4 \leftarrow \cdots$
$\quad\quad d_4 \leftarrow \cdots$
$\quad\quad (a_4 \leq d_4) \rightarrow B_6, B_8$

$B_6: \quad d_5 \leftarrow \cdots$
$\quad\quad \rightarrow B_7$

$B_7: \quad c_5 \leftarrow \phi(c_2, c_6)$
$\quad\quad d_6 \leftarrow \phi(d_5, d_4)$
$\quad\quad b_4 \leftarrow \cdots$
$\quad\quad \rightarrow B_3$

$B_8: \quad c_6 \leftarrow \cdots$
$\quad\quad \rightarrow B_7$

■ **FIGURE 9.14** Example after Renaming.

■ *Block $B_5$* After $B_4$, *Rename* pops through $B_3$ back to $B_1$. With the stacks as shown in Figure 9.13g, it recurs down into $B_1$'s final dominator-tree child, $B_5$. $B_5$ has no $\phi$-functions. *Rename* rewrites the two assignment statements and the expression in the conditional, creating new SSA names as needed. Neither of $B_5$'s CFG successors has $\phi$-functions. *Rename* next recurs on $B_5$'s dominator-tree children, $B_6$, $B_7$, and $B_8$. Finally, it pops the stacks and returns.

■ *Block $B_6$* *Rename* enters $B_6$ with the state shown in Figure 9.13h. $B_6$ has no $\phi$-functions. *Rename* rewrites the assignment to d, generating the new SSA name $d_5$. Next, it visits the $\phi$-functions in $B_6$'s CFG successor $B_7$. It rewrites the $\phi$-function arguments that correspond to the path from $B_6$ with their current names, $c_2$ and $d_5$. Since $B_6$ has no dominator-tree children, it pops the stack for d and returns.

■ *Block $B_7$* *Rename* enters $B_7$ with the state shown in Figure 9.13i. It first renames the $\phi$-function targets with new SSA names, $c_5$ and $d_6$. Next, it rewrites the assignment to b with new SSA name $b_4$. It then rewrites the $\phi$-function arguments in $B_7$'s CFG successor, $B_3$, with their current names. Since $B_7$ has no dominator-tree children, it pops the stacks and returns.

■ *Block $B_8$* *Rename* enters $B_8$ with the state shown in Figure 9.13j. $B_8$ has no $\phi$-functions. *Rename* rewrites the assignment to c with new SSA name $c_6$. It examines $B_8$'s CFG successor, $B_7$ and rewrites the corresponding $\phi$-function arguments with their current names, $c_6$ and $d_4$. Since $B_8$ has no dominator-tree children, it pops the stacks and returns.

Figure 9.14 shows the code after *Rename* halts.

### A Final Improvement

A clever implementation of *NewName* can reduce the time and the space expended on stack manipulation. The primary use of the stacks is to reset the name space on exit from a block. If a block redefines the same base name several times, *NewName* only needs to keep the most recent name. This happened with a and c in block $B_1$ of the example. *NewName* may overwrite the same stack slot multiple times within a single block.

This makes the maximum stack sizes predictable; no stack can be larger than the depth of the dominator tree. It lowers the overall space requirements, avoids the need for overflow tests on each push, and decreases the number of push and pop operations. It requires another mechanism for determining which stacks to pop on exit from a block. *NewName* can thread together the stack entries for a block. *Rename* can use the thread to pop the appropriate stacks.

## 9.3.5 Translation Out of SSA Form

Because modern processors do not implement $\phi$-functions, the compiler needs to translate SSA form back into executable code. From the examples, it is tempting to believe that the compiler can just drop the subscripts from the SSA names, revert to base names, and delete the $\phi$-functions. If the compiler simply builds SSA form and converts it back into executable code, this approach will work. If, however, the code has been rearranged or values have been renamed, this approach can produce incorrect code.

As an example, we saw in Section 8.4.1 that using SSA names could allow local value numbering (LVN) to discover and eliminate more redundancies.

| Before LVN | After LVN |
|---|---|
| a ← x + y | a ← x + y |
| b ← x + y | b ← a |
| a ← 17 | a ← 17 |
| c ← x + y | c ← x + y |

Original Name Space

| Before LVN | After LVN |
|---|---|
| $a_0 \leftarrow x_0 + y_0$ | $a_0 \leftarrow x_0 + y_0$ |
| $b_0 \leftarrow x_0 + y_0$ | $b_0 \leftarrow a_0$ |
| $a_1 \leftarrow 17$ | $a_1 \leftarrow 17$ |
| $c_0 \leftarrow x_0 + y_0$ | $c_0 \leftarrow a_0$ |

SSA Name Space

The table on the left shows a four-operation block and the results that LVN produces when it uses the code's own name space. The table on the right shows the same example using the SSA name space. Because the SSA name space gives $a_0$ a distinct name from $a_1$, LVN can replace the evaluation of $x_0 + y_0$ in the final operation with a reference to $a_0$.

$B_0$: $i_0 \leftarrow 1$
   $a_1 \leftarrow a_0$
   $b_1 \leftarrow b_0$
   $c_1 \leftarrow c_0$
   $d_1 \leftarrow d_0$
   $i_1 \leftarrow i_0$
   $\rightarrow B_1$
$B_1$: $a_2 \leftarrow \cdots$
   $c_2 \leftarrow \cdots$
   $(a_2 < c_2) \rightarrow B_2, B_5$
$B_2$: $b_2 \leftarrow \cdots$
   $c_3 \leftarrow \cdots$
   $d_2 \leftarrow \cdots$
   $a_3 \leftarrow a_2$
   $b_3 \leftarrow b_2$
   $c_4 \leftarrow c_3$
   $d_3 \leftarrow d_2$
   $\rightarrow B_3$

$B_3$: $y \leftarrow a_3 + b_3$
   $z \leftarrow c_4 + d_3$
   $i_2 \leftarrow i_1 + 1$
   $(i_2 \leq 100) \rightarrow B_9, B_4$
$B_4$: return
$B_5$: $a_4 \leftarrow \cdots$
   $d_4 \leftarrow \cdots$
   $(a_4 \leq d_4) \rightarrow B_6, B_8$
$B_6$: $d_5 \leftarrow \cdots$
   $c_5 \leftarrow c_2$
   $d_6 \leftarrow d_5$
   $\rightarrow B_7$
$B_7$: $b_4 \leftarrow \cdots$
   $a_3 \leftarrow a_4$
   $b_3 \leftarrow b_4$
   $c_4 \leftarrow c_5$
   $d_3 \leftarrow d_6$
   $\rightarrow B_3$

$B_8$: $c_6 \leftarrow \cdots$
   $c_5 \leftarrow c_6$
   $d_6 \leftarrow d_4$
   $\rightarrow B_7$
$B_9$: $a_1 \leftarrow a_3$
   $b_1 \leftarrow b_3$
   $c_1 \leftarrow c_4$
   $d_1 \leftarrow d_3$
   $i_1 \leftarrow i_2$
   $\rightarrow B_1$

■ **FIGURE 9.15** Example after Copy Insertion to Eliminate $\phi$-functions.

Notice, however, that simply dropping the subscripts on variable names produces incorrect code, since c receives the value 17. More aggressive transformations, such as code motion and copy folding, can rewrite the SSA form in ways that introduce more subtle problems.

To avoid such problems, the compiler can keep the SSA name space intact and replace each $\phi$-function with a set of copy operations—one along each incoming edge. For a $\phi$-function $x_i \leftarrow \phi(x_j, x_k)$, the compiler should insert $x_i \leftarrow x_j$ along the edge carrying the value $x_j$ and $x_i \leftarrow x_k$ along the edge carrying $x_k$.

Figure 9.15 shows the running example after $\phi$-functions have been replaced with copy operations. The four $\phi$-functions that were in $B_3$ have been replaced with a set of four copies in each of $B_2$ and $B_7$. Similarly, the two $\phi$-functions in $B_7$ induce a pair of copies in each of $B_6$ and $B_8$. In both these cases, the compiler can insert the copies into the predecessor blocks.

The $\phi$-functions in $B_1$ reveal a more complicated situation. The compiler can insert copies directly into its predecessor $B_0$, but not into its predecessor $B_3$. Since $B_3$ has multiple successors, inserting copies for the $\phi$-functions from $B_1$ at the end of $B_3$ would also cause them to execute along the path from $B_3$ to $B_4$, where they are not necessary and might produce incorrect results. To remedy this problem, the compiler can split the edge $(B_3, B_1)$, insert a new block between $B_3$ and $B_1$, and place the copies in that new

If the names defined by the copies are not LIVEIN in $B_4$, then the copies would be harmless. The compiler's strategy, however, must work if the names are LIVEIN.

block. The new block is labelled $B_9$ in Figure 9.15. After copy insertion, the example appears to have many superfluous copies. Fortunately, the compiler can remove most, if not all, of these copies with subsequent optimizations, such as copy folding (see Section 13.4.6).

**Critical edge**

In a CFG, an edge whose source has multiple successors and whose sink has multiple predecessors is called a *critical edge*.

We call an edge such as $(B_3, B_1)$ a *critical edge*. When the compiler inserts a block in the middle of a critical edge, it *splits* the critical edge. Some transformations on SSA form assume that the compiler splits all critical edges before it applies the transformation.

In out-of-SSA translation, the compiler can split critical edges to create locations for the necessary copy operations. This transformation cures most of the problems that arise during out-of-SSA translation. However, two more subtle problems can arise. The first, which we call the lost-copy problem, arises from a combination of aggressive program transformations and unsplit critical edges. The second, which we call the swap problem, arises from an interaction of some aggressive program transformations and the detailed definition of SSA form.

### The Lost-Copy Problem

Many SSA-based algorithms require that critical edges be split. Sometimes, however, the compiler cannot, or should not, split critical edges. For example, if the critical edge is the closing branch of a heavily executed loop, adding a block with one or more copy operations and a jump may have an adverse impact on execution speed. Similarly, adding blocks and edges in the late stages of compilation can interfere with regional scheduling, with register allocation, and with optimizations such as code placement.

The lost-copy problem arises from the combination of copy folding and critical edges that cannot be split. Figure 9.16 shows an example. Panel a shows the original code—a simple loop. In panel b, the compiler has converted the loop into SSA form and folded the copy from $i$ to $y$, replacing the sole use of $y$ with a reference to $i_1$. Panel c shows the code produced by straightforward copy insertion into the $\phi$-function's predecessor blocks. This code assigns the wrong value to $z_0$. The original code assigns $z_0$ the second to last value of $i$; the code in panel c assigns $z_0$ the last value of $i$. With the critical edge split, as in panel d, copy insertion produces the correct behavior. However, it adds a jump to every iteration of the loop.

The combination of an unsplit critical edge and copy folding creates the lost copy. Copy folding eliminated the assignment $y \leftarrow i$ by folding $i_1$ into the reference to $y$ in the block that follows the loop. Thus, copy folding extended the lifetime of $i_1$. Then, the copy-insertion algorithm replaced the

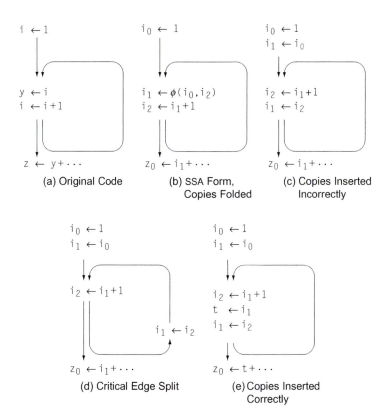

■ **FIGURE 9.16** An Example of the Lost-Copy Problem.

$\phi$-function at the top of the loop body with a copy operation in each of that block's predecessors. This inserts the copy $i_1 \leftarrow i_2$ at the bottom of the block—at a point where $i_1$ is still live.

The compiler can avoid the lost-copy problem by checking the liveness of the target name for each copy that it tries to insert during out-of-SSA translation. When it discovers a copy target that is live, it must preserve the live value in a temporary name and rewrite subsequent uses to refer to the temporary name. This rewriting step can be done with an algorithm modelled on the renaming step of the SSA construction algorithm. Figure 9.16e shows the code that this approach produces.

### *The Swap Problem*

The swap problem arises from the definition of $\phi$-function execution. When a block executes, all of its $\phi$-functions execute concurrently before any other statement in the block. That is, all the $\phi$-functions simultaneously read their

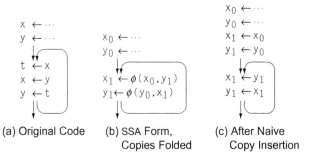

(a) Original Code | (b) SSA Form, Copies Folded | (c) After Naive Copy Insertion

■ **FIGURE 9.17** An Example of the Swap Problem.

appropriate input parameters and then simultaneously redefine their target values.

Figure 9.17 shows a simple example of the swap problem. Panel a shows the original code, a simple loop that swaps the values of $x$ and $y$. Panel b shows the code after conversion to SSA form and aggressive copy folding. In this form, with the rules for evaluating $\phi$-functions, the code retains its original meaning. When the loop body executes, the $\phi$-function parameters are read before any of the $\phi$-function targets are defined. On the first iteration, it reads $x_0$ and $y_0$ before defining $x_1$ and $y_1$. On subsequent iterations, the loop body reads $x_1$ and $y_1$ before redefining them. Panel c shows the same code, after the naive copy-insertion algorithm has run. Because copies execute sequentially, rather than concurrently, both $x_1$ and $y_1$ receive the same value, an incorrect outcome.

At first glance, it might appear that splitting the back edge—a critical edge—helps. However, splitting the edge simply places the same two copies, in the same order, in another block. The straightforward fix for this problem is to adopt a two-stage copy protocol. The first stage copies each of the $\phi$-function arguments to its own temporary name, simulating the behavior of the original $\phi$-functions. The second state then copies those values to the $\phi$-function targets.

Unfortunately, this solution doubles the number of copy operations required to translate out of SSA form. In the code from Figure 9.17a, it would require four assignments: $s \leftarrow y_1$, $t \leftarrow x_1$, $x_1 \leftarrow s$, and $y_1 \leftarrow t$. All of these assignments execute on each iteration of the loop. To avoid this loss of efficiency, the compiler should attempt to minimize the number of copies that it inserts.

In fact, the swap problem can arise without a cycle of copies; all it takes is a set of $\phi$-functions that have, as inputs, variables defined as outputs of other $\phi$-functions in the same block. In the acyclic case, in which $\phi$-functions reference the results of other $\phi$-functions in the same block, the compiler can avoid the problem by carefully ordering the inserted copies.

To solve this problem, in general, the compiler can detect cases in which $\phi$-functions reference the targets of other $\phi$-functions in the same block. For each cycle of references, it must insert a copy to a temporary that breaks the cycle. Then, it can schedule the copies to respect the dependences implied by the $\phi$-functions.

The minimal code for the example would use one extra copy; it is similar to the code in Figure 9.17a.

### 9.3.6 **Using SSA Form**

A compiler uses SSA form because it improves the quality of analysis, the quality of optimization, or both. To see how analysis over SSA form differs from the classical data-flow analysis techniques presented in Section 9.2, consider performing global constant propagation on SSA form, using an algorithm called sparse simple constant propagation (SSCP).

In the SSCP algorithm, the compiler annotates each SSA name with a value. The set of possible values forms a *semilattice*. A semilattice consists of a set $L$ of values and a meet operator, $\wedge$. The meet operator must be idempotent, commutative, and associative; it imposes an order on the elements of $L$ as follows:

$$a \geq b \quad \text{if and only if} \quad a \wedge b = b, \text{ and}$$
$$a > b \quad \text{if and only if} \quad a \geq b \text{ and } a \neq b$$

A semilattice has a bottom element, $\perp$, with the properties that

$$\forall a \in L, a \wedge \perp = \perp, \quad \text{and} \quad \forall a \in L, a \geq \perp.$$

Some semilattices also have a top element, $\top$, with the properties that

$$\forall a \in L, a \wedge \top = a \quad \text{and} \quad \forall a \in L, \top \geq a.$$

In constant propagation, the structure of the semilattice used to model program values plays a critical role in the algorithm's runtime complexity. The semilattice for a single SSA name appears in the margin. It consists of $\top$, $\perp$, and an infinite set of distinct constant values. For any two constants, $c_i$ and $c_j$, $c_i \wedge c_j = \perp$.

In SSCP, the algorithm initializes the value associated with each SSA name to $\top$, which indicates that the algorithm has no knowledge of the SSA name's value. If the algorithm subsequently discovers that SSA name $x$ has the known

**Semilattice**

a set $L$ and a *meet* operator $\wedge$ such that, $\forall a, b,$ and $c \in L,$

1. $a \wedge a = a,$

2. $a \wedge b = b \wedge a,$ and

3. $a \wedge (b \wedge c) = (a \wedge b) \wedge c$

Compilers use semilattices to model the data domains of analysis problems.

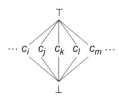

Semilattice for Constant Propagation

```
// Initialization Phase
WorkList ← Ø

for each SSA name n
    initialize Value(n) by rules specified in the text

    if Value(n) ≠ ⊤ then
        WorkList ← WorkList ∪ {n}

// Propagation Phase - Iterate to a fixed point
while (WorkList ≠ Ø)
    remove some n from WorkList          // Pick an arbitrary name

    for each operation op that uses n
        let m be the SSA name that op defines

        if Value(m) ≠ ⊥ then                  // Recompute and test for change
            t ← Value(m)
            Value(m) ← result of interpreting op over lattice values

            if Value(m) ≠ t
                then WorkList ← WorkList ∪ {m}
```

■ **FIGURE 9.18** Sparse Simple Constant Propagation Algorithm.

constant value $c_i$, it models that knowledge by assigning $Value(x)$ the semi-lattice element $c_i$. If it discovers that $x$ has a changing value, it models that fact with the value $\bot$.

The algorithm for SSCP, shown in Figure 9.18, consists of an initialization phase and a propagation phase. The initialization phase iterates over the SSA names. For each SSA name $n$, it examines the operation that defines $n$ and sets $Value(n)$ according to a simple set of rules. If $n$ is defined by a $\phi$-function, SSCP sets $Value(n)$ to $\top$. If $n$'s value is a known constant $c_i$, SSCP sets $Value(n)$ to $c_i$. If $n$'s value cannot be known—for example, it is defined by reading a value from external media—SSCP sets $Value(n)$ to $\bot$. Finally, if $n$'s value is not known, SSCP sets $Value(n)$ to $\top$. If $Value(n)$ is not $\top$, the algorithm adds $n$ to the worklist.

The propagation phase is straightforward. It removes an SSA name $n$ from the worklist. The algorithm examines each operation $op$ that uses $n$, where $op$ defines some SSA name $m$. If $Value(m)$ has already reached $\bot$, then no further evaluation is needed. Otherwise, it models the evaluation of $op$ by interpreting the operation over the lattice values of its operands. If the result is lower in the lattice than $Value(m)$, it lowers $Value(m)$ accordingly and adds $m$ to the worklist. The algorithm halts when the worklist is empty.

Interpreting an operation over lattice values requires some care. For a $\phi$-function, the result is simply the meet of the lattice values of all the $\phi$-function's arguments; the rules for meet are shown in the margin, in order of precedence. For other kinds of operations, the compiler must apply operator-specific knowledge. If any operand has the lattice value $\top$, the evaluation returns $\top$. If none of the operands has the value $\top$, the model should produce an appropriate value.

$$\top \wedge x = x \quad \forall\, x$$
$$\bot \wedge x = \bot \quad \forall\, x$$
$$c_i \wedge c_j = c_i \quad \text{if } c_i = c_j$$
$$c_i \wedge c_j = \bot \quad \text{if } c_i \neq c_j$$
Rules for Meet

For each value-producing operation in the IR, SSCP needs a set of rules that model the operands' behavior. Consider the operation $a \times b$. If $a = 4$ and $b = 17$, the model should produce the value 68 for $a \times b$. However, if $a = \bot$, the model should produce $\bot$ for any value of $b$ except 0. Because $a \times 0 = 0$, independent of $a$'s value, $a \times 0$ should produce the value 0.

## Complexity

The propagation phase of SSCP is a classic fixed-point scheme. The arguments for termination and complexity follow from the length of descending chains through the lattice that it uses to represent values, shown in Figure 9.18. The $Value$ associated with any SSA name can have one of three initial values—$\top$, some constant $c_i$ other than $\top$ or $\bot$, or $\bot$. The propagation phase can only lower its value. For a given SSA name, this can happen at most twice—from $\top$ to $c_i$ to $\bot$. SSCP adds an SSA name to the worklist only when its value changes, so each SSA name appears on the worklist at most twice. SSCP evaluates an operation when one of its operands is removed from the worklist. Thus, the total number of evaluations is at most twice the number of uses in the program.

## Optimism: The Role of Top

The SSCP algorithm differs from the data-flow problems in Section 9.2 in that it initializes unknown values to the lattice element $\top$. In the lattice for constant values, $\top$ is a special value that represents a lack of knowledge about the SSA name's value. This initialization plays a critical role in constant propagation; it allows values to propagate into cycles in the graph, which are caused by loops in the CFG.

Because it initializes unknown values to $\top$, rather than $\bot$, it can propagate some values into cycles in the graph—loops in the CFG. Algorithms that begin with the value $\top$, rather than $\bot$, are often called *optimistic* algorithms. The intuition behind this term is that initialization to $\top$ allows the algorithm to propagate information into a cyclic region, optimistically assuming that the value along the back edge will confirm this initial propagation. An initialization to $\bot$, called *pessimistic*, disallows that possibility.

$$x_0 \leftarrow 17$$

$$x_1 \leftarrow \phi(x_0, x_2)$$
$$x_2 \leftarrow x_1 + i_{12}$$

| Time | Lattice Values | | | | | |
|------|----------------|---|---|---|---|---|
| Step | Pessimistic | | | Optimistic | | |
| | $x_0$ | $x_1$ | $x_2$ | $x_0$ | $x_1$ | $x_2$ |
| 0 | 17 | $\perp$ | $\perp$ | 17 | $\top$ | $\top$ |
| 1 | 17 | $\perp$ | $\perp$ | 17 | 17 | $17 + i_{12}$ |

(a) The Code Fragment    (b) Results of Pessimistic and Optimistic Analyses

■ **FIGURE 9.19** Optimistic Constant Example.

To see this, consider the SSA fragment in Figure 9.19. If the algorithm pessimistically initializes $x_1$ and $x_2$ to $\perp$, it will not propagate the value 17 into the loop. When it evaluates the $\phi$-function for $x_1$, it computes $17 \wedge \perp$ to yield $\perp$. With $x_1$ set to $\perp$, $x_2$ also gets set to $\perp$, even if $i_{12}$ has a known value, such as 0.

If, on the other hand, the algorithm optimistically initializes unknown values to $\top$, it can propagate the value of $x_0$ into the loop. When it computes a value for $x_1$, it evaluates $17 \wedge \top$ and assigns the result, 17, to $x_1$. Since $x_1$'s value has changed, the algorithm places $x_1$ on the worklist. The algorithm then reevaluates the definition of $x_2$. If, for example, $i_{12}$ has the value 0, then this assigns $x_2$ the value 17 and adds $x_2$ to the worklist. When it reevaluates the $\phi$-function, it computes $17 \wedge 17$ and proves that $x_1$ is 17.

Consider what would happen if $i_{12}$ has the value 2, instead. Then, when SSCP evaluates $x_1 + i_{12}$, it assigns $x_2$ the value 19. Now, $x_1$ gets the value $17 \wedge 19$, or $\perp$. This, in turn, propagates back to $x_2$, producing the same final result as the pessimistic algorithm.

### The Value of SSA Form

In the SSCP algorithm, SSA form leads to a simple and efficient algorithm. To see this point, consider a classic data-flow approach to constant propagation. It would associate a set CONSTANTSIN with each block in the code, define an equation to compute CONSTANTSIN($b_i$) as a function of the CONSTANTSOUT sets of $b_i$'s predecessors, and define a procedure for interpreting the code in a block to derive CONSTANTSOUT($b_i$) from CONSTANTSIN($b_i$). In contrast, the algorithm in Figure 9.18 is relatively simple. It still has an idiosyncratic mechanism for interpreting operations, but otherwise it is a simple iterative fixed-point algorithm over a particularly shallow lattice.

In SSA form, the propagation step is sparse; it only evaluates expressions of lattice values at operations (and $\phi$-functions) that use those values. Equally important, assigning values to individual SSA names makes the optimistic initialization natural rather than contrived and complicated. In short, SSA leads to an efficient, understandable sparse algorithm for global constant propagation.

---

**SECTION REVIEW**

SSA form encodes information about both data flow and control flow in a conceptually simple intermediate form. To make use of SSA, the compiler must first transform the code into SSA form. This section focused on the algorithms needed to build *semipruned* SSA *form*. The construction is a two step process. The first step inserts $\phi$-functions into the code at join points where distinct definitions can converge. The algorithm relies heavily on dominance frontiers for efficiency. The second step creates the SSA name space by adding subscripts to the original base names during a systematic traversal of the entire procedure.

Because modern machines do not directly implement $\phi$-functions, the compiler must translate code out of SSA form before it can execute. Transformation of the code while in SSA form can complicate out-of-SSA translation. Section 9.3.5 examined both the "lost copy problem" and the "swap problem" and described approaches for handling them. Finally, Section 9.3.6 showed an algorithm that performs global constant propagation over the SSA form.

---

### Review Questions

1. Maximal SSA form includes useless $\phi$-functions that define nonlive values and redundant $\phi$-functions that merge identical values (e.g. $x_8 \leftarrow \phi(x_7, x_7)$). How does the semipruned SSA construction deal with these unneeded $\phi$-functions?

2. Assume that your compiler's target machine implements swap $r_1, r_2$, an operation that simultaneously performs $r_1 \leftarrow r_2$ and $r_2 \leftarrow r_1$. What impact would the swap operation have on out-of-SSA translation?

   swap can be implemented with the three operation sequence:

   $$r_1 \leftarrow r_1 + r_2$$
   $$r_2 \leftarrow r_1 - r_2$$
   $$r_1 \leftarrow r_1 - r_2$$

   What would be the advantages and disadvantages of using this implementation of swap in out-of-SSA translation?

---

## 9.4 INTERPROCEDURAL ANALYSIS

The inefficiencies introduced by procedure calls appear in two distinct forms: loss of knowledge in single-procedure analysis and optimization that arises from the presence of a call site in the region being analyzed and transformed and specific overhead introduced to maintain the abstractions inherent in the procedure call. Interprocedural analysis was introduced to address the former problem. We saw, in Section 9.2.4, how the compiler can compute sets that summarize the side effects of a call site. This section explores more complex issues in interprocedural analysis.

### 9.4.1 **Call-Graph Construction**

The first problem that the compiler must address in interprocedural analysis is the construction of a call graph. In the simplest case, in which every procedure call invokes a procedure named by a literal constant, as in "call foo(x, y, z)", the problem is straightforward. The compiler creates a call-graph node for each procedure in the program and adds an edge to the call graph for each call site. This process takes time proportional to the number of procedures and the number of call sites in the program; in practice, the limiting factor will be the cost of scanning procedures to find the call sites.

Source language features can make call-graph construction much harder. Even FORTRAN and C programs have complications. For example, consider the small C program shown in Figure 9.20a. Its precise call graph is shown in Figure 9.20b. The following subsections outline the language features that complicate call-graph construction.

**Procedure-Valued Variables**

If the program uses procedure-valued variables, the compiler must analyze the code to estimate the set of potential callees at each call site that invokes a procedure-valued variable. To begin, the compiler can construct the graph specified by the calls that use explicit literal constants. Next, it can track the propagation of functions as values around this subset of the call graph, adding edges as indicated.

In SSCP, initialize function-valued formals with known constant values. Actuals with the known values reveal where functions are passed through.

The compiler can use a simple analog of global constant propagation to transfer function values from a procedure's entry to the call sites that use them, using set union as its meet operation. To improve its efficiency, it can construct expressions for each parameter-valued variable used in a procedure (see the discussion of jump functions in Section 9.4.2).

As the code in Figure 9.20a shows, a straightforward analysis may overestimate the set of call-graph edges. The code calls compose to compute a(c) and b(d). A simple analysis, however, will conclude that the formal parameter g in compose can receive either c or d, and that, as a result, the program

```
int compose( int f(), int g()) {
  return f(g);
}
int a( int z() ) {
  return z();
}
int b( int z() ) {
  return z();
}
int c( ) {
  return ...;
}
int d( ) {
  return ...;
}
int main(int argc, char *argv[]) {
  return compose(a,c)
       + compose(b,d);
}
```

(a) Example C Program

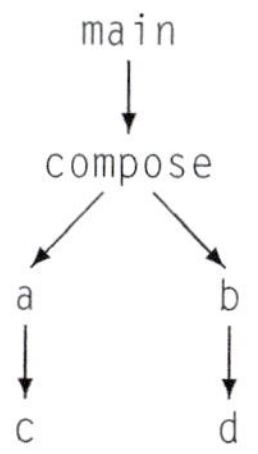

(b) Precise Call Graph

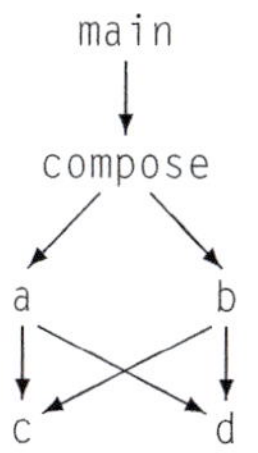

(c) Approximate Call Graph

■ **FIGURE 9.20** Building a Call Graph with Function-Valued Parameters.

might compose any of $a(c)$, $a(d)$, $b(c)$, or $b(d)$, as shown in Figure 9.20c. To build the precise call graph, it must track sets of parameters that are passed together, along the same path. The algorithm could then consider each set independently to derive the precise graph. Alternatively, it might tag each value with the path that the values travel and use the path information to avoid adding spurious edges such as $(a,d)$ or $(b,c)$.

### Contextually-Resolved Names

Some languages allow programmers to use names that are resolved by context. In object-oriented languages with an inheritance hierarchy, the binding of a method name to a specific implementation depends on the class of the receiver and the state of the inheritance hierarchy.

If the inheritance hierarchy and all the procedures are fixed at the time of analysis, then the compiler can use interprocedural analysis of the class structure to narrow the set of methods that can be invoked at any given call site. The call-graph constructor must include an edge from that call site to each procedure or method that might be invoked.

Dynamic linking, used in some operating systems to reduce virtual memory requirements, introduces similar complications. If the compiler cannot determine what code will execute, it cannot construct a complete call graph.

For a language that allows the program to import either executable code or new class definitions at runtime, the compiler must construct a conservative call graph that reflects the complete set of potential callees at each call site. One way to accomplish that goal is to construct a node in the call graph that represents unknown procedures and endow it with worst-case behavior; its MayMod and MayRef sets should be the complete set of visible names.

Analysis that reduces the number of call sites that can name multiple procedures can improve the precision of the call graph by reducing the number of spurious edges—edges for calls that cannot occur at runtime. Of equal or greater importance, any call sites that can be narrowed to a single callee can be implemented with a simple call; those with multiple callees may require runtime lookups for the dispatch of the call (see Section 6.3.3). Runtime lookups to support dynamic dispatch are much more expensive than a direct call.

### Other Language Issues

In intraprocedural analysis, we assume that the control-flow graph has a single entry and a single exit; we add an artificial exit node if the procedure has multiple returns. In interprocedural analysis, language features can create the same kinds of problems.

For example, Java has both initializers and finalizers. The Java virtual machine invokes a class initializer after it loads and verifies the class; it invokes an object initializer after it allocates space for the object but before it returns the object's hashcode. Thread start methods, finalizers, and destructors also have the property that they execute without an explicit call in the source program.

The call-graph builder must pay attention to these procedures. Initializers may be connected to sites that create objects; finalizers might be connected to the call-graph's entry node. The specific connections will depend on the language definition and the analysis being performed. MayMod analysis, for example, might ignore them as irrelevant, while interprocedural constant propagation needs information from initialization and start methods.

## 9.4.2 **Interprocedural Constant Propagation**

Interprocedural constant propagation tracks known constant values of global variables and parameters as they propagate around the call graph, both through procedure bodies and across call-graph edges. The goal of interprocedural constant propagation is to discover situations where a procedure always receives a known constant value or where a procedure always returns a known constant value. When the analysis discovers such a constant, it can specialize the code for that value.

Conceptually, interprocedural constant propagation consists of three sub-problems: discovering an initial set of constants, propagating known constant values around the call graph, and modelling transmission of values through procedures.

### Discovering an Initial Set of Constants

The analyzer must identify, at each call site, which actual parameters have known constant values. A wide range of techniques are possible. The simplest method is to recognize literal constant values used as parameters. A more effective and expensive technique might use a full-fledged global constant propagation step (see Section 9.3.6) to identify constant-valued parameters.

### Propagating Known Constant Values around the Call Graph

Given an initial set of constants, the analyzer propagates the constant values across call-graph edges and through the procedures from entry to each call site in the procedure. This portion of the analysis resembles the iterative data-flow algorithms from Section 9.2. This problem can be solved with the iterative algorithm, but the algorithm can require significantly more iterations than it would for simpler problems such as live variables or available expressions.

### Modeling Transmission of Values through Procedures

Each time it processes a call-graph node, the analyzer must determine how the constant values known at the procedure's entry affect the set of constant values known at each call site. To do so, it builds a small model for each actual parameter, called a *jump function*. A call site $s$ with $n$ parameters has a vector of jump functions, $\mathcal{J}_s = \langle \mathcal{J}_s^a, \mathcal{J}_s^b, \mathcal{J}_s^c, \ldots, \mathcal{J}_s^n \rangle$, where $a$ is the first formal parameter in the callee, $b$ is the second, and so on. Each jump function, $\mathcal{J}_s^x$, relies on the values of some subset of the formal parameters to the procedure $p$ that contains $s$; we denote that set as $Support(\mathcal{J}_s^x)$.

For the moment, assume that $\mathcal{J}_s^x$ consists of an expression tree whose leaves are all formal parameters of the caller or literal constants. We require that $\mathcal{J}_s^x$ return $\top$ if $Value(y)$ is $\top$ for any $y \in Support(\mathcal{J}_s^x)$.

### *The Algorithm*

Figure 9.21 shows a simple algorithm for interprocedural constant propagation across the call graph. It is similar to the SSCP algorithm presented in Section 9.3.6.

The algorithm associates a field $Value(x)$ with each formal parameter $x$ of each procedure $p$. (It assumes unique, or fully qualified, names for each

```
// Phase 1: Initializations
Build all jump functions and Support mappings
Worklist ← Ø

for each procedure p in the program
    for each formal parameter f to p
        Value(f) ← ⊤                        // Optimistic initial value
        Worklist ← Worklist ∪ {f}
for each call site s in the program
    for each formal parameter f that receives a value at s
        Value(f) ← Value(f) ∧ 𝒥ₛᶠ           // Initial constants factor in to 𝒥ₛᶠ

// Phase 2: Iterate to a fixed point
while (Worklist ≠ Ø)
    pick parameter f from Worklist          // Pick an arbitrary parameter
    let p be the procedure declaring f

    // Update the Value of each parameter that depends on f
    for each call site s in p and parameter x such that f ∈ Support(𝒥ₛˣ)
        t ← Value(x)
        Value(x) ← Value(x) ∧ 𝒥ₛˣ           // Compute new value
        if (Value(x) < t)
            then Worklist ← Worklist ∪ {x}

// Post-process Val sets to produce CONSTANTS
for each procedure p
    CONSTANTS(p) ← Ø
    for each formal parameter f to p
        if (Value(f) = ⊤)
            then Value(f) ← ⊥
        if (Value(f) ≠ ⊥)
            then CONSTANTS(p) ← CONSTANTS(p) ∪ {⟨f, Value(f)⟩}
```

■ **FIGURE 9.21** Iterative Interprocedural Constant Propagation Algorithm.

formal parameter.) The initialization phase optimistically sets all the *Value* fields to $\top$. Next, it iterates over each actual parameter $a$ at each call site $s$ in the program, updates the *Value* field of $a$'s corresponding formal parameter $f$ to $Value(f) \wedge \mathcal{J}_s^f$, and adds $f$ to the worklist. This step factors the initial set of constants represented by the jump functions into the *Value* fields and sets the worklist to contain all of the formal parameters.

The second phase repeatedly selects a formal parameter from the worklist and propagates it. To propagate formal parameter $f$ of procedure $p$, the analyzer finds each call site $s$ in $p$ and each formal parameter $x$ (which corresponds to an actual parameter of call site $s$) such that $f \in Support(\mathcal{J}_s^x)$. It evaluates $\mathcal{J}_s^x$ and combines it with $Value(x)$. If that changes $Value(x)$, it adds $x$ to the worklist. The worklist should be implemented with a data structure, such as a sparse set, that only allows one copy of $x$ in the worklist (see Section B.2.3).

The second phase terminates because each $Value$ set can take on at most three lattice values: $\top$, some $c_i$, and $\bot$. A variable $x$ can only enter the worklist when its initial $Value$ is computed or when its $Value$ changes. Each variable $x$ can appear on the worklist at most three times. Thus, the total number of changes is bounded and the iteration halts. After the second phase halts, a post-processing step constructs the sets of constants known on entry to each procedure.

## Jump Function Implementation

Implementations of jump functions range from simple static approximations that do not change during analysis, through small parameterized models, to more complex schemes that perform extensive analysis at each jump-function evaluation. In any of these schemes, several principles hold. If the analyzer determines that parameter $x$ at call site $s$ is a known constant $c$, then $\mathcal{J}_s^x = c$ and $Support(\mathcal{J}_s^x) = \emptyset$. If $y \in Support(\mathcal{J}_s^x)$ and $Value(y) = \top$, then $\mathcal{J}_s^x = \top$. If the analyzer determines that the value of $\mathcal{J}_s^x$ cannot be determined, then $\mathcal{J}_s^x = \bot$.

For example, $Support(\mathcal{J}_s^x)$ might contain a value read from a file, so $\mathcal{J}_s^x = \bot$.

The analyzer can implement $\mathcal{J}_s^x$ in many ways. A simple implementation might only propagate a constant if $x$ is the SSA name of a formal parameter in the procedure containing $s$. (Similar functionality can be obtained using REACHES information from Section 9.2.4.) A more complex scheme might build expressions composed of SSA names of formal parameters and literal constants. An effective and expensive technique would be to run the SSCP algorithm on demand to update the values of jump functions.

## Extending the Algorithm

The algorithm shown in Figure 9.21 only propagates constant-valued actual parameters forward along call-graph edges. We can extend it, in a straight-forward way, to handle both returned values and variables that are global to a procedure.

Just as the algorithm builds jump functions to model the flow of values from caller to callee, it can construct *return jump functions* to model the values returned from callee to caller. Return jump functions are particularly important for routines that initialize values, whether filling in a common block in FORTRAN or setting initial values for an object or class in Java. The algorithm can treat return jump functions in the same way that it handled ordinary jump functions; the one significant complication is that the implementation must avoid creating cycles of return jump functions that diverge (e.g. for a tail-recursive procedure).

To extend the algorithm to cover a larger class of variables, the compiler can simply extend the vector of jump functions in an appropriate way. Expanding the set of variables will increase the cost of analysis, but two factors mitigate the cost. First, in jump-function construction, the analyzer can notice that many of those variables do not have a value that can be modelled easily; it can map those variables onto a universal jump function that returns $\bot$ and avoid placing them on the worklist. Second, for the variables that might have constant values, the structure of the lattice ensures that they will be on the worklist at most twice. Thus, the algorithm should still run quickly.

---

**SECTION REVIEW**

Compilers perform interprocedural analysis to capture the behavior of all the procedures in the program and to bring that knowledge to bear on optimization within individual procedures. To perform interprocedural analysis, the compiler needs access to all of the code in the program. A typical interprocedural problem requires the compiler to build a call graph (or some analog), to annotate it with information derived directly from the individual procedures, and to propagate that information around the graph.

The results of interprocedural information are applied directly in intra-procedural analysis and optimization. For example, MAYMOD and MAYREF sets can be used to mitigate the impact of a call site on global data-flow analyses, or to avoid the necessity for $\phi$-functions after a call site. Information from interprocedural constant propagation can be used to initialize a global algorithm, such as SSCP or SCCP.

---

**Review Questions**

1. What features of modern software might complicate interprocedural analysis?

2. How might the analyzer incorporate MAYMOD information into inter-procedural constant propagation? What effect would you expect it to have?

---

## 9.5 **ADVANCED TOPICS**

Section 9.2 focused on iterative data-flow analysis. The text emphasizes the iterative approach because it is simple, robust, and efficient. Other approaches to data-flow analysis tend to rely heavily on structural properties of the underlying graph. Section 9.5.1 discusses flow-graph reducibility—a critical property for most of the structural algorithms.

Section 9.5.2 revisits the iterative dominance framework from Section 9.2.1. The simplicity of that framework makes it attractive; however, more specialized and complex algorithms have significantly lower asymptotic complexities. In this section, we introduce a set of data structures that make the simple iterative technique competitive with the fast dominator algorithms for flow graphs of up to several thousand nodes.

## 9.5.1 Structural Data-Flow Algorithms and Reducibility

In Chapters 8 and 9, we present the iterative algorithm because it works, in general, on any set of well-formed equations on any graph. Other data-flow analysis algorithms exist; many of these work by deriving a simple model of the control-flow structure of the code being analyzed and using that model to solve the equations. Often, that model is built by finding a sequence of transformations to the graph that reduce its complexity—by combining nodes or edges in carefully defined ways. This graph-reduction process lies at the heart of almost every data-flow algorithm *except* the iterative algorithm.

Noniterative data-flow algorithms typically work by applying a series of transformations to a flow graph; each transformation selects a subgraph and replaces it by a single node to represent the subgraph. This creates a series of derived graphs in which each graph differs from its predecessor in the series by the effect of a single transformation step. As the analyzer transforms the graph, it computes data-flow sets for the new representer nodes in each successive derived graph. These sets summarize the replaced subgraph's effects. The transformations reduce well-behaved graphs to a single node. The algorithm then reverses the process, going from the final derived graph, with its single node, back to the original flow graph. As it expands the graph back to its original form, the analyzer computes the final data-flow sets for each node.

In essence, the reduction phase gathers information from the entire graph and consolidates it, while the expansion phase propagates the effects in the consolidated set back out to the nodes of the original graph. Any graph for which such a reduction phase succeeds is deemed *reducible*. If the graph cannot be reduced to a single node, it is *irreducible*.

Figure 9.22 shows a pair of transformations that can be used to test reducibility and to build a structural data-flow algorithm. $T_1$ removes a self loop, an edge that runs from a node back to itself. The figure shows $T_1$ applied

**Reducible graph**
A flow graph is *reducible* if the two transformations, $T_1$ and $T_2$, will reduce it to a single node. If that process fails, the graph is *irreducible*.

Other tests for reducibility exist. For example, if the iterative DOM framework, using an RPO traversal order, needs more than two iterations over a graph, that graph is irreducible.

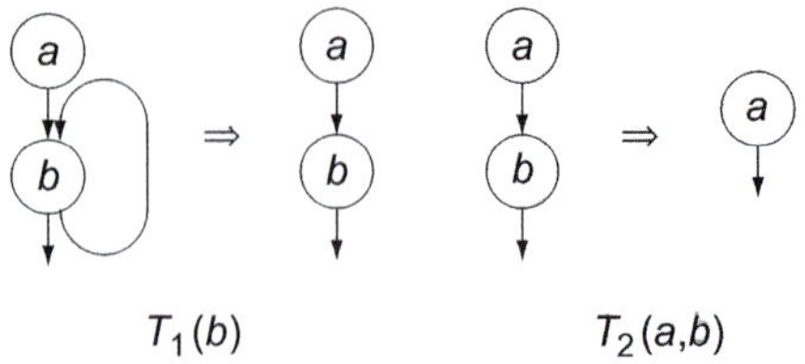

■ **FIGURE 9.22** Transformations $T_1$ and $T_2$.

to $b$, denoted $T_1(b)$. $T_2$ folds a node $b$ that has exactly one predecessor $a$ back into $a$; it removes the edge $\langle a, b\rangle$, and makes $a$ the source of any edges that originally left $b$. If this leaves multiple edges from $a$ to some node $n$, it consolidates those edges. Figure 9.22 shows $T_2$ applied to $a$ and $b$, denoted $T_2(a, b)$. Any graph that can be reduced to a single node by repeated application of $T_1$ and $T_2$ is deemed reducible. To understand how this works, consider the CFG from our continuing example. Figure 9.23a shows one sequence of applications of $T_1$ and $T_2$ that reduces it to a single-node graph. It applies $T_2$ until no more opportunities exist: $T_2(B_1, B_2)$, $T_2(B_5, B_6)$, $T_2(B_5, B_8)$, $T_2(B_5, B_7)$, $T_2(B_1, B_5)$, and $T_2(B_1, B_3)$. Next, it uses $T_1(B_1)$ to remove the loop, followed by $T_2(B_0, B_1)$ and $T_2(B_0, B_4)$ to complete the reduction. Since the final graph is a single node, the original graph is reducible.

Other application orders also reduce the graph. For example, if we start with $T_2(B_1, B_5)$, it leads to a different series of transformations. $T_1$ and $T_2$ have the finite Church-Rosser property, which ensures that the final result is independent of the order of application and that the sequence terminates. Thus, the analyzer can apply $T_1$ and $T_2$ opportunistically—finding places in the graph where one of them applies and using it.

Figure 9.23b shows what can happen when we apply $T_1$ and $T_2$ to a graph with multiple-entry loops. The analyzer uses $T_2(B_0, B_1)$ followed by $T_2(B_0, B_5)$. At that point, however, no remaining node or pair of nodes is a candidate for either $T_1$ or $T_2$. Thus, the analyzer cannot reduce the graph any further. (No other order will work either.) The graph is not reducible to a single node; it is irreducible.

The failure of $T_1$ and $T_2$ to reduce this graph arises from a fundamental property of the graph. The graph is irreducible because it contains a loop, or cycle, that has edges that enter it at different nodes. In terms of the source language, the program that generated the graph has a loop with multiple entries. We can see this in the graph; consider the cycle formed by $B_2$ and $B_3$. It has edges entering it from $B_1$, $B_4$, and $B_5$. Similarly, the cycle formed by $B_3$ and $B_4$ has edges that enter it from $B_2$ and $B_5$.

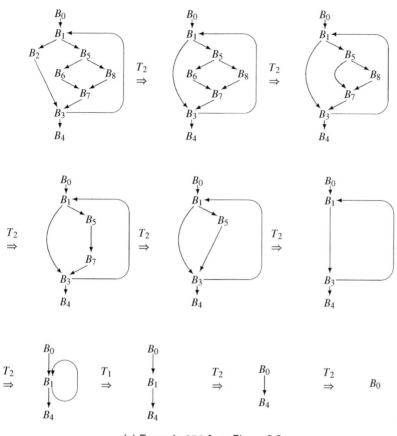

(a) Example CFG from Figure 9.2

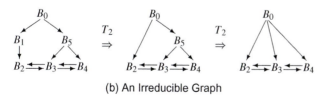

(b) An Irreducible Graph

■ **FIGURE 9.23**  Reduction Sequences for Example Graphs.

Irreducibility poses a serious problem for algorithms built on transformations like $T_1$ and $T_2$. If the reduction sequence cannot complete, producing a single-node graph, then the method must either report failure, modify the graph by splitting one or more nodes, or use an iterative approach to solve the system on the reduced graph. In general, the methods based on structurally reducing the flow graph are limited to reducible graphs. The iterative algorithm, in contrast, works correctly on an irreducible graph.

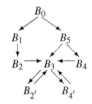

Irreducible Graph
After Node Splitting

To transform an irreducible graph to a reducible graph, the analyzer can split one or more nodes. The simplest split for the example graph, shown in the margin, clones $B_2$ and $B_4$ to create $B_{2'}$ and $B_{4'}$, respectively. The analyzer then retargets the edges $(B_3, B_2)$ and $(B_3, B_4)$ to form a complex loop, $\{B_3, B_{2'}, B_{4'}\}$. The new loop has a single entry, through $B_3$.

This transformation creates a reducible graph that executes the same sequence of operations as the original graph. Paths that, in the original graph, entered $B_3$ from either $B_2$ or $B_4$ now execute as prologues to the loop $\{B_3, B_{2'}, B_{4'}\}$. Both $B_2$ and $B_4$ have unique predecessors in the new graph. $B_3$ has multiple predecessors, but it is the sole entry to the loop and the loop is reducible. Thus, node splitting produced a reducible graph, at the cost of cloning two nodes.

Both folklore and published studies suggest that irreducible graphs rarely arise in global data-flow analysis. The rise of structured programming in the 1970s made programmers much less likely to use arbitrary transfers of control, like a `goto` statement. Structured loop constructs, such as `do`, `for`, `while`, and `until` loops, cannot produce irreducible graphs. However, transferring control out of a loop (for example, C's `break` statement) creates a CFG that is irreducible to a backward analysis. (Since the loop has multiple exits, the reverse CFG has multiple entries.) Similarly, irreducible graphs may arise more often in interprocedural analysis due to mutually recursive subroutines. For example, the call graph of a hand-coded, recursive-descent parser is likely to have irreducible subgraphs. Fortunately, an iterative analyzer can handle irreducible graphs correctly and efficiently.

### 9.5.2 Speeding up the Iterative Dominance Framework

The iterative framework for computing dominance is particularly simple. Where most data-flow problems have equations involving several sets, the equations for DOM involve computing a pairwise intersection over DOM sets and adding a single element to those sets. The simple nature of these equations presents an opportunity to use a particularly simple data-structure to improve the speed of the DOM calculation.

The iterative DOM framework uses a discrete DOM set at each node. We can reduce the amount of space required by the DOM sets by observing that the same information can be represented with a single fact at each node, its immediate dominator, or IDom. From the IDoms for the nodes, the compiler can compute all the other dominance information that it needs.

Recall our example CFG from Section 9.2.1, repeated in the margin with its dominator tree. Its IDOM sets are as follows:

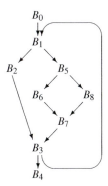

$B_0$

The Example CFG

|        | $B_0$ | $B_1$ | $B_2$ | $B_3$ | $B_4$ | $B_5$ | $B_6$ | $B_7$ | $B_8$ |
|--------|-------|-------|-------|-------|-------|-------|-------|-------|-------|
| **IDOM(n)** | ? | 0 | 1 | 1 | 3 | 1 | 5 | 5 | 5 |

Notice that the dominator tree and the IDOMs are isomorphic. IDOM($b$) is just $b$'s predecessor in the dominator tree. The root of the dominator tree has no predecessor; accordingly, its IDOM set is undefined.

The compiler can read a graph's DOM sets from its dominator tree. For a node $n$, its DOM set can be read as the set of nodes that lie on the path from $n$ to the root of the dominator tree, inclusive of the end points. In the example, the dominator-tree path from $B_7$ to $B_1$ consists of $(B_7, B_5, B_1, B_0)$, which matches the set computed for DOM($B_7$) in Section 9.2.1.

Thus, we can use the IDOM sets as a proxy for the DOM sets, provided we can provide efficient methods to initialize the sets and to intersect them. To handle the initializations, we will reformulate the iterative algorithm slightly. To intersect two DOM sets from their IDOM sets, we will use the algorithm shown in procedure `Intersect` at the bottom of Figure 9.24. It relies on two critical facts.

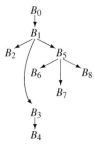

Its Dominator Tree

1. When the algorithm walks the path from a node to the root to recreate a DOM set, it encounters the nodes in a consistent order. The intersection of two DOM sets is simply the common suffix of the labels on the paths from the nodes to the root.
2. The algorithm must be able to recognize the common suffix. It starts at the two nodes whose sets are being intersected, $i$ and $j$, and walks upward from each toward the root. If we name the nodes by their RPO numbers, then a simple comparison will let the algorithm discover the nearest common ancestor—the IDOM of $i$ and $j$.

The `Intersect` algorithm in Figure 9.24 is a variant of the classic "two finger" algorithm. It uses two pointers to trace paths upward through the tree. When they agree, they both point to the node representing the result of the intersection.

```
for all nodes, b     // initialize the dominators array
    IDoms[b] ← Undefined
IDoms[b₀] ← b₀
Changed ← true
while (Changed)
    Changed ← false
    for all nodes, b, in reverse postorder (except root)
        NewIDom ← first (processed) predecessor of b   // pick one
        for all other predecessors, p, of b
            if IDoms[p] ≠ Undefined    // i.e., Doms[p] already calculated
                then NewIdom ← Intersect(p, NewIdom)
            if IDoms[b] ≠ NewIdom then
                IDoms[b] ← NewIdom
                Changed ← true


Intersect(i, j)
    finger1 ← i
    finger2 ← j
    while (finger1 ≠ finger2)
        while (RPO(finger1) > RPO(finger2))
            finger1 = IDoms[finger1]
        while (RPO(finger2) > RPO(finger1))
            finger2 = IDoms[finger2]
    return finger1
```

■ **FIGURE 9.24** The Modified Iterative Dominator Algorithm.

The algorithm assigns IDom($b_0$) the value $b_0$ to simplify the rest of the algorithm.

The top of Figure 9.24 shows a reformulated iterative algorithm that avoids the issue of initializing the IDom sets and uses the *Intersect* algorithm. It keeps the IDom information in an array, *IDoms*. It initializes the IDom entry for the root, $b_0$, to itself. It then processes the nodes in reverse postorder. In computing intersections, it ignores predecessors whose IDoms have not yet been computed.

To see how the algorithm operates, consider the graph in Figure 9.25a. Figure 9.25b shows an RPO for this graph that illustrates the problems caused by irreducibility. Using this order, the algorithm miscomputes the IDoms of $B_3$, and $B_4$ in the first iteration. It takes two iterations for the algorithm to correct those IDoms, and a final iteration to recognize that the IDoms have stopped changing.

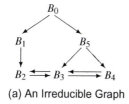

(a) An Irreducible Graph

| | $B_0$ | $B_1$ | $B_2$ | $B_3$ | $B_4$ | $B_5$ |
|---|---|---|---|---|---|---|
| RPO($n$) | 0 | 1 | 5 | 4 | 3 | 2 |

(b) A Worst-Case RPO

| | IDOM($n$) | | | | | |
|---|---|---|---|---|---|---|
| | $B_0$ | $B_1$ | $B_2$ | $B_3$ | $B_4$ | $B_5$ |
| — | 0 | ? | ? | ? | ? | ? |
| 1 | 0 | 0 | 0 | 5 | 5 | 0 |
| 2 | 0 | 0 | 0 | 0 | 5 | 0 |
| 3 | 0 | 0 | 0 | 0 | 0 | 0 |
| 4 | 0 | 0 | 0 | 0 | 0 | 0 |

(c) Progress of the IDOM Computation

■ **FIGURE 9.25** A Graph with a More Complex Shape.

This improved algorithm runs quickly. It has a small memory footprint. On any reducible graph, it halts in two passes: the first pass computes the correct IDOM sets and the second pass confirms that no changes occur. An irreducible graph will take more than two passes. In fact, the algorithm provides a rapid test for reducibility—if any IDOM entry changes in the second pass, the graph is irreducible.

## 9.6 SUMMARY AND PERSPECTIVE

Most optimization tailors general-case code to the specific context that occurs in the compiled code. The compiler's ability to tailor code is often limited by its lack of knowledge about the program's range of runtime behaviors.

Data-flow analysis allows the compiler to model the runtime behavior of a program at compile time and to draw important, specific knowledge out of the models. Many data-flow problems have been proposed; this chapter presented several of them. Many of those problems have properties that lead to efficient analyses. In particular, problems that can be expressed in iterative frameworks have efficient solutions using simple iterative solvers.

SSA form is an intermediate form that encodes both data-flow information and control-dependence information into the name space of the program. Working with SSA form often simplifies both analysis and transformation. Many modern transformations rely on the SSA form of the code.

# ■ CHAPTER NOTES

Credit for the first data-flow analysis is usually given to Vyssotsky at Bell Labs in the early 1960s [338]. Earlier work, in the original FORTRAN compiler, included the construction of a control-flow graph and a Markov-style analysis over the CFG to estimate execution frequencies [26]. This analyzer, built by Lois Haibt, might be considered a data-flow analyzer.

Iterative data-flow analysis has a long history in the literature. Among the seminal papers on this topic are Kildall's 1973 paper [223], work by Hecht and Ullman [186], and two papers by Kam and Ullman [210, 211]. The treatment in this chapter follows Kam's work.

This chapter focuses on iterative data-flow analysis. Many other algorithms for solving data-flow problems have been proposed [218]. The interested reader should explore the structural techniques, including interval analysis [17, 18, 62]; $T_1$-$T_2$ analysis [336, 185]; the Graham-Wegman algorithm [168, 169]; balanced-tree, path-compression algorithm [330, 331]; graph grammars [219]; and the partitioned-variable technique [359].

Dominance has a long history in the literature. Prosser introduced dominance in 1959 but gave no algorithm to compute dominators [290]. Lowry and Medlock describe the algorithm used in their compiler [252]; it takes at least $O(N^2)$ time, where $N$ is the number of statements in the procedure. Several authors developed faster algorithms based on removing nodes from the CFG [8, 3, 291]. Tarjan proposed an $O(N \log N + E)$ algorithm based on depth-first search and union find [329]. Lengauer and Tarjan improved this time bound [244], as did others [180, 23, 61]. The data-flow formulation for dominators is taken from Allen [12, 17]. The fast data structures for iterative dominance are due to Harvey [100]. The algorithm in Figure 9.8 is from Ferrante, Ottenstein, and Warren [145].

The SSA construction is based on the seminal work by Cytron et al. [110]. It, in turn, builds on work by Shapiro and Saint [313]; by Reif [295, 332]; and by Ferrante, Ottenstein, and Warren [145]. The algorithm in Section 9.3.3 builds semipruned SSA form [49]. The details of the renaming algorithm and the algorithm for reconstructing executable code are described by Briggs et al. [50]. The complications introduced by critical edges have long been recognized in the literature of optimization [304, 133, 128, 130, 225]; it should not be surprising that they also arise in the translation from SSA back into executable code. The sparse simple constant algorithm, SSCP, is due to Reif and Lewis [296]. Wegman and Zadeck reformulate SSCP to use SSA form [346, 347].

The IBM PL/I optimizing compiler was one of the earliest systems to perform interprocedural data-flow analysis [322]. A large body of literature has emerged on side-effect analysis [34, 32, 102, 103]. The interprocedural constant propagation algorithm is from Torczon's thesis and subsequent papers [68, 172, 263]; both Cytron and Wegman suggested other approaches to the problem [111, 347]. Burke and Torczon [64] formulated an analysis that determines which modules in a large program must be recompiled in response to a change in a program's interprocedural information. Pointer analysis is inherently interprocedural; a growing body of literature describes that problem [348, 197, 77, 238, 80, 123, 138, 351, 312, 190, 113, 191]. Ayers, Gottlieb, and Schooler described a practical system that analyzed and optimized a subset of the entire program [25].

## ■ EXERCISES

1. The algorithm for live analysis in Figure 9.2 initializes the LiveOut set of each block to $\phi$. Are other initializations possible? Do they change the result of the analysis? Justify your answer.

   Section 9.2

2. In live-variable analysis, how should the compiler treat a block containing a procedure call? What should the block's UEVar set contain? What should its VarKill set contain?

3. In the computation of available expressions, the initialization sets
   $$\text{AvailIn}(n_0) = \emptyset, \quad \text{and}$$
   $$\text{AvailIn}(n) = \{all\ expressions\}, \forall n \neq n_0$$
   Construct a small example program that shows why the latter initialization is necessary. What happens on your example if the AvailIn sets are uniformly initialized to $\emptyset$?

4. For each of the following control-flow graphs:

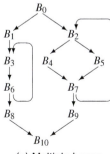

(a) Multiple Loops

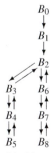

(b) Doubled Loop Body

    **a.** Compute reverse postorder numberings for the CFG and the reverse
    CFG.

    **b.** Compute reverse preorder on the CFG.

    **c.** Is reverse preorder on the CFG equivalent to postorder on the
    reverse CFG?

Section 9.3

**5.** Consider the three control-flow graphs shown below.

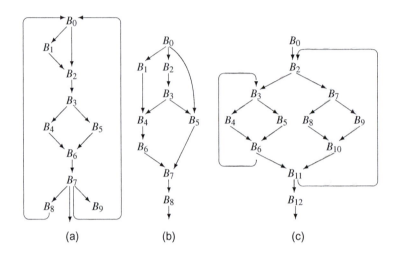

(a)           (b)           (c)

    **a.** Compute the dominator trees for CFGs a, b, and c.

    **b.** Compute the dominance frontiers for nodes 3 and 5 of CFG a,
    nodes 4 and 5 of CFG b, and nodes 3 and 11 of CFG c.

**6.** Translate the code shown in Figure 9.26 to SSA form. Show only the
final code, after both $\phi$-insertion and renaming.

**7.** Consider the set of all blocks that receive a $\phi$-function because of an
assignment $x \leftarrow \ldots$ in some block $b$. The algorithm in Figure 9.9
inserts a $\phi$-function in each block in DF($b$). Each of those blocks is
added to the worklist; they, in turn, can add nodes in their DF sets to
the worklist. The algorithm uses a checklist to avoid adding a block to
the worklist more than once. Call the set of all these blocks DF$^+$($b$).
We can define DF$^+$($b$) as the limit of the sequence

$$\text{DF}_1(b) = \text{DF}(b)$$
$$\text{DF}_2(b) = \text{DF}_1(b) \cup_{x \in \text{DF}_1(b)} \text{DF}_1(x)$$
$$\text{DF}_3(b) = \text{DF}_2(b) \cup_{x \in \text{DF}_2(b)} \text{DF}_2(x)$$
$$\cdots$$
$$\text{DF}_i(b) = \text{DF}_{i-1}(b) \cup_{x \in \text{DF}_{i-1}(b)} \text{DF}_{i-1}(x)$$

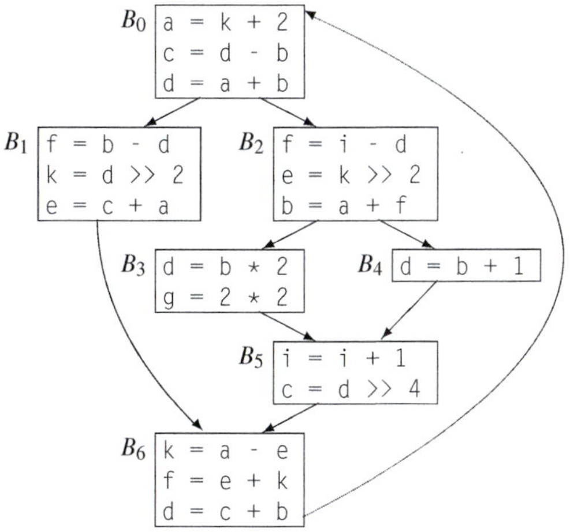

■ **FIGURE 9.26** CFG for Problem 6.

Using these extended sets, $DF^+(b)$, leads to a simpler algorithm for
inserting $\phi$-functions.
**a.** Develop an algorithm for computing $DF^+(b)$.
**b.** Develop an algorithm for inserting $\phi$-functions using these $DF^+$
sets.
**c.** Compare the overall cost of your algorithm, including the
computation of $DF^+$ sets, to the cost of the $\phi$-insertion algorithm
given in Section 9.3.3.

**8.** The maximal SSA construction is both simple and intuitive. However,
it can insert many more $\phi$-functions than the semipruned algorithm. In
particular, it can insert both redundant $\phi$-functions ($x_i \leftarrow \phi(x_j,x_j)$)
and dead $\phi$-functions—where the result is never used.
**a.** Propose a method for detecting and removing the extra $\phi$-functions
that the maximal construction inserts.
**b.** Can your method reduce the set of $\phi$-functions to just those that the
semipruned construction inserts?
**c.** Contrast the asymptotic complexity of your method against that of
the semipruned construction.

**9.** Dominance information and SSA form allow us to improve the
superlocal value numbering algorithm (SVN) from Section 8.5.1.
Assume the code is in SSA form.
**a.** For each node in the CFG with multiple predecessors, SVN begins
with an empty hash table. For such a block, $b_i$, can you use

dominance information to select a block whose facts must hold on entry to $b_i$?

**b.** On what properties of SSA form does this algorithm rely?

**c.** Assuming that the code is already in SSA form, with dominance information available, what is the extra cost of this dominator-based value numbering?

Section 9.4

10. For each of the following control-flow graphs, show whether or not it is reducible:

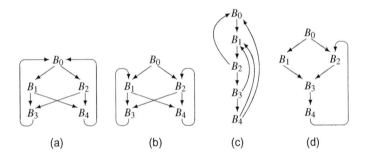

(a)        (b)        (c)        (d)

11. Prove that the following definition of a reducible graph is equivalent to the definition that uses the transformations $T_1$ and $T_2$: "A graph $G$ is reducible if and only if for each cycle in $G$, there exists a node $n$ in the cycle with the property that $n$ dominates every node in that cycle."

12. Show a sequence of reductions, using $T_1$ and $T_2$, that reduce the following graph:

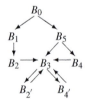

# Scalar Optimizations

## ■ CHAPTER OVERVIEW

An optimizing compiler improves the quality of the code that it generates by applying transformations that rewrite the code. This chapter builds on the introduction to optimization provided in Chapter 8 and the material on static analysis in Chapter 9 to focus on optimization of the code for a single thread of control—so-called scalar optimization. The chapter introduces a broad selection of machine-independent transformations that address a variety of inefficiencies in the compiled code.

**Keywords:** Optimization, Transformation, Machine Dependent, Machine Independent, Redundancy, Dead Code, Constant Propagation

## 10.1 INTRODUCTION

An optimizer analyzes and transforms the code with the intent to improve its performance. The compiler uses static analyses, such as data-flow analysis (see Chapter 9) to discover opportunities for transformations and to prove their safety. These analyses are preludes to transformations—unless the compiler rewrites the code, nothing will change.

Code optimization has a history that is as long as the history of compilers. The first FORTRAN compiler included careful optimization with the intent to provide performance that rivaled hand-coded assembly code. Since that first optimizing compiler in the late 1950s, the literature on optimization has grown to include thousands of papers that describe analyses and transformations.

Deciding which transformations to use and selecting an order of application for them remains one of the most daunting decisions that a compiler writer faces. This chapter focuses on *scalar optimization*, that is, optimization of

**Scalar optimization**
code improvement techniques that focus on a single thread of control

code along a single thread of control. It identifies five key sources of inefficiency in compiled code and then presents a set of optimizations that help to remove those inefficiencies. The chapter is organized around these five effects; we expect that a compiler writer choosing optimizations might use the same organizational scheme.

### *Conceptual Roadmap*

Compiler-based optimization is the process of analyzing the code to determine its properties and using the results of that analysis to rewrite the code into a more efficient or more effective form. Such improvement can be measured in many ways, including decreased running time, smaller code size, or lower processor energy use during execution. Every compiler has some set of input programs for which it produces highly efficient code. A good optimizer should make that performance available on a much larger set of inputs. The optimizer should be robust, that is, small changes in the input should not produce wild performance changes.

An optimizer achieves these goals through two primary mechanisms. It eliminates unnecessary overhead introduced by programming language abstractions and it matches the needs of the resulting program to the available hardware and software resources of the target machine. In the broadest sense, transformations can be classified as either *machine independent* or *machine dependent*. For example, replacing a redundant computation with a reuse of the previously computed value is usually faster than recomputing the value; thus, redundancy elimination is considered machine independent. By contrast, implementing a character string copy operation with the "scatter-gather" hardware on a vector processor is clearly *machine dependent*. Rewriting that copy operation with a call to the hand-optimized system routine bcopy might be more broadly applicable.

**Machine independent**
A transformation that improves code on most target machines is considered *machine independent*.

**Machine dependent**
A transformation that relies on knowledge of the target processor is considered *machine dependent*.

### *Overview*

Most optimizers are built as a series of passes, as shown in the margin. Each pass takes code in IR form as its input. Each pass produces a rewritten version of the IR code as its output. This structure breaks the implementation into smaller pieces and avoids some of the complexity that arises in large, monolithic programs. It allows the passes to be built and tested independently, which simplifies development, testing, and maintenance. It creates a natural way for the compiler to provide different levels of optimization; each level specifies a set of passes to run. The pass structure allows the compiler writer to run some passes multiple times, if desirable. In practice, some passes should run once, while others might run several times at different points in the sequence.

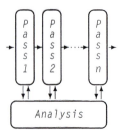

---

**OPTIMIZATION SEQUENCES**

The choice of specific transformations and the order of their application has a strong impact on the effectiveness of an optimizer. To make the problem harder, individual transformations have overlapping effects (e.g. local value numbering versus superlocal value numbering) and individual applications have different sets of inefficiencies.

Equally difficult, transformations that address different effects interact with one another. A given transformation can create opportunities for other transformations. Symmetrically, a given transformation can obscure or eliminate opportunities for other transformations.

Classic optimizing compilers provide several levels of optimization (e.g. -0, -01, -02, ...) as one way of providing the end user with multiple sequences that they can try. Researchers have focused on techniques to derive custom sequences for specific application codes, selecting both a set of transformations and an order of application. Section 10.7.3 discusses this problem in more depth.

---

In the design of an optimizer, the selection of transformations and the ordering of those transformations play a critical role in determining the overall effectiveness of the optimizer. The selection of transformations determines what specific inefficiencies in the IR program the optimizer discovers and how it rewrites the code to reduce those inefficiencies. The order in which the compiler applies the transformations determines how the passes interact.

For example, in the appropriate context ($r_2 > 0$ and $r_5 = 4$), an optimizer might replace mult $r_2$, $r_5 \Rightarrow r_{17}$ with lshiftI $r_2$, $2 \Rightarrow r_{17}$. This change replaces a multicycle integer multiply with a single-cycle shift operation and reduces demand for registers. In most cases, this rewrite is profitable. If, however, the next pass relies on commutativity to rearrange expressions, then replacing a multiply with a shift forecloses an opportunity (multiply is commutative, shift is not). To the extent that a transformation makes later passes less effective, it may hurt overall code quality. Deferring the replacement of multiplies by shifts may avoid this problem; the context needed to prove safety and profitability for this rewrite is likely to survive the intervening passes.

The first hurdle in the design and construction of an optimizer is conceptual. The optimization literature describes hundreds of distinct algorithms to improve IR programs. The compiler writer must select a subset of these transformations to implement and apply. While reading the original papers may help with the implementation, it provides little insight for the decision process, since most of the papers advocate using their own transformations.

Compiler writers need to understand both what inefficiencies arise in applications translated by their compilers and what impact those inefficiencies have on the application. Given a set of specific flaws to address, they can then select specific transformations to address them. Many transformations, in fact, address multiple inefficiencies, so careful selection can reduce the number of passes needed. Since most optimizers are built with limited resources, the compiler writer can prioritize transformations by their expected impact on the final code.

As mentioned in the conceptual roadmap, transformations fall into two broad categories: machine-independent transformations and machine-dependent transformations. Examples of machine-independent transformations from earlier chapters include local value numbering, inline substitution, and constant propagation. Machine-dependent transformations often fall into the realm of code generation. Examples include peephole optimization (see Section 11.5), instruction scheduling, and register allocation. Other machine-dependent transformations fall into the realm the optimizer. Examples include tree-height balancing, global code placement, and procedure placement. Some transformations resist classification; loop unrolling can address either machine-independent issues such as loop overhead or machine-dependent issues such as instruction scheduling.

> The distinction between the categories can be unclear. We call a transformation machine independent if it deliberately ignores target machine considerations, such as its impact on register allocation.

Chapters 8 and 9 have already presented a number of transformations, selected to illustrate specific points in those chapters. The next three chapters focus on code generation, a machine-dependent activity. Many of the techniques presented in these chapters, such as peephole optimization, instruction scheduling, and register allocation, are machine-dependent transformations. This chapter presents a broad selection of transformations, mostly machine-independent transformations. The transformations are organized around the effect that they have on the final code. We will concern ourselves with five specific effects.

- *Eliminate useless and unreachable code*  The compiler can discover that an operation is either useless or unreachable. In most cases, eliminating such operations produces faster, smaller code.
- *Move code*  The compiler can move an operation to a place where it executes fewer times but produces the same answer. In most cases, code motion reduces runtime. In some cases, it reduces code size.
- *Specialize a computation*  The compiler can use the context around an operation to specialize it, as in the earlier example that rewrote a

---

**OPTIMIZATION AS SOFTWARE ENGINEERING**

Having a separate optimizer can simplify the design and implementation of a compiler. The optimizer simplifies the front end; the front end can generate general-purpose code and ignore special cases. The optimizer simplifies the back end; the back end can focus on mapping the IR version of the program to the target machine. Without an optimizer, both the front end and back end must be concerned with finding opportunities for improvement and exploiting them.

In a pass-structured optimizer, each pass contains a transformation and the analysis required to support it. In principle, each task that the optimizer performs can be implemented once. This provides a single point of control and lets the compiler writer implement complex functions once, rather than many times. For example, deleting an operation from the IR can be complicated. If the deleted operation leaves a basic block empty, except for the block-ending branch or jump, then the transformation should also delete the block and reconnect the block's predecessors to its successors, as appropriate. Keeping this functionality in one place simplifies implementation, understanding, and maintenance.

From a software engineering perspective, the pass structure, with a clear separation of concerns, makes sense. It lets each pass focus on a single task. It provides a clear separation of concerns—value numbering ignores register pressure and the register allocator ignores common subexpressions. It lets the compiler writer test passes independently and thoroughly, and it simplifies fault isolation.

---

multiply as a shift. Specialization reduces the cost of general code sequences.

- *Eliminate a redundant computation*   The compiler can prove that a value has already been computed and reuse the earlier value. In many cases, reuse costs less than recomputation. Local value numbering captures this effect.

- *Enable other transformations*   The compiler can rewrite the code in a way that exposes new opportunities for other transformations. Inline substitution, for example, creates opportunities for many other optimizations.

This set of categories covers most machine-independent effects that the compiler can address. In practice, many transformations attack effects in more than one category. Local value numbering, for example, eliminates redundant computations, specializes computations with known constant values, and uses algebraic identities to identify and remove some kinds of useless computations.

## 10.2 ELIMINATING USELESS AND UNREACHABLE CODE

Sometimes, programs contain computations that have no externally visible effect. If the compiler can determine that a given operation does not affect the program's results, it can eliminate the operation. Most programmers do not write such code intentionally. However, it arises in most programs as the direct result of optimization in the compiler and often from macro expansion or naive translation in the compiler's front end.

**Useless**
An operation is *useless* if no operation uses its result, or if all uses of the result are, themselves dead.

**Unreachable**
An operation is *unreachable* if no valid control-flow path contains the operation.

Two distinct effects can make an operation eligible for removal. The operation can be *useless*, meaning that its result has no externally visible effect. Alternatively, the operation can be *unreachable*, meaning that it cannot execute. If an operation falls into either category, it can be eliminated. The term *dead code* is often used to mean either useless or unreachable code; we use the term to mean useless.

Removing useless or unreachable code shrinks the IR form of the code, which leads to a smaller executable program, faster compilation, and, often, to faster execution. It may also increase the compiler's ability to improve the code. For example, unreachable code may have effects that show up in the results of static analysis and prevent the application of some transformations. In this case, removing the unreachable block may change the analysis results and allow further transformations (see, for example, sparse conditional constant propagation, or SCCP, in Section 10.7.1).

Some forms of redundancy elimination also remove useless code. For instance, local value numbering applies algebraic identities to simplify the code. Examples include $x + 0 \Rightarrow x$, $y \times 1 \Rightarrow y$, and $\max(z,z) \Rightarrow z$. Each of these simplifications eliminates a useless operation—by definition, an operation that, when removed, makes no difference in the program's externally visible behavior.

Because the algorithms in this section modify the program's control-flow graph (CFG), we carefully distinguish between the terms *branch*, as in an ILOC cbr, and *jump*, as in an ILOC jump. Close attention to this distinction will help the reader understand the algorithms.

### 10.2.1 Eliminating Useless Code

An operation can set a return value in several ways, including assignment to a call-by-reference parameter or a global variable, assignment through an ambiguous pointer, or passing a return value via a return statement.

The classic algorithms for eliminating useless code operate in a manner similar to mark-sweep garbage collectors with the IR code as data (see Section 6.6.2). Like mark-sweep collectors, they perform two passes over the code. The first pass starts by clearing all the mark fields and marking "critical" operations as "useful." An operation is *critical* if it sets return values for the procedure, it is an input/output statement, or it affects the value in

```
Mark( )
 WorkList ← Ø

 for each operation i
     clear i's mark
     if i is critical then
        mark i
        WorkList ← WorkList ∪ {i}              Sweep( )
 while (WorkList ≠ Ø)                           for each operation i
     remove i from WorkList                        if i is unmarked then
      (assume i is x ← y op z)                        if i is a branch then
                                                         rewrite i with a jump
     if def(y) is not marked then                         to i's nearest marked
     mark def(y)                                          postdominator
     WorkList ← WorkList ∪ {def(y)}
     if def(z) is not marked then                     if i is not a jump then
     mark def(z)                                         delete i
     WorkList ← WorkList ∪ {def(z)}

     for each block b ∈ RDF(block(i))
        let j be the branch that ends b
        if j is unmarked then
           mark j
           WorkList ← WorkList ∪ {j}
```

|                                           |                                    |
| :---------------------------------------: | :--------------------------------: |
| (a) The `Mark` Routine                    | (b) The `Sweep` Routine            |

■ **FIGURE 10.1** Useless Code Elimination.

a storage location that may be accessible from outside the current procedure. Examples of critical operations include a procedure's prologue and epilogue code and the precall and postreturn sequences at calls. Next, the algorithm traces the operands of useful operations back to their definitions and marks those operations as useful. This process continues, in a simple worklist iterative scheme, until no more operations can be marked as useful. The second pass walks the code and removes any operation not marked as useful.

Figure 10.1 makes these ideas concrete. The algorithm, which we call `Dead`, assumes that the code is in SSA form. SSA simplifies the process because each use refers to a single definition. `Dead` consists of two passes. The first, called `Mark`, discovers the set of useful operations. The second, called `Sweep`, removes useless operations. `Mark` relies on reverse dominance frontiers, which derive from the dominance frontiers used in the SSA construction (see Section 9.3.2).

The treatment of operations other than branches or jumps is straightforward. The marking phase determines whether an operation is useful. The sweep phase removes operations that have not been marked as useful.

The treatment of control-flow operations is more complex. Every jump is considered useful. Branches are considered useful only if the execution of a useful operation depends on their presence. As the marking phase discovers useful operations, it also marks the appropriate branches as useful. To map from a marked operation to the branches that it makes useful, the algorithm relies on the notion of control dependence.

**Postdominance**

In a CFG, *j postdominates i* if and only if every path from *i* to the exit node passes through *j*.

See also the definition of dominance on page 478.

The definition of control dependence relies on *postdominance*. In a CFG, node *j* postdominates node *i* if every path from *i* to the CFG's exit node passes through *j*. Using postdominance, we can define control dependence as follows: in a CFG, node *j* is control-dependent on node *i* if and only if

1. There exists a nonnull path from *i* to *j* such that *j* postdominates every node on the path after *i*. Once execution begins on this path, it must flow through *j* to reach the CFG's exit (from the definition of postdominance).
2. *j* does not strictly postdominate *i*. Another edge leaves *i* and control may flow along a path to a node not on the path to *j*. There must be a path beginning with this edge that leads to the CFG's exit without passing through *j*.

In other words, two or more edges leave block *i*. One or more edges leads to *j* and one or more edges do not. Thus, the decision made at the branch-ending block *i* can determine whether or not *j* executes. If an operation in *j* is useful, then the branch that ends *i* is also useful.

This notion of control dependence is captured precisely by the *reverse dominance frontier* of *j*, denoted RDF(*j*). Reverse dominance frontiers are simply dominance frontiers computed on the reverse CFG. When *Mark* marks an operation in block *b* as useful, it visits every block in *b*'s reverse dominance frontier and marks their block-ending branches as useful. As it marks these branches, it adds them to the worklist. It halts when that worklist is empty.

*Sweep* replaces any unmarked branch with a jump to its first postdominator that contains a marked operation. If the branch is unmarked, then its successors, down to its immediate postdominator, contain no useful operations. (Otherwise, when those operations were marked, the branch would have been marked.) A similar argument applies if the immediate postdominator contains no marked operations. To find the nearest useful postdominator, the algorithm can walk up the postdominator tree until it finds a block that contains a useful operation. Since, by definition, the exit block is useful, this search must terminate.

After *Dead* runs, the code contains no useless computations. It may contain empty blocks, which can be removed by the next algorithm.

## 10.2.2 **Eliminating Useless Control Flow**

Optimization can change the IR form of the program so that it has useless control flow. If the compiler includes optimizations that can produce useless control flow as a side effect, then it should include a pass that simplifies the CFG by eliminating useless control flow. This section presents a simple algorithm called *Clean* that handles this task.

*Clean* operates directly on the procedure's CFG. It uses four transformations, shown in the margin. They are applied in the following order:

1. *Fold a Redundant Branch*  If *Clean* finds a block that ends in a branch, and both sides of the branch target the same block, it replaces the branch with a jump to the target block. This situation arises as the result of other simplifications. For example, $B_i$ might have had two successors, each with a jump to $B_j$. If another transformation had already emptied those blocks, then empty-block removal, discussed next, might produce the initial graph shown in the margin.

2. *Remove an Empty Block*  If *Clean* finds a block that contains only a jump, it can merge the block into its successor. This situation arises when other passes remove all of the operations from a block $B_i$. Consider the left graph of the pair shown in the margin. Since $B_i$ has only one successor, $B_j$, the transformation retargets the edges that enter $B_i$ to $B_j$ and deletes $B_i$ from $B_j$'s set of predecessors. This simplifies the graph. It should also speed up execution. In the original graph, the paths through $B_i$ needed two control-flow operations to reach $B_j$. In the transformed graph, those paths use one operation to reach $B_j$.

3. *Combine Blocks*  If *Clean* finds a block $B_i$ that ends in a jump to $B_j$ and $B_j$ has only one predecessor, it can combine the two blocks, as shown in the margin. This situation can arise in several ways. Another transformation might eliminate other edges that entered $B_j$, or $B_i$ and $B_j$ might be the result of folding a redundant branch (described previously). In either case, the two blocks can be combined into a single block. This eliminates the jump at the end of $B_i$.

4. *Hoist a Branch*  If *Clean* finds a block $B_i$ that ends with a jump to an empty block $B_j$ and $B_j$ ends with a branch, *Clean* can replace the block-ending jump in $B_i$ with a copy of the branch from $B_j$. In effect, this hoists the branch into $B_i$, as shown in the margin. This situation arises when other passes eliminate the operations in $B_j$, leaving a jump to a branch. The transformed code achieves the same effect with just a branch. This adds an edge to the CFG. Notice that $B_i$ cannot be empty, or else empty block removal would have eliminated it. Similarly, $B_i$ cannot be $B_j$'s sole predecessor, or else *Clean* would have combined the two blocks. (After hoisting, $B_j$ still has at least one predecessor.)

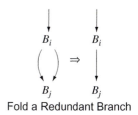
Fold a Redundant Branch

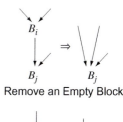
Remove an Empty Block

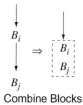
Combine Blocks

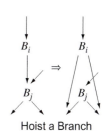
Hoist a Branch

Some bookkeeping is required to implement these transformations. Some of the modifications are trivial. To fold a redundant branch in a program represented with ILOC and a graphical CFG, *Clean* simply overwrites the block-ending branch with a jump and adjusts the successor and predecessor lists of the blocks. Others are more difficult. Merging two blocks may involve allocating space for the merged block, copying the operations into the new block, adjusting the predecessor and successor lists of the new block and its neighbors in the CFG, and discarding the two original blocks.

Many compilers and assemblers have included an ad hoc pass that eliminates a jump to a jump or a jump to a branch. *Clean* achieves the same effect in a systematic way.

*Clean* applies these four transformations in a systematic fashion. It traverses the graph in postorder, so that $B_i$'s successors are simplified before $B_i$, unless the successor lies along a back edge with respect to the postorder numbering. In that case, *Clean* will visit the predecessor before the successor. This is unavoidable in a cyclic graph. Simplifying successors before predecessors reduces the number of times that the implementation must move some edges.

In some situations, more than one of the transformations may apply. Careful analysis of the various cases leads to the order shown in Figure 10.2, which corresponds to the order in which they are presented in this section. The algorithm uses a series of *if* statements rather than an *if-then-else* to let it apply multiple transformations in a single visit to a block.

```
Clean( )
  while the CFG keeps changing
    compute postorder
    OnePass( )


OnePass( )
  for each block i, in postorder
    if i ends in a conditional branch then
        if both targets are identical then
            replace the branch with a jump          /* case 1 */
    if i ends in a jump to j then
        if i is empty then
            replace transfers to i with transfers to j    /* case 2 */
        if j has only one predecessor then
            combine i and j                         /* case 3 */
        if j is empty and ends in a conditional branch then
            overwrite i's jump with a copy of j's branch    /* case 4 */
```

■ **FIGURE 10.2** The Algorithm for *Clean*.

If the CFG contains back edges, then a pass of *Clean* may create additional opportunities—namely, unprocessed successors along the back edges. These, in turn, may create other opportunities. For this reason, *Clean* repeats the transformation sequence iteratively until the CFG stops changing. It must compute a new postorder numbering between calls to *OnePass* because each pass changes the underlying graph. Figure 10.2 shows pseudo-code for *Clean*.

*Clean* cannot, by itself, eliminate an empty loop. Consider the CFG shown in the margin. Assume that block $B_2$ is empty. None of *Clean*'s transformations can eliminate $B_2$ because the branch that ends $B_2$ is not redundant. $B_2$ does not end with a jump, so *Clean* cannot combine it with $B_3$. Its predecessor ends with a branch rather than a jump, so *Clean* can neither combine $B_2$ with $B_1$ nor fold its branch into $B_1$.

However, cooperation between *Clean* and *Dead* can eliminate the empty loop. *Dead* used control dependence to mark useful branches. If $B_1$ and $B_3$ contain useful operations, but $B_2$ does not, then the *Mark* pass in *Dead* will decide that the branch ending $B_2$ is not useful because $B_2 \notin \text{RDF}(B_3)$. Because the branch is useless, the code that computes the branch condition is also useless. Thus, *Dead* eliminates all of the operations in $B_2$ and converts the branch that ends it into a jump to its closest useful postdominator, $B_3$. This eliminates the original loop and produces the CFG labelled "After Dead" in the margin.

In this form, *Clean* folds $B_2$ into $B_1$, to produce the CFG labelled "Remove $B_2$" in the margin. This action also makes the branch at the end of $B_1$ redundant. *Clean* rewrites it with a jump, producing the CFG labelled "Fold the Branch". At this point, if $B_1$ is $B_3$'s sole remaining predecessor, *Clean* coalesces the two blocks into a single block.

This cooperation is simpler and more effective than adding a transformation to *Clean* that handles empty loops. Such a transformation might recognize a branch from $B_i$ to itself and, for an empty $B_i$, rewrite it with a jump to the branch's other target. The problem lies in determining when $B_i$ is truly empty. If $B_i$ contains no operations other than the branch, then the code that computes the branch condition must lie outside the loop. Thus, the transformation is safe only if the self-loop never executes. Reasoning about the number of executions of the self-loop requires knowledge about the run-time value of the comparison, a task that is, in general, beyond a compiler's ability. If the block contains operations, but only operations that control the branch, then the transformation would need to recognize the situation with pattern matching. In either case, this new transformation would be more

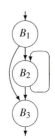

Original CFG

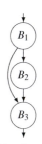

After Dead

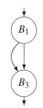

Remove $B_2$

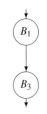

Fold the Branch

complex than the four included in *Clean*. Relying on the combination of *Dead* and *Clean* achieves the appropriate result in a simpler, more modular fashion.

### 10.2.3 Eliminating Unreachable Code

Sometimes the CFG contains code that is unreachable. The compiler should find unreachable blocks and remove them. A block can be unreachable for two distinct reasons: there may be no path through the CFG that leads to the block, or the paths that reach the block may not be executable—for example, guarded by a condition that always evaluates to false.

If the source language allows arithmetic on code pointers or labels, the compiler must preserve all blocks. Otherwise, it can limit the preserved set to blocks whose labels are referenced.

The former case is easy to handle. The compiler can perform a simple mark-sweep-style reachability analysis on the CFG. First, it initializes a mark on each block to the value "unreachable." Next, it starts with the entry and marks each CFG node that it can reach as "reachable." If all branches and jumps are unambiguous, then all unmarked blocks can be deleted. With ambiguous branches or jumps, the compiler must preserve any block that the branch or jump can reach. This analysis is simple and inexpensive. It can be done during traversals of the CFG for other purposes or during CFG construction itself.

Handling the second case is harder. It requires the compiler to reason about the values of expressions that control branches. Section 10.7.1 presents an algorithm that finds some blocks that are unreachable because the paths leading to them are not executable.

---

**SECTION REVIEW**

Code transformations often create useless or unreachable code. To determine precisely which operations are dead, however, requires global analysis. Many transformations simply leave the dead operations in the IR form of the code and rely on separate, specialized transformations, such as *Dead* and *Clean*, to remove them. Thus, most optimizing compilers include a set of transformations to excise dead code. Often, these passes run several times during the transformation sequence.

The three transformations presented in this chapter perform a thorough job of eliminating useless and unreachable code. The underlying analysis, however, can limit the ability of these transformations to prove that code is dead. The use of pointer-based values can prevent the compiler from determining that a value is unused. Conditional branches can occur in places where the compiler cannot detect the fact that they always take the same path; Section 10.8 presents an algorithm that partially addresses this problem.

**Review Questions**

1. Experienced programmers often question the need for useless code elimination. They seem certain that they do not write code that is useless or unreachable. What transformations from Chapter 8 might create useless code?

2. How might the compiler, or the linker, detect and eliminate unreachable procedures? What benefits might accrue from using your technique?

Hint: Write down the code to access A[i,j] where A is dimensioned A[1:N,1:M].

## 10.3 CODE MOTION

Moving a computation to a point where it executes less frequently than it executed in its original position should reduce the total operation count of the running program. The first transformation presented in this section, *lazy code motion*, uses code motion to speed up execution. Because loops tend to execute many more times than the code that surrounds them, much of the work in this area has focused on moving loop-invariant expressions out of loops. Lazy code motion performs loop-invariant code motion. It extends the notions originally formulated in the available expressions data-flow problem to include operations that are redundant along some, but not all, paths. It inserts code to make them redundant on all paths and removes the newly redundant expression.

Some compilers, however, optimize for other criteria. If the compiler is concerned about the size of the executable code, it can perform code motion to reduce the number of copies of a specific operation. The second transformation presented in this section, *hoisting*, uses code motion to reduce duplication of instructions. It discovers cases in which inserting an operation makes several copies of the same operation redundant without changing the values computed by the program.

### 10.3.1 Lazy Code Motion

Lazy code motion (LCM) uses data-flow analysis to discover both operations that are candidates for code motion and locations where it can place those operations. The algorithm operates on the IR form of the program and its CFG, rather than on SSA form. The algorithm use three different sets of data-flow equations and derives additional sets from those results. It produces, for each edge in the CFG, a set of expressions that should be evaluated along that edge and, for each node in the CFG, a set of expressions whose upward-exposed evaluations should be removed from the corresponding block. A simple rewriting strategy interprets these sets and modifies the code.

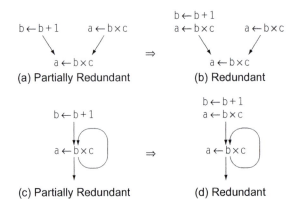

■ **FIGURE 10.3** Converting Partial Redundancies into Redundancies.

**Redundant**

An expression e is *redundant* at p if it has already been evaluated on every path that leads to p.

**Partially redundant**

An expression e is *partially redundant* at p if it occurs on some, but not all, paths that reach p.

LCM combines code motion with elimination of both redundant and partially redundant computations. Redundancy was introduced in the context of local and superlocal value numbering in Section 8.4.1. A computation is *partially redundant* at point p if it occurs on some, but not all, paths that reach p and none of its constituent operands changes between those evaluations and p. Figure 10.3 shows two ways that an expression can be partially redundant. In Figure 10.3a, a ← b × c occurs on one path leading to the merge point but not on the other. To make the second computation redundant, LCM inserts an evaluation of a ← b × c on the other path as shown in Figure 10.3b. In Figure 10.3c, a ← b × c is redundant along the loop's back edge but not along the edge entering the loop. Inserting an evaluation of a ← b × c before the loop makes the occurrence inside the loop redundant, as shown in Figure 10.3d. By making the loop-invariant computation redundant and eliminating it, LCM moves it out of the loop, an optimization called *loop-invariant code motion* when performed by itself.

The fundamental ideas that underlie LCM were introduced in Section 9.2.4. LCM computes both available expressions and anticipable expressions. Next, LCM uses the results of these analyses to annotate each CFG edge $\langle i, j \rangle$ with a set EARLIEST$(i, j)$ that contains the expressions for which this edge is the *earliest legal placement*. LCM then solves a third data-flow problem to find *later placements*, that is, situations where evaluating an expression after its earliest placement has the same effect. Later placements are desirable because they can shorten the lifetimes of values defined by the inserted evaluations. Finally, LCM computes its final products, two sets INSERT and DELETE, that guide its code-rewriting step.

In this context, *earliest* means the position in the CFG closest to the entry node.

## Code Shape

LCM relies on several implicit assumptions about the shape of the code. Textually identical expressions always define the same name. Thus, each instance of $r_i + r_j$ always targets the same $r_k$. Thus, the algorithm can use $r_k$ as a proxy for $r_i + r_j$. This naming scheme simplifies the rewriting step; the optimizer can simply replace a redundant evaluation of $r_i + r_j$ with a copy from $r_k$, rather create a new temporary name and insert copies into that name after each prior evaluation.

Notice that these rules are consistent with the register-naming rules described in Section 5.4.2.

LCM moves expression evaluations, not assignments. The naming discipline requires a second rule for program variables because they receive the values of different expressions. Thus, program variables are set by register-to-register copy operations. A simple way to divide the name space between variables and expressions is to require that variables have lower subscripts than any expression, and that in any operation other than a copy, the defined register's subscript must be larger than the subscripts of the operation's arguments. Thus, in $r_i + r_j \Rightarrow r_k$, $i < k$ and $j < k$. The example in Figure 10.4 has this property.

These naming rules allow the compiler to easily separate variables from expressions, shrinking the domain of the sets manipulated in the data-flow equations. In Figure 10.4, the variables are $r_2$, $r_4$, and $r_8$, each of which is defined by a copy operation. All the other names, $r_1$, $r_3$, $r_5$, $r_6$, $r_7$, $r_{20}$,

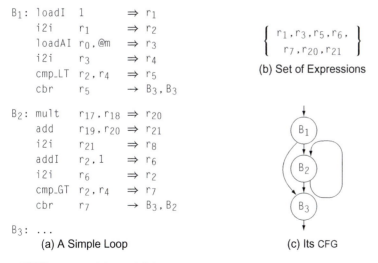

```
B1: loadI   1         ⇒ r1
    i2i     r1        ⇒ r2
    loadAI  r0,@m     ⇒ r3
    i2i     r3        ⇒ r4
    cmp_LT  r2,r4     ⇒ r5
    cbr     r5        → B3,B3

B2: mult    r17,r18   ⇒ r20
    add     r19,r20   ⇒ r21
    i2i     r21       ⇒ r8
    addI    r2,1      ⇒ r6
    i2i     r6        ⇒ r2
    cmp_GT  r2,r4     ⇒ r7
    cbr     r7        → B3,B2

B3: ...
```

(a) A Simple Loop

$$\left\{ \begin{array}{c} r_1, r_3, r_5, r_6, \\ r_7, r_{20}, r_{21} \end{array} \right\}$$

(b) Set of Expressions

(c) Its CFG

■ **FIGURE 10.4** Example for Lazy Code Motion.

and $r_{21}$, represent expressions. The following table shows the local information for the blocks in the example:

|  | $B_1$ | $B_2$ | $B_3$ |
|---|---|---|---|
| DEEXPR | $\{r_1, r_3, r_5\}$ | $\{r_7, r_{20}, r_{21}\}$ | $\emptyset$ |
| UEEXPR | $\{r_1, r_3\}$ | $\{r_6, r_{20}, r_{21}\}$ | $\emptyset$ |
| EXPRKILL | $\{r_5, r_6, r_7\}$ | $\{r_5, r_6, r_7\}$ | $\emptyset$ |

DEEXPR($b$) is the set of downward-exposed expressions in block $b$, UEEXPR($b$) is the set of upward-exposed expressions in $b$, and EXPRKILL($b$) is the set of expressions killed by some operation in $b$. We will assume, for simplicity, that the sets for $B_3$ are all empty.

### Available Expressions

The first step in LCM computes available expressions, in a manner similar to that defined in Section 9.2.4. LCM needs availability at the end of the block, so it computes AVAILOUT rather than AVAILIN. An expression $e$ is available on exit from block $b$ if, along every path from $n_0$ to $b$, $e$ has been evaluated and none of its arguments has been subsequently defined.

LCM computes AVAILOUT as follows:

$$\text{AVAILOUT}(n_0) = \emptyset$$

$$\text{AVAILOUT}(n) = \{ \text{ all expressions } \}, \forall n \neq n_0$$

and then iteratively evaluates the following equation until it reaches a fixed point:

$$\text{AVAILOUT}(n) = \bigcap_{m \in preds(n)} (\text{DEEXPR}(m) \cup (\text{AVAILOUT}(m) \cap \overline{\text{EXPRKILL}(m)}))$$

For the example in Figure 10.4, this process produces the following sets:

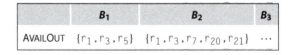

|  | $B_1$ | $B_2$ | $B_3$ |
|---|---|---|---|
| AVAILOUT | $\{r_1, r_3, r_5\}$ | $\{r_1, r_3, r_7, r_{20}, r_{21}\}$ | $\cdots$ |

LCM uses the AVAILOUT sets to help determine possible placements for an expression in the CFG. If an expression $e \in$ AVAILOUT($b$), the compiler could place an evaluation of $e$ at the end of block $b$ and obtain the result produced by its most recent evaluation on any control-flow path from $n_0$ to $b$.

If $e \notin \textsc{AvailOut}(b)$, then one of $e$'s constituent subexpressions has been modified since $e$'s most recent evaluation and an evaluation at the end of block $b$ would possibly produce a different value. In this light, $\textsc{AvailOut}()$ sets tell the compiler how far forward in the CFG it can move the evaluation of $e$, ignoring any uses of $e$.

### Anticipable Expressions

To capture information for backward motion of expressions, LCM computes anticipability. Recall, from Section 9.2.4, that an expression is anticipable at point $p$ if and only if it is computed on every path that leaves $p$ and produces the same value at each of those computations. Because LCM needs information about the anticipable expressions at both the start and the end of each block, we have refactored the equation to introduce a set $\textsc{AntIn}(n)$ which holds the set of anticipable expressions for the entrance of the block corresponding to node $n$ in the CFG. LCM initializes the $\textsc{AntOut}$ sets as follows:

$$\textsc{AntOut}(n_f) = \emptyset$$
$$\textsc{AntOut}(n) = \{ \text{ all expressions } \}, \, \forall n \neq n_f$$

Next, it iteratively computes $\textsc{AntIn}$ and $\textsc{AntOut}$ sets for each block until the process reaches a fixed point.

$$\textsc{AntIn}(m) = \textsc{UEExpr}(m) \cup (\textsc{AntOut}(m) \cap \overline{\textsc{ExprKill}(m)})$$

$$\textsc{AntOut}(n) = \bigcap_{m \in succ(n)} \textsc{AntIn}(m), \quad n \neq n_f$$

For the example, this process produces the following sets:

|        | $B_1$        | $B_2$              | $B_3$      |
|--------|--------------|--------------------|------------|
| ANTIN  | $\{r_1, r_3\}$ | $\{r_{20}, r_{21}\}$ | $\emptyset$ |
| ANTOUT | $\emptyset$  | $\emptyset$        | $\emptyset$ |

$\textsc{AntOut}$ provides information about the safety of hoisting an evaluation to either the start or the end of the current block. If $x \in \textsc{AntOut}(b)$, then the compiler can place an evaluation of $x$ at the end of $b$, with two guarantees. First, the evaluation at the end of $b$ will produce the same value as the next evaluation of $x$ along any execution path in the procedure. Second, along any execution path leading out of $b$, the program will evaluate $x$ before redefining any of its arguments.

### Earliest Placement

Given solutions to availability and anticipability, the compiler can determine, for each expression, the earliest point in the program at which it can evaluate the expression. To simplify the equations, LCM assumes that it will place the evaluation on a CFG edge rather than at the start or end of a specific block. Computing an edge placement lets the compiler defer the decision to place the evaluation at the end of the edge's source, at the start of its sink, or in a new block in the middle of the edge. (See the discussion of critical edges in Section 9.3.5.)

For a CFG edge $\langle i,j \rangle$, an expression $e$ is in EARLIEST$(i,j)$ if and only if the compiler can legally move $e$ to $\langle i,j \rangle$, and cannot move it to any earlier edge in the CFG. The EARLIEST equation encodes this condition as the intersection of three terms:

$$\text{EARLIEST}(i,j) = \text{ANTIN}(j) \cap \overline{\text{AVAILOUT}(i)} \cap (\text{EXPRKILL}(i) \cup \overline{\text{ANTOUT}(i)})$$

These terms define an earliest placement for $e$ as follows:

1. $e \in \text{ANTIN}(j)$ means that the compiler can safely move $e$ to the head of $j$. The anticipability equations ensure that $e$ will produce the same value as its next evaluation on any path leaving $j$ and that each of those paths evaluates $e$.
2. $e \notin \text{AVAILOUT}(i)$ shows that no prior computation of $e$ is available on exit from $i$. Were $e \in \text{AVAILOUT}(i)$, inserting $e$ on $\langle i,j \rangle$ would be redundant.
3. The third condition encodes two cases. If $e \in \text{EXPRKILL}(i)$, the compiler cannot move $e$ through block $i$ because of a definition in $i$. If $e \notin \text{ANTOUT}(i)$, the compiler cannot move $e$ into $i$ because $e \notin \text{ANTIN}(k)$ for some edge $\langle i,k \rangle$. If either is true, then $e$ can move no further than $\langle i,j \rangle$.

The CFG's entry node, $n_0$ presents a special case. LCM cannot move an expression earlier than $n_0$, so it can ignore the third term in the equation for EARLIEST$(n_0,k)$, for any $k$. The EARLIEST sets for the continuing example are as follows:

| | $\langle B_1,B_2 \rangle$ | $\langle B_1,B_3 \rangle$ | $\langle B_2,B_2 \rangle$ | $\langle B_2,B_3 \rangle$ |
|---|---|---|---|---|
| EARLIEST | $\{r_{20},r_{21}\}$ | $\emptyset$ | $\emptyset$ | $\emptyset$ |

### Later Placement

The final data-flow problem in LCM determines when an earliest placement can be deferred to a later point in the CFG while achieving the same effect.

Later analysis is formulated as a forward data-flow problem on the CFG with a set $\text{LATERIN}(n)$ associated with each node and another set $\text{LATER}(i,j)$ associated with each edge $\langle i,j \rangle$. LCM initializes the $\text{LATERIN}$ sets as follows:

$$\text{LATERIN}(n_0) = \emptyset$$

$$\text{LATERIN}(n) = \{ \text{ all expressions } \}, \forall \ n \neq n_0$$

Next, it iteratively computes $\text{LATERIN}$ and $\text{LATER}$ sets for each block. The computation halts when it reaches a fixed point.

$$\text{LATERIN}(j) = \bigcap_{i \in pred(j)} \text{LATER}(i,j), \quad j \neq n_0$$

$$\text{LATER}(i,j) = \text{EARLIEST}(i,j) \cup (\text{LATERIN}(i) \cap \overline{\text{UEEXPR}(i)}), \quad i \in pred(j)$$

As with availability and anticipability, these equations have a unique fixed point solution.

An expression $e \in \text{LATERIN}(k)$ if and only if every path that reaches $k$ includes an edge $\langle p,q \rangle$ such that $e \in \text{EARLIEST}(p,q)$, and the path from $q$ to $k$ neither redefines $e$'s operands nor contains an evaluation of $e$ that an earlier placement of $e$ would anticipate. The EARLIEST term in the equation for LATER ensures that $\text{LATER}(i,j)$ includes $\text{EARLIEST}(i,j)$. The rest of that equation puts $e$ into $\text{LATER}(i,j)$ if $e$ can be moved forward from $i$ ($e \in \text{LATERIN}(i)$) and a placement at the entry to $i$ does not anticipate a use in $i$ ($e \notin \text{UEEXPR}(i)$).

Given LATER and LATERIN sets, $e \in \text{LATERIN}(i)$ implies that the compiler can move the evaluation of $e$ forward through $i$ without losing any benefit—that is, there is no evaluation of $e$ in $i$ that an earlier evaluation would anticipate, and $e \in \text{LATER}(i,j)$ implies that the compiler can move an evaluation of $e$ in $i$ into $j$.

For the ongoing example, these equations produce the following sets:

| | $B_1$ | $B_2$ | $B_3$ |
|---|---|---|---|
| LATERIN | $\emptyset$ | $\emptyset$ | $\emptyset$ |

| | $\langle B_1,B_2 \rangle$ | $\langle B_1,B_3 \rangle$ | $\langle B_2,B_2 \rangle$ | $\langle B_2,B_3 \rangle$ |
|---|---|---|---|---|
| LATER | $\{r_{20},r_{21}\}$ | $\emptyset$ | $\emptyset$ | $\emptyset$ |

### Rewriting the Code

The final step in performing LCM is to rewrite the code so that it capitalizes on the knowledge derived from the data-flow computations. To drive the rewriting process, LCM computes two additional sets, INSERT and DELETE.

The INSERT set specifies, for each edge, the computations that LCM should insert on that edge.

$$\text{INSERT}(i,j) = \text{LATER}(i,j) \cap \overline{\text{LATERIN}(j)}$$

If $i$ has only one successor, LCM can insert the computations at the end of $i$. If $j$ has only one predecessor, it can insert the computations at the entry of $j$. If neither condition applies, the edge $\langle i,j \rangle$ is a critical edge and the compiler should split it by inserting a block in the middle of the edge to evaluate the expressions in INSERT$(i,j)$.

The DELETE set specifies, for a block, which computations LCM should delete from the block.

$$\text{DELETE}(i) = \text{UEEXPR}(i) \cap \overline{\text{LATERIN}(i)}, \quad i \neq n_0$$

DELETE$(n_0)$ is empty, of course, since no block precedes $n_0$. If $e \in \text{DELETE}(i)$, then the first computation of $e$ in $i$ is redundant after all the insertions have been made. Any subsequent evaluation of $e$ in $i$ that has upward-exposed uses—that is, the operands are not defined between the start of $i$ and the evaluation—can also be deleted. Because all evaluations of $e$ define the same name, the compiler need not rewrite subsequent references to the deleted evaluation. Those references will simply refer to earlier evaluations of $e$ that LCM has proven to produce the same result.

For our example, the INSERT and DELETE sets are simple.

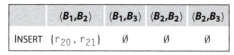

The compiler interprets the INSERT and DELETE sets and rewrites the code as shown in Figure 10.5. LCM deletes the expressions that define $r_{20}$ and $r_{21}$ from $B_2$ and inserts them on the edge from $B_1$ to $B_2$.

Since $B_1$ has two successors and $B_2$ has two predecessors, $\langle B_1, B_2 \rangle$ is a critical edge. Thus, LCM splits the edge, creating a new block $B_{2a}$ to hold the inserted computations of $r_{20}$ and $r_{21}$. Splitting $\langle B_1, B_2 \rangle$ adds an extra jump to the code. Subsequent work in code generation will almost certainly implement the jump in $B_{2a}$ as a fall through, eliminating any cost associated with it.

**Coalescing**
A pass that determines when a register to register copy can be safely eliminated and the source and destination names combined.

Notice that LCM leaves the copy defining $r_8$ in $B_2$. LCM moves expressions, not assignments. (Recall that $r_8$ is a variable, not an expression.) If the copy is unnecessary, subsequent copy coalescing, either in the register allocator or as a standalone pass, should discover that fact and eliminate the copy operation.

```
B₁: loadI  1        ⇒ r₁
    loadAI r₀, @m    ⇒ r₂
    cmp_LT r₁, r₂    ⇒ r₃
    cbr    r₃        → B₂ₐ, B₃
B₂ₐ: mult  r₁₇, r₁₈ ⇒ r₂₀
    add    r₁₉, r₂₀ ⇒ r₂₁
    jump            → B₂
B₂: i2i    r₂₁       ⇒ r₈
    addI   r₁, 1     ⇒ r₄
    i2i    r₄        ⇒ r₁
    cmp_GT rr₁, r₂   ⇒ r₅
    cbr    r₅        → B₃, B₂
B₃: ...
```

(a) The Transformed Code         (b) Its CFG

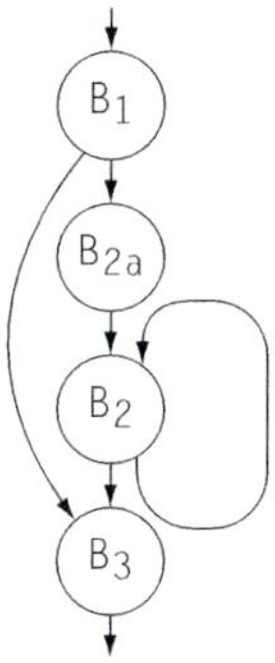

■ **FIGURE 10.5**  Example after Lazy Code Motion.

## 10.3.2 **Code Hoisting**

Code motion techniques can also be used to reduce the size of the compiled code. A transformation called *code hoisting* provides one direct way of accomplishing this goal. It uses the results of anticipability analysis in a particularly simple way.

If an expression $e \in$ ANTOUT(b), for some block $b$, that means that $e$ is evaluated along every path that leaves $b$ and that evaluating $e$ at the end of $b$ would make the first evaluation along each path redundant. (The equations for ANTOUT ensure that none of $e$'s operands is redefined between the end of $b$ and the next evaluation of $e$ along each path leaving $b$.) To reduce code size, the compiler can insert an evaluation of $e$ at the end of $b$ and replace the first occurrence of $e$ on each path leaving $b$ with a reference to the previously computed value. The effect of this transformation is to replace multiple copies of the evaluation of $e$ with a single copy, reducing the overall number of operations in the compiled code.

To replace those expressions directly, the compiler would need to locate them. It could insert $e$, then solve another data-flow problem, proving that the path from $b$ to some evaluation of $e$ is clear of definitions for $e$'s operands. Alternatively, it could traverse each of the paths leaving $b$ to find the first block where $e$ is defined—by looking in the block's UEEXPR set. Each of these approaches seems complicated.

A simpler approach has the compiler visit each block $b$ and insert an evaluation of $e$ at the end of $b$, for every expression $e \in$ ANTOUT($b$). If the compiler uses a uniform discipline for naming, as suggested in the discussion of LCM, then each evaluation will define the appropriate name. Subsequent application of LCM or superlocal value numbering will then remove the newly redundant expressions.

---

**SECTION REVIEW**

Compilers perform code motion for two primary reasons. Moving an operation to a point where it executes fewer times than it would in its original position should reduce execution time. Moving an operation to a point where one instance can cover multiple paths in the CFG should reduce code size. This section presented an example of each.

LCM is a classic example of a data-flow driven global optimization. It identifies redundant and partially redundant expressions, computes the best place for those expressions, and moves them. By definition, a loop-invariant expression is either redundant or partially redundant; LCM moves a large class of loop invariant expressions out of loops. Hoisting takes a much simpler approach; it finds operations that are redundant on every path leaving some point p and replaces all the redundant occurrences with a single instance at p. Thus, hoisting is usually performed to reduce code size.

---

The common implementation of sinking is called *cross jumping.*

**Review Questions**

1. Hoisting discovers the situation when some expression e exists along each path that leaves point *p* and each of those occurrences can be replaced safely with an evaluation of e at *p*. Formulate the symmetric and equivalent optimization, *code sinking*, that discovers when multiple expression evaluations can safely be moved forward in the code—from points that precede *p* to *p*.

2. Consider what would happen if you apply your code-sinking transformation during the linker, when all the code for the entire application is present. What effect might it have on procedure linkage code?

## 10.4 SPECIALIZATION

In most compilers, the shape of the IR program is determined by the front end, before any detailed analysis of the code. Of necessity, this produces general code that works in any context that the running program might encounter. With analysis, however, the compiler can often learn enough to narrow the contexts in which the code must operate. This creates the opportunity for the compiler to specialize the sequence of operations in ways that capitalize on its knowledge of the context in which the code will execute.

Major techniques that perform specialization appear in other sections of this book. Constant propagation, described in Sections 9.3.6 and 10.8, analyzes a procedure to discover values that always have the same value; it then folds those values directly into the computation. Interprocedural constant propagation, introduced in Section 9.4.2, applies the same ideas at the whole-program scope. Operator strength reduction, presented in Section 10.4, replaces inductive sequences of expensive computations with equivalent sequences of faster operations. Peephole optimization, covered in Section 11.5, uses pattern matching over short instruction sequences to find local improvement. Value numbering, explained in Section 8.4.1 and 8.5.1, systematically simplifies the IR form of the code by applying algebraic identities and local constant folding. Each of these techniques implements a form of specialization.

Optimizing compilers rely on these general techniques to improve code. In addition, most optimizing compilers contain specialization techniques that specifically target properties of the source languages or applications that the compiler writer expects to encounter. The rest of this section presents three such techniques that target specific inefficiencies at procedure calls: tail-call optimization, leaf-call optimization, and parameter promotion.

### 10.4.1 Tail-Call Optimization

When the last action that a procedure takes is a call, we refer to that call as a tail call. The compiler can specialize tail calls to their contexts in ways that eliminate much of the overhead from the procedure linkage. To understand how the opportunity for improvement arises, consider what happens when $o$ calls $p$ and $p$ calls $q$. When $q$ returns, it executes its epilogue sequence and jumps back to $p$'s postreturn sequence. Execution continues in $p$ until $p$ returns, at which point $p$ executes its epilogue sequence and jumps to $o$'s postreturn sequence.

If the call from $p$ to $q$ is a tail call, then no useful computation occurs between the postreturn sequence and the epilogue sequence in $p$. Thus, any code that preserves and restores $p$'s state, beyond what is needed for the return from $p$ to $o$, is useless. A standard linkage, as described in Section 6.5, spends much of its effort to preserve state that is useless in the context of a tail call.

At the call from $p$ to $q$, the minimal precall sequence must evaluate the actual parameters at the call from $p$ to $q$ and adjust the access links or the display if necessary. It need not preserve any caller-saves registers, because they cannot be live. It need not allocate a new AR, because $q$ can use $p$'s AR. It must leave intact the context created for a return to $o$, namely the return address and caller's ARP that $o$ passed to $p$ and any callee-saves registers that

$p$ preserved by writing them into the AR. (That context will cause the epilogue code for $q$ to return control directly to $o$.) Finally, the precall sequence must jump to a tailored prologue sequence for $q$.

In this scheme, $q$ must execute a custom prologue sequence to match the minimal precall sequence in $p$. It only saves those parts of $p$'s state that allow a return to $o$. The precall sequence does not preserve callee-saves registers, for two reasons. First, the values from $p$ in those registers are no longer live. Second, the values that $p$ left in the AR's register-save area are needed for the return to $o$. Thus, the prologue sequence in $q$ should initialize local variables and values that $q$ needs; it should then branch into the code for $q$.

With these changes to the precall sequence in $p$ and the prologue sequence in $q$, the tail call avoids preserving and restoring $p$'s state and eliminates much of the overhead of the call. Of course, once the precall sequence in $p$ has been tailored in this way, the postreturn and epilogue sequences are unreachable. Standard techniques such as Dead and Clean will not discover that fact, because they assume that the interprocedural jumps to their labels are executable. As the optimizer tailors the call, it can eliminate these dead sequences.

With a little care, the optimizer can arrange for the operations in the tailored prologue for $q$ to appear as the last operations in its more general prologue. In this scheme, the tail call from $p$ to $q$ simply jumps to a point farther into the prologue sequence than would a normal call from some other routine.

If the tail call is a self-recursive call—that is, $p$ and $q$ are the same procedure—then tail-call optimization can produce particularly efficient code. In a tail recursion, the entire precall sequence devolves to argument evaluation and a branch back to the top of the routine. An eventual return out of the recursion requires one branch, rather than one branch per recursive invocation. The resulting code rivals a traditional loop for efficiency.

### 10.4.2 Leaf-Call Optimization

Some of the overhead involved in a procedure call arises from the need to prepare for calls that the callee might make. A procedure that makes no calls, called a leaf procedure, creates opportunities for specialization. The compiler can easily recognize the opportunity; the procedure calls no other procedures.

The other reason to store the return address is to allow a debugger or a performance monitor to unwind the call stack. When such tools are in use, the compiler should leave the save operation intact.

During translation of a leaf procedure, the compiler can avoid inserting operations whose sole purpose is to set up for subsequent calls. For example, the procedure prologue code may save the return address from a register into a slot in the AR. That action is unnecessary unless the procedure itself makes another call. If the register that holds the return address is needed for some other purpose, the register allocator can spill the value. Similarly, if the implementation uses a display to provide addressability for nonlocal variables, as described in Section 6.4.3, it can avoid the display update in the prologue sequence.

The register allocator should try to use caller-saves registers before callee-saves registers in a leaf procedure. To the extent that it can leave callee-saves registers untouched, it can avoid the save and restore code for them in the prologue and epilogue. In small leaf procedures, the compiler may be able to avoid all use of callee-saves registers. If the compiler has access to both the caller and the callee, it can do better; for leaf procedures that need fewer registers than the caller-save set includes, it can avoid some of the register saves and restores in the caller as well.

In addition, the compiler can avoid the runtime overhead of activation-record allocation for leaf procedures. In an implementation that heap allocates ARs, that cost can be significant. In an application with a single thread of control, the compiler can allocate statically the AR of any leaf procedure. A more aggressive compiler might allocate one static AR that is large enough to work for any leaf procedure and have all the leaf procedures share that AR.

If the compiler has access to both the leaf procedure and its callers, it can allocate space for the leaf procedure's AR in each of its callers' ARs. This scheme amortizes the cost of AR allocation over at least two calls—the invocation of the caller and the call to the leaf procedure. If the caller invokes the leaf procedure multiple times, the savings are multiplied.

## 10.4.3  **Parameter Promotion**

Ambiguous memory references prevent the compiler from keeping values in registers. Sometimes, the compiler can prove that an ambiguous value has just one corresponding memory location through detailed analysis of pointer values or array subscript values, or special case analysis. In these cases, it can rewrite the code to move that value into a scalar local variable, where the register allocator can keep it in a register. This kind of transformation is often called *promotion*. The analysis to promote array references or pointer-based references is beyond the scope of this book. However, a simpler case can illustrate these transformations equally well.

**Promotion**
A category of transformations that move an ambiguous value into a local scalar name to expose it to register allocation

Consider the code generated for an ambiguous call-by-reference parameter. Such parameters can arise in many ways. The code might pass the same actual parameter in two distinct parameter slots, or it might pass a global variable as an actual parameter. Unless the compiler performs interprocedural analysis to rule out those possibilities, it must treat all reference parameters as potentially ambiguous. Thus, every use of the parameter requires a load and every definition requires a store.

If the compiler can prove that the actual parameter must be unambiguous in the callee, it can promote the parameter's value into a local scalar value, which allows the callee to keep it in a register. If the actual parameter is not modified by the callee, the promoted parameter can be passed by value. If the callee modifies the actual parameter and the result is live in the caller, then the compiler must use value-result semantics to pass the promoted parameter (see Section 6.4.1).

To apply this transformation to a procedure $p$, the optimizer must identify all of the call sites that can invoke $p$. It can either prove that the transformation applies at all of those call sites or it can clone $p$ to create a copy that handles the promoted values (see Section 10.6.2). Parameter promotion is most attractive in a language that uses call-by-reference binding.

---

**SECTION REVIEW**

Specialization includes many effective techniques to tailor general-purpose computations to their detailed contexts. Other chapters and sections present powerful global and regional specialization techniques, such as constant propagation, peephole optimization, and operator strength reduction.

This section focused on optimizations that the compiler can apply to the code entailed in a procedure call. Tail-call optimization is a valuable tool that converts tail recursion to a form that rivals conventional iteration for efficiency; it applies to nonrecursive tail calls as well. Leaf procedures offer special opportunities for improvement because the callee can omit major portions of the standard linkage sequence. Parameter promotion is one example of a class of important transformations that remove inefficiencies related to ambiguous references.

---

**Review Questions**

1. Many compilers include a simple form of strength reduction, in which individual operations that have one constant-valued operand are replaced by more efficient, less general operations. The classic example is replacing an integer multiply of a positive number by a series of shifts and adds. How might you fold that transformation into local value numbering?

2. Inline substitution might be an alternative to the procedure-call optimizations in this section. How might you apply inline substitution in each case? How might the compiler choose the more profitable alternative?

## 10.5 **REDUNDANCY ELIMINATION**

A computation $x + y$ is redundant at some point $p$ in the code if, along every path that reaches $p$, $x + y$ has already been evaluated and $x$ and $y$ have not been modified since the evaluation. Redundant computations typically arise as artifacts of translation or optimization.

We have already presented three effective techniques for redundancy elimination: local value numbering (LVN) in Section 8.4.1, superlocal value numbering (SVN) in Section 8.5.1, and lazy code motion (LCM) in Section 10.3.1. These algorithms cover the span from simple and fast (LVN) to complex and comprehensive (LCM). While all three methods differ in the scope that they cover, the primary distinction between them lies in the method that they use to establish that two values are identical. The next section explores this issue in detail. The second section presents one more version of value numbering, a dominator-based technique.

### 10.5.1 **Value Identity versus Name Identity**

LVN introduced a simple mechanism to prove that two expressions had the same value. LVN relies on two principles. It assigns each value a unique identifying number—its value number. It assumes that two expressions produce the same value if they have the same operator and their operands have the same value numbers. These simple rules allow LVN to find a broad class of redundant operations—any operation that produces a pre-existing value number is redundant.

With these rules, LVN can prove that $2 + a$ has the same value as $a + 2$ or as $2 + b$ when $a$ and $b$ have the same value number. It cannot prove that $a + a$ and $2 \times a$ have the same value because they have different operators. Similarly, it cannot prove the $a + 0$ and $a$ have the same value. Thus, we extend LVN with algebraic identities that can handle the well-defined cases not covered by the original rule. The table in Figure 8.3 on page 424 shows the range of identities that LVN can handle.

By contrast, LCM relies on names to prove that two values have the same number. If LCM sees $a + b$ and $a + c$, it assumes that they have different values because $b$ and $c$ have different names. It has relies on a lexical comparison—name identity. The underlying data-flow analyses cannot directly accommodate the notion of value identity; data-flow problems operate a predefined name space and propagate facts about those names over the CFG. The kind of ad hoc comparisons used in LVN do not fit into the data-flow framework.

As described in Section 10.6.4, one way to improve the effectiveness of LCM is to encode value identity into the name space of the code before applying LCM. LCM recognizes redundancies that neither LVN nor SVN can find. In particular, it finds redundancies that lie on paths through join points in the CFG, including those that flow along loop-closing branches, and it finds partial redundancies. On the other hand, both LVN and SVN find value-based redundancies and simplifications that LCM cannot find. Thus, encoding value identity into the name space allows the compiler to take advantage of the strengths of both approaches.

### 10.5.2 Dominator-based Value Numbering

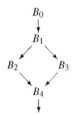

Chapter 8 presented both local value numbering (LVN) and its extension to extended basic blocks (EBBs), called superlocal value numbering (SVN). While SVN discovers more redundancies than LVN, it still misses some opportunities because it is limited to EBBs. Recall that the SVN algorithm propagates information along each path through an EBB. For example, in the CFG fragment shown in the margin, SVN will process the paths $(B_0,B_1,B_2)$ and $(B_0,B_1,B_3)$. Thus, it optimizes both $B_2$ and $B_3$ in the context of the prefix path $(B_0,B_1)$. Because $B_4$ forms its own degenerate EBB, SVN optimizes $B_4$ without prior context.

From an algorithmic point of view, SVN begins each block with a table that includes the results of all predecessors on its EBB path. Block $B_4$ has no predecessors, so it begins with no prior context. To improve on that situation, we must answer the question: on what state could $B_4$ rely? $B_4$ cannot rely on values computed in either $B_2$ or $B_3$, since neither lies on every path that reaches $B_4$. By contrast, $B_4$ can rely on values computed in $B_0$ and $B_1$, since they occur on every path that reaches $B_4$. Thus, we might extend value numbering for $B_4$ with information about computations in $B_0$ and $B_1$. We must, however, account for the impact of assignments in the intervening blocks, $B_2$ or $B_3$.

Consider an expression, $x + y$, that occurs at the end of $B_1$ and again at the start of $B_4$. If neither $B_2$ or $B_3$ redefines $x$ or $y$, then the evaluation of $x + y$ in $B_4$ is redundant and the optimizer can reuse the value computed in $B_1$. On the other hand, if either of those blocks redefines $x$ or $y$, then the evaluation of $x + y$ in $B_4$ computes a distinct value from the evaluation in $B_1$ and the evaluation is not redundant.

Fortunately, the SSA name space encodes precisely this distinction. In SSA, a name that is used in some block $B_i$ can only enter $B_i$ in one of two ways. Either the name is defined by a $\phi$-function at the top of $B_i$, or it is defined in some block that dominates $B_i$. Thus, an assignment to $x$ in either $B_2$ or $B_3$ creates a new name for $x$ and forces the insertion of a $\phi$-function for $x$ at the head of $B_4$. That $\phi$-function creates a new SSA name for $x$ and the renaming process changes the SSA name used in the subsequent computation of $x + y$. Thus, SSA form encodes the presence or absence of an intervening assignment in $B_2$ or $B_3$ directly into the names used in the expression. Our algorithm can rely on SSA names to avoid this problem.

The other major question that we must answer before we can extend SVN to larger regions is, given a block such as $B_4$, how do we locate the most recent predecessor with information that the algorithm can use? Dominance information, discussed at length in Sections 9.2.1 and 9.3.2, captures precisely this effect. $\text{DOM}(B_4) = \{B_0, B_1, B_4\}$. $B_4$'s immediate dominator, defined as the node in $(\text{DOM}(B_4) - B_4)$ that is closest to $B_4$, is $B_1$, the last node that occurs on all path from the entry node $B_0$ to $B_4$.

The dominator-based value numbering technique (DVNT) builds on the ideas behind SVN. It uses a scoped hash table to hold value numbers. DVNT opens a new scope for each block and discards that scope when they are no longer needed. DVNT actually uses SSA names as value numbers; thus the value number for an expression $a_i \times b_j$ is the SSA name defined in the first evaluation of $a_i \times b_j$. (That is, if the first evaluation occurs in $t_k \leftarrow a_i \times b_j$, then the value number for $a_i \times b_j$ is $t_k$.)

Figure 10.6 shows the algorithm. It takes the form of a recursive procedure that the optimizer invokes on a procedure's entry block. It follows both the CFG for the procedure, represented by the dominator tree, and the flow of values in the SSA form. For each block $B$, DVNT takes three steps: it processes the $\phi$-functions in $B$, if any exist, it value numbers the assignments, and it propagates information into $B$'s successors and recurs on $B$'s children in the dominator tree.

## Process the $\phi$-Functions in B

DVNT must assign each $\phi$-function $p$ a value number. If $p$ is meaningless— that is, all its arguments have the same value number—DVNT sets its value number to the value number for one of its arguments and deletes $p$. If $p$ is redundant—that is, it produces the same value number as another $\phi$-function in $B$—DVNT assigns $p$ the same value number as the $\phi$-function that it duplicates. DVNT then deletes $p$.

Otherwise, the $\phi$-function computes a new value. Two cases arise. The arguments to $p$ have value numbers, but the specific combination of arguments have not been seen before in this block, or one or more of $p$'s arguments has no value number. The latter case can arise from a back edge in the CFG.

## Process the Assignments in B

DVNT iterates over the assignments in $B$ and processes them in a manner analogous to LVN and SVN. One subtlety arises from the use of SSA names as value numbers. When the algorithm encounters a statement $x \leftarrow y \; op \; z$, it

Recall, from the SSA construction, that uninitialized names are not allowed.

```
procedure DVNT(B)
   allocate a new scope for B
   for each φ-function of the form ''n ← φ(...)'' in B
      if p is meaningless or redundant then
         VN[n] ← the value number for p
         remove p
      else
         VN[n] ← n
         Add p to the hash table

   for each assignment a of the form ''x ← y op z'' in B
      overwrite y with VN[y]
      overwrite z with VN[z]

      let expr ← ''y op z''
      if expr can be simplified to expr' then
         replace a with ''x ← expr'
         expr ← expr'

      if expr has a value number v in the hash table then
         VN[x] ← v
         remove statement a
      else
         VN[x] ← x
         add expr to the hash table with value number x

   for each successor s of B
      adjust the φ-function inputs in s
   for each child c of B in the dominator tree
      DVNT(c)
   deallocate the scope for B
```

■ **FIGURE 10.6** Dominator-based Value Numbering Technique.

can simply replace $y$ with `VN[y]` because the name in `VN[y]` holds the same
value as $y$.

### Propagate Information to B's Successors

Once DVNT has processed all the $\phi$-functions and assignments in $B$, it visits
each of $B$'s CFG successors $s$ and updates $\phi$ function arguments that correspond to values flowing across the edge $(B,s)$. It records the current value
number for the argument in the $\phi$-function by overwriting the argument's SSA
name. (Notice the similarity between this step and the corresponding step in
the renaming phase of the SSA construction.) Next, the algorithm recurs on
$B$'s children in the dominator tree. Finally, it deallocates the hash table scope
that it used for $B$.

This recursion scheme causes DVNT to follow a preorder walk on the dominator tree, which ensures that the appropriate tables have been constructed before it visits a block. This order can produce a counterintuitive traversal; for the CFG in the margin, the algorithm could visit $B_4$ before either $B_2$ or $B_3$. Since the only facts that the algorithm can use in $B_4$ are those discovered processing $B_0$ and $B_1$, the relative ordering of $B_2$, $B_3$, and $B_4$ is not only unspecified, it is also irrelevant.

---

**SECTION REVIEW**

Redundancy elimination operates on the assumption that it is faster to reuse a value than to recompute it. Building on that assumption, these methods identify as many redundant computations as possible and eliminate duplicate computation. The two primary notions of equivalence used by these transformations are value identity and name identity. These different tests for identity produce different results.

Both value numbering and LCM eliminate redundant computation. LCM eliminates redundant and partially redundant expression evaluation; it does not eliminate assignments. Value numbering does not recognize partial redundancies, but it can eliminate assignments. Some compilers use a value-based technique, such as DVNT, to discover redundancy and then encode that information into the name space for a name-based transformation such as LCM. In practice, that approach combines the strength of both ideas.

---

**Review Questions**

1. The DVNT algorithm resembles the renaming phase of the SSA construction algorithm. Can you reformulate the renaming phase so that it performs value numbering as it renames values? What impact would this change have on the size of the SSA form for a procedure?

2. The DVNT algorithm does not propagate a value along a loop-closing edge—a back edge in the call graph. LCM will propagate information along such edges. Write several examples of redundant expressions that a true "global" technique such as LCM can find that DVNT cannot.

## 10.6 ENABLING OTHER TRANSFORMATIONS

Often, an optimizer includes passes whose primary purpose is to create or expose opportunities for other transformations. In some cases, a transformation changes the shape of the code to make it more amenable to optimization. In other cases, the transformation creates a point in the code where specific conditions hold that make another transformation safe. By directly creating the necessary code shape, these enabling transformations reduce the sensitivity of the optimizer to the shape of the input code.

Several enabling transformations are described in other parts of the book. Both loop unrolling (Section 8.5.2) and inline substitution (Section 8.7.1) obtain most of their benefits by creating context for other optimization. (In each case, the transformation does eliminate some overhead, but the larger effect comes from subsequent application of other optimizations.) The tree-height balancing algorithm (Section 8.4.2) does not eliminate any operations, but it creates a code shape that can produce better results from instruction scheduling. This section presents four enabling transformations: *superblock cloning*, *procedure cloning*, *loop unswitching*, and *renaming*.

### 10.6.1 Superblock Cloning

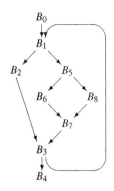

Often, the optimizer's ability to transform the code is limited by path-specific information in the code. Imagine using SVN on the CFG shown in the margin. The fact that blocks $B_3$ and $B_7$ have multiple predecessors may limit the optimizer's ability to improve code in those blocks. If, for example, block $B_6$ assigned x the value 7 and block $B_8$ assigned x the value 13, a use of x in $B_7$ would appear to receive the value $\perp$, even though the value is known and predictable along each path leading to $B_7$.

In such circumstances, the compiler can clone blocks to create code that is better suited for the transformation. In this case, it might create two copies of $B_7$, say $B_{7a}$ and $B_{7b}$, and redirect the incoming edges as $\langle B_6, B_{7a}\rangle$ and $\langle B_8, B_{7b}\rangle$. With this change, the optimizer could propagate the value 7 for x into $B_{7a}$ and the value 13 for x into $B_{7b}$.

As an additional benefit, since $B_{7a}$ and $B_{7b}$ both have unique predecessors, the compiler can actually merge the blocks to create a single block from $B_6$ and $B_{7a}$ and another from $B_8$ and $B_{7b}$. This transformation eliminates the block-ending jump in $B_6$ and $B_8$ and, potentially, allows for further improvement in optimization and in instruction scheduling.

**Backward branch**
a CFG edge whose destination has a lower depth-first number than its source, with respect to some depth-first traversal of the CFG

An issue in this kind of cloning is, when should the compiler stop cloning? One cloning technique, called *superblock cloning*, is widely used to create additional context for instruction scheduling inside loops. In superblock cloning, the optimizer starts with a loop head—the entry to a loop—and clones each path until it reaches a backward branch.

Applying this technique to the example CFG produces the modified CFG shown in the margin. $B_1$ is the loop header. Each of the nodes in the loop body has a unique predecessor. If the compiler applies a superlocal optimization (one based on extended basic blocks), every path that it finds will encompass a single iteration of the loop body. (To find longer paths, the optimizer would need to unroll the loop so that superblock cloning encompassed multiple iterations.)

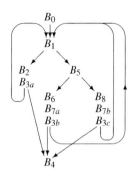

Superblock cloning can improve the results of optimization in three principal ways.

1. *It creates longer blocks* Longer blocks let local optimization handle more context. In the case of value numbering, the superlocal and dominator versions are as strong as the local version. For some techniques, however, this is not the case. For instruction scheduling, for example, superlocal and dominator versions are weaker than the local method. In that case, cloning, followed by local optimization, can produce better code.

2. *It eliminates branches* Combining two blocks eliminates a branch between them. Branches take time to execute. They also disrupt some of the performance-critical mechanisms in the processor, such as instruction fetching and many of the pipelined functions. The net effect of removing branches is to shorten execution time, by eliminating operations and by making hardware mechanisms for predicting behavior more effective.

3. *It creates points where optimization can occur* When cloning eliminates a control-flow merge point, it creates new points in the program where the compiler can derive more precise knowledge about the runtime context. The transformed code may present opportunities for specialization and redundancy elimination that exist nowhere in the original code.

Of course, cloning has costs, too. It creates multiple copies of individual operations, which leads to larger code. The larger code may run more quickly because it avoids some end-of-block jumps. It may run more slowly if its size causes additional instruction cache misses. In applications where the user cares more about code space than runtime speed, superblock cloning may be counterproductive.

## 10.6.2 **Procedure Cloning**

Inline substitution, described in Section 8.7.1 on page 458, has effects similar to superblock cloning. For a call from $p$ to $q$, it creates a unique copy of $q$ and merges it with the call site in $p$. The same effects that arise with superblock cloning arise with inline substitution, including specialization to a particular context, elimination of some control-flow operations, and increased code size.

```
                              do i = 1 to n          if (x > y) then
                                if (x > y)             do i = 1 to n
                                  then a(i) = b(i) * x      a(i) = b(i) * x
                                  else a(i) = b(i) * y   else
                                                         do i = 1 to n
                                                           a(i) = b(i) * y
```

(a) Original Loop                    (b) Unswitched Version

■ **FIGURE 10.7**  Unswitching a Short Loop.

In some cases, the compiler can achieve some of the benefits of inline substitution with less code growth by cloning the procedure. The idea is analogous to the block cloning that occurs in superblock cloning. The compiler creates multiple copies of the callee and assigns some of the calls to each instance of the clone.

*main*

$P_0$  $P_1$  $P_2$

$P_3$

Original Call Graph

Careful assignment of calls to clones can create situations where every call has a similar context for optimization. Consider, for example, the simple call graph shown in the margin. Assume that $P_3$ is a library routine whose behavior depends strongly on one of its input parameters; for a value of one, the compiler can generate code that provides efficient memory access, while for other values, it produces much larger, slower code. Further, assume that $P_0$ and $P_1$ both pass it the value 1, while $P_2$ passes it the value 17.

*main*

$P_0$  $P_1$  $P_2$

$P_{3a}$  $P_{3b}$

After Cloning $P_3$

Constant propagation across the call graph does not help here because it must compute the parameter as $1 \wedge 1 \wedge 17 = \bot$. With constant propagation alone, the compiler must still generate the fully general code for $P_3$. Procedure cloning can create a place where the parameter is always 1; $P_{3a}$ in the graph in the margin. The call that inhibits optimization, $(P_2,P_3)$ in the original call graph, is assigned to $P_{3b}$. The compiler can generate optimized code for $P_{3a}$ and the general code for $P_{3b}$.

### 10.6.3 Loop Unswitching

Loop unswitching hoists loop-invariant control-flow operations out of a loop. If the predicate in an if-then-else construct is loop invariant, then the compiler can rewrite the loop by pulling the if-then-else out of the loop and generating a tailored copy of the loop inside each half of the new if-then-else. Figure 10.7 shows this transformation for a short loop.

Unswitching is an enabling transformation; it allows the compiler to tailor loop bodies in ways that are otherwise hard to achieve. After unswitching, the remaining loops contain less control flow. They execute fewer branches and other operations to support those branches. This can lead to better scheduling, better register allocation, and faster execution. If the original loop contained loop-invariant code that was inside the `if-then-else`, then LCM could not move it out of the loop. After unswitching, LCM easily finds and removes such redundancies.

Unswitching also has a simple, direct effect that can improve a program: it moves the branching logic that governs the loop-invariant conditional out of the loop. Moving control flow out of loops is difficult. Techniques based on data-flow analysis, like LCM, have trouble moving such constructs because the transformation modifies the CFG on which the analysis relies. Techniques based on value numbering can recognize cases where the predicates controlling `if-then-else` constructs are identical, but typically cannot remove the construct from a loop.

### 10.6.4 **Renaming**

Most scalar transformations rewrite or reorder the operations in the code. We have seen, at several points in the text, that the choice of names can either obscure or expose opportunities for improvement. For example, in LVN, converting the names in a block to the SSA name space exposed some opportunities for reuse that would otherwise be difficult to capture.

For many transformations, careful construction of the "right" name space can expose additional opportunities, either by making more facts visible to analysis or by avoiding some of the side effects that arise from reuse of storage. As an example, consider LCM. Because it relies on data-flow analysis to identify opportunities, the analysis relies on a notion of lexical identity—redundant operations must have the same operation and their operands must have the same names. Thus, LCM cannot discover that $x + x$ and $2 \cdot x$ have the same value, or that $x + x$ and $x + y$ have the same value when $x = y$.

To improve the results of LCM, the compiler can encode value identity into the name space before it applies LCM. The compiler would use a value-based redundancy technique, such as DVNT, and then rewrite the name space so that equivalent values share the same name. By encoding value identity into lexical identity, the compiler exposes more redundancy to LCM and makes it more effective.

In a similar way, names matter to instruction scheduling. In a scheduler, names encode the data dependences that constrain the placement of operations in the scheduled code. When the reuse of a name reflects the actual flow of values, that reuse provides critical information required for correctness. If reuse of a name occurs because a prior pass has compressed the name space, then the reuse may unnecessarily constrain the schedule. For example, the register allocator places distinct values into the same physical register to improve register utilization. If the compiler performs allocation

The illusion of a constraint introduced by naming is often called *false sharing*.

before scheduling, the allocator can introduce apparent constraints on the scheduler that are not required by the original code.

Renaming is a subtle issue. Individual transformations can benefit from name spaces with different properties. Compiler writers have long recognized that moving and rewriting operations can improve programs. In the same way, they should recognize that renaming can improve optimizer effectiveness. As SSA has shown, the compiler need not be bound by the name space introduced by the programmer or by the compiler's front end. Renaming is a fertile ground for future work.

---

**SECTION REVIEW**

As we saw in Chapter 7, the shape of the IR for a procedure has an effect on the code that the compiler can generate for it. The techniques discussed in this section create opportunities for other optimizations by changing the shape of the code. They use replication, selective rewriting, and renaming to create places in the code that are amenable to improvement by specific transformations.

Cloning, at the block level or the procedure level, achieves its effects by eliminating the deleterious effects that occur at control-flow merge points. As it eliminates edges, in either the CFG or the call graph, cloning also creates opportunities to merge code. Loop unswitching performs specialized code motion of control structures, but its primary benefit derives from creating simpler loops that do not contain conditional control flow. This latter benefit improves results from transformations that range from LCM to instruction scheduling. Renaming is a powerful idea with widespread application; the specific case of encoding value identity into lexical identity has proven itself in several well-known compilers.

---

**Review Questions**

1. Superblock cloning creates new opportunities for other optimizations. Consider tree-height balancing. How much can superblock cloning help? Can you envision a transformation to follow superblock cloning that would expose more opportunities for tree-height balancing? For SVN, how might the results of using SVN after cloning compare to the results of running LCM on the same code?

2. Procedure cloning attacks some of the same inefficiencies as inline substitution. Is there a role for both of these transformations in a single compiler? What are the potential benefits and risks of each transformation? How might a compiler chose between them?

**THE SSA GRAPH**

In some algorithms, viewing the SSA form of the code as a graph simplifies either the discussion or the implementation. The algorithm for strength reduction interprets the SSA form of the code as a graph.

In SSA form, each name has a unique definition, so that a name specifies a particular operation in the code that computed its value. Each use of a name occurs in a specific operation, so the use can be interpreted as a chain from the use to its definition. Thus, a simple lookup table that maps names to the operations that define them creates a chain from each use to the corresponding definition. Mapping a definition to the operations that use it is slightly more complex. However, this map can easily be constructed during the renaming phase of the SSA construction.

We draw SSA graphs with edges that run from a use to its corresponding definition. This indicates the relationship implied by the SSA names. The compiler needs to traverse the edges in both directions. Strength reduction moves, primarily, from uses to definitions. The SCCP algorithm transmits values from definitions to uses. The compiler writer can easily add the data structures needed to allow traversal in both directions.

## 10.7  ADVANCED TOPICS

Most of the examples in this chapter have been chosen to illustrate a specific effect that the compiler can use to speed up the executable code. Sometimes, performing two optimizations together can produce results that cannot be obtained with any combination of applying them separately. The next subsection shows one such example: combining constant propagation with unreachable code elimination. Section 10.7.2 presents a second, more complex example of specialization: operator strength reduction with linear function test replacement. The algorithm that we present, *OSR*, is simpler than previous algorithms because it relies on properties of SSA form. Finally, Section 10.7.3 discusses some of the issues that arise in choosing a specific application order for the optimizer's set of transformations.

### 10.7.1  Combining Optimizations

Sometimes, reformulating two distinct optimizations in a unified framework and solving them jointly can produce results that cannot be obtained by any combination of the optimizations run separately. As an example, consider the sparse simple constant propagation (SSCP) algorithm described in Section 9.3.6. It assigns a lattice value to the result of each operation in the

SSA form of the program. When it halts, it has tagged every definition with a lattice value that is either $\top$, $\bot$, or a constant. A definition can have the value $\top$ only if it relies on an uninitialized variable or it occurs in an unreachable block.

SSCP assigns a lattice value to the operand used by a conditional branch. If the value is $\bot$, then either branch target is reachable. If the value is neither $\bot$ nor $\top$, then the operand must have a known value and the compiler can rewrite the branch with a jump to one of its two targets, simplifying the CFG. Since this removes an edge from the CFG, it may make the block that was the branch target unreachable. Constant propagation can ignore any effects of an unreachable block. SSCP has no mechanism to take advantage of this knowledge.

We can extend the SSCP algorithm to capitalize on these observations. The resulting algorithm, called *sparse conditional constant propagation* (SCCP), appears in Figures 10.8, 10.9, and 10.10.

In concept, SCCP operates in a straightforward way. It initializes the data structures. It iterates over two graphs, the CFG and the SSA graph. It propagates reachability information on the CFG and value information on the SSA graph. It halts when the value information reaches a fixed point; because the constant propagation lattice is so shallow, it halts quickly. Combining these two kinds of information, SCCP can discover both unreachable code and constant values that the compiler simply could not discover with any combination of the SSCP and unreachable code elimination.

To simplify the explanation of SCCP, we assume that each block in the CFG represents just one statement, plus some optional $\phi$-functions. A CFG node with a single predecessor holds either an assignment statement or a conditional branch. A CFG node with multiple predecessors holds a set of $\phi$-functions, followed by an assignment or a conditional branch.

In detail, SCCP is much more complex than either SSCP or unreachable code elimination. Using two graphs introduces additional bookkeeping. Making the flow of values depend on reachability introduces additional work to the algorithm. The result is a powerful but complex algorithm.

The algorithm proceeds as follows. It initializes each *Value* field to $\top$ and marks each CFG edge as "unexecuted." It initializes two worklists, one for CFG edges and the other for SSA graph edges. The CFG worklist receives the set of edges that leave the procedure's entry node, $n_0$. The SSA worklist receives the empty set.

```
CFGWorkList ← { edges leaving n₀ }
SSAWorkList ← ∅

for each edge e in the CFG
    mark e as unexecuted

for each def and each use, x, in the procedure
    Value(x) ← ⊤

while (CFGWorkList ≠ ∅ or SSAWorkList ≠ ∅)

    if CFGWorkList ≠ ∅ then
        remove an edge e = (m,n) from CFGWorkList
        if e is marked as unexecuted then
            mark e as executed
            EvaluateAllPhisInBlock((m,n))
            if no other edge entering n is marked as executed then
                if n is an assignment
                    EvaluateAssign(n)
                    let o be n's CFG successor
                    add (n,o) to CFGWorkList
                else EvaluateConditional(n)

    if SSAWorkList ≠ ∅ then
        remove an edge e = (s,d) from SSAWorkList
        c ← CFG node that uses d
        if any edge entering c is marked as executed then
            if d is a φ function argument
                then EvaluatePhi((s,d))
            else if c is an assignment then
                EvaluateAssign(c)
            else EvaluateConditional(c)
```

■ **FIGURE 10.8** Sparse Conditional Constant Propagation.

After the initialization phase, the algorithm repeatedly picks an edge from one of the two worklists and processes that edge. For a CFG edge $(m,n)$, SCCP determines if the edge is marked as executed. If $(m,n)$ is so marked, SCCP takes no further action for $(m,n)$. If $(m,n)$ is marked as unexecuted, then SCCP marks it as executed and evaluates all of the $\phi$-functions at the start of block $n$. Next, SCCP determines if block $n$ has been previously entered along another edge. If it has not, then SCCP evaluates the assignment or conditional branch in $n$. This processing may add edges to either worklist.

In this discussion, a block is *reachable* if and only if some CFG edge that enters it is marked as executable.

```
EvaluateAssign(m) /* m is a CFG node */
    for each value y used by the expression in m
        let (x,y) be the SSA edge that supplies y
        Value(y) ← Value(x)

    let d be the name of the value produced by m
    if Value(d) ≠ ⊥ then
        v ← evaluation of m over lattice values
        if v ≠ Value(d) then
            Value(d) ← v
            for every SSA edge (d,u)
                add (d,u) to SSAWorkList


EvaluateConditional(m) /* m is a CFG node */
    let (s,d) be the SSA edge referenced in m

    if Value(d) ≠ ⊥ then

        if Value(d) ≠ Value(s) then
            Value(d) ← Value(s)
            if Value(d) = ⊥ then
                for each CFG edge (m,n)
                    add (m,n) to CFGWorkList

            else
                let (m,n) be the CFG edge that
                    matches Value(d)
                add (m,n) to CFGWorkList
```

■ **FIGURE 10.9** Evaluating Assignments and Conditionals.

For an SSA edge, the algorithm first checks if the destination block is reachable. If the block is reachable, SCCP calls one of *EvaluatePhi*, *EvaluateAssign*, or *EvaluateConditional*, based on the kind of operation that uses the SSA name. When SCCP must evaluate an assignment or a conditional over the lattice of values, it follows the same scheme used in SSCP, discussed in Section 9.3.6 on page 515. Each time the lattice value for a definition changes, all the uses of that name are added to the SSA worklist.

Because SCCP only propagates values into blocks that it has already proved executable, it avoids processing unreachable blocks. Because each value propagation step is guarded by a test on the executable flag for the entering edge, values from unreachable blocks do not flow out of those blocks. Thus, values from unreachable blocks have no role in setting the lattice values in other blocks.

After the propagation step, a final pass is required to replace operations that have operands with *Value* tags other than ⊥. It can specialize many of these

```
EvaluatePhi((s,d)) /* (s,d) is an SSA graph edge */
    let p be the φ function that uses d
    EvaluateOperands(p)
    EvaluateResult(p)

EvaluateAllPhisInBlock((m,n)) /* (m,n) is a CFG edge */
    for each φ function p in block n
        EvaluateOperands(p)

    for each φ function p in block n
        Evaluate Result(p)

EvaluateOperands(phi)
    let x be the name defined by φ function phi
    if Value(x) ≠ ⊥ then
        for each parameter p of φ function phi
            let c be the CFG edge corresponding to p
            let (x,y) be the SSA edge ending in p
            if c is marked as executed
                then Value(y) ← Value(x)

EvaluateResult(phi)
    let x be the name defined by φ function phi
    if Value(x) ≠ ⊥ then
        v ← evaluation of phi over lattice values

        if Value(x) ≠ v then
            Value(x) ← v

            for each SSA graph edge (x,y)
                add (x,y) to SSAWorkList
```

■ **FIGURE 10.10** Evaluating $\phi$ Functions.

operations. It should also rewrite branches that have known outcomes with the appropriate jump operations. Later passes can remove the unreachable code (see Section 10.2). The algorithm cannot rewrite the code until the propagation completes.

### Subtleties in Evaluating and Rewriting Operations

Some subtle issues arise in modeling individual operations. For example, if the algorithm encounters a multiply operation with operands $\top$ and $\bot$, it might conclude that the operation produces $\bot$. Doing so, however, is premature. Subsequent analysis might lower the $\top$ to the constant 0, so that the multiply produces a value of 0. If SCCP uses the rule $\top \times \bot \rightarrow \bot$, it introduces the potential for nonmonotonic behavior—the multiply's value might follow the sequence $\top, \bot, 0$, which would increase the running time of SCCP. Equally important, it might incorrectly drive other values to $\bot$ and cause SCCP to miss opportunities for improvement.

To address this, SCCP should use three rules for multiplies that involve $\bot$, as follows: $\top \times \bot \rightarrow \top$, $\alpha \times \bot \rightarrow \bot$ for $\alpha \neq \top$ and $\alpha \neq 0$, and $0 \times \bot \rightarrow 0$. This same effect occurs for any operation for which the value of one argument can completely determine the result. Other examples include a shift by more than the word length, a logical AND with zero, and a logical OR with all ones.

Some rewrites have unforeseen consequences. For example, replacing $4 \times s$, for nonnegative $s$, with a shift replaces a commutative operation with a noncommutative operation. If the compiler subsequently tries to rearrange expressions using commutativity, this early rewrite forecloses an opportunity. This kind of interaction can have noticeable effects on code quality. To choose when the compiler should convert $4 \times s$ into a shift, the compiler writer must consider the order in which optimizations will be applied.

### Effectiveness

SCCP can find constants that the SSCP algorithm cannot. Similarly, it can discover unreachable code that no combination of the algorithms in Section 10.2 can discover. It derives its power from combining reachability analysis with the propagation of lattice values. It can eliminate some CFG edges because the lattice values are sufficient to determine which path a branch takes. It can ignore SSA edges that arise from unreachable operations (by initializing those definitions to $\top$) because those operations will be evaluated if the block becomes marked as reachable. The power of SCCP arises from the interplay between these analyses—constant propagation and reachability.

If reachability did not affect the final lattice values, then the same effects could be achieved by performing constant propagation (and rewriting constant-valued branches as jumps) followed by unreachable-code elimination. If constant propagation played no role in reachability, then the same effects could be achieved by the other order—unreachable-code elimination followed by constant propagation. The power of SCCP to find simplifications beyond those combinations comes precisely from the fact that the two optimizations are interdependent.

### 10.7.2 Strength Reduction

Operator strength reduction is a transformation that replaces a repeated series of expensive ("strong") operations with a series of inexpensive ("weak") operations that compute the same values. The classic example

```
    loadI  0        ⇒ r_s0
    loadI  1        ⇒ r_i0                loadI  0          ⇒ r_s0
    loadI  100      ⇒ r_100              loadI  @a         ⇒ r_t6
l1: phi   r_i0,r_i2 ⇒ r_i1               addI   r_t6,396   ⇒ r_lim
    phi   r_s0,r_s2 ⇒ r_i1          l1:  phi    r_t6,r_t8  ⇒ r_t7
    subI  r_i1,1    ⇒ r_1                 phi    r_s0,r_s2  ⇒ r_s1
    multI r_1,4     ⇒ r_2                 load   r_t7       ⇒ r_4
    addI  r_2,@a    ⇒ r_3                 add    r_s1,r_4   ⇒ r_s2
    load  r_3       ⇒ r_4                 addI   r_t7,4     ⇒ r_t8
    add   r_s1,r_4  ⇒ r_s2                cmp_LE r_t8,r_lim ⇒ r_5
    addI  r_i1,1    ⇒ r_s2                cbr    r_5        → l1,l2
    cmp_LE r_i2,r_100 ⇒ r_5         l2:  ...
    cbr   r_5       → l1,l2
l2: ...
```

|                  (a) Original Code                  |    (b) Strength-Reduced Code    |

■ **FIGURE 10.11** Strength Reduction Example.

replaces integer multiplications based on a loop index with equivalent additions. This particular case arises routinely from the expansion of array and structure addresses in loops. Figure 10.11a shows the ILOC that might be generated for the following loop:

$$\text{sum} \leftarrow 0$$
$$\text{for } i \leftarrow 1 \text{ to } 100$$
$$\text{sum} \leftarrow \text{sum} + a(i)$$

The code is in semipruned SSA form; the purely local values ($r_2$, $r_2$, $r_3$, and $r_4$) have neither subscripts nor $\phi$-functions. Notice how the reference to $a(i)$ expands to four operations—the subI, multI, and addI that compute $(i-1) \times 4 - @a$ and the load that defines $r_4$.

For each iteration, this sequence of operations computes the address of $a(i)$ from scratch as a function of the loop index variable $i$. Consider the sequences of values taken on by $r_{i_1}$, $r_1$, $r_2$, and $r_3$.

$$r_{i_1}: \{\, 1, 2, 3, \ldots, 100 \,\}$$
$$r_1: \{\, 0, 1, 2, \ldots, 99 \,\}$$
$$r_2: \{\, 0, 4, 8, \ldots, 396 \,\}$$
$$r_3: \{\, @a, @a+4, @a+8, \ldots, @a+396 \,\}$$

The values in $r_1$, $r_2$, and $r_3$ exist solely to compute the address for the load operation. If the program computed each value of $r_3$ from the preceding one, it could eliminate the operations that define $r_1$ and $r_2$. Of course, $r_3$ would then need an initialization and an update. This would make it a nonlocal name, so it would also need a $\phi$-function at both $l_1$ and $l_2$.

Figure 10.11b shows the code after strength reduction, linear-function test replacement, and dead-code elimination. It computes those values formerly in $r_3$ directly into $r_{t_7}$ and uses $r_{t_7}$ in the load operation. The end-of-loop test, which used $r_1$ in the original code, has been modified to use $r_{t_8}$. This makes the computations of $r_1$, $r_2$, $r_3$, $r_{i_0}$, $r_{i_1}$, and $r_{i_2}$ all dead. They have been removed to produce the final code. Now, the loop contains just five operations, ignoring $\phi$-functions, while the original code contained eight. (In translating from SSA form back to executable code, the $\phi$-functions become copy operations that the register allocator can usually remove.)

If the multI operation is more expensive than an addI, the savings will be larger. Historically, the high cost of multiplication justified strength reduction. However, even if multiplication and addition have equal costs, the strength-reduced form of the loop may be preferred because it creates a better code shape for later transformations and for code generation. In particular, if the target machine has an autoincrement addressing mode, then the addI operation in the loop can be folded into the memory operation. This option simply does not exist for the original multiply.

The rest of this section presents a simple algorithm for strength reduction, which we call OSR, followed by a scheme for linear function test replacement that shifts end-of-loop tests away from variables that would otherwise be dead. OSR operates on the SSA form of the code, considered as a graph. Figure 10.12 shows the code for our example, alongside its SSA graph.

### Background

Strength reduction looks for contexts in which an operation, such as a multiply, executes inside a loop and its operands are (1) a value that does not vary in that loop, called a *region constant*, and (2) a value that varies systematically from iteration to iteration, called an *induction variable*. When it finds this situation, it creates a new induction variable that computes the same sequence of values as the original multiplication in a more efficient way. The restrictions on the form of the multiply operation's operands ensure that this new induction variable can be computed using additions, rather than multiplications.

**Region constant**
A value that does not vary within a given loop is a *region constant* for that loop.

**Induction variable**
A value that increases or decreases by a constant amount in each iteration of a loop is an *induction variable*.

$$x \leftarrow c \times i$$
$$x \leftarrow i \times c$$
$$x \leftarrow c + i$$
$$x \leftarrow i + c$$
$$x \leftarrow i - c$$
Candidate Operations

We call an operation that can be reduced in this way a *candidate operation*. To simplify the presentation of OSR, we consider only candidate operations that have one of the five forms shown in the margin, where c is a region constant and i is an induction variable. The key to finding and reducing candidate operations is efficient identification of region constants and induction

```
        loadI   0          ⇒ r_{s_0}
        loadI   1          ⇒ r_{i_0}
        loadI   100        ⇒ r_{100}
l_1:    phi     r_{i_0}, r_{i_2}  ⇒ r_{i_1}
        phi     r_{s_0}, r_{s_2}  ⇒ r_{i_1}
        subI    r_{i_1}, 1   ⇒ r_1
        multI   r_1, 4     ⇒ r_2
        addI    r_2, @a    ⇒ r_3
        load    r_3        ⇒ r_4
        add     r_{s_1}, r_4  ⇒ r_{s_2}
        addI    r_{i_1}, 1   ⇒ r_{s_2}
        cmp_LE  r_{i_2}, r_{100}  ⇒ r_5
        cbr     r_5          → l_1, l_2
l_2:    ...
```

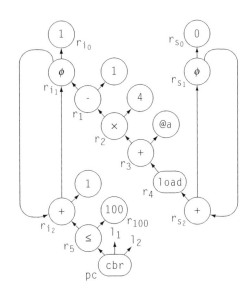

(a) Example in ILOC SSA Form          (b) Corresponding SSA Graph

■ **FIGURE 10.12** Relating SSA in ILOC to the SSA Graph .

variables. An operation is a candidate if and only if it has one of these forms, including the restrictions on operands.

A region constant can either be a literal constant, such as 10, or a loop-invariant value, that is, one not modified inside the loop. With the code in SSA form, the compiler can determine if an argument is loop invariant by checking the location of its sole definition—its definition must dominate the entry to the loop that defines the induction variable. OSR can check both of these conditions in constant time. Performing LCM and constant propagation before strength reduction may expose more region constants.

Intuitively, an induction variable is a variable whose values in the loop form an arithmetic progression. For the purposes of this algorithm, we can use a much more specific and restricted definition: an induction variable is a strongly connected component (SCC) of the SSA graph in which each operation that updates its value is one of (1) an induction variable plus a region constant, (2) an induction variable minus a region constant, (3) a $\phi$-function, or (4) a register-to-register copy from another induction variable. While this definition is much less general than conventional definitions, it is sufficient to enable the OSR algorithm to find and reduce candidate operations. To identify induction variables, OSR finds SCCs in the SSA graph and iterates over them to determine if each operation in the SCC is of one of these four types.

Because *OSR* defines induction variables in the SSA graph and region constants relative to a loop in the CFG, the test to determine if a value is constant relative to the loop containing a specific induction variable is complicated. Consider an operation $o$ of the form $x \leftarrow i \times c$, where $i$ is an induction variable. For $o$ to be a candidate for strength reduction, $c$ must be a region constant with respect to the outermost loop in which $i$ varies. To test whether $c$ has this property, *OSR* must relate the SCC for $i$ in the SSA graph back to a loop in the CFG.

*OSR* finds the SSA graph node with the lowest reverse postorder number in the SCC defining $i$. It considers this node to be the header of the SCC and records that fact in the header field of each node of the SCC. (Any node in the SSA graph that is not part of an induction variable has its header field set to *null*.) In SSA form, the induction variable's header is the $\phi$-function at the start of the outermost loop in which it varies. In an operation $x \leftarrow i \times c$, where $i$ is an induction variable, $c$ is a region constant if the CFG block that contains its definition dominates the CFG block that contains $i$'s header. This condition ensures that $c$ is invariant in the outermost loop in which $i$ varies. To perform this test, the SSA construction must produce a map from each SSA node to the CFG block where it originated.

The header field plays a critical role in determining whether or not an operation can be strength reduced. When *OSR* encounters an operation $x \leftarrow y \times z$, it can determine if $y$ is an induction variable by following the SSA graph edge to $y$'s definition and inspecting its header field. A *null* header field indicates that $y$ is not an induction variable. If both $y$ and $z$ have *null* header fields, the operation cannot be strength reduced.

If one of $y$ or $z$ has a non-*null* header field, then *OSR* uses that header field to determine if the other operand is a region constant. Assume $y$'s header is not *null*. To find the CFG block for the entry to the outermost loop where $y$ varies, *OSR* consults the SSA-to-CFG map, indexed by $y$'s header. If the CFG block containing $z$'s definition dominates the CFG block of $y$'s header, then $z$ is a region constant relative to the induction variable $y$.

### The Algorithm

To perform strength reduction, *OSR* must examine each operation and determine if one of its operands is an induction variable and the other is a region constant. If the operation meets these criteria, *OSR* can reduce it by creating a new induction variable that computes the needed values and replacing the operation with a register-to-register copy from this new induction variable. (It should avoid creating duplicate induction variables.)

```
OSR(G)
  nextNum ← 0

  while there is an unvisited n ∈ G
    DFS(n)

DFS(n)
  n.Num ← nextNum++
  n.Visited ← true
  n.Low ← n.Num
  push(n)

  for each operand o of n
    if o.Visited = false then
      DFS(o)
      n.Low ← min(n.Low,o.Low)

    if o.Num < n.Num and
       o is on the stack
      then n.Low ← min(n.Low,o.Num)

  if n.Low = n.Num then
    SCC ← ∅
    until x = n do
      x ← pop( )
      SCC ← SCC ∪ { x }
    Process(SCC)
```

```
Process(N)
  if N has only one member n
    then if n is a candidate operation
           then Replace(n,iv,rc)
           else n.Header ← null
    else ClassifyIV(N)

ClassifyIV(N)
  IsIV ← true
  for each node n ∈ N
    if n is not a valid update for
       an induction variable
      then IsIV ← false

  if IsIV then
    header ← n ∈ N with the
              lowest RPO number
    for each node n ∈ N
      n.Header ← header
  else
    for each node n ∈ N
      if n is a candidate operation
        then Replace(n,iv,rc)
        else n.Header ← null
```

■ **FIGURE 10.13** Operator Strength Reduction Algorithm.

Based on the preceding discussion, we know that *OSR* can identify induction variables by finding sccs in the ssa graph. It can discover a region constant by examining the value's definition. If the definition results from an immediate operation, or its cfg block dominates the cfg block of the induction variable's header, then the value is a region constant. The key is putting these ideas together into an efficient algorithm.

*OSR* uses Tarjan's strongly connected region finder to drive the entire process. As shown in Figure 10.13, *OSR* takes an ssa graph as its argument and repeatedly applies the strongly connected region finder, *DFS*, to it. (This process stops when *DFS* has visited every node in *G*.)

*DFS* performs a depth-first search of the ssa graph. It assigns each node a number, corresponding to the order in which it visits the node. It pushes each node onto a stack and labels the node with the lowest depth-first number on a node that can be reached from its children. When it returns from processing the children, if the lowest node reachable from *n* has *n*'s number, then *n* is the header of an scc. *DFS* pops nodes off the stack until it reaches *n*; all of those nodes are members of the scc.

*DFS* removes sccs from the stack in an order that simplifies the rest of *OSR*. When an scc is popped from the stack and passed to *Process*, *DFS* has already visited all of its children in the ssa graph. If we interpret the ssa graph so that its edges run from uses to definitions, as shown in the ssa graph in Figure 10.12, then candidate operations are encountered only after their operands have been passed to *Process*. When *Process* encounters an operation that is a candidate for strength reduction, its operands have already been classified. Thus, *Process* can examine operations, identify candidates, and invoke *Replace* to rewrite them in strength-reduced form during the depth-first search.

$$x \leftarrow c \times i$$
$$x \leftarrow i \times c$$
$$x \leftarrow c + i$$
$$x \leftarrow i + c$$
$$x \leftarrow i - c$$

Candidate Operations

When *Process* identifies *n* as a candidate operation, it finds both the induction variable, *iv* and the region constant, *rc*.

*DFS* passes each scc to *Process*. If the scc consists of a single node *n* that has the form of a candidate operation, shown in the margin, *Process* passes *n* to *Replace*, along with its induction variable, *iv*, and its region constant, *rc*. *Replace* rewrites the code, as described in the next section. If the scc contains multiple nodes, *Process* passes the scc to *ClassifyIV* to determine whether or not it is an induction variable.

*ClassifyIV* examines each node in the scc to check it against the set of valid updates for an induction variable. If all the updates are valid, the scc is an induction variable, and *Process* sets each node's header field to contain the node in the scc with the lowest reverse postorder number. If the scc is not an induction variable, *ClassifyIV* revisits each node in the scc to test it as a candidate operation, either passing it to *Replace* or setting its header to show that it is not an induction variable.

### Rewriting the Code

The remaining piece of *OSR* implements the rewriting step. Both *Process* and *ClassifyIV* call *Replace* to perform the rewrite. Figure 10.14 shows the code for *Replace* and its support functions *Reduce* and *Apply*.

*Replace* takes three arguments, an ssa graph node *n*, an induction variable *iv*, and a region constant *rc*. The latter two are operands to *n*. *Replace* calls *Reduce* to rewrite the operation represented by *n*. Next, it replaces *n* with a copy operation from the result produced by *Replace*. It sets *n*'s header field, and returns.

*Reduce* and *Apply* do most of the work. They use a hash table to avoid inserting duplicate operations. Since *OSR* works on ssa names, a single global hash table suffices. It can be initialized in *OSR* before the first call to *DFS*. *Insert* adds entries to the hash table; *Lookup* queries the table.

```
Replace(n, iv, rc)                      Apply(op, o1, o2)
    result ← Reduce(n.op, iv, rc)           result ← Lookup(op, o1, o2)
    replace n with a copy from result       if result is "not found" then
    n.header ← iv.header                         if o1 is an induction variable
                                                     and o2 is a region constant
Reduce(op,iv,rc)                                 then result ← Reduce(op, o1, o2)
    result ← Lookup(op, iv, rc)
    if result is "not found" then                else if o2 is an induction variable
        result ← NewName()                               and o1 is a region constant
        Insert(op, iv, rc,result)                    then result ← Reduce(op, o2, o1)

        newDef ← Clone(iv, result)               else
        newDef.header ← iv.header                    result ← NewName()
                                                     Insert(op, o1, o2,result)
        for each operand o of newDef
            if o.header = iv.header                  Find block b dominated by the
            then rewrite o with                          definitions of o1 and o2
                    Reduce(op, o, rc)
                                                     Create "op o1, o2 ⇒ result"
            else if op is × or                           at the end of b and set its
                    newDef.op is φ                        header to null
                then replace o with
                    Apply(op, o, rc)         return result
    return result
```

■ **FIGURE 10.14** Algorithm for the Rewriting Step.

The plan for *Reduce* is simple. It takes an opcode and its two operands and either creates a new induction variable to replace the computation or returns the name of an induction variable previously created for the same combination of opcode and operands. It consults the hash table to avoid duplicate work. If the desired induction variable is not in the hash table, it creates the induction variable in a two-step process. First, it calls *Clone* to copy the definition for $iv$, the induction variable in the operation being reduced. Next, it recurs on the operands of this new definition.

These operands fall into two categories. If the operand is defined inside the scc, it is part of $iv$, so *Reduce* recurs on that operand. This forms the new induction variable by cloning its way around the scc of the original induction variable $iv$. An operand defined outside the scc must be either the initial value of $iv$ or a value by which $iv$ is incremented. The initial value must be a $\phi$-function argument from outside the scc; *Reduce* calls *Apply* on each such argument. *Reduce* can leave an induction-variable increment alone, unless the candidate operation is a multiply. For a multiply, *Reduce* must compute a new increment as the product of the old increment and the original region constant $rc$. It invokes *Apply* to generate this computation.

*Apply* takes an opcode and two operands, locates an appropriate point in the code, and inserts that operation. It returns the new SSA name for the result of that operation. A few details need further explanation. If this new operation is, itself, a candidate, *Apply* invokes *Reduce* to handle it. Otherwise, *Apply* gets a new name, inserts the operation, and returns the result. (If both *o1* and *o2* are constant, *Apply* can evaluate the operation and insert an immediate load.) It locates an appropriate block for the new operation using dominance information. Intuitively, the new operation must go into a block dominated by the blocks that define its operands. If one operand is a constant, *Apply* can duplicate the constant in the block that defines the other operand. Otherwise, both operands must have definitions that dominate the header block, and one must dominate the other. *Apply* can insert the operation immediately after this later definition.

### Back to the Example

Consider what happens when *OSR* encounters the example in Figure 10.12. Assume that it begins with the node labelled $r_{s_2}$ and that it visits left children before right children. It recurs down the chain of operations that define $r_4$, $r_3$, $r_2$, $r_1$, and $r_{i_1}$. At $r_{i_1}$, it recurs on $r_{i_2}$ and then $r_{i_0}$. It finds the two single-node SCCs that contain the literal constant one. Neither is a candidate, so *Process* marks them as noninduction variables by setting their headers to *null*.

The first nontrivial SCC that *DFS* discovers contains $r_{i_1}$ and $r_{i_2}$. All the operations are valid updates for an induction variable, so *ClassifyIV* marks each node as an induction variable by setting its header field to point to the node with the lowest depth-first number in the SCC—the node for $r_{i_1}$.

Now, *DFS* returns to the node for $r_1$. Its left child is an induction variable and its right child is a region constant, so it invokes *Reduce* to create an induction variable. In this case, $r_1$ is $r_{i_1} - 1$, so the induction variable has an initial value equal to one less than the initial value of the old induction variable, or zero. The increment is the same. Figure 10.15 shows the SCC that *Reduce* and *Apply* create, under the label "for $r_1$." Finally, the definition of $r_1$ is replaced with a copy operation, $r_1 \leftarrow r_{t_1}$. The copy operation is marked as an induction variable.

Next, *DFS* discovers the SCC that consists of the node labelled $r_2$. *Process* discovers that it is a candidate because its left operand (the copy that now defines $r_1$) is an induction variable and its right operand is a region constant. *Process* invokes *Replace* to create an induction variable that has the value

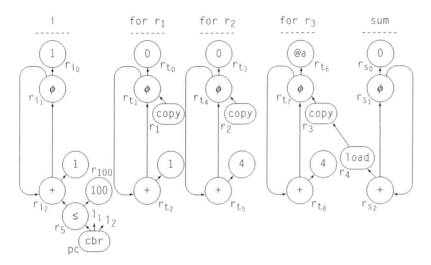

■ **FIGURE 10.15** Transformed ssa Graph for the Example.

$r_1 \times 4$. *Reduce* and *Apply* clone the induction variable for $r_1$, adjust the increment since the operation is a multiply, and add a copy to $r_2$.

*DFS* next passes the node for $r_3$ to *Process*. This creates another induction variable with @a as its initial value and copies its value to $r_3$.

*Process* handles the load, followed by the scc that computes the sum. It finds that none of these operations are candidates.

Finally, *OSR* invokes *DFS* on the unvisited node for the cbr. *DFS* visits the comparison, the previously marked induction variable, and the constant 100. No further reductions occur.

The ssa graph in Figure 10.15 shows all of the induction variables created by this process. The induction variables labelled "for $r_1$" and "for $r_2$" are dead. The induction variable for i would be dead, except that the end-of-loop test still uses it. To eliminate this induction variable, the compiler can apply linear-function test replacement to transfer the test to the induction variable for $r_3$.

### Linear-Function Test Replacement

Strength reduction often eliminates all uses of an induction variable, except for an end-of-loop test. In that case, the compiler may be able to rewrite the end-of-loop test to use another induction variable found in the loop. If the compiler can remove this last use, it can eliminate the original induction variable as dead code. This transformation is called linear-function test replacement (LFTR).

To perform LFTR, the compiler must (1) locate comparisons that rely on otherwise unneeded induction variables, (2) locate an appropriate new induction variable that the comparison could use, (3) compute the correct region constant for the rewritten test, and (4) rewrite the code. Having LFTR cooperate with $OSR$ can simplify all of these tasks to produce a fast, effective transformation.

The operations that LFTR targets compare the value of an induction variable against a region constant. $OSR$ examines each operation in the program to determine if it is a candidate for strength reduction. It can easily and inexpensively build a list of all the comparison operations that involve induction variables. After $OSR$ finishes its work, LFTR should revisit each of these comparisons. If the induction-variable argument of a comparison was strength reduced by $OSR$, LFTR should retarget the comparison to use the new induction variable.

To facilitate this process, $Reduce$ can record the arithmetic relationship it uses to derive each new induction variable. It can insert a special LFTR edge from each node in the original induction variable to the corresponding node in its reduced counterpart and label it with the operation and region constant of the candidate operation responsible for creating that induction variable. Figure 10.16 shows the SSA graph with these additional edges in black. The sequence of reductions in the example create a chain of labelled edges. Starting from the original induction variable, we find the labels $-1$, $\times 4$, and $+@a$.

When LFTR finds a comparison that should be replaced, it can follow the edges from its induction-variable argument to the final induction variable that resulted from a chain of one or more reductions. The comparison should use this induction variable with an appropriate new region constant.

The labels on the LFTR edges describe the transformation that must be applied to the original region constant to derive the new region constant. In the example, the trail of edges leads from $r_{i_2}$ to $r_{t_8}$ and produces the value $(100 - 1) \times 4 + @a$ for the transformed test. Figure 10.16 shows the edges and the rewritten test.

This version of LFTR is simple, efficient, and effective. It relies on close collaboration with $OSR$ to identify comparisons that might be retargeted and to record the reductions as it applies them. Using these two data structures, LFTR can find comparisons to retarget, find the appropriate place to retarget

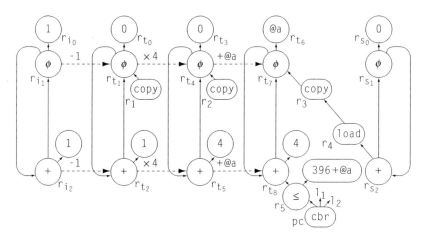

■ **FIGURE 10.16** Example after LFTR.

them, and find the necessary transformation for the comparison's constant argument.

### 10.7.3 Choosing an Optimization Sequence

The effectiveness of an optimizer on any given code depends on the sequence of optimizations that it applies to the code—both the specific transformations that it uses and the order in which it applies them. Traditional optimizing compilers have offered the user the choice of several sequences (e.g. -0, -01, -02, ... ). Those sequences provide a tradeoff between compile time and the amount of optimization that the compiler attempts. Increased optimization effort, however, does not guarantee improvement.

**Optimization sequence**
a set of optimizations and an order for their application

The optimization sequence problem arises because the effectiveness of any given transformation depends on several factors.

1. Does the opportunity that the transformation targets appear in the code? If not, the transformation cannot improve the code.
2. Has a prior transformation hidden or obscured that opportunity? For example, the optimization of algebraic identities in LVN can convert $2 \times a$ into a shift operation, which replaces a commutative operation with a faster non-commutative optimization. Any transformation that needs commutativity to effect its improvement might see opportunities vanish from prior application of LVN.
3. Has any other transformation already eliminated the inefficiency? Transformations have overlapping and idiosyncratic effects; for example, LVN achieves some of the effects of global constant

propagation and loop unrolling achieves effects similar to superblock cloning. The compiler writer might include both transformations for their nonoverlapping effects.

The interactions between transformations makes it difficult to predict the improvement from the application of any single transformation or any sequence of transformations.

Some research compilers attempt to discover good optimization sequences. The approaches vary in granularity and in technique. The various systems have looked for sequences at the block level, at the source-file level, and at the whole-program level. Most of these systems have used some kind of search over the space of optimization sequences.

The space of potential optimization sequences is huge. For example, if the compiler chooses a sequence of length 10 from a pool of 15 transformations, it has $10^{15}$ possible sequences that it can generate—an impractically large number for the compiler to explore. Thus, compilers that search for good sequences use heuristic techniques to sample smaller portions of the search space. In general, these techniques fall into three categories: (1) genetic algorithms adapted to act as intelligent searches, (2) randomized search algorithms, and (3) statistical machine learning techniques. All three approaches have shown promise.

In this context, a *good* sequence is one that produces results within 5% of the best results.

Despite the huge size of the search spaces, well-tuned search algorithms can find good optimization sequences with 100 to 200 probes of the search space. While that number is not yet practical, further refinement may reduce the number of probes to a practical level.

One interesting application of these techniques is to derive the sequences used by the compiler's command line flags, such as -02. The compiler writer can use an ensemble of representative applications to discover good general sequences and then apply those sequences as the compiler's default sequences. A more aggressive approach, used in several systems, is to derive a handful of good sequences for different application ensembles and have the compiler try each of those sequences and retain the best result.

## 10.8  SUMMARY AND PERSPECTIVE

The design and implementation of an optimizing compiler is a complex undertaking. This chapter has introduced a conceptual framework for thinking about transformations—the taxonomy of effects. Each category in the taxonomy is represented by several examples, either in this chapter or elsewhere in the book.

The challenge for the compiler writer is to select a set of transformations that work well together to produce good code—code that meets the user's needs. The specific transformations implemented in a compiler determine, to a large extent, the kinds of programs for which it will produce good code.

## ■ CHAPTER NOTES

While the algorithms presented in this chapter are modern, many of the basic ideas were well known in the 1960s and 1970s. Dead-code elimination, code motion, strength reduction, and redundancy elimination are all described by Allen [11] and by Cocke and Schwartz [91]. A number of survey papers provide overviews of the state of the field at different points in time [16, 28, 30, 316]. Books by Morgan [268] and Muchnick [270] both discuss the design, structure, and implementation of optimizing compilers. Wolfe [352] and Allen and Kennedy [20] focus on dependence-based analysis and transformations.

*Dead* implements a mark-sweep style of dead-code elimination that was introduced by Kennedy [215, 217]. It is reminiscent of the Schorr-Waite marking algorithm [309]. *Dead* is specifically adapted from the work of Cytron et al. [110, Section 7.1]. *Clean* was developed and implemented in 1992 by Rob Shillner [254].

LCM improves on Morel and Renvoise's classic algorithm for partial redundancy elimination [267]. That paper inspired many improvements, including [81, 130, 133, 321]. Knoop, Rüthing, and Steffen's LCM [225] improved code placement; the formulation in Section 10.3 uses equations from Drechsler and Stadel [134]. Bodik, Gupta, and Soffa combined this approach with replication to find and remove all redundant code [43]. The DVNT algorithm is due to Briggs [53]. It has been implemented in a number of compilers.

Hoisting appears in the Allen-Cocke catalogue as a technique for reducing code space [16]. The formulation using anticipability appears in several places, including Fischer and LeBlanc [147]. Sinking or cross-jumping is described by Wulf et al. [356].

Both peephole optimization and tail-recursion elimination date to the early 1960s. Peephole optimization was first described by McKeeman [260]. Tail-recursion elimination is older; folklore tells that McCarthy described it at the chalkboard during a talk in 1963. Steele's thesis [323] is a classic reference for tail-recursion elimination.

Superblock cloning was introduced by Hwu et al. [201]. Loop optimizations such as unswitching and unrolling have been studied extensively [20, 28]; Kennedy used unrolling to avoid copy operations at the end of a loop [214].

Cytron, Lowrey, and Zadeck present an interesting alternative to unswitching [111]. McKinley et al. give practical insight into the impact of memory optimizations on performance [94, 261].

Combining optimizations, as in sccp, often leads to improvements that cannot be obtained by independent application of the original optimizations. Value numbering combines redundancy elimination, constant propagation, and simplification of algebraic identities [53]. lcm combines elimination of redundancies and partial redundancies with code motion [225]. Click and Cooper [86] combine Alpern's partitioning algorithm [21] with sccp [347]. Many authors have combined register allocation and instruction scheduling [48, 163, 269, 276, 277, 285, 308].

The sccp algorithm is due to Wegman and Zadeck [346, 347]. Their work clarified the distinction between optimistic and pessimistic algorithms; Click discusses the same issue from a set-building perspective [84].

Operator strength reduction has a rich history. One family of strength-reduction algorithms developed out of work by Allen, Cocke, and Kennedy [19, 88, 90, 216, 256]. The *OSR* algorithm is in this family [107]. Another family of algorithms grew out of the data-flow approach to optimization exemplified by the lcm algorithm; a number of sources give techniques in this family [127, 129, 131, 178, 209, 220, 226]. The version of *OSR* in Section 10.7.2 only reduces multiplications. Allen et al. show the reduction sequences for many other operators [19]; extending *OSR* to handle these cases is straightforward. A weaker form of strength reduction rewrites integer multiplies with faster operations [243].

## ■ EXERCISES

**Section 10.1**

1. One of the primary functions of an optimizer is to remove overhead that the compiler introduced during the translation from source language into ir.
   a. Give four examples of inefficiencies that you would expect an optimizer to improve, along with the source-language constructs that give rise to them.
   b. Give four examples of inefficiencies that you would expect an optimizer to miss, even though they can be improved. Explain why an optimizer would have difficulty improving them.

**Section 10.2**

2. Figure 10.1 shows the algorithm for *Dead*. The marking pass is a classic fixed-point computation.
   a. Explain why this computation terminates.
   b. Is the fixed-point that it finds unique? Prove your answer.
   c. Derive a tight time bound for the algorithm.

**3.** Consider the algorithm `Clean` from Section 10.2. It removes useless control flow and simplifies the CFG.
   **a.** Why does the algorithm terminate?
   **b.** Give an overall time bound for the algorithm.

**4.** LCM uses data-flow analysis to find redundancy and to perform code motion. Thus, it relies on a lexical notion of identity to find redundancy—two expressions can only be redundant if the data-flow analysis maps them to the same internal name. By contrast, value numbering computes identity based on values.
   **a.** Give an example of a redundant expression that LCM will discover but a value-based algorithm (say a global version of value numbering) will not.
   **b.** Give an example of a redundant expression that LCM will not discover but a value-based algorithm will.

Section 10.3

**5.** Redundancy elimination has a variety of effects on the code that the compiler generates.
   **a.** How does LCM affect the demand for registers in the code being transformed? Justify your answer.
   **b.** How does LCM affect the size of the code generated for a procedure? (You can assume that demand for registers is unchanged.)
   **c.** How does hoisting affect the demand for registers in the code being transformed? Justify your answer.
   **d.** How does hoisting affect the size of the code generated for a procedure? (Use the same assumptions.)

**6.** A simple form of operator strength reduction replaces a single instance of an expensive operation with a sequence of operations that are less expensive to execute. For example, some integer multiply operations can be replaced with a sequence of shifts and adds.
   **a.** What conditions must hold to let the compiler safely replace an integer operation $x \leftarrow y \times z$ with a single shift operation?
   **b.** Sketch an algorithm that replaces a multiplication of a known constant and an unsigned integer with a sequence of shifts and adds in cases where the constant is not a power of two.

Section 10.4

**7.** Both tail-call optimization and inline substitution attempt to reduce the overhead caused by the procedure linkage.
   **a.** Can the compiler inline a tail call? What obstacles arise? How might you work around them?
   **b.** Contrast the code produced from your modified inlining scheme with that produced by tail-call optimization.

Section 10.5

**8.** A compiler can find and eliminate redundant computations in many different ways. Among these are DVNT and LCM.
   **a.** Give two examples of redundancies eliminated by DVNT that cannot be found byLCM.
   **b.** Give an example that LCM finds that is missed by DVNT.

Section 10.6

**9.** Develop an algorithm to rename the value in a procedure to that encodes value identity into variable names.

**10.** Superblock cloning can cause significant code growth.
   **a.** How might the compiler mitigate code growth in superblock cloning while retaining as much of the benefit as possible?
   **b.** What problems might arise if the optimizer allowed superblock cloning to continue across a loop-closing branch? Contrast your approach with loop unrolling.

Hint: Think back to the block-placement algorithm in Chapter 8.

# Instruction Selection

## ■ CHAPTER OVERVIEW

The compiler's front end and optimizer both operate on the code in its IR form. Before the code can execute on a target processor, the IR form of the code must be rewritten into the processor's instruction set. The process of mapping IR operations into target machine operations is called instruction selection.

This chapter introduces two different approaches to instruction selection. The first uses the technology of tree-pattern matching algorithms. The second builds on the classic late-stage transformation, peephole optimization. Both have found widespread use in real compilers.

**Keywords:** Instruction Selection, Tree-Pattern Matching, Peephole Optimization

## 11.1 INTRODUCTION

To translate a program from an intermediate representation such as an abstract syntax tree or a low-level linear code into executable form, the compiler must map each IR construct into a corresponding and equivalent construct in the target processor's instruction set. Depending on the relative levels of abstraction in the IR and the target machine's ISA, this translation can involve elaborating details that are hidden in the IR program or it can involve combining multiple IR operations into a single machine instruction. The specific choices that the compiler makes have an impact on the overall efficiency of the compiled code.

The complexity of instruction selection derives from the large number of alternative implementations that a typical ISA provides for even simple operations. In the 1970s, the DEC PDP-11 had a small and compact instruction set; thus a good compiler such as the BLISS-11 compiler could perform instruction selection with a simple hand-coded pass. As processor ISAS expanded, the number of possible encodings for each program grew unmanageable. This explosion led to systematic approaches for instruction selection, such as those presented in this chapter.

### Conceptual Roadmap

Instruction selection, which maps the compiler's IR into the target ISA, is a pattern-matching problem. At its simplest, the compiler could provide a single target ISA sequence for each IR operation. The resulting selector would provide a template-like expansion that would produce correct code. Unfortunately, that code might make poor use of target machine resources. Better approaches consider many possible code sequences for each IR operation and choose the sequence that has the lowest expected cost.

This chapter presents two approaches to instruction selection: one based on tree-pattern matching and one based on peephole optimization. The former approach relies on a high-level tree notation for both the compiler's IR and the target machine's ISA. The latter approach translates the compiler's ISA into a low-level linear IR, systematically improves that IR, and then maps it into the target ISA. Each of these techniques can produce high-quality code that takes into account local context. Each has been incorporated into tools that take a target machine description and produce a working instruction selector.

### Overview

Systematic approaches to code generation make it easier to retarget a compiler. The goal of such work is to minimize the effort required to port the compiler to a new processor or system. Ideally, the front end and the optimizer need minimal changes, and much of the back end can be reused as well. This strategy makes good use of the investment in building, debugging, and maintaining the common parts of the compiler.

In practice, a new language often needs some new operations in the IR. The goal, however, is to extend the IR, rather than to reinvent it.

Much of the responsibility for handling diverse targets rests on the instruction selector. A typical compiler uses a common IR for all targets and, to the extent possible, for all source languages. It optimizes the intermediate form based on a set of assumptions that hold true on most, if not all, target machines. Finally, it uses a back end in which the compiler writer has tried to isolate and extract the target-dependent details.

While the scheduler and register allocator need target-dependent information, good design can isolate that knowledge into a concrete description of the target machine and its ISA. Such a description might include register-set sizes; the number, capabilities, and operation latencies of the functional units; memory alignment restrictions; and the procedure-call convention. The algorithms for scheduling and allocation are then parameterized by those system characteristics and reused across different ISAs and systems.

Thus, the key to retargetability lies in the implementation of the instruction selector. A retargetable instruction selector consists of a pattern-matching engine coupled to a set of tables that encode the needed knowledge about mapping from the IR to the target ISA. The selector consumes the compiler's IR and produces assembly code for the target machine. In such a system, the compiler writer creates a description of the target machine and runs the back-end generator (sometimes called a *code generator*). The back-end generator, in turn, uses the specification to derive the tables needed by the pattern matcher. Like a parser generator, the back-end generator runs offline during compiler development. Thus, we can use algorithms to create the tables that require more time than algorithms typically employed in a compiler.

While the goal is to isolate all machine-dependent code in the instruction selector, scheduler, and register allocator, the reality almost always falls somewhat short of this ideal. Some machine-dependent details creep, unavoidably, into earlier parts of the compiler. For example, the alignment restrictions on activation records may differ among target machines, changing offsets for values stored in activation records (ARS). The compiler may need to represent features such as predicated execution, branch delay slots, and multiword memory operations explicitly if it is to make good use of them. Still, pushing target-dependent details into instruction selection can reduce the number of changes to other parts of the compiler that are needed to port it to a new target processor.

This chapter examines two approaches to automating the construction of instruction selectors. Section 11.3 revisits the simple treewalk scheme from Chapter 7 and uses it as a detailed introduction to the complexities of instruction selection. The following two sections present different ways to apply pattern-matching techniques to transform IR sequences to assembly sequences. The first technique, in Section 11.4, builds on algorithms for matching tree patterns against trees. The second technique, in Section 11.5, builds on ideas from peephole optimization. Both of these methods are description based. The compiler writer writes a description of the target ISA; a tool then constructs a selector for use at compile time. Both methods have been used in successful portable compilers.

**SELECTION, SCHEDULING, AND ALLOCATION**

The three major processes in the back end are instruction selection, scheduling, and register allocation. All three processes have a direct impact on the quality of the generated code, and they all interact with each other.

Selection directly changes the scheduling process. Selection dictates both the time required for an operation and the functional units on which it can execute. Scheduling might affect instruction selection. If the code generator can implement an IR operation with either of two assembly operations, and those operations use different resources, the code generator might need to understand the final schedule to ensure the best choice.

Selection interacts with register allocation in several ways. If the target processor has a uniform register set, then the instruction selector can assume an unlimited supply of registers and rely on the allocator to insert the loads and stores needed to fit the values into the register set. If, on the other hand, the target machine has rules that restrict register usage, then the selector must pay close attention to specific physical registers. This can complicate selection and predetermine some or all of the allocation decisions. In this situation, the code generator might use a coroutine to perform local register allocation during instruction selection.

Keeping selection, scheduling, and allocation separate—to the extent possible—can simplify implementation and debugging of each process. However, since each of these processes can constrain the others, the compiler writer must take care to avoid adding unnecessary constraints.

## 11.2 CODE GENERATION

The compiler's back end must solve three problems to generate executable code for a program in IR form. It must convert the IR operations into operations in the target processor's ISA, a process called *instruction selection*, which is the subject of this chapter. It must select an order in which those operations should execute, a process called *instruction scheduling*, which is the subject of Chapter 12. It must determine, at each point in the final code, which values should reside in registers and which values should reside in memory, a process called *register allocation*, which is the subject of Chapter 13. Most compilers handle these three processes separately. These three distinct but related processes are often lumped together in the term "code generation," even though the instruction selector has the primary responsibility for generating target-machine instructions.

Each of these three problems is, on its own, a computationally hard problem. While it is not clear how to define optimal instruction selection, the problem of generating the fastest code sequence for a CFG with control flow involves a huge number of alternatives. Instruction scheduling is NP-complete for a basic block under most realistic execution models; moving to larger regions of code does not simplify the problem. Register allocation is, in its general form, also NP-complete in procedures with control flow. Most compilers handle these three problems independently.

The level of exposed detail in the IR program matters. An IR with a higher level of abstraction than the ISA requires the instruction selector to supply additional detail. (Mechanical generation of such detail at this late stage in compilation can lead to template-like code with a low level of customization.) An IR with a lower level of abstraction than the ISA allows the selector to tailor its selections accordingly. Compilers that perform little or no optimization generate code directly from the IR produced by the front end.

The complexity of instruction selection arises from the fact that a typical processor provides many distinct ways to perform the same computation. Abstract away, for the moment, the issues of instruction scheduling and register allocation; we will return to them in the next two chapters. If each IR operation had just one implementation on the target machine, the compiler could simply rewrite each IR operation with the equivalent sequence of machine operations. In most contexts, however, a target machine provides multiple ways to implement each IR construct.

Consider, for example, an IR construct that copies a value from one general-purpose register, $r_i$, to another, $r_j$. Assume that the target processor uses ILOC as its native instruction set. As we shall see, even ILOC has enough complexity to expose many of the problems of code generation. The obvious implementation of $r_i \rightarrow r_j$ uses $\text{i2i } r_i \Rightarrow r_j$; such a register-to-register copy is typically one of the least-expensive operations that a processor provides. However, other implementations abound. These include, for example, each of the following operations:

```
addI  rᵢ,0  ⇒ rⱼ    subI    rᵢ,0 ⇒ rⱼ    multI   rᵢ,1 ⇒ rⱼ
divI  rᵢ,1  ⇒ rⱼ    lshiftI rᵢ,0 ⇒ rⱼ    rshiftI rᵢ,0 ⇒ rⱼ
and   rᵢ,rᵢ ⇒ rⱼ    orI     rᵢ,0 ⇒ rⱼ    xorI    rᵢ,0 ⇒ rⱼ
```

Still more possibilities exist. If the processor maintains a register whose value is always 0, another set of operations works, using add, sub, lshift, rshift, or, and xor. A larger set of two-operation sequences, including a store followed by a load, also works.

A human programmer would rapidly discount most, if not all, of these alternate sequences. Using i2i is simple, fast, and obvious. An automated process, however, may need to consider all the possibilities and make the appropriate choices. The ability of a specific ISA to accomplish the same effect in multiple ways increases the complexity of instruction selection. For ILOC, the ISA provides only a few, simple, low-level operations for each particular effect. Even so, it supports myriad ways to implement register-to-register copy.

Real processors are more complex than ILOC. They may include higher-level operations and addressing modes that the code generator should consider. While these features allow a skilled programmer or a carefully crafted compiler to create more efficient programs, they also increase the number of choices that the instruction selector confronts—they make the space of potential implementations larger.

Each alternate sequence has its own costs. Most modern machines implement simple operations, such as i2i, add, and lshift, so that they execute in a single cycle. Some operations, like integer multiplication and division, may take longer. The speed of a memory operation depends on many factors, including the detailed current state of the computer's memory system.

In some cases, the actual cost of an operation might depend on context. If, for example, the processor has several functional units, it might be better to perform a register-to-register copy using an operation other than copy that will execute on an underutilized functional unit. If the unit would otherwise be idle, the operation is, effectively, free. Moving it onto the underutilized unit might actually speed up the entire computation. If the code generator must rewrite the copy to a specific operation that executes only on the underutilized unit, this is a selection problem. If the same operation can run on any unit, it is a scheduling problem.

In most cases, the compiler writer wants the back end to produce code that runs quickly. However, other metrics are possible. For example, if the final code will run on a battery-powered device, the compiler might consider the typical energy consumption of each operation. (Individual operations may consume different amounts of energy.) The costs in a compiler that tries to optimize for energy may be radically different than the costs that a speed metric would involve. Processor energy consumption depends heavily on details of the underlying hardware and, thus, may change from one implementation of a processor to another. Similarly, if code space is critical, the compiler writer might assign costs based solely on sequence length. Alternatively, the compiler writer might simply exclude all multioperation sequences that achieve the same effect as a single-operation sequence.

Since a shorter code sequence fetches fewer bytes from RAM, reducing code space may also reduce energy consumption.

To further complicate matters, some ISAs place additional constraints on specific operations. An integer multiply might need to take its operands from a subrange of the registers. A floating-point operation might need its operands in even-numbered registers. A memory operation might only execute on one of the processor's functional units. A floating-point unit might include an operation that computes the sequence $(r_i \times r_j) + r_k$ more quickly than the individual multiply and add operations. Load-multiple and store-multiple operations might require contiguous registers. The memory system might deliver its best bandwidth and latency for doubleword or quadword loads, rather than singleword loads. Restrictions such as these constrain instruction selection. At the same time, they increase the importance of finding a solution that uses the best operation at each point in the input program.

When the level of abstraction of the IR and the target ISA differ significantly, or the underlying computation models differ, instruction selection can play a critical role in bridging that gap. The extent to which instruction selection can map the computations in the IR program efficiently to the target machine will often determine the efficiency of the generated code. For example, consider three scenarios for generating code from an ILOC-like IR.

1. *A simple, scalar RISC machine*  The mapping from IR to assembly is straightforward. The code generator might consider only one or two assembly-language sequences for each IR operation.
2. *A CISC processor*  To make effective use of a CISC instruction set, the compiler may need to aggregate several IR operations into one target-machine operation.
3. *A stack machine*  The code generator must translate from the register-to-register computational style of ILOC to a stack-based style with its implicit names and, in some cases, destructive operations.

Moving from one-address code to three-address code entails similar problems.

As the gap in abstraction between the IR and the target ISA grows, so does the need for tools to help build code generators.

While instruction selection can play an important role in determining code quality, the compiler writer must keep in mind the enormous size of the search space that the instruction selector might explore. As we shall see, even moderately sized instruction sets can produce search spaces that contain hundreds of millions of states. Clearly, the compiler cannot afford to explore such spaces exhaustively. The techniques that we describe explore the space of alternative code sequences in a disciplined fashion and either limit their searching or precompute enough information to make a deep search efficient.

## 11.3 EXTENDING THE SIMPLE TREEWALK SCHEME

To make the discussion concrete, consider the issues that can arise in generating code for an assignment statement such as $a \leftarrow b - 2 \times c$. It might be represented by an abstract syntax tree (AST), as shown on the left, or by a table of quadruples, as shown on the right.

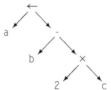

| Op | Arg₁ | Arg₂ | Result |
|----|------|------|--------|
| × | 2 | c | t |
| - | b | t | a |

Instruction selection must produce an assembly-language program from IR representations like these two. For the sake of discussion, assume that it must generate operations in the ILOC subset shown in Figure 11.1.

In Chapter 7, we saw that a simple treewalk routine could generate code from the AST for an expression. The code in Figure 7.5 handled the binary operators, +, -, ×, and ÷ applied to variables and numbers. It generated naive code for the expression and was intended to illustrate an approach that might be used to generate either a low-level, linear IR or assembly code for a simple RISC machine.

The simple treewalk approach generates the same code for every instance of a particular AST node type. While this produces correct code, it never capitalizes on the opportunity to tailor the code to specific circumstances and context. If a compiler performs significant optimization after instruction selection, this may not be a problem. Without subsequent optimization, however, the final code is likely to contain obvious inefficiencies.

Consider, for example, the way that the simple treewalk routine handles variables and numbers. The code for the relevant cases is

```
case IDENT:                          case NUM:
    t1 ← base(node);                     result ← NextRegister();
    t2 ← offset(node);                   emit (loadI, val(node),
    result ← NextRegister();                 none, result);
    emit (loadA0, t1, t2, result);   break;
    break;
```

For variables, it relies on two routines, *base* and *offset*, to get the base address and offset into registers. It then emits a loadA0 operation that adds these two values to produce an effective address and retrieves the contents of the memory location at that address. Because the AST does not differentiate between the storage classes of variables, *base* and *offset* presumably consult the symbol table to obtain the additional information that they need.

**CODE LAYOUT**

Before it begins emitting code, the compiler has the opportunity to lay out the basic blocks in memory. If each branch in the IR has two explicit branch targets, as ILOC does, then the compiler can choose either of a block's logical successors to follow it in memory. If branches have only one explicit branch target, then rearranging blocks may require rewriting branches—swapping the taken branch and the fall-through branch.

Two architectural considerations should guide this decision. On some processors, taking the branch requires more time than falling through to the next operation. On machines with cache memory, blocks that execute together should be located together. Both of these favor the same strategy for layout. If block *a* ends in a branch that targets *b* and *c*, the compiler should place the more frequently taken target after *a* in memory.

Of course, if a block has multiple predecessors in the control-flow graph, only one of them can immediately precede it in memory. The others will require a branch or jump to reach it (see Section 8.6.2).

| **Arithmetic Operations** | | **Memory Operations** | |
|---|---|---|---|
| add | $r_1, r_2 \Rightarrow r_3$ | store | $r_1 \Rightarrow r_2$ |
| addI | $r_1, c_2 \Rightarrow r_3$ | storeAO | $r_1 \Rightarrow r_2, r_3$ |
| sub | $r_1, r_2 \Rightarrow r_3$ | storeAI | $r_1 \Rightarrow r_2, c_3$ |
| subI | $r_1, c_2 \Rightarrow r_3$ | loadI | $c_1 \Rightarrow r_3$ |
| rsubI | $r_2, c_1 \Rightarrow r_3$ | load | $r_1 \Rightarrow r_3$ |
| mult | $r_1, r_2 \Rightarrow r_3$ | loadAO | $r_1, r_2 \Rightarrow r_3$ |
| multI | $r_1, c_2 \Rightarrow r_3$ | loadAI | $r_1, c_2 \Rightarrow r_3$ |

■ **FIGURE 11.1** The ILOC Subset.

Extending this scheme to a more realistic set of cases, including variables that have different-sized representations, call-by-value and call-by-reference parameters, and variables that reside in registers for their entire lifetimes, would require writing explicit code to check all of the cases at each reference. This would make the code for the *IDENT* case much longer (and much slower). It eliminates much of the appealing simplicity of the hand-coded treewalk scheme.

The code to handle numbers is equally naive. It assumes that a number should be loaded into a register in every case, and that *val* can retrieve the number's value from the symbol table. If the operation that uses the number (its parent in the tree) has an immediate form on the target machine and the constant has a value that fits into the immediate field, the compiler should use the immediate form, since it uses one fewer register. If the number is of a type not supported by an immediate operation, the compiler must arrange to store the value in memory and generate an appropriate memory reference to load the value into a register. This, in turn, may create opportunities for further improvement, such as keeping the constant in a register.

Consider the three multiply operations shown in Figure 11.2. The symbol-table annotations appear below the leaf nodes in the trees. For an identifier, this consists of a name, a label for the base address (or ARP to indicate the current activation record), and an offset from the base address. Below each tree are two code sequences—the code generated by the simple treewalk evaluator and the code we would like the compiler to generate. In the first case, $e \times f$, the inefficiency comes from the fact that the treewalk scheme does not generate loadAI operations. More complicated code in the *IDENT* case can cure this problem.

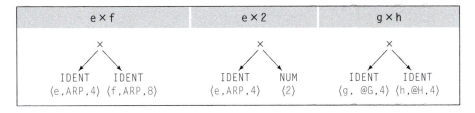

| $e \times f$ | $e \times 2$ | $g \times h$ |
|---|---|---|
| ×  <br> IDENT   IDENT <br> ⟨e,ARP,4⟩ ⟨f,ARP,8⟩ | ×  <br> IDENT   NUM <br> ⟨e,ARP,4⟩   ⟨2⟩ | ×  <br> IDENT   IDENT <br> ⟨g, @G,4⟩ ⟨h,@H,4⟩ |

| Generated Code | | |
|---|---|---|
|  |  | loadI  @G      ⇒ $r_5$ |
| loadI   4        ⇒ $r_5$ | loadI   4        ⇒ $r_5$ | loadI  4       ⇒ $r_6$ |
| loadAO $r_{arp}$,$r_5$ ⇒ $r_6$ | loadAO $r_{arp}$,$r_5$ ⇒ $r_6$ | loadAO $r_5$,$r_6$   ⇒ $r_7$ |
| loadI   8        ⇒ $r_7$ | loadI   2        ⇒ $r_7$ | loadI  @H      ⇒ $r_8$ |
| loadAO $r_{arp}$,$r_7$ ⇒ $r_8$ | mult    $r_6$,$r_7$   ⇒ $r_8$ | loadI  4       ⇒ $r_9$ |
| mult    $r_6$,$r_8$   ⇒ $r_9$ |  | loadAO $r_8$,$r_9$   ⇒ $r_{10}$ |
|  |  | mult   $r_7$,$r_{10}$  ⇒ $r_{11}$ |

| Desired Code | | |
|---|---|---|
|  |  | loadI   4        ⇒ $r_5$ |
| loadAI $r_{arp}$,4 ⇒ $r_5$ | loadAI $r_{arp}$,4 ⇒ $r_5$ | loadAI $r_5$,@G ⇒ $r_6$ |
| loadAI $r_{arp}$,8 ⇒ $r_6$ | multI   $r_5$,2    ⇒ $r_6$ | loadAI $r_5$,@H ⇒ $r_7$ |
| mult    $r_5$,$r_6$   ⇒ $r_7$ |  | mult    $r_6$,$r_7$  ⇒ $r_8$ |

■ **FIGURE 11.2** Variations on Multiply.

The second case, $e \times 2$, is harder. The code generator could implement the multiply with a `multI` operation. To recognize this fact, however, the code generator must look beyond the local context. To work this into the treewalk scheme, the case for $\times$ might recognize that one subtree evaluates to a constant. Alternatively, the code that handles the *NUM* node might determine that its parent can be implemented with an immediate operation. Either way, it requires nonlocal context that violates the simple treewalk paradigm.

The third case, $g \times h$, has another nonlocal problem. Both subtrees of $\times$ refer to a variable at offset 4 from its base address. The references have different base addresses. The original treewalk scheme generates an explicit `loadI` operation for each constant—@G, 4, @H, and 4. A version amended to use `loadAI`, as previously mentioned, would either generate separate `loadI`s for @G and @H or it would generate two `loadI`s for 4. (Of course, the lengths of the values of @G and @H come into play. If they are too long, then the compiler must use 4 as the immediate operand to the `loadAI` operations.)

The fundamental problem with this third example lies in the fact that the final code contains a common subexpression that was hidden in the AST. To discover the redundancy and handle it appropriately, the code generator would require code that explicitly checks the base address and offset values of subtrees and generates appropriate sequences for all the cases. Handling one case in this fashion would be clumsy. Handling all the similar cases that can arise would require a prohibitive amount of additional coding.

A better way of catching this kind of redundancy is to expose the redundant details in the IR and let the optimizer eliminate them. For the example assignment, $a \leftarrow b - 2 \times c$, the front end might produce the low-level tree shown in Figure 11.3. This tree has several new kinds of nodes. A `Val` node represents a value known to reside in a register, such as the ARP in $r_{arp}$.

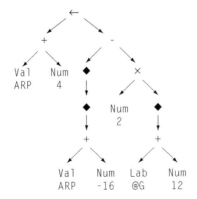

■ **FIGURE 11.3** Low-Level AST for a $\leftarrow b - 2 \times c$.

---

**OPTIMAL CODE GENERATION**

The treewalk scheme for selecting instructions produces the same code sequence each time it encounters a particular kind of AST node. More realistic schemes consider multiple patterns and use cost models to choose among them. This leads, naturally, to the question: Can a compiler make optimal choices?

If each operation has an associated cost, and we ignore the effects of instruction scheduling and register allocation, then optimal instruction selection is possible. The tree-pattern-matching code generators described in Section 11.4 produce locally optimal sequences—that is, each subtree is computed by a minimal-cost sequence.

The difficulty of capturing runtime behavior in a single cost number calls into question the importance of such a claim. The impact of execution order, bounded hardware resources, and context-sensitive behavior in the memory hierarchy all complicate the problem of determining the actual cost of any specific code sequence.

In practice, most modern compilers largely ignore scheduling and allocation during instruction selection and assume that the costs associated with various rewrite rules are accurate. Given these assumptions, the compiler looks for locally optimal sequences—those that minimize the estimated cost for an entire subtree. The compiler then performs scheduling and allocation in one or more postpasses over the code produced by instruction selection.

---

A Lab node represents a relocatable symbol, typically an assembly-level label used for either code or data. A ◆ node signifies a level of indirection; its child is an address and it produces the value stored at that address. These new node types require the compiler writer to specify more matching rules. In return, however, additional detail can be optimized, such as the duplicate references to 4 in g × h.

This version of the tree exposes details at a lower level of abstraction than the target ILOC instruction set. Inspecting this tree reveals, for instance, that a is a local variable stored at offset 4 from the ARP, that b is a call-by-reference parameter (note the two ◆ nodes), and that c is stored at offset 12 from label @G. Furthermore, the additions that are implicit in loadAI and storeAI operations appear explicitly in the tree—as a subtree of a ◆ node or as the left child of an ← node.

Exposing more detail in the AST should lead to better code. Increasing the number of target-machine operations that the code generator considers should also lead to better code. Together, however, these factors create a situation in which the code generator can discover many different ways to implement a given subtree. The simple treewalk scheme had one option for each AST node type. To make effective use of the target machine's instruction set, the code generator should consider as many possibilities as is practical.

This increased complexity does not arise from a particular methodology or a specific matching algorithm; rather, it reflects a fundamental aspect of the underlying problem—any given machine might provide multiple ways to implement an IR construct. When the code generator considers multiple possible matches for a given subtree, it needs a way to choose among them. If the compiler writer can associate a cost with each pattern, then the matching scheme can select patterns in a way that minimizes the costs. If the costs truly reflect performance, this sort of cost-driven instruction selection should lead to good code.

The compiler writer needs tools that help to manage the complexity of code generation for real machines. Rather than writing code that explicitly navigates the IR and tests the applicability of each operation, the compiler writer should specify rules, and the tools should produce the code required to match those rules with the IR form of the code. The next two sections explore two different approaches to managing the complexity that arises for the instruction set of a modern machine. The next section explores the use of tree-pattern matching techniques. These systems fold the complexity into the process of constructing the matcher, in the same way that scanners fold their choices into the transition tables of DFAS. The following section examines the use of peephole optimization for instruction selection. The peephole-based systems move the complexity of choice into a uniform scheme for low-level simplification followed by pattern matching to find the appropriate instructions. To keep the cost of matching low, these systems limit their scope to short segments of code—two or three operations at a time.

---

**SECTION REVIEW**

If the compiler is to take full advantage of the complexities of the target machine, it must expose those complexities in the IR and consider them during instruction selection. Many compilers expand their IR into a detailed low-level form before selecting instructions. Such detailed IRs can be structural, as with our low-level AST, or they can be linear, as we will see in Section 11.5. In either case, the instruction selector must match the details of the IR form of the code to sequences of instructions on the target machine. This section showed that we can expand an ad hoc, treewalk evaluator to perform the task; it also exposed some of the issues that the instruction selector must handle. The next two sections show more general approaches to the problem.

## 11.4 INSTRUCTION SELECTION VIA TREE-PATTERN MATCHING

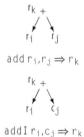

$r_k +$

$r_i$ $r_j$

add $r_i,r_j \Rightarrow r_k$

$r_k +$

$r_i$ $c_j$

addI $r_i,c_j \Rightarrow r_k$

The compiler writer can use tree-pattern-matching tools to attack the complexity of instruction selection. To transform code generation into tree-pattern matching, both the IR form of the program and the target machine's instruction set must be expressed as trees. As we have seen, the compiler can use a low-level AST as a detailed model of the code being compiled. It can use similar trees to represent the operations available on the target processor. For example, ILOC's addition operations might be modelled by operation trees like those shown in the left margin. By systematically matching operation trees with subtrees of an AST, the compiler can discover all the potential implementations for the subtree.

To work with tree patterns, we need a more convenient notation for describing them. Using a prefix notation, we can write the operation tree for add as $+(r_i,r_j)$ and addI as $+(r_i,c_j)$. Of course, $+(c_i,r_j)$ is the commutative variant of $+(r_i,c_j)$. The leaves of the operation tree encode information about the storage types of the operands. For example, in $+(r_i,c_j)$, the symbol r denotes an operand in a register and the symbol c denotes a known constant operand. Subscripts are added to ensure uniqueness, just as we did in the rules for an attribute grammar. If we rewrite the AST from Figure 11.3 in prefix form, it becomes:

$$\leftarrow(+(Val_1,Num_1),$$
$$-(\blacklozenge(\blacklozenge(+(Val_2,Num_2))),$$
$$\times(Num_3,\blacklozenge(+(Lab_1,Num_4)))))$$

While the drawing of the tree may be more intuitive, this linear prefix form contains the same information.

Given an AST and a collection of operation trees, the goal is to map the AST to operations by constructing a *tiling* of the AST with operation trees. A tiling is a collection of ⟨*ast-node,op-tree*⟩ pairs, where *ast-node* is a node in the AST and *op-tree* is an operation tree. The presence of an ⟨*ast-node,op-tree*⟩ pair in the tiling means that the target-machine operation represented by *op-tree* could implement *ast-node*. Of course, the choice of an implementation for *ast-node* depends on the implementations of its subtrees. The tiling will specify, for each of *ast-node*'s subtrees, an implementation that "connects" with *op-tree*.

A tiling *implements* the AST if it implements every operation and each tile connects with its neighbors. We say that a tile, ⟨*ast-node,op-tree*⟩, connects with its neighbors if *ast-node* is covered by a leaf in another *op-tree* in the tiling, unless *ast-node* is the root of the AST. Where two such trees overlap (at *ast-node*), they must agree on the storage class of their common node. For example, if both assume that the common value resides in a register, then the code sequences for the two *op-trees* are compatible. If one assumes that the value resides in memory and the other that it resides in a register, the code sequences are incompatible, since they will not correctly transmit the value from the lower tree to the upper tree.

Given a tiling that implements an AST, the compiler can easily generate assembly code in a bottom-up walk. Thus, the key to making this approach practical lies in algorithms that quickly find good tilings for an AST. Several efficient techniques have emerged for matching tree patterns against low-level ASTs. All these systems associate costs with the operation trees and produce minimal cost tilings. They differ in the technology used for matching—tree matching, text matching, and bottom-up rewrite systems—and in the generality of their cost models—static fixed costs versus costs that can vary during the matching process.

## 11.4.1 **Rewrite Rules**

The compiler writer encodes the relationships between operation trees and subtrees in the AST as a set of *rewrite rules*. The rule set includes one or more rules for every kind of node in the AST. A rewrite rule consists of a production in a tree grammar, a code template, and an associated cost. Figure 11.4 shows a set of rewrite rules for tiling our low-level AST with ILOC operations.

Consider rule 16, which corresponds to the tree drawn in the margin. (Its result, at the + node, is implicitly a Reg.) The rule describes a

| | Production | | Cost | Code Template | | |
|---|---|---|---|---|---|---|
| 1 | Goal | $\rightarrow$ Assign | 0 | | | |
| 2 | Assign | $\rightarrow$ $\leftarrow$ (Reg$_1$,Reg$_2$) | 1 | store | $r_2$ | $\Rightarrow r_1$ |
| 3 | Assign | $\rightarrow$ $\leftarrow$ (+ (Reg$_1$,Reg$_2$),Reg$_3$) | 1 | storeAO | $r_3$ | $\Rightarrow r_1,r_2$ |
| 4 | Assign | $\rightarrow$ $\leftarrow$ (+ (Reg$_1$,Num$_2$),Reg$_3$) | 1 | storeAI | $r_3$ | $\Rightarrow r_1,n_2$ |
| 5 | Assign | $\rightarrow$ $\leftarrow$ (+ (Num$_1$,Reg$_2$),Reg$_3$) | 1 | storeAI | $r_3$ | $\Rightarrow r_2,n_1$ |
| 6 | Reg | $\rightarrow$ Lab$_1$ | 1 | loadI | $l_1$ | $\Rightarrow r_{new}$ |
| 7 | Reg | $\rightarrow$ Val$_1$ | 0 | | | |
| 8 | Reg | $\rightarrow$ Num$_1$ | 1 | loadI | $n_1$ | $\Rightarrow r_{new}$ |
| 9 | Reg | $\rightarrow$ ◆ (Reg$_1$) | 1 | load | $r_1$ | $\Rightarrow r_{new}$ |
| 10 | Reg | $\rightarrow$ ◆ (+ (Reg$_1$,Reg$_2$)) | 1 | loadAO | $r_1,r_2$ | $\Rightarrow r_{new}$ |
| 11 | Reg | $\rightarrow$ ◆ (+ (Reg$_1$,Num$_2$)) | 1 | loadAI | $r_1,n_2$ | $\Rightarrow r_{new}$ |
| 12 | Reg | $\rightarrow$ ◆ (+ (Num$_1$,Reg$_2$)) | 1 | loadAI | $r_2,n_1$ | $\Rightarrow r_{new}$ |
| 13 | Reg | $\rightarrow$ ◆ (+ (Reg$_1$,Lab$_2$)) | 1 | loadAI | $r_1,l_2$ | $\Rightarrow r_{new}$ |
| 14 | Reg | $\rightarrow$ ◆ (+ (Lab$_1$,Reg$_2$)) | 1 | loadAI | $r_2,l_1$ | $\Rightarrow r_{new}$ |
| 15 | Reg | $\rightarrow$ + (Reg$_1$,Reg$_2$) | 1 | add | $r_1,r_2$ | $\Rightarrow r_{new}$ |
| 16 | Reg | $\rightarrow$ + (Reg$_1$,Num$_2$) | 1 | addI | $r_1,n_2$ | $\Rightarrow r_{new}$ |
| 17 | Reg | $\rightarrow$ + (Num$_1$,Reg$_2$) | 1 | addI | $r_2,n_1$ | $\Rightarrow r_{new}$ |
| 18 | Reg | $\rightarrow$ + (Reg$_1$,Lab$_2$) | 1 | addI | $r_1,l_2$ | $\Rightarrow r_{new}$ |
| 19 | Reg | $\rightarrow$ + (Lab$_1$,Reg$_2$) | 1 | addI | $r_2,l_1$ | $\Rightarrow r_{new}$ |
| 20 | Reg | $\rightarrow$ - (Reg$_1$,Reg$_2$) | 1 | sub | $r_1,r_2$ | $\Rightarrow r_{new}$ |
| 21 | Reg | $\rightarrow$ - (Reg$_1$,Num$_2$) | 1 | subI | $r_1,n_2$ | $\Rightarrow r_{new}$ |
| 22 | Reg | $\rightarrow$ - (Num$_1$,Reg$_2$) | 1 | rsubI | $r_2,n_1$ | $\Rightarrow r_{new}$ |
| 23 | Reg | $\rightarrow$ × (Reg$_1$,Reg$_2$) | 1 | mult | $r_1,r_2$ | $\Rightarrow r_{new}$ |
| 24 | Reg | $\rightarrow$ × (Reg$_1$,Num$_2$) | 1 | multI | $r_1,n_2$ | $\Rightarrow r_{new}$ |
| 25 | Reg | $\rightarrow$ × (Num$_1$,Reg$_2$) | 1 | multI | $r_2,n_1$ | $\Rightarrow r_{new}$ |

■ **FIGURE 11.4** Rewrite Rules for Tiling the Low-Level Tree with ILOC.

tree that computes the sum of a value located in a Reg and an immediate value in a Num. The left side of the table gives the tree pattern for the rule, Reg $\rightarrow$ + (Reg$_1$,Num$_2$). The center column lists its cost, one. The right column shows an ILOC operation that implements the rule, addI $r_1,n_2 \Rightarrow r_{new}$. The operands in the tree pattern, Reg$_1$ and Num$_2$, correspond to the operands $r_1$ and $n_2$ in the code template. The compiler must rewrite the field $r_{new}$ in the code template with the name of a register allocated to hold the result of the addition. This register name will, in turn, become a leaf in the subtree that connects to this subtree. Notice that rule 16 has a commutative variant, rule 17. An explicit rule is needed to match subtrees such as the one drawn in the margin.

The rules in Figure 11.4 form a tree grammar similar to the grammars that we used to specify the syntax of programming languages. Each rewrite rule, or production, has a nonterminal symbol as its left-hand side. In rule 16, the nonterminal is Reg. Reg represents a collection of subtrees that the tree grammar can generate, in this case using rules 6 through 25. The right-hand side of a rule is a linearized tree pattern. In rule 16, that pattern is $+ (Reg_1, Num_2)$, representing the addition of two values, a Reg and a Num.

The rules in Figure 11.4 use Reg as both a terminal and a nonterminal symbol in the rules set. This fact reflects an abbreviation in the example. A complete set of rules would include a set of productions that rewrite Reg with a specific register name, such as $Reg \rightarrow r_0$, $Reg \rightarrow r_1, \ldots$, and $Reg \rightarrow r_k$.

The nonterminals in the grammar allow for abstraction. They serve to connect the rules in the grammar. They also encode knowledge about where the corresponding value is stored at runtime and what form it takes. For example, Reg represents a value produced by a subtree and stored in a register, while Val represents a value already stored in register. A Val might be a global value, such as the ARP. It might be the result of a computation performed in a disjoint subtree—a common subexpression.

The cost associated with a production should provide the code generator with a realistic estimate of the runtime cost of executing the code in the template. For rule 16, the cost is one to reflect the fact that the tree can be implemented with a single operation that requires just one cycle to execute. The code generator uses the costs to choose among the possible alternatives. Some matching techniques restrict the costs to numbers. Others allow costs that vary during matching to reflect the impact of previous choices on the cost of the current alternatives.

Tree patterns can capture context in a way that the simple treewalk code generator cannot. Rules 10 through 14 each match two operators (◆ and +). These rules express the conditions in which the ILOC operators loadAO and loadAI can be used. Any subtree that matches one of these five rules can be tiled with a combination of other rules. A subtree that matches rule 10 can also be tiled with the combination of rule 15 to produce an address and rule 9 to load the value. This flexibility makes the set of rewrite rules ambiguous. The ambiguity reflects the fact that the target machine has several ways to implement this particular subtree. Because the treewalk code generator matches one operator at a time, it cannot directly generate either of these ILOC operations.

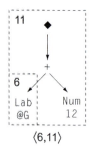

■ **FIGURE 11.5** A Simple Tree Rewrite Sequence.

To apply these rules to a tree, we look for a sequence of rewriting steps that reduces the tree to a single symbol. For an AST that represents a complete program, that symbol should be the goal symbol. For an interior node, that symbol typically represents the value produced by evaluating the subtree rooted at the expression. The symbol also must specify where the value exists—typically in a register, in a memory location, or as a known constant value.

Figure 11.5 shows a rewrite sequence for the subtree that references the variable c in Figure 11.3. (Recall that c was at offset 12 from the label @G.) The leftmost panel shows the original subtree. The remaining panels show one reduction sequence for that subtree. The first match in the sequence recognizes that the left leaf (a Lab node) matches rule 6. This allows us to rewrite it as a Reg. The rewritten tree now matches the right-hand side of rule 11, ◆ (+ (Reg$_1$,Num$_2$)), so we can rewrite the entire subtree rooted at ◆ as a Reg. This sequence, denoted ⟨6,11⟩, reduces the entire subtree to a Reg.

To summarize such a sequence, we will use a drawing like the one shown in the margin. The dashed boxes show the specific right-hand sides that matched the tree, with the rule number recorded in the upper left corner of each box. The list of rule numbers below the drawing indicates the sequence in which the rules were applied. The rewrite sequence replaces the boxed subtree with the final rule's left-hand side.

Notice how the nonterminals ensure that the operation trees connect appropriately at the points where they overlap. Rule 6 rewrites a Lab as a Reg. The left leaf in rule 11 is a Reg. Viewing the patterns as rules in a grammar folds all of the considerations that arise at the boundaries between operation trees into the labelling of nonterminals.

For this trivial subtree, the rules generate many rewrite sequences, reflecting the ambiguity of the grammar. Figure 11.6 shows eight of these sequences. All the rules in our scheme have a cost of one, except for rules 1 and 7. Since none of the rewrite sequences use these rules, their costs are equal to

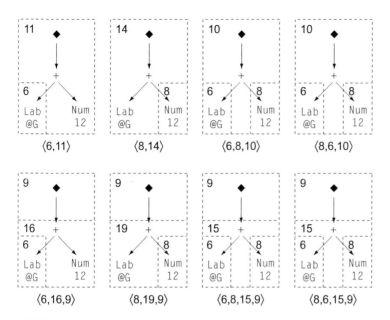

■ **FIGURE 11.6** Potential Matches.

their sequence length. The sequences fall into three categories by cost. The first pair of sequences, $\langle 6,11 \rangle$ and $\langle 8,14 \rangle$, each have cost two. The next four sequences, $\langle 6,8,10 \rangle$, $\langle 8,6,10 \rangle$, $\langle 6,16,9 \rangle$, and $\langle 8,19,9 \rangle$, each have cost three. The final sequences, $\langle 6,8,15,9 \rangle$ and $\langle 8,6,15,9 \rangle$, each have cost four.

To produce assembly code, the selector uses the code templates associated with each rule. A rule's code template consists of a sequence of assembly-code operations that implements the subtree generated by the production. For example, rule 15 maps the tree pattern + $(\text{Reg}_1,\text{Reg}_2)$ to the code template add $r_1, r_2 \Rightarrow r_{new}$. The selector replaces each of $r_1$ and $r_2$ with the register name holding the result of the corresponding subtree. It allocates a new virtual register name for $r_{new}$. A tiling for an AST specifies which rules the code generator should use. The code generator uses the associated templates to generate assembly code in a bottom-up walk. It supplies names, as needed, to tie the storage locations together and emits the instantiated operations corresponding to the walk.

The instruction selector should choose a tiling that produces the lowest-cost assembly-code sequence. Figure 11.7 shows the code that corresponds to each potential tiling. Arbitrary register names have been substituted where appropriate. Both $\langle 6,11 \rangle$ and $\langle 8,14 \rangle$ produce the lowest cost—two. They lead to different, but equivalent code sequences. Because they have identical

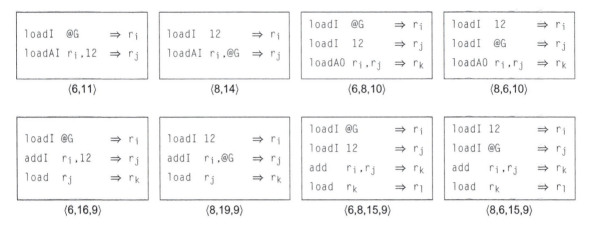

**FIGURE 11.7** Code Sequences for the Matches.

costs, the selector is free to choose between them. The other sequences are, as expected, more costly.

If loadAI only accepts arguments in a limited range, the sequence ⟨8,14⟩ might not work, since the address that eventually replaces @G may be too large for the immediate field in the operation. To handle this kind of restriction, the compiler writer can introduce into the rewriting grammar the notion of a constant with an appropriately limited range of values. It might take the form of a new terminal symbol that can only represent integers in a given range, such as $0 \leq i < 4096$ for a 12-bit field. With such a distinction, and code that checks each instance of an integer to classify it, the code generator could avoid the sequence ⟨8,14⟩, unless @G falls in the allowable range for an immediate operand of loadAI.

The cost model drives the code generator to select one of the better sequences. For example, notice that the sequence ⟨6,8,10⟩ uses two loadI operations, followed by a loadA0. The code generator prefers the lower-cost sequences, each of which avoids one of the loadI operations and issues fewer operations. Similarly, the cost model avoids the four sequences that use an explicit addition—preferring, instead, to perform the addition implicitly in the addressing hardware.

## 11.4.2 Finding a Tiling

To apply these ideas to code generation, we need an algorithm that can construct a good tiling, that is, a tiling that produces efficient code. Given a set of rules that encode the operator trees and relate them to the structure of an AST, the code generator should discover an efficient tiling for a specific AST.

Several techniques for constructing such a tiling exist. They are similar in concept, but differ in detail.

To simplify the algorithm, we make two assumptions about the form of the rewrite rules. First, each operation has, at most, two operands. Extending the algorithm to handle the general case is straightforward, but the details complicate the explanation. Second, a rule's right-hand side contains at most one operation. This restriction simplifies the matching algorithm, at no loss in generality. A simple, mechanical procedure can transform the unrestricted case to this simpler case. For a production $\alpha \rightarrow \text{op}_1(\beta, \text{op}_2(\gamma, \delta))$, rewrite it as $\alpha \rightarrow \text{op}_1(\beta, \alpha')$ and $\alpha' \rightarrow \text{op}_2(\gamma, \delta)$, where $\alpha'$ is a new symbol that only occurs in these two rules. The resulting growth is linear in the size of the original grammar.

To make this concrete, consider rule 11, $\text{Reg} \rightarrow \blacklozenge \;(+(\text{Reg}_1, \text{Num}_2))$. The transformation rewrites it as $\text{Reg} \rightarrow \blacklozenge \;(\text{R11P2})$ and $\text{R11P2} \rightarrow +(\text{Reg}_1, \text{Num}_2)$, where R11P2 is a new symbol. Notice that the new rule for R11P2 duplicates rule 16 for addI. The transformation adds another ambiguity to the grammar. However, tracking and matching the two rules independently lets the pattern matcher consider the cost of each. The pair of rules that replaces rule 11 should have a cost of one, the cost of the original rule. (Each rule might have fractional cost, or one of them might have zero cost.) This reflects the fact that rewriting with rule 16 produces an addI operation, while the rule for R11P2 folds the addition into the address generation of a loadAI operation. The two rule combination, with its lower cost, will guide the pattern matcher to the loadAI code sequence when possible—specializing the code to capitalize on the inexpensive addition provided in the AI address mode.

The goal of tiling is to label each node in the AST with a set of patterns that the compiler can use to implement it. Since rule numbers correspond directly to right-hand-side patterns, the code generator can use them as a shorthand for the patterns. The compiler can compute sequences of rule numbers, or patterns, for each node in a postorder traversal of the tree. Figure 11.8 sketches an algorithm, *Tile*, that finds tilings for a tree rooted at node *n* in the AST. It annotates each AST node *n* with a set *Label(n)* that contains all the rule numbers that can be used to tile the tree rooted at node *n*. It computes the *Label* sets in a postorder traversal to ensure that it labels a node's children before it labels the node.

Consider the inner loop for the case of a binary node. To compute *Label(n)*, it examines each rule *r* that implements the operation specified by *n*. It uses the functions *left* and *right* to traverse both the AST and the tree patterns (or right-hand sides of the rules). Because *Tile* has already labelled

Each rule specifies an operator and at most two children. Thus, for a rule *r*, *left(r)* and *right(r)* have clear meanings.

```
Tile(n)
  Label(n) ← Ø
  if n is a binary node then
    Tile(left(n))
    Tile(right(n))
    for each rule r that matches n's operation
      if left(r) ∈ Label(left(n)) and right(r) ∈ Label(right(n))
        then Label(n) ← Label(n) ∪ {r}
  else if n is a unary node then
    Tile(left(n))
    for each rule r that matches n's operation
      if left(r) ∈ Label(left(n))
        then Label(n) ← Label(n) ∪ {r}
  else /* n is a leaf */
    Label(n) ← {all rules that match the operation in n}
```

■ **FIGURE 11.8** Compute *Label* Sets to Tile an AST.

$n$'s children, it can use a simple membership test to compare $r$'s children against $n$'s children. If $left(r) \in Label(left(n))$, then $Tile$ has already discovered that it can generate code for $n$'s left subtree in a way that is compatible with using $r$ to implement $n$. A similar argument holds for the right subtrees of both $r$ and $n$. If both subtrees match, then $r$ belongs in $Label(n)$.

A tree-pattern matching code generator built from this algorithm will spend most of its time in the two for loops—computing matches for binary operators or for unary operators. To speed up the code generator, the compiler writer can precompute all the possible matches and store the results in a three-dimensional table, indexed by an operation ($n$ in the algorithm) and the label sets of its left and right children. If we replace each of the for loops with a simple table lookup, the algorithm becomes a linear cost walk over the tree.

The tables in this scheme can grow to be large. For example, the lookup table for binary operators has size $|operation\ trees| \times |label\ sets|^2$. The table for unary operators has only two dimensions, with size $|operation\ trees| \times |label\ sets|$. The label sets are bounded in size. If R is the number of rules, then $|Label(n)| \leq R$, and there can be no more than $2^R$ distinct label sets.

For a machine with 200 operations and a grammar with 1024 distinct label sets (R = 10), the resulting table has over 200,000,000 entries. Because the structure of the grammar rules out many possibilities, the tables constructed for this purpose are sparse and can be encoded efficiently. In fact, finding ways to build and encode these tables efficiently was one of the key advances that made tree-pattern matching a practical tool for code generation.

### *Finding the Low-Cost Matches*

The algorithm in Figure 11.8 finds all of the matches possible within the pattern set. In practice, we want the code generator to find the lowest-cost match. While it could derive the lowest-cost match from the set of all matches, there are more efficient ways to compute the match.

Conceptually, the code generator can discover the lowest-cost match for each subtree in a bottom-up pass over the AST. A bottom-up traversal can compute the cost of each alternative match—the cost of the matched rule plus the costs of the associated subtree matches. In principle, it can discover matches as in Figure 11.8 and retain the lowest-cost ones, rather than all the matches. In practice, the process is slightly more complex.

The cost function depends, inherently, on the target processor; it cannot be derived automatically from the grammar. Instead, it must encode properties of the target machine and reflect the interactions that occur between operations in an assembly program—particularly the flow of values from one operation to another.

A value in the compiled program may have different forms and reside in different locations. For example, a value might reside in a memory location or a register; alternatively, it might be a constant that is small enough to fit into some or all of the immediate operations. (An immediate operand resides in the instruction stream.) Choices among forms and locations matter to the instruction selector because they change the set of target-machine operations that can use the value.

When the instruction selector constructs the set of matches for a particular subtree, it must know the cost of evaluating each of that subtree's operands. If those operands may be in different storage classes—such as registers, memory locations, or immediate constants—the code generator needs to know the cost of evaluating the operand into each of those storage classes. Thus, it must track the lowest-cost sequences that generate each of these storage classes. As it makes the bottom-up traversal to compute costs, the code generator can easily determine the lowest-cost match for each storage class. This adds a small amount of space and time to the process, but the increase is bounded by a factor equal to the number of storage classes—a number that depends entirely on the target machine, and not on the number of rewrite rules.

A careful implementation can accumulate these costs while tiling the tree. If, at each match, the code generator retains the lowest-cost matches, it will

**Local optimality**
A scheme in which the compiler has no better alternative, at each point in the code, is considered *locally optimal*.

produce a locally optimal tiling. That is, at each node, no better alternative exists, given the rule set and the cost functions. This bottom-up accumulation of costs implements a dynamic-programming solution to finding the minimal-cost tiling.

If we require that the costs be fixed, the cost computation can be folded into the construction of the pattern matcher. This strategy moves computation from compile time into the construction algorithm and almost always produces a faster code generator. If we allow the costs to vary and account for the context in which a match is made, then the cost computation and comparison must be done at compile time. While this scheme may slow down the code generator, it allows more flexibility and precision in the cost functions.

### 11.4.3 **Tools**

As we have seen, a tree-oriented, bottom-up approach to code generation can produce efficient instruction selectors. There are several ways that the compiler writer can implement code generators based on these principles.

1. The compiler writer can hand code a matcher, similar to *Tile*, that explicitly checks for matching rules as it tiles the tree. A careful implementation can limit the set of rules that must be examined for each node. This avoids the large sparse table and leads to a compact code generator.
2. Since the problem is finite, the compiler writer can encode it as a finite automaton—a tree-matching automaton—and obtain the low-cost behavior of a DFA. In this scheme, the lookup table encodes the transition function of the automaton, implicitly incorporating all the required state information. Several different systems have been built that use this approach, often called bottom-up rewrite systems (BURS).
3. The grammar-like form of the rules suggests using parsing techniques. The parsing algorithms must be extended to handle the highly ambiguous grammars that result from machine descriptions and to choose least-cost parses.
4. By linearizing the tree into a prefix string, the problem can be translated to a string-matching problem. Then, the compiler can use algorithms from string-pattern matching to find the potential matches.

Tools are available that implement each of the last three approaches. The compiler writer produces a description of a target machine's instruction set, and a code generator creates executable code from the description.

The automated tools differ in details. The cost per emitted instruction varies with the technique. Some are faster, some are slower; none is slow enough that it has a major impact on the speed of the resulting compiler. The approaches allow different cost models. Some systems restrict the compiler writer to a fixed cost for each rule; in return, they can perform some or all of the dynamic programming during table generation. Others allow more general cost models that may vary the cost during the matching process; these systems must perform the dynamic programming during code generation. In general, however, all these approaches produce code generators that are both efficient and effective.

---

**SECTION REVIEW**

Instruction selection via tree-pattern matching relies on the simple fact that trees are a natural representation for both the operations in a program and the operations in the target machine's ISA. The compiler writer develops a library of tree patterns that map constructs in the compiler's IR into operations on the target ISA. Each pattern consists of a small IR tree, a code template, and a cost. The selector finds a low-cost tiling for the tree; in a postorder walk of the tiled tree, it generates code from the templates of the selected tiles.

Several technologies have been used to implement tiling passes. These include hand-coded matchers such as the one shown in Figure 11.8, parser-based matchers operating on ambiguous grammars, linear matchers based on algorithms for fast string matching of the linearized forms, and automata-based matchers. All of these technologies have worked well in one or more systems. The resulting instruction selectors run quickly and produce high-quality code.

---

**Review Questions**

1. Tree-pattern matching seems natural for use in a compiler with a tree-like IR. How might sharing in the tree—that is, using a directed acyclic graph (DAG) rather than a tree—affect the algorithm? How might you apply it to a linear IR?

2. Some systems based on tree-pattern matching require that the costs associated with a pattern be fixed, while others allow dynamic costs— costs computed at the time the match is considered. How might the compiler use dynamic costs?

---

## 11.5 INSTRUCTION SELECTION VIA PEEPHOLE OPTIMIZATION

Another technique for performing the matching operations that lie at the heart of instruction selection builds on a technology developed for late-stage optimization, called *peephole optimization*. To avoid encoding complexity in the code generator, this approach combines systematic local optimization on a low-level IR with a simple scheme for matching the IR to target-machine operations. This section introduces peephole optimization, explores its use as a mechanism for instruction selection, and describes the techniques that have been developed to automate construction of peephole optimizers.

### 11.5.1 **Peephole Optimization**

The basic premise of peephole optimization is simple: the compiler can efficiently find local improvements by examining short sequences of adjacent operations. As originally proposed, the peephole optimizer ran after all other steps in compilation. It both consumed and produced assembly code. The optimizer had a sliding window, or "peephole," that it moved over the code. At each step, it examined the operations in the window, looking for specific patterns that it could improve. When it recognized a pattern, it would rewrite it with a better instruction sequence. The combination of a limited pattern set and a limited area of focus led to fast processing.

A classic example pattern is a store followed by a load from the same location. The load can be replaced by a copy.

$$
\begin{array}{l}
\text{storeAI } r_1 \quad \Rightarrow r_{arp},8 \\
\text{loadAI } \ r_{arp},8 \Rightarrow r_{15}
\end{array}
\quad \Rightarrow \quad
\begin{array}{l}
\text{storeAI } r_1 \Rightarrow r_{arp},8 \\
\text{i2i} \qquad r_1 \Rightarrow r_{15}
\end{array}
$$

If the peephole optimizer recognized that this rewrite made the store operation dead (that is, the load was the sole use for the value stored in memory), it could also eliminate the store operation. In general, however, recognizing dead stores requires global analysis that is beyond the scope of a peephole optimizer. Other patterns amenable to improvement by peephole optimization include simple algebraic identities, such as

$$
\begin{array}{l}
\text{addI } r_2,0 \ \Rightarrow r_7 \\
\text{mult } r_4,r_7 \Rightarrow r_{10}
\end{array}
\quad \Rightarrow \quad
\text{mult } r_4,r_2 \Rightarrow r_{10}
$$

and cases where the target of a branch is, itself, a branch

$$
\begin{array}{l}
\text{jumpI } \rightarrow l_{10} \\
l_{10}\text{: jumpI } \rightarrow l_{11}
\end{array}
\quad \Rightarrow \quad
\begin{array}{l}
\text{jumpI } \rightarrow l_{11} \\
l_{10}\text{: jumpI } \rightarrow l_{11}
\end{array}
$$

If this eliminates the last branch to $l_{10}$, the basic block beginning at $l_{10}$ becomes unreachable and can be eliminated. Unfortunately, proving that the operation at $l_{10}$ is unreachable takes more analysis than is typically available during peephole optimization (see Section 10.2.2).

**TREE-PATTERN MATCHING ON QUADS?**

The terms used to describe these techniques—*tree-pattern matching and peephole optimization*—contain implicit assumptions about the kinds of IR to which they can be applied. BURS theory deals with rewriting operations on trees. This creates the impression that BURS-based code generators require tree-shaped IRs. Similarly, peephole optimizers were first proposed as a final assembly-to-assembly improvement pass. The idea of a moving instruction window strongly suggests a linear, low-level IR for a peephole-based code generator.

Both techniques can be adapted to fit most IRs. A compiler can interpret a low-level linear IR like ILOC as trees. Each operation becomes a tree node; the edges are implied by the reuse of operands. Similarly, if the compiler assigns a name to each node, it can interpret trees as a linear form by performing a postorder treewalk. A clever implementor can adapt the methods presented in this chapter to a wide variety of actual IRs.

Early peephole optimizers used a limited set of hand-coded patterns. They used exhaustive search to match the patterns but ran quickly because of the small number of patterns and the small window size—typically two or three operations.

Peephole optimization has progressed beyond matching a small number of patterns. Increasingly complex ISAs led to more systematic approaches. A modern peephole optimizer breaks the process into three distinct tasks: expansion, simplification, and matching. It replaces the pattern-driven optimization of early systems with a systematic application of symbolic interpretation and simplification.

Structurally, this looks like a compiler. The expander recognizes the input code in IR form and builds an internal representation. The simplifier performs some rewriting operations on that IR. The matcher transforms the IR into target-machine code, typically assembly code (ASM). If the input and output languages are the same, this system is a peephole optimizer. With different languages as input and output, the same algorithms can perform instruction selection, as we shall see in Section 11.5.2.

The expander rewrites the IR, operation by operation, into a sequence of lower-level IR (LLIR) operations that represents all the direct effects of an operation—at least, all of those that affect program behavior. If the operation add $r_i, r_j \Rightarrow r_k$ sets the condition code, then its LLIR representation must include operations that assign $r_i + r_j$ to $r_k$ and that set the condition code to the appropriate value. Typically, the expander has a simple structure. Operations can be expanded individually, without regard to context. The process uses a template for each IR operation and substitutes appropriate register names, constants, and labels in the templates.

The simplifier makes a pass over the LLIR, examining the operations in a small window on the LLIR and systematically trying to improve them. The basic mechanisms of simplification are forward substitution, algebraic simplification (for example, $x + 0 \Rightarrow x$), evaluating constant-valued expressions (for example, $2 + 17 \Rightarrow 19$), and eliminating useless effects, such as the creation of unused condition codes. Thus, the simplifier performs limited local optimization on the LLIR in the window. This subjects all the details exposed in the LLIR (address arithmetic, branch targets, and so on) to a uniform level of local optimization.

In the final step, the matcher compares the simplified LLIR against the pattern library, looking for the pattern that best captures all the effects in the LLIR. The final code sequence may produce effects beyond those required by the LLIR sequence; for example, it might create a new, albeit useless, condition-code value. It must, however, preserve the effects needed for correctness. It cannot eliminate a live value, regardless of whether the value is stored in memory, in a register, or in an implicitly set location such as the condition code.

Figure 11.9 shows how this approach might work on the example from Section 11.3. It begins, in the upper left, with the quadruples for the low-level AST shown in Figure 11.3. (Recall that the AST computes a ← b - 2 × c, with a stored at offset 4 in the local AR, b stored as a call-by-reference parameter whose pointer is stored at offset –16 from the ARP, and c at offset 12 from the label @G.) The expander creates the LLIR shown on the upper right. The simplifier reduces this code to produce the LLIR code in the bottom right. From this LLIR fragment, the matcher constructs the ILOC code in the lower left.

The key to understanding this process lies in the simplifier. Figure 11.10 shows the successive sequences that the peephole optimizer has in its window as it processes the low-level IR for the example. Assume that it has a three-operation window. Sequence 1 shows the window with the first three operations. No simplification is possible. The optimizer rolls the first

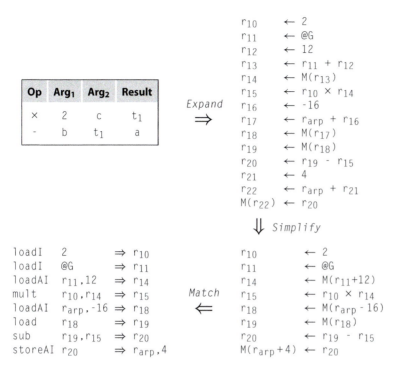

| Op | Arg₁ | Arg₂ | Result |
|----|------|------|--------|
| × | 2 | c | t₁ |
| - | b | t₁ | a |

*Expand* $\Rightarrow$

$r_{10} \leftarrow 2$
$r_{11} \leftarrow @G$
$r_{12} \leftarrow 12$
$r_{13} \leftarrow r_{11} + r_{12}$
$r_{14} \leftarrow M(r_{13})$
$r_{15} \leftarrow r_{10} \times r_{14}$
$r_{16} \leftarrow \text{-}16$
$r_{17} \leftarrow r_{arp} + r_{16}$
$r_{18} \leftarrow M(r_{17})$
$r_{19} \leftarrow M(r_{18})$
$r_{20} \leftarrow r_{19} \text{ - } r_{15}$
$r_{21} \leftarrow 4$
$r_{22} \leftarrow r_{arp} + r_{21}$
$M(r_{22}) \leftarrow r_{20}$

$\Downarrow$ *Simplify*

```
loadI   2           ⇒ r₁₀
loadI   @G          ⇒ r₁₁
loadAI  r₁₁,12      ⇒ r₁₄
mult    r₁₀,r₁₄     ⇒ r₁₅
loadAI  rarp,-16    ⇒ r₁₈
load    r₁₈         ⇒ r₁₉
sub     r₁₉,r₁₅     ⇒ r₂₀
storeAI r₂₀         ⇒ rarp,4
```

*Match* $\Leftarrow$

$r_{10} \leftarrow 2$
$r_{11} \leftarrow @G$
$r_{14} \leftarrow M(r_{11}+12)$
$r_{15} \leftarrow r_{10} \times r_{14}$
$r_{18} \leftarrow M(r_{arp} - 16)$
$r_{19} \leftarrow M(r_{18})$
$r_{20} \leftarrow r_{19} \text{ - } r_{15}$
$M(r_{arp}+4) \leftarrow r_{20}$

■ **FIGURE 11.9** *Expand, Simplify,* and *Match* Applied to the Example.

operation, defining $r_{10}$, out of the window and brings in the definition of $r_{13}$. In this window, it can substitute $r_{12}$ forward into the definition of $r_{13}$. Because this makes $r_{12}$ dead, the optimizer discards the definition of $r_{12}$ and pulls another operation into the bottom of the window to reach sequence 3. Next, it folds $r_{13}$ into the memory reference that defines $r_{14}$, producing sequence 4.

No simplification is possible on sequence 4, so the optimizer rolls the definition of $r_{11}$ out of the window. It cannot simplify sequence 5, either, so it rolls the definition of $r_{14}$ out of the window, too. It can simplify sequence 6 by forward substituting -16 into the addition that defines $r_{17}$. That action produces sequence 7. The optimizer continues in this manner, simplifying the code when possible and advancing when it cannot. When it reaches sequence 13, it halts because it cannot further simplify the sequence and it has no additional code to bring into the window.

Returning to Figure 11.9, compare the simplified code with the original code. The simplified code consists of those operations that roll out the top of the window, plus those left in the window when simplification halts. After

$$\boxed{\begin{array}{l} r_{10} \leftarrow 2 \\ r_{11} \leftarrow @G \\ r_{12} \leftarrow 12 \end{array}}$$
Sequence 1

$$\boxed{\begin{array}{l} r_{11} \leftarrow @G \\ r_{12} \leftarrow 12 \\ r_{13} \leftarrow r_{11} + r_{12} \end{array}}$$
Sequence 2

$$\boxed{\begin{array}{l} r_{11} \leftarrow @G \\ r_{13} \leftarrow r_{11} + 12 \\ r_{14} \leftarrow M(r_{13}) \end{array}}$$
Sequence 3

$$\boxed{\begin{array}{l} r_{11} \leftarrow @G \\ r_{14} \leftarrow M(r_{11} + 12) \\ r_{15} \leftarrow r_{10} \times r_{14} \end{array}}$$
Sequence 4

$$\boxed{\begin{array}{l} r_{14} \leftarrow M(r_{11} + 12) \\ r_{15} \leftarrow r_{10} \times r_{14} \\ r_{16} \leftarrow -16 \end{array}}$$
Sequence 5

$$\boxed{\begin{array}{l} r_{15} \leftarrow r_{10} \times r_{14} \\ r_{16} \leftarrow -16 \\ r_{17} \leftarrow r_{arp} + r_{16} \end{array}}$$
Sequence 6

$$\boxed{\begin{array}{l} r_{15} \leftarrow r_{10} \times r_{14} \\ r_{17} \leftarrow r_{arp} - 16 \\ r_{18} \leftarrow M(r_{17}) \end{array}}$$
Sequence 7

$$\boxed{\begin{array}{l} r_{15} \leftarrow r_{10} \times r_{14} \\ r_{18} \leftarrow M(r_{arp} - 16) \\ r_{19} \leftarrow M(r_{18}) \end{array}}$$
Sequence 8

$$\boxed{\begin{array}{l} r_{18} \leftarrow M(r_{arp} - 16) \\ r_{19} \leftarrow M(r_{18}) \\ r_{20} \leftarrow r_{19} - r_{15} \end{array}}$$
Sequence 9

$$\boxed{\begin{array}{l} r_{19} \leftarrow M(r_{18}) \\ r_{20} \leftarrow r_{19} - r_{15} \\ r_{21} \leftarrow 4 \end{array}}$$
Sequence 10

$$\boxed{\begin{array}{l} r_{20} \leftarrow r_{19} - r_{15} \\ r_{21} \leftarrow 4 \\ r_{22} \leftarrow r_{arp} - r_{21} \end{array}}$$
Sequence 11

$$\boxed{\begin{array}{l} r_{20} \leftarrow r_{19} - r_{15} \\ r_{22} \leftarrow r_{arp} + 4 \\ M(r_{22}) \leftarrow r_{20} \end{array}}$$
Sequence 12

$$\boxed{\begin{array}{l} r_{20} \leftarrow r_{19} - r_{15} \\ M(r_{arp} + 4) \leftarrow r_{20} \end{array}}$$
Sequence 13

■ **FIGURE 11.10** Sequences Produced by the Simplifier.

simplification, the computation takes 8 operations, instead of 14. It uses 7 registers (other than $r_{arp}$), instead of 13.

Several design issues affect the ability of a peephole optimizer to improve code. The ability to detect when a value is dead plays a critical role in simplification. The handling of control-flow operations determines what happens at block boundaries. The size of the peephole window limits the optimizer's ability to combine related operations. For example, a larger window would let the simplifier fold the constant 2 into the multiply operation. The next three subsections explore these issues.

### Recognizing Dead Values

$$\begin{array}{l} r_{12} \leftarrow 2 \\ r_{14} \leftarrow r_{12} + r_{12} \end{array}$$

When the simplifier confronts a sequence such as the one shown in the margin, it can fold the value 2 in place of the use of $r_{12}$ in the second operation. It cannot, however, eliminate the first operation unless it knows that $r_{12}$ is not live after the use in the second operation—that is, the value is dead. Thus, the ability to recognize when a value is no longer live plays a critical role in the simplifier's operation.

The compiler can compute LiveOut sets for each block and then, in a backward pass over the block, track which values are live at each operation. As an alternative, it can use the insight that underlies the semipruned SSA form; it can identify names that are used in more than one block and consider any such name live on exit from each block. This alternative strategy avoids the expense of live analysis; it will correctly identify any value that is strictly local to the block where it is defined. In practice, the effects introduced by the expander are strictly local so the less expensive approach produces good results.

Given either LiveOut sets or the set of global names, the expander can mark last uses in the LLIR. Two observations make this possible. First, the expander can process a block from bottom to top; the expansion is a simple template-driven process. Second, as it walks the block from bottom to top, the expander can build a set of values that are live at each operation, LiveNow.

**Last use**
a reference to a name after which the value
represented by that name is no longer live

The computation of LiveNow is simple. The expander sets the initial value for LiveNow equal to the LiveOut set for the block. (In the absence of LiveOut sets, it can set LiveNow to contain all the global names.) Now, as it processes an operation $r_i \leftarrow r_j$ op $r_k$, the algorithm adds $r_j$ and $r_k$ to LiveNow and deletes $r_i$. This algorithm produces, at each step, a LiveNow set that is as precise as the initial information used at the bottom of the block.

On a machine that uses a condition code to control conditional branches, many operations set the condition code's value. In a typical block, many of those condition code values are dead. The expander must insert explicit assignments to the condition code. The simplifier must understand when the condition code's value is dead because extraneous assignments to the condition code may prevent the matcher from generating some instruction sequences.

For example, consider the computation $r_i \times r_j + r_k$. If both $\times$ and $+$ set the condition code, the two-operation sequence might generate the following LLIR:

$$
\begin{aligned}
r_{t1} &\leftarrow r_i \times r_j \\
cc &\leftarrow f_\times(r_i, r_j) \\
r_{t2} &\leftarrow r_{t1} + r_k \\
cc &\leftarrow f_+(r_{t1}, r_k)
\end{aligned}
$$

The first assignment to cc is dead. If the simplifier eliminates that assignment, it can combine the remaining operations into a multiply-add operation, assuming the target machine has such an instruction. If it cannot eliminate

$cc \leftarrow f_x(r_i, r_j)$, however, the matcher cannot use multiply-add because it cannot set the condition code twice.

### Control-Flow Operations

The presence of control-flow operations complicates the simplifier. The easiest way to handle them is to clear the simplifier's window when it reaches a branch, a jump, or a labelled instruction. This keeps the simplifier from moving effects onto paths where they were not present.

The simplifier can achieve better results by examining context around branches, but it introduces several special cases to the process. If the input language encodes branches with a single target and a fall-through path, then the simplifier should track and eliminate dead labels. If it eliminates the last use of a label and the preceding block has a fall-through exit, then it can remove the label, combine the blocks, and simplify across the old boundary. If the input language encodes branches with two targets, or the preceding block ends with a jump, then a dead label implies an unreachable block that can be completely eliminated. In either case, the simplifier should track the number of uses for each label and eliminate labels that can no longer be referenced. (The expander can count label references, allowing the simplifier to use a simple reference-counting scheme to track the number of remaining references.)

A more aggressive approach might consider the operations on both sides of a branch. Some simplifications may be possible across the branch, combining effects of the operation immediately before the branch with those of the operation at the branch's target. However, the simplifier must account for *all* the paths reaching the labelled operation.

Predicated operations require some of these same considerations. At runtime, the predicate values determine which operations actually execute. In effect, the predicates specify a path through a simple CFG, albeit one without explicit labels or branches. The simplifier must recognize these effects and treat them in the same cautious fashion that it uses for labelled operations.

### Physical versus Logical Windows

The discussion, so far, has focused on a window containing adjacent operations in the low-level IR. This notion has a nice physical intuition and makes the concept concrete. However, adjacent operations in the low-level IR may not operate on the same values. In fact, as target machines offer more instruction-level parallelism, a compiler's front end and optimizer must generate IR programs that have more independent and interleaved computations to keep the target machine's functional units busy. In this case, the peephole optimizer may find very few opportunities for improving the code.

To improve this situation, the peephole optimizer can use a logical window rather than a physical window. With a logical window, it considers operations that are connected by the flow of values within the code—that is, it considers together operations that define and use the same value. This creates the opportunity to combine and simplify related operations, even if they are not adjacent in the code.

During expansion, the optimizer can link each definition with the next use of its value in the block. The simplifier uses these links to fill its window. When the simplifier reaches operation $i$, it constructs a window for $i$ by pulling in operations linked to $i$'s result. (Since simplification relies, in large part, on forward substitution, there is little reason to consider the next physical operation, unless it uses $i$'s result.) Using a logical window within a block can make the simplifier more effective, reducing both compile time required and the number of operations remaining after simplification. In our example, a logical window would let the simplifier fold the constant 2 into the multiplication.

Extending this idea to larger scopes adds some complication. The compiler can attempt to simplify operations that are logically adjacent but too far apart to fit in the peephole window together—either within the same block or in different blocks. This requires a global analysis to determine which uses each definition can reach (that is, reaching definitions from Section 9.2.4). Additionally, the simplifier must recognize that a single definition may reach multiple uses, and a single use might refer to values computed by several distinct definitions. Thus, the simplifier cannot simply combine the defining operation with one use and leave the remaining operations stranded. It must either limit its consideration to simple situations, such as a single definition and a single use, or multiple uses with a single definition, or it must perform some careful analysis to determine whether a combination is both safe and profitable. These complications suggest applying a logical window within a local or superlocal context. Moving the logical window beyond an extended basic block adds significant complications to the simplifier.

## 11.5.2 **Peephole Transformers**

The advent of more systematic peephole optimizers, as described in the previous section, created the need for more complete pattern sets for a target machine's assembly language. Because the three-step process translates all operations into LLIR and tries to simplify all the LLIR sequences, the matcher needs the ability to translate arbitrary LLIR sequences back into assembly code for the target machine. Thus, these modern peephole systems have much larger pattern libraries than earlier, partial systems. As computers moved from 16-bit instructions to 32-bit instructions, the explosion in the

**RISC, CISC, AND INSTRUCTION SELECTION**

Early proponents of RISC architectures suggested that RISCs would lead to simpler compilers. Early RISC machines, like the IBM 801, had many fewer addressing modes than contemporary CISC machines (like DEC's VAX-11). They featured register-to-register operations, with separate load and store operations for moving data between registers and memory. In contrast, the VAX-11 accommodated both register and memory operands; many operations were supported in both two-address and three-address forms.

The RISC machines did simplify instruction selection. They offered fewer ways to implement a given operation. They had fewer restrictions on register use. However, their load-store architectures increased the importance of register allocation.

In contrast, CISC machines have operations that encapsulate more complex functionality into a single operation. To make effective use of these operations, the instruction selector must recognize larger patterns over larger code fragments. This increases the importance of systematic instruction selection; the automated techniques described in this chapter are more important for CISC machines, but equally applicable to RISC machines.

number of distinct assembly operations made hand-generation of the patterns problematic. To handle this explosion, most modern peephole systems include a tool that automatically generates a matcher from a description of a target machine's instruction set.

The advent of tools to generate the large pattern libraries needed to describe a processor's instruction set has made peephole optimization a competitive technology for instruction selection. One final twist further simplifies the picture. If the compiler already uses the LLIR for optimization, then the compiler does not need an explicit expander. Similarly, if the compiler optimized the LLIR, the simplifier need not worry about dead effects; it can assume that the optimizer will remove them with its more general techniques for dead-code elimination.

This scheme also reduces the work required to retarget a compiler. To change target processors, the compiler writer must (1) provide an appropriate machine description to the pattern generator so that it can produce a new instruction selector; (2) change the LLIR sequences generated by earlier phases so that they fit the new ISA; and (3) modify the instruction scheduler and register allocator to reflect the characteristics of the new ISA. While this encompasses a significant amount of work, the infrastructure for describing, manipulating, and improving the LLIR sequences remains intact. Put another way, the LLIR sequences for radically different machines must capture their differences; however, the base language in which those sequences are written remains the same. This allows the compiler writer to build a set of tools that are useful across many architectures and to produce a machine-specific compiler by generating the appropriate low-level IR for the target ISA and providing an appropriate set of patterns for the peephole optimizer.

The other advantage of this scheme lies in the simplifier. This stripped-down peephole transformer still includes a simplifier. Systematic simplification of code, even when performed in a limited window, provides a significant advantage over a simple hand-coded pass that walks the IR and rewrites it into assembly language. Forward substitution, application of simple algebraic identities, and constant folding can produce shorter, more efficient LLIR sequences. These, in turn, may lead to better code for a target machine.

Several important compiler systems have used this approach. The best known may be the Gnu compiler system (GCC). GCC uses a low-level IR known as register-transfer language (RTL) for some of its optimizations and for code generation. The back end uses a peephole scheme to convert RTL into assembly code for target computers. The simplifier is implemented using systematic symbolic interpretation. The matching step in the peephole optimizer actually interprets the RTL code as trees and uses a simple tree-pattern matcher built from a description of the target machine. Other systems, such as Davidson's VPO, construct a grammar from the machine description and generate a small parser that processes the RTL in a linear form to perform the matching step.

---

**SECTION REVIEW**

The technology of peephole optimization has been adapted to perform instruction selection. The classic peephole-based instruction selector consists of a template-based expander that translates the compiler's IR into a more detailed form with a level of abstraction below the target ISA's level of abstraction; a simplifier that uses forward substitution, algebraic simplification, constant propagation, and dead-code elimination within a three or four operation scope; and a matcher that maps the optimized low-level IR onto the target ISA.

The strength of this approach lies in the simplifier; it removes interoperation inefficiencies that the expansion from compiler IR to low-level IR introduces. Those opportunities involve values that are local in scope; they cannot be seen at earlier stages of translation. The resulting improvements can be surprising. The final matching phase is straightforward; technologies ranging from hand-coded matchers to LR() parsers have been used.

--------------------------------------------------------------------

**Review Questions**

1. Sketch a concrete algorithm for the simplifier that applies forward substitution, algebraic simplification, and local constant propagation. What is the complexity of your algorithm? How does the size of the peephole window affect the cost of running your algorithm over a block?

2. The example shown in Figure 11.10 on page 626 demonstrates one weakness of peephole-based selectors. The assignment of $2$ to $r_{10}$ is too far from the use of $r_{10}$ to allow the simplifier to fold the constant and simplify the multiply (into either a `multI` or an `add`). What techniques might you use to expose this opportunity to the simplifier?

--------------------------------------------------------------------

## 11.6 ADVANCED TOPICS

Both BURS-based and peephole-based instruction selectors have been designed for compile-time efficiency. Both techniques are limited, however, by the knowledge contained in the patterns that the compiler writer provides. To find the best instruction sequences, the compiler writer might consider using search techniques. The idea is simple. Combinations of instructions sometimes have surprising effects. Because the results are unexpected, they are rarely foreseen by a compiler writer and, therefore, are not included in the specification produced for a target machine.

Two distinct approaches that use exhaustive search to improve instruction selection have appeared in the literature. The first involves a peephole-based system that discovers and optimizes new patterns as it compiles code. The second involves a brute-force search of the space of possible instructions.

### 11.6.1 Learning Peephole Patterns

A major issue that arises in implementing or using a peephole optimizer is the tradeoff between the time spent specifying the target machine's instruction set and the speed and quality of the resulting optimizer or instruction selector. With a complete pattern set, the cost of both simplification and matching can be kept to a minimum by using an efficient pattern-matching technique. Of course, someone must generate all those patterns. On the other hand, systems that interpret the rules during simplification or matching have a larger overhead per LLIR operation. Such a system can operate with a much smaller set of rules. This makes the system easier to create. However, the resulting simplifier and matcher run more slowly.

One effective way to generate the explicit pattern table needed by a fast, pattern-matching peephole optimizer is to pair it with an optimizer that has a symbolic simplifier. In this scheme, the symbolic simplifier records all the patterns it simplifies. Each time it simplifies a pair of operations, it records the initial pair and the simplified pair. Then, it can record the resulting pattern in the lookup table to produce a fast, pattern-matching optimizer.

By running the symbolic simplifier on a training set of applications, the optimizer can discover most of the patterns it needs. Then, the compiler can use the table as the basis of a fast pattern-matching optimizer. This lets the compiler writer expend computer time during design to speed up routine use of the compiler. It greatly reduces the complexity of the patterns that must be specified.

Increasing the interaction between the two optimizers can further improve code quality. At compile time, the fast pattern matcher will encounter some LLIR pairs that match no pattern in its table. When this occurs, it can invoke the symbolic simplifier to search for an improvement, bringing the power of search to bear only on the LLIR pairs for which it has no pre-existing pattern.

To make this approach practical, the symbolic simplifier should record both successes and failures. This allows it to reject previously seen LLIR pairs without the overhead of symbolic interpretation. When it succeeds in improving a pair, it should add the new pattern to the optimizer's pattern table, so that future instances of that pair will be handled by the more efficient mechanism.

This learning approach to generating patterns has several advantages. It applies effort only on previously unseen LLIR pairs. It compensates for holes in the training set's coverage of the target machine. It provides the thoroughness of the more expensive system while preserving most of the speed of the pattern-directed system.

In using this approach, however, the compiler writer must determine when the symbolic optimizer should update the pattern tables and how to accommodate those updates. Allowing an arbitrary compilation to rewrite the pattern table for all users seems unwise; synchronization and security issues are sure to arise. Instead, the compiler writer might opt for periodic updates—storing the newly found patterns away so they can be added to the table as a routine maintenance action.

> The simplifier must check a proposed pattern against the machine description to ensure that the proposed simplification is broadly applicable.

## 11.6.2 Generating Instruction Sequences

The learning approach has an inherent bias: it assumes that the low-level patterns should guide the search for an equivalent instruction sequence. Some compilers have taken an exhaustive approach to the same basic problem.

Instead of trying to synthesize the desired instruction sequence from a low-level model, they adopt a generate-and-test approach.

The idea is simple. The compiler, or compiler writer, identifies a short sequence of assembly-language instructions that should be improved. The compiler then generates all assembly-language sequences of cost one, substituting the original arguments into the generated sequence. It tests each one to determine if it has the same effect as the target sequence. When it has exhausted all sequences of a given cost, it increments the cost of the sequences and continues. This process continues until (1) it finds an equivalent sequence, (2) it reaches the cost of the original target sequence, or (3) it reaches an externally imposed limit on either cost or compile time.

While this approach is inherently expensive, the mechanism used for testing equivalence has a strong impact on the time required to test each candidate sequence. A formal approach, using a low-level model of machine effects, is clearly needed to screen out subtle mismatches, but a faster test can catch the gross mismatches that occur most often. If the compiler simply generates and executes the candidate sequence, it can compare the results against those obtained from the target sequence. This simple approach, applied to a few well-chosen inputs, should eliminate most of the inapplicable candidate sequences with a low-cost test.

This approach is, obviously, too expensive to use routinely or to use for large code fragments. In some circumstances, however, it merits consideration. If the application writer or the compiler can identify a small, performance-critical section of code, the gains from an outstanding code sequence may justify the cost of exhaustive search. For example, in some embedded applications, the performance-critical code consists of a single inner loop. Using exhaustive search for small code fragments—to improve either speed or space—may be worthwhile.

Similarly, exhaustive search has been applied as part of the process of retargeting a compiler to a new architecture. This application uses exhaustive search to discover particularly efficient implementations for IR sequences that the compiler routinely generates. Since the cost is incurred when the compiler is ported, the compiler writer can justify the use of search by amortizing that cost over the many compilations that are expected to use the new compiler.

## 11.7 SUMMARY AND PERSPECTIVE

At its heart, instruction selection is a pattern-matching problem. The difficulty of instruction selection depends on the level of abstraction of the compiler's IR, the complexity of the target machine, and the quality of code desired from the compiler. In some cases, a simple treewalk approach will produce adequate results. For harder instances of the problem, however, the systematic search conducted by either tree-pattern matching or peephole optimization can yield better results. Creating a handcrafted treewalk code generator that achieves the same results would take much more work. While these two approaches differ in almost all their details, they share a common vision—the use of pattern matching to find a good code sequence among the myriad sequences possible for any given IR program.

Tree-pattern matchers discover low-cost tilings by taking the low-cost choice at each decision point. The resulting code implements the computation specified by the IR program. Peephole transformers systematically simplify the IR program and match what remains against a set of patterns for the target machine. Because they lack explicit cost models, no argument can be made for their optimality. They generate code for a computation with the same effects as the IR program, rather than a literal implementation of the IR program. Because of this subtle distinction in the two approaches, we cannot directly compare the claims for their quality. In practice, excellent results have been obtained with each approach.

The practical benefits of these techniques have been demonstrated in real compilers. Both LCC and GCC run on many platforms. The former uses tree-pattern matching; the latter uses a peephole transformer. The use of automated tools in both systems has made them easy to understand, easy to retarget, and, ultimately, widely accepted in the community.

Equally important, the reader should recognize that both families of automatic pattern matchers can be applied to other problems in compilation. Peephole optimization originated as a technique for improving the final code produced by a compiler. In a similar way, the compiler can apply tree-pattern matching to recognize and rewrite computations in an AST. BURS technology can provide a particularly efficient way to recognize and improve simple patterns, including the algebraic identities recognized by value numbering.

## ■ CHAPTER NOTES

Most early compilers used hand-coded, ad hoc techniques to perform instruction selection [26]. With sufficiently small instruction sets, or large enough compiler teams, this worked. For example, the Bliss-11 compiler generated excellent code for the PDP-11, with its limited repertoire of operations [356]. The small instruction sets of early computers and minicomputers let researchers and compiler writers ignore some of the problems that arise on modern machines.

For example, Sethi and Ullman [311], and, later, Aho and Johnson [5] considered the problem of generating optimal code for expression trees. Aho, Johnson, and Ullman extended their ideas to expression DAGs [6]. Compilers based on this work used ad hoc methods for the control structures and clever algorithms for expression trees.

In the late 1970s, two distinct trends in architecture brought the problem of instruction selection to the forefront of compiler research. The move from 16- to 32-bit architectures precipitated an explosion in the number of operations and address modes that the compiler had to consider. For a compiler to explore even a large fraction of the possibilities, it needed a more formal and powerful approach. At the same time, the nascent Unix operating system began to appear on multiple platforms. This sparked a natural demand for C compilers and increased interest in retargetable compilers [206]. The ability to easily retarget the instruction selector plays a key role in determining the ease of porting a compiler to new architectures. These two trends started a flurry of research on instruction selection that started in the 1970s and continued well into the 1990s [71, 72, 132, 160, 166, 287, 288].

The success of automation in scanning and parsing made specification-driven instruction selection an attractive idea. Glanville and Graham mapped the pattern matching of instruction selection onto table-driven parsing [160, 165, 167]. Ganapathi and Fischer attacked the problem with attribute grammars [156].

Tree-pattern-matching code generators grew out of early work in table-driven code generation [9, 42, 167, 184, 240] and in tree-pattern matching [76, 192]. Pelegri Llopart formalized many of these notions in the theory of BURS [281]. Subsequent authors built on this work to create a variety of implementations, variations, and table-generation algorithms [152, 153, 288]. The Twig system combined tree-pattern matching and dynamic programming [2, 334].

The first peephole optimizer appears to be McKeeman's system [260]. Bagwell [30], Wulf et al. [356], and Lamb [237] describe early peephole systems. The cycle of expand, simplify, and match described in Section 11.5.1 comes from Davidson's work [115, 118]. Kessler also worked on deriving peephole optimizers directly from low-level descriptions of target architectures [222]. Fraser and Wendt adapted peephole optimization to perform code generation [154, 155]. The machine learning approach described in Section 11.6.1 was described by Davidson and Fraser [116].

Massalin proposed the exhaustive approach described in Section 11.6.2 [258]. It was applied in a limited way in GCC by Granlund and Kenner [170].

## ■ EXERCISES

Section 11.2

1. The treewalk code generator shown in Figure 7.2 uses a `loadI` for every number. Rewrite the treewalk code generator so that it uses `addI`, `subI`, `rsubI`, `multI`, `divI` and `rdivI`. Explain any additional routines or data structures that your code generator needs.

Section 11.3

2. Using the rules given in Figure 11.5, generate two tilings for the AST shown in Figure 11.4.

3. Build a low-level AST for the following expressions, using the tree in Figure 11.4 as a model:

   **a.** y ← a × b + c × d
   **b.** w ← a × b × c - 7

   Use the rules given in Figure 11.5 to tile these trees and generate ILOC.

4. Tree-pattern matching assumes that its input is a tree.
   **a.** How would you extend these ideas to handle DAGs, where a node can have multiple parents?
   **b.** How do control-flow operations fit into this paradigm?

5. In any treewalk scheme for code generation, the compiler must choose an evaluation order for the subtrees. That is, at some binary node $n$, does it evaluate the left subtree first or the right subtree first?
   **a.** Does the choice of order affect the number of registers required to evaluate the entire subtree?
   **b.** How can this choice be incorporated into the bottom-up tree-pattern matching schemes?

Section 11.4

6. A real peephole optimizer must deal with control-flow operations, including conditional branches, jumps, and labelled statements.
   **a.** What should a peephole optimizer do when it brings a conditional branch into the optimization window?
   **b.** Is the situation different when it encounters a jump?
   **c.** What happens with a labelled operation?
   **d.** What can the optimizer do to improve this situation?

7. Write down concrete algorithms for performing the simplification and matching functions of a peephole transformer.
   **a.** What is the asymptotic complexity of each of your algorithms?
   **b.** How is the running time of the transformer affected by a longer input program, by a larger window, and by a larger pattern set (both for simplification and for matching)?

8. Peephole transformers simplify the code as they select a concrete implementation for it. Assume that the peephole transformer runs

before either instruction scheduling or register allocation and that the transformer can use an unlimited set of virtual register names.

**a.** Can the peephole transformer change the demand for registers?

**b.** Can the peephole transformer change the set of opportunities that are available to the scheduler for reordering the code?

# Instruction Scheduling

## ◼ CHAPTER OVERVIEW

The execution time of a set of operations depends heavily on the order in which they are presented for execution. Instruction scheduling attempts to reorder the operations in a procedure to improve its running time. In essence, it tries to execute as many operations per cycle as possible.

This chapter introduces the dominant technique for scheduling in compilers: greedy list scheduling. It then presents several methods for applying list scheduling to larger scopes than a single basic block.

**Keywords:** Instruction Scheduling, List Scheduling, Trace Scheduling, Software Pipelining

## 12.1 INTRODUCTION

On many processors, the order in which operations are presented for execution has a significant effect on the length of time it takes to execute a sequence of instructions. Different operations take different lengths of time. On a typical commodity microprocessor, integer addition and subtraction require less time than integer division; similarly, floating-point division takes longer than floating-point addition or subtraction. Multiplication usually falls between the corresponding addition and division operations. The time required to complete a load from memory depends on where in the memory hierarchy the value resides at the time that the load is issued.

The task of ordering the operations in a block or a procedure to make effective use of processor resources is called *instruction scheduling*. The scheduler takes as input a partially ordered list of operations in the target machine's assembly language; it produces as output an ordered version of the same list. The scheduler assumes that the code has already been optimized and it does not try to duplicate the optimizer's work. Instead, it packs operations into the available cycles and functional unit issue slots so that the code will run as quickly as possible.

### Conceptual Roadmap

The order in which the processor encounters operations has a direct impact on the speed of execution of compiled code. Thus, most compilers include an instruction scheduler that reorders the final operations to improve performance. The scheduler's choices are constrained by the flow of data, by the delays associated with individual operations, and by the capabilities of the target processor. The scheduler must account for all these factors if it is to produce a correct and efficient schedule for the compiled code.

The dominant technique for instruction scheduling is a greedy heuristic called list scheduling. List schedulers operate on straightline code and use a variety of priority ranking schemes to guide their choices. Compiler writers have invented a number of frameworks to schedule over larger regions in the code than basic blocks; these regional and loop schedulers simply create conditions where the compiler can apply list scheduling to a longer sequence of operations.

### Overview

On most modern processors, the order in which instructions appear has an impact on the speed with which the code executes. Processors overlap the execution of operations, issuing successive operations as quickly as possible given the finite (and small) set of functional units. In principle this strategy makes good utilization of hardware resources and decreases execution time by overlapping the execution of successive operations. The difficulty arises when an operation issues before its operands are ready.

**Stall**

the delay caused by a hardware *interlock* that prevents a value from being read until its defining operation completes

An *interlock* is the mechanism that detects the premature issue and creates the actual delay.

**Statically scheduled**

A processor that relies on compiler insertion of NOPs for correctness is a *statically scheduled* processor.

**Dynamically scheduled**

A processor that provides interlocks to ensure correctness is a *dynamically scheduled* processor.

Processor designs handle this situation in one of two ways. The processor can *stall* the premature operation until its operands are available. On a machine that stalls premature operations, the scheduler reorders the operations in an attempt to minimize the number of such stalls. Alternatively, the processor can execute the premature operation, albeit with the incorrect operands. This approach relies on the scheduler to maintain enough distance between a value's definition and its various uses to maintain correctness. If insufficient useful operations are available to cover the delay associated with some operation, the scheduler must insert nops to fill the gap.

Commodity microprocessors often have operations that have different latencies. Typical values might be one cycle for an integer add or subtract, three for an integer multiply or a floating-point add or subtract, five for a floating-point multiply, 12 to 18 for a floating-point divide, and 20 to 40 for an integer divide. As a further complication, some operations have variable latencies. The latency of a `load` depends on where in the memory hierarchy it finds the value; those latencies can range from a few cycles, say one to five for the nearest cache, to tens or hundreds of cycles for values in main memory. Arithmetic operations can have variable latencies as well. For example, floating-point multiply and divide units may take an early exit when they recognize that the actual operands render some stages of processing irrelevant (e.g. multiply by zero or one).

To further complicate matters, many commodity processors have the property that they can initiate execution of more than one operation in each cycle. So-called *superscalar* processors exploit parallelism at the instruction level—independent operations that can run concurrently without conflict. In a superscalar environment, the scheduler's job is to keep as many functional units busy as possible. Because the instruction dispatch hardware has a limited amount of lookahead, the scheduler may need to pay attention to both the cycle in which each operation issues and the relative ordering of operations within each cycle.

**Superscalar**
A processor that can issue distinct operations to multiple distinct functional units in a single cycle is considered a *superscalar* processor.

**Instruction level parallelism (ILP)**
the availability of independent operations that can execute concurrently

Consider, for example, a simple processor with one integer functional unit and one floating-point functional unit. The compiler wants to schedule a loop that consists of 100 integer operations and 100 floating-point operations. If the compiler orders the operations so that the first 75 operations are integer operations, the floating-point unit will sit idle until the processor finally reaches some work for it. If all the operations are independent (an unrealistic assumption), the best order might be to alternate operations between the two units.

Informally, instruction scheduling is the process whereby a compiler reorders the operations in the compiled code in an attempt to decrease its running time. Conceptually, an instruction scheduler looks like:

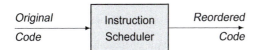

The instruction scheduler takes as input a partially ordered list of instructions; it produces as output an ordered list of instructions constructed from the same set of operations. The scheduler assumes a fixed set of operations; it does not rewrite the code (other than adding `nops` to maintain correct execution). The scheduler assumes a fixed allocation of values to registers; while it may rename registers, it does not change allocation decisions.

**MEASURING RUNTIME PERFORMANCE**

The primary goal of instruction scheduling is to improve the running time of the generated code. Discussions of performance use many different metrics; the two most common are

*Instructions per second* The metric commonly used to advertise computers and to compare system performance is the number of instructions executed in a second. This can be measured as instructions issued per second or instructions retired per second.

*Time to complete a fixed task* This metric uses one or more programs whose behavior is known and compares the time required to complete these fixed tasks. This approach, called *benchmarking*, provides information about overall system performance, both hardware and software, on a particular workload.

No single metric contains enough information to allow evaluation of the quality of code generated by the compiler's back end. For example, if the measure is instructions per second, does the compiler get extra credit for leaving extraneous (but independent) instructions in code? The simple timing metric provides no information about what is achievable for a given program. Thus, it allows one compiler to do better than another but fails to show the distance between the generated code and what is optimal for that code on the target machine.

Numbers that the compiler writer might want to measure include the percentage of executed instructions whose results are actually used and the percentage of cycles spent in stalls and interlocks. The former gives insight into some aspects of predicated execution, while the latter directly measures some aspects of schedule quality.

The instruction scheduler has three primary goals. First, it must preserve the meaning of the code that it receives as input. Second, it should minimize execution time by avoiding stalls or nops. Third, it should avoid increasing value lifetimes past the point where additional register spills are necessary. Of course, the scheduler should operate efficiently.

Many processors can issue multiple operations per cycle. While the mechanisms vary across architectures, the underlying challenge for the scheduler is the same: make good utilization of the hardware resources. In a very long instruction word (VLIW) processor, the processor issues an operation for each functional unit in each cycle, all gathered into a single fixed-format instruction. (The scheduler packs nops into the slots for idle functional units.) A packed VLIW machine avoids many of these nops with a variable-length instruction.

Superscalar processors look over a small window in the instruction stream, pick out operations that can execute on available units, and assign them to functional units. A dynamically scheduled processor considers operand availability; a statically scheduled processor only considers functional unit availability. An out-of-order superscalar processor uses a much larger window to scan for operations to execute; the window might be a hundred or more instructions.

This diversity of hardware dispatch mechanisms blurs the distinction between an operation and an instruction. On VLIW and packed VLIW machines, an instruction contains multiple operations. On superscalar machines, we usually refer to a single operation as an instruction and describe these machines as issuing multiple instructions per cycle. Throughout this book, we have used the term *operation* to describe a single opcode and its operands. We use the term *instruction* only to refer to an aggregation of one or more operations that all issue in the same cycle.

In deference to tradition, we still refer to this problem as *instruction scheduling*, although it might be more precisely called *operation scheduling*. On a VLIW or packed VLIW architecture, the scheduler packs operations into instructions that execute in a given cycle. On a superscalar architecture, either in order or out of order, the scheduler reorders operations to let the processor issue as many as possible in each cycle.

This chapter examines scheduling and the tools and techniques that compilers use to perform it. Section 12.2 provides a detailed introduction to the problem. Section 12.3 introduces the standard framework used for instruction scheduling: the list-scheduling algorithm. Section 12.4 presents several techniques that compilers use to extend the range of operations over which they can apply list scheduling. The "Advanced Topics" section presents an approach to loop scheduling.

## 12.2 THE INSTRUCTION-SCHEDULING PROBLEM

Consider the small example code shown in Figure 12.1; it reproduces an example used in Section 1.3. The column labelled "Start" shows the cycle in which each operation begins execution. Assume that the processor has a single functional unit, loads and stores take three cycles, a multiply takes two cycles, and all other operations complete in a single cycle. With these assumptions, the original code, shown on the left, takes 22 cycles.

The scheduled code, in Figure 12.1b, executes in many fewer cycles. It separates long-latency operations from operations that reference their results. This separation allows operations that do not depend on these results to

| Start | Operations | | |
|---|---|---|---|
| 1 | loadAI | r_arp,@a | ⇒ r_1 |
| 4 | add | r_1,r_1 | ⇒ r_1 |
| 5 | loadAI | r_arp,@b | ⇒ r_2 |
| 8 | mult | r_1,r_2 | ⇒ r_1 |
| 10 | loadAI | r_arp,@c | ⇒ r_2 |
| 13 | mult | r_1,r_2 | ⇒ r_1 |
| 15 | loadAI | r_arp,@d | ⇒ r_2 |
| 18 | mult | r_1,r_2 | ⇒ r_1 |
| 20 | storeAI | r_1 | ⇒ r_arp,@a |

(a) Original Code

| Start | Operations | | |
|---|---|---|---|
| 1 | loadAI | r_arp,@a | ⇒ r_1 |
| 2 | loadAI | r_arp,@b | ⇒ r_2 |
| 3 | loadAI | r_arp,@c | ⇒ r_3 |
| 4 | add | r_1,r_1 | ⇒ r_1 |
| 5 | mult | r_1,r_2 | ⇒ r_1 |
| 6 | loadAI | r_arp,@d | ⇒ r_2 |
| 7 | mult | r_1,r_3 | ⇒ r_1 |
| 9 | mult | r_1,r_2 | ⇒ r_1 |
| 11 | storeAI | r_1 | ⇒ r_arp,@a |

(b) Scheduled Code

■ **FIGURE 12.1** Example Block from Chapter 1.

execute concurrently with the long-latency operations. The code issues load operations in the first three cycles; the results are available in cycles 4, 5, and 6, respectively. This schedule requires an extra register, $r_3$, to hold the result of the third concurrently executing load operation, but it allows the processor to perform useful work while waiting for the first arithmetic operand to arrive. The overlap among operations effectively hides the latency of the memory operations. The same idea, applied throughout the block, hides the latency of the mult operation. The reordering reduces the running time to 13 cycles, a 41 percent improvement.

All of the examples we have seen so far deal, implicitly, with a target machine that issues a single operation in each cycle. Almost all commodity processors have multiple functional units and issue several operations in each cycle. We will introduce the list-scheduling algorithm for a single-issue machine and point out how to extend the basic algorithm to handle multioperation instructions.

**Dependence graph**

For a block $b$, its dependence graph $\mathcal{D} = (N, E)$ has a node for each operation in $b$. An edge in $\mathcal{D}$ connects two nodes $n_1$ and $n_2$ if $n_2$ uses the result of $n_1$.

The instruction scheduling problem is defined over the *dependence graph* $\mathcal{D}$ of a basic block. $\mathcal{D}$ is sometimes called a *precedence graph*. Edges in $\mathcal{D}$ represent the flow of values in the block. Additionally, each node has two attributes, an *operation type* and a *delay*. For a node $n$, the operation corresponding to $n$ must execute on a functional unit specified by its operation type; it requires $delay(n)$ cycles to complete. Figure 12.2b shows the dependence graph for the code in our running example. We have substituted concrete numbers for @a, @b, @c, and @d to avoid confusion with the labels used to identify operations.

Nodes with no predecessors in $\mathcal{D}$, such as $a$, $c$, $e$, and $g$ in the example, are called *leaves* of the graph. Since the leaves depend on no other operations,

| | | |
|---|---|---|
| *a*: | loadAI | r$_{arp}$,@a $\Rightarrow$ r$_1$ |
| *b*: | add | r$_1$,r$_1$ $\Rightarrow$ r$_1$ |
| *c*: | loadAI | r$_{arp}$,@b $\Rightarrow$ r$_2$ |
| *d*: | mult | r$_1$,r$_2$ $\Rightarrow$ r$_1$ |
| *e*: | loadAI | r$_{arp}$,@c $\Rightarrow$ r$_3$ |
| *f*: | mult | r$_1$,r$_2$ $\Rightarrow$ r$_1$ |
| *g*: | loadAI | r$_{arp}$,@d $\Rightarrow$ r$_2$ |
| *h*: | mult | r$_1$,r$_2$ $\Rightarrow$ r$_1$ |
| *i*: | storeAI | r$_1$ $\Rightarrow$ r$_{arp}$,@a |

(a) Example Code                (b) Its Dependence Graph

■ **FIGURE 12.2** Dependence Graph for the Example.

they can be scheduled as early as possible. Nodes with no successors in $\mathcal{D}$, such as *i* in the example, are called *roots* of the graph. The roots are, in some sense, the most constrained nodes in the graph because they cannot execute until all of their ancestors have executed. With this terminology, it appears that we have drawn $\mathcal{D}$ upside down—at least with regard to the trees, ASTs, and DAGs used earlier in the book. Placing the leaves at the top of the figure, however, creates a rough correspondence between placement in the drawing and eventual placement in the scheduled code. A leaf is at the top of the tree because it can execute early in the schedule. A root is at the bottom of the tree because it must execute after each of its ancestors.

> $\mathcal{D}$ is not a tree. It is a forest of DAGs. Thus, nodes can have multiple parents and $\mathcal{D}$ can have multiple roots.

Given a dependence graph $\mathcal{D}$ for a code fragment, a schedule $S$ maps each node $n \in N$ to a nonnegative integer that denotes the cycle in which it should be issued, assuming that the first operation issues in cycle 1. This provides a clear and concise definition of an instruction, namely, the $i^{th}$ instruction is the set of operations $\{n \mid S(n) = i\}$. A schedule must meet three constraints.

1. $S(n) \geq 1$, for each $n \in N$. This constraint forbids operations that issue before execution starts. A schedule that violates this constraint is not well formed. For the sake of uniformity, the schedule must also have at least one operation $n'$ with $S(n') = 1$.
2. If $(n_1, n_2) \in E$ then $S(n_1) + delay(n_1) \leq S(n_2)$. This constraint enforces correctness. An operation cannot issue until its operands have been defined. A schedule that violates this rule changes the flow of data in the code and is likely to produce incorrect results on a statically-scheduled machine.

**3.** Each instruction contains no more operations of each type $t$ than the target machine can issue in a cycle. This constraint enforces feasibility, since a schedule that violates it contains instructions that the target machine cannot possibly issue. (On a typical VLIW machine, the scheduler must fill unused slots in an instruction with nops.)

The compiler should only produce schedules that meet all three constraints.

Given a well-formed schedule that is both correct and feasible, the length of the schedule is simply the cycle number in which the last operation completes, assuming the first instruction issues in cycle 1. Schedule length can be computed as:

$$L(S) = \max_{n \in N} \ (S(n) + delay(n)).$$

If we assume that *delay* captures all the operational latencies, schedule $S$ should execute in $L(S)$ time. With a notion of schedule length comes the notion of a *time-optimal* schedule. A schedule $S_i$ is time optimal if $L(S_i) \leq L(S_j)$ for all other schedules $S_j$ that contain the same set of operations.

**Critical path**
the longest latency path through a dependence graph

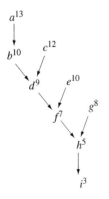

Dependence Graph
Annotated with Latencies

The dependence graph captures important properties of the schedule. Computing the total delay along the paths through the graph exposes additional detail about the block. Annotating the dependence graph $\mathcal{D}$ for our example with information about cumulative latency yields the graph shown in the margin. The path length from a node to the end of the computation is shown as a superscript on the node. The values clearly show that the path *abdfhi* is longest—it is the *critical path* that determines overall execution time for this example.

How, then, should the compiler schedule this computation? An operation can only be scheduled into an instruction when its operands are available. Since $a$, $c$, $e$, and $g$ have no predecessors in the graph, they are the initial candidates for scheduling. The fact that $a$ lies on the critical path strongly suggests that it be scheduled into the first instruction. Once $a$ has been scheduled, the longest path remaining in $\mathcal{D}$ is *cdefhi*, suggesting that $c$ be scheduled as the second instruction. With the schedule $ac$, $b$ and $e$ tie for the longest path. However, $b$ needs the result of $a$, which will not be available until the fourth cycle. This makes $e$ followed by $b$ the better choice. Continuing in this fashion leads to the schedule *acebdgfhi*. This matches the schedule shown in Figure 12.1b.

However, the compiler cannot simply rearrange the instructions into the proposed order. Recall that both $c$ and $e$ define $r_2$ and $d$ uses the value that $c$ stores in $r_2$. The scheduler cannot move $e$ before $d$ unless it renames the

**LIMITATIONS TO SCHEDULING**

The scheduler cannot cure all problems with instruction order. Consider the following code to compute $a^{16}$

| Start | Operations | | |
|---|---|---|---|
| 1 | loadAI | $r_{arp},@a$ | $\Rightarrow r_1$ |
| 4 | mult | $r_1,r_1$ | $\Rightarrow r_1$ |
| 6 | mult | $r_1,r_1$ | $\Rightarrow r_1$ |
| 8 | mult | $r_1,r_1$ | $\Rightarrow r_1$ |
| 10 | mult | $r_1,r_1$ | $\Rightarrow r_1$ |
| 12 | storeAI | $r_1$ | $\Rightarrow r_{arp}.@x$ |

The mult operations each need two cycles. The chain of dependences, shown on the left below, between the multiplies prevents the scheduler from improving the code. (If other independent operations are available, the scheduler could place them between the multiplies.)

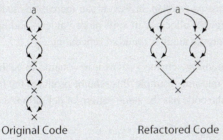

Original Code          Refactored Code

The issue is one of code shape that must be addressed earlier in compilation. If the optimizer refactors or reshapes the code into $(a^2)^2 \cdot (a^2)^2$, as shown on the right, the scheduler can overlap some of the multiplications and achieve a shorter schedule. If the processor can only issue one multiply per cycle, the refactored schedule saves one cycle. If the processor can issue two multiplies per cycle, it saves two cycles.

result of $e$ to avoid the conflict with $c$'s definition of $r_2$. This constraint arises not from the flow of data, as with the dependences modelled by edges in $\mathcal{D}$. Instead, it prevents an assignment that would change the flow of data. These constraints are often called *antidependences*. We denote the antidependence between $e$ and $d$ as $e \rightarrow d$.

**Antidependence**
Operation $x$ is *antidependent* on operation $y$ if $x$ precedes $y$ and $y$ defines a value used in $x$. Reversing their order of execution could cause $x$ to compute a different value.

The scheduler can produce correct code in at least two different ways. It can discover the antidependences that are present in the input code and respect them in the final schedule, or it can rename values to avoid them. The example contains four antidependences, namely, $e \rightarrow c$, $e \rightarrow d$, $g \rightarrow e$, and $g \rightarrow f$. All of them involve redefinition of $r_2$. (Constraints exist based on $r_1$ as well, but each antidependence on $r_1$ duplicates a dependence based on the flow of values.)

Respecting antidependences changes the set of schedules that the compiler can produce. For example, it cannot move $e$ before $c$ or $d$. This forces it to produce a schedule such as *acbdefghi*, which requires 18 cycles. While this schedule is an 18 percent improvement over the unscheduled code (*abcdefghi*), it is not competitive with the 41 percent improvement obtained by renaming to produce *acebdgfhi*, as shown on the right side of Figure 12.1.

As an alternative, the scheduler can systematically rename the values in the block to eliminate antidependences before it schedules the code. This approach frees the scheduler from the constraints imposed by antidependences, but it creates the potential for problems if the scheduled code requires spill code. Renaming does not change the number of live variables; it simply changes their names and helps the scheduler avoid violating antidependences. Increasing overlap, however, can increase demand for registers and force the register allocator to spill more values—adding long-latency operations and forcing another round of scheduling.

The simplest renaming scheme assigns a new name to each value as it is produced. In the ongoing example, this scheme produces the following code. This version of the code has the same pattern of definitions and uses.

```
a:  loadAI   rarp,@a  ⇒ r1
b:  add      r1,r1    ⇒ r2
c:  loadAI   rarp,@b  ⇒ r3
d:  mult     r2,r3    ⇒ r4
e:  loadAI   rarp,@c  ⇒ r5
f:  mult     r4,r5    ⇒ r6
g:  loadAI   rarp,@d  ⇒ r7
h:  mult     r6,r7    ⇒ r8
i:  storeAI  r8       ⇒ rarp,@a
```

However, the dependence relationships are expressed unambiguously in the code. It contains no antidependences, so naming constraints cannot arise.

## 12.2.1 Other Measures of Schedule Quality

Schedules can be measured in terms other than time. Two schedules $S_i$ and $S_j$ for the same block might produce different demands for registers—that is, the maximum number of live values in $S_j$ may be less than in $S_i$. If the processor requires the scheduler to insert nops for idle functional units, then $S_i$ might have fewer operations than $S_j$ and might fetch fewer instructions as a result. This need not depend solely on schedule length. For example, on a

**INTERACTIONS BETWEEN SCHEDULING AND ALLOCATION**

Antidependences between operations can limit the scheduler's ability to reorder operations. The scheduler can avoid antidependences by renaming; however, renaming creates a need for the compiler to perform register allocation after scheduling. This example is but one of the interactions between instruction scheduling and register allocation.

The core function of the scheduler is to reorder operations. Since most operations both use and define values, changing the relative order of two operations *x* and *y* can change the lifetimes of values. Moving *y* from below *x* to above *x* lengthens the lifetime of the value *y* defines. If one of *x*'s operands is a last use, moving *x* below *y* lengthens its lifetime. Symmetrically, if one of *y*'s operands is a last use, moving *y* above *x* shortens its lifetime.

The net effect of reordering *x* and *y* depends on the details of both *x* and *y*, as well as the surrounding code. If none of the uses involved is a last use, then the swap has no net effect on demand for registers. (Each operation defines a register; swapping them changes the lifetimes of specific registers, but not the aggregate demand for registers.)

In a similar way, register allocation can change the instruction-scheduling problem. The core functions of a register allocator are to rename references and to insert memory operations when demand for registers is larger than the register set. Both these functions affect the ability of the scheduler to produce fast code. When the allocator maps a large virtual name space to the name space of target-machine registers, it can introduce antidependences that constrain the scheduler. Similarly, when the allocator inserts spill code, it adds operations to the code that must, themselves, be scheduled into instructions.

We know, mathematically, that solving these problems together might produce solutions that cannot be obtained by running the scheduler followed by the allocator or the allocator followed by the scheduler. However, both problems are complex enough that most real-world compilers treat them separately.

processor with a variable-cycle nop, bunching nops together produces fewer operations and, potentially, fewer instructions. Finally, $S_j$ might require less energy than $S_i$ to execute on the target system because it never uses one of the functional units, it fetches fewer instructions, or it causes fewer bit transitions in the processor's fetch and decode logic.

## 12.2.2 **What Makes Scheduling Hard?**

The fundamental operation in scheduling is gathering operations together into groups based on the cycle in which those operations will begin execution. For each operation, the scheduler must choose a cycle. For each cycle, the scheduler must choose a set of operations. In balancing these two viewpoints, it must ensure that each operation issues only when its operands are available.

When the scheduler places an operation $i$ in cycle $c$, that decision affects the earliest possible placement of any operation that relies on the result of $i$—any operation in $\mathcal{D}$ that is reachable from $i$. If more than one operation can legally execute in cycle $c$, then the scheduler's choice can change the earliest placement of many operations—all those operations dependent (either directly or transitively) on each of the possible choices.

Local instruction scheduling is NP-complete for all but the simplest architectures. In practice, compilers produce approximate solutions to scheduling problems using greedy heuristics. Almost all the scheduling algorithms used in compilers are based on a single family of heuristic techniques, called *list scheduling*. The following section describes list scheduling in detail. Subsequent sections show how to extend the paradigm to larger scopes.

---

**SECTION REVIEW**

A local instruction scheduler must assign an execution cycle to each operation. (These cycles are numbered from the entry to the basic block.) In the process, it must ensure that no cycle in the schedule has more operations than the hardware can issue in a single cycle. On a statically scheduled processor, it must ensure that each operation issues only after its operands are available; that may require it to insert nops into the schedule. On a dynamically scheduled processor, it should minimize the expected number of stalls that execution will cause.

The key data structure for instruction scheduling is the dependence graph for the block being processed. It represents the flow of data in the block. It is easily annotated with information about operation-by-operation delays. The annotated dependence graph exposes important information about constraints and critical paths in the block.

---

### Review Questions

1. What parameters of the target processor might the scheduler need? Find these parameters for the processor in your own computer.

2. It is well known and widely appreciated that instruction scheduling interacts with register allocation. How does instruction scheduling interact with instruction selection? Are there modifications to the instruction selection process that we might make to simplify scheduling?

## 12.3 **LOCAL LIST SCHEDULING**

List scheduling is a greedy, heuristic approach to scheduling the operations in a basic block. It has been the dominant paradigm for instruction scheduling since the late 1970s, largely because it discovers reasonable schedules and it adapts easily to changes in computer architectures. However, list scheduling is an approach rather than a specific algorithm. Wide variation exists in how it is implemented and how it attempts to prioritize instructions for scheduling. This section explores the basic framework of list scheduling, as well as a couple of variations on the idea.

### 12.3.1 **The Algorithm**

Classic list scheduling operates on a single basic block. Limiting our consideration to straightline sequences of code allows us to ignore situations that can complicate scheduling. For example, when the scheduler considers multiple blocks, an operand might depend on prior definitions in different blocks, which creates uncertainty about when the operand is available for use. Code motion across block boundaries creates another set of complications. It can move an operation onto a path where it did not previously exist; it can also remove an operation from a path where it is necessary. Restricting our consideration to the single-block case avoids these complications. Section 12.4 explores cross-block scheduling.

To apply list scheduling to a block, the scheduler follows a four-step plan.

1. *Rename to avoid antidependences* To reduce the set of constraints on the scheduler, the compiler renames values. Each definition receives a unique name. This step is not strictly necessary. However, it lets the scheduler find some schedules that the antidependences would have prevented and it simplifies the scheduler's implementation.

2. *Build a dependence graph, $\mathcal{D}$* To build the dependence graph, the scheduler walks the block from bottom to top. For each operation, it constructs a node to represent the newly created value. It adds edges from that node to each node that uses the value. Each edge is annotated with the latency of the current operation. (If the scheduler does not perform renaming, $\mathcal{D}$ must represent antidependences as well.)

3. *Assign priorities to each operation* The scheduler uses these priorities as a guide when it picks from the set of available operations at each step. Many priority schemes have been used in list schedulers. The scheduler may compute several different scores for each node, using one as the primary ordering and the others to break ties between equally ranked nodes. One classic priority scheme uses the length of the longest

```
Cycle ← 1
Ready ← leaves of D
Active ← Ø

while (Ready ∪ Active ≠ Ø)
    for each op ∈ Active
        if S(op) + delay(op) < Cycle then
            remove op from Active
            for each successor s of op in D
                if s is ready
                    then add s to Ready

    if Ready ≠ Ø then
        remove an op from Ready
        S(op) ← Cycle
        add op to Active

    Cycle ← Cycle + 1
```

■ **FIGURE 12.3** List-Scheduling Algorithm.

latency-weighted path from the node to a root of $D$. Other priority schemes are described in Section 12.3.4.

4. *Iteratively select an operation and schedule it* To schedule operations, the algorithm starts in the block's first cycle and chooses as many operations as possible to issue in that cycle. It then increments its cycle counter, updates its notion of which operations are ready to execute, and schedules the next cycle. It repeats this process until each operation has been scheduled. Clever use of data structures makes this process efficient.

Renaming and building $D$ are straightforward. Typical priority computations traverse the dependence graph $D$ and compute some metric on it. The heart of the algorithm, and the key to understanding it, lies in the final step—the scheduling algorithm. Figure 12.3 shows the basic framework for this step, assuming that the target has a single functional unit.

The scheduling algorithm performs an abstract simulation of the block's execution. It ignores the details of values and operations to focus on the timing constraints imposed by edges in $D$. To track time, it maintains a simulation clock, in the variable `Cycle`. It initializes `Cycle` to 1 and increments it as it proceeds through the block.

The algorithm uses two lists to track operations. The `Ready` list holds all the operations that can execute in the current cycle. If an operation is in `Ready`, all of its operands have been computed. Initially, `Ready` contains all the leaves of $\mathcal{D}$, since they do not depend on other operations in the block. The `Active` list holds all operations that were issued in an earlier cycle but have not yet finished. Each time the scheduler increments `Cycle`, it removes from `Active` any operation `op` that finishes before `Cycle`. It then checks each successor of `op` in $\mathcal{D}$ to determine if it can move onto the `Ready` list—that is, if all its operands are available.

The list-scheduling algorithm follows a simple discipline. At each time step, it accounts for any operations completed in the previous cycle, it schedules an operation for the current cycle, and it increments `Cycle`. The process terminates when the simulated clock indicates that every operation has completed. If all the times specified by *delay* are accurate and all operands of the leaves of $\mathcal{D}$ are available in the first cycle, this simulated running time should match the actual execution time. A simple postpass can rearrange the operations and insert `nops` as needed.

The algorithm must respect one final constraint. Any block-ending or jump must be scheduled so that the program counter does not change before the block ends. So, if $i$ is the block-ending branch, it cannot be scheduled earlier than cycle $L(S) + 1 - delay(i)$. Thus, a single-cycle branch must be scheduled in the last cycle of the block, and a two-cycle branch must be scheduled no earlier than the second to last cycle in the block.

The quality of the schedule produced by this algorithm depends primarily on the mechanism used to pick an operation from the `Ready` queue. Consider the simplest scenario, where the `Ready` list contains at most one item in each iteration. In this restricted case, the algorithm must generate an optimal schedule. Only one operation can execute in the first cycle. (There must be at least one leaf in $\mathcal{D}$, and our restriction ensures that there is exactly one.) At each subsequent cycle, the algorithm has no choices to make— either `Ready` contains an operation and the algorithm schedules it, or `Ready` is empty and the algorithm schedules nothing to issue in that cycle. The difficulty arises when, in some cycle, the `Ready` queue contains multiple operations.

When the algorithm must choose among several ready operations, that choice is critical. The algorithm should take the operation with the highest priority score. In the case of a tie, it should use one or more other criteria to break the tie (see Section 12.3.4). The metric suggested earlier, the longest latency-weighted distance to a root in $\mathcal{D}$, corresponds to always choosing the node on the critical path for the current cycle in the schedule being constructed. To the extent that the impact of a scheduling priority is predictable, this scheme should provide balanced pursuit of the longest paths.

```
for each load operation, l, in the block
    delay(l) ← 1

for each operation i in D
    let Dᵢ be the nodes and edges in D independent of i
    for each connected component C of Dᵢ do
        find the maximal number of loads, N, on any path through C
        for each load operation l in C
            delay(l) ← delay(l) + delay(i) / N
```

■ **FIGURE 12.4** Computing Delays for Load Operations.

## 12.3.2 Scheduling Operations with Variable Delays

Memory operations often have uncertain and variable delays. A load operation on a machine with multiple levels of cache memory might have an actual delay ranging from zero cycles to hundreds or thousands of cycles. If the scheduler assumes the worst-case delay, it risks idling the processor for long periods. If it assumes the best-case delay, it will stall the processor on a cache miss. In practice, the compiler can obtain good results by calculating an individual latency for each load based on the amount of instruction-level parallelism available to cover the load's latency. This approach, called *balanced scheduling*, schedules the load with regard to the code that surrounds it rather than the hardware on which it will execute. It distributes the locally available parallelism across loads in the block. This strategy mitigates the effect of a cache miss by scheduling as much extra delay as possible for each load. It will not slow down execution in the absence of cache misses.

Figure 12.4 shows the computation of delays for individual loads in a block. The algorithm initializes the delay for each load to one. Next, it considers each operation $i$ in the dependence graph $D$ for the block. It finds the computations in $D$ that are independent of $i$, called $D_i$. Conceptually, this task is a reachability problem on $D$. We can find $D_i$ by removing from $D$ every node that is a transitive predecessor of $i$ or a transitive successor of $i$, along with any edges associated with those nodes.

The algorithm then finds the connected components of $D_i$. For each component $C$, it finds the maximum number $N$ of loads on any single path through $C$. $N$ is the number of loads in $C$ that can share operation $i$'s delay, so the algorithm adds $delay(i)/N$ to the delay of each load in $C$. For a given load $l$, the operation sums the fractional share of each independent operation $i$'s delay that can be used to cover the latency of *l*. Using this value as *delay(l)* produces a schedule that shares the slack time of independent operations evenly across all loads in the block.

### 12.3.3 Extending the Algorithm

The list-scheduling algorithm, as presented, makes several assumptions that may not hold true in practice. The algorithm assumes that only one operation can issue per cycle; most processors can issue multiple operations per cycle. To handle this situation, we must expand the `while` loop so that it looks for an operation for each functional unit in each cycle. The initial extension is straightforward—the compiler writer can add a loop that iterates over the functional units.

The complexity arises when some operations can execute on multiple functional units and others cannot. The compiler writer may need to choose an order for the functional units that schedules the more-constrained units first and the less-constrained units later. On a processor with a partitioned register set, the scheduler may need to place an operation in the partition where its operands reside or schedule it into a cycle where the inter-partition transfer apparatus is idle.

At block boundaries, the scheduler needs to account for the fact that some operands computed in predecessor blocks may not be available in the first cycle. If the compiler invokes the list scheduler on the blocks in reverse postorder on the CFG, then the compiler can ensure that the scheduler knows how many cycles into the block it must wait on operands entering the block along forward edges in the CFG. (This solution does not help with a loop-closing branch; see Section 12.5 for a discussion of loop scheduling.)

### 12.3.4 Tie Breaking in the List-Scheduling Algorithm

The complexity of instruction scheduling causes compiler writers to use relatively inexpensive heuristic techniques—variants of the list-scheduling algorithm—rather than solving the problem to optimality. In practice, list scheduling produces good results; it often builds optimal or near-optimal schedules. However, as with many greedy algorithms, its behavior is not robust—small changes in the input may make large differences in the solution.

The methodology used to break ties has a strong impact on the quality of schedules produced by list scheduling. When two or more items have the same rank, the scheduler should break the tie based on another priority ranking. A good scheduler might have two or three tie-breaking priority ranks for each operation; it applies them in some consistent order. In addition to the latency-weighted path length described earlier, the scheduler might use the following:

- A node's rank is the number of immediate successors it has in $\mathcal{D}$. This metric encourages the scheduler to pursue many distinct paths through the graph—closer to a breadth-first approach. It tends to keep more operations on the *Ready* queue.
- A node's rank is the total number of descendants it has in $\mathcal{D}$. This metric amplifies the effect of the previous ranking. Nodes that compute critical values for many other nodes are scheduled early.
- A node's rank is equal to its *delay*. This metric schedules long-latency operations as soon as possible. It pushes them early in the block when more operations remain that might be used to cover their latency.
- A node's rank is equal to the number of operands for which this operation is the last use. As a tie breaker, this metric moves last uses closer to their definitions, which may decrease demand for registers.

Unfortunately, none of these priority schemes dominates the others in terms of overall schedule quality. Each excels on some examples and does poorly on others. Thus, there is little agreement about which rankings to use or in which order to apply them.

### 12.3.5 **Forward versus Backward List Scheduling**

The list-scheduling algorithm, as presented in Figure 12.3, works over the dependence graph from its leaves to its roots and creates the schedule from the first cycle in the block to the last. An alternate formulation of the algorithm works over the dependence graph in the opposite direction, scheduling from roots to leaves. The first operation scheduled is the last to issue and the last operation scheduled is the first to issue. This version of the algorithm is called *backward list scheduling*, and the original version is called *forward list scheduling*.

List scheduling is not an expensive part of compilation. Thus, some compilers run the scheduler several times with different combinations of heuristics and keep the best schedule. (The scheduler can reuse most of the preparatory work—renaming, building the dependence graph, and computing some of the priorities.) In such a scheme, the compiler should consider using both forward and backward scheduling.

In practice, neither forward scheduling nor backward scheduling always wins. The difference between forward and backward list scheduling lies

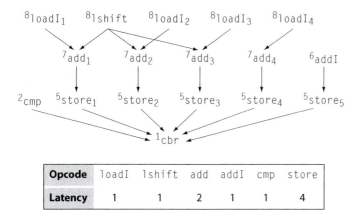

■ **FIGURE 12.5** Dependence Graph for a Block from go.

in the order in which the scheduler considers operations. If the schedule depends critically on the careful ordering of some small set of operations, the two directions may produce noticeably different results. If the critical operations occur near the leaves, forward scheduling seems more likely to consider them together, while backward scheduling must work its way through the remainder of the block to reach them. Symmetrically, if the critical operations occur near the roots, backward scheduling may examine them together, while forward scheduling sees them in an order dictated by decisions made starting at the other end of the block.

To make this latter point more concrete, consider the example shown in Figure 12.5. It shows the dependence graph for a basic block found in the SPEC 95 benchmark program go. The compiler added dependences from the store operations to the block-ending branch to ensure that the memory operations complete before the next block begins execution. (Violating this assumption could produce an incorrect value from a subsequent load operation.) Superscripts on nodes in the dependence graph give the latency from the node to the end of the block; subscripts differentiate among similar operations. The example assumes operation latencies that appear in the table below the dependence graph.

This example demonstrates the difference between forward and backward list scheduling. It came to our attention in a study of list scheduling; the compiler was targeting an ILOC machine with two integer functional units and one unit to perform memory operations. The five store operations take most of the time in the block. The schedule that minimizes execution time must begin executing stores as early as possible.

Forward list scheduling, using latency to the end of the block for priority, executes the operations in priority order, except for the comparison. It schedules the five operations with rank eight, then the four rank seven operations and the rank six operation. It begins on the operations with rank five, and slides the cmp in alongside the stores, since the cmp is a leaf. If ties are broken arbitrarily by taking left-to-right order, this produces the schedule shown in Figure 12.6a. Notice that the memory operations begin in cycle 5, producing a schedule that issues the branch in cycle 13.

Using the same priorities with backward list scheduling, the compiler first places the branch in the last slot of the block. The cmp precedes it by one cycle, determined by *delay*(cmp). The next operation scheduled is $store_1$ (by the left-to-right tie-breaking rule). It is assigned the issue slot on the memory unit that is four cycles earlier, determined by *delay*(store). The scheduler fills in successively earlier slots on the memory unit with the other store operations, in order. It begins filling in the integer operations, as they become ready. The first is $add_1$, two cycles before $store_1$. When the algorithm terminates, it has produced the schedule shown in Figure 12.6b.

The backward schedule takes one fewer cycle than the forward schedule. It places the addI earlier in the block, allowing $store_5$ to issue in cycle 4— one cycle earlier than the first memory operation in the forward schedule. By considering the problem in a different order, using the same underlying priorities and tie breakers, the backward algorithm finds a different result.

|    | Integer | Integer | Memory |
|----|---------|---------|--------|
| 1  | $loadI_1$ | lshift | — |
| 2  | $loadI_2$ | $loadI_3$ | — |
| 3  | $loadI_4$ | $add_1$ | — |
| 4  | $add_2$ | $add_3$ | — |
| 5  | $add_4$ | addI | $store_1$ |
| 6  | cmp | — | $store_2$ |
| 7  | — | — | $store_3$ |
| 8  | — | — | $store_4$ |
| 9  | — | — | $store_5$ |
| 10 | — | — | — |
| 11 | — | — | — |
| 12 | — | — | — |
| 13 | cbr | — | — |

(a) Forward Schedule

|    | Integer | Integer | Memory |
|----|---------|---------|--------|
| 1  | $loadI_4$ | — | — |
| 2  | addI | lshift | — |
| 3  | $add_4$ | $loadI_3$ | — |
| 4  | $add_3$ | $loadI_2$ | $store_5$ |
| 5  | $add_2$ | $loadI_1$ | $store_4$ |
| 6  | $add_1$ | — | $store_3$ |
| 7  | — | — | $store_2$ |
| 8  | — | — | $store_1$ |
| 9  | — | — | — |
| 10 | — | — | — |
| 11 | cmp | — | — |
| 12 | cbr | — | — |

(b) Backward Schedule

■ **FIGURE 12.6** Schedules for the Block from go.

**WHAT ABOUT OUT-OF-ORDER EXECUTION?**

Some processors include hardware support for executing instructions out of order (OOO). We refer to such processors as *dynamically scheduled* machines. This feature is not new; for example, it appeared on the IBM 360/91. To support OOO execution, a dynamically scheduled processor looks ahead in the instruction stream for operations that can execute before they would in a statically scheduled processor. To do this, the dynamically scheduled processor builds and maintains a portion of the dependence graph at runtime. It uses this piece of the dependence graph to discover when each instruction can execute and issues each instruction at the first legal opportunity.

When can an out-of-order processor improve on the static schedule? If runtime circumstances are better than the assumptions made by the scheduler, then the OOO hardware might issue an operation earlier than its position in the static schedule. This can happen at a block boundary, if an operand is available before its worst-case time. It can happen with a variable-latency operation. Because it knows actual runtime addresses, an OOO processor can also disambiguate some load-store dependences that the scheduler cannot.

OOO execution does not eliminate the need for instruction scheduling. Because the lookahead window is finite, bad schedules can defy improvement. For example, a lookahead window of 50 instructions will not let the processor execute a string of 100 integer instructions followed by 100 floating-point instructions in interleaved (integer, floating-point) pairs. It may, however, interleave shorter strings, say of length 30. OOO execution helps the compiler by improving good, but nonoptimal, schedules.

A related processor feature is dynamic register renaming. This scheme provides the processor with more physical registers than the ISA allows the compiler to name. The processor can break antidependences that occur within its lookahead window by using additional physical registers that are hidden from the compiler to implement two references connected by an antidependence.

Why does this happen? The forward scheduler must place all the rank-eight operations in the schedule before any rank-seven operations. Even though the `addI` operation is a leaf, its lower rank causes the forward scheduler to defer it. By the time the scheduler runs out of rank-eight operations, other rank-seven operations are available. In contrast, the backward scheduler places the `addI` before three of the rank-eight operations—a result that the forward scheduler could not consider.

## 12.3.6 **Improving the Efficiency of List Scheduling**

To pick an operation from the Ready list, as described so far, requires a linear scan over Ready. This makes the cost of creating and maintaining Ready approach $O(n^2)$. Replacing the list with a priority queue can reduce the cost of these manipulations to $O(n \log_2 n)$, for a minor increase in the difficulty of implementation.

A similar approach can reduce the cost of manipulating the Active list. When the scheduler adds an operation to Active, it can assign it a priority equal to the cycle in which the operation completes. A priority queue that seeks the smallest priority will push all the operations completed in the current cycle to the front, for a small increase in cost over a simple list implementation.

Further improvement is possible in the implementation of Active. The scheduler can maintain a set of separate lists, one for each cycle in which an operation can finish. The number of lists required to cover all the operation latencies is *MaxLatency* $= \max_{n \in \mathcal{D}}$ delay($n$). When the compiler schedules operation $n$ in Cycle, it adds $n$ to WorkList[(Cycle + delay($n$)) mod *MaxLatency*]. When it goes to update the Ready queue, all of the operations with successors to consider are found in WorkList[Cycle mod *MaxLatency*]. This scheme uses a small amount of extra space; the sum of operations in the WorkLists is the same as in the Active list. The individual WorkLists will have a small amount of overhead space. It uses a little more time on each insertion into a WorkList, to calculate which WorkList it should use. In return, it avoids the quadratic cost of searching Active and replaces it with a linear walk through a smaller WorkList.

---

**SECTION REVIEW**

List scheduling has been the dominant paradigm that compilers have used to schedule operations for many years. It computes, for each operation, the cycle in which it should issue. The algorithm is reasonably efficient; its complexity relates directly to the underlying dependence graph. This greedy heuristic approach, in its forward and backward forms, produces excellent results for single blocks.

Algorithms that perform scheduling over larger regions in the CFG use list scheduling to order operations. Its strengths and weaknesses carry over to those other domains. Thus, any improvements made to local list scheduling have the potential to improve the regional scheduling algorithms, as well.

**Review Questions**

1. You are asked to implement a list scheduler for a compiler that will produce code for your laptop. What metric do you use as your primary ranking for the ready list and how do you break ties? Provide a rationale for your choices.

2. Different priority metrics cause the scheduler to consider the operations in different orders. Could you apply randomization to achieve similar effects?

## 12.4 REGIONAL SCHEDULING

As with value numbering, moving from single basic blocks to larger scopes can improve the quality of code that the compiler generates. For instruction scheduling, many different approaches have been proposed for regions larger than a block but smaller than a whole procedure. Almost all of those approaches use the basic list-scheduling algorithm as the engine for reordering instructions. They surround that algorithm with an infrastructure that lets it consider longer (e.g. multi-block) sequences of code. In this section, we will examine three ideas for improving schedule quality by changing the context in which the compiler applies list scheduling.

### 12.4.1 Scheduling Extended Basic Blocks

Recall from Section 8.3 that an extended basic block (EBB) consists of a set of blocks $B_1, B_2, \ldots, B_n$ in which $B_1$ has multiple predecessors and every other block $B_i$ has exactly one predecessor, some $B_j$ in the EBB. The compiler can identify EBBs in a simple pass over the CFG. Consider the simple code fragment shown in the margin. It has one large EBB, $\{B_1, B_2, B_3, B_4\}$, and two trivial EBBs, $\{B_5\}$ and $\{B_6\}$. The large EBB has two paths, $\langle B_1, B_2, B_4 \rangle$, and $\langle B_1, B_3 \rangle$, The paths share $B_1$ as a common prefix.

To obtain a larger context for list scheduling, the compiler can treat paths in an EBB, such $\langle B_1, B_2, B_4 \rangle$, as if they are single blocks, provided it accounts for the shared path prefixes, such as $B_1$, which occurs in both $\langle B_1, B_2, B_4 \rangle$ and $\langle B_1, B_3 \rangle$, and the premature exits, such as $B_1 \rightarrow B_3$ and $B_2 \rightarrow B_5$. (We saw this same concept in the superlocal value numbering algorithm in Section 8.5.1.) This approach lets the compiler apply its highly effective scheduling engine—list scheduling—to longer sequences of operations. The effect is to increase the fraction of code that is scheduled together, which should improve execution times.

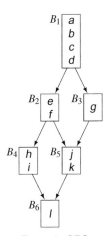

Example CFG

To see how shared prefixes and premature exits complicate list scheduling, consider the possibilities for code motion in the path $\langle B_1, B_2, B_4 \rangle$ in the example from the margin. Such code motion may require that the scheduler insert *compensation code* to maintain correctness.

**Compensation code**

code inserted into a block $B_i$ to counteract the effects of cross-block code motion along a path that does not include $B_i$

- The compiler can move an operation forward—that is, later on the path. For example, it might move operation $c$ from $B_1$ into $B_2$. While that decision might speed execution along the path $\langle B_1, B_2, B_4 \rangle$, it changes the computation performed along the path $\langle B_1, B_3 \rangle$. Moving $c$ forward out of $B_1$ means that the path $\langle B_1, B_3 \rangle$ no longer executes $c$. Unless $c$ is dead along all paths leading from $B_3$, the scheduler must correct this situation.

  To fix this problem, the scheduler must insert a copy of $c$ into $B_3$. If it was legal to move $c$ past $d$ on $\langle B_1, B_2, B_4 \rangle$, it must be legal to move $c$ past $d$ on $\langle B_1, B_3 \rangle$ as well, since the dependences that could prevent that motion are wholly contained in $B_1$. The new copy of $c$ does not lengthen execution along the path $\langle B_1, B_3 \rangle$ but it does increase the overall size of the code fragment.

- The compiler can move an operation backward—that is, earlier on the path. For example, it might move $f$ from $B_2$ to $B_1$. While that decision might speed execution along the path $\langle B_1, B_2, B_4 \rangle$, it inserts a computation of $f$ into the path $\langle B_1, B_3 \rangle$. That action has two consequences. First, it lengthens the execution of $\langle B_1, B_3 \rangle$. Second, it may produce incorrect code along $\langle B_1, B_3 \rangle$.

  If $f$ kills some value used in $B_3$, renaming the result of $f$ can avoid the problem. If the value is live after $B_4$, the scheduler may need to copy it back to its original name after $B_4$.

  If $f$ has a side effect that changes the values produced along any path leading from $B_3$, then the scheduler must rewrite the code to undo that effect in $B_3$. In some cases, renaming can cure the problem; in other cases, it must insert one or more compensating operations into $B_3$. These operations further slow execution along the path $\langle B_1, B_3 \rangle$.

The issue of compensation code also makes clear the order in which the scheduler should consider paths in an EBB. Since the first path scheduled receives little or no compensation code, the scheduler should choose paths in order of their likely execution frequency. It can either use profile data or estimates, in the same way that the global code-placement algorithm in Section 8.6.2 does.

The scheduler can take steps to mitigate the impact of compensation code. It can use live information to avoid some of the compensation code suggested by forward motion. If the result of the moved operation is not live on entry to the off-path block, no compensation code is needed in that block. It can avoid all of the compensation code needed by backward motion by simply prohibiting backward motion across block boundaries. While this restriction limits the scheduler's ability to improve the code, it avoids lengthening other paths and still allows the scheduler some opportunity for improvement.

The mechanics of EBB scheduling are straightforward. To schedule an EBB path, the scheduler performs renaming, if necessary, over the region. Next, it builds a single dependence graph for the entire path, ignoring any premature exits. It computes the priority metrics needed to select among ready operations and to break ties. Finally, it applies list scheduling, as for a single block. Each time it assigns an operation to a specific instruction in a specific cycle of the schedule, it inserts any compensation code necessitated by that choice.

In this scheme, the compiler schedules each block once. In our example, the scheduler might first process the path $\langle B_1, B_2, B_4 \rangle$. The next path is $\langle B_1, B_3 \rangle$. Since $B_1$'s schedule is already fixed, it will use knowledge of $B_1$'s schedule as an initial condition when it processes $B_3$, but it will not change the schedule for $B_1$. Finally, it schedules the trivial EBBs, $B_5$ and $B_6$.

### 12.4.2 **Trace Scheduling**

Trace scheduling extends the basic concept of scheduling paths beyond the range of a path through an EBB. Instead of focusing on EBBs, trace scheduling constructs maximal-length acyclic paths through the CFG and applies the list-scheduling algorithm to those paths, or *traces*. Because trace scheduling has the same issues with compensation code as EBB scheduling, the compiler should choose traces in a way that ensures that hot paths—the most frequently executed paths—are scheduled before colder paths.

**Trace**
an acyclic path through the CFG, selected using profile information

To build traces for scheduling, the compiler needs access to profile information for the edges in the CFG. The diagram in the margin shows our example with execution counts on each edge. To build a trace, the scheduler can use a simple greedy approach. It begins a trace by selecting the most frequently executed edge in the CFG. In our example, it would select the edge $\langle B_1, B_2 \rangle$ to create an initial trace of $\langle B_1, B_2 \rangle$. It then examines the edges entering the first node of the trace or leaving the last node of the trace and chooses the edge with the highest execution count. In the example, it chooses $\langle B_2, B_4 \rangle$ over $\langle B_2, B_5 \rangle$ to make the trace $\langle B_1, B_2, B_4 \rangle$. Since $B_4$ has just one successor, $B_6$, it chooses $\langle B_4, B_6 \rangle$ as its next edge and produces the trace $\langle B_1, B_2, B_4, B_6 \rangle$.

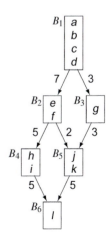

Trace construction stops when the algorithm either runs out of possible edges, as in our example, or encounters a loop-closing branch. The latter condition prevents the scheduler from constructing a trace that moves operations out of a loop. The assumption is that earlier optimization will have performed loop-invariant code motion (e.g. lazy code motion in Section 10.3.1) and that the scheduler should not put itself in the position to insert compensation code on the loop-closing branch.

Given a trace, the scheduler applies the list-scheduling algorithm to the entire trace, in the same way that EBB scheduling applies it to a path through an EBB. With an arbitrary trace, one additional opportunity for compensation code occurs; the trace may have interim entry points—blocks in mid-trace that have multiple predecessors.

- Forward code motion of an operation $i$ across an interim entry point may add $i$ to the off-trace path. If $i$ redefines a value that is also live across the interim entry, some combination of renaming or recomputation may be necessary. The alternative is to either prohibit forward motion across the interim entry or to use cloning to avoid this situation (see Section 12.4.3).
- Backward code motion of an operation $i$ across an interim entry point may necessitate adding $i$ to the off-trace path. This situation is straightforward, since $i$ already occurred on the off-trace path (albeit later in execution). Because the scheduler must correct for any naming issues introduced by the on-trace backward motion, the off-trace compensation code can simply define the same name.

To schedule the entire procedure, the trace scheduler constructs a trace and schedules it. It then removes the blocks in the trace from consideration, and selects the next most frequently executed trace. This trace is scheduled, with the requirement that it respect any constraints imposed by previously scheduled code. The process continues, picking a trace, scheduling it, and removing it from consideration, until all the blocks have been scheduled.

EBB scheduling can be considered a degenerate case of trace scheduling in which interim entries to the trace are prohibited.

### 12.4.3 Cloning for Context

In our continuing example, join points in the CFG limit the opportunities for either EBB scheduling or trace scheduling. To improve the results, the compiler can clone blocks to create longer join-free paths. Superblock cloning has exactly this effect (see Section 10.6.1). For EBB scheduling, it increases the size of the EBB and the length of some of the paths through the EBB. For trace scheduling, it avoids the complications caused by interim entry points in the trace. In either case, cloning also eliminates some of the branches and jumps in the EBB.

The figure in the margin shows the CFG that might result from cloning in our continuing example. Block $B_5$ has been cloned to create separate instances for the path from $B_2$ and the path from $B_3$. Similarly, $B_6$ has been cloned twice to create a unique instance for each path that enters it. Taken together, these actions eliminate all join points in the CFG.

After cloning, the entire graph forms one single EBB. If the compiler decides that $\langle B_1, B_2, B_4, B_6 \rangle$ is the hot path, it will schedule $\langle B_1, B_2, B_4, B_6 \rangle$ first. At that point, it has two other paths to schedule. It can schedule $\langle B_5, B_6' \rangle$ using the scheduled $\langle B_1, B_2 \rangle$ as a prefix. It can schedule $\langle B_3, B_5', B_6'' \rangle$ using the scheduled $B_1$ as a prefix. In the cloned CFG, neither of these latter choices interferes with the other.

Contrast this result with the simple EBB scheduler. It scheduled $B_3$ with respect to $B_1$ and scheduled both $B_5$ and $B_6$ without prior context. Because $B_5$ and $B_6$ have multiple predecessors and inconsistent context, the EBB scheduler cannot do better than local scheduling. Cloning these blocks to give the scheduler extra context costs one copy of statements $j$ and $k$ and two copies of statement $l$.

In practice, the compiler can simplify the CFG by combining pairs of blocks such as $B_4$ and $B_6$ that are linked by an edge where the source has no other successors and the sink has no other predecessors. Combining such blocks eliminates the end-of-block jump in the first block of the pair.

A second situation where cloning merits consideration arises in tail-recursive programs. Recall from Sections 7.8.2 and 10.4.1 that a program is tail recursive if its last action is a recursive self-invocation. When the compiler detects a tail call, it can convert the call to a jump back to the procedure's entry. From the scheduler's point of view, cloning may improve the situation.

The first diagram shown in the margin shows the abstracted CFG graph for a tail-recursive routine, after the tail call has been optimized. Block $B_1$ is entered along two paths, the path from the procedure entry and the path from $B_2$. This forces the scheduler to use worst-case assumptions about what precedes $B_1$. By cloning $B_1$ as shown in the lower diagram, the compiler can make control enter $B_{1'}$ along only one edge, which may improve the results of regional scheduling. To further simplify the situation, the compiler might coalesce $B_{1'}$ onto the end of $B_2$, creating a single-block loop body. The resulting loop can be scheduled with either a local scheduler or a loop scheduler, as appropriate.

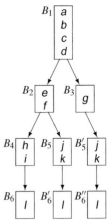

Example After Cloning

Tail Recursion After
Tail Call Optimization

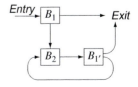

After Cloning

---

**SECTION REVIEW**

Regional scheduling techniques use a variety of methods to construct longer segments of straightline code for list scheduling. The quality of the code produced by these methods is, to some extent, determined by the quality of the underlying scheduler. The infrastructure of regional scheduling simply provides more context and more operations to the list scheduler, in an attempt to provide that scheduler with more freedom and more opportunities.

All three techniques examined in this section must deal with compensation code. While compensation code introduces complications into the algorithms and may introduce delays along some paths, experience suggests that the benefits of regional scheduling outweigh the complications.

---

**Review Questions**

1. In EBB scheduling, the compiler must schedule some blocks with respect to their already-scheduled prefixes. A naive implementation might reanalyze the prescheduled blocks and rebuild their dependence graphs. What data structures could your compiler use to avoid this extra work?

2. Both trace scheduling and cloning for context try to improve on the results of EBB scheduling. Compare and contrast these approaches. How would you expect the results to differ?

## 12.5 **ADVANCED TOPICS**

Compiler optimization has, since the first FORTRAN compiler, focused on improving code in loops. The reason is simple: code inside loops executes more frequently than code outside of loops. This observation has led to the development of specialized scheduling techniques that attempt to decrease the total running time of a loop. The most widely used technique is called *software pipelining* because it builds a schedule that mimics the behavior of a hardware pipeline.

### 12.5.1 **The Strategy of Software Pipelining**

Specialized loop-scheduling techniques can create schedules that improve on the results of local scheduling, EBB scheduling, and trace scheduling for one simple reason: they can account for the flow of values around the entire loop, including the loop-closing branch. Specialized loop-scheduling techniques make sense only when the default scheduler is unable to produce compact and efficient code for the loop. If the loop body, after scheduling, contains no stalls, interlocks, or `nops`, then a loop scheduler is unlikely to improve its performance. Similarly, if the loop body is long enough that the end-of-loop effects are a tiny fraction of its running time, a specialized loop scheduler is unlikely to show significant improvement.

Still, many small, computationally intensive loops benefit from loop scheduling. Typically, these loops have too few operations relative to the length of their critical paths to keep the underlying hardware busy. A software pipelined loop overlaps the execution of successive iterations of the loop; in a given cycle, the loop might issue operations from two or three different iterations. These pipelined loops consist of a fixed length *kernel*, along with a prologue and an epilogue to handle the initialization and finalization of the loop. The combined effect is analogous to that of a hardware pipeline, which has distinct operations in process concurrently.

**Loop kernel**
The central portion of a software pipelined loop; the *kernel* executes most of the loop's iterations in an interleaved fashion.

For a pipelined loop to execute correctly, the code must first execute a prologue section that fills up the pipeline. If the kernel executes operations from three iterations of the original loop, then each kernel iteration processes roughly one-third of each active iteration of the original loop. To start execution, the prologue must perform enough work to prepare for the last third of iteration 1, the second third of iteration 2, and the first third of iteration 3. After the loop kernel completes, a corresponding epilogue is needed to complete the final iterations—emptying the pipeline. In the example, it would need to execute the final two-thirds of the penultimate iteration and the final third of the last iteration. The prologue and epilogue sections increase code size. While the specific increase is a function of the loop and the number of iterations that the kernel executes concurrently, it is not unusual for the prologue and epilogue to double the amount of code required for the loop.

To make these ideas concrete, consider the following loop, written in C:

```
for (i=1; i < 200; i++)
    z[i] = x[i] * y[i];
```

Figure 12.7 shows the code that a compiler might generate for this loop, after optimization. In this case, both operator strength reduction and linear function test replacement have been applied (see Section 10.4), so the address expressions for $x$, $y$, and $z$ are updated with `addI` operations and the end of loop test has been rewritten in terms of the offset in $x$, eliminating the need to maintain a value for $i$.

The code in Figure 12.7 has been scheduled for a machine with one functional unit, assuming that loads and stores take three cycles, multiplies takes two cycles, and all other operations take one cycle. The first column shows cycle counts, normalized to the first operation in the loop (at label $L_1$).

| Cycle | Functional Unit 0 | | | Comments |
|-------|-------|-------|-------|----------|
| −4 | loadI | @x | ⇒ $r_{@x}$ | Set up the loop |
| −3 | loadI | @y | ⇒ $r_{@y}$ | with initial loads |
| −2 | loadI | @z | ⇒ $r_{@z}$ | |
| −1 | addI | $r_{@x}$, 792 | ⇒ $r_{ub}$ | |
| 1 | $L_1$: loadAO | $r_{arp}$, $r_{@x}$ | ⇒ $r_x$ | Get x[i] & y[i] |
| 2 | loadAO | $r_{arp}$, $r_{@y}$ | ⇒ $r_y$ | |
| 3 | addI | $r_{@x}$, 4 | ⇒ $r_{@x}$ | Bump the pointers |
| 4 | addI | $r_{@y}$, 4 | ⇒ $r_{@y}$ | in shadow of loads |
| 5 | mult | $r_x$, $r_y$ | ⇒ $r_z$ | The actual work |
| 6 | cmp_LT | $r_{@x}$, $r_{ub}$ | ⇒ $r_{cc}$ | Shadow of mult |
| 7 | storeAO | $r_z$ | ⇒ $r_{arp}$, $r_{@z}$ | Save the result |
| 8 | addI | $r_{@z}$, 4 | ⇒ $r_{@z}$ | Bump z's pointer |
| 9 | cbr | $r_{cc}$ | → $L_1$, $L_2$ | Loop-closing branch |
| | $L_2$: ... | | | |

■ **FIGURE 12.7** Example Loop Scheduled for One Functional Unit.

The preloop code initializes a pointer for each array ($r_{@x}$, $r_{@y}$, and $r_{@z}$). It computes an upper bound for the range of $r_{@x}$ into $r_{ub}$; the end-of-loop test uses $r_{ub}$. The loop body loads x and y, performs the multiply, and stores the result into z. The scheduler has filled all of the issue slots in the shadow of long-latency operations with other operations. During the load latencies, the schedule updates $r_{@x}$ and $r_{@y}$. It performs the comparison in the multiply's shadow. It fills the slots after the store with the update of $r_{@z}$ and the branch. This produces a tight schedule for a one-functional-unit machine.

Consider what happens if we run this same code on a superscalar processor with two functional units and the same latencies. Assume that loads and stores must execute on unit 0, that functional units stall when an operation issues before its operands are ready, and that the processor cannot issue operations to a stalled unit. Figure 12.8 shows the execution trace of the loop's first iteration. The mult in cycle 3 stalls because neither $r_x$ nor $r_y$ is ready. It stalls in cycle 4 waiting for $r_y$, begins executing again in cycle 5, and produces $r_z$ at the end of cycle 6. This forces the storeAO to stall until the start of cycle 7. Assuming that the hardware can tell that $r_{@z}$ contains an address that is distinct from $r_{@x}$ and $r_{@y}$, the processor can issue the first loadAO for the second iteration in cycle 7. If not, then the processor will stall until the store completes.

Using two functional units improved the execution time. It cut the preloop time in half, to two cycles. It reduced the time between the start of successive iterations by one-third, to six cycles. The critical path executes as quickly as

| Cycle | Functional Unit 0 | | | Functional Unit 1 | | |
|---|---|---|---|---|---|---|
| -2 | | loadI | @x ⇒ $r_{@x}$ | loadI | @y | ⇒ $r_{@y}$ |
| -1 | | loadI | @z ⇒ $r_{@z}$ | addI | $r_{@x}$,792 | ⇒ $r_{ub}$ |
| 1 | $L_1$: | loadAO | $r_{arp}$,$r_{@x}$ ⇒ $r_x$ | *no operation issued* | | |
| 2 | | loadAO | $r_{arp}$,$r_{@y}$ ⇒ $r_y$ | addI | $r_{@x}$,4 | ⇒ $r_{@x}$ |
| 3 | | addI | $r_{@y}$,4 ⇒ $r_{@y}$ | mult | $r_x$,$r_y$ | ⇒ $r_z$ |
| 4 | | cmp_LT | $r_{@x}$,$r_{ub}$ ⇒ $r_{cc}$ | *stall on* $r_y$ | | |
| 5 | | storeAO | $r_z$ ⇒ $r_{arp}$,$r_{@z}$ | addI | $r_{@z}$,4 | ⇒ $r_{@z}$ |
| 6 | | *stall on* $r_z$ | | cbr | $r_{cc}$ | → $L_1$,$L_2$ |
| 7 | | *. . . start of next iteration* . . . | | | | |

This figure shows an *execution trace*, not the scheduled code.

■ **FIGURE 12.8** Execution Trace on a Two-Unit Superscalar Processor.

| Cycle | Functional Unit 0 | | | Functional Unit 1 | | |
|---|---|---|---|---|---|---|
| -2 | | loadI | @x ⇒ $r_{@x}$ | loadI | @y | ⇒ $r_{@y}$ |
| -1 | | loadI | @z ⇒ $r_{@z}$ | addI | $r_{@x}$,788 | ⇒ $r_{ub}$ |
| 1 | $L_1$: | loadAO | $r_{arp}$,$r_{@x}$ ⇒ $r_x$ | addI | $r_{@x}$,4 | ⇒ $r_{@x}$ |
| 2 | | loadAO | $r_{arp}$,$r_{@y}$ ⇒ $r_y$ | addI | $r_{@y}$,4 | ⇒ $r_{@y}$ |
| 3 | | cmp_LT | $r_{@x}$,$r_{ub}$ ⇒ $r_{cc}$ | nop | | |
| 4 | | storeAO | $r_z$ ⇒ $r_{arp}$,$r_{@z}$ | addI | $r_{@z}$,4 | ⇒ $r_{@z}$ |
| 5 | | cbr | $r_{cc}$ → $L_1$,$L_2$ | mult | $r_x$,$r_y$ | ⇒ $r_z$ |
| +1 | $L_2$: | nop | | nop | | |
| +2 | | storeAO | $r_z$ ⇒ $r_{arp}$,$r_{@z}$ | nop | | |
| +3 | | . . . | | . . . | | |

■ **FIGURE 12.9** Example Loop after Software Pipelining.

we can expect; the multiply issues before $r_y$ is available and executes as soon as possible. The store proceeds as soon as $r_z$ is available. Some issue slots are wasted (unit 0 in cycle 6 and unit 1 in cycles 1 and 4).

Reordering the linear code can change the execution schedule. For example, moving the update of $r_{@x}$ in front of the load from $r_{@y}$ allows the processor to issue the updates of $r_{@x}$ and $r_{@y}$ in the same cycles as the loads from those registers. This lets some of the operations issue earlier in the schedule, but it does nothing to speed up the critical path. The net result is the same—a six-cycle loop. Pipelining the code can reduce the time needed for each iteration, as shown in Figure 12.9. In this case, it reduces the number of cycles per iteration from six to five. The next subsection presents the algorithm that generated this schedule.

## 12.5.2 **An Algorithm for Software Pipelining**

To create a software pipelined loop, the scheduler follows a simple plan. First, it estimates the number of cycles in the kernel, called the *initiation interval*. Second, it tries to schedule the kernel; if that process fails, it increases the kernel size by one and tries again. (This process must halt because scheduling will succeed before the kernel size exceeds the size of the nonpipelined loop.) As the final step, the scheduler generates prologue and epilogue code to match the scheduled kernel.

### *Estimating Kernel Size*

As an initial estimate for kernel size, the loop scheduler can compute lower bounds on the number of cycles that must be in the loop kernel.

■ The compiler can estimate the minimum number of cycles in the kernel from a simple observation: every operation in the loop body must issue. It can compute the number of cycles required to issue all the operations as follows:

$$RC = max_u(\lceil I_u/N_u \rceil)$$

where $u$ varies over all functional unit types $u$, $I_u$ is the number of operations of type $u$ in the loop and $N_u$ is the number of functional units of type $u$. We call $RC$ the resource constraint.

**Recurrence**

a loop-based computation that creates a cycle in the dependence graph

A recurrence must span multiple iterations.

■ The compiler can estimate the minimum number of cycles in the kernel from another simple observation: the initiation interval must be long enough to allow each recurrence to complete. It can compute the a lower bound from recurrence lengths as follows:

$$DC = max_r(\lceil d_r/k_r \rceil)$$

where $r$ ranges over all recurrences in the loop body, $d_r$ is the cumulative *delay* around recurrence $r$, and $k_r$ is the number of iterations that $r$ spans. We call $DC$ the dependence constraint.

The scheduler can use $ii = max(RC, DC)$ as its first initiation interval. In our example loop, all computations are of the same type. Since the loop body contains nine operations for two functional units, that suggests a resource constraint of $\lceil 9/2 \rceil = 5$. However, the loadA0 and storeA0 operations can only execute on unit 0, so we must also compute $\lceil 3/1 \rceil = 3$ as the constraint for unit 0. Since $5 > 3$, $RC$ is 5. From the dependence graph in Figure 12.10b, the recurrences are on $r_{@x}$, $r_{@y}$, and $r_{@z}$. All three have *delay* of one and span a single iteration, so $DC$ is one. Taking the larger of $RC$ and $DC$, the algorithm finds an initial value for $ii$ as 5.

```
a:        loadI    @x         ⇒ r@x
b:        loadI    @y         ⇒ r@y
c:        loadI    @z         ⇒ r@z
d:        addI     r@x,792    ⇒ rub

e:  L1:   loadAO   rarp,r@x   ⇒ rx
f:        loadAO   rarp,r@y   ⇒ ry
g:        addI     r@x,4      ⇒ r@x
h:        addI     r@y,4      ⇒ r@y
i:        mult     rx,ry      ⇒ rz
j:        cmp_LT   r@x,rub    ⇒ rcc
k:        storeAO  rz         ⇒ rarp,r@z
l:        addI     r@z,4      ⇒ r@z
m:        cbr      rcc        → L1,L2

n:  L2:   ...
```

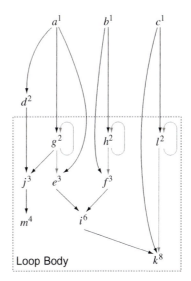

| (a) Code for Example Loop | (b) Dependence Graph |
|---|---|

■ **FIGURE 12.10** Dependence Graph for the Example Loop in Figure Figure 12.7.

## Scheduling the Kernel

To schedule the kernel, the compiler uses list scheduling with a fixed-length schedule of *ii* slots. Updates to the scheduling clock, `Cycle` in Figure 12.3, are performed modulo *ii*. Loop scheduling introduces a complication that cannot arise in straightline code (e.g. a block, an EBB, or a trace): cycles in the dependence graph.

**Modulo scheduling**
List scheduling with a cyclic clock is sometimes called *modulo scheduling*.

The scheduler must recognize that loop-carried dependences, such as $(g, e)$, do not constrain the first iteration of the loop. (Loop-carried dependences are drawn in gray in Figure 12.10b.) In the first iteration, only operations *e* and *f* depend solely on values computed before the loop.

**Loop-carried dependence**
a dependence that represents a value carried along the CFG edge for the loop-closing branch

The loop-carried dependences also expose antidependences. In the example, an antidependence runs from *e* to *g*; the code cannot update $r_{@x}$ before using it in the load operation. Similar antidependences from *f* to *h* and from *k* to *l*. If we assume that an operation reads its operands at the start of the cycle when it issues and writes its result at the end of the cycle when the operation finishes, then the delay on an antidependence is zero. Thus scheduling the operation at the source of the antidependence satisfies the constraint from the antidependence. We will see this behavior in the example below.

Modulo scheduling the dependence graph for the loop into a five-cycle, two-functional-unit schedule produces the kernel schedule shown in Figure 12.11. In cycle 1, with an initial ready list of $(e, f)$, the scheduler

| Cycle | Functional Unit 0 | | | Functional Unit 1 | | |
|---|---|---|---|---|---|---|
| 1 | $L_1$: loadAO | $r_{arp}, r_{@x}$ | $\Rightarrow r_x$ | addI | $r_{@x}, 4$ | $\Rightarrow r_{@x}$ |
| 2 | loadAO | $r_{arp}, r_{@y}$ | $\Rightarrow r_y$ | addI | $r_{@y}, 4$ | $\Rightarrow r_{@y}$ |
| 3 | cmp_LT | $r_{@x}, r_{ub}$ | $\Rightarrow r_{cc}$ | nop | | |
| 4 | storeAO | $r_z$ | $\Rightarrow r_{arp}, r_{@z}$ | addI | $r_{@z}, 4$ | $\Rightarrow r_{@z}$ |
| 5 | cbr | $r_{cc}$ | $\rightarrow L_1, L_2$ | mult | $r_x, r_y$ | $\Rightarrow r_z$ |

■ **FIGURE 12.11** Kernel Schedule for the Pipelined Loop.

chooses $e$, using some tie breaker, and schedules $e$ on unit 0. Scheduling $e$ satisfies the antidependence to $g$. Since the only dependences entering $g$ from inside the loop are loop-carried dependences, $g$ is now ready and can be scheduled into unit 1 in cycle 1.

Advancing the cycle counter to 2, the ready list contains $f$ and $j$. The scheduler selects $f$, breaking the tie in favor of the operation with the longer latency. It schedules $f$ onto unit 0. This action satisfies the antidependence from $f$ to $h$; the scheduler immediately places $h$ on unit 1 in cycle 2.

In cycle 3, the ready list contains just $j$. The scheduler places it on unit 0. In cycle 4, the dependence from $j$ to $m$ is satisfied; however, the additional constraint that keeps a block-ending branch at the end of the block delays it for a cycle.

In cycle 4, the ready list is empty. When the cycle counter advances to cycle 5, both $m$ and $i$ are ready. The scheduler places them on units 0 and 1.

When the counter advances beyond cycle 5, it wraps to cycle 1. The ready list is empty, but the active list is not, so the scheduler bumps the cycle counter. In cycle 2, operation $i$ has finished and operation $k$ is ready. Operation $k$ is a store, which must execute on unit 0. Unit 0 is busy in cycles 2 and 3, so the scheduler keeps bumping the cycle counter looking for a slot where it can place operation $k$. Finally, in cycle 4, it finds an issue slot for operation $k$.

Kernel scheduling fails when it does not find an issue slot for some operation. If that happens, the algorithm increments *ii* and tries again.

Scheduling operation $k$ in cycle 4 satisfies the antidependence from $k$ to $l$. The scheduler immediately schedules $l$ onto unit 1 in cycle 4. The scheduler then bumps the counter until both these operations come off the active list. Since neither has any descendents in the dependence graph, both ready and active become empty and the algorithm halts.

### Generating Prologue and Epilogue Code

In principle, generating the prologue and epilogue code is simple. The key insight, in both cases, is that the compiler can use the dependence graph as its guide.

To generate the prologue code, the compiler starts from each upward exposed use in the loop and follows the dependence graph in a backward scheduling phase. For each upward exposed use, it must generate the chain of operations that generate the necessary value, properly scheduled to cover their latencies. To generate the epilogue, the compiler starts from each downward exposed use in the loop and follows the dependence graph in a forward scheduling phase.

The example loop has particularly simple prologue and epilogue code, because the initiation interval is large relative to the delays in the loop. Exercise 9 at the end of the chapter shows a version of the same code with a tighter loop body and, hence, a more complex prologue and epilogue.

## 12.6 SUMMARY AND PERSPECTIVE

To obtain reasonable performance on a modern processor, the compiler must schedule operations carefully. Almost all modern compilers use some form of list scheduling. The algorithm is easily adapted and parameterized by changing priority schemes, tie-breaking rules, and even the direction of scheduling. List scheduling is robust, in the sense that it produces good results across a wide variety of codes. In practice, it often finds a time-optimal schedule.

Variations on list scheduling that operate over larger regions address problems that arise, at least in part, from the increased complexity of modern processors. Techniques that schedule EBBs and loops are, in essence, responses to the increase in both the number of pipelines that the compiler must consider and their individual latencies. As machines have become more complex, schedulers have needed more scheduling context to discover enough instruction-level parallelism to keep the machines busy. Software pipelining provides a way of increasing the number of operations issued per cycle and decreasing total time for executing a loop. Trace scheduling was developed for VLIW architectures, for which the compiler needed to keep many functional units busy.

## ■ CHAPTER NOTES

Scheduling problems arise in many domains, ranging from construction, through industrial production, through service delivery, to getting payloads onto the space shuttle. A rich literature has grown up about scheduling, including many specialized variants of the problem. Instruction scheduling has been studied as a distinct problem since the 1960s.

Algorithms that guarantee optimal schedules exist for simple situations. For example, on a machine with one functional unit and uniform operation latencies, the Sethi-Ullman labelling algorithm creates an optimal schedule for an expression tree [311]. It can be adapted to produce good code for expression DAGs. Fischer and Proebsting built on the labelling algorithm to derive an algorithm that produces optimal or near optimal results for small memory latencies [289]. Unfortunately, it has trouble when latencies rise or the number of functional units grows.

Much of the literature on instruction scheduling deals with variants on the list-scheduling algorithm described in this chapter. Landskov et al. is often cited as the definitive work on list scheduling [239], but the algorithm goes back, at least, to Heller in 1961 [187]. Other papers that build on list scheduling include Bernstein and Rodeh [39], Gibbons and Muchnick [159], and Hennessy and Gross [188]. Krishnamurthy et al. provide a high-level survey of the literature for pipelined processors [234, 320]. Kerns, Lo, and Eggers developed balanced scheduling as a way to adapt list scheduling to uncertain memory latencies [221, 249]. Schielke's RBF algorithm explored the use of randomization and repetition as an alternative to multilayered priority schemes [308].

Many authors have described regional scheduling algorithms. The first automated regional technique was Fisher's trace-scheduling algorithm [148, 149]. It has been used in several commercial systems [137, 251] and numerous research systems [318]. Hwu et al. proposed *superblock* scheduling as an alternative [201]; inside a loop, it clones blocks to avoid join points, in a fashion similar to that shown in Section 12.4.3. Click proposed a global scheduling algorithm based on the use of a global value graph [85]. Several authors have proposed techniques to make use of specific hardware features [303, 318]. Other approaches that use replication to improve scheduling include Ebcioğlu and Nakatani [136] and Gupta and Soffa [174]. Sweany and Beaty proposed choosing paths based on dominance information [327]; others have looked at various aspects of that approach [105, 199, 326].

Software pipelining has been explored extensively. Rau and Glaeser introduced the idea in 1981 [294]. Lam developed the scheme for software pipelining presented here [236]; the paper includes a hierarchical scheme for handling control flow inside a loop. Aiken and Nicolau developed a similar approach, called *perfect pipelining* [10] at the same time as Lam's work.

The example for backward versus forward scheduling in Figure 12.5 was brought to our attention by Philip Schielke [308]. He took it from the SPEC 95 benchmark program go. It captures, concisely, an effect that has caused many compiler writers to include both forward and backward schedulers in their compilers' back ends.

## ■ EXERCISES

Section 12.2

1. Develop an algorithm that builds the dependence graph for a basic block. Assume that the block is written in ILOC and that any values defined outside the block are ready before execution of the block begins.

2. If the primary use for a dependence graph is instruction scheduling, then accurate modeling of actual delays on the target machine is critical.
   a. How should the dependence graph model the uncertainty caused by ambiguous memory references?
   b. In some pipelined processors, write-after-read delays can be shorter than read-after-write delays. For example, the sequence

   $$[ \ add \ r_{10}, r_{12} \Rightarrow r_2 \ | \ sub \ r_{13}, r_{11} \Rightarrow r_{10} \ ]$$

   would read the value from $r_{10}$ for use in the add before writing the result of the sub into $r_{10}$. How can a compiler represent antidependences in a dependence graph for such an architecture?
   c. Some processors bypass memory to reduce read-after-write delays. On these machines, a sequence such as

   ```
   storeAI r21    ⇒ rarp,16
   loadAI  rarp,16 ⇒ r12
   ```

   forwards the value of the store (in $r_{21}$ at the beginning of the sequence) directly to the result of the load ($r_{12}$). How can the dependence graph reflect this hardware bypass feature?

Section 12.3

3. Extend the local list-scheduling algorithm from Figure 12.3 to handle multiple functional units. Assume that all functional units have identical capabilities.

4. A critical aspect of any scheduling algorithm is the mechanism for setting initial priorities and for breaking ties when several operations with the same priority are ready at the same cycle. Some alternative tiebreakers might be:
   a. Take the operations with register-based operands in preference to operations with immediate operands.
   b. Take the operation whose operands were most recently defined.
   c. Take a randomly chosen operation from the ready list.
   d. Take a load before any computation.
   For each tiebreaker, suggest a rationalization—a guess as to why someone suggested it. Which tiebreaker would you use first? Which would you use second? Justify (or rationalize) your answers.

5. Some operations, such as a register-to-register copy, can execute on almost any functional unit, albeit with a different opcode. Can the scheduler capitalize on these alternatives? Suggest modifications to the basic list-scheduling framework that allow it to use "synonyms" for a basic operation such as a copy.

6. Most modern microprocessors have *delay slots* on some or all branch operations. With a single delay slot, the operation immediately following the branch executes while the branch processes; thus, the ideal slot for scheduling a branch is in the second-to-last cycle of a basic block. (Most processors have a version of the branch that does not execute the delay slot, so that the compiler can avoid generating a nop instruction in an unfilled delay slot.)

   **a.** How would you adapt the list-scheduling algorithm to improve its ability to "fill" delay slots?

   **b.** Sketch a post-scheduling pass that would fill delay slots.

   **c.** Propose a creative use for the branch-delay slots that cannot be filled with useful operations.

**Section 12.4**

7. The order in which operations occur determines when values are created and when they are used for the last time. Taken together, these effects determine the lifetime of the value.

   **a.** How can the scheduler reduce the demand for registers? Suggest concrete tiebreaking heuristics that would fit into a list scheduler.

   **b.** What is the interaction between these register-oriented tiebreakers and the scheduler's ability to produce short schedules?

8. Software pipelining overlaps loop iterations to create an effect that resembles hardware pipelining.

   **a.** What impact will software pipelining have on the demand for registers?

   **b.** How can the scheduler use predicated execution to reduce the code-space penalty for software pipelining?

**Section 12.5**

9. The example code in Figure 12.7 generates a five-cycle software pipelined kernel because it contains nine operations. If the compiler chose a different scheme for generating the addresses of x, y, and z, it could further reduce the operation count in the loop body.

| Cycle | | Functional Unit 0 | | | Comments |
|---|---|---|---|---|---|
| −5 | | addI | $r_{arp}$,@x | $\Rightarrow r_{@x}$ | Set up the loop |
| −4 | | addI | $r_{arp}$,@y | $\Rightarrow r_{@y}$ | with initial loads |
| −3 | | addI | $r_{arp}$,@z | $\Rightarrow r_{@z}$ | |
| −2 | | loadI | 0 | $\Rightarrow r_{ctr}$ | |
| −1 | | loadI | 792 | $\Rightarrow r_{ub}$ | |
| 1 | $L_1$: | loadAO | $r_{ctr}$,$r_{@x}$ | $\Rightarrow r_x$ | Get x[i] & y[i] |
| 2 | | loadAO | $r_{ctr}$,$r_{@y}$ | $\Rightarrow r_y$ | |
| 3 | | mult | $r_x$,$r_y$ | $\Rightarrow r_z$ | The actual work |
| 4 | | cmp_LT | $r_{ctr}$,$r_{ub}$ | $\Rightarrow r_{cc}$ | Shadow of mult |
| 5 | | storeAO | $r_z$ | $\Rightarrow r_{ctr}$,$r_{@z}$ | Save the result |
| 6 | | addI | $r_{ctr}$,4 | $\Rightarrow r_{@z}$ | Bump the offset counter |
| 7 | | cbr | $r_{cc}$ | $\rightarrow L_1$,$L_2$ | Loop-closing branch |
| | $L_2$: | ... | | | |

This figure shows the *scheduled* code.

This scheme uses one more register, $r_{ctr}$, than the original version. Thus, depending on context, it might need spill code where the original did not.

**a.** Compute *RC* and *DC* for this version of the loop.

**b.** Generate the software pipelined loop body.

**c.** Generate the prologue and epilogue code for your pipelined loop body.

# Register Allocation

## ■ CHAPTER OVERVIEW

The code generated by a compiler must make effective use of the limited resources of the target processor. Among the most constrained resources is the set of hardware registers. Thus, most compilers include a pass that both allocates and assigns hardware registers to program values.

This chapter focuses on global register allocation and assignment via graph coloring; it describes the problems that occur at smaller scopes as a means of motivating a global allocator.

**Keywords:** Register Allocation, Register Spilling, Copy Coalescing, Graph-Coloring Allocators

## 13.1 INTRODUCTION

Registers are the fastest locations in the memory hierarchy. Often, they are the only memory locations that most operations can access directly. The proximity of registers to the functional units makes good use of registers a critical factor in runtime performance. In a compiler, responsibility for making good use of the target machine's register set lies with the register allocator.

The register allocator determines, at each point in the program, which values will reside in registers and which register will hold each of those values. If the allocator cannot keep a value in a register throughout its lifetime, the value must be stored in memory for some or all of its lifetime. The allocator might relegate a value to memory because the code contains more live values than the target machine's register set can hold. Alternatively, the value might be kept in memory between uses because the allocator cannot prove that it can safely reside in a register.

### Conceptual Roadmap

Conceptually, the register allocator takes as its input a program that uses some arbitrary number of registers and produces. It takes as output an equivalent program that fits into the finite register set of the target machine.

The allocator may need to insert loads and stores to move values between registers and memory. The goal of register allocation is to make effective use of the target machine's register set and to minimize the number of loads and stores that the code must execute.

Register allocation plays a direct role in creating executable code that executes quickly, for the simple reason that register accesses are faster than memory accesses. At the same time, the algorithmic problems that underlie register allocation are hard—in their general form, they defy optimal solution. A good register allocator computes an effective approximate solution to a hard problem, and does it quickly.

### Overview

To simplify the earlier parts of the compiler, most compilers use an IR in which the name space is not tied to either the address space of the target processor or its register set. To translate the IR code into assembly code for the target machine, these names must be mapped into the name space used in the target machine's ISA. Values stored in memory in the IR program must be turned into static coordinates that, in turn, map to runtime addresses using techniques such as those described in Section 6.4.3. Values stored in virtual registers in the IR must be mapped into the processors physical registers.

If the IR models computation with a memory-to-memory storage model, then the register allocator promotes memory-bound values into registers in the regions where they are heavily used. In this model, register allocation is an optimization that improves program performance by eliminating memory operations.

On the other hand, if the IR models the code with a register-to-register storage model, the register allocator must decide, at each point in the code, which virtual registers should reside in physical registers and which ones can live in memory. It constructs a map from virtual registers in the IR into some combination of physical registers and memory locations and rewrites the code to reflect that mapping. In this model, register allocation is required to create a correct target-machine program; it inserts loads and stores into the code and tries to place them where they will least hurt performance.

In general, the register allocator tries to minimize the impact of the loads and stores that it adds to the code, called *spill code*. That impact includes the time needed to execute the spill code, the code space that it occupies, and the data space occupied by the spilled values. A good register allocator tries to minimize all three.

The next section reviews some of the background issues that create the environment in which register allocators operate. Subsequent sections explore algorithms for register allocation and assignment in both local and global scopes.

**Spill code**

Loads and stores inserted by the register allocator are *spill code*.

## 13.2 BACKGROUND ISSUES

The register allocator takes as input code that is almost completely compiled—the code has been scanned, parsed, checked, analyzed, optimized, rewritten as target-machine code, and, perhaps, scheduled. The allocator must fit that code into the register set of the target machine by renaming values and inserting operations that move values between registers and memory. Many decisions made in earlier phases of the compiler affect the allocator's task, as do properties of the target machine's instruction set. This section explores several factors that play a role in shaping the role of the register allocator.

### 13.2.1 Memory versus Registers

The compiler writer's choice of a memory model defines many details of the allocation problem that the allocator must address (see Section 5.4.3). With a register-to-register model, earlier phases in the compiler directly encode their knowledge about ambiguous memory references into the shape of the IR; they place unambiguous values in virtual registers. Therefore, values stored in memory are assumed to be ambiguous (see Section 7.2), so the allocator leaves them in memory.

In a memory-to-memory model, the allocator does not have this code shape hint, because the IR program keeps all values in memory. In this model, the allocator must determine which values can be kept safely in registers—that is, which values are unambiguous. Next, it must determine whether keeping them in registers is profitable. In this model, the code that the allocator receives as input typically uses fewer registers and executes more memory operations than the equivalent register-to-register code. To obtain good performance, the allocator must promote as many of the memory-based values into registers as it can.

Thus, the choice of memory model fundamentally determines the allocator's task. In both scenarios, the allocator's goal is to reduce the number of loads and stores that the final code executes to move values back and forth between registers and memory. In a register-to-register model, allocation is a necessary part of the process that produces legal code; it ensures that the final code fits into the target machine's register set. The allocator inserts load and store operations to move some register-based values into memory—presumably in regions where demand for registers exceeds supply. The allocator tries to minimize the impact of the load and store operations that it inserts.

In contrast, in a compiler with a memory-to-memory model, the compiler performs register allocation as an optimization. The code is legal before allocation; allocation merely improves performance by keeping some memory-based values in registers and eliminating the loads and stores used to access them. The allocator tries to remove as many loads and stores as possible, since this can significantly improve the final code's performance.

Thus, lack of knowledge—limitations in the compiler's analysis—may keep the compiler from allocating a variable to a register. It can also occur when a single code sequence inherits different environments along different paths. These limitations on what the compiler may know tend to favor the register-to-register model. The register-to-register model provides a mechanism for other parts of the compiler to encode knowledge about ambiguity and uniqueness. This knowledge might come from analysis, it might come from understanding the translation of a complex construct, or it might even be derived from the source text in the parser.

## 13.2.2 Allocation versus Assignment

In a modern compiler, the register allocator solves two distinct problems— register allocation and register assignment—that have sometimes been handled separately in the past. These problems are related but distinct.

1. *Allocation* Register allocation maps an unlimited name space onto the register set of the target machine. In a register-to-register model, register allocation maps virtual registers to a new set of names that models the physical register set and spills values that do not fit in the register set. In a memory-to-memory model, it maps some subset of the memory locations to a set of names that models the physical register set. Allocation ensures that the code will fit the target machine's register set at each instruction.

2. *Assignment* Register assignment maps an allocated name set to the physical registers of the target machine. Register assignment assumes that allocation has been performed, so the code will fit into the set of physical registers provided by the target machine. Thus, at each

instruction in the generated code, no more than $k$ values are designated as residing in registers, where $k$ is the number of physical registers. Assignment produces the actual register names required by the executable code.

Register allocation is a hard problem. General formulations of the problem are NP-complete. For a single basic block, with one size of data value, optimal allocation can be done in polynomial time, if every value must be stored to memory at the end of its lifetime and the cost of storing those values is uniform. Almost any additional complexity in the problem makes it NP-complete. For example, adding a second size of data item, such as a register pair that holds a double-precision floating-point number, makes the problem NP-complete. Alternately, adding a memory model with nonuniform access costs, or the distinction that some values, such as constants, need not be stored at the end of their lifetime, makes the problem NP-complete. Extending the scope of allocation to include control flow and multiple blocks also makes the problem NP-complete. In practice, one or more of these issues arise in compiling for any real system. In many cases, all of them arise.

Register assignment, in many cases, can be solved in polynomial time. Assume a machine with one kind of register. Given a feasible allocation for a basic block—that is, one in which the demand for physical registers at each instruction does not exceed the number of physical registers—an assignment can be produced in linear time using an analog of *interval-graph* coloring. The related problem for an entire procedure can be solved in polynomial time—that is, if, at each instruction, the demand for physical registers does not exceed the number of physical registers, then the compiler can construct an assignment in polynomial time.

**Interval graph**

An *interval graph* represents the overlap between multiple intervals on the real line. It has a node for each interval and an edge $(i,j)$ if and only if $i$ and $j$ have a non-empty intersection.

The distinction between allocation and assignment is both subtle and important. In seeking to improve a register allocator's performance, the compiler writer must understand whether the weakness lies in allocation or assignment and direct effort to the appropriate part of the algorithm.

## 13.2.3 **Register Classes**

The physical registers provided by most processors do not form a homogenous pool of interchangeable resources. Most processors have distinct classes of registers for different kinds of values.

For example, most modern computers have both *general-purpose registers* and *floating-point registers*. The former hold integer values and memory addresses, while the latter hold floating-point values. This dichotomy is not new; the early IBM 360 machines had 16 general-purpose registers and four floating-point registers. Modern processors may add more classes.

For example, the PowerPC has a separate register class for condition codes, and the Intel IA-64 has additional classes for predicate registers and branch-target registers. The compiler must place each value in a register of the appropriate class.

If the interactions between two register classes are limited, the compiler may allocate registers for them independently. On most processors, general-purpose registers and floating-point registers are not used to hold the same kinds of values. Thus, the compiler can allocate the floating-point registers independently from the general-purpose registers. The fact that the compiler uses general-purpose registers to spill floating-point registers means that it should allocate the floating-point registers first. Breaking allocation into smaller problems in this way reduces the size of the data structures, and may produce faster compile times.

The values in floating-point registers have a different source-language type, so they are disjoint from the values stored in general-purpose registers.

If, on the other hand, different register classes overlap, the compiler must allocate them together. The common practice of using the same registers for single and double precision floating-point numbers forces the allocator to handle them as a single allocation problem—whether a double-precision value uses two single-precision registers or a single-precision value uses one-half of a double-precision register. A similar problem arises on architectures that allow values of different length to be stored in general-purpose registers. For example, the ISAs derived from the Intel x86 allow some 32-bit registers to hold one 32-bit value, two 16-bit values, or four 8-bit values. The allocator must model both potential uses and conflicts between those uses.

## 13.3 LOCAL REGISTER ALLOCATION AND ASSIGNMENT

As an introduction to register allocation, consider the problems that arise in producing a good allocation for a single basic block—local allocation, to use the terminology from optimization (see Section 8.3). A local allocator operates on one block.

To simplify the discussion, we assume that the block is the entire program. It loads the values that it needs from memory. It stores the values that it produces to memory. The input block uses a single class of general-purpose registers; the techniques extend easily to handle multiple disjoint register classes. The target machine provides a single set of $k$ physical registers.

The code shape encodes information about which values can legally reside in a register for nontrivial amounts of time. The code keeps any value that can legally reside in a register in a register. It uses as many virtual registers as needed to encode this information; thus, the input block may name more than $k$ virtual registers.

The input block contains a series of three-address operations $o_1, o_2, o_3, \ldots, o_N$. Each operation, $o_i$, has the form $op_i \ vr_{i_1}, vr_{i_2} \Rightarrow vr_{i_3}$. From a high-level view, the goal of local register allocation is to create an equivalent block in which each reference to a virtual register is replaced with a reference to a specific physical register. If the number of virtual registers is greater than $k$, the allocator may need to insert loads and stores to fit the code into the $k$ physical registers. An alternative statement of this property is that the output code can have no more than $k$ values in registers at any point in the block.

> We use $vr_i$ to denote a virtual register and $r_i$ to denote a physical register.

This section explores two approaches to local allocation. The first approach counts the number of references to a value in the block and uses these "frequency counts" to determine which values reside in registers. Because it relies on externally derived information—the frequency counts—to prioritize the allocation of virtual to physical registers, we consider this a top-down approach. The second approach relies on detailed, low-level knowledge of the code to make its decisions. It walks over the block and determines, at each operation, whether or not a spill is needed. Because it synthesizes and combines many low-level facts to drive its decision-making process, we consider this a bottom-up approach.

### 13.3.1 **Top-Down Local Register Allocation**

The top-down local allocator works from a simple principle: the most heavily used values should reside in registers. To implement this heuristic, it finds the number of times that each virtual register appears in the block. Then, it allocates virtual registers to physical registers in descending order by frequency count.

If there are more virtual registers than physical registers, the allocator must reserve enough physical registers to allow it to load, store, and use the values that are not kept in registers. The precise number of registers that it needs depends on the processor. A typical RISC machine might need two to four registers. We will refer to this machine-specific number as $\mathcal{F}$.

> $\mathcal{F}$
> On any given ISA, $\mathcal{F}$ is the number of registers needed to generate code for values that live in memory. We pronounce $\mathcal{F}$ "feasible."

If the block uses fewer than $k$ virtual registers, allocation is trivial and the compiler can simply assign each $vr$ to its own physical register. In this case, the allocator does not need to set aside the $\mathcal{F}$ physical registers for spill code. If the block uses more than $k$ virtual registers, the compiler applies the following simple algorithm:

1. *Compute a priority for each virtual register* In a linear pass over the operations in the block, the allocator tallies the number of times each

virtual register appears. This frequency count is the virtual register's priority.

2. *Sort the virtual registers into priority order* Priorities vary between two and the block length, so the best sorting algorithm depends on block length.

3. *Assign registers in priority order* Assign the first $k - \mathcal{F}$ virtual registers to physical registers.

4. *Rewrite the code* In a linear pass over the code, the allocator rewrites the code. It replaces virtual register names with physical register names. Any reference to a virtual register name with no allocated physical register is replaced with a short sequence that uses one of the reserved register and performs the appropriate load or store operation.

Top-down local allocation keeps heavily used virtual registers in physical registers. Its primary weakness lies in its approach to allocation—it dedicates a physical register to one virtual register for the entire basic block. Thus, a value that sees heavy use in the first half of the block and no use in the second half of the block effectively wastes that register through the second half of the block. The next section presents a technique that addresses this problem. It takes a fundamentally different approach to allocation—a bottom-up, incremental approach.

### 13.3.2 **Bottom-Up Local Register Allocation**

The key idea behind the bottom-up local allocator is to focus on the details of how values are defined and used on an operation-by-operation basis. The bottom-up local allocator begins with all the registers unoccupied. For each operation, the allocator needs to ensure that its operands are in registers before it executes. It must also allocate a register for the operation's result. Figure 13.1 shows its basic algorithm, along with three support routines that it uses.

The bottom-up allocator iterates over the operations in the block, making allocation decisions on demand. There are, however, some subtleties. By considering $vr_{i_1}$ and $vr_{i_2}$ in order, the allocator avoids using two physical registers for an operation with a repeated operand, such as add $r_y, r_y \Rightarrow r_z$. Similarly, trying to free $r_x$ and $r_y$ before allocating $r_z$ avoids spilling a register to hold an operation's result when the operation actually frees a register. Most of the complications in the algorithm occur in the routines *Ensure*, *Allocate*, and *Free*.

The routine *Ensure* is conceptually simple. It takes two arguments, a virtual register, $vr$, holding the desired value, and a representation for the

```
/* the bottom-up local allocator */        Ensure(vr,class)
for each operation, i, in order from 1         if (vr is already in class)
    to N where i has the form                     then result ← vr's physical register
        op vr_{i_1} vr_{i_2} ⇒ vr_{i_3}        else
    r_x ← Ensure(vr_{i_1}, class(vr_{i_1}))          result ← Allocate(vr,class)
    r_y ← Ensure(vr_{i_2}, class(vr_{i_2}))          emit code to move vr into result
    if vr_{i_1} is not needed after i          return result
        then Free(r_x, class(r_x))
    if vr_{i_2} is not needed after i        Allocate(vr,class)
        then Free(r_y, class(r_y))              if (class.StackTop ≥ 0)
    r_z ← Allocate(vr_{i_3}, class(vr_{i_3}))       then i ← pop(class)
    rewrite i as op_i r_x,r_y ⇒ r_z         else
    if vr_{i_1} is needed after i                   i ← j that maximizes class.Next[j]
        then class.Next[r_x] ← Dist(vr_{i_1})       store contents of j
    if vr_{i_2} is needed after i              class.Name[i] ← vr
        then class.Next[r_y] ← Dist(vr_{i_2})  class.Next[i] ← −1
    class.Next[r_z] ← Dist(vr_{i_3})           class.Free[i] ← false
                                                return i
```

■ **FIGURE 13.1**  The Bottom-Up, Local Register Allocator.

appropriate register class, $class$. If $vr$ already occupies a physical register, *Ensure*'s job is done. Otherwise, it allocates a physical register for $vr$ and emits code to move $vr$'s value into that physical register. In either case, it returns the physical register.

*Allocate* and *Free* expose the details of the allocation problem. To understand them, we need a concrete representation for a register class, shown in the C code to the left. A class has $Size$ physical registers, each of which is represented by a virtual register name ($Name$), an integer that indicates the distance to its next use ($Next$), and a flag indicating whether or not that physical register is currently in use ($Free$). To initialize the class structure, the compiler sets each register to an unallocated state (say, $class.Name$ as an invalid name, $Class.Next$ as $\infty$, and $class.Free$ as true), and pushes each of them onto the class' stack.

```
struct Class {
  int Size;
  int Name[Size];
  int Next[Size];
  int Free[Size];
  int Stack[Size];
  int StackTop;
}
```

At this level of detail, both *Allocate* and *Free* are straightforward. Each class has a stack of free physical registers. *Allocate* returns a physical register from the free list of $class$, if one exists. Otherwise, it selects the value stored in $class$ that is used farthest in the future, spills it, and reallocates the corresponding physical register to *vr*. *Allocate* sets the *Next* field to −1 to ensure that this register is not chosen for the other operand in the current operation. The allocator resets this field after it finishes with the current operation. *Free* simply needs to push the freed register onto the stack and reset its fields to their initial values. The function *Dist(vr)* returns the index in the block of the next reference to *vr*. The compiler can precompute this information in a backward pass over the block.

The bottom-up local allocator operates in an intuitive way. It assumes that the physical registers are initially empty and it places them all on a free list. It satisfies demand for registers from the free list, until that list is exhausted. After that, it satisfies demand by spilling some value to memory and reusing that value's register. It always spills the value whose next use is farthest in the future. Intuitively, it selects the register that would otherwise be unreferenced for the longest period of time. In some sense, it maximizes the benefit obtained for the cost of the spill.

In practice, this algorithm produces excellent local allocations. Indeed, several authors have argued that it produces optimal allocations. However, complications arise that cause it to produce suboptimal allocations. At any point in the allocation, some values in registers may need to be stored on a spill, while others may not. For example, if the register contains a known constant value, the store is superfluous since the allocator can recreate the value without a copy in memory. Similarly, a value that was created by a load from memory need not be stored. A value that need not be stored is called *clean*, while a value that needs a store is called *dirty*.

To produce an optimal local allocation, the allocator must take into account the difference in cost between spilling clean values and spilling dirty values. Consider, for example, allocation on a two-register machine, where the values $x_1$ and $x_2$ are already in the registers. Assume that $x_1$ is clean and $x_2$ is dirty. If the reference string for the remainder of the block is $x_3$ $x_1$ $x_2$, the allocator must spill one of $x_1$ or $x_2$. Since $x_2$'s next use lies farthest in the future, the bottom-up local algorithm would spill it, producing the sequence of memory operations shown on the left. If, instead, the allocator spills $x_1$, it produces the shorter sequence of memory operations shown on the right.

```
store x₂
load  x₃
load  x₂
```

Spill Dirty Value

```
load  x₃   (overwriting x₁)
load  x₁
```

Spill Clean Value

This scenario suggests that the allocator should preferentially spill clean values over dirty values. The answer is not that simple.

Consider another reference string, $x_3$ $x_1$ $x_3$ $x_1$ $x_2$, with the same initial conditions. Consistently spilling the clean value produces the sequence of four memory operations on the left. In contrast, consistently spilling the dirty value produces the sequence on the right, which requires fewer memory operations.

```
        load x₃
        load x₁                     store x₂
        load x₃                     load  x₃
        load x₁                     load  x₂
     Spill Clean Value           Spill Dirty Value
```

Thepresence of both clean and dirty values makes optimal local allocation NP-hard. Still, the bottom-up local allocator produces good local allocations in practice. The allocations tend to be better than those produced by the top-down algorithm.

In local allocation, "optimal" means the allocation with the fewest spills.

### 13.3.3 **Moving Beyond Single Blocks**

We have seen how to build good allocators for single blocks. Working top down, we arrived at the frequency-count allocator. Working bottom up, we arrived at an allocator based on distance to the next use. However, local allocation does not capture the reuse of values across multiple blocks. Because such reuse occurs routinely, we need allocators that extend their scope across multiple blocks.

Unfortunately, moving from a single block to multiple blocks adds many complications. For example, our local allocators assumed implicitly that values do not flow between blocks. The primary reason for moving to a larger scope for allocation is to account for the flow of values between blocks and to generate allocations that handle such flows efficiently. The allocator must correctly handle values computed in previous blocks, and it must preserve values for use in following blocks. To accomplish this, the allocator needs a more sophisticated way of handling "values" than the local allocators use.

#### *Liveness and Live Ranges*

Regional and global allocators try to assign values to registers in a way that coordinates their use across multiple blocks. We saw, in both the top-down allocator and in the earlier discussion of ssa form (see Section 9.3), that the compiler can sometimes compute a new name space that better serves

**Live range**
a closed set of related definitions and uses that serves as the base name space for register allocation

the purposes of a given algorithm. Regional and global allocators rely on this observation; they compute a name space that reflectsthe actual patterns of definitions and uses for each value. Rather than allocating variables or values to registers, these allocators compute a name space that is defined in terms of *live ranges*.

A single live range consists of a set of definitions and uses that are related to each other because their values flow together. That is, a live range contains a set of definitions and a set of uses. This set is self-contained in the sense that, for each use, every definition that can reach that use is in the same live range as the use. Similarly, for each definition, every use that can refer to the result of the definition is in the same live range as the definition.

The term *live range* relies, implicitly, on the notion of *liveness*, as described in Section 8.6.1. Recall that a variable $v$ is *live* at point $p$ if it has been defined along a path from the procedure's entry to $p$ and there exists a path from $p$ to a use of $v$ along which $v$ is not redefined. Anywhere that $v$ is live, its value must be preserved because subsequent execution might use $v$. Remember, $v$ can be either a source-program variable or a compiler-generated temporary.

The set of live ranges is distinct from the set of variables and the set of values. Every value computed in the code is part of some live range, even if it has no name in the original source code. Thus, the intermediate results produced by address computations are live ranges, as do programmer-named variables, array elements, and addresses loaded for use as branch targets. A single source-language variable may form multiple live ranges. An allocator that works on live ranges can place distinct live ranges in different registers. Thus, a source-language variable might reside in different registers at distinct points in the executing program.

In straightline code, we can represent a live range as an interval [$i,j$] where operation $i$ defines it and operation $j$ is its last use.

For live ranges that span multiple blocks, we need a more complex notation.

To make these ideas concrete, first consider the problem of finding live ranges in a single basic block. Figure 13.2 repeats the ILOC code that we first encountered in Figure 1.3, with the addition of an initial operation that defines $r_{arp}$. The table on the right side shows the distinct live ranges in the block. In straightline code, we can represent a live range as an interval. Notice that each operation defines a value and, thus, starts a live range. Consider $r_{arp}$. It is defined in operation 1. Every other reference to $r_{arp}$ is a use. Thus, the block uses just one value for $r_{arp}$, which is live over the interval [1,11].

In contrast, $r_a$ has several live ranges. Operation 2 defines it; operation 7 uses the value from operation 2. Operations 7, 8, 9, and 10 each define a new value for $r_a$; in each case, the following operation uses the value. Thus,

| | | | | Register | Interval |
|---|---|---|---|---|---|
| 1 | loadI | ⋯ | ⇒ $r_{arp}$ | | |
| 2 | loadAI | $r_{arp}$,@a | ⇒ $r_a$ | 1 $r_{arp}$ | [1,11] |
| 3 | loadI | 2 | ⇒ $r_2$ | 2 $r_a$ | [2,7] |
| 4 | loadAI | $r_{arp}$,@b | ⇒ $r_b$ | 3 $r_a$ | [7,8] |
| 5 | loadAI | $r_{arp}$,@c | ⇒ $r_c$ | 4 $r_a$ | [8,9] |
| 6 | loadAI | $r_{arp}$,@d | ⇒ $r_x$ | 5 $r_a$ | [9,10] |
| 7 | mult | $r_a$,$r_2$ | ⇒ $r_a$ | 6 $r_a$ | [10,11] |
| 8 | mult | $r_a$,$r_b$ | ⇒ $r_a$ | 7 $r_2$ | [3,7] |
| 9 | mult | $r_a$,$r_c$ | ⇒ $r_a$ | 8 $r_b$ | [4,8] |
| 10 | mult | $r_a$,$r_d$ | ⇒ $r_a$ | 9 $r_c$ | [5,9] |
| 11 | storeAI | $r_a$ | ⇒ $r_{arp}$,@a | 10 $r_d$ | [6,10] |

■ **FIGURE 13.2** Live Ranges in a Basic Block.

the value named $r_a$ in the original code corresponds to five distinct live ranges: [2,7], [7,8], [8,9], [9,10], and [10,11]. A register allocator need not keep these distinct live ranges in the same physical register. Instead, it can treat each live range in the block as an independent value for allocation and assignment.

To find live ranges in larger regions, the allocator must understand when a value is live past the end of the block that defines it. LIVEOUT sets, as computed in Section 8.6.1, encode precisely this knowledge. At any point in the code, only live values need registers. Thus, LIVEOUT sets play a key role in register allocation.

### Complications at Block Boundaries

A compiler that uses local register allocation might compute LIVEOUT sets for each block as a necessary prelude to provide the local allocator with information about the status of values at the block's entry and exit. LIVEOUT sets allows the allocator to handle the end-of-block conditions correctly. Any value in LIVEOUT($b$) must be stored to its assigned location in memory after its last definition in $b$ to ensure that the correct value is available in a subsequent block. In contrast, a value that is not in LIVEOUT($b$) can be discarded without a store after its last use in $b$.

While LIVEOUT information allows the local allocator to produce correct code, that code will contain stores and loads whose sole purpose is to connect values across block boundaries. Consider the example shown in the margin. The local allocator has assigned the variable x to different registers

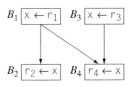

in each block: $r_1$ in $B_1$, $r_2$ in $B_2$, $r_3$ in $B_3$, and $r_4$ in $B_4$. The only local mechanism to resolve these conflicting assignments is to store $x$ at the end of $B_1$ and $B_3$ and to load it at the start of $B_2$ and $B_4$, as shown. This solution passes the value of $x$ through memory to move it into its assigned register in $B_2$ and $B_4$.

Along the control-flow edges $(B_1, B_2)$ and $(B_3, B_4)$, the compiler could replace the store-load pair with a register-to-register copy operation in the appropriate place: the start of $B_2$ for $(B_1, B_2)$ and the end of $B_3$ for $(B_3, B_4)$. However, edge $(B_1, B_4)$ does not have a location where the compiler can place the copy because it is a critical edge, as discussed in Section 9.3.5. Placing the copy at the end of $B_1$ produces an incorrect assignment for $B_2$, while placing it at the start of $B_4$ produces an incorrect result on edge $(B_3, B_4)$.

The local allocator cannot, in general, use copy operations to connect the flow of values between blocks. It cannot know, when processing $B_1$, the allocation and assignment decisions made in subsequent blocks. Thus, it must resort to passing the values through memory. Even if the allocator knew the assignments in $B_2$ and $B_4$ when it processed $B_1$, it still cannot resolve the problem with $(B_1, B_4)$ unless it changes the control-flow graph. Alternately, the allocator could avoid these problems by coordinating the assignment process across all the blocks. At that point, however, the allocator would no longer be a local allocator.

Similar effects arise with allocation. What if $x$ were not referenced in $B_2$? Even if we could coordinate assignment globally, to ensure that $x$ was always in some register, say $r_2$, when it was used, the allocator would need to insert a load of $x$ at the end of $B_2$ to let $B_4$ avoid the initial load of $x$. Of course, if $B_2$ had other successors, they might not reference $x$ and might need another value in $r_2$.

A second issue, both more subtle and more problematic, arises when we try to stretch the local-allocation paradigms beyond single blocks. Consider the situation that would arise when performing bottom-up local allocation on block $B_1$ of the example shown in the margin. If, after the use of $x$ in $B_1$, the allocator needs an additional register, it must compute the distance to the next use of $x$. In a single block that next reference is unique, as is its distance. With multiple successor blocks, the distance will depend on the path taken at runtime, $(B_1, B_2)$ or $(B_1, B_3, B_4)$. Thus, it is not well defined. Even if all the subsequent uses of $x$, are equidistant before allocation, local spilling in one block might increase the distances on one or more paths. As the basic metric that underlies the bottom-up local method is multivalued, the algorithm's effects become harder to understand and to justify.

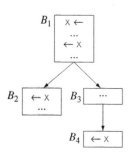

The effects at block boundaries can be complex. They do not fit into a local allocator because they deal with phenomena that are entirely outside a local allocator's scope. All of these problems suggest that a different approach is needed to move beyond local allocation to regional or global allocation. Indeed, successful global allocation algorithms bear little resemblance to local ones.

---

**SECTION REVIEW**

Local register allocation looks at a single basic block. That limited context simplifies the analysis and the algorithm. This section presented both a top-down and a bottom-up algorithm for local allocation. The top-down algorithm prioritizes values by the number of references to that value in the block. It assigns the highest priority values to registers. It reserves a small set of registers to handle those values that do not receive registers. The bottom-up allocator assigns values to registers as it encounters them in a forward pass over the block. When it needs an additional register, it spills the value whose next use is farthest in the future.

The top-down and bottom-up allocators presented here differ in how they treat individual values. When the top-down algorithm allocates a register for some value, it reserves that register for the entire block. When the bottom-up algorithm allocates a register for some value, it reserves that register until it encounters a more immediate need for the register. The bottom-up algorithm's ability to use a single register for multiple values allows it to produce better allocations than the top-down algorithm. The allocation paradigms in these two algorithms begin to break down when we try to apply them to larger regions.

---

**Review Questions**

1. For each of the two allocators, answer the following questions: Which step in the allocator has the worst asymptotic complexity? How might the compiler writer limit its impact on compile time?

2. The top-down allocator aggregates frequency counts by virtual register names and performs allocation by virtual register names. Sketch an algorithm that renames virtual registers in a way that improves the results of the top-down algorithm.

## 13.4 GLOBAL REGISTER ALLOCATION AND ASSIGNMENT

Register allocators try to minimize the impact of the spill code that they must insert. That impact can take at least three forms: execution time for the spill code, code space for the spill operations, and data space for the spilled values. Most allocators focus on the first of these effects—minimizing the execution time of spill code.

Global register allocators cannot guarantee an optimal solution to the problem of minimizing spill code execution time. The difference between two different allocations for the same code lies in both the number of loads, stores, and copy operations that the allocator inserts and their placement in the code. The number of operations matters, both in code space and execution time. The placement of operations matters because different blocks execute different numbers of times and those execution frequencies vary from run to run.

Global allocation differs from local allocation in two fundamental ways.

1. The structure of a global live range can be more complex than that of a local live range. A local live range is an interval in straightline code. A global live range is a web of definitions and uses found by taking the closure of two relationships. For a use $u$ in live range $LR_j$, $LR_j$ must include every definition $d$ that reaches $u$. Similarly, for each definition $d$ in $LR_j$, $LR_j$ must include every use $u$ that $d$ reaches.
   Global allocators create a new name space in which each live range has a distinct name. Allocation then maps live-range names to either a physical register or a memory location.
2. Within a global live range $LR_j$, the distinct references may execute different numbers of times. In a local live range, all references execute once per execution of the block (unless an exception occurs). Thus, the cost of local spilling is uniform. In a global allocator, the cost of spilling depends on where the spill code occurs. The problem of choosing a value to spill is, thus, much more complex in the global case than in the local case.
   Global allocators annotate each reference with an estimated execution frequency, derived from static analysis or from profile data. Allocation then uses these annotations to guide decisions about both allocation and spilling.

Any global allocator must address both these issues. Each of these issues makes global allocation substantially more complex than local allocation.

Global allocators make decisions about both allocation and assignment. They decide, for each live range, whether or not it will reside in a register. They decide, for each enregistered live range, whether or not it can share a register with other live ranges. They choose, for each enregistered live range, a specific physical register for that live range.

**GRAPH COLORING**

Many global register allocators use *graph coloring* as a paradigm to model the underlying allocation problem. For an arbitrary graph *G*, a coloring of *G* assigns a color to each node in *G* so that no pair of adjacent nodes have the same color. A coloring that uses *k* colors is termed a *k*-coloring, and the smallest such *k* for a given graph is called the graph's *chromatic number*. Consider the following graphs:

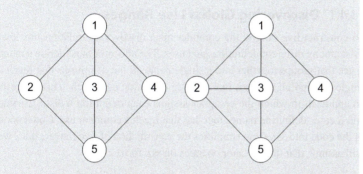

The graph on the left is two-colorable. For example, we can assign *blue* to nodes 1 and 5, and *red* to nodes 2, 3, and 4. Adding the edge (2,3), as shown on the right, makes the graph three-colorable, but not two-colorable. (Assign *blue* to nodes 1 and 5, *red* to nodes 2 and 4, and *yellow* to node 3.)

For a given graph, the problem of finding its chromatic number is NP-complete. Similarly, the problem of determining if a graph is *k*-colorable, for some fixed *k*, is NP-complete. Algorithms that use graph coloring as a paradigm to allocate resources use approximate methods to find colorings that fit the set of available resources.

To make these decisions, many compilers perform register allocation using an analogy to graph coloring. Graph-coloring allocators build a graph, called the *interference graph*, to model the conflicts between live ranges. They attempt to construct a *k*-coloring for that graph, where *k* is the number of physical registers available to the allocator. (Some physical registers, such as the ARP, may be dedicated to other purposes.) A *k*-coloring for the interference graph translates directly into an assignment of the live ranges to physical registers. If the compiler cannot directly construct a *k*-coloring for the graph, it modifies the underlying code by spilling some values to memory and tries again. Because spilling simplifies the graph, this process is guaranteed to halt.

**Interference graph**
a graph where the nodes represent live ranges and an edge $(i,j)$ indicates that $LR_i$ and $LR_j$ cannot share a register

Different coloring allocators handle spilling (or allocation) in different ways. We will look at top-down allocators that use high-level information to make allocation decisions and at bottom-up allocators that use low-level information to make those decisions. Before examining these two approaches, however, we explore some of the subproblems that the allocators have in common: discovering live ranges, estimating spill costs, and building an interference graph.

### 13.4.1 **Discovering Global Live Ranges**

To construct live ranges, the compiler must discover the relationships that exist among different definitions and uses. The allocator must derive a name space that groups together into a single name all the definitions that reach a single use and all the uses that a single definition can reach. This suggests an approach in which the compiler assigns each definition a distinct name and merges definition names together that reach a common use. Conversion of the code into SSA form simplifies the construction of live ranges; thus, we will assume that the allocator operates on SSA form.

The SSA form of the code provides a natural starting point for this construction. Recall that in SSA form, each name is defined once, and each use refers to one definition. The $\phi$-functions inserted to reconcile these two rules record the fact that distinct definitions on different paths in the control-flow graph reach a single reference. An operation that references the name defined by a $\phi$-function uses the value of one of its arguments; which argument depends on how control flow reached the $\phi$-function. All those definitions should reside in the same register and, thus, belong in the same live range. The $\phi$-functions allow the compiler to build live ranges efficiently.

The compiler can represent global live ranges as a set of one or more SSA names.

To build live ranges from SSA form, the allocator uses the disjoint-set union-find algorithm and makes a single pass over the code. The allocator treats each SSA name, or definition, as a set in the algorithm. It examines each $\phi$-function in the program, and unions together the sets associated with each $\phi$-function parameter and the set for the $\phi$-function result. After all the $\phi$-functions have been processed, the resulting sets represent the live ranges in the code. At this point, the allocator can either rewrite the code to use live-range names or it can create and maintain a mapping between SSA names and live-range names.

Figure 13.3a shows a code fragment in semipruned SSA form that involves source-code variables, a, b, c, and d. To find the live ranges, the allocator assigns each SSA name a set containing its name. It unions together the sets associated with names used in the $\phi$-function, $\{d_0\} \cup \{d_1\} \cup \{d_2\}$. This gives a final set of four live ranges: $LR_a$ that contains $\{a_0\}$, $LR_b$ that contains $\{b_0\}$,

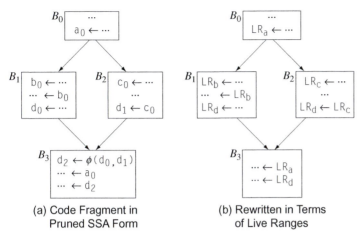

(a) Code Fragment in
Pruned SSA Form

(b) Rewritten in Terms
of Live Ranges

■ **FIGURE 13.3** Discovering Live Ranges.

LR$_c$ that contains$\{c_0\}$, and LR$_d$ that contains $\{d_0, d_1, d_2\}$. Figure 13.3b shows the code rewritten to use live-range names.

In Section 9.3.5, we saw that transformations applied to the SSA form can introduce complications into this rewriting process. If the allocator builds SSA form, uses it to find live ranges, and rewrites the code without performing other transformations, then it can simply replace SSA names with live-range names. On the other hand, if the allocator uses SSA form that has already been transformed, the rewrite process must deal with the complications described in Section 9.3.5. Since most compilers will perform allocation after instruction selection and, possibly, instruction scheduling, the code that the allocator consumes will not be in SSA form. This forces the allocator to build SSA form for the code and ensures that the rewriting process is straightforward.

### 13.4.2 Estimating Global Spill Costs

To make informed spill decisions, the global allocator needs an estimate of the cost of spilling each value. The cost of a spill has three components: the address computation, the memory operation, and an estimated execution frequency.

The compiler writer can choose where in memory to keep spilled values. Typically, they reside in a designated register-save area in the current activation record (AR) to minimize the cost of the address computation (see Figure 6.4). Storing spilled values in the AR lets the allocator generate operations such as a loadAI or storeAI relative to r$_{arp}$ for the spill. Such operations usually avoid the need for additional registers to compute the memory address of a spilled value.

**Scratchpad memory**

Dedicated, noncached, local memory is sometimes called *scratchpad* memory.

Scratchpad memory is a feature in some embedded processors.

The cost of the memory operation is, in general, unavoidable. For each spilled value, the compiler must generate a store after each definition and a load before each use. As memory latencies rise, the costs of these spill operations grow. If the target processor has a fast scratchpad memory, the compiler might lower the cost of spill operations by spilling to the scratchpad memory. To make matters worse, the allocator inserts spill operations into regions where demand for registers is high. In those regions, lack of free registers may constrain the scheduler's ability to hide the memory latency. Thus, the compiler writer must hope that spill locations stay in the cache. (Paradoxically, those locations stay in the cache only if they are accessed often enough to avoid replacement—suggesting that the code is executing too many spill operations.)

### Accounting for Execution Frequencies

To account for the different execution frequencies of the basic blocks in the control-flow graph, the compiler should annotate each block with an estimated execution count. The compiler can derive these estimates from profile data or from heuristics. Many compilers simply assume that each loop executes 10 times. This assumption assigns a weight of 10 to a load inside one loop, 100 to a load inside two nested loops, and so on. An unpredictable if-then-else would decrease the estimated frequency by half. In practice, these estimates ensure a bias toward spilling in outer loops rather than inner loops.

To estimate the cost of spilling a single reference, the allocator adds the cost of the address computation to the cost of the memory operation and multiplies that sum by the estimated execution frequency of the reference. For each live range, it sums the costs of the individual references. This requires a pass over all the blocks in the code. The allocator can precompute these costs for all live ranges, or it can wait to compute them until it discovers that it must spill at least one value.

### Negative Spill Costs

A live range that contains a load, a store, and no other uses should receive a negative spill cost if the load and store refer to the same address. (Such a live range can result from transformations intended to improve the code; for example, if the use were optimized away and the store resulted from a procedure call rather than the definition of a new value.) Sometimes, spilling a live range may eliminate copy operations with a higher cost than the spill operations; such a live range also has a negative cost. Any live range with a negative spill cost should be spilled, since doing so decreases demand for registers *and* removes instructions from the code.

### Infinite Spill Costs

Some live ranges are so short that spilling them does not help. Consider the short live range shown in the left margin. If the allocator tries to spill $vr_i$, it will insert a store after the definition and a load before the use, creating two new live ranges. Neither of these new live ranges uses fewer registers than the original live range, so the spill produces no benefit. The allocator should assign the original live range a spill cost of infinity, ensuring that the allocator does not try to spill it. In general, a live range should have infinite spill cost if no other live range ends between its definitions and its uses. This condition stipulates that availability of registers does not change between the definitions and uses.

$$vr_i \qquad \leftarrow \cdots$$
$$Mem[vr_j] \leftarrow vr_i$$

A Live Range With
Infinite Spill Cost

### 13.4.3 **Interferences and the Interference Graph**

The fundamental effect that a global register allocator must model is the competition among values for space in the processor's register set. Consider two distinct live ranges, $LR_i$ and $LR_j$. If there is an operation in the program during which both $LR_i$ and $LR_j$ are live, they cannot reside in the same register. (In general, a physical register can hold just one value at a time.) We say that $LR_i$ and $LR_j$ *interfere*.

**Interference**
Two live ranges, $LR_i$ and $LR_j$ *interfere* if one is live at the definition of the other and they have different values.

To model the allocation problem, the compiler can build an interference graph $I = (N,E)$, in which nodes in $N$ represent individual live ranges and edges in $E$ represent interferences between live ranges. Thus, an undirected edge $(n_i, n_j) \in I$ exists if and only if the corresponding live ranges $LR_i$ and $LR_j$ interfere. Figure 13.4 shows the code from Figure 13.3b along with its interference graph. As the graph shows, $LR_a$ interferes with each of the other live ranges. The rest of the live ranges, however, do not interfere with each other.

If the compiler can color $I$ with $k$ or fewer colors, then it can map the colors directly onto physical registers to produce a legal allocation. In the example, $LR_a$ cannot receive the same color as $LR_b$, $LR_c$, or $LR_d$ because it interferes with each of them. However, the other three live ranges can all share a single color because they do not interfere with each other. Thus, the interference graph is two-colorable, and the code can be rewritten to use just two registers.

Consider what would happen if another phase of the compiler reordered the two operations at the end of $B_1$. This change makes $LR_b$ live at the definition of $LR_d$. The allocator must add the edge $(LR_b, LR_d)$ to $E$, which makes

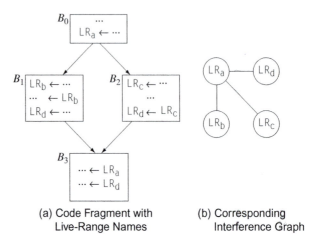

(a) Code Fragment with
Live-Range Names

(b) Corresponding
Interference Graph

■ **FIGURE 13.4** Live Ranges and Interference.

it impossible to color the graph with just two colors. (The graph is small enough to prove this by enumeration.) To handle this graph, the allocator has two options: to use three registers, or, if the target machine has only two registers, to spill one of $LR_b$ or $LR_a$ before the definition of $LR_d$ in $B_1$. Of course, the allocator could also reorder the two operations and eliminate the interference between $LR_b$ and $LR_d$. Typically, register allocators do not reorder operations. Instead, allocators assume a fixed order of operations and leave ordering questions to the instruction scheduler (see Chapter 12.)

### Building the Interference Graph

Once the allocator has built global live ranges and annotated each basic block in the code with its LIVEOUT set, it can construct the interference graph in a simple linear pass over each block. Figure 13.5 shows the basic algorithm. As it walks the block, from bottom to top, the allocator computes LIVENOW, the set of values that are live at the current operation. (We saw LIVENOW in Section 11.5.1.) At the last operation in the block, LIVEOUT and LIVENOW must be identical. As the algorithm walks backward through the block, it adds the appropriate interference edges to the graph and updates the LIVENOW set to reflect the operation's impact.

The algorithm implements the definition of interference given earlier: $LR_i$ and $LR_j$ interfere only if one is live at a definition of the other. This definition allows the compiler to build the interference graph by adding, at each operation, an interference between the target of the operation, $LR_c$, and each live range that is live after the operation.

Copy operations require special treatment. A copy $LR_i \Rightarrow LR_j$ does not create an interference between $LR_i$ and $LR_j$ because the two live ranges have the

```
for each LRᵢ
    create a node nᵢ ∈ N
for each basic block b
    LIVENOW ← LIVEOUT(b)
        for each operation opₙ, opₙ₋₁, opₙ₋₂, ...op₁ in b
            with form opᵢ LRₐ, LR_b ⇒ LR_c
                for each LRⱼ ∈ LIVENOW
                    add (LR_c, LRⱼ) to E
                remove LR_c from LIVENOW
                add LRₐ and LR_b to LIVENOW
```

■ **FIGURE 13.5** Constructing the Interference Graph.

same value and therefore can occupy the same register. Thus, the operation should not induce an edge $(LR_i, LR_j)$ in $E$. If subsequent context creates an interference between these live ranges, that operation will create the edge. Likewise, a $\phi$-function does not create an interference between any of its arguments and its result. Treating copies and $\phi$-functions in this way creates an interference graph that precisely captures when $LR_i$ and $LR_j$ can occupy the same register.

To improve the allocator's efficiency, the compiler should build both a lower-diagonal bit matrix and a set of adjacency lists to represent $E$. The bit matrix allows a constant-time test for interference, while the adjacency lists allows efficient iteration over a node's neighbors. The two-representation strategy uses more space than a single representation would, but pays off in reduced allocation time. As suggested in Section 13.2.3, the allocator can build separate graphs for disjoint register classes, which reduces the maximum graph size.

### Building an Allocator

To build a global allocator based on the graph-coloring paradigm, the compiler writer needs two additional mechanisms. First, the allocator needs an efficient technique to discover $k$-colorings. Unfortunately, the problem of determining if a $k$-coloring exists for a particular graph is NP-complete. Thus, register allocators use fast approximations that are not guaranteed to find a $k$-coloring. Second, the allocator needs a strategy that handles the case when no color remains for a specific live range. Most coloring allocators approach this by rewriting the code to change the allocation problem. The allocator picks one or more live ranges to modify. It either spills or *splits* the chosen live ranges. Spilling turns the chosen live range into sets of tiny

**Live-range splitting**
If the allocator cannot keep a live range in one register, it can break the live range into smaller pieces, connected by copies or by loads and stores. The new smaller live ranges may fit into registers.

live ranges, one at each definition or use of the original live range. Splitting breaks the chosen live range into smaller, but nontrivial, pieces. In either case, the transformed code performs the same computation but has a different interference graph. If the changes are effective, the new interference graph is $k$-colorable. If they are not, the allocator must spill or split more live ranges.

### 13.4.4 **Top-Down Coloring**

A top-down graph-coloring global register allocator uses low-level information to assign colors to individual live ranges and high-level information to select the order in which it colors live ranges. To find a color for a specific live range $LR_i$ the allocator tallies the colors already assigned to $LR_i$'s neighbors in $I$. If the set of neighbors' colors is incomplete—that is, one or more colors are not used—the allocator can assign an unused color to $LR_i$. If the set of neighbors' colors is complete, then no color is available for $LR_i$ and the allocator must use its strategy for uncolored live ranges.

The top-down allocators try to color the live ranges in an order determined by some ranking function. The priority-based, top-down allocators assign each node a rank that is the estimated runtime savings that accrue from keeping that live range in a register. These estimates are analogous to the spill costs described in Section 13.4.2. The top-down global allocator uses registers for the most important values, as identified by these rankings.

The allocator considers the live ranges in rank order and attempts to assign a color to each of them. If no color is available for a live range, the allocator invokes the spilling or splitting mechanism to handle the uncolored live range. To improve the process, the allocator can partition the live ranges into two sets—constrained live ranges and unconstrained live ranges. A live range is *constrained* if it has $k$ or more neighbors—that is, it has degree $\geq k$ in $I$. Constrained live ranges are colored first, in rank order. After all constrained live ranges have been handled, the unconstrained live ranges are colored, in any order. Because an unconstrained live range has fewer than $k$ neighbors, the allocator can always find a color for it; no assignment of colors to its neighbors can use all $k$ colors.

We denote "degree of $LR_i$" as $LR_i^\circ$. $LR_i$ is constrained if and only if $LR_i^\circ \geq k$.

By handling constrained live ranges first, the allocator avoids some potential spills. The alternative, working in a straight priority order, would let the allocator assign all available colors to unconstrained, but higher priority, neighbors of $LR_i$. This approach could force $LR_i$ to remain uncolored, even though colorings of its unconstrained neighbors that leave a color for $LR_i$ must exist.

### Handling Spills

When the top-down allocator encounters a live range that cannot be colored, it must either spill or split some set of live ranges to change the problem. Since all previously colored live ranges were ranked higher than the uncolored live range, it makes sense to spill the uncolored live range rather than a previously colored one. The allocator can consider recoloring one of the previously colored live ranges, but it must exercise care to avoid the full generality and cost of backtracking.

To spill $LR_i$, the allocator inserts a store after every definition of $LR_i$ and a load before each use of $LR_i$. If the memory operations need registers, the allocator can reserve enough registers to handle them. (For example, a register is needed to hold the spilled value when it is loaded before a use.) The number of registers needed for this purpose is a function of the target machine's instruction set architecture. Reserving these registers simplifies spilling.

An alternative to reserving registers for spill code is to look for free colors at each definition and use; if no color is available, the allocator must retroactively spill a live range that has already colored. In this scheme, the allocator would insert the spill code, which removes the original live range and creates a new short live range, $s$. It would recompute interferences in the neighborhood of the spill site and tally the colors assigned to the neighbors of $s$. If this process does not discover an available color for $s$, the allocator spills the lowest-priority neighbor of $s$.

Of course, this scheme has the potential to spill previously colored live ranges recursively. This feature has led most implementors of top-down, priority-based allocators to reserve spill registers instead. The paradox, of course, is that reserving registers for spilling may itself cause spills by effectively lowering $k$.

### Live-Range Splitting

Spilling changes the coloring problem. An uncolored live range is broken into a series of tiny live ranges, one at each definition or use. Another way to change the problem is to split an uncolored live range into new live ranges—subranges that contain several references. If the new live ranges interfere with fewer live ranges than did the original live range, they may receive colors. For example, some of the new live ranges may be unconstrained. Live-range splitting can avoid spilling the original live range at every reference; with well-chosen split points, it can isolate the portions of the live range that the allocator must spill.

The first top-down, priority-based coloring allocator, built by Chow, broke the uncolored live range into single-block live ranges, counted interferences for each resulting live range, and then recombined live ranges from adjacent blocks if the combined live range remained unconstrained. It placed an arbitrary upper limit on the number of blocks that a split live range could span. It inserted a load at the starting point of each split live range and a store at the live range's ending point. The allocator spilled any split live ranges that remained uncolored.

### 13.4.5 **Bottom-Up Coloring**

Bottom-up graph-coloring register allocators use many of the same mechanisms as top-down global allocators. These allocators discover live ranges, build an interference graph, attempt to color it, and generate spill code when needed. The major distinction between top-down and bottom-up allocators lies in the mechanism used to order live ranges for coloring. While a top-down allocator uses high-level information to select an order for coloring, a bottom-up allocator computes an order from detailed structural knowledge about the interference graph. Such an allocator constructs a linear order in which to consider the live ranges and assign colors in that order.

To order the live ranges, a bottom-up, graph-coloring allocator relies on the fact that unconstrained live ranges are trivial to color. It assigns colors in an order where every node has fewer than $k$ colored neighbors. The algorithm computes the coloring order for a graph $I = (N, E)$ as follows:

```
initialize stack to empty
while (N ≠ ∅)
    if ∃ n ∈ N with n° < k
        then node ← n
        else node ← n picked from N
    remove node and its edges from I
    push node onto stack
```

The allocator repeatedly removes a node from the graph and places the node on a stack. It uses two distinct mechanisms to select the node to remove next. The first clause takes a node that is unconstrained in the graph from which it is removed. Because these nodes are unconstrained, the order in which they are removed does not matter. Removing an unconstrained node decreases the degree of each of its neighbors and may make them unconstrained. The second clause, invoked only when every remaining node is constrained, picks a node using some external criteria. Any node removed by this clause has more than $k$ neighbors and, thus, may not receive a color during the assignment phase. The loop halts when the graph is empty. At that point, the stack contains all the nodes in order of removal.

To color the graph, the allocator rebuilds the interference graph in the order represented by the stack—the reverse of the order in which the allocator removed them from the graph. It repeatedly pops a node $n$ from the stack, inserts $n$ and its edges back into $I$, and picks a color for $n$. The algorithm is:

```
while (stack ≠ Ø)
    node ← pop(stack)
    insert node and its edges into I
    color node
```

To pick a color for node $n$, the allocator tallies the colors of $n$'s neighbors in the current approximation to $I$ and assigns $n$ an unused color. To pick a specific color, it can search in a consistent order each time, or it can assign colors in a round-robin fashion. (In our experience, the mechanism used for color choice has little practical impact.) If no color remains for $n$, it is left uncolored.

When the stack is empty, $I$ has been rebuilt. If every node has a color, the allocator declares success and rewrites the code, replacing live-range names with physical registers. If any node remains uncolored, the allocator either spills the corresponding live range or splits it into smaller pieces. At this point, the classic bottom-up allocators rewrite the code to reflect the spills and splits and repeat the entire process—finding live ranges, building $I$, and coloring it. The process repeats until every node in $I$ receives a color. Typically, the allocator halts in a couple of iterations. Of course, a bottom-up allocator could reserve registers for spilling, as the top-down allocator does. This strategy would allow it to halt after a single pass.

### Why Does This Work?

The bottom-up allocator inserts each node back into the graph from which it was removed. If the reduction algorithm removes the node representing $LR_i$ from $I$ through its first clause (because it was unconstrained at the time of removal), then it reinserts $LR_i$ into a graph in which it is also unconstrained. Thus, when the allocator inserts $LR_i$, a color must be available for $LR_i$. The only way that a node $n$ can fail to receive a color is if $n$ was removed from $I$ using the spill metric. Such a node is inserted into a graph in which it has $k$ or more neighbors. However, a color may still be available for $n$. Assume that $n° > k$ when the allocator inserts it into $I$. Its neighbors cannot all have distinct colors, since they can have at most $k$ colors. If they have precisely $k$ colors, then the allocator finds no color for $n$. If, instead, they use fewer than $k$ colors, then the allocator finds a color available for $n$.

The reduction algorithm determines the order in which nodes are colored. This order is crucial, in that it determines whether or not colors are available. For nodes removed from the graph because they are unconstrained, the order is unimportant with respect to the remaining nodes. The order may be important with respect to nodes already on the stack; after all, the current node may have been constrained until some of the earlier nodes were removed. For nodes removed from the graph using the `else` clause, the order is crucial. This clause executes only when every remaining node is constrained. Thus, the remaining nodes form one or more heavily connected subgraphs of $I$.

The heuristic used by the else clause to pick a node is often called the *spill metric*. The original bottom-up graph-coloring allocator, built by Chaitin et al., used a simple spill metric. It picked a node that minimized the ratio of $\frac{cost}{degree}$, where *cost* is the estimated spill cost and *degree* is the node's degree in the current graph. This metric balances between spill cost and the number of nodes whose degree will decrease.

Other spill metrics have been tried. These include $\frac{cost}{degree^2}$, which emphasizes the impact on neighbors; straight cost, which emphasizes runtime speed; and counting the spill operations, which decreases code size. The first two, $\frac{cost}{degree}$ and $\frac{cost}{degree^2}$, attempt to balance cost and impact; the latter two, cost and spill operations, aim to optimize specific criteria. In practice, no single heuristic dominates the others. Since the actual coloring process is fast relative to building $I$, the allocator can try several colorings, each using a different spill metric, and retain the best result.

### 13.4.6 **Coalescing Copies to Reduce Degree**

The compiler writer can use the interference graph to determine when two live ranges that are connected by a copy can be *coalesced*, or combined. Consider the operation i2i $LR_i \Rightarrow LR_j$. If $LR_i$ and $LR_j$ do not otherwise interfere, the operation can be eliminated and all references to $LR_j$ rewritten to use $LR_i$. Combining these live ranges has several beneficial effects. It eliminates the copy operation, making the code smaller and, potentially, faster. It reduces the degree of any $LR_k$ that interfered with both $LR_i$ and $LR_j$. It shrinks the set of live ranges, making $I$ and many of the data structures

```
add  LRt , LRu  ⇒ LRa  ⌐a          add  LRt , LRu   ⇒ LRab  ⌐ab
                                                            
     . . .                              . . .               
                                                            
i2i LRa       ⇒ LRb   ⌐b                                    
                                   i2i LRab        ⇒ LRc    
i2i LRa       ⇒ LRc   │   ⌐c                           ⌐c  
                      │                 . . .               
     . . .            │                                     
                      │            add  LRab , LRw  ⇒ LRx   
add  LRb , LRw ⇒ LRx  └                                     
                                   add  LRc , LRy   ⇒ LRz   
add  LRc , LRy ⇒ LRz  └
```

|  (a) Before Coalescing | (b) After Coalescing LRa and LRb |

■ **FIGURE 13.6** Coalescing Live Ranges.

related to $I$ smaller. (In his thesis, Briggs shows examples where coalescing eliminates up to one-third of the live ranges.) Because these effects help in allocation, compilers often perform coalescing before the coloring stage in a global allocator.

Figure 13.6 shows an example. The original code appears in panel a, with lines to the right of the code that indicate the regions where each of the relevant values, $LR_a$, $LR_b$, and $LR_c$ are live. Even though $LR_a$ overlaps both $LR_b$ and $LR_c$, it interferes with neither of them because the source and destination of a copy do not interfere. Since $LR_b$ is live at the definition of $LR_c$, they do interfere. Both copy operations are candidates for coalescing.

Figure 13.6b shows the result of coalescing $LR_a$ and $LR_b$ to produce $LR_{ab}$. Since $LR_c$ is defined by a copy from $LR_{ab}$, they do not interfere. Combining $LR_a$ and $LR_b$ to form $LR_{ab}$ lowered the degree of $LR_c$. In general, coalescing two live ranges cannot increase the degrees of any of their neighbors. It can decrease their degrees or leave their degrees unchanged, but it cannot increase their degrees.

To perform coalescing, the allocator walks each block and examines each copy operation in the block. Consider a copy i2i $LR_i$ ⇒ $LR_j$. If $LR_i$ and $LR_j$ do not interfere $(LR_i , LR_j) \notin E$, the allocator combines them, eliminates the copy, and updates $I$ to reflect the combination. The allocator can conservatively update $I$ by moving all edges from the node for $LR_j$ to the node for $LR_i$—in effect, using $LR_i$ as $LR_{ij}$. This update is not precise, but it lets the allocator continue coalescing. In practice, allocators coalesce every live range allowed by $I$, then rewrite the code, rebuild $I$, and try again. The process typically halts after a couple of rounds of coalescing.

The example illustrates the imprecision inherent in this conservative update to $I$. The update would leave an interference between $LR_{ab}$ and $LR_C$ when, in fact, that interference does not exist. Rebuilding $I$ from the transformed code produces the precise interference graph, with no edge between $LR_{ab}$ and $LR_C$, and allows the allocator to coalesce $LR_{ab}$ and $LR_C$.

Because coalescing two live ranges can prevent subsequent coalescing of other live ranges, the order of coalescing matters. In principle, the compiler should coalesce the most frequently executed copies first. Thus, the allocator might coalesce copies in order by the loop nesting depth of the block where the copies are found. To implement this, the allocator can consider the basic blocks in order from most deeply nested to least deeply nested.

In practice, the cost of building the interference graph for the first round of coalescing dominates the overall cost of the graph-coloring allocator. Subsequent passes through the build-coalesce loop process a smaller graph and, therefore, run more quickly. To reduce the cost of coalescing, the compiler can build a subset of the reduced interference graph—one that only includes live ranges involved in a copy operation. This observation applies the insight from semipruned SSA form to interference graph construction—only include names that matter.

### 13.4.7 Comparing Top-Down and Bottom-Up Global Allocators

Both the top-down and the bottom-up coloring allocators have the same basic structure, shown in Figure 13.7. They find live ranges, build the inter-

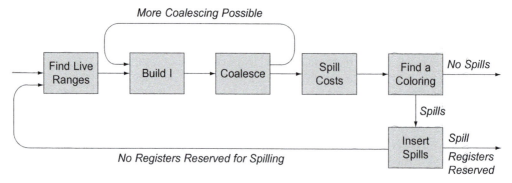

■ **FIGURE 13.7** Structure of the Coloring Allocators.

ference graph, coalesce live ranges, compute spill costs on the coalesced version of the code, and attempt a coloring. The build-coalesce process is repeated until it finds no more opportunities. After coloring, one of two situations occurs. If it assigns every live range a color, then it rewrites the code using physical register names, and allocation terminates. If some live ranges remain uncolored, then it inserts spill code.

If the allocator has reserved registers for spilling, then it uses those registers in the spill code, rewrites the colored registers with their physical register names, and the process terminates. Otherwise, the allocator invents new virtual register names to use in spilling and inserts the necessary loads and stores to accomplish the spills. This changes the coloring problem slightly, so the entire allocation process is repeated on the transformed code. When each live range has a color, the allocator maps colors onto real registers and rewrites the code in its final form.

Of course, a top-down allocator could adopt the spill-and-iterate philosophy used in the bottom-up allocator. This would eliminate the need to reserve registers for spilling. Similarly, a bottom-up allocator could reserve several registers for spilling and eliminate the need for iterating the entire allocation process. Spill-and-iterate trades additional compile time for an allocation that, potentially, uses less spill code. Reserving registers produces an allocation that, potentially, contains more spills but requires less compile time to produce.

The top-down allocator uses its priority ranking to order all the constrained nodes. It colors the unconstrained nodes in arbitrary order, since the order cannot change the fact that they receive a color. The bottom-up allocator constructs an order in which most nodes are colored in a graph where they are unconstrained. Every node that the top-down allocator classifies as unconstrained is colored by the bottom-up allocator, since it is unconstrained in the original graph and in each graph derived by removing nodes and edges from $I$. The bottom-up allocator also classifies some nodes as unconstrained that the top-down allocator treats as constrained. These nodes may also be colored in the top-down allocator; there is no clear way of comparing their performance on these nodes without implementing both algorithms and running them.

The truly hard-to-color nodes are those that the bottom-up allocator removes from the graph with its spill metric. The spill metric is invoked only when every remaining node is constrained. These nodes form a strongly connected subgraph of $I$. In the top-down allocator, these nodes will be colored in an order determined by their rank or priority. In the bottom-up allocator,

---

**LINEAR SCAN ALLOCATION**

Linear scan allocators begin from the assumption that they can represent global live ranges with a simple interval $[i,j]$ as we did in local allocation. This representation overestimates the extent of the live range to ensure that it includes both the earliest and the latest operation where the live range is live. The overestimate ensures that the resulting interference graph is an interval graph.

Interval graphs are much simpler than the general graphs that arise in global register allocation; for example, the interference graph of a single block is always an interval graph. From a complexity standpoint, interval graphs offer advantages to the allocator. While the problem of determining if an arbitrary graph is $k$-colorable is NP-complete, the same problem is solvable in linear time on an interval graph.

The interval representation is less expensive to build than the precise interference graph. Interval graphs lends themselves to allocation algorithms, such as the bottom-up local algorithm, that are simpler than the global allocators. Because both allocation and assignment can be performed in a single linear pass over the code, this approach is called *linear scan allocation*.

Linear scan allocators avoid building the complex precise global interference graph—the most expensive step in graph-coloring global allocators—as well as the $O(N^2)$ loop to choose spill candidates. Thus, they use much less compile time than do global graph-coloring allocators. In some applications, such as just-in-time compilers (JITs), the tradeoff between speed of allocation and increase in spill code makes these linear scan allocators attractive.

Linear scan allocation has all of the subtlety seen in the global allocators. For example, using the top-down local algorithm in a linear scan allocator spills a live range everywhere it occurs, while using the bottom-up local algorithm spills it at precisely those points where the spill is needed. The imprecise notion of interference means that these allocators must use other mechanisms to coalesce copies.

---

the spill metric uses that same ranking, moderated by a measurement of how many other nodes have their degree lowered by each choice. Thus, the top-down allocator chooses to spill low-priority, constrained nodes, while the bottom-up allocator spills nodes that are still constrained after all unconstrained nodes have been removed. From this latter set it picks nodes that minimize the spill metric.

## 13.4.8 **Encoding Machine Constraints in the Interference Graph**

Register allocation must deal with idiosyncratic properties of the target machine and its calling convention. Some of the constraints that arise in practice can be encoded in the coloring process.

### *Multiregister Values*

Consider a target machine that requires an aligned pair of adjacent registers for each double-precision floating-point value and a program with two single-precision live ranges $LR_a$ and $LR_b$ and one double-precision live range $LR_c$.

With interferences $(LR_a, LR_c)$ and $(LR_b, LR_c)$, the techniques described in Section 13.4.3 produce the graph shown in the margin. Three registers, $r_0, r_1$, and $r_2$, with a single aligned pair, $(r_0, r_1)$, should suffice for this graph. $LR_a$ and $LR_b$ can share $r_2$, leaving the pair $(r_0, r_1)$ for $LR_c$. Unfortunately, this graph does not adequately represent the actual constraints on allocation.

Given $k = 3$, the bottom-up coloring allocator assigns colors in arbitrary order since no node has degree $\geq k$. If the allocator considers $LR_c$, first it will succeed, since $(r_0, r_1)$ is free to hold $LR_c$. If either $LR_a$ or $LR_b$ is colored first, the allocator might use either $r_0$ or $r_1$, creating a situation in which the aligned register pair is not available for $LR_c$.

To force the desired order, the allocator can insert two edges to represent an interference with a value that needs two registers. This produces the graph at left. With this graph and $k = 3$, the bottom-up allocator must remove one of $LR_a$ or $LR_b$ first, since $LR_c$ has degree 4. This ensures that two registers are available for $LR_c$.

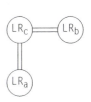

The doubled edges produce a correct allocation because they match the degree of nodes that interfere with $LR_c$ with the actual resource requirements. It does not ensure that an adjacent pair is available for $LR_c$. Poor assignment can leave $LR_c$ without a pair. For example, in the coloring order $LR_a, LR_c, LR_b$, the allocator might assign $LR_a$ to $r_1$. The compiler writer might bias the coloring order in favor of $LR_c$ by choosing single-register values first among unconstrained nodes (the first clause in the graph-reduction algorithm). Another approach the allocator can take is to perform limited recoloring among $LR_c$'s neighbors if an appropriate pair is not available when it tries to assign colors.

### Specific Register Placement

The register allocator must also deal with requirements for the specific placement of live ranges. These constraints arise from several sources. The linkage convention dictates the placement of values that are passed in registers; this can include the ARP some or all of the actual parameters, and the return value. Some operations may require their operands in particular registers; for example, the short unsigned multiply on the Intel x86 machines always writes its result into the $ax$ register.

As an example of the complications that arise from assigned registers in the procedure linkage, consider the typical convention on a PowerPC processor. By convention, the return value of a function is left in $r_3$. Suppose that the code being compiled has a function call and that the code represents the return value as $vr_i$. The allocator can force $vr_i$ into $r_3$ by adding edges from $vr_i$ to each physical register except $r_3$; this modification of the interference graph ensures that the color corresponding to $r_3$ is the only color available for $vr_i$. This solution, however, can overconstrain the interference graph.

To see the problem, assume that the code being compiled has two function calls and that the code represents those return values as $vr_i$ and $vr_j$. If $vr_i$ is live across the other call, the final code cannot keep both $vr_i$ and $vr_j$ in $r_3$. Constraining both virtual registers to map into $r_3$ will force one or both of them to spill.

The solution to this problem is to rely on code shape. The compiler can create a short live range for the return value at each call; say it uses $vr_1$ at the first call and $vr_2$ at the second call. It can constrain both $vr_1$ and $vr_2$ so that they map exclusively into $r_3$. It can add copy operations, $vr_1 \Rightarrow vr_i$ and $vr_2 \Rightarrow vr_j$. This approach creates correct code that decouples $vr_i$ and $vr_j$ from $r_3$. Of course, the allocator must constrain the coalescing mechanism to avoid combining live ranges with conflicting physical register constraints; in practice, the compiler might avoid coalescing any live range that has explicit interferences with physical registers.

As an example of the physical register constraints that an ISA can impose, consider the one-address integer multiply operation on an Intel x86 processor. It use the $ax$ register as its implicit second argument and as its result register. Consider mapping the IR sequence shown in the margin into x86 code. The compiler might constrain $vr_2$, $vr_1$, and $vr_5$ so that they map into the $ax$ register. In that case, the process might produce a code sequence similar to the pseudo-assembly code at the left, with the virtual register names, $vr_i$, replaced with their actual runtime locations. As long as the live ranges mapped to $ax$ are short, this strategy can produce high-quality code. Again, coalescing must be constrained on any live ranges that overlap other operations that require $ax$.

$vr_1 \leftarrow vr_2 \times vr_3$
$vr_5 \leftarrow vr_1 \times vr_4$

```
mov ax,vr2
imul vr3
imul vr4
```

**SECTION REVIEW**

Global register allocators consider the longer and more complex live ranges that arise from control-flow graphs that contain multiple blocks. Accordingly, global allocation is harder than local allocation. Most global allocators operate by analogy to graph coloring. The allocator builds a graph that represents the interferences between live ranges, and then it attempts to find a *k*-coloring for that graph, where *k* is the number of registers available to the allocator.

Graph-coloring allocators vary in the precision in their definition of a live range, in the precision with which they measure interference, in the algorithm used to find a *k*-coloring, and in the technique that they use to select values for spilling or splitting. In general, these allocators produce reasonable allocations with acceptable amounts of spill code. The major opportunities for improvement appear to be in the areas of spill choice, spill placement, and in live-range splitting.

**Review Questions**

1. The original top-down, priority-driven register allocator used a different notion of interference than that presented in Section 13.4.3. It added an edge $(LR_i, LR_j)$ to the graph if $LR_i$ and $LR_j$ were live in the same basic block. What impact would that definition have on the allocator? On register coalescing?

2. The bottom-up global allocator chooses values to spill by finding the value that minimizes some ratio, such as $\frac{spill\ cost}{degree}$. When the algorithm runs, it sometimes must choose several live ranges to spill before it makes any other live range unconstrained. Explain how this situation can happen. Can you envision a spill metric that avoids this problem?

## 13.5 ADVANCED TOPICS

Because the cost of a misstep during register allocation can be high, algorithms for register allocation have received a great deal of attention. Many variations on the basic graph-coloring allocation techniques have been published. Section 13.5.1 describes several of these approaches. Section 13.5.2 sketches another promising approach: using SSA names as live ranges in a global allocators.

### 13.5.1 Variations on Graph-Coloring Allocation

Many variations on these two basic styles of graph-coloring register allocation have appeared in the literature. This section describes several of these improvements. Some address the cost of allocation. Others address the quality of allocation.

### Imprecise Interference Graphs

Chow's top-down, priority-based allocator used an imprecise notion of inter-ference: live ranges $LR_i$ and $LR_j$ interfere if both are live in the same basic block. This makes building the interference graph faster. However, the imprecise nature of the graph overestimates the degree of some nodes and prevents the allocator from using the interference graph as a basis for coalescing. (In an imprecise graph, two live ranges connected by a useful copy interfere because they are live in the same block.) The allocator also included a prepass to perform local allocation on values that are live in only one block.

### Breaking the Graph into Smaller Pieces

If the interference graph can be separated into components that are not connected, those disjoint components can be colored independently. Since the size of the bit matrix is $\mathbf{O}(N^2)$, breaking it into independent compo-nents saves both space and time. One way to split the graph is to consider nonoverlapping register classes separately, as with floating-point registers and integer registers. A more complex alternative for large procedures is to discover clique separators, connected subgraphs whose removal divides the interference graph into several disjoint pieces. For large enough graphs, using a hash table instead of the bit matrix may improve both speed and space.

### Conservative Coalescing

**Conservative coalescing**
a form of coalescing that only combines $LR_i$ and $LR_j$ if $LR_{ij}$ receives a color

When the allocator coalesces two live ranges, $LR_i$ and $LR_j$, the new live range, $LR_{ij}$, may be more constrained than either $LR_i$ or $LR_j$. If $LR_i$ and $LR_j$ have distinct neighbors, then $LR_{ij}^\circ > \max(LR_i^\circ, LR_j^\circ)$. If $LR_{ij}^\circ < k$, then creating $LR_{ij}$ is strictly beneficial. However, if $LR_i^\circ < k$ and $LR_j^\circ < k$, but $LR_{ij}^\circ \geq k$, then coalescing $LR_i$ and $LR_j$ can make $I$ harder to color without spilling. To avoid this problem, the compiler writer can use a limited form of coalescing called *conservative coalescing*. In this scheme, the allocator only combines $LR_i$ and $LR_j$ if $LR_{ij}$ has fewer than $k$ neighbors of "significant" degree—that is, neighbors in $I$ that themselves have $k$ or more neighbors. This restriction ensures that coalescing $LR_i$ and $LR_j$ does not make $I$ harder to color.

If the allocator uses conservative coalescing, another improvement is possi-ble. When the allocator reaches a point at which every remaining live range is constrained, the basic algorithm selects a spill candidate. An alternative approach is to reapply coalescing at this point. Live ranges that were not coalesced because of the degree of the resulting live range may well coa-lesce in the reduced graph. Coalescing at this point may reduce the degree of nodes that interfere with both the source and destination of the copy. This style of *iterated coalescing* can remove additional copies and reduce the degrees of nodes. It may create one or more unconstrained nodes and allow coloring to proceed. If iterated coalescing does not create any unconstrained nodes, spilling proceeds as before.

*Biased coloring* is another approach to coalescing copies without making the graph harder to color. In this approach, the allocator tries to assign the same color to live ranges that are connected by a copy. In picking a color for $LR_i$, it first tries colors that have been assigned to live ranges connected to $LR_j$ by a copy operation. If it can assign them both the same color, the allocator eliminates the copy. With a careful implementation, this adds little or no expense to the color selection process.

### Spilling Partial Live Ranges

As described, both approaches to global allocation spill entire live ranges. This approach can lead to overspilling if the demand for registers is low through most of the live range and high in a small region. More sophisticated spilling techniques find the regions where spilling a live range is productive—that is, the spill frees a register in a region where a register is truly needed. The splitting scheme described for the top-down allocator achieved this result by considering each block in the spilled live range separately. A bottom-up allocator can achieve similar results by spilling only in the region where interference occurs. One technique, called *interference-region spilling*, identifies a set of live ranges that interfere in the region of high demand and limits spilling to that region. The allocator can estimate the cost of several spilling strategies for the interference region and compare those costs against the standard spill-everywhere approach. By letting the alternatives compete on an estimated-cost basis, the allocator can improve overall allocation.

### Live-Range Splitting

Breaking a live range into pieces can improve the results of coloring-based register allocation. In principle, splitting harnesses two distinct effects. If the split live ranges have lower degrees than the original one, they may be easier to color—possibly even unconstrained. If some of the split live ranges have high degree and, therefore, spill, then splitting may prevent spilling other portions of the same live range that have lower degree. As a final, pragmatic effect, splitting introduces spills at the points where the live range is broken. Careful selection of the split points can control the placement of some spill code—for example, outside loops rather than inside them.

Many approaches to splitting have been tried. Section 13.4.4 describes one that breaks a live range into blocks and coalesces them back together if doing so does not change the allocator's ability to assign a color. Several approaches that use properties of the control-flow graph to choose splitting points have been tried. Briggs showed that many have been inconsistent [45]; however, two particular techniques show promise. A method called *zero-cost splitting* capitalizes on nops in the instruction schedule to split live ranges and improve both allocation and scheduling. A technique called *passive splitting* uses a directed interference graph to determine where splits should occur and selects between splitting and spilling based on their estimated costs.

### Rematerialization

Some values cost less to recompute than to spill. For example, small integer constants should be recreated with a load immediate rather than being retrieved from memory with a load. The allocator can recognize such values and rematerialize them rather than spill them.

Modifying a bottom-up graph-coloring allocator to perform rematerialization takes several small changes. The allocator must identify and tag SSA names that can be rematerialized. For example, any operation whose arguments are always available is a candidate. It can propagate these rematerialization tags over the code using the constant-propagation algorithm described in Chapter 9. In forming live ranges, the allocator should only combine SSA names that have identical rematerialization tags.

The compiler writer must make the spill-cost estimation handle rematerialization tags correctly, so that these values have accurate spill-cost estimates. The spill-code insertion process must also examine the tags and generate the appropriate lightweight spills for rematerializable values. Finally, the allocator should use conservative coalescing to avoid prematurely combining live ranges with distinct rematerialization tags.

### Ambiguous Values

In code that makes heavy use of ambiguous values, whether derived from source-language pointers, array references, or object references whose class cannot be determined at compile time, the allocator's ability or inability to keep such values in registers is a serious performance issue. To improve allocation of ambiguous values, several systems have included transformations that rewrite the code to keep unambiguous values in scalar local variables, even when their "natural" home is inside an array element or a pointer-based structure. Scalar replacement uses array-subscript analysis to identify reuse of array-element values and to introduce scalar temporary variables that hold reused values. Register promotion uses data-flow analysis of pointer values to determine when a pointer-based value can safely be kept in a register throughout a loop nest and to rewrite the code so that the value is kept in a newly introduced temporary variable. Both of these transformations encode the results of analysis into the shape of the code, making it obvious to the register allocator that these values can be kept in registers. These transformations can increase the demand for registers. In fact, promoting too many values can produce spill code whose cost exceeds the the cost of the memory operations that the transformation is intended to avoid. Ideally, these techniques should be integrated into the allocator in which realistic estimates of the demand for registers can be used to determine how many values to promote.

### 13.5.2 **Global Register Allocation over SSA Form**

The complexity of global register allocation shows up in many ways. In the graph-coloring formulation, that complexity exhibits itself in the fact that the problem of determining if a $k$-coloring of a general graph exists is NP-complete. For restricted classes of graphs, the coloring problem has polynomial-time solutions. For example, the interval graphs generated by a basic block can be colored in time linear in the size of the graph. To capitalize on this fact, linear scan allocators approximate global live ranges with simple intervals that produce an interval graph.

If the compiler builds an interference graph from SSA names rather than live ranges, the resulting graph is a *chordal graph*. The problem of $k$-coloring a chordal graph can be solved in $\mathbf{O}(|V| + |E|)$ time. This observation has sparked interest in global register allocation over the SSA form of the code.

**Chordal graph**
a graph in which every cycle of more than three nodes has a *chord*—an edge that joins two nodes that are not adjacent in the cycle

Working from SSA form simplifies some parts of the register allocator. The allocator can compute an optimal coloring for its interference graph, rather than relying on heuristic approaches to coloring. The optimal coloring may use fewer registers than the heuristic coloring would.

If the graph needs more than $k$ colors, the allocator still must spill one or more values. While SSA form does not lower the complexity of spill choice, it may offer some benefits. Global live ranges tend to have longer lifetimes than SSA names, which are broken by $\phi$-functions at appropriate places in the code, such as loop headers and blocks that follow loops. These breaks give the allocator the chance to spill values over smaller regions than it might have with global live ranges.

Unfortunately, SSA-based allocation leaves the code in SSA form. The allocator, or a postpass, must translate out of SSA form, with all of the complications discussed in Section 9.3.5. That translation may increase demand for registers. (If the translation must break a cycle of concurrent copies, it needs an additional register to do so.) An SSA-based allocator must be prepared to handle this situation.

Equally important, that translation inserts copy operations into the code; some of those copies may be extraneous. The allocator cannot coalesce away copies that implement the flow of values corresponding to a $\phi$-function; to do so would destroy the chordal property of the graph. Thus, an SSA-based allocator would probably use a coalescing algorithm that is not based on the interference graph. Several strong algorithms exist.

It is difficult to asses the merits of an SSA-based allocator versus an allocator based on traditional global live ranges. The SSA-based allocator has the potential to obtain a better coloring than the traditional allocator, but it does so on a different graph. Both allocators must address the problems of spill choice and spill placement, which may contribute more to performance than the actual coloring. The two allocators use different techniques for copy coalescing. As with any register allocator, the actual low-level details of the implementation will matter.

## 13.6  **SUMMARY AND PERSPECTIVE**

Because register allocation is an important part of a modern compiler, it has received much attention in the literature. Strong techniques exist for both local and global allocation. Because many of the underlying problems are NP-hard, the solutions tend to be sensitive to small decisions, such as how ties between identically ranked choices are broken.

Progress in register allocation has come from the use of paradigms that provide intellectual leverage on the problem. Thus, graph-coloring allocators have been popular, not because register allocation is identical to graph coloring, but rather because coloring captures some of the critical aspects of the global allocation problem. In fact, many of the improvements to coloring allocators have come from attacking the points where the coloring paradigm does not accurately reflect the underlying problem, such as better cost models and improved methods for live-range splitting. In effect, these improvements have made the paradigm more closely fit the real problem.

# ■ CHAPTER NOTES

Register allocation dates to the earliest compilers. Backus reports that Best invented the bottom-up local algorithm in the mid-1950s, during the development of the original FORTRAN compiler [26, 27]. Best's algorithm has been rediscovered and reused in many contexts over the years [36, 117, 181, 246]. Its best-known incarnation is as Belady's offline page-replacement algorithm [36]. The complications that arise from having a combination of clean values and dirty values are described by Horwitz [196] and by Kennedy [214]. Liberatore et al. suggest spilling clean values before dirty values as a practical compromise [246]. The example on page 688 and 689 was suggested by Ken Kennedy.

The connection between graph coloring and storage-allocation problems was suggested by Lavrov [242] many years earlier; the Alpha project used coloring to pack data into memory [140, 141]. The first complete graph-coloring allocator to appear in the literature was an allocator built by Chaitin and his colleagues for IBM's PL.8 compiler [73, 74, 75]. Schwartz describes early algorithms by Ershov and by Cocke [310] that focus on reducing the number of colors and ignore spilling.

Top-down graph coloring begins with Chow [81, 82, 83]. His implementation worked from a memory-to-memory model, used an imprecise interference graph, and performed live-range splitting as described in Section 13.4.4. It uses a separate optimization pass to coalesce copies [81]. Chow's algorithm was used in several prominent compilers. Larus built a top-down, priority-based allocator for SPUR LISP that used a precise interference graph and operated from a register-to-register model [241]. The top-down allocation in Section 13.4.4 roughly follows Larus' plan.

The bottom-up allocator in Section 13.4.5 follows Chaitin's plan with Briggs' modifications [51, 52, 56]. Chaitin's contributions include the fundamental definition of interference and the algorithms for building the interference graph, for coalescing, and for handling spills. Briggs presented an SSA-based algorithm for live range construction, an improved coloring heuristic, and several approaches to live-range splitting [51]. Other significant improvements in bottom-up coloring have included better methods for spilling [37, 38], rematerialization of simple values [55], stronger coalescing methods [158, 280], and methods for live-range splitting [98, 106, 235]. Gupta, Soffa, and Steele suggested shrinking the graph with clique separators [175], while Harvey proposed splitting it by register classes [101].

Chaitin, Nickerson, and Briggs all discuss adding edges to the interference graph to model specific constraints on assignment [54, 75, 275]. Smith et al. present a clear treatment of how to handle register classes [319]. Both scalar replacement [67, 70] and register promotion [250, 253, 306] rewrite the code to increase the set of values that the allocator can keep in registers.

The observation that SSA names form a chordal graph was made independently by several authors [58, 177, 283]. Both Hack and Bouchez built on the original observation with in-depth treatments of SSA-based global allocation [47, 176].

### ■ EXERCISES

Section 13.3

1. Consider the following ILOC basic block. Assume that $r_{arp}$ and $r_i$ are live on entry to the block.

   ```
   loadAI    r_arp, 12  ⇒ r_a
   loadAI    r_arp, 16  ⇒ r_b
   add       r_i, r_a   ⇒ r_c
   sub       r_b, r_i   ⇒ r_d
   mult      r_c, r_d   ⇒ r_e
   multI     r_b, 2     ⇒ r_f
   add       r_e, r_f   ⇒ r_g
   storeAI   r_g        ⇒ r_arp, 8
   jmp                  → L_003
   ```

   a. Show the result of using the top-down local algorithm on it to allocate registers. Assume a target machine with four registers.
   b. Show the result of using the bottom-up local algorithm on it to allocate registers. Assume a target machine with four registers.

2. The top-down local allocator is somewhat naive in its handling of values. It allocates one value to a register for the entire basic block.
   a. An improved version might calculate live ranges within the block and allocate values to registers for their live ranges. What modifications would be necessary to accomplish this?
   b. A further improvement might be to split the live range when it cannot be accommodated in a single register. Sketch the data structures and algorithmic modifications that would be needed to (1) break a live range around an instruction (or range of instructions) where a register is not available and to (2) reprioritize the remaining pieces of the live range.
   c. With these improvements, the frequency count technique should generate better allocations. How do you expect your results to

compare with using the bottom-up local algorithm? Justify your answer.

3. Consider the following control-flow graph:

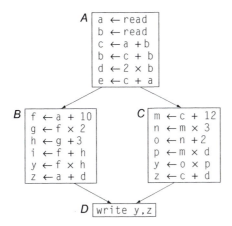

Assume that read returns a value from external media and that write transmits a value to external media.

a. Compute the LIVEIN and LIVEOUT sets for each block.

b. Apply the bottom-up local algorithm to each block, A, B, and C. Assume that three registers are available to the computation. If block *b* defines a name *n* and $n \in$ LIVEOUT($b$), the allocator must store *n* back to memory so that its value is available in subsequent blocks. Similarly, if block *b* uses name *n* before any local definition of *n*, it must load *n*'s value from memory. Show the resulting code, including all loads and stores.

c. Suggest a scheme that would allow some of the values in LIVEOUT($A$) to remain in registers, avoiding their initial loads in the successor blocks.

4. Consider the following interference graph:

Section 13.4

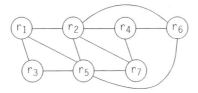

Assume that the target machine has just three registers.

a. Apply the bottom-up global coloring algorithm to the graph. Which virtual registers are spilled? Which are colored?

**b.** Does the choice of spill node make a difference?

**c.** Earlier coloring allocators spilled any live range that is constrained when it is selected. Rather than applying the algorithm shown in Figure 13.8, they used the following method:

```
initialize stack to empty
while (N ≠ ∅)
    if ∃ n∈N with n° <k then
        remove n and its edges from I
        push n onto stack
    else
        pick a node n from N
        mark n to be spilled
```

If this marks any node for spilling, the allocator inserts spill code and repeats the allocation process on the modified program. If no node is marked for spilling, it proceeds to assign colors in the manner described for the bottom-up global allocator.

What happens when you apply this algorithm to the example interference graph? Does the mechanism used to choose a node for spilling change the result?

**5.** After register allocation, a careful analysis of the code may discover that, in some stretches of the code, there are unused registers. In a bottom-up, graph-coloring, global allocator, this occurs because of detailed shortcomings in the way that live ranges are spilled.

**a.** Explain how this situation can arise.

**b.** How might the compiler discover if this situation occurs and where it occurs?

**c.** What might be done to use these unused registers, both within the global framework and outside of it?

**6.** When a graph-coloring allocator reaches the point where no color is available for a particular live range, $LR_i$, it spills or splits that live range. As an alternative, it might attempt to recolor one or more of $LR_i$'s neighbors. Consider the case where $(LR_i, LR_j) \in I$ and $(LR_i, LR_k) \in I$, but $(LR_j, LR_k) \notin I$. If $LR_j$ and $LR_k$ have already been colored, and have received different colors, the allocator might be able to recolor one of them to the other's color, freeing up a color for $LR_i$.

**a.** Sketch an algorithm that discovers if a legal and productive recoloring exists for $LR_i$.

**b.** What is the impact of your technique on the asymptotic complexity of the register allocator?

**c.** If the allocator cannot recolor $LR_k$ to the same color as $LR_j$ because one of $LR_k$'s neighbors has the same color as $LR_j$, should the allocator consider recursively recoloring $LR_k$'s neighbors? Explain your rationale.

**7.** The description of the bottom-up global allocator suggests inserting spill code for *every* definition and use in the spilled live range. The top-down global allocator first breaks the live range into block-sized pieces, then combines those pieces when the result is unconstrained and, finally, assigns them a color.

**a.** If a given block has one or more free registers, spilling a live range multiple times in that block is wasteful. Suggest an improvement to the spill mechanism in the bottom-up global allocator that avoids this problem.

**b.** If a given block has too many overlapping live ranges, then splitting a spilled live range does little to address the problem in that block. Suggest a mechanism (other than local allocation) to improve the behavior of the top-down global allocator inside blocks with high demand for registers.

**8.** Consider spilling in the bottom-up global allocator. When the allocator must spill, it chooses the value that minimizes the ratio $\frac{spill\ cost}{degree}$.

In a procedure with a single long block, or a single long block inside a loop nest, the spill cost for a live range approximates its frequency count. Thus, a live range that is heavily used at the beginning and ends of the long block, but unreferenced in the middle, ties up a register for the entire block.

How might you modify the bottom-up allocator so that its spill behavior on long blocks more closely resembled the behavior of the bottom-up local algorithm than the top-down local algorithm?

# ILOC

## ■ CHAPTER OVERVIEW

ILOC is the assembly code for a simple abstract machine. It was originally designed as a low-level, linear IR for use in an optimizing compiler. We use it throughout the book as an example IR. We also use it as a simplified target language in the chapters that discuss code generation. This appendix serves as a reference on ILOC.

**Keywords:** Intermediate Representation, Three-Address Code, ILOC

## A.1 INTRODUCTION

ILOC is the linear assembly code for a simple abstract RISC machine. The ILOC used in this book is a simplified version of the intermediate representation that was used in the Massively Scalar Compiler Project at Rice University. For example, ILOC as presented here assumes one generic data type, an integer without a specific length; in the compiler, the IR supported a broad variety of data types.

The ILOC abstract machine has an unlimited number of registers. It has three-address, register-to-register operations, load and store operations, comparisons, and branches. It supports just a few simple addressing modes—direct, address + offset, address + immediate, and immediate. Source operands are read at the beginning of the cycle when the operation issues. Result operands are defined at the end of the cycle in which the operation completes.

Other than its instruction set, the details of the machine are left unspecified. Most of the examples assume a simple machine, with a single functional unit that executes ILOC operations in their order of appearance. When other models are used, we discuss them explicitly.

An ILOC program consists of a sequential list of instructions. Each instruction may be preceded by a label. A label is just a textual string; it is separated from the instruction by a colon. By convention, we limit ourselves to labels of the form $[a–z] ([a–z] | [0–9] | −)*$. If some instruction needs more than one label, we insert an instruction that only contains a nop before it, and place the extra label on the nop. To define an ILOC program more formally,

$$
\begin{array}{rcl}
\textit{IlocProgram} & \rightarrow & \textit{InstructionList} \\
\textit{InstructionList} & \rightarrow & \textit{Instruction} \\
& | & \texttt{label} : \textit{Instruction} \\
& | & \textit{Instruction InstructionList}
\end{array}
$$

Each instruction contains one or more operations. A single-operation instruction is written on a line of its own, while a multioperation instruction can span several lines. To group operations into a single instruction, we enclose them in square brackets and separate them with semicolons. More formally,

$$
\begin{array}{rcl}
\textit{Instruction} & \rightarrow & \textit{Operation} \\
& | & \texttt{[} \;\; \textit{OperationList} \;\; \texttt{]} \\
\textit{OperationList} & \rightarrow & \textit{Operation} \\
& | & \textit{Operation} \; ; \; \textit{OperationList}
\end{array}
$$

An ILOC operation corresponds to a machine-level instruction that might be issued to a single functional unit in a single cycle. It has an opcode, a sequence of comma-separated source operands, and a sequence of comma-separated target operands. The sources are separated from the targets by the symbol $\Rightarrow$, pronounced "into."

$$
\begin{array}{rcl}
\textit{Operation} & \rightarrow & \textit{NormalOp} \\
& | & \textit{ControlFlowOp} \\
\textit{NormalOp} & \rightarrow & \textit{Opcode OperandList} \Rightarrow \textit{OperandList} \\
\textit{OperandList} & \rightarrow & \textit{Operand} \\
& | & \textit{Operand} \; , \; \textit{OperandList} \\
\textit{Operand} & \rightarrow & \texttt{register} \\
& | & \texttt{num} \\
& | & \texttt{label}
\end{array}
$$

The nonterminal *Opcode* can be any ILOC operation, except cbr, jump, and jumpI. Unfortunately, as in a real assembly language, the relationship between an opcode and the form of its operands is less than systematic. The easiest way to specify the form of the operands for each opcode is in a tabular form. The tables that occur later in this appendix show the number of operands and their types for each ILOC opcode used in the book.

*Operand*s may be one of three types: `register`, `num`, and `label`. The type of each operand is determined by the opcode and the position of the operand in the operation. In the examples, we use both numerical ($r_{10}$) and symbolic ($r_i$) names for registers. Numbers are simple integers, signed if necessary. We always begin a label with an `l` to make its type obvious. This is a convention rather than a rule. ILOC simulators and tools should treat any string of the form described above as a potential label.

Most operations have a single target operand; some of the `store` operations have multiple target operands, as do the branches. For example, `storeAI` has a single source operand and two target operands. The source must be a register, and the targets must be a register and an immediate constant. Thus, the ILOC operation

$$\text{storeAI } r_i \Rightarrow r_j, 4$$

computes an address by adding 4 to the contents of $r_j$ and stores the value found in $r_i$ into the memory location specified by the address. In other words,

$$\text{MEMORY } (r_j + 4) \leftarrow \text{CONTENTS } (r_i)$$

Control-flow operations have a slightly different syntax. Since these operations do not define their targets, we write them with the single arrow $\rightarrow$, instead of $\Rightarrow$.

$$
\begin{array}{lllll}
\textit{ControlFlowOp} & \rightarrow & \text{cbr} & \text{register} & \rightarrow & \text{label , label} \\
& | & \text{jumpI} & & \rightarrow & \text{label} \\
& | & \text{jump} & & \rightarrow & \text{register}
\end{array}
$$

The first operation, `cbr`, implements a conditional branch. The other two operations are unconditional branches, called jumps.

## A.2 NAMING CONVENTIONS

The ILOC code in the text examples uses a simple set of naming conventions.

1. Memory offsets for variables are represented symbolically by prefixing the variable name with the @ character.

2. The user can assume an unlimited supply of registers. These are named with simple integers, as in $r_{1776}$, or with symbolic names, as in $r_i$.
3. The register $r_{arp}$ is reserved as a pointer to the current activation record. Thus, the operation

$$\text{loadAI } r_{arp}, @x \Rightarrow r_1$$

loads the contents of the variable x, stored at offset @x from the ARP, into $r_1$.

ILOC comments begin with the string // and continue until the end of a line. We assume that these are stripped out by the scanner; thus, they can occur anywhere in an instruction and are not mentioned in the grammar.

## A.3 INDIVIDUAL OPERATIONS

The examples in the book use a limited set of ILOC operations. The tables at the end of this appendix shows the set of all ILOC operations used in the book, except for the alternate branch syntax used in Chapter 7 to discuss the impact of different forms of branching constructs.

### A.3.1 Arithmetic

To express arithmetic, ILOC has three-address, register-to-register operations.

| Opcode | Sources | Targets | Meaning |
|--------|---------|---------|---------|
| add | $r_1, r_2$ | $r_3$ | $r_1 + r_2 \Rightarrow r_3$ |
| sub | $r_1, r_2$ | $r_3$ | $r_1 - r_2 \Rightarrow r_3$ |
| mult | $r_1, r_2$ | $r_3$ | $r_1 \times r_2 \Rightarrow r_3$ |
| div | $r_1, r_2$ | $r_3$ | $r_1 \div r_2 \Rightarrow r_3$ |
| addI | $r_1, c_2$ | $r_3$ | $r_1 + c_2 \Rightarrow r_3$ |
| subI | $r_1, c_2$ | $r_3$ | $r_1 - c_2 \Rightarrow r_3$ |
| rsubI | $r_1, c_2$ | $r_3$ | $c_2 - r_1 \Rightarrow r_3$ |
| multI | $r_1, c_2$ | $r_3$ | $r_1 \times c_2 \Rightarrow r_3$ |
| divI | $r_1, c_2$ | $r_3$ | $r_1 \div c_2 \Rightarrow r_3$ |
| rdivI | $r_1, c_2$ | $r_3$ | $c_2 \div r_1 \Rightarrow r_3$ |

All these operations read their source operands from registers or constants and write their result back to a register. Any register can serve as a source or destination operand.

The first four operations are standard register-to-register operations. The next six operations specify an immediate operand. The noncommutative operations, sub and div, have two immediate forms to allow the immediate operand on either side of the operator. The immediate forms are useful to express the results of certain optimizations, to write down examples more concisely, and to record obvious ways to reduce demand for registers.

Note that a real ILOC-based processor would need more than one data type. This would lead to typed opcodes or to polymorphic opcodes. We would prefer a family of typed opcodes—an integer add, a floating-point add, and so on. The research compiler where ILOC originated has distinct arithmetic operations for integer, single-precision floating-point, double-precision floating-point, complex, and pointer data, but not for character data.

### A.3.2 **Shifts**

ILOC supports a set of arithmetic shift operations—to the left and to the right, in both register and immediate forms.

| Opcode | Sources | Targets | Meaning |
|--------|---------|---------|---------|
| lshift | $r_1, r_2$ | $r_3$ | $r_1 \ll r_2 \Rightarrow r_3$ |
| lshiftI | $r_1, c_2$ | $r_3$ | $r_1 \ll c_2 \Rightarrow r_3$ |
| rshift | $r_1, r_2$ | $r_3$ | $r_1 \gg r_2 \Rightarrow r_3$ |
| rshiftI | $r_1, c_2$ | $r_3$ | $r_1 \gg c_2 \Rightarrow r_3$ |

### A.3.3 **Memory Operations**

To move values between memory and registers, ILOC supports a full set of load and store operations. The load and cload operations move data items from memory to registers.

| Opcode | Sources | Targets | Meaning |
|--------|---------|---------|---------|
| load | $r_1$ | $r_2$ | MEMORY $(r_1) \Rightarrow r_2$ |
| loadAI | $r_1, c_2$ | $r_3$ | MEMORY $(r_1 + c_2) \Rightarrow r_3$ |
| loadAO | $r_1, r_2$ | $r_3$ | MEMORY $(r_1 + r_2) \Rightarrow r_3$ |
| cload | $r_1$ | $r_2$ | character load |
| cloadAI | $r_1, c_2$ | $r_3$ | character loadAI |
| cloadAO | $r_1, r_2$ | $r_3$ | character loadAO |

The operations differ in the addressing modes that they support. The load and cload forms assume that the full address is in the single register operand. The loadAI and cloadAI forms add an immediate value to the contents of the register to form an immediate address before performing the load. We call these *address-immediate* operations. The loadAO and cloadAO forms add the contents of two registers to compute an effective address before performing the load. We call these *address-offset* operations.

As a final form of load, ILOC supports a simple load immediate operation. It takes an integer from the instruction stream and places it in a register.

| Opcode | Sources | Targets | Meaning |
|--------|---------|---------|---------|
| loadI | $c_1$ | $r_2$ | $c_1 \Rightarrow r_2$ |

A complete, ILOC-like IR should have a load immediate for each distinct kind of value that it supports.

The store operations match the load operations. ILOC supports both numerical stores and character stores in its simple register form, in the address-immediate form, and in the address-offset form.

| Opcode | Sources | Targets | Meaning |
|--------|---------|---------|---------|
| store | $r_1$ | $r_2$ | $r_1 \Rightarrow$ MEMORY $(r_2)$ |
| storeAI | $r_1$ | $r_2, c_3$ | $r_1 \Rightarrow$ MEMORY $(r_2 + c_3)$ |
| storeAO | $r_1$ | $r_2, r_3$ | $r_1 \Rightarrow$ MEMORY $(r_2 + r_3)$ |
| cstore | $r_1$ | $r_2$ | character store |
| cstoreAI | $r_1$ | $r_2, c_3$ | character storeAI |
| cstoreAO | $r_1$ | $r_2, r_3$ | character storeAO |

There is no store immediate operation.

## A.3.4 **Register-to-Register Copy Operations**

To move values between registers, without going though memory, ILOC includes a set of register-to-register copy operations.

| Opcode | Sources | Targets | Meaning |
|--------|---------|---------|---------|
| i2i | $r_1$ | $r_2$ | $r_1 \Rightarrow r_2$ for integers |
| c2c | $r_1$ | $r_2$ | $r_1 \Rightarrow r_2$ for characters |
| c2i | $r_1$ | $r_2$ | convert character to integer |
| i2c | $r_1$ | $r_2$ | convert integer to character |

The first two operations, i2i and c2c, copy a value from one register to another, with no conversion. The former is for use with integer values, while the latter is for characters. The last two operations perform conversions between characters and integers, replacing a character by its ordinal position in the ASCII character set and replacing an integer with the corresponding ASCII character.

## A.4 CONTROL-FLOW OPERATIONS

In general, the ILOC comparison operators take two values and return a boolean value. If the specified relationship holds between its operands, the comparison sets the target register to the value true; otherwise the target register receives false.

| Opcode | Sources | Targets | Meaning | |
|---|---|---|---|---|
| cmp_LT | $r_1, r_2$ | $r_3$ | true $\Rightarrow r_3$ <br> false $\Rightarrow r_3$ | if $r_1 < r_2$ <br> otherwise |
| cmp_LE | $r_1, r_2$ | $r_3$ | true $\Rightarrow r_3$ <br> false $\Rightarrow r_3$ | if $r_1 \leq r_2$ <br> otherwise |
| cmp_EQ | $r_1, r_2$ | $r_3$ | true $\Rightarrow r_3$ <br> false $\Rightarrow r_3$ | if $r_1 = r_2$ <br> otherwise |
| cmp_GE | $r_1, r_2$ | $r_3$ | true $\Rightarrow r_3$ <br> false $\Rightarrow r_3$ | if $r_1 \geq r_2$ <br> otherwise |
| cmp_GT | $r_1, r_2$ | $r_3$ | true $\Rightarrow r_3$ <br> false $\Rightarrow r_3$ | if $r_1 > r_2$ <br> otherwise |
| cmp_NE | $r_1, r_2$ | $r_3$ | true $\Rightarrow r_3$ <br> false $\Rightarrow r_3$ | if $r_1 \neq r_2$ <br> otherwise |
| cbr | $r_1$ | $l_2, l_3$ | $l_2 \rightarrow$ PC <br> $l_3 \rightarrow$ PC | if $r_1 =$ true <br> otherwise |

The conditional branch operation, cbr, takes a boolean as its argument and transfers control to one of two target labels. The first label is selected if the boolean is true; the second is selected if the boolean is false. Because the two branch targets are not "defined" by the instruction, we change the syntax slightly. Rather than use the arrow $\Rightarrow$, we write branches with the single arrow $\rightarrow$.

All branches in ILOC have two labels. This approach eliminates a branch followed by a jump and makes the code more concise. It also eliminates any "fall-through" paths; by making those paths explicit, it removes any positional dependence and simplifies construction of the control-flow graph.

## A.4.1 **Alternate Comparison and Branch Syntax**

To discuss code shape on processors that use a condition code, we must introduce an alternate comparison and branch syntax. The condition code scheme simplifies the comparison and pushes the complexity into the conditional branch operation.

| Opcode | Sources | Targets | Meaning | |
|--------|---------|---------|---------|---|
| comp | $r_1, r_2$ | $cc_3$ | sets $cc_3$ | |
| cbr_LT | $cc_1$ | $l_2, l_3$ | $l_2 \rightarrow$ PC | if $cc_3 = $ LT |
| | | | $l_3 \rightarrow$ PC | otherwise |
| cbr_LE | $cc_1$ | $l_2, l_3$ | $l_2 \rightarrow$ PC | if $cc_3 = $ LE |
| | | | $l_3 \rightarrow$ PC | otherwise |
| cbr_EQ | $cc_1$ | $l_2, l_3$ | $l_2 \rightarrow$ PC | if $cc_3 = $ EQ |
| | | | $l_3 \rightarrow$ PC | otherwise |
| cbr_GE | $cc_1$ | $l_2, l_3$ | $l_2 \rightarrow$ PC | if $cc_3 = $ GE |
| | | | $l_3 \rightarrow$ PC | otherwise |
| cbr_GT | $cc_1$ | $l_2, l_3$ | $l_2 \rightarrow$ PC | if $cc_3 = $ GT |
| | | | $l_3 \rightarrow$ PC | otherwise |
| cbr_NE | $cc_1$ | $l_2, l_3$ | $l_2 \rightarrow$ PC | if $cc_3 = $ NE |
| | | | $l_3 \rightarrow$ PC | otherwise |

Here, the comparison operator, comp, takes two values and sets the condition code appropriately. We always designate the target of comp as a condition-code register by writing it as $cc_i$. The corresponding conditional branch has six variants, one for each comparison result.

## A.4.2 **Jumps**

ILOC includes two forms of the jump operation. The form used in almost all of the examples is an immediate jump that transfers control to a literal label. The second, a jump-to-register operation, takes a single register operand. It interprets contents of the register as a runtime address and transfers control to that address.

| Opcode | Sources | Targets | Meaning |
|--------|---------|---------|---------|
| jumpI | — | $l_1$ | $l_1 \rightarrow$ PC |
| jump | — | $r_1$ | $r_1 \rightarrow$ PC |

The jump-to-register form is an ambiguous control-flow transfer. Once it has been generated, the compiler may be unable to deduce the correct set of target labels for the jump. For this reason, the compiler should avoid using jump to register, if possible.

Sometimes, the gyrations needed to avoid a jump to register are so complex that jump to register becomes attractive, despite its problems. For example, FORTRAN includes a construct that jumps to a label variable; implementing it with immediate branches would require logic similar to a case statement— a series of immediate branches, along with code to match the runtime value of the label variable against the set of possible labels. In such circumstances, the compiler should probably use a jump to register.

To reduce the loss of information from jump to register, ILOC includes a pseudo-operation that lets the compiler record the set of possible labels for a jump to register. The tbl operation has two arguments, a register and an immediate label.

| Opcode | Sources | Targets | Meaning |
|--------|---------|---------|---------|
| tbl | $r_1, l_2$ | — | $r_1$ might hold $l_2$ |

A tbl operation can occur only after a jump. The compiler interprets a set of one or more tbls as naming all the possible labels for the register. Thus, the following code sequence asserts that the jump targets one of L01, L03, L05, or L08:

```
jump              →r_i
tbl      r_i, L01
tbl      r_i, L03
tbl      r_i, L05
tbl      r_i, L08
```

## A.5 REPRESENTING SSA FORM

When a compiler constructs the SSA form of a program from its IR version, it needs a way to represent $\phi$-functions. In ILOC, the natural way to write a $\phi$-function is as an ILOC operation. Thus, we will sometimes write

$$\text{phi } r_i, r_j, r_k \Rightarrow r_m$$

for the $\phi$-function $r_m \leftarrow \phi (r_i, r_j, r_k)$. Because of the nature of SSA form, the phi operation may take an arbitrary number of sources. It always defines a single target.

| ILOC Opcode Summary | | | |
|---|---|---|---|
| **Opcode** | **Sources** | **Targets** | **Meaning** |
| nop | *none* | *none* | Used as a placeholder |
| add | $r_1, r_2$ | $r_3$ | $r_1 + r_2 \Rightarrow r_3$ |
| sub | $r_1, r_2$ | $r_3$ | $r_1 - r_2 \Rightarrow r_3$ |
| mult | $r_1, r_2$ | $r_3$ | $r_1 \times r_2 \Rightarrow r_3$ |
| div | $r_1, r_2$ | $r_3$ | $r_1 \div r_2 \Rightarrow r_3$ |
| addI | $r_1, c_2$ | $r_3$ | $r_1 + c_2 \Rightarrow r_3$ |
| subI | $r_1, c_2$ | $r_3$ | $r_1 - c_2 \Rightarrow r_3$ |
| rsubI | $r_1, c_2$ | $r_3$ | $c_2 - r_1 \Rightarrow r_3$ |
| multI | $r_1, c_2$ | $r_3$ | $r_1 \times c_2 \Rightarrow r_3$ |
| divI | $r_1, c_2$ | $r_3$ | $r_1 \div c_2 \Rightarrow r_3$ |
| rdivI | $r_1, c_2$ | $r_3$ | $c_2 \div r_1 \Rightarrow r_3$ |
| lshift | $r_1, r_2$ | $r_3$ | $r_1 \ll r_2 \Rightarrow r_3$ |
| lshiftI | $r_1, c_2$ | $r_3$ | $r_1 \ll c_2 \Rightarrow r_3$ |
| rshift | $r_1, r_2$ | $r_3$ | $r_1 \gg r_2 \Rightarrow r_3$ |
| rshiftI | $r_1, c_2$ | $r_3$ | $r_1 \gg c_2 \Rightarrow r_3$ |
| and | $r_1, r_2$ | $r_3$ | $r_1 \wedge r_2 \Rightarrow r_3$ |
| andI | $r_1, c_2$ | $r_3$ | $r_1 \wedge c_2 \Rightarrow r_3$ |
| or | $r_1, r_2$ | $r_3$ | $r_1 \vee r_2 \Rightarrow r_3$ |
| orI | $r_1, c_2$ | $r_3$ | $r_1 \vee c_2 \Rightarrow r_3$ |
| xor | $r_1, r_2$ | $r_3$ | $r_1 \textit{ xor } r_2 \Rightarrow r_3$ |
| xorI | $r_1, c_2$ | $r_3$ | $r_1 \textit{ xor } c_2 \Rightarrow r_3$ |
| loadI | $c_1$ | $r_2$ | $c_1 \Rightarrow r_2$ |
| load | $r_1$ | $r_2$ | MEMORY $(r_1) \Rightarrow r_2$ |
| loadAI | $r_1, c_2$ | $r_3$ | MEMORY $(r_1 + c_2) \Rightarrow r_3$ |
| loadAO | $r_1, r_2$ | $r_3$ | MEMORY $(r_1 + r_2) \Rightarrow r_3$ |
| cload | $r_1$ | $r_2$ | character load |
| cloadAI | $r_1, c_2$ | $r_3$ | character loadAI |
| cloadAO | $r_1, r_2$ | $r_3$ | character loadAO |
| store | $r_1$ | $r_2$ | $r_1 \Rightarrow$ MEMORY $(r_2)$ |
| storeAI | $r_1$ | $r_2, c_3$ | $r_1 \Rightarrow$ MEMORY $(r_2 + c_3)$ |
| storeAO | $r_1$ | $r_2, r_3$ | $r_1 \Rightarrow$ MEMORY $(r_2 + r_3)$ |
| cstore | $r_1$ | $r_2$ | character store |
| cstoreAI | $r_1$ | $r_2, c_3$ | character storeAI |
| cstoreAO | $r_1$ | $r_2, r_3$ | character storeAO |
| i2i | $r_1$ | $r_2$ | $r_1 \Rightarrow r_2$ for integers |
| c2c | $r_1$ | $r_2$ | $r_1 \Rightarrow r_2$ for characters |
| c2i | $r_1$ | $r_2$ | convert character to integer |
| i2c | $r_1$ | $r_2$ | convert integer to character |

| **ILOC Control-Flow Operations** | | | | |
|---|---|---|---|---|
| **Opcode** | **Sources** | **Targets** | **Meaning** | |
| jump | — | $r_1$ | $r_1 \rightarrow PC$ | |
| jumpI | — | $l_1$ | $l_1 \rightarrow PC$ | |
| cbr | $r_1$ | $l_2, l_3$ | $l_2 \rightarrow PC$ | if $r_1 = \text{true}$ |
| | | | $l_3 \rightarrow PC$ | otherwise |
| tbl | $r_1, l_2$ | — | $r_1$ might hold $l_2$ | |
| cmp_LT | $r_1, r_2$ | $r_3$ | $\text{true} \Rightarrow r_3$ | if $r_1 < r_2$ |
| | | | $\text{false} \Rightarrow r_3$ | otherwise |
| cmp_LE | $r_1, r_2$ | $r_3$ | $\text{true} \Rightarrow r_3$ | if $r_1 \leq r_2$ |
| | | | $\text{false} \Rightarrow r_3$ | otherwise |
| cmp_EQ | $r_1, r_2$ | $r_3$ | $\text{true} \Rightarrow r_3$ | if $r_1 = r_2$ |
| | | | $\text{false} \Rightarrow r_3$ | otherwise |
| cmp_GE | $r_1, r_2$ | $r_3$ | $\text{true} \Rightarrow r_3$ | if $r_1 \geq r_2$ |
| | | | $\text{false} \Rightarrow r_3$ | otherwise |
| cmp_GT | $r_1, r_2$ | $r_3$ | $\text{true} \Rightarrow r_3$ | if $r_1 > r_2$ |
| | | | $\text{false} \Rightarrow r_3$ | otherwise |
| cmp_NE | $r_1, r_2$ | $r_3$ | $\text{true} \Rightarrow r_3$ | if $r_1 \neq r_2$ |
| | | | $\text{false} \Rightarrow r_3$ | otherwise |
| comp | $r_1, r_2$ | $cc_3$ | sets $cc_3$ | |
| cbr_LT | $cc_1$ | $l_2, l_3$ | $l_2 \rightarrow PC$ | if $cc_3 = LT$ |
| | | | $l_3 \rightarrow PC$ | otherwise |
| cbr_LE | $cc_1$ | $l_2, l_3$ | $l_2 \rightarrow PC$ | if $cc_3 = LE$ |
| | | | $l_3 \rightarrow PC$ | otherwise |
| cbr_EQ | $cc_1$ | $l_2, l_3$ | $l_2 \rightarrow PC$ | if $cc_3 = EQ$ |
| | | | $l_3 \rightarrow PC$ | otherwise |
| cbr_GE | $cc_1$ | $l_2, l_3$ | $l_2 \rightarrow PC$ | if $cc_3 = GE$ |
| | | | $l_3 \rightarrow PC$ | otherwise |
| cbr_GT | $cc_1$ | $l_2, l_3$ | $l_2 \rightarrow PC$ | if $cc_3 = GT$ |
| | | | $l_3 \rightarrow PC$ | otherwise |
| cbr_NE | $cc_1$ | $l_2, l_3$ | $l_2 \rightarrow PC$ | if $cc_3 = NE$ |
| | | | $l_3 \rightarrow PC$ | otherwise |

# Data Structures

## ■ CHAPTER OVERVIEW

Compilers execute so many times that the compiler writer must pay attention to the efficiency of each pass in the compiler. Both asymptotic complexity and expected complexity matter. This appendix presents background material on algorithms and data structures used to address problems in different phases of the compiler.

**Keywords:** Set Representation, Intermediate Representations, Hash Tables, Lexically Scoped Symbol Tables

## B.1 INTRODUCTION

Crafting a successful compiler requires attention to many details. This appendix explores some of the algorithmic issues that arise in compiler design and implementation. In most cases, these details would distract from the relevant discussion in the body of the text. We have gathered them together into this appendix, where they can be considered as needed.

This appendix focuses on the infrastructure to support compilation. Many engineering issues arise in the design and implementation of that infrastructure; the manner in which the compiler writer resolves those issues has a large impact on both the speed of the resulting compiler and the ease of extending and maintaining the compiler. As an example of the issues that arise, the compiler cannot know the size of its inputs until it has read them; thus, the front end must be designed to expand the size of its data structures gracefully in order to accommodate large input files. As a corollary, however, the compiler should know the approximate sizes needed for most of its internal data structures when it invokes the passes that follow the front end. Having generated an IR program with 10,000 names, the compiler should not begin its second pass with a symbol table sized for 1024 names. Any file that contains IR should begin with a specification of the rough sizes of major data structures.

Similarly, the later passes of a compiler can assume that the IR program presented to them was generated by the compiler. While they should do a complete job of error detection, the implementor need not spend as much time explaining errors and trying to correct them as might be expected in the front end. A common strategy is to build a validation pass that performs a thorough check on the IR program and can be inserted for debugging purposes, and to rely on less-strenuous error detection and reporting when not debugging the compiler. Throughout the process, however, the compiler writers should remember that they are the people most likely to look at the code between passes. Effort spent to make the external forms of the IR more readable often reward the very people who invested the time and effort in it.

## B.2 REPRESENTING SETS

Many different problems in compilation are formulated in terms that involve sets. They arise at many points in the text, including the subset construction (Chapter 2), the construction of the canonical collection of LR(1) items (Chapter 3), data-flow analysis (Chapters 8 and 9), and worklists such as the ready queue in list scheduling (Chapter 12). In each context, the compiler writer must select an appropriate set representation. In many cases, the efficiency of the algorithm depends on careful selection of a set representation. (For example, the *IDoms* data structure in the dominance computation represents all the dominator sets, as well as the immediate dominators, in one compact array.)

A fundamental difference between building a compiler and building other kinds of systems software—such as an operating system—is that many problems in compilation can be solved offline. For example, the bottom-up local algorithm for register allocation described in Section 13.3.2 was proposed in the mid-1950s for the original FORTRAN compiler. It is better known as Belady's MIN algorithm for offline page replacement, which has long been used as a standard against which to judge the effectiveness of online page-replacement algorithms. In an operating system, the algorithm is of only academic interest because it is an offline algorithm. Since the operating system cannot know what pages will be needed in the future, it cannot use an offline algorithm. On the other hand, the offline algorithm is practical for a compiler because the compiler can look through an entire block before making decisions.

The offline nature of compilation allows the compiler writer to use a broad variety of set representations. Many representations for sets have been explored. In particular, offline computation often lets us restrict the members of a set $S$ to a fixed-size universe $U$ ($S \subseteq U$). This, in turn, lets us use more efficient set representations than are available in an online situation where the size of $U$ is discovered dynamically.

Common set operations include *member*, *insert*, *delete*, *clear*, *select*, *cardinality*, *forall*, *copy*, *compare*, *union*, *intersect*, *difference*, and *complement*. A specific application typically uses only a small subset of these operations. The cost of individual set operations depends on the particular representation chosen. In selecting an efficient representation for a particular application, it is important to consider how frequently each type of operation will be used. Other factors to consider include the memory requirements of the set representation and the expected sparsity of $S$ relative to $U$.

The rest of this section focuses on three efficient set representations that have been employed in compilers: ordered linked lists, bit vectors, and sparse sets.

### B.2.1  Representing Sets as Ordered Lists

In cases in which the size of each set is small, it sometimes makes sense to use a simple linked-list representation. For a set $S$, this representation consists of a linked list and a pointer to the first element in the list. Each node in the list contains a representation for a single element of $S$ and a pointer to the next element of the list. The final node on the list has its pointer set to a standard value indicating the end of the list. With a linked-list representation, the implementation can impose an order on the elements to create an ordered list. For example, an ordered linked list for the set $S = \{i, j, k\}, i < j < k$ might look like this:

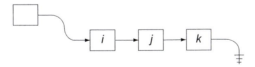

The elements are kept in ascending order. The size of $S$'s representation is proportional to the number of elements in $S$, not the size of $U$. If $|S|$ is much smaller than $|U|$, the savings from representing just the elements present in $S$ may more than offset the extra cost incurred for a pointer in each element.

The list representation is particularly flexible. Because nothing in the list relies on either the size of $U$ or the size of $S$, it can be used in situations in which the compiler is discovering $U$ or $S$ or both, such as the live-range-finding portion of a graph-coloring register allocator.

The table in Figure B.1 shows the asymptotic complexities of common set operations using this representation. Most common set operations on ordered

| Operation | Ordered Linked List | Bit Vector | Sparse Set |
|---|---|---|---|
| member | $\mathbf{O}(|S|)$ | $\mathbf{O}(1)$ | $\mathbf{O}(1)$ |
| insert | $\mathbf{O}(|S|)$ | $\mathbf{O}(1)$ | $\mathbf{O}(1)$ |
| delete | $\mathbf{O}(|S|)$ | $\mathbf{O}(1)$ | $\mathbf{O}(1)$ |
| clear | $\mathbf{O}(1)$ | $\mathbf{O}(|U|)$ | $\mathbf{O}(1)$ |
| select | $\mathbf{O}(1)$ | $\mathbf{O}(|U|)$ | $\mathbf{O}(1)$ |
| cardinality | $\mathbf{O}(|S|)$ | $\mathbf{O}(|U|)$ | $\mathbf{O}(1)$ |
| forall | $\mathbf{O}(|S|)$ | $\mathbf{O}(|U|)$ | $\mathbf{O}(|S|)$ |
| copy | $\mathbf{O}(|S|)$ | $\mathbf{O}(|U|)$ | $\mathbf{O}(|S|)$ |
| compare | $\mathbf{O}(|S|)$ | $\mathbf{O}(|U|)$ | $\mathbf{O}(|S|)$ |
| union | $\mathbf{O}(|S|)$ | $\mathbf{O}(|U|)$ | $\mathbf{O}(|S|)$ |
| intersect | $\mathbf{O}(|S|)$ | $\mathbf{O}(|U|)$ | $\mathbf{O}(|S|)$ |
| difference | $\mathbf{O}(|S|)$ | $\mathbf{O}(|U|)$ | $\mathbf{O}(|S|)$ |
| complement | — | $\mathbf{O}(|U|)$ | $\mathbf{O}(|U|)$ |

■ **FIGURE B.1** Asymptotic Time Complexities of Set Operations.

linked lists are $\mathbf{O}(|S|)$ because it is necessary to walk the linked lists to perform the operations. If deallocation does not require walking the list to free the nodes for individual elements, as in some garbage-collected systems or an arena-based system, *clear* takes constant time.

A variant on this idea makes sense when the universe is unknown, and the sets can grow reasonably large, as in interference-graph construction (see Chapter 13). Making each node hold a fixed number (greater than 1) of set elements significantly reduces the overhead in both space and time. With $k$ elements per node, building a set of $n$ elements requires $\lceil \frac{n}{k} \rceil$ allocations and $\lceil \frac{n}{k} \rceil + 1$ pointers, while a set with single-element nodes would take $n$ allocations and $n + 1$ pointers. This scheme retains the easy expansion of the list representation but reduces the space overhead. Insertion and deletion move more data than with a single element per node; however their asymptotic complexity is still $\mathbf{O}(|S|)$.

Keeping the extra space at the front of the list rather than at the end can simplify *insert* and *delete*, assuming a singly linked list.

The *IDoms* array used in the fast dominance computation (see Section 9.5.2) is a clever application of the list representation of sets to a very special case. In particular, the compiler knows the size of the universe and the number of sets. The compiler also knows that, using ordered sets, they will have the peculiar property that if $e \in S_1$ and $e \in S_2$ then every element after $e$ in $S_1$ is also in $S_2$. Thus, the elements starting with $e$ can be shared. By using an array representation, the element names can be used as pointers, too. This enables a single array of $n$ elements to represent $n$ sparse sets as ordered lists. It also produces a fast intersection operator for those sets.

## B.2.2 **Representing Sets as Bit Vectors**

Compiler writers often use *bit vectors* to represent sets, particularly those used in data-flow analysis (see Sections 8.6.1 and 9.2). For a bounded universe $U$, a set $S \subseteq U$ can be represented with a bit vector of length $|U|$, called the *characteristic vector* for $S$. For each $i \in U$, $0 \le i < |U|$; if $i \in S$, the $i^{th}$ element of the characteristic vector equals one. Otherwise, the $i^{th}$ element is zero. For example, the characteristic vector for the set $S \subseteq U$, where $S = \{i,j,k\}$, $i < j < k$ is as follows:

| 0 | | $i-1$ | $i$ | $i+1$ | | $j-1$ | $j$ | $j+1$ | | $k-1$ | $k$ | $k+1$ | | $|U|-1$ |
|---|---|---|---|---|---|---|---|---|---|---|---|---|---|---|
| 0 | $\cdots$ | 0 | 1 | 0 | $\cdots$ | 0 | 1 | 0 | $\cdots$ | 0 | 1 | 0 | $\cdots$ | 0 |

The bit-vector representation always allocates enough space to represent all elements in $U$; thus, this representation can be used only in an application where $U$ is known—an offline application.

The table in Figure B.1 lists the asymptotic complexities of common set operations with this representation. Although many of the operations are $\mathbf{O}(|U|)$, they can still be efficient if $U$ is small. A single word holds many elements; the representation gains a constant-factor improvement over representations that need one word per element. Thus, for example, with a word size of 32 bits, any universe of 32 or fewer elements has a single-word representation.

The compactness of the representation carries over into the speed of operations. With single-word sets, many of the set operations become single machine instructions; for example *union* becomes a logical-or operation and *intersection* becomes a logical-and operation. Even if the sets take multiple words to represent, the number of machine instructions required to perform many of the set operations is reduced by a factor of the machine's word size.

## B.2.3 **Representing Sparse Sets**

For a fixed universe $U$ and a set $S \subseteq U$, $S$ is a sparse set if $|S|$ is much smaller than $|U|$. Some of the sets encountered in compilation are sparse. For example, the LiveOut sets used in register allocation are typically sparse. Compiler writers often use bit vectors to represent such sets, due to their efficiency in time and space. With enough sparsity, however, more time-efficient representations are possible, especially in situations in which a large percentage of the operations can be supported in either $\mathbf{O}(1)$ or $\mathbf{O}(|S|)$ time. By contrast, bit vector sets take either $\mathbf{O}(1)$ or $\mathbf{O}(|U|)$ time on these operations. If $|S|$ is smaller than $|U|$ by a factor greater than the word size, then bit vectors may be the less efficient choice.

One sparse-set representation that has these properties uses two vectors of length $|U|$ and a scalar to represent the set. The first vector, $sparse$, holds a sparse representation of the set; the other vector, $dense$, holds a dense representation of the set. The scalar, $next$, holds the index of the location in $dense$ where the next new element of the set can be inserted. Of course, $next$ also holds the set's cardinality.

Neither vector needs to be initialized when a sparse set is created; set membership tests ensure the validity of each entry as it is accessed. The $clear$ operation simply sets $next$ back to zero, its initial value. To add a new element $i \in U$ to $S$, the code (1) stores $i$ in the $next$ location in $dense$, (2) stores the value of $next$ in the $i^{th}$ location in $sparse$, and (3) increments $next$ so that it is the index of the next location where an element can be inserted in $dense$.

If we began with an empty sparse set $S$ and added the elements $j$, $i$, and $k$, in that order, where $i < j < k$, the set would look like this:

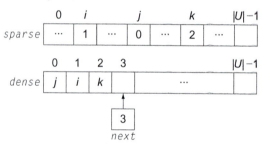

Note that the sparse-set representation requires enough space to represent all of $U$. Thus, it can be used only in offline situations in which the compiler knows the size of $U$.

Because valid entries for an element $i$ in $sparse$ and $dense$ must point to each other, membership can be determined with the following tests:

$$0 \leq sparse\,[i] < next \quad \text{and} \quad dense\,[sparse[i]] = i$$

The table in Figure B.1 lists the asymptotic complexities of common set operations. Because this scheme includes both a sparse and a dense representation of the set, it has some of the advantages of each. Individual elements of the set can be accessed in $\mathbf{O}(1)$ time through $sparse$, while set operations that must traverse the set can use $dense$ to obtain $\mathbf{O}(|S|)$ complexity.

Both space and time complexities should be considered when choosing between bit-vector and sparse-set representations. The sparse-set representation requires two vectors of length $|U|$ and a scalar. In contrast, a bit-vector representation requires a single bit-vector of length $|U|$. As shown in Figure B.1, the sparse-set representation dominates the bit-vector representation in terms of asymptotic time complexity. However, because of the efficient implementations possible for bit-vector set operations, bit vectors are preferred in situations where $S$ is not sparse. When choosing between the two representations, it is important to consider the sparsity of the represented set and the relative frequency of the set operations employed.

## B.3 IMPLEMENTING INTERMEDIATE REPRESENTATIONS

After choosing a specific style of IR, the compiler writer must decide how to implement it. At first glance, the choices seem obvious. DAGs are easily represented as nodes and edges, using pointers and heap-allocated data structures. Quadruples fall naturally into a $4 \times k$ array. As with sets, however, choosing the best implementation requires a deeper understanding of how the compiler will use the data structures.

### B.3.1 Graphical Intermediate Representations

Compilers use a variety of graphical IRs, as discussed in Chapter 5. Tailoring the implementation of a graph to the needs of the compiler can improve both the time and space efficiency of the compiler. This section describes some of the issues that arise with trees and graphs.

#### Representing Trees

The natural representation for trees, in most languages, is as a collection of nodes connected by pointers. A typical implementation allocates the nodes on demand, as the compiler builds the tree. The tree may include nodes of several sizes—for example, varying the number of children in the node and some of the data fields. Alternatively, the tree might be built with a single kind of node, allocated to fit the largest possible node.

Another way to represent the same tree is as an array of node structures. In this representation, pointers are replaced with integer indices and pointer-based references become standard array and structure references. This implementation forces a one-size-fits-all node, but is otherwise similar to the pointer-based implementation.

Each of these schemes has strengths and weaknesses.

■ The pointer scheme handles arbitrarily large ASTs. The array scheme requires code to expand the array when the AST grows beyond its initially allocated size.

- The pointer scheme requires an allocation for each node, while the array scheme simply increments a counter (unless it must expand the array). Techniques, like arena-based allocation (see the sidebar "Arena-Based Allocation," in Chapter 6), can reduce the cost of allocation and reclamation.

- The pointer scheme has locality of reference that depends entirely on the behavior of the allocator at run time. The array technique uses consecutive memory locations. One or the other may be desirable on a particular system.

- The pointer scheme is harder to optimize because of the comparatively poor quality of static analysis on pointer-intensive code. By contrast, many of the optimizations developed for dense linear-algebra codes apply to an array scheme. When the compiler is compiled, these optimizations may produce faster code for the array scheme than for the pointer scheme.

- The pointer scheme may be harder to debug than the array implementation. Programmers seem to find array indices more intuitive than memory addresses.

- The pointer system requires a way to encode pointers if the AST must be written to external media. Presumably, this includes traversing the nodes, following the pointers. The array system uses offsets relative to the start of the array, so no translation is required. On many systems, this can be accomplished with a large, block I/O operation.

There are many other tradeoffs. Each must be evaluated in context.

### *Mapping Trees to Binary Trees*

A straightforward implementation of abstract syntax trees might support nodes with many different numbers of children. For example, a typical for loop header

$$\text{for } i = 1 \text{ to } n \text{ by } 2$$

might have a node in the AST with five children, like the one shown in Figure B.2.a. The node labelled body represents the subtree for the body of the for loop.

For some constructs, no fixed number of children will work. To represent a procedure call, the AST must either custom allocate nodes based on the number of parameters, or use a single child that holds a list of parameters. The former approach complicates all the code that traverses the AST; the variable-sized nodes must hold numbers to indicate how many children they have, and the traversal must contain code to read those numbers and

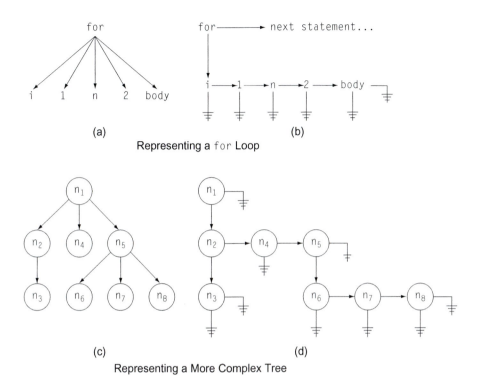

(a)

(b)

Representing a for Loop

(c)

(d)

Representing a More Complex Tree

■ **FIGURE B.2**  Mapping Arbitrary Trees onto Binary Trees.

modify its behavior accordingly. The latter approach separates the AST's implementation from its strict adherence to the source but uses a well-understood construct, the list, to represent those places where a fixed-arity node is inappropriate.

To simplify the implementation of trees, the compiler writer can take this separation of form and meaning one step further. Any arbitrary tree can be mapped onto a binary tree—a tree in which each node has precisely two children. In this mapping, the left-child pointer is designated for the leftmost child, and the right-child pointer is designated for the next sibling at the current level. Figure B.2.b shows the five-child for node mapped onto a binary tree. Since each node is binary, this tree has null pointers in each leaf node. It also has a sibling pointer in the for node; in the version on the left, that pointer occurs in the for node's parent. Parts c and d in the figure show a more complex example.

Using binary trees introduces additional null pointers into the trees, as the two examples show. In return, it simplifies the implementation in several ways. Memory allocation can be done simply, with an arena-based allocator or a custom one. The compiler writer can also implement the tree as an array of structures. The code that deals with the binary tree is somewhat simpler than the code required for a tree with nodes of many different arities.

### Representing Arbitrary Graphs

Several structures that a compiler must represent are arbitrary graphs, rather than trees. Examples include the control-flow graph and the data-precedence graph. A simple implementation might use heap-allocated nodes, with pointers to represent the edges. The left side of Figure B.3 shows a simple CFG. Clearly, it needs three nodes. The difficulty arises with the edges: how many incoming and outgoing edges does each node need? Each node could maintain a list of outgoing edges; this leads to an implementation that might look like the one shown on the right side of the figure.

In the diagram, the rectangles represent nodes, and the ovals represent edges. This representation makes it easy to walk the graph in the direction of the edges. It does not provide for random access to any of the nodes; to remedy this, we can add an array of node pointers, indexed by the nodes' integer names. With this minor addition (not shown), the graph is suitable for solving forward data-flow problems. It provides a fast means for finding all the successors of a node.

Unfortunately, compilers often need to traverse the CFG against the direction of the edges. This occurs, for example, in backward data-flow problems, where the algorithm needs a fast predecessor operation. To adapt this graph structure for backward traversal, we would need to add another pointer

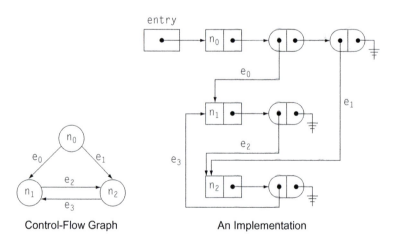

Control-Flow Graph · · · · · · · · · · · · · · · · · · · · · An Implementation

■ **FIGURE B.3** An Example Control-Flow Graph.

to each node and create a second set of edge structures to represent the predecessors of a node. This approach will certainly work, but the data structure becomes complicated to draw, implement, and debug.

An alternative, as with trees, is to represent the graph as a pair of tables—one for the nodes and one for the edges. The node table has two fields: one for the first edge to a successor and one for the first edge to a predecessor. The edge table has four fields: the first pair hold the source and sink of the edge being represented, and the other pair holds the next successor of the source and the next predecessor of the sink. Using this scheme, the tables for our example CFG are shown in Figure B.4. This representation provides quick access to successors, predecessors, and individual nodes and edges by their names (assuming that the names are represented by small integers).

The tabular representation works well for traversing the graph and finding predecessors and successors. If the application makes heavy use of other operations on the graph, better representations can be found. For example, the dominant operations in a graph-coloring register allocator are testing for an edge's presence in the interference graph and iterating over a node's neighbors. To support these operations, most implementations use two different graph representations (see Section 13.4.3). To answer membership questions—is the edge $(i, j)$ in the graph?—these implementations use a bit matrix. Since the interference graph is undirected, a lower-diagonal bit matrix will suffice, saving roughly half the space required for a full bit matrix. To iterate quickly over a node's neighbors, a set of adjacency vectors is used.

Because interference graphs are both large and sparse, space for the adjacency vectors can become an issue. Some implementations use two passes to build the graph—the first pass computes the size of each adjacency vector and the second pass builds the vectors, each with the minimal required size. Other implementations use a variant of the list representation for sets from Section B.2.1—the graph is built in a single pass, using an unordered list for the adjacency vector, with multiple edges per list node.

**Node Table**

| Name | Successor | Predecessor |
|------|-----------|-------------|
| $n_0$ | $e_0$ | — |
| $n_1$ | $e_2$ | $e_0$ |
| $n_2$ | $e_3$ | $e_1$ |

**Edge Table**

| Name | Source | Sink | Next Successor | Next Predecessor |
|------|--------|------|----------------|------------------|
| $e_0$ | $n_0$ | $n_1$ | $e_1$ | $e_3$ |
| $e_1$ | $n_0$ | $n_2$ | — | $e_2$ |
| $e_2$ | $n_1$ | $n_2$ | — | — |
| $e_3$ | $n_2$ | $n_1$ | — | — |

■ **FIGURE B.4** Tabular Representation of a CFG.

## B.3.2 **Linear Intermediate Forms**

Part of the conceptual appeal of linear intermediate forms, like ILOC, is that they have a simple, obvious implementation as an array of structures. For example, an ILOC program has an immediate mapping to a FORTRAN-style array—$n$ ILOC operations map onto an $(n \times 4)$-element array of integers. The opcode determines how to interpret each of the operands. Of course, any design decision has its advantages and disadvantages, and a compiler writer who wants to use a linear IR should consider representations other than a simple array.

### *Fortran-Style Array*

Using a single array of integers to hold the IR ensures fast access to individual opcodes and operands and low overhead for both allocation and access. The passes that manipulate the IR should run quickly, since all of the array accesses can be improved using the standard analyses and transformations developed to improve dense linear-algebra programs. A linear pass through the code has predictable memory locality; since consecutive operations occupy consecutive memory locations, they cannot conflict in the cache. If the compiler must write the IR to external media (between passes, for example), it can use efficient block I/O operations.

There are, however, disadvantages to the array implementation. If the compiler needs to insert an operation into the code, it must create space for the new operation. Similarly, deletions should contract the code. Any kind of code motion runs into some version of this problem. A naive implementation would create the space by shuffling operations; a compiler that takes this approach will often leave empty slots in the array—after branches and jumps—to reduce the amount of shuffling needed.

An alternative strategy is to use a detour operator that directs any traversal of the IR to an out-of-line code segment. This approach lets the compiler thread control through out-of-line segments, so an insertion can be done by overwriting an existing operation with a detour, putting the inserted code and the overwritten operation at the end of the array, and following it with a detour back to the operation after the first detour. The final piece of strategy is to linearize the detours occasionally—for example, at the end of each pass, or any time the fraction of detours exceeds some threshold.

Another complication with the array implementation arises from the need for an occasional operation, such as a $\phi$-function that takes a variable number of operands. In the compiler from which our ILOC is derived, procedure calls are represented by a single complicated operation. The call operation has an operand for each formal parameter, an operand for the return value (if any), and two operands that are lists of values potentially modified by the call and potentially used by the call. This operation does not fit the mold of an $n \times 4$-element array, unless the operands are interpreted as pointers to lists of parameters, modified variables, and used variables.

### List of Structures

An alternative to the array implementation is to use a list of structures. In this scheme, each operation has an independent structure, along with a pointer to the next operation. Since the structures can be allocated individually, the program representation expands easily to arbitrary size. Since order is imposed by the pointers that link operations, operations can be inserted or removed with straightforward pointer assignments—no shuffling or copying is required. Variable-length operations, like the call operation previously described, are handled by using variant structures; in fact, short operations such as `loadI` and `jump` can also use a variant to save small amounts of space.

Of course, using individually allocated structures increases the overhead from allocation—the array needed one initial allocation, while the list scheme needs one allocation per IR operation. The list pointers increase the space required. Since all the compiler passes that manipulate the IR must include many pointer-based references, the code for those passes may be slower than code that uses a simple array implementation, because pointer-based code is often harder to analyze and optimize than array-intensive code. Finally, if the compiler writes the IR to external media between passes, it must traverse the list as it writes and reconstruct the list as it reads. This slows down the I/O.

These disadvantages can be ameliorated, to some extent, by implementing the list of structures inside either an arena or an array. With an arena-based allocator, the cost of allocations drops to a test and an addition in the typical case. The arena also produces roughly the same locality as a simple array implementation.

In any pass other than the first one, the compiler should have a fairly accurate notion of how big the IR is. Thus, it can allocate an arena that holds both the IR and some space for growth and avoid the more expensive case of expanding the arena.

Implementing the list in an array achieves the same goals, with the additional advantage that all the pointers become integer indices. Experience suggests that this simplifies debugging; it also makes it possible to use a block I/O operation to write and read the IR.

## B.4 **IMPLEMENTING HASH TABLES**

The two central problems in hash-table implementation are ensuring that the hash function produces an even distribution of integers (at all the table sizes that will be used) and handling collisions in an efficient way. Finding good hash functions is difficult. Fortunately, hashing has been in use long enough that many good functions have been described in the literature.

The rest of this section describes design issues that arise in implementing hash tables. Section B.4.1 describes two hash functions that, in practice, produce good results. The next two sections present the two most widely used strategies for resolving collisions. Section B.4.2 describes *open hashing* (sometimes called *bucket hashing*), while Section B.4.3 presents an alternative scheme called *open addressing* or *rehashing*. Section B.4.4 discusses storage management issues for hash tables, while Section B.4.5 shows how to incorporate the mechanisms for lexical scoping into these schemes. The final section deals with a practical issue that arises in a compiler-development environment, namely, frequent changes to the hash-table definition.

### B.4.1 **Choosing a Hash Function**

The importance of a good hash function cannot be overemphasized. A hash function that produces a bad distribution of index values directly increases the average cost of inserting items into the table and finding such items later. Fortunately, many good hash functions have been documented in the literature, including the multiplicative hash functions described by Knuth and the universal hash functions described by Cormen et al.

### *Multiplicative Hash Functions*

A *multiplicative hash function* is deceptively simple. The programmer chooses a single constant $C$ and uses it in the following formula:

$$h(key) = \lfloor TableSize \cdot ((C \cdot key) \bmod 1) \rfloor$$

where $C$ is the constant, *key* is the integer being used as a key into the table, and *TableSize* is, rather obviously, the current size of the hash table. Knuth suggests the following value for $C$:

$$0.6180339887 \approx \frac{\sqrt{5}-1}{2}$$

## ORGANIZING A SYMBOL TABLE

In designing a symbol table, the first decision that the compiler writer faces concerns the organization of the table and its search algorithm. As in many other applications, the compiler writer has several choices.

### Linear List

A linear list can expand to arbitrary size. The search algorithm is a single, small, tight loop. Unfortunately, the search algorithm requires $O(n)$ probes per lookup, on average, where $n$ is the number of symbols in the table. This single disadvantage almost always outweighs the simplicity of implementation and expansion. To justify using a linear list, the compiler writer needs strong evidence that the procedures being compiled have very few names, as might occur for an object-oriented language.

### Binary Search

To retain the easy expansion of the linear list while improving search time, the compiler writer might use a balanced binary tree. Ideally, a balanced tree should allow lookup in $O(\log_2 n)$ probes per lookup; this is a considerable improvement over the linear list. Many algorithms have been published for balancing search trees. (Similar effects can be achieved by using a binary search of an ordered table, but the table makes insertion and expansion more difficult.)

### Hash Table

A hash table may minimize access costs. The implementation computes a table index directly from the name. As long as that computation produces a good distribution of indices, the average access cost should be $O(1)$. The worst case, however, can devolve to linear search. The compiler writer can take steps to decrease the likelihood of this happening, but pathological cases may still occur. Many hash-table implementations have inexpensive schemes for expansion.

### Multiset Discrimination

To avoid worst-case behavior, the compiler writer can use an offline technique called *multiset discrimination*. It creates a distinct index for each identifier, at the cost of an extra pass over the source text. This technique avoids the possibility of pathological behavior that always exists with hashing. (See the sidebar "An Alternative to Hashing," in Chapter 5 for more details.)

Of these organizations, the most common choice appears to be the hash table. It provides better compile-time behavior than the linear list or binary tree, and the implementation techniques have been widely studied and taught.

The effect of the function is to compute $C \cdot key$, take its fractional part with the mod function, and multiply the result by the size of the table.

### Universal Hash Functions

To implement a *universal hash function*, the programmer designs a family of functions that can be parameterized by a small set of constants. At execution time, a set of values for the constants is chosen at random—either using random numbers for the constants or selecting a random index into a set of previously tested constants. (The same constants are used throughout a single execution of the program that uses the hash function, but the constants vary from execution to execution.) By varying the hash function in each execution of the program, a universal hash function produces different distributions in each run of the program. In a compiler, if the input program produced pathological behavior in some particular compilation, it is unlikely to produce the same behavior in subsequent compilations. To implement a universal version of the multiplicative hash function, the compiler writer can randomly generate an appropriate value for $C$ at the start of compilation.

### B.4.2 **Open Hashing**

*Open hashing*, also called *bucket hashing*, assumes that the hash function $h$ produces collisions. It relies on $h$ to partition the set of input keys into a fixed number of sets, or *buckets*. Each bucket contains a linear list of records, one record per name. `LookUp(n)` walks the linear list stored in the bucket indexed by $h(n)$ to find $n$. Thus, `LookUp` requires one evaluation of $h(n)$ and the traversal of a linear list. Evaluating $h(n)$ should be fast; the list traversal will take time proportional to the length of the list. For a table of size $S$, with $N$ names, the cost per lookup should be roughly $\mathbf{O}\left(\frac{N}{S}\right)$. As long as $h$ distributes names fairly uniformly and the ratio of names to buckets is small, this cost approximates our goal: $\mathbf{O}(1)$ time for each access.

Figure B.5 shows a small hash table implemented with this scheme. It assumes that $h(\mathtt{a}) = h(\mathtt{d}) = 3$ to create a collision. Thus, $\mathtt{a}$ and $\mathtt{d}$ occupy the same slot in the table. The list structure links them together. `Insert` should add to the front of the list for efficiency.

Open hashing has several advantages. Because it creates a new node in one of the linked lists for every inserted name, it can handle an arbitrarily large number of names without running out of space. An excessive number of entries in one bucket does not affect the cost of access in other buckets. Because the concrete representation for the set of buckets is usually an array of pointers, the overhead for increasing $S$ is small—one pointer for each

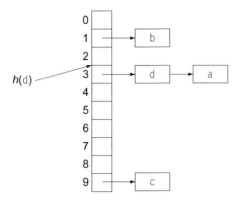

■ **FIGURE B.5**  Open-Hashing Table.

added bucket. (This makes it less expensive to keep $\frac{N}{S}$ small. The cost per name is constant.) Choosing $S$ as a power of two reduces the cost of the inevitable mod operation required to implement $h$.

The primary drawbacks for open hashing relate directly to these advantages. Both can be managed.

1. Open hashing can be allocation intensive. Each insertion allocates a new record. When implemented on a system with heavy-weight memory allocation, this may be noticeable. Using a lighter-weight mechanism, such as arena-based allocation (see the sidebar in Chapter 6), can alleviate this problem.

2. If any particular set gets large, *LookUp* degrades to linear search. With a reasonably behaved hash function, this occurs only when $N$ is much larger than $S$. The implementation should detect this problem and enlarge the array of buckets. Typically, this involves allocating a new array of buckets and reinserting each entry from the old table into the new table.

A well-implemented open hash table provides efficient access with low overhead in both space and time.

To improve the behavior of the linear search performed in a single bucket, the compiler can dynamically reorder the chain. Rivest and others [302, 317] describe two effective strategies: move a node up the chain by one position on each lookup, or move it to the front of the list on each lookup. More complex schemes to organize each bucket can be used as well. However, the compiler writer should assess the total amount of time lost in traversing a bucket before investing much effort in this problem.

**THE PERILS OF POOR HASH FUNCTIONS**

The choice of a hash function has a critical impact on the cost of table insertions and lookups. This is a case in which a small amount of attention can make a large difference.

Many years ago, we saw a student implement the following hash function for character strings: (1) break the key into 4-byte chunks, (2) exclusive-or them together, and (3) take the resulting number, $e$, modulo the table size, as the index. The function is relatively fast. It has a straightforward, efficient implementation. For some table sizes, it produces adequate distributions.

When the student inserted this implementation into a system that performed source-to-source translation on FORTRAN programs, several independent facts combined to create an algorithmic disaster. First, the implementation language padded character strings with blanks to the right to reach a 4-byte boundary. Second, the student chose an initial table size of 2048. Finally, FORTRAN programmers use many one- and two-character variable names, such as i, j, k, x, y, and z.

All the short variable names fit in a single word, avoiding any effect from the exclusive-or. However, taking $e$ mod 2048 masks out all but the final 11 bits of $e$. Thus, all short variable names produce the same index—the last 11 bits of a pair of blanks. The hash search instantly devolves into linear search. While this particular hash function is far from ideal, simply changing the table size to 2047 eliminates the most noticeable negative effects.

## B.4.3 Open Addressing

*Open addressing*, also called *rehashing*, handles collisions by computing an alternative index for the names whose normal slot, at $h(n)$, is already occupied. In this scheme, $LookUp(n)$ computes $h(n)$ and examines that slot. If the slot is empty, $LookUp$ fails. If $LookUp$ finds $n$, it succeeds. If it finds a name other than $n$, it uses a second function $g(n)$ to compute an increment for the search. This leads it to probe the table at $(h(n) + g(n))$ mod $S$, then at $(h(n) + 2 \times g(n))$ mod $S$, then at $(h(n) + 3 \times g(n))$ mod $S$, and so on, until it either finds $n$, finds an empty slot, or returns to $h(n)$ a second time. (The table is numbered from 0 to $S-1$, which ensures that mod $S$ will return a valid table index.) If $LookUp$ finds an empty slot, or it returns to $h(n)$ a second time, it fails.

Figure B.6 shows a small hash table implemented with this scheme. It uses the same data as Figure B.5. As before, $h(a) = h(d) = 3$, while $h(b) = 1$ and $h(c) = 9$. When d was inserted, it produced a collision with a. The secondary hash function $g(d)$ produced 2, so *Insert* placed d at index 5 in the table. In effect, open addressing builds chains of items similar to those used in

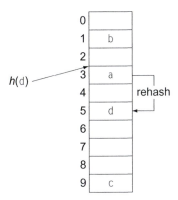

■ **FIGURE B.6** Open-Addressing Table.

open hashing. In open addressing, however, the chains are stored directly in the table, and a single table location can serve as the starting point for multiple chains, each with a different increment produced by $g$.

This scheme makes a subtle tradeoff of space against speed. Since each key is stored in the table, $S$ must be larger than $N$. If collisions are infrequent, because $h$ and $g$ produce good distributions, then the rehash chains stay short and access costs stay low. Because it can recompute $g$ inexpensively, this scheme need not store pointers to form the rehash chains—a savings of $N$ pointers. This saved space goes into making the table larger, and the larger table improves performance by lowering the collision frequency. The primary advantage of open addressing is simple: lower access costs through shorter rehash chains.

Open addressing has two primary drawbacks. Both arise as $N$ approaches $S$ and the table becomes full.

1. Because rehash chains thread through the index table, a collision between $n$ and $m$ can interfere with a subsequent insertion of some other name $p$. If $h(n) = h(m)$ and $(h(m) + g(m)) \bmod S = h(p)$, then inserting $n$, followed by $m$, fills $p$'s slot in the table. When the scheme behaves well, this problem has a minor impact. As $N$ approaches $S$, it can become pronounced.
2. Because $S$ must be at least as large as $N$, the table must be expanded if $N$ grows too large. (Similarly, the implementation may expand $S$ when some chain becomes too long.) Expansion is needed for correctness; with open hashing, it is a matter of efficiency.

Some implementations use a constant function for $g$. This simplifies the implementation and reduces the cost of computing secondary indices. However, it creates a single rehash chain for each value of $h$ and has the effect of merging rehash chains whenever a secondary index encounters an already occupied table slot. These two disadvantages outweigh the cost of evaluating a second hash function. A more reasonable choice is to use two multiplicative hash functions with different constants, selected randomly at startup from a table of constants, if possible.

The table size $S$ plays an important role in open addressing. $LookUp$ must recognize when it reaches a table slot that it has already visited; otherwise, it will not halt on failure. To make this efficient, the implementation should ensure that it eventually returns to $h(n)$. If $S$ is a prime number, then any choice of $0 < g(n) < S$ generates a series of probes, $p_1, p_2, \ldots, p_S$ with the property that $p_1 = p_S = h(n)$ and $p_i \neq h(n), \forall i$ such that $1 < i < S$. That is, $LookUp$ will examine every slot in the table before it returns to $h(n)$. Since the implementation may need to expand the table, it should include a table of appropriately sized prime numbers. A small set of primes will suffice, due to the realistic limits on both program size and memory available to the compiler.

### B.4.4 **Storing Symbol Records**

Neither open hashing nor open addressing directly addresses the issue of how to allocate space for the information associated with each hash table entry. With open hashing, the temptation is to allocate the records directly in the nodes that implement the chains. With open addressing, the temptation is to avoid pointers and make each entry in the index table be a symbol record. Both these approaches have drawbacks. We may achieve better results by using a separately allocated stack to hold the records.

Figure B.7 depicts this implementation. In an open-hashing implementation, the chain lists themselves can be implemented on the stack. This

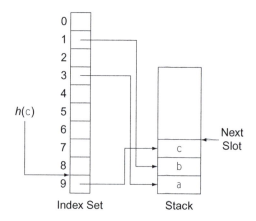

■ **FIGURE B.7** Stack Allocation for Records.

lowers the cost of allocating individual records—particularly if allocation is a heavy-weight operation. In an open-addressing implementation, the rehash chains are still implicit in the index set, preserving the space saving that motivated the idea.

When the actual records are stored in a stack, they form a dense table, which is better for external I/O. For heavyweight allocation, this scheme amortizes the cost of a large allocation over many records. With a garbage collector, it decreases the number of objects that must be marked and collected. In either case, having a dense table makes it more efficient to iterate over the symbols in the table—an operation that the compiler uses to perform tasks such as assigning storage locations.

As a final advantage, this scheme drastically simplifies the task of expanding the index set. To expand the index set, the compiler discards the old index set, allocates a larger set, and then reinserts the records into the new table, working from the bottom of the stack to the top. This eliminates the need to have, temporarily, both the old and new table in memory. Iterating over the dense table takes less work, in general, than chasing the pointers to traverse the lists in open hashing. It avoids iterating over empty table slots, as can happen when open addressing expands the index set to keep the chains short.

The compiler need not allocate the entire stack as a single object. Instead, the stack can be implemented as a chain of nodes that each hold $k$ records, for some reasonable $k$. When a node becomes full, the implementation allocates a new node, adds it to the end of the chain, and continues. This provides the compiler writer with fine-grained control over the tradeoff between allocation cost and wasted space.

### B.4.5 **Adding Nested Lexical Scopes**

Section 5.5.3 describes the issues that arise in creating a symbol table to handle nested lexical scopes. It describes a simple implementation that creates a sheaf of symbol tables, one per level. While that implementation is conceptually clean, it pushes the overhead of scoping into *LookUp*, rather than into *InitializeScope*, *FinalizeScope*, and *Insert*. Since the compiler invokes *LookUp* many more times than it invokes these other routines, other implementations deserve consideration.

Consider again the code in Figure 5.10. It generates the following actions:

$\uparrow$ ⟨w,0⟩ ⟨x,0⟩ ⟨example,0⟩ $\uparrow$ ⟨a,1⟩ ⟨b,1⟩ ⟨c,1⟩

$\uparrow$ ⟨b,2⟩ ⟨z,2⟩ $\downarrow$ $\uparrow$ ⟨a,2⟩ ⟨x,2⟩ $\uparrow$ ⟨c,3⟩, ⟨x,3⟩ $\downarrow$ $\downarrow$ $\downarrow$ $\downarrow$

where $\uparrow$ represents a call to *InitializeScope*, $\downarrow$ a call to *FinalizeScope*, and ⟨name, $n$⟩ represents a call to *Insert* that adds name at level $n$.

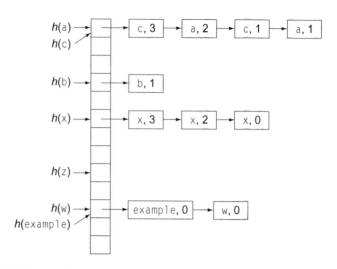

**■ FIGURE B.8** Lexical Scoping in an Open-Hashing Table.

### Adding Lexical Scopes to Open Hashing

Consider what might happen in an open-hashing table if we simply add a lexical-level field to the record for each name and insert each new name at the front of its chain. *Insert* could then check for duplicates by comparing both names and lexical levels. *LookUp* would return the first record that it discovered for a given name. *InitializeScope* would simply bump a counter for the current lexical level. This scheme pushes the complications into *FinalizeScope*, which must not only decrement the current lexical level, but also must remove the records for any names inserted in the scope being deallocated.

If open hashing is implemented with individually allocated nodes for its chains, as shown in Figure B.5, then *FinalizeScope* must find all records for the scope being discarded and remove them from their respective chains. If they will not be used later in the compiler, *FinalizeScope* must deallocate them; otherwise, it must chain them together to preserve them. Figure B.8 shows the table that this approach would produce, at the assignment statement in Figure 5.10.

With stack-allocated records, *FinalizeScope* can iterate from the top of the stack downward until it reaches a record for some level below the level being discarded. For each record, it updates the index-set entry with the record's pointer to the next item on the chain. If the records are being discarded, *FinalizeScope* resets the pointer to the next available slot; otherwise, the

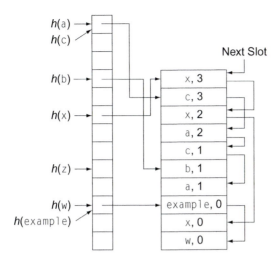

■ **FIGURE B.9** Lexical Scoping in a Stack-Allocated Open-Hashing Table.

records are preserved together on the stack. Figure B.9 shows the symbol table for our example at the assignment statement.

With a little care, dynamic reordering of the chain can be added to this scheme. Since *FinalizeScope* uses the stack ordering, rather than the chain ordering, it will still find all the top-level names at the top of the stack. With reordered chains, the compiler either needs to walk the chain to remove each deleted name record, or to doubly link the chains to allow quicker deletion.

### Adding Lexical Scopes to Open Addressing

With an open-addressing table, the situation is slightly more complex. Slots in the table are a critical resource; when all the slots are filled, the table must be expanded before further insertion can occur. Deletion from a table that uses rehashing is difficult; the implementation cannot easily tell if the deleted record falls in the middle of some rehash chain. Thus, marking the slot empty breaks any chain that passes through that location (rather than ending there). This argues against storing discrete records for each variant of a name in the table. Instead, the compiler should link only one record per name into the table; it can create a chain of superseded records for older variants. Figure B.10 depicts this situation for the continuing example.

This scheme pushes most of the complexity into *Insert* and *FinalizeScope*. *Insert* creates a new record on top of the stack. If it finds an older declaration of the same name in the index set, it replaces that reference with a reference to the new record and links the older reference to the

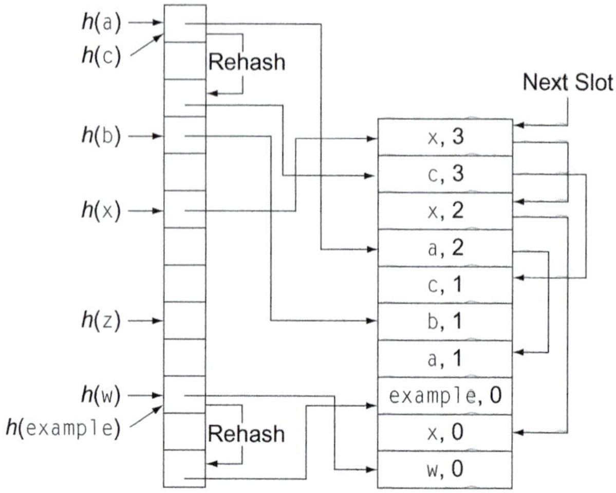

■ **FIGURE B.10**  Lexical Scoping in an Open-Addressing Table.

new record. *FinalizeScope* iterates over the top items on the stack, as in open hashing. To remove a record that has an older variant, it simply relinks the index set to point to the older variant. To remove the final variant of a name, it must insert a reference to a specially designated record that denotes a deleted reference. *LookUp* must recognize the deleted reference as occupying a slot in the current chain. *Insert* must know that it can replace a deleted reference with any newly inserted symbol.

This scheme, in essence, creates separate chains for collisions and for redeclarations. Collisions are threaded through the index set. Redeclarations are threaded through the stack. This should reduce the cost of *LookUp* slightly, since it avoids examining more than one record for any single name.

Consider a bucket in open hashing that contains seven declarations for $x$ and a single declaration for $y$ at level zero. *LookUp* might encounter all seven records for $x$ before finding $y$. With the open-addressing scheme, *LookUp* encounters one record for $x$ and one record for $y$.

## B.5  A FLEXIBLE SYMBOL-TABLE DESIGN

Most compilers use a symbol table as a central repository for information about the various names that arise in the source code, in the IR, and in the generated code. During compiler development, the set of fields in the symbol table seems to grow monotonically. Fields are added to support new passes and to communicate information between passes. When the need for a field disappears, it may or may not be removed from the symbol-table definition.

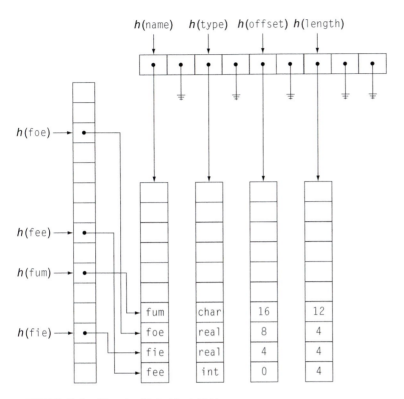

■ **FIGURE B.11**  Two-Dimensional Hashed Symbol Table.

As each field is added, the symbol table swells in size and any parts of the compiler with direct access to the symbol table must be recompiled.

We encountered this problem in the implementation of the $\mathcal{R}^n$ and Para-Scope programming environments. The experimental nature of these systems led to a situation where additions and deletions of symbol-table fields were common. To address the problem, we implemented a more complex but more flexible structure for the symbol table—a *two-dimensional hash table*. This eliminated almost all changes to the symbol-table definition and its implementation.

The two-dimensional table, shown in Figure B.11, uses two distinct hash index tables. The first, shown along the left edge of the drawing, corresponds to the sparse index table from Figure B.7. The implementation uses this table to hash on symbol names. The second, shown along the top of the drawing, is a hash table for field names. The programmer references individual fields by both their textual name and the name of the symbol; the implementation hashes the symbol name to obtain an index and the field name to select a vector of data. The desired attribute is stored in the vector under the symbol's index. It behaves as if each field has its own hash table, implemented as shown in Figure B.7.

While this seems complex, it is not particularly expensive. Each table access requires two hash computations rather than one. The implementation need not allocate storage for a given field until a value is stored in it; this avoids the space overhead of unused fields. It allows individual developers to create and delete symbol-table fields without interfering with other programmers.

Our implementation provided entry points for setting initial values for a field (by name), for deleting a field (by name), and for reporting statistics on field use. This scheme allows individual programmers to manage their own symbol-table use in a responsible and independent way, without interference from other programmers and their code.

As a final issue, the implementation should be abstract with respect to a specific symbol table. That is, it should always take a table instance as a parameter. This allows the compiler to reuse the implementation in many cases, such as the superlocal or dominator-based value numbering algorithms in Chapter 8.

## ■  APPENDIX NOTES

Many of the algorithms in a compiler manipulate sets, maps, tables, and graphs. The underlying implementations directly affect the space and time that those algorithms require and, ultimately, the usability of the compiler itself [57]. Algorithms and data-structure textbooks cover many of the issues that this appendix brings together [231, 4, 195, 109, 41].

Our research compilers have used almost all the data structures described in this appendix. We have seen performance problems from data-structure growth in several areas.

- Abstract syntax trees, as mentioned in the sidebar in Chapter 5, can grow unreasonably large. The technique of mapping an arbitrary tree onto a binary tree simplifies the implementation and seems to keep overhead low [231].
- The tabular representation of a graph, with lists of successors and predecessors, has been reinvented many times. It works particularly well for CFGs, for which the compiler iterates over both successors and predecessors. We first used this data structure in the PFC system in 1980.
- The sets in data-flow analysis can grow to occupy hundreds of megabytes. Because allocation and deallocation are performance issues at that scale, we routinely use Hanson's arena-based allocator [179].

- The size and sparsity of interference graphs makes them another area that merits careful consideration. We use the ordered-list variant with multiple set elements per node to keep the cost of building the graph low while managing the space overhead [101].

Symbol tables play a central role in the way that compilers store and access information. Much attention has been paid to the organization of these tables. Reorganizing lists [302, 317], balanced search trees [109, 41] and hashing [231, vol. 3] all play a role in making access to these tables efficient. Knuth [231, vol. 3] and Cormen [109] describe the multiplicative hash function in detail.

# Bibliography

[1] P.S. Abrams, An APL Machine, PhD thesis, Stanford University, Stanford, CA, 1970. Technical Report SLAC-R-114, Stanford Linear Accelerator Center, Stanford University, February 1970.

[2] A.V. Aho, M. Ganapathi, S.W.K. Tjiang, Code generation using tree matching and dynamic programming, ACM Trans. Program. Lang. Syst. 11 (4) (1989) 491–516.

[3] A.V. Aho, J.E. Hopcroft, J.D. Ullman, On finding lowest common ancestors in trees, in: Conference Record of the Fifth Annual ACM Symposium on Theory of Computing (STOC), ACM, New York, 1973, pp. 253–265.

[4] A.V. Aho, J.E. Hopcroft, J.D. Ullman, The Design and Analysis of Computer Algorithms, Addison-Wesley, Reading, MA, 1974.

[5] A.V. Aho, S.C. Johnson, Optimal code generation for expression trees, J. ACM 23 (3) (1976) 488–501.

[6] A.V. Aho, S.C. Johnson, J.D. Ullman, Code generation for expressions with common subexpressions, in: Conference Record of the Third ACM Symposium on Principles of Programming Languages, Atlanta, GA, ACM, New York, 1976, pp. 19–31.

[7] A.V. Aho, R. Sethi, J.D. Ullman, Compilers: Principles, Techniques, and Tools, Addison-Wesley, Reading, MA, 1986.

[8] A.V. Aho, J.D. Ullman, The Theory of Parsing, Translation, and Compiling, Prentice-Hall, Englewood Cliffs, NJ, 1973.

[9] P. Aigrain, S.L. Graham, R.R. Henry, M.K. McKusick, E. Pelegri-Llopart, Experience with a Graham-Glanville style code generator, SIGPLAN Not. 19 (6) (1984) 13–24. Proceedings of the ACM SIGPLAN '84 Symposium on Compiler Construction.

[10] A. Aiken, A. Nicolau, Optimal loop parallelization, SIGPLAN Not. 23 (7) (1988) 308–317. Proceedings of the ACM SIGPLAN '88 Conference on Programming Language Design and Implementation.

[11] F.E. Allen, Program optimization, in: M. Halpern, C. Shaw (Eds.), Annual Review in Automatic Programming, vol. 5, Pergamon Press, Oxford, England, 1969, pp. 239–307.

[12] F.E. Allen, Control flow analysis, SIGPLAN Not. 5 (7) (1970) 1–19. Proceedings of a Symposium on Compiler Optimization.

[13] F.E. Allen, A basis for program optimization, in: Proceedings of Information Processing 71, North-Holland Publishing Company, Amsterdam, 1971, pp. 385–390.

[14] F.E. Allen, The history of language processor technology in IBM, IBM J. Res. Dev. 25 (5) (1981) 535–548.

[15] F.E. Allen, Private communication, Dr. Allen noted that Beatty described live analysis in a document titled 'Optimization Methods for Highly Parallel, Multiregister Machines' dated September 1968, April 2009.

[16] F.E. Allen, J. Cocke, A catalogue of optimizing transformations, in: R. Rustin (Ed.), Design and Optimization of Compilers, Prentice-Hall, Englewood Cliffs, NJ, 1972, pp. 1–30.

[17] F.E. Allen, J. Cocke, Graph-Theoretic Constructs for Program Flow Analysis, Technical Report RC 3923 (17789), IBM Thomas J. Watson Research Center, Yorktown Heights, NY, 1972.

[18] F.E. Allen, J. Cocke, A program data flow analysis procedure, Commun. ACM 19 (3) (1976) 137–147.

[19] F.E. Allen, J. Cocke, K. Kennedy, Reduction of operator strength, in: S.S. Muchnick, N.D. Jones (Eds.), Program Flow Analysis: Theory and Applications, Prentice-Hall, Englewood Cliffs, NJ, 1981, pp. 79–101.

[20] J.R. Allen, K. Kennedy, Optimizing Compilers for Modern Architectures, Morgan Kaufmann, San Francisco, CA, 2001.

[21] B. Alpern, F.B. Schneider, Verifying temporal properties without temporal logic, ACM Trans. Program. Lang. Syst. 11 (1) (1989) 147–167.

[22] B. Alpern, M.N. Wegman, F.K. Zadeck, Detecting equality of variables in programs, in: Proceedings of the Fifteenth Annual ACM Symposium on Principles of Programming Languages, San Diego, CA, ACM, New York, 1988, pp. 1–11.

[23] S. Alstrup, D. Harel, P.W. Lauridsen, M. Thorup, Dominators in linear time, SIAM J. Comput. 28 (6) (1999) 2117–2132.

[24] M.A. Auslander, M.E. Hopkins, An overview of the PL.8 compiler, SIGPLAN Not. 17 (6) (1982) 22–31. Proceedings of the ACM SIGPLAN '82 Symposium on Compiler Construction.

[25] A. Ayers, R. Gottlieb, R. Schooler, Aggressive inlining, SIGPLAN Not. 32 (5) (1997) 134–145. Proceedings of the ACM SIGPLAN '97 Conference on Programming Language Design and Implementation.

[26] J.W. Backus, The history of FORTRAN I, II, and III, in: R.L. Wexelblat (Ed.), History of Programming Languages, Academic Press, New York, 1981, pp. 25–45.

[27] J.W. Backus, R.J. Beeber, S. Best, R. Goldberg, L.M. Haibt, H.L. Herrick, et al., The FORTRAN automatic coding system, in: Proceedings of the Western Joint Computer Conference, Institute of Radio Engineers, New York, 1957, pp. 188–198.

[28] D.F. Bacon, S.L. Graham, O.J. Sharp, Compiler transformations for high-performance computing, ACM Comput. Surv. 26 (4) (1994) 345–420.

[29] J.-L. Baer, D.P. Bovet, Compilation of arithmetic expressions for parallel computation, in: Proceedings of 1968 IFIP Congress, North-Holland Publishing Company, Amsterdam, 1969, pp. 340–346.

[30] J.T. Bagwell Jr., Local optimizations, SIGPLAN Not. 5 (7) (1970) 52–66. Proceedings of a Symposium on Compiler Optimization.

[31] J.E. Ball, Predicting the effects of optimization on a procedure body, in: SIGPLAN '79: Proceedings of the 1979 SIGPLAN Symposium on Compiler Construction, ACM, New York, 1979, pp. 214–220,

[32] J. Banning, An efficient way to find side effects of procedure calls and aliases of variables, in: Conference Record of the Sixth Annual ACM Symposium on Principles of Programming Languages, San Antonio, TX, ACM, New York, 1979, pp. 29–41.

[33] W.A. Barrett, J.D. Couch, Compiler Construction: Theory and Practice, Science Research Associates, Inc., Chicago, IL, 1979.

[34] J.M. Barth, An interprocedural data flow analysis algorithm, in: Conference Record of the Fourth ACM Symposium on Principles of Programming Languages, Los Angeles, CA, ACM, New York, 1977, pp. 119–131.

[35] A.M. Bauer, H.J. Saal, Does APL really need run-time checking? Softw. Pract. Experience 4 (2) (1974) 129–138.

[36] L.A. Belady, A study of replacement algorithms for a virtual storage computer, IBM Syst. J. 5 (2) (1966) 78–101.

[37] P. Bergner, P. Dahl, D. Engebretsen, M.T. O'Keefe, Spill code minimization via interference region spilling, SIGPLAN Not. 32 (5) (1997) 287–295. Proceedings of the ACM SIGPLAN '97 Conference on Programming Language Design and Implementation.

[38] D. Bernstein, D.Q. Goldin, M.C. Golumbic, H. Krawczyk, Y. Mansour, I. Nahshon, et al., Spill code minimization techniques for optimizing compilers, SIGPLAN Not. 24 (7) (1989) 258–263. Proceedings of the ACM SIGPLAN '89 Conference on Programming Language Design and Implementation.

[39] D. Bernstein, M. Rodeh, Global instruction scheduling for superscalar machines, SIGPLAN Not. 26 (6) (1991) 241–255. Proceedings of the ACM SIGPLAN '91 Conference on Programming Language Design and Implementation.

[40] R.L. Bernstein, Producing good code for the case statement, Softw. Pract. Experience 15 (10) (1985) 1021–1024.

[41] A. Binstock, J. Rex, Practical Algorithms for Programmers, Addison-Wesley, Reading, MA, 1995.

[42] P.L. Bird, An implementation of a code generator specification language for table driven code generators, SIGPLAN Not. 17 (6) (1982) 44–55. Proceedings of the ACM SIGPLAN '82 Symposium on Compiler Construction.

[43] R. Bodík, R. Gupta, M.L. Soffa, Complete removal of redundant expressions, SIGPLAN Not. 33 (5) (1998) 1–14. Proceedings of the ACM SIGPLAN '98 Conference on Programming Language Design and Implementation.

[44] H.-J. Boehm, Space efficient conservative garbage collection, SIGPLAN Not. 28 (6) (1993) 197–206. Proceedings of the ACM SIGPLAN '93 Conference on Programming Language Design and Implementation.

[45] H.-J. Boehm, A. Demers, Implementing Russell, SIGPLAN Not. 21 (7) (1986) 186–195. Proceedings of the ACM SIGPLAN '86 Symposium on Compiler Construction.

[46] H.-J. Boehm, M. Weiser, Garbage collection in an uncooperative environment, Softw. Pract. Experience 18 (9) (1988) 807–820.

[47] F. Bouchez, A Study of Spilling and Coalescing in Register Allocation As Two Separate Phases, PhD thesis, École Normale Supérieure de Lyon, Lyon, France, 2009.

[48] D.G. Bradlee, S.J. Eggers, R.R. Henry, Integrating register allocation and instruction scheduling for RISCs, SIGPLAN Not. 26 (4) (1991) 122–131. Proceedings of the Fourth International Conference on Architectural Support for Programming Languages and Operating Systems (ASPLOS-IV).

[49] P. Briggs, Register Allocation via Graph Coloring, PhD thesis, Department of Computer Science, Rice University, Houston, TX, 1992. Technical Report TR92-183, Computer Science Department, Rice University, 1992.

[50] P. Briggs, K.D. Cooper, T.J. Harvey, L.T. Simpson, Practical improvements to the construction and destruction of static single assignment form, Softw. Pract. Experience 28 (8) (1998) 859–881.

[51] P. Briggs, K.D. Cooper, K. Kennedy, L. Torczon, Coloring heuristics for register allocation, SIGPLAN Not. 24 (7) (1989) 275–284. Proceedings of the ACM SIGPLAN '89 Conference on Programming Language Design and Implementation.

[52] P. Briggs, K.D. Cooper, K. Kennedy, L. Torczon, Digital computer register allocation and code spilling using interference graph coloring, United States Patent 5,249,295, March 1993.

[53] P. Briggs, K.D. Cooper, L.T. Simpson, Value numbering, Softw. Pract. Experience 27 (6) (1997) 701–724.

[54] P. Briggs, K.D. Cooper, L. Torczon, Coloring register pairs, ACM Lett. Program. Lang. Syst. 1 (1) (1992) 3–13.

[55] P. Briggs, K.D. Cooper, L. Torczon, Rematerialization, SIGPLAN Not. 27 (7) (1992) 311–321. Proceedings of the ACM SIGPLAN '92 Conference on Programming Language Design and Implementation.

[56] P. Briggs, K.D. Cooper, L. Torczon, Improvements to graph coloring register allocation, ACM Trans. Program. Lang. Syst. 16 (3) (1994) 428–455.

[57] P. Briggs, L. Torczon, An efficient representation for sparse sets, ACM Lett. Program. Lang. Syst. 2 (1–4) (1993) 59–69.

[58] P. Brisk, F. Dabiri, J. Macbeth, M. Sarrafzadeh, Polynomial time graph coloring register allocation, in: $14^{th}$ International Workshop on Logic and Synthesis, Lake Arrowhead, CA, 2005, pp. 447–454.

[59] K. Brouwer, W. Gellerich, E. Ploedereder, Myths and facts about the efficient implementation of finite automata and lexical analysis, in: Proceedings of the International Conference on Compiler Construction CC'1998, vol. 1883 of LNCS, Springer-Verlag, Berlin, Heidelberg, 1998, pp. 1–15.

[60] J.A. Brzozowski, Canonical regular expressions and minimal state graphs for definite events, in: Mathematical Theory of Automata, vol. 12 of MRI Symposia Series, Polytechnic Press, Polytechnic Institute of Brooklyn, New York, 1962, pp. 529–561.

[61] A.L. Buchsbaum, H. Kaplan, A. Rogers, J.R. Westbrook, Linear-time pointer-machine algorithms for least common ancestors, MST verification, and dominators, in: Proceedings of the Thirtieth Annual ACM Symposium on Theory of Computing (STOC), Dallas, TX, ACM, New York, 1998, pp. 279–288.

[62] M. Burke, An interval-based approach to exhaustive and incremental interprocedural data-flow analysis, ACM Trans. Program. Lang. Syst. 12 (3) (1990) 341–395.

[63] M. Burke, J.-D. Choi, S. Fink, D. Grove, M. Hind, V. Sarkar, et al., The Jalapeño dynamic optimizing compiler for Java$^{TM}$, in: Proceedings of the ACM 1999 Conference on Java Grande, San Francisco, CA, ACM, New York, 1999, pp. 129–141.

[64] M. Burke, L. Torczon, Interprocedural optimization: eliminating unnecessary recompilation, ACM Trans. Program. Lang. Syst. 15 (3) (1993) 367–399.

[65] J. Cai, R. Paige, Using multiset discrimination to solve language processing problems without hashing, Theor. Comput. Sci. 145 (1–2) (1995) 189–228.

[66] B. Calder, D. Grunwald, Reducing branch costs via branch alignment, SIGPLAN Not. 29 (11) (1994) 242–251. Proceedings of the Sixth International Conference on Architectural Support for Programming Languages and Operating Systems (ASPLOS-VI).

[67] D. Callahan, S. Carr, K. Kennedy, Improving register allocation for subscripted variables, SIGPLAN Not. 25 (6) (1990) 53–65. Proceedings of the ACM SIGPLAN '90 Conference on Programming Language Design and Implementation.

[68] D. Callahan, K.D. Cooper, K. Kennedy, L. Torczon, Interprocedural constant propagation, SIGPLAN Not. 21 (7) (1986) 152–161. Proceedings of the ACM SIGPLAN '86 Symposium on Compiler Construction.

[69] L. Cardelli, Type systems, in: A.B. Tucker Jr. (Ed.), The Computer Science and Engineering Handbook, CRC Press, Boca Raton, FL, 1996, pp. 2208–2236.

[70] S. Carr, K. Kennedy, Scalar replacement in the presence of conditional control flow, Softw. Pract. Experience 24 (1) (1994) 51–77.

[71] R.G.G. Cattell, Automatic derivation of code generators from machine descriptions, ACM Trans. Program. Lang. Syst. 2 (2) (1980) 173–190.

[72] R.G.G. Cattell, J.M. Newcomer, B.W. Leverett, Code generation in a machine-independent compiler, SIGPLAN Not. 14 (8) (1979) 65–75. Proceedings of the ACM SIGPLAN '79 Symposium on Compiler Construction.

[73] G.J. Chaitin, Register allocation and spilling via graph coloring, SIGPLAN Not. 17 (6) (1982) 98–105. Proceedings of the ACM SIGPLAN '82 Symposium on Compiler Construction.

[74] G.J. Chaitin, Register allocation and spilling via graph coloring, United States Patent 4,571,678, February 1986.

[75] G.J. Chaitin, M.A. Auslander, A.K. Chandra, J. Cocke, M.E. Hopkins, P.W. Markstein, Register allocation via coloring, Comput. Lang. 6 (1) (1981) 47–57.

[76] D.R. Chase, An improvement to bottom-up tree pattern matching, in: Proceedings of the Fourteenth Annual ACM Symposium on Principles of Programming Languages, Munich, Germany, ACM, New York, 1987, pp. 168–177,

[77] D.R. Chase, M. Wegman, F.K. Zadeck, Analysis of pointers and structures, SIGPLAN Not. 25 (6) (1990) 296–310. Proceedings of the ACM SIGPLAN '90 Conference on Programming Language Design and Implementation.

[78] J.B. Chen, B.D.D. Leupen, Improving instruction locality with just-in-time code layout, in: Proceedings of the First USENIX Windows NT Workshop, Seattle, WA, The USENIX Association, Berkeley, CA, 1997, pp. 25–32.

[79] C.J. Cheney, A nonrecursive list compacting algorithm, Commun. ACM 13 (11) (1970) 677–678.

[80] J.-D. Choi, M. Burke, P.R. Carini, Efficient flow-sensitive interprocedural computation of pointer-induced aliases and side effects, in: Proceedings of the Twentieth Annual ACM SIGPLAN-SIGACT Symposium on Principles of Programming Languages, Charleston, SC, ACM, New York, 1993, pp. 232–245.

[81] F.C. Chow, A Portable Machine-Independent Global Optimizer—Design and Measurements, PhD thesis, Department of Electrical Engineering, Stanford University, Stanford, CA, 1983. Technical Report CSL-TR-83-254, Computer Systems Laboratory, Stanford University, December 1983.

[82] F.C. Chow, J.L. Hennessy, Register allocation by priority-based coloring, SIGPLAN Not. 19 (6) (1984) 222–232. Proceedings of the ACM SIGPLAN '84 Symposium on Compiler Construction.

[83] F.C. Chow, J.L. Hennessy, The priority-based coloring approach to register allocation, ACM Trans. Program. Lang. Syst. 12 (4) (1990) 501–536.

[84] C. Click, Combining Analyses, Combining Optimizations, PhD thesis, Department of Computer Science, Rice University, Houston, TX, 1995. Technical Report TR95-252, Computer Science Department, Rice University, 1995.

[85] C. Click, Global code motion/global value numbering, SIGPLAN Not. 30 (6) (1995) 246–257. Proceedings of the ACM SIGPLAN '95 Conference on Programming Language Design and Implementation.

[86] C. Click, K.D. Cooper, Combining analyses, combining optimizations, ACM Trans. Program. Lang. Syst. 17 (2) (1995) 181–196.

[87] J. Cocke, Global common subexpression elimination, SIGPLAN Not. 5 (7) (1970) 20–24. Proceedings of a Symposium on Compiler Optimization.

[88] J. Cocke, K. Kennedy, An algorithm for reduction of operator strength, Commun. ACM 20 (11) (1977) 850–856.

[89] J. Cocke, P.W. Markstein, Measurement of program improvement algorithms, in: S.H. Lavington (Ed.), Proceedings of IFIP Congress 80, Information Processing 80, North Holland, Amsterdam, Netherlands, 1980, pp. 221–228.

[90] J. Cocke, P.W. Markstein, Strength reduction for division and modulo with application to accessing a multilevel store, IBM J. Res. Dev. 24 (6) (1980) 692–694.

[91] J. Cocke, J.T. Schwartz, Programming Languages and Their Compilers: Preliminary Notes, Technical Report, Courant Institute of Mathematical Sciences, New York University, New York, 1970.

[92] J. Cohen, Garbage collection of linked structures, ACM Comput. Surv. 13 (3) (1981) 341–367.

[93] R. Cohn, P.G. Lowney, Hot cold optimization of large Windows/NT applications, in: Proceedings of the Twenty-Ninth IEEE/ACM Annual International Symposium on Microarchitecture (MICRO-29), Paris, France, ACM, New York, 1996, pp. 80–89.

[94] S. Coleman, K.S. McKinley, Tile size selection using cache organization and data layout, SIGPLAN Not. 30 (6) (1995) 279–290. Proceedings of the ACM SIGPLAN '95 Conference on Programming Language Design and Implementation.

[95] G.E. Collins, A method for overlapping and erasure of lists, Commun. ACM 3 (12) (1960) 655–657.

[96] M.E. Conway, Design of a separable transition diagram compiler, Commun. ACM 6 (7) (1963) 396–408.

[97] R.W. Conway, T.R. Wilcox, Design and implementation of a diagnostic compiler for PL/I, Commun. ACM 16 (3) (1973) 169–179.

[98] K.D. Cooper, J. Eckhardt, Improved passive splitting, in: Proceedings of the 2005 International Conference on Programming Languages and Compilers, Computer Science Research, Education, and Applications (CSREA) Press, Athens, Georgia, 2005, pp. 1155–1122.

[99] K.D. Cooper, M.W. Hall, L. Torczon, An experiment with inline substitution, Softw. Pract. Experience 21 (6) (1991) 581–601.

[100] K.D. Cooper, T.J. Harvey, K. Kennedy, A Simple, Fast Dominance Algorithm, Technical Report TR06-38870, Rice University Computer Science Department, Houston, TX, 2006.

[101] K.D. Cooper, T.J. Harvey, L. Torczon, How to build an interference graph, Softw. Pract. Experience 28 (4) (1998) 425–444.

[102] K.D. Cooper, K. Kennedy, Interprocedural side-effect analysis in linear time, SIGPLAN Not. 23 (7) (1988) 57–66. Proceedings of the ACM SIGPLAN '88 Conference on Programming Language Design and Implementation.

[103] K.D. Cooper, K. Kennedy, Fast interprocedural alias analysis, in: Proceedings of the Sixteenth Annual ACM Symposium on Principles of Programming Languages, Austin, TX, ACM, New York, 1989, pp. 49–59.

[104] K.D. Cooper, K. Kennedy, L. Torczon, The impact of interprocedural analysis and optimization in the Rn programming environment, ACM Trans. Program. Lang. Syst. 8 (4) (1986) 491–523.

[105] K.D. Cooper, P.J. Schielke, Non-local instruction scheduling with limited code growth, in: F. Mueller, A. Bestavros (Eds.), Proceedings of the 1998 ACM SIG-PLAN Workshop on Languages, Compilers, and Tools for Embedded Systems (LCTES), Lecture Notes in Computer Science 1474, Springer-Verlag, Heidelberg, Germany, 1998, pp. 193–207.

[106] K.D. Cooper, L.T. Simpson, Live range splitting in a graph coloring register allocator, in: Proceedings of the Seventh International Compiler Construction Conference (CC '98), Lecture Notes in Computer Science 1383, Springer-Verlag, Heidelberg, Germany, 1998, pp. 174–187.

[107] K.D. Cooper, L.T. Simpson, C.A. Vick, Operator strength reduction, ACM Trans. Program. Lang. Syst. 23 (5) (2001) 603–625.

[108] K.D. Cooper, T. Waterman, Understanding energy consumption on the C62x, in: Proceedings of the 2002 Workshop on Compilers and Operating Systems for Low Power, Charlottesville, VA, 2002, pp. 4-1–4-8.

[109] T.H. Cormen, C.E. Leiserson, R.L. Rivest, Introduction to Algorithms, MIT Press, Cambridge, MA, 1992.

[110] R. Cytron, J. Ferrante, B.K. Rosen, M.N. Wegman, F.K. Zadeck, Efficiently computing static single assignment form and the control dependence graph, ACM Trans. Program. Lang. Syst. 13 (4) (1991) 451–490.

[111] R. Cytron, A. Lowry, F.K. Zadeck, Code motion of control structures in high-level languages, in: Conference Record of the Thirteenth Annual ACM Symposium on Principles of Programming Languages, St. Petersburg Beach, FL, ACM, New York, 1986, pp. 70–85.

[112] J. Daciuk, Comparison of construction algorithms for minimal, acyclic, deterministic finite-state automata from sets of strings, in: Seventh International Conference on Implementation and Application of Automata, CIAA 2002, vol. 2068 of LNCS, Springer-Verlag, Berlin, Heidelberg, 2003, pp. 255–261.

[113] M. Das, Unification-based pointer analysis with directional assignments, SIGPLAN Not. 35 (5) (2000) 35–46. Proceedings of the ACM SIGPLAN '00 Conference on Programming Language Design and Implementation.

[114] J. Davidson, S. Jinturkar, Aggressive loop unrolling in a retargetable optimizing compiler, in: Proceedings of the 6th International Conference on Compiler Construction (CC '96), Linköping, Sweden, April 24–26, Springer-Verlag, London, 1996, pp. 59–73.

[115] J.W. Davidson, C.W. Fraser, The design and application of a retargetable peephole optimizer, ACM Trans. Program. Lang. Syst. 2 (2) (1980) 191–202.

[116] J.W. Davidson, C.W. Fraser, Automatic generation of peephole optimizations, SIGPLAN Not. 19 (6) (1984) 111–116. Proceedings of the ACM SIGPLAN '84 Symposium on Compiler Construction.

[117] J.W. Davidson, C.W. Fraser, Register allocation and exhaustive peephole optimization, Softw. Pract. Experience 14 (9) (1984) 857–865.

[118] J.W. Davidson, C.W. Fraser, Automatic inference and fast interpretation of peephole optimization rules, Softw. Pract. Experience 17 (11) (1987) 801–812.

[119] J.W. Davidson, A.M. Holler, A study of a C function inliner, Softw. Pract. Experience 18 (8) (1988) 775–790.

[120] A.J. Demers, M. Weiser, B. Hayes, H. Boehm, D. Bobrow, S. Shenker, Combining generational and conservative garbage collection: framework and implementations, in: Proceedings of the Seventeenth Annual ACM Symposium on Principles of Programming Languages, San Francisco, CA, ACM, New York, 1990, pp. 261–269.

[121] F. DeRemer, Simple LR(k) grammars, Commun. ACM 14 (7) (1971) 453–460.

[122] F. DeRemer, T.J. Pennello, Efficient computation of LALR(1) look-ahead sets, SIGPLAN Not. 14 (8) (1979) 176–187. Proceedings of the ACM SIGPLAN '79 Symposium on Compiler Construction.

[123] A. Deutsch, Interprocedural May-Alias analysis for pointers: beyond $k$-limiting, SIGPLAN Not. 29 (6) (1994) 230–241. Proceedings of the ACM SIGPLAN '94 Conference on Programming Language Design and Implementation.

[124] L.P. Deutsch, An Interactive Program Verifier, PhD thesis, Computer Science Department, University of California, Berkeley, CA, 1973. Technical Report CSL-73-1, Xerox Palo Alto Research, May 1973.

[125] L.P. Deutsch, D.G. Bobrow, An efficient, incremental, automatic, garbage collector, Commun. ACM 19 (9) (1976) 522–526.

[126] L.P. Deutsch, A.M. Schiffman, Efficient implementation of the Smalltalk-80 system, in: Conference Record of the Eleventh Annual ACM Symposium on Principles of Programming Languages, Salt Lake City, UT, ACM, New York, 1984, pp. 297–302.

[127] D.M. Dhamdhere, On algorithms for operator strength reduction, Commun. ACM 22 (5) (1979) 311–312.

[128] D.M. Dhamdhere, A fast algorithm for code movement optimisation, SIGPLAN Not. 23 (10) (1988) 172–180.

[129] D.M. Dhamdhere, A new algorithm for composite hoisting and strength reduction, Int. J. Comput. Math. 27 (1) (1989) 1–14.

[130] D.M. Dhamdhere, Practical adaptation of the global optimization algorithm of Morel and Renvoise, ACM Trans. Program. Lang. Syst. 13 (2) (1991) 291–294.

[131] D.M. Dhamdhere, J.R. Isaac, A composite algorithm for strength reduction and code movement optimization, Int. J. Comput. Inf. Sci. 9 (3) (1980) 243–273.

[132] M.K. Donegan, R.E. Noonan, S. Feyock, A code generator generator language, SIGPLAN Not. 14 (8) (1979) 58–64. Proceedings of the ACM SIGPLAN '79 Symposium on Compiler Construction.

[133] K.-H. Drechsler, M.P. Stadel, A solution to a problem with Morel and Renvoise's "Global optimization by suppression of partial redundancies," ACM Trans. Program. Lang. Syst. 10 (4) (1988) 635–640.

[134] K.-H. Drechsler, M.P. Stadel, A variation of Knoop, Rüthing, and Steffen's "lazy code motion," SIGPLAN Not. 28 (5) (1993) 29–38.

[135] J. Earley, An efficient context-free parsing algorithm, Commun. ACM 13 (2) (1970) 94–102.

[136] K. Ebcioğlu, T. Nakatani, A new compilation technique for parallelizing loops with unpredictable branches on a VLIW architecture, in: Selected Papers of

the Second Workshop on Languages and Compilers for Parallel Computing (LCPC '89), Pitman Publishing, London, 1990, pp. 213–229.

[137] J.R. Ellis, Bulldog: A Compiler for VLIW Architectures, The MIT Press, Cambridge, MA, 1986.

[138] M. Emami, R. Ghiya, L.J. Hendren, Context-sensitive interprocedural points-to analysis in the presence of function pointers, SIGPLAN Not. 29 (6) (1994) 242–256. Proceedings of the ACM SIGPLAN '94 Conference on Programming Language Design and Implementation.

[139] A.P. Ershov, On programming of arithmetic expressions, Commun. ACM 1 (8) (1958) 3–6. The figures appear in volume 1, number 9, page 16.

[140] A.P. Ershov, Reduction of the problem of memory allocation in programming to the problem of coloring the vertices of graphs, Sov. Math. 3 (1962) 163–165. Originally published in Doklady Akademii Nauk S.S.S.R. 142 (4) (1962).

[141] A.P. Ershov, Alpha: an automatic programming system of high efficiency, J. ACM 13 (1) (1966) 17–24.

[142] R. Farrow, Linguist-86: yet another translator writing system based on attribute grammars, SIGPLAN Not. 17 (6) (1982) 160–171. Proceedings of the ACM SIGPLAN '82 Symposium on Compiler Construction.

[143] R. Farrow, Automatic generation of fixed-point-finding evaluators for circular, but well-defined, attribute grammars, SIGPLAN Not. 21 (7) (1986) 85–98. Proceedings of the ACM SIGPLAN '86 Symposium on Compiler Construction.

[144] R.R. Fenichel, J.C. Yochelson, A LISP garbage-collector for virtual-memory computer systems, Commun. ACM 12 (11) (1969) 611–612.

[145] J. Ferrante, K.J. Ottenstein, J.D. Warren, The program dependence graph and its use in optimization, ACM Trans. Program. Lang. Syst. 9 (3) (1987) 319–349.

[146] C.N. Fischer, R.J. LeBlanc Jr., The implementation of run-time diagnostics in Pascal, IEEE Trans. Software Eng. SE-6 (4) (1980) 313–319.

[147] C.N. Fischer, R.J. LeBlanc Jr., Crafting a Compiler with C, Benjamin/Cummings, Redwood City, CA, 1991.

[148] J.A. Fisher, Trace scheduling: a technique for global microcode compaction, IEEE Trans. Comput. C-30 (7) (1981) 478–490.

[149] J.A. Fisher, J.R. Ellis, J.C. Ruttenberg, A. Nicolau, Parallel processing: a smart compiler and a dumb machine, SIGPLAN Not. 19 (6) (1984) 37–47. Proceedings of the ACM SIGPLAN '84 Symposium on Compiler Construction.

[150] R.W. Floyd, An algorithm for coding efficient arithmetic expressions, Commun. ACM 4 (1) (1961) 42–51.

[151] J.M. Foster, A syntax improving program, Comput. J. 11 (1) (1968) 31–34.

[152] C.W. Fraser, D.R. Hanson, T.A. Proebsting, Engineering a simple, efficient code generator generator, ACM Lett. Program. Lang. Syst. 1 (3) (1992) 213–226.

[153] C.W. Fraser, R.R. Henry, Hard-coding bottom-up code generation tables to save time and space, Softw. Pract. Experience 21 (1) (1991) 1–12.

[154] C.W. Fraser, A.L. Wendt, Integrating code generation and optimization, SIGPLAN Not. 21 (7) (1986) 242–248. Proceedings of the ACM SIGPLAN '86 Symposium on Compiler Construction.

[155] C.W. Fraser, A.L. Wendt, Automatic generation of fast optimizing code generators, SIGPLAN Not. 23 (7) (1988) 79–84. Proceedings of the ACM SIGPLAN '88 Conference on Programming Language Design and Implementation.

[156] M. Ganapathi, C.N. Fischer, Description-driven code generation using attribute grammars, in: Conference Record of the Ninth Annual ACM Symposium on Principles of Programming Languages, Albuquerque, NM, ACM, New York, 1982, pp. 108–119.

[157] H. Ganzinger, R. Giegerich, U. Möncke, R. Wilhelm, A truly generative semantics-directed compiler generator, SIGPLAN Not. 17 (6) (1982) 172–184. Proceedings of the ACM SIGPLAN '82 Symposium on Compiler Construction.

[158] L. George, A.W. Appel, Iterated register coalescing, in: Proceedings of the Twenty-Third ACM SIGPLAN-SIGACT Symposium on Principles of Programming Languages, St. Petersburg Beach, FL, ACM, New York, 1996, pp. 208–218.

[159] P.B. Gibbons, S.S. Muchnick, Efficient instruction scheduling for a pipelined architecture, SIGPLAN Not. 21 (7) (1986) 11–16. Proceedings of the ACM SIGPLAN '86 Symposium on Compiler Construction.

[160] R.S. Glanville, S.L. Graham, A new method for compiler code generation, in: Conference Record of the Fifth Annual ACM Symposium on Principles of Programming Languages, Tucson, AZ, ACM, New York, 1978, pp. 231–240.

[161] N. Gloy, M.D. Smith, Procedure placement using temporal-ordering information, ACM Trans. Program. Lang. Syst. 21 (5) (1999) 977–1027.

[162] A. Goldberg, D. Robson, Smalltalk-80: The Language and Its Implementation, Addison-Wesley, Reading, MA, 1983.

[163] J.R. Goodman, W.-C. Hsu, Code scheduling and register allocation in large basic blocks, in: Proceedings of the Second International Conference on Supercomputing, ACM, New York, 1988, pp. 442–452.

[164] E. Goto, Monocopy and Associative Operations in Extended Lisp, Technical Report 74-03, University of Tokyo, Tokyo, Japan, 1974.

[165] S.L. Graham, Table-driven code generation, IEEE Comput. 13 (8) (1980) 25–34.

[166] S.L. Graham, M.A. Harrison, W.L. Ruzzo, An improved context-free recognizer, ACM Trans. Program. Lang. Syst. 2 (3) (1980) 415–462.

[167] S.L. Graham, R.R. Henry, R.A. Schulman, An experiment in table driven code generation, SIGPLAN Not. 17 (6) (1982) 32–43. Proceedings of the ACM SIGPLAN '82 Symposium on Compiler Construction.

[168] S.L. Graham, M. Wegman, A fast and usually linear algorithm for global flow analysis, in: Conference Record of the Second ACM Symposium on Principles of Programming Languages, Palo Alto, CA, ACM, New York, 1975, pp. 22–34.

[169] S.L. Graham, M. Wegman, A fast and usually linear algorithm for global flow analysis, J. ACM 23 (1) (1976) 172–202.

[170] T. Granlund, R. Kenner, Eliminating branches using a superoptimizer and the GNU C compiler, SIGPLAN Not. 27 (7) (1992) 341–352. Proceedings of the ACM SIGPLAN '92 Conference on Programming Language Design and Implementation.

[171] D. Gries, Compiler Construction for Digital Computers, John Wiley & Sons, New York, 1971.

[172] D. Grove, L. Torczon, Interprocedural constant propagation: a study of jump function implementations, in: Proceedings of the ACM SIGPLAN 93 Conference on Programming Language Design and Implementation (PLDI), ACM, New York, 1993, pp. 90–99. Also published as SIGPLAN Not. 28 (6) (1993).

[173] R. Gupta, Optimizing array bound checks using flow analysis, ACM Lett. Program. Lang. Syst. (LOPLAS) 2 (1993) 135–150.

[174] R. Gupta, M.L. Soffa, Region scheduling: an approach for detecting and redistributing parallelism, IEEE Trans. Software Eng. SE-16 (4) (1990) 421–431.

[175] R. Gupta, M.L. Soffa, T. Steele, Register allocation via clique separators, SIGPLAN Not. 24 (7) (1989) 264–274. Proceedings of the ACM SIGPLAN '89 Conference on Programming Language Design and Implementation.

[176] S. Hack, Register Allocation for Programs in SSA Form, PhD thesis, Universität Karlsruhe, Karlsruhe, Germany, 2007.

[177] S. Hack, G. Goos, Optimal register allocation for SSA-form programs in polynomial time, Inf. Process. Lett. 98 (4) (2006) 150–155.

[178] M. Hailperin, Cost-optimal code motion, ACM Trans. Program. Lang. Syst. 20 (6) (1998) 1297–1322.

[179] D.R. Hanson, Fast allocation and deallocation of memory based on object lifetimes, Softw. Pract. Experience 20 (1) (1990) 5–12.

[180] D. Harel, A linear time algorithm for finding dominators in flow graphs and related problems, in: Proceedings of the Seventeenth Annual ACM Symposium on Theory of Computing (STOC), ACM, New York, 1985, pp. 185–194.

[181] W.H. Harrison, A Class of Register Allocation Algorithms, Technical Report RC-5342, IBM Thomas J. Watson Research Center, Yorktown Heights, NY, 1975.

[182] W.H. Harrison, A new strategy for code generation: the general purpose optimizing compiler, IEEE Trans. Software Eng. SE-5 (4) (1979) 367–373.

[183] A.H. Hashemi, D.R. Kaeli, B. Calder, Efficient procedure mapping using cache line coloring, in: Proceedings of the ACM SIGPLAN 1997 Conference on Programming Language Design and Implementation, ACM, New York, 1997, pp. 171–182. Also appeared as SIGPLAN Not. 32 (5).

[184] P.J. Hatcher, T.W. Christopher, High-quality code generation via bottom-up tree pattern matching, in: Conference Record of the Thirteenth Annual ACM Symposium on Principles of Programming Languages, St. Petersburg Beach, FL, ACM, New York, 1986, pp. 119–130.

[185] M.S. Hecht, J.D. Ullman, Characterizations of reducible flow graphs, J. ACM 21 (3) (1974) 367–375.

[186] M.S. Hecht, J.D. Ullman, A simple algorithm for global data flow analysis problems, SIAM J. Comput. 4 (4) (1975) 519–532.

[187] J. Heller, Sequencing aspects of multiprogramming, J. ACM 8 (3) (1961) 426–439.

[188] J.L. Hennessy, T. Gross, Postpass code optimization of pipeline constraints, ACM Trans. Program. Lang. Syst. 5 (3) (1983) 422–448.

[189] V.P. Heuring, The automatic generation of fast lexical analysers, Softw. Pract. Experience 16 (9) (1986) 801–808.

[190] M. Hind, M. Burke, P. Carini, J.-D. Choi, Interprocedural pointer alias analysis, ACM Trans. Program. Lang. Syst. 21 (4) (1999) 848–894.

[191] M. Hind, A. Pioli, Which pointer analysis should I use? ACM SIGSOFT Software Eng. Notes 25 (5) (2000) 113–123. In Proceedings of the International Symposium on Software Testing and Analysis.

[192] C.M. Hoffmann, M.J. O'Donnell, Pattern matching in trees, J. ACM 29 (1) (1982) 68–95.

[193] J.E. Hopcroft, An $n \log n$ algorithm for minimizing states in a finite automaton, in: Z. Kohavi, A. Paz (Eds.), Theory of Machines and Computations: Proceedings, Academic Press, New York, 1971, pp. 189–196.

[194] J.E. Hopcroft, J.D. Ullman, Introduction to Automata Theory, Languages, and Computation, Addison-Wesley, Reading, MA, 1979.

[195] E. Horowitz, S. Sahni, Fundamentals of Computer Algorithms, Computer Science Press, Inc., Potomac, MD, 1978.

[196] L.P. Horwitz, R.M. Karp, R.E. Miller, S. Winograd, Index register allocation, J. ACM 13 (1) (1966) 43–61.

[197] S. Horwitz, P. Pfeiffer, T. Reps, Dependence analysis for pointer variables, SIG-PLAN Not. 24 (7) (1989) 28–40. Proceedings of the ACM SIGPLAN '89 Conference on Programming Language Design and Implementation.

[198] S. Horwitz, T. Teitelbaum, Generating editing environments based on relations and attributes, ACM Trans. Program. Lang. Syst. 8 (4) (1986) 577–608.

[199] B.L. Huber, Path-Selection Heuristics for Dominator-Path Scheduling, Master's thesis, Computer Science Department, Michigan Technological University, Houghton, MI, 1995.

[200] W. Hunt, B. Maher, K. Coons, D. Burger, K.S. McKinley, Optimal Huffman tree-height reduction for instruction level parallelism, unpublished manuscript, provided by authors, 2006.

[201] W.-M.W. Hwu, S.A. Mahlke, W.Y. Chen, P.P. Chang, N.J. Warter, R.A. Bringmann, et al., The superblock: an effective technique for VLIW and superscalar compilation, J. Supercomputing—Special Issue on Instruction Level Parallelism 7 (1–2) (1993) 229–248.

[202] E.T. Irons, A syntax directed compiler for Algol 60, Commun. ACM 4 (1) (1961) 51–55.

[203] M. Jazayeri, K.G. Walter, Alternating semantic evaluator, in: Proceedings of the 1975 Annual Conference of the ACM, ACM, New York, 1975, pp. 230–234.

[204] M.S. Johnson, T.C. Miller, Effectiveness of a machine-level, global optimizer, SIGPLAN Not. 21 (7) (1986) 99–108. Proceedings of the ACM SIGPLAN '86 Symposium on Compiler Construction.

[205] S.C. Johnson, Yacc: Yet Another Compiler-Compiler, Technical Report 32 (Computing Science), AT&T Bell Laboratories, Murray Hill, NJ, 1975.

[206] S.C. Johnson, A tour through the portable C compiler, in: Unix Programmer's Manual, seventh ed., vol. 2b, AT&T Bell Laboratories, Murray Hill, NJ, 1979.

[207] W.L. Johnson, J.H. Porter, S.I. Ackley, D.T. Ross, Automatic generation of efficient lexical processors using finite state techniques, Commun. ACM 11 (12) (1968) 805–813.

[208] D.W. Jones, How (not) to code a finite state machine, ACM SIGPLAN Not. 23 (8) (1988) 19–22.

[209] S.M. Joshi, D.M. Dhamdhere, A composite hoisting-strength reduction transformation for global program optimization, Int. J. Comput. Math. 11 (1) (1982) 21–44 (part I); 11 (2) 111–126 (part II).

[210] J.B. Kam, J.D. Ullman, Global data flow analysis and iterative algorithms, J. ACM 23 (1) (1976) 158–171.

[211] J.B. Kam, J.D. Ullman, Monotone data flow analysis frameworks, Acta Informatica 7 (1977) 305–317.

[212] T. Kasami, An efficient recognition and syntax analysis algorithm for context-free languages, Scientific Report AFCRL-65-758, Air Force Cambridge Research Laboratory, Bedford, MA, 1965.

[213] K. Kennedy, A global flow analysis algorithm, Int. J. Comput. Math. Sect. A 3 (1971) 5–15.

[214] K. Kennedy, Global Flow Analysis and Register Allocation for Simple Code Structures, PhD thesis, Courant Institute of Mathematical Sciences, New York University, New York, 1971.

[215] K. Kennedy, Global dead computation elimination, SETL Newsletter 111, Courant Institute of Mathematical Sciences, New York University, New York, 1973.

[216] K. Kennedy, Reduction in strength using hashed temporaries, SETL Newsletter 102, Courant Institute of Mathematical Sciences, New York University, New York, 1973.

[217] K. Kennedy, Use-definition chains with applications, Comput. Lang. 3 (3) (1978) 163–179.

[218] K. Kennedy, A survey of data flow analysis techniques, in: N.D. Jones, S.S. Muchnik (Eds.), Program Flow Analysis: Theory and Applications, Prentice-Hall, Englewood Cliffs, NJ, 1981, pp. 5–54.

[219] K. Kennedy, L. Zucconi, Applications of graph grammar for program control flow analysis, in: Conference Record of the Fourth ACM Symposium on Principles of Programming Languages, Los Angeles, CA, ACM, New York, 1977, pp. 72–85.

[220] R. Kennedy, F.C. Chow, P. Dahl, S.-M. Liu, R. Lo, M. Streich, Strength reduction via SSAPRE, in: Proceedings of the Seventh International Conference on Compiler Construction (CC '98), Lecture Notes in Computer Science 1383, Springer-Verlag, Heidelberg, Germany, 1998, pp. 144–158.

[221] D.R. Kerns, S.J. Eggers, Balanced scheduling: instruction scheduling when memory latency is uncertain, SIGPLAN Not. 28 (6) (1993) 278–289. Proceedings of the ACM SIGPLAN '93 Conference on Programming Language Design and Implementation.

[222] R.R. Kessler, Peep: an architectural description driven peephole optimizer, SIGPLAN Not. 19 (6) (1984) 106–110. Proceedings of the ACM SIGPLAN '84 Symposium on Compiler Construction.

[223] G.A. Kildall, A unified approach to global program optimization, in: Conference Record of the ACM Symposium on Principles of Programming Languages, Boston, MA, ACM, New York, 1973, pp. 194–206.

[224] S.C. Kleene, Representation of events in nerve nets and finite automata, in: C.E. Shannon, J. McCarthy (Eds.), Automata Studies, Annals of Mathematics Studies, vol. 34, Princeton University Press, Princeton, NJ, 1956, pp. 3–41.

[225] J. Knoop, O. Rüthing, B. Steffen, Lazy code motion, SIGPLAN Not. 27 (7) (1992) 224–234. Proceedings of the ACM SIGPLAN '92 Conference on Programming Language Design and Implementation.

[226] J. Knoop, O. Rüthing, B. Steffen, Lazy strength reduction, Int. J. Program. Lang. 1 (1) (1993) 71–91.

[227] D.E. Knuth, A history of writing compilers, Comput. Autom. 11 (12) (1962) 8–18. Reprinted in Compiler Techniques, B.W. Pollack (Ed.), Auerbach, Princeton, NJ, 1972, pp. 38–56.

[228] D.E. Knuth, On the translation of languages from left to right, Inf. Control 8 (6) (1965) 607–639.

[229] D.E. Knuth, Semantics of context-free languages, Math. Syst. Theory 2 (2) (1968) 127–145.

[230] D.E. Knuth, Semantics of context-free languages: correction, Math. Syst. Theory 5 (1) (1971) 95–96.

[231] D.E. Knuth, The Art of Computer Programming, Addison-Wesley, Reading, MA, 1973.

[232] D.C. Kozen, Automata and Computability, Springer-Verlag, New York, 1997.

[233] G. Krasner (Eds.), Smalltalk-80: Bits of History, Words of Advice. Addison-Wesley, Reading, MA, 1983.

[234] S.M. Krishnamurthy, A brief survey of papers on scheduling for pipelined processors, SIGPLAN Not. 25 (7) (1990) 97–106.

[235] S.M. Kurlander, C.N. Fischer, Zero-cost range splitting, SIGPLAN Not. 29 (6) (1994) 257–265. Proceedings of the ACM SIGPLAN '94 Conference on Programming Language Design and Implementation.

[236] M. Lam, Software pipelining: an effective scheduling technique for VLIW machines, SIGPLAN Not. 23 (7) (1988) 318–328. Proceedings of the ACM SIGPLAN '88 Conference on Programming Language Design and Implementation.

[237] D.A. Lamb, Construction of a peephole optimizer, Softw. Pract. Experience 11 (6) (1981) 639–647.

[238] W. Landi, B.G. Ryder, Pointer-induced aliasing: a problem taxonomy, in: Proceedings of the Eighteenth Annual ACM Symposium on Principles of Programming Languages, Orlando, FL, ACM, New York, 1991, pp. 93–103.

[239] D. Landskov, S. Davidson, B. Shriver, P.W. Mallett, Local microcode compaction techniques, ACM Comput. Surv. 12 (3) (1980) 261–294.

[240] R. Landwehr, H.-S. Jansohn, G. Goos, Experience with an automatic code generator generator, SIGPLAN Not. 17 (6) (1982) 56–66. Proceedings of the ACM SIGPLAN '82 Symposium on Compiler Construction.

[241] J.R. Larus, P.N. Hilfinger, Register allocation in the SPUR Lisp compiler, SIGPLAN Not. 21 (7) (1986) 255–263. Proceedings of the ACM SIGPLAN '86 Symposium on Compiler Construction.

[242] S.S. Lavrov, Store economy in closed operator schemes, J. Comput. Math. Math. Phys. 1 (4) (1961) 687–701. English translation in U.S.S.R. Computational Mathematics and Mathematical Physics 3 (1962) 810–828.

[243] V. Lefévre, Multiplication By an Integer Constant, Technical Report 4192, INRIA, Lorraine, France, 2001.

[244] T. Lengauer, R.E. Tarjan, A fast algorithm for finding dominators in a flowgraph, ACM Trans. Program. Lang. Syst. 1 (1) (1979) 121–141.

[245] P.M. Lewis, R.E. Stearns, Syntax-directed transduction, J. ACM 15 (3) (1968) 465–488.

[246] V. Liberatore, M. Farach-Colton, U. Kremer, Evaluation of algorithms for local register allocation, in: Proceedings of the Eighth International Conference on Compiler Construction (CC '99), Lecture Notes in Computer Science 1575, Springer-Verlag, Heidelberg, Germany, 1999, pp. 137–152.

[247] H. Lieberman, C. Hewitt, A real-time garbage collector based on the lifetimes of objects, Commun. ACM 26 (6) (1983) 419–429.

[248] B. Liskov, R.R. Atkinson, T. Bloom, J.E.B. Moss, C. Schaffert, R. Scheifler, et al., CLU Reference Manual, Lecture Notes in Computer Science 114, Springer-Verlag, Heidelberg, Germany, 1981.

[249] J.L. Lo, S.J. Eggers, Improving balanced scheduling with compiler optimizations that increase instruction-level parallelism, SIGPLAN Not. 30 (6) (1995) 151–162.

Proceedings of the ACM SIGPLAN '95 Conference on Programming Language Design and Implementation.

[250] R. Lo, F. Chow, R. Kennedy, S.-M. Liu, P. Tu, Register promotion by sparse partial redundancy elimination of loads and stores, SIGPLAN Not. 33 (5) (1998) 26–37. Proceedings of the ACM SIGPLAN '98 Conference on Programming Language Design and Implementation.

[251] P.G. Lowney, S.M. Freudenberger, T.J. Karzes, W.D. Lichtenstein, R.P. Nix, J.S. O'Donnell, et al., The multiflow trace scheduling compiler, J. Supercomputing—Special Issue 7 (1–2) (1993) 51–142.

[252] E.S. Lowry, C.W. Medlock, Object code optimization, Commun. ACM 12 (1) (1969) 13–22.

[253] J. Lu, K.D. Cooper, Register promotion in C programs, SIGPLAN Not. 32 (5) (1997) 308–319. Proceedings of the ACM SIGPLAN '97 Conference on Programming Language Design and Implementation.

[254] J. Lu, R. Shillner, Clean: removing useless control flow, unpublished manuscript, Department of Computer Science, Rice University, Houston, TX, 1994.

[255] P. Lucas, The structure of formula-translators, ALGOL Bull. (Suppl. 16) (1961) 1–27. [Die strukturanalyse von formelübersetzern, Elektronische Rechenanlagen 3 (4) (1961) 159–167.]

[256] P.W. Markstein, V. Markstein, F.K. Zadeck, Reassociation and strength reduction. Unpublished book chapter.

[257] V. Markstein, J. Cocke, P. Markstein, Optimization of range checking, in: Proceedings of the 1982 SIGPLAN Symposium on Compiler Construction, ACM, New York, 1982, pp. 114–119. Also published as SIGPLAN Not. 17 (6) (1982).

[258] H. Massalin, Superoptimizer: a look at the smallest program, SIGPLAN Not. 22 (10) (1987) 122–126. Proceedings of the Second International Conference on Architectural Support for Programming Languages and Operating Systems (ASPLOS-II).

[259] J. McCarthy, Lisp: notes on its past and future, in: Proceedings of the 1980 ACM Conference on Lisp and Functional Programming, Stanford University, Stanford, CA, 1980, pp. v–viii.

[260] W.M. McKeeman, Peephole optimization, Commun. ACM 8 (7) (1965) 443–444.

[261] K.S. McKinley, S. Carr, C.-W. Tseng, Improving data locality with loop transformations, ACM Trans. Program. Lang. Syst. 18 (4) (1996) 424–453.

[262] R. McNaughton, H. Yamada, Regular expressions and state graphs for automata, IRE Trans. Electron. Comput. EC-9 (1) (1960) 39–47.

[263] R. Metzger, S. Stroud, Interprocedural constant propagation: an empirical study, ACM Lett. Program. Lang. Syst. (LOPLAS) 2 (1–4) (1993) 213–232.

[264] T.C. Miller, Tentative Compilation: A Design for an APL Compiler, PhD thesis, Yale University, New Haven, CT, 1978. See also the paper of the same title in the Proceedings of the International Conference on APL: Part 1, New York, 1979, pp. 88–95.

[265] R. Milner, M. Tofte, R. Harper, D. MacQueen, The Definition of Standard ML—Revised, MIT Press, Cambridge, MA, 1997.

[266] J.S. Moore, The Interlisp Virtual Machine Specification, Technical Report CSL 76-5, Xerox Palo Alto Research Center, Palo Alto, CA, 1976.

[267] E. Morel, C. Renvoise, Global optimization by suppression of partial redundancies, Commun. ACM 22 (2) (1979) 96–103.

[268] R. Morgan, Building an Optimizing Compiler, Digital Press (an imprint of Butterworth–Heineman), Boston, MA, 1998.

[269] R. Motwani, K.V. Palem, V. Sarkar, S. Reyen, Combining Register Allocation and Instruction Scheduling, Technical Report 698, Courant Institute of Mathematical Sciences, New York University, New York, 1995.

[270] S.S. Muchnick, Advanced Compiler Design & Implementation, Morgan Kaufmann, San Francisco, CA, 1997.

[271] F. Mueller, D.B. Whalley, Avoiding unconditional jumps by code replication, SIGPLAN Not. 27 (7) (1992) 322–330. Proceedings of the ACM SIGPLAN '92 Conference on Programming Language Design and Implementation.

[272] T.P. Murtagh, An improved storage management scheme for block structured languages, ACM Trans. Program. Lang. Syst. 13 (3) (1991) 372–398.

[273] P. Naur (Ed.), J.W. Backus, F.L. Bauer, J. Green, C. Katz, J. McCarthy, et al., Revised report on the algorithmic language Algol 60, Commun. ACM 6 (1) (1963) 1–17.

[274] E.K. Ngassam, B.W. Watson, D.G. Kourie, Hardcoding finite state automata processing, in: Proceedings of SAICSIT 2003 Annual Conference of the South African Insitute of Computer Scientists and Information Technologists, Republic of South Africa, 2003, pp. 111–121.

[275] B.R. Nickerson, Graph coloring register allocation for processors with multi-register operands, SIGPLAN Not. 25 (6) (1990) 40–52. Proceedings of the ACM SIGPLAN '90 Conference on Programming Language Design and Implementation.

[276] C. Norris, L.L. Pollock, A scheduler-sensitive global register allocator, in: Proceedings of Supercomputing '93, Portland, OR, ACM, New York, 1993, pp. 804–813.

[277] C. Norris, L.L. Pollock, An experimental study of several cooperative register allocation and instruction scheduling strategies, in: Proceedings of the Twenty-Eighth Annual International Symposium on Microarchitecture (MICRO-28), Ann Arbor, MI, IEEE Computer Society Press, Los Alamitos, CA, 1995, pp. 169–179.

[278] K. Nygaard, O.-J. Dahl, The development of the SIMULA languages, SIGPLAN Not. 13 (8) (1978) 245–272. Proceedings of the First ACM SIGPLAN Conference on the History of Programming Languages.

[279] M. Paleczny, C.A. Vick, C. Click, The Java HotSpot[TM] Server Compiler, in: Proceedings of the First Java[TM] Virtual Machine Research and Technology Symposium (JVM '01), Monterey, CA, The USENIX Association, Berkeley, CA, 2001, pp. 1–12.

[280] J. Park, S.-M. Moon, Optimistic register coalescing, in: Proceedings of the 1998 International Conference on Parallel Architecture and Compilation Techniques (PACT), IEEE Computer Society, Washington, DC, 1998, pp. 196–204.

[281] E. Pelegrí-Llopart, S.L. Graham, Optimal code generation for expression trees: an application of BURS theory, in: Proceedings of the Fifteenth Annual ACM Symposium on Principles of Programming Languages, San Diego, CA, ACM, New York, 1988, pp. 294–308.

[282] T.J. Pennello, Very fast LR parsing, SIGPLAN Not. 21 (7) (1986) 145–151. Proceedings of the ACM SIGPLAN '86 Symposium on Compiler Construction.

[283] F.M.Q. Pereira, J. Palsberg, Register allocation via coloring of chordal graphs, in: Proceedings of the Asian Symposium on Programming Languages and Systems (APLAS '05), Springer-Verlag, Berlin, Heidelberg, 2005, pp. 315–329.

[284] K. Pettis, R.C. Hansen, Profile guided code positioning, SIGPLAN Not. 25 (6) (1990) 16–27. Proceedings of the ACM SIGPLAN '90 Conference on Programming Language Design and Implementation.

[285] S.S. Pinter, Register allocation with instruction scheduling: a new approach, SIGPLAN Not. 28 (6) (1993) 248–257. Proceedings of the ACM SIGPLAN '93 Conference on Programming Language Design and Implementation.

[286] G.D. Plotkin, Call-by-name, call-by-value and the $\lambda$-calculus, Theor. Comput. Sci. 1 (2) (1975) 125–159.

[287] T.A. Proebsting, Simple and efficient BURS table generation, SIGPLAN Not. 27 (7) (1992) 331–340. Proceedings of the ACM SIGPLAN '92 Conference on Programming Language Design and Implementation.

[288] T.A. Proebsting, Optimizing an ANSI C interpreter with superoperators, in: Proceedings of the Twenty-Second ACM SIGPLAN-SIGACT Symposium on Principles of Programming Languages, San Francisco, CA, ACM, New York, 1995, pp. 322–332.

[289] T.A. Proebsting, C.N. Fischer, Linear-time, optimal code scheduling for delayed-load architectures, SIGPLAN Not. 26 (6) (1991) 256–267. Proceedings of the ACM SIGPLAN '91 Conference on Programming Language Design and Implementation.

[290] R.T. Prosser, Applications of boolean matrices to the analysis of flow diagrams, in: Proceedings of the Eastern Joint Computer Conference, Institute of Radio Engineers, New York, 1959, pp. 133–138.

[291] P.W. Purdom Jr., E.F. Moore, Immediate predominators in a directed graph [H], Commun. ACM 15 (8) (1972) 777–778.

[292] M.O. Rabin, D. Scott, Finite automata and their decision problems, IBM J. Res. Dev. 3 (2) (1959) 114–125.

[293] B. Randell, L.J. Russell, Algol 60 Implementation: The Translation and Use of Algol 60 Programs on a Computer, Academic Press, London, 1964.

[294] B.R. Rau, C.D. Glaeser, Some scheduling techniques and an easily schedulable horizontal architecture for high performance scientific computing, in: Proceedings of the Fourteenth Annual Workshop on Microprogramming (MICRO-14), Chatham, MA, IEEE Press, Piscataway, NJ, 1981, pp. 183–198,

[295] J.H. Reif, Symbolic programming analysis in almost linear time, in: Conference Record of the Fifth Annual ACM Symposium on Principles of Programming Languages, Tucson, AZ, ACM, New York, 1978, pp. 76–83.

[296] J.H. Reif, H.R. Lewis, Symbolic evaluation and the global value graph, in: Conference Record of the Fourth ACM Symposium on Principles of Programming Languages, Los Angeles, CA, ACM, New York, 1977, pp. 104–118.

[297] T. Reps, Optimal-time incremental semantic analysis for syntax-directed editors, in: Conference Record of the Ninth Annual ACM Symposium on Principles of Programming Languages, Albuquerque, NM, ACM, New York, 1982, pp. 169–176.

[298] T. Reps, B. Alpern, Interactive proof checking, in: Conference Record of the Eleventh Annual ACM Symposium on Principles of Programming Languages, Salt Lake City, UT, ACM, New York, 1984, pp. 36–45.

[299] T. Reps, T. Teitelbaum, The Synthesizer Generator: A System for Constructing Language-Based Editors, Springer-Verlag, New York, 1988.

[300] M. Richards, The portability of the BCPL compiler, Softw. Pract. Experience 1 (2) (1971) 135–146.

[301] S. Richardson, M. Ganapathi, Interprocedural analysis versus procedure integration, Inf. Process. Lett. 32 (3) (1989) 137–142.

[302] R. Rivest, On self-organizing sequential search heuristics, Commun. ACM 19 (2) (1976) 63–67.

[303] A. Rogers, K. Li, Software support for speculative loads, SIGPLAN Not. 27 (9) (1992) 38–50. Proceedings of the Fifth International Conference on Architectural Support for Programming Languages and Operating Systems (ASPLOS-V).

[304] B.K. Rosen, M.N. Wegman, F.K. Zadeck, Global value numbers and redundant computations, in: Proceedings of the Fifteenth Annual ACM Symposium on Principles of Programming Languages, San Diego, CA, ACM, New York, 1988, pp. 12–27.

[305] D.J. Rosenkrantz, R.E. Stearns, Properties of deterministic top-down grammars, Inf. Control 17 (3) (1970) 226–256.

[306] A.V.S. Sastry, R.D.C. Ju, A new algorithm for scalar register promotion based on SSA form, SIGPLAN Not. 33 (5) (1998) 15–25. Proceedings of the ACM SIGPLAN '98 Conference on Programming Language Design and Implementation.

[307] R.G. Scarborough, H.G. Kolsky, Improved optimization of FORTRAN object programs, IBM J. Res. Dev. 24 (6) (1980) 660–676.

[308] P.J. Schielke, Stochastic Instruction Scheduling, PhD thesis, Department of Computer Science, Rice University, Houston, TX, 2000. Technical Report TR00-370, Computer Science Department, Rice University, 2000.

[309] H. Schorr, W.M. Waite, An efficient machine-independent procedure for garbage collection in various list structures, Commun. ACM 10 (8) (1967) 501–506.

[310] J.T. Schwartz, On Programming: An Interim Report on the SETL Project, Installment II: The SETL Language and Examples of Its Use, Technical Report, Courant Institute of Mathematical Sciences, New York University, New York, 1973.

[311] R. Sethi, J.D. Ullman, The generation of optimal code for arithmetic expressions, J. ACM 17 (4) (1970) 715–728.

[312] M. Shapiro, S. Horwitz, Fast and accurate flow-insensitive points-to analysis, in: Proceedings of the Twenty-Fourth ACM SIGPLAN-SIGACT Symposium on Principles of Programming Languages, Paris, France, ACM, New York, 1997, pp. 1–14.

[313] R.M. Shapiro, H. Saint, The Representation of Algorithms, Technical Report CA-7002-1432, Massachusetts Computer Associates, Wakefield, MA, 1970.

[314] P.B. Sheridan, The arithmetic translator-compiler of the IBM FORTRAN automatic coding system, Commun. ACM 2 (2) (1959) 9–21.

[315] M. Sipser, Introduction to the Theory of Computation, PWS Publishing Co., Boston, MA, 1996.

[316] R.L. Sites, D.R. Perkins, Universal P-code Definition, Version 0.2, Technical Report 78-CS-C29, Department of Applied Physics and Information Sciences, University of California at San Diego, San Diego, CA, 1979.

[317] D.D. Sleator, R.E. Tarjan, Amortized efficiency of list update and paging rules, Commun. ACM 28 (2) (1985) 202–208.

[318] M.D. Smith, M. Horowitz, M.S. Lam, Efficient superscalar performance through boosting, SIGPLAN Not. 27 (9) (1992) 248–259. Proceedings of the Fifth

International Conference on Architectural Support for Programming Languages
and Operating Systems (ASPLOS-V).

[319] M.D. Smith, N. Ramsey, G. Holloway, A generalized algorithm for graph-coloring
register allocation, in: Proceedings of the ACM SIGPLAN 2004 Conference on
Programming Language Design and Implementation, ACM, New York, 2004,
pp. 277–288. Also appeared as SIGPLAN Not. 39 (6).

[320] M. Smotherman, S.M. Krishnamurthy, P.S. Aravind, D. Hunnicutt, Efficient
DAG construction and heuristic calculation for instruction scheduling, in: Proceedings of the Twenty-Fourth Annual IEEE/ACM International Symposium
on Microarchitecture (MICRO-24), Albuquerque, NM, ACM, New York, 1991,
pp. 93–102.

[321] A. Sorkin, Some comments on "A solution to a problem with Morel and
Renvoise's 'Global optimization by suppression of partial redundancies,'" ACM
Trans. Program. Lang. Syst. 11 (4) (1989) 666–668.

[322] T.C. Spillman, Exposing side-effects in a PL/I optimizing compiler, in: C.V.
Freiman, J.E. Griffith, J.L. Rosenfeld (Eds.), Proceedings of IFIP Congress '71,
Information Processing 71, North-Holland, Amsterdam, Netherlands, 1972,
pp. 376–381.

[323] G.L. Steele Jr., Rabbit: A Compiler for Scheme, Technical Report AI-TR-474,
MIT Artificial Intelligence Laboratory, Massachusetts Institute of Technology,
Cambridge, MA, 1978.

[324] G.L. Steele Jr., R.P. Gabriel, History of Programming Languages—II, "The
Evolution of LISP," ACM Press, New York, 1996, pp. 233–330.

[325] M. Stephenson, S. Amarasinghe, Predicting unroll factors using supervised classification, in: CGO '05: Proceedings of the International Symposium on Code
Generation and Optimization, IEEE Computer Society, Washington, DC, 2005,
pp. 123–134.

[326] P.H. Sweany, S.J. Beaty, Post-compaction register assignment in a retargetable compiler, in: Proceedings of the Twenty-Third Annual International Symposium and Workshop on Microprogramming and Microarchitecture
(MICRO-23), Orlando, FL, IEEE Computer Society Press, Los Alamitos, CA,
1990, pp. 107–116.

[327] P.H. Sweany, S.J. Beaty, Dominator-path scheduling: a global scheduling method,
ACM SIGMICRO Newsl. 23 (1–2) (1992) 260–263. Proceedings of the Twenty-
Fifth Annual International Symposium on Microarchitecture (MICRO-25).

[328] D. Tabakov, M.Y. Vardi, Experimental evaluation of classical automat constructions, in: Proceedings of the 12th International Conference on Logic for Programming, Artificial Intelligence, and Reasoning (LPAR '05), Lecture Notes in
Compuer Science 3835, Springer-Verlag, Berlin, Heidelberg, 2005, pp. 371–386.

[329] R.E. Tarjan, Testing flow graph reducibility, J. Comput. Syst. Sci. 9 (3) (1974)
355–365.

[330] R.E. Tarjan, Fast algorithms for solving path problems, J. ACM 28 (3) (1981)
594–614.

[331] R.E. Tarjan, A unified approach to path problems, J. ACM 28 (3) (1981) 577–593.

[332] R.E. Tarjan, J.H. Reif, Symbolic program analysis in almost-linear time, SIAM
J. Comput. 11 (1) (1982) 81–93.

[333] K. Thompson, Programming techniques: regular expression search algorithm,
Commun. ACM 11 (6) (1968) 419–422.

[334] S.W.K. Tjiang, Twig Reference Manual, Technical Report CSTR 120, Computing Sciences, AT&T Bell Laboratories, Murray Hill, NJ, 1986.

[335] L. Torczon, Compilation Dependences in an Ambitious Optimizing Compiler, PhD thesis, Department of Computer Science, Rice University, Houston, TX, 1985.

[336] J.D. Ullman, Fast algorithms for the elimination of common subexpressions, Acta Informatica 2 (3) (1973) 191–213.

[337] D. Ungar, Generation scavenging: a non-disruptive high performance storage reclamation algorithm, ACM SIGSOFT Software Eng. Notes 9 (3) (1984) 157–167. Proceedings of the First ACM SIGSOFT/SIGPLAN Software Engineering Symposium on Practical Software Development Environments.

[338] V. Vyssotsky, P. Wegner, A Graph Theoretical FORTRAN Source Language Analyzer, Manuscript, AT&T Bell Laboratories, Murray Hill, NJ, 1963.

[339] W. Waite, G. Goos, Compiler Construction, Springer-Verlag, New York, 1984.

[340] W.M. Waite. The cost of lexical analysis, Softw. Pract. Experience 16 (5) (1986) 473–488.

[341] D.W. Wall, Global register allocation at link time, in: Proceedings of the 1986 ACM SIGPLAN Symposium on Compiler Construction, ACM, New York, 1986, pp. 264–275.

[342] S.K. Warren, The Coroutine Model of Attribute Grammar Evaluation, PhD thesis, Department of Mathematical Sciences, Rice University, Houston, TX, 1976.

[343] B. Watson, A fast new semi-incremental algorithm for the construction of minimal acyclic DFAs, in: Third International Workshop on Implementing Automata, WIA '98, vol. 1660 of LNCS, Springer-Verlag, Berlin, Heidelberg, 1999, pp. 121–132.

[344] B.W. Watson, A taxonomy of deterministic finite automata minimization algorithms, Computing Science Report 93/44, Eindhoven University of Technology, Department of Mathematics and Computing Science, Eindhoven, The Netherlands, 1993.

[345] B.W. Watson, A fast and simple algorithm for constructing minimal acyclic deterministic finite automata, J. Univers. Comput. Sci. 8 (2) (2002) 363–367.

[346] M.N. Wegman, F.K. Zadeck, Constant propagation with conditional branches, in: Conference Record of the Twelfth Annual ACM Symposium on Principles of Programming Languages, New Orleans, LA, ACM, New York, 1985, pp. 291–299.

[347] M.N. Wegman, F.K. Zadeck, Constant propagation with conditional branches, ACM Trans. Program. Lang. Syst. 13 (2) (1991) 181–210.

[348] W.E. Weihl, Interprocedural data flow analysis in the presence of pointers, procedure variables, and label variables, in: Conference Record of the Seventh Annual ACM Symposium on Principles of Programming Languages, Las Vegas, NV, ACM, New York, 1980, pp. 83–94.

[349] C. Wiedmann, Steps toward an APL compiler, ACM SIGAPL APL Quote Quad 9 (4) (1979) 321–328. Proceedings of the International Conference on APL.

[350] P.R. Wilson, Uniprocessor garbage collection techniques, in: Proceedings of the International Workshop on Memory Management, Lecture Notes in Computer Science 637, Springer-Verlag, Heidelberg, Germany, 1992, pp. 1–42.

[351] R.P. Wilson, M.S. Lam, Efficient context-sensitive pointer analysis for C programs, SIGPLAN Not. 30 (6) (1995) 1–12. Proceedings of the ACM SIGPLAN '95 Conference on Programming Language Design and Implementation.

[352] M. Wolfe, High Performance Compilers for Parallel Computing, Addison Wesley, Redwood City, CA, 1996.

[353] D. Wood, The theory of left-factored languages, part 1, Comput. J. 12 (4) (1969) 349–356.

[354] D. Wood, The theory of left-factored languages, part 2, Comput. J. 13 (1) (1970) 55–62.

[355] D. Wood, A further note on top-down deterministic languages, Comput. J. 14 (4) (1971) 396–403.

[356] W. Wulf, R.K. Johnsson, C.B. Weinstock, S.O. Hobbs, C.M. Geschke, The Design of an Optimizing Compiler, Programming Languages Series, Elsevier, New York, 1975.

[357] C. Young, D.S. Johnson, D.R. Karger, M.D. Smith, Near-optimal intraprocedural branch alignment, SIGPLAN Not. 32 (5) (1997) 183–193. Proceedings of the ACM SIGPLAN '97 Conference on Programming Language Design and Implementation.

[358] D.H. Younger, Recognition and parsing of context-free languages in time $n^3$, Inf. Control 10 (2) (1967) 189–208.

[359] F.K. Zadeck, Incremental data flow analysis in a structured program editor, SIGPLAN Not. 19 (6) (1984) 132–143. Proceedings of the ACM SIGPLAN '84 Symposium on Compiler Construction.

# Index